INTERNATIONAL HUMAN RIGHTS

Text and Materials

PHILIP ALSTON

*John Norton Pomeroy Professor of Law at
New York University School of Law*

Citation. Philip Alston, *International Human Rights* (New York, NYU Law, 2024).

ISBN. 9798335545587 (Part I Sections A, B & C)
 Imprint. Independently published.

www.humanrightstextbook.org

PREFACE

This is a substantially revised edition of a human rights textbook newly-designed to be accessible to all, both in whole, or in its various parts, everywhere in the world. It is presented free of charge for all users, including students, teachers, activists and practitioners, and will be updated on an annual basis. It is also available in a hard copy, print-on-demand format priced at cost, to ensure affordability. The author aims to update the materials annually to ensure that they are timely and reflect key current developments.

This book is a successor to previous volumes entitled *International Human Rights in Context* (1996, 2000 and 2008) and *International Human Rights: Text and Materials* (2013). All four volumes were published by Oxford University Press. After lengthy discussions, the Press generously agreed to revert all rights to the author in order to enable this Open Access publication.

While I was a co-author for all of these editions, the lead author for the first three was Professor Henry Steiner, who founded Harvard Law School's Human Rights Program in 1984 and directed it until 2005. Henry was the driving force behind those three volumes, and they stand as a tribute to his depth of understanding, his endlessly probing intellect and his vision of how human rights should be taught. The 2008 and 2013 editions were also jointly authored with Professor Ryan Goodman whose major contributions continue to be reflected in this new edition. I am deeply grateful to both Henry and Ryan for their expertise, insights, friendship, and support.

Basic purposes

Almost eight decades after the human rights regime began to emerge out of the disasters of the Second World War, human rights norms and institutions deeply inform the rhetoric, practice and theory of international law and politics, as well as the internal constitutional structures of many states. Although the frailties and shortcomings of human rights as an ideal, an ideology or practice are all too evident today, the concept of human rights has become a part of modern consciousness, a lens through which to see the world and a universal if inevitably contested discourse. The course book uses the term 'human rights regime' to include post-1945 governmental, intergovernmental and nongovernmental institutions and practices in both national and international contexts in the recognition and protection of human rights.

Although the human rights regime now forms an indelible part of our legal, political and moral landscape, and indeed perhaps precisely because of that status, recent years have witnessed some of the deepest challenges to the foundations upon which the regime has been built, its aspirations to universality, and its claims of growing success in spreading and realizing its message. In response to these challenges, the book seeks to examine the regime's failures as well as triumphs and dilemmas in seeking to achieve human rights ideals across the world's many histories and cultures.

The book aims to enable readers to see the 'big picture', to understand the history, doctrine and institutional structures of the regime, and above all, to think critically about the subject. The book seeks to describe, analyze, criticize and propose, by drawing from a diverse range of political, cultural, moral and geopolitical perspectives. It tries not to impose any single dogma, direction or method for thinking about the history or the future of human rights.

Principal features of the book

The conceptual framework for the book consists, in sequence, of the historical development and character of human rights discourse and basic norms; the dilemmas of rights and duties, and of universalism and cultural relativism; the architecture of international institutions as well as their functions, powers and interplay with norms; and the interaction of states with international law and organizations as well as with each other. Certain major themes run through the different parts of the book — for example, the colonial and imperial objectives often pursued in the name of human rights, evolving notions of autonomy and sovereignty, the changing configuration of the public-private divide in human rights ordering, the escalating tensions between international human rights and national security, and the striking evolution of ideas about the nature and purposes of the regime itself.

The book emphasizes the *international dimensions* of the human rights system, while also exploring the vital relationships between that system and states' internal orders. It provides more than a doctrinal understanding of human rights, particularly by including materials from a range of disciplines other than law. For those who do not have any background knowledge of international law, the first two or three chapters provide an introduction to basic concepts, sources, processes and norms of that field.

Practical details on materials

Most of the materials have been sharply edited in order to make them as compact as possible. Omissions (except for footnotes) are indicated by the conventional use of ellipses. Retained footnotes are renumbered within the consecutive footnote numbering of each chapter. When a final page number is not available for a publication, these materials list it as 000. The book uses British rather than American spelling, primarily because previous editions were published in the United Kingdom.

The choice of materials, and particularly the length of excerpts, is significantly dependent on the willingness of publishers to grant permission. Some publishers refuse to participate in any Open Access work available free online, others require exorbitant fees which cannot be accommodated in an enterprise that generates no royalties.

Acknowledgements

Many people have helped to shape this book. In addition to Henry Steiner and Ryan Goodman, successive generations of students have been sharp and discerning critics. Various research assistants have made invaluable contributions over the years to the course from which the book draws. For assistance in the preparation of this edition, I am especially grateful to Lucy Forbes, Katarina Sydow, Jackson Gandour, Brianne Cuffe, Matthew Scarfo, and Youssef Farhat. Among my academic colleagues, Hélène Tigroudja was extraordinarily generous and wise with her advice, and Fionnuala Ní Aoláin, Steven Ratner and César Rodriguez-Garavito provided very helpful comments. Sally Engle Merry offered important guidance. Gráinne de Búrca was a constant and indispensable source of advice, inspiration and support.

Philip Alston
New York University School of Law, July 2024

Table of Contents

PART A: INTRODUCTION TO THE INTERNATIONAL HUMAN RIGHTS REGIME **26**

    Chapter 1. Human Rights Concepts and Discourse **27**

      A. Global Snapshots 27

      B. Human Rights Discourse: Capital Punishment 27

        1.   The Rapidly Changing Law on Capital Punishment 28

          Arguments about Justifications for Continuing or Abolishing the Death Penalty 28

          State v. Makwanyane 29

          Francis Karioko Muruatetu v. Republic 36

        2. The Death Penalty in India 39

          The Nirbhaya Gang-rape Case 40

          Mukesh & Anr. v. State For Nct of Delhi & Ors. 40

          Economic and Political Weekly, Deadly Errors in Judgment 43

        3. Drugs and the Death Penalty 44

        4. The Death Penalty in the United States 46

          Roper v. Simmons 46

          Austin Sarat, The Death Penalty on the Ballot: 55

          Life Without Parole 56

    Chapter 2. The Human Rights Regime: International Law Framework and Origins **57**

      A. The Law of Armed Conflict and Customary International Law 60

        The Paquete Habana 60

      1. International Humanitarian Law 65

      2. The Role of Custom 67

        Relationships between Treaties and Custom 68

        Martti Koskenniemi, The Pull of the Mainstream 69

      3. The Changing Character of Customary International Law 71

        Anthea Roberts, Traditional and Modern Approaches to Customary International Law 72

        Hugh Thirlway, The Sources of International Law 73

        B.S. Chimni, 'Customary International Law: A Third World Perspective' 75

      B. General Principles and Natural Law: State Responsibility 77

      The *Chattin* Case 79

          State Responsibility Today 82

      General Principles 83

        Oscar Schachter, International Law in Theory and Practice 83

      The Teachings of Publicists 86

      C. Slavery, The Interwar Minorities Regime and the Role of Treaties 87

      1. Treaties and the Abolition of Slavery 87

      2. The Minorities Regime after the First World War 89

Minority Schools in Albania...91

Further Aspects of the Minority Treaties 96

3. Treaties...97

Duties Imposed by Treaty Law 98

Treaty Formation 99

Consent 99

Reservations...99

Violations of and Changes in Treaties 99

Treaty Interpretation...100

Başak Çali, Specialized Rules of Treaty Interpretation: Human Rights 101

4. The ILO...103

D. Judgment at Nuremberg...104

The Nuremberg Trial 104

Judgment of Nuremberg Tribunal 107

Views of Commentators 111

Genocide...116

Eric D. Weitz, A World Divided: The Global Struggle for Human Rights in the Age of Nation-States..118

**PART B: NORMATIVE FOUNDATIONS OF INTERNATIONAL HUMAN RIGHTS ....
120**

Chapter 3. Civil and Political Rights...121

A. The Charter, UDHR and Origins of the Human Rights Regime......................................121

Charter Provisions 122

The Universal Declaration...122

Other UN Organs Related to Human Rights 124

Historical Sequence and Typology of Instruments...124

The Aspiration to Universality 125

E. H. Carr, Rights and Obligations...128

Roland Burke, Decolonization, Development, and Identity...128

Lauterpacht and the UDHR 130

Hersch Lauterpacht, International Law and Human Rights 130

Impact of the UDHR...133

B. The International Covenant on Civil and Political Rights...134

The Relationship between the UDHR and the ICCPR...134

Indivisibility and *Jus Cogens*..137

Withdrawal from the ICCPR 143

C. Women's Rights and CEDAW 144

1. Background to Women's Rights 144

Initial Report of Guatemala to the CEDAW Committee 146

Human Development Perspectives, Tackling Social Norms: 147

2. CEDAW: Provisions and Committee 151

    CEDAW'S Substantive Provisions 152

        Substantive Equality 155

    Types of State Duties Imposed by Human Rights Treaties 156

    The Committee on the Elimination of Discrimination Against Women 159

    Andrew Byrnes, The Committee on the Elimination of Discrimination Against Women 159

        State Reporting..162

    CEDAW Committee, Concluding Observations on the Eighth Periodic Report of The Republic of Türkiye 162

3. The Public/Private Divide: 'Private' Violence Against Women 164

    Velásquez Rodríguez Case 166

    General Recommendations..168

    CEDAW Committee, General Recommendation No. 19 on Violence Against Women 168

    CEDAW Committee, General Recommendation No. 35 on Gender-Based Violence Against Women... 169

        Follow-up 172

        The Inquiry Procedure..173

        The Complaints Procedure..174

    N. A. E. v. Spain, Views of the Committee 175

4. Affirmative Action and Quotas 178

    Political Representation..179

5. Sexual and Reproductive Rights..181

    Manuela et al. v. El Salvador.. 184

    Conscientious Objection to Abortion 189

    Sentence C-055/22.. 189

6. Reservations: CEDAW and Other Treaties..194

    a. U.S. Treaty Ratification and Reservations...194

    Christopher N. J. Roberts, The Contentious History of the International Bill of Human Rights 194

        The ICCPR..196

    Proposals by Bush Administration of Reservations to International Covenant on Civil and Political Rights...196

    b. CEDAW and Reservations..199

        Reservations 200

        Objections 201

    The Effect of Treaty Reservations...203

    Human Rights Committee, General Comment No. 24................................ 204

    International Law Commission, Guide to Practice on Reservations to Treaties....................... 205

    Reactions to General Comment No. 24...208

7. The Impact of CEDAW 209

    D. Evolution of Human Rights: Sexual Orientation Discrimination...213

        National and Transnational Social and Legal Change...214

            The Road to Formal Recognition at the International Level........................214

            Regional Systems...217

            Inter-American Court of Human Rights, Gender Identity, and Equality and Non-Discrimination of Same-Sex Couples 217

        Gender Identity Cases..219

            Children's Rights..220

            Case of Bayev and Others v. Russia..220

            The Right to Bodily Autonomy and Physical Integrity.........................223

            Resolution on the Promotion and Protection of the Rights of Intersex Persons in Africa 224

        Pushback or Backlash Against LQBTQI and Women's Rights 225

            a. International Law Critique 225

            Li-Ann Thio, Equality and Non-Discrimination in International Human Rights Law..............225

            b. 'Gender Ideology'..226

                Islamic Countries' Response..227

            c. 'Traditional Values' Debate..228

            Human Rights Council, Protection of the Family....................................228

            d. Neoliberalism 229

            e. National-Level Cultural Responses...230

    E. Torture..234

        1. Norm Regression: The Torture Prohibition...234

            International Instruments Prohibiting Torture..235

            Public Committee Against Torture in Israel v. Government of Israel............................236

            David Kretzmer and Yaël Ronen, The Occupation of Justice: 240

            Debating the Merits 242

        2. U.S. Law and Policy on Torture after September 11 244

            Senate Select Committee on Intelligence, Committee Study of the Central Intelligence Agency's Detention and Interrogation Program...245

            The Impact of U.S. Policies on the Norm against Torture 248

Chapter 4. Economic, Social, and Cultural Rights...249

    Overview...249

        Philip Alston, The Parlous State of Poverty Eradication 252

    A. The Historical Origins of ESR...254

        Excerpts from the ICESR..257

    1. Differentiating the Rights 258

    2. Implementation: the ESCR Committee..259

        Hamid Saydawi and Masir Farah v. Italy, ...260

        ESCR Committee, General Comment No. 15: The Right to Water.............................261

    3. Responses to General Comment No. 15 262

B. Competing Perspectives on ESR 266

   1. Ambivalence towards ESR 267

      Kenneth Roth, Defending Economic, Social and Cultural Rights: 269

   2. Historical Perspectives 270

      Samuel Moyn, Not Enough: Human Rights in an Unequal World 271

      Philip Alston, The Past and Future of Social Rights 272

   3. Philosophical Perspectives 274

      Friedrich Hayek, Justice and Individual Rights 275

      Aryeh Neier, Social and Economic Rights: A Critique 275

      David Kelley, A Life of One's Own: Individual Rights and the Welfare State 277

      James Griffin, The Presidential Address 278

      James W. Nickel, Poverty and Rights 279

      Amartya Sen, The Idea of Justice 280

C. The Relationship between the Two Sets of Rights 281

      Philip Alston, Report of the Special Rapporteur on Extreme Poverty and Human Rights on his
      Mission to the United States of America 282

D. 'Available Resources' 284

   The Response of the UN Committee on ESCR 285

      Committee on ESCR, General Comment No. 3: The Nature of state Parties Obligations 285

      Committee on ESCR, General Comment No. 11: Plans of Action for Primary Education 285

      Committee on ESCR, An Evaluation of the Obligation to Take Steps to the 'Maximum of
      Available Resources' Under an Optional Protocol to the Covenant 287

      Committee on ESCR, General Comment No. 19: The Right to Social Security 288

E. Constitutions, Courts and Other Remedies 288

      Committee on ESCR, General Comment No. 9 289

   ESR Litigation in Specific Constitutional Settings 290

   1. India: Public Interest Litigation 291

      Olga Tellis v. Bombay Municipal Corporation 292

      Dipika Jagatram Sahani v. Union of India and Others 295

      Responses to India's PIL 296

   2. South Africa and Kenya 298

      Soobramoney v. Minister of Health (Kwazulu-Natal) 300

      Government of South Africa v. Grootboom 302

      Treatment Action Campaign v. Minister of Health 305

      Mazibuko v. City of Johannesburg 308

      City of Johannesburg Metropolitan Municipality v. Blue Moonlight Properties 39 (Pty) Ltd and Another ... 312

      General Comments on the Right to Housing 314

      Mitu-Bell Welfare Society v. The Kenya Airports Authority et al. 315

      William Musembi v. The Moi Educational Centre Co. Ltd. 319

The Relationship Between Housing and Property Rights 319

   3. ESR in the Inter-American Convention 322

     The Maya Kaqchikel Indigenous Peoples of Sumpango et al. v. Guatemala 322

   4. Assessing ESR Litigation 324

F. ESR: Beyond Constitutions and Litigation 327

  Accountability 329

    Spain 329

    United Kingdom 330

G. The Political Economy of Human Rights 332

  1. Austerity 332

    R (On the Application of SC, CB and 8 Children) v. Secretary of State for Work and Pensions 334

  2. Privatization 335

  3. Inequality 337

  4. Fiscal Policy Responses 338

    Alex Cobham, Fariya Mohiuddin and Liz Nelson, Global Tax Justice and Human Rights 339

    The Impact of Tax Avoidance and Evasion on ESR 340

    The Role of International Law 343

Chapter 5. National Security, Terrorism and International Humanitarian Law 345

A. Terrorism: Definitions and Institutional Responses 346

    Ben Saul, The Legal Black Hole in United Nations Counterterrorism 347

  The Role of the UN Security Council 349

    Security Council Resolution 2462 349

    Statement by the President of the Security Council 350

    Fionnuala Ní Aoláin, 'Soft Law', Informal Lawmaking and 'New Institutions' in the Global
    Counter-Terrorism Architecture 352

  Selected Issues 354

B. The Legal Framework 362

  1. Emergencies and Derogation 362

    Joan Fitzpatrick, Human Rights in Crisis 363

    Human Rights Committee, States of Emergency, General Comment 29 (On Article 4) 364

    Venice Commission, Opinion on Emergency Decree Laws Nos. 667-676 367

    Pişkin v. Turkey 369

    COVID-19 373

    Ghana, Imposition of Restrictions Act, 2020 375

  2. International Humanitarian Law and its Relationship to Human Rights 377

    The Structure and Content of IHL 377

    The Relationship Between the Two Bodies of Law 379

C. Renditions 384

    Ryan Goodman, The Laws of War in the Age of Terror 385

Husayn (Abu Zubaydah) v. Poland..388

United States v. Husayn, Aka Zubaydah, et al....390

D. Detention 392

A And Others v. United Kingdom..394

The House of Lords Judgment in A and Others 397

E. Fair Trials..400

Ibrahim and Others v. The United Kingdom...401

Military Tribunals 405

Inter-American Commission on Human Rights, Report on Terrorism and Human Rights..... 405

Human Rights Committee, Article 14: Right to Equality Before Courts and Tribunals and to a Fair Trial, General Comment 32 406

İncal v. Turkey..407

Öcalan v. Turkey 409

U. S. Military Commissions 410

Guantánamo...411

PART C: RIGHTS, DUTIES AND DILEMMAS OF UNIVERSALISM **413**

Chapter 6. Rights versus Duties **414**

A. Rights and Rights Rhetoric..414

Martti Koskenniemi, Rights, History, Critique 415

Henry Steiner, Some Characteristics of the Liberal Political Tradition 417

Charles Beitz, The Idea of Human Rights 420

Paul O'connell, On the Human Rights Question 421

Wendy Brown, Suffering the Paradoxes of Rights...422

David Kennedy, The International Human Rights Movement: Part of the Problem?............ 424

Paul O'connell, On the Human Rights Question 426

Frédéric Mégret, The Anthropocentrism of Human Rights 427

Lorenzo Cotula, Between Hope and Critique: Human Rights, Social Justice and Re-Imagining International Law from the Bottom Up..430

B. Duty-Based Social Orders..434

1. Duties...434

Robert Cover, Obligation: A Jewish Jurisprudence of the Social Order 434

Jomo Kenyatta, Facing Mount Kenya: The Tribal Life of the Gikuyu...................436

Christopher N.J. Roberts, The Contentious History of the International Bill of Human Rights 437

2. Duty Provisions of National Constitutions 438

China..438

Ecuador 438

Uganda..439

3. Rights and Duties in the African Charter 439

Makau Mutua, Human Rights and the African Fingerprint 441

4. Recent Debates over Duties and Responsibilities 445

Chapter 7. Conflict in Culture, Tradition and Practices: Challenges to Universalism **450**

A. Universalism and Cultural Relativism 450

American Anthropological Association, Statement on Human Rights 453

Sally Engle Merry, Human Rights and Gender Violence 454

Vernacularization 457

Sally Engle Merry and Peggy Levitt, The Vernacularization of Women's Human Rights 458

Harri Englund, Prisoners of Freedom: Human Rights and the African Poor 459

Abdullahi Ahmed An-Na'im, Human Rights in the Muslim World 462

Comments on Cultural Relativism 469

B. Dissonance and Conflict: Illustrations 470

1. Gender 471

Sindiso Mnisi and Aninka Claassens, Rural Women Redefining Land Rights in the Context of Living Customary Law 472

Dianne Otto, Feminist Approaches to International Law 473

Female Genital Mutilation/Cutting (FGM/C) 474

World Health Organization, Female Genital Mutilation – Fact Sheet 475

Inquiry Concerning Mali Under Article 8 of the Optional Protocol to CEDAW 476

A Kenyan Case Study 478

Kamau v. Attorney-General et al 478

Male Circumcision 482

Re B and G (Children) (Care Proceedings) 484

2. Religion 488

a. Comparative Perspectives among States 489

W. Cole Durham, Patterns of Religion State Relations 489

Tobias Cremer, Nations Under God 492

Benjamin Lawrence, Saffron Suffrage 493

Songfeng Li, Freedom in Handcuffs: Religious Freedom in the Constitution of China 494

b. International Law Perspectives 495

Declaration on the Elimination of All Forms of Intolerance and of Discrimination Based on Religion or Belief 496

Human Rights Committee, General Comment No. 22: The Right to Freedom of Thought, Conscience and Religion 499

Reports of the Special Rapporteur on Freedom of Religion or Belief 500

Defining Antisemitism 503

c. Proselytism 506

Kokkinakis v. Greece 506

Makau Mutua, Human Rights, Religion, and Proselytism 511

    Mukesh Kumar and Garima Yadav, Anxieties of the Dominant.. 513

3. Dress and Symbols, Migration and Multiculturalism...514

    Timothy Savage, Europe and Islam: Crescent Waxing, Cultures Clashing 515

    Leyla Şahin v. Turkey... 517

    a. Headscarves in France...521

    Samira Achbita v. G4S Secure Solutions NV 522

    S.A.S. v. France... 524

    Yaker v. France.. 530

    b. Crucifixes in Italian Classrooms...533

    Lautsi v. Italy.. 533

4. Freedom of Speech 538

    Hate Speech...539

    The Jersild and Jallow Decisions.. 540

    Jallow v. Denmark.. 541

        Hate Speech in Conflict Situations...544

        Sexual Orientation Hate Speech 545

        Gendered Hate Speech 547

        Regulation of Hate Speech 548

    Faurisson v. France... 550

    Mona Elbahtimy, The Right to Be Free from the Harm of Hate Speech 554

    Note on the United States.. 556

    Blasphemy..557

    The Danish Cartoons and Defamation of Religion 559

    Ronald Dworkin, Even Bigots and Holocaust Deniers Must Have Their Say 563

PART A: INTRODUCTION TO THE INTERNATIONAL HUMAN RIGHTS REGIME

This book examines the world of contemporary human rights, including legal norms, political contexts and moral ideals. It takes us into diverse realms, including humanitarian laws of war, human rights discourse, state interests, international relations and institutions, governmental (state) and nongovernmental (non-state) actors, social policy, and climate change. The boundaries of the subject have steadily expanded as the human rights regime that emerged after the Second World War has become an indelible part of our legal, political and moral landscape. Given the breadth and complexity of the regime, including its engagement with law, politics, morals and radically different cultures, the book necessarily includes materials from a range of disciplines.

Three principal themes — law, politics and morals — are interrelated, indeed inseparable, for an understanding of the regime. The political and moral aspects of international human rights are self-evident; it is the international legal aspect that is novel. The rules and standards of contemporary human rights are expressed not only through states' constitutions, laws and practices, but also through treaties and international custom, as well as the work products (decisions about action, forms of adjudication, studies, investigative reports, resolutions, recommendations) of diverse international institutions and organs.

This regime is relatively young and the task of students and others committed to its ideals is to see themselves not as apprentices learning about an established, even static, framework of ideas and institutions, but rather as shapers and architects of the regime's ongoing evolution. The book aims not only to train students to work effectively within existing structures and boundaries, but also to impart a broad as well as critical understanding, and to provoke ideas about the directions in which the regime may be or ought to be heading.

Chapter 1. Human Rights Concepts and Discourse

This introductory chapter assumes no special knowledge about the foundations or content of rights, human rights and international human rights. Rather it is meant to spur thoughts about a range of issues that later chapters examine.

The two sections of the chapter explore some fundamental questions from complementary perspectives. Section A involves using media reports to explore current and pressing human rights issues. In many of the relevant situations, courts are likely to have played at best a marginal role.

In Section B, by contrast, the focus is on the way that courts from different states address and argue about alleged violations of rights. The section explores challenges to the legality of capital punishment under state laws and in light of developing international human rights law. These materials illustrate the growing attention by national courts to foreign law, whether constitutional, statutory, or judicial, to learn how other countries reason and decide about the permissibility of capital punishment (and many other issues). Those inquiries lead us to what is often described as the special situation of the United States with respect to human rights (and other fields), that involves so-called U.S. exceptionalism or unilateralism.

A. GLOBAL SNAPSHOTS

One way for teachers to introduce the issues dealt with in this book is to identify a range of current media reports describing some of the diverse human rights problems that the world confronts, and ask students to identify how they think human rights might be implicated. When reading such reports, consider the following questions:

- What is the source of the rules or standards under which governmental, inter-governmental and nongovernmental organizations evaluate and criticize a state?
- What different roles do the types of organizations referred to in these reports seem to play?
- How would you identify the alleged human rights violation in each story? Is it clear from each story that (if the reported facts are true) there has been a violation?
- In addition to the rights of individuals, are there cases that implicate the rights of groups?
- Are (international) human rights violations committed only by states, or are corporations, nongovernmental forces, and individuals also accused of such violations?
- What steps, if any, seem to be, or perhaps could be, taken to bring an end to the violations?

B. HUMAN RIGHTS DISCOURSE: CAPITAL PUNISHMENT

Section A drew attention to media accounts to illustrate the range of issues implicated in human rights doctrine and discourse. For the most part, the role of courts is likely to have been limited.

Section 1 below differs in several respects. It examines one broad issue, capital punishment, either in general or with respect to a particular category of criminal defendants. And it examines some illustrative judicial decisions to explore the argument of courts, and the evolving character of human rights discourse in the hands of courts, those most 'legal' of institutions. It is important to bear in mind that much of the invocation of rights and many of the arguments in these decisions are phenomena of the last seventy or so years. Many of the international institutions to which these courts refer simply did not exist before then and such extensive consideration by courts of case law from other jurisdictions was rare.

Section 2 considers the degree to which these courts and other national and international organs (parliaments, UN or regional bodies) form part of a global framework of interaction and discourse. Among the questions raised are the following: do many national courts look to international law, or to the law in foreign states, whether judicial or legislative or constitutional in form, as part of their inquiry and research into a concrete human rights issue? Do they ask (even if not formally bound by a treaty or customary law): what does international law have to say about this, or what do other states have to say about this? In a broader sense, to what extent can we say that some form of world community is developing among the judiciaries or legislatures of many states with respect to human rights issues, at least with respect to interest in what other states are saying about common issues?

Section 3 takes a look at the United States, and at the critical and sceptical stance that it has taken for many years towards international law and decisions of other states on controverted human rights issues. This stance goes by many terms that carry different shades of meaning, such as 'unilateralism', or 'exceptionalism'. Sections 1 and 2 provide pertinent background for the readings about and inquiry into these terms. Indeed, Section B in its entirety raises questions that reappear and continue to be troubling in later chapters of this book.

1. The Rapidly Changing Law on Capital Punishment

In 1965 only 25 countries had abolished the death penalty, and by 1998 only 35 countries had done so. But by 2020 the abolitionist movement had been so influential that only 54 out of some 190 countries imposed death sentences, and only 18 actually carried them out. One factor in such dramatic progress was a series of international treaties requiring states to abolish the death penalty. They include the 1989 Second Optional Protocol to the International Covenant on Civil and Political Rights (ICCPR) (90 states parties in 2024), the 1990 Protocol to the American Convention on Human Rights to Abolish the Death Penalty (13 states); and Protocols 6 (1983) and 13 (2002) to the European Convention on Human Rights (46 and 44 states respectively).

Amnesty International tracks the number of people executed around the world each year. For 2022 it recorded 883 executions (up from 579 in 2021) in 20 countries, with the most executions taking place in China, Iran, Saudi Arabia, and Egypt. China is believed to execute thousands each year, but the data are classified as a state secret. North Korea and Vietnam are also considered to have high executions rates, but are also very secretive.[1]

In 2004, the Chinese Government told the UN that abolition of the death penalty 'must proceed in pace with the respective stages in the development of a society; if it is decided to abolish the death penalty before a society has reached the necessary level of development, this may cause a number of social problems … . Each country should decide whether to retain or abolish the death sentence on the basis of its own actual circumstances and the aspirations of its people. (UN Doc. E/CN.4/2004/7/Add.1 (24 March 2004), para. 69. Soon thereafter, China greatly limited the range of crimes for which the death penalty can be imposed, and gave the Supreme Court oversight of all death sentences.

In 2007 the UN General Assembly adopted a heavily contested resolution calling for a global 'moratorium on executions with a view to abolishing the death penalty'. 104 states supported the resolution. By 2022 the biennial resolution garnered 125 votes in favor, 37 against and 22 abstaining (Res. 77/222).

The Nuremberg and related trials after the Second World War imposed the death sentence on certain defendants. But the maximum penalty for persons convicted of war crimes, crimes against humanity, or genocide by the International Criminal Tribunals created by the UN Security Council for the Former Yugoslavia and for Rwanda, or by the International Criminal Court, is life imprisonment, and in practice the various courts have sought to develop global norms that are less punitive than most national jurisdictions.

Arguments about Justifications for Continuing or Abolishing the Death Penalty

For centuries, philosophers, religious figures, law enforcement agencies, defence counsel, criminologists, and the general public have argued about this issue from many different perspectives. To take one early example, Cesare Beccaria wrote in *An Essay on Crimes and Punishments* (1764), chapter XXVIII:

> What right … have men to cut the throats of their fellow-creatures? Certainly not that on which the sovereignty and laws are founded. … Did anyone ever give to others the right of taking away his life? …

> …

---

[1] Amnesty International, *Death Sentences and Executions 2022* (2023).

> [The death penalty is] a war of a whole nation against a citizen, whose destruction they consider as necessary or useful to the general good. ...
>
> The death of a citizen cannot be necessary but in one case. When, though deprived of his liberty, he has such power and connections as may endanger the security of the nation; when his existence may produce a dangerous revolution in the established form of government. ...
>
> [T]he punishment of death has never prevented determined men from injuring society ....
>
> It is not the intenseness of the pain that has the greatest effect on the mind, but its continuance ... .

In response to especially heinous or sensational crimes, demands to reinstate the death penalty are often heard. Just as retentionists value the principle of 'an eye for an eye' in response to atrocious crimes, so too have abolitionists tended to treat the death penalty as a litmus test for humane policies across the board.

The South African judicial decision below, issued at the very start of the post-apartheid regime, rehearses many of the leading contemporary arguments. Advocates and courts cast those arguments both in terms of justice and fairness, and in instrumental terms that take into account the effects/consequences of capital punishment on the incidence of crime and other matters. The arguments often fall within the broadly invoked categories of retribution, fairness (including the issue of discrimination) and deterrence. This is followed by a Kenyan case that shows a more reticent bench nonetheless relying on international precedents to eliminate the mandatory death penalty. Finally, consideration is given to a recent resurgence of judicial support for the death penalty in India, primarily in response to very serious sexual crimes.

STATE V. MAKWANYANE
CONSTITUTIONAL COURT OF THE REPUBLIC OF SOUTH AFRICA, CASE NO. CCT/3/94, [1995] 1 LRC 269

[The two appellants were convicted of murder, and sentenced to death by the Witwatersrand Local Division of the Supreme Court. The Appellate Division postponed hearing of the appeals against the death sentence until the new, post-apartheid Constitutional Court decided the question of its constitutionality under the transitional 1993 Constitution. The eleven individual opinions of the Justices of the Constitutional Court were unanimous in holding that the death sentence was unconstitutional, but focused on different constitutional provisions and arguments. The excerpts below are from the opinion of Chief Justice Chaskalson.]

Relevant provisions of the Constitution

[7] The Constitution

> ... provides a historic bridge between the past of a deeply divided society characterised by strife, conflict, untold suffering and injustice, and a future founded on the recognition of human rights, democracy and peaceful co-existence and development opportunities for all South Africans, irrespective of colour, race, class, belief or sex.

It is a transitional constitution but one which itself establishes a new order in South Africa; an order in which human rights and democracy are entrenched and in which the Constitution:

> ... shall be the supreme law of the Republic and any law or act inconsistent with its provisions shall, unless otherwise provided expressly or by necessary implication in this Constitution, be of no force and effect to the extent of the inconsistency.

[8] Chapter Three of the Constitution sets out the fundamental rights to which every person is entitled under the Constitution and also contains provisions dealing with the way in which the Chapter is to be interpreted by the Courts. It does not deal specifically with the death penalty, but in section 11(2), it prohibits 'cruel, inhuman or degrading treatment or punishment' ...

...

[10] ... [S]*ection* 11(2) of the Constitution must not be construed in isolation, but in its context, which includes the history and background to the adoption of the Constitution, other provisions of the Constitution itself and, in particular, the provisions of Chapter Three of which it is part. It must also be construed in a way which secures for 'individuals the full measure' of its protection. Rights with which *section* 11(2) is associated in Chapter Three of the Constitution, and which are of particular importance to a decision on the constitutionality of the death penalty are included *in section* 9, 'every person shall have the right to life', *section* 10, 'every person shall have the right to respect for and protection of his or her dignity', and *section* 8, 'every person shall have the right to equality before the law and to equal protection of the law'. Punishment must meet the requirements of *sections* 8, 9 and 10; and this is so, whether these sections are treated as giving meaning to *Section* 11(2) or as prescribing separate and independent standards with which all punishments must comply.

[11] Mr. Bizos, who represented the South African government at the hearing of this matter, informed us that the government accepts that the death penalty is a cruel, inhuman and degrading punishment and that it should be declared unconstitutional. The Attorney General of the Witwatersrand, whose office is independent of the government, took a different view, and contended that the death penalty is a necessary and acceptable form of punishment and that it is not cruel, inhuman or degrading within the meaning of section 11(2) ... .

...

[27] The principal arguments advanced by counsel for the accused in support of their contention that the imposition of the death penalty for murder is a 'cruel, inhuman or degrading punishment', were that the death sentence is an affront to human dignity, is inconsistent with the unqualified right to life entrenched in the Constitution, cannot be corrected in case of error or enforced in a manner that is not arbitrary, and that it negates the essential content of the right to life and the other rights that flow from it. The Attorney General argued that the death penalty is recognised as a legitimate form of punishment in many parts of the world, it is a deterrent to violent crime, it meets society's need for adequate retribution for heinous offences, and it is regarded by South African society as an acceptable form of punishment ... .

International and foreign comparative law

[33] ... The movement away from the death penalty gained momentum during the second half of the present century with the growth of the abolitionist movement. In some countries it is now prohibited in all circumstances, in some it is prohibited save in times of war, and in most countries that have retained it as a penalty for crime, its use has been restricted to extreme cases. ...

[34] ... The international and foreign authorities are of value because they analyze arguments for and against the death sentence and show how courts of other jurisdictions have dealt with this vexed issue. For that reason alone they require our attention. They may also have to be considered because of their relevance to section 35(1) of the Constitution, which states:

> In interpreting the provisions of this Chapter a court of law shall promote the values
> which underlie an open and democratic society based on freedom and equality and shall,
> where applicable, have regard to public international law applicable to the protection of
> the rights entrenched in this Chapter, and may have regard to comparable foreign case
> law.

[35] ... In the context of *section* 35(1), public international law would include non-binding as well as binding law. They may both be used under the section as tools of interpretation. International agreements and customary international law accordingly provide a framework within which Chapter Three can be evaluated and understood, and for that purpose, decisions of tribunals dealing with comparable instruments, such as the United Nations Committee on Human Rights, the Inter-American Commission on Human Rights, the Inter-American Court of Human Rights, the European Commission on Human Rights, and the European Court of Human Rights, and in appropriate cases, reports of specialized agencies such as the International Labour Organization may provide guidance as to the correct interpretation of particular provisions of Chapter Three.

[36] Capital punishment is not prohibited by public international law, and this is a factor that has to be taken into account in deciding whether it is cruel, inhuman or degrading punishment within the meaning of *section*

11(2). International human rights agreements differ, however, from our Constitution in that where the right to life is expressed in unqualified terms they either deal specifically with the death sentence, or authorize exceptions to be made to the right to life by law ... .

...

[40] ... From the beginning, the United States Constitution recognized capital punishment as lawful. The Fifth Amendment (adopted in 1791) refers in specific terms to capital punishment and impliedly recognizes its validity. The Fourteenth Amendment (adopted in 1868) obliges the states, not to 'deprive any person of life, liberty, or property, without due process of law' and it too impliedly recognizes the right of the states to make laws for such purposes. The argument that capital punishment is unconstitutional was based on the Eighth Amendment, which prohibits cruel and unusual punishment ... . [In a brief discussion of U.S. constitutional law, the Court noted that the federal constitutionality of capital punishment was affirmed, subject to conditions stated, in *Gregg v. Georgia*, 428 U.S. 153 (1976).]

...

[43] ... Mr Trengove contended on behalf of the accused that the imprecise language of section 277, and the unbounded discretion vested by it in the Courts, make its provisions unconstitutional.

...

[45] Under our court system questions of guilt and innocence, and the proper sentence to be imposed on those found guilty of crimes, are not decided by juries. In capital cases, where it is likely that the death sentence may be imposed, judges sit with two assessors who have an equal vote with the judge on the issue of guilt and on any mitigating or aggravating factors relevant to sentence; but sentencing is the prerogative of the judge alone. The Criminal Procedure Act allows a full right of appeal to persons sentenced to death ... .

[46] Mitigating and aggravating factors must be identified by the Court, bearing in mind that the onus is on the State to prove beyond reasonable doubt the existence of aggravating factors, and to negative beyond reasonable doubt the presence of any mitigating factors relied on by the accused. Due regard must be paid to the personal circumstances and subjective factors which might have influenced the accused person's conduct, and these factors must then be weighed up with the main objects of punishment, which have been held to be: deterrence, prevention, reformation, and retribution. In this process '[e]very relevant consideration should receive the most scrupulous care and reasoned attention', and the death sentence should only be imposed in the most exceptional cases, where there is no reasonable prospect of reformation and the objects of punishment would not be properly achieved by any other sentence.

[47] There seems to me to be little difference between the guided discretion required for the death sentence in the United States, and the criteria laid down by the Appellate Division for the imposition of the death sentence ... .

[48] The argument that the imposition of the death sentence under *section* 277 is arbitrary and capricious does not, however, end there. It also focuses on what is alleged to be the arbitrariness inherent in the application of *section* 277 in practice. Of the thousands of persons put on trial for murder, only a very small percentage are sentenced to death by a trial court, and of those, a large number escape the ultimate penalty on appeal. At every stage of the process there is an element of chance. The outcome may be dependent upon factors such as the way the case is investigated by the police, the way the case is presented by the prosecutor, how effectively the accused is defended, the personality and particular attitude to capital punishment of the trial judge and, if the matter goes on appeal, the particular judges who are selected to hear the case. Race and poverty are also alleged to be factors.

[49] Most accused facing a possible death sentence are unable to afford legal assistance, and are defended under the *pro deo* system. The defending counsel is more often than not young and inexperienced, frequently of a different race to his or her client, and if this is the case, usually has to consult through an interpreter. *Pro deo* counsel are paid only a nominal fee for the defence, and generally lack the financial resources and the infrastructural support to undertake the necessary investigations and research, to employ expert witnesses to give advice, including advice on matters relevant to sentence, to assemble witnesses, to bargain with the prosecution, and generally to conduct an effective defence. Accused persons who have the money to do so, are able to retain experienced attorneys and counsel, who are paid to undertake the necessary investigations and research, and as a result they are less likely to be sentenced to death than persons similarly placed who are unable to pay for such services.

...

[54] The differences that exist between rich and poor, between good and bad prosecutions, between good and bad defence, between severe and lenient judges, between judges who favour capital punishment and those who do not, and the subjective attitudes that might be brought into play by factors such as race and class, may in similar ways affect any case that comes before the courts, and is almost certainly present to some degree in all court systems... . Imperfection inherent in criminal trials means that error cannot be excluded; it also means that persons similarly placed may not necessarily receive similar punishment. This needs to be acknowledged ... .

...

[56] ... The acceptance by a majority of the United States Supreme Court of the proposition that capital punishment is not per se unconstitutional, but that in certain circumstances it may be arbitrary, and thus unconstitutional, has led to endless litigation. Considerable expense and interminable delays result from the exceptionally-high standard of procedural fairness set by the United States courts in attempting to avoid arbitrary decisions. The difficulties that have been experienced in following this path ... persuade me that we should not follow this route.

The right to dignity

[57] Although the United States Constitution does not contain a specific guarantee of human dignity, it has been accepted by the United States Supreme Court that the concept of human dignity is at the core of the prohibition of 'cruel and unusual punishment' by the Eighth and Fourteenth Amendments ... .

[58] Under our constitutional order the right to human dignity is specifically guaranteed. It can only be limited by legislation which passes the stringent test of being 'necessary' ... .

[59] In Germany, the Federal Constitutional Court has stressed this aspect of punishment.

> Respect for human dignity especially requires the prohibition of cruel, inhuman, and degrading punishments. [The state] cannot turn the offender into an object of crime prevention to the detriment of his constitutionally protected right to social worth and respect.

[60] That capital punishment constitutes a serious impairment of human dignity has also been recognized by judgments of the Canadian Supreme Court. [In *Kindler v Canada* (1992) 6 CRR (2d) SC 4, involving murder, three] of the seven judges who heard the cases expressed the opinion that the death penalty was cruel and unusual:

> It is the supreme indignity to the individual, the ultimate corporal punishment, the final and complete lobotomy and the absolute and irrevocable castration. [It is] the ultimate desecration of human dignity.

> ...

[61] Three other judges [concluded that] the death penalty cannot, except in exceptional circumstances, be justified ... .

...

The International Covenant on Civil and Political Right

[63] [The two defendants in *Kindler v Canada*,] *Ng* and *Kindler* took their cases to the [UN] Human Rights Committee, contending that Canada had breached its obligations under the International Covenant on Civil and Political Rights. Once again, there was a division of opinion within the tribunal. In [*Ng v. Canada*, Communication No. 469/1991, 5 Nov. 1993] it was said:

> The Committee is aware that, by definition, every execution of a sentence of death may be considered to constitute cruel and inhuman treatment within the meaning of article 7 of the covenant.

[64] There was no dissent from that statement. But [Article 6 of] the International Covenant contains provisions permitting, with some qualifications, the imposition of capital punishment for the most serious crimes. In view

of these provisions, the majority of the Committee were of the opinion that the extradition of fugitives to a country which enforces the death sentence in accordance with the requirements of the International Covenant, should not be regarded as a breach of the obligations of the extraditing country ... .

...

[The opinion considered the decision by the European Court of Human Rights in *Soering v. United Kingdom* (1989) 11 EHRR 439, involving the question whether the United Kingdom would violate the provisions on inhuman and degrading treatment or punishment in Article 3 of the Convention, by extraditing a fugitive to the United States to face murder charges that were subject to capital punishment. In the circumstances, including the experience of 'death row' in the U.S. prisons and possible extradition of the fugitive by the United Kingdom for trial in another country that had abolished the death sentence, the European Court concluded that extradition to the United States would violate Article 3.

The opinion next examined a 1980 decision of the Indian Supreme Court holding that capital punishment did not violate the Indian Constitution. It distinguished the Indian decision partly by emphasizing the different wording of relevant provisions in the Constitutions of the two countries].

The right to life

[80] The unqualified right to life vested in every person by *section 9* of our Constitution is another factor crucially relevant to the question whether the death sentence is cruel, inhuman or degrading punishment within the meaning of *section 11(2)* of our Constitution. In this respect our Constitution differs materially from the Constitutions of the United States and India. It also differs materially from the European Convention and the International Covenant. Yet in the cases decided under these constitutions and treaties there were judges who dissented and held that notwithstanding the specific language of the constitution or instrument concerned, capital punishment should not be permitted.

...

[83] An individual's right to life has been described as '[t]he most fundamental of all human rights', and was dealt with in that way in the judgments of the Hungarian Constitutional Court declaring capital punishment to be unconstitutional ... .

...

Public opinion

[87] ... It was disputed whether public opinion, properly informed of the different considerations, would in fact favour the death penalty. I am, however, prepared to assume that it does and that the majority of South Africans agree that the death sentence should be imposed in extreme cases of murder. The question before us, however, is not what the majority of South Africans believe a proper sentence for murder should be. It is whether the Constitution allows the sentence.

[88] Public opinion may have some relevance to the enquiry, but in itself, it is no substitute for the duty vested in the Courts to interpret the Constitution and to uphold its provisions without fear or favour. If public opinion were to be decisive there would be no need for constitutional adjudication. The protection of rights could then be left to Parliament, which has a mandate from the public, and is answerable to the public for the way its mandate is exercised, but this would be a return to parliamentary sovereignty, and a retreat from the new legal order established by the 1993 Constitution... . The very reason for establishing the new legal order, and for vesting the power of judicial review of all legislation in the courts, was to protect the rights of minorities and others who cannot protect their rights adequately through the democratic process. Those who are entitled to claim this protection include the social outcasts and marginalized people of our society. It is only if there is a willingness to protect the worst and the weakest amongst us, that all of us can be secure that our own rights will be protected.

...

Cruel, inhuman and degrading punishment

...

[94] Proportionality is an ingredient to be taken into account in deciding whether a penalty is cruel, inhuman or degrading. No Court would today uphold the constitutionality of a statute that makes the death sentence a

competent sentence for the cutting down of trees or the killing of deer, which were capital offences in England in the 18th Century. But murder is not to be equated with such 'offences'. The wilful taking of an innocent life calls for a severe penalty, and there are many countries which still retain the death penalty as a sentencing option for such cases. Disparity between the crime and the penalty is not the only ingredient of proportionality; factors such as the enormity and irredeemable character of the death sentence in circumstances where neither error nor arbitrariness can be excluded, the expense and difficulty of addressing the disparities which exist in practice between accused persons facing similar charges, and which are due to factors such as race, poverty, and ignorance, and the other subjective factors which have been mentioned, are also factors that can and should be taken into account in dealing with this issue. It may possibly be that none alone would be sufficient under our Constitution to justify a finding that the death sentence is cruel, inhuman or degrading. But these factors are not to be evaluated in isolation. They must be taken together, and in order to decide whether the threshold set by *section* 11(2) has been crossed they must be evaluated with other relevant factors, including the two fundamental rights on which the accused rely, the right to dignity and the right to life.

[95] The carrying out of the death sentence destroys life, which is protected without reservation under *section* 9 of our Constitution, it annihilates human dignity which is protected under *section* 10, elements of arbitrariness are present in its enforcement and it is irremediable. Taking these factors into account, as well as the assumption that I have made in regard to public opinion in South Africa, and giving the words of *section* 11(2) the broader meaning to which they are entitled at this stage of the enquiry, rather than a narrow meaning, I am satisfied that in the context of our Constitution the death penalty is indeed a cruel, inhuman and degrading punishment.
...

Section 33 and limitation of rights

[98] *Section* 33(1) of the Constitution provides, in part, that:
The rights entrenched in this Chapter may be limited by law of general application, provided that such limitation—
    (a) shall be permissible only to the extent that it is—
        (i)   reasonable; and
        (ii) justifiable in an open and democratic society based on freedom and equality; and
    (b) shall not negate the essential content of the right in question.

[99] *Section* 33(1)(b) goes on to provide that the limitation of certain rights, including the rights referred to in *section* 10 and *section* 11 'shall, in addition to being reasonable as required in paragraph (a)(I), also be necessary'.

[100] Our Constitution deals with the limitation of rights through a general limitations clause... . [T]his calls for a 'two-stage' approach, in which a broad rather than a narrow interpretation is given to the fundamental rights enshrined in Chapter Three, and limitations have to be justified through the application of section 33. In this it differs from the Constitution of the United States, which does not contain a limitation clause, as a result of which courts in that country have been obliged to find limits to constitutional rights through a narrow interpretation of the rights themselves. Although the 'two-stage' approach may often produce the same result as the 'one-stage' approach, this will not always be the case.
...

[102] Under our Constitution, ... [the question] is whether the infliction of death as a punishment for murder has been shown to be both reasonable and necessary, and to be consistent with the other requirements of *section* 33 ... .
...

[106] Although there is a rational connection between capital punishment and the purpose for which it is prescribed, the elements of arbitrariness, unfairness and irrationality in the imposition of the penalty, are factors that would have to be taken into account in the application of the first component of this test. As far as the second component is concerned, the fact that a severe punishment in the form of life imprisonment is available as an alternative sentence, would be relevant to the question whether the death sentence impairs the right as little as possible.
...

Deterrence

[116] The Attorney General attached considerable weight to the need for a deterrent to violent crime. He argued that the countries which had abolished the death penalty were on the whole developed and peaceful countries in which other penalties might be sufficient deterrents. We had not reached that stage of development, he said. If in years to come we did so, we could do away with the death penalty. Parliament could decide when that time has come ... .

[117] ... Without law, individuals in society have no rights. The level of violent crime in our country has reached alarming proportions. It poses a threat to the transition to democracy, and the creation of development opportunities for all, which are primary goals of the Constitution ... .
...

[119] The cause of the high incidence of violent crime cannot simply be attributed to the failure to carry out the death sentences imposed by the courts ... .

[120] Homelessness, unemployment, poverty and the frustration consequent upon such conditions are other causes of the crime wave ... .

[121] We would be deluding ourselves if we were to believe that the execution of the few persons sentenced to death during this period, and of a comparatively few other people each year from now onwards will provide the solution to the unacceptably high rate of crime ... .

[122] The greatest deterrent to crime is the likelihood that offenders will be apprehended, convicted and punished. It is that which is presently lacking in our criminal justice system; and it is at this level and through addressing the causes of crime that the State must seek to combat lawlessness.
...

Retribution

[129] Retribution is one of the objects of punishment, but it carries less weight than deterrence. The righteous anger of family and friends of the murder victim, reinforced by the public abhorrence of vile crimes, is easily translated into a call for vengeance. But capital punishment is not the only way that society has of expressing its moral outrage at the crime that has been committed. We have long outgrown the literal application of the biblical injunction of 'an eye for an eye, and a tooth for a tooth'. Punishment must to some extent be commensurate with the offence, but there is no requirement that it be equivalent or identical to it... . A very long prison sentence is also a way of expressing outrage and visiting retribution upon the criminal.
...

Conclusion

[144] The rights to life and dignity are the most important of all human rights, and the source of all other personal rights in Chapter Three. ... And this must be demonstrated by the State in everything that it does, including the way it punishes criminals ...
...

[146] ... Taking [all the described] factors into account, as well as the elements of arbitrariness and the possibility of error in enforcing the death penalty, the clear and convincing case that is required to justify the death sentence as a penalty for murder, has not been made out. The requirements of section 33(1) have accordingly not been satisfied, and it follows that the provisions of section 277(1)(a) of the Criminal Procedure Act, 1977 must be held to be inconsistent with section 11(2) of the Constitution ... .

FRANCIS KARIOKO MURUATETU V. REPUBLIC
SUPREME COURT OF KENYA [2017] EKLR

[The two petitioners were convicted of murder and sentenced to death pursuant to Section 204 of the Penal Code which states that 'any person convicted of murder shall be sentenced to death'. Before the Supreme Court they challenged the constitutionality of the mandatory death penalty that removes all judicial discretion in sentencing.[2] In 2023, 158 people were reportedly on death row, but no executions had occurred since 1987.]

…

E. ISSUES FOR DETERMINATION

[25] … [T]he following issues [arise] for determination:

a) Whether the mandatory nature of the death penalty provided for in the Penal Code under section 204 is unconstitutional …

F. ANALYSIS

[The Court observed that it would not consider the constitutionality of the death sentence, since the issue did not arise in this appeal.]

i. Violation of the right to fair trial

[27] … [T]he constitutionality of the mandatory nature of the death penalty has engaged many court in various jurisdiction globally. It is the major issue in this appeal. It has also engaged the High Court and the Court of Appeal in many cases in this country resulting in divergent opinions. It started with the Mutiso case … in which the Court of Appeal opined that as it denied an accused person right to fair trial [and was thus] arbitrary and unconstitutional. … [The] Court observed that:

"… section 204 of the Penal Code which provides for a mandatory death sentence is antithetical to the Constitutional provisions on protection against inhuman or degrading punishment or treatment and fair trial. … We declare Section 204 … to the extent it provides that the death penalty is the only sentence in respect of the crime of murder is inconsistent with the letter and spirit of the Constitution …".

[28] That remained the position until the Mwaura case in which the Court of Appeal changed it holding that by the use of the word 'shall' Section 204 of the Penal Code was couched in mandatory terms leaving the court with no discretion but to impose the death penalty. …
…
[Various lower courts subsequently followed this approach.]

[30] … Some Kenyan courts have even observed that mitigating factors in such cases were at best, superfluous in terms of the sentence provided. It therefore serves no purpose for the trial judges to hear mitigating factors from convicts in such cases.

[31] On the international arena, however, most jurisdictions have declared not only the mandatory but also the discretionary death penalty unconstitutional. In *Roberts v. Louisiana*, 431 U.S. 633 (1977) a Louisiana statute provided for the mandatory imposition of the death sentence. Upon challenge, the US Supreme Court declared it unconstitutional since the statute allowed for no consideration of particularized mitigating factors in deciding whether the death sentence should be imposed. In [*Reyes v. the Queen* (2002)], the Privy Council was of the view that a statutory provision that denied the offender an opportunity to persuade the Court why the death sentence should not be passed, denied such an offender his basic humanity. And in *Spence v The Queen; Hughes v the Queen (Spence & Hughes)* (unreported, 2 April 2001) where the constitutionality of the mandatory death sentence for the offence of murder was challenged, the Privy Council held that such sentence did not take into account that

---

[2] See L. Chenwi, 'The Downfall of the Mandatory Death Penalty in Kenya', 63 *J. Af. L.* (2019) 25.

persons convicted of murder could have committed the crime with varying degrees of gravity and culpability. In the words of Byron CJ:

"In order to be exercised in a rational and non-arbitrary manner, the sentencing discretion should be guided by legislative or judicially-prescribed principles and standards, and should be subject to effective judicial review, all with a view to ensuring that the death penalty is imposed in only the most exceptional and appropriate circumstances. There should be a requirement for individualized sentencing in implementing the death penalty."

[32] Two Indian decisions also merit mention. In *Mithu v State of Punjab*, ... 1980, the Indian Supreme Court held that "a law that disallowed mitigation and denied a judicial officer discretion in sentencing was harsh, unfair and just" while in *Bachan Singh v The State of Punjab* ... [1980], it was held that "It is only if the offense is of an exceptionally depraved and heinous character, and constitutes on account of its design and manner of its execution a source of grave danger to the society at large, the Court may impose the death sentence."

[33] The UN ...Human Rights Committee has also had occasion to consider the mandatory death penalty. In case of Eversley Thomson v St. Vincent, Communication No. 806/ 1998U.N. Doc. CCPR/70/806/1998 (2000), it stated that such sentence constituted a violation of Article 26 of the Covenant, since the mandatory nature of the death sentence did not allow the judge to impose a lesser sentence taking into account any mitigating circumstances and denied the offender the most fundamental of right, the right to life, without considering whether this exceptional form of punishment was appropriate in the circumstances of his or her case.

Interrogating Section 204 of the Penal Code

...

[35] To determine the [constitutionality of Section 204 of the Penal Code], it is imperative to consider certain constitutional provisions in relation to the above section. [The court then made reference to: Article 19 (3) (a) which provides that the rights contained in the Bill of Rights "belong to each and every individual and are not granted by the State;" Article 20 stating that the Bill of Rights "applies to all law and binds all state organs and all persons"; Article 28 recognizing every person's inherent dignity; Article 48 mandating "the State to ensure justice for all persons"; Article 50 (1) providing that "Every person has a right to have any dispute that can be resolved by the application of law decided in a fair and public hearing before a court or if appropriate another independent and impartial tribunal or body"; and Article 50 (2) according every accused person the right to a fair trial, including the right "if convicted, to appeal to, or apply for review by, a higher court as prescribed by Law."

[38] Kenya is a signatory to the International Covenant on Civil and Political Rights (ICCPR) since May 1972. ...

[39] The [UN] Commission on Human Rights has recommended the abolition of the death sentence as a mandatory sentence in ... Resolution 2005/59 [urging] all States that still maintain the death penalty:

'...(d) Not to impose the death penalty for any but the most serious crimes ...;

...

... (f) To ensure also that the notion of "most serious crimes" does not go beyond intentional crimes with lethal or extremely grave consequences and that the death penalty is not imposed for non-violent acts such as financial crimes, religious practice or expression of conscience and sexual relations between consenting adults nor as a mandatory sentence.'

[40] These ... provisions ... bring to the fore a number of principles. Firstly, the rights and fundamental freedoms belong to each individual. Secondly, the bill of rights applies to all law and binds all persons. Thirdly, all persons have inherent dignity which must be respected and protected. Fourthly, the State must ensure access to justice to all. Fifthly, every person is entitled to a fair hearing and lastly, the right to a fair trial is non-derogable. For Section 204 of the Penal Code to stand, it must be in accord with these provisions.

[41] It is evident that the trial process does not stop at convicting the accused. ... [T]he principle of fair trial must be accorded to the sentencing stage too.

[42] Pursuant to [the] Laws of Kenya, mitigation is a part of the trial process. ... Section 329 of the Criminal Procedure Code provides:

The court may, before passing sentence, receive such evidence as it thinks fit in order to inform itself as to the proper sentence to be passed.

[43] Therefore, ... the Court ought to take into account the evidence, the nature of the offence and the circumstances of the case in order to arrive at an appropriate sentence. It is not lost on us that these provisions are couched in permissive terms. However, the Court of Appeal has consistently reiterated on the need for noting down mitigating factors. Not only because they might affect the sentence but also for futuristic endeavors such as when the appeal is placed before another body for clemency.
...
[45] [W]hat Section 204 the Penal Code is essentially saying to a convict is that he or she cannot be heard on why, in all the circumstances of his or her case, the death sentence should not be imposed on him or her ... . [W]e cannot decipher the possible rationale for this provision. We think that a person facing the death sentence is most deserving to be heard in mitigation because of the finality of the sentence.

[46] We are of the view that mitigation is an important congruent element of fair trial. The fact that mitigation is not expressly mentioned as a right in the Constitution does not deprive it of its necessity and essence in the fair trial process. In any case, the rights pertaining to fair trial of an accused pursuant to Article 50(2) of the Constitution are not exhaustive.

[47] Indeed the right to fair trial is not just a fundamental right. It is one of the inalienable rights enshrined in Article 10 of the Universal Declaration of Human Rights, and in ... Article 25(c) of the Constitution ... . The right to fair trial is one of the cornerstones of a just and democratic society, without which the Rule of Law and public faith in the justice system would inevitably collapse.

[48] Section 204 of the Penal Code deprives the Court of the use of judicial discretion in a matter of life and death. Such law can only be regarded as harsh, unjust and unfair. The mandatory nature deprives the Courts of their legitimate jurisdiction to exercise discretion not to impose the death sentence in appropriate cases. Where a court listens to mitigating circumstances but has, nonetheless, to impose a set sentence, the sentence imposed fails to conform to the tenets of fair trial ... .
...
[51] The dignity of the person is ignored if the death sentence, which is final and irrevocable is imposed without the individual having any chance to mitigate. We say so because we cannot shut our eyes to the distinct possibility of the differing culpability of different murderers. ... To our minds a formal equal penalty for unequally wicked crimes and criminals is not in keeping with the tenets of fair trial.
...
[54] A fair trial has many facets, and includes mitigation and, the right to appeal or apply for review by a higher Court as prescribed by law. ...

[55] [Michael Edwards] petitioned the Inter-American Commission on Human Rights. He challenged the mandatory death penalty on the basis, inter alia, that his rights to equality before the law and a fair trial enshrined in the American Declaration of the Rights and Duties of Man had been violated. The Commission held at paragraph 137:

" ... Moreover, by reason of its compulsory and automatic application, a mandatory death sentence cannot be the subject of review by a higher court. Once a mandatory sentence is imposed, all that remains for a higher court to review is whether the defendant was found guilty of the crime for which the sentence is mandated."

[56] [Based on the decision of the Inter-American Commission on Human Rights in *Edwards v The Bahamas* (Report No. 48/01, 4th April 2001) [we consider] that Section 204 violates Article 50 (2) (q) of the Constitution

as convicts under it are denied the right to have their sentence reviewed by a higher Court – their appeal is in essence limited to conviction only. …

…

[58] [A]ny law or procedure which when executed culminates in termination of life, ought to be just, fair and reasonable. As a result, due process is made possible by a procedure which allows the Court to assess the appropriateness of the death penalty in relation to the circumstances of the offender and the offence. We are of the view that the mandatory nature of this penalty runs counter to constitutional guarantees enshrining respect for the rule of law.

…

[65] A generous and purposive interpretation is to be given to constitutional provisions that protect human rights. …

…

[67] It is to be noted that the mandatory nature of the death sentence provided for under Section 204 of the Penal Code long predates any international agreements for the protection of Human Rights. … [I]t is indeed a colonial relic that has no place in Kenya today. …

…

[69] Consequently, we find that Section 204 of the Penal Code is inconsistent with the Constitution and invalid … For the avoidance of doubt, this decision does not outlaw the death penalty, which is still applicable as a discretionary maximum punishment.

QUESTION

What are the advantages and disadvantages of basing opposition to the death penalty on (i) the rule of law, (ii) the prohibition of cruel, inhuman, or degrading punishment, or (iii) human dignity?

---

2. The Death Penalty in India

The case of India illustrates a different trajectory from that in South Africa and Kenya. The death penalty dates back to colonial times and, despite many challenges to its legality, it continues to be applied for a variety of crimes. Juveniles and those suffering serious mental illness or insanity are not subject to execution. In practice, relatively few convicted prisoners have actually been executed. For example, in 2016, India imposed 136 new death sentences, had 397 prisoners on death row, and carried out no executions. In the same year, the Supreme Court confirmed the imposition of the death penalty in none of the seven cases it considered. Out of 1,810 death sentences imposed between 2000 and 2014, only four people had been executed as of 2016, and 95 per cent of the sentences had been overturned or commuted by higher courts. A third of death sentences given by trial courts resulted in acquittals at a later stage.[3]

Economic vulnerability and a lack of education are hallmarks of those on death row. The National Law University's *Death Penalty in India Report* found that, of 385 persons on death row nationwide in 2016, almost two-thirds belonged to the 'backward classes,' religious minorities, Dalits and Adivasis. The same number were classified as economically vulnerable sections and over 80 per cent of them had not completed school. A large majority of them had been tortured in custody; less than half could understand legal proceedings; and nearly 70 per cent of them said they hardly had any interaction with their lawyers when their cases were in the higher courts. Only 8 per cent had a prior criminal conviction and 25 per cent were juveniles or very young at the time of the offence. Some 77 per cent said that they had never met their lawyers out of court, and that their interactions in court were 'perfunctory'. Legal aid lawyers were said to have tried to extort money from the families of death-row prisoners, and threatened not to turn up for hearings unless they were paid.

In 2021, the number of prisoners on death row increased by 21 per cent from 2020. The Supreme Court, however, did not confirm any sentences and applied demanding scrutiny in assessing lower court decisions.

---

[3] National Law University, *Death Penalty in India: Annual Statistics Report 2016* (March 2017).

Sexual offences accounted for 54 per cent of all death penalty sentences.[4] In 2015, the Law Commission of India had proposed the abolition of the death penalty in a phased manner, beginning by limiting it to terrorism-related offences.

The Nirbhaya Gang-rape Case

At 9.30 pm on December 16, 2012, a 23-year-old physiotherapy student named Jyoti Singh (originally given the pseudonym of 'Nirbhaya' to protect her identity), and her male companion, were waiting at a bus stop, after having seen a movie. An off-duty charter bus stopped and they boarded. When the man objected that a different route had been taken and the lights in the bus turned off, a fight broke out. The man was severely beaten, the woman was brutally gang-raped by the six occupants of the bus, including being sexually assaulted with an iron rod, their possessions were stolen, they were thrown out of the bus half naked and the bus attempted to run them over. They were found at 11 p.m. by a passerby and taken to hospital. The victim remained in a critical condition until her death on December 29, in Singapore where she had been taken for further treatment.

In response to the incident, massive protests erupted throughout India, and police used water cannons, teargas, and baton charges to control crowds. Metro stations and roads were closed and a limited curfew was imposed. The leader of the parliamentary opposition called for the rapists to be hanged and the Chief Minister of Delhi referred to the city as India's 'rape capital'.

On December 23, 2012, the Government appointed a committee headed by former Chief Justice J. S. Verma, to recommend amendments to the criminal law to provide for quicker trial and enhanced punishment for criminals accused of committing sexual assault against women. It reported one month later, after receiving over 80,000 submissions from civil society. It made wide-ranging recommendations for reform, but it recommended a maximum penalty of life imprisonment for rape, based on considerable evidence that the death penalty did not deter serious crimes.

The committee proposed including new offences relating to stalking, voyeurism and intentional touching, higher penalties for rape and a definition of gang rape in the law. It advocated the punishment of marital rape, as well as gender sensitization measures and police and electoral reforms.[5]

Of the original six defendants, one was tried and sentenced as a juvenile. One committed suicide while awaiting trial, and the remaining four were convicted and sentenced to death in September 2013. Following the rejection of an appeal to the Supreme Court, the four convicted men were hanged on 20 March 2020.

MUKESH & ANR. V. STATE FOR NCT OF DELHI & ORS.
SUPREME COURT OF INDIA (2017) 6 SCC 1

DIPAK MISRA, J. [FOR HIMSELF AND ASHOK BHUSHAN, J.]

…

331. … [In Bachan Singh v. State of Punjab (1980) 2 SCC 684], the Court held thus:

"(a) The normal rule is that the offence of murder shall be punished with the sentence of life imprisonment. …

(b) While considering the question of sentence … the court must have regard to every relevant circumstance relating to the crime as well as the criminal. If the court finds, but not otherwise, that the offence is of an exceptionally depraved and heinous character and constitutes, on account of its design and the manner of its execution, a source of grave danger to the society at large, the court may impose the death sentence."

332. [The Court took note of a list of aggravating circumstances proposed by counsel but concluded that] we would prefer not to fetter judicial discretion by attempting to make an exhaustive enumeration one way or the other."

---

[4] Project 39A, *Death Penalty in India, Annual Statistics Report 2021* (2022) 7.
[5] 'Nirbhaya gangrape case 2012: A look at what all has happened over the years,' *Indian Express*, May 5, 2017.

333. Thereafter, the Court referred to the suggestions pertaining to mitigating circumstances:
...

    (1) That the offence was committed under the influence of extreme mental or emotional disturbance.
    (2) The age of the accused. If the accused is young or old, he shall not be sentenced to death.
    (3) The probability that the accused would not commit criminal acts of violence as would constitute a continuing threat to society.
    (4) The probability that the accused can be reformed and rehabilitated. ...
    (5) ... [T]he accused believed that he was morally justified in committing the offence.
    (6) That the accused acted under the duress or domination of another person.
    (7) That the condition of the accused showed that he was mentally defective ......

334. In the said case, the Court has also held thus:

"... A real and abiding concern for the dignity of human life postulates resistance to taking a life through law's instrumentality. That ought not to be done save in the rarest of rare cases when the alternative option is unquestionably foreclosed."

335. In [Machhi Singh and Ors. v. State of Punjab (1983) 3 SCC 470], a three-Judge Bench has explained the concept of 'rarest of the rare cases' by observing thus:

"The reasons why the community as a whole does not endorse the humanistic approach reflected in 'death sentence-in-no-case' doctrine are not far to seek. In the first place, the very humanistic edifice is constructed on the foundation of 'reverence for life' principle. When a member of the community violates this very principle by killing another member, the society may not feel itself bound by the shackles of this doctrine. Secondly, it has to be realised that every member of the community is able to live with safety without his or her own life being endangered because of the protective arm of the community and on account of the rule of law enforced by it. The very existence of the rule of law and the fear of being brought to book operates as a deterrent for those who have no scruples in killing others if it suits their ends. Every member of the community owes a debt to the community for this protection."

336. Thereafter, the Court [added that the death penalty may be imposed] 'in the rarest of rare cases' when its collective conscience is so shocked that it will expect the holders of the judicial power centre to inflict death penalty irrespective of their personal opinion as regards desirability or otherwise of retaining death penalty."

337. [In Macchi Singh], stress was laid on certain aspects, namely, the manner of commission of the murder, the motive for commission of the murder, anti-social or socially abhorrent nature of the crime, magnitude of the crime and personality of the victim of murder.

338. [The Court concluded that] ...

(iv) A balance sheet of aggravating and mitigating circumstances has to be drawn up and in doing so the mitigating circumstances have to be accorded full weightage and a just balance has to be struck between the aggravating and the mitigating circumstances before the option is exercised."
...

356. It is necessary to state here that in the instant case, the brutal, barbaric and diabolic nature of the crime is evincible from the acts committed by the accused persons, ... [T]he gross sadistic and beastly instinctual pleasures came to the forefront when they, after ravishing her, thought it to be just a matter of routine to throw her along with her friend out of the bus and crush them. The casual manner with which she was treated and the devilish manner in which they played with her identity and dignity is humanly inconceivable. It sounds like a story from a different world where humanity has been treated with irreverence. The appetite for sex, the hunger for violence, the position of the empowered and the attitude of perversity, to say the least, are bound to shock the collective conscience which knows not what to do. It is manifest that the wanton lust, the servility to absolutely unchained carnal desire and slavery to the loathsome beastiality of passion ruled the mindset of the

appellants to commit a crime which can summon with immediacy "tsunami" of shock in the mind of the collective and destroy the civilised marrows of the milieu in entirety.

357. When we cautiously, consciously and anxiously weigh the aggravating circumstances and the mitigating factors, we are compelled to arrive at the singular conclusion that the aggravating circumstances outweigh the mitigating circumstances …. Therefore, we conclude and hold that the High Court has correctly confirmed the death penalty … .

R. BANUMATHI, J. [CONCURRING]

[1.] … I entirely agree with the reasoning [and conclusions above]. However, in view of the … role of Judiciary in addressing crime against women, I would prefer to give my additional reasoning for concurrence.
…

146. … The present case clearly comes within the category of 'rarest of rare case' … . … If the dreadfulness displayed by the accused in committing the gang-rape, unnatural sex, insertion of iron rod in the private parts of the victim does not fall in the 'rarest of rare category', then one may wonder what else would fall in that category. …

147. The incident of gang-rape … causes ripples in the conscience of society and serious doubts are raised as to whether we really live in a civilized society and whether both men and women feel the same sense of liberty and freedom … . [A]n unknown sense of insecurity and helplessness grabs the entire society, women in particular, and the only succour people look for, is the State to take command of the situation and remedy it effectively.

148. The statistics of National Crime Records Bureau … show that despite the progress made by women in education and in various fields and changes brought in ideas of women's rights, respect for women is on the decline and crimes against women are on the increase. … [I]t becomes important to ensure that gender justice does not remain only on paper.

149. We have a responsibility to set good values and guidance for posterity. … Crime against women not only affects women's self esteem and dignity but also degrades the pace of societal development. I hope that this gruesome incident … will be an eye-opener for a mass movement "to end violence against women" and "respect for women and her dignity" and sensitizing public at large on gender justice. … The battle for gender justice can be won only with strict implementation of legislative provisions, sensitization of public, taking other pro-active steps at all levels for combating violence against women and ensuring widespread attitudinal changes and comprehensive change in the existing mind set. …

RESPONSES TO THE NIRBHAYA CASE[6]

In an article titled 'Justice?: Why Death Penalty is a Weak Response to Structural Violence' posted on the Youth Ki Awaaz website on 25 March 2020[7], a contributor with the username pinjratod highlighted the gendered and other structural assumptions that underpin reactions to sexual violence and demands for the death penalty to be imposed:

> … Though this execution is using the trope of women's safety and rights, we need to understand that the popular outrage against rape in this case and generally in society is often rooted not so much in respecting the bodily integrity of women but the notions of honour and chastity of women. This chastity is seen to be 'defiled' by the act of rape. Rape is, therefore, exceptionalised and produces greater outrage than other acts of violence on women, which may be equally brutal and life-threatening.

---

[6] See generally B. Rajan, D. Kundu, and S. Sarkar, 'Rape, Popular Culture, and Nirbhaya: A Study of *India's Daughter and Delhi Crime*', J. Commun. Inq. (2022).

[7] Available at https://www.youthkiawaaz.com/2020/03/justice-is-not-retribution-oppose-the-death-penalty-in-the-name-of-womens-security/

Therefore, during the public outrage in 2012, feminist voices asking for understanding and dealing with the structural nature of sexual violence on women were drowned by the clamour of demands for the death penalty, castration, etc. To satisfy this sense of public outrage or 'collective conscience', a death sentence was pronounced for the convicts, which was justified by the kind brutality meted out to the victim.

…

The demand for the death penalty for the rape convicts operates on the principle of externalising the problem of sexual violence in our everyday structures and lives and locates it on a handful of convicts identified in the most publicised and brutal rape cases. As if, on exterminating these convicts can rid us of the problem of rape altogether.

Yet rape continues unabated and only becomes more brutal. Are such exemplary punishments not just a Band-Aid for a larger structural problem done to ease public rage over an issue or to reaffirm public faith in the State that refuses to take any effective structural measures for ensuring safety and well being of women?

… [T]he crime which is considered worthy of being treated as 'rarest of the rare' is constituted more by social and political exigencies than by any real response to pain and brutality inflicted.

…

Demands for death penalty are seldom made if the perpetrators are from socially and politically powerful backgrounds and more often enjoy state impunity … .

…

The Muslim lorry driver, the security guard or the migrant worker becomes the "other", the villain from whom the women need to be protected—completely glossing over the statistical evidence that in most cases of sexual violence the perpetrators are known to the victims.

An earlier editorial addressing the acquittal of six men, sentenced to death in a separate case, opined on the legal errors and faulty evidence that are endemic in court cases awarding the death penalty, and on the extent to which capital sentences fall disproportionately on the dispossessed:

ECONOMIC AND POLITICAL WEEKLY, DEADLY ERRORS IN JUDGMENT VOL. 54, NO. 11 (16 MARCH 2019)

… [T]he Supreme Court has set aside its own judgment that had confirmed the conviction of and death penalty for the accused in *Ankush Maruthi Shinde v State of Maharashtra*.

The litany of deadly horrors in this case is long. A poverty-stricken family is set upon by unknown assailants who rob, assault, and murder them over the course of one horrific night. The police … concoct an entirely false case against six innocent men, only because they belong to a "criminal tribe." No actual evidence is unearthed to link them to the scene of the crime or their remote involvement in the matter. "Eyewitnesses" repeatedly change their statements as the circumstance warrants. Yet, shockingly, the trial court, the high court, and the Supreme Court confirm their convictions on the basis of this thin and unreliable "evidence."

The men are on death row for more than a decade, living solitary, tortured, and pitiable lives in jails. … When three of them find their death sentences commuted by the Bombay High Court, the Supreme Court overturns such commutation and awards the death penalty without hearing them at all. The Supreme Court then dismisses their review petitions without an open court hearing.

It was only when the curative petition in the Supreme Court was placed before a totally different bench and the "error" was discovered that the wheels of justice finally began to turn. ... In the end, the Supreme Court has acquitted all the accused, directed the state of Maharashtra to pay compensation to them, and attempted to hold the police accountable for this callous lapse. What it has not done is offer any sort of mea culpa for its own failings in this case.

While the Supreme Court is fond of justifying the death penalty on the grounds that it must be applied only in the "rarest of rare cases" and after carefully weighing all mitigating and aggravating factors in a case, in reality it has been happy to discard the law at the drop of a hat. The judgment awarding the death penalty to the convicts in the "Nirbhaya" case, for example, is long on impassioned rhetoric and short on the law when it comes to awarding the death penalty. ...

... [I]t is safe to assume that a large number of such death penalties have been awarded by the courts in cases with grievously faulty trials.

And, yet, this hardly seems to inform bloodthirsty calls in the public for increasing the imposition of death penalty by the courts. Politicians of all stripes are happy to accede to these demands, which are ignorant or unconcerned about the vagaries of a broken criminal justice system that only ends up creating more victims than punishing any hardened criminals. ...

With the criminal justice system being what it is, it is hard to see the death penalty as anything but an institutionalised form of murder, one that unerringly chooses its victims from the oppressed and disenfranchised sections of society. ...

3. Drugs and the Death Penalty

In 2018, the ICCPR Committee adopted General Comment No. 36 on the right to life. Article 6 of the ICCPR provides, inter alia, that: '1. Every human being has the inherent right to life. This right shall be protected by law. No one shall be arbitrarily deprived of his life.'; '2. In countries which have not abolished the death penalty, sentence of death may be imposed only for the most serious crimes ...'; and '5. Sentence of death shall not be imposed for crimes committed by persons below eighteen years of age and shall not be carried out on pregnant women.' The relevant part of the Committee's analysis follows:

33. ... Given the anomalous nature of regulating the application of the death penalty in an instrument enshrining the right to life, the contents of paragraph 2 have to be narrowly construed.

34. ... States parties that have abolished the death penalty cannot deport, extradite or otherwise transfer persons to a country in which they are facing criminal charges that carry the death penalty, unless credible and effective assurances against the imposition of the death penalty have been obtained. ...

35. The term "the most serious crimes" must be read restrictively and appertain only to crimes of extreme gravity involving intentional killing. Crimes not resulting directly and intentionally in death, such as attempted murder, corruption and other economic and political crimes, armed robbery, piracy, abduction, drug and sexual offences, although serious in nature, can never serve as the basis, within the framework of article 6, for the imposition of the death penalty. In the same vein, a limited degree of involvement or of complicity in the commission of even the most serious crimes, such as providing the physical means for the commission of murder, cannot justify the imposition of the death penalty. ...

36. Under no circumstances can the death penalty ever be applied as a sanction against conduct the very criminalization of which violates the Covenant,

> including adultery, homosexuality, apostasy, establishing political opposition
> groups or offending a head of State. …

In 2022, the UN reported that at least 35 states and territories retained the death penalty for drug-related offences (UN Doc. A/77/274 (2022)) and Amnesty International noted that 325 people were executed for drug-related offences in 2022, or 37% of known global executions. There were 255 in Iran, 57 in Saudi Arabia and 11 in Singapore.

Eight out of eleven Southeast Asian countries retain the death penalty for drug offences, although the majority do not generally carry it out. The most common arguments in favour of it are that it succeeds as a deterrent and that public opinion demands it. British entrepreneur, Richard Branson, described Singapore's April 2022 execution of a Malaysian man who had attempted to smuggle the equivalent of three tablespoons of heroin, as 'a serious stain on Singapore's reputation'. Critics alleged, and the government denied, that the man had learning difficulties. A story in *The Guardian* (Rebecca Ratcliffe, 'Richard Branson refuses Singapore invitation to debate death penalty', 31 October 2022) reported that Branson was subsequently invited by the Ministry of Home Affairs to debate the Minister live on television.

The Ministry was quoted as saying that, while Branson's views may be widely held in the UK, 'we do not accept that Mr. Branson or others in the west are entitled to impose their values on other societies. Nor do we believe that a country that prosecuted two wars in China in the 19th century to force the Chinese to accept opium imports has any moral right to lecture Asians on drugs'. It added that its 'priority is to protect Singapore and Singaporeans from the scourge of drugs'.

Branson declined the offer, saying that: '[a] television debate – limited in time and scope, always at risk of prioritising personalities over issues – cannot do the complexity of the death penalty any service. It reduces nuanced discourse to soundbites, turns serious debate into spectacle.' Instead, he called on the government to engage Singaporean activists and human rights lawyers in such a debate, rather than ignoring or harassing them. The story noted that following the execution, 'more than 400 people turned out for a rare protest in April at Speakers' Corner at Hong Lim Park, the only place where demonstrations are permitted in Singapore, to call for executions to be halted.' It added that '[a]t least 10 death row inmates have since been executed. Death penalty cases are rarely reported in any detail in Singapore's tightly controlled media.'

A survey of public opinion in Singapore, reported in Wing-Cheong Chan et al., 'How Strong Is Public Support for the Death Penalty in Singapore?', 13 *Asian Criminology* (2018) 91, at 101 concluded that:

> … Singaporeans apparently favoured the death penalty despite admitting that they knew
> very little about it, [were] not interested in it and could not give an accurate estimate of
> the number of persons executed. …

> … There was a much lower support for the death penalty when respondents were faced
> with scenarios of cases—all of which would have merited the mandatory sentence under
> the current Singapore law—than the proportion who said they favoured it in the abstract.
> This was particularly so for drug trafficking and firearm offences. This finding is
> consistent with surveys in other places which also showed that support for the death
> penalty dropped when respondents were given alternative sentencing options …

Another analysis, focused on Vietnam, concluded that although the government had made a number of incremental changes to move closer to the goal of abolition of the death penalty for drug offences, abolition remained far away. Noting that the number of people executed each year remains a state secret, the authors called on Vietnam to 'make its statistics and data on the death penalty publicly available and accessible' and to facilitate both national and international discourse. The latter would 'give the impression of a responsible nation trying to bring its legislation in line with universally recognised standards.' They also called for 'a nationwide survey on drug control measures in relation to three capital drug crimes' since existing surveys are outdated and do not focus on the death penalty (Tien Duc Nguyen and Thu Thuy Thi Tran, 'The Limits of Vietnam's Incrementalism towards the Abolition of Capital Punishment for Drug Offenses', *Asian J. Comp. L.* (2022) 1).

QUESTIONS

1. What weight should courts accord to public opinion in relation to the imposition of the death penalty? Compare the approaches in Makwanyane and Mukesh. How important is transparency and informed public debate?

2. Does the concept of the 'rarest of the rare' provide a meaningful safeguard against the arbitrary imposition of the death penalty?

3. Is the Human Rights Committee's interpretation of 'the most serious crimes' too strict? Should weight be given to different value systems in that context?

---

4. The Death Penalty in the United States

In 2021, 18 people were sentenced to death. Five states (Alabama, Mississippi, Missouri, Oklahoma and Texas) and the federal government carried out 11 executions in 2021, the fewest since 1988. The federal executions included persons with severe mental illness, intellectual disability, and unexamined evidence of innocence. At the state level, all but one of those executed had significant impairments such as serious mental illness; brain injury or damage; an IQ in the intellectually disabled range; or chronic serious childhood trauma, neglect and abuse.

The majority of those sentenced to death in 2021 (10 of 18, 55.6 per cent) were Black or Latinx; 56 per cent of those executed (6 of 11) were Black. 83.3 per cent of the death sentences and half of the executions involving Black men were for interracial offenses, as were three of the four new death sentences imposed on Latino defendants. Since 1972, 186 wrongfully-convicted people have been exonerated from death row, amounting to one exoneration for every 8.3 executions.[8]

The following opinion of the U.S. Supreme Court makes clear how dramatically the United States differs from most other states.

ROPER V. SIMMONS
SUPREME COURT OF THE UNITED STATES, 543 U.S. 551 (2005)

OPINION OF JUSTICE KENNEDY FOR THE COURT:

This case requires us to address ... whether it is permissible under the Eighth and Fourteenth Amendments to the Constitution of the United States to execute a juvenile offender who was older than 15 but younger than 18 when he committed a capital crime. In *Stanford v. Kentucky*, 492 U.S. 361 (1989), a divided Court rejected the proposition that the Constitution bars capital punishment for juvenile offenders in this age group. We reconsider the question.

[Simmons committed murder at age 17 when a junior (the penultimate year) in secondary school. He was sentenced to death when he was 18. The murder was callous and premeditated. At trial, the judge instructed the jury that it could consider Simmons's age as a mitigating factor in sentencing. The jury recommended the death penalty, which the trial judge imposed. The Missouri Supreme Court affirmed.]

After these proceedings in Simmons' case had run their course, this Court held that the Eighth and Fourteenth Amendments prohibit the execution of a mentally retarded person. *Atkins v. Virginia*, 536 U.S. 304 (2002). Simmons filed a new petition for state postconviction relief, arguing that the reasoning of *Atkins* established

---

[8] Death Penalty Information Center, *The Death Penalty in 2021: Year End Report* (2022).

that the Constitution prohibits the execution of a juvenile who was under 18 when the crime was committed. [The Missouri Supreme Court agreed, and resentenced Simmons to 'life imprisonment without eligibility for probation, parole, or release except by act of the Governor'.]

The Eighth Amendment provides: "Excessive bail shall not be required, nor excessive fines imposed, nor cruel and unusual punishments inflicted." The provision is applicable to the States through the Fourteenth Amendment. As the Court explained in *Atkins*, the Eighth Amendment guarantees individuals the right not to be subjected to excessive sanctions. The right flows from the basic "precept of justice that punishment for crime should be graduated and proportioned to [the] offense." 536 U.S. at 311. By protecting even those convicted of heinous crimes, the Eighth Amendment reaffirms the duty of the government to respect the dignity of all persons.

The prohibition against "cruel and unusual punishments," like other expansive language in the Constitution, must be interpreted according to its text, by considering history, tradition, and precedent, and with due regard for its purpose and function in the constitutional design. To implement this framework we have established the propriety and affirmed the necessity of referring to "the evolving standards of decency that mark the progress of a maturing society" to determine which punishments are so disproportionate as to be cruel and unusual. *Trop v. Dulles*, 356 U.S. 86, 100–101 (1958) (plurality opinion).

In *Thompson v. Oklahoma*, 487 U.S. 815 (1988), a plurality of the Court determined that our standards of decency do not permit the execution of any offender under the age of 16 at the time of the crime. The plurality opinion explained that no death penalty State that had given express consideration to a minimum age for the death penalty had set the age lower than 16. The plurality also observed that "[t]he conclusion that it would offend civilized standards of decency to execute a person who was less than 16 years old at the time of his or her offense is consistent with the views that have been expressed by respected professional organizations, by other nations that share our Anglo-American heritage, and by the leading members of the Western European community." The opinion further noted that juries imposed the death penalty on offenders under 16 with exceeding rarity; the last execution of an offender for a crime committed under the age of 16 had been carried out in 1948, 40 years prior.

Bringing its independent judgment to bear on the permissibility of the death penalty for a 15-year-old offender, the *Thompson* plurality stressed that "[t]he reasons why juveniles are not trusted with the privileges and responsibilities of an adult also explain why their irresponsible conduct is not as morally reprehensible as that of an adult." According to the plurality, the lesser culpability of offenders under 16 made the death penalty inappropriate as a form of retribution, while the low likelihood that offenders under 16 engaged in "the kind of cost-benefit analysis that attaches any weight to the possibility of execution" made the death penalty ineffective as a means of deterrence ... .

The next year, in *Stanford v. Kentucky* [*supra*], the Court, over a dissenting opinion joined by four Justices, referred to contemporary standards of decency in this country and concluded the Eighth and Fourteenth Amendments did not proscribe the execution of juvenile offenders over 15 but under 18. The Court noted that 22 of the 37 death penalty States permitted the death penalty for 16-year-old offenders, and, among these 37 States, 25 permitted it for 17-year-old offenders. These numbers, in the Court's view, indicated there was no national consensus "sufficient to label a particular punishment cruel and unusual." ...

The same day the Court decided *Stanford*, it held that the Eighth Amendment did not mandate a categorical exemption from the death penalty for the mentally retarded. *Penry v. Lynaugh*, 492 U.S. 302 (1989). In reaching this conclusion it stressed that only two States had enacted laws banning the imposition of the death penalty on a mentally retarded person convicted of a capital offense. According to the Court, "the two state statutes prohibiting execution of the mentally retarded, even when added to the 14 States that have rejected capital punishment completely, [did] not provide sufficient evidence at present of a national consensus."

Three Terms ago the subject was reconsidered in *Atkins*. We held that standards of decency have evolved since *Penry* and now demonstrate that the execution of the mentally retarded is cruel and unusual punishment. The Court noted objective indicia of society's standards, as expressed in legislative enactments and state practice with respect to executions of the mentally retarded. When *Atkins* was decided only a minority of States permitted the practice, and even in those States it was rare. On the basis of these indicia the Court determined that executing mentally retarded offenders "has become truly unusual, and it is fair to say that a national consensus has developed against it."

... The *Atkins* Court ... returned to the rule, established in decisions predating *Stanford*, that "the Constitution contemplates that in the end our own judgment will be brought to bear on the question of the acceptability of the death penalty under the Eighth Amendment." Mental retardation, the Court said, diminishes personal culpability even if the offender can distinguish right from wrong. The impairments of mentally retarded offenders make it less defensible to impose the death penalty as retribution for past crimes and less likely that the death penalty will have a real deterrent effect ... .

...

III

A

The evidence of national consensus against the death penalty for juveniles is similar, and in some respects parallel, to the evidence *Atkins* held sufficient to demonstrate a national consensus against the death penalty for the mentally retarded. When *Atkins* was decided, 30 States prohibited the death penalty for the mentally retarded. This number comprised 12 that had abandoned the death penalty altogether, and 18 that maintained it but excluded the mentally retarded from its reach. By a similar calculation in this case, 30 States prohibit the juvenile death penalty, comprising 12 that have rejected the death penalty altogether and 18 that maintain it but, by express provision or judicial interpretation, exclude juveniles from its reach. *Atkins* emphasized that even in the 20 States without formal prohibition, the practice of executing the mentally retarded was infrequent... . In the present case, too, even in the 20 States without a formal prohibition on executing juveniles, the practice is infrequent ... .

... Impressive in *Atkins* was the rate of abolition of the death penalty for the mentally retarded. Sixteen States that permitted the execution of the mentally retarded at the time of Penry [*supra*] had prohibited the practice by the time we heard *Atkins*. By contrast, the rate of change in reducing the incidence of the juvenile death penalty, or in taking specific steps to abolish it, has been slower. Five States that allowed the juvenile death penalty at the time of *Stanford* have abandoned it in the intervening 15 years — four through legislative enactments and one through judicial decisions.

Though less dramatic ... we still consider the change from *Stanford* to this case to be significant... . [T]he same consistency of direction of change has been demonstrated ... .

...

B

A majority of States have rejected the imposition of the death penalty on juvenile offenders under 18, and we now hold this is required by the Eighth Amendment.

Because the death penalty is the most severe punishment, the Eighth Amendment applies to it with special force... . Capital punishment must be limited to those offenders who commit "a narrow category of the most serious crimes" and whose extreme culpability makes them "the most deserving of execution." This principle is implemented throughout the capital sentencing process ... .

Three general differences between juveniles under 18 and adults demonstrate that juvenile offenders cannot with reliability be classified among the worst offenders. First, as any parent knows and as the scientific and sociological studies respondent and his *amici* cite tend to confirm, "[a] lack of maturity and an underdeveloped sense of responsibility are found in youth more often than in adults and are more understandable among the young. These qualities often result in impetuous and ill-considered actions and decisions." ... It has been noted that "adolescents are overrepresented statistically in virtually every category of reckless behavior." ...

The second area of difference is that juveniles are more vulnerable or susceptible to negative influences and outside pressures, including peer pressure... .

The third broad difference is that the character of a juvenile is not as well formed as that of an adult. The personality traits of juveniles are more transitory, less fixed.

... The reality that juveniles still struggle to define their identity means it is less supportable to conclude that even a heinous crime committed by a juvenile is evidence of irretrievably depraved character. From a moral standpoint it would be misguided to equate the failings of a minor with those of an adult, for a greater possibility exists that a minor's character deficiencies will be reformed ... .

Once the diminished culpability of juveniles is recognized, it is evident that the penological justifications for the death penalty apply to them with lesser force than to adults ... .

As for deterrence, it is unclear whether the death penalty has a significant or even measurable deterrent effect on juveniles, as counsel for the petitioner acknowledged at oral argument... . [I]t is worth noting that the punishment of life imprisonment without the possibility of parole is itself a severe sanction, in particular for a young person.

Drawing the line at 18 years of age is subject, of course, to the objections always raised against categorical rules... . The age of 18 is the point where society draws the line for many purposes between childhood and adulthood. It is, we conclude, the age at which the line for death eligibility ought to rest.

...

IV

Our determination that the death penalty is disproportionate punishment for offenders under 18 finds confirmation in the stark reality that the United States is the only country in the world that continues to give official sanction to the juvenile death penalty. This reality does not become controlling, for the task of interpreting the Eighth Amendment remains our responsibility. Yet at least from the time of the Court's decision in *Trop* [*supra*], the Court has referred to the laws of other countries and to international authorities as instructive for its interpretation of the Eighth Amendment ...

... Article 37 of the United Nations Convention on the Rights of the Child, which every country in the world has ratified save for the United States and Somalia, contains an express prohibition on capital punishment for crimes committed by juveniles under 18. ... Parallel prohibitions are contained in other significant international covenants. See [ICCPR], Art. 6(5), 999 U.N.T.S., at 175 (prohibiting capital punishment for anyone under 18 at the time of offense) (signed and ratified by the United States subject to a reservation regarding Article 6(5) ... .

... [O]nly seven countries other than the United States have executed juvenile offenders since 1990: Iran, Pakistan, Saudi Arabia, Yemen, Nigeria, the Democratic Republic of Congo, and China. Since then each of these countries has either abolished capital punishment for juveniles or made public disavowal of the practice. In sum, it is fair to say that the United States now stands alone in a world that has turned its face against the juvenile death penalty.

... [T]he United Kingdom abolished the juvenile death penalty before [the UN] covenants came into being. The United Kingdom's experience bears particular relevance here in light of the historic ties between our countries and in light of the Eighth Amendment's own origins. The Amendment was modeled on a parallel provision in the English Declaration of Rights of 1689, which provided: "[E]xcessive Bail ought not to be required nor excessive Fines imposed; nor cruel and unusuall Punishments inflicted." ...

It is proper that we acknowledge the overwhelming weight of international opinion against the juvenile death penalty... . The opinion of the world community, while not controlling our outcome, does provide respected and significant confirmation for our own conclusions.

... It does not lessen our fidelity to the Constitution or our pride in its origins to acknowledge that the express affirmation of certain fundamental rights by other nations and peoples simply underscores the centrality of those same rights within our own heritage of freedom.

...

JUSTICE O'CONNOR (DISSENTING)

...

... [T]he evidence of an international consensus does not alter my determination that the Eighth Amendment does not, at this time, forbid capital punishment of 17-year-old murderers in all cases.

Nevertheless, I disagree with Justice Scalia's contention that foreign and international law have no place in our Eighth Amendment jurisprudence. Over the course of nearly half a century, the Court has consistently referred to foreign and international law as relevant to its assessment of evolving standards of decency. This inquiry reflects the special character of the Eighth Amendment, which, as the Court has long held, draws its meaning directly from the maturing values of civilized society... . But this Nation's evolving understanding of human dignity certainly is neither wholly isolated from, nor inherently at odds with, the values prevailing in other countries. On the contrary, we should not be surprised to find congruence between domestic and international values, especially where the international community has reached clear agreement — expressed in international law or in the domestic laws of individual countries — that a particular form of punishment is inconsistent with fundamental human rights. At least, the existence of an international consensus of this nature can serve to confirm the reasonableness of a consonant and genuine American consensus. The instant case presents no such domestic consensus, however ... .

...

JUSTICE SCALIA (WITH WHOM THE CHIEF JUSTICE AND JUSTICE THOMAS JOIN, DISSENTING)

...

Though the views of our own citizens are essentially irrelevant to the Court's decision today, the views of other countries and the so-called international community take center stage.

...

More fundamentally, however, the basic premise of the Court's argument — that American law should conform to the laws of the rest of the world — ought to be rejected out of hand. In fact the Court itself does not believe it. In many significant respects the laws of most other countries differ from our law — including not only such explicit provisions of our Constitution as the right to jury trial and grand jury indictment, but even many interpretations of the Constitution prescribed by this Court itself. The Court-pronounced exclusionary rule, for example, is distinctively American ... .

...

... I do not believe that approval by "other nations and peoples" should buttress our commitment to American principles any more than (what should logically follow) disapproval by "other nations and peoples" should weaken that commitment. More importantly, however, the Court's statement flatly misdescribes what is going on here. Foreign sources are cited today, *not* to underscore our "fidelity" to the Constitution, our "pride in its origins," and "our own [American] heritage." To the contrary, they are cited to *set aside* the centuries-old American practice — a practice still engaged in by a large majority of the relevant States — of letting a jury of 12 citizens decide whether, in the particular case, youth should be the basis for withholding the death penalty. What these foreign sources "affirm," rather than repudiate, is the Justices' own notion of how the world ought to be, and their diktat that it shall be so henceforth in America ... .

...

* * *

Justice Scalia's argument, reiterated in many other contexts, has drawn strong criticism. The Supreme Court has, over the course of many decades, referred to foreign law and no objection was raised until 1988. But Jeremy Waldron, in 'Foreign Law and the Modern *Ius Gentium*', in M. Andenas and D. Fairgrieve (eds.), *Courts and Comparative Law* (2015) 550, has also pointed out that 'the Supreme Court in *Roper* failed to articulate any general ideas or standards by which its use of foreign law might be evaluated.' His own analysis acknowledges that '[n]o crisp or precise litmus test defines the sort of international consensus that makes up ius gentium [the law of nations] on any particular subject.' Because interpretation thus inevitably plays an important role, cherry-picking of favorable foreign cases is always a risk. But, for Waldron, it depends on how law is understood:

The real contrast between those who oppose and those who defend the use of foreign law in American legal reasoning is not that jurists in the first group are parochial and the second cosmopolitan. It is rather this contrast between law as will and law as reason. Those who approach the law as a matter of will do not see any reason why expressions of will elsewhere in the world should affect our expressions of will in America. But those who see law as a matter of reason may well be willing to approach it in a scientific spirit that relies not just on our own reasoning but on some rational relation between what we are wrestling with and what others have figured out.

In the same volume, Thomas Graziano, in 'Is it Legitimate and Beneficial for Judges to Compare?' (at 26) lists several other commonly invoked arguments against the use of foreign law. They include: (i) foreign law lacks democratic legitimacy; (ii) invoking foreign law undermines the intrinsic coherence of any given national legal system; (iii) courts weigh a range of factors that are specific to the national situation and the resulting decisions are not readily transferable; (iv) 'legal science' is a distinctively national science; and (v) judges lack adequate knowledge of foreign law and foreign languages.

Based on a survey of the practice of courts, particularly supreme courts, Graziano identifies the following uses of a comparative approach (at 52):

- in order to demonstrate that the domestic law is fully in line with modern international trends;

- to complement the historical method of interpretation of domestic law;

- to discover and demonstrate the diversity of solutions from which the courts may choose;

- to benefit from experiences made abroad and to avoid reinventing the wheel again and again;

- to sharpen one's own understanding of certain legal problems and to compare the national solution with differing foreign solutions in order to highlight the particularities of the domestic law;

- to counter arguments that a given solution will lead to harmful or disastrous results;

- to find legal support for a value judgment by the court; and finally,

- to justify changes to domestic case law or to confront new problems, introduce new institutions or remedies.

In his Hamlin Lectures, Lord Bingham, former Lord Chief Justice of England and Wales (Thomas Bingham, *Widening Horizons: The Influence of Comparative Law and International Law on Domestic Law* (2010) 6), commented that '[i]n no other field of intellectual endeavor – be it science, medicine, philosophy, literature, architecture, art, music, engineering or sociology – would ideas or insights be rejected simply because they were of foreign origin … [I]t would be strange if in this field alone practitioners and academics were obliged to ignore developments elsewhere, or at least to regard them as of no practical consequence. Such an approach can only impoverish our law; it cannot enrich it.' Bingham concluded his lectures (at 83) by quoting Nobel laureate Amartya Sen: 'Even though contemporary attacks on intellectual globalisation tend to come not only from traditional isolationists but also from modern separatists, we have to recognize that our global civilization is a world heritage – not just a collection of disparate local cultures.'

QUESTIONS

1. How would you explain the contrast between the reluctance of most U.S. Supreme Court justices to invoke international standards or foreign judgments and the apparent enthusiasm of courts in South Africa, Kenya and elsewhere to do so?9

2. How do you react to the idea that finding 'consensus' is very helpful or indispensable to concluding that capital punishment is unconstitutional in a given context? Why are the 50 states the appropriate accounting units (as opposed, say, to the total population in states going one or the other way on the issue)? How large a majority (of states, population, etc.) constitutes a consensus? Is not a trend over a few decades more compelling than the 'consensus' at a given moment? Why should consensus be decisive for a justice who follows a different approach to the question of constitutionality?

Racial and Cultural Underpinnings of the Death Penalty

The materials that follow are designed to put the death penalty debate in a broader perspective. Carol Steiker and Jordan Steiker trace the deep role played by racism in the American context, and David Garland asks why the death penalty has been so enduring when so few people are ever actually executed in the United States. Finally, Austin Sarat compares U.S. policy in this area with European approaches. But first, the Death Penalty Information Center's report, *Facts about the Death Penalty* (April 10, 2024) takes an instrumentalist approach, in the hope that those who might otherwise support the death penalty will conclude that it is simply too costly:

- Capital trials cost more than non-capital cases because of higher costs for prosecution and defense lawyers; time consuming pre-trial investigation; lengthy jury selection process for death-qualification; enhanced security requirements; longer trials because of bifurcated proceedings; solitary confinement incarceration; and necessary appeals to ensure fairness.

- An economic analysis of independent research studies completed in 15 death penalty states from 2001-2017 found that the average difference in case-level costs for seeking the death penalty was just over $700,000. …

- Oklahoma capital cases cost, on average, 3.2 times more than non-capital cases. …

- Defense costs for death penalty trials in Kansas averaged about $400,000 per case, compared to $100,000 per case when the death penalty was not sought.

- A study in California revealed that the cost of the death penalty in the state has been over $4 billion since 1978. …

- A report by the Administrative Office of the U.S. Courts in 2010 found that seeking a federal death sentence costs 8 times more than seeking a life sentence.

A historical perspective on the role of race is provided by Carol S. Steiker and Jordan M. Steiker, in 'The Rise, Fall, and Afterlife of the Death Penalty in the United States', 3 *Annual Rev. Criminol.* (2020) 299 at 304:

> Capital punishment in the antebellum South was an essential part of maintaining the slave economy … Whereas the vast majority of whites executed in the antebellum South were punished for murder, blacks were also frequently executed for rape, slave revolt, attempted murder, burglary, and arson. Owners of executed slaves were compensated by

---

9 For a comparison of the United States and South Africa, see M. Ndulo, 'International and Foreign Law in Domestic Constitutional Law', in A. L. Cantillo, et al (eds.), *Constitutionalism: Old Dilemmas, New Insights* (2021) 373.

the state to discourage shielding their slaves from the harsh, racialized criminal justice system.

Following the adoption of the Fourteenth Amendment in 1868, lynching replaced official executions in many Southern states. Reduced resort to lynching in the early twentieth century led to an increase in official executions, although the distinction between the two phenomena was sometimes blurred. Steiker and Steiker note that mobs sometimes assembled 'at the court-house steps, or even in the courtroom, insisting on the swift declaration of a death sentence … . These "legal lynchings" prompted the Supreme Court to begin to regulate state capital systems.'

An important advocacy role was played by the National Association for the Advancement of Colored People, founded in 1909 by W. E. B. Du Bois and others. Its Legal Defense Fund (LDF), created in 1939, played a major role in linking the death penalty to racial discrimination and in bringing cases to the Supreme Court. In *Furman v. Georgia* (1972), the court held that under certain circumstances the death penalty could violate the Eighth Amendment prohibition of cruel and unusual punishment. After a temporary national moratorium, followed by significant reforms at the state level, the court effectively reinstated the death penalty in *Gregg v. Georgia* (1976) which held that it could be an appropriate punishment for murder. In *Coker v. Georgia* (1977), the imposition of a death sentence for rape was found to violate the Eighth Amendment.

In 1983 the Baldus study,[10] , commissioned by the NAACP, examined over 2,000 murder cases since the *Furman* decision in 1972. use of the death penalty. It found that cases involving white victims were at least four times more likely to generate death sentences than cases with minority victims. In *McCleskey v. Kemp* (1987), the court accepted the study's methodological soundness but rejected the argument that system-wide racial discrimination, rather than case-specific discrimination, was sufficient to warrant relief. According to Steiker and Steiker:

> *McCleskey* is a remarkable decision in acknowledging the presence of racial disparities and suggesting that they are not susceptible to judicial remediation. *McCleskey's* legacy remains contested. Although it possibly strengthened the political case against the death penalty by highlighting the failure of legislatures and courts to curtail its discriminatory administration, the decision may reflect a broader reluctance to engage the death penalty on racial terms, thereby contributing to a diminished role for race in contemporary abolitionist discourse.

> Since *McCleskey*, the Supreme Court has focused on more discrete instances of alleged racial discrimination and misconduct. …

> Racial discrimination appears to permeate all phases of capital litigation, including investigation, charging decisions, jury selection, and sentencing. Such discrimination appears to influence not only which inmates are sentenced to death but also which are actually executed. …

In a 2020 update, Scott Phillips and Justin Marceau, in 'Whom the State Kills', 55 *Harv. Civ. Rights-Civ. Lib. L. Rev* (2020) 585, supplemented the sentencing data in Baldus's study with their own original execution data. They concluded that 'the overall execution rate is substantially greater for defendants convicted of killing a white victim than for those convicted of killing a Black victim. Specifically, 2.26% (22/972) of the defendants who were convicted of killing a white victim were ultimately executed, compared to just 0.13% (2/1503) of the defendants convicted of killing a Black victim. Thus, the overall execution rate is a staggering seventeen times greater for defendants convicted of killing a white victim'.

Various authors have sought to explain why the death penalty has survived in the United States when most of its peer countries have long since abolished it. Consider this analysis by David Garland, in *Peculiar Institution: America's Death Penalty in an Age of Abolition* (2010):

---

[10] David Baldus, Charles Pulaski, and George Woodworth, 'Comparative Review of Death Sentences: An Empirical Study of the Georgia Experience', 74 *J. Crim. Law & Criminology* (1983) 661.

The American capital punishment system has not survived into the twenty-first century because death sentences are more necessary or more functional in the United States than elsewhere. ...

[The survival of the death penalty in America] has little to do with its instrumental value for governmental or penal purposes and everything to do with the institutional difficulty of securing abolition in the face of majority public opinion. But ... the institution has been used by groups and actors who have seized the opportunities that it provides to advance their interests or meet their needs. These actors have taken the death penalty and made it work for them, using it sometimes to express their sense of justice, sometimes to enhance their power, their profit, and their casual pleasure.

... The day-to-day uses of the American death penalty are grounded in the microphysics of local politics — of group relations and status competition, professional rivalry and ambition, and the venal give-and-take of political exchange — rather than being connected to the great ends of state. ...

...

The system of capital punishment that exists in America today is primarily a communication system. ... [The system] is about mounting campaigns, taking polls, passing laws, bringing charges, bargaining pleas, imposing sentences, and rehearing cases. It is about threats rather than deeds, anticipated deaths rather than actual executions. ...

Capital punishment in America today operates primarily on the plane of the imaginary, and the great majority of its deaths are imagined ones. But the political and economic effects of these grim fantasies are no less real for being imagined. In American criminal sentencing, the availability of the death penalty permits very lengthy sentences of imprisonment, even life imprisonment without parole, to appear comparatively humane, thereby contributing to the nation's extraordinary rates of imprisonment. In the American political system and in the entertainment zone of popular culture, talk about death permits symbolic acts, exchanges, and representations that are used by groups and individuals in their pursuit of power, profit, and pleasure. That the death penalty is increasingly declaratory and discursive makes it no less powerful in its political, legal, and cultural effects. Nor is it any less lethal for the more than twelve hundred men and women who have been put to their deaths since executions resumed three decades ago.

Focusing on U.S. exceptionalism more broadly, the same author, David Garland, in 'Penal Controls and Social Controls: Toward a Theory of American Penal Exceptionalism', 22 *Punishment & Society* (2020) 321, at 336, explains why America is characterized by exceptional levels of both violence and disorder and of punishment:

... [Structural] reasons ... make social policy programs less likely than penal responses. Social policy interventions are generally more long-term and more expensive—even if they would work out cheaper in the end—and their impact upon crime is less targeted and less direct. Given powerful resistance to taxation, Republican opposition to social spending, the short-termism of election cycles, popular hostility toward ex-prisoners and people on welfare, and a division of political power that allows numerous opportunities to veto controversial legislation, American governments are generally predisposed to reject preventative social investments and rely instead upon post facto responses. Given this settled disposition, efforts to mount social interventions often require novel forms of expertise, personnel, and agencies—and a willingness to engage in long-term investment and institution-building on the part of government. In contrast, there is a ready-made resort to police, prosecution, and imprisonment that makes penal control the path of least resistance. Political barriers are lower too, since proposals to increase punishments rarely meet with organized opposition.

...

... [There is thus a] settled political preference for penal rather than social measures, especially where poor minorities are concerned. But I want to suggest that the resort to penal controls is also determined by limits of *state capacity*: that America's ultra-liberal political economy has produced a welfare state that is much less expansive and much less enabling. That, as compared to other nations, the US state (at the national, state, and local levels) has a more limited capacity for remedial social action. ...

... America's meagre welfare state is less well equipped with the kinds of soft power—the social services, personnel, infrastructure, and capacity for positive, co-ordinated action—that other nations use to deal with crime and disorders. As a consequence, it lacks social reach and effectiveness. When American politicians, policy-makers, and judicial actors are faced with urgent demands to stem the tide of criminal violence, they have fewer options at their disposal and those they have are mostly repressive. As a result, American criminal justice is charged with tasks that other nations allocate to social service agencies. Jails are America's biggest mental health facilities— a task for which they are singularly ill-suited. And America's police—relatively ill-trained as they are—are expected to manage the social and health problems of poor communities in addition to the work of law enforcement.

AUSTIN SARAT, THE DEATH PENALTY ON THE BALLOT: AMERICAN DEMOCRACY AND THE FATE OF CAPITAL PUNISHMENT (2019) 1

... Over the course of the twentieth and into the twenty-first centuries, death penalty ballot campaigns [at the state level in the US] served to mobilize affect, appeal to group thinking, and stoke fears. Images of capital punishment and its role in society have been carefully crafted and marketed, and voters have repeatedly been asked to choose sides on one of America's most charged and divisive issues.

The European Comparison

Putting important public policy questions, like whether to retain or abolish the death penalty, on the ballot exemplifies what James Whitman calls the "weakness" of the American state in comparison with European states.[11] Those states, he says, are both "relatively powerful and autonomous ... They are autonomous in the sense that they are steered by bureaucracies that are relatively immune from the vagaries of public opinion." The strength of the state allowed nations like Germany and France to abolish capital punishment when a majority of their citizens continued to support it. Describing abolition in those countries, Whitman observes that "government actors initiate abolition and slowly bring public opinion around."

In Germany, the post-war "Basic Law" (Grundgesetz), ratified in 1949, contained Article 102, a simple four-word article that in English reads "capital punishment is abolished." This constitutional provision reflected Germany's "revulsion at the large number of death sentences carried out in the last few years" and symbolized the state's commitment to distancing itself from the atrocities of the Holocaust. Since its enactment, there have been numerous attempts to reinstate capital punishment. One, which occurred when the Deutsche Partei filed a motion to reintroduce capital punishment in 1952, illustrates the way German political leaders think about their role in the face of public agitation to restore the death penalty. Thomas Dehler of the Free Democratic Party urged government officials to ignore the German people's preference for capital punishment. As Dehler put it, "one fails to recognize the true meaning of democracy when one believes that the parliament is the executor of the people's will." Elected representatives, he argued, were required to demonstrate "greater insight, understanding, and responsibility than the great mass of citizens" and were called upon to respect human dignity, uphold a modern justice system, and firmly reject the contempt for human life previously exhibited by the Nazi Party.

In France, after a series of highly publicized brutal crimes fueled an increased fear of crime and pushed public sentiment in favor of capital punishment in the 1970s, abolitionists claimed that ending capital punishment was

---

[11] J. Q. Whitman, *Harsh Justice: Criminal Punishment and the Widening Divide Between America and Europe* (2003) 13–14.

the "next urgent step in the march of human progress." Spearheaded by legal scholar and activist Robert Badinter and by François Mitterand, France's president and leader of the Socialist Party, the French Parliament voted to end the death penalty in September 1981 by a vote of 333 to 117. In 2007 the French Constitution was amended to say, "No one can be sentenced to death." As historian Robert A. Nye observes, "The abolition of capital punishment in France was accomplished as a coup d'etat by a political and intellectual elite against the clearly established sentiments of the vast majority of the public."

While European political elites "had the legal capacity and political opportunity to pass laws that abolished ... (the death penalty) once and for all," America's political system divides and fragments power and prevents such uniform action. The vulnerability of the American state, Whitman argues, is particularly consequential in the domain of crime and punishment, where the public tends to be more punitive in its dispositions than state officials and elites. The death penalty persists in the United States because lawmakers responsible for criminal justice policy are much more responsive to the public than are their counterparts in Europe and because the public plays a larger role in legislating about capital punishment.

What sets America apart, Whitman argues, "is the relatively easy translation of majority sentiment into policy." When courts, legislators, or executives have been willing to face the political consequences of trying to abolish the death penalty, the public used initiative and referendum processes, like those in California, Nebraska, and Oklahoma in 2016, to parry those efforts. European "voters can exercise only gradual influence over the broad outlines of criminal justice policy, by voting for different political parties"; Americans can use initiatives and referenda to pass criminal laws as direct legislation.

…

Life Without Parole

One of the unintended consequences of the abolition of the death penalty has been the increased popularity of life without parole (LWOP) sentences. Every state in the USA, except Alaska, permits LWOP as a possible sentence. In *Graham v. Florida*, 130 S. Ct. 2011 (2010) the US Supreme Court held that the sentence of life without parole for a non-homicide offense committed by a juvenile violated the Eighth Amendment's prohibition against cruel and unusual punishments. In *Miller v. Alabama and Jackson v. Hobbs*, 132 S.Ct. 2455 (2012) this was extended to apply to convictions for all offences, including homicide.

As countries like India and China come under increased pressure to reduce or eliminate capital punishment, there has been a marked increase in the number of LWOP sentences.[12] And even countries that do not provide for such sentences per se use surrogates such as imposing ten cumulative life sentences. Between 2000 and 2014 there was an 80 percent rise in life sentences globally. In the U.S. the number increased by almost 70 percent, to 56,000, between 2003 and 2020. One in 7 people in U.S. prisons is serving a life sentence, either life without parole (LWOP), life with parole (LWP) or virtual life (50 years or more), totaling 203,865 people, according to The Sentencing Project, *No End in Sight: America's Enduring Reliance on Life Imprisonment* (2021). Over two-thirds of those serving life sentences are people of color.

---

[12] See generally, Dirk van Zyl Smit and Catherine Appleton, *Life Imprisonment: A Global Human Rights Analysis* (2019).

Chapter 2. The Human Rights Regime: International Law Framework and Origins

In its discussion of the legality of the death penalty and related issues, Chapter 1(B) concentrated on the law — often the constitutional law — of different states. The selected opinions of state courts devoted most of their analyses to their own and to foreign legal systems. International law figured through relevant treaty provisions, but in a subsidiary way. It was not at centre stage.

Chapters 2 to 4, on the other hand, concentrate on the international law aspects of the human rights regime. Why has this path been followed? After all, it is possible to study human rights issues not at the international level but in the detailed contexts of different states' histories, socio-economic and political structures, legal systems, religions, cultures, and so on. With respect to its legal dimension, a human rights course that was so organized would stress the internal law of states as well as foreign and comparative law. It would engage in a contextual and comparative analysis of bodies of domestic law, perhaps devoting its full attention to states like China, Saudi Arabia, Nigeria, Italy, the United States, or Guatemala. It could focus on liberal constitutionalism or on recent trends towards 'democratic' or non-democratic authoritarianism.[13] For such a study of human rights, international law could play a peripheral role, relevant only when it exerted some clear influence on the national scene or had a place in the basic logic of a judicial decision.

The attractiveness of such an approach becomes more apparent when one contrasts with international human rights many other international subjects where international law occupies, indeed must occupy, a central position. Imagine, for example, that this book's interest was not human rights but the humanitarian law of war as applied to interstate conflicts, or the regulation of fisheries, or immunities of diplomats from arrest, or the regulation of trade barriers like tariffs. Each of those fields is inherently, intrinsically, international in character. Each involves relations between states or between citizens of different states. We could not profitably examine any one of them without examining international custom and treaties, and international institutions and processes.

Violations of human rights are different. Not only are they generally rooted within states rather than in interstate engagements, but they need not on their surface involve any international consequences whatsoever. Of course, systemic and severe human rights violations that appear to be 'internal' matters — for example, recurrent violence against an ethnic minority — could well have international consequences, perhaps by leading to refugee flows abroad or by angering other states whose populations are related by ethnicity to the oppressed minority. In typical instances of violations, the police of state X torture defendants to extract confessions; the government of X shuts the opposition press as elections approach; access to housing or health care is denied to particular groups; prisoners are raped by their guards; courts decide cases according to executive command; women or a minority group are barred from education or certain work. Each of these events could profitably be studied entirely within a state's (or region's, culture's) internal framework, just as law students in many countries traditionally concentrate on the internal legal–political system, including that system's provision for civil liberties and human rights.

Nonetheless, since the Second World War it would be inadequate, even misleading, to develop a framework for the study of human rights in many countries without including as a major ingredient the international legal and political aspects of the field: laws, processes, and institutions. In today's world, human rights is characteristically imagined as a regime involving international law and institutions, as well as a movement supported by civil society actors. Internal developments in many states have been much influenced by international law and institutions, as well as by pressures from other states trying to uphold international law.

Internal or comparative approaches to human rights law and the truly international aspects of human rights are now broadly recognized to be complexly intertwined and reciprocally influential with respect to the growth of human rights norms, the causes and effects of their violations, the reactions and sanctions of intergovernmental bodies or other states, the transformations of internal orders and so on. By the same token it is important to recognize, as subsequent chapter do, that the international law framework has been the subject of far-reaching

---

[13] Freedom House, *Freedom in the World 2022: The Global Expansion of Authoritarian Rule.*

critiques by scholars grounded in diverse areas such as feminism, critical race studies, radical ecology, and many other perspectives. For example, Antony Anghie, in 'Rethinking International Law: A TWAIL Retrospective', 34 *Eur. J. Int'l L.* (2023) 7, at 80-81, outlines the ways in which scholars linked to the 'Third World Approaches to International Law' movement (TWAIL) have addressed human rights. Some have 'sought to amend and adapt human rights law to make it more effective and more sensitive to the realities of those societies and the particular harms suffered by minorities and women' and 'explored how people in the Third World have innovated to develop and expand human rights in ways that would protect human dignity more widely conceived'. Some have argued 'that the "universal human being" posited as the foundation of international human rights law is a human being that is essentially European, white and male'. Others have argued that it 'may replicate forms of colonialism'. A different approach has been to explore 'affinities between human rights and the teachings of various religious and cultural traditions that have shaped non-Western societies. Finally, there has also been a critical focus on the political economy of rights and the extent to which they have been linked to neoliberal regimes of international trade and investment law that 'have had an enormous impact on the everyday lives of people in the Third World.' All of these critiques are considered in the pages below.

From another perspective as well it would be impossible to grasp the character of the human rights regime without a basic knowledge about international law and its contributions to it. The regime's aspirations to universal validity are necessarily rooted in that body of law. Many of the distinctive organizations intended to help to realize those aspirations are creations of international law.

For such reasons, this book frequently examines but does not concentrate on the internal law and politics of states. It relates throughout this 'horizontal' strand of the human rights movement, as constitutionalism spreads among states, to the 'vertical' strand of the new international law that is meant to bind states and that is implemented by the new international institutions. Both the horizontal and vertical dimensions are vital to an understanding of the human rights regime. But the truly novel developments of the last 70 years have involved primarily this second dimension.

Chapter 2 has several functions. It sketches the doctrines and principles in an older international law that served as background to and precedents for the human rights regime that took root and developed immediately after the Second World War. They provide the background against which the Universal Declaration of Human Rights was drafted between 1946 and 1948 and adopted on 10 December 1948. The chapter uses national and international decisions of courts and other tribunals not only to present basic doctrines and principles, but also to convey an understanding of international law: its so-called 'sources', its processes of growth, particularly with respect to customary and treaty law. The two tasks are interrelated. By what means or methods have the international rules and standards of the human rights regime developed? By what processes are international legal rules made, elaborated, applied, and changed?

Several of the opinions and scholarly writings in the chapter draw on Article 38 of the Statute of the International Court of Justice (ICJ), the judicial organ of the United Nations that was created by the UN Charter of 1945.[14] That article has long served as a traditional point of departure for examining questions about the 'sources' of international law. It repeats (largely in identical language) the similar provisions of the 1921 Statute of its predecessor court, the Permanent Court of International Justice that was linked to the League of Nations and effectively died during the Second World War. It reads:

> 1. The Court, whose function is to decide in accordance with international law such disputes as are submitted to it, shall apply:
>
>   a. international conventions, whether general or particular, establishing rules expressly recognized by the contesting states;
>
>   b. international custom, as evidence of a general practice accepted as law;

---

[1] The Court can only hear cases to which states are parties: Article 34 of the Statute. A state's consent is necessary for the Court to exercise jurisdiction over it. That consent generally refers to the Court's adjudicating all 'legal disputes' concerning the 'interpretation of a treaty', a 'question of international law', the existence of a fact which, if established 'would constitute a breach of an international obligation' and the reparation to be made for breach of an international obligation: Article 36. Statute of the International Court of Justice, T.S. No. 993 (at p. 25) (U.S.).

   c.   the general principles of law recognized by civilized nations;

   d.   subject to the provisions of Article 59 [stating that decisions of the
        Court have no binding force except between the parties to the case],
        judicial decisions and the teachings of the most highly qualified publicists
        of the various nations, as subsidiary means for the determination of rules
        of law.

Although Article 38 formally instructs this particular Court about the method of applying international law to resolve disputes, its influence has extended to other international tribunals, to national courts, and indeed generally to argument based on international law that is made in settings other than courts.

The Article takes a positivist perspective. It defines the task of the Court in terms of its *application* of an identifiable body of international law that in one or another sense, has been consented to ('expressly recognized', 'accepted as law', 'recognized') directly or indirectly by states. Its skeletal list expresses a formal conception of the judicial function that is radically different from that of, say, a legal realist. Consider the following comments on Article 38. The first is by José Alvarez, *International Organizations as Law Makers*, at 46 (2005):

> Public international lawyers, through at least the greater part of the 20th century, have
> sought to define their field as relatively autonomous from either politics or morality.
> Their endeavor turned many, particularly in Europe and North America, towards legal
> positivism....
>
> ...
>
> Nothing embodies these central positivist tenets in international law as much as the
> doctrine of sources. For most international lawyers trained in the West, article 38 of the
> Statute of the International Court of Justice remains the "constitution" of the
> international community. Its enumerated sources of international law — treaties, custom,
> and general principles of law — remain, for most, the exclusive means for generating legal
> obligations on states. Through the doctrine of sources, international lawyers define (and
> defend) their field as characteristically legal. Thanks to sources doctrine, international
> lawyers argue that international law, like domestic law, also has a circumscribed set of
> sources and rules for interpreting them; thanks to article 38, international law is
> distinguished from morality or politics. Thanks to sources, international rules have a
> distinctive either/or quality, essential to distinguish mere wishful thinking (*lex ferenda*)
> from black letter obligation (*lex lata*): something either is or is not within one of the
> recognized sources of international law and someone with the requisite skill, like a judge,
> can do so....
>
> ... The doctrine of sources then, has a dual agenda: it tells the lawyer where to find the law
> in an objective fashion because it is ostensibly based in the concrete practice of states but
> it also seeks to provide a normatively constraining code for states... .

The second comment is by Hilary Charlesworth, 'Law-Making and Sources', in James Crawford and Martti Koskenniemi (eds.), *The Cambridge Companion to International Law* (2012), 187, at 189.

> [Art. 38] allows international lawyers to sidestep complex debates about the function of
> international law and the relative legitimacies of state consent and claims of justice. It is a
> pithy mantra that offers a quasi-scientific formula for practitioners of international law,
> postponing (possibly indefinitely) discussion of the politics of the designated sources. The
> formal nature of article 38(1) obscures the fact that international law is generated by a
> multi-layered process of interactions, instruments, pressures and principles.

A. THE LAW OF ARMED CONFLICT AND CUSTOMARY INTERNATIONAL LAW

The following decision in *The Paquete Habana* deals with an earlier period in the development of the law of armed conflict, now more commonly called international humanitarian law (IHL) or the laws of war (here, naval warfare), and with a theme that became central in the later treaty development of this field — the protection of noncombatant civilians and their property (here, civilian fishing vessels) against the ravages of war. Within the framework of the law of armed conflict, this case involves *jus in bello*, the ways in which war ought to be waged, the rules of war itself, rather than the related but distinct *jus ad bellum*, the determination of those conditions (if any) in which a *just* or justified war can be waged, conditions in which (under contemporary international law) going to war is legal.

In its analysis of the question before it, the US Supreme Court here illustrates a classical understanding of customary international law — an understanding that, we shall see, is today open to substantial challenge and reformation. In reading the opinion, keep in mind two questions. What method does the majority opinion employ to conclude that a relevant, indeed decisive, rule of customary international law has developed? Does the dissent differ as to the method itself or as to its application in this case?

THE PAQUETE HABANA
SUPREME COURT OF THE UNITED STATES, 175 U.S. 677 (1900)

MR. JUSTICE GRAY DELIVERED THE OPINION OF THE COURT

These are two appeals from decrees of the district court of the United States for the southern district of Florida condemning two fishing vessels and their cargoes as prize of war.

Each vessel was a fishing smack, running in and out of Havana, and regularly engaged in fishing on the coast of Cuba; sailed under the Spanish flag; was owned by a Spanish subject of Cuban birth, living in the city of Havana; was commanded by a subject of Spain also residing in Havana; and her master and crew had no interest in the vessel, but were entitled to shares, amounting in all to two thirds, of her catch, the other third belonging to her owner. Her cargo consisted of fresh fish, caught by her crew from the sea, put on board as they were caught, and kept and sold alive. Until stopped by the blockading squadron she had no knowledge of the existence of the war or of any blockade. She had no arms or ammunition on board, and made no attempt to run the blockade after she knew of its existence, nor any resistance at the time of the capture.

...

Both the fishing vessels were brought by their captors into Key West. A libel for the condemnation of each vessel and her cargo as prize of war was there filed on April 27, 1898; a claim was interposed by her master on behalf of himself and the other members of the crew, and of her owner; evidence was taken, showing the facts above stated; and on May 30, 1898, a final decree of condemnation and sale was entered, 'the court not being satisfied that as a matter of law, without any ordinance, treaty, or proclamation, fishing vessels of this class are exempt from seizure'.

Each vessel was thereupon sold by auction; the Paquete Habana for the sum of $490; and the Lola for the sum of $800. There was no other evidence in the record of the value of either vessel or of her cargo....

...

We are then brought to the consideration of the question whether, upon the facts appearing in these records, the fishing smacks were subject to capture by the armed vessels of the United States during the recent war with Spain.

By an ancient usage among civilized nations, beginning centuries ago, and gradually ripening into a rule of international law, coast fishing vessels, pursuing their vocation of catching and bringing in fresh fish, have been recognized as exempt, with their cargoes and crews, from capture as prize of war.

This doctrine, however, has been earnestly contested at the bar; and no complete collection of the instances illustrating it is to be found, so far as we are aware, in a single published work, although many are referred to and discussed by the writers on international law, notable in 2 Ortolan, *Règles Internationales et Diplomatie de la Mer* (4th ed.) …; in 4 Calvo, *Droit International* (5th ed.) …; in De Boeck, *Propriété Privé Ennemie sous Pavillon Ennemie*, …; and in Hall, *International Law* (4th ed.) … . It is therefore worth the while to trace the history of the rule, from the earliest accessible sources, through the increasing recognition of it with occasional setbacks, to what we may now justly consider as its final establishment in our own country and generally throughout the civilized world.

The earliest acts of any government on the subject, mentioned in the books, either emanated from, or were approved by, a King of England.

In 1403 and 1406 Henry IV issued orders to his admirals and other officers, entitled 'Concerning Safety for Fishermen … . By an order of October 26, 1403, reciting that it was made pursuant to a treaty between himself and the King of France; and for the greater safety of the fishermen of either country, and so that they could be, and carry on their industry, the more safely on the sea, and deal with each other in peace; and that the French King had consented that English fishermen should be treated likewise, — it was ordained that French fishermen might, during the then pending season for the herring fishery, safely fish for herrings and all other fish, from the harbor of Gravelines and the island of Thanet to the mouth of the Seine and the harbor of Hautoune … .

The same custom would seem to have prevailed in France until towards the end of the seventeenth century. For example, in 1675, Louis XIV and the States General of Holland by mutual agreement granted to Dutch and French fishermen the liberty, undisturbed by their vessels of war, of fishing along the coasts of France, Holland, and England … .

The doctrine which exempts coast fishermen, with their vessels and cargoes, from capture as prize of war, has been familiar to the United States from the time of the War of Independence.

…

In the treaty of 1785 between the United States and Prussia, article 23.… provided that, if war should arise between the contracting parties, 'all women and children, scholars of every faculty, cultivators of the earth, artisans, manufacturers, and fishermen, unarmed and inhabiting unfortified towns, villages, or places, and in general all others whose occupations are for the common subsistence and benefit of mankind, shall be allowed to continue their respective employments, and shall not be molested in their persons, nor shall their houses or goods be burnt or otherwise destroyed, nor their fields wasted by the armed force of the enemy, into whose power, by the events of war, they may happen to fall; but if anything is necessary to be taken from them for the use of such armed force, the same shall be paid for at a reasonable price'.…

Since the United States became a nation, the only serious interruptions, so far as we are informed, of the general recognition of the exemption of coast fishing vessels from hostile capture, arose out of the mutual suspicions and recriminations of England and France during the wars of the French Revolution.

…

On January 24, 1798, the English government by express order instructed the commanders of its ships to seize French and Dutch fishermen with their boats.… After the promulgation of that order, Lord Stowell (then Sir William Scott) in the High Court of Admiralty of England condemned small Dutch fishing vessels as prize of war. In one case the capture was in April, 1798, and the decree was made November 13, 1798. *The Young Jacob and Johanna* … .

On March 16, 1801, the Addington Ministry, having come into power in England, revoked the orders of its predecessors against the French fishermen; maintaining, however, that 'the freedom of fishing was nowise founded upon an agreement, but upon a simple concession', that 'this concession would be always subordinate to the convenience of the moment', and that 'it was never extended to the great fishery, or to commerce in oysters or in fish'. And the freedom of the coast fisheries was again allowed on both sides.…

Lord Stowell's judgment in *The Young Jacob and Johanna*, … was much relied on by the counsel for the United States, and deserves careful consideration.

The vessel there condemned is described in the report as 'a small Dutch fishing vessel taken April, 1798, on her return from the Dogger bank to Holland'; and Lord Stowell, in delivering judgment, said: 'In former wars it has not been usual to make captures of these small fishing vessels; but this rule was a rule of comity[15] only, and not of legal decision; it has prevailed from views of mutual accommodation between neighbouring countries, and from tenderness to a poor and industrious order of people. In the present war there has, I presume, been sufficient reason for changing this mode of treatment; and as they are brought before me for my judgment they must be referred to the general principles of this court; they fall under the character and description of the last class of cases; that is, of ships constantly and exclusively employed in the enemy's trade'. And he added: 'it is a further satisfaction to me, in giving this judgment, to observe that the facts also bear strong marks of a false and fraudulent transaction'.

Both the capture and the condemnation were within a year after the order of the English government of January 24, 1798, instructing the commanders of its ships to seize French and Dutch fishing vessels, and before any revocation of that order. Lord Stowell's judgment shows that his decision was based upon the order of 1798, as well as upon strong evidence of fraud. Nothing more was adjudged in the case.

But some expressions in his opinion have been given so much weight by English writers that it may be well to examine them particularly. The opinion begins by admitting the known custom in former wars not to capture such vessels; adding, however, 'but this was a rule of comity only, and not of legal decision'. Assuming the phrase 'legal decision' to have been there used, in the sense in which courts are accustomed to use it, as equivalent to 'judicial decision', it is true that so far as appears, there had been no such decision on the point in England. The word 'comity' was apparently used by Lord Stowell as synonymous with courtesy or goodwill. But the period of a hundred years which has since elapsed is amply sufficient to have enabled what originally may have rested in custom or comity, courtesy or concession, to grow, by the general assent of civilized nations, into a settled rule of international law....

The French prize tribunals, both before and after Lord Stowell's decision, took a wholly different view of the general question....

The English government [by Orders in Council of 1806 and 1810] unqualifiedly prohibited the molestation of fishing vessels employed in catching and bringing to market fresh fish....

Wheaton, in his Digest of the Law of Maritime Captures and Prizes, published in 1815, wrote: 'It has been usual in maritime wars to exempt from capture fishing boats and their cargoes, both from views of mutual accommodation between neighboring countries, and from tenderness to a poor and industrious order of people. This custom, so honorable to the humanity of civilized nations, has fallen into disuse; and it is remarkable that both France and England mutually reproach each other with that breach of good faith which has finally abolished it'. Wheaton, Captures, chap. 2,18.

This statement clearly exhibits Wheaton's opinion that the custom had been a general one, as well as that it ought to remain so. His assumption that it had been abolished by the differences between France and England at the close of the last century was hardly justified by the state of things when he wrote, and has not since been borne out.
...
In the war with Mexico, in 1846, the United States recognized the exemption of coast fishing boats from capture....

In the treaty of peace between the United States and Mexico, in 1848, were inserted the very words of the earlier treaties with Prussia, already quoted, forbidding the hostile molestation or seizure in time of war of the persons, occupations, houses, or goods of fishermen. ...
...
France in the Crimean war in 1854, and in her wars with Italy in 1859 and with Germany in 1870, by general orders, forbade her cruisers to trouble the coast fisheries, or to seize any vessel or boat engaged therein, unless naval or military operations should make it necessary.
...

---

[15] A modern-day American definition of comity is 'deference to foreign government actors that is not required by international law but is incorporated in domestic law.' William S. Dodge, 'International Comity in American Law,' 115 *Colum. L. Rev.* (2015) 2071.

Since the English orders in council of 1806 and 1810... in favor of fishing vessels employed in catching and bringing to market fresh fish, no instance has been found in which the exemption from capture of private coast fishing vessels honestly pursuing their peaceful industry has been denied by England or by any other nation. And the Empire of Japan (the last state admitted into the rank of civilized nations), by an ordinance promulgated at the beginning of its war with China in August, 1894, established prize courts, and ordained that 'the following enemy's vessels are exempt from detention', including in the exemption 'boats engaged in coast fisheries', as well as 'ships engaged exclusively on a voyage of scientific discovery, philanthropy, or religious mission'. Takahashi, *International Law*, 11, 178.

International law is part of our law, and must be ascertained and administered by the courts of justice of appropriate jurisdiction as often as questions of right depending upon it are duly presented for their determination. For this purpose, where there is no treaty and no controlling executive or legislative act or judicial decision, resort must be had to the customs and usages of civilized nations, and, as evidence of these, to the works of jurists and commentators who by years of labor, research, and experience have made themselves peculiarly well acquainted with the subjects of which they treat. Such works are resorted to by judicial tribunals, not for the speculations of their authors concerning what the law ought to be, but for trustworthy evidence of what the law really is. *Hilton v. Guyot*, 159 U.S. 113 ... .

...

Chancellor Kent says: 'In the absence of higher and more authoritative sanctions, the ordinances of foreign states, the opinions of eminent statesmen, and the writings of distinguished jurists, are regarded as of great consideration on questions not settled by conventional law. In cases where the principal jurists agree, the presumption will be very great in favor of the solidity of their maxims; and no civilized nation that does not arrogantly set all ordinary law and justice at defiance will venture to disregard the uniform sense of the established writers on international law'. 1 Kent, Com. 18.

It will be convenient, in the first place, to refer to some leading French treatises on international law, which deal with the question now before us, not as one of the law of France only, but as one determined by the general consent of civilized nations ...

[Discussion of French treatises omitted.]

...

No international jurist of the present day has a wider or more deserved reputation than Calvo, who, though writing in French, is a citizen of the Argentine Republic, employed in its diplomatic service abroad. In the fifth edition of his great work on international law, published in 1896, he observes ... that the international authority of decisions in particular cases by the prize courts of France, of England, and of the United States is lessened by the fact that the principles on which they are based are largely derived from the internal legislation of each country; and yet the peculiar character of maritime wars, with other considerations, gives to prize jurisprudence a force and importance reaching beyond the limits of the country in which it has prevailed. He therefore proposes here to group together a number of particular cases proper to serve as precedents for the solution of grave questions of maritime law in regard to the capture of private property as prize of war. Immediately ... he goes on to say: 'Notwithstanding the hardships to which maritime wars subject private property, notwithstanding the extent of the recognized rights of belligerents, there are generally exempted, from seizure and capture, fishing vessels'....

The modern German books on international law, cited by the counsel for the appellants, treat the custom by which the vessels and implements of coast fishermen are exempt from seizure and capture as well established by the practice of nations. Heffter, 137; 2 Kalterborn, 237, p. 480; Bluntschli, 667; Perels, 37, p. 217.

...

Two recent English text-writers cited at the bar (influenced by what Lord Stowell said a century since) hesitate to recognize that the exemption of coast fishing vessels from capture has now become a settled rule of international law. Yet they both admit that there is little real difference in the views, or in the practice, of England and of other maritime nations; and that no civilized nation at the present day would molest coast fishing vessels so long as they were peaceably pursuing their calling and there was no danger that they or their crews might be of military use to the enemy....

But there are writers of various maritime countries, not yet cited, too important to be passed by without notice....

[The opinion quotes from writing from the Netherlands, Spain, Austria, Portugal and Italy.]

This review of the precedents and authorities on the subject appears to us abundantly to demonstrate that at the present day, by the general consent of the civilized nations of the world, and independently of any express treaty or other public act, it is an established rule of international law, founded on considerations of humanity to a poor and industrious order of men, and of the mutual convenience of belligerent states, that coast fishing vessels, with their implements and supplies, cargoes and crews, unarmed and honestly pursuing their peaceful calling of catching and bringing in fresh fish, are exempt from capture as prize of war....

...

This rule of international law is one which prize courts administering the law of nations are bound to take judicial notice of, and to give effect to, in the absence of any treaty or other public act of their own government in relation to the matter.

...

To this subject in more than one aspect are singularly applicable the words uttered by Mr. Justice Strong, speaking for this court: 'Undoubtedly no single nation can change the law of the sea. The law is of universal obligation and no statute of one or two nations can create obligations for the world. Like all the laws of nations, it rests upon the common consent of civilized communities. It is of force, not because it was prescribed by any superior power, but because it has been generally accepted as a rule of conduct. Whatever may have been its origin, whether in the usages of navigation, or in the ordinances of maritime states, or in both, it has become the law of the sea only by the concurrent sanction of those nations who may be said to constitute the commercial world....Of [these facts] we may take judicial notice.

Foreign municipal laws must indeed be proved as facts, but it is not so with the law of nations'. ... *Sears v. The Scotia*, 20 L.Ed. 822 ... .

The position taken by the United States during the recent war with Spain was quite in accord with the rule of international law, now generally recognized by civilized nations, in regard to coast fishing vessels.

On April 21, 1898, the Secretary of the Navy gave instructions to Admiral Sampson, commanding the North Atlantic Squadron, to 'immediately institute a blockade of the north coast of Cuba, extending from Cardenas on the east to Bahia Honda on the west'. Bureau of Navigation Report of 1898, appx. 175. The blockade was immediately instituted accordingly. On April 22 the President issued a proclamation declaring that the United States had instituted and would maintain that blockade, 'in pursuance of the laws of the United States, and the law of nations applicable to such cases'. ... And by the act of Congress of April 25, 1898, chap. 189, it was declared that the war between the United States and Spain existed on that day, and had existed since and including April 21. ...

On April 26, 1898, the President issued another proclamation which, after reciting the existence of the war as declared by Congress, contained this further recital: 'It being desirable that such war should be conducted upon principles in harmony with the present views of nations and sanctioned by their recent practice'. This recital was followed by specific declarations of certain rules for the conduct of the war by sea, making no mention of fishing vessels. ... But the proclamation clearly manifests the general policy of the government to conduct the war in accordance with the principles of international law sanctioned by the recent practice of nations....

Upon the facts proved in either case, it is the duty of this court, sitting as the highest prize court of the United States, and administering the law of nations, to declare and adjudge that the capture was unlawful and without probable cause; and it is therefore, in each case, –

Ordered, that the decree of the District Court be reversed, and the proceeds of the sale of the vessel, together with the proceeds of any sale of her cargo, be restored to the claimant, with damages and costs.

MR. CHIEF JUSTICE FULLER, WITH WHOM CONCURRED MR. JUSTICE HARLAN AND MR. JUSTICE MEKENNA, DISSENTING

The district court held these vessels and their cargoes liable because not 'satisfied that as a matter of law, without any ordinance, treaty, or proclamation, fishing vessels of this class are exempt from seizure'.

This court holds otherwise, not because such exemption is to be found in any treaty, legislation, proclamation, or instruction granting it, but on the ground that the vessels were exempt by reason of an established rule of international law applicable to them, which it is the duty of the court to enforce.

I am unable to conclude that there is any such established international rule, or that this court can properly revise action which must be treated as having been taken in the ordinary exercise of discretion in the conduct of war.
...
This case involves the capture of enemy's property on the sea, and executive action, and if the position that the alleged rule *proprio vigore* limits the sovereign power in war be rejected, then I understand the contention to be that, by reason of the existence of the rule, the proclamation of April 26 must be read as if it contained the exemption in terms, or the exemption must be allowed because the capture of fishing vessels of this class was not specifically authorized.

The preamble to the proclamation stated, it is true, that it was desirable that the war 'should be conducted upon principles in harmony with the present views of nations and sanctioned by their recent practice', but the reference was to the intention of the government 'not to resort to privateering, but to adhere to the rules of the Declaration of Paris'; and the proclamation spoke for itself. The language of the preamble did not carry the exemption in terms, and the real question is whether it must be allowed because not affirmatively withheld, or, in other words, because such captures were not in terms directed.
...
It is impossible to concede that the Admiral ratified these captures in disregard of established international law and the proclamation, or that the President, if he had been of opinion that there was any infraction of law or proclamation, would not have intervened prior to condemnation.

In truth, the exemption of fishing craft is essentially an act of grace, and not a matter of right, and it is extended or denied as the exigency is believed to demand.

It is, said Sir William Scott, 'a rule of comity only, and not of legal decision'.
...
It is difficult to conceive of a law of the sea of universal obligation to which Great Britain has not acceded. And I am not aware of adequate foundation for imputing to this country the adoption of any other than the English rule.
...
It is needless to review the speculations and repetitions of the writers on international law. Ortolan, De Boeck, and others admit that the custom relied on as consecrating the immunity is not so general as to create an absolute international rule; Heffter, Calvo, and others are to the contrary. Their lucubrations may be persuasive, but not authoritative.

In my judgment, the rule is that exemption from the rigors of war is in the control of the Executive. He is bound by no immutable rule on the subject. It is for him to apply, or to modify, or to deny altogether such immunity as may have been usually extended.
...

1. International Humanitarian Law

The opinion in *The Paquete Habana* has the aura of a humane world in which, if war occurs, the fighting should be as compassionate in spirit as possible. It rests the rule of exemption of coastal fishing vessels 'on considerations of humanity to a poor and industrious order of men, and [on] the mutual convenience of fishing vessels'. The intricate body of international humanitarian law considered by the Supreme Court grew out of centuries of primarily customary law, although custom was supplemented, informed and developed centuries ago by selective bilateral treaties. To this day, custom remains essential to argument about IHL, including to the norms considered by international criminal tribunals examined in Chapter 16 and potentially to assessments of military measures to combat terrorism examined in Chapter 5. Like many other areas of international law, this field is increasingly dominated by multilateral instruments that have both codified customary standards and rules and developed new ones. Multilateral declarations and treaties started to achieve prominence in the second half of the nineteenth century. The treaties now include The Hague Conventions concluded around the turn of the century, the four Geneva Conventions of 1949 (as well as two significant protocols of 1977 to those conventions), and several more recent discrete treaties banning particular weapons and protecting cultural property. But in an increasingly fractious world, the prospects of successfully negotiating new multilateral treaties are diminished, which again highlights the importance of customary law.

In 2005 the ICRC published a major compendium of customary law rules and practices, which is now regularly updated (https://ihl-databases.icrc.org/customary-ihl/eng/docs/home). A scholarly evaluation of its impact (Marko Milanovic and Sandesh Sivakumaran, 'Assessing the Authority of the ICRC Customary IHL Study', 920 *Int'l Rev Red Cross* (2022) 1856) concludes that it has been highly influential as a result of its rigour, the ICRC's special mandate and expertise, and because there is no readily accessible alternative source.

In Chapter 5, we introduce IHL in greater depth. For now, it is important to know that the basic Geneva Conventions (which have now obtained universal ratification) and the two Protocols (Protocol I, 174 parties; Protocol II, 169 parties) cover a vast range of problems stemming from land, air and naval warfare, including the protection of wounded combatants, prisoners of war, civilian populations and civilian objects, and medical and religious personnel and buildings. As suggested by this list, the provisions of the four Conventions and the two Protocols constitute the principal contemporary regulation of *jus in bello*, that is, how war ought to be waged.

This entire corpus of custom and treaties has as its broad purpose, in the words of the landmark St. Petersburg Declaration of 1868, 'alleviating as much as possible the calamities of war'. Here lies the tension, even contradiction, within this body of law. Putting aside the question of a war's legality (an issue central to the Judgment of the International Military Tribunal at Nuremberg (see Ch. 2D, below), and today governed by the UN Charter), a war fought in compliance with the standards and rules of the laws of war permits — one might say authorizes or legitimates — massive intentional killing or wounding and massive other destruction that, absent a war, would violate the most fundamental human rights norms.

Hence all these standards and rules stand at some perilous and problematic divide between brutality and destruction (1) that is permitted or privileged and (2) that is illegal and subject to sanction. Broad standards like 'proportionality' in choosing military means or like the avoidance of 'unnecessary suffering' are employed to help to draw the line. The powerful ideal of reducing human suffering that animates international humanitarian law thus is countered by the goal of state parties to a war — indeed, in the eyes of states, the paramount goal — of gaining military objectives and victory while reducing as much as possible the losses to one's own armed forces.

The generous mood of *The Paquete Habana* toward the civilian population and its food-gathering needs was reflected in the various Hague Conventions regulating land and naval warfare that were adopted during the ensuing decade. Note Article 3 of The Hague Convention of 1907 on Certain Restrictions with Regard to the Exercise of the Right to Capture in Naval War, which proclaimed in 1910: 'Vessels used exclusively for fishing along the coast... are exempt from capture ...'.

The efforts to protect civilian populations and their property took on renewed vigor after the Second World War through the Geneva Conventions of 1949 and the Protocols of 1977. Consider Article 48 of Protocol I to the Geneva Conventions. Article 48 enjoins the parties to a conflict to 'distinguish between the civilian population and combatants and between civilian objects and military objectives'. Military attacks are to be directed 'only against military objectives'. Article 52 defines military objectives to be 'objects which, by their nature, location, purposes or use make an effective contribution to military action and whose total or partial destruction, capture or neutralization, in the circumstances ruling at the time, offers a definite military advantage'. Article 54 is entitled, 'Protection of Objects Indispensable to the Survival of the Civilian Population'. It states that '[s]tarvation of civilians as a method of warfare is prohibited'. Specifically, parties are prohibited from attacking or removing 'objects indispensable to the survival of the civilian population, such as foodstuffs ... for the specific purpose of denying them for their sustenance value to the civilian population or to the adverse

Party....' An exception is made for objects used by an adverse party as sustenance 'solely' for its armed forces or 'in direct support of military action'.

In relation to *The Paquete Habana*, note:

(a) the emphasis on the fact that the Supreme Court here sat as a *prize court* administering the law of nations, and note its references to the international character of the law maritime. Indeed, the Court almost assumed the role of an international tribunal, a consideration stressed in the excerpts from the scholar Calvo. Nonetheless, the Court's statement that 'international law is part of our law' and must be 'ascertained and administered by courts of justice' as often as 'questions of right' depending on it are presented for determination, has been drawn on in many later judicial decisions in the United States involving unrelated international law issues.

(b) An antiquarian aspect of the decision and period is that the naval personnel who captured the fishing vessels participated in the judicial proceedings, for at the time of the war captors were entitled to share in the proceeds of the sale of lawful prizes. That practice has ended and proceeds are now paid into the Treasury.

(c) The Court looked to a relatively small number of countries for evidence of state practice, dominantly in Western Europe. It referred to Japan as 'the last state admitted into the rank of civilized nations'. Even at the start of the twentieth century, the world community creating international law was a small and relatively cohesive one; today's total of almost 200 states offers a striking contrast. Consider the multinational and multicultural character of an assembly of states today drafting a convention on the laws of war or a human rights convention, and imagine the range of states to which references might be made in a contemporary judicial opinion considering the customary law of international human rights.

2. The Role of Custom

The Supreme Court decision in *The Paquete Habana* raises basic questions about custom, which has been referred to as the oldest and original source of international law. Customary law remains indispensable to an adequate understanding of human rights law. It figures in many fora, from scholarship about the content of human rights law, to the broad debates about human rights within the United Nations, to the arguments of counsel before an international or national tribunal. As this chapter later indicates, the character of such argument today differs in significant respects from the character a century ago at the time of this decision.

Customary law refers to conduct, or the conscious abstention from certain conduct, of states that becomes in some measure a part of international legal order. By virtue of a developing custom, particular conduct may be considered to be permitted or obligatory in legal terms, or abstention from particular conduct may come to be considered a legal duty.

Consider the 1950 statement of a noted scholar describing the character of the state practice that can build a customary rule of international law: (1) 'concordant practice' by a number of states relating to a particular situation; (2) continuation of that practice 'over a considerable period of time'; (3) a conception that the practice is required by or consistent with international law; and (4) general acquiescence in that practice by other states.[16] Other scholars have contested some of these observations, and today many authorities contend that custom has long been a less rigid, more flexible and dynamic force in law-making.

Clause (b) of Article 38(1) of the Statute of the ICJ states that the Court shall apply 'international custom, as evidence of a general practice accepted as law'. The phrase is as confusing as it is terse. Contemporary formulations of custom have overcome some difficulties in understanding it, but three of the terms there used remain contested and vexing: 'general', 'practice' and 'accepted as law'.

In 1987 the *Restatement (Third), Foreign Relations Law of the United States*, sought to clarify some of these issues, but it also did not shy away from the obstacles:

---

[16] M. Hudson, Working Paper on Article 24 of the Statute of the International Law Commission, UN Doc. A/CN.4/16, 3 Mar. 1950, at 5.

> Each element in attempted definitions has raised difficulties. There have been philosophical debates about the very basis of the definition: how can practice build law? Most troublesome conceptually has been the circularity in the suggestion that law is built by practice based on a sense of legal obligation: how, it is asked, can there be a sense of legal obligation before the law from which the legal obligation derives has matured? Such conceptual difficulties, however, have not prevented acceptance of customary law essentially as here defined. (From the Reporter's Notes to Section 102).

The most recent attempt to shed light on the concept is a thorough study on the 'identification of customary international law', by the International Law Commission (ILC). The ILC was set up in 1947 to promote 'the progressive development of international law and its codification'. Its expert membership of 34 is supposed to reflect 'the main forms of civilization and … the principal legal systems of the world'. After appointing Sir Michael Wood as Special Rapporteur on the subject (2012-2018), the ILC submitted its draft conclusions to the General Assembly which took note and drew them to the attention of States and other actors 'who may be called upon to identify rules of customary international law' (Res. 73/203 (2018)).

The ILC's starting point is the need to ascertain whether there is a general practice and whether that practice is 'accepted as law'. The latter formulation is the Commission's way of presenting the conventional Latin phrase *opinio juris*, which in turn is an abbreviation of *opinio juris sive necessitatis*, meaning 'an opinion of law or necessity.' The two elements are to be separately ascertained. Practice is primarily that of states, and sometimes that of international organizations. It does not include the conduct of other (non-state) actors, although that may be relevant in assessing the practice of states or international organizations. Practice includes 'both physical and verbal acts' and possibly inaction:

> Forms of State practice include, but are not limited to: diplomatic acts and correspondence; conduct in connection with resolutions adopted by an international organization or at an intergovernmental conference; conduct in connection with treaties; executive conduct, including operational conduct "on the ground"; legislative and administrative acts; and decisions of national courts. (Conclusion 6(2)).

The practice must be 'sufficiently widespread and representative, as well as consistent,' but 'no particular duration is required.' *Opinio juris* 'means that the practice in question must be undertaken with a sense of legal right or obligation', and is 'to be distinguished from mere usage or habit.' (Conclusion 9). In addition to positive evidence of *opinio juris*, 'failure to react over time to a practice may serve as evidence …, provided that States were in a position to react and the circumstances called for some reaction' (Conclusion 10). A resolution of an international organization or intergovernmental conference 'cannot, of itself, create a rule of customary international law', but it might reflect a customary norm or provide evidence relating to one.

The ILC confirms the concept of a 'persistent objector' (criticized by Chimni below) in the following terms:

1. Where a State has objected to a rule of customary international law while that rule was in the process of formation, the rule is not opposable to the State concerned for so long as it maintains its objection.
2. The objection must be clearly expressed, made known to other States, and maintained persistently. (Conclusion 15).

Relationships between Treaties and Custom

Thus far we have considered custom independently of treaties (whose elements are described in Ch. 2C, below). But these two 'sources' or law-making processes of international law are complexly interrelated. For example, the question often arises of the extent to which a treaty should be read in the light of pre-existing custom. A treaty norm of great generality may naturally be interpreted against the background of relevant state practice or policies. In such contexts, the question whether the treaty is intended to be 'declaratory' of pre-existing customary law or to change that law may become relevant.

Moreover, treaties may give birth to rules of customary law. Assume a succession of bilateral treaties among many states, each containing a provision giving indigent aliens who are citizens of the other state party, the right to counsel at the government's expense in a criminal prosecution. The question may arise whether these bilateral treaties create a custom that would bind a state not party to any of them. Polar arguments will likely be developed by parties to such a dispute, for example: (1) The nonparty state cannot be bound by those treaties since it has not consented. The series of bilateral treaties simply constitutes special exceptions to the traditional customary law that leaves the state's discretion unimpaired on this matter. Indeed, the necessity that many states saw for treaties underscores that no obligation existed under customary law. (2) A solution worked out among many states should be considered relevant or persuasive for the development of a customary law setting standards for all countries. Similarly, the network of treaties may have become dense enough, and state practice consistent with the treaty may have become general enough, to build a customary norm binding all states. Article 38 of the Vienna Convention on the Law of Treaties signals rather than resolves this issue by stating that nothing in its prior articles providing generally that a treaty does not create obligations for a third state precludes a rule set forth in a treaty from becoming binding on a third state 'as a customary rule of international law, recognized as such'.

In contemporary international law, broadly ratified multilateral treaties are more likely than a series of bilateral treaties to generate the argument that treaty rules have become customary law binding nonparties. Some of the principal human rights treaties, for example, have from around 150 to 196 states parties from all parts of the world. Of course, one must distinguish between substantive norms in multilateral treaties that are alleged to constitute customary law that binds nonparties, and institutional arrangements created by the treaties in which parties have agreed, for example, to submit reports or disputes to a treaty organ.

MARTTI KOSKENNIEMI, THE PULL OF THE MAINSTREAM
88 MICH. L. REV. (1990) 1946

... [I]nternational lawyers have had difficulty accounting for rules of international law that do not emanate from the consent of the states against which they are applied. In fact, most modern lawyers have assumed that international law is not really binding unless it can be traced to an agreement or some other meeting of wills between two or more sovereign states. Once the idea of a natural law is discarded, it seems difficult to justify an obligation that is not voluntarily assumed.

...

The matter is particularly important in regard to norms intended to safeguard basic human rights and fundamental freedoms. If the only states bound to respect such rights and freedoms are the states that have formally become parties to the relevant instruments ... then many important political values would seem to lack adequate protection. It is inherently difficult to accept the notion that states are legally bound not to engage in genocide, for example, only if they have ratified and not formally denounced the 1948 Genocide Convention. Some norms seem so basic, so important, that it is more than slightly artificial to argue that states are legally bound to comply with them simply because there exists an agreement between them to that effect, rather than because, in the words of the International Court of Justice (ICJ), noncompliance would 'shock[] the conscience of mankind' and be contrary to 'elementary considerations of humanity'.

...

... Although it seems clear that not all international law can be based upon agreement, it seems much less clear what else, then, it may be founded upon.... A Grotian lawyer would not, of course, perceive a great difficulty. He would simply say that some norms exist by force of natural reason or social necessity. Such an argument, however, is not open to a modern lawyer or court, much less an international court, established for the settlement of disputes between varying cultures, varying traditions, and varying conceptions of reason and justice. Such conceptions seem to be historically and contextually conditioned, so that imposing them on a nonconsenting state seems both political and unjustifiable as such.

It is, I believe, for this reason — the difficulty of justifying conceptions of natural justice in modern society — that lawyers have tended to relegate into 'custom' all those important norms that cannot be supported by treaties. In this way, they might avoid arguing from an essentially naturalistic — and thus suspect — position. 'Custom' may seem both less difficult to verify and more justifiable to apply than abstract maxims of international justice.

...

Professor Meron [an authority on humanitarian law whose book is here under review by Koskenniemi] follows this strategy. Although he accepts the category of 'general principles' as a valid way to argue about human rights and humanitarian norms, he does not use this argumentative tack. Nor does he examine whether, or to what extent, such norms might be valid as natural law. His reason for so doing is clearly stated: he wishes to 'utilize irreproachable legal methods' to enhance 'the credibility of the norms' for which he argues. The assumption here is that to argue in terms of general principles or natural justice is to engage in a political debate and to fall victim to bias and subjectivism. Following his rationalistic credo, Meron hopes to base human rights and humanitarian norms on something more tangible, something that jurists can look at through a distinct (objective, scientific) method and thus ground their conclusions in a more acceptable way — a way that would also better justify their application against nonconsenting states.

The starting point — hoping to argue nontreaty-based human rights and humanitarian norms as custom — however, does not fare too well in Professor Meron's careful analysis of pertinent case law and juristic opinion. He accepts the orthodox 'two-element theory' of custom (*i.e.*, for custom to exist, there must be both material practice to that effect and the practice must have been motivated by a belief that it is required by law (p. 3)), yet case law contains little to actually support such a theory, although passages paying lip service to it are abundant....
...
... [The rest of material practice and the *opinio juris*] is useless, first, because the interpretation of 'state behavior' or 'state will' is not an automatic operation but involves the choice and use of conceptual matrices that are controversial and that usually allow one to argue either way. But it is also, and more fundamentally, useless because ... it is really our certainty that genocide or torture is illegal that allows us to understand state behavior and to accept or reject its legal message, not state behavior itself that allows us to understand that these practices are prohibited by law. It seems to me that if we are uncertain of the latter fact, then there is really little in this world we can feel confident about.

In other words, finding juristic evidence (a precedent, a habitual behaviour, a legal doctrine) to support such a conclusion adds little or nothing to our reasons for adopting it. To the contrary, it contains the harmful implication that it is *only* because this evidence is available that we can justifiably reach our conclusion. It opens the door for disputing the conclusion by disputing the presence of the evidence, or for requiring the same evidence in support of some other equally compelling conclusion, when that evidence might not be so readily available.

It is, of course, true that people are uncertain about right and wrong. The past two hundred years since the Enlightenment and the victory of the principle of arbitrary value have done nothing to teach us about how to know these things or how to cope with our strong moral intuitions. But one should not pretend that this uncertainty will vanish if only one is methodologically 'rigorous'. If the development of the human sciences has taught us anything during its short history, it is that the effort to replace our loss of faith in theories about the right and the good with an absolute faith in our ability to understand human life as a matter of social 'facts' has been a failure. We remain just as unable to derive norms from the facts of state behavior as Hume was. And we are just as compelled to admit that everything we know about norms which are embedded in such behavior is conditioned by an anterior — though at least in some respects largely shared — criterion of what is right and good for human life.
...

QUESTIONS

1. Does the US Supreme Court's method of 'ascertaining' the customary rule appear consistent with some of the observations about the nature of custom and the processes for its development in the preceding readings? Consider, for example, how the Supreme Court deals with:

(a) the issue of *opinio juris*, and its relation to comity, grace, concession or discretion;
(b) the relevance of treaties, as expressing a customary norm or as special rules (*lex specialis*) negating the existence of a custom; and

(c) the departure from the rule of exemption during the Napoleonic wars, as a temporary interruption of or as aborting an emerging custom.

About which of these three aspects of the opinion does the dissenting opinion differ? How would you have argued against the Court's resolution of these three aspects?

2. How do you assess Koskenniemi's argument about customary law and natural law? How would you make the argument that the decision in *The Paquete Habana* in fact supports Koskenniemi's view of what underlies argument about customary law and what indeed should be brought to the forefront of argument?

3. Advocates acting on behalf of prisoners sentenced to death have argued in a number of countries that the death penalty is now barred by customary international law. Based on the materials in Chapter 1(B), and in light of the preceding discussions of custom, how would you develop the argument that customary international law bars capital punishment? How would you make the opposing argument? In developing your arguments, take account of the evidence of state practice and of *opinio juris*, and of the major difference between (a) ascertaining customary law through interaction between two states or between citizens of one state and the government of another state in a case like *The Paquete Habana*, and (b) ascertaining customary international law in a death penalty case.

3. The Changing Character of Customary International Law

The Paquete Habana exemplifies a practice of relying on bilateral rather than multilateral agreements. Since the Second World War, the international legal arena has experienced an extraordinary growth of multilateral instruments, many of them creating inter-governmental organizations (IGOs). So many fields of international law — human rights, peacekeeping, the use of force, monetary and trade agreements, environmental treaties, criminal law — contributed to this significant trend from bilateral to multilateral agreements and institutions as the preferred means by which to address some of the problems of the day. Inevitably these treaties and organizations so changed the international law context and the relationships between states and international law as well as between each other as to influence some basic concepts and doctrines, including doctrinal understanding of the sources of international law.

As we will see in the following chapters, the Universal Declaration of Human Rights (UDHR) and the major human rights treaties suggest the importance of this phenomenon for the evolution of the human rights regime. Not only do the basic duties of the state run towards its internal social and political order and population, but other states — independently or as members of various international human rights organizations — become involved in the process of attempting to assure the observance by delinquent states of those duties. IGOs become to one or another degree independent actors working toward treaties' goals. Or at least the scheme so suggests, for this book's later materials explore how far shy of that 'assurance' the system has in fact progressed.

These and other phenomena, ranging from the development of national and international human rights nongovernmental organizations (NGOs) to globalization embracing multiple cultures, have influenced the very paths of 'making' international law. For example, even outside the world of states and IGOs, there are today so many more voices and places contributing statements, resolutions, declarations, draft codes and other types of instruments about the content of international law — what it 'is', what it 'ought to be'. The UDHR, for example, has evolved from its early status as an aspirational statement to a body of norms in which many provisions are widely accepted as authoritative — as, for example, part of customary international law, or as an authoritative interpretation of the Charter's human rights provisions. Which individuals, which groups, which institutions, which states served as agents of this process? Do those who understand the UDHR, or important parts of it, as authoritative international law, as much so as a treaty, rely on the traditional criteria of customary law to support their understanding? Do UN General Assembly resolutions approved with large majorities occupy a special status? Are different criteria for the formation of custom developing, and becoming widely accepted? Such questions, addressed not only to global and regional IGOs but also to human rights NGOs, to international associations of lawyers and judges, and to a broad range of other non-state groups issuing proposals about human rights, have led to the concept of 'soft law', which is now another, often perplexing ingredient in the multi-faceted evolution of international law. Although of direct relevance in the present context, we examine soft law in Ch. 5A, below.

ANTHEA ROBERTS, TRADITIONAL AND MODERN APPROACHES TO CUSTOMARY INTERNATIONAL LAW: A RECONCILIATION
95 AM. J. INT'L. L. (2001) 757

... [C]ustom has become an increasingly significant source of law in important areas such as human rights obligations. Codification conventions, academic commentary, and the case law of the [ICJ] have also contributed to a contemporary resurrection of custom. These developments have resulted in two apparently opposing approaches, which I term "traditional custom" and "modern custom." ...

... Custom is generally considered to have two elements: state practice and *opinio juris*.... This distinction is problematic because it is difficult to determine what states believe as opposed to what they say. Whether treaties and declarations constitute state practice or *opinio juris* is also controversial. For the sake of clarity, this article adopts Anthony D'Amato's distinction between action (state practice) and statements (*opinio juris*). Thus, actions can form custom only if accompanied by an articulation of the legality of the action. *Opinio juris* concerns statements of belief rather than actual beliefs. Further, treaties and declarations represent *opinio juris* because they are statements about the legality of action, rather than examples of that action....

What I have termed traditional custom results from general and consistent practice followed by states from a sense of legal obligation. It focuses primarily on state practice in the form of interstate interaction and acquiescence. *Opinio juris* is a secondary consideration invoked to distinguish between legal and nonlegal obligations. Traditional custom is evolutionary and is identified through an *inductive* process in which a general custom is derived from specific instances of state practice....

By contrast, modern custom is derived by a *deductive* process that begins with general statements of rules rather than particular instances of practice. This approach emphasizes *opinio juris* rather than state practice because it relies primarily on statements rather than actions. Modern custom can develop quickly because it is deduced from multilateral treaties and declarations by international fora such as the General Assembly, which can declare existing customs, crystallize emerging customs, and generate new customs.... A good example of the deductive approach is the Merits decision in *Military and Paramilitary Activities in and against Nicaragua* [1986 ICJ Rep. 14]. The Court paid lip service to the traditional test for custom but derived customs of non-use of force and nonintervention from statements such as General Assembly resolutions. The Court did not make a serious inquiry into state practice, holding that it was sufficient for conduct to be generally consistent with statements of rules, provided that instances of inconsistent practice had been treated as breaches of the rule concerned rather than as generating a new rule....

...

Traditional custom is closely associated with descriptive accuracy because norms are constructed primarily from state practice — working from practice to theory. Reliance on state practice provides continuity with past actions and reliable predictions of future actions. It results in practical and achievable customs that can actually regulate state conduct. By contrast, modern custom demonstrates a predilection for substantive normativity rather than descriptive accuracy. Modern custom derives norms primarily from abstract statements of *opinio juris* — working from theory to practice. Whereas state practice is clearly descriptive, *opinio juris* is inherently ambiguous in nature because statements can represent *lex lata* (what the law is, a descriptive characteristic) or *lex ferenda* (what the law should be, a normative characteristic). The Court has held that only statements of *lex lata* can contribute to the formation of custom. However, modern custom seems to be based on normative statements of *lex ferenda* cloaked as *lex lata*, for three reasons.

...

[Third], treaties and resolutions often use mandatory language to prescribe a model of conduct and provide a catalyst for the development of modern custom. Treaties and declarations do not merely photograph or declare the current state of practice on moral issues. Rather, they often reflect a deliberate ambiguity between actual and desired practice, designed to develop the law and to stretch the consensus on the text as far as possible. For example, some rights set out in the Universal Declaration of Human Rights of 1948 are expressed in mandatory terms and have achieved customary status even though infringements are 'widespread, often gross and generally tolerated by the international community.' As a result, modern custom often represents progressive development of the law masked as codification by phrasing *lex ferenda* as *lex lata*.

...

The moral content of modern custom explains the strong tendency to discount the importance of contrary state practice in the modern approach. Irregularities in description can undermine a descriptive law, but a normative law may be broken and remain a law because it is not premised on descriptive accuracy. For example, *jus cogens* norms prohibit fundamentally immoral conduct and cannot be undermined by treaty arrangement or inconsistent state practice. Since the subject matter of modern customs is not morally neutral, the international community is not willing to accept any norm established by state practice. Modern custom involves an almost teleological approach, whereby some examples of state practice are used to justify a chosen norm, rather than deriving norms from state practice.... Thus, the importance of descriptive accuracy varies according to the facilitative or moral content of the rule involved.

...

A critique of modern custom.... Deriving customs primarily from treaties and declarations, rather than state practice, is potentially more democratic because it involves practically all states. Most states can participate in the negotiation and ratification of treaties and declarations of international fora, such as the United Nations General Assembly. The notion of sovereign equality (one state, one vote) helps to level the playing field between developed and developing countries. While formal equality cannot remedy all inequalities in power, international fora provide less powerful states with a cost-efficient means of expressing their views. ... [V]otes in the General Assembly usually receive little media scrutiny and are generally not intended to make law. For example, the General Assembly resolution on torture was adopted unanimously, while a much smaller number of states ratified the Convention Against Torture and others entered significant reservations to it.

...

The greatest criticism of modern custom is that it is descriptively inaccurate because it reflects ideal, rather than actual, standards of conduct. The normative nature of modern custom leads to an enormous gap between asserted customs and state practice. For example, customary international law prohibits torture, yet torture is endemic. A similar criticism is made of the 'emptiness' of *jus cogens* norms, which are often flouted in practice. These laws lack efficacy because states have not internalized them as standards of behavior to guide their actions and judge the behavior of others. The regulatory function of modern custom is doubtful because it appears merely to set up aspirational aims rather than realistic requirements about action.... Some theorists characterize modern customs as 'soft laws' or sublegal obligations that do not amount to law. Indeed, norms that are honored in the breach do not yield reliable predictions of future conduct and are likely to bring themselves, and possibly custom as a whole, into disrepute.

...

HUGH THIRLWAY, THE SOURCES OF INTERNATIONAL LAW (2ND ED., 2019) 75

The concept of States 'specially affected' has provoked considerable controversy in recent years, sparked by the inclusion of that concept in the studies prepared by the ILC Special Rapporteur ... . Vociferous opposition by a number of States led ultimately to such mention being excluded from the draft Conclusions ... . Essentially, the opposition was based on the belief that 'specially affected States' meant, or would be interpreted to mean, the more powerful States, those of the 'global North' as distinct from those of the 'global South' ... . However the concept remains available for use in negotiation over the validity of a particular alleged customary rule, and may well be judicially re-endorsed in due course.

A further indication as to the required generality and consistency of practice is given by the ICJ decision in the case of Military and Paramilitary Activities in and against Nicaragua. The Court observed that '[i]t is not to be expected that in the practice of States the application of the [customary] rules in question should have been perfect, in the sense that States should have [acted] with complete consistency ...'. [The Court added that it:]

> ... deems it sufficient that the conduct of States should, in general, be consistent with
> such rules, and that instances of State conduct inconsistent with a given rule should

generally have been treated as breaches of that rule, not as indications of the recognition of a new rule.

While frequent repetition lends weight to a custom, the degree of frequency has to be weighed against the frequency with which the circumstances arise in which the action constituting practice has to be taken, or is appropriate. If the circumstances are such that they only present themselves from time to time, all that can be required is that the response to them has been, overall, consistent; and the fact that there have in sum been only a handful of instances is irrelevant. ...

In the view of most authors, and on the basis of ICJ jurisprudence, while the formation of a custom normally requires a more or less lengthy period of development, the transition from 'regular practice not yet binding as a custom' to 'binding rule of customary law' is something that happens at a particular moment, and in that sense is instantaneous. The word 'crystallization' is often used to refer to this decisive moment. It has, however, been suggested that the normativity of a rule in *statu nascendi* (coming to birth) could be a matter of degree: that its binding quality could 'harden', as it were, as time went by. This may be conceivable, or even probable, as a matter of theory; but the function of law being to settle disputes, at any moment it ought to be possible to say whether a rule in course of formation does or does not exist as a binding rule. ... The essence of custom, in the traditional view, is that its provisions have been hammered out in the resolution of conflicts of interests, or disputes, between States in their day-to-day relations. As has been well observed by Simma and Alston: '[A]n element of interaction—in a broad sense—is intrinsic to, and essential to, the kind of State practice leading to the formation of customary international law ... [T]he processes of customary international law can only be triggered, and continue working, in situations in which States interact, where they apportion or delimit in some tangible way.' ...

...

Turning to the second problem mentioned above, the concept of custom suggests that its rules emerge from the interaction of all States, all sovereign and equal, contributing to its establishment by their action or their reaction (or lack of it): a democratic means of arriving at rules applicable, and acceptable, to all. Even today, this is not necessarily an accurate picture, and that it has been less so in the past is notorious. Certain States have at all times been more powerful and influential, and have been able either to control the practice to be noted as relevant to custom, or to dominate the prevailing *opinio*, so as to influence what becomes established as 'international custom': custom is not necessarily democratic. It has been suggested that the practice hitherto invoked to support the assertion of the existence of a customary rule, has been too limited, being confined to the practice of a certain category of States, and neglecting that of the remainder. But is the fact of bias due the influence of powerful States necessarily a reason for challenging what is law, essentially merely because the observer would have preferred it to be otherwise? A customary norm is, of its nature, not a rule devised by and for an ideal community; it was devised by and for an actual community, and necessarily took into account (inter alia) the power relations within that community.

The relevant distinction between States is sometimes defined in terms of 'strong/weak', but a key element is also whether the practice of the State comes to the attention of the international community, in particular through its recording in the publications of, or within, the State itself. The contention is that this leads to an unbalanced picture of what the general international practice comprises, thus distorting the consequent vision of the law (and, incidentally, conflicting with the principle of sovereign equality of States). There is justice in this criticism, but it is perhaps over-simple. State practice is normally bilateral (at least): if action by a State does not have any impact on its fellows, this is probably because it is within its sovereignty, or at any rate is of no particular significance for the development of the law. If there is contact—not to say conflict—between an 'invisible' State and a 'visible' State, the outcome (which is what matters for custom-development) will become visible in the publications of the 'visible' State. What may remain invisible is the contention of the 'losing' side in the controversy (which will not necessarily be the 'invisible' State), but if it was put forward to no avail it does not generate 'practice'. It is only in the relations between two (or more) 'invisible' States that significant practice might develop, yet remain out of view.

B.S. CHIMNI, 'CUSTOMARY INTERNATIONAL LAW: A THIRD WORLD PERSPECTIVE'
112 AM. J. INT'L L. (2018) 1, 43.

…

VII. Conclusion

The principal aim of the present article is to offer an alternative account of the historical evolution of CIL. It was argued that the doctrine of CIL originated in nineteenth century Europe in the period of the industrial revolution that saw the emergence of a shared legal consciousness and, in its second half, high imperialism. It was also the period in which the positivist method came to dominate the study of international law. Yet, at this point, the inextricable relationship between "formal" and "material" sources of CIL[17] was transparent and undeniable as these developments had roots in the European cultural, social, and political order. The imperial order of the times meant that CIL played a key role in facilitating the colonial project—its rules in the field of state responsibility being a case in point.

The first serious challenge to the Eurocentric doctrine of CIL came after the October revolution. The Soviet Union expressed deep skepticism about CIL as a source of international law as it reflected the practices and *opinio juris* of the leading capitalist powers. Later, the traditional doctrine of CIL came to be actively questioned by the newly independent states advancing a justice critique. These states contended that the traditional doctrine was fashioned by the ideology, interests, and power of metropolitan states. The two critiques necessitated a fresh look at the doctrine of CIL in order to advance a more sustainable theory of CIL that reflected changed times.

A first generation of efforts of western scholars to reformulate the doctrine of CIL appeared in the 1960s and 1970s. These formulations posited a distinction between "formal" and "material" sources of CIL that was given its blessings by the ICJ in the North Sea Continental Shelf case. A principal objective of this distinction was to salvage the doctrine of CIL from its historical condition—of being associated with the colonial and neocolonial projects. Besides the fact that the doctrine of CIL was a western construct, its rules came to be derived from western state practice on which the dominant positivist method placed great stress. Even today the lack of the ready availability of state practice in the instance of postcolonial states means that western states carry the day. Any talk of generality of practice or representative practice in the formation of CIL by default became a reference to the practice of western states. The absence of writings of postcolonial scholars contesting the divide between "formal" and "material" sources of CIL further reduced the possibility of supporting the claims of third world states. But western scholars did not allow matters to rest there. The possibility that postcolonial states could use their numerical strength to give rise to a particular rule of CIL that advanced their interests (as in the case of creating a NIEO) led to the invention of the persistent objector rule to offer a possible escape route to western nations from being compelled to undertake obligations that were not in their interest. Defection was made possible only through producing evidence of objection over time. The persistent objector rule did not require deliberative reasons to be considered. There was thus no room for debating the justice of CIL rules. But as has been pointed out, if "conscientious objection" is not permitted "then the parties are entitled to doubt the bona fides of those who insist on the customs as binding in the name of the community as a whole." On the flip side, a dominant majority of members of the community must be in a position to claim that certain practices that advance the global common good have given rise to norms of CIL.

A second generation of attempts to theorize CIL began as the Cold War neared its end and the neoliberal globalization process gathered momentum. The collapse of the Soviet Union and the diminished opposition of postcolonial states in this period saw the distinction between "formal" and "material" sources emphatically endorsed by ILA and later ILC. But this phase also saw the emergence of the idea of "modern" CIL with its inclusive understanding of "state practice" and greater stress on the element of *opinio juris*. The move permitted relatively rapid development in the fields of [international investment, human rights, humanitarian, criminal and environmental law] and the greater use of CIL norms by domestic courts and international tribunals. The essential aim of the "modern" doctrine of CIL is the generation of norms that safeguard the systemic interests of the global capitalist system. These norms sought to make the international legal order responsive in the era of neoliberal globalization to the concerns of the subaltern states, peoples and groups on the one hand and

---

[17] Following Pellet, the formal sources are 'the processes through which international law rules become legally relevant,' while the material sources are 'the political, sociological, economic, moral or religious origins of the legal rules.' A. Pellet, 'Article 38', in A. Zimmermann et al., (eds.), *The Statute of the International Court of Justice: A Commentary*, (2nd ed., 2012), 731, at 774.

ravaged nature on the other. But the idea of "modern" CIL has caused much anxiety among western realist scholars of international law who are conscious of its negative impact on the ability of advanced capitalist states to realize short-term interests. These scholars are concerned that given the growing internalization of "modern" CIL by domestic courts, the domestic and foreign policies of states may be unduly constrained. In voicing this anxiety, realist scholars like Bradley, Goldsmith, and Posner do not appreciate the salience of "modern" CIL in sustaining the stability and legitimacy of the global capitalist system in the long run.

The ILA and ILC have responded in different ways to the anxiety of realist critics. The ILA has been more sympathetic to the realist view and therefore emphasized the element of state practice in the formation of CIL, even as it has conceded that "where it can be shown that an *opinio juris* exists about a practice that will be sufficient." However, the ILC has given importance to both the elements, leaving room for the expedient invoking of either of them for the rapid development of CIL. From a third world perspective, both the ILA and ILC do not assign sufficient weight to the fact that the state practice of weak states is not easily available and that their *opinio juris* is trumped by the invented doctrines of "specially affected states" and "persistent objectors." Meanwhile, if decision-makers and scholars of weak states are not vigorously contesting the idea of "modern" CIL it is because the rules embody hegemonic ideas and beliefs. The hegemony of ideas and beliefs is, among other things, the function of the growing coincidence of interests between the elites of the first and the third worlds brought about by the ascendance of a transnational capitalist class. It is not that "modern" CIL does not contribute to the global common good, but it does so in an inadequate manner. Its norms can also be turned against subaltern states and actors, as in the case of the doctrine of responsibility to protect. Of course, the role of ideas and beliefs is present even when power and coercion are used to give rise to a norm of CIL. But in such cases, there is more active resistance to them.

In conclusion, it was asked whether a postmodern doctrine of CIL can be advanced to help promote the global common good and safeguard our common humanity. It was submitted that an alternative doctrine must have its roots in a decolonized, self-determined, and plural cultural and political international order in which deliberative reason plays a central role. A postmodern doctrine must therefore, to begin with, rest on the recognition that CIL has historically been an undemocratic source of international law. Indeed, it has been shorthand for norms that accommodate the reality of imperialism. If the dark past of CIL is acknowledged, the distinction between formal and material sources of CIL, endorsed by the ICJ, ILA, and ILC, should be rejected as it veils the harm done to subaltern peoples and actors. A postmodern doctrine would also address the democratic deficit that characterizes the conceptualization and formation of CIL norms. The deficit flows from, among other things, the absence of availability of state practice of third world states, the paucity of writings of its publicists, the lack of adequate weight given to qualifying resolutions of international organizations, and the nonrecognition of the practices of the global civil society. A postmodern doctrine would also distinguish between *opinio juris* as a constituent element of CIL and *opinio juris communis* representing universal conscience in order to inject progressive content into the international legal order. In the final analysis, a postmodern doctrine would redefine the epistemology and ontology of CIL formation in order to help work toward a just world order. Such a doctrine can only be given life through the sustained effort of those social forces that are dissatisfied with the current global order. In this process, the role of critical theories of international law will be crucial as new doctrines are in the final analysis shaped by scholars of international law.

We will return in a later session to examine the concept of jus cogens norms which, in the view of most commentators, are closely related to customary international law. This session focuses first on the categories of 'the general principles of law'.

QUESTION

Compare and contrast the perspectives on customary international law reflected in the articles by Roberts, Thirlway, and Chimni.

B. GENERAL PRINCIPLES AND NATURAL LAW: STATE RESPONSIBILITY

The *Chattin* case described below was decided under a 1923 General Claims Convention between the United States and Mexico, 43 Stat. 1730, T.S. No. 678. That treaty provided that designated claims against Mexico of US citizens (and vice versa) for losses or damages suffered by persons or by their properties that (in the case of the US citizens) had been presented to the US Government for interposition with Mexico and that had remained unsettled 'shall be submitted to a Commission consisting of three members for decision in accordance with the principles of international law, justice and equity'. Each state was to appoint one member, and the presiding third commissioner was to be selected by mutual agreement (and by stipulated procedures failing agreement).

These arbitrations grew out of and further developed the law of state responsibility for injuries to aliens, a branch of international law that was among the important predecessors to contemporary human rights law. That body of law addressed only certain kinds of conflicts — not including, for example, conflicts originating in the first instance in a dispute between a claimant state (X) and a respondent state (Y). Thus it did not cover a dispute, say, based on a claim by X that Y had violated international law by its invasion of X's territory or by its imprisonment of X's ambassador.

Rather, the claims between states that were addressed by the law of state responsibility for injuries to aliens grew out of disputes arising in the first instance between a citizen-national of X and the government of Y. For example, respondent state Y allegedly imprisoned a citizen of claimant state X without hearing or trial, or seized property belonging to citizens of X — allegations which, if true, could show violations of international law. Note that these illustrations involve action leading to injury of X's citizens by governmental officials or organs (executive, legislative, judicial) of Y. The law of state responsibility required that the conduct complained of be that of the state or, in less clear and more complex situations, be ultimately attributable to the state.

In the normal case, the citizen of X would seek a remedy within Y, probably through its judiciary — release from jail, return of the seized property or compensation for it. Indeed, before invoking the aid of his own government, the citizen of X would generally be required under the relevant treaty to pursue such a path, to 'exhaust local remedies'. But that path could prove to be fruitless, because of lack of recourse to Y's judiciary, because that judiciary was corrupt, or because of Y's law adverse to the citizen of X that would certainly be applied by its judiciary. In such circumstances, the injured person may turn to his own government X for diplomatic protection.

The 1924 decision of the Permanent Court of International Justice in the *Mavrommatis Palestine Concessions (Jurisdiction)* case, P.C.I.J., Ser. A, No. 2, gave classic expression to such diplomatic protection. It pointed out that when a state took up the cause of one of its subjects (citizens-nationals) in a dispute originating between that subject and respondent state, the dispute:

> entered upon a new phase; it entered the domain of international law, and became a dispute between two States.... It is an elementary principle of international law that a State is entitled to protect its subjects, when injured by acts contrary to international law committed by another State, from whom they have been unable to obtain satisfaction through the ordinary channels. By taking up the case of one of its subjects and by resorting to diplomatic action or international judicial proceedings on his behalf, a State is in reality asserting its own rights — its right to ensure, in the person of its subjects, respect for the rules of international law.

Precisely what action to take, what form of diplomatic protection to extend, lay within the discretion of the claimant state. If it decided to intervene and thereby make the claim its own, it might espouse the claim through informal conversations with the respondent state, or make a formal diplomatic protest, or exert various economic and political pressures to encourage a settlement (extending at times to military intervention), or, if these strategies failed, have recourse to international tribunals. Such recourse was infrequent. International tribunals to whose jurisdiction states had consented for the resolution of disputes between them were rare. Moreover, states were reluctant to raise controversies between their citizens and foreign states to the level of interstate conflict before an international tribunal except where a clear national interest gave reason to do so.

An arbitral tribunal to which the claimant state turned may have been created by agreement between the disputing states to submit to it designated types of disputes. That agreement may have been part of a general arbitration treaty (which after the Second World War found scant use) covering a broad range of potential disputes between the two parties. Or it may have been a so-called 'compromissory clause' (*compromis*) in a treaty dealing with a specific subject that bound the parties to submit to arbitration disputes that might arise under that treaty. Of course, two states could always agree to submit specified disputes to arbitration, as in the 1923 General Claims Convention between the United States and Mexico under which *Chattin* was decided.

In 1921, ad hoc arbitral tribunals were first supplemented by an international court, the Permanent Court of International Justice provided for in the Covenant of the League of Nations. Again, problems of states' consent to jurisdiction and states' reluctance to start interstate litigation limited the role of that court (and indeed the role of its successor, the International Court of Justice created under the Charter of the United Nations) in developing the law of state responsibility (or, today, in developing the international law of human rights).

The growth in the nineteenth and twentieth centuries of the law of state responsibility for injury to aliens was the product of and evidenced by a range of state interactions — diplomatic protests and responses, negotiated settlements, arbitral decisions — and the writings of scholars. Before the Second World War, there was little attempt at formal codification or creative development of this body of law through treaties — that is, treaties spelling out the content of what international law required of a state in its treatment of aliens.

As it developed, the international law of state responsibility reflected the more intense identification of the individual with his state (or later, the identification of the corporation with the state of its incorporation, or of most of its shareholders) that accompanied the nationalistic trends of that era. This body of law would not have developed so vigorously but for Western colonialism and economic imperialism that reached their zenith during this period.[18] Transnational business operations centred in Europe, and later in the United States as well, penetrated those regions now known as the Third World or developing countries. The protection afforded aliens under international law had obvious importance for the foreign operations of transnational corporations that were often directed by foreign nationals.

In such circumstances, given the links between the success and wealth of corporations in their foreign ventures and national wealth and power, the security of the person and property of a national or corporation operating in a foreign part of the world became a concern of his or its government. That concern manifested itself in the vigorous assertion of diplomatic protection and in the enhanced activity of arbitral tribunals. In the late nineteenth and early twentieth centuries, some such arbitrations occurred under the pressure of actual or threatened military force by the claimant states, particularly against Latin American governments.

A statement in an arbitral proceeding in 1924 by Max Huber, a Judge of the Permanent Court of International Justice, cogently expressed some basic principles of that era's consensus (among states of the developed world) about the law of state responsibility:[19]

> ... It is true that the large majority of writers have a marked tendency to limit the responsibility of the State. But their theories often have political inspiration and represent a natural reaction against unjustified interventions in the affairs of certain nations....

> ... The conflicting interest with respect to the problem of compensation of aliens are, on the one hand, the interest of a State in exercising its public power in its own territory without interference or control of any nature by foreign States and, on the other hand, the interest of the State in seeing the rights of its nationals established in foreign countries respected and well protected.

> Three principles are hardly debatable:

---

[18] See A. Tzvika Nissel, Merchants of Legalism: A History of State Responsibility (1870–1960) (2024).
[19] Judge Huber delivered these remarks in his role as a Reporter (in effect, arbitrator) in a dispute between Great Britain and Spain. *British Claims in the Spanish Zone of Morocco*, 2 U.N.R.I.A.A. (1924) 615, at 639.

...

(2) In general, a person established in a foreign country is subject to the territorial legislation for the protection of his person and his property, under the same conditions as nationals of that country.

(3) A State whose national established in another State is deprived of his rights has a right to intervene if the injury constitutes a violation of international law....

... The territorial character of sovereignty is so essential a trait of contemporary public law that foreign intervention in relationships between a territorial State and individuals subject to its sovereignty can be allowed only in extraordinary cases....

... This right of intervention has been claimed by all States; only its limits are under discussion. By denying this right, one would arrive at intolerable results: international law would become helpless in the face of injustices tantamount to the negation of human personality, for that is the subject which every denial of justice touches.

... No police or other administration of justice is perfect, and it is doubtless necessary to accept, even in the best administered countries, a considerable margin of tolerance. However, the restrictions thus placed on the right of a State to intervene to protect its nationals assume that the general security in the country of residence does not fall below a certain standard....

How was it determined whether, in Huber's words, an 'injury' to an alien 'constitutes a violation of international law', or whether the administration of justice in a given country fell below 'a certain standard'? To what materials would, for example, an arbitral tribunal turn for help in defining the content of that standard? What types of argument and justifications would inform the development of this body of international law? Decisions in the many arbitrations, including the *Chattin* case below, shed light on these questions.

The *Chattin* Case

The *Chattin* case[20] is among the more interesting of the arbitral decisions. Chattin, a US citizen, was a conductor on a railroad in Mexico from 1908 to 1910, when he was arrested for embezzlement of fares. His trial was consolidated with those of several other Americans and Mexicans who had been arrested on similar charges. In February 1911, he was convicted and sentenced to two years' imprisonment. His appeal was rejected in July 1911. In the meantime the inhabitants of Mazatlán, during a political uprising, threw open the doors of the jail and Chattin escaped to the United States. In asserting Chattin's claims, the United States argued that the arrest was illegal, that Chattin was mistreated while in prison, that his trial was unreasonably delayed, and that there were irregularities in the trial. It claimed that Chattin suffered injuries worth $50,000 in compensation.

Of the three members of the Claims Commission, one came from the United States (Nielsen) and another from Mexico (MacGregor). Each wrote an opinion. Excerpts from the opinion of the third Commissioner follow:

COMMISSIONER VAN VOLLENHOVEN

This opinion examined a range of complaints about the conduct of the trial. The Commissioner gave particular attention to three such complaints.

(1) Chattin claimed that he had not been duly informed of the charges. The opinion concluded that this claim was 'proven by the record, and to a painful extent'. The principal complainant, an American manager of the railroad company, made full statements to the Court 'without ever being confronted with the accused and his colleagues', and indeed was 'allowed to submit to the Court a series of anonymous written accusations....It is not shown that the confrontation between Chattin and his

---

[20] *United States of America (B.E. Chattin) v. United Mexican States*, United States–Mexican Claims Commission, 1927. Opinions of Commissioners under the 1923 Convention between the United States and Mexico (1927) 4 U.N.R.I.A.A. 282.

accusers amounted to anything like an effort on the Judge's part to find out the truth'. Nonetheless Chattin was generally aware of the details of the investigation.

(2) Van Vollenhoven dismissed Chattin's charge that witnesses were not sworn as irrelevant, 'as Mexican law does not require an "oath" (it is satisfied with a solemn promise, *protesta*, to tell the truth), nor do international standards of civilization'.

(3) Van Vollenhoven found the charge that the hearings in open court lasted only five minutes was proven by the record. That hearing was 'a pure formality', in which written documents were confirmed and defence counsel said only a word or two. The opinion concludes that 'the whole of the proceedings discloses a most astonishing lack of seriousness on the part of the Court', and cites instances where the judge failed to follow leads or examine certain people. Excerpts follow:

> Neither during the investigations nor during the hearings in open court was any such thing as an oral examination or cross-examination of any importance attempted. It seems highly improbable that the accused have been given a real opportunity during the hearings in open court, freely to speak for themselves. It is not for the Commission to endeavor to reach from the record any conviction as to the innocence or guilt of Chattin and his colleagues; but even in case they were guilty, the Commission would render a bad service to the Government of Mexico if it failed to place the stamp of its disapproval and even indignation on a criminal procedure so far below international standards of civilization as the present one.

Nonetheless, the opinion found the record sufficient to warrant a conviction of Chattin and rejected a charge that the court was biased against American citizens, since four Mexicans were also convicted.

> ... Since this is a case of alleged responsibility of Mexico for injustice committed by its judiciary, it is necessary to inquire whether the treatment of Chattin amounts even to an outrage, to bad faith, to wilful neglect of duty, or to an insufficiency of governmental action recognizable by every unbiased man ... and the answer here again can only be in the affirmative.

Taking all these factors into account, the opinion allowed damages in the sum of $5,000.

COMMISSIONER NIELSEN (CONCURRING)
Nielsen observed that counsel for Mexico had stressed that during the period of investigation a Mexican judge was at liberty to receive anything placed before him, including anonymous accusations. Although European procedure allowed 'a similar measure of latitude' for judges, there was one essential difference: after proceedings before a judge of investigation, the case is taken over by another judge who conducts the actual trial. Thus, said Nielsen, under the French law of the period

> the preliminary examination does not serve as a foundation for the verdict of the judge who decided as to the guilt of the accused. The examination allows the examining judge to determine whether there is ground for formal charge, and in case there is, to decide upon the jurisdiction. ... [The trial of the accused] is before a judge whose functions are of a more judicial character than those of a judge of investigation employing inquisitorial methods in the nature of those used by a prosecutor ....

Nielsen, 'having further in mind the peculiarly delicate character of an examination of judicial proceedings by an international tribunal, as well as the practical difficulties inherent in such examination', concluded that the Commission should render a small award based on the mistreatment of Chattin during the period of investigation.

COMMISSIONER MACGREGOR (DISSENTING)
In his dissent, Commissioner MacGregor referred to the charge that the trial proper lasted only five minutes, 'implying thereby that there was really no trial and that Chattin was convicted without being heard'. This was an 'erroneous criticism which arises from the difference between Anglo-Saxon procedure and that of other countries'. Mexican criminal procedure consisted of two parts: preliminary proceedings (sumario) and plenary

proceedings (plenario). In the sumario, evidence is gathered, investigations occur, the judge or defendant can cross examine. When the judge concludes that there are sufficient facts to establish a case, the sumario ends as the record is given to all parties to be certain that they do not request more testimony and so that they can make final pleas. Then a public hearing (plenario) is held 'in which the parties very often do not have anything further to allege'. That hearing is formal, and serves little new function. Such occurred in the *Chattin* case.

> In view of the foregoing explanation, I believe that it becomes evident that the charge, that there was no trial proper, can not subsist, for, in Mexican procedure, it is not a question of a trial in the sense of Anglo-Saxon law, which requires that the case be always heard in plenary proceedings, before a jury, adducing all the circumstances and evidence of the cause, examining and cross-examining all the witnesses, and allowing the prosecuting attorney and counsel for the defense to make their respective allegations. International law insures that a defendant be judged openly and that he be permitted to defend himself, but in no manner does it oblige these things to be done in any fixed way, as they are matters of internal regulation and belong to the sovereignty of States. ...

> ...

> ... It is hardly of any use to proclaim in theory respect for the judiciary of a nation, if, in practice, it is attempted to call the judiciary to account for its minor acts. It is true that sometimes it is difficult to determine when a judicial act is internationally improper and when it is so from a domestic standpoint only. In my opinion the test which consists in ascertaining if the act implies damage, wilful neglect, or palpable deviation from the established customs becomes clearer by having in mind the damage which the claimant could have suffered. There are certain defects in procedure that can never cause damage which may be estimated separately, and that are blotted out or disappear, to put it thus, if the final decision is just. There are other defects which make it impossible for such decision to be just. The former, as a rule, do not engender international liability; the latter do so, since such liability arises from the decision which is iniquitous because of such defects. To prevent an accused from defending himself, either by refusing to inform him as to the facts imputed to him or by denying him a hearing and the use of remedies; to sentence him without evidence, or to impose on him disproportionate or unusual penalties, to treat him with cruelty and discrimination; are all acts which per se cause damage due to their rendering a just decision impossible. But to delay the proceedings somewhat, to lay aside some evidence, there existing other clear proofs, to fail to comply with the adjective law in its secondary provisions and other deficiencies of this kind, do not cause damage nor violate international law. Counsel for Mexico justly stated that to submit the decisions of a nation to revision in this respect was tantamount to submitting her to a régime of capitulations. All the criticism which has been made of these proceedings, I regret to say, appears to arise from lack of knowledge of the judicial system and practice of Mexico, and, what is more dangerous, from the application thereto of tests belonging to foreign systems of law. For example, in some of the latter the investigation of a crime is made only by the police magistrates and the trial proper is conducted by the Judge. Hence the reluctance in accepting that one same judge may have the two functions and that, therefore, he may have to receive in the preliminary investigation (instrucción) of the case all kinds of data, with the obligation, of course, of not taking them into account at the time of judgment, if they have no probative weight.... [T]he foreign-law procedure is used to understand what is a trial or open trial imagining at the same time that it must have the sacred forms of common-law and without remembering that the same goal is reached by many roads. And the same can be said when speaking of the manner of taking testimony of witnesses, of cross-examination, of holding confrontations, etc.... In view of the above considerations, I am of the opinion that this claim should be disallowed.

STATE RESPONSIBILITY TODAY

The opinions of the Commissioners underscore the methodological problems in developing a minimum international standard of criminal procedure out of such diverse materials — a diversity that was restricted in *Chattin* to Europe and Latin America, hence far less perplexing than today's worldwide diversity of legal cultures and criminal processes. A treaty was relevant to *Chattin*, but as indicated above, it addressed the scope and structure of the arbitration between the United States and Mexico rather than the international norms of criminal procedure to be applied. The only reference of the General Claims Convention to applicable norms was the terse provision in Article 1 that claims should be submitted to the tripartite Commission 'for decision in accordance with the principles of international law, justice and equity'.

Today a dispute like that in *Chattin* could draw on a human rights treaty, the International Covenant on Civil and Political Rights (ICCPR), to be discussed later, that in 2024 had 173 state parties. Article 14 of that Covenant dealing with criminal trials provides in relevant part:

1. All persons shall be equal before the courts.... [E]veryone shall be entitled to a fair and public hearing by [an] impartial tribunal....

2. Everyone ... shall have the right to be presumed innocent until proved guilty according to law.

3. [E]veryone shall be entitled to the following minimum guarantees ...:

    d. To be tried in his presence and to defend himself in person or through legal assistance of his own choosing ... .

    e. To examine, or have examined, the witnesses against him and to obtain the attendance and examination of witnesses on his behalf. ...

The International Court of Justice confirmed in 2007 that the scope of international law protection 'governing alleged violations of the minimum standard of treatment of aliens, has subsequently widened to include, inter alia, internationally guaranteed human rights.'[21] The fact that this body of law now goes well beyond the protection of aliens was also reflected in the International Law Commission's Draft Articles on Responsibility of States for Internationally Wrongful Acts (2001). As a result, state responsibility today encapsulates a broad set of 'secondary' rules that determine such matters as when a state is responsible for an internationally wrongful act and the remedies for a state's breach of 'primary' or substantive rules of international law (such as the prohibition on genocide). For present purposes, we provide a rough sketch of these secondary rules. They include the following subjects:

1. **Attribution**: This set of rules determine when conduct consisting of the acts or omissions of state officials or other groups and individuals can be considered the responsibility of the state. These rules are relevant in the human rights context, for example, in determining the conditions under which a state is responsible for extraterritorial human rights violations by corporations and when a state is responsible for human rights violations committed by armed opposition groups that the state supports.

2. **Circumstances Precluding Wrongfulness**: This set of rules provide defences that preclude the wrongfulness of state conduct that is not in conformity with the state's international obligations. These rules include duress, force majeure, necessity and self-defence. In the human rights context, for example, necessity may allow a state to suspend obligations that implicate human rights but forecloses that defence if the state contributed to bringing about the condition of necessity.

3. **Consequences that follow when a state breaches an international obligation**: These rules set forth remedies that a state must provide for violation of an international obligation. The remedies include cessation, reparations, restitution, compensation, satisfaction and assurances of non-repetition. In the human rights context, these rules are relevant, for example, in determining what actions by a

---

[21] *Ahmadou Sadio Diallo (Republic of Guinea v. Democratic Republic of the Congo)*, Preliminary Objections, Judgment, I.C.J. Reports 2007 (II) 599, para. 39.

state are sufficient when it has subject a foreign national to execution without access to their foreign consul in violation of an international agreement.

4. **Countermeasures**: These rules regulate the permissible range of responses to another state's breach of international law. In the human rights context, these rules may be important in determining whether and to what degree a state may employ sanctions in response to another state's human rights violations. Notably, these rules also preclude states from taking countermeasures in other contexts that would affect 'obligations for the protection of fundamental human rights' or 'obligations of a humanitarian character prohibiting reprisals' (Art. 50).[22]

It is important to note two additional features of this area of law. First, state responsibility exists side by side with treaty law, including those treaties governing human rights. However, when the latter constitute *lex specialis*, or special rules, they take priority if there is any inconsistency. Second, the articles of state responsibility are highly focused on state-to-state interactions. That feature limits their value for human rights law. Admittedly, Article 33 (pertaining to consequences of a breach) provides that the obligations set forth by these rules can be owed to another state 'or to the international community as a whole'; and Article 33 also provides that nothing in the rules should prejudice any rights arising from the international responsibility of a state that would 'accrue directly to any person'. Nevertheless, many of the rules are framed in terms of an injury to another state and the actions that states may take in response to being unlawfully injured.

QUESTIONS

1. Why is international law relevant to this decision? Were there any international factors in the trial and conviction and, if so, how do they compare with the international factors in *The Paquete Habana*?

2. How would you identify the most serious problem in the judicial process leading to Chattin's conviction — say, on the basis of a comparison with judicial processes in other legal systems?

3. How do the Commissioners approach the task of identifying an 'international standard of civilization' (or, within the terms of the 1923 Convention, the relevant 'international law, justice and equity') against which they are to test the legality of the conviction? Do they resort to customary international law?

4. Would the tribunal's task have been much simpler if there had been a treaty between the United States and Mexico regulating treatment of aliens that reflected Article 14 of the ICCPR? Would Article 14 have resolved the basic issues on its face?

General Principles

OSCAR SCHACHTER, INTERNATIONAL LAW IN THEORY AND PRACTICE (1991) 50

Chapter IV: General Principles and Equity

...

The Broad Expanse of General Principles of Law

We can distinguish five categories of general principles that have been invoked and applied in international law discourse and cases. Each has a different basis for its authority and validity as law. They are:

(1) The principles of municipal law 'recognized by civilized nations'.

---

[22] See J. Crawford, *The International Law Commission's Articles on State Responsibility: Introduction Text and Commentaries* (2002).

(2) General principles of law 'derived from the specific nature of the international community'.
(3) Principles 'intrinsic to the idea of law and basic to all legal systems'.
(4) Principles 'valid through all kinds of societies in relationships of hierarchy and co-ordination'.
(5) Principles of justice founded on 'the very nature of man as a rational and social being'.

Although these five categories are analytically distinct, it is not unusual for a particular general principle to fall into more than one of the categories. For example, the principle that no one shall be a judge in his own cause or that a victim of a legal wrong is entitled to reparation are considered part of most if not all, systems of municipal law and as intrinsic to the basic idea of law.

Our first category, general principles of municipal law, has given rise to a considerable body of writing and much controversy. Article 38(1)(c) of the Statute of Court does not expressly refer to principles of national law but rather general principles 'recognized by civilized nations'.... Elihu Root, the American member of the drafting committee, prepared the text finally adopted and it seemed clear that his amendment was intended to refer to principles 'actually recognized and applied in national legal systems'. The fact that the subparagraph was distinct from those on treaty and custom indicated an intent to treat general principles as an independent source of law, and not as a subsidiary source. As an independent source, it did not appear to require any separate proof that such principles of national law had been 'received' into international law.

However, a significant minority of jurists holds that national law principles, even if generally found in most legal systems, cannot *ipso facto* be international law. One view is that they must receive the *imprimatur* of State consent through custom or treaty in order to become international law. The strict positivist school adheres to that view. A somewhat modified version is adopted by others to the effect that rules of municipal law cannot be considered as recognized by civilized nations unless there is evidence of the concurrence of States on their status as international law. Such concurrence may occur through treaty, custom or other evidence of recognition. This would allow for some principles, such as *res judicata*, which are not customary law but are generally accepted in international law....

...

... The most important limitation on the use of municipal law principles arises from the requirement that the principle be appropriate for application on the international level. Thus, the universally accepted common crimes — murder, theft, assault, incest — that apply to individuals are not crimes under international law by virtue of their ubiquity....

At the same time, I would suggest a somewhat more positive approach for the emergent international law concerned with the individual, business companies, environmental dangers and shared resources. In as much as these areas have become the concern of international law, national law principles will often be suitable for international application. This does not mean importing municipal rules 'lock, stock and barrel', but it suggests that domestic law rules applicable to such matters as individual rights, contractual remedies, liability for extra-hazardous activities, or restraints on use of common property, have now become pertinent for recruitment into international law. In these areas, we may look to representative legal systems not only for the highly abstract principles of the kind referred to earlier but to more specific rules that are sufficiently widespread as to be considered 'recognized by civilized nations'....

The second category of general principles included in our list comprises principles derived from the specific character of the international community. The most obvious candidates for this category of principles are ... the necessary principles of co-existence. They include the principles of *pacta sunt servanda*, non-intervention, territorial integrity, self-defence and the legal equality of States. Some of these principles are in the United Nations Charter and therefore part of treaty law, but others might appropriately be treated as principles required by the specific character of a society of sovereign independent members.

...

The foregoing comments are also pertinent to the next two categories of general principles. The idea of principles *'jus rationale'* 'valid through all kinds of human societies' ... is associated with traditional natural law doctrine. At the present time its theological links are mainly historical as far as international law is concerned, but its principal justification does not depart too far from the classic natural law emphasis on the nature of 'man', that is, on the human person as a rational and social creature.

The universalist implication of this theory — the idea of the unity of the human species — has had a powerful impetus in the present era. This is evidenced in at least three significant political and legal developments. The first is the global movements against discrimination on grounds of race, colour and sex. The second is the move toward general acceptance of human rights. The third is the increased fear of nuclear annihilation. These three developments strongly reinforce the universalistic values inherent in natural law doctrine. They have found expression in numerous international and constitutional law instruments as well as in popular movements throughout the world directed to humanitarian ends. Clearly, they are a 'material source' of much of the new international law manifested in treaties and customary rules.

In so far as they are recognized as general principles of law, many tend to fall within our fifth category — the principles of natural justice. This concept is well known in many municipal law systems (although identified in diverse ways). 'Natural justice' in its international legal manifestation has two aspects. One refers to the minimal standards of decency and respect for the individual human being that are largely spelled out in the human rights instruments. We can say that in this aspect, 'natural justice' has been largely subsumed as a source of general principles by the human rights instruments....

* * *

Different Views

The views of commentators on the role of general principles vary considerably. Alain Pellet and Daniel Müller, 'Article 38', in Andreas Zimmermann and Christian Tams. (eds.), *The Statute of the International Court of Justice: A Commentary* (2019) 819, at 941, downplay their significance. They observe that the Court 'will usually only resort to them in order to fill a gap in the treaty or customary rules available to settle a particular dispute' and 'will decline to invoke them when other rules exist'. They explain this marginality by noting that 'general principles are difficult to handle', that they must 'be discovered in domestic rules' which are not formally a source of international law, and that they are inevitably transitory in the sense that their repeated use will transform them into custom.

In contrast, Mads Andenas and Ludovica Chiussi in Andenas et al. (eds.), *General Principles and the Coherence of International Law* (2019) 34 attribute three 'decisive roles' to general principles: (1) as 'a cohesive force certifying the systemic nature of international law'; (2) as a centripetal force 'providing a common ground for interaction' among different bodies of law; and (3) reducing the separation between international law and municipal legal systems'. Similarly, a former President of the ICJ (Abdulqawi A Yusuf, 'Concluding Remarks', in Andenas et al (above) 458), has identified three ways in which general principles promote coherence in the international legal system: (1) 'a small number of general principles can be said to underlie the conscience of humanity generally'; (2) they may reflect 'the common views of the international community on matters that belong – to borrow Judge Cançado Trindade's terminology – to "the domain of superior … human values, to be safeguarded, [yet] not sufficiently worked upon in international case law and doctrine"'; and (3) they may 'also reflect relatively uncontroversial common values regarding … the proper functioning of the legal system.'

In 2019, the International Law Commission began working on the topic of general principles. Its Special Rapporteur, Marcelo Vázquez-Bermúdez, has identified two different categories: those 'derived from national legal systems', and those 'formed within the international legal system'. The latter reflects a principle that: 'is widely acknowledged in treaties and other international instruments; underlies general rules of conventional or customary international law; or is inherent in the basic features and fundamental requirements of the international legal system' (UN Doc. A/CN.4/741 (2020) para. 119). In his 2022 report (UN Doc. A/CN.4/753) the rapporteur argues that, in addition to filling gaps, general principles can constitute an independent basis for rights and obligations (para. 110), may serve to clarify certain aspects of customary international law (para. 138), and may serve to ensure overall coherence not just through gap-filling but 'by establishing substantive rights and obligations, secondary rules, procedural rules or interpretative rules' (para. 146).

The Teachings of Publicists

The final source referred to in Article 38 is 'the teachings of the most highly qualified publicists of the various nations'. In the era of *The Paquete Habana* this concept was readily translatable into the major treatises produced in various countries, to which the U.S. Supreme Court referred. Today, however, there are vastly more treatises and a great many other means through which leading 'publicists' express their views. Using the ICJ as the lens through which to make an assessment of the importance of this source, Pellet and Müller (see above), minimizes its formal significance:

> 338 If the influence of the doctrinal views on the Court's decisions were to be evaluated according to the number of citations in the judgments and advisory opinions, it would be very proximate to nil … . [T]he Court seems to have only referred (and rarely) to 'the teachings of legal authorities', 'legal doctrine', 'the opinions of writers', or 'legal thinking' in general. In the Lotus case, the Permanent Court referred to the 'teachings of publicists' leaving expressly apart 'the question as to what their value may be from the point of view of establishing the existence of a rule of customary law'.

> 339 It is not illogical that the weight of the legal doctrine, so eminently influential in laying the foundations of international law, decreases with the growth of international judicial activity, the development of the case law of the Court and the new means to gain knowledge of State practice. However, the scarce avowed use of the 'teachings of publicists' in the Court's case law probably does not accurately reflect the influence these 'teachings' still have. A sign of this is given by the fairly abundant references to the opinions of writers in the opinions of the individual judges: this suggests that these views have probably been discussed during the deliberation.

> 340 Be this as it may, there is no doubt that the practice of the Court not to refer expressly to particular authors is wise and appropriate. The intrinsic scientific value and reliability of the doctrine is extremely variable, probably as much as is the exploitability of the works of scholars who, quite often, take delight in abstract discussions which can only be of little help in the adjucating process. International law is a 'small world' not exempt from jealousy and envy and the Court is certainly well-advised not to distribute good or bad marks. Moreover, one must admit that, as unfortunate as it is, the main doctrinal 'production' still comes from the North and more particularly from a handful of countries where international law has gained a rather high degree of sophistication; too much emphasis on the 'teachings of publicists' by the Court would unavoidably throw light on this unfortunate situation while, at the same time, showing that 'the different nations', in principle required by the text of Article 38, para. 1 (d), are not so 'different'.

A very different perspective is offered by Sandesh Sivakumaran, 'The Influence of Teachings of Publicists on the Development of International Law', 66 *I. C. L. Q.* (2017) 1. He defines the category more broadly:

> … Insofar as publicists are concerned, it includes entities that have been empowered by States to produce teachings; expert groups, standing and ad hoc; and ordinary publicists. Teachings are also made up of different types, and include digests, treatises, textbooks, monographs, commentaries, journal articles and blog posts. All are of different types, have different goals in mind, and appeal to different audiences. Teachings of publicists should thus not be limited either to the individual publicist or to the repository of State practice.

> The influence of teachings of publicists is difficult to assess. It includes, but is not limited to, an assessment of citation by courts and tribunals. Citation is one useful measure of determining influence, but citation does not necessarily mean influence and lack of citation certainly does not mean lack of influence. More importantly for present purposes, focus on citation by courts and tribunals privileges the role of these bodies in the development of international law and downplays the role of other actors, such as States, international organizations and treaty bodies. It also understates the more pervasive

influence of teachings, such as on the structure of the discipline, and on students of international law, who constitute later generations of international lawyers. Instead, influence should be assessed by reference to how all the actors within the community of international lawyers use or do not use the teachings of publicists. Individual publicists do not create law by themselves. Rather, they constitute a part of the community that does create the law. Thus, it is the interaction between teachings and the members of the community of international lawyers that is determinative of influence.

> ... it is evident that teachings of publicists continue to have an important influence on the making and shaping of international law. The precise nature of the influence varies considerably. It includes the publicist as the originator of ideas, as the finessor of norms, and as the 'grammarian'. The influence also varies by publicist. The balance between the influence of teachings of State-empowered entities and ordinary publicists has changed, with the former proving particularly significant. Ordinary publicists continue to play a crucial role, but their role is different to times past. Ultimately, as Wolfke put it: 'the influence of doctrine on the formation of international law in general is certainly rather behind-the-scenes and anonymous. To disregard it would, however, be to say the least, unjustified.'

In 2010, Singapore's highest court, in examining the legality of the mandatory death penalty, took into account the views expressed on the matter by two UN Special Rapporteurs. It did so on the basis that they were part of 'the teachings of the most highly qualified publicists of the various nations', as provided for in Article 38 of the ICJ Statute. The Court concluded that while the opinions were relevant, 'they are not in themselves sources of CIL. Instead, they are a subsidiary means for determining the existence or otherwise of rules of CIL.'[23]

C. SLAVERY, THE INTERWAR MINORITIES REGIME AND THE ROLE OF TREATIES

1. Treaties and the Abolition of Slavery

Slavery is one of the most heinous violations of human rights. While it has existed in different forms since ancient times, it was not until the early nineteenth-century that those seeking its abolition began to use the tools of international law for that purpose. Up until then, international law, partly reflecting Roman law, had been an important factor in facilitating and legitimizing the slave trade.[24] Treaties were to play an important role in achieving eventual abolition.

The following analysis traces the evolution of the nineteenth-century treaty-making.

> ... Between 1501 and 1867, 10.7 million people were enslaved and transported from Africa to the Western Hemisphere — an average of over 34,000 persons every year for over three and a half centuries. The process was inhuman at every step of the way. Large numbers died en route from their homes to the ports on the African coast. The conditions on the slave ships were atrocious. Holds were packed full with men, women, and children lying "spooned" tight behind one another for five weeks or more in urine- and feces-drenched squalor. On average, fifteen percent of the "cargo" died. And conditions upon arrival, especially on the plantations in the West Indies, were generally appalling. ...

> ... [By 1814 Britain] was estimated to have had over one million slaves in the Caribbean ..., and British territories were producing more than fifty percent of Europe's sugar

---

[23] *Yong Vui Kong v. Public Prosecutor* [2010] 2 Singapore Law Reports 192, para. 97, Court of Appeal.
[24] A. Martineau, 'Georges Scelle's Study of the Slave Trade: French Solidarism Revisited,' 27 *Eur. J. Int'l L.* (2017) 1131.

imports. At the end of the eighteenth century, British slave traders continued to land fifty thousand slaves annually in the New World.

The rise of the [British] abolition movement was surprisingly rapid and greatly assisted by the use of highly innovative techniques. Specifically, the movement relied on pamphleteering and other public relations tools, the gathering of mass petitions on a scale previously unseen, and consumer boycotts. Quaker and other activists succeeded in mobilizing diverse constituencies, and women emerged as important players. Starting in 1789, an abolition bill was put before Parliament every year for eighteen years until finally both houses of Parliament passed the 1807 Act for the Abolition of the Slave Trade.

The campaign that culminated in this Act is familiar territory. Less well known is the network of treaties that were negotiated and the mixed commissions that were established to implement the ban. Since the British legislation could apply only to British ships, it was essential that Britain find ways to extend the application of the ban or the slack would simply be taken up by ships trading under other flags. Initially, the Napoleonic Wars provided a legal justification to board ships on the high seas in order to ascertain whether they were either enemy ships or others providing de facto support to the enemy. Although the war was over by 1815, and peacetime searches were illegal, the practice continued until the British courts began in 1817 to invalidate the resulting seizures of alleged slave ships of other nations. The British government then initiated a series of long-drawn-out negotiations designed to create a network of bilateral treaties with the key trading states. In 1814, treaties were signed with both the Netherlands and the United States, although the treaty with the latter contained no enforcement provision. Negotiations with France and Spain stalled, but in 1815 Britain "succeeded through a combination of bribery and threats" in getting Portugal to sign a treaty that included enforcement provisions, although this did not apply to the trade south of the equator. In order to assuage fears that mutual inspection arrangements would, in practice, license the British and their own judicial system at the expense of other nations' sovereignty, Britain proposed bilateral arrangements to create specialized tribunals. These "mixed commissions" were set up pursuant to bilateral treaties signed with Portugal, Spain, and the Netherlands in 1817–18. Eventually Sweden, Argentina, Uruguay, Bolivia, and Ecuador also signed such treaties. But France never did, and until the Civil War the United States resisted all enforcement arrangements. ...[25]

Assessments of the importance of these early treaties vary. Jenny Martinez has argued strongly that while the treaties and tribunals 'did not alone end the slave trade, they played an important role in consolidating the consensus against the slave trade and provided a mechanism for cooperation between nations.'[26] Samuel Moyn, in contrast, dismisses them as 'a minor episode in the history of anti-slavery.'[27] In examining factors leading to abolition, most historians tend to focus more on the role of slave revolutions and uprising, on-board slave rebellions, the changing economics of slavery, and imperial self-interest, than on the treaties.

Nevertheless, soft law declarations and treaties did lay the foundations for abolition. Among the former was the declaration by major European powers at the 1815 Congress of Vienna that the slave trade was 'repugnant to the principles of humanity and universal morality' and that they wished to end 'a scourge, which has so long desolated Africa, degraded Europe, and afflicted humanity'. Much later, towards the end of the nineteenth century, 17 states adopted the Convention Relative to the Slave Trade and Importation into Africa of Firearms, Ammunition, and Spiritous Liquors (1890) which stated that it would 'put an end to Negro Slave Trade by land as well as by sea' and 'improve the moral and material conditions of existence of the native races.' In 1926, the League of Nations adopted the Slavery Convention, 1926 which aimed to achieve 'the complete suppression' and 'the abolition of slavery and the slave trade'. In Article 1 it defined slavery as 'the status or condition of a person over whom any or all of the powers attaching to the right of ownership are exercised,' and the slave trade was defined to include 'all acts involved in the capture, acquisition or disposal of a person with intent to

[25] P. Alston, 'Does the Past Matter? On the Origins of Human Rights,'126 *Harvard Law Review* (2013) 2043, at 2045
[26] J. S. Martinez, 'The Anti-Slavery Movement and the Rise of International Non-Governmental Organizations,' in D. Shelton (ed.), *The Oxford Handbook of International Human Rights Law* (2013) 222, at 238.
[27] S. Moyn, 'Of Deserts and Promised Lands: The Dream of Global Justice,' *Nation,* 29 February 2012.

reduce him to slavery; all acts involved in the acquisition of a slave with a view to selling or exchanging him; all acts of disposal by sale or exchange of a slave acquired with a view to being sold or exchanged, and, in general, every act of trade or transport in slaves.'

Thus, the Convention sought not only to end slavery and the slave trade in fact, but also in law: to abolish laws which allowed for such enslavement.[28] The Convention is wider in scope than its title suggests, as it addresses not only slavery but also compulsory or forced labour, and the slave trade. Pre-dating the establishment of international human rights law, the Slavery Convention is an instrument of penal law, mandating that the High Contracting Parties 'adopt the necessary measures in order that severe penalties' be imposed. The Convention creates differing obligations as between the slave trade, which requires States to 'prevent and suppress', and slavery where the Parties were given time to 'bring about, progressively and as soon as possible, the complete abolition of slavery in all its forms'. Where forced labour is concerned, the obligation set out by the Convention is to 'take all necessary measures to prevent compulsory or forced labour from developing into conditions analogous to slavery'. In 1956 the UN adopted the Supplementary Convention on the Abolition of Slavery, the Slave Trade, and Institutions and Practices Similar to Slavery.

2. The Minorities Regime after the First World War

The *Minority Schools in Albania* opinion, which follows, illustrates treaties as a source and major expression of international law, and introduces another field of international law that influenced the growth of the human rights regime. The background to the minorities question is noted by Will Kymlicka:

> The rise of the nation-state has often been catastrophic for ethnic and religious minorities. Consider the Balkans and the Middle East. For some 1,500 years, a panoply of ethnic, linguistic, and religious communities lived side by side under both the Byzantine and Ottoman empires. Yet ever since these empires were replaced with nation-states, we have witnessed a terrible "unmixing of peoples," due to civil wars, ethnic cleansing, genocide, and forced assimilation. Inter-communal relations of tolerance and conviviality that had survived for centuries were torn apart in a few short decades under the nation-state.
>
> These conflicts are often described as evidence of "ancient ethnic hatreds," but in fact they are the result of the rise of the modern nation-state, whose very logic turns "minorities" into a "problem." It is worth noting that none of the ethnic or religious groups in the Byzantine and Ottoman empires were considered "minorities," in part because there was no "majority." These empires did not rule in the name of a particular majority nation, but rather ruled as a dynasty over all their diverse subjects. These multi-ethnic dynastic empires have now been swept away by the rise of nation-states, each of which claims to rule in the name of a particular people or nation. (What was once the territory of the Ottoman empire now comprises 43 such nation-states.) …
>
> … Minorities pose a persistent existential threat to state legitimacy. Each nation-state's claim to sovereignty flows from the claim that it represents "the people" in whose name it governs. It is therefore destabilizing of a state's legitimacy to have a group within the boundaries of the state who think of themselves as forming or belonging to a distinct people.[29]

Treaties and other special regimes to protect minorities have a long history in international law dating from the emergence in the seventeenth century of the modern form of the political state, sovereign within its territorial boundaries. Within Europe, religious issues became a strong concern since states often included more than one religious denomination, and abuse by a state of a religious minority could lead to intervention by other states where that religion was dominant. Hence peace treaties sometimes included provisions on religious minorities. In the eighteenth and nineteenth centuries, the precarious situation of Christian minorities within the Ottoman

---

[28] For a strong critique of the way in which this regime has been implemented see C. Gevers, 'Refiguring Slavery Through International Law: The 1926 Slavery Convention, the "Native Labor Code" and Racial Capitalism', 25 *J. Int. Econ. Law* (2022) 312.

[29] W. Kymlicka, 'Minority Rights', in C. Brown and R. Eckersley (eds.), *The Oxford Handbook of International Political Theory* (2018) 166.

Empire and of religious minorities in newly independent East European or Balkan states led to outbreaks of violence and to sporadic treaty regulation.

The First World War ushered in an era of heightened attention to problems of racial, religious or linguistic minorities. The collapse of the great Austro-Hungarian and Ottoman multinational empires, and the chaos as the Russian empire of the Romanoffs was succeeded by the Soviet Union, led to much redrawing of maps and the creation of new states. President Wilson's Fourteen Points, however compromised they became in the Versailles Treaty and later arrangements, nonetheless exerted influence on the postwar settlements. In it and other messages, Wilson stressed the ideals of the freeing of minorities and the related 'self-determination' of peoples or nationalities. That concept of self-determination, so politically powerful and open to such diverse interpretations, continues to this day to be much disputed and to have profound consequences. It not only appears in the UN Charter but is given a position of high prominence in the two principal human rights covenants.

From concepts like 'self-determination', and out of the legacy of nineteenth-century liberal nationalism that saw the development of nation-states like Germany and Italy, the principle of nationalities took on a new force. Here was another ambiguous and disputed concept — the 'nation' or 'nationality' as distinct from the political state, the nation (often identified with a 'people') defined in cultural or historical terms, often defined more concretely in racial, linguistic and religious terms. One goal in displacing the old empires with new or redrawn states was to identify the nation with the state — ideally, to give each 'nation' its own state. Membership in a 'nation' would ideally be equivalent to membership in a 'state' consisting only or principally of that nation.

Within the pure realization of this ideal, all 'Poles', for example, would be situated in Poland; there would be no 'Polish' national minority in other states, and other 'nationalities' would not be resident in Poland. Indeed, the detaching of Poland after the First World War from the empires and states that had absorbed different parts of it represented one of the few instances of relatively strict congruence between the 'nation' and 'state'. There were polar moves; for example, the creation of Yugoslavia as a multiethnic state that after 70 years has had such tragic consequences.

Of course the goal of total identification of state with nation — a goal itself disputed and in contradiction with other conceptions of the political state that did not emphasize cultural homogeneity or ethnic purity — could not be realized. Life and history were and remain too various and complex for such precise correlation. The nineteenth-century examples of Germany and Italy, for instance, were far from unitary; each had its national, ethnic, linguistic and religious minorities. National or ethnic homogeneity could be achieved in the vast majority of the world's states only by the compulsory and massive migrations of minority groups, migrations far more systematic and coercive than were some of the population movements and exchanges after the First World War. A 'nation' defined, say, in linguistic-religious terms would generally transcend national boundaries and be located in the territories of two or several sovereign states in the new world created by the postwar settlements. A Greek-speaking Christian minority would, for example, be present in the reconfigured Muslim Albania.

Bear in mind another confusing linguistic usage. The term 'national' is generally used in international law to signify the subjects or citizens of a state. Hence members of the 'German' nation (in the sense of a 'people' and' culture') living in Poland could be Polish 'nationals' in the sense of being citizens of Poland. Or they could possess only German citizenship and be alien residents in Poland. In the *Minority Schools in Albania* case that follows, members of the Greek-speaking Christian minority (part of a 'nation' in the cultural or ethnic sense) in Muslim Albania were 'nationals' (citizens) of Albania. One can imagine the ambiguity attending the frequent usage of the term 'national minorities', which could mean at least (1) a group in a state belonging in the cultural or ethnic sense to a 'nation' that constituted a minority in that state, or (2) all minorities in a state who were 'nationals' (citizens) of that state.

After the First World War, the victorious powers and the new League of Nations sought to address this situation. They confronted the impossibility, even if it were desirable, of creating ethnically homogeneous states. Hence, they had to deal with the continuing presence in states of minorities which had frequently been abused in ways ranging from economic discrimination to pogroms and other violence that could implicate other states, spill across international boundaries and lead to war. The immediate trigger for the outbreak of the First World War in the tormented Balkans was fresh in memory.

President Wilson had proposed that the Covenant of the League of Nations include norms governing the protection of minorities that would have embraced all members of the League. The other major powers rejected this approach, preferring discrete international arrangements to handle discrete problems of minorities in particular states of Central-East Europe and the Balkans rather than a universal treaty system. This compromise led to the regime of the so-called 'Minorities Treaties' that were imposed on the new or reconfigured states of Central-East Europe and the Balkans.

For some states like Austria and Hungary, provisions for minority protection were included in the peace treaties. Other states like Poland or Greece signed minority protection treaties with the allied and associated powers. Some states like Albania and Lithuania made minority protection declarations as a condition for their membership in the League of Nations. There were also bilateral treaties protecting minorities such as one between Germany and Poland. Note that one of the features of this new regime was to insulate the victorious powers from international regulation of their treatment of their own citizens belonging to minorities.

Although there were significant variations among these treaties and declarations, many provisions were common. The 1919 Minorities Treaty between the Principal Allied and Associated Powers and Poland served as a model for later treaties and declarations. It provided for protection of life and liberty and religious freedom for all 'inhabitants of Poland'. All Polish nationals (citizens) were guaranteed equality before the law and the right to use their own language in private life and judicial proceedings. Members of racial, religious or linguistic minorities were guaranteed 'the same treatment and security in law and in fact' as other Polish nationals, and the right to establish and control at their expense their own religious, social and educational institutions. In areas of Poland where a 'considerable proportion' of Polish nationals belonged to minorities, an 'equitable share' of public funds would go to such minority groups for educational or religious purposes. In view of the particular history of oppression and violence, there were specific guarantees for Jews.

Like other minority treaties and declarations, the Polish treaty's provisions were placed under the guarantee of the League of Nations to the extent that 'they affect persons belonging to' minority groups. The League developed procedures to implement its duties, including a right of petition to it by beleaguered minorities claiming that a treaty regime or declaration had been violated, and including a minorities committee given the task of seeking negotiated solutions to such disputes. As shown by the *Minority Schools in Albania* case, the Council of the League could invoke in accordance with its usual procedures the advisory opinion jurisdiction of the Permanent Court of International Justice (PCIJ), the first international court (supplementing ad hoc arbitral tribunals as in the *Chattin* case). The Court was created by the League in 1921, became dormant in the Second World War, and was then succeeded by the International Court of Justice created under the UN Charter.

MINORITY SCHOOLS IN ALBANIA
ADVISORY OPINION, PERMANENT COURT OF INTERNATIONAL JUSTICE
SER. A/B, NO. 64 (1935)

[In 1920, the Assembly of the League of Nations adopted a recommendation requesting that, if Albania were admitted into the League, it 'should take the necessary measures to enforce the principles of the Minorities Treaties' and to arrange the 'details required to carry this object into effect' with the Council of the League. Albania was admitted to membership a few days later. In 1921 the Council included on its agenda the question of protection of minorities in Albania.

The Greek Government, in view of the presence of a substantial Christian minority of Greek origin in (dominantly Muslim) Albania, communicated to the League proposals for provisions going beyond the Minorities Treaties that were related to Christian worship and to education in the Greek language. The Council commissioned a report, and the reporter submitted to it a draft Declaration to be signed by Albania and formally communicated to the Council. The Declaration was signed by Albania and submitted to the Council in 1921, with basic similarities to but some differences from the typical clauses of the Minorities Treaties. The Council decided that the stipulations in the Declaration about minorities should be placed under the guarantee of the League from the date of the Declaration's ratification by Albania, which took place in 1922.

The first paragraph of Article 5 of the Declaration, at the core of the dispute that later developed, provided as follows:

> Albanian nationals who belong to racial, linguistic or religious minorities, will enjoy the same treatment and security in law and in fact as other Albanian nationals. In particular, they shall have an equal right to maintain, manage and control at their own expense or to establish in the future, charitable, religious and social institutions, schools and other educational establishments, with the right to use their own language and to exercise their religion freely therein.

Over the years, numerous changes in the laws and practices of the Albanian Government led to questions about compliance with the Declaration. In 1933, the Albanian National Assembly modified Articles 206 and 207 of the Constitution, which had provided that 'Albanian subjects may found private schools' subject to government regulation, to state:

> The instruction and education of Albanian subjects are reserved to the State and will be given in State schools. Primary education is compulsory for all Albanian nationals and will be given free of charge. Private schools of all categories at present in operation will be closed.

The new provisions affecting Greek-language and other private schools led to petitions and complaints to the League from groups including the Greek minority in Albania. Acting within its regular powers, the Council requested the PCIJ in 1935 to give an advisory opinion whether, in light of the 1921 Declaration as a whole, Albania was justified in its position that it had acted in conformity with 'the letter and the spirit' of Article 5 because (as Albania argued) its abolition of private schools was a general measure applicable to the majority as well as minority of Albanian nationals.

There follow excerpts from the opinion for the PCIJ and from a dissenting opinion. For present purposes, the Albanian Declaration can be understood as tantamount to a treaty. The opinions draw no relevant distinction between the two, and refer frequently to the Minorities Treaties to inform their interpretation of the Declaration.]

The contention of the Albanian Government is that the above-mentioned clause imposed no other obligation upon it, in educational matters, than to grant to its nationals belonging to racial, religious, or linguistic minorities a right equal to that possessed by other Albanian nationals. Once the latter have ceased to be entitled to have private schools, the former cannot claim to have them either. This conclusion, which is alleged to follow quite naturally from the wording of paragraph I of Article 5, would, it is contended, be in complete conformity with the meaning and spirit of the treaties for the protection of minorities, an essential characteristic of which is the full and complete equality of all nationals of the State, whether belonging to the majority or to the minority. On the other hand, it is argued, any interpretation which would compel Albania to respect the private minority schools would create a privilege in favour of the minority and run counter to the essential idea of the law governing minorities. Moreover, as the minority régime is an extraordinary régime constituting a derogation from the ordinary law, the text in question should, in case of doubt, be construed in the manner most favourable to the sovereignty of the Albanian State.

According to the explanations furnished to the Court by the Greek Government, the fundamental idea of Article 5 of the Declaration was on the contrary to guarantee freedom of education to the minorities by granting them the right to retain their existing schools and to establish others, if they desired; equality of treatment is, in the Greek Government's opinion, merely an adjunct to that right, and cannot impede the purpose in view, which is to ensure full and effectual liberty in matters of education. Moreover, the application of the same régime to a majority as to a minority, whose needs are quite different, would only create an apparent equality, whereas the Albanian Declaration, consistently with ordinary minority law, was designed to ensure a genuine and effective equality, not merely a formal equality.

...

As the Declaration of October 2nd, 1921, was designed to apply to Albania the general principles of the treaties for the protection of minorities, this is the point of view which, in the Court's opinion, must be adopted in construing paragraph 1 of Article 5 of the said Declaration.

The idea underlying the treaties for the protection of minorities is to secure for certain elements incorporated in a State, the population of which differs from them in race, language or religion, the possibility of living peaceably alongside that population and co-operating amicably with it, while at the same time preserving the characteristics which distinguish them from the majority, and satisfying the ensuing special needs.

In order to attain this object, two things were regarded as particularly necessary, and have formed the subject of provisions in these treaties.

The first is to ensure that nationals belonging to racial, religious or linguistic minorities shall be placed in every respect on a footing of perfect equality with the other nationals of the State.

The second is to ensure for the minority elements suitable means for the preservation of their racial peculiarities, their traditions and their national characteristics.

These two requirements are indeed closely interlocked, for there would be no true equality between a majority and a minority if the latter were deprived of its own institutions, and were consequently compelled to renounce that which constitutes the very essence of its being as a minority.

In common with the other treaties for the protection of minorities, and in particular with the Polish Treaty of June 28th, 1919, the text of which it follows, so far as concerns the question before the Court, very closely and almost literally, the Declaration of October 2nd, 1921, begins by laying down that no person shall be placed, in his relations with the Albanian authorities, in a position of inferiority by reason of his language, race or religion....
...

In all these cases, the Declaration provides for a régime of legal equality for all persons mentioned in the clause; in fact no standard of comparison was indicated, and none was necessary, for at the same time that it provides for equality of treatment the Declaration specifies the rights which are to be enjoyed equally by all.
...

It has already been remarked that paragraph 1 of Article 5 consists of two sentences, the second of which is linked to the first by the words *in particular*: for a right apprehension of the second part, it is therefore first necessary to determine the meaning and the scope of the first sentence. This sentence is worded as follows:

> Albanian nationals who belong to racial, linguistic or religious minorities, will enjoy the
> same treatment and security in law and in fact as other Albanian nationals.

The question that arises is what is meant by the *same treatment and security in law and in fact*.

It must be noted to begin with that the equality of all Albanian nationals before the law has already been stipulated in the widest terms in Article 4. As it is difficult to admit that Article 5 set out to repeat in different words what had already been said in Article 4, one is led to the conclusion that 'the same treatment and security in law and in fact' which is provided for in Article 5 is not the same notion as the equality before the law which is provided for in Article 4.
...

This special conception finds expression in the idea of an equality in fact which in Article 5 supplements equality in law. All Albanian nationals enjoy the equality in law stipulated in Article 4; on the other hand, the equality between members of the majority and of the minority must, according to the terms of Article 5, be an equality in law and in fact.

It is perhaps not easy to define the distinction between the notions of equality in fact and equality in law; nevertheless, it may be said that the former notion excludes the idea of a merely formal equality; that is indeed what the Court laid down in its Advisory Opinion of September 10th, 1923, concerning the case of the German settlers in Poland (Opinion No. 6), in which it said that:

> There must be equality in fact as well as ostensible legal equality in the sense of the absence of discrimination in the words of the law.

Equality in law precludes discrimination of any kind; whereas equality in fact may involve the necessity of different treatment in order to attain a result which establishes an equilibrium between different situations.

It is easy to imagine cases in which equality of treatment of the majority and of the minority, whose situation and requirements are different, would result in inequality in fact; treatment of this description would run counter to the first sentence of paragraph 1 of Article 5. The equality between members of the majority and of the minority must be an effective, genuine equality; that is the meaning of this provision.

The second sentence of this paragraph provides as follows:

> In particular they shall have an equal right to maintain, manage and control at their own expense or to establish in the future, charitable, religious and social institutions, schools and other educational establishments, with the right to use their own language and to exercise their religion freely therein.

This sentence of the paragraph being linked to the first by the words 'in particular', it is natural to conclude that it envisages a particularly important illustration of the application of the principle of identical treatment in law and in fact that is stipulated in the first sentence of the paragraph. For the institutions mentioned in the second sentence are indispensable to enable the minority to enjoy the same treatment as the majority, not only in law but also in fact. The abolition of these institutions, which alone can satisfy the special requirements of the minority groups, and their replacement by government institutions, would destroy this equality of treatment, for its effect would be to deprive the minority of the institutions appropriate to its needs, whereas the majority would continue to have them supplied in the institutions created by the State.

Far from creating a privilege in favour of the minority, as the Albanian Government avers, this stipulation ensures that the majority shall not be given a privileged situation as compared with the minority.

It may further be observed that, even disregarding the link between the two parts of paragraph 1 of Article 5, it seems difficult to maintain that the adjective 'equal', which qualifies the word 'right', has the effect of empowering the State to abolish the right, and thus to render the clause in question illusory; for, if so, the stipulation which confers so important a right on the members of the minority would not only add nothing to what has already been provided in Article 4, but it would become a weapon by which the State could deprive the minority régime of a great part of its practical value. …

…

The idea embodied in the expression 'equal right' is that the right thus conferred on the members of the minority cannot in any case be inferior to the corresponding right of other Albanian nationals. In other words, the members of the minority must always enjoy the right stipulated in the Declaration, and, in addition, any more extensive rights which the State may accord to other nationals....

…

The Court, having thus established that paragraph 1 of Article 5 of the Declaration, both according to its letter and its spirit, confers on Albanian nationals of racial, religious or linguistic minorities the right that is stipulated in the second sentence of that paragraph, finds it unnecessary to examine the subsidiary argument adduced by the Albanian Government to the effect that the text in question should in case of doubt be interpreted in the sense that is most favourable to the sovereignty of the State.

…

For these reasons,

The Court is of opinion, by eight votes to three,

that the plea of the Albanian Government that, as the abolition of private schools in Albania constitutes a general measure applicable to the majority as well as to the minority, it is in conformity with the letter and spirit of the stipulations laid down in Article 5, first paragraph, of the Declaration of October 2nd, 1921, is not well founded.

...

DISSENTING OPINION BY SIR CECIL HURST, COUNT ROSTWOROWSKI, AND MR. NEGULESCO

The undermentioned are unable to concur in the opinion rendered by the Court. They can see no adequate reason for holding that the suppression of the private schools effected in Albania in virtue of Articles 206 and 207 of the Constitution of 1933 is not in conformity with the Albanian Declaration of October 2nd, 1921.

...

The construction of the paragraph is clear and simple. The first sentence stipulates for the treatment and the security being the same for the members of the minority as for the other Albanian nationals. The second provides that as regards certain specified matters the members of the minority shall have an equal right. The two sentences are linked together by the words 'In particular' (*notamment*). These words show that the second sentence is a particular application of the principle enunciated in the first. If the rights of the two categories under the first sentence are to be the same, the equal right provided for in the second sentence must indicate equality between the same two categories, viz. the members of the minority and the other Albanian nationals. The second sentence is added because the general principle laid down in the first sentence mentions only 'treatment and security in law and in fact' — a phrase so indefinite that without further words of precision it would be doubtful whether it covered the right to establish and maintain charitable, religious and social institutions and schools and other educational establishments, but the particular application of the general principle of identity of treatment and security remains governed by the dominating element of equality as between the two categories.

The word 'equal' implies that the right so enjoyed must be equal in measure to the right enjoyed by somebody else. *'They shall have an equal right'* means that the right to be enjoyed by the people in question is to be equal in measure to that enjoyed by some other group. A right which is unconditional and independent of that enjoyed by other people cannot with accuracy be described as an 'equal right'. 'Equality' necessarily implies the existence of some extraneous criterion by reference to which the content is to be determined.

If the text of the first paragraph of Article 5 is considered alone, it does not seem that there could be any doubt as to its interpretation. It is, however, laid down in the Opinion from which the undersigned dissent that if the general purpose of the minority treaties is borne in mind and also the contents of the Albanian Declaration taken as a whole, it will be found that the 'equal right' provided for in the first paragraph of Article 5 cannot mean a right of which the extent is measured by that enjoyed by other Albanian nationals, and that it must imply an unconditional right, a right of which the members of the minority cannot be deprived.

...

As the opinion of the Court is based on the general purpose which the minorities treaties are presumed to have had in view and not on the text of Article 5, paragraph 1, of the Albanian Declaration, it involves to some extent a departure from the principles hitherto adopted by this Court in the interpretation of international instruments, that in presence of a clause which is reasonably clear the Court is bound to apply it as it stands without considering whether other provisions might with advantage have been added to it or substituted for it, and this even if the results following from it may in some particular hypothesis seem unsatisfactory.

...

Furthermore, the suppression of the private schools — even if it may prejudice to some appreciable extent the interests of a minority — does not oblige them to abandon an essential part of the characteristic life of a minority. In interpreting Article 5, the question whether the possession of particular institutions may or may not be *important* to the minority cannot constitute the decisive consideration. There is another consideration entitled to equal weight. That is the extent to which the monopoly of education may be of importance to the

State. The two considerations cannot be weighed one against the other: Neither of them — in the absence of a clear stipulation to that effect — can provide an objective standard for determining which of them is to prevail.

International justice must proceed upon the footing of applying treaty stipulations impartially to the rights of the State and to the rights of the minority, and the method of doing so is to adhere to the terms of the treaty — as representing the common will of the parties — as closely as possible.

...

If the intention of the second sentence: 'In particular they [the minority] shall have an equal right ...', had been that the right so given should be universal and unconditional, there is no reason why the draftsman should not have dealt with the right to establish institutions and schools in the earlier articles [of the Declaration that set up fixed and universal standards for all Albanians on matters like protection of life and free exercise of religion]. The draftsman should have dealt with the liberty to maintain schools and other institutions on lines similar to those governing the right to the free exercise of religion, which undoubtedly is conferred as a universal and unconditional right. Instead of doing so the right conferred upon the minority is an 'equal' right....

...

Further Aspects of the Minority Treaties

The *Minority Schools in Albania* opinions address many current issues that remain vexing. The discussions about the nature of 'equality' and assurances thereof, in particular about equality 'in law' and 'in fact', inform contemporary human rights law as well as constitutional and legislative debates in many states with respect to issues like equal protection and affirmative action. The question whether the Declaration and the Court's opinion recognized only the rights of individual members of a minority, or also the right of the minority itself as a collective or group, remains one that vexes the discussion of minority rights. Protection aiming at the cultural survival of minorities continues to raise the troubling issue of which types of minorities merit such protection, and whether assurance of equal protection (with the majority) is sufficient for the purpose.

But if the issues debated within the minorities regime remain, that particular regime disappeared. Over the next two decades, its norms were roundly violated. Its international machinery within the League of Nations proved to be ineffectual, partly for the same lack of political will that led to other disastrous events in the interwar period. As Susan Pedersen notes in relation to Iraq whose minorities were notoriously persecuted, League of Nations Council members had little interest in that aspect: they 'were more concerned to protect the privileges of their own citizens and their access to Iraq's lucrative resources and contracts.'[30] Laura Robson is even more damning in presenting the whole exercise around the minorities treaties as having very little to do with minority protection and instead being primarily 'designed to enshrine the idea that minority communities represented a legitimate site of external intervention into the affairs of the newly defined postwar European and Middle Eastern nations that housed so many Allied economic interests.'[31]

The failure of the regime was tragic in its consequences. Its stated purposes were distorted or blunted or ignored as Europe of the 1930s moved toward the horrors of the Second World War, the Holocaust and the brutalization and slaughter of so many other minorities. The settlements, norms and institutions after the Second World War designed to prevent further savagery against minorities stressed different principles and created radically different institutions, principally within the universal human rights system built in and around the United Nations.

Nonetheless, it is important to recognize the distinctive dilemmas and advances as well as the shortcomings of this minorities regime. Sovereignty in the sense of a state's (absolute) internal control over its own citizens was to some extent eroded. Treaties-declarations subjected aspects of the state's treatment of its own citizens to international law and international processes — that is, citizens who were members of a racial, religious or linguistic minority. Although the norms were expressed in bilateral treaties or declarations, the regime took on a multilateral aspect through its incorporation into the League as well as through the large number of nearly simultaneous treaties and declarations. The whole scheme was informed by multilateral planning, in contrast with the centuries-old examples of sporadic bilateral treaties protecting (usually religious) minorities. Minorities

---

[30] S. Pedersen, *The Guardians: The League of Nations and the Crisis of Empire* (2015) 282.
[31] L. Robson, 'Capitulations Redux: The Imperial Genealogy of the Post–World War I "Minority" Regimes', 23 *Am. Historical Rev.* (2021) 978 at 1000.

became a matter of formal international concern, the treaties-declarations fragmented the state into different sections of its citizens, and international law reached beyond the law of state responsibility to protect some of a state's own citizens.

In the 1960s, international efforts began again to grapple with the status of minorities. The 1960 UNESCO Convention against Discrimination in Education, for example, addressed the precise issue raised in the Albanian case. Domestically, assimilationist assumptions began to be replaced by the notion of multiculturalism, which accepted that the members of minority groups were entitled to maintain and practice their distinctive collective identities. Post World War II decolonization as well as post-1989 developments put a renewed spotlight on minority rights. The result was the adoption of a range of new declarations and treaties, including the UN Declaration on the Rights of Persons Belonging to National or Ethnic, Religious or Linguistic Minorities (1992), the Council of Europe Framework Convention for the Protection of National Minorities (1995), and the UN Declaration on the Rights of Indigenous Peoples (2007).

3. Treaties

Treaties have inevitably figured in this chapter's prior discussions — for example, the bilateral treaties whose relevance to custom was debated in *The Paquete Habana*, or the convention underlying the *Chattin* litigation. As noted above, the Albanian Declaration can be understood for present purposes as tantamount to a treaty, for the opinions do not distinguish between the two and refer to the Minorities Treaties to advance their interpretation of the Declaration. Hence this Comment, and particularly its sections on issues like interpretation, is relevant here.

In Article 38(1) of the Statute of the International Court of Justice, the Court is instructed in clause (a) to apply 'international conventions, whether general or particular, establishing rules expressly recognized by the contesting states'. Treaties thus head the list. They have become the primary expression of international law and, particularly when multilateral, the most effective if not the only path toward international regulation of many contemporary problems. Multilateral treaties have been the principal means for development of the human rights regime. One striking advantage of treaties over custom should be noted. Only treaties can create, and define the powers and jurisdiction of, international institutions in which state parties participate and to which they may owe duties.

The terminology for this voluminous and diverse body of international law varies. International agreements are referred to as pacts, protocols (generally supplemental to another agreement), covenants, conventions, charters, and exchanges of notes, as well as treaties — terms that are more or less interchangeable in legal significance. Within the internal law of some countries such as the United States, the term 'treaty' (as contrasted, say, with international executive agreement) has a particular constitutional significance.

Consider the different purposes that treaties serve. Some concerning vital national security interests have a basic political character: alliances, peace settlements, control of nuclear weapons. Others, outside the scope of national security, also involve relationships between governments and affect private parties only indirectly: agreements on foreign aid, cooperation in the provision of governmental services such as the mails. But treaties often have a direct and specific impact upon private parties. For many decades, tariff accords, income tax conventions, and treaties of friendship, commerce and navigation have determined the conditions under which the nationals or residents of one signatory can export to, or engage in business activities within, the other signatory's territory. Most significant for this book's purposes, human rights treaties have sought to extend protection to all persons against governmental abuse.

Domestic analogies to the treaty help to portray its distinctive character: contract and legislation. Some treaties settling particular disputes between states resemble an accord and satisfaction under contract law: an agreement over boundaries, an agreement to pay a stated sum as compensation for injury to the receiving nation or its nationals. Others are closer in character to private contracts of continuing significance or to domestic legislation because they regulate recurrent problems by defining rights and obligations of the parties and their nationals: agreements over rules of navigation, income taxation or the enforcement of foreign judgments. The term 'international legislation' to describe treaties has accordingly gained some currency particularly with respect to multilateral treaties such as human rights agreements that impose rules on states intended to regulate their conduct. The Albanian Declaration and the many bilateral treaties that formed part of the minorities regime of the period come within this description.

Nonetheless, domestic legislation differs in several critical respects from the typical treaty. A statute is generally enacted by the majority of a legislature and binds all members of the relevant society. Even changes in a constitution, which usually require approval by the legislature and other institutions or groups, can be accomplished over substantial dissent. The ordinary treaty, on the other hand, is a consensual arrangement. With few exceptions, such as Article 2(6) of the UN Charter, it purports to bind or benefit only parties. Alteration of its terms by one state party generally requires the consent of all.

Consider the institution of contract. Like the treaty, a contract can be said to make or create law between the parties: within the facilitative framework of governing law and subject to that law's mandatory norms and constraints, courts recognize and enforce contract-created duties. The treaty shares a contract's consensual basis, but treaty law lacks the breadth and relative inclusiveness of a national body of contract law. It has preserved a certain Roman law flavour (*'pacta sunt servanda', 'rebus sic stantibus'*) acquired during the long period from the Renaissance to the nineteenth century, when continental European scholars dominated the field. But treaty law often reflects the diversity of approaches to domestic contract law that lawyers bring to the topic, a diversity that is particularly striking on issues of treaty interpretation.

Duties Imposed by Treaty Law

Whatever its purpose or character, an international agreement is generally recognized from the perspective of international law as an authoritative starting point for legal reasoning about any dispute to which it is relevant. The maxim *'pacta sunt servanda'* is at the core of treaty law. It embodies a widespread recognition that commitments publicly, formally and (more or less) voluntarily made by a nation should be honoured. As stated in Article 26 of the Vienna Convention on the Law of Treaties: 'Every treaty in force is binding upon the parties to it and must be performed by them in good faith'.

Whatever the jurisprudential or philosophical basis for this norm, one can readily perceive the practical reasons for and the national interests served by adherence to the principle of *pacta sunt servanda*. The treaty represents one of the most effective means for bringing some order to relationships among states or their nationals, and for the systematic development of new principles responsive to the changing needs of the international community. It is the prime legal form through which that community can realize some degree of predictability and seek to institutionalize ideals like peaceful settlement of disputes and the protection of human rights. Often such goals can be achieved only through international organizations whose powers, structure, membership and purposes will be set forth in the treaties that bring them into existence. Treaties then are the basic instruments underlying much contemporary international regulation.

Acceptance of the primary role of the treaty does not, however, mean that a problem between two countries is adequately solved from the perspective of legal ordering simply by execution of a treaty with satisfactory provisions. A body of law has necessarily developed to deal with questions analogous to those addressed by domestic contract law — for example, formation of a treaty, its interpretation and performance, remedies for breach, and amendment or termination. But that body of law is often fragmentary and vague, reflecting the scarcity of decisions of international tribunals and the political tensions which some aspects of treaty law reflect.

There have been recurrent efforts to remedy this situation through more or less creative codification of the law of treaties. The contemporary authoritative text grows out of a UN Conference on the Law of Treaties that adopted in 1969 the Vienna Convention on the Law of Treaties. That Convention became effective in 1980 and (as of 2024) had been ratified by 116 states. Excerpts from it appear in the Documents Supplement. For reasons stemming largely from tensions between the Executive and the Congress over authority over different types of international agreements, the United States has not ratified the Vienna Convention. Nonetheless, in its provisions on international agreements, the *Restatement (Third), Foreign Relations Law of the United States* (1987) 'accepts the Vienna Convention as, in general, constituting a codification of the customary international law governing international agreements, and therefore as foreign relations law of the United States ...'. All other major industrial countries have ratified the Convention. And the United States has signed it.

Treaty Formation

A treaty is formed by the express consent of its parties. Although there are no precise requirements for execution or form, certain procedures have become standard. By choice of the parties, or in order to comply with the internal rules of a signatory country that are considered in Chapter 12, it may be necessary to postpone the effectiveness of the agreement until a national legislative body has approved it and national executive authorities have ratified it. Instruments of ratification for bilateral agreements are then exchanged. In the case of multilateral treaties, such instruments are deposited with the national government or international organization that has been designated as the custodian of the authentic text and of all other instruments relating to the treaty, including subsequent adhesions by nations that were not among the original signatories. Thereafter a treaty will generally be proclaimed or promulgated by the executive in each country.

Consent

Given the established principle that treaties are consensual, what rules prevail as to the character of that consent? Do domestic law contract principles about the effect of duress carry over to the international field?

In a domestic legal system, a party cannot enforce a contract which was signed by a defendant at gunpoint. One could argue that victorious nations cannot assert rights under a peace treaty obtained by a whole army. It is not surprising that the large powers are reluctant to recognize that such forms of duress can invalidate a treaty. If duress were a defence, it would be critical to define its contours, for many treaties result from various forms of military, political or economic pressure. The paucity of and doubts about international institutions with authority to develop answers to such questions underscore the reluctance to open treaties to challenge on these grounds. Article 52 of the Vienna Convention states: 'A treaty is void if its conclusion has been procured by the threat or use of force in violation of the principles of international law embodied in the Charter of the United Nations'. Attempts at Vienna to broaden the scope of coercion to include economic duress failed, although they resulted in a declaration condemning the use of such practices.

Reservations

Problems of consent that have no precise parallel in national contract law arise in connection with reservations to treaties, i.e., unilateral statements made by a state accepting a treaty 'whereby it purports to exclude, or vary the legal effect of certain provisions of the treaty in their application to a state' (Art. 2(1)(d) of the Vienna Convention). With bilateral treaties, no conceptual difficulties arise: ratification with reservations amounts to a counteroffer; the other state may accept (or reject) explicitly or may be held to have tacitly accepted it by proceeding with its ratification process or with compliance with the treaty. With multilateral treaties the problems may be quite complex. The traditional rule held that acceptance by all parties was required. The expanding number of states has required more flexibility.

Given the increased number of reservations, some of great significance, that many states are attaching to their ratifications of basic human rights treaties, questions about those reservations' validity under general treaty law or under the terms of a specific treaty have become matters of high concern within the human rights regime. We discuss the issue of reservation at greater length in Chapter 3.

Violations of and Changes in Treaties

Violation of a treaty may lead to diplomatic protests and a claim before an international tribunal. But primarily because of the limited and qualified consent of states to the jurisdiction of international tribunals, the offended party will usually resort to other measures. In a national system of contract law, well-developed rules govern such measures. They may distinguish between a minor breach not authorizing the injured party to terminate its own performance, and a material breach providing justification for such a move. Article 60 of the Vienna Convention provides that a material breach (as defined) of a bilateral treaty entitles the other party to terminate the treaty or suspend its performance in whole or in part. These rules necessarily grow more complex for multilateral treaties, but they also entitle a party affected the material breach of another party to terminate or suspend its obligations under certain conditions. Article 60, however, explains that termination or suspension 'do[es] not apply to provisions relating to the protection of the human person contained in treaties of a humanitarian character'. That said, it might very well apply to treaties that only indirectly affect human rights (e.g. an agreement on pharmaceutical patents; a multilateral peace agreement).

Amendments raise additional problems. The treaty's contractual aspect suggests that the consent of all parties is necessary. Parties may however agree in advance (see Art. 108 of the UN Charter) to be bound with respect to certain matters by the vote of a specified number. Such provisions in a multilateral treaty bring it closer in character to national legislation. They may be limited to changes which do not impose new obligations upon a dissenting party, although a state antagonistic to an amendment could generally withdraw. Absent such provisions, a treaty might aggravate rather than resolve a fundamental problem of international law: how to achieve in a peaceful manner changes in existing arrangements that are needed to adapt them to developing political, social or economic conditions.

One of the most contentious issues in treaty law is whether the emergence of conditions that were unforeseeable or unforeseen at the time of the treaty's conclusion terminates or modifies a party's obligation to perform. This problem borders the subject of treaty interpretation, considered below, since it is often described as a question whether an implied condition or an escape clause should be read into a treaty. Mature municipal legal systems have developed rules for handling situations where the performance of one party is rendered impossible or useless by intervening conditions. 'Impossibility', 'frustration', 'force majeure' and 'implied conditions' are the concepts used in Anglo-American law.

At the international level, possibilities of changes in conditions that upset assumptions underlying an agreement are enhanced by the long duration of many treaties, the difficulty in amending them and the rapid political, economic and social vicissitudes in modern times. Thus, nations have occasionally used *rebus sic stantibus* as the basis for declaring treaties no longer effective. Article 62 of the Vienna Convention states that a 'fundamental change of circumstances' which was not foreseen by the parties may not be invoked as a ground for terminating a treaty unless 'the existence of those circumstances constituted an essential basis of the consent of the parties to transform the extent of obligations still to be performed under the treaty'; and 'the effect of the change is radically to transform the extent of obligations still to be performed under the treaty.'

Treaty Interpretation

There is no shortcut to a reliable sense of how a given treaty will be construed. Even immersion in a mass of diplomatic correspondence and cases would not develop such a skill. In view of the variety of treaties and of approaches to their interpretation, such learning would more likely shed light on the possibilities than provide a particular answer to any given question.

One obstacle to reliable generalization about treaty interpretation is the variety of purposes which treaties serve. Different approaches are advisable for treaties that lay down rules for a long or indefinite period, in contrast with those settling past or temporally limited disputes. The long-term treaty must rest upon a certain flexibility and room for development if it is to survive changes in circumstances and relations between the parties. Changes in conditions like those that make *rebus sic stantibus* an attractive doctrine may lead a court or executive official to interpret a treaty flexibly so as to give it a sensible application to new circumstances. The type of problem that a treaty addresses will influence the approach of an official charged with interpreting it. Certain categories, such as income tax conventions, lend themselves to a detailed draftsmanship that will often be impractical and undesirable in a constitutional document such as the UN Charter. Conventions such as those relating to human rights will, for some matters, necessarily use broad terms and standards like fairness or *ordre public*. As a formal matter, a general rule of interpretation holds that a treaty should be interpreted in light of 'its object and purpose'.

Maxims similar to those found in domestic fields exist for treaties as well. The Vienna Convention contains several. Article 31 provides that a 'treaty shall be interpreted in good faith in accordance with the ordinary meaning to be given to the terms of the treaty in their context'. Article 32 goes on to add that recourse may be had to supplementary means — including *travaux préparatoires* (literally, 'preparatory work', and analogous to legislative history) — if interpretation produces a meaning that is 'ambiguous or obscure' or an outcome 'manifestly absurd or unreasonable'. A standard form of interpretation also takes into account the subsequent practice of states in the application of the treaty.

One way to build a framework for construing treaties is to consider the continuum which lies between 'strict' interpretation according to the 'plain meaning' of the treaty, and interpretation according to the interpreter's view of the best means of implementing the purposes or realizing the principles expressed by the treaty. Of course, both extremes of the spectrum are untenanted. One cannot wholly ignore the treaty's words, nor can one always find an unambiguous and relevant text that resolves the immediate issue.

Part of the difficulty is that treaties may be drafted in several languages. If domestic courts deem it unwise to 'make a fortress out of the dictionary', it would seem particularly unwise when interpreters need to resort to dictionaries in several languages (and in different legal systems according different meanings to linguistically similar terms). Sometimes corresponding words in the different versions may shed more light on the intended meaning; at other times, they generate greater ambiguity.

Reliance upon literal construction or 'strict' interpretation may however be an attractive method or technique to an international tribunal that is sensitive to its weak political foundation. It may be tempted to take refuge in the position that its decision is the ineluctable outcome of the drafters' intention expressed in clear text, and not a choice arrived at on the basis of the tribunal's understanding of policy considerations or relevant principles that may resolve a dispute over interpretation. Reliance on *travaux préparatoires* can achieve the same result of placing responsibility on the drafters. The charge of 'judicial legislation' evokes strong reactions in some political and legal cultures; it inevitably influences judges of international tribunals and heightens the temptation to take refuge in the dictionary.

BAŞAK ÇALI, SPECIALIZED RULES OF TREATY INTERPRETATION: HUMAN RIGHTS D. HOLLIS (ED.), THE OXFORD GUIDE TO TREATIES (2ND ED., 2020) 504

…

I. International Human Rights Treaty Interpretation: Exceptional or Specialized?

Does international human rights treaty interpretation have its own interpretive scheme distinct and separate from the general principles of treaty interpretation codified in the VCLT? Or, is it a specialized regime due to the subject matter it regulates, but one nevertheless located within the confines of Article 31 of the VCLT?

There are supporters of both views. On the one hand, scholars argue that the sui generis nature of human rights calls for an interpretative practice that disregards traditional principles of general international law. On the other hand, there are those who say that the interpretation of human rights treaties are specialized and that this is an inevitable development in international law. On this latter view, international human rights treaty interpretation may be no more specialized than, for example, international trade law or investment law. In terms of practice, there is no evidence to suggest that UN treaty bodies, regional human rights courts, the ICJ, the ILC, or domestic courts have systematically advocated either of these views. In fact, the evidence shows that these bodies cite the VCLT as a guide to interpretation and that regional human rights courts, in particular, are creating their own specialized rules and doctrines in the course of interpreting specific provisions of human rights treaties.

Differences in opinion on this preliminary question are better conceived as disagreements on the rules of treaty interpretation in international law rather than disagreements on the correct interpretations of human rights treaties. …

…

Even though the order in which interpretive techniques should be employed is made clear between Articles 31 and 32, it has long been debated how Article 31's tripartite interpretive formula of wording, context, and object and purpose should be understood. Some commentators have understood Article 31 as imposing a literal ordering, where wording, context and object and purpose should be employed as interpretive tools in the order they appear. This formula, associated with McNair, suggested a 'sliding scale' approach to what interpretation entails. Interpretation is only required when the wording of the treaty is not clear. In that sense, the more literally unclear a provision becomes, the more necessary it is to refer to context. If context does not bring clarity, object and purpose should be employed as a last resort.

Since 1969, however, there has been wider support for a holistic approach to Article 31. This approach emphasizes the importance of an interpreter's judgment as to how the wording, context, and object and purpose interact with each other. The original source for this perspective lies with ILC Commentaries on the draft VCLT describing treaty interpretation as a 'single combined operation' where wording, context, and object and purpose are 'thrown into a crucible', which subsequently led this approach to be called the 'crucible approach'.

…

Such strong overlap between wording and object and purpose, however, is not often the case in human rights treaty provisions—hence the controversy about the relevant regime of interpretation. This is primarily because the provisions of human rights treaties often do not lend themselves easily to tight wording. They state rights in abstract ways without stating in detail what they require for their application. One obvious explanation for this is the treaty negotiation process and the difficulties of getting agreements on certain words or concepts. Commentators in other fields of international law would concur, however, that this is not necessarily a problem sui generis with respect to human rights treaties, but generally permeates all international law treaty-drafting processes.

There is, however, a deeper explanation for the frequent lack of clear fit between the ordinary wording of human rights treaties, their context, and their object and purpose, which makes human rights treaties a demanding case for interpretation. This explanation is based on the very nature of the conceptual structure of these treaty provisions. As many commentators have noted, human rights treaties do not create reciprocal obligations between States parties, but instead create obligations for States in relation to their treatment of individuals under their jurisdiction. …

…

… [N]either the exact scope of States' rights nor their duties are specified in detail in human rights treaties. This lack of precision is a function of the non-mechanical context in which human rights claims arise. Human rights treaties apply to a much larger universe of situations than many other international treaties. By their very nature, human rights provisions need to be interpreted in the light of changing political, social, and economic justifications of State policies. Human rights treaty law interpreters have to decide which interests of specific individuals are so important that they need to be safeguarded from policies that seem to respect or make better-off the majority of individuals under a particular jurisdiction. The key trigger for the interpretative task to start is a claim on behalf of an individual that her situation is within the scope of a human rights treaty, ie that she has a claim grounded in human rights law against the State. Does the lack of access to disabled facilities in a police detention centre constitute degrading treatment with respect to a disabled detainee even if there is no such intention to mistreat on the part of the authorities? Does handing out leaflets in a privatized shopping mall that has been historically a public space come under the scope of freedom of assembly? What responsibility does a State have with respect to actions of non-State military forces acting in its territory? None of these questions can be resolved solely by analysing (respectively) the text of the right to be free from torture, inhuman, or degrading treatment; the right to freedom of assembly; or the right to life provisions in various human rights treaties.

…

III. Specialized Interpretive Principles in the Field of Human Rights Treaty Law

…

A. The effectiveness approach and human rights treaties

Even though all human rights treaties have their own distinct context and wording, there is nevertheless significant convergence around the notion that the core interpretive task for any interpreter is to make human rights treaty provisions 'effective, real, and practical' for individuals as right-holders under international law. This is sometimes called the principle of effectiveness … . Effectiveness is an overarching approach to human rights treaty interpretation. It animates a range of other more fine- grained, specific interpretive principles developed in the context of each human rights treaty. Examples include the interpretive principles of 'autonomous concepts', 'living instrument', and 'practicality' in the ECtHR context; the 'responsiveness to African circumstances' in the case of the African Commission on Human and People's Rights; the consideration of the 'real situation' in the case of the Inter-American Court of Human Rights; and the 'dynamic instrument doctrine' put forward by the Committee against All Forms of Discrimination against Women. These principles all derive from the interpretive consensus that interpretations that are devoid of actual effect for human rights protections do not cohere with good faith interpretations of the wording and context of human rights treaties in the light of their object and purpose.

...[T]he principle of effectiveness has two aspects. The first aspect directs the interpreter to give meaning to each and every treaty provision so that each term has effect rather than no effect. This aspect comes from the good faith requirement of Article 31. The second aspect involves taking a teleological approach to interpretation and this is associated with the demands of the treaty's object and purpose. In human rights treaty interpretation we find that interpreters have developed both aspects of effectiveness, often in tandem with each other.

QUESTIONS

1. The types of protections or assurances given by treaty to a distinctive group within a larger polity can be categorized in various ways, including the following. The assurance can be *absolute* (fixed, unconditional) or *contingent* (dependent on some reference group). For example, treaties of commerce between two states may reciprocally grant to citizens of each state the right to reside (for business purposes) and do business (as aliens) in the other state. Some assurances in such treaties will be absolute — for example, citizens of each state are given the right to buy or lease real property for residential purposes in the other state. Other assurances will be contingent — for example, citizens of each state are given the right to organize a corporation and qualify to do business in the other state on the same terms as citizens of that other state (so called 'national treatment'). Within this framework, how would you characterize the rights given to members of a designated minority by the Albanian Declaration? Do the majority and dissenting opinions differ about how to characterize them?

2. If you were a member of the Greek-speaking Christian minority, would you have been content with a Declaration that contained no more than a general equal protection clause? If not, why not? How would you justify your argument for more protection?

3. Would Albania have been justified in imposing some control on the Greek schools, such as defining subjects to be taught and censoring teaching materials that, say, urged independence from Albania?

4. Why do the opinions refer to this minorities regime as 'extraordinary'? In what respects does it depart from classical conceptions of international law, or differ from the law of state responsibility?

5. Consider how close to or distant from the minorities regime Article 27 of the International Covenant on Civil and Political Rights appears on its face to be. It provides:

"In those States in which ethnic, religious or linguistic minorities exist, persons belonging to such minorities shall not be denied the right, in community with the other members of their group, to enjoy their own culture, to profess and practice their own religion, or to use their own language."

---

4. The ILO

Another important early twentieth-century development that was to contribute to the post-World War II international human rights regime was the creation of the International Labour Organization in 1919. It was partly a response to the Communist Revolution in Russia in 1917:

> The Governments of Europe were nervous in the face of a rising industrial unrest, with unknown Bolshevist possibilities, with menacing fires of revolution in Germany and with at least one or two of the Governments represented at Paris daily in danger of being overthrown. As a result, the Allied Governments had to offer to labor some definite and formal recognition ..., both to justify themselves with reference to the war in the past,

and to hold forth the hope of a larger measure of international labor agreements in the future.[32]

The ILO was created to abolish the 'injustice, hardship, and privation' which workers suffered and to guarantee 'fair and humane conditions of labour.' It made extensive use of law-making techniques, including the adoption of treaties. At its first session, in 1919, it adopted Conventions under which ratifying states undertook to: limit hours of work in industry, closely monitor unemployment rates, provide maternity protection for working mothers, prohibit night-work by women and children under 18 except in family enterprises, and not employ children under 14 in industrial undertakings. It also produced an array of non-binding 'recommendations' dealing with unemployment, reciprocity of treatment, anthrax prevention, the dangers of lead poisoning to women and children, labor inspection, and white phosphorus. In its early years, it also proved to be a pioneer in developing various techniques for promotion and supervision of its standards, which the UN system partially emulated several decades later. Its adoption of standards was so prolific that, in 1951, it launched the 'International Labour Code' bringing together 100 Conventions and 92 Recommendations adopted since 1919. Wilfred Jenks of the ILO presented this as a 'Codex of social justice',[33] and argued that virtually all of the standards should be 'regarded as measures for the implementation of the right to just and favourable conditions of work affirmed' in the UDHR and the ICESCR.[34]

D. JUDGMENT AT NUREMBERG

The Nuremberg Trial

The trial at Nuremberg in 1945–1946 of major war criminals among the Axis powers, dominantly Nazi party leaders and military officials, gave the nascent human rights movement a powerful impulse. The UN Charter that became effective in 1945 included a few broad human rights provisions. But they were more programmatic than operational, more a programme to be realized by states over time than a system in place for application to states. Nuremberg, on the other hand, was concrete and applied: prosecutions, convictions, punishment. The prosecution and the Judgment of the International Military Tribunal in this initial, weighty trial for massive crimes committed during the war years were based on concepts and norms, some of which had deep roots in international law and some of which represented a significant development of that law that opened the path toward the later formulation of fundamental human rights norms.

We do not address below the International Military Tribunal for the Far East, known as the Tokyo trial. Between May 1946 and November 1948, judges from 11 countries tried 28 wartime Japanese leaders.[35] The court heard 419 witnesses, and built a 50,000-page transcript. For many reasons, Gary J. Bass argues in *Judgment at Tokyo: World War II on Trial and the Making of Modern Asia* (2023) 10-11, that it 'misfired and fizzled':

> Unlike Nuremberg, whose verdict has over the decades taken on an almost sacred status in democratic Germany and its neighbors, Tokyo is an ongoing source of bitter controversy across East Asia today. … [T]here is no Japanese equivalent of the near universal national repentance and grief that are at the core of current German politics and society. …

The striking aspect of Nuremberg was that the trial and Judgment applied international law doctrines and concepts to impose criminal punishment on individuals for their commission of any of the three types of crimes under international law that are described below. The notion of crimes against the law of nations for which violators bore an individual criminal responsibility was itself an older one, but it had operated in a restricted field. As customary international law developed from the time of Grotius, certain conduct came to be considered a violation of the law of nations — in effect, a universal crime. Piracy on the high seas was long the classic example of this limited category of crimes. Given the common interest of all nations in protecting

---

[32] J.T. Shotwell, 'The International Labour Organization as an Alternative to Violent Revolution', 166 *The Annals of the American Academy of Political and Social Science* (1933) 18.

[33] C.W. Jenks, *Law, Freedom and Welfare* (1963) 102. On the ILO generally see G. F. Sinclair, *To Reform the World: International Organizations and the Making of Modern States* (2017).

[34] C.W. Jenks, 'Human Rights, Social Justice and Peace', in A. Eide and A. Schou (eds.), *International Protection of Human Rights* (1968) 235-36.

[35] N. Boister and R. Cryer, *Documents on the Tokyo International Military Tribunal: Charter, Indictment, and Judgments* (2008).

navigation against interference on the high seas outside the territory of any state, it was considered appropriate for the state apprehending a pirate to prosecute in its own courts. Since there was no international criminal tribunal, prosecution in a state court was the only means of judicial enforcement. To the extent that the state courts sought to apply the customary international law defining the crime of piracy, either directly or as it had become absorbed into national legislation, the choice of forum became less significant, for state courts everywhere were in theory applying the same law.

One specialized field, the humanitarian laws of war, had long included rules regulating the conduct of war, the so-called *'jus in bello'*. This body of law imposed sanctions against combatants who committed serious violations of the restrictive rules. Such application of the laws of war, and its foundation in customary norms and in treaties, figure in the Judgment, *infra*. But the concept of individual criminal responsibility was not systematically developed. It achieved a new prominence and a clearer definition after the Nuremberg Judgment, primarily through the Geneva Conventions of 1949 and their 1977 Protocols. Gradually other types of conduct have been added to this small list of individual crimes under international law — for example, slave trading long prior to Nuremberg and genocide thereafter. Recent years have seen the creation of the International Criminal Tribunals for the former Yugoslavia and for Rwanda in the 1990s and the initiation of the International Criminal Court in 2002, all discussed in Chapter 16.

As the Second World War came to an end, the Allied Powers held several conferences to determine what policies they should follow towards the Germans responsible for the war and for the systematic barbarity and annihilation of the period. The wartime destruction and civilian losses were known. The nature and extent of the Holocaust were first becoming widely known. These conferences culminated in the London Agreement of 8 August 1945, 59 Stat. 1544, E.A.S. No. 472, in which the United States, the USSR, Britain and France determined to constitute 'an International Military Tribunal for the trial of war criminals'. The Charter annexed to the Agreement provided for the composition and basic procedures of the Tribunal and stated the criminal provisions for the trials in its three critical articles:

<u>Article 6</u>

> The Tribunal established by the Agreement referred to in Article 1 hereof for the trial and punishment of the major war of the criminals European Axis countries shall have the power to try and punish persons who, acting in the interests of the European Axis countries, whether as individuals or as members of organizations, committed any of the following crimes.
>
> The following acts, or any of them, are crimes coming within the jurisdiction of the Tribunal for which there shall be individual responsibility:
>
> (a) *Crimes Against Peace*: namely, planning, preparation, initiation or waging of a war of aggression, or a war in violation of international treaties, agreements or assurances, or participation in a common plan or conspiracy for the accomplishment of any of the foregoing;
>
> (b) *War Crimes*: namely, violations of the laws or customs of war. Such violations shall include, but not be limited to, murder, ill-treatment or deportation to slave labor or for any other purpose of civilian population of or in occupied territory, murder or ill-treatment of prisoners of war or persons on the seas, killing of hostages, plunder of public or private property, wanton destruction of cities, towns or villages, or devastation not justified by military necessity;
>
> (c) *Crimes Against Humanity*: namely, murder, extermination, enslavement, deportation, and other inhumane acts committed against any civilian population, before or during the war, or persecutions on political, racial or religious grounds in execution of or in connection with any crime within the jurisdiction of the Tribunal, whether or not in violation of the domestic law of the country where perpetrated.

Leaders, organizers, instigators and accomplices participating in the formulation or execution of a common plan or conspiracy to commit any of the foregoing crimes are responsible for all acts performed by any persons in execution of such plan.

Article 7

The official position of defendants, whether as Heads of State or responsible officials in Government Departments, shall not be considered as freeing them from responsibility or mitigating punishment.

Article 8

The fact that the Defendant acted pursuant to order of his Government or of a superior shall not free him from responsibility, but may be considered in mitigation of punishment if the Tribunal determines that justice so requires.

Note the innovative character of these provisions. Although the Tribunal consisted of only four judges, one from each of the victorious Allied Powers, it nonetheless had an international character in its formation and composition, and to that extent was radically different from the national military courts before which the laws of war had to that time generally been enforced. At the core of the Charter lay the concept of international crimes for which there would be 'individual responsibility', a sharp departure from the then-existing customary law or conventions which stressed the duties of (and sometimes sanctions against) states. Moreover, in defining crimes within the Tribunal's jurisdiction, the Charter went beyond the traditional 'war crimes' (para. (b) of Art. 6) in two ways.

First, the Charter included the war-related 'crimes against peace' — so-called '*jus ad bellum*', in contrast with the category of war crimes or *jus in bello*. International law had for a long time been innocent of such a concept. After a slow departure during the post-Reformation period from earlier distinctions of philosophers, theologians and writers on international law between 'just' and 'unjust' wars, the European nations moved towards a conception of war as an instrument of national policy, much like any other, to be legally regulated only with respect to *jus in bello*, the manner of its conduct. The Covenant of the League of Nations did not frontally challenge this principle, although it attempted to control aggression through collective decisions of the League. The interwar period witnessed some fortification of the principles later articulated in the Nuremberg Charter, primarily through the Kellogg-Briand Pact of 1927 that is referred to in the Judgment. Today, the UN Charter requires members (Art. 2(4)) to 'refrain in their international relations from the threat or use of force' against other states, while providing (Art. 51) that nothing shall impair 'the inherent right of individual or collective self-defence if an armed attack occurs against a Member ...' When viewed in conjunction with the Nuremberg Charter, those provisions suggest the contemporary effort to distinguish not between 'just' and 'unjust' wars but between the permitted 'self-defence' and the forbidden 'aggression' — the word used in defining 'crimes against peace' in Article 6(a) of that Charter.

Second, Article 6(c) represented an important innovation. There were few precedents for use of the phrase 'crimes against humanity' as part of a description of international law, and its content was correspondingly indeterminate. On its face, paragraph (c) might have been read to include the entire programme of the Nazi government to exterminate Jews and other civilian groups, in and outside Germany, whether 'before or during the war', and thus to include not only the Holocaust but also the planning for and early persecution of Jews and other groups preceding the Holocaust. Moreover, that paragraph appeared to bring within its scope the persecution or annihilation by Germany of Jews who were German nationals as well as those who were aliens. This would represent a great advance on the international law of state responsibility to aliens as described in Ch. 2B, above. Note, however, how the Judgment of the Tribunal interpreted Article 6(c) with respect to these observations.

In other respects as well, the concept of 'crimes against humanity', even in this early formulation, developed earlier international law. War crimes could cover discrete as well as systematic action by a combatant — an isolated murder of a civilian by a combatant as well a systematic policy of wanton destruction of towns. Crimes against humanity were directed primarily to planned conduct, to systematic conduct.

In defining the charges against the major Nazi leaders tried at Nuremberg and its successor tribunals, the Allied Powers took care to exclude those types of conduct which had not been understood to violate existing custom or conventions and in which they themselves had engaged — for example, the massive bombing of cities with necessarily high tolls of civilians that was indeed aimed at demoralization of the enemy. [36]

JUDGMENT OF NUREMBERG TRIBUNAL
INTERNATIONAL MILITARY TRIBUNAL, NUREMBERG (1946)

...

[The Law of the Charter]

The jurisdiction of the Tribunal is defined in the [London] Agreement and Charter, and the crimes coming within the jurisdiction of the Tribunal, for which there shall be individual responsibility, are set out in Article 6. The law of the Charter is decisive, and binding upon the Tribunal.

The making of the Charter was the exercise of the sovereign legislative power by the countries to which the German Reich unconditionally surrendered; and the undoubted right of these countries to legislate for the occupied territories has been recognized by the civilized world. The Charter is not an arbitrary exercise of power on the part of the victorious Nations, but in the view of the Tribunal, as will be shown, it is the expression of international law existing at the time of its creation; and to that extent is itself a contribution to international law.

The Signatory Powers created this Tribunal, defined the law it was to administer, and made regulations for the proper conduct of the Trial. In doing so, they have done together what any one of them might have done singly; for it is not to be doubted that any nation has the right thus to set up special courts to administer law. With regard to the constitution of the Court, all that the defendants are entitled to ask is to receive a fair trial on the facts and law.

The Charter makes the planning or waging of a war of aggression or a war in violation of international treaties a crime; and it is therefore not strictly necessary to consider whether and to what extent aggressive war was a crime before the execution of the London Agreement. But in view of the great importance of the questions of law involved, the Tribunal has heard full argument from the Prosecution and the Defence, and will express its view on the matter.

It was urged on behalf of the defendants that a fundamental principle of all law — international and domestic — is that there can be no punishment of crime without a pre-existing law. '*Nullum crimen sine lege, nulla poena sine lege.*' It was submitted that *ex post facto* punishment is abhorrent to the law of all civilized nations, that no sovereign power had made aggressive war a crime at the time that the alleged criminal acts were committed, that no statute had defined aggressive war, that no penalty had been fixed for its commission, and no court had been created to try and punish offenders.

In the first place, it is to be observed that the maxim *nullum crimen sine lege* is not a limitation of sovereignty, but is in general a principle of justice. To assert that it is unjust to punish those who in defiance of treaties and assurances have attacked neighboring states without warning is obviously untrue, for in such circumstances the attacker must know that he is doing wrong, and so far from it being unjust to punish him, it would be unjust if his wrong were allowed to go unpunished ... .

This view is strongly reinforced by a consideration of the state of international law in 1939, so far as aggressive war is concerned. The General Treaty for the Renunciation of War of 27 August 1928, more generally known as the Pact of Paris or the Kellogg-Briand Pact, was binding on 63 nations, including Germany, Italy and Japan at the outbreak of war in 1939. ...

... The nations who signed the Pact or adhered to it unconditionally condemned recourse to war for the future as an instrument of policy, and expressly renounced it. After the signing of the Pact, any nation resorting to war

---

[36] See J. von Bernstorff and E. Mensching, 'The Dark Legacy of Nuremberg', 36 *Leiden J. Int'l L.* (2023) 1117.

as an instrument of national policy breaks the Pact. In the opinion of the Tribunal, the solemn renunciation of war as an instrument of national policy necessarily involves the proposition that such a war is illegal in international law; and that those who plan and wage such a war, with its inevitable and terrible consequences, are committing a crime in so doing. War for the solution of international controversies undertaken as an instrument of national policy certainly includes a war of aggression, and such a war is therefore outlawed by the Pact. ...

... The Hague Convention of 1907 prohibited resort to certain methods of waging war. These included the inhumane treatment of prisoners, the employment of poisoned weapons, the improper use of flags of truce, and similar matters. Many of these prohibitions had been enforced long before the date of the Convention; but since 1907 they have certainly been crimes, punishable as offenses against the law of war; yet the Hague Convention nowhere designates such practices as criminal, nor is any sentence prescribed, nor any mention made of a court to try and punish offenders. For many years past, however, military tribunals have tried and punished individuals guilty of violating the rules of land warfare laid down by this Convention. In the opinion of the Tribunal, those who wage aggressive war are doing that which is equally illegal, and of much greater moment than a breach of one of the rules of the Hague Convention.... The law of war is to be found not only in treaties, but in the customs and practices of states which gradually obtained universal recognition, and from the general principles of justice applied by jurists and practised by military courts. This law is not static, but by continual adaptation follows the needs of a changing world. Indeed, in many cases treaties do no more than express and define for more accurate reference the principles of law already existing.
...

All these expressions of opinion, and others that could be cited, so solemnly made, reinforce the construction which the Tribunal placed upon the Pact of Paris, that resort to a war of aggression is not merely illegal, but is criminal. The prohibition of aggressive war demanded by the conscience of the world, finds its expression in the series of pacts and treaties to which the Tribunal has just referred.
...

... That international law imposes duties and liabilities upon individuals as well as upon States has long been recognized. ... Crimes against international law are committed by men, not by abstract entities, and only by punishing individuals who commit such crimes can the provisions of international law be enforced.
...

The authors of these acts cannot shelter themselves behind their official position in order to be freed from punishment in appropriate proceedings. Article 7 of the Charter expressly declares:

> The official position of Defendants, whether as heads of State, or responsible officials in Government departments, shall not be considered as freeing them from responsibility, or mitigating punishment.

On the other hand, the very essence of the Charter is that individuals have international duties which transcend the national obligations of obedience imposed by the individual state. He who violates the laws of war cannot obtain immunity while acting in pursuance of the authority of the state if the state in authorizing action moves outside its competence under international law.

It was also submitted on behalf of most of these defendants that in doing what they did they were acting under the orders of Hitler, and therefore cannot be held responsible for the acts committed by them in carrying out these orders. The Charter specifically provides in Article 8:

> The fact that the Defendant acted pursuant to order of his Government or of a superior shall not free him from responsibility, but may be considered in mitigation of punishment.

The provisions of this article are in conformity with the law of all nations. That a soldier was ordered to kill or torture in violation of the international law of war has never been recognized as a defense to such acts of brutality, though, as the Charter here provides, the order may be urged in mitigation of the punishment. The true test, which is found in varying degrees in the criminal law of most nations, is not the existence of the order, but whether moral choice was in fact possible.

…

War Crimes and Crimes against Humanity

… War Crimes were committed on a vast scale, never before seen in the history of war. They were perpetrated in all the countries occupied by Germany, and on the High Seas, and were attended by every conceivable circumstance of cruelty and horror. There can be no doubt that the majority of them arose from the Nazi conception of 'total war', with which the aggressive wars were waged. For in this conception of 'total war,' the moral ideas underlying the conventions which seek to make war more humane are no longer regarded as having force or validity. Everything is made subordinate to the overmastering dictates of war. Rules, regulations, assurances, and treaties all alike are of no moment; and so, freed from the restraining influence of international law, the aggressive war is conducted by the Nazi leaders in the most barbaric way. Accordingly, War Crimes were committed when and wherever the Führer and his close associates thought them to be advantageous. They were for the most part the result of cold and criminal calculation.

…

… Prisoners of war were ill-treated and tortured and murdered, not only in defiance of the well-established rules of international law, but in complete disregard of the elementary dictates of humanity. Civilian populations in occupied territories suffered the same fate. Whole populations were deported to Germany for the purposes of slave labor upon defense works, armament production, and similar tasks connected with the war effort. Hostages were taken in very large numbers from the civilian populations in all the occupied countries, and were shot as suited the German purposes. Public and private property was systematically plundered and pillaged in order to enlarge the resources of Germany at the expense of the rest of Europe. Cities and towns and villages were wantonly destroyed without military justification or necessity.

…

Murder and Ill-Treatment of Civilian Population

Article 6(b) of the Charter provides that 'ill-treatment … of civilian population of or in occupied territory … killing of hostages … wanton destruction of cities, towns, or villages' shall be a war crime. In the main, these provisions are merely declaratory of the existing laws of war as expressed by the Hague Convention, Article 46....

…

One of the most notorious means of terrorizing the people in occupied territories was the use of concentration camps … [which] became places of organized and systematic murder, where millions of people were destroyed.

In the administration of the occupied territories the concentration camps were used to destroy all opposition groups....

A certain number of the concentration camps were equipped with gas chambers for the wholesale destruction of the inmates, and with furnaces for the burning of the bodies. Some of them were in fact used for the extermination of Jews as part of the 'final solution' of the Jewish problem....

…

Slave Labor Policy

Article 6(b) of the Charter provides that the 'ill-treatment or deportation to slave labor or for any other purpose, of civilian population of or in occupied territory' shall be a War Crime. The laws relating to forced labor by the inhabitants of occupied territories are found in Article 52 of the Hague Convention.... The policy of the German occupation authorities was in flagrant violation of the terms of this convention.... [T]he German occupation authorities did succeed in forcing many of the inhabitants of the occupied territories to work for the German war effort, and in deporting at least 5,000,000 persons to Germany to serve German industry and agriculture.

…

Persecution of the Jews

The persecution of the Jews at the hands of the Nazi Government has been proved in the greatest detail before the Tribunal. It is a record of consistent and systematic inhumanity on the greatest scale. Ohlendorf, Chief of Amt III in the RSHA from 1939 to 1943, and who was in command of one of the Einsatz groups in the campaign against the Soviet Union testified as to the methods employed in the extermination of the Jews....

When the witness Bach Zelewski was asked how Ohlendorf could admit the murder of 90,000 people, he replied: 'I am of the opinion that when, for years, for decades, the doctrine is preached that the Slav race is an inferior race, and Jews not even human, then such an outcome is inevitable'.

...

... The Nazi Party preached these doctrines throughout its history, *Der Stürmer* and other publications were allowed to disseminate hatred of the Jews, and in the speeches and public declarations of the Nazi leaders, the Jews were held up to public ridicule and contempt.

... By the autumn of 1938, the Nazi policy towards the Jews had reached the stage where it was directed towards the complete exclusion of Jews from German life. Pogroms were organized, which included the burning and demolishing of synagogues, the looting of Jewish businesses, and the arrest of prominent Jewish business men....

It was contended for the Prosecution that certain aspects of this anti-Semitic policy were connected with the plans for aggressive war. The violent measures taken against the Jews in November 1938 were nominally in retaliation for the killing of an official of the German Embassy in Paris. But the decision to seize Austria and Czechoslovakia had been made a year before. The imposition of a fine of one billion marks was made, and the confiscation of the financial holdings of the Jews was decreed, at a time when German armament expenditure had put the German treasury in difficulties, and when the reduction of expenditure on armaments was being considered....

It was further said that the connection of the anti-Semitic policy with aggressive war was not limited to economic matters....

The Nazi persecution of Jews in Germany before the war, severe and repressive as it was, cannot compare, however, with the policy pursued during the war in the occupied territories.... In the summer of 1941, however, plans were made for the 'final solution' of the Jewish question in Europe. This 'final solution' meant the extermination of the Jews....

The plan for exterminating the Jews was developed shortly after the attack on the Soviet Union....

...

... Adolf Eichmann, who had been put in charge of this program by Hitler, has estimated that the policy pursued resulted in the killing of 6 million Jews, of which 4 million were killed in the extermination institutions.

The Law Relating to War Crimes and Crimes against Humanity

...

The Tribunal is of course bound by the Charter, in the definition which it gives both of War Crimes and Crimes against Humanity. With respect to War Crimes, however, as has already been pointed out, the crimes defined by Article 6, Section (b), of the Charter were already recognized as War Crimes under international law. They were covered by Articles 46, 50, 52, and 56 of the Hague Convention of 1907, and Articles 2, 3, 4, 46, and 51 of the Geneva Convention of 1929. That violation of these provisions constituted crimes for which the guilty individuals were punishable is too well settled to admit of argument.

But it is argued that the Hague Convention does not apply in this case, because of the 'general participation' clause in Article 2 of the Hague Convention of 1907. That clause provided:

> The provisions contained in the regulations (Rules of Land Warfare) referred to in Article
> 1 as well as in the present Convention do not apply except between contracting powers,
> and then only if all the belligerents are parties to the Convention.

Several of the belligerents in the recent war were not parties to this Convention.

In the opinion of the Tribunal it is not necessary to decide this question. The rules of land warfare expressed in the Convention undoubtedly represented an advance over existing international law at the time of their adoption. But the Convention expressly stated that it was an attempt 'to revise the general laws and customs of war', which it thus recognized to be then existing, but by 1939 these rules laid down in the Convention were recognized by all civilized nations, and were regarded as being declaratory of the laws and customs of war which are referred to in Article 6(b) of the Charter.

...

With regard to Crimes against Humanity there is no doubt whatever that political opponents were murdered in Germany before the war, and that many of them were kept in concentration camps in circumstances of great horror and cruelty. The policy of terror was certainly carried out on a vast scale, and in many cases was organized and systematic. The policy of persecution, repression, and murder of civilians in Germany before the war of 1939, who were likely to be hostile to the Government, was most ruthlessly carried out. The persecution of Jews during the same period is established beyond all doubt. To constitute Crimes against Humanity, the acts relied on before the outbreak of war must have been in execution of, or in connection with, any crime within the jurisdiction of the Tribunal. The Tribunal is of the opinion that revolting and horrible as many of these crimes were, it has not been satisfactorily proved that they were done in execution of, or in connection with, any such crime. The Tribunal therefore cannot make a general declaration that the acts before 1939 were Crimes against Humanity within the meaning of the Charter, but from the beginning of the war in 1939 War Crimes were committed on a vast scale, which were also Crimes against Humanity; and insofar as the inhumane acts charged in the Indictment, and committed after the beginning of the war, did not constitute War Crimes, they were all committed in execution of, or in connection with, the aggressive war, and therefore constituted Crimes against Humanity.

[The opinion considered individually each of the 22 defendants at this first trial of alleged war criminals. It found 19 of the defendants guilty of one or more counts of the indictment. It imposed 12 death sentences. Most convictions were for war crimes and Crimes Against Humanity, the majority of those convicted being found guilty of both crimes.]

NOTE

Note the following statement in Ian Brownlie, *Principles of Public International Law* (4th edn. 1990), at 562:

> But whatever the state of the law in 1945, Article 6 of the Nuremberg Charter has since come to represent general international law. The Agreement to which the Charter was annexed was signed by the United States, United Kingdom, France, and USSR, and nineteen other states subsequently adhered to it. In a resolution adopted unanimously on 11 December 1946, the General Assembly affirmed 'the principles of international law recognized by the Charter of the Nuremberg Tribunal and the judgment of the Tribunal'.

Views of Commentators

There follow a number of authors' observations about the charges, the Judgment and the principles in the Nuremberg trials.[37]

(1) In a review of a book by Sheldon Glueck entitled *The Nuremberg Trial and Aggressive War* (1946), the reviewer George Finch, 47 *Am. J. Int'l. L.* (1947) 334, makes the following arguments:

> As the title indicates, this book deals with the charges at Nuremberg based upon the planning and waging of aggressive war. The author has written it because in his previous volume he expressed the view that he did not think such acts could be regarded as 'international crimes'. He has now changed his mind and believes 'that for the purpose of conceiving aggressive war to be an international crime, the Pact of Paris may, together with other treaties and resolutions, be regarded as evidence of a sufficiently developed *custom* to be accepted as international law' (pp. 4–5)....

[37] For a comprehensive collection, see G. Mettraux (ed.), *Perspectives on the Nuremberg Trial* (2008).

The reviewer fully agrees with the author in regard to the place of custom in the development of international law. He regards as untenable, however, the argument not only of the author but of the prosecutors and judges at Nuremberg that custom can be judicially established by placing interpretations upon the words of treaties which are refuted by the acts of the signatories in practice, by citing unratified protocols or public and private resolutions of no legal effect, and by ignoring flagrant and repeated violations of non-aggression pacts by one of the prosecuting governments which, if properly weighed in the evidence, would nullify any judicial holding that a custom outlawing aggressive war had been accepted in international law....

(2) In his article, 'The Nurnberg Trial', 33 *Va. L. Rev.* (1947) 679, at 694, Francis Biddle, the American judge on the Tribunal, commented on the definition of 'crimes against humanity' in Article 6(c) of the Charter:

... The authors of the Charter evidently realized that the crimes enumerated were essentially domestic and hardly subject to the incidence of international law, unless partaking of the nature of war crimes. Their purpose was evidently to reach the terrible persecution of the Jews and liberals within Germany before the war. But the Tribunal held that 'revolting and horrible as many of these crimes were', it had not been established that they were done 'in execution of, or in connection with' any crime within its jurisdiction. After the beginning of the war, however, these inhumane acts were held to have been committed in execution of the war, and were therefore crimes against humanity.

...

Crimes against humanity constitute a somewhat nebulous conception, although the expression is not unknown to the language of international law.... With one possible exception ... crimes against humanity were held [in the Judgment of the Tribunal] to have been committed only where the proof also fully established the commission of war crimes. Mr. Stimson suggested [that the Tribunal eliminate from its jurisdiction matters related to pre-war persecution in Germany], which involved 'a reduction of the meaning of crimes against humanity to a point where they became practically synonymous with war crimes'. I agree. And I believe that this inelastic construction is justified by the language of the Charter and by the consideration that such a rigid interpretation is highly desirable in this stage of the development of international law.

(3) Hans Kelsen, in 'Will the Judgment in the Nuremberg Trial Constitute a Precedent in International Law?' 1 *Int'l. L. Q.* (1947) 153, at 164, was critical of several aspects of the London Agreement and the Judgment. But with respect to the question of retroactivity of criminal punishment, he wrote:

The objection most frequently put forward — although not the weightiest one — is that the law applied by the judgment of Nuremberg is an ex post facto law. There can be little doubt that the London Agreement provides individual punishment for acts which, at the time they were performed were not punishable, either under international law or under any national law.... However, this rule [against retroactive legislation] is not valid at all within international law, and is valid within national law only with important exceptions. [Kelsen notes several exceptions, including the rule's irrelevance to 'customary law and to law created by a precedent, for such law is necessarily retroactive in respect to the first case to which it is applied....']

A retroactive law providing individual punishment for acts which were illegal though not criminal at the time they were committed, seems also to be an exception to the rule against ex post facto laws. The London Agreement is such a law. It is retroactive only in so far as it established individual criminal responsibility for acts which at the time they were committed constituted violations of existing international law, but for which this law has provided only collective responsibility.... Since the internationally illegal acts for which the London Agreement established individual criminal responsibility were certainly also morally most objectionable, and the persons who committed these acts were certainly aware of their immoral character, the retroactivity of the law applied to them can hardly be considered as absolutely incompatible with justice.

(4) In his biography entitled *Harlan Fiske Stone: Pillar of the Law* (1956), Alpheus Thomas Mason discussed Chief Justice Stone's views about the involvement of Justices of the US Supreme Court in extrajudicial assignments and, in particular, Stone's views about President Truman's appointment of Justice Robert Jackson to be American Prosecutor at the trials. The following excerpts (at 715) are all incorporations by Mason in his book of quotations of Chief Justice Stone's remarks:

> So far as the Nuremberg trial is an attempt to justify the application of the power of the victor to the vanquished because the vanquished made aggressive war, ... I dislike extremely to see it dressed up with a false facade of legality. The best that can be said for it is that it is a political act of the victorious States which may be morally right.... It would not disturb me greatly.... if that power were openly and frankly used to punish the German leaders for being a bad lot, but it disturbs me some to have it dressed up in the habiliments of the common law and the Constitutional safeguards to those charged with crime. Jackson is away conducting his high-grade lynching party in Nuremberg.... I don't mind what he does to the Nazis, but I hate to see the pretense that he is running a court and proceeding according to common law. This is a little too sanctimonious a fraud to meet my old-fashioned ideas.

(5) Herbert Wechsler, in 'The Issues of the Nuremberg Trial', 62 *Pol. Sci. Q.* (1947) 11, at 23 observed:

> ... [M]ost of those who mount the attack [on the Judgment on contentions including *ex post facto* law] hasten to assure us that their plea is not one of immunity for the defendants; they argue only that they should have been disposed of politically, that is, dispatched out of hand. This is a curious position indeed. A punitive enterprise launched on the basis of general rules, administered in an adversary proceeding under a separation of prosecutive and adjudicative powers is, in the name of law and justice, asserted to be less desirable than an ex parte execution list or a drumhead court-martial constituted in the immediate aftermath of the war.... Those who choose to do so may view the Nuremberg proceeding as 'political' rather than 'legal' — a program calling for the judicial application of principles of liability politically defined. They cannot view it as less civilized an institution than a program of organized violence against prisoners, whether directed from the respective capitals or by military commanders in the field.

(6) Mark Osiel, in *Mass Atrocity, Collective Memory, and the Law* (1997), comments on charges against the defeated states (at 122):

> For the Nuremberg and Tokyo courts, it mattered little to the validity of criminal proceedings against Axis leadership that Allied victors had committed vast war crimes of their own. Unlike the law of tort, criminal law has virtually no place for 'comparative fault', no doctrinal device for mitigating the wrongdoing or culpability of the accused in light of the accusers'.... For the public, however, ... it mattered *greatly* in gauging the legitimacy of the trials that they seemed tendentiously selective, aimed at focusing memory in partisan ways. It mattered for such listeners that the defendants ... had constituted only a single side to a two- or multi-sided conflict, one in which other parties had similarly committed unlawful acts on a large scale. This unsavory feature of the Nuremberg judgment has undermined its authority in the minds of many, weakening its normative weight.

(7) David Luban, in *Legal Modernism* (1994), describes what he sees as a confusion in the Nuremberg charges (at 336):

> This idea that Nuremberg was to be the Trial to End All Wars seems fantastic and naïve forty years (and 150 wars) later. It has also done much to vitiate the real achievements of the trial, in particular the condemnation of crimes against humanity. To end all war, the authors of the Nuremberg Charter were led to incorporate an intellectual confusion into

it. The Charter criminalized aggression; and by criminalizing aggression, the Charter erected a wall around state sovereignty and committed itself to an old-European model of unbreachable nation-states. But crimes against humanity are often, even characteristically, carried out by states against their own subjects. The effect, and great moral and legal achievement, of criminalizing such acts and assigning personal liability to those who order them and carry them out is to pierce the veil of sovereignty. As a result, Article 6(a) pulls in the opposite direction from Articles 6(c), 7 and 8, leaving us ... with a legacy that is at best equivocal and at worst immoral.

(8) Thane Rosenbaum, in 'The Romance of Nuremberg and the Tease of Moral Justice', 27 *Cardozo L. Rev.* (2006) 1731, argues about legal and moral justice (at 1736):

When it came to the Nazis, jurisdictional concerns, retroactive punishments, standard causation requirements, and freedom of association principles, were not going to impede moral justice and the development of international law. No one seemed to mind during Nuremberg that these constitutional principles were being upended, and that a strict adherence to constitutional safeguards seemingly did not make the trip to Germany. Given the enormity of the Nazis' crimes and the moral implications of acquitting them on procedural grounds, the Constitution, as a document, apparently was deemed not fit for travel and therefore was left behind. There was little ambivalence among the American prosecutors, including a sitting Supreme Court justice, about applying this new path to justice, one that looked legal but tilted in an entirely moral direction.

(9) Mahmood Mamdani, in 'Beyond Nuremberg: The Historical Significance of the Post-Apartheid Transition in South Africa', Makerere Institute of Social Research, Working Paper No. 23 (2015) at 27, argues that following the logic of Nuremberg has been deeply problematic for the human rights movement:

As interpreted by the human rights movement, the lesson of Nuremberg is twofold: one, that responsibility for mass violence must be ascribed to individual agents; and, two, that criminal justice is the only politically viable and morally acceptable response to mass violence. Turned into the founding moment of the new human rights movement, Nuremberg is today the model for the ICC and is held as the fitting antidote to every incident of mass violence.

To de-ideologize Nuremberg is to recognize that the logic of Nuremberg flowed from the context of inter-state war, one that ended in victory for one side, which then put the losers on trial. The logic of a court trial is zero sum: you are either innocent or guilty. This kind of logic ill fits the context of a civil war. Victims and perpetrators in civil wars often trade places in ongoing cycles of violence. No one is wholly innocent and none wholly guilty. Each side has a narrative of victimhood. Victims' justice is the flip side of victors' justice: both demonize the other side and exclude it from participation in the new political order. A civil war can end up either as a renegotiated union or as a separation between states. The logic of Nuremberg drives parties in the civil war to the latter conclusion: military victory and the separation of yesterday's perpetrators and victims into two separate political communities. ...

The contemporary human rights movement is permeated with the logic of Nuremberg. Human rights groups focus on atrocities for which they seek individual criminal responsibility. Their method of work has a formalized name: Naming and Shaming. The methodology involves a succession of clearly defined steps: catalogue atrocities, identify victims and perpetrators, name and shame the perpetrators, and demand that they be held criminally accountable. ... [C]ontext is considered a distraction from establishing the universality of human rights.

This is problematic if one recognizes that political violence is often not a standalone incident but part of a cycle of violence.[38]

(10) Michael Walzer, in 'The Legacy of Nuremberg', 48 *Philosophia* (2020) 1291, characterizes Nuremberg as having come at a 'moment' 'of world government – when powerful states, ... perhaps together with organizations ..., succeed in constructing the legislative basis, the executive power, and the judicial authority necessary for a strong international response to wars and massacres'. For him, this does not 'mean that all postwar justice is "victor's justice," but it is, to some degree, great power justice.'

He contrasts that type of moment with the International Criminal Court's indictment of President Bashir of Sudan for crimes against humanity in 2009:

> ... the ICC was acting like the judicial arm of a world government when there was no world government. This is an example of what I have called in another place "the politics of pretending." The ICC had no way of bringing Bashir to trial; nor could it control events in Darfur. Its decision put people at risk, and the court was unable to protect them. When Bashir expelled all aid organizations from the Sudan, he was retaliating against Darfurians for the ICC's action against him; he was deliberately provoking a humanitarian crisis or, more accurately, intensifying the crisis that already existed. And there was nothing that the court could do—or that any international agency could do in the name of the court. The ICC, most simply, had no executive arm, but it acted as if it did. Pretending that there is an effective system of global justice, that there is some kind of world government, when no such thing exists or will exist in the foreseeable future seems to me an example of moral and political irresponsibility.

> ...

QUESTIONS

1. Recall clause (c) of Article 38(1) of the Statute of the ICJ, and the comments thereon by Oscar Schachter, above. Should the Tribunal have relied on that clause to respond to charges of *ex post facto* application of Article 6(c) to individuals who were responsible for the murder of groups of Germans or aliens?

2. Do you agree with the Tribunal's restrictive interpretation of Article 6(c)? Consider the commentary above by Francis Biddle.

3. How do you evaluate the criticism by Finch of the Tribunal's use of treaties in deciding whether customary international law included a given norm? Recall the comments about the growth of customary law by Schachter.

4. How do you evaluate the criticism of the Nuremberg trial by Chief Justice Stone? By Osiel? By Luban? By Rosenbaum?

5. How do you assess the significance and consequences of Nuremberg? Even if you agree with some or several of the criticisms above, do you nonetheless conclude that the trial and judgment were justified in their actual historical forms? If so, why?

---

[38] For a strong rebuttal of Mamdani's approach, see Jonas Bens, Ch. 16B, below.

Genocide

There has been considerable expansion in the definitions of the crimes set out in Article 6. The field of individual criminal responsibility for war crimes has been broadened and clarified, through the Geneva Conventions of 1949 and the 1998 Rome Statute for the International Criminal Court (ICC). The provisions for 'grave breaches' in these conventions are discussed later. The concept of crimes against humanity has expanded greatly in coverage since Nuremberg, and is examined in Chapter 16 below. And since 2018, the ICC has been enabled to prosecute 'crimes against peace' under the rubric of the crime of aggression.

The problem of *ex post facto* trials is addressed in Article 15(1) of the International Covenant on Civil and Political Rights, which states that: 'No one shall be held guilty of any criminal offence on account of any act or omission which did not constitute a criminal offence, under national or international law, at the time when it was committed.'

Compare with the Nuremberg Judgment the following provisions of the Convention on the Prevention and Punishment of the Crime of Genocide (153 parties in 2024) bearing on personal responsibility. The treaty parties 'confirm' in Article I that genocide 'is a crime under international law which they undertake to prevent and to punish'. Article 2 defines genocide:

> In the present Convention, genocide means any of the following acts committed with intent to destroy, in whole or in part, a national, ethnical, racial or religious group, as such:
>
> (a) Killing members of the group;
>
> (b) Causing serious bodily or mental harm to members of the group;
>
> (c) Deliberately inflicting on the group conditions of life calculated to bring about its physical destruction in whole or in part;
>
> (d) Imposing measures intended to prevent births within the group;
>
> (e) Forcibly transferring children of the group to another group.

Persons committing acts of genocide 'shall be punished, whether they are constitutionally responsible rulers, public officials or private individuals' (Art. IV). The parties agree (Art. V) to enact the necessary legislation to give effect to the Convention and 'to provide effective penalties for persons guilty of genocide'. Under Article VI, persons charged with genocide are to be tried by a tribunal 'of the State in the territory of which the act was committed, or by such international penal tribunal as may have jurisdiction with respect to those Contracting Parties which shall have accepted its jurisdiction'. One of the perceived weaknesses of the Convention was its lack of a monitoring mechanism like a treaty body. Instead it provides in Article IX that:

> Disputes between the Contracting Parties relating to the interpretation, application or fulfilment of the present Convention, including those relating to the responsibility of a State for genocide or for any of the other acts enumerated in article III, shall be submitted to the International Court of Justice at the request of any of the parties to the dispute.

As will be seen below this provision has unexpectedly and belatedly taken on major importance as various states have filed cases before the International Court of Justice (ICJ) alleging acts of genocide by other states parties. These include, most recently, cases brought by The Gambia, Ukraine, South Africa and Nicaragua.

The first conviction for genocide by an international court came in 1998 in the *Akayesu* case before the International Criminal Tribunal for Rwanda (Ch. 16A, below). Today, the crime of genocide falls under the jurisdiction of the ICC, and has also been litigated on a number of occasions in the ICJ.

In 2007, the ICJ held in the *Bosnia Genocide* case that the obligation 'to prevent' in Article I created independent and territorially unlimited obligations for states, based on their capacity to influence a specific situation. The obligation arises 'at the instant that the State learns of, or should normally have learned of, the existence of a serious risk that genocide will be committed.' This might be thought of as a form of 'due diligence' obligation.[39]

In August 2019, an independent fact-finding commission on Myanmar, appointed by the UN Human Rights Council, reported that it had 'reasonable grounds to conclude that there is a strong inference of genocidal intent on the part of the State, that there is a serious risk that genocidal actions may recur, and that Myanmar is failing in its obligation to prevent genocide, to investigate genocide and to enact effective legislation criminalizing and punishing genocide' (UN Doc. A/HRC/42/50 (2019), para. 90). It also welcomed efforts by states to bring a case against Myanmar before the ICJ under the Genocide Convention.

In a November 2019 application to the court, The Gambia accused Myanmar of genocidal acts against members of the Rohingya group, described as a 'distinct ethnic, racial and religious group that resides primarily in Myanmar's Rakhine State'. Provisional measures were also sought to preserve the Rohingya's rights pending the court's final decision. In its January 2020 Order in response to this request, the court recalled that 'The Gambia contends that Myanmar's military and security forces and persons or entities acting on its instructions or under its direction and control have been responsible, inter alia, for killings, rape and other forms of sexual violence, torture, beatings, cruel treatment, and for the destruction or denial of access to food, shelter and other essentials of life, all with the intent to destroy the Rohingya group, in whole or in part' (*The Gambia v. Myanmar*, Request for the Indication of Provisional Measures, Order of 23 January 2020, para. 29). Myanmar denied committing any of the alleged violations of the Genocide Convention, and claimed that there was no genocidal intent. Based in part on the UN report, the ICJ concluded that 'there is a real and imminent risk of irreparable prejudice to the rights invoked by The Gambia (para. 75)' and ordered Myanmar to 'take all measures within its power to prevent the commission of all acts within the scope of Article II of this Convention' (para. 86).

One issue of particular relevance for this Chapter is the issue of standing to sue.[40] In the subsequent phase of the case, Myanmar alleged that The Gambia lacked standing because it was not an 'injured' or 'specially affected' state, and had not demonstrated an 'individual legal interest'. The court rejected the relevance of these criteria and held, by a vote of 14 to 1, that 'All the States parties to the Genocide Convention … have a common interest to ensure the prevention, suppression and punishment of genocide, [which] implies that the obligations in question are owed by any State party to all the other States parties to the relevant convention; they are obligations *erga omnes partes*, in the sense that each State party has an interest in compliance with them in any given case …' (*The Gambia v. Myanmar*, Judgment of 22 July 2022, para. 107). In dissent, Judge Xue noted that the concept of *erga omnes* obligations had not been an established part of international law when the Genocide Convention was adopted, and she concluded that the court's reliance on that concept in a series of cases since 1970 exceeded 'the reasonable expectations of the States parties' and was not conducive 'to the security and stability of treaty relations' (dissenting opinion, para. 25).[41]

* * *

This chapter has had two main goals. It has provided an illustrative survey of different forms or sources of international law (custom, general principles, treaties) and it has surveyed the principal areas in which human rights issues have featured in traditional international law topics (laws of war, state responsibility, labour rights, slavery, minorities, and international criminal law). While the historiography of human rights has exploded as a field of study over the past two decades, generating a contentious but rich and instructive literature, the materials in this chapter provide some of the essential background to the study of the post-Second World War human rights regime. The following excerpt from the conclusion to one major historical survey helps to make the transition.

---

[39] L. van den Herik and E. Irving, 'Due Diligence and the Obligation to Prevent Genocide and Crimes Against Humanity,' in H. Krieger, A. Peters, and L. Kreuzer (eds.), *Due Diligence in the International Legal Order* (2020) 200.
[40] See B. Simma, 'From Bilateralism to Community Interest in International Law', 250 *Collected Courses of the Hague Academy of International Law* (1984) 233.
[41] O. Hathaway, A. Hachem and J. Cole, 'A New Tool for Enforcing Human Rights: Erga Omnes Partes Standing', 61 *Colum. J. Transnat'l L.* (2024) 259.

ERIC D. WEITZ, A WORLD DIVIDED: THE GLOBAL STRUGGLE FOR HUMAN RIGHTS IN THE AGE OF NATION-STATES
(2019) 427

Conclusion

…

In the twenty-first century the stream of human rights politics runs far more deeply and broadly than ever before. Skeptics abound. Some charge that human rights are mere veneers that enable states to protect themselves while they carry out all sorts of inhumane acts. Others condemn human rights as mere rhetoric or evidence of Western neo-imperialism. …

Indeed, … we see a tidal wave of right-wing populist and extreme nationalist movements in the United States and Europe. Authoritarian dictators around the globe firm up their power and hold on to their offices for years on end. Some crisis situations, as in Syria, go on with no resolution in sight while the population endures bombardments, displacements, and malnutrition, the utter shattering of their society. Wars rage elsewhere as well, and civilians, perhaps more than ever, bear the brunt of their furies. Since the passage of the Genocide Convention in 1948, genocides have taken place in Burundi and Rwanda …, Guatemala, the former Yugoslavia, Darfur in Sudan, among Yazidis in Iraq and Rohingya in Myanmar. The Chinese government has launched a vast "reeducation" campaign of Uighur, placing tens of thousands of them in detention. Much of the world still lives under dictatorial regimes and in conditions of extreme inequality. On a global scale, democracy seems to be in retreat. And we are witnessing today the largest refugee crisis in history.

But perhaps it is too early to sound the death knell of the human rights era. After all, who could have predicted, in the early eighteenth century, the abolition of slavery? In the early nineteenth century, the triumph of the idea of human rights? Or in late 1961, the Helsinki Final Act, the fall of the Berlin Wall, and the collapse of communism?

[H]uman rights have never proceeded in a straight line. They are complex and move in crooked paths. A future in which human rights reign supreme and we all live in peace and fellowship is a chimera. Utopian sentiments are only good insofar as they project the possibility of a better life upon humane principles. Without those hopes, we stagnate in the present without any path forward.

The very term "human rights" has moved into the center of politics at all levels—local, national, and international. It provides a powerful motivating force for people to demand lives of liberty and security. From the mothers of the disappeared in Argentina to Soviet dissidents, anti-apartheid activists in South Africa, and women all around the globe—all of them have adopted the rhetoric of human rights to rally support and make their claims in the streets, in the halls of governance, and on the floor of the UN General Assembly. The meaning of human rights has expanded over two and one-half centuries, and now includes social and economic as well as political rights.

Amid all these developments, the nation-state remains. It has shown its mettle and commands power and loyalty. It will not disappear anytime in the foreseeable future. In the best of circumstances, the nation-state is our protector if we live within the charmed circle of rights-bearing citizens. It is also our greatest threat, the powerful violator of human rights and the exclusion-enforcing institution that drives out, removes, forcibly assimilates, and kills those denied the right to have rights within its borders.

Since the 1940s, human rights have been proclaimed for everyone regardless of citizenship status. Human rights protections have moved—in part—to the international plane. The UDHR, the Genocide Convention, international tribunals, the ICC—all the measures and conventions and resolutions discussed [in this book] infringe on the absolute sovereignty of the nation-state. Thankfully so. Anything that moves the conception and enforcement of human rights to the international level moves us beyond the nation-state as the sole enforcer (and violator) of rights, and that is progress.

The nation-state remains; so do our identities as individuals of particular nationalities, ethnicities, religions (or the lack thereof), and genders. The Enlightenment fiction of an abstract individual, stripped of all markers, is just that—a fiction. A system of human rights built on that understanding will always be flawed and easily subject to attack by the heralds of an exclusive, supposedly timeless culture of nation or race or of the essential differences between men and women. Yet diversity of all sorts is the intractable reality of human existence. How we live with that difference is the critical issue. Those who somehow differ from a dominant group may be subordinated, driven out, or killed, or they may be recognized as fellow humans and accorded the same rights as everyone else—without being required to dispense with their identities.

For all the partial advances, for all the contradictions, all the sheer opposition—human rights remain our best hope for the future. Their advocates sometimes espouse utopian aspirations. A restrained perspective is more appropriate and effective. Human rights will never be implemented in the all-embracing fashion of declarations like the UDHR; they will always face opponents, some quite strong. Yet human rights provide a powerful affirmation of the human spirit. They require that people be respected and afforded recognition no matter what their specific gender, nationality, or race. They demand that all people have access to the basic necessities of life, and have the freedom to express themselves, to work and build and create as they wish, to join with others as they desire, and to be free of the scourge of violence and forced displacement. Those are our fundamental human rights. We should demand nothing less from the worlds we inhabit.

QUESTIONS

1. In Weitz's analysis, the nation-state takes centre stage. But he concludes that '[a]nything that moves the conception and enforcement of human rights to the international level moves us beyond the nation-state as the sole enforcer (and violator) of rights, and that is progress.' To what extent does that framing seem helpful or realistic in light of what has been discussed so far about the international human rights regime?

2. Samuel Moyn, in 'Human rights have lost their monopoly as a framework for reform', *Open Global Rights*, May 19, 2021, poses a challenge to Weitz's optimism. He argues that human rights have lost much of their appeal, particularly 'for young people who did not experience human rights as the morality of the obsolescence of ideological alternatives, and 'in many places around the world, where different forms of ideology and different forms of social mobilization than generally characterize human rights, have begun to beckon.' He does 'not believe the record of human rights law or movements justify much confidence that they can' take on more tasks, which would open them up to 'the risk of failing even more comprehensively'. Instead they should 'claim less and allow other movements to surge'. What might those other movements be, and what role would human rights then play?

PART B: NORMATIVE FOUNDATIONS OF INTERNATIONAL HUMAN RIGHTS

Chapter 3. Civil And Political Rights

The Nuremberg trial and several provisions of the United Nations Charter of 1945 were the major elements of the incipient human rights regime until 1948, when the UN General Assembly approved the Universal Declaration of Human Rights (UDHR). For 28 years, the UDHR occupied centre stage. The two fundamental human rights treaties, the International Covenant on Civil and Political Rights (ICCPR) and the International Covenant on Economic, Social and Cultural Rights (ICESCR), both became effective in 1976. (Note: only these two human rights treaties bear the solemn title of 'Covenant'.)

Together with the Declaration, the Covenants form the International Bill of Human Rights, which now stands at the core of the universal human rights system — universal in the sense that membership is open to states from all parts of the world. Chapter 11 examines three regional human rights systems, each open to members only from the designated part of the world: the European Convention for the Protection of Human Rights and Fundamental Freedoms (known as the 'European Convention on Human Rights'), the American Convention on Human Rights and the African Charter on Human and Peoples' Rights. Each of these treaties is supported and developed (in different ways) by an intergovernmental body that in most cases is created by the treaty itself. The central institutional participants in the human rights regime also include other intergovernmental bodies, national governments and national human rights institutions, nongovernmental human rights groups, corporate actors, and a range of labour, environmental, religious, development, and other organizations.

This chapter opens with a focus on the Charter and Declaration, before undertaking an in-depth examination of civil and political rights, and economic and social rights respectively. The Declaration includes both categories. These categories are far from airtight. Many treaties declare rights that straddle the two, or that fall clearly within the domains of both of them. Many rights are hard to categorize. Nonetheless, at their core, the conventional distinctions are clear, whatever the relationships and interdependency between the two. Freedom from torture, equal protection, due process and the right to form political associations fall within the first category; the right to health or food or education come within the second.

The remaining sections of this chapter introduce basic ideas and instruments of the universal human rights regime that concern civil and political rights; the next chapter addresses economic and social rights. Section B below examines the ICCPR.

Section C then turns to the Convention on the Elimination of All Forms of Discrimination against Women (CEDAW) a major treaty that took form several decades after work on drafting the ICCPR began, and that reveals different concerns, goals and strategies of the human rights regime. Comparison of the ICCPR and CEDAW offers insight into the evolution and changing character of civil and political rights and their implementation.
In Section D we focus on efforts designed to prohibit discrimination on the grounds of sexual orientation and to protect the rights of gay, lesbian, bisexual and transgender persons in order to illustrate the evolution of new norms within the international system.

Section E makes for a contrast with Section D by looking at threats posed in recent years, primarily in the context of counter-terrorism activities, to the long-established and seemingly well-entrenched norm against torture.

A. THE CHARTER, UDHR AND ORIGINS OF THE HUMAN RIGHTS REGIME

The human rights regime is not simply a systematic ordering, through treaties and customary law, of fundamental postulates, ideologies and norms (that is, 'oughts' in the form of rules, standards, and principles). To the contrary, these basic elements are imbedded in institutions, some of them state and some international, some governmental or intergovernmental and some nongovernmental and in related international processes. It is impossible to grasp this regime adequately without an appreciation of its close relation to and reliance on international organizations. For example, the basic instruments of the universal system were drafted within the different organs of the United Nations and adopted by its General Assembly, before (in the case of the treaties) being submitted to states for ratification. UN organs play a major role in monitoring, officially commenting on, and applying sanctions to state behaviour.

The United Nations Charter itself first gave formal and authoritative expression to the human rights regime that began at the end of the Second World War. Since its birth in 1945, the UN has served as a vital institutional spur to the development of the regime, as well as serving as a major forum for many-sided debates about it. The purpose of the present section is to call attention to aspects of the UN and its Charter that bear particularly on the human rights regime.

Readers should now become familiar with the provisions of the Charter that are referred to below, and of the UDHR.

Charter Provisions

Consider first the Charter's radical transformation of the branch of the laws of war concerning *jus ad bellum*. Recall that for several centuries that body of law had addressed almost exclusively *jus in bello*, the rules regulating the conduct of warfare rather than the justice or legality of the waging of war. The International Military Tribunal at Nuremberg was empowered to adjudicate 'crimes against peace', part of *jus ad bellum* and the most disputed element of that Tribunal's mandate.

The Charter builds on the precedents to which the Nuremberg Judgment refers and states the UN's basic purpose of securing and maintaining peace. It does so by providing in Article 2(4) that UN members 'shall refrain in their international relations from the threat or use of force against the territorial integrity or political independence of any state', a rule qualified by Article 51's provision that nothing in the Charter 'shall impair the inherent right of individual or collective self-defence if an armed attack occurs' against a member.

The Charter's references to human rights are scattered, terse, even cryptic. The term 'human rights' appears infrequently. Note its occurrence in the following provisions: second paragraph of the Preamble, Article 1(3), Article 13(1)(b), Articles 55 and 56, Article 62(2) and Article 68.

Several striking characteristics of these provisions emerge. Many have a promotional or programmatic character, for they refer principally to the purposes or goals of the UN or to the competences of different UN organs: 'encouraging respect for human rights', 'assisting in the realization of human rights', 'promote ... universal respect for, and observance of, human rights'. Not even a provision such as Article 56, which refers to action of the member states rather than of the UN, contains the language of obligation. It notes only that states 'pledge themselves' to action 'for the achievement' of purposes including the promotion of observance of human rights. Note that only one substantive human right, the right to equal protection, receives specific mention in the Charter (Arts. 1(3), 13(1)(b) and 55).

In retrospect, Louis Henkin, in *International Law: Politics, Values and Functions*, 216 Collected Courses of The Hague Academy of International Law (Vol. IV, 1989), at 215, argued that there has been a tendency to exaggerate what the Charter did for human rights:

> The Charter made the promotion of human rights a purpose of the United Nations; perhaps without full appreciation of the extent of the penetration of Statehood that was involved, it thereby recognized and established that relations between a State and its own inhabitants were a matter of international concern. But the Charter did not erode State autonomy and the requirement of State consent to new human rights law. ...

The Universal Declaration

Despite proposals to the contrary, the Charter stopped shy of incorporating a bill of rights. Instead, there were proposals for developing one through the work of a special commission that would give separate attention to the issue. That commission was contemplated by Charter Article 68, which provides that one of the UN organs, the Economic and Social Council (ECOSOC), 'shall set up commissions in economic and social fields and for the promotion of human rights'. In 1946, ECOSOC established the Commission on Human Rights (referred to in this book as the UN Commission), which evolved over the decades to become the world's single most important (and perhaps most disputed) human rights organ. At its inception, the new Commission was charged primarily with submitting reports and proposals on an international bill of rights. (The UN Commission was displaced by a newly created Human Rights Council in 2006. Chapter 8 examines the work of both the Commission and Council.)

The UN Commission first met in its present form early in 1947, composed of the representatives of states. The United States was represented by Eleanor Roosevelt. Some representatives urged that the draft bill of rights under preparation should take the form of a declaration — that is, a recommendation by the General Assembly to Member States (see Charter Art. 13) that would exert a moral and political influence on states rather than constitute a legally binding instrument. Other representatives urged the Commission to prepare a draft convention containing a bill of rights that would, after adoption by the General Assembly, be submitted to states for their ratification.

The first path was followed. In 1948, the UN Commission adopted a draft Declaration, which in turn was adopted by the General Assembly that year as the Universal Declaration of Human Rights (UDHR), with 48 states voting in favour and eight abstaining — Saudi Arabia, South Africa and the Soviet Union, together with four East European states and a Soviet republic whose votes it controlled. (It is something of a jolt to realize today, in a decolonized and fragmented world with 193 UN member states, that that number stood at only 56 states in 1948.)

The UDHR was meant to precede more detailed and comprehensive provisions in a single convention that would be approved by the General Assembly and submitted to states for ratification. After all, within the prevailing concepts of human rights at that time, the UDHR seemed to cover most of the field, including economic and social rights (see Arts. 22–26) as well as civil and political rights. But during the years of drafting — years in which the Cold War took harsher and more rigid form, and in which the United States strongly qualified the nature of its commitment to the universal human rights regime — these matters became more contentious.[42] The human rights regime was buffeted by ideological conflict and the formal differences of approach in a polarized world. One consequence was the decision in 1952 to build on the UDHR by dividing its provisions between two treaties, one on civil and political rights, the other on economic, social and cultural rights.

The plan to use the Universal Declaration as a springboard to treaties triumphed, but not as quickly as anticipated. The two principal treaties — the ICCPR and the ICESCR — made their ways through the drafting and amendment processes in the Commission, the Third Committee and the General Assembly, where they were approved only in 1966. Another decade passed before the two Covenants achieved in 1976 the number of ratifications necessary to enter into force.

During the 28 years between 1948 and 1976, a number of specialized human rights treaties such as the Genocide Convention entered into force. But not until the two principal Covenants became effective did a treaty achieve as broad coverage of human rights topics as the Universal Declaration. It was partly for this reason that the UDHR became so widely known and frequently invoked. During these intervening years, it was the only broad-based human rights instrument available. To this day, it:

> … has retained its place of honor in the human rights movement. No other document
> has so caught the historical moment, achieved the same moral and rhetorical force, or
> exerted as much influence on the movement as a whole.... [T]he Declaration expressed in
> lean, eloquent language the hopes and idealism of a world released from the grip of
> World War II. However self-evident it may appear today, the Declaration bore a more
> radical message than many of its framers perhaps recognized. It proceeded to work its

---

[42]See, for example, O. Barsalou, 'The United States and Human Rights Marginalization at the International Court of Justice, 1945–1950', 24 *J. Hist. Int'l L.* (2022) 102.

subversive path though many rooted doctrines of international law, forever changing the discourse of international relations on issues vital to human decency and peace.[43]

As a declaration voted in the General Assembly, the UDHR lacked the formal authority of a treaty that binds its parties under international law. Nonetheless, it remains in some sense the constitution of the entire regime, as well as the single most cited human rights instrument.

Other UN Organs Related to Human Rights

Together with the UN Commission, other UN organs have played major roles in developing universal human rights. Their full significance with respect to drafting and approving treaties or declarations, monitoring, censuring, and authorizing or ordering state action becomes apparent in later chapters. A brief description follows.

Chapter IV of the Charter sets forth the composition and powers of the General Assembly. Those powers are described in Articles 10–14 in terms such as 'initiate studies', 'recommend', 'promote', 'encourage' and 'discuss'. Particularly relevant are Articles 10 and 13. Article 10 authorizes the General Assembly to 'discuss any questions or any matters within the scope of the present Charter [and] ... make recommendations to the Members of the United Nations ... on any such questions or matters'. Article 13 authorizes the GA to 'make recommendations' for the purpose of, *inter alia*, 'assisting in the realization of human rights'. Throughout its history, the GA has been active in voting resolutions related to human rights issues.

Contrast the stronger and more closely defined powers of the Security Council under Chapter VII. Those powers range from making recommendations to states parties about ending a dispute, to the power to authorize and take military action 'to maintain or restore international peace and security' (Art. 42) after the Council 'determine[s] the existence of any threat to the peace, breach of the peace, or act of aggression' (Art. 39). Under Article 25, member states 'agree to accept and carry out' the Security Council's 'decisions' on these and other matters. No such formal obligation of states attaches to recommendations or resolutions of the General Assembly. As Chapter 9 indicates, the Security Council has in recent years used its powers to address situations involving major human rights violations.

Two of the six Main Committees of the General Assembly — committees of the whole, for all UN members are entitled to be represented on them — have also participated in drafting or other processes affecting human rights. The Social, Humanitarian and Cultural Committee (Third Committee) and the Legal Committee (Sixth Committee) have reviewed drafts of proposed declarations or conventions and often added their comments to the document submitted to the plenary General Assembly for its ultimate approval.

Historical Sequence and Typology of Instruments

That part of the universal human rights regime consisting of intergovernmental instruments — that is, excluding for present purposes both national laws and nongovernmental institutions forming part of the regime — can be imagined as a four-tiered normative edifice, the tiers described generally in the order of their chronological appearance.

(1) The UN Charter, at the pinnacle of the human rights system, has relatively little to say about the subject. But what it does say has been accorded great significance. Through interpretation and extrapolation, as well as frequent invocation, the sparse text has constituted a point of departure for inventive development of the entire regime.

(2) The UDHR, viewed by some as an elaboration of the brief references to human rights in the Charter, occupies in important ways the primary position of constitution of the entire regime. Today many understand the UDHR — or more specifically, numbers of its provisions — to have gained formal legal force by becoming a part of customary international law.

[43] H. Steiner, 'Securing Human Rights: The First Half-Century of the Universal Declaration, and Beyond', *Harvard Magazine* (Sept.–Oct. 1998) 45.

(3) The two principal covenants, which alone among the universal treaties have broad coverage of human rights topics, develop in more detail the basic categories of rights that figure in the Universal Declaration, and include additional rights as well

(4) A host of multilateral human rights treaties (usually termed 'conventions', for there are only the two basic 'covenants'), as well as resolutions or declarations with a more limited or focused subject than the comprehensive International Bill of Rights, have grown out of the United Nations (drafting by UN organs, approval by the General Assembly) and (in the case of treaties) have been ratified by large numbers of states. They develop further the content of rights that are more tersely described in the two covenants or, in some cases, that escape mention in them. This fourth tier consists of a network of treaties, most but not all of which became effective after the two Covenants. They include: the Convention on the Prevention and Punishment of the Crime of Genocide (153 states parties as of 2024), the International Convention on the Elimination of all Forms of Racial Discrimination (182 parties), the Convention on the Elimination of all Forms of Discrimination against Women (189 parties), the Convention against Torture and other Cruel, Inhuman or Degrading Treatment or Punishment (173 parties), the Convention on the Rights of the Child (196 parties), and the Convention on the Rights of Persons with Disabilities (188 parties).

This book discusses to one or another degree most of these instruments.

QUESTION

Compare the premises, character and provisions of the UDHR with the prior illustrations in Chapter 2 of the relevant doctrines in international law that constitute the 'background' to the post-war human rights regime. In what respects (putting aside its legal character as a declaration rather than a treaty) does the UDHR stand out as strikingly different, as resting on premises that were not simply alien to but close to heresies within the preceding international law?

The Aspiration to Universality

From the start, the human rights regime had universal aspirations. It was not to address only the developed countries of the West/North but rather all regions and all states, whatever their form of government, socio-economic situation or religious–cultural traditions. After all, the key document at the very start of the regime was entitled the *Universal* Declaration of Human Rights (UDHR). Its language, like that of many later human rights treaties, speaks abstractly of 'everyone', or 'no person'. It communicates no sense of differentiation among its subjects based on religion, gender, colour, ethnicity, national origin, wealth, region, education. To the contrary, the human rights texts fasten on equality and non-discrimination as cardinal concepts.

Over the decades, the question of how 'universal' the postwar catalogue of human rights are or should seek to become has assumed greater prominence. The 'universal' is often contrasted with the 'particular' or 'culturally specific', or 'cultural relativism'. The different meanings of these concepts and illustrations of their significance for a number of human rights topics figure as a central theme in Chapters 6 and 7. In this Chapter we focus on conflicting views on the question of its universality and on the political and ethical traditions that inform it.

The issue of universality, per se, was not prominent on the agenda of the drafters of the UDHR, although there were major philosophical differences within the group. In February 1947, the UN Commission on Human Rights appointed a three-person Drafting Committee from among the governmental representatives on the Commission. The following month, it was enlarged to make it more representative (UN Doc. E/383 (1947)). It consisted of Eleanor Roosevelt (United States) Chairperson, and Alexandre Bogomolov (USSR), René Cassin (France), Peng-chun Chang (China), Charles Dukes (United Kingdom), William Hodgson (Australia), Charles Malik (Lebanon), and Hernán Santa Cruz (Chile). Hansa Mehta (India) and Carlos Romulo (The Philippines) also played important roles in the process, as did John Humphrey, the Canadian director of the UN Secretariat who compiled the first draft.

There were a great many inputs into the drafting process and contemporary debates outside the Commission context also shed light on some of the controversies. Lawyers, especially from the United States and Latin America, contributed important draft documents reflecting domestic constitutional traditions. Of particular importance were the American Law Institute's *Statement of Essential Human Rights* (1945), and the Institut de Droit International's report entitled *Les droits fondamentaux de l'homme, base d'une restauration du droit international* (1947).

The most significant philosophical foray at the time was undertaken by a group of philosophers and other prominent public figures convened by the United Nations Educational, Scientific and Cultural Organization (UNESCO) in 1947 to give their views as to what could or should be covered in a proposed declaration of rights. The group, somewhat haphazardly chosen, almost entirely male, and fa r from being truly representative in cultural or philosophical terms, made it clear that there could be no consensus beyond a very thin set of shared formulations.[44] For example, a University of Chicago political scientist, Charles Merriam, insisted that 'the basic right is the right to life', without which 'the other so-called rights lose their meaning'. Mahatma Gandhi recalled that he had learned from his 'illiterate but wise mother that all rights to be deserved and preserved came from duty well done.' As a result, every right that did not correspond to some 'duty to be first performed … can be shown to be a usurpation hardly worth fighting for.' And the British author, Aldous Huxley, warned that 'mere paper restrictions, designed to curb the abuse of a power already concentrated in a few hands, are but the mitigation of an existing evil', adding that 'personal liberty can be made secure only by abolishing the evil altogether'.

In introducing the UNESCO survey, the French Catholic philosopher, Jacques Maritain, argued that while fundamental ideological and philosophical differences could never be bridged, this did not preclude the emergence of 'a sort of common denominator, … at the point where in practice the most widely separated theoretical ideologies and mental traditions converge.' This, he said, would require a pragmatic approach and the recasting of accepted formulae in order that they would be acceptable 'as points of convergence in practice, however opposed the theoretic viewpoints.' He concluded by observing that, despite 'the clash of theory' reflected in the views of the various contributors, one could nevertheless hope that 'a few scanty features of … a practical ideology … are in the course of taking root in the conscience of the nations'.[45]

Subsequently, the Chairman of the 'UNESCO Committee on the theoretical bases of Human Rights', the prominent British historian E. H. Carr, characterized the UDHR as being 'pale, eclectic and unconvincing'. In his view, it reflected the outcome of a 'political sparring match' rather than a 'common agreement among men of good will'. He lamented its striking 'emptiness' and the fact that 'political expediency' had led the drafters to keep the 'real issues' 'decently out of sight.'[46]

Many anthropologists also had deep misgivings, as reflected in the statement submitted by the American Anthropological Association to the UDHR drafters that adopted a strong relativist position. While the statement was apparently written solely by Melville Herskovits, who was also a contributor to the UNESCO volume,[47] it nonetheless reflected a view held by many anthropologists at the time.

And prominent economists were also divided on the question of whether economic justice should form part of a declaration of rights. The emphasis on 'freedom from want', proclaimed in the 1941 Atlantic Charter outlining the allied war aims, and again in President Franklin Delano Roosevelt's 1944 proposal for a second Bill of Rights in the United States, was strongly supported by many. But early neoliberal economists were strongly critical. In the Mont Pèlerin Society's 1947 Statement of Aims, Friedrich von Hayek, Ludwig von Mises, and others saw 'danger in the expansion of government, not least in the welfare state, in the power of trade unions and business monopoly …'.[48] Hayek considered social justice to be a mirage and the term itself to be both 'nonsense' and 'empty and meaningless'.[49] He reserved particular scorn for the economic and social rights recognized in the

---

[44] *Human Rights: Comments and Interpretations*, a symposium edited by Unesco, with an Introduction by Jacques Maritain, UNESCO Doc. UNESCO/PHS/3 (rev), 25 July 1948, available at https://unesdoc.unesco.org/ark:/48223/pf0000155042
[45] Ibid,
[46] E. H. Carr, 'Rights and Obligations', *The Times Literary Supplement*, No. 2943, November 11, 1949, p. 725-26.
[47] M Goodale, *Anthropology and Law: A Critical Introduction* (New York, New York University Press, 2017) 99.
[48] Statement of Aims (April 8, 1947) at https://www.montpelerin.org/statement-of-aims/
[49] A. Lister, 'The Mirage of "Social Justice": Hayek Against (and For) Rawls', 25 *Critical Review* (2013) 409, at 410.

UDHR, arguing that they were fundamentally incompatible with civil rights, were incapable of being meaningfully designed, and would require a totalitarian system for their implementation.[50] Von Mises shared this contempt for so-called 'basic economic rights'.[51]

Some commentators have staunchly defended the UDHR's universality. In particular, Mary Ann Glendon, in *A World Made New* (2001) at 227, argued that:

> The Declaration ... was far more influenced by the modern dignitarian rights tradition of continental Europe and Latin America than by the more individualistic documents of Anglo-American lineage. ...

> Dignitarian rights instruments, with their emphasis on the family and their greater attention to duties, are more compatible with Asian and African traditions. In these documents, rights bearers tend to be envisioned within families and communities; rights are formulated so as to make clear their limits and their relation to one another as well as to the responsibilities that belong to citizens and the state ...

Glendon interprets 'the Declaration's "Everyone" [as] an individual who is constituted ... by and through relationships with others':

> There is little doubt about how the principal framers of the Universal Declaration would have responded to the charge of "Western-ness." What was crucial for them — indeed, what made universal human rights possible — was the *similarity* among all human beings. Their starting point was the simple fact of the common humanity shared by every man, woman, and child on earth, a fact that, for them, put linguistic, racial, religious. and other differences into their proper perspective.

But Makau Mutua, also cited in Glendon's book, takes a fundamentally different position about the origin and character of the UDHR:[52]

> ... Non-Western philosophies and traditions particularly on the nature of man and the purposes of political society were either unrepresented or marginalized during the early formulation of human rights.... There is no doubt that the current human rights corpus is well meaning. But that is beside the point.... International human rights fall within the historical continuum of the European colonial project in which whites pose as the saviors of a benighted and savage non-European world. The white human rights zealot joins the unbroken chain that connects her to the colonial administrator, the Bible-wielding missionary, and the merchant of free enterprise.... Thus human rights reject the cross-fertilization of cultures and instead seek the transformation of non-Western cultures by Western cultures.

Glendon (at p. 221) also interpreted the UNESCO philosophers' conclusions as indicating that 'a core of fundamental principles was widely shared' across cultures and countries. But Mark Goodale, in *Letters to the Contrary: A Curated History of the UNESCO Human Rights Survey* (2018), at 30, concludes that 'if any "common convictions" can be said to emerge [from the views of the philosophers], they would be those that either doubt the value of the entire project of human rights itself, or prefer to understand it as a temporary, historically contingent, reaction to the horrors of world war ...'. E. H. Carr, Chair of the UNESCO Committee, also reached conclusions that were very different from Glendon's.

---

[50] 'Justice and Individual Rights: Appendix to Chapter Nine', in F. A. von Hayek, *Law, Legislation, and Liberty: A New Statement of the Liberal Principles of Justice and Political Economy* (1982 rev. ed.), at 101-106.

[51] L. von Mises, *Socialism: An Economic and Sociological Analysis* (1951) 56-63.

[52] M. Mutua, 'The Complexity of Universalism in Human Rights', in A. Sajó (ed.), *Human Rights with Modesty* (2004) 51.

E. H. CARR, RIGHTS AND OBLIGATIONS
THE TIMES LITERARY SUPPLEMENT, NO. 2493 (11 NOVEMBER 1949) 725

…

No political party would venture to appeal to the electorate of the most orthodox democracy to-day without inscribing in its programme the right to work, the right to a living wage, and the right to care and maintenance in infancy, old age, ill-health or unemployment. These rights today – far more than the right to vote or freedom of speech and assembly – make up the popular conception of the rights of man. We have moved on from the age of bourgeois individualism to the age of mass industrial civilization. The rights of man, the things which he most wants from society, have changed with the times.

But does this mean that the new social and political rights can simply be added to the old political rights, so that we have merely broadened our conception of the rights of man in general? Things are not quite so easy as this. The fact of juxtaposition produces a process of interaction between different rights which must end by altering their character. The dilemma of reconciling political equality with political liberty was always resolved, down to the time of J. S. Mill, by defining liberty as freedom to do everything that did not restrict the liberty of others. But when equality comes to mean economic equality or – at any rate some enforced mitigation of economic inequality – and when liberty comes to mean something like liberty of opportunity, or free and equal access to the good things which society has to offer, the relation between equality and liberty takes on a much more baffling complexion. To claim that "freedom from want" is merely an extension of the older conceptions of freedom, that without freedom from want no other freedom can be real, is plausible enough. But the fact remains that "freedom from want" is not only an emanation from the old freedoms, but is incompatible with some of them; it is, for example, incompatible with the freedom of a *laissez-faire* society. The present conflict about human rights does represent to some extent the difficult choice between incompatible alternatives. Both sides are to this extent insincere when they pretend to offer a formula that makes the best of all worlds.

… The second problem is older and more familiar; for at no period of history has the correlation between rights and obligations been denied. Any definition of the rights of man is a definition of the relation between the individual and society; and this relation necessarily involves rights and obligations on both sides. … The modern revolution comes at the end of a long period of buoyant and almost unrestrained individual enterprise, when the individual has tended more and more to claim his rights against society and to forget the corresponding weight of his social obligations. The wheel has come round; the leaders of liberal democracies, no less than of totalitarian States, are finding it to-day increasingly necessary to dwell on what the citizen owes to the community of which he forms a part.

The truth that rights cannot be divorced from obligations would seem trite if it had not been so often overlooked in recent years. … [The obligation attached to political rights is sometimes describes as being mainly passive, or] being confined to loyalty to the political order. This is not wholly correct. Liberal democracy worked because a sufficient number of those who profited by its privileges recognized the positive obligation to play their part in making it work. The tradition of public service-and even of unpaid public service-was one of its essential attributes. It is doubtful whether western democracy has given sufficient attention to the problem of transferring this conception of individual public service to the conditions of mass civilization. …

…

Human rights, though in principle rights recognized as valid for mankind as a whole, are generally discussed … as the rights of the citizen. [Attention should thus be given to the rights of outcasts from society, such as "law-breakers" and "primitive peoples".] … To remove racial discrimination is here the beginning, but certainly not the end, of wisdom.

…

ROLAND BURKE, DECOLONIZATION, DEVELOPMENT, AND IDENTITY:
THE EVOLUTION OF THE ANTICOLONIAL HUMAN RIGHTS CRITIQUE, 1948-1978
J. QUATAERT AND L. WILDENTHAL (EDS.), THE ROUTLEDGE HISTORY OF HUMAN RIGHTS (2020) 222

…

… In the peak years of the anticolonial movement, human rights were embraced as a language integral to opposing empire. Liberal nationalist movements which, in the late 1940s through early 1960s, were the principal force for decolonization, saw their own aspirations in the precepts of the [UDHR]. Universalistic, promising the full swathe of freedoms - civil and political, economic and social - human rights were at once the answer to patronizing imperial claims of civilizational tutelage, the foremost weapon against colonial authoritarianism, and the most fundamental rejoinder to racial discrimination.

For around a decade, harmony prevailed between anticolonial nationalism and the form of human rights enunciated in the post-war period, which presumed the properly constituted sovereign state as the premier guarantor of freedom. If anything, the main dissenters to the incipient global human rights order were the European imperial powers, who guarded their own sovereign prerogative across overseas territories, and in a more elemental sense, the moral legitimacy of colonial rule. ... Initially, ... anticolonial critiques were limited in extent, and only episodically florid in expression. Nevertheless, by the mid-1960s, human rights, as they were understood in the late 1940s and early 1950s, were the subject of growing skepticism and even outright hostility from post-independence governments and a number of African, Asian, Arab, and Western intellectuals. Emphatic on the urgency of national mobilizations, the equilibrium between individual and state agreed at in 1948 no longer seemed sufficient for many in this later generation of anticolonial voices.

With the radical expansion of the human rights NGO movement in the 1970s, with its center of gravity firmly within the political West, anticolonialism and the new transnational human rights movement drew further apart. ... Amnesty and Human Rights Watch in particular, championed a quite different interpretation of human rights even to that posited in 1948. Their "human rights" was avowedly anti-statist in inflexion - at precisely the moment when strengthening the state was the priority concern of the Third World. Stung by the more confrontational style of the 1970s NGOs, post-independence governments began to issue strident defensive critique to specific, condemnatory NGO reports, notably those from Amnesty International. Alongside the usual dissembling characteristic of most governments indicted by an NGO denunciation, Third World states now began to repudiate key elements of universalism, and advanced subversive, particularistic, schemes of regional, religious, and traditionalist re-definition. In their rejections of NGO scrutiny, Third World governments denounced the authority of Western activists, which formed much of the early transnational human rights movement. Yet these states - and numerous others, notably apartheid South Africa - went further than debating substantive merit of NGO criticisms: they began to attack those concepts of universality, indivisibility, and inherence, the very features which had subtended the power of human rights as an anti-imperial discourse. In the rhetoric of many post-colonial regimes, human rights scrutiny was increasingly dismissed as a new mode of imperialism.

[In focusing on] ... the dissents that emerged from the Third World [this chapter looks at] the emergence and growing acceptance of pleas for a temporary exception - an allowance for the exigencies of development, which were often an extension of imperial pleas for gradualism. These calls, which had once been treated - properly - with scorn when recited by British and French legations, were the first wave of anticolonial arguments against universality in the mid-to-late 1950s advanced by new national leaders. By the later 1960s, these arguments for a caveated and deferred universality had migrated to the center of international human rights conversation. Invoking very real imperatives for economic development, this wave of critique opened the first major, sustained breach in the conceptual foundation of the UDHR. Tension between state mobilization for material well-being, and individual civil and political freedoms, was a latent site of rupture from the late 1940s. Differences in capacity between the developed and underdeveloped had been raised repeatedly during the formulation of the UDHR, and a principal factor in the division of the human rights covenant that followed it. ...

However, the radicalization of these arguments, typically from the wave of repressive rulers that arrived after the first hopeful moment of independence, turned good faith recognition of a problem into a bald dismissal of universal human rights in any practical sense. Conditions themselves also altered the terrain of the debate - the sheer duration of the Third World's economic misery obscured any appreciable difference between transient and reluctant variation of an accepted norm - and transmuted into a permanent assertion of essential difference. The later accretion of cultural and traditionalist identity particularism, which were grafted on to the original core of developmental claims, further foreclosed the sweeping universality of 1948.

The ... divergence between anticolonialism and human rights was mutual - the former changed dramatically in character, and the latter acquired a narrower set of emphases in the 1970s. While there were doubtlessly areas of radical transformation which cut across this dynamic, exemplified by a revivified international women's rights movement, the most prominent human rights NGOs had built much of their campaign on a sparing set of priority concerns. Their human rights minimalism - which devoted much effort to the most primordial subjects, torture and extra-judicial killing - was a language of limited capacity to inspire. The more radical transformations envisaged in the 1940s and 1950s, of economic sovereignty, the welfare state, and a redistribution of global power, which had been at least part of the appeal of human rights for anticolonial movements, were much less readily set in this new architecture. A logic of the least worst, and the most that could be hoped, which often seemed a breviary of the philosophy under which groups like Amnesty International operated, was a world away from revolutionary promises of a New International Economic Order. This conflict produced a deep confusion in the language, and an erosion of its normative power, as numerous hostile species of human rights proliferated. Human rights, for a substantial bloc of post-colonial states, became commingled with another project, the augmentation and development of their own states, and a repartitioning of global economic power along more equitable lines. For many Western NGOs, the state, once recognized as a vital pillar for realizing an ambitious vision of human rights, was recast as the prime enemy of a much more austere set of freedoms. Both had departed from the UDHR, while simultaneously proclaiming their fealty to it. Each variant of "human rights" was deployed to attack the other. Human rights critique was, by the 1980s, almost always conducted in the name of another "human rights."

…

QUESTIONS

1. As a principle of interpretation, in what direction (if any) would Glendon's understanding of the UDHR's 'dignitarian' tradition point with respect to, say, (a) a question of freedom of speech as applied to hate speech, (b) a question of individual liberty in relation to the right of others to an adequate standard of living, (c) a question of equal protection in relation to a claim for gay marriage?

2. Based on Glendon's argument in these excerpts, how do you react to her position that the UDHR was at its origin and is now properly understood as having universal validity?

3. What conclusions would you draw from Burke's historical overview?

Lauterpacht and the UDHR

Understandings of the Universal Declaration have inevitably changed over time. Appreciation of earlier ideas at the start of the human rights regime illuminates its general evolution as well as suggests how perceptions of it and, more broadly, international law have developed over 75 years. There follow some excerpts from an influential book by a preeminent scholar of international law of his generation, Hersch Lauterpacht. At the time of the book's publication, the Declaration was two years old and untested as to its character and significance. His comments on the place of natural law in this context remain pertinent.[53]

HERSCH LAUTERPACHT, INTERNATIONAL LAW AND HUMAN RIGHTS (1950) 61

Chapter 4: The Subjects of the Law of Nations, the Function of International Law, and the Rights of Man

…

What have been the reasons which have prompted the changes in the matter of subjects of international law, with regard both to international rights and to international duties? These causes have been numerous and manifold. They have included, with reference to the recognition of the individual as a subject of international

---

[53] See generally T. Angier, I, Benson and M. Retter (eds.), *The Cambridge Handbook of Natural Law and Human Rights* (2022).

rights, the acknowledgment of the worth of human personality as the ultimate unit of all law; the realisation of the dangers besetting international peace as the result of the denial of fundamental human rights; and the increased attention paid to those already substantial developments in international law in which, notwithstanding the traditional dogma, the individual is in fact treated as a subject of international rights. Similarly, in the sphere of international duties there has been an enhanced realisation of the fact that the direct subjection of the individual to the rule of international law is an essential condition of the strengthening of the ethical basis of international law and of its effectiveness in a period of history in which the destructive potentialities of science and the power of the machinery of the State threaten the very existence of civilised life.

Above all, with regard to both international rights and international duties the decisive factor has been the change in the character and the function of modern international law. The international law of the past was to a large extent of a formal character. It was concerned mainly with the delimitation of the jurisdiction of States.... In traditional international law the individual played an inconspicuous part because the international interests of the individual and his contacts across the frontier were rudimentary. This is no longer the case ... .
...
... [I]t is in relation to State sovereignty that the question of subjects of international law has assumed a special significance. Critics of the traditional theory have treated it as an emanation of the doctrine of sovereignty. In their view it is State sovereignty — absolute, petty, and overbearing — which rejects, as incompatible with the dignity of States, the idea of individuals as units of that international order which they have monopolised and thwarted in its growth. It is the sovereign State, with its claim to exclusive allegiance and its pretensions to exclusive usefulness that interposes itself as an impenetrable barrier between the individual and the greater society of all humanity....
...
... [T]he recognition of the individual, by dint of the acknowledgment of his fundamental rights and freedoms, as the ultimate subject of international law, is a challenge to the doctrine which in reserving that quality exclusively to the State tends to a personification of the State as a being distinct from the individuals who compose it, with all that such personification implies. That recognition brings to mind the fact that, in the international as in the municipal sphere, the collective good is conditioned by the good of the individual human beings who comprise the collectivity. It denies, by cogent implication, that the corporate entity of the State is of a higher order than its component parts....

... International law, which has excelled in punctilious insistence on the respect owed by one sovereign State to another, henceforth acknowledges the sovereignty of man. For fundamental human rights are rights superior to the law of the sovereign State.... [T]he recognition of inalienable human rights and the recognition of the individual as a subject of international law are synonymous. To that vital extent they both signify the recognition of a higher, fundamental law not only on the part of States but also, through international law, on the part of the organized international community itself. That fundamental law, as expressed in the acknowledgment of the ultimate reality and the independent status of the individual, constitutes both the moral limit and the justification of the a international legal order....

Chapter 5: The Idea of Natural Rights in Legal and Political Thought
...
... The law of nature and natural rights can never be a true substitute for the positive enactments of the law of the society of States. When so treated they are inefficacious, deceptive and, in the long run, a brake upon progress.... The law of nature, even when conceived as an expression of mere ethical postulates, is an inarticulate but powerful element in the interpretation of existing law. Even after human rights and freedoms have become part of the positive fundamental law of mankind, the ideas of natural law and natural rights which underlie them will constitute that higher law which must forever remain the ultimate standard of fitness of all positive law, whether national or international...

[Lauterpacht then turns to historical antecedents of 'the notion and the doctrine of natural, inalienable rights of man pre-existent to and higher than the positive law of the State'. He observes that 'ideas of the law of nature date back to antiquity', and briefly describes such ideas and notions of natural right in Greek philosophy and the Greek state, in Roman thought, in the Middle Ages and in the Reformation and the period of Social Contract. Lauterpacht then addresses 'fundamental rights in modern constitutions'.]

In the nineteenth and twentieth centuries the recognition of the fundamental rights of man in the constitutions of States became, in a paraphrase of Article 38 of the Statute of the Permanent Court of International Justice, a general principle of the constitutional law of civilised States. It became part of the law of nearly all European States....

... [T]here is one objection to the notion of natural rights which, far from invalidating the essential idea of natural rights, is nevertheless in a sense unanswerable. It is a criticism which reveals a close and, indeed, inescapable connexion between the idea of fundamental rights on the one hand and the law of nature and the law of nations on the other. That criticism is to the effect that, in the last resort, such rights are subject to the will of the State: that they may — and must — be regulated, modified, and if need be taken away by legislation and, possibly, by judicial interpretation; that, therefore, these rights are in essence a revocable part of the positive law of a sanctity and permanence no higher than the constitution of the State either as enacted or as interpreted by courts and by subsequent legislation....

...

Chapter 17: The Universal Declaration of Human Rights

The Universal Declaration of Human Rights ... has been hailed as an historic event of profound significance and as one of the greatest achievements of the United Nations.... Mrs. Roosevelt, Chairman of the Commission on Human Rights and the principal representative of the United States on the Third Committee, said: 'It [the Declaration] might well become the international Magna Carta of all mankind.... Its proclamation by the General Assembly would be of importance comparable to the 1789 proclamation of the Declaration of the Rights of Man, the proclamation of the rights of man in the Declaration of Independence of the United States of America, and similar declarations made in other countries'....

...

The practical unanimity of the Members of the United Nations in stressing the importance of the Declaration was accompanied by an equally general repudiation of the idea that the Declaration imposed upon them a legal obligation to respect the human rights and fundamental freedoms which it proclaimed. The debates in the General Assembly and in the Third Committee did not reveal any sense of uneasiness on account of the incongruity between the proclamation of the universal character of the human rights forming the subject matter of the Declaration and the rejection of the legal duty to give effect to them. The delegates gloried in the profound significance of the achievement whereby the nations of the world agree as to what are the obvious and inalienable rights of man ... but they declined to acknowledge them as part of the law binding upon their States and Governments....

... [T]he representative of the United States, in the same statement before the General Assembly in which she extolled the virtues of the Declaration, said: 'In giving our approval to the declaration today, it is of primary importance that we keep clearly in mind the basic character of the document. It is not a treaty; it is not an international agreement. It is not and does not purport to be a statement of law or of legal obligation....'

...

... It is now necessary to consider the view, expressed in various forms, that, somehow, the Declaration may have an indirect legal effect.

In the first instance, it may be said — and has been said — that although the Declaration in itself may not be a legal document involving legal obligations, it is of legal value inasmuch as it contains an authoritative interpretation of the 'human rights and fundamental freedoms' which do constitute an obligation, however imperfect, binding upon the Members of the United Nations. It is unlikely that any tribunal or other authority administering international law would accept a suggestion of that kind. To maintain that a document contains an authoritative interpretation of a legally binding instrument is to assert that that former document itself is as legally binding and as important as the instrument which it is supposed to interpret....

... [T]here would seem to be no substance in the view that the provisions of the Declaration may somehow be of importance for the interpretation of the Charter as a formulation, in this field, of the 'general principles of law recognized by civilised nations'. The Declaration does not purport to embody what civilized nations generally recognize as law.... The Declaration gives expression to what, in the fullness of time, ought to become principles of law generally recognized and acted upon by States Members of the United Nations....

...

Undoubtedly the Declaration will occasionally be invoked by private and official bodies, including the organs of the United Nations. But it will not — and cannot — properly be invoked as a source of legal obligation....

Not being a legal instrument, the Declaration would appear to be outside international law. Its provisions cannot form the subject matter of legal interpretation. There is little meaning in attempting to elucidate, by reference to accepted canons of construction and to preparatory work, the extent of an obligation which is binding only in the sphere of conscience....

The fact that the Universal Declaration of Human Rights is not a legal instrument expressive of legally binding obligations is not in itself a measure of its importance. It is possible that, if divested of any pretence to legal authority, it may yet prove, by dint of a clear realisation of that very fact, a significant landmark in the evolution of a vital part of international law ... .

...

The moral authority and influence of an international pronouncement of this nature must be in direct proportion to the degree of the sacrifice of the sovereignty of States which it involves. Thus conceived, the fundamental issue in relation to the moral authority of the Declaration can be simply stated: That authority is a function of the degree to which States commit themselves to an effective recognition of these rights guaranteed by a will and an agency other than and superior to their own ... .

Its moral force cannot rest on the fact of its universality — or practical universality — as soon as it is realised that it has proved acceptable to all for the reason that it imposes obligations upon none. ...

... [C]ompare the Declaration of 1948 with that of [the French Declaration of] 1789 and similar constitutional pronouncements. These may not have been endowed, from the very inception, with all the remedies of judicial review and the formal apparatus of enforcement. But they became, from the outset, part of national law and an instrument of national action. They were not a mere philosophical pronouncement.... One of the governing principles of the Declaration — a principle which was repeatedly affirmed and which is a juridical heresy — is that it should proclaim rights of individuals while scrupulously refraining from laying down the duties of States. To do otherwise, it was asserted, would constitute the Declaration a legal instrument. But there are, in these matters, no rights of the individual except as a counterpart and a product of the duties of the State. There are no rights unless accompanied by remedies. That correlation is not only an inescapable principle of juridical logic. Its absence connotes a fundamental and decisive ethical flaw in the structure and conception of the Declaration.
... [54]

* * *

Impact of the UDHR

The UDHR features prominently throughout this book. Note different reactions to its impact. Samuel Moyn has described it variously as 'a funeral wreath laid on the grave of wartime hopes'. 'death by birth', and 'a stillborn project'.[55] Christopher N. J. Roberts, in *The Contentious History of the International Bill of Human Rights* (2014) 225, calls the UDHR an 'incredible achievement' but traces the ways in which states like the United States and the United Kingdom fought successfully to circumvent its impact. In the former, those who 'opposed the new social order implied by human rights renewed the rights and duties of the ... states vis-à-vis the federal government; they updated the obligations and privileges of US sovereignty in the face of a new communist enemy; they defended the prerogatives of racial supremacy amidst "forced integration from abroad"; and they reasserted the rights and duties associated with a free market.'

---

[54] For a survey of the many ways of conceptualizing the role of the individual in international law today, see generally T. Sparks and A. Peters (eds.), *The Individual in International Law: History and Theory* (2024). For a critical perspective see, in that volume, B. S. Chimni, 'The Status of the Individual in International Law: A TWAIL Perspective', p. 231 at 248:

> The focus of any assessment of whether an individual is a subject of international law should not merely be on the atomistic individual or legal materials but on internal and global social relations as these impose structural constraints on realising the goal of human dignity.

[55] Quoted in S. Jensen, *The Making of International Human Rights: The 1960s, Decolonization and the Reconstruction of Global Values* (2016) 20-21.

Based on an extensive empirical analysis, Zachary Elkins and Tom Ginsburg, in 'Imagining a World Without the Universal Declaration of Human Rights', 74 *World Politics* (2022) 327 discern a major impact:

> … How would the world's constitutions look if the UDHR had never been declared? Our conclusion is that subsequent national constitutions— the principal legal device for enforcing rights—would be much different: they would likely include fewer rights, a smaller core of consensual rights, and, outside the core, a different cast of elective rights. It could also be that the societies governed by these rights are today very different places to live because of the rights. …

> …

> … Writing down a set of universal rights and then grandly proclaiming them through the auspices of the United Nations, the newly created arbiter of the world order, has had strong globalizing effects. The fabric of human rights law in most countries is noticeably different from what it would have been. But this isn't to say that the UDHR was an exogenous force. Quite the contrary. We find that the UDHR clearly represented the values and trends of a new, modern world clambering over the wreckage of a human rights catastrophe. In this sense, the UDHR importantly reinforced and accelerated the uptake of these values. In other words, the document was both a reflection of its times and highly formative of what was to come. …

B. THE INTERNATIONAL COVENANT ON CIVIL AND POLITICAL RIGHTS

The Relationship between the UDHR and the ICCPR

You should now become familiar with the substantive part (Arts. 1–27) of the International Covenant on Civil and Political Rights. The comparisons below between the UDHR and the ICCPR assume that familiarity. One basic similarity informs all of the following discussion; each instrument aspires to universality. The UDHR was supported by the great majority of states of its time; the ICCPR now includes the great majority of the world's states. This section's examination of the ICCPR is brief; Chapter 9 examines the Covenant more intensively through the work of the treaty body that it creates, the Human Rights Committee.

(1) Under international law, approval by the General Assembly of a declaration like the UDHR has a different consequence from a treaty that has become effective through the required number of ratifications. Of course the declaration will have solemn effects as the formal act of a deliberative body of global importance. Its subject matter, like that of the UDHR, may be of the greatest significance. But when approved or adopted, it is hortatory and aspirational, recommendatory rather than, in a formal sense, binding.

The Covenant, on the other hand, binds the states parties in accordance with its terms and with international law, subject to such formal matters as reservations and the kinds of exceptional circumstances described in the examination of treaties, above. Of course this statement of international law doctrine and its basic postulate, *pacta sunt servanda* (agreements must be kept), does not end discussion. The content of important provisions of a treaty may long remain in dispute among the states parties. Differences over interpretation will likely arise; some states will disagree with others as to what even basic provisions of the Covenant (such as, in the case of the ICCPR, the 'right to life') mean and require. What indeed is the 'commitment'? Absent a consensus over meaning, which state party or international institution can provide an interpretation that most parties will view as authoritative and decisive? Even if there is a widespread consensus, one must confront the question of whether states will honour this 'binding' commitment and, if not, whether the UN or some member states will apply pressure against violators sufficient to persuade them to comply. Does or should the probability of enforcement against violators have any bearing on the legally binding character of an international agreement?

In the case of the UDHR, the years have further blurred the threshold contrast between 'binding' and 'hortatory' instruments. The countless references to and invocations of the Declaration as the fountainhead or constitution or grand statement of the human rights regime has affected how it is viewed — perhaps as shy of 'binding', but somehow relevant to norm formation and influential with respect to state behaviour as so-called 'soft law'(see Ch. 5, below). Moreover, broadly supported arguments have developed for viewing all or parts of this Declaration as legally binding, either as a matter of customary international law or as an authoritative interpretation of the UN Charter.

(2) A resolution of the General Assembly (such as that approving the Universal Declaration) with the formal status of a recommendation will not generally seek to create an international institution with defined membership, structure and powers. Neither can customary international law. A treaty can and often does. The Charter creates numerous organs, some organically part of the UN and some distinct from but related to it. The ICCPR creates an ongoing institution, a so-called 'treaty body': the Human Rights Committee. That organ gives institutional support to the Covenant's norms, for the Covenant imposes on states parties formal obligations (such as the submission of periodic reports) to the Committee. This Committee is charged with the performance of the tasks defined both in the Covenant (173 states parties as of 2024) and in its Optional Protocol (116 parties).

(3) Both the UDHR and ICCPR are terse about their derivations or foundations in moral and political thought. Such statements as are made that have the character of foundational assumptions, justifications or explanations appear in the preambles (with a few exceptions such as Article 21 of the UDHR and Article 25 of the ICCPR). But clearly these instruments differ radically from, say, a tax treaty that expresses a compromise and temporary convergence of interests among its states parties. They speak to matters deep, lasting, purportedly universal. What then are the intuitions that shape them, their sources in intellectual history or moral or religious thought, the important guides to their interpretation and evolution?

(4) Many rights declared in the Covenant closely resemble the provisions of the Universal Declaration, although they are stated in considerably greater detail. Compare, for example, the requirements for criminal trials in Articles 10 and 11 of the Declaration with the analogous provisions in Articles 14 and 15 of the Covenant.

(5) *Individual* rights characterize these instruments. Group or collective rights — that is, rights that pertain to and are exercised by the collectivity as such, perhaps by vote but more likely through representatives — are rare. In a few cases, they are either asserted or hinted at in the Covenant, most directly in Articles 1 (on self-determination of peoples) and 27 (on survival of cultures). The Universal Declaration lacks such provisions. Both the UDHR and the ICCPR refer to the family as the 'natural and fundamental group unit of society'. On the other hand, it should be kept in mind that rights cast in terms of the individual, such as the right to equal protection or the right to practice one's religion or participate in associations, have an inherent group character, either in the sense that the identity at issue in denials of equal protection is a group identity (race, ethnicity, gender, religion) or in the sense that the right is generally practised in community with others (as suggested by ICCPR Art. 27).

(6) In both instruments the idea of *rights* dominates with respect to individuals. Duties characteristically attach to the state. Article 29(1) of the Declaration does provide that everyone 'has duties to the community in which alone the free and full development of his personality is possible'. The Covenant contains no article referring to individuals' *duties*, though its Preamble has such a clause.

(7) Article 17 of the Declaration on the 'right to own property' and protection against arbitrary deprivation thereof does not figure among the rights declared in the Covenant. Ideological disputes between East and West, and disputes between the West and the South over the nationalization of industries and other resources made agreement on a consensus formulation impossible.

(8) The UDHR goes little beyond declaring that everyone has the 'right to an effective remedy by the competent national tribunals' for violations of fundamental rights (Art. 8). The remedial structure of the ICCPR reaches much further. In Article 2, states parties agree to 'ensure' to all persons within their

territory the rights recognized by the Covenant, and to adopt such legislative or other measures as may be necessary to achieve that goal. Moreover, the parties undertake to 'ensure' that any person whose rights are violated 'shall have an effective remedy', and that 'the competent authorities shall enforce such remedies when granted'. They undertake in particular 'to develop the possibilities of judicial remedy'.

(9) Two types of provisions in the ICCPR limit states' obligations thereunder:

    a.   Under closely stated conditions and limits, Article 4 dealing with a public emergency ('which threatens the life of the nation and the existence of which is officially proclaimed') permits a *derogation*, in the sense of a temporary adjustment to or suspension of the operation of some of the rights declared by the Covenant. Thus states may consciously, purposively depart from such rights as those in Article 9 relating to arrest and detention. Note that under Article 4(2) certain rights are non-derogable. This issue of derogation becomes a major concern in Chapter 5, which deals with national security issues.

    b.   Several articles include *limitation clauses* — that is, provisions indicating that a given right is not absolute but may be adapted to take account of a state's need to protect public safety, order, health or morals, or national security. See, for example, Articles 18 and 19. In Articles 21 and 22, the limitation clause is phrased in terms of permitting those restrictions on a right 'which are necessary in a democratic society'. Compare the broad provision of Article 29(2) of the UDHR, which is not linked to a specific right. Note that the limitation clauses may overlap with but are not identical with the common problem of resolving conflicts between *rights* (such as rights to speech and to privacy, as accommodated in the law of defamation) that also may lead to a 'limitation', in this case of one right to give space to the other.

(10) Article 5 of the UDHR bans 'cruel, inhuman or degrading' punishment, but that instrument does not refer to capital punishment as such. See Article 6(2) of the ICCPR. The Second Optional Protocol to the ICCPR, aiming at abolition of the death penalty, had 90 states parties as of 2024. Article 1 provides that 'No one within the jurisdiction of a State Party to the present Protocol shall be executed ... . Each State Party shall take all necessary measures to abolish the death penalty within its jurisdiction'. Recall the discussion about measures affecting capital punishment in Chapter 1.

One can organize or classify the rights declared in the Declaration and Covenant in various ways, depending on the purpose of the typology. Consider the adequacy of the following scheme that embraces most of the Covenant's rights, although it excludes such distinctive provisions as ICCPR Article 1 on the self-determination of peoples and Article 27 on the enjoyment by minorities of their own cultures:

    a)   protection of the individual's physical integrity, as in provisions on torture, arbitrary arrest and arbitrary deprivation of life;

    b)   procedural fairness when government deprives an individual of liberty, as in provisions on arrest, trial procedure and conditions of imprisonment;

    c)   equal protection norms defined in racial, religious, gender and other terms;

    d)   freedoms of belief, speech and association, such as provisions on political advocacy, the practice of religion, press freedom, and the right to hold an assembly and form associations; and

    e)   the right to political participation.

These five categories of rights can be imagined as on a spectrum. At one extreme lie killing or torture over which there exists a broad formal-verbal consensus among states (whatever the degree of ongoing violation of the relevant rights by many states). At the other extreme lie rights whose purposes, basic meanings and even validity are formally disputed. For example, few if any states (even those that practise it) formally justify torture (see below). A good number of states, however, may justify some form of religious or gender discrimination stemming from religious belief or customary practices, and argue that such practices should be viewed as consistent with the goals of the human rights regime — perhaps because (the argument goes) in such circumstances, equal protection rights should not be viewed as 'universal' so as to bind local cultures or practices or traditions that differ. Or states that reject the core practices of political democracy may justify different forms of political organization ranging from hereditary or elite (say, 'vanguard') leadership to a theocracy.

Among the intergovernmental organs or institutions referred to in this Chapter, some such as the UN Human Rights Council are mandated by the UN Charter, others such as the Human Rights Committee by distinct treaties (in this case, the ICCPR). As a matter of convenience, the first set is often referred to as 'Charter-based' organs/institutions, and the second set as 'treaty-based' organs/institutions or 'treaty bodies' (i.e., treaties other than the Charter).

But the human rights treaties adopted since the Charter are distinct from it only up to a point. Thus, the ICCPR and other human rights treaties noted all grew within the UN, from the time that they were first drafted in an organ like the UN Commission on Human Rights (now the Human Rights Council) to their final approval by the General Assembly and submission to states for ratification. Typically for such treaties, the ICCPR provides for a number of ongoing links to the UN. Article 45 indicates that the Annual Report of the ICCPR Committee should be submitted to the General Assembly. Note also the provisions for amendment of the ICCPR in Article 51. Moreover, each of these separate treaty regimes like the ICCPR depends for funding on the regular biennial budget adopted by the General Assembly.

QUESTIONS

1. Relying only on the preambles and texts of the UDHR and the ICCPR, how would you identify the reasons for those instruments, their justifications in moral and political thought, the moral and political traditions from which they derive? Why do you suppose there was such a sparse statement of reasons or justifications in these instruments?

2. Do you see in either of these instruments any departure from 'universal' premises, rights and related obligations of states? That is, are there concessions in any provisions to different cultures or regions that would allow those cultures or regions to privilege their own practices and traditions rather than follow these instruments' rules — for example, by inflicting certain severe modes of criminal punishment, or governing by theocracy or inherited rule, or imposing restrictions on minority religions or on activities of women?

3. Article 2 of the ICCPR includes states' undertakings 'to respect and to ensure to all individuals' the recognized rights. States parties must 'ensure' that persons whose rights are violated have an 'effective remedy'. Competent authorities 'shall enforce such remedies when granted'.

(a) Is it accurate to say that rights are borne by individuals, and duties are borne only by states since the ICCPR is concerned only with state violations? Who may violate, say, your right to bodily security? Who may violate your right to political participation under Article 25, or your right to procedural due process under Article 14?

(b) Is it accurate to say that the duties of the state are entirely 'negative', in the sense of requiring no more than that the state generally keep its 'hands off' individuals, and refrains from certain conduct such as torture, discrimination, or repression of hostile (to it) political opinion? Is it accurate to say that fulfilment by the state of its duties would then be cost-free?

Indivisibility and *Jus Cogens*

The 1993 Vienna World Conference on Human Rights famously concluded that:

> All human rights are universal, indivisible and interdependent and interrelated. The international community must treat human rights globally in a fair and equal manner, on the same footing, and with the same emphasis.

This is referred to as the indivisibility or non-subordination doctrine. The following readings explore this issue of equality or hierarchy, with Eric Heinze arguing that free speech is 'the most human right', and Theodor Meron pointing to the pitfalls of any such hierarchical ordering. The readings then introduce the separate, but closely related, concept of *jus cogens*, or peremptory norms of international law.

Eric Heinze begins his book, *The Most Human Right: Why Free Speech is Everything* (2022) by asking '[w]hat distinguishes human rights as a system of justice?'. His answer is that:

> … [T]he only thing that can turn government-managed human goods into citizen-directed human rights is free speech. In order for a human rights system to come into being, free speech cannot count as just another right on the Universal Declaration's checklist. Free speech within a safe and robust public sphere furnishes a necessary prior condition for the existence of human rights … .

> … Some would argue that all or most of the rights set forth in the Universal Declaration cannot be secure without all or most of the others, so no one right can be said to found all the others. They accept that free speech is as important as those other goods, but reject any suggestion that it is more important. Yet my point will not be that free speech is more "important" than life, protections from torture, fair trials, availability of food and water, and other goods. … My aim is not to rank human goods, but only to ask … what turns human goods into human rights?

> …

> Free speech within the public sphere is the only thing that can render human rights different from other models of justice.

> …

> *Conclusion*

> …

> …[T]he official policy remains that of "indivisibility," or at least "nonsubordination," whereby no one right is deemed to be more important than any others. That principle would pose no problems if all rights were cost free, but … all rights presuppose considerable costs if they are to be reliably implemented.

> Yet given that all states operate under financial constraints, non-subordination becomes financially impossible. Indeed, the opposite policy becomes compulsory: a policy of tradeoffs, which we find everywhere practiced but nowhere formally acknowledged, as the myth of non-subordination continues to be upheld. …

> …

> …Free speech within a safe and robust public sphere stands as the ultimate recourse for individuals who, rightly or wrongly, believe their rights have been violated or neglected. Only within that sphere of public discourse can state-managed human goods become objects of citizen-directed human rights. …

Compare Heinze's approach with that of Theodor Meron, 'On a Hierarchy of International Human Rights', 80 *Am. J. Int'l. L.* (1986) 1, at 21:

> … Hierarchical terms constitute a warning sign that the international community will not accept any breach of those rights. Historically, the notions of 'basic rights of the human person' and 'fundamental rights' have helped establish the *erga omnes* principle, which is so crucial to ensuring respect for human rights. Eventually, they may contribute to the crystallization of some rights, through custom or treaties, into hierarchically superior norms, as in the more developed national legal systems.

Yet the balance of pros and cons does not necessarily weigh clearly on the side of the pros. Resort to hierarchical terms has not been matched by careful consideration of their legal significance. Few criteria for distinguishing between ordinary rights and higher rights have been agreed upon. There is no accepted system by which higher rights can be identified and their content determined. Nor are the consequences of the distinction between higher and ordinary rights clear. Rights not accorded quality labels, i.e., the majority of human rights, are relegated to inferior, second-class, status. Moreover, rather than grapple with the harder questions of rationalizing human rights lawmaking and distinguishing between rights and claims, some commentators are resorting increasingly to superior rights in the hope that no state will dare — politically, morally and perhaps even legally — to ignore them. In these ways, hierarchical terms contribute to the unnecessary mystification of human rights, rather than to their greater clarity.

Caution should therefore be exercised in resorting to a hierarchical terminology. Too liberal an invocation of superior rights such as 'fundamental rights' and 'basic rights,' as well as *jus cogens*, may adversely affect the credibility of human rights as a legal discipline.

Some international lawyers have long advocated the notion of a hierarchy of norms with *jus cogens* (Latin for 'compelling norms') at the apex. For most commentators, these peremptory norms build upon custom, while for others they represent transcendent values, perhaps closer to natural law. They have featured prominently in recent years in international legal discourse, but their real-world impact is contested. The sources of international law are not ranked hierarchically, so there is no equivalent of constitutional norms at the domestic level. Nonetheless, arguments have long been made that certain rules should enjoy a superior status. The 1969 Vienna Convention on the Law of Treaties (VCLT) brought a breakthrough in this regard by recognizing a 'peremptory norm of general international law', or a norm of *jus cogens*, defined as one 'accepted and recognized by the international community of States as a whole as a norm from which no derogation is permitted and which can be modified only by a subsequent norm of general international law having the same character' (Art. 53). Although the same article provided that 'a treaty is void if, at the time of its conclusion, it conflicts with' such a peremptory norm, the VCLT included no list of *jus cogens* norms and specified no procedure for identifying them.

Robert Kolb, in *Peremptory International Law – Jus Cogens: A General Inventory* (2015) observes that 'there is a greater amount of uncertainty in the context of *jus cogens* than in almost any other cardinal concept of the legal order – with the exception, perhaps, of sovereignty.' He is critical of 'mainstream' definitions which see *jus cogens* as 'a sort of new constitutional legal order of the international community, or as a series of substantive norms of international law of fundamental importance to the collectivity.' In his view it should not be understood as 'a class of norms of international law with specific qualities, such as being "superior" in a hierarchy or centred on concerns of the international community.' Rather than being 'a series of substantive norms … it is a quality of certain legal norms, a quality engrafted upon them in order not to allow the operation of the *lex specialis* principle in respect of them.' They thus prevail, even over norms that would otherwise be privileged under the *lex specialis* rule, according to which more specific rules will prevail over more general rules.

Proponents often seek to endow these 'highly cherished' rules 'with an unlimited number of miraculous legal consequences in the form of super-norms'. But Kolb warns in conclusion that States 'must be able to live in peace with the concept and its ramifications.' This means that 'if the notion is pushed too far, it will backfire. The danger of a "do-gooder" *jus cogens* is that it may discredit the concept entirely and allow power politics to exact an all too easy revenge.'

Compare this cautionary approach with that of Antonio Cassese in 'A Plea for a Global Community Grounded in the Core of Human Rights', in *ibid.* (ed.), *Realizing Utopia: The Future of International Law* (2012) 137:

> We should first of all draw a distinction between (i) a core of fundamental values which must be common to all nations, states, and individuals and may not, therefore, be derogated from and (ii) other values, the application of which may need to take into account national conditions. The fundamental values of the world society are those enshrined in that core of rules that constitute the international *jus cogens* … .

...

With this [evolution of thinking after the late 1960s] came a clear understanding that *jus cogens* rules included norms concerning human rights: those banning genocide, slavery, racial discrimination, and forcible denial of self-determination. Over the years national or international bodies have suggested that other international rules also enjoy the status of peremptory norms: the ban on torture, the prohibition of the slave trade, the right to life, the right of access to justice, the right of any person arrested or detained to be brought promptly before a judge (the so-called habeas corpus right), the ban on *refoulement* (refusal of entry of refugees at the frontier), the prohibition of collective penalties, and the principle of personal responsibility in criminal matters. I would also add the right to a fair trial. Other norms are likely gradually to rise to the level of *jus cogens* through a process of accretion. This normative process unfolds through judicial decisions (be they national or international), pronouncements by collective bodies such as the UN General Assembly, and declarations of states and other international legal subjects. ...

... [P]eremptory norms ... can be considered as those which have universal scope and bearing. They must be obeyed by all nations, states, and individuals of the planet. Other values, consecrated instead in international rules deprived of the nature of *jus cogens*, although still important, can be restrained in their incidence and scope by individual states, or adjusted to some extent to national conditions — as long as, however, such interpretation or adjustment does not appear to be absolutely arbitrary or unwarranted to other states or the relevant international bodies.

The existence of two different sets of values and corresponding international norms can make allowance for the coexistence of a core of indispensable and absolute values and a set of other, less imperative values. The gradual expansion over time of the first group of norms might eventually lead in the future to the formation of a global community where all the basic norms on human rights must be equally respected by everyone in any part of the planet.

Scholars have long differed on the foundations of these norms. Bruno Simma, writing before he became a judge of the ICJ, endorsed the view expressed by Serge Sur that, rather than being a 'strengthened form of custom', *jus cogens* norms emerge from 'an autonomous, original mode of formation, which perhaps does not form part of practice'. In his view, 'once recognition by the "international community as a whole" can be established, the question from which formal source rules of peremptory law can flow is more or less irrelevant. Persistent objection is to be regarded as inadmissible ... .' The 'peremptory quality' of the norms results from 'the universal recognition that these rules consecrate values which are not at the disposal of individual States (any more).'

Antonio Cassese, at p. 165, argued that 'no consistent practice of states and other international legal subjects (usus) is necessary'. Dinah Shelton in *Jus Cogens* (2021) predicts that environmental, territorial and other challenges are likely to generate new claims of *jus cogens* norms and observes that many will feel that the 'international community cannot afford a consensual regime' in order to address such problems.

In 2002, the U.S. Supreme Court held that an undocumented Mexican migrant worker was not permitted to receive back pay owed to him after being laid off for union-organizing activities, because he was present and working in the U.S illegally (*Hoffman Plastic Compounds v. National Relations Labor Board*, 535 US 137 (2002)). With 6 million Mexicans working outside the country, some 2.5 million of whom were undocumented and most working in the U.S., the Mexican Government turned to the Inter-American Court of Human Rights. Because the U.S. is not a party to the American Convention, no case could be brought against it, but Mexico was entitled to seek an advisory opinion. It asked the court whether depriving migrant workers of certain labour rights was compatible with the Organization of American States (OAS) Member States' obligation 'to ensure the principles of legal equality, non-discrimination and the equal and effective protection of the law' as embodied in international human rights instruments. The Advisory Opinion squarely addressed the *jus cogens* dimension of the issue:[56]

---

[56] Inter-American Court of Human Rights Advisory Opinion OC-18/03 of September 17, 2003.

101. [T]his Court considers that the principle of equality before the law, equal protection before the law and non-discrimination belongs to *jus cogens*, because the whole legal structure of national and international public order rests on it and it is a fundamental principle that permeates all laws. Nowadays, no legal act that is in conflict with this fundamental principle is acceptable, and discriminatory treatment of any person, owing to gender, race, color, language, religion or belief, political or other opinion, national, ethnic or social origin, nationality, age, economic situation, property, civil status, birth or any other status is unacceptable. …

In strong contrast, Alain Pellet and Daniel Müller, in 'Article 38', in Andreas Zimmermann *et al* (eds.), *The Statute of the International Court of Justice: A Commentary* (2019) 819, at 936 argue that '[j]*us cogens* is not a 'new' category of formal sources of international law. It describes a particular quality of certain norms, usually of a customary nature, the existence of which is proven by an 'intensified *opinio juris*' which has to be established by following the same method as that relevant for demonstrating the existence of an 'ordinary' customary rule.' The fact that these norms are peremptory 'does not contradict the principle that the various sources of international law are not in a hierarchical position with regard to one another—but rather means that some norms, parts of a still rudimentary international public order, are, intrinsically, because of their content, superior to all others (whatever their source).' They also note that the ICJ has only rarely recognized the existence of such norms and even more rarely 'drawn consequences from them'.

In 1993, Hilary Charlesworth and Christine Chinkin in 'The Gender of *Jus cogens*', 15 *Hum. Rts Q.* (1993) 63, at 74, criticized *jus cogens* norms as being highly gendered:

> Fundamental norms designed to protect individuals should be truly universal in application as well as rhetoric, and operate to protect both men women from those harms they are in fact most likely to suffer. They should be genuine human rights, not male rights. The very human rights principles that are most frequently designated as *jus cogens* do not in fact operate equally upon men and women. They are gendered and not therefore of universal validity. Further, the choices that are typically made of the relevant norms and the interpretation of what harms they are designed to prevent reflect male choices which frequently bear no relevance to women's lives. On the other hand, the violations that women do most need guarantees against do not receive this same protection or symbolic labelling. The priorities asserted are male-oriented and are given a masculine interpretation. Taking women's experiences into account in the development of *jus cogens* norms will require a fundamental rethinking of every aspect.

Earlier in the analysis, they had addressed the question of what a feminist jurisprudence of *jus cogens* could look like:

> … [One aspect] is to challenge the gendered dichotomy between public and private worlds and to reshape doctrines based on it. For example, existing human rights law can be redefined to transcend the distinction between public and private spheres and truly take into account women's lives as well as men's. Considerations of gender should be fundamental to an analysis of international human rights law.

> Feminist rethinking of *jus cogens* would also give prominence to a range of other human rights; the right to sexual equality, to food, to reproductive freedom, to be free from fear of violence and oppression, and to peace. … [There is a] dissonance between women's experiences and international legal principles generally. In the particular context of the concept of *jus cogens*, which has an explicitly promotional and aspirational character, it should be possible for even traditional international legal theory to accommodate rights that are fundamental to the existence and dignity of half the world's population. …

> …

In 2022, after seven years of debate, the International Law Commission adopted a set of draft conclusions on *jus cogens* (UN Doc. A//77/10):

Conclusion 2 …

[A *jus cogens* norm is one] accepted and recognized by the international community of States as a whole as a norm from which no derogation is permitted and which can be modified only by a subsequent norm of general international law having the same character.

Conclusion 3 …

[*Jus cogens* norms] reflect and protect fundamental values of the international community, are hierarchically superior to other rules of international law and are universally applicable.

…

Conclusion 5 …

1. Customary international law is the most common basis for [*jus cogens*].

2. Treaty provisions and general principles of law may also serve as bases … .

…

Conclusion 7 …

1. It is the acceptance and recognition by the international community of States as a whole that is relevant for the identification of [*jus cogens*].

2. Acceptance and recognition by a very large majority of States is required …; acceptance and recognition by all States is not required.

3. While the positions of other actors may be relevant in providing context and for assessing acceptance and recognition by the international community of States as a whole, these positions cannot, in and of themselves, form part of such acceptance and recognition.

Conclusion 8 …

1. Evidence of acceptance and recognition [of *jus cogens* norms] may take a wide range of forms.

2. Such forms of evidence include, but are not limited to: public statements made on behalf of States; official publications; government legal opinions; diplomatic correspondence; legislative and administrative acts; decisions of national courts; treaty provisions; and resolutions adopted by an international organization or at an intergovernmental conference.

…

Conclusion 23…

Without prejudice to the existence or subsequent emergence of other peremptory norms …, a non-exhaustive list of norms that the International Law Commission has previously referred to as having that status is to be found in the annex to the present draft conclusions.

Annex

(a) The prohibition of aggression;

(b) The prohibition of genocide;

(c) The prohibition of crimes against humanity;

(d) The basic rules of international humanitarian law;

(e) The prohibition of racial discrimination and apartheid;

(f) The prohibition of slavery;

(g) The prohibition of torture;

(h) The right of self-determination.

QUESTIONS

1. Cassese divides human rights into two categories: fundamental and intransgressible; and flexible and contingent. What are the arguments for and against such an approach?

2. Does the ILC draft give a clear indication as to the normative foundations of jus cogens? Compare Conclusions 2 and 3.

3. In the 80 pages of the ILC's 2022 final report on jus cogens, there is not a single reference to the words 'women' or 'gender', although there are two footnote references to the article by Charlesworth and Chinkin. What factors might account for this omission?

Withdrawal from the ICCPR

The issue arose in the 1990s of a state party's right to withdraw from the ICCPR which, unlike many treaties, has no provision about termination of obligations. The Human Rights Committee issued its General Comment No. 26 (1997) on this question. Excerpts follow:

> 1. ... [T]he possibility of termination, denunciation or withdrawal must be considered in the light of applicable rules of customary international law which are reflected in the Vienna Convention on the Law of Treaties. . . .
>
> ...
>
> 3. ... [I]t is clear that the Covenant is not the type of treaty which, by its nature, implies a right of denunciation. Together with the simultaneously prepared and adopted International Covenant on Economic, Social and Cultural Rights, the Covenant codifies in treaty form the universal human rights enshrined in the Universal Declaration of Human Rights, the three instruments together often being referred to as the 'International Bill of Human Rights'. As such, the Covenant does not have a temporary character typical of treaties where a right of denunciation is deemed to be admitted, notwithstanding the absence of a specific provision to that effect.
>
> 4. The rights enshrined in the Covenant belong to the people living in the territory of the State party. The Human Rights Committee has consistently taken the view ... that once the people are accorded the protection of the rights under the Covenant, such protection devolves with territory and continues to belong to them, notwithstanding change in government of the State party, including dismemberment in more than one State or State succession. ...

5. The Committee is therefore firmly of the view that international law does not permit a State which has ratified or acceded or succeeded to the Covenant to denounce it or withdraw from it. …

C. WOMEN'S RIGHTS AND CEDAW

The study of women's rights illustrates the trajectory, ambition, breadth and complexity of the human rights regime.[57] We see a proliferation of instruments and institutions, but also growing conflicts about premises and goals within the women's movement itself. The feminist literature relevant to human rights assumptions, goals and strategies has moved adventurously in many directions, sometimes polar directions; its engagement with the human rights regime has enriched and deepened thought about the entire project. The complexity and different currents of advocacy and criticism, idealism and scepticism, views of sexuality and gender, and indeed views of equality are captured in the different responses to an innovative and ambitious treaty adopted in 1979, the Convention on the Elimination of All Forms of Discrimination against Women, known as CEDAW (189 states parties as of 2024). Only seven UN Member States have failed to ratify the treaty: Iran, Palau, Somalia, Sudan, Tonga, the Holy See, and the United States.[58]

Of the several blind spots in the early development of the human rights regime, none is as striking as the failure to accord violations of women's (human) rights the attention they require. It is not only that these problems adversely affect half of the world's population. They affect everyone, for a deep change in women's circumstances and possibilities produces change throughout social, economic and political life.

The materials in this section suggest the complexly interwoven socio-economic, legal, political and cultural strands to the problem of women's subordination and the content of women's rights. Although a systematic study of economic and social rights must await Chapter 4, this section demonstrates in many ways the interrelationships and functional interdependence of civil and political rights (CPR) and economic and social rights (ESR). CEDAW's title uses a classic CPR lens — discrimination — but the content of its rights and the work of its Committee range much more broadly. Moreover, when one focuses specifically on what are often presented as 'women's issues,' links with other aspects of social order and disorder appear pervasive and the inter-relationship of all issues is apparent.

1. Background to Women's Rights

In 1991, Hilary Charlesworth, Christine Chinkin and Shelley Wright published a path-breaking analysis entitled 'Feminist Approaches to International Law', 85 *Am. J. Int'l L.* (1991) 613. They argued that 'international legal structures and principles … are more accurately described as international men's law':

> Modern international law is not only androcentric, but also Euro-centered in its origins, and has assimilated many assumptions about law and the place of law in society from western legal thinking. These include essentially patriarchal legal institutions, the assumption that law is objective, gender neutral and universally applicable, and the societal division into public and private spheres, which relegates many matters of concern to women to the private area regarded as inappropriate for legal regulation. …

> … A feminist transformation of international law would involve more than simply refining or reforming existing law. It could lead to the creation of international regimes that focus on structural abuse and the revision of our notions of state responsibility. It could also lead to a challenge to the centrality of the state in international law and to the traditional sources of international law.

---

[57] R. Cook (ed.), *Frontiers of Gender Equality: Transnational Legal Perspectives* (2023).

[58] In relation to the United States, see R. de Silva de Alwis and M. Verveer, '"Time Is a-Wasting": Making the Case for CEDAW Ratification by the United States', 60 *Colum. J. Transnat'l L.* (2021) 1; and A. Comstock, 'Signing CEDAW and Women's Rights: Human Rights Treaty Signature and Legal Mobilization', 48 *Law and Soc. Inquiry* (2023) 1.

Charlesworth and Chinkin elaborated on their critique in *The Boundaries of International Law* (2000). Their central argument was 'that the absence of women in the development of international law has produced a narrow and inadequate jurisprudence that has … legitimated the unequal position of women around the world rather than challenged it.' They criticized the neglect of women's rights by mainstream human rights institutions, the ineffective implementation of women's rights, the negative impact of many reservations to CEDAW, the neglect of underlying structures and power relations in 'equal treatment' approaches, the lack of scrutiny given to the human rights consequences of actions by corporate and religious actors, and the disappointing results of gender mainstreaming. In the second edition of their book in 2022, Charlesworth and Chinkin look back at their earlier work and note their assumption that 'once the gendered nature of the international legal system was exposed, change would follow. Twenty years later, we see that apparent progress can be quickly unraveled and today the boundaries of international law remain largely unchanged.'

The same conclusion was reached by the World Economic Forum in its *Global Gender Gap Report 2022*, which noted that 'progress towards gender parity is stalling', and that this is 'a catastrophe for the future of our economies, societies and communities.' The report estimated that, at the current rate of progress, it will take 132 years to reach full parity. While 'health and survival' and 'educational attainment' rates were around 95% parity globally, the rate for 'economic participation and opportunity' was 60% and for 'political empowerment' it is 22%.

The following materials suggest the complex relationships among diverse phenomena that bear on women's rights. Several themes recur in the readings.

(1) Legal norms capture and reinforce deep cultural norms and community practices. They entrench ideas and help give them the sense of being natural, part of the inevitable order of things.

(2) Reformers and advocates of deep legal and cultural transformation insist that change is possible, so that what was seen as natural or inevitable comes to be understood as socially constructed and thus contingent, open to change.

(3) Property rights and economic dependence interact with patterns of authority within family and workplace, and with vital issues like education, health, and political participation.

(4) Major economic and political programmes, particularly those linked to neoliberalism, such as austerity, deregulation, privatization, or tax-cutting, may impose particular and severe costs on women that are not acknowledged or immediately apparent.

(5) The statistics and indexes created by bureaucracies or scholars structure and confine the imagination. They are often viewed as objective data, without awareness of the disputable methods and categories that determine their formulation. What they record, as well as what they do not record, influences policies as well as perceptions.

The status of women within the international human rights regime and the task of ensuring human rights for women are incomprehensible without taking into account the social and economic conditions that characterize women's lives around the world.[59] Later readings underscore the degree to which rights abuses are strongly correlated to women's slight social and economic power, and hence their limited political power. Those most vulnerable to human rights abuses often lack the favour or protection of the state, as well as the power within their communities to protect and further their basic needs and interests.

According to virtually every indicator of social well-being and status — political participation, legal capacity, access to economic resources and employment, wage differentials, levels of education and health care — women fare significantly and sometimes dramatically worse than men. The following materials reflect some of these dimensions.

---

[59] For an important survey, see R. Cook (ed.), Frontiers of Gender Equality; Transnational Legal Perspectives (2023).

A 1991 report by Guatemala to the CEDAW Committee opens a window into the status of women in that country and many others at the time.[60]

INITIAL REPORT OF GUATEMALA TO THE CEDAW COMMITTEE
CEDAW/C/GUA/1–2 (2 APRIL 1991)

...

46. Guatemala is a multi-ethnic, multi-cultural and multilingual country with traditional, cultural patterns that reinforce the subordination of women on the social, cultural, economic and political planes. Extended Guatemalan families in the country and nuclear families in the city are governed by a patriarchal system in which decisions are taken by men (husband, father or eldest son), who are considered the heads of the household, a role assumed by women only in their absence.

47. In Guatemalan society the man is expected to be the breadwinner, the legal representative, the repository of authority; the one who must 'correct' the children, while the mother is relegated to their care and upbringing, to household tasks, and to 'waiting on' or looking after her husband or partner. These roles often have to be performed in addition to engaging in some profitable activity which generates earnings that are always regarded as 'complementary'.

48. For their childhood, little boys and girls are guided towards work considered 'masculine' or 'feminine'; for example, boys play at working outside the home as carpenters, mechanics, farmers or pilots, and in all those jobs that are considered 'tough' or that require physical strength. Girls, on the other hand, are taught to interest themselves in cooking, weaving, sewing, washing, ironing, or cleaning the house and, especially, caring for the children and helping the mother, as a responsibility and duty more than just a game.

49. Care of the children is strictly considered the responsibility of the mother, grandmother, and/or sister ... .

...

51. Notwithstanding what has been said, the woman is the chief social agent in the majority of spheres of action. An empirical profile of a Guatemalan woman may cover the following characteristics.

52. She is responsible for family health and hygiene and for the supervision of the formal and informal upbringing of the children in the home; she organizes and maintains living and sanitary conditions and a supply of water for domestic use. ... [S]he is the one in charge of the purchase, preparation, stocking and distribution of food within the home. In addition, she manages the family income ... .

53. She takes responsibility for generating additional income or for producing consumer goods when her partner's income does not cover the minimum family requirements.

54. In the case of an irresponsible father, the entire responsibility for the support of the children devolves upon her, reflected in particular by a considerable increase in her hours of work.

55. Her work is poorly paid or not paid at all and is generally of low productivity owing to lack of access to capital.

56. It is falsely assumed that the man is the one who makes the principal economic contributions to the family, for which reason he is the owner and beneficiary of all payments and services.

57. The educational level of the woman is low, which reflects on the effectiveness of her efforts to maintain and improve the health, feeding, housing and other living conditions of her family.

58. In the paid work that she does, her salary is inferior to a man's and her instability in the sense of a job is greater.

...

---

[60] See generally, J. E. Alvarez and J. Bauder, *Women's Property Rights under CEDAW* (2024).

190.The woman's rights and responsibilities in marriage are as follows:

...

(2) The husband owes his wife protection and assistance, and must provide her with all the means necessary to maintain the household, in accordance with his financial resources. The woman has a special right and duty to nurture and care for her children during their minority, and to take charge of domestic affairs.

...

    (5) The woman may be employed or ply a trade, occupation, public office or business, where she is able to do so without endangering the interests and the care of her children, or other needs of her household.

...

197.Married women are restricted in representing the marriage and in administration of marital assets, roles which are assigned by law to the husband, and this constitutes a relative incapacity.

198.Parental authority is a right which is virtually forbidden to women, since it is assigned to the father. Women only come to exercise this right when the father is imprisoned or legally barred from such.

...

201. The legal context allows the husband to object to the wife engaging in activities outside the home, thus barring her from the right and freedom to work. The legal context restricts her right to personal fulfillment in areas outside her function as mother and housewife and restricts her personal liberty.

...

203. A judicial declaration of paternity in cases of rape, rape of juveniles and abduction is dependent on the conduct of the mother, based on what the law terms 'notoriously disorderly conduct', an express form of discrimination against women and the product of conception resulting from forced intercourse.

...

209. Adultery defined as an 'offence against honour' protects the legal right of filiation and 'the interests of the family', but makes a clear distinction concerning the gravity of the act, depending on whether it involves the man or the woman, providing a tougher sentence for the woman; the proof and the procedure are different in the two cases, so that in practice it is only applied to women.

...

211. With regard to the offence of rape, the punishment is graded according to the age of the victim and the relationship of authority which may exist between the victim and the offender. ...

212. Maltreatment of women and children and domestic violence are not defined as offences against the person and in practice are lumped together with injuries, coercion and threats, causing serious difficulties with regard to proof and other procedural problems.

HUMAN DEVELOPMENT PERSPECTIVES, TACKLING SOCIAL NORMS: A GAME CHANGER FOR GENDER INEQUALITIES
UNDP (2020)

Gender disparities are a persistent form of inequality in every country. Despite remarkable progress in some areas, no country in the world— rich or poor— has achieved gender equality. All too often, women and girls are discriminated against in health, in education, at home and in the labour market— with negative repercussions for their freedoms.

...

The world is not on track to achieve gender equality by 2030. The *Human Development Report's* Gender Inequality Index (GII)— a measure of women's empowerment in health, education and economic status— shows that overall progress in gender inequality has been slowing in recent years. For instance, based on current trends, it would take 257 years to close the gender gap in economic opportunity. The number of female heads of government is lower today than five years ago, with only 10 women in such positions among 193 countries (down from 15 in 2014).

Beyond what is measured, there are unaccounted burdens behind the achievements: the double shift at home, the harassment in public transportation, the discrimination in workplaces, and the multiple hidden constraints that women face. New social movements are emerging all around the world. Different forms of demonstration— including online campaigns, women marches and street performances— demand new ways of looking at gender equality and women's empowerment. The #MeToo movement gives voice to many silence breakers, uncovering abuse and vulnerability. In India the #IWillGoOut movement demands equal rights for women in public spaces. In Latin America the #NiUnaMenos movement sheds light on femicides and violence against women from Argentina to Mexico. A movement born in Chile created a hymn named "a rapist in your way," ... demanding that society stop blaming the victims of rape.

Why is progress towards some aspects of gender equality getting slower and more difficult? Are there hidden dimensions of gender inequality? ...

Social norms are central to the understanding of these dynamics. For example, societies often tell their girls that they can become anything they want and are capable of, while investing in their education. But the same societies tend to block their access to power positions without giving them a fair chance. ...

The situation of women: an inequality plateau?

There has been remarkable progress on gender equality. Over the past century, women in most countries were granted basic political, economic and social rights. Restrictions to vote, go to school and work in different economic areas were lifted, with the principle of equality typically granted in constitutions. The trend gained global momentum in the second half of the 20th century.
...

Are social norms and power imbalances shifting?
...
Social norms cover several aspects of an individual's identity—age, gender, ability, ethnicity, religion and so on—that are heterogeneous and multidimensional. Discriminatory social norms and stereotypes reinforce gendered identities and determine power relations that constrain women's and men's behaviour in ways that lead to inequality. Norms influence expectations for masculine and feminine behaviour considered socially acceptable or looked down on. So they directly affect individuals' choices, freedoms and capabilities.
...

Widespread biases and backlash

... 91 percent of men and 86 percent of women show at least one clear bias against gender equality in areas such as politics, economic, education, intimate partner violence and women's reproductive rights.

About 50 percent of men and women interviewed across 75 countries say they think men make better political leaders than women, while more than 40 percent felt that men made better business executives. Almost 30 percent of people agree it is justifiable for a man to beat his partner.
...
Globally close to 50 percent of men agree men should have more right to a job than women. This coincides with the fact that professional women currently face a challenge in finding a partner that will support their career.

More worrying, despite decades of progress in advancing women's rights, bias against gender equality is increasing in some countries, with evidence of a backlash in attitudes among both men and women. ...
...

What causes change—and what determines its nature?

How can practices and behaviours either change or sustain traditional gender roles? Norms can change as economies develop, with changes in communications technology, with new laws, policies or programmes, with social and political activism and with exposure to new ideas and practices through formal and informal channels (education, role models and media). Policymakers often focus on the tangible—on laws, policies, spending commitments, public statements and so on. This is driven partly by the desire to measure impact and by sheer impatience with the slow pace of change. Yet neglecting the invisible power of norms would miss a deeper understanding of social change.

Consider the subtle differences between descriptive and injunctive norms. Descriptive norms are beliefs about what is considered a normal practice in a social group or an area. Injunctive norms state what people in a community should do. This distinction is important for practice, as it can lead to an understanding of why some aspects of gender norms and relations shift faster than others.

The family sets norms, and experiences from childhood create an unconscious gender bias. Parents' attitudes towards gender influence children through mid-adolescence, and children at school perceive gender roles. …
…
Social convention refers to how compliance with gender social norms is internalized in individual values reinforced by rewards or sanctions. Rewards use social or psychological approvals, while sanctions can range from exclusion from the community to violence or legal action. Stigma can limit what is considered normal or acceptable and be used to enforce stereotypes and social norms about appropriate behaviours. A social norm will be stickiest when individuals have the most to gain from complying with it and the most to lose from challenging it. Social norms have enough power to keep women from claiming their legal rights due to pressure to conform to societal expectations.
…

Restricted choices and power imbalances—a lifecycle perspective

Gender inequality within households and communities is characterized by inequality across multiple dimensions, with a vicious cycle of powerlessness, stigmatization, discrimination, exclusion and material deprivation all reinforcing each other. Human development is about expanding substantive freedoms and choices, and too often women face heavily restricted or even "tragic" choices.

Examples of restricted choices can be identified in a lifecycle approach. Some represent blatant limits to basic freedoms and human rights, and others, subtle manifestations of gender biases. Social norms can affect girls even before they are born since some countries deeply prefer bearing sons over daughters. In 1990, when only few countries had access to technology to … determine a baby's gender, only 6 countries had imbalanced sex rations at birth—today it is 21 countries.

Discrimination continues through the way households share resources. Girls and women sometimes eat last and least in the household. The gender politics of food—nurtured by assumptions, norms and practices about women needing fewer calories—can push women into perpetual malnutrition and protein deficiency.

Among children attending school, determinants of occupational choices appear very early. Girls are less likely to study subjects such as science, technology, engineering and mathematics, while boys are a minority of those studying health and education. …

Early marriage condemns girls to live a life with heavily restricted choices—every year 12 million girls are victims of forced marriage. By region, the highest rates are registered in Sub-Saharan Africa, with 36 percent of women marrying before their 18th birthday, and South Asia, with 29 percent.

The disparities of childhood and adolescence are amplified when women reach adulthood. For unpaid care work, women bear a bigger burden, on average spending about 2.5 times more than men do. This affects women's labor force participation, which is consistently lower than for men, both globally and by human development grouping. In 2018 the global labour force participation rate was around 75 percent for men and 48 percent for women. …

Older women's challenges accumulate through the life course. They are less likely than men to have access to pensions, even though they can expect to live three years longer. Along the way, social norms and path dependence—how outcomes today affect outcomes tomorrow—interact to form a highly complex system of structural gender gaps.

…

The Impact of COVID-19

Covid-19 has exacerbated many pre-existing problems. In 2022, UN Women and UNDP surveyed the consequences in *Government Responses to COVID-19: Lessons on Gender Equality for a World in Turmoil:*

> Since COVID-19 was declared a pandemic in March 2020, it has claimed more than 6 million lives, destroyed countless livelihoods and forced the global economy to its knees. With an end still not in sight, the crisis has taken a disproportionate toll on women and girls. As countries locked down, violence against women and girls intensified. …
>
> ### Rising economic insecurity
>
> Even before the pandemic, progress in closing the global gender gap in labour force participation rates had stalled, occupational segregation and gender wage gaps remained pervasive and the majority of the world's working women were stuck in informal and precarious jobs with few rights and protections. COVID-19 exacerbated these trends, taking a disproportionate toll on women's jobs and livelihoods. …
>
> … New projections estimate that in 2022, 124 women aged 25-34 are living in extreme poverty for every 100 men of the same age. …
>
> Many of these problems were exacerbated for the world's 740 million women working in the informal economy. Indeed, women informal workers experienced even sharper declines and slower recovery in working days and earnings than their male counterparts; and this pattern was more pronounced among women workers who experienced a parallel increase in unpaid care responsibilities. At the same time, these workers were least likely to enjoy access to social protection, resulting in severe economic hardship. Largescale loss of income and limited access to social protection quickly ushered in rising food insecurity, which is affecting women disproportionately.
>
> ### Increasing demand for unpaid care
>
> While business activities ground to a halt, paid and unpaid care work increased in intensity and significance. COVID-19 exposed the extent to which the care economy relies on women's unpaid and underpaid labour as never before.
>
> …
>
> With the mass closure of schools, nurseries and day-care centres, families witnessed a huge shift of childcare responsibilities into their homes. …
>
> That unpaid care work is provided for free does not mean that it comes without costs— to economic security and financial independence, mental health and well-being—that have been borne disproportionately by women. …

In a 2022 European Union poll, 77% of women identified a pandemic-led increase in physical and emotional violence against women in their country.[61]

---

[61] A. Brysk, 'Pandemic Patriarchy: The Impact of a Global Health Crisis on Women's Rights', 21 *J. Hum. Rts.* (2022) 283.

2. CEDAW: Provisions and Committee

Early efforts to promote women's rights, beyond the very basic provisions of the UDHR, involved participants from around the world. Before examining CEDAW, the following snapshots provide some background to the events of the 1950s and 1960s.

A defining early moment in Global South solidarity was the 1955 Bandung Conference, in Indonesia. It led to the founding of the Non-Aligned Movement (NAM) in 1961. Today the NAM has 120 member states which proclaim that they are not formally aligned with any major power bloc. Aziza Ahmed, in 'Bandung's Legacy: Solidarity and Contestation in Global Women's Rights', in Luis Eslava, Michael Fakhri, and Vasuki Nesiah (eds.), *Bandung, Global History, and International Law: Critical Pasts and Pending Futures* (2017) 450 describes its importance for women's rights:

> While the Final [Bandung] Communiqué speaks to human rights, it makes no mention of women, gender, or women's rights. … [Nevertheless,] the momentum and critique generated by Bandung and NAM enabled feminists of the Global South (GS) and their allies in the Global North (GN) to take a broader structural approach to addressing issues facing women and girls. This included acknowledging the centrality of race, colonialism, and economic inequality in struggles for women's rights.

> …

> Early agitation for women's rights by the few women present at the founding meetings of the UN resulted in a UN Charter calling for equality between men and women and the Commission on the Status of Women. Through the 1950s and 1960s, the Commission worked on a range of formal equality issues, including women's suffrage and a declaration specifically addressing women's rights. The 1970s were a turning point. The rise of NAM, as well as the reemergence of human rights in international law … provided a new framework in which women could push for the centrality of women … . As argued by Devaki Jain and Shubha Chacko [in *Women, Development and the UN: A Sixty-Year Quest for Equality and Justice* (2005)]:

> The Non-Aligned Movement's idea of the path to women's equality departed from UN strategies. The UN system at this time saw "women's status" largely as a social development issue and did not strongly connect it to the larger context of international development. Within the UN, women were still viewed as resources whose potential could be tapped. But the NAM gatherings offered a space where women from former colonies could reassert the standpoint that they were active agents in their nations, contributors to their country's progress, and not mere consumers of social services.

> …

> … The UN Decade on Women, which began with the First World Conference on Women held in Mexico City in 1975, inspired the formation of a global movement of women's rights activists who sought to engage UN mechanisms. GN and GS activists collaborated to push the agenda for women's rights. The initial organizing was rooted in second-wave feminist ideas of achieving women's equality through ending women's subordination to men.

> Tensions emerged, however, as feminists began to challenge the assumptions of universality in the experiences of women within the context of human rights struggles. Writing … from the GS, Gita Sen and Caren Grown reflected on the divisions between feminists in the mid-1980s: "While gender subordination has universal elements, feminism cannot be based on a rigid concept of universality that negates the wide variation in women's experience." Feminists of the GS also noted that the early organizing of Western feminists did not take into account the "shocks of the world economy" generated by the rise of neoliberalism and the negative impact of structural

adjustment programs on women's well being. For GS feminists, gender was simply one category in a broader analysis of inequalities perpetuated by the legacy of colonialism and the international development agenda. Unlike the largely identity-based struggles of second-wave feminism in the GN, feminists situated in the context of NAM also framed their struggles against colonialism, capitalism, and imperialism.

During this period, the UN Commission on the Status of Women (CSW) played a central role in drafting treaties on issues such as the political status of women and the nationality of married women, while the International Labour Organization and the International Committee of the Red Cross also promoted important standards relating to women in armed conflict and in the workplace. Roland Burke, in 'Universal Human Rights for Women: UN Engagement with Traditional Abuses, 1948–1965', in Rebecca Adami and Dan Plesch (eds.), *Women and the UN: A New History of Women's International Human Rights* (2022) 71, describes how a treaty on the age of marriage came to be adopted in 1962:

> In December 1954, … the General Assembly proclaimed a sweeping programme against "ancient customs" which prevented the realization of the UDHR for women. Resolution 843 affirmed the supremacy of the UDHR over any custom, and demanded "elimination of such customs, ancient laws and practices," notably in marriage and family law, which were "inconsistent" with the precepts set down in 1948. By 1961, the animating spirit of Resolution 843 was set into a draft treaty, adopted a year later as the Convention on Consent, Minimum Age, and Registration for Marriage. …

> …

> … [T]he animating impulse was a profoundly hopeful vision of universality, advanced by a small but effective cohort of women, many from the newly independent states. The Marriage Convention, its precursors, and their associated sentiments represented an effort to translate the grand abstractions of 1948 into lived reality. …

> Unlike many other forums of the UN, the human rights and humanitarian arena was a place where women found sustained presence, and substantial influence. …

> While still grossly unequal, the role and impact of women in the UN's human rights enterprise was much greater than in the notionally masculinist forums of the Security Council, and the economic components of the new international organization. The bespoke forum for women's rights, the Commission on the Status of Women (CSW), … was well-regarded for its commitment [and independence]. …

> [The author describes the key role played by women from the Global South]. In their proximity to the community, the local, this Third World cohort were somewhat closer to the balance of interests that would become more characteristic of the 1970s and early 1980s, across the various International Women's Year Conferences, and their NGO Tribunes, in Mexico City, Copenhagen, and Nairobi.

In 1963, the UN General Assembly, on the initiative of developing and socialist states, called for a UDHR-like declaration focused specifically on women's rights. CSW took the lead and the key drafters were women. In 1967, the Assembly adopted the non-binding Declaration on the Elimination of Discrimination against Women. It took another 12 years for the declaration to be developed into a binding treaty. More states have entered reservations to their ratification of CEDAW than to any other human rights treaty. Some reservations seriously qualify a state's commitment, particularly those that base the reservation on conflicting principles or rules in a religion or culture. This is addressed in greater detail below, including examples of reservations that are examined in the context of a discussion about universalism and cultural relativism.

CEDAW'S Substantive Provisions

The Convention is among the many that elaborate in one particular field the norms and ideals that are generally and tersely stated in the Universal Declaration, and stated somewhat more amply in the ICCPR. Its preamble suggests how far-reaching the issues are and that the norms of this Convention must be placed in a broader transformative context. It recognizes 'that a change in the traditional role of men as well as the role of women in society and in the family is needed to achieve full equality between men and women'.

The reader should be familiar with the provisions of the Convention, a few of which are addressed by the following comments.

Article 1

> For the purposes of the present Convention, the term "discrimination against women" shall mean any distinction, exclusion or restriction made on the basis of sex which has the effect or purpose of impairing or nullifying the recognition, enjoyment or exercise by women, irrespective of their marital status, on a basis of equality of men and women, of human rights and fundamental freedoms in the political, economic, social, cultural, civil or any other field.'

Note three vital characteristics of the definition. (a) The reference to *effect* as well as *purpose*, thus directing attention to the consequences of governmental measures as well as the intentions underlying them. (b) The definition is not limited to discrimination through 'state action' or action by persons acting under colour of law. (c) The definition's range is further expanded by the concluding phrase, 'or any other field'.

Article 2

> States Parties condemn discrimination against women in all its forms, agree to pursue by all appropriate means and without delay a policy of eliminating discrimination against women and, to this end, undertake:
>
> (a) To embody the principle of the equality of men and women in their national constitutions or other appropriate legislation if not yet incorporated therein and to ensure, through law and other appropriate means, the practical realization of this principle;
>
> (b) To adopt appropriate legislative and other measures, including sanctions where appropriate, prohibiting all discrimination against women;
>
> (c) To establish legal protection of the rights of women on an equal basis with men and to ensure through competent national tribunals and other public institutions the effective protection of women against any act of discrimination;
>
> (d) To refrain from engaging in any act or practice of discrimination against women and to ensure that public authorities and institutions shall act in conformity with this obligation;
>
> (e) To take all appropriate measures to eliminate discrimination against women by any person, organization or enterprise;
>
> (f) To take all appropriate measures, including legislation, to modify or abolish existing laws, regulations, customs and practices which constitute discrimination against women;
>
> (g) To repeal all national penal provisions which constitute discrimination against women.

Consider the possible meanings of key terms such as 'appropriate', 'without delay', 'equality' in clause (a), and 'any act of discrimination' in clause (c). Note the breadth of clauses (e) and (f) with respect to the private, nongovernmental sectors of society, particularly in relation to the definition in Article 1. Note throughout the Convention the blurred lines between the private and public spheres of life, and the range of obligations on states to intervene in the private sector, to go beyond 'respect' in order to 'protect', 'ensure' and 'promote'.

Article 3

States Parties shall take in all fields, in particular in the political, social, economic and cultural fields, all appropriate measures, including legislation, to ensure the full development and advancement of women, for the purpose of guaranteeing them the exercise and enjoyment of human rights and fundamental freedoms on a basis of equality with men.

Note the grand goal set forth for states, and consider whether the other human rights instruments examined contain a similar conception for any group, or for people in general.

Article 4

1. Adoption by States Parties of temporary special measures aimed at accelerating de facto equality between men and women shall not be considered discrimination as defined in the present Convention, but shall in no way entail as a consequence the maintenance of unequal or separate standards; these measures shall be discontinued when the objectives of equality of opportunity and treatment have been achieved.

2. Adoption by States Parties of special measures, including those measures contained in the present Convention, aimed at protecting maternity shall not be considered discriminatory.

This 'affirmative action' clause, duly qualified, appears as well in the Convention on the Elimination of all Forms of Racial Discrimination, but not in the ICCPR. Consider this article in relation to Article 2(e) and (f), and Article 11.

Article 5

States Parties shall take all appropriate measures: (a) To modify the social and cultural patterns of conduct of men and women, with a view to achieving the elimination of prejudices and customary and all other practices which are based on the idea of the inferiority or the superiority of either of the sexes or on stereotyped roles for men and women;

(b) To ensure that family education includes a proper understanding of maternity as a social function and the recognition of the common responsibility of men and women in the upbringing and development of their children, it being understood that the interest of the children is the primordial consideration in all cases.

The breadth and aspiration of this article are striking. Other human rights treaties lack a similar provision, although Article 2 of the Racial Discrimination Convention comes close. Consider the arguments for and against including such an ambitious and far-reaching provision.

Articles 6–16: These articles evidence how a treaty devoted to one set of problems — here, ending discrimination against women and achieving equality — makes possible discrete, disaggregated treatment of the different issues relevant to these problems. Clearly the variety and detail in these articles would have been out of place, indeed impossible, in a treaty of general scope like the ICCPR. Note the great range of verbs that are used throughout these articles to define states parties' duties, including: eliminate, provide, encourage, protect, introduce, accord, ensure.

Article 6 is typical of many provisions in requiring a state party to regulate specific nongovernmental activity.

Articles 7–9, to the contrary, deal with the traditional notion of state action, here barring discrimination by the state.

Article 10 concerns a particular field, education, and lists specific goals which, in their totality, take on a programmatic character. Note paragraph (h) on family planning and its relationship to three other provisions: Articles 12(1), 14(2)(b) and 16(e). The Convention does not address, as such, the question of abortion.

Article 12 together with a number of other provisions indicate the degree to which CEDAW involves and interrelates the classical categories of civil-political rights and economic-social rights. It imposes a limited duty to provide free health care.

Article 14 disaggregates women's problems in regional and functional terms. It underscores strategies for realizing goals that permeate the entire Convention, such as mobilization through functional grass roots groups and participation in local decision-making. CEDAW is not a convention in which solutions are to be provided only by the central authority of the state.

Article 16 orders the states to sweep away a large number of fundamental, traditional discriminations against and forms of subordination of women. Like several other articles, it could be understood as a complement to, as one specification of, the broad goals stated in Article 5.

SUBSTANTIVE EQUALITY

While the treaty covers a broad range of issues, the notion of discrimination remains central. It is thus critical to understand how international law has sought to achieve the goal of substantive equality based on this departure point. The path-breaking work done by Sandra Fredman in books such as *Human Rights Transformed* (2008) and *Discrimination Law* (2nd ed, 2011) has been reflected in various UN reports[62] and in the following excerpt from a Concurring Opinion by Arif Bulkan and Hélène Tigroudja in *Eugénie Chakupewa et al. v. Democratic Republic of the Congo* (UN Doc. CCPR/C/131/D/2835/2016 (2021), Annex I). The case involved the follow up to gang rapes carried out by soldiers in South Kivu. Five persons were subsequently sentenced 'to penal servitude (imprisonment) for life, with no mitigating circumstances, for the crime against humanity of mass rape'. The tribunal also 'ruled that the defendants were liable *in solidum* with the State party to pay each author [complainant] US$ 50,000 in damages for the harm suffered.' But no such payments were ever made.

1. We anticipate … questions … based on an argument that the authors have not demonstrated that male victims have been compensated in domestic proceedings while female victims have not. …

2. International human rights law has been critiqued as androcentric because of its general orientation towards male interests, an assessment thrown into sharp relief by formal approaches to sex discrimination that insist upon identifying a similarly situated male comparator who is treated more favourably. …

3. The sterility of a purely formal analysis of discrimination, particularly in circumstances where there is no factual equivalence, is graphically illustrated by the argument of the State party in one case where it denied that the criminalization of abortion could amount to sex discrimination since any differentiation of treatment inevitably resulted from biological differences between men and women [*Mellet v. Ireland*, (CCPR/C/116/D/2324/2013)]. Likewise, the woman who complains of obstetric violence can never find a male comparator to demonstrate the inequality of treatment she may have received, [See *N. A. E. v. Spain*, below] so the importance of adopting a broader approach to claims of gender discrimination is self-evident.

4. … The "intensely individualistic" nature of formal notions of equality, whereby the disadvantage associated with the particular status or group is not factored in the analysis, has been noted [by Fredman]. The problem with merely seeking equivalence between men and women is that doing so ignores the structural differences that account for inequality in the first place and perpetuates the

---

[62] S. Fredman and B. Goldblatt, *Gender Equality and Human Rights* (UN Women, 2015).

disadvantage associated with the group. For this reason, the alternative model is one that proceeds upon a substantive notion of equality that seeks a more transformative outcome, in other words the elimination of social disadvantage.

5. … Women and girls are subjected to violence precisely because they are women and girls, a longstanding disadvantage that is buttressed by societal attitudes and systematically tolerated by institutional structures. …

6. …

7. … [I]n the context of what were grave crimes, the obdurate refusal of the national authorities to pay the compensation ordered is indicative of the social disadvantage and oppression the authors face as women. … [T]he climate of impunity that inevitably results from failing to enforce judgments in cases of violence in turn encourages or at least facilitates repetition of the conduct. …

Types of State Duties Imposed by Human Rights Treaties

To understand the significance and implications of the rights stated in the ICCPR, CEDAW and other human rights treaties, it is helpful to examine the related duties/obligations of states — even though human rights conventions rarely talk of duties. Attention to such duties clarifies the significance and even content of the related rights. It also points to strategies to realize a right, as by persuading the state to change its behaviour in one or another respect. The effort, then, is to deconstruct a right into its related state duties, perhaps duties that an advocate seeks to have imposed on the state.

Some of these duties can fairly be called correlative (corresponding) to the right — for example, implying from your right not to be tortured the state's correlative duty not to torture you. These may be the duties that come most promptly and naturally to the mind of the rights-holder. As a practical matter and from a functional perspective, other duties may be necessary implications from the nature of a given right even if they are not spelled out in treaty text — for example, a state's duty to create and operate electoral institutions and processes if the citizen's right to vote is to be realized.

Different rights may point to different types of state duties. All depends on the nature of the right, on the problems that it was meant to overcome or to prevent. Some types of state duties described below are more prominent in the ICCPR, some in CEDAW, some in the International Covenant on Economic, Social and Cultural Rights discussed in Chapter 4, or in other human rights treaties. Identifying the multiple duties that may be relevant to any one right sharpens an understanding of what is distinctive to and necessary to realize that right.

Two points should be kept in mind as we examine different kinds of rights from the perspective of related variable state duties.

First, at the start of the human rights regime, much weight was given to a distinction between so-called 'negative' and 'positive' rights. The negative rights basically imposed a duty of 'hands-off', a duty of a state not to interfere with, say, an individual's physical security. The illustration of torture noted above fits well here. Thus, the right not to be tortured was imagined to impose only such a negative duty — the state's correlative duty not to torture. Positive rights, on the other hand, imposed affirmative (positive) duties on the state — in the classic case, a duty to provide food (food stamps/subsidies and so on) if such provision was essential to satisfy the right to food. Thus economic and social rights such as the right to food were considered positive rights, which frequently required financial expenditures by the state, unlike the classic negative rights that were thought to require merely abstention from unjustified interference with another person. It will be important to consider how much of this negative-positive distinction remains valid in the light of the illustrations and analysis below, and whether it clarifies or confuses the issues before us.

Consider the following classic presentation of this distinction in Maurice Cranston, 'Are There Any Human Rights?', in 112 (4) *Daedalus* (1983) 1, at 12:

> The traditional political and civil rights are not difficult to institute. For the most part, they require governments, and other people generally, to leave a man alone. ... Do not injure, arrest, or imprison him. To respect a man's right to life, liberty, and property is not a very costly exercise. As Locke and others have explained, it requires a system of law that recognizes those rights to protect those rights. But rulers are not called upon to do anything that it is unreasonable to expect of them. ... Political ... rights can be secured by fairly simple legislation. Since those rights are largely rights against government interference, the greatest effort will be directed toward restraining the government's own executive arm. But this is no longer the case where economic and social rights are concerned. ...

Second, rights are not static. They evolve. They broaden or contract over time. One way of understanding an expansion of the content of a given right (to speech, to food) is to examine the duties related to that right, and to inquire whether and how they have expanded. The argument for a broader construction of a given right often amounts to the claim that further duties ought to be imposed on the state in order to satisfy the right. Consider some examples. The right to speech implies at a minimum the government's correlative duty not to interfere with it. It should not enjoin or penalize the rights-holder who indeed speaks. A modest expansion of this 'hands off' right imposes the further duty on government to protect a speaker against deliberate interference by non-state actors. Your right to speak loses meaning if others are permitted to block you in various ways from publishing or orally communicating your ideas. An argument for further expansion can be based on the claim that government must facilitate speech by assuring access of political groups to the media (that is, to newspapers or electronic media whether or not owned or controlled by the state). Such arguments for expansion of the kinds of state duties can constitute a strategy of change. So attention to duties, how they differ among rights within a treaty and among treaties, and how they change over time is one vital way of examining and fostering change in the human rights regime as a whole.

The following scheme of five types of state duties is a variation on a typology that emerged in the 1980s, often expressed as the 'respect, protect, fulfill' framework.[63] The Constitution of South Africa, 1996 (Article 7(2)), for example provides that '[t]he state must respect, protect, promote and fulfil the rights in the Bill of Rights.'

(1) Respect Rights of Others

This duty requires the state to treat persons equally, to respect their individual dignity and worth, and hence not to interfere with or impair their declared rights. It is often described as 'negative' in the sense of being a 'hands-off' duty. The observance by states of this duty would itself, without the possibility of any further state duties, lead to a vast improvement in the human condition. In this sense, the duty of respect can be seen to lie at the core of the human rights regime. Compliance with it would avoid many of the worst calamities: genocides, massacres, torture.

For most rights, the duty of respect reaches beyond states to obligate individuals and non-state entities. A person's right to bodily security or to vote imposes a correlative duty on all other persons to refrain from interfering with it. Under human rights treaties, individuals or non-state entities are generally not considered to bear direct duties to protect other individuals. This section covers only state duties.

(2) Create Institutional Machinery Essential to Realization of Rights

Some rights may be impaired or effectively annulled not only by government's direct interference with them (torture, preventing a citizen from expressing ideas or voting), but also by its failure to put in place the institutional machinery essential for the realization or practice of the right. Political participation offers a simple illustration. A citizen's right to vote means little unless a government maintains fair electoral machinery that

---

[63] See H. Shue, *Basic Rights* (2nd edn. 1996); G. J. H. van Hoof, 'The Legal Nature of Economic, Social and Cultural Rights', in P. Alston and K. Tomasevski (eds.), *The Right to Food* (1984) 97; and D. Karp, 'What is the Responsibility to Respect Human Rights? Reconsidering the "Respect, Protect, and Fulfill" Framework', 12 *Int'l Theory* (2020) 83.

makes possible the act of voting, counting of ballots and so on. The negative–positive distinction is inadequate to describe this duty.

(3) Protect Rights/Prevent Violations

Several human rights treaties make explicit the state's duty to protect against and to prevent violations of rights. For this, institutional machinery is required. In the ICCPR, the state's duty in Article 2 is to 'ensure to all individuals' the recognized rights. Surely states must provide a police force to protect people against violations of their rights (to physical security, or free speech, or property) either by state or non-state ('private') actors. They must create normative systems like tort or criminal law, as well as institutions like courts or jails, processes like civil suits or criminal prosecutions, in order to maintain a system of justice that provides remedies for violations and imposes sanctions on violators. This duty to protect has been vital to the development of CEDAW and women's rights.

As in category (2) above, the state's duty to protect/prevent involves state expenditures. Again, the negative-positive rights distinction is not helpful. The classic 'negative' rights here demand the classic 'positive' protection. It is difficult to imagine a right for which this is not true.

(4) Provide Goods and Services to Satisfy Rights

The state's duty here is primarily to provide material resources to the rights-bearer, like housing or food or health care. Resources provided by the state may go directly from it to the individual rights-bearer, as by providing food stamps or subsidized public housing, or it may go indirectly to the ultimate beneficiary through, say, subsidies to construction firms that will then offer low-rent housing. Unlike the duty of respect (do not worsen the situation of the rights-bearer), this duty to provide generally is meant to improve the situation of the rights-bearer.

The state must expend public funds to meet its duties. It is for this reason that state duties related to welfare rights have most frequently been described as affirmative (positive). Unlike categories (2) and (3) above, both of which also involve state expenditures, these expenditures are the very essence of the individual right.

On the other hand, the realization of economic and social rights need not depend on 'direct' or 'indirect' provision by the state. Other, radically different policies may achieve the goal of satisfying a right to, say, food, such as a programme of expropriation and land reform that would increase employment and yield and thereby make more people self-sufficient with respect to food. Again, monetary or fiscal policy designed to lower unemployment and hence malnutrition and homelessness could reduce the need for direct provision of funds or goods. Such characteristic policies of the modern welfare state may then make the direct or indirect provision of funds or goods measures of last rather than first resort.

(5) Promote Rights

This state duty refers to bringing about changes in public consciousness or perception or understanding about a given problem or issue. It generally requires the state to expend funds and create the institutions necessary to promote acceptance of the right. It often involves public education — for example, school education or public campaigns meant to change attitudes about violence towards women or children. Promotion to achieve such types of cultural change plays a vital role in CEDAW. Promotion underscores the point that these categories of duties are not discrete. They are often complexly interrelated, and indeed overlap.

QUESTIONS

1. Consider CEDAW's stress on eliminating discrimination to achieve equality between men and women, as well as its means for realizing that equality. The phrase 'on the basis of equality of men and women' recurs in many of its articles. Compare the notion of equality in the ICCPR — say, in ICCPR Article 3 ('to ensure the equal rights of men and women to the enjoyment of all civil and political rights' in that covenant), or ICCPR Article 26 ('All persons are equal before the law and are entitled

without any discrimination to the equal protection of the law'). Are the two treaties' conceptions of equality identical, similar, very different?

2. Do the provisions of CEDAW on their face make any concession to cultural relativism, to cultural diversity in regional, ethnic, religious or other terms? Or do they insist throughout on universal application of its norms without variation, no matter what the cultural context, history or circumstances of the state involved?

3. Under Article 2, states parties agree to pursue the required policies, 'by all appropriate means and without delay'. Contrast the description of state obligations in Article 2 of the Covenant on Economic, Social and Cultural Rights: 'achieving progressively the full realization' of the recognized rights. Is this textual contrast accurate with respect to CEDAW? How do you understand the question of CEDAW's 'time frame' in comparison, say, with the ICCPR?

The Committee on the Elimination of Discrimination Against Women

Before the CEDAW Committee was set up in 1981, the main UN institution focused on women's rights was the UN Commission on the Status of Women. Created in 1946 and composed of governments, its contribution has been important, but has also varied considerably over the years.[64] The Committee is a 'treaty organ' rather than a 'Charter organ'.. Chapter 9 will examine the ICCPR Committee. You should now read Articles 17–21 of the Convention.

ANDREW BYRNES, THE COMMITTEE ON THE ELIMINATION OF DISCRIMINATION AGAINST WOMEN
FRÉDÉRIC MÉGRET AND PHILIP ALSTON (EDS.), THE UN AND HUMAN RIGHTS (2020) 393

...
... The Committee and its work: an overview

... In its early years the Committee existed in geographical, institutional and substantive isolation from the Geneva-based human-rights organs of the UN and the other treaty bodies ... . During this period the Committee included a significant number of Eastern European members and the influence of Cold War politics meant that conservative attitudes tended to prevail over attempts to take expansive or innovative approaches to the Committee's work.
...
The early 1990s saw an increased momentum in efforts to put gender perspectives on the international human rights agenda. ...
...
By the early 2000s, the increase in the number of ratifications brought the Convention close to universal ratification, and the Committee began its work under the Optional Protocol. The Committee continued to become more closely integrated into the human-rights framework of the United Nations, with close attention to developments elsewhere in the system, driven in part by the efforts towards harmonization of the human rights treaty bodies, and the Committee's move to Geneva from New York in early 2008.

In the last decade, the Committee has continued to develop its jurisprudence in the form of wide-ranging general recommendations and under the complaints and inquiry procedures of the Optional Protocol. ...

... The composition of the Committee

---

[64] See Z. Arat, 'The Commission on the Status of Women', in F. Mégret and P. Alston (eds.), *The UN and Human Rights* (2020) 253.

... [The 23 member expert committee] is established '[f]or the purpose of considering the progress made in the implementation of the Convention'. The Convention assumes that this task will be discharged through the examination of the reports submitted by States parties. ...

The members of the Committee are nominated and elected by the States parties from among their nationals for four-year terms, with no restriction on re-election. The members are to be 'experts of high moral standing and competence in the field covered by the Convention'; they serve in their personal capacity, not as representatives of states. The Convention requires that in the election of the members 'consideration be ... given to equitable geographical distribution and the representation of different forms of civilization and the principal legal systems.'

The geographical distribution of the Committee's membership has broadly conformed with the criteria laid down in the Convention. ...

The backgrounds of Committee members have been diverse. They include sociology, medicine, dentistry, international relations, education, political science, psychology, communications, law, and government and foreign service. Nearly all the members of the Committee have been active in promoting gender equality ... .
... [I]n the last decade the number of lawyers has climbed back to around half of the committee members.

The range of professional backgrounds has made available to the Committee a breadth of knowledge that is important for assessing the implementation of the Convention. The smaller proportion of lawyers on the Committee during the 1990s was a mixed blessing. On the one hand, it meant that less attention was devoted to what might be considered sterile procedural matters (sometimes as a proxy for restricting the scope of the Committee's activities), with the Committee tending to focus on substantive issues. On the other hand, it meant that the Committee was slow to come to the view that, as a body charged with the supervision of an international human rights treaty, it had an important legal role to play in its interpretation of the Convention and the development of jurisprudence under it.
...
The presence on the Committee of members who are government officials has also given rise to concern among some observers and civil society groups. For a period in the 2000s, the number of diplomats and government officials nominated and elected to CEDAW and other treaty bodies increased, with roughly a third of the Committee membership falling into this category (not counting judges). Many of these came from equal opportunity offices or women's ministries. Of particular concern has been the presence of diplomats or high-level political appointees ... .
...
All but six of the members of the Committee have been women. This is perhaps no surprise, since the membership of treaty bodies reflects one national selection process multiplied many times, and in most countries there is likely to be a higher percentage of women than men working on issues relating to women's equality, thus making it more likely that a woman will be nominated. ...

... The reporting procedure

... The reporting process will have the greatest impact in a state if a number of conditions are fulfilled. These include the regular submission of good quality substantive reports, the availability to the Committee of independent information (whether from NGOs, specialized agencies, NHRIs, or through other channels), a critical analysis of the report to identify deficiencies in the implementation of the Convention, a frank discussion with an appropriately qualified government delegation, the production by the Committee of detailed substantive recommendations to the state, wide publicity for the process at the national level, and the broad dissemination of the results of the hearings, and follow-up and monitoring at the national level as well as at the international level.

The procedures of the Committee for the examination of reports have changed significantly over the years to reflect the increase in the number of reports being submitted, the fact that nearly all the reports submitted are now periodic reports, the greater involvement of NGOs and other actors in the review process, the need to make as efficient use as possible of its meeting time, and the move towards greater harmonization of the procedures of all the UN human rights treaty bodies.

...

... Before the dialogue

After the Committee has received a state report, it schedules the report for consideration at a future session, appoints a country rapporteur, and schedules the report for initial consideration by its pre-sessional working group. The [latter] ... prepares a list of questions which is sent to the State party. The working group is normally made up of five members meeting for one week following each session. The working group meets in private and considers material put before it by the country rapporteur, and the secretariat, as well as written material provided by specialized agencies, national human rights institutions (NHRIs), and NGOs. The working group also meets with representatives of UN entities who wish to appear, as well as with NGOs and NHRIs who wish to meet the working group to brief it on the situation in a particular country; it also draws on information provided by UN country teams. The list of not more than thirty questions is sent to the State party, which is asked to respond (in no more than 25–30 pages) within six weeks, in time for the material to be translated and circulated before the review.

... Consideration of reports

The review of a state's report by the Committee takes place in a public meeting to which representatives of the State party are invited and which they are expected to attend, though the Committee has made use of video-conferencing to allow delegations (and NGOs) to participate in a review. The procedure is not intended to be a judicial or quasi-judicial process ... . Rather, it is an occasion for the state [and the Committee to engage] in what has become known in UN jargon as a 'constructive dialogue'.

... Both in individual comments and in the Committee's collective concluding observations on a report, extremely critical assessments have been made, although the Committee seeks to express a balanced view. At the same time there is a perception among some observers that the Committee has been too often uncritical in its praise ... .

...

The Committee schedules two sessions for each initial and periodic report. Country representatives are permitted up to thirty minutes to introduce the report. Questioning then follows by country task force members, who are limited in the number and duration of interventions they may make. ...

The quality of the discussions is directly influenced by the nature of the delegation sent by a state. ... The Committee is generally less than impressed where the delegation consists only of the local diplomatic representatives, who may have no particular expertise in the areas covered by the Convention. ...

...

The Committee stated in 2008 that its objective was 'to formulate detailed concluding observations, with concrete, achievable, but non-prescriptive recommendations'. They ... encapsulate the Committee's view of the priority areas for action in the implementation of the Convention in the country concerned, as well as providing detailed recommendations for action. It is this document which NGOs at the national level can use to lobby governments, legislatures and other decision-makers to adopt the changes recommended by the Committee.

... Follow-up procedure on Concluding Observations

...

In 2008 the Committee decided to introduce a follow-up procedure for Concluding Observations. This involves requesting that States parties implement specified recommendations in the Concluding Observations and report within two years on the steps taken to do so. The Committee also appointed a Rapporteur for Follow-up, who reports to the Committee on the responses received, and writes to (and may meet with) States which are overdue with their responses. The process is transparent, with the States parties' responses and the Committee's replies being made available on the Committee's website.

The Committee's follow-up procedure has provided an opportunity for the dialogue between the Committee and the State party (and other stakeholders such as NGOs, who have also submitted material under the procedure) to continue beyond the one-off engagement that otherwise culminates in the public hearings. In the period 2011 to 2016, 92 of the requested 120 follow-up reports were received ... .

The Committee assesses whether the relevant recommendations have been 'Implemented', 'Substantially implemented', 'Partially Implemented', or 'Not implemented', or concludes that there is a 'Lack of information received to make an assessment'; or more recently that 'Information or measures taken are contrary to or reflect rejection of the recommendation'. The Committee may then request further information or clarification or recommend technical assistance. In its assessment of the 2011–2016 period, the Committee considered that 18 per cent of the recommendations had been implemented, 37 per cent had been partially implemented, 26 per cent had not been implemented, and in 20 per cent of cases insufficient information had been received to allow an assessment. This is something of a mixed record, though the procedure has had the effect of keeping pressure on states; whether it achieves real change is something that can be better assessed over a longer period. …

… Developing a jurisprudence of the Convention

…

The challenge facing CEDAW has been to ensure that the Convention continues to address contemporary violations of women's human rights. The Committee is able to interpret the Convention in a dynamic fashion through its questioning of States parties during its consideration of reports, the adoption of General recommendations, and in its work under the Optional Protocol. …

…

… NGOs and the work of the Committee

The Convention accords non-governmental organizations no formal role in the review of the reports of States parties … . [R]epresentatives of NGOs are not permitted to speak at meetings at which the Committee is considering a State report, and NGO documents submitted to the Committee are not translated or circulated as official documents (though most of them now appear on the OHCHR website). Nor does the Convention envisage any role for NGOs in the other work of the Committee. …

…

STATE REPORTING

We start our study of the Committee by looking at its function of monitoring states parties with respect to their compliance with the Convention. It does so through its examination of the periodic reports on compliance that states parties are required to submit. The Committee's recommendations are printed in bold. In June 2022, a delegation from Turkey, led by the Minister of Family and Social Services and including representatives of seven government ministries, responded to questions from the Committee, leading to the adoption of the following conclusions.

CEDAW COMMITTEE, CONCLUDING OBSERVATIONS ON THE EIGHTH PERIODIC REPORT OF THE REPUBLIC OF TÜRKIYE UN DOC. CEDAW/C/TUR/CO/8 (4 JULY 2022)

E. Principal areas of concern and recommendations

General context

8. The Committee expresses deep concern about the measures taken by the State party during the two-year state of emergency applied following the 2016 attempted coup against the Government, which ended in principle on 18 July 2018. It is particularly concerned about the impact that the government's various repressive counter-terrorism measures have had on women's human rights and the rule of law in the State party [including measures] that led to the dismissal of thousands of women from their occupations, including civil servants, judges, military personnel, and academics. …

…

10. … [T]he Committee reiterates its deep regret and concern about the decision of the State party [in March 2021] to withdraw from the [Council of Europe's Istanbul Convention on Preventing and Combating Violence against Women and Domestic Violence]. … [I]t regrets … that the decision … was taken without a parliamentary debate and reportedly without wider consultation with civil society

... . [The denunciation] constitutes a retrogressive measure that reduces the scope of protection of women's human rights and is inconsistent with the State party's due diligence obligations under the [CEDAW] ... .

11. ... [T]he Committee invites the State party to reconsider its decision ... .

...

12. The Committee takes note of the measures taken by the State party to implement gender-responsive recovery strategies related to [COVID-19] and targeted measures to alleviate the negative economic and social effects of the pandemic on women and girls. Nevertheless, [it] is concerned about the high prevalence of gender-based violence against women in the State party, including domestic violence, the longest shutdown of educational institutions globally due to the pandemic and the feminization of poverty, which disproportionately affects women and girls belonging to disadvantaged and marginalized groups, who already faced multiple and intersecting forms of discrimination and whose condition further deteriorated during the pandemic.

...

15. ... [T]he Committee recommends that the State party:
    (a) Disseminate and give more visibility to the Convention and the Committee's concluding observations, its jurisprudence under the Optional Protocol and its general recommendations;
    (b) Consider establishing a comprehensive mechanism for the implementation of the present concluding observations and involve non-governmental organizations ...;
    (c) Raise awareness among women of their rights under the Convention and the legal remedies available to them to claim violations of such rights ... .

...

18. The Committee is concerned about the negative impact that the adoption of the 2017 constitutional amendments had on the State party's judiciary, further undermining its ability to independently discharge its mandate. It is also concerned that the changes in the structure of both the Turkish Constitutional Court and the Council of Judges and Prosecutors, the body responsible for ensuring self-governance of the judiciary, seriously undermine the independence of the judiciary by positioning it under close oversight by the Executive. The Committee ... [is] concerned:
    (a) About the dismissal of approximately 20 percent of active judges and prosecutors during the state of emergency on grounds of "association with terrorism" and the failure of the State party to reinstate judges, including women, dismissed following the attempted coup despite their acquittal of criminal charges;
    (b) At the climate of fear of reprisals that these dismissals have created among incumbent judges and prosecutors;
    (c) That the dismissed judges and prosecutors have reportedly been largely replaced with often inexperienced judges and prosecutors facing an already heavy caseload ...;
    ...
    (f) About open rejection and failure to implement judgments of the European Court of Human Right by the State party, including in cases brought by women applicants.

...

20. The Committee remains concerned about persisting barriers to women's access to justice, including:
    (a) Legal illiteracy among many women and girls;
    (b) The limited scope of legal aid, both economically and substantively, resulting in non-eligibility for legal aid of women earning the minimum wage, the cumbersome procedure to prove eligibility, and language barriers faced by women seeking justice, in particular Kurdish women, women belonging to other minorities and refugee women;
    (c) Limited knowledge of women's rights on the part of law enforcement officials and legal practitioners.

21. ... [T]he Committee recommends that the State party:
    (a) Enhance women and girls' awareness of their rights and their means of enforcing them, placing particular emphasis on the integration into curricula at all levels of education on women's rights and gender equality, including legal literacy programmes, and emphasizing the crucial role of women's access to justice;

(b) Ensure that free legal aid and interpretation in Kurdish and Arabic, is made available to women without sufficient means, including those earning the minimum wage, for example through the establishment of legal aid clinics in rural and remote areas ...;

...

24. The Committee remains concerned about the persistence of deep-rooted discriminatory stereotypes and State party's official declarations concerning the roles and responsibilities of women and men in the family and in society, which overemphasize the traditional role of women as mothers and wives, thereby undermining women's social status, autonomy, educational opportunities and professional careers, as well as constituting an underlying cause of gender-based violence against women. It notes with concern that patriarchal attitudes persist within State authorities and society, and that the principle of gender equality is increasingly being replaced by a vaguely defined concept of "gender justice".

25. ... [T]he Committee recommends that the State party adopt a comprehensive strategy based on women's rights and empowerment aiming at eliminating patriarchal attitudes and stereotypes that discriminate against women. ...

26. The Committee remains concerned about:
    (a) The ongoing practice, especially in rural and remote areas, of giving girls as brides to settle blood feuds, and the continued payment of "bride prices" in certain regions;
    (b) The significant number of child marriages, especially in deprived rural areas, their wide acceptance in society and the insufficient efforts made by the State party to prevent them and adequately punish perpetrators.

27. ... [T]he Committee recommends that the State party:
    (a) Ensure that any form of sale or exchange of women and girls for the purpose of dispute settlement is criminalized, investigated and prosecuted and that perpetrators are adequately punished;
    (b) Effectively implement the prohibition of child marriage, and strengthen awareness-raising efforts regarding the harmful effects of child marriage on the health and development of girls.
    ...

28. ... The Committee reiterates its concern about the persistence of systematic and widespread gender-based violence against women in the State party, including sexual violence, and that:
    (a) At least 3,175 femicides in the State party have been reported between 2010 and 2020 and that more than 300 women were murdered in 2021, mostly by their intimate or former intimate partners or husbands or members of their families;
    (b) Official data on violence against women demonstrate that in 8.5 percent of cases of women killed between 2016 and 2021, the woman had obtained a protection order that was valid at the time of her death. In 2021 this percentage increased to 12 percent;
    (c) Gender-based violence against women and girls is considerably underreported owing to victims' stigmatization, fear of reprisals, economic dependence on the perpetrator, legal illiteracy, language barriers and/or lack of trust in the law enforcement authorities;

...

3. The Public/Private Divide: 'Private' Violence Against Women

In classical terms human rights obligations are assumed by, or imposed upon, the state. The resulting duties are 'public' or governmental. Some treaties, such as the Torture Convention, are exclusively state-centric, focusing only on actions taken 'by or at the instigation of or with the consent or acquiescence of a public official or other person acting in an official capacity'. CEDAW, on the other hand, is explicit in also addressing conduct attributable not to the state ('public' actors) but to non-state/nongovernmental ('private') actors. The resulting divide between what is public and what is private thus becomes an especially prominent theme in relation to women's rights, although it has important ramifications in other areas as well.[65]

---

[65] For example, the Convention on the Rights of Persons with Disabilities makes several explicit references to private actors.

The gendered boundary between 'public' and 'private' spheres correlated with two different kinds of claims to social resources, one based on market labor, and the other based upon family ties. (This gendered public/private dichotomy thus links to another public/private dichotomy: that between the state and the market, both arenas dominated by men.) In the 'male' sphere contractual relations of exchange flourished. Such relations existed between individuals who were presupposed to be free and independent and in control of their objects of exchange. This 'possessive individualism' correlated with the idea of self-ownership. Coverture [the legal doctrine according to which a married woman's legal rights and obligations are subsumed by those of her husband], ... like slavery, rationalized subjection of those who could not claim their labor power as their own, separating the universe into those who were free citizens, and those who were not.

... [E]ligibility for paid work outside the home was an explicit criterion for citizenship. Relegated exterior to citizenship were the degraded and enslaved, as well as the citizen's dependents, whose field of action was confined to the domestic sphere of the intimate family. In that sphere, resources were to flow through blood and sentiment, unlinked to any public circuit of exchange. Single mothers who faced difficulty providing such care and who became the recipients of 'mother's pensions' in the United States, so that the state stepped in for the absent male wage, were 'pitied but not entitled.' Care work was perceived to be a product of 'charity,' rather than of 'contract.' Otherwise articulated, the public sphere was characterized as the realm of rights and the pursuit of self-interest, while the private was perceived as the realm of needs, bonds, and selflessness of family.[66]

In the human rights context, the terms 'public' and 'private' can refer to either actors or contexts, and the divide is often not straightforward. Thus a government official might act in ways that are entirely outside her legitimate public functions, as a result of which her actions will be deemed private. Or conduct by a private individual might be characterized as public because the state was in some way complicit, as in the acts of death squads operating with governmental connivance. And, of particular importance in the present context, a government might become liable for the entirely private acts of private individuals if it can be shown that it did not do all it could or should have to prevent such actions, or to investigate and punish them after the event.

This section examines some of the issues arising out of the public/private divide, including the practical, political and ideological significance of the divide; the shifting boundary line between the two as conceptions of their significance and content change; the degree to which human rights treaties should require states parties to regulate the relevant conduct of private (in the sense of non-state) actors; and the degree to which human rights treaties should directly regulate the relevant conduct of such private actors and impose sanctions on such actors for violations of their duties within the regulatory scheme.

We use the fight to eliminate violence against women as the lens through which to explore these issues, while highlighting both the central role of CEDAW and the interaction among key institutional actors to achieve a crucial degree of normative and policy consensus around dealing with the problem.

[O]ne third of women— and more than two-thirds in some countries— have experienced physical or sexual violence inflicted by an intimate partner or sexual violence inflicted by a non-partner. Some 20 percent of women experienced sexual violence as children. Nearly a quarter of girls ages 15–19 worldwide reported having been victims of violence after turning 15. Violence against women can be perpetuated through social norms. For example, female genital mutilation and cutting remain widespread. ... Acid attacks against women are a heinous form of violence common in communities where patriarchal gender orders are used to justify violence against women. ... In some societies women are also targets of honour-based violence, where the concept of honour and shame is fundamentally bound up with the expected behaviours of women, as dictated by their families or societies.[67]

[66] L. Volpp, 'Feminist, Sexual, and Queer Citizenship,' in A. Shachar, et al. (eds.), *The Oxford Handbook of Citizenship* (2017) 156-57.
[67] UNDP, *Human Development Report 2016: Human Development for Everyone* (2017) 58-9.

The immense gap between the evolving normative framework and the reality on the ground is illustrated by an overview report on rape (UN Doc. A/HRC/47/26), presented in 2021 by Dubravka Šimonović, UN Special Rapporteur on violence against women and girls, its causes and consequences:

> Globally, … 1 in 10 girls has been a victim of rape. Rape has been criminalized in a large number of States and yet it remains one of the most widespread crimes, with the majority of perpetrators enjoying impunity and the majority of women victims not reporting it.

> 9. Currently, the international human rights framework and jurisprudence recognizes rape as a human rights violation and a manifestation of gender-based violence against women and girls that could amount to torture. Under international humanitarian law and international criminal law, rape can constitute a war crime, a crime against humanity, or a constitutive act with respect to genocide when the other elements of the crimes are present.

> 10. However, these international standards have not been fully incorporated at the national level. States criminalize rape using different definitions (based on force or on lack of consent), protecting different persons (only women or all persons), including or excluding marital rape, covering different types of penetrations, prescribing different aggravating and mitigating circumstances, setting different lengths of sentences, prescribing ex officio or ex parte prosecution of rape, and providing or not providing at all for different statutes of limitation for its prosecution.

> 11. Additionally, their implementation is influenced by the surrounding general context of different forms of discrimination and gender-based violence against women, myths and gender-based stereotyping on rape by the media and the criminal justice system.

> 12. All these factors contribute to the fact that rape is frequently not reported. If rape is reported, it is seldom prosecuted; if prosecuted, the prosecution is rarely pursued in a gender-sensitive manner and often leads to very few convictions, the revictimization of survivors and high attrition rates, resulting in a normalization of rape, a culture of rape or silence on rape, stigmatization of victims and impunity for perpetrators.

But the issue of violence against women remained largely 'invisible' prior to the 1979 adoption of the CEDAW Convention, which contains not a single reference to it. World Conferences on Women in 1980 and 1985 alluded to the problem, but the first serious steps in the UN context came with resolutions by the ECOSOC in 1984 and the General Assembly in 1985 (GA Res. 40/36 (29 Nov. 1985)). These led to a path-breaking UN study on 'Violence against Women in the Family' (UN Doc. ST/CSDHA/2 (1989)), and a more detailed General Assembly resolution in 1990 (GA Res. 45/114). These developments occurred at the same time as the Inter-American Court of Human Rights adopted a judgment that was to become a classic in the field because of its clarification of a state's duties with respect to violence committed by non-state actors.

VELÁSQUEZ RODRÍGUEZ CASE
INTER-AMERICAN COURT OF HUMAN RIGHTS, SER. C, NO. 4 (1988)

[A petition against Honduras was received by the Inter-American Commission of Human Rights, alleging that Velásquez Rodríguez was arrested without warrant by Honduran national security units. Knowledge of his whereabouts was consistently denied by police and security forces. Velásquez had disappeared. Petitioners argued that through this conduct, Honduras had violated several articles of the American Convention on Human Rights. After hearings and conclusions, the Commission referred the matter to the Inter-American Court of Human Rights, whose contentious jurisdiction had been recognized by Honduras. The Court concluded that Honduras had violated the Convention.

In the excerpts below, the Court addresses the issue of just what the obligations of Honduras were under the Convention. Was Honduras obligated only to 'respect' individual rights and not directly violate them, as by torture or illegal arrest? Or was Honduras obligated to take steps, within reasonable limits, to protect people like Velásquez from seizure even by non-state, private persons? In an earlier portion of the opinion (above), the Court had found that the Honduran state was implicated in the arrest and disappearance, and that the acts of those arresting Velásquez could be imputed to the state. In the present excerpts, the Court reviews that information, and considers what might be the responsibility of Honduras even if the seizure and disappearance of Velásquez were caused by private persons unconnected with the government.]

161. Article 1(1) of the Convention provides:

> 1. The States Parties to this Convention undertake to respect the rights and freedoms recognized herein and to ensure to all persons subject to their jurisdiction the free and full exercise of those rights and freedoms. . . .

...

164. Article 1(1) is essential in determining whether a violation of the human rights recognized by the Convention can be imputed to a State Party. In effect, that article charges the States Parties with the fundamental duty to respect and guarantee the rights recognized in the Convention. Any impairment of those rights which can be attributed under the rules of international law to the action or omission of any public authority constitutes an act imputable to the State, which assumes responsibility in the terms provided by the Convention itself.

165. The first obligation assumed by the States Parties under Article 1(1) is 'to respect the rights and freedoms' recognized by the Convention. ...

166. The second obligation of the States Parties is to ['ensure'] the free and full exercise of the rights recognized by the Convention to every person subject to its jurisdiction. This obligation implies the duty of the States Parties to organize the governmental apparatus and, in general, all the structures through which public power is exercised, so that they are capable of juridically ensuring the free and full enjoyment of human rights. As a consequence of this obligation, the States must prevent, investigate and punish any violation of the rights recognized by the Convention and, moreover, if possible attempt to restore the rights violated and provide compensation as warranted for damages resulting from the violation.

...

169. According to Article 1(1), any exercise of public power that violates the rights recognized by the Convention is illegal. ...

170. This conclusion is independent of whether the organ or official has contravened provisions of internal law or overstepped the limits of his authority. Under international law a State is responsible for the acts of its agents undertaken in their official capacity and for their omissions, even when those agents act outside the sphere of their authority or violate internal law.

...

172. Thus, in principle, any violation of rights recognized by the Convention carried out by an act of public authority or by persons who use their position of authority is imputable to the State. However, this does not define all the circumstances in which a State is obligated to prevent, investigate and punish human rights violations, nor all the cases in which the State might be found responsible for an infringement of those rights. An illegal act which violates human rights and which is initially not directly imputable to a State (for example, because it is the act of a private person or because the person responsible has not been identified) can lead to international responsibility of the State, not because of the act itself, but because of the lack of due diligence to prevent the violation or to respond to it as required by the Convention.

...

174. The State has a legal duty to take reasonable steps to prevent human rights violations and to use the means at its disposal to carry out a serious investigation of violations committed within its jurisdiction, to identify those responsible, impose the appropriate punishment and ensure the victim adequate compensation.

175. This duty to prevent includes all those means of a legal, political, administrative and cultural nature that promote the safeguard of human rights and ensure that any violations are considered and treated as illegal acts,

which, as such, may lead to the punishment of those responsible and the obligation to indemnify the victims for damages. It is not possible to make a detailed list of all such measures, as they vary with the law and the conditions of each State Party. Of course, while the State is obligated to prevent human rights abuses, the existence of a particular violation does not, in itself, prove the failure to take preventive measures. ...

...

177. In certain circumstances, it may be difficult to investigate acts that violate an individual's rights. The duty to investigate, like the duty to prevent, is not breached merely because the investigation does not produce a satisfactory result. Nevertheless, it must be undertaken in a serious manner. ... Where the acts of private parties that violate the Convention are not seriously investigated, those parties are aided in a sense by the government, thereby making the State responsible on the international plane.

178. In the instant case, the evidence shows a complete inability of the procedures of the State of Honduras, which were theoretically adequate, to ensure the investigation of the disappearance of Manfredo Velásquez and the fulfillment of its duties to pay compensation and punish those responsible, as set out in Article 1(1) of the Convention.

179. As the Court has verified above, the failure of the judicial system to act upon the writs brought before various tribunals in the instant case has been proven. Not one writ of habeas corpus was processed. No judge had access to the places where Manfredo Velásquez might have been detained. The criminal complaint was dismissed.

180. Nor did the organs of the Executive Branch carry out a serious investigation to establish the fate of Manfredo Velásquez. There was no investigation of public allegations of a practice of disappearances nor a determination of whether Manfredo Velásquez had been a victim of that practice. The Commission's requests for information were ignored to the point that the Commission had to presume, under Article 42 of its Regulations, that the allegations were true...

...

182. The Court is convinced, and has so found, that the disappearance of Manfredo Velásquez was carried out by agents who acted under cover of public authority. However, even had that fact not been proven, the failure of the State apparatus to act, which is clearly proven, is a failure on the part of Honduras to fulfill the duties it assumed under Article 1(1) of the Convention, which obligated it to guarantee Manfredo Velásquez the free and full exercise of his human rights.

...

General Recommendations

As observed above, one of most important techniques available to the CEDAW Committee involves the adoption of General Recommendations, through which it explains its understanding of a particular right or issue that arises under the Convention.

CEDAW COMMITTEE, GENERAL RECOMMENDATION NO. 19 ON VIOLENCE AGAINST WOMEN
UN DOC. A/47/38 (1992)

6. ... The definition of discrimination includes gender-based violence, that is, violence that is directed against a woman because she is a woman or that affects women disproportionately. It includes acts that inflict physical, mental or sexual harm or suffering, threats of such acts, coercion and other deprivations of liberty. Gender-based violence may breach specific provisions of the Convention, regardless of whether those provisions expressly mention violence.

7. Gender-based violence, which impairs or nullifies the enjoyment by women of human rights and fundamental freedoms under general international law or under human rights conventions, is discrimination within the meaning of article 1 of the Convention. [The rights violated by gender-based violence amounting to discrimination include the right to life, to liberty and security of the person, to equality in the family, to the highest standard attainable of physical and mental health, and to just and favourable conditions of work.]

...

9. ... [D]iscrimination under the Convention is not restricted to action by or on behalf of Governments (see articles 2(e), 2(f) and 5). ... Under general international law and specific human rights covenants, States may also be responsible for private acts if they fail to act with due diligence to prevent violations of rights or to investigate and punish acts of violence, and for providing compensation.

...

11. Traditional attitudes by which women are regarded as subordinate to men or as having stereotyped roles perpetuate widespread practices involving violence or coercion, such as family violence and abuse, forced marriage, dowry deaths, acid attacks and female circumcision. Such prejudices and practices may justify gender-based violence as a form of protection or control of women. The effect of such violence on the physical and mental integrity of women is to deprive them of the equal enjoyment, exercise and knowledge of human rights and fundamental freedoms. While this comment addresses mainly actual or threatened violence, the underlying consequences of these forms of gender-based violence help to maintain women in subordinate roles and contribute to their low level of political participation and to their lower level of education, skills and work opportunities.

...

20. In some States there are traditional practices perpetuated by culture and tradition that are harmful to the health of women and children. These practices include dietary restrictions for pregnant women, preference for male children and female circumcision or genital mutilation.

...

23. Family violence is one of the most insidious forms of violence against women. It is prevalent in all societies.

...

[The Committee recommends that states parties should (among other measures) take a range of steps to 'overcome all forms of gender-based violence, whether by public or private act', provide adequate protective and support services for victims of family violence and provide gender-sensitive training to police and judges, take measures 'to ensure that the media respect and promote respect for women', take measures to eliminate prejudices and attitudes that lead to violence, and ensure that women need not resort to illegal abortion 'because of lack of appropriate services in regard to fertility control'.]

CEDAW COMMITTEE, GENERAL RECOMMENDATION NO. 35 ON GENDER-BASED VIOLENCE AGAINST WOMEN, UPDATING GENERAL RECOMMENDATION NO. 19 UN DOC. CEDAW/C/GC/35 (2017)

...

I. Introduction

...

2. For over 25 years, the practice of States parties has endorsed the Committee's interpretation [in general recommendation No. 19]. The *opinio juris* and State practice suggest that the prohibition of gender-based violence against women has evolved into a principle of customary international law. General recommendation No. 19 has been a key catalyst for this process.

...

4. The Committee acknowledges that civil society, especially women's non- governmental organisations, have prioritised the elimination of gender- based violence against women; their activities have had a profound social and political impact, contributing to the recognition of gender-based violence against women as a human rights violation and to the adoption of laws and policies to address it.

5. The Committee's concluding observations and their follow up procedures, general recommendations, statements and views and recommendations following communications and inquiries under the Optional Protocol to the Convention condemn gender-based violence against women, in all its forms, wherever it occurs. They also clarify standards for eliminating this violence and the obligations of States parties in this regard.

6. Despite these advances, gender-based violence against women … remains pervasive in all countries of the world, with high levels of impunity. It manifests in a continuum of multiple, interrelated and recurring forms, in a range of settings, from private to public, including technology-mediated settings and in the contemporary globalized world it transcends national boundaries.

7. In many states, legislation addressing gender–based violence against women remains non-existent, inadequate and/or poorly implemented. An erosion of legal and policy frameworks to eliminate gender-based discrimination or violence, often justified in the name of tradition, culture, religion or fundamentalist ideologies, and significant reductions in public spending, often as part of "austerity measures" following economic and financial crises, further weaken the state responses. In the context of shrinking democratic spaces and consequent deterioration of the rule of law, all these factors allow for the pervasiveness of gender-based violence against women and lead to a culture of impunity.

…

II. Scope

…

15. Women's right to a life free from gender-based violence is indivisible from and interdependent with other human rights, including the right to life, health, liberty and security of the person, the right to equality and equal protection within the family, freedom from torture, cruel, inhumane or degrading treatment, freedom of expression, movement, participation, assembly and association.

16. Gender-based violence against women, may amount to torture or cruel, inhuman or degrading treatment in certain circumstances, including in cases of rape, domestic violence or harmful practices, among others. In some cases, some forms of gender-based violence against women may also constitute international crimes.

17. The Committee endorses the view of other human rights treaty bodies and special procedures mandate-holders that in making the determination of when acts of gender-based violence against women amount to torture or cruel, inhuman or degrading treatment, a gender sensitive approach is required to understand the level of pain and suffering experienced by women, and that the purpose and intent requirement of torture are satisfied when acts or omissions are gender specific or perpetrated against a person on the basis of sex.

18. Violations of women's sexual and reproductive health and rights, such as forced sterilizations, forced abortion, forced pregnancy, criminalisation of abortion, denial or delay of safe abortion and post-abortion care, forced continuation of pregnancy, abuse and mistreatment of women and girls seeking sexual and reproductive health information, goods and services, are forms of gender-based violence that, depending on the circumstances, may amount to torture or cruel, inhuman or degrading treatment.

19. The Committee regards gender-based violence against women to be rooted in gender-related factors such as the ideology of men's entitlement and privilege over women, social norms regarding masculinity, the need to assert male control or power, enforce gender roles, or prevent, discourage or punish what is considered to be unacceptable female behaviour. These factors also contribute to the explicit or implicit social acceptance of gender-based violence against women, often still considered as a private matter, and to the widespread impunity for it.

20. Gender-based violence against women occurs in all spaces and spheres of human interaction, whether public or private. These include the family, the community, the public spaces, the workplace, leisure, politics, sport, health services, educational settings and their redefinition through technology-mediated environments, such as contemporary forms of violence occurring in the Internet and digital spaces. In all these settings, gender-based violence against women can result from acts or omissions of State or non-State actors, acting territorially or extraterritorially, including extraterritorial military action of States, individually or as members of international or intergovernmental organizations or coalitions, or extraterritorial actions by private corporations.

III. General obligations of States parties under the Convention relating to gender-based violence against women

21. Gender-based violence against women constitutes discrimination against women under article 1 and therefore engages all of the obligations in the Convention. Article 2 establishes that the overarching obligation

of States parties is to pursue by all appropriate means and without delay a policy of eliminating discrimination against women, including gender-based violence against women. This is an obligation of an immediate nature; delays cannot be justified on any grounds, including on economic, cultural or religious grounds. ...

Responsibility for acts or omissions of State actors

22. Under the Convention and general international law, a State party is responsible for acts and omissions by its organs and agents that constitute gender-based violence against women. These include the acts or omissions of officials in its executive, legislative and judicial branches. Article 2 (d) of the Convention requires that States parties, and their organs and agents, refrain from engaging in any act or practice of direct or indirect discrimination against women and ensure that public authorities and institutions act in conformity with this obligation. Besides ensuring that laws, policies, programmes and procedures do not discriminate against women, according to article 2 (c) and (g), States parties must have an effective and accessible legal and services framework in place to address all forms of gender-based violence against women committed by State agents, on their territory or extraterritorially.

23. States parties are responsible for preventing these acts or omissions by their own organs and agents – including through training and the adoption, implementation and monitoring of legal provisions, administrative regulations and codes of conduct- and to investigate, prosecute and apply appropriate legal or disciplinary sanctions as well as provide reparation in all cases of gender-based violence against women, including those constituting international crimes, as well as in cases of failure, negligence or omission on the part of public authorities. In so doing, women's diversity and the risks of intersectional discrimination stemming from it should be taken into consideration.

Responsibility for acts or omissions of non-State actors

24. Under general international law, as well as under international treaties, a private actor's acts or omissions may engage the international responsibility of the State in certain cases. These include:

a) *Acts and omissions by non-state actors attributable to the States.* The acts or omissions of private actors empowered by the law of that State to exercise elements of the governmental authority, including private bodies providing public services, such as healthcare or education, or operating places of detention, shall be considered as acts attributable to the State itself, as well as the acts or omissions of private agents in fact acting on the instructions of, or under the direction or control of that State, including when operating abroad.

b) *Due diligence obligations for acts and omissions of non-State actors.* Article 2(e) of the Convention explicitly provides that States parties are required to take all appropriate measures to eliminate discrimination against women by any person, organisation or enterprise. This obligation, frequently referred to as an obligation of due diligence, underpins the Convention as a whole and accordingly States parties will be responsible if they fail to take all appropriate measures to prevent as well as to investigate, prosecute, punish and provide reparation for acts or omissions by non-State actors which result in gender-based violence against women. This includes actions by corporations operating extraterritorially. In particular, States Parties are required to take necessary steps to prevent human rights violations abroad by corporations over which they may exercise influence, whether by regulatory means or by the use of incentives, including economic incentives. Under the obligation of due diligence, States parties have to adopt and implement diverse measures to tackle gender-based violence against women committed by non-State actors. They are required to have laws, institutions and a system in place to address such violence. Also, States parties are obliged to ensure that these function effectively in practice, and are supported and diligently enforced by all State agents and bodies. The failure of a State party to take all appropriate measures to prevent acts of gender-based violence against women when its authorities know or should know of the danger of violence, or a failure to investigate, prosecute and punish, and to provide reparation to victims/survivors of such acts, provides tacit permission or encouragement to acts of gender-based violence against women. These failures or omissions constitute human rights violations.

...

IV. Recommendations

...

28. The Committee also recommends that States parties take the following measures in the areas of prevention, protection, prosecution, punishment and redress; data collection and monitoring and international cooperation to accelerate elimination of gender-based violence against women. All these measures should be implemented with a victim/survivor-centred approach, acknowledging women as subjects of rights and promoting their agency and autonomy, including the evolving capacity of girls, from childhood to adolescence. Also, these measures should be designed and implemented with the participation of women and taking into account the particular situation of women affected by intersecting forms of discrimination.

...

QUESTION

1. While acknowledging the overall importance of General Recommendation No. 35, Ramona Vijeyarasa in 'CEDAW's General Recommendation No. 35: A Quarter of a Century of Evolutionary Approaches to Violence against Women', 19 *J. Hum. Rts* (2020) 153 has called it a 'shopping list' that reflects a cut-and-paste exercise rather than new thinking. In her view, 'many issues are dealt with in too cursory a manner and ... fall short of providing concrete guidance to states ...'. How detailed and specific should such a document be?

2. How would you respond to critiques by various authors that the emphasis on violence against women has: (i) reflected a conservative agenda that reinforces the gendered distinction between victims and protectors; (ii) encouraged a focus on violence as opposed to the inequalities that generate it; and (iii) promoted a narrow focus on sexual violence that reinforces a restrictive ideal of female sexuality?[68]

FOLLOW-UP

CEDAW's 1992 General Recommendation was followed soon after by the UN General Assembly's adoption of the Declaration on the Elimination of Violence against Women (GA Res. 48/104 (20 December 1993)) which, in practice, amounted to endorsement by governments of the Committee's approach. The Declaration defined violence against women as meaning 'any act of gender-based violence that results in, or is likely to result in, physical, sexual or psychological harm or suffering to women, including threats of such acts, coercion or arbitrary deprivation of liberty, whether occurring in public or in private life' (Art. 1). The formally non-binding Declaration stated that 'States should condemn violence against women and should not invoke any custom, tradition or religious consideration to avoid their obligations with respect to its elimination. States should pursue by all appropriate means and without delay a policy of eliminating violence against women. ...' (Art. 4).

The legacy of the *Velásquez Rodríguez Case*, combined with the developments traced above was solidly entrenched through the Inter-American Commission on Human Rights decision in *Jessica Lenahan (Gonzales) et al. v. United States* (Report No. 80/11, Case 12.626, 21 July 2011). Ms. Lenahan had obtained a restraining order against her ex-husband and claimed that the police failed to adequately respond to her repeated and urgent calls seeking help in response to the father's subsequent abduction of their children. They were later found dead in his truck after he exchanged gunfire with the police. Investigations into the deaths of the children were entirely inadequate and no effective judicial remedies were available. The Commission noted the 'broad international consensus over the use of the due diligence principle to interpret ... State legal obligations' in such contexts and 'the link between the duty to act with due diligence and the obligation of States to guarantee access to adequate and effective judicial remedies for victims and their family members when they suffer acts of violence (paras. 123 and 127).'

In 1994, the UN Commission on Human Rights appointed a Special Rapporteur 'on violence against women, its causes and consequences,' who was authorized to undertake field missions and submit analytical and other reports to the Commission. Successive rapporteurs (Radhika Coomaraswamy,1994–2003; Yakin Ertürk, 2003–

---

[68] H. Charlesworth, 'Feminist Futures in Human Rights', in N. Bhuta (ed.), *Human Rights in Transition* (2024) 182, at 200-01.

2009; Rashida Manjoo, 2009–2015; Dubravka Šimonović, 2015–2021; and Reem Alsalem, 2021-) have undertaken detailed studies on a wide range of issues affecting women in annual reports to both the Human Rights Council and the General Assembly.

For its part, the CEDAW Committee, having played the crucial role of catalyst in developing the initial normative consensus, has continued to deepen the understanding of the issue and its implications through the use of two other techniques, in addition to state reporting and General Recommendations. They are the undertaking of 'inquiries' and the consideration of 'communications' (complaints). Both of these procedures are laid down in an Optional Protocol to CEDAW (the 'OP'), adopted in 1999. The OP is open to ratification only by parties to CEDAW itself, and is a way in which they can extend, or deepen, their commitments to cooperate with the Committee. As of 2024, 115 states had agreed to the OP, compared with 189 parties to CEDAW itself. (Chapter 9, below, on the Human Rights Committee created by the ICCPR examines in more detail the work of that Committee under a similar OP to the ICCPR, which also enables it to examine complaints.)

THE INQUIRY PROCEDURE

This procedure under the OP begins with a submission to the Committee, most likely by an NGO, of 'reliable information indicating grave or systematic violations by a State Party of rights set forth in the Convention'. The government concerned is then asked to comment on the information before the Committee decides whether or not to 'designate one or more of its members to conduct an inquiry and to report urgently to the Committee.' The OP provides that '[w]here warranted and with the consent of the State Party, the inquiry may include a visit to its territory.' The inquiry is conducted confidentially, ideally with the government's cooperation at all stages. The resulting report, including recommendations, is sent to the government, which is invited to respond and the issues can subsequently be pursued under the Convention's regular reporting procedures. As of 2024, the Committee has published reports on inquiries undertaken in relation to Mexico, the Philippines, Canada, Kyrgyzstan, the United Kingdom (twice), Mali, and South Africa.

The Canadian inquiry was requested by the Feminist Alliance for International Action and the Native Women's Association of Canada. These organizations claimed that 'aboriginal women and girls experience extremely high levels of violence in Canada, as shown by the high number of disappearances and murders of aboriginal women in particular; they report rates of violence, including domestic violence and sexual assault, that are 3.5 times higher than those for non-aboriginal women; young aboriginal women are five times more likely than other Canadian women of the same age to die as a result of violence; and aboriginal women and girls experience high levels of sexual abuse and violence in their families and communities and in society at large.' In response, the Committee found (para. 214) 'that the measures taken to protect aboriginal women from disappearance and murder have been insufficient and inadequate, that the weaknesses in the justice and law enforcement system have resulted in impunity and that no efforts have been made to bring about any significant compensation or reparation.' It made a series of recommendation to the government, including that a national inquiry be established. In 2016 an inquiry was set up.[69] The resulting 2019 report (*Reclaiming Power and Place: The Final Report of the National Inquiry into Missing and Murdered Indigenous Women and Girls*) 'is comprised of the truths of more than 2,380 family members, survivors of violence, experts and Knowledge Keepers shared over two years of cross-country public hearings and evidence gathering. It delivers 231 individual Calls for Justice directed at governments, institutions, social service providers, industries and all Canadians.'

The South African inquiry was triggered by information submitted in 2013 by 11 organizations claiming that the high levels of domestic violence in South Africa and the state's failure to comply with its due diligence obligation to protect women from such violence amounted to grave or systematic violations of the Convention. They also pointed to exacerbating factors including: (a) The prevalence of harmful practices such as *ukuthwala* (i.e., elopement leading to child and forced marriages) and polygamy; (b) Persistent stereotypes that legitimize domestic violence and discourage women from reporting such violence; (c) The lack of statistical data and research; and (d) The lack of public awareness-raising and capacity-building for law enforcement agencies and health and social workers. After considering the information, the Committee invited the government to

[69] Report of the inquiry concerning Canada of the Committee on the Elimination of Discrimination against Women under article 8 of the Optional Protocol, UN Doc. CEDAW/C/OP.8/CAN/1 (30 March 2015).

respond, which it did in 2015. In 2019, it agreed to a country visit. Two members of the Committee spent 12 days in South Africa in September 2019. In the resulting report (UN Doc. CEDAW/C/ZAF/IR/1 (14 May 2021)), the Committee found the State party responsible for:

(a) Grave violations of rights under the Convention, considering that the State party has failed to protect a significant number of women and girls from domestic violence and to provide adequate access to justice, protection and support to enable women to leave abusive domestic relationships, thereby exposing them to or unnecessarily prolonging their severe physical and mental suffering;

(b) Systematic violations of rights under the Convention, considering that the State party has knowingly omitted to take effective measures:

(i) To address patriarchal attitudes and social norms that legitimize domestic violence and to destigmatize victims;

(ii) To specifically criminalize domestic violence and femicide, enforce and monitor civil remedies against perpetrators, repeal provisions that tolerate harmful practices giving rise to domestic violence, enforce general criminal law provisions punishing domestic violence and prosecute ex officio domestic violence and rape;

(iii) To establish appropriate institutional arrangements, oversight and accountability measures to protect victims of and prevent domestic violence;

(iv) To remove the economic and social barriers faced by victims of domestic violence and create a supportive environment that enables victims to obtain access to justice.

117. The Committee considers that the State party has knowingly accepted these omissions, which are not a random occurrence, as evidenced by the extremely high levels of domestic violence in the State party. They constitute elements of systematic violations of rights under the Convention.

The Committee made a large number of detailed recommendations to the State Party.

THE COMPLAINTS PROCEDURE

Under this procedure, states parties to the OP agree to recognize the competence of the Committee 'to receive and consider communications'. Individuals or 'groups of individuals' under the 'jurisdiction' of a state party may submit communications to the Committee, 'claiming to be victims of a violation [by the state] of any of the rights set forth in the Convention'. Communications must meet certain conditions and criteria to be judged admissible — for example, submission following exhaustion of domestic remedies. The Committee brings the communication confidentially to the attention of the state party involved. After finding the communication admissible and examining it, the Committee transmits its 'views' on the communication, 'together with its recommendations', to the concerned parties. The state party 'shall give due consideration' to the Committee's views and recommendations. By February 2023, 194 communications had been registered, with 46 of those awaiting the Committee's consideration (UN Doc. A/78/38). Most emanated from European states. Under the Committee's communications follow-up procedure, a Committee member seeks to engage with the State party in relation to each communication to ensure implementation of the decision. Information is also sought from victims, NGOs and others and the resulting information is reflected in the Committee's annual reports, thus seeking to maintain pressure for compliance.

N. A. E. V. SPAIN, VIEWS OF THE COMMITTEE … IN RESPECT OF COMMUNICATION NO. 149/2019, UN DOC. CEDAW/C/82/D/149/2019 (27 JUNE 2022)

…

1.1 The author of the communication is N.A.E., a Spanish national born on 12 September 1986. The author maintains that Spain violated her rights under articles 2, 3, 5 and 12 of the [CEDAW] owing to the obstetric violence she experienced in hospital during childbirth. …

1.2 … [T]he Committee received 11 submissions from third parties, which were transmitted to both parties for their comments.

Facts as submitted by the author

…

2.1 During the 25-year-old author's first pregnancy, which had been monitored and healthy throughout, she and her partner submitted a birth plan to the public hospital … . [T] hey stated that they did not want drugs to be administered to induce or accelerate labour, that any decisions taken by the medical staff should have their consent, that, if a caesarean section were necessary, the baby should be with its mother immediately following birth … and that the baby should not be bottle-fed.

2.2 At 8 a.m. on 9 July 2012, at 38 weeks of pregnancy, the author went to the hospital because her waters had broken. …

2.3 The hospital's protocol sets out a waiting period of 24 hours before inducing labour. At 4 p.m. the same day, however, a gynaecologist informed the author that labour would be induced because, in the gynaecologist's words, "we do not induce at night". The author claims that there was no medical need to induce labour [and that the decision was] for the convenience of the attendants. …

2.4 The author did not consent to the induction of labour; her repeated requests for information on the risks and alternatives went unanswered.

2.5 Before labour was medically induced, the author requested permission to eat, which was denied by the hospital despite the fact that the Spanish Ministry of Health … guidelines … recommends that food be provided … to ensure maternal and fetal well-being.

…

2.8 At 9.30 a.m. on 10 July 2012 … despite the fact that the fetal monitoring recordings were fine, the midwife informed the author that a caesarean section was being considered because the labour was supposedly "stalled". …When the doctors arrived, however, they had already made the decision, stating "yes, a caesarean section and that's that". When the author asked for information, the doctor did not provide any, but rather spoke to her like a child, replying "calm down, I'm going to take care of you".

2.9 At 10 a.m., the students began the operation without the author's consent. The doctors did not allow the author's husband to be present. According to the author:

> I was placed on the operating table like a doll. No one introduced themselves; no one spoke to me; no one looked me in the face. No one bothered to try to calm me down. I was crying a lot. They placed my arms out to the sides. The operating room was full of people … . I was there alone and naked, and people were coming and going … . They were talking among themselves about … what they had done over the weekend … .

…

2.11 The author's son was born at 10.12 a.m. After the caesarean section had been performed, the protocol was once again not followed. According to the protocol, the newborn should remain with its mother from the moment she is responsive in order to initiate breastfeeding and skin-to-skin contact between mother and child, which improves the baby's heart rate, temperature, blood glucose, immune system and sleep. However, the baby was separated from his mother to be taken to the paediatrician for no reason, and the author had no opportunity to have skin-to-skin contact with him; she caught a glimpse of him only from afar. … The author requested that the baby be given to his father and was told: "Calm down, little girl, it's all over." The author could hear instructions on how to sew her up being given to the students. They finished without saying a word to her.

2.12 Over the next few hours, the author asked for the baby to be brought to her, but he was not, contrary to the recommendations of the Spanish Paediatric Association on care and assistance for healthy newborns.

2.13 … [T]he baby was bottle-fed, despite the parents' having stated that they wanted him to be breastfed. …

2.14 Later, the author suffered from abdominal pain in the caesarean scar and lower abdomen and from urinary incontinence. …

2.15 … In a report dated 7 June 2013 … the author was diagnosed with post-partum post-traumatic stress disorder, anticipatory distress and anxiety, emotional instability and reactive depression … .
…

Consideration of the merits
…
15.2 The Committee notes that the author claims that [the problems described above] … were the result of structural discrimination based on gender stereotypes regarding childbirth. The author maintains that these stereotypes were perpetuated in the administrative and judicial proceedings. The judge did not take into account the disregard of the protocols, the reports provided by the author to prove malpractice or the reports submitted concerning the diagnosis of post-partum post-traumatic stress disorder, but rather described the injuries suffered by the author as a mere matter of perception. …

15.3 The Committee recalls that, according to its general recommendation No. 24 (1999) on women and health, quality health-care services are those that are delivered in a way that ensures that a woman gives her fully informed consent, respects her dignity, guarantees her confidentiality and is sensitive to her needs and perspectives. …

15.4 The Committee also [takes note of the phenomenon described of obstetric violence as used to refer to violence suffered by women during childbirth in health-care settings, which is widespread and systematic. According to the UN Special Rapporteur on violence against women 'it is part of a continuum of the violations that occur in the wider context of structural inequality, discrimination and patriarchy, and also the result of a lack of proper education and training, as well as lack of respect for women's equal status and human rights'.]
…
…
15.6 The Committee recalls that it is generally for the authorities of States parties to evaluate the facts and evidence and the application of national law in a particular case, unless it can be established that the evaluation was conducted in a manner that was biased, based on gender stereotypes that constitute discrimination against women or clearly arbitrary or that amounted to a denial of justice. … According to the gynaecological and obstetric clinical reports provided by the author, both to the domestic courts and to the Committee, the medical personnel did not comply with *lex artis*, namely, the protocols were not followed, not enough time had elapsed before performing a caesarean section, a diagnosis of stalled labour had been made in haste, there were alternatives to the caesarean section and there are no consent forms for the induction of labour or the caesarean section as required by the Patient Autonomy Act. As the reports make very clear, had the applicable standards and protocols been followed, the author was very likely to have experienced a normal birth. … [T]he Committee notes that … the national authorities did not carry out an exhaustive analysis of these elements of the evidence … … ….

15.7 … [None of the principal allegations] has been contested by the State party … .

15.8 … [U]nder articles 2 (f) and 5, States parties have the obligation to take all appropriate measures to modify or abolish … customs and practices that constitute discrimination against women. The Committee considers that stereotyping affects the right of women to be protected against gender-based violence, in this case obstetric violence, and that the authorities responsible for analysing responsibility for such acts should exercise particular caution in order not to reproduce stereotypes. … [I]n the present case, the State party's administrative and judicial authorities applied stereotypical and therefore discriminatory notions, for example by assuming that it is the doctor who decides whether or not to perform a caesarean section without duly analysing the evidence and reports submitted by the author which point to there having been alternative courses of action to a caesarean section, or by assuming that the psychological injuries suffered by the author were a matter of mere perception.

15.9 … [T]he Committee is of the view that the facts before it reveal a violation of the rights of the author under articles 2 (b), (c), (d) and (f), 3, 5 and 12 of the Convention.

16 … [It] makes the following recommendations to the State party:
(a) Concerning the author: provide her with the appropriate reparation, including adequate financial compensation for the damage that she suffered to her physical and psychological health;
…

(b) General:

(i) Ensure women's rights to safe motherhood and access to appropriate obstetric services, in accordance with general recommendation No. 24 (1999) on women and health; and, in particular, provide women with adequate information at each stage of childbirth and establish a requirement for their free, prior and informed consent to be obtained for any invasive treatment performed during childbirth, thereby respecting their autonomy and their capacity to make informed decisions about their reproductive health;

(ii) Conduct research into obstetric violence in the State party in order to shed light on the situation and thus provide guidance for public policies to combat such violence;

(iii) Provide obstetricians and other health workers with adequate professional training on women's reproductive health rights;

(iv) Ensure access to effective remedies in cases in which women's reproductive health rights have been violated, including in cases of obstetric violence, and provide specialized training to judicial and law enforcement personnel.

(v) Establish, publicize and implement a Patients' Bill of Rights.

…

QUESTIONS

1. Why would such a case be taken to the CEDAW Committee rather than elsewhere?

2. What sort of evidence base should the Committee have to ground such a decision? How would you respond to the assertion that it is not for some UN committee to be shaping Spanish obstetrics policy?

3. Eva Brems, in 'UN Human Rights Treaty Bodies Talking to Domestic Adjudicators Through Their Quasi-judicial Work: An Examination of CERD and CEDAW', 45 *Hum. Rts. Q.* (2023) 568, argues that *N. E. A. v. Spain* exemplifies the Committee's failure to provide 'generalizable interpretations' which would 'offer guidance to domestic monitoring bodies on how to address' the issue of obstetric violence.' Discuss.

4. Affirmative Action and Quotas

Nigeria ratified CEDAW in 1985. Following the 2023 national elections women occupied 3 percent of seats in the Senate and 4 percent in the House of Representatives. Only 10 percent of candidates were female. Such statistics provide an indication of why CEDAW explicitly endorses the need for affirmative action or what are termed 'temporary special measures'. This includes measures designed to enhance women's participation in the political process. The CEDAW Committee has adopted expansive interpretations of Article 4 of the CEDAW Convention in particular ('Adoption by States Parties of temporary special measures aimed at accelerating de facto equality between men and women shall not be considered discrimination …').

In General Recommendation No. 23: Political and Public Life (1997) the Committee noted (para. 5) that:

> Article 7 obliges States parties to take all appropriate measures to eliminate discrimination against women in political and public life and to ensure that they enjoy equality with men in political and public life. … The political and public life of a country is a broad concept. It refers to the exercise of political power, in particular the exercise of legislative, judicial, executive and administrative powers. The term covers all aspects of public administration and the formulation and implementation of policy at the international, national, regional and local levels. The concept also includes many aspects of civil society, including public boards and local councils and the activities of organizations such as political parties, trade unions, professional or industry associations, women's organizations, community-based organizations and other organizations concerned with public and political life.
>
> …
>
> 16. … Research demonstrates that if women's participation reaches 30 to 35 per cent (generally termed a "critical mass"), there is a real impact on political style and the content of decisions, and political life is revitalized.
>
> …
>
> 22. The system of balloting, the distribution of seats in Parliament, the choice of district, all have a significant impact on the proportion of women elected to Parliament. Political parties must embrace the principles of equal opportunity and democracy and endeavour to balance the number of male and female candidates.
>
> …
>
> 29. Measures that have been adopted by a number of States parties in order to ensure equal participation by women in senior cabinet and administrative positions and as members of government advisory bodies include: adoption of a rule whereby, when potential appointees are equally qualified, preference will be given to a woman nominee; the adoption of a rule that neither sex should constitute less than 40 per cent of the members of a public body; a quota for women members of cabinet and for appointment to public office; and consultation with women's organizations to ensure that qualified women are nominated for membership in public bodies and offices and the development and maintenance of registers of such women in order to facilitate the nomination of women for appointment to public bodies and posts. …
>
> …
>
> 31. Examination of the reports of States parties also demonstrates that in certain cases the law excludes women from exercising royal powers, from serving as judges in religious or traditional tribunals vested with jurisdiction on behalf of the State or from full participation in the military. These provisions discriminate against women, deny to society the advantages of their involvement and skills in these areas of the life of their communities and contravene the principles of the Convention.

32. ... Political parties should be encouraged to adopt effective measures to ... ensure that women have an equal opportunity in practice to serve as party officials and to be nominated as candidates for election.

33. Measures that have been adopted by some political parties include setting aside for women a certain minimum number or percentage of positions on their executive bodies, ensuring that there is a balance between the number of male and female candidates nominated for election, and ensuring that women are not consistently assigned to less favourable constituencies or to the least advantageous positions on a party list. ...

34. Other organizations such as trade unions and political parties have an obligation to demonstrate their commitment to the principle of gender equality in their ... memberships with gender-balanced representation on their executive boards so that these bodies may benefit from the full and equal participation of all sectors of society and from contributions made by both sexes. ...

...

39. The globalization of the contemporary world makes the inclusion of women and their participation in international organizations, on equal terms with men, increasingly important. The integration of a gender perspective and women's human rights into the agenda of all international bodies is a government imperative. ...

...

In General Recommendation No. 25: Temporary Special Measures (2004), the Committee noted that:

...

8. ... [T]he Convention requires that women be given an equal start and that they be empowered by an enabling environment to achieve equality of results. It is not enough to guarantee women treatment that is identical to that of men. Rather, biological as well as socially and culturally constructed differences between women and men must be taken into account. Under certain circumstances, non-identical treatment of women and men will be required in order to address such differences. ...

...

10. ... [M]easures [must be] adopted towards a real transformation of opportunities, institutions and systems so that they are no longer grounded in historically determined male paradigms of power and life patterns.

...

14. ... [T]he application of temporary special measures in accordance with the Convention is one of the means to realize de facto or substantive equality for women, rather than an exception to the norms of nondiscrimination and equality.

The Committee plans to adopt its 40th General Recommendation in October 2024 dealing with 'the equal and inclusive representation of women in decision-making systems'. Its goal is to spell out an approach to 'governance based on parity as a core principle and a leading force for transformative change.'

Political Representation

In 2023, according to UN Women (*Facts and figures: Women's leadership and political participation*) 15 countries had a woman Head of State, and 16 had a woman Head of Government. Less than 23 percent of government ministers were women and very often they held ministries assumed to be of particular relevance to women such as family, environment, labour, and women's affairs. In 1995, 11 percent of all national parliamentarians were women, but by 2021 the figure was 26.5 percent. Six countries had 50 percent or more women in parliament in single or lower houses: Rwanda (61), Cuba (53), Nicaragua (52), Mexico (50), New Zealand (50) and the United Arab Emirates (50). In 22 countries, women accounted for less than 10 percent of lower house parliamentarians.

In the United States, in 2023, women held 29 percent of seats in the House of Representatives, and 25 percent in the Senate. No woman has been elected President and only one has held the Vice-Presidency. Twelve of 50 governors were women and 33 percent of legislators at the state level were women (five times as many as in 1971).

Before the adoption of CEDAW in 1979, only a handful of countries had adopted quotas to promote women's representation in the political arena. Today, over 100 countries have such quotas. There are three main forms: (1) parliamentary seats reserved by law for women (20 percent of countries with quotas have this type — mostly in South Asia and Africa); (2) legal quotas requiring a percentage of political party nominees to be women (38 percent, mainly in Latin America and Africa); and (3) voluntary quotas adopted by the political parties themselves (61 percent, mainly in Western Europe). Quotas might apply at the local, regional or national levels; they might set a low or a high percentage; and they might be weakly or strongly enforced.

Scholars have identified a range of benefits linked to quotas. They 'raise awareness about the underrepresentation of women in politics', 'send a clear signal that a persistent imbalance is a social problem that exists and must be redressed', and increase public support for more women in politics.[70] Empirical studies show that 'quotas are followed by greater legislative attention to the interests and priorities of women as a group', especially in relation to women's rights, public health, and poverty alleviation. Quotas 'send cues to all officeholders, prompting broad changes in legislator behavior, and by bringing more women into legislatures, they increase women's ability to collectively influence legislative decisions.'[71]

But quotas are not without controversy. Krook points out that both feminist and non-feminist actors might promote quotas for 'distinct and even contradictory reasons', and she cites four concerns held by at least some feminists: 'that quotas further neoliberal projects, demobilize women's movements, result in the election of non-feminist women, promote a static view of "women" as a group, and decrease the effectiveness of women as political actors.'[72]

A different concern centres around the concept of 'autocratic genderwashing' which 'occurs when autocrats take credit for advances in gender equality in order to turn attention away from persistent nondemocratic practices, such as violations of electoral integrity and human rights. In doing so, they exploit the often simplistic association between gender equality and democracy to seek legitimacy and achieve regime stability.'[73] Consistent with this critique, it has been claimed that dictatorships have vigorously enacted gender-related legislation, at a rate that surpasses democracies in the developing world. This enables them to signal adherence to international norms by demonstrating progress on gender equality, while maintaining authoritarian rule. It also ensures access to certain forms of foreign aid and enables avoidance of more politically costly reforms.[74] Rwanda, where women occupied 61 percent of seats in the Chamber of Deputies after 2018, is often cited by way of example.

Another perspective on gender quotas is provided by Ruth Rubio Marín, in 'A New European Parity-Democracy Sex Equality Model and Why It Won't Fly in the United States', 60 *Am. J. Comp. L.* (2012) 99. She contrasts the European model with reluctance in the United States to address such issues directly. One reason is the shadow cast by 'the political underrepresentation or disempowerment of blacks and other minorities.' Another is that 'conservative forces in the United States, often mobilized by Christian religious fundamentalism, have historically succeeded in presenting every instance of affirmation of women's rights and fight for equality as a threat to the family.' In Europe, gender parity has been promoted on instrumental grounds that it is better for society and the economy and as a matter of justice. But a very different approach has prevailed in the United States:

---

[70] J. Fernández and C. Valiente, 'Gender Quotas and Public Demand for Increasing Women's Representation in Politics: An Analysis of 28 European Countries', 13 *Eur. Pol. Sci. Rev.* (2021) 351.

[71] A. Clayton, 'How Do Electoral Gender Quotas Affect Policy?', 24 *Annu. Rev. Political Sci.* (2021) 235.

[72] M. L. Krook, 'Quota Laws for Women in Politics: Implications for Feminist Practice', 15 *Social Politics* (2008) 345, at 360.

[73] E. Bjarnegård and P. Zetterberg, 'How Autocrats Weaponize Women's Rights', 33 *J. of Democracy* (2022) 60.

[74] D. Donno, S. Fox and J. Kaasik, 'International Incentives for Women's Rights in Dictatorships', 55 *Comparative Political Studies* (2022) 451.

Underlying the U.S. rejection of strict and mandatory gender quotas is of course the critical understanding that quotas on the basis of sex violate formal equality and a gender neutral reading of the Equal Protection Clause. … [S]trict quotas are not uncontroversial in Europe either because despite the prevalent substantive equality model and the application of indirect discrimination as a constitutional doctrine, the formal equality principle still exists forcing a proportionality analysis. Such analysis is more likely to succeed with regard to measures that are less invasive than strict quotas and closer to the ideal of ensuring equal opportunities but not equal results. …

The greater resistance towards the enactment of legislative measures to ensure women's access to positions of power in both the political and the economic domains is also related to the stronger U.S. individualist tradition and its faith in both autonomy and meritocracy as expressed through the free functioning of the market and of social forces, including capital and political parties, that constitutional provisions such as First Amendment associational rights of political parties help to protect. In Europe, the social or welfare state tradition with its post-World War II constitutional embedding has less difficulty advancing the notion that political and economic imbalances of powers may require positive corrections by the State to protect the more vulnerable. …

D. Anti-essentialism and Anti-stereotyping

… In Europe, quotas have been defended both by those who believe that women can add a distinctive way of ruling (more collaborative, less competitive or ego driven) and those who sustain that this is ultimately irrelevant because the point is simply treating women as equal citizens. In contrast, in the United States, quotas would most likely be seen as rigid and essentializing, and the affirmation of the difference that women can make is likely to be controversial enough to prevent feminists of different strands from joining forces to support the initiative.

QUESTIONS

1. How do you react to the provisions in both General Recommendations on affirmative action, either by the state or by political parties? As a member of the Committee, which if any of these provisions would you oppose? Is it consistent with Article 25 of the ICCPR, guaranteeing the right to vote? How do you react to paragraph 31 of General Recommendation No. 23?

2. If the United States were to ratify CEDAW would it need to lodge a reservation in relation to Article 7 of the Convention ('States Parties shall take all appropriate measures to eliminate discrimination against women in the political and public life of the country … .')?

3. Is it problematic that CEDAW norms affect states differently, depending on whether the international community can exert pressure through development assistance and other forms of influence?

---

5. Sexual and Reproductive Rights

The sexual and reproductive health rights of women and girls have long been a battleground in society at large, and within the international human rights regime. The U.S. Supreme Court's overruling in 2022 of the constitutional right to abortion, previously recognized in *Roe v. Wade*, further elevated the prominence of the issue. The UN Human Rights Council's Working Group on discrimination against women has observed that these rights 'are systematically neglected, not because of a lack of resources or technical knowledge but because of the widespread disregard for women's dignity, bodily integrity and autonomy. Sexual and reproductive health matters are intrinsic to every woman and girl and tied to their ability to live with dignity and exercise their agency' (UN Doc. A/HRC/47/38 (2021)). According to the group:

> 16. ... An estimated 810 maternal deaths occur each day globally, and 25 million unsafe abortions take place annually, resulting in approximately 47,000 deaths every year, primarily in developing countries and among members of socioeconomically disadvantaged and marginalized populations. Every 16 seconds there is a stillbirth. More than 200 million women who want to avoid pregnancy are not using modern contraception, due to a range of barriers. Millions of women and girls are denied the ability to manage their monthly menstrual cycle safely and with dignity.
>
> ...
>
> 18. ... A woman's right to control her fertility is central to the realization of those rights and to her autonomy and agency. States are obligated to ensure that sexual and reproductive health services are available, accessible, affordable, acceptable and of good quality. The distinct sexual and reproductive health needs of women and girls must be addressed to ensure substantive equality. ...

The most contentious issue in this context is the right to safe and legal abortion. World Health Organization statistics paint a grim picture (WHO, *Preventing Unsafe Abortion*, 25 September 2020). Each year between 2015 and 2019 there were 73 million induced (safe and unsafe) abortions worldwide. This amounted to 39 induced abortions per 1000 women aged between 15 and 49 years. Three out of ten of all pregnancies, and 6 out of 10 of all unintended pregnancies, ended in an induced abortion. Estimates from 2010 to 2014 showed that around 45 percent of all abortions were unsafe.

The CEDAW Convention is silent on contraception and abortion rights, a lacuna that Martha C. Nussbaum, 'Women's Progress and Women's Human Rights', in Bardo Fassbender and Knut Traisbach (eds.), *The Limits of Human Rights* (2020) 231 has described as a notorious defect:

> ... [T]he Roman Catholic Church, together with some conservative religious authorities in other religions, made specific language on these points impossible. Access to reliable contraception is surely of the greatest importance to women's equality. The issue is mentioned in CEDAW, but in an evasive way. In Article 16, subsection (e), women are accorded 'The same rights to decide freely and responsibly on the number and spacing of their children and to have access to the information, education, and means to enable them to exercise those rights.' The same as men, that is. This surely stops well short of guaranteeing access to legal artificial contraception, since a nation could totally ban contraception for both women and men equally without running afoul of this section. Or, more likely, it could decide that what is permissible is education in 'natural' methods of contraception, such as the so- called 'rhythm method', but continue to ban all artificial contraception. It's obvious that conservative religious leaders could be happy with this section.
>
> Abortion rights are simply not mentioned at all ... [and] the subsequent recommendations of the Committee are also quite vague. ...
>
> Was there any purpose of the vague language of Article 16? Would it not have been better to leave this out? The women's movement could reasonably regard this article as a placeholder for their urgent concerns. Had these concerns not been mentioned at all, it would seem that the movement had capitulated to external pressures and agreed simply to remove them from consideration. As it is, the document makes it evident that control over family planning is an important issue for women's full equality. ... In terms of the further development of the international women's movement, it is an important statement: we may have encountered an obstacle, but we are here to stay and are not backing down.

In fact, most human rights treaties steer clear of these issues. When drafting the UDHR, a proposal to state that the right to life begins 'from the moment of conception' was rejected by six votes to two (UN Doc. E/CN.4/AC.1/SR.35 (1948), 6). The phrase was, however, included in the American Convention on Human Rights (Article 4(1)) which states that: [e]very person has the right to have his life respected. This right shall be protected by law and, in general, from the moment of conception. No one shall be arbitrarily deprived of his life.' While a preambular paragraph of the Convention on the Rights of the Child states that 'the child, by reason of his physical and mental immaturity, needs special safeguards and care, including appropriate legal protection, before as well as after birth', most commentators do not consider this to restrict abortion rights.[75]

In interpreting relevant rights, most UN treaty bodies have addressed the issue of abortion. The Committee on Economic, Social and Cultural Rights, in General Comment No. 22 (2016), paragraph 28, states that:

> … Preventing unintended pregnancies and unsafe abortions requires States to adopt legal and policy measures to guarantee all individuals access to affordable, safe and effective contraceptives and comprehensive sexuality education, including for adolescents; to liberalize restrictive abortion laws; to guarantee women and girls access to safe abortion services and quality post-abortion care, including by training health-care providers; and to respect the right of women to make autonomous decisions about their sexual and reproductive health. …

Similarly, in General Comment No. 20 (2016) the Committee on the Rights of the Child in paragraph 60:

> …urges States to decriminalize abortion to ensure that girls have access to safe abortion and post-abortion services, review legislation with a view to guaranteeing the best interests of pregnant adolescents and ensure that their views are always heard and respected in abortion-related decisions.

The most detailed, and nuanced treatment is the Human Rights Committee's General Comment No. 36 (2019):

> 8. Although States parties may adopt measures designed to regulate voluntary terminations of pregnancy, such measures must not result in violation of the right to life of a pregnant woman or girl, or her other rights under the Covenant. Thus, restrictions on the ability of women or girls to seek abortion must not, inter alia, jeopardize their lives, subject them to physical or mental pain or suffering which violates article 7, discriminate against them or arbitrarily interfere with their privacy. States parties must provide safe, legal and effective access to abortion where the life and health of the pregnant woman or girl is at risk, and where carrying a pregnancy to term would cause the pregnant woman or girl substantial pain or suffering, most notably where the pregnancy is the result of rape or incest or is not viable. In addition, States parties may not regulate pregnancy or abortion in all other cases in a manner that runs contrary to their duty to ensure that women and girls do not have to undertake unsafe abortions, and they should revise their abortion laws accordingly. For example, they should not take measures such as criminalizing pregnancies by unmarried women or apply criminal sanctions against women and girls undergoing abortion or against medical service providers assisting them in doing so, since taking such measures compel women and girls to resort to unsafe abortion. States parties should not introduce new barriers and should remove existing barriers that deny effective access by women and girls to safe and legal abortion, including barriers caused as a result of the exercise of conscientious objection by individual medical providers. States parties should also effectively protect the lives of women and girls against the mental and physical health risks associated with unsafe abortions. In particular, they should ensure access for women and men, and, especially, girls and boys, to quality and evidence-based information and education about sexual and reproductive health and to a wide range of affordable contraceptive methods, and prevent the stigmatization of women and girls seeking abortion. States parties should ensure the

---

[75] D. Archard and J. Tobin, 'Art.1 The Definition of a Child', in J. Tobin (ed.), *The UN Convention on the Rights of the Child: A Commentary* (2019) 24.

availability of, and effective access to, quality prenatal and post-abortion health care for women and girls, in all circumstances, and on a confidential basis.

In 2018, an on-site 'inquiry' by the CEDAW Committee, pursuant to Article 8 of the Optional Protocol, examined the situation relating to abortion in Northern Ireland (UN Doc. CEDAW/C/OP.8/GBR/1). It concluded that:

> 83. The Committee finds that the State party is responsible for:
>
> (a) Grave violations of rights under the Convention considering that the State party's criminal law compels women in cases of severe foetal impairment, including FFA, and victims of rape or incest to carry pregnancies to full term, thereby subjecting them to severe physical and mental anguish, constituting gender-based violence against women; and
>
> (b) Systematic violations of rights under the Convention considering that the State party deliberately criminalises abortion and pursues a highly restrictive policy on accessing abortion, thereby compelling women to: (i) carry pregnancies to full term; (ii) travel outside NI to undergo legal abortion; or (iii) self-administer abortifacients.

The United Kingdom Government subsequently adopted the *Abortion (Northern Ireland) (No. 2) Regulations 2020,* which permit abortions up to 12 weeks, and beyond 12 weeks under certain circumstances.

In recent years, abortion law reform has led to decriminalization and safe access in countries such as Chile, Colombia, Gabon, Gambia, India, Ireland and South Korea. But the U.S. Supreme Court's decision in *Dobbs v. Jackson Women's Health Organization*, 597 U.S. 215 (2022) to end the constitutional right to abortion that had been recognized since 1973, and to entrust the respective states to decide on appropriate regulation, has generated even greater contention around the issue.

One of the countries with the strictest laws against abortion is El Salvador, in which it is 'illegal under all circumstances. Women face two to eight years in prison for having an abortion. Providers face prison sentences of 6 months to 12 years.' Women 'who suffered miscarriages or obstetric emergencies, have been sentenced to up to 40 years in prison' (*Human Rights Watch World Report 2022*). One such case began with a complaint to the Inter-American Commission on Human rights, which in turn referred it to the Inter-American Court.

MANUELA ET AL. V. EL SALVADOR
INTER-AMERICAN COURT OF HUMAN RIGHTS, JUDGMENT, 2 NOVEMBER 2021

…

VII - Facts

A. Factual framework

35. In 1998, a new Criminal Code …eliminated the grounds for non-punishable abortion, and also the classification as mitigated homicide for cases in which a "mother kills her child during the delivery or within the following seventy- two hours."

…

37. [In 1999, the Constitution was amended to recognize as a human person] "every human being from the moment of conception."

38. … Article 37 [of the Health Code provides that] [p]rofessional secrecy is an obligation derived from the very essence of the profession. …

…

40. [But the Criminal Code provides that physicians and other health professionals are obliged to report if they] "become aware […] [of actionable offenses] while providing the care required by their profession … ". …

B. Factual context

41. In its Merits Report, the Commission included information on the criminalization of abortion in El Salvador and the alleged effect that this has had in cases of obstetric emergencies and infanticide. Even though the criminal laws on abortion were not applied in this case, the Court notes that this information relates to the alleged criminalization of women who have suffered obstetric emergencies in El Salvador. ...

42. [The Court takes note of the relevant jurisprudence of the Human Rights Committee, the Committee on Economic, Social and Cultural Rights, and the CEDAW Committee.]
...
45. ... A report ... revealed that, between 1998 and 2003, 80% of obstetric gynecologists in El Salvador believed that reporting obstetric emergencies was compulsory in all cases.

46. Lastly, the Court notes that most of the women prosecuted for such facts had few if any financial resources, came from rural or marginalized urban areas and had little schooling. In addition, many of them were detained and handcuffed while receiving medical care.

C. Manuela and her family unit

47. [Manuela was born in 1977, married in 1997, and had two children. Her husband left her and she lived with her family.] Neither Manuela nor her parents knew how to read or write.

48. On August 24, 2006, Manuela went to the Cacaopera Health Unit because she was suffering from a headache, nausea, pain in the pit of her stomach and tiredness. She was diagnosed with acute gastritis. On May 14, 2007, Manuela visited the unit again due to headaches and it was recorded that she had what "appeared to be a painful lump behind her ear"; she was diagnosed with cervical adenitis and was prescribed analgesics. Manuela then developed several lumps in her neck, which were visible and caused her pain; therefore, she had further appointments in June and August 2007 and was then diagnosed with right neck lymphadenopathy and referred to the San Francisco Gotera National Hospital. The case file does not reveal whether the presumed victim went to that hospital or whether she received treatment there.

D. Manuela's pregnancy

...
50.   On February 26, 2008, Manuela [who was pregnant] was washing clothes in the river with her elder son, when she fell heavily and injured her pelvic area. ...

E. The medical treatment of the obstetric emergency

52.   On February 27, 2008, at 3:25 p.m., Manuela was admitted to [hospital]. ... [T]he preoperative diagnosis was "delivery outside the hospital, retained placenta and perineal tear."

53. [The hospital record stated] that she was admitted due to abortion. [It quoted] Manuela indicating: "I don't know if it fell to the floor or if the umbilical cord broke, or if my mother cut it. My sister says that my mother cut the cord and buried the baby; my sister told me that the baby was born dead." ... [S]he was advised that the prosecution service would be notified.
...
56. The report does not mention the lumps on Manuela's neck [which had been misdiagnosed during treatment in 2006 and 2007].

F. The criminal prosecution of Manuela

57. On February 27, 2008, the physician ... filed a complaint against Manuela with the ... Prosecution Service ..., and this initiated the criminal proceedings ... .

58. [The physician told the police that the [information provided by the patient did not match the clinical picture … …..

59. … [At 9 a.m., a forensic physician reported:]

Umbilical cord […] with a clean cut, not ruptured. Based on the foregoing, the patient gave birth outside a hospital, if not full-term at least very nearly … .

60. [On the same date, Manuela's house was searched based on a warrant and the body of a 'full-term newborn' was found inside a septic tank.]
…

62. The case file also includes a statement by Manuela's father, in which he indicated that he "felt ashamed because [his daughter's] husband is […] in the United States, but […] his daughter told him that she got pregnant from another man" and that "he was sorry for his daughter, but this would never have made her get rid of the child." This statement bears a fingerprint because the presumed victim's father does not know how to read or write.

63. Subsequently, Manuela's father indicated that the police "put pressure on him and made him sign a piece of paper" and "threatened him until placed his fingerprint." …

G. The presumed victim's detention and subsequent investigation procedures

64. [Hospital records show that Manuela was arrested in hospital on February 28, 2008, and] detained in flagrante delicto "for the crime of the murder of her newborn son …'. The record indicates that Manuela refused to sign it….
…

68. On February 29, 2008, the Prosecutor General issued an order requiring a formal investigation with the provisional detention of Manuela for the crime of the aggravated homicide of a newborn. He indicated that the detention was necessary "to ensure that this case does not remain unpunished and that the normal outcome of the proceedings is not frustrated …". …
…

[After various hearings, on August 11, 2008 Manuela was sentenced to 30 years' imprisonment for the crime of aggravated homicide. No appeal was filed. In February 2009 she was diagnosed with Hodgkin's lymphoma, and she died in hospital on April 30, 2010.]

VIII - Merits

91. In the instant case, there is no dispute regarding the facts that Manuela was pregnant, gave birth and suffered from preeclampsia [which constitutes] an obstetric emergency.

92. What is in dispute is the State's alleged responsibility for the detention, prosecution and conviction of the presumed victim for aggravated homicide following the obstetric emergency that she suffered, and also for the medical care that the presumed victim received, and the alleged violation of professional secrecy by the medical staff who attended her. Bearing in mind that this case does not refer to the occurrence of a therapeutic abortion, the context established above will only be taken into account to the extent that it relates to the purpose of the dispute.
…

VIII-1 - Rights to personal liberty and presumption of innocence …

A. Arguments of the parties and the Commission
….

95. The representatives argued that "Manuela's detention was unlawful and arbitrary because: (a) she was detained by application of a presumption of in flagrante delicto which is contrary to the object and purpose of

the treaty; (b) she was not informed of the reasons for her detention and the charges against her; (c) her pretrial detention was ordered based on a legal presumption of guilt; (d) her criminal trial was conducted in contravention of judicial guarantees and judicial protection, and (e) the laws applied were contrary to the principle of the legality of criminal proceedings." They emphasized that the pretrial detention ordered against the presumed victim was based on the court's presumption of guilt and also argued that the presumed victim had no remedy to contest the imposition of pretrial detention.

96. The State pointed out that the initial detention was in keeping with the Code of Criminal Procedure. ...

B. Considerations of the Court

...
112. Taking into account that the order of pretrial detention against the presumed victim was arbitrary because it did not contain a reasoned and objective legal justification for its admissibility, and also its duration of more than five months without its pertinence having been duly reviewed by the judicial authorities, the Court declares that El Salvador violated Manuela's right to the presumption of innocence established in Article 8(2) of the American Convention ... .

VIII-2 - Rights to judicial guarantees, personal integrity and equality ...

A. Arguments of the parties and the Commission

...
115. The representatives argued that the criminal trial was conducted in violation of judicial guarantees and judicial protection because: (i) the minimum conditions for the rigorous determination of Manuela's criminal responsibility were not provided; (ii) Manuela gave a statement before she was notified of the charges brought against her; (iii) she did not have a suitable State-appointed defense counsel, in violation of the right to adequate time to prepare her defense, to communicate freely and privately with her legal counsel, and to have a public defender; iv) there was no effective remedy available to appeal the first instance judgment, and (v) Manuela was never heard at her trial, ... because she was prevented from doing so by the public defender on call that she had for the hearings.
...

B. Considerations of the Court

...
119.   In this case, a series of violations of judicial guarantees has been alleged. The Court only has sufficient evidence to examine: (1) the right to defense; (2) the use of gender stereotypes and judicial guarantees, and (3) the sentence imposed on Manuela.

B.1 The right to defense

...
130.   The Court considers that ... the actions of the public defender harmed Manuela's rights and interests, leaving her defenseless, which constituted a violation of the essential right to be assisted by legal counsel. [Her] substantive right to defense was also violated because she was prevented from defending her interests. ... .

B.2 The use of gender stereotypes and judicial guarantees

131. Article 8(1) of the Convention establishes that every person has the right to be tried by an impartial court.
...

B.2.a The investigations

146. ... [T]he Court considers that Manuela's guilt was presumed from the very start of the investigation. Moreover, little effort was made to determine the truth of what happened and to take into account the probative elements that could have disproved the thesis of the presumed victim's guilt. This attitude was also encouraged by the investigators' prejudices against women who do not comply with the role of self-sacrificing mothers who must always seek to protect their children. The prejudices and negative gender stereotyping affected the

objectivity of the agents in charge of the investigations, closing possible lines of investigation into the actual circumstances. The Court also notes [the failure to investigate] the possibility that the mother is not responsible for causing the death of which she is accused.

B.2.b The reasoning behind the guilty verdict

147. … [This court's] purpose is not to determine Manuela's innocence or guilt, but rather to decide whether the judicial authorities violated obligations established in the Convention; particularly, the obligation to provide the reasons for a decision, the principle of presumption of innocence, and the right to be tried by an impartial court.
…
155. … [T]his Court notes that the reasoning provided by the Trial Court demonstrates that gender stereotypes were used to supplement the court's lack of sufficient evidence. Thus, the judgment convicting Manuela suffers from all the prejudices inherent in a patriarchal system and downplays the factual circumstances and motivations. It reprimands Manuela as if she had violated duties considered inherent in her gender and indirectly criticizes her sexual conduct. It minimizes and disregards that a possible reason for the desire to conceal her supposed error was to evade the disapproval of an environment created by traditional androcentric values. Consequently, it constituted a violation of the right to presumption of innocence, the right to be tried by an impartial court, and the obligation to state the reasons for judicial decisions.
…
159. … The application of those stereotypes was only possible because Manuela was a woman; and the impact was exacerbated because she was poor and illiterate and lived in a rural area. Therefore, the Court considers that the distinction made in the application of the criminal law was arbitrary and, consequently, discriminatory.
…

B.4 Conclusion

173. Based on all the above considerations, the Court concludes that the investigation and trial to which the presumed victim was subjected did not comply with the right to defense, the right to be tried by an impartial court, the presumption of innocence, the duty to provide the reasons for a decision, the obligation not to apply laws in a discriminatory manner, the right not to be subjected to cruel, inhuman or degrading punishment and the obligation to ensure that the purpose of punishments consisting in deprivation of liberty is the reform and social readaptation of prisoners. Consequently, the State violated Articles 8(1), 8(2), 8(2)(d), 8(2)(e), 24, 5(2) and 5(6) of the Convention, in relation to Articles 1(1) and 2 of this instrument, to the detriment of Manuela.
…

[Reparations]

[The Court, in paragraph 327, required the State to, inter alia: publicly acknowledge international responsibility; grant scholarships to Manuela's sons; provide medical, psychological and/or psychiatric treatment to Manuela's parents; regulate the obligation of medical professional secrecy and the confidentiality of medical records; elaborate an action protocol for the treatment of women who require emergency medical attention for obstetric emergencies; adapt its regulations on pretrial detention; implement an awareness-raising and training course for judicial officials, as well as the health personnel of the Rosales National Hospital; adapt its regulation concerning the dosimetry of the sentence for infanticide; implement an education program on sexuality and reproduction; ensure comprehensive care in cases of obstetric emergencies; pay compensation for pecuniary and non-pecuniary damage and reimburse costs and expenses; and, within one year of the judgment, report back to the Court on measures taken to comply with it.]

* * *

In a comparable case, *Camila v. Peru*, the UN Committee on the Rights of the Child (Communication No. 136/2021 of 13 June 2023) considered the case of a 13-year-old Peruvian indigenous victim of rape and incest starting at the age of nine. Her request for access to legal therapeutic abortion was ignored. Following a spontaneous abortion, she was prosecuted and convicted for self-abortion, although later acquitted on appeal:

> 8.15. … The Committee notes that the author, an Indigenous girl living in a rural area
> who was the victim of rape, was repeatedly revictimized in both police and health-care
> contexts when her request for an abortion was repeatedly ignored and her privacy was

invaded at both her home and her school, resulting in the harassment of the author by her family and community. Lastly, the Committee considers that the author's lack of access to safe abortion and her subsequent prosecution for self-abortion constituted in themselves differential treatment based on the author's gender, as she was denied access to a service that was essential for her health and was punished for not complying with gender-based stereotypes relating to her reproductive role. In the light of the foregoing, the Committee concludes that the facts before it disclose discrimination against the author on the basis of age, gender, ethnic origin and social status, in violation of article 2 of the Convention.

Conscientious Objection to Abortion

In situations in which women are legally entitled to obtain an abortion, some states recognize that a health care worker, or perhaps an institution, can refuse to provide relevant services on the grounds of conscience or religious belief. In *R. R. v. Poland* (App. No. 2761/04 (2011)) the European Court of Human Rights observed that, in such situations '[s]tates are obliged to organize the health services system in such a way as to ensure that an effective exercise of the freedom of conscience of health professionals in the professional context does not prevent patients from obtaining access to services to which they are entitled under the applicable legislation' (paragraph 206).

But especially in predominantly Catholic countries, such as Argentina, Ireland, Italy, and Mexico, the legalization of abortion has been accompanied by widespread invocation of conscientious objections by medical personnel, thereby making it extremely difficult to actually obtain an abortion in practice.[76] The Colombian Constitutional Court addressed this issue, among others, in an important 2022 judgment.

SENTENCE C-055/22
CONSTITUTIONAL COURT OF COLOMBIA (21 FEBRUARY 2022)
[UNOFFICIAL, ELECTRONIC, TRANSLATION]

The Full Chamber of the Constitutional Court ... decides on the complaint filed by the citizens of the reference in exercise of the public action of unconstitutionality ... against Article 122 of Law 599 of 2000 (Criminal Code), the text of which is as follows:

...

> "Article 122. Abortion. A woman who causes her own abortion or allows another to cause it shall be sentenced to [16 to 54] months' imprisonment.
>
> The same penalty shall apply to anyone who, with the woman's consent, engages in the conduct referred to in the preceding subparagraph.
>
> *This article was declared conditionally constitutional by the Constitutional Court in Ruling C-355 of May 10, 2006, "on the understanding that the crime of abortion is not committed when, with the woman's consent, the pregnancy is terminated in the following cases: (i) When the continuation of the pregnancy constitutes danger to the life or health of the woman, certified by a physician; (ii) When there is serious malformation of the fetus that makes its life unviable, certified by a physician; and, (iii) When the pregnancy is the result of conduct, duly reported, constituting carnal access or sexual act without consent, abusive or non-consensual artificial insemination or transfer of fertilized egg, or incest."*

II. The Claim

---

[76] 'In Argentina and Mexico, abortion is not a crime. But many women struggle to access the procedure', *New York Times* (21 February 2022).

1. The plaintiffs seek a declaration of the total unenforceability of the impugned provision. In their view, it violates [16 different provisions] of the Political Constitution [and various provisions of the UDHR and the American Convention on Human Rights].

[Because the Court had already ruled on related issues, the doctrine of *res judicata* meant that it was necessary to show that this challenge was materially different.]
...

247. [A substantive pronouncement in the present case is warranted because of several changes in the normative context relevant to Article 122].

248. First, the issuance of the 2015 Statutory Health Law. In [relation to] the Criminal Code, health is presented as an autonomous and inalienable fundamental right, individually and collectively, while in the review developed in Ruling C-355 of 2006 health was considered as a "fundamental right by connection with life".
...

250. The autonomous justifiability of the right to health requires that the institutions, rules, procedures, participants and actors in the system focus on the dignity of individuals as the cornerstone ... . [T]he challenged provision has been introduced in a new regulatory context of health insurance ... .

251. Second, subsequent to Judgment C-355 of 2006, multiple international organizations, including the [Committee on Economic, Social and Cultural Rights], the Special Rapporteur on the right to health, and the CEDAW Committee, have raised the need to decriminalize abortion as a measure in favor of the sexual and reproductive health and rights of this population, as well as a way to act against violence against women. ... [T]here are international documents of varying normative value that have advocated for the decriminalization of abortion beyond the three grounds defined in Ruling C-355 of 2006 and, therefore, have an impact on a new constitutional understanding of the phenomenon.

252. Third, criminal policy has seen a reassessment of the meaning of proportionality and the purposes of punishment.
...

11.... [T]he freedom of conscience of women, girls and pregnant women ...
...

11.2. Constitutional characterization of freedom of conscience

376. ... [T]he concept of conscience [enshrined in Article 18 of the Constitution] ... refers to the power of each person to discern between what is morally right or wrong ..., without any of such determinations being encouraged or subject to disproportionate intervention by the State or third parties. ...

379. This freedom protects three fundamental guarantees: first, the right to keep one's convictions secret ... . Secondly, once the thoughts are expressed or communicated, the guarantee extends to not being pressured or disturbed by the manifestation of such convictions. Finally, it protects the prerogative of not being forced to act against one's intimate personal convictions ... .
...

385. ... [C]onscientious objection ... can be based on religious, moral, ethical, humanitarian or similar grounds. However, it is possible for the legislator to establish restrictions to this right, as long as they are reasonable and proportionate ... . [T]he general principle is that, given the silence of the Legislator in relation to the characteristics of beliefs, any profound conviction that opposes the legal good guaranteed by the norm that establishes a legal duty to act or refrain from acting, can be adduced to excuse oneself from its fulfillment. Conscientious objection, however, cannot be invoked by judicial authorities and notaries in the performance of public functions or, in some cases, by physicians in cases of voluntary termination of pregnancy, among other events.
...

394. The decision to assume motherhood, therefore, is (i) highly personal, because it has an impact on the life project of the woman, girl, adolescent or pregnant person who decides to continue and carry a pregnancy to

term ...; (ii) individual, due to the physical and emotional impact that the development of the pregnancy has on her life experience and her own existence; and (iii) non-transferable, because the autonomy of the decision to assume motherhood cannot be transferred to a third party, except in exceptional cases ... . [T]his is a decision that cannot be appropriated by the State or other individuals ... .

...

VII. Summary of the Decision

...

650. The Court found that there was a tension of constitutional relevance between, on the one hand, the protection of life in gestation ... and, on the other hand, the rights to health and reproductive rights; the equality of women in vulnerable situations and in irregular migratory situations; freedom of conscience; and the constitutional purpose of general prevention of punishment ... .

651. ... [T]his constitutional tension cannot be resolved by giving preference to one of the guarantees in tension, since this would entail the absolute sacrifice of the others. For this reason, it considered it necessary to adopt a formula that recognizes the constitutional relevance of each of these guarantees, in such a way that, as opposed to subtracting protection from them -because of the result that would follow from giving preference to one of them- a greater realization of all the rights, principles, and values in conflict is achieved.

652. The Court resolved this tension ... by identifying an optimal point in the term of gestation that, in the abstract, avoids the wide margins of lack of protection for the dignity and rights of women ... and, at the same time, protects as much as possible the life in gestation, based on three elements:

653. The first is constituted by the three "extreme hypotheses of affectation of [the] dignity" of women, as evidenced by the Court in Judgment C-355 of 2006.

654. The second, constituted by the concept of "autonomy," which allows for the abstract maximization of the goods in tension, since it refers to the moment in which it is possible to demonstrate that the dependence of the life in formation on the pregnant person is broken, which justifies its reinforced protection by criminal law in the current normative context. In effect, to totally decriminalize abortion with consent, without the existence of alternative measures for the protection of life in gestation, would place the Colombian State in a situation of non-compliance with its constitutional and international obligation to adopt measures for this purpose. ...

655. The third, promotes a dialogue in the bodies of democratic representation, so that ... they formulate and implement a comprehensive public policy that avoids the wide margins of lack of protection for the dignity and rights of pregnant women, ... [and] gradually and incrementally protects life in gestation, without intensely affecting such guarantees.

...

VIII. Decision
[The Court]
RESOLVES
FIRST: [In applying Article 122 of the Penal Code, abortion] shall only be punishable when it is performed after the twenty-fourth (24) week of gestation and, in any case, this time limit shall not apply to the three cases in which Ruling C-355 of 2006 established that abortion is not a crime ... .

SECOND. TO EXHORT the Congress of the Republic and the national government, without prejudice to the immediate compliance with this judgment, to formulate and implement, as soon as possible, a comprehensive public policy ... . This policy must contain, at a minimum, (i) clear disclosure of the options available to pregnant women during and after pregnancy, (ii) the elimination of any obstacle to the exercise of the sexual and reproductive rights recognized in this decision, (iii) the existence of instruments for the prevention of pregnancy and planning, (iv) the development of education programs on sexual and reproductive education for all persons, (v) support measures for pregnant mothers that include adoption options, among others, and (vi) measures that guarantee the rights of those born in the circumstances of pregnant women who wish to have an abortion.

...

Responses

Responses to the Court's ruling have varied. One anti-abortion group expressed satisfaction that the court: did not characterize abortion as a fundamental right; did not obligate 'the health system to perform abortions'; and did recognize 'the need to protect the right to life of the unborn legally'.[77] On the other hand, a pro-choice group argued that the court 'should have considered complete decriminalization, with regulations on abortion approached as health care' and characterized the fact that abortion beyond 24 weeks could still be punished 'as a symbolic and patriarchal punishment of the reproductive autonomy of women.'[78]

Douglas NeJaime and Reva Siegel, in 'Conscience Wars in the Americas', 5 *Lat. Am. L. Rev.* (2020) 1, note that in paradigmatic cases, religious accommodation has been recognized to individuals 'from a minority faith to engage in ritual observance or religiously-motivated dress or grooming that runs afoul of generally applicable laws'. But, in recent years, religious conscience claims have increasingly been invoked in 'culture wars', especially in relation to issues of sexuality such as LGBTQI+ rights, or reproductive rights. In the case of abortion, conservative religious groups argue first for comprehensive criminalization and, when that fails, seek to invoke a wide-ranging right to conscientious objection on the part not just of physicians but of all healthcare workers.

The authors note that the latter claims differ from the paradigmatic cases, such as Sikh men being permitted to wear turbans or Jewish men to wear the yarmulke when others may not cover their heads, in that culture war conscience claims are asserted to defend majority rather than minority norms and may inflict significant harms on other citizens. In line with the approach reflected in the work of several UN treaty bodies, in order for a legal system to avoid aligning itself with the belief system of the objector and against the rights to which the objector objects, a system that seeks to accommodate objections should also apply principled limits, including:

1. **Protecting Patients**
   Laws can endeavour to protect conscience while providing for the patient's welfare by, first and foremost, prioritizing the health and safety of the individual seeking services. Accommodation regimes can be designed in ways that require institutions to anticipate problems and ensure patient access. Some laws require objectors to identify themselves to their employers or to the government in advance. The government or employer must ensure that willing providers are available and that the patient does not endure a stigmatizing encounter with an objecting provider.

2. **Limiting Accommodation of Complicity Objections**
   Laws can also differentiate between those directly involved in the objected-to service and those who object on the basis of indirect involvement. … Complicity claims can be constrained by limiting the range of actors who can claim conscience exemptions, as well as the range of acts subject to conscience exemptions.

3. **Ensuring Alternative Access**
   Legal systems may be able to afford affected individuals with an alternate source of goods and services by requiring objectors to provide information and refer patients to willing providers. …

4. **Limiting Conscientious Objection to Individuals**
   Institutions, including hospitals and other religiously affiliated organizations, assert rights of conscientious objection—raising conceptual questions given that … conscientious objection is premised on an individual ethical imperative.

This institutional dimension assumes particular importance in an era of widespread privatization. Elizabeth Sepper and James Nelson, in 'Government's Religious Hospitals', 109 *Va. L. Rev* (2023) 61 note that under the U.S. Constitution, 'States are not supposed to own or operate religious institutions, but they now do' as a result of the merging of the public and the private, which results in 'public' hospitals being treated for certain purposes as private religious institutions. These 'government religious hospitals' threaten religious freedom and equal citizenship. For example, 'State Medicaid contracts go to religiously affiliated insurers that refuse to cover

---

[77] R. Gómez, 'The Reality of Abortion in Colombia up to 24 Weeks', *Americans United for Life* (August 25, 2022).
[78] Center for Reproductive Rights, Colombia: Historic Advancement in the Decriminalization of Abortion (2022), at 5.

reproductive healthcare for the many women of childbearing age covered by the public program.' In other sectors as well, 'faith-based organizations are sole providers of emergency shelter for unhoused people, a service funded by and often explicitly the duty of local governments. … Legislatures delegate public functions – ranging from policing to child welfare – to religious entities.' They conclude that litigation will not resolve the problems and that 'creative solutions—from fostering competition to developing public options—will be required …'.

In October 2022, the World Medical Association revised the provisions relating to conscientious objection in the International Code of Medical Ethics:

> 29. This Code represents the physician's ethical duties. However, on some issues there are profound moral dilemmas concerning which physicians and patients may hold deeply considered but conflicting conscientious beliefs.
>
> The physician has an ethical obligation to minimise disruption to patient care. Physician conscientious objection to provision of any lawful medical interventions may only be exercised if the individual patient is not harmed or discriminated against and if the patient's health is not endangered.
>
> The physician must immediately and respectfully inform the patient of this objection and of the patient's right to consult another qualified physician and provide sufficient information to enable the patient to initiate such a consultation in a timely manner.

Given the backlash against women's reproductive rights in the United States, what role should be played by international law in domestic debates? Frédéric Mégret, in 'Overturning of *Roe v Wade*: Time to Rethink US Engagement With International Human Rights Law?', *Int'l J. Const. L. Blog* (8 July 2022) argues that, in the aftermath of *Dobbs v. Jackson Women's Health Organization*,[79] U.S. lawyers should use international law because it provides 'a sophisticated framework to understand what might be wrong with outright bans and thus a clear opening for some access to abortion.' He argues that 'the international system is a pluralistic one marked by national and regional differences of appreciation about the scope of certain rights that does not mandate a single, one-size fits all approach, all the more so on an internationally divided issue such as abortion.'

Mégret suggests three reasons justifying the use of international law-based arguments in the domestic context. First, 'international human rights law provides a particularly pared down version of the argument about abortion, unencumbered by domestic idiosyncrasies. Precisely because it is universal and not implicated in the local constitution of the political, it acts as a kind of abstract dramatization of the human stakes'. Second, 'internationalizing the debate is sometimes simply the only option when a system has become stubbornly rigged against the rights of some. A fragile democracy facing major backsliding of key rights and whose judiciary shows significant problems of bias, the US is in some ways an excellent test case of the supra-constitutional utility of international human rights. Its situation highlights the importance of anchoring human rights commitments to international obligations as a guarantee against rollback.' And third, it 'expresses the global dimensions of the abortion issue. If nothing else, US dynamics stand to have an outsize impact on other countries' abortion debates, as they have had quite perniciously for example through the global "gag rule"', that has in the past prohibited US aid to any international family planning groups that are even indirectly involved with clinics providing or promoting abortion.'

In November 2023, the UN Human Rights Committee's 'concluding observations' on the United States expressed alarm at post-*Dobbs* developments including 'the criminalization of various actors linked to their role in providing or seeking abortion care, including health care providers, persons who assist women to procure an abortion, notably family members, and the pregnant women seeking an abortion' as well as 'restrictions to inter-state travel, bans on medication abortion, and surveillance of women seeking abortion care through their digital data for prosecution purposes' (UN Doc. CCPR/C/USA/CO/5 (2023) para. 28).

---

[79] See generally D.S. Cohen, G. Donley and R. Rebouché, 'The New Abortion Battleground', 123 *Colum. L. Rev.* (2023) 1.

QUESTIONS

1. How would you describe the current state of international law in relation to a 'right to abortion'?

2. What criteria would you use to evaluate the different impacts that CEDAW has had at the national and international levels?

---

6. Reservations: CEDAW and Other Treaties

The CEDAW treaty has been ratified with more reservations than any other human rights treaty. In the materials that follow we look at: (1) the general practice of the United States in relation to treaty ratification; (2) reservations to CEDAW, and United States policy in that regard; and (3) questions of international law relating to the effect of treaty reservations.

a. U.S. Treaty Ratification and Reservations

In comparison with other democratic states, and even with many one-party and authoritarian states that are persistent violators of human rights, the United States has a low record of ratification of human rights treaties. In theory, that comparison could be interpreted in two very different ways. One would be to say that the United States has a lesser commitment to and concern for international human rights standards than do many (say, European and Commonwealth) states of a roughly similar political and economic character. As the world's leading power, its lesser commitment necessarily weakens the human rights normative regime. The other would be to argue that the United States does not engage in the hypocrisy of many states in ratifying and then ignoring treaties. If it ratifies, it means to comply, and hence will take a careful look to be certain that full compliance is possible.

But neither of these 'pure' explanations captures the complexity of the arguments within the Executive Branch and the Senate about ratification of these treaties. Consider a very different account.

CHRISTOPHER N. J. ROBERTS, THE CONTENTIOUS HISTORY OF THE INTERNATIONAL BILL OF HUMAN RIGHTS
(2014) 225

After World War II, the structures that protected America's post–Civil War racial and social hierarchies were in danger of crumbling. The federal government expanded dramatically and the United States plunged itself into international affairs. Yet there were those that wished to preserve the social status quo. Amidst a changing world, proponents of a "traditional" social order were forced to reinvent the arguments about limited government, states' rights, and isolationism that they had used in the past. During battles over human rights, those that opposed the new social order implied by human rights renewed the rights and duties of the several states vis-à-vis the federal government; they updated the obligations and privileges of US sovereignty in the face of a new communist enemy; they defended the prerogatives of racial supremacy amidst "forced integration from abroad"; and they reasserted the rights and duties associated with a free market.

… Between 1951 and 1953 there were at least four Senate resolutions for constitutional amendments restricting the president's treaty-making powers, motivated by those who, for various reasons, sought to maintain the existing constellation of social relationships. By January of 1953, Senator John Bricker of Ohio – the leader of this movement – announced that he had garnered enough support among his colleagues for one such proposed amendment to pass. A February 1953 State Department memo dryly summed up the situation:

> The Covenants are under attack by large and important groups in this country such as the
> American Bar Association and a number of members of the U.S. Senate. For the

administration to press ahead with the Covenants would tend to keep alive and strengthen support for the Bricker amendments to the Constitution.

... [T]he State Department outlined ... [three] options. ... First, the United States could just end its support for the Covenants altogether. This might quell the rising tide of domestic opposition and quiet the push for a constitutional amendment ... . Second, the United States could focus only on the [ICCPR], ignore the [ICESCR], and work on shaping the former in the image of the US Bill of Rights. To a certain extent, ... [this] had always been a part of the US strategy – this angle of attack though, probably would not placate Bricker and company. The initial option would be to stall the creation of the Covenants indefinitely by employing delay tactics.

In the spring of 1953, Eisenhower chose to quit the Covenants: the United States would not attempt to ratify the Covenants, but it would continue to take part in their drafting. ...

...

... During the drafting of the International Bill of Human Rights, Great Britain and the United States were often forced to act on two conflicting imperatives: the first was to support certain human rights in the international sphere for the sake of geopolitical interests and friendly relations between states. But the very human rights principles that fostered international unity, also threatened their domestic spheres with monumental upheaval. As a result, the second imperative was to prevent human rights from redefining the human relationships in specific areas of society. From these imperatives came lasting solutions that were integrated into the very foundation of the modern international system of human rights.

Both the United States and Great Britain responded to the dual imperative to simultaneously confirm and contest human rights through a campaign to develop a human rights framework that could flip back and forth between alternate, conflicting modes of social organization. If "successful," this had the power to not only neutralize the prerogatives of the human rights instrument, but also, through various legal mechanisms, to allow entirely contrary practices to flourish amidst a state's apparent support for a human rights treaty.

Such successes are evident in the Reservations, Understandings, and Declarations (RUDs) that accompanied the international treaties. RUDs are legal footnotes that can limit, alter, or negate entire portions of the treaty's text with respect to a particular signatory. From a social reading, they also identify where the boundaries of the lost struggles exist.

...

... [T]he United States incorporated a series of RUDs to go along with its ratification of the ICCPR. One such reservation is [the federal-state clause]. ...

...

... [This] represents a framework in which a social relationship defined by racial inequality could flourish while others social relationships – for example, those embodying racial equality – would falter. The intensity of debate over the colonial clause and the federal-state clause reveal the social battles that were fought through legal proxy. The now-accepted division between socioeconomic rights, on the one hand, and civil and political rights on the other is not in any way natural and inevitable. ... [I]t is the product of a series of struggles over how to organize global and domestic relations.

* * *

In the years that followed, the United States did ratify a few human rights treaties, including the Slavery Convention, the Protocol Relating to the Status of Refugees, the Convention on the Political Rights of Women and the four Geneva Conventions on the laws of war. But it was not until the Carter Administration in the late 1970s that a President sought the Senate's consent for ratification of a number of major treaties (including the two Covenants).

The United States became a party to the Genocide Convention in 1988 (with one of its reservations stating that 'nothing in the Convention requires or authorizes legislation or other action by the United States of America prohibited by the Constitution of the United States as interpreted by the United States.'), the ICCPR in 1992, the Convention against Torture in 1994 (with detailed and controversial reservations), and the International Convention on the Elimination of All Forms of Racial Discrimination (CERD), also in 1994. But there has never been sustained debate in the Senate or broader political debate in the country about participation in other major and widely ratified treaties, including CEDAW, the American Convention on Human Rights, ICESCR, the Convention on the Rights of the Child (CRC), or the Convention on the Rights of Persons with Disabilities (CRPD).

THE ICCPR

In 1978, the Carter Administration proposed a list of reservations, understandings and declarations (RUDs) when it submitted four human rights treaties to the Senate. The treaties were the ICCPR, ICESCR, CERD and the American Convention on Human Rights. The Senate approved none of them. In 1991, the Bush Administration revived the ICCPR alone among the four treaties, noting that '[s]ubject to a few essential reservations and understandings, [the Covenant] is entirely consonant with the fundamental principles incorporated in our own Bill of Rights. U.S. ratification would also strengthen our ability to influence the development of appropriate human rights principles in the international community'. In its submission to the Senate Foreign Relations Committee it explained its reasons for proposing several of the RUDs. The treaty was subsequently ratified on the basis of these caveats.

PROPOSALS BY BUSH ADMINISTRATION OF RESERVATIONS TO INTERNATIONAL COVENANT ON CIVIL AND POLITICAL RIGHTS
REP. OF S. COMM. FOR. REL. TO ACCOMPANY EXEC. E, 95–2 (1992) [10]

General Comments

In general, the substantive provisions of the Covenant are consistent with the letter and spirit of the United States Constitution and laws, both state and federal ... .

In a few instances, however, it is necessary to subject U.S. ratification to reservations, understandings or declarations in order to ensure that the United States can fulfill its obligations under the Covenant in a manner consistent with the United States Constitution, including instances where the Constitution affords greater rights and liberties to individuals than does the Covenant. Additionally, a few provisions of the Covenant articulate legal rules which differ from U.S. law and which, upon careful consideration, the Administration declines to accept in preference to existing law. ...

Formal Reservations

1. Free Speech (Article 20)
Although Article 19 of the Covenant specifically protects freedom of expression and opinion, Article 20 directly conflicts with the First Amendment by requiring the prohibition of certain forms of speech and expression which are protected under the First Amendment to the U.S. Constitution (i.e., propaganda for war and advocacy of national, racial or religious hatred that constitutes incitement to discrimination, hostility or violence). The United States cannot accept such an obligation.

Accordingly, the following reservation is recommended:

> Article 20 does not authorize or require legislation or other action by the United States
> that would restrict the right of free speech and association protected by the Constitution
> and laws of the United States.

...

2. Article 6 (capital punishment)

Article 6, paragraph 5 of the Covenant prohibits imposition of the death sentence for crimes committed by persons below 18 years of age and on pregnant women. In 1978, a broad reservation to this article was proposed in order to retain the right to impose capital punishment on any person duly convicted under existing or future laws permitting the imposition of capital punishment. The Administration is now prepared to accept the prohibition against execution of pregnant women. However, in light of the recent reaffirmation of U.S. policy towards capital punishment generally, and in particular the Supreme Court's decisions upholding state laws permitting the death penalty for crimes committed by juveniles aged 16 and 17, the prohibition against imposition of capital punishment for crimes committed by minors is not acceptable. Given the sharply differing view taken by many of our future treaty partners on the issue of the death penalty (including what constitutes 'serious crimes' under Article 6(2)), it is advisable to state our position clearly.

Accordingly, we recommend the following reservation to Article 6:

> The United States reserves the right, subject to its Constitutional constraints, to impose capital punishment on any person (other than a pregnant woman) duly convicted under existing or future laws permitting the imposition of capital punishment, including such punishment for crime committed by persons below eighteen years of age.

3. Article 7 (torture/punishment)

[Proposed reservation:]

> That the United States considers itself bound by Article 7 to the extent that "cruel, inhuman or degrading treatment or punishment" means the cruel and unusual treatment or punishment prohibited by the Fifth, Eighth and/or Fourteenth Amendments to the Constitution of the United States.

4. Article 15(1) (post-offense reductions in penalty)

Article 15, paragraph 1 ... [provides]: 'If, subsequent to the commission of the offense, provision is made by law for the imposition of the lighter penalty, the offender shall benefit thereby.' Current federal law, as well as the law of most states, does not require such relief and in fact contains a contrary presumption that the penalty in force at the time the offense is committed will be imposed, although post-sentence reductions are permitted ... and are often granted in practice when there have been subsequent statutory changes. Upon consideration, there is no disposition to require a change in U.S. law to conform to the Covenant. [A reservation was proposed.]

Understandings

1. Article 2(1), 4(1) and 26 (non-discrimination)

The very broad anti-discrimination provisions contained in the above articles do not precisely comport with long-standing Supreme Court doctrine in the equal protection field. In particular, Articles 2(1) and 26 prohibit discrimination not only on the bases of 'race, colour, sex, language, religion, political or other opinion, national or social origin, property, birth' but also on any 'other status.' Current U.S. civil rights law is not so open-ended: discrimination is only prohibited for specific statuses, and there are exceptions which allow for discrimination. For example, under the Age Discrimination Act of 1975, age may be taken into account in certain circumstances. In addition, U.S. law permits additional distinctions, for example between citizens and non-citizens and between different categories of non-citizens, especially in the context of the immigration laws.

...

Notwithstanding the very extensive protections already provided under U.S. law and the Committee's interpretive approach to the issue, we recommend [an understanding that expresses the preceding concerns.] [Eds.: The text of that understanding is here omitted.]

4. Article 14 (right to counsel, compelled witness, and double jeopardy)

In a few particular aspects, this Article could be read as going beyond existing U.S. domestic law... .Under the Constitution, double jeopardy attaches only to multiple prosecutions by the same sovereign and does not prohibit trial of the same defendant for the same crime in, for example, state and federal courts or in the courts of two states. See *Burton v. Maryland*, 395 U.S. 784 (1969).

To clarify our reading of the Covenant with respect to these issues, we recommend the following understanding, similar to the one proposed in 1978:

> ... The United States understands the prohibition upon double jeopardy in paragraph 7 to apply only when the judgment of acquittal has been rendered by a court of the same governmental unit, whether the Federal Government or a constituent unit, as is seeking a new trial for the same cause.

Declarations

1. Non-self-executing Treaty

For reasons of prudence, we recommend including a declaration that the substantive provisions of the Covenant are not self-executing. The intent is to clarify that the Covenant will not create a private cause of action in U.S. courts. As was the case with the Torture Convention, existing U.S. law generally complies with the Covenant; hence, implementing legislation is not contemplated.

We recommend the following declaration ...

> The United States declares that the provisions of Articles 1 through 27 of the Covenant are not self-executing.

...

3. Article 41 (state-to-state complaints)

Under Article 41, States Party to the Covenant may accept the competence of the Human Rights Committee to consider state-to-state complaints by means of a formal declaration to that effect....

Accordingly, we recommend informing the Senate of our intent, subject to its approval, to make an appropriate declaration under Article 41 at the time of ratification, as follows:

> The United States declares that it accepts the competence of the Human Rights Committee to receive and consider communications under Article 41 in which a State Party claims another State Party is not fulfilling its obligations under the Covenant.

...

* * *

The proposed RUDs were accepted by the Senate and conveyed to the UN when the US ratified the ICCPR on 8 June 1992.

QUESTIONS

1. Several NGOs participating in the Senate hearings on ratification of the ICCPR opposed the proposed (and later adopted) non-self-executing declaration. Note the following comments by Human Rights Watch and the ACLU:[80]

"... Americans would have been able to enforce the treaty in U.S. courts either if it had been declared to be self-executing or if implementing legislation had been enacted to create causes of action under the treaty. The Bush administration rejected both routes. The result was that ratification became an empty act for Americans: the endorsement of the most important treaty for the protection of civil rights yielded not a single additional enforceable right to citizens and residents of the United States."

---

[80] Human Rights Watch and American Civil Liberties Union, (1993), at 2.

Do you agree with these observations about the need for a self-executing Covenant? What arguments would you make against this position?

2. Consider the following warning by Jack Goldsmith in 2001 against the incorporation of the ICCPR in US domestic law:

"[A] domesticated ICCPR would generate enormous litigation and uncertainty, potentially changing domestic civil rights law in manifold ways. Human rights protections in the United States are not remotely so deficient as to warrant these costs. Although there is much debate around the edges of domestic civil and political rights law, there is a broad consensus about the appropriate content and scope of this law. This consensus has built up slowly over the past century. It is the product of years of judicial interpretation of domestic statutory and constitutional law, various democratic processes, lengthy and varied experimentation, and a great deal of practical local experience. Domestic incorporation of the ICCPR would threaten to upset this balance. It would constitute a massive, largely standardless delegation of power to federal courts to rethink the content and scope of nearly every aspect of domestic human rights law.[81]"

3. Ratification by the United States of the ICCPR Optional Protocol does not seem to have been discussed. No such proposal was put to the Senate. (a) Why do you suppose this to have been the case? (b) As a member of the State Department, would you have argued for or against joining the Optional Protocol? (c) Would ratification of the Optional Protocol have been the correct solution, preferable to making the ICCPR self-executing?

b. CEDAW and Reservations

Of the 189 States parties to CEDAW, as of 2024, 79 had entered reservations or declarations to parts of the treaty (though some of those were simply to Article 29 providing for arbitration and adjudication by the ICJ). And 24 states had registered objections to the reservations of one or more other states. A considerable number of the original reservations have since been withdrawn. The CEDAW Committee has consistently urged states to do so and it has been suggested that the Universal Periodic Review process (Ch. 8, below) has also played an important part in this regard.[82]

Unlike the ICCPR, which is silent on the issue, CEDAW addresses reservations in Article 28(2), which prohibits those incompatible with the 'object and purpose' of the Convention. Tolerance of reservations has been urged on various grounds — for example, the desirability of securing widespread participation in treaties serving a 'purely humanitarian and civilizing purpose' (in the words of the Genocide Convention Advisory Opinion), and hence the reluctance to view a ratification as invalid because of reservations. Another reason is to protect states' freedom to maneuver.

Some commentators have characterized reservations to Article 2 of CEDAW as 'manifestly incompatible' with the object and purpose of the Convention, and other states have objected that some of them threaten the integrity of the Convention and the human rights regime in general. Reservations that purport to be consistent with Article 28(2) of CEDAW raise issues of religious intolerance and of cultural relativism. The net result is said to have been the diffuse and widespread view that international obligations assumed through the ratification of CEDAW are somehow 'separate and distinct' from and less binding than those of other human rights treaties.[83]

Selected illustrations of the reservations and objections follow.

---

[81] J. Goldsmith, 'Should International Human Rights Law Trump US Domestic Law', 1 *Chi. J. Int'l L.* (2000) 327, at 332.
[82] F. Cowell, 'Reservations to Human Rights Treaties in Recommendations from the Universal Periodic Review: An Emerging Practice?', 25 *Int'l J. Hum. Rts.* (2021) 274.
[83] B. Clark, 'The Vienna Convention Reservations Regime and the Convention on the Discrimination Against Women', 85 *Am. J. Int'l L.* (1991) 281.

RESERVATIONS

Austria (subsequently withdrawn)

Austria reserves its right to apply the provision of article 7(b) as far as service in the armed forces is concerned, and the provision of article 11 as far as night work of women and special protection of working women is concerned, within the limits established by national legislation.

Bahrain

[The original reservations submitted in 2002 were subsequently 'edited' so that in 2014 the formulation was:] The Kingdom of Bahrain is committed to implement the provisions of Articles 2, 15 paragraph 4 and 16 of [CEDAW] without breaching the provisions of the Islamic Shariah.

Bangladesh (subsequently withdrawn with respect to Articles 13(a); 16(1)(c) and (f))

… Bangladesh does not consider as binding upon itself the provisions of articles 2, 13(a) and 16(1)(c) and (f) as they conflict with Shariah law based on Holy Koran and Sunna.

Belgium (subsequently withdrawn)

The application of article 7 shall not affect the validity of the provisions of the Constitution …which reserves for men the exercise of royal powers … .

Brazil (subsequently withdrawn)

The Government of the Federative Republic of Brazil hereby expresses its reservations to article 15, paragraph 4, and to article 16, paragraph 1(a), (c), (g) and (f)....

Brunei Darussalam

The Government of Brunei Darussalam expresses its reservations regarding those provisions of the said Convention that may be contrary to the Constitution of Brunei Darussalam and to the beliefs and principles of Islam, the official religion of Brunei Darussalam and, without prejudice to the generality of the said reservations, expresses its reservations regarding paragraph 2 of Article 9 and paragraph 1 of Article 29 of the Convention.

Egypt

Reservation to the text of article 9, paragraph 2, concerning the granting to women of equal rights with men with respect to the nationality of their children, without prejudice to the acquisition by a child born of a marriage of the nationality of his father … . [Reservation withdrawn in 2008.]

Reservation to the text of article 16 concerning the equality of men and women in all matters relating to marriage and family relations during the marriage and upon its dissolution, without prejudice to the Islamic Shariah provisions whereby women are accorded rights equivalent to those of their spouses so as to ensure a just balance between them. This is out of respect for the sacrosanct nature of the firm religious beliefs which govern marital relations in Egypt and which may not be called in question and in view of the fact that one of the most important bases of these relations is an equivalency of rights and duties so as to ensure complementarity which guarantees true equality between the spouses, not a quasi-equality that renders the marriage a burden on the wife... .The provisions of the Shariah lay down that the husband shall pay bridal money to the wife and maintain her fully and shall also make a payment to her upon divorce, whereas the wife retains full rights over her property and is not obliged to spend anything on her keep. The Shariah therefore restricts the wife's rights to divorce by making it contingent on a judge's ruling, whereas no such restriction is laid down in the case of the husband.

The Arab Republic of Egypt is willing to comply with the content of [Article 2], provided that such compliance does not run counter to the Islamic Shariah.

France

[Declarations:] The Government of the French Republic declares that article 9 of the Convention must not be interpreted as precluding the application of the second paragraph of article 96 of the code of French nationality.

...

The Government of the French Republic declares that no provision of the Convention must be interpreted as prevailing over provisions of French legislation which are more favourable to women than to men.

Ireland

[Re Article 16(1)(d) and (f)] Ireland is of the view that the attainment in Ireland of the objectives of the Convention does not necessitate the extension to men of rights identical to those accorded to women in respect of the guardianship, adoption and custody of children born out of wedlock and reserves the right to implement the Convention subject to that understanding.

Malta

The Government of Malta does not consider itself bound by subparagraph (e) of Article 16, insofar as the same may be interpreted as imposing an obligation on Malta to legalize abortion.

Oman

1. All provisions of the Convention not in accordance with the provisions of the Islamic sharia and legislation in force in the Sultanate of Oman;

...

Singapore

In the context of Singapore's multi-racial and multi-religious society and the need to respect the freedom of minorities to practise their religious and personal laws, the Republic of Singapore reserves the right not to apply the provisions of articles 2 and 16 where compliance with these provisions would be contrary to their religious or personal laws.

Singapore interprets article 11, paragraph 1, in the light of the provisions of article 4, paragraph 2 as not precluding prohibitions, restrictions or conditions on the employment of women in certain areas, or on work done by them where this is considered necessary or desirable to protect the health and safety of women or the human foetus. ...

Turkey

The Government of the Republic of Turkey [makes reservations] with regard to the articles of the Convention dealing with family relations which are not completely compatible with the provisions of the Turkish Civil Code.

...

OBJECTIONS

Germany

The Federal Republic of Germany considers that the reservations made by Egypt regarding article 2, article 9, paragraph 2, and article 16, by Bangladesh regarding article 2, article 13 (a) and article 16, paragraph 1 (c) and (f), by Brazil regarding article 15, paragraph 4, and article 16, paragraph 1 (a), (c), (g) and (h), by Jamaica regarding article 9, paragraph 2, by the Republic of Korea regarding article 9 and article 16, paragraph 1 (c), (d), (f) and (g), and by Mauritius regarding article 11, paragraph 1 (b) and (d), and article 16, paragraph 1 (g), are incompatible with the object and purpose of the Convention (article 28, paragraph 2) and therefore objects to them. In relation to the Federal Republic of Germany, they may not be invoked in support of a legal practice which does not pay due regard to the legal status afforded to women and children in the Federal Republic of Germany in conformity with the above-mentioned articles of the Convention.

This objection shall not preclude the entry into force of the Convention as between Egypt, Bangladesh, Brazil, Jamaica, the Republic of Korea, Mauritius and the Federal Republic of Germany.

QUESTIONS

1. Which of the preceding reservations do you view as objectionable within the criteria of the Vienna Convention? Consider the reservations of Egypt. What arguments would you make for the validity of its reservations under the criteria stated in the Vienna Convention and CEDAW?

2. Which of the reservations raise issues of cultural relativism? Only those based on a state's local custom or religion?

3. Why do you suppose that CEDAW has attracted more reservations by states than other human rights treaties?

Ratification has been considered by the United States on several occasions. In 1994, the Senate Committee on Foreign Relations, after hearings, recommended ratification to the Senate, by a vote of 13–5, subject to various reservations, understandings and declarations, including the following:

> [T]he Constitution and laws of the United States establish extensive protections against discrimination, reaching all forms of governmental activity as well as significant areas of non-governmental activity. However, individual privacy and freedom from governmental interference in private conduct are also recognized as among the fundamental values of our free and democratic society. The United States understands that by its terms the Convention requires broad regulation of private conduct, in particular under Articles 2, 3 and 5. The United States does not accept any obligation under the Convention to enact legislation or to take any other action with respect to private conduct except as mandated by the Constitution and laws of the United States. [84]

The Committee also proposed reservations to the right to equal pay understood as comparable worth, the right to paid maternity leave, and any obligation under Articles 5, 7, 8 and 13 of the Convention that might restrict constitutional rights to speech, expression and association.

Five senators (a Republican minority) on the Committee objected to ratification. In their Minority Views they endorsed the goal of eliminating discrimination against women, but felt that CEDAW was not the best means of pursuing that objective. The Minority Views made the following points:

(1) CEDAW may enable ratifying states to generate 'political capital', but is 'unlikely to convince governments to make policy changes they would otherwise avoid'.

(2) Countries like the United States 'must guard against treaties that overreach', and must not promise 'more than we can deliver or we risk diluting the moral suasion that undergirds existing covenants'.

(3) More than 30 states, including Islamic states, had made significant and sometimes problematic reservations when ratifying CEDAW. The statement questioned 'whether such behavior does not, in fact, "cheapen the coin" of human rights treaties generally'. These reservations suggest that CEDAW 'may reach beyond the necessarily restrictive scope of an effective human rights treaty'.

---

[84] See S384–10, Exec. Rep. Sen. Comm. on For. Rel., 3 October 1994. The text of all proposed reservations is in 89 Am. J. Int'l. L. (1995) 102.

(4) 'Improvement in the status of women in countries such as India, China, and Sudan will ultimately be made in those countries, not in the United States Senate'.

(5) Evolution of 'internationally accepted norms' on human rights must 'take place within an international system of sovereign nations with differing cultural, religious and political systems. Pushing a normative agenda beyond that system's ability to incorporate it leads, we believe, to what is represented by this convention.' ...

The Convention was not brought to a vote in the full Senate. Since 1994 there has been little action.[85] In 1998, President Clinton sought congressional support for gaining Senate consent to ratification. In 2002, the Senate Foreign Relations Committee held a brief hearing on CEDAW and voted 12–7 for ratification, subject to most of the earlier proposed reservations, understandings and declarations, plus two additional ones. Democratic Senator Biden, chairman of the Committee, sponsored an understanding to the effect that 'the CEDAW Committee has no authority to compel parties to follow its recommendations'. Republican Senator Jesse Helms proposed an understanding that 'nothing in this Convention shall be construed to reflect or create any right to abortion and in no case should abortion be promoted as a method of family planning.'[86]

In October 2020, the Trump administration signed the 'Geneva Consensus Declaration', calling on states to promote women's rights and health, but without access to abortion.[87]

The Effect of Treaty Reservations

Following U.S. ratification of the ICCPR, a number of states parties objected to one or more of the U.S. reservations. Several states — including Belgium, Denmark, Finland, France, Germany, Italy, the Netherlands, Norway, Portugal, Spain and Sweden — objected to the reservation regarding Article 6, paragraph 5, prohibiting the imposition of the death sentence for crimes committed by persons below 18 years of age, and found that reservation incompatible with the object and purpose of the Covenant. Most of these states also objected to other reservations (or to understandings), particularly the one relating to Article 7. The objections, however, stressed that (to take one illustration) the state's position on the relevant reservations 'does not constitute an obstacle to the entry into force of the Covenant between the Kingdom of Spain and the United States of America'. Compare in this respect Articles 20–21 of the Vienna Convention on the Law of Treaties.

In objecting to three reservations and three understandings, Sweden observed that under international treaty law, the name 'assigned to a statement' that excluded or modified the effect of certain treaty provisions:

> [D]oes not determine its status as a reservation to the treaty. Thus, the Government considers that some of the understandings made by the United States in substance constitute reservations to the Covenant.

> A reservation by which a State modifies or excludes the application of the most fundamental provisions of the Covenant, or limits its responsibilities under that treaty by invoking general principles of national law, may cast doubts upon the commitment of the reserving State to the object and purpose of the Covenant. The reservations made by the United States of America include both reservations to essential and non-derogable provisions, and general references to national legislation. Reservations of this nature contribute to undermining the basis of international treaty law. All States parties share a common interest in the respect for the object and purpose of the treaty to which they have chosen to become parties.

Two legal analyses are of particular relevance in assessing the question of the legal effect of reservations. The first is a General Comment by the Human Rights Committee and the second is the outcome of work by the

---

[85] In 2010, the Senate Judiciary Committee's Subcommittee on Human Rights and the Law held CEDAW hearings, at which the Obama Administration expressed support for ratification.

[86] See generally, Congressional Research Service, The U.N. Convention on the Elimination of All Forms of Discrimination Against Women (CEDAW): Issues in the U.S. Ratification Debate (August 7, 2009 – July 23, 2015).

[87] J. Borger, 'US signs anti-abortion declaration with group of largely authoritarian governments', *The Guardian,* 22 October 2020.

International Law Commission. You should notice, as you read, several points of agreement and disagreement between the two texts.

HUMAN RIGHTS COMMITTEE, GENERAL COMMENT NO. 24
CCPR/C/21/REV. 1/ADD. 6 (2 NOVEMBER 1994)

[This General Comment focuses 'on issues relating to reservations made upon ratification of accession to the Covenant or the Optional Protocols thereto, or in relation to declarations under article 41 of the Covenant.' It was adopted after the United States' ratification of the ICCPR, and before the Committee considered the United States' first periodic report in 1995. It refers to the provisions of the Vienna Convention on the Law of Treaties.

The General Comment notes that 46 of the then 127 states parties to the ICCPR had entered a total of 150 reservations, ranging from exclusion of the duty to provide particular rights, to insistence on the 'paramountcy of certain domestic legal provisions' and to limitations on the competence of the Committee. Those reservations 'tend to weaken respect' for obligations and 'may undermine the effective implementation of the Covenant'. The Committee felt compelled to act, partly under the necessity of clarifying for states parties just what obligations had been undertaken, a clarification that would require the Committee to determine 'the acceptability and effects' of reservations.

The General Comment observed that the ICCPR itself makes no reference to reservations (as is true also for the First Optional Protocol; the Second Optional Protocol limits reservations), and that the matter of reservations is governed by international law. It found in Article 19(3) of the Vienna Convention on the Law of Treaties 'relevant guidance'. Therefore, that article's 'object and purpose test ... governs the matter of interpretation and acceptability of reservations'.]

8. Reservations that offend peremptory norms would not be compatible with the object and purpose of the Covenant. Although treaties that are mere exchanges of obligations between States allow them to reserve *inter se* application of rules of general international law, it is otherwise in human rights treaties, which are for the benefit of persons within their jurisdiction. Accordingly, provisions in the Covenant that represent customary international law (and *a fortiori* when they have the character of peremptory norms) may not be the subject of reservations. Accordingly, a State may not reserve the right to engage in slavery, to torture, to subject persons to cruel, inhuman or degrading treatment or punishment, to arbitrarily deprive persons of their lives, to arbitrarily arrest and detain persons, to deny freedom of thought, conscience and religion, to presume a person guilty unless he proves his innocence, to execute pregnant women or children, to permit the advocacy of national, racial or religious hatred, to deny to persons of marriageable age the right to marry, or to deny to minorities the right to enjoy their own culture, profess their own religion, or use their own language. And while reservations to particular clauses of Article 14 may be acceptable, a general reservation to the right to a fair trial would not be.

9. Applying more generally the object and purpose test to the Covenant, the Committee notes that, for example, ... a State [may not] reserve an entitlement not to take the necessary steps at the domestic level to give effect to the rights of the Covenant (Article 2(2)).

10. ... [I]t falls for consideration as to whether reservations to the non-derogable provisions of the Covenant are compatible with its object and purpose ... . One reason for certain rights being made non-derogable is because their suspension is irrelevant to the legitimate control of the state of national emergency (for example, no imprisonment for debt, in article 11)... .At the same time, some provisions are non-derogable exactly because without them there would be no rule of law. A reservation to the provisions of article 4 itself, which precisely stipulates the balance to be struck between the interests of the State and the rights of the individual in times of emergency, would fall in this category. And some non-derogable rights, which in any event cannot be reserved because of their status as peremptory norms, are also of this character [e.g., torture] ... . While there is no automatic correlation between reservations to non-derogable provisions, and reservations which offend against the object and purpose of the Covenant, a State has a heavy onus to justify such a reservation.

11. ... The Committee's role under the Covenant, whether under article 40 or under the Optional Protocols, necessarily entails interpreting the provisions of the Covenant and the development of a jurisprudence.

Accordingly, a reservation that rejects the Committee's competence to interpret the requirements of any provisions of the Covenant would also be contrary to the object and purpose of that treaty.

12. ... Domestic laws may need to be altered properly to reflect the requirements of the Covenant; and mechanisms at the domestic level will be needed to allow the Covenant rights to be enforceable at the local level. Reservations often reveal a tendency of States not to want to change a particular law. And sometimes that tendency is elevated to a general policy. Of particular concern are widely formulated reservations which essentially render ineffective all Covenant rights which would require any change in national law to ensure compliance with Covenant obligations. No real international rights or obligations have thus been accepted. And when there is an absence of provisions to ensure that Covenant rights may be sued on in domestic courts, and, further, a failure to allow individual complaints to be brought to the Committee under the first Optional Protocol, all the essential elements of the Covenant guarantees have been removed.

...

17. ... [Human rights] treaties, and the Covenant specifically, are not a web of inter-State exchanges of mutual obligations ... . Because the operation of the classic rules on reservations is so inadequate for the Covenant, States have often not seen any legal interest in or need to object to reservations. The absence of protest by States cannot imply that a reservation is either compatible or incompatible with the object and purpose of the Covenant ... .

18. It necessarily falls to the Committee to determine whether a specific reservation is compatible with the object and purpose of the Covenant ... . Because of the special character of a human rights treaty, the compatibility of a reservation with the object and purpose of the Covenant must be established objectively, by reference to legal principles, and the Committee is particularly well placed to perform this task. The normal consequence of an unacceptable reservation is not that the Covenant will not be in effect at all for a reserving party. Rather, such a reservation will generally be severable, in the sense that the Covenant will be operative for the reserving party without benefit of the reservation.

19. Reservations must be specific ... . States should not enter so many reservations that they are in effect accepting a limited number of human rights obligations, and not the Covenant as such. So that reservations do not lead to a perpetual non-attainment of international human rights standards, reservations should not systematically reduce the obligations undertaken only to the presently existing in less demanding standards of domestic law. Nor should interpretative declarations or reservations seek to remove an autonomous meaning to Covenant obligations, by pronouncing them to be identical, or to be accepted only insofar as they are identical, with existing provisions of domestic law.

...

INTERNATIONAL LAW COMMISSION, GUIDE TO PRACTICE ON RESERVATIONS TO TREATIES

[In 2011, the International Law Commission (ILC) adopted the Guide to Practice on Reservations to Treaties. The Guide was the culmination of 17 years of work by Special Rapporteur, Alain Pellet. As with other ILC documents of its kind, early drafts of the guidelines were scrutinized annually by the UN General Assembly's Sixth Committee, a body of governmental representatives, which gave states an opportunity to express their views on the general endeavour and specific details. Through this process of governmental review and continued refinement of the text, the Guide increased its legitimacy and support among states. Accompanying the publication of the Guide, the Commission also published a lengthy (nearly 600 pages) set of Commentaries.[88] The following excerpts from the Guide and Commentaries include sections that are relevant to important areas of international human rights law and practice.]

3.1.5 Incompatibility of a reservation with the object and purpose of the treaty

A reservation is incompatible with the object and purpose of the treaty if it affects an essential element of the treaty that is necessary to its general tenour, in such a way that the reservation impairs the *raison d'être* of the treaty.

---

[88] See UN Docs. A/CN.4/SER.A/2011/Add.1 (Part 2), and Add.2 (Part 3).

Commentary

[N]either the object — defined as the actual content of the treaty — still less the purpose — the outcome sought — remain immutable over time …

…

… [I]n an endeavour to avoid too high a 'threshold', the Commission chose the adjective 'necessary' in preference to the stronger term 'indispensable', and decided on the verb 'impair' (rather than 'deprive') to apply to the '*raison d'être*' of the treaty, it being understood ... that the question could even arise of whether the *raison d'être* might change over time.

3.1.5.2 Vague or general reservations

A reservation shall be worded in such a way as to allow its meaning to be understood, in order to assess in particular its compatibility with the object and purpose of the treaty.

Commentary

Since, under article 19 (c) of the Vienna Conventions, ... a reservation must be compatible with the object and purpose of the treaty, and since other States are required, under article 20, to take a position on this compatibility, it must be possible for them to do so. This will not be the case if the reservation in question is worded in such a way as to preclude any determination of its scope, in other words, if it is vague or general ... .

…

…

[The problem that the 'text of the reservation does not allow its meaning to be understood'] often happens when a reservation invokes the internal law of the State that has formulated it without identifying the provisions in question or specifying whether they are to be found in its constitution or its civil or criminal code. In such cases, it is not the reference to the domestic law of the reserving State *per se* that is the problem, but rather the frequent vagueness and generality of the reservations referring to domestic law, which make it impossible for the other States parties to take a position on them ... .

…

The same applies when a State reserves the general right to have its constitution prevail over a treaty, as for instance in the reservation by the United States of America to the Convention on the Prevention and Punishment of the Crime of Genocide: '... nothing in the Convention requires or authorizes legislation or other action by the United States of America prohibited by the Constitution of the United States as interpreted by the United States.'

Some of the so-called 'sharia reservations' give rise to the same objection, a case in point being the reservation by which Mauritania approved the 1979 [CEDAW] 'in each and every one of its parts which are not contrary to Islamic sharia'. Here again, the problem lies not in the fact that Mauritania is invoking a law of religious origin which it applies, but, rather that, as Denmark noted, 'the general reservations with reference to the provisions of Islamic law are of unlimited scope and undefined character'. …

3.1.5.3 Reservations to a provision reflecting a customary rule

The fact that a treaty provision reflects a rule of customary international law does not in itself constitute an obstacle to the formulation of a reservation to that provision.

Commentary

… Guideline 3.1.5.3 therefore sets out the principle that a reservation to a treaty rule which reflects a customary rule is not *ipso jure* incompatible with the object and purpose of the treaty, even if due account must be taken of that element in assessing such compatibility.

On occasion States parties to a treaty have objected to reservations and challenged their compatibility with its object and purpose on the pretext that they were contrary to well established customary rules. …

…

- Customary rules are binding on States, independently of their expression of consent to a treaty rule but, unlike the case of peremptory norms, States may opt out by agreement inter se; it is not clear why they could not do so through a reservation ...;

- A reservation concerns only the expression of the rule in the context of the treaty, not its existence as a customary rule, even if, in some cases, it may cast doubt on the rule's general acceptance 'as law' ...;

- If the customary nature of the rule is well-established, States remain bound by it, independently of the treaty;
  ...

- And, lastly, a reservation may be the means by which a 'persistent objector' manifests the persistence of its objection; the objector may certainly reject the application, through a treaty, of a rule which cannot be invoked against it under general international law.

The question has been raised, however, whether this solution can be transposed to the field of human rights... .[The Commission finds no reason to make a distinction on this basis.]

...

The Commission did not consider it necessary to draft a specific guideline on reservations to a treaty provision reflecting a peremptory norm of general international law (*jus cogens*). Such a norm is, in almost all cases, customary in nature. It follows that the reasoning applicable to reservations to treaty provisions reflecting 'normal' customary rules can be transposed to reservations to provisions reflecting *jus cogens* norms.

...

3.1.5.4 Reservations to provisions concerning rights from which no derogation is permissible under any circumstances

A State or an international organization may not formulate a reservation to a treaty provision concerning rights from which no derogation is permissible under any circumstances [Eds.: e.g., Article 5 of the ICCPR], unless the reservation in question is compatible with the essential rights and obligations arising out of that treaty. In assessing that compatibility, account shall be taken of the importance which the parties have conferred upon the rights at issue by making them non-derogable.

3.1.5.7 Reservations to treaty provisions concerning dispute settlement or the monitoring of the implementation of the treaty

A reservation to a treaty provision concerning dispute settlement or the monitoring of the implementation of the treaty is not, in itself, incompatible with the object and purpose of the treaty, unless:

(i)   the reservation purports to exclude or modify the legal effect of a provision of the treaty essential to its *raison d'être*

...

3.2 Assessment of the permissibility of reservations

The following may assess, within their respective competences, the permissibility of reservations to a treaty formulated by a State or an international organization:

- contracting States or contracting organizations;
- dispute settlement bodies;
- treaty monitoring bodies.

Commentary

In the first place ... it must be acknowledged that the treaty bodies could not carry out their mandated functions if they could not be sure of the exact extent of their jurisdiction vis-à-vis the States concerned, whether in their consideration of complaints by States or individuals or of periodic reports, or in their exercise of an advisory function; it is therefore part of their functions to assess the permissibility of reservations ... . Secondly, in so doing, they have neither more nor less authority than in any other area: the Human Rights Committee and the other international human rights treaty bodies which do not have decision-making power do not acquire it in the area of reservations ... [T]hirdly ... they may not substitute their own judgement for the State's consent to be bound by the treaty. It goes without saying that the powers of the treaty bodies do not affect the power of States or organizations to accept reservations or object to them, as established and regulated under articles 20, 21 and 23 of the Vienna Conventions.

...

3.2.3 Consideration of the assessments of treaty monitoring bodies

States and international organizations that have formulated reservations to a treaty establishing a treaty monitoring body shall give consideration to that body's assessment of the permissibility of the reservations.

Commentary

[T]here is no question but that [treaty bodies] may assess the permissibility of reservations to treaties whose observance they are required to monitor. On the other hand, they may not ...[t]ake the place of the author of the reservation, in any case, in determining the consequences to be drawn from the impermissibility of a reservation ... .

* * *

Reactions to General Comment No. 24

France, the United Kingdom and the United States submitted observations to the ICCPR Committee on General Comment No. 24. The U.S. Government stated that the General Comment 'appears to go much too far' and that the ICCPR does not 'impose on States Parties an obligation to give effect to the Committee's interpretations or confer on the Committee the power to render definitive interpretations of the Covenant.' The observations stated that paragraphs 16–20 of the General Comment 'appear to reject the established rules of interpretation of treaties' in the Vienna Convention and in customary international law. It criticized the General Comment's condemnation of the types of reservations that the United States had entered.

The observations were particularly critical of paragraph 18, which stated that in the indicated circumstances, 'the Covenant will be operative for the reserving party without benefit of the reservations'. This conclusion is 'completely at odds with established legal practice and principles ... .' If it were determined that any one or more of the U.S. reservations were Ineffective, the consequence would be that the ratification as a whole could thereby be nullified, and the United States would not be party to the Covenant. France and the United Kingdom submitted similar observations. On the severability question, France 'reject[ed] this entire analysis ... . [I]f these reservations are deemed incompatible with the purpose and object of the treaty, the only course open is to declare that this consent is not valid and decide that these States cannot be considered parties to the instrument in question.' On this point of law, the UK Government stated similar concerns and added a pragmatic one: 'questions of principle aside, an approach as outlined in ... the General Comment would risk discouraging States from ratifying human rights conventions (since they would not be in a position to reassure their national Parliaments as to the status of treaty provisions on which it was felt necessary to reserve).'

Despite these responses, other treaty bodies subsequently endorsed General Comment No. 24, and the Human Rights Committee employed its severability approach. In a communication submitted to the ILC, the chairpersons of the treaty bodies stated: 'The Chairpersons express ... their firm support for the approach reflected in General Comment No. 24 of the Human Rights Committee and they urge ... that the conclusions proposed by the International Law Commission should be adjusted accordingly to reflect that approach.' Shortly thereafter, the Human Rights Committee applied its severability approach in a First Optional Protocol proceeding involving a death row inmate. See *Kennedy v. Trinidad and Tobago*, Communication No 845/1999, 31

Dec. 1999, UN Doc. CCPR/C/67/D/845/1999. For a detailed analysis of the question of severability, see Ryan Goodman, 'Human Rights Treaties, Invalid Reservations, and State Consent', 96 *Am. J. Int. L.* (2002) 531.

QUESTIONS

1. Why was there near unanimity among the states parties to the ICCPR that objected to the reservations by the United States about the particular reservation concerning Article 6, paragraph 5 (death sentence)? Did that reservation raise a special problem under the Covenant? On the other hand, was there special reason for the United States to reserve as to that provision?

2. In light of General Comment No. 24, if you were a Senator committed to U.S. ratification of the major human rights instruments, would you have voted for any reservation? Did any one of the reservations have a special justification?

3. Is General Comment No. 24 consistent with the spirit of the Genocide Convention Advisory Opinion described above? Using that opinion, how would you argue that the reservations of the United States should be accepted in their entirety as valid under international law?

4. The ILC Commentary admits that, if every treaty body and various other institutions all have the authority to assess the permissibility of a reservation, multiple conflicting decisions may result. Nevertheless, the Commentary concludes that 'it is probably better to have too much assessment than no assessment at all' (Commentary to 3.2). Do you agree? Is the comparison to 'no assessment at all' the correct one? Is there a point — and if so, what is it — whereby the costs of multiple venues of assessment would undermine the goals of the human rights regime?

5. The Vienna Convention on the Law of Treaties does not include an express prohibition on 'vague' or 'general' reservations. Did the ILC Commentary go too far in developing this doctrine and in describing the reservations that it would discredit or does this section of the Commentary seem well tethered to existing law and practice?

---

7. The Impact of CEDAW

It is notoriously difficult to evaluate the impact of human rights treaties or of different forms of human rights advocacy. Any 'victory' will have multiple authors, and disaggregating the local, national, and international elements is likely to be impossible. Governments rarely ever acknowledge that change was driven by human rights advocacy, and the interaction between normative statements (or treaty obligations) and the many ways in which they might influence key social movements, or political and other actors is often indirect and subtle.

The impact of CEDAW is, inevitably, contested. Martha Nussbaum, in *The Cosmopolitan Tradition: A Noble but Flawed Ideal* (2019), at 220, acknowledges that, in some areas of women's rights, there has been great progress around the world in recent decades:

> ... [I]nternational agreements are important parts of international movements, and the moral work that is done in international society is often enormously important, bringing people together around a common set of demands and complaints, and giving them opportunities to meet, exchange ideas, and reinforce one another. ... The various women's congresses have built a valuable type of solidarity and ferment, and this energy has surely contributed greatly to the progress of women in most nations of the world.

> ...

[While CEDAW's ratification gave new impetus to domestic political efforts, it] accomplished little directly. It is also a deeply flawed document, skirting around some of the most important issues, such as access to artificial contraception and counting women's work as work in national income accounts. It has also not altered the relentlessly male-centered perspective of other human-rights documents. As Eleanor Roosevelt warned from the beginning, giving women a separate lobby and a separate document is a double-edged sword, possibly sidelining women's energies, which might have been used to fight in the more inclusive forum. In this case, however, there is no doubt that, despite the efforts of many, the United Nations has always been and remains a profoundly patriarchal institution, hostile to women's equality. Fighting in the more inclusive forum would have been frustrating and probably doomed, whereas the mobilization of women worldwide to create a text that stands before all the world, affirming women's equality, has proved politically and strategically valuable, no matter what the defects of the document and the yet greater defects of its implementation, which basically amounts to a handful of domestic court cases in countries with woman-friendly judiciaries (India and Botswana) in which the fact that the nation ratified the treaty has been used to effect legal change.

In short, … international documents are not legally enforced and do not amount to a world constitution. That is actually good … . It is more appropriate that these documents remain sources of persuasive norms, to be enforced through domestic policies, including constitution-making, legislation, and judicial interpretation—occasionally citing the document itself, but more often influenced by the arguments and the persuasive climate of the international community that led to and received additional impetus from the document. International society remains primarily a moral realm of persuasion, and only becomes a truly political realm occasionally. This does not mean, however, that the process of creating and ratifying documents is useless: it creates solidarity and a sense of common goals, enabling powerful transnational movements to arise and to influence national policies.

Fareda Banda, in 'The Limits of Law: A Response to Martha C. Nussbaum', in Bardo Fassbender and Knut Traisbach (eds.), *The Limits of Human Rights* (2019) 267, at 278, pushes back against some of Nussbaum's critique:

While true that CEDAW as drafted is a thin version and vision of women's rights, the Committee has not allowed itself to be constrained by its drafting. As the human rights corpus has grown, so too has CEDAW's framing of the problems. It has worked with other agencies. Its influence can be seen in the lobbying work of civil society, in interactions with governments in national and international forums. Moreover, its widespread citation in domestic case law points to its growing legitimacy and persuasive power. Of all the international human rights instruments, CEDAW, more than any other, has demonstrated its efficacy.

Other scholars have argued that CEDAW has had an important impact in relation to abortion policies. According to Kate Hunt and Mike Gruszczynski in 'The Ratification of CEDAW and the Liberalization of Abortion Laws', 15 *Politics & Gender* (2019) 722, at 741:

… states that ratify CEDAW without reservations have more liberal abortion laws. These effects are stable and consistent, remaining the same regardless of the state's level of democracy, number of women in parliament, GDP per capita, and percentage of the population that is Catholic, Protestant, or Muslim. … [T]hese results suggest that CEDAW is an important factor in explaining cross-national liberalization of abortion laws and therefore could be an important factor in explaining when states are likely to create policy change in order to respect other rights of women as outlined in that treaty.

One positive impact assessment comes from Mala Htuny and Francesca R. Jensenius, in 'Expressive Power of Anti-Violence Legislation: Changes in Social Norms on Violence Against Women in Mexico', 74 *World Politics* (2022) 1:

There are reasons to believe that violence against women legislation, and other rights enacted by transitioning and consolidating democracies, have little impact. States adopted many new laws quickly in order to look good abroad and gain legitimacy at home, without developing the bureaucratic infrastructure required for effective enforcement. The problem is not just low state capacity. Many social groups lack the resources to compel state actors to enforce the law, while groups with resources – such as politicians and upper classes – often have little interest in abiding by legal rules themselves and imposing the law on others. Sticky social norms that uphold power hierarchies and inequality among groups and individuals also reduce compliance with equal rights laws. The result is that in much of the Global South there is a large gap between the letter of the law and behavior on the ground.

In this paper, we propose that violence against women legislation, even when weakly enforced and unevenly implemented, may nonetheless change social relations through the mechanism of normative expression. …

Expressive law theory implies that legal changes will be associated with changes in social norms to align with the law. To empirically measure the norm changes associated with legal changes, we operationalize Richard McAdam's proposed conditions for the emergence of a new norm. We argue that if norm change on violence against women is occurring, we should see it in four patterns: a gradual reduction in experiences of violence, a decline in shares of people with attitudes that condone violence, a rise in shares of women who speak about their experiences to public authorities and people in the local community, and widespread knowledge of women's rights. …

In contrast to skepticism about VAW laws as 'window dressing' institutions that look good but are otherwise inconsequential, and the view that the problem of violence is getting worse, armed by frightful accounts of femicides in the Mexican media and nationwide strikes against violence by hundreds of thousands of women, the data reveal a sharp decline in abuse by intimate partners. Between 2003 and 2016, … the share of women who say they had experienced some form of domestic abuse during the previous year drops from 40.7% to 27.4%. At the same time, there is a sharp reduction in the share of women saying that a man has the right to hit his partner, that a woman must obey her spouse, and that the violence they have experienced is "unimportant." The share of women victims who report episodes of violence to the authorities increased, there is growth in the share of women who speak about their experiences with friends or family, and most women claim familiarity with the 2007 VAW Law.

Our findings support a cautiously optimistic assessment of current trends on violence against women in Mexico, the ability of laws on violence to change norms, and the law's power to undermine societal resistance to the egalitarian principles upheld by consolidating democracies. Our argument does not exclude the possibility that laws affect society in other ways, such as through enforcement and implementation by state actors. Nor do we rule out that economic growth and the global diffusion of ideas contribute to the changes we observe over the four waves of survey data. However, by comparing the empirical implications of our own argument with the implications of alternative explanations, we show that these other explanations do not, on their own, seem to account for the major behavioral and attitudinal changes we see across the survey waves.
…

Janice K. Gallagher also finds room for hope in the struggle against disappearances in Mexico. In *Bootstrap Justice: The Search for Mexico's Disappeared* (2022) 228 she describes impunity as the status quo equilibrium in Mexico which means that in the normal course of events 'crimes will not be investigated; perpetrators will not be punished; and no steps will be taken to provide redress to victims or to prevent disappearances in the future.' But she nevertheless concludes that impunity 'has been meaningfully challenged by the sustained mobilization of the family members of the disappeared' who as a result 'became rights-claiming, and ultimately rights-bearing citizens.'

An analysis by Cosette Creamer and Beth Simmons, 'The Dynamic Impact of Periodic Review on Women's Rights', 81 *Law and Contemporary Problems* (2018) 31, assesses the impact of the CEDAW process, especially in Latin American countries. The authors are responding to oft-heard criticism 'that UN treaty bodies constitute a bloated, toothless bureaucracy that is unable to contribute much to rights protections' (at 32). They conclude that:

> [S]elf-reporting and dialogue between state representatives and international experts ... generates new ideas, advice, and domestic pressure for change in practice. The periodic review process may well have been important to making improvements in law and in practice to guarantee full political and economic rights for women in many societies ... .
>
> ... The number and the density of reports and reviews are crucial to the process of rights improvements. This is certainly far more realistic a finding than to expect last year's reporting cycle to yield one-shot improvements in women's political and economic rights in the following year or so. Reporting and review histories have had a causal influence on the probability of improved women's rights, in law and in practice. ...
>
> [There are] three mutually reinforcing pathways through which the self-reporting process encourages domestic actors to demand and implement change. Domestic shadow reports are on the rise and indicate local CSOs follow the process closely and provide information that supplements and sometimes contradicts government reports. Media reports about the CEDAW spike during the reporting and review process, signifying the penetration of information about the Geneva process to local stakeholders. And finally, legislatures pay attention to the review process and specific [CEDAW Committee] recommendations do have an impact on the lawmaking process. Taken together, the evidence points to the catalytic role of self-reporting and review in putting important women's rights issues on national agendas, thereby creating an occasion for their national discussion.
>
> ... CEDAW may be consequential for its influence on a number of channels, from influencing donor's development assistance policies to clarifying violations through the optional individual complaint process. States have quite heterogeneous experiences in their interactions with the [Committee], and no amount of dialogue can or should create homogeneous outcomes. The quality of interactions as well as the legal, cultural, and political context can be expected to produce quite different results across states.

The evidence supporting the contribution of constructive dialogue to rights improvements is reasonably strong. One reason is that the review process sparks shadow reporting and gains a domestic audience through the national media. ... The national media in Latin America, for example, is replete with discussions and debates about what governments are telling the experts, how shadow reports shape the conversations, what [the Committee] has asked, and how governments have responded. There is plenty of official excuse-making going on, but a surprising amount of criticism as well. Legislators take up these themes in official sessions. These patterns are consistent with a theory that treaties matter because discussing human rights engages interested domestic publics, who are in a better position, armed with legal rights and better information, to hold their governments accountable.

It might be useful to move away from conceptions of the treaty body report- and-review process as a strong enforcement measure, and instead to think of the whole process as more of a dialogue, or as Zwingel puts it, "a constant process of negotiating and re-negotiating norms." ...

Finally, the reporting regime is not a comprehensive solution to the world's worst human rights abuses. Even though CEDAW ratification is now nearly universal, it has proved impossible to coerce a meaningful conversation out of unwilling states. Constructive dialogue only has effects when it actually takes place. …

Finally, Hilary Charlesworth and Christine Chinkin, in 'Between the Margins and the Mainstream: The Case of Women's Rights', in Bardo Fassbender and Knut Traisbach (eds.), *The Limits of Human Rights* (2019) note that:

> 'CEDAW's broad notion of equality … is limited conceptually by its general requirement of a male comparator. … [T]he Convention's standard of equality is that of male lives and experience. This account of equality thus excludes human rights violations that have no counterpart in men's lives, such as women's reproductive rights. Another normative limitation is that the exclusive focus on the categories of men and women emphasizes the significance of biological sex and heterosexual relations.

…

IV. Conclusion

… There appears to be an unruly array of agendas for women's rights, implicating many different types of legal standards, instruments, and institutions. Specialist regimes promote focused attention to women's lives, but allow the mainstream to proceed undisturbed: human rights remain men's rights and women's rights become issues of development or 'special cases' in light of women's 'special needs'. When women's human rights are mainstreamed, as in the WPS [the UN's Women, Peace and Security agenda, described in Ch. 8D, below], they quickly lose their bite. This can occur through their focus on only fragments of women's lives and experiences, or by being co-opted into serving other political agendas, or simply by being ignored or overlooked. Despite all the activity, there is little attention given to the structural causes of human rights abuses against women. The movement between the areas of human rights and WPS shows that the locations of both margins and mainstream are fluid, changing, and contingent. Indeed, there are locations at which margins and mainstream meet, merge, and separate again.

The oscillation between the margins and the mainstream is echoed in debates in the feminist international legal literature about whether feminist scholars should aim for the margins or the centre of the discipline. The margin is often understood as the place we want to leave behind as we head for the centre, the mainstream, where, it is assumed, power resides and all the action takes place. However, the periphery also has its pleasures and virtues. It can be an attractive vantage point, offering a sense of adventure, of originality, of solidarity with the (often vaguely defined) oppressed against those with power.

Feminist scholarship pays attention to the locations of power within a society. Power is often dispersed and is not always concentrated in a centre. Patriarchal power exists at the level of the state, but it also shapes local communities and family relationships. Power is thus best understood as a network, operating in complex and inconsistent ways. For this reason, although international women's groups have long campaigned for enhanced legal regulation, one might conclude that international law will always be an imperfect tool to unravel patriarchal power and will be most effective when it is woven with other forms of regulation and influence.

D. EVOLUTION OF HUMAN RIGHTS: SEXUAL ORIENTATION DISCRIMINATION

In this section we turn to the evolution of new norms, and consider the particular case of lesbian, gay, bisexual, transgender, queer, and intersex (LGBTQI) rights. These rights are very important in themselves, but they also illustrate important issues for the understanding of international human rights law more generally. For example, how does a new human rights norm emerge? What relationship might it have to the existing legal framework? How does it overcome strong political resistance from different corners of the globe? How do like-minded states work strategically to promote the wider recognition of a new norm? What are the consequences of normative evolution being driven by elites rather than reflecting popular opinion?

National and Transnational Social and Legal Change

Formal recognition of LGBTQI rights at the international level began in the 1980s, in response to fundamental social change at the national level. Efforts to forge a new legal regime were galvanized, in particular, by two key developments. In England, a government-appointed expert commission issued a report in 1957 (the Wolfenden Report), which recommended that 'homosexual behaviour between consenting adults in private should no longer be a criminal offence'. The ensuing public debate culminated in legal reforms and substantial (though incomplete) decriminalization of same-sex conduct in 1967. In the United States, a new social movement began with an uprising among gay residents in New York City in response to systematic police harassment. A flashpoint occurred at a gay bar, the Stonewall Inn, in 1969. The following year on the anniversary of the 'Stonewall Riots', the first Gay Pride marches took place in major cities of the United States. These social changes were also emboldened by changes within the medical establishment, and especially the 1973 decision of the American Psychiatric Association (APA) to no longer classify homosexuality as a mental disorder. This gave an important impetus to social change in the United States (and globally). At the same time, leading NGOs such as the American Civil Liberties Union became active in this area. In 1973 the ACLU set up a Sexual Privacy Project (later renamed the Lesbian, Gay, Bisexual, Transgender and AIDS Project), and the Lambda Legal Defense and Education Fund was established as the first legal organization dedicated to achieving equal rights for lesbian and gay people. Not until 1990, however, did the World Health Organization follow the lead of the APA.

These social and legal changes soon acquired a transnational dimension. LGBTQI organizations formed in multiple countries, advocating decriminalization of same-sex conduct. Between 1965 and 2005, almost 80 countries decriminalized sodomy.

The Road to Formal Recognition at the International Level

At the international level, the formal recognition of LGBTQI rights has been advanced in diverse fora. In general, international bodies composed of judges and independent experts — rather than state officials or representatives — led the way. The European Court of Human Rights was the first with its landmark 1981 decision in *Dudgeon v. United Kingdom*. It held that sodomy laws violated the right to privacy under the European Convention,[89] a finding subsequently reaffirmed in cases arising out of Ireland in 1988 and Cyprus in 1993. Beginning in 1994, the United Nations High Commissioner for Refugees recognized that individuals persecuted for their sexual orientation qualified as a 'particular social group' eligible for protection under international refugee law. Also in 1994, the UN Human Rights Committee, the supervisory body of the ICCPR, concluded that Tasmania's local sodomy law violated the ICCPR (*Toonen v. Australia*, Ch. 9, below). Its reasoning rested primarily on the right to privacy but it also invoked the right to equality. In 1995, after reviewing the report of the United States, the Committee expressed its concern 'at the serious infringement of private life' due to US sodomy statutes. By 2001, four of the other five universal human rights treaties were interpreted by their respective supervisory organs to cover sexual orientation discrimination (CEDAW in 1999, CESCR in 2000, CRC in 2000 and CAT in 2001).

At the Fourth World Conference on Women, in Beijing in 1995, explicit references to sexual orientation supported by various states remained in the draft until the very final hours of the conference. At 4 a.m. on the final day the drafting group eliminated all such references in response to significant opposition. A provision was also inserted in the final report explaining that the word 'gender' was not being used in any way that expanded the sense in which it had previously been used in other UN settings. Over 25 states objected to the deletion and some indicated that they would interpret particular parts of the final text to include sexual orientation.

---

[89] In contrast, the Inter-American Court of Human Rights decided its first case recognizing LGBTQI rights only in 2012.

Also in the 1990s, independent experts working under UN mandates on violence against women and extrajudicial executions took up the issue of discrimination based on sexual orientation. Others followed in the early 2000s, including those dealing with torture, arbitrary detention, human rights defenders (all in 2001); the independence of judges and lawyers (2002), minority issues (2006), housing (2010) and health (2009).

These efforts were complemented by a second wave of international endeavours, especially in Europe. In 1997, the Amsterdam Treaty (amending the Treaty of the European Union) became the first international agreement to prohibit discrimination based on 'sexual orientation'. Similarly, states applying to join the EU had to agree to decriminalize homosexual conduct and eliminate laws violating LGBTQI rights.

Early efforts in the UN General Assembly to promote state recognition of LGBTQI rights were led by Brazil, France, and South Africa. Starting in the mid-1990s, the UN Commission on Human Rights passed an annual resolution calling for strictly circumscribing, and eventually abolishing, the death penalty. In 2002, the text was extended to urge states to ensure that 'the death penalty is not imposed for-non-violent acts such as ... sexual relations between consenting adults'.

In the same year, the biennial General Assembly resolution on extrajudicial executions called 'upon Governments concerned to investigate promptly and thoroughly ... all killings committed for any discriminatory reason, including sexual orientation'. By 2010, however, at the committee stage, a coalition of African, Arab, and Islamic states successfully proposed the deletion of this provision (79 in favour, 70 against and 17 abstentions). Before the final plenary vote, then UN Secretary-General Ban Ki-moon made an uncharacteristically passionate plea for the rejection of discrimination based on sexual orientation and gender identity, and the U.S. Ambassador also pushed a proposal to restore the reference to 'sexual orientation' in the text. In a major victory, the final vote was 93-55-27.

At the same time, efforts to get the UN Human Rights Commission to adopt a specific resolution on sexual orientation began with a Brazil-sponsored resolution in 2003. Although also supported by 18 European countries and Canada, strong opposition led to the withdrawal of the proposal in both 2003 and 2004. With international NGOs becoming more active on this issue an initiative by a group of 29 international human rights experts led to the adoption in 2006 of the 'Yogyakarta Principles on the Application of Human Rights Law in relation to Sexual Orientation and Gender Identity' which invoked existing legal standards in support of a wide range of LGBTQI rights. A decade later, these principles were updated and significantly extended.[90]

In 2008, at the UN General Assembly, 66 states called for abolition of criminal penalties based on sexual orientation or gender identity' and the investigation and prosecution of human rights violations based on sexual orientation or gender identity. A second group, of 57 states led by Syria, promptly issued a response expressing serious concern about two problematic notions:

> The notion of orientation spans a wide range of personal choices that expand way beyond the individual's sexual interest in copulatory behavior with normal consenting adult human beings, thereby ushering in the social normalization and possibly the legitimization of many deplorable acts including pedophilia. The second [notion attributes] particular sexual interests or behaviors to genetic factors, a matter that has been scientifically rebuffed repeatedly.
>
> ...
>
> ... We note with concern the attempts to create "new rights" or "new standards" by misinterpreting the Universal Declaration and international treaties to include such notions that were never articulated nor agreed by the general membership. These attempts ... seriously jeopardize the entire international human rights framework.

Notwithstanding this pushback, the Human Rights Council adopted the UN's first ever resolution on 'human rights, sexual orientation and gender identity' in 2011 by a vote of 23-19-3 (Res. 17/19). Its main thrust was to request the OHCHR to conduct a study 'to document discriminatory laws and practices and acts of violence

---

[90] A. Park, 'Yogyakarta Plus 10: A Demand for Recognition of SOGIESC', 44 *North Carolina J. Int'l L.* (2019) 223.

against individuals based on their sexual orientation and gender identity, in all regions of the world'. During the Council debate, Nigeria noted that 'more than 90 per cent of the African people did not support this draft resolution,' and urged that notions of 'sexual orientation should not be imposed on countries'. Saudi Arabia argued that it 'was not appropriate to impose values without considering them as counter to Sharia in Islam, and other religions.' Bahrain said the Council was attempting 'to create new standards and new human rights by misinterpreting the existing international human rights standards.'

When the resulting report was debated the following year, most Arab and African nations walked out. The Vatican representative was 'seriously concerned at the use 'of terms such as "sexual orientation" and "gender identity" which do not enjoy mention in binding [UN] documents [and] lack specific definition in international Human Rights instruments.' He added that the Council risked 'demeaning the sacred and time-honoured legal institution of marriage between man and woman, between husband and wife … . If marriage were to be re-defined in a way that makes other relationships equivalent to it, … the institution of marriage, and consequently the natural family itself, will be both devalued and weakened.'[91]

In 2016, the Council established the position of 'Independent Expert on protection against violence and discrimination based on sexual orientation and gender identity' (Res. 32/2), and renewed the mandate three years later (Res. 41/18) by a vote of 27-12-7, with Afghanistan, Bahrain, Bangladesh, China, Egypt, Eritrea, Iraq, Nigeria, Pakistan, Qatar, Saudi Arabia, and Somalia voting against. In 2020, Austria made a formal statement to the Council on behalf of 32 states[92] (four more later subscribed) calling on all States "as a matter of urgency, to protect the autonomy of intersex adults and children and their rights to health, and to physical and mental integrity so that they live free from violence and harmful practices".

In a statement to the Copenhagen Human Rights Forum on 17 August 2021, the UN High Commissioner for Human Rights welcomed the fact that over 70 countries have decriminalized consensual same-sex relations, but she added that '69 countries continue to have discriminatory laws today. These are laws used to arrest, harass, blackmail, and exclude on the basis of the perceived sexual orientation, and often, the gender identity of individuals. In five of these countries, these laws are so extreme as to include the death penalty.'

In 2021, the Independent Expert, Victor Madrigal-Borloz, reported to the Human Rights Council (UN Doc. A/HRC/47/27) on aspects of 'gender theory'. He framed the report in these terms:

> 1. The notion that there is a gender norm, from which identities and expressions vary or depart, is based on a series of preconceptions that must be challenged … . Among these … is the idea that it is a legitimate societal objective that persons adopt roles, forms of expression and behaviours that are considered entitlements or burdens according to their sex assigned at birth. Only by acknowledging the stereotypes, power asymmetries, inequality and fundamental violence that lies at the foundation of this system does the State comply with its obligation … .

In concluding his analysis, the expert called for the recognition of 'two fundamental duties of the State':

> (a) To prevent, prosecute and punish violence and discrimination on the basis of sexual orientation, gender identity and gender expression and, if relevant, provide reparation to the victims;
>
> (b) To recognize every human being's freedom to determine the confines of their existence, including their gender identity and expression.
>
> …
>
> 79. Gender describes a sociocultural construct that ascribes certain roles, behaviours, forms of expression, activities and attributes determined to be appropriate according to the meaning given to biological sex characteristics. Under this definition, gender and sex do not

---

[91] 9 March 2012, at www.radiovaticana.org/EN1/Articolo.asp?c=569943.

[92] Note that voting in the Council is restricted to the 47 elected members, whereas any state can endorse a statement or co-sponsor a resolution.

substitute each other, and gender identity and gender expression are inextricably linked to them as practices of concern in anti-discrimination analysis.

80. The use of the terms gender and gender identity and expression in international human rights law includes all persons, communities and populations. Whether self-defining into a specific gender, or remaining gender-fluid, across binaries, gender is in operation through the work of naming things as masculine and feminine. The concepts of gender, sex, and gender identity and expression are related, but can be applied independently as protected grounds.

81. The work of addressing and ultimately eradicating violence and discrimination based on sexual orientation and gender identity demands the adoption of intersectional analysis, the sites of which include laws and policies which claim to be gender-neutral or are gender-specific (and may discriminate both against cisgender hetero- and lesbian-identified women and trans and other gender-nonconforming women and men).

82. Legal recognition of gender identity, and protection from violence and discrimination related to it, to gender expression and to sexual orientation, are inextricably connected with bodily autonomy. ...

...

Regional Systems

In 2008, the OAS unanimously adopted a resolution expressing concern about 'acts of violence and related human rights violations committed against individuals because of their sexual orientation and gender identity'. In 2014, the Inter-American Commission on Human Rights appointed a Rapporteur on the Rights of Lesbian, Gay, Bisexual, Trans and Intersex Persons. The Inter-American Court has adopted several important judgments on these issues.

INTER-AMERICAN COURT OF HUMAN RIGHTS, GENDER IDENTITY, AND EQUALITY AND NON-DISCRIMINATION OF SAME-SEX COUPLES, ADVISORY OPINION OC-24/17, 24 NOVEMBER 2017

[Costa Rica requested an Advisory Opinion from the Court in relation to several questions, including:
- Does the Convention imply that states must 'recognize and facilitate the name change of an individual in accordance with his or her gender identity';
- Is it contrary to the Convention if those interested in changing their given name have access only to a judicial rather than an administrative procedure;
- Does the Convention require states to recognize all the patrimonial (economic) rights deriving from a same-sex relationship;
- Must there be a legal institution that regulates same sex relationships for the state to recognize those rights.]

78. ... [S]exual orientation and gender identity, as well as gender expression, are categories protected by the Convention. ...

79. With regard to gender expression, this Court has indicated that a person may be discriminated against on the grounds of the perception that others have of his or her relationship with a social sector or group, regardless of whether this corresponds to the reality or to the self-identification of the victim. ...

...

116. ... [T]he answer to the first question raised by Costa Rica ... [is]:

The change of name, the rectification of the image and the rectification of the sex or gender in the public records and identity documents, so that they correspond to the self-perceived gender identity is a right protected by Article 18 (Right to a Name), but also by Articles 3 (Right to Recognition of Juridical Personality), 7(1) (Right to Personal Liberty), and 11(2) (Right to Privacy) of the American Convention. Consequently, pursuant to the obligation to respect and ensure rights without any discrimination (Articles 1(1) and 24 of the Convention), and the obligation to adopt domestic legal provisions (Article 2 of the Convention), States are obliged to recognize, regulate and establish the appropriate procedure to this end.

...

160. ... [T]he answer to the second question ... [is]:

States may determine and establish, in keeping with the characteristics of each context and their domestic law, the most appropriate procedures for the [required changes] ..., regardless of whether these are of an administrative or judicial nature. However, these procedures should comply with the following requirements established in this Opinion: (a) these should be centered on the complete rectification of the self-perceived gender identity; (b) these should be based solely on the free and informed consent of the applicant without involving requirements such as medical and/or psychological or other certifications that could be unreasonable or pathologizing; (c) these should be confidential, and the changes, corrections or amendments to the records and on the identity documents should not reflect the changes made based on the gender identity; (d) these should be prompt and, insofar as possible, cost-free, and (e) these should not require evidence of surgery and/or hormonal therapy.

...

182. [Although Article 17(2)] ... recognizes the "right of men and women of marriageable age to marry and to raise a family," this wording does not propose a restrictive definition of how marriage should be understood or how a family should be based. In the opinion of this Court, Article 17(2) is merely establishing, expressly, the treaty-based protection of a specific model of marriage. In the Court's opinion, this wording does not necessarily mean either that this is the only form of family protected by the American Convention.

...

189. [A] restrictive interpretation of the concept of "family" that excludes the emotional ties between a same-sex couple from the inter-American protection would defeat the object and purpose of the Convention. ...

...

192. ... [T]he Court agrees with its European counterpart in that it would be "artificial to maintain the view that, in contrast to a different-sex couple, a same-sex couple cannot enjoy 'family life.'" ...

...

199. [In response to Costa Rica's fourth question] ... the Court concludes that:

... [T]he American Convention protects the family ties that may derive from a relationship between persons of the same sex. The Court also finds that all the patrimonial rights derived from a protected family relationship between a same-sex couple must be protected ... .

...

224. ... [T] here would be no sense in creating an institution that produces the same effects and gives rise to the same rights as marriage, but that is not called marriage except to draw attention to same-sex couples by the use of a label that indicates a stigmatizing difference or that, at the very least, belittles them. ... [T]he existence of two types of formal unions ... would create a distinction based on an individual's sexual orientation that would be discriminatory and, therefore, incompatible with the American Convention.

225. In addition, as already indicated, the Court understands that the principle of human dignity derives from the complete autonomy of the individual to choose with whom he or she wishes to enter into a permanent and marital relationship, whether it be a natural one (de facto union) or a formal one (marriage). ... [T]he Court is not diminishing the institution of marriage but, to the contrary, considers marriage necessary to recognize equal dignity to those persons who belong to a human group that has historically been oppressed and discriminated against.

226. ... [T]his Court cannot ignore the possibility that some States must overcome institutional difficulties to adapt their domestic law ... . [T]he Court urges those States to promote, in good faith, the legislative, administrative and judicial reforms required to adapt their domestic laws, and internal interpretations and practice.

227. That said, States that do not yet ensure the right of access to marriage to same-sex couples are obliged not to violate the provisions that prohibit discriminating against them … .

…

Gender Identity Cases

Note also two cases involving violence against LGBTQI individuals in which the Court has broken important ground. The first is *Azul Rojas Marín et al. v. Peru*, Inter-American Court of Human Rights, Judgment of March 12, 2020. Azul Rojas Marín was born in 1981. When arrested in 2008 she self-identified as a gay man but as of 2020 identified herself as a woman. She was arrested after midnight by police who used disparaging terms referring to her sexual orientation. At the police station she was forcibly undressed, beaten, and a police baton was inserted in her anus. The arrest was not recorded. Prosecutions against the responsible officers were dismissed.

The Court found the detention to be unlawful, discriminatory and arbitrary, concluded that the abuse and aggression suffered by Azul Rojas Marín, including rape, constituted an act of torture by state agents, and found that the State failed to act with due diligence in investigating the sexual torture. In addition to reparations for the individual concerned, the State was ordered: to adopt a protocol for the investigation and the administration of justice in criminal proceedings in cases involving members of the LGBTQI community who are victims of violence; to create and implement a plan to raise awareness and provide training on violence against members of the LGBTQI community; to design and implement a system for producing and compiling statistics on such violence; and to eliminate the goal of eradicating 'homosexuals and transvestites' from Public Security Plans.

The second case, *Vicky Hernández et al. v. Honduras*, Judgment of 26 March 2021, involved a transgender woman who was a sex worker and a recognized trans activist. On 28 June 2009, a police patrol tried to arrest Vicky Hernández and two companions. The women fled, but the next day Hernández's body was found with a bullet wound in the head. Based on the evidence, including a context of discrimination and police violence against LGBTQI persons, and particularly against transwomen sex workers, the Court concluded that agents of the State were responsible, and that the violence was committed due to her gender expression or gender identity. The Court found violations of the rights to recognition as a person before the law, to liberty, to privacy, to freedom of expression, to a name, and to equality and non-discrimination. The right to gender identity was violated at the time of her killing, in the subsequent investigation, and in the State's general legal framework which denied her the opportunity to reflect her gender identity and her chosen name on her identity card, thus fostering discrimination and social exclusion.

Among the more innovative reparations ordered, the State was required to make an audiovisual documentary on the discrimination and violence experienced by trans women in Honduras; and to create a 'Vicky Hernández' educational scholarship for trans women.

The Court also held that the State had violated its obligations under the Convention of Belém do Pará (on the Prevention, Punishment, and Eradication of Violence against Women). In a partially dissenting opinion, the President of the Court, Judge Elizabeth Odio Benito, insisted on the need to distinguish 'gender identity' from sex.

40. … [V]iolence against women derives from the social hierarchy established according to the gender roles assigned on the basis of biological sex, while the violence that was directed against Ms. Hernández … was due to her nonconformity and act of resistance against the social and cultural impositions of the heteropatriarchy. …

41. … [If the Court fails to recognize this] distinction, there is a risk that violence against women becomes invisible or is diluted in the face of other violence and violations and is not adequately analyzed within policies as a structural phenomenon linked to the system of domination and gender stereotypes against women. On the contrary, the analysis of violence against transgender people from a perspective that only analyzes violence against women because they are women, while not going to the origin of the specific violence suffered by this group, is clearly counterproductive and ineffective.

Children's Rights

A major area in which international law has brought significant transformation is the rights of the child, especially as spelled out in the 1989 UN Convention on the Rights of the Child. The following materials survey the approaches taken by different UN and regional bodies, especially in the context of LGBTQI persons.

CASE OF BAYEV AND OTHERS V. RUSSIA
EUROPEAN COURT OF HUMAN RIGHTS (THIRD SECTION)
20 JUNE 2017

[The cases were brought by three different applicants, described by the Court as gay rights activists, who had each been found guilty of the administrative offence of "public activities aimed at the promotion of homosexuality among minors." concerning regional laws prohibiting public activities aimed at the promotion of homosexuality among minors. The first had demonstrated outside a secondary school in 2009 with banners stating "Homosexuality is normal" and "I am proud of my homosexuality". In 2012 the second and the third applicants demonstrated in front of a children's library. One held a banner stating "Russia has the world's highest rate of teenage suicide. This number includes a large proportion of homosexuals. They take this step because of the lack of information about their nature. Deputies are child-killers. Homosexuality is good!" The other applicant's banner stated "Children have the right to know. Great people are also sometimes gay; gay people also become great. Homosexuality is natural and normal." The Constitutional Court of the Russian Federation rejected challenges to the applicants' convictions.]

…

2. The Court's assessment

(a) Whether there was interference with the exercise of the applicants' freedom of expression

61. … [T]he central issue in this case is the very existence of a legislative ban on promotion of homosexuality or non-traditional sexual relations among minors … . The applicants complained about the general impact of these laws on their lives, in that it not only prevented them from campaigning for LGBT rights but in effect required them to be aware of the presence of minors in their daily activities, in order to conceal their sexual orientation from them. …

…

(b) Whether the interference was justified

…

63. … [T]he Court's assessment in this case will focus on the necessity of the impugned laws as general measures … .

(i) Justification on the grounds of protection of morals

65. … [T]he Government … alleged that an open manifestation of homosexuality was an affront to the mores prevailing among the religious and even non-religious majority of Russians and was generally seen as an obstacle to instilling traditional family values.

66. The Court would generally accept a wider margin of appreciation in the absence of consensus among member States where the subject matter may be linked to sensitive moral or ethical issues. In the instant case, however, the Court notes that there is a clear European consensus about the recognition of individuals' right to openly identify themselves as gay, lesbian or any other sexual minority, and to promote their own rights and freedoms. …

67. … [T]he Government advanced the alleged incompatibility between maintaining family values as the foundation of society and acknowledging the social acceptance of homosexuality. The Court sees no reason to consider these elements as incompatible, especially in view of the growing general tendency to include

relationships between same-sex couples within the concept of "family life" and the acknowledgement of the need for their legal recognition and protection. ... . The Government failed to demonstrate how freedom of expression on LGBT issues would devalue or otherwise adversely affect actual and existing "traditional families" or would compromise their future.

68. The Court has consistently declined to endorse policies and decisions which embodied a predisposed bias on the part of a heterosexual majority against a homosexual minority ... .

69. The legislation at hand is an example of such predisposed bias, unambiguously highlighted by its domestic interpretation and enforcement, and embodied in formulas such as "to create a distorted image of the social equivalence of traditional and non-traditional sexual relationships" ... Even more unacceptable are the attempts to draw parallels between homosexuality and paedophilia ... .

70. The Court takes note of the Government's assertion that the majority of Russians disapprove of homosexuality and resent any display of same-sex relations. ... The Court reiterates that it would be incompatible with the underlying values of the Convention if the exercise of Convention rights by a minority group were made conditional on its being accepted by the majority. ...

71. In view of the above considerations, the Court rejects the Government's claim that regulating public debate on LGBT issues may be justified on the grounds of the protection of morals.

(ii) Justification on the grounds of protection of health

72. ... [T]he Government have not demonstrated that the applicants' messages advocated reckless behaviour or any other unhealthy personal choices. In any event, the Court considers it improbable that a restriction on potential freedom of expression concerning LGBT issues would be conducive to a reduction of health risks. ...
...

(iii) Justification on the grounds of protection of the rights of others

74. Finally, the Government's third line of argument focused on the need to shield minors from information which could convey a positive image of homosexuality, as a precaution against their conversion to a "homosexual lifestyle" which would be detrimental to their development and make them vulnerable to abuse.
...
...
78. The position of the Government ... remains unsubstantiated. The Government were unable to provide any explanation of the mechanism by which a minor could be enticed into "[a] homosexual lifestyle", let alone science-based evidence that one's sexual orientation or identity is susceptible to change under external influence. The Court therefore dismisses these allegations as lacking any evidentiary basis.

79. In so far as the Government alleged a risk of exploitation and corruption of minors, referring to the latter's vulnerability, the Court upholds the applicants' objection to the effect that protection against such risks should not be limited to same-sex relationships; the same positive obligation should, as a matter of principle, be equally relevant with regard to opposite-sex relationships. ...
...
81. Even assuming that the authorities' obligation to respect parents' religious or philosophical views may be interpreted as requiring them to take measures beyond setting the curricula of educational institutions, it would be unrealistic to expect that parents' religious or philosophical views would have to be given automatic priority in every situation, particularly outside school. The Court reiterates in this context that the Convention does not guarantee the right not to be confronted with opinions that are opposed to one's own convictions ... .

82. In sensitive matters such as public discussion of sex education, where parental views, educational policies and the right of third parties to freedom of expression must be balanced, the authorities have no choice but to

resort to the criteria of objectivity, pluralism, scientific accuracy and, ultimately, the usefulness of a particular type of information to the young audience. ...

(c) Conclusion

83. ... [T]he Court finds that the legal provisions in question do not serve to advance the legitimate aim of the protection of morals, and that such measures are likely to be counterproductive in achieving the declared legitimate aims of the protection of health and the protection of rights of others. ...]B]y adopting such laws the authorities reinforce stigma and prejudice and encourage homophobia, which is incompatible with the notions of equality, pluralism and tolerance inherent in a democratic society.

...

DISSENTING OPINION OF JUDGE DEDOV

...

Vulnerability of children

This element of privacy was not seriously taken into consideration by the Court. The ... Convention on the Rights of the Child (CRC) ... provides that the child, by reason of his physical and mental immaturity, needs special safeguards and care. The CRC obliges the States to respect the right of the child to preserve his or her identity without unlawful interference. ... States should take measures to prevent the inducement or coercion of a child to engage in any unlawful sexual activity (Articles 8, 9 and 34).

Mental immaturity is a decisive element of vulnerability. It is well known that children are vulnerable and credulous because of their lack of experience and incapacity to judge. Children may easily become interested in any information or ideas, especially in homosexual relations, without understanding their nature. The idea that same-sex sexual relations are normal indeed creates a situation where they are ready to engage in such relations, just because of the curiosity which is an integral part of a child's mind. This is how the dissemination of ideas works *vis-à-vis* children. ...

...

I would agree with the applicants that this is just a neutral dissemination of information if the problem of paedophilia were completely resolved. According to the statistics, every year up to 50,000 children in Russia are subjected to sexual abuse ... . [S]ame-sex violence constitutes a significant part of such cases, so that it deserves to be taken into consideration by making a special reference to same-sex relations in the law.

...

Freedom of expression

The Court, in the present case, did not seriously take into account the fact that the private life of children is more important than the freedom of expression of homosexuals.

It appears from the circumstances of the case that all the demonstrations were held in order to promote non-traditional sexual relations (which is not itself an issue of public interest); they were not held to express opinions on issues of public interest such as same-sex marriage or adoption. ...

...

Conclusion

... Until now, the Council of Europe has favoured unrestricted public recognition of non-traditional sexual relations, even in sensitive areas such as the vulnerability of a particular group of persons (children) owing to their immaturity, the religious and philosophical convictions of their parents (on how the family should be organised), the national traditions and values including maternity, the national demographic policy and the sensitivity of sexuality education.

* * *

Prior to the CRC's adoption in 1989, many states accorded very few rights to children and treated them in some respects as though they were the property of their parents or guardians. The CRC recognizes that children enjoy the full range of rights and that '[i]n all actions concerning children, whether undertaken by public or private social welfare institutions, courts of law, administrative authorities or legislative bodies, the best interests of the child shall be a primary consideration' (Article 3). In its General Comment No. 20 (2016) on the implementation of the rights of the child during adolescence (UN Doc. CRC/C/GC/20), the Committee on the Rights of the Child takes a very different approach to adolescence:

> 1. The [CRC] defines a child as every human being below the age of 18 years unless under the law applicable to the child majority is attained earlier … . … [T]he implementation of rights should take account of children's development and their evolving capacities. Approaches adopted to ensure the realization of the rights of adolescents differ significantly from those adopted for younger children.
>
> …
>
> Lesbian, gay, bisexual, transgender and intersex adolescents
>
> …
>
> 34. The Committee emphasizes the rights of all adolescents to freedom of expression and respect for their physical and psychological integrity, gender identity and emerging autonomy. It condemns the imposition of so-called "treatments" to try to change sexual orientation and forced surgeries or treatments on intersex adolescents. It urges States to eliminate such practices, repeal all laws criminalizing or otherwise discriminating against individuals on the basis of their sexual orientation, gender identity or intersex status and adopt laws prohibiting discrimination on those grounds. States should also take effective action to protect all lesbian, gay, bisexual, transgender and intersex adolescents from all forms of violence, discrimination or bullying by raising public awareness and implementing safety and support measures.

The Right to Bodily Autonomy and Physical Integrity

International human rights bodies have also recognized that the rights of LGBTQI people extend beyond freedom from the more obvious forms of discrimination and violence. The right to bodily autonomy and physical integrity informs the rights of trans, gender-diverse and intersex people, including children, to make decisions about their gender expression and medical care. This includes the right to access gender-affirming care without abusive or invasive requirements, as well as the right not to be subjected to 'conversion therapy' or (in the case of intersex people) 'normalising' medical interventions.

Gender-diverse people are often denied these rights due to the dominance of societal sex and gender norms in legal and medical spaces. In 2021, the UN Independent Expert on Sexual Orientation and Gender Identity described early surgeries on intersex children as 'a blatant and cruel effect of gender binary norms' and called on states:

> to protect the right to bodily integrity, autonomy and self-determination of intersex children by prohibiting what are heinously called "normalising" medical procedures. The definition of bodily autonomy is also of fundamental importance for trans persons who face cruel, inhuman and degrading treatment, and possible torture, in the form of abusive requirements for gender recognition such as medical certification, surgery, treatment, sterilization or divorce. It is the State's duty to confer every human being with the freedom to determine the confines of their existence - that means establishing no invasive preconditions to legally recognize a person's gender identity by way of self-determination.

The Inter-American Commission on Human Rights (OEA/Ser.L/V/II., Doc. 239 (7 August 2020)) has also emphasized the way in which pathologization of gender diversity by legislative and medical institutions – for example, requirements for trans persons to obtain a diagnosis of 'gender dysphoria' before accessing gender-affirming care or changing their identity documents – impacts their rights to health, bodily autonomy and physical integrity.

One of the most far-reaching statements on the rights of intersex persons was adopted by the African Commission on Human and Peoples' Rights:

RESOLUTION ON THE PROMOTION AND PROTECTION OF THE RIGHTS OF INTERSEX PERSONS IN AFRICA – ACHPR/RES.552 (LXXIV) 2023

Considering that Article 5 of the Protocol to the African Charter on Human and Peoples' Rights on the Rights of Women in Africa and Article 21 of the African Charter on the Rights and Welfare of the Child prohibit harmful social and cultural practices;

Recognizing that intersex persons, who are born naturally with a chromosomal abnormality and reproductive or sexual anatomy that does not appear to fit the typical definitions of female or male, exist in all African societies;

Recognizing that intersexuality is an inherent handicap at birth and that it should not be considered a taboo in all African societies;

Recognizing also that non-consensual and unnecessary surgical and other genital normalization procedures performed on intersex persons, in a medical or other setting, may cause them lifelong physical and psychological suffering, permanent sterility, incontinence, and loss of sexual pleasure;

Further recognizing that the above-mentioned non-consensual and unnecessary surgical and other genital normalization procedures have irreversible consequences similar to genital mutilation and can be considered as such;

Concerned about human rights violations against intersex persons ...;

...

The Commission calls on States Parties to:

1. Promote and protect the rights of intersex persons on the continent;

2. Stop non-consensual genital normalization practices on intersex persons, such as surgical, hormonal and sterilization procedures that alter the sexual characteristics of intersex persons and ensure respect for their rights to make their own decisions regarding their bodily integrity, physical autonomy and self-determination;

3. Ensure that any action concerning an intersex minor is carried out with the permission of the parents and after medical analysis, taking strict account of the best interests of the child;

4. End human rights violations against intersex persons, such as infanticide and abandonment of intersex children;

5. Prohibit discrimination based on intersex traits and characteristics or intersex status ...;

...

7. Incorporate intersex education into prenatal counselling and support services, and provide training for health care personnel ...;

8. Enact enabling legislation and institutionalize administrative processes that allow intersex persons to change the gender designation on their birth certificates and other official documents, based on decision taken through medical intervention;

...

Pushback or Backlash Against LQBTQI and Women's Rights

The relative success of efforts to promote the rights of LGBTQI people, alongside the deepening of the women's rights agenda, has prompted significant pushback from a variety of actors.[93] The following materials provide examples relating to the response of different legal, religious, cultural, and political groups

a. International Law Critique

LI-ANN THIO, EQUALITY AND NON-DISCRIMINATION IN INTERNATIONAL HUMAN RIGHTS LAW
THE HERITAGE FOUNDATION, SPECIAL REPORT NO. 240, 31 DECEMBER 2020

... [T]he original understanding underlying "non-discrimination" in [the UDHR has] evolved through the expansive and contested interpretations of human rights bodies as a method of standard-setting, which has been criticized as advancing a subjective ideological agenda ... .

...

Human Rights Treaty Law

...

Many human rights bodies with cosmopolitan drives have sought to promote their vision of substantive equality by expansively interpreting what equality and non-discrimination requires or by a radical interpretation of the text not contemplated by the authors of an instrument. ...

To read sexual orientation into "sex" is a method that has no basis in historical intent or, indeed, the conventional method of treaty interpretation ... . The point is to detect the parties' intention, not to supplant them, as U.N. bureaucrats do not have legislative powers to speak for the international community— nor do U.N. monitoring bodies have determinative power to declare what the treaty means. ...

...

Argument by Reiteration

...

... Various regional human rights courts and U.N. bureaucrats appear to favor reading human rights treaties as "living instruments,"—discounting historical intent—and allow their preferred value-laden interpretations to be advanced. This renders texts infinitely malleable, enlisted to serve whatever the interpreter deems a worthy cause. The strategy of reiteration is to keep repeating opinions until they achieve actual or perceived canonical status, with successive iterations relying for authority mostly upon one another. Each victory is celebrated as the acme of progressivism, and dissenting views are silenced through intimidation, shaming, and slurs. ...

...

Soft-Law Instruments

...

[The Yogyakarta Principles] are not the product of government negotiation and agreement, but of a group of self-selecting experts, U.N. bureaucrats, and LGBT ... pressure groups attempting to present a radical social policy vision as binding norms. Some states have utilized it as a tool ... .

...

Clash of Rights: Sexual-Orientation Discrimination and the Assault on the Human Rights and Fundamental Freedoms

...

Principles of SOGI discrimination in particular, have far-reaching and negative effects on public discourse— and threaten to diminish other human rights. ...

---

[93] C. Roggeband, 'International Women's Rights: Progress Under Attack?', in H. Krieger and A. Liese (eds.) *Tracing Value Change in the International Legal Order: Perspectives from Legal and Political Science* (2023) 252.

Right to Education. Demands that governments should promote tolerance and respect for diverse sexual orientations through public education programs aimed against "homophobia" and "transphobia" through "comprehensive sexuality education" violate the human right of parents to instill values in their children. ...

...

Freedom of Religion and Expression. Expansive readings of non-discrimination on grounds like sexual orientation promotes liberty and equality for some at the expense of equality and liberty for others—particularly in relation to freedom of religion, conscience and expression ... .

...

Recommendations

...

... *[P]olicymakers should recognize a global margin of appreciation* to respect principles of pluralism, subsidiary and the democratic will of national societies. While some jurisdictions may, for example, recognize same-sex marriage as part of privacy or equality rights, whether based on the democratic views of that society or their courts, policymakers should respect the political independence of other states by letting their societies decide what they wish their social fabric and sense of social morality to be—without external coercion, pressure, or intervention.

Conclusion

Human rights law is not made by the pronouncements of human rights experts or monitoring bodies. Though they wield considerable influence in shaping human rights discourse, they have no authority to impose a moral diktat by declaring a controversial political claim to be a legal human right. ...

b. 'Gender Ideology'

During the 1990s a coalition led by the Vatican, with strong support from other predominantly Christian and Muslim states, opposed the use of the term 'gender' in the context of the 1995 Fourth World Conference on Women and the 1994 International Conference on Population and Development. Juan Marco Vaggione in 'The Conservative Uses of Law: The Catholic Mobilization against Gender Ideology', 67 *Social Compass* (2020) 252, describes how for 'the Catholic Church, legal reforms allowing contraception, abortion, assisted reproductive methods, same-sex partnerships, or gender identity are not only immoral but also illegal and should be resisted by believers and citizens worldwide.' Much of the Church's advocacy is based on the idea of 'gender ideology' as 'a conceptual tool that, despite the absence of a clear definition ..., provides an effective frame to capture (while reducing) the complex politics of feminist and LGBTQI movements. According to this frame, these movements are actively seeking to impose an agenda contrary to scientific rationality and Christian values.'

Law is a key focus of this struggle, and human rights debates have become a favoured battleground. Populist leaders in a range of countries have taken up the rallying cry against 'gender ideology' and Vaggione argues that it is being used to demand public action 'in order to defend a series of values, such as family, life, national sovereignty and human rights'. 'In Latin America, this fight is being waged through three linked actors who constitute the neoconservative movement: factions of the Catholic and evangelical hierarchies, pro-life/pro-family NGO's, and anti-gender politicians. This movement, which transcends the religious secular dichotomy, is changing the political map of the Latin American region'.

Ruth Rubio-Marín, in 'On Constitutionalism and Women's Citizenship', 74 *Current Legal Problems* (2021) 361, describes the implications of different types of constitutionalism for 'women's equal citizenship: (1) exclusionary constitutionalism, which locks in the separation between public and private spheres; (2) inclusive constitutionalism, which grants equal rights to women; (3) participatory constitutionalism, which emphasizes the importance of women's equal participation in a broadly conceived public sphere; and (4) transformative constitutionalism, which not only incorporates women in the public sphere but also reinterprets the domestic sphere in a way that disestablishes gender roles. But across these different approaches, recent years have seen an alliance between religious and far-right actors who have promoted:

> 'constitutional reforms to (re)entrench the traditional family order in the constitutions (*constitutional entrenchment*); constitutional litigation to invalidate or reduce previously granted rights in favour of women, and sexual and gender minorities (*constitutional erosion*); and *constitutional co-option*, which ... co-opts the discourse of rights to preserve majority

values from their perceived erosion. Since the last two rely on judicial activity they can certainly prosper with governments that, suspicious of what they denounce as "gender ideology", pack the court system in ways they deem fit to offer resistance.

...

[C]onstitutional co-option ... uses victimization narratives which describe an 'oppressed majority' allegedly threatened by a totalitarian 'gender ideology' and combines the subversion of the constitutional logic of fundamental rights with the supra-ordination of religious freedom or freedom of conscience, to limit or even de facto empty the rights and freedoms granted to women and sexual and gender minorities by claiming protection for conscientious objection. Thus, if originally the accommodation of religious exemptions had been able to serve to protect religious minorities (in the observance of their practices, food or dress standards), now religious and ideological exemptions are affirmed as a way of preserving majority religious values to the detriment of the constitutional equality of women and sexual minorities. Conscientious objections in relation to the right to abortion are the subject of constitutional litigation in several countries ... . Objections are also raised against the sale and coverage by insurers of abortion and contraceptive methods, including emergency contraception. And they have also become a key mode of objection to LGBT rights, mainly in relation to same-sex marriage and antidiscrimination policies. 'Invoking freedom of conscience, religious pluralism, and non-discrimination', rather than religious doctrine itself, 'opponents of women's reproductive rights and LGBT equality seek more persuasive justification for their positions and partly disable liberals from objecting' [Quoting NeJaime and Siegel].

ISLAMIC COUNTRIES' RESPONSE

The Independent Permanent Human Rights Commission of the Organization of Islamic Cooperation undertook a study in 2017 to consider the implications of the SOGI agenda in light of 'Islamic interpretations'.94 The study described the 'natural family, composed of a father, mother and children' as being 'under assault by those who are attempting to radically redefine it to include ... *'same-sex unions'*. It characterized the efforts of the LGBT community 'to practice their way of life as normal families' as 'the most controversial subject that continue [sic] to pitch traditional societies in the Muslim and most African countries as well as many of the religious communities against Western societies'. It warned of 'disastrous consequences of this suicidal social experiment' if the LGBT community is successful, noting that 'there is a real danger that other groups, citing genetic predisposition claims, would also be encouraged to demand legalizing incest, bestiality and other such deviant sexual behaviors and personal choices as a matter of "human right"'.

The study relied on several arguments to show 'that the concept of sexual orientation does not fall into the purview of international human rights law:'

i. ... [P]roponents of sexual rights falsely claim that such rights are covered under the existing rights of equality, non-discrimination and sexual and reproductive health. But the fact remains that none of the above has ever been defined or accepted in any of the human rights instruments or UN documents by consensus.

ii. ... [A]ny attempt to introduce such concepts or notions, that have no legal foundation in international human rights law and directly impinge on the socio-cultural and religious sensitivities of a large group of UN countries, would only lead to further polarization and undermining of the cooperative and consensual nature of the international human rights architecture;

...

---

94 OIC-IPHRC Study on Sexual Orientation and Gender Identity in the Light of Islamic Interpretations and International Human Rights Framework (May 2017, Jeddah).

v. While reaffirming commitment to combating all forms of violence and discrimination against any person or group on any ground, attempts to universalize SOGI are clearly meant to imposing [sic] one set of values and preferences on the rest of the world, which counteracts the fundamentals of universal human rights that call for respecting diversity, national and regional particularities and various historical, cultural and religious backgrounds, as clearly set out in various international human rights instruments;

...

vii. While attempting to implement such controversial concepts, the international community must accord respect for the sovereign right of each country as well as its national laws, development priorities, the various religious and ethical values and cultural backgrounds of its people in full conformity with universally recognized international human rights ... .

c. 'Traditional Values' Debate

Beginning in 2009, the Russian Government, with strong domestic support from the Russian Orthodox Church, began promoting an agenda within UN fora focusing on 'traditional values' and 'protection of the family'.[95] The text of the latter appears below. McCrudden observes that these resolutions aim to have concepts such as '"dignity", "freedom" and "responsibility"', interpreted through the lens of the idea of "traditional values", which is left undefined.' He argues that although the resolutions are 'rightly regarded with suspicion' given the darker side of the ways in which traditional values and religious faith have been used in political and legal affairs, and 'threaten to further divide rather than unite', they also raise important issues because 'they indicate a deep unease with aspects of the human rights project that needs to be taken seriously. ... Reorientation of the human rights project towards concern for the exploited, drawing on traditional values embedded in societies and cultures throughout the world, could be an important way in which the traditional values debate produces a more positive outcome ...'.[96]

Stoeckl and Medvedeva are more skeptical, suggesting that the Russian initiative has succeeded in putting a 'specific group of actors into a situation of an argumentative double bind. Some religious NGOs from Western countries overlap with the traditionalist agenda on functional grounds, but disagree on strategy and political implications. Moderate conservative actors express puzzlement to find themselves on one side with Russia, against liberal democratic governments they otherwise support.' In their view, the political motivation behind Russia's 'traditionalist agenda ... appears to be polarisation, not advancement on topics of common concern'.[97]

HUMAN RIGHTS COUNCIL, PROTECTION OF THE FAMILY ...
RESOLUTION 29/22 (3 JULY 2015)

The Human Rights Council,

...

4.   Reaffirms that the family is the natural and fundamental group unit of society and is entitled to protection by society and the State;

...

6.   Recognizes that the family, while respect for the rights of its members is ensured, is a strong force for social cohesion and integration, intergenerational solidarity and social development, and that the family plays a crucial role in the preservation of cultural identity, traditions, morals, heritage and the values system of society;

7.   Conscious that families are sensitive to strain caused by social and economic changes, and expresses deep concern that conditions have worsened for many families owing to economic and financial crises, lack of

---

[95] K. Stoeckl, 'Traditional Values, Family, Homeschooling: The Role of Russia and the Russian Orthodox Church in Transnational Moral Conservative Networks and their Efforts at Reshaping Human Rights', 21 *Int'l J. Const. L.* (2023) 224.

[96] C. McCrudden, 'Human Rights and Traditional Values', in U. Baxi, C. McCrudden, and A. Paliwala (eds.), *Law's Ethical, Global and Theoretical Contexts* (2015) 38.

[97] K. Stoeckl and K. Medvedeva, 'Double Bind at the UN: Western Actors, Russia, and the Traditionalist Agenda', 7 *Global Constitutionalism* (2018) 383, at 412.

job security, temporary employment and lack of regular income and gainful employment, as well as measures taken by Governments seeking to balance their budget by reducing social expenditure;

8. Recognizes that the family unit is facing increasing vulnerabilities;

…

10. Reaffirms the need to promote and protect the rights of the child, and in this regard calls upon States to render appropriate assistance to parents and legal guardians in the performance of their child-rearing responsibilities …;

11. Stresses that equality between women and men, women's equal participation in employment and shared parental responsibility are essential elements of a policy on the family;

12. Regrets that women's social and economic contributions to the welfare of the family and the social significance of maternity and paternity continue to be inadequately addressed and that women continue on many occasions to bear a disproportionate share of household responsibilities and the care of children, the sick and elderly, and in this regard emphasizes the need to consistently address such imbalances and to ensure that maternity, motherhood, parenting and the role of women in procreation is not a basis for discrimination nor for restricting the full participation of women in society;

…

16. Stresses that persons with disabilities and their family members should receive the necessary protection and assistance … ;

17. Recognizes the positive impact that policies and measures to protect the family can have on protecting and promoting the human rights of its members and can contribute to, inter alia, decreasing drop-out rates from educational institutions, achieving equality between women and men and girls and boys, empowering women and girls and enhancing the protection against violence, abuses, sexual exploitation, harmful practices and the worst forms of child labour …;

…

[Adopted by a vote of 29-14-4:

d. Neoliberalism

Judith Butler, in 'Anti-Gender Ideology and Mahmood's Critique of the Secular Age', 87 *J. Am. Acad. of Religion* (2019) 955, locates the backlash against feminist and LGBTQI approaches partly in the needs of a neoliberal economy.

> The platform of the anti-gender ideology alliance of right-wing Catholics and Evangelicals is clear: they oppose feminism, LGBTQI rights, especially gay marriage and trans legal and medical rights, single mothers, gay parents, and more. My wager is that as neoliberal economic policies devastate the work lives and the sense of futurity for many people who face contingent labor and unpayable debt, the turn against "gender" is a way of shoring up a traditional sense of place and privilege. It also draws the line between public and private, walling off the family and its patriarchal privilege from the market, where humiliation and dispensability have become the norm. Both the nationalist and traditionalist investment in prohibiting gay marriage, gay and lesbian families and adoption rights, trans and *travestis* rights, single parent adoption and access to reproductive technology, gender inequality, and the concept of "gender" itself follows from the fact that the heteronormative family is now being defended, sometimes violently, as the sole defense against devastating market forces. …
>
> … [T]he withdrawal of state support for families, dependent children, and social services has shifted the burden of basic support back to families, which is one reason why the fierce rehabilitation of the traditional family has taken place at the same time as its financial stability has been severely challenged. The authority of the Evangelical Church has stepped in, as it were, not just to give moral order to the family, without which the economy cannot function, but to aid and abet free market economics. … Moreton argues that white Christian women who constitute the driving force of the evangelical movement

understand quite clearly that "family values are an indispensable element of the global service economy, not a distraction from it". Indeed, the evangelical church is itself part of free enterprise, or what some call Christian enterprise, and this convergence is consistently claimed to be the only alternative to socialism or communism or to elites on campus. ... Just as family values are indispensable to maintaining the service economy, as only the free labor of the family can render its economic terms even marginally livable, so faith-based welfare networks are indispensable to the withdrawal of government from the mandate to provide social services to those in need. In departing from the basic ideals of social democracy, the private realm of the family and of religion assume a more central role in the economic and political functioning of society.

...

e. National-Level Cultural Responses

In 2015, the US Supreme Court held that the Constitution grants same-sex couples the right to marry, thus effectively overturning a ban that had persisted in 13 of the 50 states. In 1996 only 27 percent of Americans approved of same-sex marriage, but by 2020 polls put the figure at 70 percent. Globally in 2021 same-sex marriage is legal in 28 countries, and various others recognise civil partnership for same-sex couples. But most of these countries are in Europe or the Americas. In 2023, the Indian Supreme Court ruled that it was for Parliament, not the courts, to recognize same-sex marriage.

There has been especially strong resistance in some African countries, often based on an appeal to traditional values. In 2021 a Ghanaian Member of Parliament introduced the Promotion of Proper Human Sexual Rights and Ghanaian Family Values Bill, 2021 aiming 'to provide for proper human sexual rights and Ghanaian family values; proscribe LGBTQ+ and related activities; proscribe propaganda of, advocacy for, or promotion of LGBTTQQIAAP+ and related activities; provide for the protection of, and support for, children, persons who are victims or accused of LGBTTQQIAAP+ and related activities and other persons; and related matters.' Penalties of three to five years in prison were prescribed for any non-heterosexual sex acts. A 'grossly indecent act', with a penalty of 6-12 months in prison, included any 'public show of amorous relations between or among persons of the same sex'. In July 2023 the Supreme Court dismissed a legal challenge to the Bill and the President announced that a modified version would be adopted by the Government.

Z. Z. Devji, in 'Forging Paths for the African Queer: Is There an "African" Mechanism for Realizing LGBTIQ Rights?,' 60 *J. African L.* (2016) 343, highlights the contrast between South Africa's very progressive constitutional law in this area, and societal values:

> The recognition of queer rights in the law of South Africa is perhaps one of the most advanced in the world. The language of the country's 1996 constitution, which included the sexual orientation of individuals as a class towards whom discrimination was prohibited, drove the recognition of queer rights. In 2006, South Africa was the first country in Africa to extend full marriage rights to same sex couples. Prior to ruling that the state's refusal to recognize marriage for same sex couples was unconstitutional, South African courts also overturned the prohibitions against sodomy, held that permanent same sex partners of South Africans should receive the same benefits as heterosexual spouses, legalized same sex adoptions, recognized the right to change one's sex, and invalidated a provision of the Children's Status Act that classified children born to same sex couples, through the aid of artificial insemination, as illegitimate. All these fundamental victories for the South African queer population were achieved under the constitution's equality provision. In addition to establishing concrete rights, the Constitutional Court has interpreted the term "sexual orientation" broadly, by defining it as erotic attraction ... .

> ... [T]he court broadly reads the proscription of discrimination based on sexual orientation to outlaw discrimination based on conduct, as well as discrimination based on sexual identification.

However, despite progressive policies and interpretations of the South African Constitution, public opinion and majoritarian sentiments are largely contrary to the liberal nature of the law. "The vast majority of South Africans condemn [the queer]." One South African constitutional law scholar offers three explanations for why the law was able to progress in South Africa, despite public opinion: the rise of queer visibility during key moments of transitional justice; the dominant ideology of the liberation movements, which was grounded in prohibiting discrimination and promoting equality; and the actual process of drafting the constitution, which allowed for its approval despite a lack of public support.

… Thus, although the constitution gives a strong legal basis for queer rights, South Africa remains a deeply conservative country that highly values heteronormativity. … [T]he South African case study serves to demonstrate that good policies and progressive constitutions are not enough to shape a society's values and sustain the clear rule of law.

Sylvia Tamale, in 'Confronting the Politics of Nonconforming Sexualities in Africa', 56 *African Studies Rev.* (2013) 31 argues that 'nonconforming sexualities have been instrumentalized to entrench dictatorships and to weaken democracy' and that 'homophobia has become a political tool used by conservative politicians to promote self-serving agendas.' But she is also very critical of western responses to African homophobia:

When the Anti-Homosexuality Bill was [first] introduced in Uganda, a number of Western government leaders called on Uganda to recognize the sexual citizenship of all its people. Overnight this was turned into a "conditionality" for aid to government and nongovernmental human rights organizations alike. Prior to this debacle, Ugandan activists had shouted themselves hoarse regarding rigged elections, detentions without trial, abuses of media freedoms, corruption, and many other human rights violations. But Western governments failed to respond, and instead dubbed [Ugandan President] Museveni one of only a handful of a "new breed" of African leaders. The selective conditionality when it comes to the rights of LGBTI individuals therefore smacks of hypocrisy.

In 2014 Uganda's Parliament adopted the Anti-Homosexuality Act, but it was subsequently annulled by the Supreme Court on procedural grounds. In May 2023, Uganda's President, Yoweri Museveni, signed into law the Anti-Homosexuality Act. All but two of Uganda's 389 Members of Parliament voted in favor of the law. Its stated purpose is 'to prohibit any form of sexual relations between persons of the same sex; to prohibit the promotion or recognition of sexual relations between persons of the same sex; and for related matters.' Some excerpts follow:

<u>Article 2</u>

(1) A person commits the offence of homosexuality if the person performs a sexual act or allows a person of the same sex to perform a sexual act on him or her.

(2) A person who commits the offence of homosexuality is liable, on conviction, to imprisonment for life.

…

<u>Article 3</u>

(1) A person who commits the offence of homosexuality in any of the circumstances specified in subsection (2), commits the offence of aggravated homosexuality and is liable, on conviction, to suffer death.

(2) The circumstances referred to in subsection (1) are where—

(a) the person against whom the offence is committed is a child;

(b) the offender is a parent, guardian or relative of the person against whom the offence is committed;

(c) the person against whom the offence is committed contracts a terminal illness as a result of the sexual act;

...

(i) the sexual act is committed against a person by means of threats, force, fear of bodily harm, duress or undue influence, intimidation of any kind, or through misrepresentation as to the nature of the act; ...

...

Article 11

(1) A person who promotes homosexuality commits an offence and is liable, on conviction, to imprisonment for a period not exceeding twenty years.

(2) A person promotes homosexuality where the person—

(a) encourages or persuades another person to perform a sexual act or to do any other act that constitutes an offence under this Act;

(b) knowingly advertises, publishes, prints, broadcasts, distributes or causes the advertisement, publication, printing, broadcasting or distribution by any means, including the use of a computer, information system or the internet, of any material promoting or encouraging homosexuality or the commission of an offence under this Act;

(c) provides financial support, whether in kind or cash, to facilitate activities that encourage homosexuality or the observance or normalisation of conduct prohibited under this Act;

(d) knowingly leases or subleases, uses or allows another person to use any house, building or establishment for the purpose of undertaking activities that encourage homosexuality or any other offence under this Act; or

(e) operates an organisation which promotes or encourages homosexuality or the observance or normalisation of conduct prohibited under this Act.

...

Kapya Kaoma, in Christianity, Globalization, and Protective Homophobia: Democratic Contestation of Sexuality in Sub-Saharan Africa (2018) 171 explores the religious and colonial roots of 'protective homophobia' in Africa:

The growing influence of Christianity amidst the challenges of globalization and democracy is directly related to the resurgence of protective homophobia in sub-Saharan African politics. ...

...

... [T]he claim of battling "the global homosexual agenda" is established on the continent. This conspiracy presents Africa and the youth as helpless victims to be rescued from this evil agenda. ...

The contestation of sexuality, however, is not new to the continent—in Christian Africa, it dates to the seventeenth- to nineteenth-century colonial and the Christianization projects. At that time Africans contested the Victorian sexual norms that sought to displace sexuality from its central place in their worldviews. After many years of resistance, these Victorian norms were re-appropriated—the Victorian sexual norms became African and so did Christianity. ...

...

... [C]ultural, religious, and postcolonial predispositions inform sexuality politics in Africa. The history of colonialism, Christianization, and civilization/globalization is the lens through which sexuality is debated. Since sexuality revolves around social and religious values, Christian sexual norms become the basis for public policy. For this very reason, African sexual politics is a contest between localized religiously informed norms and the globalized human rights cultures. Paradoxically, both the defense of cultural values and sexual orientation and gender identity are acknowledged human rights.

...

Domestically, the claim that homosexuality is a donor-driven agenda gives African religious and political leaders ammunition to oppose sexual rights. Because politicians understand the frustration of many Africans over supposed global injustices, they package their anti-gay messages as defending an African cultural identity and religion. Moreover, by defining homosexuality as a Western imposition, politicians negatively define the West. In doing so, they attract support from the overtly religious electorate, while negatively projecting Africa's socio-economic plight on the West. Yet the growing visibility of sexual minorities also destabilizes the hetero-sexualization of the African identity. Through the politics of being, sexual minorities are not just reclaiming their political and to some extent cultural space, but also reforming and informing the public deliberations on sexuality.

...

... The contestation of sexuality by pro-gay and anti-gay rights advocates is interpreted as exercising one's democratic rights of expression and freedom of associations which are fundamental to human rights cultures. In short, both groups are active political actors in sexual rights democratic deliberations—they know that they can influence public policy through social activism.

...

... [T]he emphasis placed on same-sex sexual acts as opposed to sexual minorities' humanity robs them of their authentic humanity or *ubuntu*. Sexual minorities are not just fighting for the rights to have sex—despite the emphasis placed on it. They are fighting for the rights to exist as human beings with equal rights to other vehicles of social life— employment, legal protection, and accessing health services, among many others. ...

QUESTIONS

1. Discuss the following comment on the dissent of Judge Odio Benito in Hernández v Honduras:

"To insist ... on a static definition of woman as "female" serves to maintain a binary system of gender that oppresses those who defy it. Odio Benito's interpretation does not seek to understand in structural terms the situation of gender-based oppression, but instead to attach intrinsic characteristics to some persons and from there to infer legal results. ...

By contrast, a progressive interpretation of rights must be situated, open, and possibilistic, and the categories on which it is based must be "explicitly tentative, relational, and unstable." One must understand how social hierarchies operate in different contexts and historical moments in order to, on the one hand, recognize persons who suffer oppression and, on the other, try to dismantle the body of prejudices, stereotypes, and violence which work to maintain said system of domination. In this sense, cis (biological) and trans women both suffer patriarchal gender-based violence. ...[98]"

2. How should states and international organizations respond to laws like that adopted in Uganda? According to Outright International, in 2023 the World Bank was providing $US 5.5 billion in multi-year financing to the Ugandan government, whose total annual expenditure budget is $US 13 billion. On 8 August 2023 the Bank announced that the Act 'fundamentally contradicts' its values. 'We believe our vision to eradicate poverty on a livable planet can only succeed if it includes everyone irrespective of race, gender, or sexuality. This law undermines those efforts.' It added that there would be no new public financing for Uganda until unspecified measures have been implemented and tested for efficacy. The Bank has no such general policy in place and it has long argued that, because its Articles of Agreement prohibit it from interfering in the political affairs of member states, it can take no position on human rights obligations. The United States imposed sanctions against Uganda, but after the President of Burundi suggested in December 2023 that gay people should be taken to a stadium and stoned, the U.S. said only that it was 'deeply troubled'.

E. TORTURE
1. Norm Regression: The Torture Prohibition

If one were to ask an average group of people to rank rights in order of importance, torture would be near the top of the list. It could be said, 'If anything is a human right, then it's the right not to be tortured.' Consider its prominence in human rights texts. Article 5 of the UDHR states that no one shall be subject 'to torture or to cruel, inhuman or degrading treatment or punishment'. Article 7 of the ICCPR restates this language. An entire treaty — the Convention against Torture and other Cruel, Inhuman or Degrading Treatment or Punishment — addresses the problem of state-inflicted torture. As of 2024, that treaty had 173 states parties. The regional conventions reveal the same emphasis on the prohibition, in both general and torture-specific treaties.

Nonetheless, despite this broad normative consensus over prohibition of torture by states, its incidence remains significant and widespread. It is more common in authoritarian than liberal regimes and in the developing than the developed world, but occurs in developed and democratic countries as well. Some amount of torture by the state will stem from truly aberrational conduct by an official, in violation of state policy and possibly attracting sanctions for unlawful conduct. But torture by the state predominantly takes place because of state policies expressly allowing or requiring it or because authorities quietly tolerate violations of formal policy. Undoubtedly, sheer venality — the satisfaction of sexual and sadistic desires or the desire to humiliate and exercise total physical dominion over another's body — has always played its role. It appears that periods of mass violence of horrific proportions weaken inherent or acquired inhibitions against vile behaviour so as to make commonplace the torture of helpless civilian populations and prisoners. Such abominations, themselves often fostered by state propaganda to enlist the participation of non-state actors in the savaging of the target population, may constitute both a response to and heightening of the process of dehumanization that underlies mass violence, to the extreme of genocide.

Torture by state officials is, then, rarely gratuitous or attributable simply to aberrational conduct stemming from the dark side of human nature. It generally serves as a means to some further goal, as in a broad sense dehumanization serves a genocidal programme. A state, for example, may systematically employ torture as a

---

[98] A. M. Alterio, 'Latin American Feminists, Gender, and the Binary System of Human Rights Protection', 116 *Am. J. Int'l L. Unbound* (2022) 390.

method for terrorizing a population and discouraging dissent or other behaviour condemned by the government.[99]

Torture as broadly understood today has figured in many cultures as a part of punishment itself after the criminal process has ended in a conviction. The historical punishments of being drawn and quartered, placed on the rack, or burned at the stake, provide classic illustrations. Today few such formal institutions of punishment remain, though dispute continues over methods of capital punishment used in many countries, and over methods of punishment that may be religiously based such as amputation of limbs. In the West, however, torture served for hundreds of years another, related, function. It had long been a routine, formal and judicially sanctioned part of criminal procedure, used in many European states to investigate a suspect once some threshold of facts leading to suspicion had been uncovered. It was employed (subject to certain safeguards designed to heighten the credibility of what was revealed or confessed) both to extract incriminating information and to achieve a confession that, despite the coercion, was used by courts to establish guilt. The interrogative function of torture was largely abolished by the eighteenth century, but its legacy remains.

While progress has been made, principally in normative terms but also in the diminishing incidence of torture as part of a broad system of investigation or punishment, the debates that unfolded after the attacks on the United States on 11 September 2001 showed that the prohibitions of state conduct once thought settled as a matter of normative consensus could be abruptly re-opened for debate, leading many commentators, especially in the United States, to again contemplate either the legality or the inevitability, or both, of officially-sanctioned torture.[100] Interrogations of suspected terrorists were carried out, and defended, on the grounds that the information thereby obtained could bring heinous killers to justice and prevent attacks from occurring that could cost thousands of lives. This section focuses almost exclusively on United States policies since 2001 and on their impact on the global anti-torture regime.[101]

International Instruments Prohibiting Torture

The following illustrations are drawn from treaties and listed in chronological order.

Universal Declaration of Human Rights, 1948

Article 5: 'No one shall be subjected to torture or to cruel, inhuman or degrading treatment or punishment.'

Geneva Conventions, 1949

All four Geneva Conventions of 1949 prohibit torture. In addition, 'torture or inhuman treatment, including biological experiments, wilfully causing great suffering or serious injury to body or health' are classified as 'grave breaches', which must be the subject of 'effective penal sanctions' in national law.

European Convention for the Protection of Human Rights and Fundamental Freedoms, 1950

Article 3: 'No one shall be subjected to torture or to inhuman or degrading treatment or punishment.'

International Covenant on Civil and Political Rights, 1966

Article 7: contains the same text as in the UDHR. Article 4(2) provides that no derogation may be made from Article 7.

African (Banjul) Charter on Human and Peoples' Rights, 1981

Article 5: '... All forms of exploitation and degradation of man particularly slavery, slave trade, torture, cruel, inhuman or degrading punishment and treatment shall be prohibited.'

---

[99] See generally, R. Hassner, *Anatomy of Torture* (2022); and D. Rejali, *Torture and Democracy* (2007).

[100] E. Kearns and J. Young, *Tortured Logic: Why Some Americans Support the Use of Torture in Counterterrorism* (2020).

[101] Note that many other governments also used or covered up torture during these years. In relation to the United Kingdom, see R. Blakeley and S. Raphael, 'Accountability, Denial and the Future-proofing of British Torture', 96 *Int'l Aff.* (2020) 691.

Convention against Torture and Other Cruel, Inhuman or Degrading Treatment or Punishment, 1984

Article 1(1): 'For the purposes of this Convention, the term 'torture' means any act by which severe pain or suffering, whether physical or mental, is intentionally inflicted on a person for such purposes as obtaining from him or a third person information or a confession, punishing him for an act he or a third person has committed or is suspected of having committed, or intimidating or coercing him or a third person, or for any reason based on discrimination of any kind, when such pain or suffering is inflicted by or at the instigation of or with the consent or acquiescence of a public official or other person acting in an official capacity. It does not include pain or suffering arising only from, inherent in or incidental to lawful sanctions.'

Article 2(2): 'No exceptional circumstances whatsoever, whether a state of war or a threat of war, internal political instability or any other public emergency, may be invoked as a justification of torture.'

Article 4(1): 'Each State Party shall ensure that all acts of torture are offences under its criminal law.'

Article 16: 'Each State Party shall undertake to prevent in any territory under its jurisdiction other acts of cruel, inhuman or degrading treatment or punishment which do not amount to torture as defined in article 1.'

Inter-American Convention to Prevent and Punish Torture, 1985

Article 2: 'For the purposes of this Convention, torture shall be understood to be any act intentionally performed whereby physical or mental pain or suffering is inflicted on a person for purposes of criminal investigation, as a means of intimidation, as personal punishment, as a preventive measure, as a penalty, or for any other purpose. Torture shall also be understood to be the use of methods upon a person intended to obliterate the personality of the victim or to diminish his physical or mental capacities, even if they do not cause physical pain or mental anguish.

The concept of torture shall not include physical or mental pain or suffering that is inherent in or solely the consequence of lawful measures, provided that they do not include the performance of the acts or use of the methods referred to in this article.'

Article 5(1): 'The existence of circumstances such as a state of war, threat of war, state of siege or of emergency, domestic disturbance or strife, suspension of constitutional guarantees, domestic political instability, or other public emergencies or disasters shall not be invoked or admitted as justification for the crime of torture.'

Rome Statute for the International Criminal Court, 1998

Article 7(1): 'For the purpose of this Statute, "crime against humanity" means any of the following acts when committed as part of a widespread or systematic attack directed against any civilian population, with knowledge of the attack:
....
(f) Torture;
...
(2): For the purpose of paragraph 1: ...
(e) "Torture" means the intentional infliction of severe pain or suffering, whether physical or mental, upon a person in the custody or under the control of the accused; except that torture shall not include pain or suffering arising only from, inherent in or incidental to, lawful sanctions.'

PUBLIC COMMITTEE AGAINST TORTURE IN ISRAEL V. GOVERNMENT OF ISRAEL SUPREME COURT OF ISRAEL, H.C. 5100/94 (6 SEPTEMBER 1999)

[The applications for relief brought before the Court concerned interrogation methods used by the General Security Service (GSS) to investigate individuals suspected of committing crimes against Israel's security. The

Court noted the 'unceasing struggle' of Israel for its existence and security, in particular the combat against terrorist organizations committed to Israel's annihilation. Terrorist attacks that included suicide bombings against civilian and military targets led to 121 deaths and 707 injured people from 1996 to May 1998.]

PRESIDENT A. BARAK:
Shaking

9. A number of applicants claimed that the shaking method was used against them. … [This] is defined as the forceful shaking of the suspect's upper torso, back and forth, repeatedly, in a manner which causes the neck and head to dangle and vacillate rapidly. According to an expert opinion submitted in one of the applications, the shaking method is likely to cause serious brain damage, harm the spinal cord, cause the suspect to lose consciousness, vomit and urinate uncontrollably and suffer serious headaches.

… To [the State's] contention, there is no danger to the life of the suspect inherent to shaking; … In any event, they argue, doctors are present. …

All agree that in one particular case the suspect in question expired after being shaken. … [T]he State argues … that the shaking method is … a last resort. The interrogation directives define the appropriate circumstances for its application and the rank responsible for authorizing its use. … [It claims] shaking is indispensable to fighting and winning the war on terrorism. … Its use in the past has lead to the thwarting of murderous attacks.

Waiting in the "Shabach" Position

10. … [A] suspect investigated under the "Shabach" position has his hands tied behind his back. He is seated on a small and low chair, whose seat is tilted forward, towards the ground. One hand is tied behind the suspect, and placed inside the gap between the chair's seat and back support. His second hand is tied behind the chair, against its back support. The suspect's head is covered by an opaque sack, falling down to his shoulders. Powerfully loud music is played in the room. … [S]uspects are detained in this position for a prolonged period of time, awaiting interrogation at consecutive intervals.
…
[The opinion described three additional 'physical means' included in the applications: (1) the 'frog crouch', consecutive, periodical crouches on tip toes each crouch lasting five minutes, (2) excessive tightening of hand or leg cuffs, allegedly leading to serious injuries, and (3) sleep deprivation while being tied in the 'Shabach' position, involving long interrogations without breaks.]

Applicants' Arguments

14. … [Applicants] argue that the physical means employed by GSS investigators not only infringe upon … human dignity…, but … constitute criminal offences. These methods, argue the applicants, are in violation of International Law as they constitute "Torture," which is expressly prohibited under International Law. Thus, the GSS investigators are not authorized to conduct these interrogations. …

We asked the applicants' attorneys whether the "ticking time bomb" rationale was not sufficiently persuasive to justify the use of physical means, for instance, when a bomb is known to have been placed in a public area and will undoubtedly explode causing immeasurable human tragedy if its location is not revealed at once. This question elicited a variety of responses from the various applicants before the Court. There are those convinced that physical means are not to be used under any circumstances; the prohibition on such methods to their mind is absolute, whatever the consequences may be. On the other hand, there are others who argue that even if it is perhaps acceptable to employ physical means in most exceptional "ticking time bomb" circumstances, these methods are in practice used even in absence of the "ticking time bomb" conditions. The very fact that, in most cases, the use of such means is illegal provides sufficient justification for banning their use altogether, even if doing so would inevitably absorb those rare cases in which physical coercion may have been justified. …

The State's Arguments

15. ... [T]he State argues that these [methods] do not violate International Law ... [and] cannot be qualified as "torture," "cruel and inhuman treatment" or "degrading treatment" ... .

Moreover, the State argues that these means are equally legal under Israel's internal (domestic) law. This is due to the "necessity" defence outlined in article 34(11) of the Penal Law (1977). ...

The [Landau] Commission of Inquiry's Report [1987]

16. ... The Commission approved the use of "a moderate degree of physical pressure" with various stringent conditions including directives that were set out in the second (and secret) part of the Report, and for the supervision of various elements both internal and external to the GSS. The Commission's recommendations were duly approved by the government.

[The Court explored bases for the authority of the GSS to conduct interrogations and concluded that it was so authorized.]

The Means Employed for Interrogation Purposes

21. [The state] argued before this Court that some of the physical means employed by the GSS investigators are permitted by the "law of interrogation" itself. ...

22. ... In crystallizing the interrogation rules, two values or interests clash. *On the one hand*, lies the desire to uncover the truth, thereby fulfilling the public interest in exposing crime and preventing it. *On the other hand*, is the wish to protect the dignity and liberty of the individual being interrogated. This having been said, these interests and values are not absolute. A democratic, freedom-loving society does not accept that investigators use any means for the purpose of uncovering the truth. ... At times, the price of truth is so high that a democratic society is not prepared to pay it. To the same extent however, a democratic society, desirous of liberty seeks to fight crime and to that end is prepared to accept that an interrogation may infringe upon the human dignity and liberty of a suspect provided it is done for a proper purpose and that the harm does not exceed that which is necessary. ...

...

23. [The Court identifies] a number of general principles ...:

First, a reasonable investigation is necessarily one free of torture, free of cruel, inhuman treatment of the subject and free of any degrading handling whatsoever. ... This conclusion is in perfect accord with (various) International Law treaties — to which Israel is a signatory ... . These prohibitions are "absolute". There are no exceptions to them and there is no room for balancing. Indeed, violence directed at a suspect's body or spirit does not constitute a reasonable investigation practice. The use of violence during investigations can potentially lead to the investigator being held criminally liable. *Second*, a reasonable investigation is likely to cause discomfort; It may result in insufficient sleep; The conditions under which it is conducted risk being unpleasant. ... In the end result, the legality of an investigation is deduced from the propriety of its purpose and from its methods. ...

From the General to the Particular

24. ... Plainly put, shaking is a prohibited investigation method. ... [T]here is no doubt that shaking is not to be resorted to in cases outside the bounds of "necessity" or as part of an "ordinary" investigation.

...

Physical Means and the "Necessity" Defence

33. ... [A]n explicit authorization permitting GSS to employ physical means is not to be found in our law. An authorization of this nature can, in the State's opinion, be obtained in specific cases by virtue of the criminal law defense of "necessity", prescribed in [Article 34 (1) of] the Penal Law. ...

A person will not bear criminal liability for committing any act immediately necessary for the purpose of saving the life, liberty, body or property, of either himself or his fellow person, from substantial danger of serious harm, imminent from the particular state of things [circumstances], at the requisite timing, and absent alternative means for avoiding the harm.

The State's position is that by virtue of this "defence" to criminal liability, GSS investigators are also authorized to apply physical means, such as shaking, in the appropriate circumstances, in order to prevent serious harm to human life or body, in the absence of other alternatives. ... It is choosing the lesser evil. Not only is it legitimately permitted to engage in the fighting of terrorism, it is our moral duty to employ the necessary means for this purpose. ... [T]here is no obstacle preventing the investigators' superiors from instructing and guiding them with regard to when the conditions of the "necessity" defence are fulfilled and the proper boundaries in those circumstances. From this flows the legality of the directives with respect to the use of physical means in GSS interrogations. In the course of their argument, the State's attorneys submitted the "ticking time bomb" argument. ... Is a GSS investigator authorized to employ physical means in order to elicit information regarding the location of the bomb in such instances? The State's attorneys answer in the affirmative.

34. We are prepared to assume that — although this matter is open to debate — the "necessity" defence is open to all, particularly an investigator, acting in an organizational capacity of the State in interrogations of that nature. Likewise, we are prepared to accept — although this matter is equally contentious — that the "necessity" exception is likely to arise in instances of "ticking time bombs", and that the immediate need ("necessary in an immediate manner" for the preservation of human life) refers to the imminent nature of the act rather than that of the danger. ...

...

35. ... This however, is not the issue before this Court. ... The question before us is whether it is possible to infer the authority to, in advance, establish permanent directives setting out the physical interrogation means that may be used under conditions of "necessity". ...

36. In the Court's opinion ... [the nature of the] "necessity" defence does not ... allow it to serve as the source of a general administrative power. ... The very fact that a particular act does not constitute a criminal act (due to the "necessity" defence) does not in itself authorize the administration to carry out this deed, and in doing so infringe upon human rights. The Rule of Law (both as a formal and substantive principle) requires that an infringement on a human right be prescribed by statute, authorizing the administration to this effect. ...

37. ... If the State wishes to enable GSS investigators to utilize physical means in interrogations, they must seek the enactment of legislation for this purpose. This authorization would also free the investigator applying the physical means from criminal liability. ...

38. Our conclusion is therefore the following: According to the existing state of the law, neither the government nor the heads of security services possess the authority to establish directives and bestow authorization regarding the use of liberty infringing physical means during the interrogation of suspects suspected of hostile terrorist activities, beyond the general directives which can be inferred from the very concept of an interrogation. Similarly, the individual GSS investigator — like any police officer — does not possess the authority to employ physical means which infringe upon a suspect's liberty during the interrogation, unless these means are inherently accessory to the very essence of an interrogation and are both fair and reasonable.

An investigator who insists on employing these methods, or does so routinely, is exceeding his authority. His responsibility shall be fixed according to law. His potential criminal liability shall be examined in the context of the "necessity" defence, and according to our assumptions, the investigator may find refuge under the "necessity" defence's wings (so to speak), provided this defence's conditions are met by the circumstances of the case. ...

A Final Word

39. This decision opens with a description of the difficult reality in which Israel finds herself security wise. We shall conclude this judgment by re-addressing that harsh reality. We are aware that this decision does not ease dealing with that reality. This is the destiny of democracy, as not all means are acceptable to it, and not all practices employed by its enemies are open before it. ... Preserving the Rule of Law and recognition of an

individual's liberty constitutes an important component in its understanding of security. At the end of the day, they strengthen its spirit and its strength and allow it to overcome its difficulties. ... If it will nonetheless be decided that it is appropriate for Israel, in light of its security difficulties to sanction physical means in interrogations ... this is an issue that must be decided by the legislative branch which represents the people. We do not take any stand on this matter at this time. ...

40. Deciding these applications weighed heavy on this Court. True, from the legal perspective, the road before us is smooth. We are, however, part of Israeli society. Its problems are known to us and we live its history. We are not isolated in an ivory tower. We live the life of this country. We are aware of the harsh reality of terrorism in which we are, at times, immersed. Our apprehension ... that this decision will hamper the ability to properly deal with terrorists and terrorism, disturbs us. We are, however, judges. Our brethren require us to act according to the law. ...

...

Consequently ... we declare that the GSS does not have the authority to "shake" a man, hold him in the "Shabach" position ... force him into a "frog crouch" position and deprive him of sleep in a manner other than that which is inherently required by the interrogation. ...

[Seven Justices agreed with the opinion. Justice J'Kedmi accepted the opinion's conclusion but would have suspended the judgment's effectiveness for one year.]

DAVID KRETZMER AND YAËL RONEN, THE OCCUPATION OF JUSTICE: THE SUPREME COURT OF ISRAEL AND THE OCCUPIED TERRITORIES (2ND EDN., 2021) 359

... First, when asked in earlier cases to intervene in real time on the basis of the same arguments that it eventually accepted in the PCATI case, the Court desisted. In [PCATI, it] was not required to intervene in an ongoing interrogation. ...

Second, ... [the] Court referred to standards of international human rights law ... but refrained from ruling whether all, or any, of the interrogation methods mentioned in the judgment were covered by this prohibition. ...
...

Finally, ... the Court ... left a loophole for extreme cases. ...
...
... [T]he PCATI judgment ... led to creation of a new term, namely 'necessity interrogations'.

3.3 Aftermath of the PCATI Case

... [T]he judgment ... had an immediate and dramatic effect on the interrogation practices of the ISA. Some of the specific practices that the Court had ruled out—shaking detainees, tying them to a low chair, and playing extremely loud noise—were abandoned. However, soon after the judgment was delivered the Attorney General followed the 'advice' included in the judgment and issued guidelines under which interrogators would not face criminal prosecution ...:

> In cases in which, during an interrogation, an interrogator has used means of interrogation that were needed immediately in order to gain essential information for the purpose of preventing a concrete danger of severe harm to state security, human life, liberty or bodily integrity, where in the circumstances there was no other reasonable way of immediately obtaining the information, and where the means of interrogation used were reasonable in the circumstances to prevent the harm, the Attorney General will consider not opening criminal proceedings.

...

... [T]he Attorney General's guidelines ... clearly open the road for an institutional mechanism that allows interrogators to exceed their authority on the strength of the expectation that they will not be subject to criminal liability if they do so. In this situation the lack of legal authority to employ the 'special methods of interrogation' becomes a meaningless formality.

[The authors then analyse two major cases in which the Court considered the legitimacy of 'necessity interrogations': *Abu Ghosh v. Attorney General*, HCJ 5722/12 (2017) and *Tbeish v. Attorney General*, HCJ 9018/17 (2018)]

4. Assessment

...

... [W]hat is abundantly clear from the Court's judgments is that it has granted judicial imprimatur to the use of means of interrogation that the ISA is not authorised to use, and that are prohibited by criminal law. How can we explain this?

... [First, faced] with claims that if the security authorities' hands are tied they will not be able to protect the public from real security risks, domestic courts are notoriously reluctant to intervene in the actions of those authorities. ...

... [Second is] the notion of 'Israeli exceptionalism', namely the notion that Israel's situation is unique, and this uniqueness justifies departing from accepted norms. ... [I]n the *Tbeish (No 1)* case ... Justice Elron stated:

> The 'necessity' which was the basis for the interrogation of the petitioner does not exist in a vacuum. One must understand and interpret it in light of the complex security reality of the State of Israel. The petitioner was active in a terrorist organisation, which carried out, and continues to carry out, serious terrorist attacks, including murder in cold blood, with great cruelty and no mercy on innocent men, women and children, solely because they are Israelis.

This dictum reflects the way the Court has decontextualised the problem, and perceives only the Israelis as victims without any awareness of the nature of the occupation.

...

... [We are] faced with the fundamental question ...: What has been the main function of the Court—legitimising the practices of the military and security authorities, or mitigating them as much as it thought possible?

* * *

International human rights law played a minor part in the PCATI judgment. But a broader review of its role in the jurisprudence of the Israeli Supreme Court is provided by Natalie Davidson and Tamar Hostovsky Brandes, in 'Israeli Courts and the Paradox of International Human Rights Law', *33 Eur. J. Int'l L.* (2022) 1243:

Existing studies of the Supreme Court have pointed to the pre-eminence of the European Convention on Human Rights in citation practices, to the deployment of IHRL to develop doctrine in the area of social rights and to an overall superficial engagement with IHRL. In addition, they have found a practice of invoking IHRL to justify state action. We find that courts refer to IHRL primarily with respect to children's rights and due process, seldom invoking IHRL in relation to ethnic and gender equality. That is, Israeli courts refer to IHRL predominantly in relation to those issues and actors least challenging to the political order in Israel ... .

QUESTIONS

1. Is allowing the defence of 'necessity' consistent with an 'absolute' view of protection against torture, such that exceptions and balancing are both forbidden (see para. 23)? How would you state the criteria for and the conditions to a 'necessity' defence?

2. What is the relationship between, on the one hand, a required standard of reasonableness and fairness in the policies and practices of the state during interrogations, and on the other hand, an absolute protection against torture? Would you expect a consensus among states about what kind of conduct in what circumstances would clearly violate an absolute ban, but might be viewed as permissible within the reasonableness standard?

3. How would you answer Kretzmer and Ronen's final question?

Debating The Merits

A couple of years after the events of 9/11, and as a vibrant public debate occurred over the merits and legality of torture, Sanford Levinson edited *Torture: A Collection* (2004). Consider some of the reflections it contained.

Jean Bethke Elshtain, 'Reflection on the Problem of "Dirty Hands"', at 77:

> …
>
> Let's sum up this unhappy subject. Far greater moral guilt falls on a person in authority who permits the deaths of hundreds of innocents rather than choosing to "torture" one guilty or complicit person. One hopes and prays such occasions emerge only rarely. Were I the parent or grandparent of a child whose life might be spared, I confess, with regret, that I would want officials to rank their moral purity as far less important in the overall scheme of things than eliciting information that might spare my child or grandchild and all those other children and grand-children. But I do not want a law to "cover" such cases, for, truly, hard cases do make bad laws. Instead, we work with a rough rule of thumb in circumstances in which we believe an informant might have information that would probably spare the lives of innocents. In a world of such probabilities, we should demur from Torture 1 — the extreme forms of physical torment. But Torture 2 ['torture lite'], for which we surely need a different name, like coercive interrogation, may, with regret, be used. This is a distinction with a difference.

Oren Gross, 'The Prohibition on Torture and the Limits of Law', at 229:

> …
>
> I peg my belief on the twin notions of *pragmatic absolutism and official disobedience*. … [T]he way to reconcile that absolute ban on torture with the necessities of the catastrophic case is not through any means of legal accommodation (such as recognizing an explicit legal exception to the ban on torture that applies to catastrophic cases) but rather through a mechanism of extralegal action that I would term *official disobedience:* in circumstances amounting to a catastrophic case, the appropriate method of tackling extremely grave national dangers and threats *may* entail going outside the legal order, at times even violating otherwise accepted constitutional principles.
>
> Going completely outside the law in appropriate cases preserves, rather than undermines, the rule of law in a way that bending the law to accommodate for catastrophes does not. … [T]o say that governments are going to use preventive interrogational torture in the catastrophic case is not the same as saying that they should be authorized to do so through a priori, ex ante legal rules. It is extremely dangerous to provide for such eventualities and such awesome powers within the framework of the existing legal system because of the large risks of contamination and manipulation of that system and the deleterious message involved in legalizing such actions … .
>
> Instead, my proposal calls on public officials having to deal with the catastrophic case to consider the possibility of acting outside the legal order while openly acknowledging their actions and the extralegal nature of such actions. Those officials must assume the risks involved in acting extralegally. … Society retains the role of making the final determination whether the actor ought to be punished and rebuked or rewarded and commended for her actions. …

... [T]he acting official may ... for example, need to resign her position, face criminal charges or civil suits, or be subjected to impeachment proceedings. Alternatively, the people may approve the actions and ratify them. ... [L]egal modes of ratification may include exercising prosecutorial discretion not to bring criminal charges against persons accused of using torture, jury nullification where criminal charges are brought, executive pardoning or clemency where criminal proceedings result in conviction, or governmental indemnification of state agents who are found liable for damages to persons who were tortured. ...

Alan Dershowitz, 'Tortured Reasoning', at 257:

...

... I sought a debate [after September 11]: ... if torture would, *in fact* be employed by a democratic nation under the circumstances, would the rule of law and principles of accountability require that any use of torture be subject to some kind of judicial (or perhaps executive) oversight (or control)? ... My answer, unlike that of the Supreme Court of Israel, is yes. To elaborate, I have argued that unless a democratic nation is prepared to have a proposed action governed by the rule of law, it should not undertake, or authorize, that action. As a corollary, if it needs to take the proposed action, then it must subject it to the rule of law. Suggesting that an after-the-fact "necessity defense" might be available in extreme cases is not an adequate substitute for explicit advance approval

... In explaining my preference for a warrant, I [earlier] wrote the following.

...

There is, of course, a downside: legitimating a horrible practice that we all want to see ended or minimized. Thus we have a triangular conflict unique to democratic societies: If these horrible practices continue to operate below the radar screen of accountability, there is no legitimation, but there is continuing and ever expanding *sub rosa* employment of the practice. If we try to control the practice by demanding some kind of accountability, then we add a degree of legitimation to it while perhaps reducing its frequency and severity. If we do nothing, and a preventable act of nuclear terrorism occurs, then the public will demand that we constrain liberty even more. There is no easy answer.

...

The strongest argument against my preference for candor and accountability is the claim that it is better for torture — or any other evil practice deemed necessary during emergencies — to be left to the low-visibility discretion of low-level functionaries than to be legitimated by high-level, accountable decision-makers. Posner makes this argument:

> Dershowitz believes that the occasions for the use of torture should be regularized — by requiring a judicial warrant for the needle treatment, for example. But he overlooks an argument for leaving such things to executive discretion. If rules are promulgated permitting torture in defined circumstances, some officials are bound to want to explore the outer bounds of the rules. Having been regularized, the practice will become regular. Better to leave in place the formal and customary prohibitions, but with the understanding that they will not be enforced in extreme circumstances.

...

QUESTION

Which approach do you prefer, out of the PCATI judgment, Gross, or Dershowitz?

2. U.S. Law and Policy on Torture after September 11

The events of 11 September 2001 led the Administration at the time to develop and institutionalize a broad policy of counter-terrorism. It proposed, and Congress enacted, broad legislation like the Patriot Act. In important part, the Administration also proceeded through the Executive Branch, independently of Congress — for example, in establishing interpretations of both domestic legislation and treaties that bore on vital matters including the question of prohibited methods of interrogation of persons detained on suspicion of participation in terrorism.

When it ratified the Convention against Torture in 1994, the U.S. entered a reservation:

> That the United States considers itself bound by the obligation under Article 16 to prevent "cruel, inhuman or degrading treatment or punishment," only insofar as [that] term ... means the cruel, unusual and inhumane treatment or punishment prohibited by the Fifth, Eighth, and/or Fourteenth Amendments to the Constitution of the United States.

> A similarly worded reservation was made when the U.S. ratified the ICCPR in 1992. The ratification of the Convention against Torture was also made subject to the following 'understanding':

> That with reference to Article 1, the United States understands that, in order to constitute torture, an act must be specifically intended to inflict severe physical or mental pain or suffering and that mental pain or suffering refers to prolonged mental harm caused by or resulting from: (1) the intentional infliction or threatened infliction of severe physical pain or suffering; (2) the administration or application, or threatened administration or application, of mind altering substances or other procedures calculated to disrupt profoundly the senses or the personality; (3) the threat of imminent death; or (4) the threat that another person will imminently be subjected to death, severe physical pain or suffering, or the administration or application of mind altering substances or other procedures calculated to disrupt profoundly the senses or personality.

On 1 August 2002, Assistant Attorney General Jay Bybee sent a Memorandum to Alberto Gonzales, Counsel to the President, analyzing standards of conduct for interrogating detainees outside the United States under the Torture Act (18 U.S.C. §§2340–2340A) which implemented the Convention against Torture (CAT) and the provisions for grave breaches in the Geneva Conventions. It separately analysed the statute and treaty. It quoted part of Section 2340:

> (1) 'torture' means an act committed by a person acting under the color of law specifically intended to inflict severe physical or mental pain or suffering (other than pain or suffering incidental to lawful sanctions) upon another person within his custody or physical control;

> ...

Bybee observed that the statute did not define the critical word 'severe'. Turning to dictionary definitions to identify the 'ordinary or natural meaning' of that term, the memo concludes that 'the pain or suffering must be of such a high level of intensity that the pain is difficult for the subject to endure'. Turning to other statutes using the term 'severe' such as those defining an emergency medical condition for the purpose of providing health care, Bybee understood them to suggest that 'severe' pain in Section 2340:

> must rise to a similarly high level — the level that would ordinarily be associated with a sufficiently serious physical condition or injury such as death, organ failure, or serious impairment of body functions — in order to constitute torture.

The memo then refers to the statute's four-part definition of severe 'mental' pain or suffering, and summarizes its views:

Each component of the definition emphasizes that torture is not the mere infliction of pain or suffering on another, but is instead a step well removed. The victim must experience intense pain or suffering of the kind that is equivalent to the pain that would be associated with serious physical injury so severe that death, organ failure, or permanent damage resulting in a loss of significant body function will likely result. If that pain or suffering is psychological, that suffering must result from one of the acts set forth in the statute. In addition, these acts must cause long-term mental harm.

The memo recalled that CAT distinguishes between 'torture' and 'cruel, inhuman or degrading treatment or punishment which does not amount to torture as defined in Article 1.' It argued that CAT's text, ratification history and negotiating history confirmed that torture 'is a step far-removed from other cruel, inhuman or degrading treatment or punishment'. CAT reaches only 'the most heinous acts'. Such an interpretation gave the Executive Branch more leeway in deciding on methods of interrogation seeking information from suspected terrorists that were shy of the ultimate prohibition of torture.

The memorandum also considers 'defenses', including that of 'necessity'. Such a defence could eliminate criminal liability even if the statutory definition of torture was found to have been violated. The memo stresses two factors: (1) The greater the certainty of government officials that the person under interrogation has information needed to prevent a serious attack, the more necessary the interrogation. (2) The greater the likelihood that a terrorist attack will occur, and the greater the damage expected from such an attack, the more the interrogation would be necessary. Much then depends on the knowledge of the government official conducting the interrogation. 'While every interrogation that might violate Section 2340A does not trigger a necessity defense, we can say that certain circumstances would support such a defense.'

A subsequent Memorandum, on 30 December 2004, from Daniel Levin, Acting Assistant Attorney General indicated that the August 2002 Memorandum had been 'withdrawn', but also suggested that specific interrogation methods previously approved would still be valid even under more restrictive legal definitions adopted. It was later revealed that another (Top Secret) 1 August 2002 Memorandum by Bybee had discussed and approved a wide range of specific techniques including 'waterboarding' — forcibly pouring water down the throat of a restrained individual to create the uncontrollable physiological sensation of drowning — sleep deprivation, throwing an individual against a flexible false wall, and confining the individual inside a box and introducing an insect into the box. In 2005, the Office of Legal Counsel issued an opinion stating explicitly — and explaining in detail — that these techniques, including waterboarding, were consistent with the 2004 Memorandum by Levin and thus did not constitute torture.

Following the widespread publication of graphic photos depicting the abuse of detainees in the Abu Ghraib prison facility in Iraq, President Bush stated on 26 June 2004 that on the UN 'International Day in Support of Victims of Torture, the United States reaffirms its commitment to the worldwide elimination of torture. … Freedom from torture is an inalienable human right, and we are committed to building a world where human rights are respected and protected by the rule of law. … We will investigate and prosecute all acts of torture and undertake to prevent other cruel and unusual punishment in all territory under our jurisdiction.'

SENATE SELECT COMMITTEE ON INTELLIGENCE, COMMITTEE STUDY OF THE CENTRAL INTELLIGENCE AGENCY'S DETENTION AND INTERROGATION PROGRAM APPROVED 13 DECEMBER 2012, UPDATED FOR RELEASE 3 APRIL 2014, DECLASSIFICATION REVISIONS 3 DECEMBER 2014

…

Findings and Conclusions

#1: The CIA's use of its enhanced interrogation techniques was not an effective means of acquiring intelligence or gaining cooperation from detainees.

…

While being subjected to the CIA's enhanced interrogation techniques and afterwards, multiple CIA detainees fabricated information, resulting in faulty intelligence. ...
...

#2: The CIA's justification for the use of its enhanced interrogation techniques rested on inaccurate claims of their effectiveness.
...
The Committee reviewed 20 of the most frequent and prominent examples of purported counterterrorism successes that the CIA has attributed to the use of its enhanced interrogation techniques, and found them to be wrong in fundamental respects. ...
...

#3: The interrogations of CIA detainees were brutal and far worse than the CIA represented to policymakers and others.

... The waterboarding technique was physically harmful, inducing convulsions and vomiting. Abu Zubaydah, for example, became "completely unresponsive, with bubbles rising through his open, full mouth." ...

Sleep deprivation involved keeping detainees awake for up to 180 hours, usually standing or in stress positions, at times with their hands shackled above their heads. ...
...

#4: The conditions of confinement for CIA detainees were harsher than the CIA had represented to policymakers and others.

... CIA detainees at the COBALT detention facility [in Afghanistan] were kept in complete darkness and constantly shackled in isolated cells with loud noise or music and only a bucket to use for human waste. ...

At times, the detainees ... were... subjected to what was described as a "rough takedown," in which approximately five CIA officers would scream at a detainee, drag him outside of his cell, cut his clothes off, and secure him with Mylar tape. The detainee would then be hooded and dragged up and down a long corridor while being slapped and punched.
...
Throughout the program, multiple CIA detainees ... exhibited psychological and behavioral issues, including hallucinations, paranoia, insomnia, and attempts at self-harm and self-mutilation. ...

[The next sections of the report addressed these issues, *inter alia*: #5: The CIA repeatedly provided inaccurate information to the Department of Justice ...; #6: The CIA has actively avoided or impeded congressional oversight of the program; #7: The CIA impeded effective White House oversight and decision-making; ...[and] #9: The CIA impeded oversight by the CIA's Office of Inspector General.]

#12: The CIA's management and operation of its Detention and Interrogation Program was deeply flawed ...

... The CIA kept few formal records of the detainees [at COBALT] ... . Untrained CIA officers at the facility conducted frequent, unauthorized, and unsupervised interrogations of detainees using harsh physical interrogation techniques that were not-and never became-part of the CIA's formal "enhanced" interrogation program. ...

#13: Two contract psychologists devised the CIA's enhanced interrogation techniques and played a central role in the operation, assessments, and management of the CIA's Detention and Interrogation Program. By 2005, the CIA had overwhelmingly outsourced operations related to the program.

The CIA contracted with two psychologists to develop, operate, and assess its interrogation operations. ... Neither psychologist had any experience as an interrogator, nor did either have specialized knowledge of al-Qa'ida, a background in counterterrorism, or any relevant cultural or linguistic expertise.

On the CIA's behalf, the contract psychologists developed ... the list of enhanced interrogation techniques that was approved for use against Abu Zubaydah and subsequent CIA detainees. The psychologists personally conducted interrogations ... [and] evaluated ... detainees' psychological state ... . The psychologists carried out inherently governmental functions, such as acting as liaison between the CIA and foreign intelligence services, assessing the effectiveness of the interrogation program, and participating in the interrogation of detainees in held in foreign government custody.

…

In 2006, the value of the CIA's base contract with the company formed by the psychologists with all options exercised was in excess of $180 million; … . In 2007, the CIA provided a multi-year indemnification agreement to protect the company and its employees from legal liability … .

…

* * *

For over two decades after 9/11, a large number of UN bodies and the Inter-American Commission on Human Rights challenged U.S. conduct. Two recent examples follow:

In 2022, the UN Human Rights Council's Working Group on Arbitrary Detention gave its assessment (Opinion No. 66/2022, UN Doc. A/HRC/WGAD/2022/66) of a complaint brought by Abu Zubaydah against the United States and states that had 'hosted' CIA detainees (Pakistan, Thailand, Poland, Morocco, Lithuania, Afghanistan and the United Kingdom).

The report states that Abu Zubaydah is a Palestinian, born in 1971, who grew up in Saudi Arabia. He was captured in Pakistan in March 2002, and was wounded in the process. Following medical attention, he was flown by the CIA to a secret detention site in Thailand. The U.S. identified him as a key terrorist threat and a 'member of Usama bin Laden's inner circle'. These allegations, based on torture-induced information, were recanted in 2002. The CIA's own documentation did not support those claims and the 'Agency was informed on 10 August 2002 that it was highly unlikely that Mr. Zubaydah had the intelligence sought'. In February 2008, the U.S. conceded that he was not a member of Al-Qaida. In 2017, the U.S. removed him from the sanctions list. The U.S. nonetheless continued 'to assert its right to detain him indefinitely'.

Between 4 and 23 August 2002, Mr. Zubaydah was subjected to combined enhanced interrogation techniques almost 24 hours a day. During this time, he spent 266 hours in a coffin-size confinement box and 29 hours in a small confinement box. He was threatened with death and waterboarded at least 83 times. He was previously kept in isolation for 47 days and subjected to sensory manipulation. He was also subjected to ice baths, rectal rehydration, forced nudity and sexual violence. The UN Working Group held that the U.S. and the other countries involved had violated a wide range of human rights.

In 2023, the UN Special Rapporteur on human rights and counter-terrorism, Fionnuala Ní Aoláin, reported on a visit to the Guantánamo Bay detention facility. For over two decades, the U.S. had denied full access to the camp to a range of UN experts. The Rapporteur expressed gratitude to the Biden Administration and noted certain improvements in treatment over the preceding 22 years. She noted (para. 15) that 780 Muslim men had been held in Guantánamo and reaffirmed previous UN findings of 'structured, discriminatory, and systematic rendition, secret detention, and torture and ill-treatment at multiple (including black) sites and at Guantánamo Bay.' She reaffirmed that the prohibition of arbitrary detention and torture are *jus cogens* norms and that the U.S. Government has a continuing obligation to 'complete thorough, independent, and effective investigations' to 'sanction those responsible' and to provide reparations. None of these steps had yet been taken.

In terms of the right to a fair trial (para. 44) she observed that 'of the 30 men remaining at Guantánamo, 19 men have **never** been charged with a single crime' and observed (para. 48) not only that the U.S. had failed to respect fair trial guarantees, but that it had 'severely impeded the detainees' access to justice'.

The Impact of U.S. Policies on the Norm against Torture

In the same report, the Rapporteur concluded (para. 67) that 'the exceptionalism, discrimination, securitization, and anti-terror discourse perpetuated by the continuing existence of and justification for Guantánamo have ... [had] enormous human rights consequences in multiple countries.' Adopting a broader perspective, Averell Schmidt and Kathryn Sikkink, in 'Breaking the Ban? The Heterogeneous Impact of US Contestation of the Torture Norm', 4 *J. Glob. Sec. Stud.* (2019) 105 conclude that 'US actions presented a direct challenge to the laws, treaties, and values that constitute the core of the norm against torture, especially its status as a nonderogable norm. ... [S]tates that participated with the United States in its torture program later showed increased levels of physical integrity rights violations ... .' In their view, U.S. actions 'damaged the torture norm's robustness by injecting a greater degree of legal and cultural acceptance for the situational use of torture and by disregarding the obligation of accountability.'

But, perhaps surprisingly, each of three scholars writing in H. Krieger and A. Liese (eds.) *Tracing Value Change in the International Legal Order: Perspectives from Legal and Political Science* (2023) concluded that the torture norm had been unexpectedly resilient in response to U.S. policies.

(1) Wayne Sandholtz, in 'Is Winter Coming? Norm Challenges and Norm Resilience' (*ibid*, 47) noted that U.S. torture 'triggered vigorous pro-norm arguments from other governments, NGOs, civil society, and from segments of the United States government itself' as well as 'efforts by activists, lawyers, and legislators within the United States'. In his view, 'the anti-torture norm may well have emerged strengthened internationally.'

(2) Max Lesch and Lisbeth Zimmermann, in 'There's Life in the Old Dog Yet: Assessing the Strength of the International Torture Prohibition' (*ibid*, 115), identify three factors that enabled the norm to 'weather the storm': (i) 'anti- norm arguments' put forward by Israel and the United States contested only the application rather than the validity of the norm; (ii) the norm is deeply embedded in many parts of the international legal system; and (iii) domestic and international legal institutions played a crucial role. In particular, the UN Committee against Torture 'was able to sort out the disputes and contribute to a stabilization of *opinio juris'.*

(3) Dominik Steiger, in '*Ex iniuria ius oritur*? Norm Change and Norm Erosion of the Prohibition of Torture' (*ibid*, 118) concludes that because the legal and institutional regimes are so embedded, the norm 'is very hard to erode', in part because even the many states that use torture continue to assert their 'continued support for the prohibition of torture'.

QUESTION

Is the prohibition of torture unique among human rights norms in being so resilient? If so, what do you think explains its strengths? Could the same be said of the norm of gender equality discussed earlier?

Chapter 4. Economic, Social, and Cultural Rights

OVERVIEW

The Universal Declaration of Human Rights recognizes two sets of human rights: the 'traditional' civil and political rights (CPR), as well as economic, social and cultural rights (ESCR). In transforming the Declaration's provisions into legally binding obligations, the United Nations adopted two separate International Covenants which, taken together, constitute the bedrock of the international normative regime for human rights. The issues raised in earlier chapters concentrated on CPR, although ESCR have a clear and direct relevance in relation to women's rights and even the death penalty. This chapter explores the rights recognized in the International Covenant on Economic, Social and Cultural Rights (ICESCR).

While cultural rights are of major importance (Article 15(1) recognizes 'the right of everyone ... to take part in cultural life'), and are dealt with in a range of cases elsewhere in this coursebook (including Chapter 7), their practical implementation has tended to raise issues that make them much closer to CPR than ESR (bans on the use of cultural symbols, exclusion of certain languages from official sanction, ethnicity-based forms of discrimination, and forced cultural assimilation). They have thus tended to be dealt with under the ICCPR, including its non-discrimination clause (Art. 2(1)), the minorities provision (Art. 27) or specific rights such as freedoms of expression, religion and association and the right to 'take part in the conduct of public affairs'. Thus, except for the case from the Inter-American Court of Human Rights, in Sec. E, below, most of this chapter focuses on economic and social rights (ESR). These form a reasonably coherent category, even if all of the classifications reflected in the dichotomy between the two sets of rights are somewhat arbitrary, as explained below.

The 'official' UN position, dating back to the Universal Declaration and reaffirmed in innumerable resolutions since that time, is that the two covenants and sets of rights are, in the words adopted by the 1993 second World Conference on Human Rights in Vienna, 'universal, indivisible and interdependent and interrelated. The international community must treat human rights globally in a fair and equal manner, on the same footing, and with the same emphasis' (Vienna Declaration, para. 5). But this oft-restated formal consensus masks a deep and enduring disagreement over the proper status of ESCR. At one extreme lies the view that these rights are superior to civil and political rights in terms of an appropriate value hierarchy and in chronological terms. Of what use is the right to free speech to those who are starving and illiterate? The homeless cannot register to vote, the illiterate cannot fully exercise their political rights, and those living in poverty are systematically discriminated against. At the other extreme we find the view that economic and social rights do not constitute rights (as properly understood) at all. Treating them as rights undermines the enjoyment of individual freedom, distorts the functioning of free markets by justifying state intervention in the economy, and provides an excuse to downgrade the importance of civil and political rights. And a democratic society will inevitably ensure respect for ESR.

The complexity of the political and other challenges in implementing ESR as human rights is well illustrated by comparing the positions of the two nations that are currently the main protagonists in UN human rights debates, China and the United States. China ratified the ICESCR in 2001. In official 'White Papers' and 'Human Rights Action Plans' it consistently states that its top priority is to safeguard citizen's ESCR. It also prioritizes and champions these rights in its international diplomacy. But while the list of 'fundamental rights and duties of citizens' in Chapter 2 of the 1982 Constitution addresses *issues* dealt with in the ICESCR, the Chinese Constitution uses generic rather than rights-based formulations and omits some ESR altogether. And the provisions of the Covenant have not been transformed into domestic law, which means courts cannot apply them. Nor have these rights generally been reflected as human rights in Chinese legislation.[102]

In China, implementation arrangements for ESR are largely absent. There is no national human rights institution because, according to the government, numerous departments already perform the relevant functions. This explanation has been rejected by the UN Committee on ESCR. There are almost no effective accountability mechanisms that would enable individual citizens to claim their ESR. One commentator put it succinctly: 'the

---

[102] P. Alston, Report of the Special Rapporteur on extreme poverty and human rights on his mission to China, UN Doc. A/HRC/35/26/ Add.2 (2017).

authorities have sought to close down rhetoric (constitutionalism), channels (court trials) and social forces (lawyers) that activists had used to mobilize greater changes.'[103] Writing about China, Amartya Sen has highlighted the 'serious fragility in any authoritarian system of governance, since there is little recourse or remedy when the government leaders alter their goals or suppress their failures.'[104] This was vividly demonstrated in relation to policies for responding to Covid-19 in 2020-22.

The United States, on the other hand has, since the advent of the Reagan Administration in 1981, rejected the idea that ESR are full-fledged human rights, and contested the notion that it is bound to implement such rights. While Jimmy Carter signed the ICESCR in 1978, the U.S. has never ratified it, nor has the Senate ever really debated doing so. Significantly, despite its immense wealth, a 2018 report showed that about 40 million Americans lived in poverty, 18.5 million in extreme poverty, and 5.3 million in absolute poverty. It has the highest youth poverty rate in the Organization for Economic Cooperation and Development (OECD), and the highest infant mortality rates among comparable OECD States. Its citizens live shorter and sicker lives compared to those living in all other rich democracies, it has the world's highest incarceration rate, one of the lowest levels of voter registrations among OECD countries, and the highest rate of income inequality among Western countries.[105] Yet its diplomats continue to contest ESR whenever they arise in international forums.

Although variations on these extreme positions vis-à-vis ESR have dominated both diplomatic and academic discourse, most other governments have taken some sort of intermediate position. In general, that position has involved (1) support for the equal status and importance of ESR (as of 2024, 172 states were parties to the ICESCR, compared with 174 parties to the ICCPR), together with (2) failure to take steps to entrench those rights constitutionally, to adopt legislative or administrative provisions based explicitly on the recognition of specific ESR as international human rights, or to provide effective means of redress to individuals or groups alleging violations of those rights. Nevertheless, the importance of ESR in domestic legal systems has clearly grown in recent years. In particular, the impact of COVID-19, rapidly growing inequality, and sustained inflation have compelled greater attention to the consequences of their neglect.

Even before the final adoption of the UDHR, the debate over the relationship between the two sets of rights had become a casualty of the Cold War: Communist countries abstained from voting on its adoption by the General Assembly on the grounds that the ESR provisions were inadequate, and Western states were so keen to cabin ESR that they insisted that there should be two Covenants rather than a single integrated one. Since the 1970s, the debate has also taken on important North-South dimensions. These sometimes include claims that developing countries should not necessarily be held to the same ESR standards, and that respect for rights by poorer states must be linked to international aid, trade and other concessions. To a significant extent, the debates and policy initiatives that are so urgently needed at the international level have been replaced by futile ideological contestation. At the national level, neoliberal economic policies have replaced ideals of community solidarity with notions of individual responsibility, diminished government revenues, and substituted governmental responsibility with corporate control over vast areas of economic and social policy.

In a statement to the Vienna World Conference in 1993, the UN Committee on Economic, Social and Cultural Rights (hereafter the ESCR Committee) drew attention to:

> [t]he shocking reality ... that States and the international community as a whole continue to tolerate all too often breaches of [ESCR] which, if they occurred in relation to civil and political rights, would provoke expressions of horror and outrage and would lead to concerted calls for immediate remedial action. In effect, despite the rhetoric, violations of [CPR] continue to be treated as though they were far more serious, and more patently intolerable, than massive and direct denials of [ESCR] ... .
>
> ... Statistical indicators of the extent of deprivation, or breaches, of economic, social and cultural rights have been cited so often that they have tended to lose their impact. The magnitude, severity and constancy of that deprivation have provoked attitudes of

---

[103] C. Minzner, 'China at the Tipping Point? The Turn against Legal Reform', 24 *J. of Democ.* (2013) 69.
[104] A. Sen, 'Quality of life: India vs. China', *The New York Review of Books* (12 May 2011).
[105] P. Alston, Report of the Special Rapporteur on extreme poverty and human rights on his mission to the United States of America, UN Doc. A/HRC/38/33/Add.1 (2018), para. 4.

resignation, feelings of helplessness and compassion fatigue. Such muted responses are facilitated by a reluctance to characterize the problems that exist as gross and massive denials of [ESCR]. Yet it is difficult to understand how the situation can realistically be portrayed in any other way.[106]

In the UN and in the international 'development' context, ESR have been marginalized by an overwhelming preoccupation with the Sustainable Development Goals (SDGs), adopted by the UN General Assembly in 2015. The stated aim of the SDGs is to provide a 'shared blueprint for peace and prosperity' and they have become the dominant framework through which poverty eradication efforts and development policy are structured globally. This is a partial list:

Goal 1. End poverty in all its forms everywhere

Goal 2. End hunger, achieve food security and improved nutrition and promote sustainable agriculture

Goal 3. Ensure healthy lives and promote well-being for all at all ages

Goal 4. Ensure inclusive and equitable quality education and promote lifelong learning opportunities for all

Goal 5. Achieve gender equality and empower all women and girls

Goal 6. Ensure availability and sustainable management of water and sanitation for all

Goal 7 Ensure access to affordable, reliable, sustainable and modern energy for all

Goal 8. Promote sustained, inclusive and sustainable economic growth, full and productive employment and decent work for all

Goal 9. Build resilient infrastructure, promote inclusive and sustainable industrialization and foster innovation

Goal 10. Reduce inequality within and among countries

…

Goal 16. Promote peaceful and inclusive societies for sustainable development, provide access to justice for all and build effective, accountable and inclusive institutions at all levels

Goal 17. Strengthen the means of implementation …

While huge efforts have been made to promote these goals, progress has been deeply disappointing. The *Sustainable Development Report 2023* concluded that the 'SDGs are seriously off track'. 'At current trends, based on simple projections, there is a risk that the gap in SDG outcomes between HICs [high-income countries] and LICs [low-income countries] will be wider in 2030 … than it was in 2015 … … … If we look at each of the 17 individual SDGs, not a single SDG is projected to be met at the global level.'

Every four years, the UN publishes a *Global Sustainable Development Report*. The 2023 report notes that:

… In 2023, the situation is much more worrisome … . For Goals where progress was too slow in 2019, countries have not accelerated enough, and for others, including food security, climate action and protecting biodiversity, the world is still moving in the wrong direction. In addition, recent crises including the ongoing COVID-19 pandemic, cost-of-living increases, armed conflict and natural disasters have wiped out years of progress on some SDGs including eradication of extreme poverty. Progress has slowed down on

---

[106] UN Doc. E/1993/22, Annex III, paras. 5 and 7.

targets including ending preventable deaths under 5, vaccine coverage and access to energy.

These crises are not independent events: they are entwined through multiple environmental, economic, and social strands, each fuelling the other's intensities. …

…

Compounding the effects of the pandemic is the highest level of state-based armed conflict since 1945. By the end of 2020, around two billion people were living in conflict-affected countries. In 2021, the number of refugees and internally displaced persons was the highest on record at 89 million, and, for the first time, global military expenditure exceeded $2 trillion.

While the SDGs contain preambular references to human rights, specific rights and rights-based targets are largely absent from the agenda, as a result of strong resistance during the drafting process. Jaye Ellis and Dylan Edmonds, in 'Coming to Terms with the SDGs: A Perspective from Legal Scholarship', 36 *Leiden J. Int'l L.* (2023) 251, at 253, criticize the technocratic approach reflected in the SDGs:

The passive voice in which the Goals are communicated strengthens the impression of a turn to technocracy, and this may be deliberate: by drawing attention away from agency, this presentation suggests that progress towards goals will depend to a much greater extent on scientific – and therefore, presumably, objective, universally valid – expertise, rather than being subjected to the vagaries of political will. …

In terms of ESR, ending poverty and reducing inequality are among the key SDGs. But it has been argued that the approach adopted to each is problematic:

PHILIP ALSTON, THE PARLOUS STATE OF POVERTY ERADICATION REPORT OF THE SPECIAL RAPPORTEUR ON EXTREME POVERTY AND HUMAN RIGHTS, UN DOC. A/HRC/44/40 (2020)

[SDG 1] begins with a call for an end to poverty in all its forms everywhere. Yet the targets set do not actually seek to eliminate poverty. The first target is aimed at ending poverty as measured by the World Bank's international poverty line, at best a bare subsistence goal that, even if met, would leave billions facing serious deprivation. The second calls for reducing the proportion of people living in poverty under national measures by just half, a failure of ambition in a period of unparalleled wealth and inequality. …

… [SDG] 10 calls for reducing inequality within and among countries … . In reality, as Oxfam has noted, "economic inequality is out of control". …

… [But] the targets and indicators set for realizing [SDG] 10 are weak by design. They set an agenda of "shared prosperity", focusing on inclusive growth rather than actual reduction of inequalities. Target 10.1, for example, focuses entirely on the rate of income growth within the bottom 40 per cent of the population – ignoring the situation of the wealthiest. This conveniently sidesteps necessary questions around wealth redistribution, elite capture of economic gains, growth achieved through carbon emissions, and inequitable fiscal policies. It treats inequality reduction as a problem to be solved through overall income growth, which flies in the face of recent history and is even more deeply problematic in light of the impacts of COVID-19 and climate change. And despite the importance of tackling gender inequality, at the current rate of economic growth, closing the gender gap in economic opportunity is projected to take 257 years.

[The biggest problem is that the SDGs marginalize the key components of a viable theory of change in this area, which are empowerment, funding, partnership and accountability.]

Empowerment

The [SDGs] are replete with references to transformation, empowerment, collaboration and inclusion. But these concepts are illusory if people are unable to exercise their human rights. Despite almost 20 mentions of human rights in the text, there is not a single reference to any specific civil and political right, and human rights in general remain marginal and often invisible in the overall [SDG] context. …

Most SDG reports by the [UN] and the World Bank pay little heed to rights, with the exception of gender. They rarely discuss substantively the impact of discrimination, the absence of rights-respecting institutional decision-making structures, or the development consequences of even egregious rights violations. At a time when civil society is under sustained attack in many countries around the world, and space for meaningful democratic engagement is shrinking dramatically, in one 2020 report, the Department of Economic and Social Affairs limply observes that "some countries are providing support to non-state actors to build their capacities for engagement on the 2030 Agenda, establishing funding mechanisms to empower their actions and engagement". Unfortunately, [SDG] reporting too often tends to describe the glass as being one-fifth full rather than four-fifths empty.

Funding and partnership

The success of the [SDGs] relies heavily on adequate funding, but … "international economic and financial systems are not only failing to deliver" …, but there has also been "substantial backsliding in key action areas". …

The response of the international community has been to rely ever more heavily on private sector funding, which is increasingly presented as the only viable way forward. … The Secretary-General stated that business must "move further and faster … to meet the global goals" … .

The central strategy is "to use public funds more sparingly [and] ensure a better mobilization of private capital". But there are many problems with this approach. First, it begs the crucial question as to whether privatization in its various forms is capable of achieving many of the [SDGs], especially for the most vulnerable, whose inclusion may not be profitable. There are powerful reasons to doubt this. Second, it recasts the overall [SDG] enterprise as one focused largely on the building of infrastructure and prioritizes an enabling business environment over empowering people. Third, the role of Governments is downplayed, often relegated to insuring private investments. Fourth, all too little is done to promote domestic revenue mobilization, leaving in place destructive fiscal policies, systematic tax avoidance strategies, and illicit outflows that entrench poverty and inequality. Fifth, the commitment in the 2030 Agenda to "a revitalized Global Partnership", promoting "solidarity with the poorest and with people in vulnerable situations", is lost in the fog of an overriding focus on public-private partnerships with troubling track records.

Accountability

The drafters of the 2030 Agenda explicitly rejected the concepts of monitoring and accountability in designing the [SDG] follow-up and review processes. The resulting system is characterized by its voluntary nature, deference to national choices, and institutional arrangements that minimize opportunities for sustained scrutiny. …

…

Instead of promoting empowerment, funding, partnerships and accountability, too much of the energy surrounding the [SDG] process has gone into generating portals, dashboards, stakeholder engagement plans, bland reports and colourful posters. Official assessments are rarely critical or focused, and they often hide behind jargon.

* * *

In other words, there is a huge gap between the idea of legally binding governmental obligations to ensure ESR for their populations and the entirely voluntary and heavily outsourced aggregate targets of the SDGs.

A. THE HISTORICAL ORIGINS OF ESR

The historical origins of the recognition of ESR are diffuse. Those rights have drawn strength from the injunctions expressed in different religious traditions to care for those in need and those who cannot look after themselves. In Catholicism, papal encyclicals have long promoted the importance of the right to subsistence with dignity, while 'liberation theology' has sought to build upon this 'preferential option for the poor'. Virtually all major religions manifest comparable concern for the poor and oppressed. Other sources include philosophical analyses and political theory from authors as diverse as Thomas Paine, Karl Marx, Immanuel Kant and John Rawls; the political programmes of the nineteenth-century Fabian socialists in Britain, Chancellor Bismarck in Germany (who introduced social insurance schemes in the 1880s) and the New Dealers in the United States; and constitutional precedents such as the Mexican Constitution of 1917, the first and subsequent Soviet Constitutions, and the 1919 Constitution of the Weimar Republic (embodying the *Wohlfahrtsstaat* concept).

This comment concentrates on the evolution of these ideas in international human rights law. The most appropriate starting point is the International Labour Organization (ILO). Established by the Treaty of Versailles in 1919 to abolish the 'injustice, hardship and privation' which workers suffered and to guarantee 'fair and humane conditions of labour', it was conceived as the response of Western countries to the ideologies of Bolshevism and Socialism arising out of the Russian Revolution.[107]

In the interwar years, the ILO adopted international minimum standards in relation to a wide range of matters which now fall under the rubric of ESR. They included, *inter alia*, conventions dealing with freedom of association and the right to organize trade unions, forced labour, minimum working age, hours of work, weekly rest, sickness protection, accident insurance, invalidity and old-age insurance, and freedom from discrimination in employment. The Great Depression of the early 1930s underscored the need for social protection of those who were unemployed and gave a strong impetus to full employment policies such as those advocated by Keynes in his *General Theory of Employment, Interest and Money* (1936).

Partly as a result of these developments, various proposals were made during the drafting of the UN Charter for the inclusion of provisions enshrining the maintenance of 'full employment' as a commitment to be undertaken by member states. The strongest version, known after its principal proponents as the 'Australian Pledge', committed UN members to take action to secure 'improved labour standards, economic advancement, social security, and employment for all who seek it'.[108]

Despite significant support, the United States opposed the proposal on the grounds that any such undertaking would involve interference in the domestic economic and political affairs of states. Ultimately agreement was reached on Article 55(a) of the Charter, which simply states that the United Nations shall promote 'higher standards of living, full employment, and conditions of economic and social progress and development' but does not call for specific follow-up at the international level.

U.S. opposition in this context did not signify the rejection of ESR *per se*. Indeed, in 1941 President Roosevelt had nominated 'freedom from want' as one of the four freedoms that should characterize the future world order. In his 1944 State of the Union address, he called for a second Bill of Rights.[109]

> We have come to a clear realization of the fact that true individual freedom cannot exist
> without economic security and independence. 'Necessitous men are not free men.' People
> who are out of a job are the stuff of which dictatorships are made.
>
> In our day these economic truths have become accepted as self-evident. We have
> accepted, so to speak, a second bill of rights, under which a new basis of security and
> prosperity can be established for all — regardless of station, race, or creed.

---

[107] J. T. Shotwell, 'The International Labor Organization as an Alternative to Violent Revolution', 166 *Annals Am. Acad. Pol. & Soc. Sci.* (1933) 18.

[108] See generally R. Russell and J. Muther, *A History of the United Nations Charter: The Role of the United States 1940–1945* (1958), at 786.

[109] Eleventh Annual Message to Congress (11 January 1944), in F. L. Israel (ed.), *The State of the Union Messages of the President 1790-1966* (Vol. 3, 1966) at 2881.

Among these are:

The right to a useful and remunerative job in the industries, or shops, or farms, or mines of the Nation;

The right to earn enough to provide adequate food and clothing and recreation;

The right of every farmer to raise and sell his products at a return which will give him and his family a decent living;

The right of every businessman, large and small, to trade in an atmosphere of freedom from unfair competition and domination by monopolies at home or abroad;

The right of every family to a decent home;

The right to adequate medical care and the opportunity to achieve and enjoy good health;

The right to adequate protection from the economic fears of old age, sickness, accident, and unemployment;

The right to a good education.

All of these rights spell security. And after this war is won we must be prepared to move forward, in the implementation of these rights, to new goals of human happiness and well-being.

This approach was subsequently reflected in a draft international Bill of Rights, completed in 1944, by a Committee appointed by the American Law Institute. In addition to listing the rights contained in the U.S. Bill of Rights (the first ten amendments to the Constitution), the Institute's proposal advocated international recognition of a range of rights and acceptance of the correlative duties in relation to education, work, reasonable conditions of work, adequate food and housing, and social security.[110] In relation to each of the proposed rights, a Comment by the Committee drew attention to the fact that it had already been recognized in the 'current or recent constitutions' of many countries; e.g., 40 countries in the case of the right to education; nine for the right to work; 11 for the right to adequate housing; 27 for the right to social security.

Although these proposals of the Committee were never formally endorsed by the American Law Institute, they were submitted to the United Nations and were to prove highly influential in the preparation of the first draft of the Universal Declaration in 1947. In the drafting of Articles 22–28 of the UDHR, strong support for the inclusion of ESR came from the United States (a delegation led by Eleanor Roosevelt), Egypt, several Latin American countries (particularly Chile) and from the (Communist) countries of Eastern Europe. The United Kingdom opposed their inclusion,[111] as did South Africa, which objected first that 'a condition of existence does not constitute a fundamental human right merely because it is eminently desirable for the fullest realization of all human potentialities' and second that if the proposed economic rights were to be taken seriously it would be 'necessary to resort to more or less totalitarian control of the economic life of the country'.[112]

After the adoption of the Universal Declaration in 1948, the next step was to translate the rights it recognized in Articles 22–28 into binding treaty obligations. This took until 1966 as a result of Cold War tensions, developing U.S. domestic opposition to the principle of international human rights treaties, and the scope and complexity of the proposed obligations. By 1955, the main lines of what was to become the ICESCR were agreed.

Between 1949 and 1951 the Commission on Human Rights worked on a single draft covenant dealing with both categories of rights. But in 1951 the General Assembly, under pressure from the Western-dominated

---

[110] See Statement of Essential Human Rights, UN Doc. A/148 (1947), Arts. 11–15.
[111] See B. Saul, D. Kinley and J. Mowbray, The International Covenant on Economic, Social and Cultural Rights: Commentary, Cases and Materials (2014); and J. Morsink, *The Universal Declaration of Human Rights: Origins, Drafting and Intent* (1999) Chs. 5–6.
[112] UN Doc. E/CN.4/82/Add.4 (1948), at 11, 13.

Commission, agreed to draft two separate covenants. A contemporaneous UN account (UN Doc. A/2929 (1955)) captures the main ESCR-related dilemmas and controversies during the drafting process:

> 6 ... [T]he goal was for the two covenants] to contain 'as many similar provisions as possible' and to be approved and opened for signature simultaneously, in order to emphasize the unity of purpose.
>
> ...
>
> 8. Those who were in favour of drafting a single covenant maintained that human rights could not be clearly divided into different categories, nor could they be so classified as to represent a hierarchy of values. All rights should be promoted and protected at the same time. Without [ESCR], [CPR] might be purely nominal in character; without [CPR], [ESCR] could not be long ensured ... .
>
> 9. Those in favour of drafting two separate covenants argued that [CPR] were enforceable, or justiciable, or of an 'absolute' character, while [ESCR] were not or might not be; that the former were immediately applicable, while the latter were to be progressively implemented; and that, generally speaking, the former were rights of the individual 'against' the State, that is, against unlawful and unjust action of the State, while the latter were rights which the State would have to take positive action to promote. Since the nature of [CPR] and that of [ESCR], and the obligations of the State in respect thereof, were different, it was desirable that two separate instruments should be prepared.
>
> 10. The question of drafting one or two covenants was intimately related to the question of implementation. If no measures of implementation were to be formulated, it would make little difference whether one or two covenants were to be drafted. Generally speaking, [CPR] were thought to be 'legal' rights and could best be implemented by the creation of a good offices committee, while [ESCR] were thought to be 'programme' rights and could best be implemented by the establishment of a system of periodic reports. Since the rights could be divided into two broad categories, which should be subject to different procedures of implementation, it would be both logical and convenient to formulate two separate covenants.
>
> 11. However, it was argued that not in all countries and territories were all [CPR] 'legal' rights, nor all [ESCR] 'programme' rights. A [CPR] might well be a 'programme' right under one régime, an [ESCR] a 'legal' right under another. A covenant could be drafted in such a manner as would enable States, upon ratification or accession, to announce, each in so far as it was concerned, which civil, political, economic, social and cultural rights were 'legal' rights, and which 'programme' rights, and by which procedures the rights would be implemented.

The ICESCR was adopted by the General Assembly in Res. 2200A (XXI) of 16 December 1966 and entered into force on 3 January 1976. It is divided into five 'Parts'. Part I (like Part I of the ICCPR) recognizes the right of peoples to self-determination; Part II defines the general nature of states parties' obligations; Part III enumerates the specific substantive rights; Part IV deals with international implementation; and Part V contains typical final provisions of a human rights treaty. In terms of substantive rights, the right to property, although recognized in the Universal Declaration, was not included, primarily because of the inability of governments to agree on a formulation governing public takings and the compensation therefor.

ESR are not to be found only in the ICESCR. To the contrary, they figure in most of the other major treaties, albeit in different forms. While it is essential to read the full text of the Covenant, the following excerpts from Parts II and III provide a flavour of some of the key issues. Later materials explore the meaning of Article 2.

EXCERPTS FROM THE ICESCR

...

PART II

Article 2

1. Each State Party to the present Covenant undertakes to take steps, individually and through international assistance and co-operation, especially economic and technical, to the maximum of its available resources, with a view to achieving progressively the full realization of the rights recognized in the present Covenant by all appropriate means, including particularly the adoption of legislative measures ... .

PART III

Article 6

1. The States Parties to the present Covenant recognize the right to work, which includes the right of everyone to the opportunity to gain his living by work which he freely chooses or accepts, and will take appropriate steps to safeguard this right.

2. The steps to be taken by a State Party to the present Covenant to achieve the full realization of this right shall include technical and vocational guidance and training programmes, policies and techniques to achieve steady economic, social and cultural development and full and productive employment under conditions safeguarding fundamental political and economic freedoms to the individual.

Article 7

The States Parties to the present Covenant recognize the right of everyone to the enjoyment of just and favourable conditions of work which ensure, in particular:

    (a) Remuneration which provides all workers, as a minimum, with:

        (i) Fair wages and equal remuneration for work of equal value ...;

        (ii) A decent living for themselves and their families ...;

    (b) Safe and healthy working conditions;

    ...

    (d) Rest, leisure and reasonable limitation of working hours and periodic holidays with pay, as well as remuneration for public holidays ... .

Article 9

The States Parties to the present Covenant recognize the right of everyone to social security, including social insurance.

...

Article 11

1. The States Parties to the present Covenant recognize the right of everyone to an adequate standard of living for himself and his family, including adequate food, clothing and housing, and to the continuous improvement of living conditions ... .

2. The States Parties to the present Covenant, recognizing the fundamental right of everyone to be free from hunger, shall take, individually and through international co-operation, the measures, including specific programmes, which are needed:

    (a) To improve methods of production, conservation and distribution of food ...;

...

Article 12

1. The States Parties to the present Covenant recognize the right of everyone to the enjoyment of the highest attainable standard of physical and mental health.

2. The steps to be taken by the States Parties to the present Covenant to achieve the full realization of this right shall include those necessary for:

  (a) The provision for the reduction of the stillbirth-rate and of infant mortality and for the healthy development of the child;
  (b) The improvement of all aspects of environmental and industrial hygiene;
  (c) The prevention, treatment and control of epidemic, endemic, occupational and other diseases;
  (d) The creation of conditions which would assure to all medical service and medical attention in the event of sickness.

Article 13

1. The States Parties to the present Covenant recognize the right of everyone to education ... .

2. The States Parties to the present Covenant recognize that, with a view to achieving the full realization of this right:

  (a) Primary education shall be compulsory and available free to all;
  (b) Secondary education ... shall be made generally available and accessible to all by every appropriate means, and in particular by the progressive introduction of free education;
  (c) Higher education shall be made equally accessible to all, on the basis of capacity, by every appropriate means, and in particular by the progressive introduction of free education;

...

1. Differentiating the Rights

The two Covenants use different terminology in relation to each right. Thus where the ICCPR contains terms such as 'everyone has the right to ...' or 'no one shall be ...', the ICESCR usually employs the formula 'States Parties recognize the right of everyone to ...'. There are major differences in terms of the general obligations clause. Article 2(1) provides that these are subject to the availability of resources ('to the maximum of its available resources'), and that the obligation is one of progressive realization ('with a view to achieving progressively').

This language has been subject to conflicting critiques. On the one hand, it is sometimes suggested that the nature of the obligation under the ICESCR is so onerous that virtually no government would be able to comply. Developing countries, in particular, are seen to confront an impossible challenge. On the other hand, it is argued that the relative open-endedness of the concept of progressive realization, particularly in light of the qualification about availability of resources, renders the obligation devoid of meaningful content. Governments can present themselves as defenders of ESR without international imposition of any precise constraints on their policies and behaviour. A related criticism is that the Covenant imposes only 'programmatic' obligations upon governments — that is, obligations to be fulfilled incrementally through the ongoing execution of a programme. It therefore becomes difficult if not impossible to determine when those obligations ought to, or have been, met.

Another problematic distinction is that between the different categories of ESCR. Which are economic, which are social, and which are cultural? The ICESCR does not make explicit any distinction in this regard Commentators differ as to their characterization of each of the declared rights,[113] or ignore the distinction. The

---

[113] E.g., H. Steiner, 'Social Rights and Economic Development: Converging Discourses?', 4 *Buffalo Hum. Rts. L. Rev.* (1998) 25.

original drafting rationale was an essentially bureaucratic one: the rights of concern to the ILO (Arts. 6–9) were assumed to be 'economic', those relevant to UN agencies such as the Food and Agriculture Organization and the World Health Organization (Arts. 10–12) were treated as 'social', and those that fell within the sphere of interest of UNESCO (Arts. 13–15) were designated as 'cultural'. In practice, however, most such distinctions are difficult to maintain. Education, for example, can arguably be classified as belonging to all of the relevant categories — economic, social and cultural, not to mention civil and political.

2. Implementation: the ESCR Committee

The greatest challenge is to identify effective approaches to implementation — i.e., to the means by which ESCR can be given effect and governments can be held accountable to fulfil their obligations. The Covenant says only that governments must use 'all appropriate means' to work towards the stated ends. Such means may be universally valid or relevant or may be quite specific to a particular culture or legal system. The Covenant gives no further pointers, beyond noting that 'appropriate means' includes 'particularly the adoption of legislative measures'. It is clear, however, that neither legislation nor effective remedies of a judicial nature, which are both central to the domestic implementation framework contained in the ICCPR (Art. 2), will play the same roles or *per se* be sufficient in relation to the ICESCR.

In terms of international procedures designed to promote accountability, the UN Human Rights Council has several relevant mechanisms. One is the Universal Periodic Review process (Ch. 8B, below), and another relates to the scrutiny provided by commissions of inquiry and other reporting mechanisms (Ch. 8C, below). Neither of these has so far been very focused or effective in relation to ESR. The most significant contribution has been made by the group of Special Procedures appointed by the Council (Ch. 8B, below). This now includes Special Rapporteurs and independent experts focused specifically on the rights to culture, education, environment, food, health, and housing, as well as on a range of thematic issues such as disability, discrimination, and poverty. Examples of country reporting on ESR are provided below (Sec. F, below).

The principal UN body concerned specifically with ESCR is the Committee on Economic, Social and Cultural Rights (the 'ESCR Committee'). The creation of the Committee was not foreseen in the text of the Covenant. It first met in 1987, having been established by a 1985 resolution of the Economic and Social Council after earlier monitoring arrangements had failed. The Committee has 18 independent expert members, elected for four-year terms on the basis of equitable geographic representation. In most respects it functions along the same lines as the ICCPR Committee, the work of which is analysed in detail in Chapter 9, below, and the CEDAW Committee discussed in Chapter 3, above. For that reason, little detail as to procedures is provided in the present context.[114] Its task is to supervise compliance by states parties with their obligations under the ICESCR. It does this on the basis of regular reports they submit in accordance with its 'reporting guidelines'. An initial report by each state party is due within two years, and subsequent reports which respond to a list of country-specific issues drawn up by the Committee are required at roughly five to eight year intervals. The examination of a state's report by the Committee culminates in the adoption of the Committee's 'concluding observations', following the same sort of approach as we saw earlier in relation to the CEDAW Committee (Ch. 3C, above).

In addition to its reporting function, the 2008 Optional Protocol established a complaints procedure.[115] It entered into force on 5 May 2013 and, as of 2024, has 29 States Parties.[116] By the beginning of 2024, the Committee had registered 339 communications, resulting in the adoption of 16 Views (13 of which found violations); 27 declared inadmissible; 75 discontinued or withdrawn; and 221pending consideration (UN Doc. E/2024/22, para. 106). Most complaints have involved housing rights.[117] An example follows:

---

[114] See P. Alston, 'The Committee on Economic, Social and Cultural Rights', in F. Mégret and P. Alston (eds.), *The United Nations and Human Rights: A Critical Appraisal* (2nd ed., 2021) 439.

[115] See M. Langford, B. Porter, R. Brown and J. Rossi (eds.), The Optional Protocol to the International Covenant on Economic, Social and Cultural Rights: A Commentary (2016).

[116] S. Liebenberg, 'Reasonableness Review', in M. Langford and K. Young (eds.), *The Oxford Handbook of Economic and Social Rights* (2022) 000; and *ibid*, 'Between Sovereignty and Accountability: The Emerging Jurisprudence of the United Nations Committee on Economic, Social and Cultural Rights Under the Optional Protocol', 42 *Hum. Rts. Q.* (2020) 48.

[117] Nils-Hendrik Grohmann, 'Tracing the Development of the Proportionality Analysis in Relation to Forced Evictions under the ICESCR', 22 *Hum. Rts. L. Rev.* (2022).

HAMID SAYDAWI AND MASIR FARAH V. ITALY, COMMUNICATIONS NO. 226/2021 AND NO. 227/2021, VIEWS OF 13 MARCH 2024

[The applicants had lived in two houses with their families since 2000 and 2005 respectively. They had renovated the houses and registered the houses as their place of residence and the State party 'condoned' their actions. In 2008, the houses were acquired by the Italian State railway company, which initiated eviction proceedings in 2012, leading to a firm eviction order in March 2021.]

...

7.5 The authors do not have the financial means to find adequate alternative housing on the private market. They requested social housing in 2021, and the authorities have been aware of their need for alternative housing since 2011. The only alternative offered by the State party consisted of temporary emergency shelter, which would have led to a separation of each family, through a separation of the men from the women.

7.6 The authors claim that evicting them and their families without alternative and adequate accommodation would amount to a violation of their right to adequate housing under article 11 (1) of the Covenant.

...

D. Conclusion and recommendations

11.1 On the basis of all the information provided and in the particular circumstances of the present cases, the Committee considers that the eviction of the authors and their families without an adequate proportionality test by the judicial authorities, in the absence of a consideration of the disproportionate impact that the eviction might have on the authors and their families and of the best interests of the child, and without respecting the procedural guarantees of adequate and genuine consultation, would constitute a violation of the authors' right to adequate housing.

11.2   The Committee ... makes the following recommendations to the State party.

Recommendations in respect of the authors

12. The State party is under an obligation to provide the authors with an effective remedy, in particular by: (a) reassessing, if they are not currently in adequate housing, their state of necessity and their place on the waiting list ...; (b) providing the authors with financial compensation ...; and (c) reimbursing the authors for [their] legal costs ... .

General recommendations

13. ... [T]he State party has an obligation:

(a) To ensure that its normative framework allows persons in respect of whom an eviction order is issued and who might consequently be at risk of destitution or of violation of their Covenant rights ... to challenge the decision before a judicial or other impartial and independent authority with the power to order the cessation of the violation and to provide an effective remedy so that such authorities can examine the proportionality of the measure in the light of the criteria for limiting the rights enshrined in the Covenant under the terms of article 4;

(b) To take the necessary measures to ensure that evictions affecting persons who do not have the means of obtaining alternative housing are carried out only within the framework of proceedings involving genuine and effective consultation with the persons concerned, in which all available alternative housing (whether belonging to such persons or made available by the relevant State agencies) is assessed and only after the State has taken all essential steps, to the maximum of its available resources, to ensure that evicted persons have alternative housing, especially in cases involving families, older persons, children and/or other persons in vulnerable situations. If the group to be evicted includes children, the proceedings must guarantee their right to be heard;

(c) To take the necessary measures to solve the problems caused by the failure of the courts and social services to coordinate their efforts, which can result in an evicted person's being left without adequate accommodation;

(d) To develop and implement, to the maximum of its available resources, a comprehensive plan to guarantee the right to adequate housing for low-income persons, in keeping with general comment No. 4 (1991). This plan should provide for the necessary resources, indicators, time frames and evaluation criteria to guarantee these individuals' right to housing in a reasonable, timely and measurable manner.

...

* * *

The Optional Protocol also includes provision for an inquiry procedure, similar to that of CEDAW discussed in Ch. 3 above. Only a handful of States Parties have accepted the Committee's role in that regard and no inquiries have yet been undertaken. The Committee holds a 'day of general discussion' at most of its sessions to enable experts from civil society, academia, international agencies and elsewhere to discuss key issues relating to ESCR.

Finally, the Committee has also been active in producing General Comments,[118] a term that describes a function very similar to that performed by the CEDAW Committee's General Recommendations. The Committee's General Comment on the right to water illustrates the strengths as well as some of the problems inherent in this process. Recall that the ICESCR makes no reference to water, let alone a right thereto.

ESCR COMMITTEE, GENERAL COMMENT NO. 15: THE RIGHT TO WATER (2002)

1. ... The human right to water is indispensable for leading a life in human dignity. It is a prerequisite for the realization of other human rights ... .

2. The human right to water entitles everyone to sufficient, safe, acceptable, physically accessible and affordable water for personal and domestic uses. An adequate amount of safe water is necessary to prevent death from dehydration, to reduce the risk of water-related disease and to provide for consumption, cooking, personal and domestic hygienic requirements.

3. [Covenant Article 11(1)] specifies a number of rights emanating from, and indispensable for, the realization of the right to an adequate standard of living 'including adequate food, clothing and housing'. The use of the word 'including' indicates that this catalogue of rights was not intended to be exhaustive. The right to water clearly falls within the category of guarantees essential for securing an adequate standard of living, particularly since it is one of the most fundamental conditions for survival ... .

...

10. The right to water contains both freedoms and entitlements. The freedoms include the right to maintain access to existing water supplies necessary for the right to water, and the right to be free from interference, such as the right to be free from arbitrary disconnections or contamination of water supplies. By contrast, the entitlements include the right to a system of water supply and management that provides equality of opportunity for people to enjoy the right to water.

11. The elements of the right to water must be *adequate* for human dignity, life and health... . The adequacy of water should not be interpreted narrowly, by mere reference to volumetric quantities and technologies. Water should be treated as a social and cultural good, and not primarily as an economic good ... .

12. While the adequacy of water required for the right to water may vary according to different conditions, the following factors apply in all circumstances:

---

[118] Between 1989 and 2023 the ESCR Committee adopted 21 General Comments. They are: No. 1: Reporting by States parties (1989); No. 2: International technical assistance (1990); No. 3: The nature of States parties' obligations (1990); No. 4: Right to adequate housing (1991); No. 5: Persons with disabilities (1994); No. 6:ESCR of older persons (1995); No. 7: Forced evictions (1997); No. 8: Economic sanctions and ESCR (1997); No.9:Domestic application of the Covenant (1998); No. 10: National human rights institutions and ESCR (1998); No. 11: Plans of action for primary education (1999); No. 12: Right to adequate food (1999); No. 13: Right to education (1999); No. 14: Right to health (2000); No. 15: Right to water (2002); No.16: Equal right of men and women to ESCR (2005); No. 17: Authorial rights under Art. 15(1)(c); No. 18: Right to work (2005); No. 19: The right to social security (2008); No. 20: Non-discrimination in ESCR (2009); No. 21: Right of everyone to take part in cultural life (2009); No. 22: Right to sexual and reproductive health (2016); No. 23: Right to just and favourable conditions of work (2016); No. 24; State obligations in the context of business activities (2017); No. 25: Science and ESCR (2020); and No. 26: Land and ESCR (2022).

Availability. The water supply for each person must be sufficient and continuous for personal and domestic uses ...;

Quality. The water required for each personal or domestic use must be safe, therefore free from micro-organisms, chemical substances and radiological *hazards* that constitute a threat to a person's health. Furthermore, water should be of an acceptable colour, odour and taste for each personal or domestic use.

Accessibility. Water and water facilities and services have to be accessible to *everyone* without discrimination, within the jurisdiction of the State party ... .

...

International obligations

30. [ICESCR Articles 2(1), 11(1) and 23] require that States parties recognize the essential role of international cooperation and assistance and take joint and separate action to achieve the full realization of the right to water.

31. To comply with their international obligations in relation to the right to water, States parties have to respect the enjoyment of the right in other countries. International cooperation requires States parties to refrain from actions that interfere, directly or indirectly, with the enjoyment of the right to water in other countries. Any activities undertaken within the State party's jurisdiction should not deprive another country of the ability to realize the right to water for persons in its jurisdiction.

32. States parties should refrain at all times from imposing embargoes or similar measures, ...

33. Steps should be taken by States parties to prevent their own citizens and companies from violating the right to water of individuals and communities in other countries ... .

34. Depending on the availability of resources, States should facilitate realization of the right to water in other countries, for example through provision of water resources, financial and technical assistance, and provide the necessary aid when required ... .

35. ... States parties should take steps to ensure that [any international agreements to which they are parties] do not adversely impact upon the right to water. Agreements concerning trade liberalization should not curtail or inhibit a country's capacity to ensure the full realization of the right to water.

...

3. Responses to General Comment No. 15

Some governments expressed strong reservations.[119] Canada, for example, argued that while governments owe a responsibility to their own people to provide access to water and sanitation, this did not translate into a human right. But other governments and many NGOs enthusiastically embraced the right and in 2008 the Human Rights Council appointed an 'Independent Expert on the issue of human rights obligations related to access to safe drinking water and sanitation'. The Expert, Catarina de Albuquerque, subsequently presented a series of reports that helped to persuade states of the importance and validity of the right and in 2010 the UN General Assembly (in Res. 64/292) recognized 'the right to safe and clean drinking water and sanitation as a human right that is essential for the full enjoyment of life and all human rights'.

The resolution was adopted with 122 votes in favour, 0 against and 41 abstentions. Among the abstainers were many Western governments, including the United States and the United Kingdom. The latter argued that 'there was no sufficient legal basis for declaring or recognizing water or sanitation as freestanding human rights, nor was there evidence that they existed in customary law.' Despite this reluctance on the part of 41 states, several

---

[119] See generally, M. Satterthwaite, 'Assessing the Rights to Water and Sanitation: Between Institutionalization and Radicalization', 52 *Geo. J. Int'l L.* (2021) 315; M. Davis, 'Freedom from Thirst: A Right to Basic Household Water', 42 *Cardozo L. Rev.* (2021) 879; and N. Reiners, 'States as Bystanders of Legal Change: Alternative Paths for the Human Rights to Water and Sanitation in International Law', 37 *Leiden J. Int'l L* (2024) 22.

months later the Council adopted a resolution, without a vote (i.e., with no formal objections) recalling the Assembly's resolution and affirming 'that the human right to safe drinking water and sanitation is derived from the right to an adequate standard of living and inextricably related to the right to the highest attainable standard of physical and mental health, as well as the right to life and human dignity' (HRC Res. 15/9 (2010)). Six months later the Council 'upgraded' the title of the Independent Expert to that of Special Rapporteur on the human right to safe drinking water and sanitation. The transformation of the right – from unmentioned in the ICESCR and strongly opposed by key governments, to uncontested recognition and the appointment of a Special Rapporteur to move it forward – was thus complete.

It still remained to clarify whether a single right encompasses both water and sanitation or whether these are two separate rights. The latter understanding was confirmed by the UN General Assembly in 2015 (Res. 70/169):

> … the human right to sanitation entitles everyone, without discrimination, to have physical and affordable access to sanitation, in all spheres of life, that is safe, hygienic, secure, socially and culturally acceptable and that provides privacy and ensures dignity, while reaffirming that both rights are components of the right to an adequate standard of living; …

According to the former Special Rapporteur, Léo Heller, in *The Human Rights to Water and Sanitation* [HRtWS] (2022) 2, there are 2 billion people worldwide without access to an adequate water supply, 1.4 billion of whom live in rural areas. 4.2 billion people lacked access to safely managed sanitation services, of which 494 million were still practicing open defecation. 584 million children did not have a basic water service at school, with 31 percent of schools worldwide lacking these services, and 698 million children were without basic sanitation services at school, accounting for 37 percent of schools worldwide.

Somewhat surprisingly, the response of UN agencies to these developments has been unenthusiastic, in Heller's view (at 370):

> UN-Water itself generally does not emphasize the theme or HRtWS, even when its focus is on water and sanitation services. Its annual World Water Development Reports, which have an important impact in the area, are often focused on technological issues or on topics with little proximity to more social or human rights concerns.

The reluctance of these agencies might be partly explained by the United States' continuing *de facto* opposition. On 15 November 2021, it explained its position on the relevant General Assembly resolution in these terms:

> … While we respect the importance of promoting access to sanitation and water and that efforts to do so can involve distinctive approaches, we understand this resolution's references to human rights to water and sanitation to refer to the right derived from [ESCR] contained in the [ICESCR]. The United States is not a party to the ICESCR, and the rights contained therein are not justiciable in U.S. courts. …
>
> We disagree with any assertion that the right to safe drinking water and sanitation is inextricably related to or otherwise essential to enjoyment of other human rights, such as the right to life [under the ICCPR]. To the extent that access to safe drinking water and sanitation is derived from the right to an adequate standard of living, it is addressed under the ICESCR, which imposes a different standard of implementation than that contained in the ICCPR. We do not believe that a State's duty to protect the right to life by law would extend to addressing general conditions in society or nature that may eventually threaten life or prevent individuals from enjoying an adequate standard of living.[120]

---

[120] United States Mission to the United Nations, Explanation of Position for the Human Rights to Safe Drinking Water and Sanitation Resolution (15 November 2021).

This reticence in turn can perhaps be understood as a result of ongoing debates within the United States. A well-known case, in which four UN Special Rapporteurs became involved,[121] was the contamination of drinking water in Flint, Michigan by as much as 100 times the legal level of lead. In response to lawsuits:

> … the state of Michigan and city of Flint [argued] that clean water is not a constitutional right. This would mean they would not be liable for the lead-poisoned water, when they decided in 2014 to draw the city's water supply from the Flint River without having the water properly treated. It would also mean they are not liable for the impact the dangerously tainted water had on people in Flint, including the 9,000 children known to have been exposed to it.[122]

In Lowndes County, Alabama, a majority of residents live without properly functioning, legal, basic sanitation infrastructure, and must instead rely on a series of ditches or crudely constructed piping systems to guide human waste away from their residences. Both Flint and Lowndes County are home to a large percentage of low-income Black residents. Following a widely publicized visit by a UN Special Rapporteur,[123] and strong local activism,[124] the U.S. Justice Department investigated whether the Alabama authorities were engaging in race discrimination in violation of the Civil Rights Act. In May 2023, an 'interim resolution' was announced that would suspend the investigation on the condition that clearly specified remedial measures were taken by the Alabama authorities. Many other such cases where access to water and sanitation were impacted by racial discrimination have been documented in the United States and in other wealthy countries.[125]

By contrast, courts in India have long acknowledged a right to sanitation facilities. Already in 1980, the Indian Supreme Court, in *Municipal Council, Ratlam vs Shri Vardhichand & Ors* 1980 AIR 1622, had lamented that:

> … the grievous failure of local authorities to provide the basic amenity of public conveniences drives the miserable slum-dwellers to ease in the streets, on the sly for a time, and openly thereafter … . A responsible municipal council constituted for the precise purpose of preserving public health and providing better finances cannot run away from its principal duty by pleading financial inability. Decency and dignity are non-negotiable facets of human rights and are a first charge on local self-governing bodies.

The Court ordered that:

> 2. The Municipal Council shall, within six months from to-day, construct a sufficient number of public latrines for use by men and women separately, provide water supply and scavenging service morning and evening so as to ensure sanitation.
>
> …
>
> 4. The municipality will not merely construct the drains but also fill up cesspools and other pits of filth and use its sanitary staff to keep the place free from accumulations of filth. After all, what it lays out on prophylactic sanitation is a gain on its hospital budget.
>
> …
>
> … [T]he court will not sit idly by and allow municipal government to become a statutory mockery. The law will relentlessly be enforced and the plea of poor finance will be poor alibi when people in misery cry for justice.

In *Milun Saryajani v. Pune Municipal Commissioner*, C.A. (Bom.) (2015), the Bombay High Court relied on Article 21 (the right to life) and Article 47 (State's duty to improve public health) of the Indian Constitution, along with

---

[121] 'Flint: "Not just about water, but human rights"', OHCHR Press Release (3 May 2016).

[122] A. Klasing, 'Water Is a Human Right – in Flint, in Michigan, and the US', *Human Rights Watch Dispatch* (11 July 2018); and N. Gaber, 'Mobilizing Health Metrics for the Human Right to Water in Flint and Detroit, Michigan', 21 *Health and Hum. Rts.* (2019) 179.

[123] UN Doc. A/HRC/38/33/Add.1 (2018) para. 69; and PBS Newshour, 'The story of American poverty, as told by one Alabama county', *PBS* (7 July 2018).

[124] J. Carrera and C. Flowers, 'Sanitation Inequity and the Cumulative Effects of Racism in Colorblind Public Health Policies', 77 *Am. J. Econ. & Sociol.* (2018) 941.

[125] J. Brown et al., 'The Effects of Racism, Social Exclusion, and Discrimination on Achieving Universal Safe Water and Sanitation in High-Income Countries', 11 *The Lancet Global Health* (2023) e606.

references to the ICESCR, in a case which focused specifically on the absence of toilet facilities for 'women walking on the streets'. The Court noted that there were 180 urinals for 1.7 million women and that 'not a single farthing/penny' of the budget for new construction had been spent. It focused specifically on the gendered implications of these failures:

> 42. … the consequence of not going to the toilet and controlling the bladder results in urinary tract infection, kidney stone, interstitial cystitis and swelling of the bladder.

> 44. … women have the right to have safe and clean toilets at all convenient places, which in a way impacts their right to live with human dignity. One of the paramount duty of the State and the Corporations is to improve public health by providing toilets for women at all convenient places.

> …

> ORDER

> [50.] (i) All Municipal Corporations shall formulate a comprehensive scheme for construction of toilets/urinals/ restrooms/ privies for women walking on the streets. The Corporations shall constitute a Committee [within four weeks, to oversee the entire process.]

> (ii) … The Committee shall formulate a comprehensive scheme from the identification of the spot to construction of such toilets which shall include the management and maintenance of the toilets. …

* * *

Inspired by such precedents, along with the almost total absence of public restrooms in the United States, one commentator has called for U.S. state courts to recognize a right to public toilets as part of their constitutional public health obligations.[126] But while courts have a potentially important role, Margaret Satterthwaite, in 'The Rights to Water and Sanitation', in Malcolm Langford and Katharine Young (eds.), *The Oxford Handbook on Economic and Social Rights* (2023) 000, draws attention to an indispensable ingredient in most such struggles:

> A technocratic approach to the right to water can make some changes possible by giving policymakers tools to analyze needed government actions, regulatory imperatives and failures, and the limits of commodification and financialization. However, the kinds of thoroughgoing changes required in the face of extreme inequality, global pandemics, and climate change require creative, contextually relevant, and dogged political action connected to broader social movements for global justice. …

QUESTIONS

1. Is the ESCR Committee skating over important terminological issues when it claims that we tolerate 'breaches of economic, social and cultural rights which, if they occurred in relation to civil and political rights, would provoke expressions of horror and outrage'?

2. Consider the following issues in relation to the excerpts from the ICESCR: does the right to work amount to a guarantee of employment? Is Article 7 on working conditions utopian or relevant only to an advanced industrial economy? Is the much-derided 'right to holidays with pay' defensible?[127] How

---

[126] R. Weinmeyer, 'Lavatories of Democracy: Recognizing a Right to Public Toilets through International Human Rights and State Constitutional Law', 26 *U. Pa. J. Const. L.* (forthcoming, 2024).
[127] The United States is the only advanced economy that does not guarantee paid holidays for workers. A. Maye, *No Vacation Nation, Revised* (2019).

could the right to social security be meaningful in a poor developing country? Why is the right to health not formulated in terms of a right of access to health care? Is the vision of the right to education in Article 13 outdated?

3. Craven has argued that a 'desire to conserve the status quo may involve occasionally reading an instrument such as the Covenant in a 'teleological' or 'evolutive' manner, just as a desire to transform or change social relations may involve reading it 'literally'.'[128] What interpretive strategy does the Committee use to justify its conclusion that there is a right to water, and how persuasive is it?

4. Mechlem has criticized the ESCR Committee for claiming, in its General Comment No. 12 on the Right to Food, that international organizations such as the FAO and the World Bank have 'international obligations' under the Covenant. She notes that there is no mention of any such obligations in the text and that these organizations cannot become parties to the treaty:

"Disconnected from any methodological basis, its conclusions seem to have been reached at random. Because statements rather than arguments are offered, it is also difficult to reconstruct the train of thought of the CESCR... .

The CESCR pays a price for its endorsement of forward-looking human rights thinking. Because this endorsement cannot be based on a legally sound interpretation of the ICESCR, it undermines the credibility and legitimacy of its overall interpretation output.[129]"

Is this a valid criticism? If so, what are the implications for the Committee's approach to the right to water? If not, what are the limits to the Committee's 'creativity' in proclaiming new norms and obligations?

5. Should there be a 'right to pee', as Indian NGOs have long advocated? How do you assess the United States' position that 'the right to safe drinking water and sanitation is [not] inextricably related to or otherwise essential to enjoyment of other human rights'?

B. COMPETING PERSPECTIVES ON ESR

In the following materials we examine some of the philosophical, religious, economic and legal challenges that are frequently posed by the critics of ESR, both at the national and international levels. The materials tend to emphasize the U.S. debate, partly because the United States still tends to be the key player on these issues in international fora and partly because U.S.-style economic liberalism has been widely adopted elsewhere.

But before reviewing the various critiques it is important to note that there are many settings in which ESR are widely accepted in both theory and practice. The right to education, at least at primary school level, is almost universally accepted and has achieved extensive constitutional recognition. When people are forcibly evicted from their homes and have nowhere else to live, most legal systems recognize some dimensions of their right to shelter or housing. The deliberate denial of access to food — whether in relation to detainees, displaced persons, disfavoured ethnic or racial groups, or in the context of an embargo — is widely acknowledged to violate basic human rights norms. When states fail to establish and enforce basic minimal health and safety protections for workers the international community considers a violation of labour rights to have occurred. But despite such examples, there remain many challenges to these rights, as the following readings indicate.

---

[128] M. Craven, 'Some Thoughts on the Emergent Right to Water', in E. Riedel and P. Rothen (eds.), *The Human Right to Water* (2006) 37, at 39.
[129] K. Mechlem, 'Treaty Bodies and the Interpretation of Human Rights', 42 *Vand. J. Transnat'l. L.* (2009) 905.

1. Ambivalence towards ESR

Despite almost universal rhetorical commitment by governments to the doctrine that ESR and CPR are of equal importance, many governments and human rights NGOs continue to be ambivalent towards ESR. Thus, for example, in terms of formal commitments:

- While all 46 member states of the Council of Europe are parties to the European Convention on Human Rights and thus to its complaints procedure (indeed its acceptance is a prerequisite to membership), only one-third of them (16) have accepted the collective complaints system under the European Social Charter (which is the Convention's counterpart in the field of ESR).

- The Additional Protocol to the American Convention on Human Rights in the Area of Economic, Social and Cultural Rights, of 1988 (the 'Protocol of San Salvador'), has only been ratified by 18 countries, compared with the 25 parties to the Convention itself.

- While the Optional Protocol to the ICCPR providing for the submission of complaints has been ratified by 116 States, the equivalent for the ICESCR has only 29 States Parties.

The only open hostility to this group of rights has come from the United States, whose attitude has varied considerably from one administration to another.[130] Eleanor Roosevelt, who represented the Truman Administration, was a strong proponent of ESR. The United States, under President Johnson, voted in the General Assembly in 1966 to adopt both Covenants. Although neither the Nixon nor Ford Administrations were opposed to these rights, neither actively promoted them. The Carter Administration adopted a different approach, epitomized by Secretary of State Cyrus Vance's 'Law Day Speech' at the University of Georgia in which he defined human rights as including:

> First, ... the right to be free from governmental violation of the integrity of the person ... .
> Second, ... the right to the fulfilment of such vital needs as food, shelter, health care and
> education ... . Third, ... the right to enjoy civil and political liberties ... .[131]

In 1978, President Carter signed the Covenant and sent it to the Senate for its advice and consent with a view to ratification. At the time, however, no action was taken by the Senate, even in Committee. The Reagan and George H. W. Bush Administrations reversed official policy and opposed the concept of ESR on the grounds that, while:

> the urgency and moral seriousness of the need to eliminate starvation and poverty from
> the world are unquestionable ... the idea of economic and social rights is easily abused by
> repressive governments which claim that they promote human rights even though they
> deny their citizens the basic ... civil and political rights.[132]

In 1993, the Clinton Administration committed to move towards ratification of the Covenant, but did not do so and continued to oppose the inclusion of all references to rights such as the right to adequate housing and the right to adequate food in international diplomatic settings. The Administration of George W. Bush remained unsympathetic but became open to formal acknowledgement of ESR while insisting that they were very different in nature. Thus it characterized the right to food as 'a goal or aspiration to be realized progressively' that translates into 'the opportunity to secure food; [and] not a guaranteed entitlement'.[133]

The Obama Administration announced a 'major policy shift' in 2011, rejecting the concerns of previous administrations that: (1) recognition of ESCR would obligate the United States to provide increased foreign assistance; (2) such rights might become justiciable; (3) states' rights and prerogatives would be threatened; and (4) recognition would play into the hands of those who use ESR to justify neglect of CPR. It announced that it would 'work constructively with like-minded delegations to adopt fair and well-reasoned resolutions at the UN'

---

[130] P. Alston, 'Putting Economic, Social, and Cultural Rights Back on the Agenda of the United States', in William F. Shulz (ed.), *The Future of Human Rights: US Policy for a New Era* (2008) 120.

[131] 76 Dept. of State Bulletin (1977) 505.

[132] Introduction, U.S. Dept. of State, Country Reports on Human Rights Practices for 1992, 5.

[133] See www.fao.org/DOCREP/MEETING/005/Y7106E/y7106e03.htm.

on ESCR that 'are consistent with our own laws and policies'.[134] In practice, little changed. And both the Trump and Biden administrations have systematically followed the traditional policy approach of downgrading ESCR at every opportunity. The State Department's annual *Country Reports on Human Rights Practices* still do not address ESR, although they do include a range of labour rights, the definition of which 'is informed by internationally recognized labor rights and standards', but in fact tracks U.S. domestic law much more closely.[135]

One striking anomaly in the U.S. position should be noted. Alone among ESR, the right to education is addressed, albeit in different ways, in the constitutions of many of the 50 component states. In 1954, in the landmark case of *Brown v. Board of Education* (347 U.S. 483), a unanimous Supreme Court recognized 'education [as] perhaps the most important function of state and local governments' and declared it to be 'a right which must be made available to all on equal terms'. But, almost two decades later, in *San Antonio Independent School District v. Rodriguez* (411 U.S. 1 (1973)) the Court took a very different approach. While much of the 5–4 majority decision was concerned with the finer points of U.S. equal protection law, the Court also considered whether education was a constitutionally protected fundamental right. It insisted that such a right could not be derived from arguments about the 'relative societal significance of education' but only from the text of the Constitution. And it found that, despite dramatic differences in the funding provided for education from one district to another, there was no 'absolute denial of educational opportunities to any' children. It also expressed concerns that a finding of a right to education might logically lead to findings relating to issues such as denials of 'decent food and shelter'. The silver lining of the Supreme Court's abdication has been that it helped provoke extensive litigation in state courts, resulting in some surprisingly strong affirmations of the right to education.[136]

But the United States and China, as discussed above, are not alone in their ambivalence. Although formal support for ESCR has been near universal, in practice no group of states has consistently followed up its rhetorical support at the international level with practical and sustained programmes of implementation. West European social democracies would seem best placed to promote the importance of these rights. But, while being consistently supportive of initiatives, they have been generally cautious, in part because the rights are often not accorded full constitutional or other recognition as rights *per se in their own domestic orders,* and in part because of domestic political constituencies calling for reductions in the scope of the European welfare state.[137]

Australia, for example, has no bill of rights but a number of major inquiries have been held to consider whether one should be adopted and a key question has always concerned the possible but much contested inclusion of ESCR. In 2024 a federal Parliamentary Committee recommended the adoption of a Human Rights Act, drafted so as to:

> [capture] the immediately realisable aspects of economic, social and cultural rights, including obligations to ensure people enjoy rights without discrimination; satisfy certain minimum aspects of these rights; and not take backwards steps (or 'retrogressive measures') with respect to these rights; …[138]

Developing countries continue to be the most vocal proponents of these rights, but they have made few concrete proposals beyond calling for more attention to be accorded to them. Cuba, for example, was so reluctant to treat these rights as individually enforceable that it initially resisted the appointment of any special rapporteurs to investigate ESCR.[139]

Finally, some of the most prominent international NGOs have also been ambivalent towards ESR. Until 1993 Human Rights Watch (HRW)[140] definitively eschewed ESCR, and Amnesty International effectively did so until 2001. Since then both organizations have sought to develop a coherent strategy in relation to these rights, albeit with rather limited success. At the same time, a number of more specialized groups such as Physicians for Human Rights, ESCR-Net, the Center for Economic and Social Rights and the National Economic and Social

---

[134] M. Posner, 'The Four Freedoms Turn 70: Ensuring Economic, Political, and National Security in the 21st Century', U.S. Dept. of State, 24 March 2011.
[135] https://www.state.gov/reports/2022-country-reports-on-human-rights-practices/ (2023) Appendix B.
[136] M. Kaufman, Badges and Incidents: A Transdisciplinary History of the Right to Education in America (2019).
[137] C. O'Cinneide, 'The Present Limits and Future Potential of European Social Constitutionalism', in K. Young (ed.), *The Future of Economic and Social Rights* (2019) 324.
[138] Parliamentary Joint Committee on Human Rights, *Inquiry into Australia's Human Rights Framework* (May 2024) p. xxi and Ch. 6.
[139] UN Doc. E/CN.4/1998/25, para. 16.
[140] See generally P. Alston, *Human Rights Watch Inc.* (2025).

Rights Initiative, along with the International Commission of Jurists, have made important contributions to enhanced understanding of these rights.[141] The justification put forward by Kenneth Roth, Executive Director of HRW from 1993 to 2022, was that the 'methodologies' they have developed for CPR are difficult to apply in relation to ESR:

KENNETH ROTH, DEFENDING ECONOMIC, SOCIAL AND CULTURAL RIGHTS: PRACTICAL ISSUES FACED BY AN INTERNATIONAL HUMAN RIGHTS ORGANIZATION 26 HUM. RTS. Q. (2004) 63

...

In my view, the most productive way for international human rights organizations, like Human Rights Watch, to address ESC rights is by building on the power of our methodology. The essence of that methodology ... is not the ability to mobilize people in the streets, to engage in litigation, to press for broad national plans, or to provide technical assistance. Rather, the core of our methodology is our ability to investigate, expose, and shame. We are at our most effective when we can hold governmental (or, in some cases, nongovernmental) conduct up to a disapproving public ... .

... [T]o shame a government effectively — to maximize the power of international human rights organizations like Human Rights Watch — clarity is needed around three issues: violation, violator, and remedy. We must be able to show persuasively that a particular state of affairs amounts to a violation of human rights standards, that a particular violator is principally or significantly responsible, and that a widely accepted remedy for the violation exists. If any of these three elements is missing, our capacity to shame is greatly diminished ... .

...

Broadly speaking, [these elements are] clearest when it is possible to identify arbitrary or discriminatory governmental conduct that causes or substantially contributes to an ESC rights violation. These three dimensions are less clear when the ESC shortcoming is largely a problem of distributive justice. If all an international human rights organization can do is argue that more money be spent to uphold an ESC right — that a fixed economic pie be divided differently — our voice is relatively weak. We can argue that money should be diverted from less acute needs to the fulfillment of more pressing ESC rights, but little reason exists for a government to give our voice greater weight than domestic voices. On the other hand, if we can show that the government (or other relevant actor) is contributing to the ESC shortfall through arbitrary or discriminatory conduct, we are in a relatively powerful position to shame: we can show a violation (the rights shortfall), the violator (the government or other actor through its arbitrary or discriminatory conduct), and the remedy (reversing that conduct).

...

To conclude, let me offer a hypothesis about the conduct of international human rights organizations working on ESC rights. It has been clear for many years that the movement would like to do more in the ESC realm. Yet despite repeated professions of interest, its work in this area remains limited. Part of the reason, of course, is expertise; the movement must staff itself somewhat differently to document shortfalls in such matters as health or housing than to record instances of torture or political imprisonment. But much of the reason, I suspect, is a sense of futility. International human rights activists see how little impact they have in taking on matters of pure distributive justice so they have a hard time justifying devoting scarce institutional resources for such limited ends ... .

QUESTIONS

1. Given the reticence of many states, how would you explain the fact that ESR continue to occupy an important place within the international regime? What factors might lead any given government to be strongly supportive of the concept and practice of such rights? Why would the U.S. Government be so keen to address labour rights in its annual reports?

---

[141] See especially various interpretive guides adopted by civil society groups, such as (1) the Limburg Principles on the Implementation of the International Covenant on Economic, Social and Cultural Rights (1986), 9 *Hum. Rts. Q.* 122 (1987); (2) the Maastricht Guidelines on Violations of Economic, Social and Cultural Rights (1997), 20 *Hum. Rts Q.* (1998) 691; (3) the Montréal Principles on Women's Economic, Social and Cultural Rights (2002), 26 *Hum. Rts. Q.* (2004) 760; (4) the Maastricht Principles on Extraterritorial Obligations of States in the Area of [ESCR] (2013); and (5) the Maastricht Principles on The Human Rights of Future Generations (2023).

2. If China has done so well in recent years in lifting vast numbers out of poverty, is there any reason to worry about the fact that it has few significant accountability mechanisms in place in relation to ESR?

3. Lee Kuan Yew, the former Prime Minister of Singapore, adopted an ESR policy which has been described in the following terms:

"[It is government policy] not to provide direct funds to individuals in its 'welfare' programs. Instead, much is spent on education, public housing, health care and infrastructure build-up as human capital investments to enable the individual and the nation as a whole to become economically competitive in a capitalist world ... . For those who fall through the economic net ... public assistance is marginal and difficult to obtain ... . The government's position is that 'helping the needy' is a moral responsibility of the community itself and not just of the state. So construed, the recipients of the moral largesse of the community are to consider themselves privileged and bear the appropriate sense of gratitude."

Does such an approach give priority to ESR or does it instead put economic growth ahead of both sets of rights? If Singapore were to decide to become a party to the ICESCR, would it need to change such policies?

4. Are ESR matters of 'pure distributive justice', and if so, does this make them any less human rights than civil and political rights?

2. Historical Perspectives

The phrase 'not enough' was famously used by Anthony Crosland in his book *The Future of Socialism* (1956) to which Samuel Moyn refers in his own book entitled *Not Enough*. But while Crosland was arguing that equality of opportunity was 'not enough', Moyn's critique is that ESR are insufficient because they fall short of undefined goals such as 'full-fledged distributive justice', 'material equality', and 'distributive equality'.

Mila Versteeg, in 'Can Rights Combat Economic Inequality?', 133 *Harv. L. Rev.* (2020) 2017 provides an overview of Moyn's thesis:[142]

> ... As Moyn puts it, human rights have been "unambitious in theory and ineffectual in practice in the face of market fundamentalism's success". While human rights "have occupied the global imagination," they have "contributed little of note, merely nipping at the heels of the neoliberal giant". Even worse, the human rights movement has been tainted by association with unconstrained capitalism because the movement gained prominence while laissez-faire policies were gaining favor globally. Moyn believes that ... "even perfectly realized human rights ... are compatible with ... radical inequality".
>
> Moyn acknowledges that some advocacy efforts have addressed social rights, such as the rights to healthcare, to social security, and to education. But these efforts are not enough either, as they have focused only on *sufficiency*: a minimum of resources for the poorest of the poor, rather than comparable resources for all. For Moyn, there exists a crucial distinction between the former, that is, "sufficiency," and the latter, what he calls "material equality" (also "distributive equality", "economic justice", or just "equality"). Sufficiency captures "how far an individual is from having nothing and how well she is doing in relation to some minimum of provision of the good things in life". In contrast, material equality "concerns how far individuals are from one another in the portion of those good things they get". A commitment to material equality therefore effectively requires limiting inequality in any given country and a "commitment to a universal middle

---

[142] For an update by Moyn himself, see Samuel Moyn, 'Sufficiency, Equality, and Human Rights', in Malcolm Langford and Katharine G. Young (eds.), *The Oxford Handbook of Economic and Social Rights* (2023) 000.

class". Moyn believes that promoting sufficiency is not enough to achieve equality: even if we realize higher levels of sufficiency for more people, the rich can still become richer.

… Moyn concludes that human rights law is actually the wrong vehicle for promoting material equality. One reason is that human rights law — with its individualistic premise of constraining the state from committing human rights abuses against discrete persons — is simply a bad fit for the task of effecting material equality. "[W]henever inequality has been limited," he says, "it was never on the sort of individualistic and often antistatist basis that human rights share with their market fundamentalist *Doppelgänger*". Another, related reason is that human rights law's toolkit — litigation and "naming and shaming" violators — is ill-equipped to promote economic justice. According to Moyn, "When it comes to mobilizing support for economic fairness, the chief tool[] of the human rights movement — playing informational politics to stigmatize the repressions of states … — [is] simply not fit for use". …

… Moyn's primary objective is to force redistribution and cap inequality. To accomplish that, he argues, we need not only to provide a basic minimum of subsistence but also to set an income ceiling, lift up the middle classes, prevent the dismantling of existing social welfare states, and build new ones…. The end goal is a strong social welfare state, preferably extended to the global level. …

SAMUEL MOYN, NOT ENOUGH: HUMAN RIGHTS IN AN UNEQUAL WORLD (2018)

…

The distinction between sufficiency and equality allows us to see how profoundly the age of human rights … has mainly been a golden age for the rich. The meaning of human rights has slowly transformed as egalitarian aspiration has fallen. … The French Revolution's dream of a welfare state offering sufficient provision as well as egalitarian citizenship returned—at least in some places—when the Great Depression and World War II ushered in new kinds of national communities. In that era, human rights partook of the ideal of distributive equality within nations. In our day, human rights have instead become associated (along with the excesses of terrible leaders and the horrors of heartrending atrocity) with global sufficiency alone. … To a startling extent, human rights have become prisoners of the contemporary age of inequality. …

…

… The human rights revolution of our time is bound up with a global concern for the "wretched of the earth," but not in the egalitarian sense that the socialist and postcolonial promoters of that phrase originally meant.

Instead of global justice, market fundamentalism triumphed starting in the 1970s … . …

The companionship between human rights and market fundamentalism was not inevitable. … The attempt to mobilize economic and social rights has remained unimpressive since the end of the Cold War … . [H]uman rights lost their original connection with a larger egalitarian aspiration, focusing on sufficient provision instead.

…

There is no reason for human rights ideals to continue the accommodating relationship they have had with market fundamentalism and unequal outcomes. Human rights may well serve to indirectly indict the consequences of inequality when it threatens the minimum standards of liberty, security, and provision that human rights protect. This does not mean, however, that either human rights norms or the kinds of movements we have learned to associate with those norms—engaging in an informational politics of "naming and shaming," operating in the professional mode, and prizing judges as ideal enforcers of basic norms—are up to the challenge of supplementing sufficiency with equality in theory or practice. …

…

PHILIP ALSTON, THE PAST AND FUTURE OF SOCIAL RIGHTS
STEVEN L. B. JENSEN AND CHARLES WALTON (EDS.), SOCIAL RIGHTS AND THE POLITICS OF OBLIGATION IN HISTORY (2022) 308

Equality and non-discrimination were always among the key tenets of international human rights law. The issues were high on the UN's agenda in the early years after the adoption of the Universal Declaration of Human Rights (UDHR), but the focus was primarily on racial equality and equality between men and women. The structural dimensions underpinning these forms of discrimination were very much present at the outset but, as Steven L. B. Jensen has shown, key Western governments carried out a very successful effort to marginalise and all but erase them from both the human rights and the development agendas in the 1940s and 1950s, in part because they raised unpleasant and unwanted questions about the impact and aftermath of colonialism. Inequality issues subsequently made their way back on to the international human rights agenda in different forms [especially through the 1973 Ganji Report on social rights, which focused heavily on inequality at the national level and the New International Economic Order demands in the mid-1970s]. Again, these efforts were assiduously, and ultimately effectively, blocked by Western nations, but it would be a misrepresentation to suggest that the corpus of human rights law was inherently incapable of saying anything about material inequality. …

…

Inequality is so central to Moyn's thesis [in his book *Not Enough*] that the terms 'equality' or 'inequality' appear an astonishing 525 times in his book. The principal themes that he develops can be distilled down for present purposes to the following:

(a) Human rights have 'nothing to say about material inequality' because they neglect the need for a 'ceiling on inequality'.

(b) Social rights as understood in the post-war era reflected a commitment to egalitarian citizenship that was later lost.

(c) The UDHR was originally a 'template' or 'charter' for 'national welfare states'.

(d) Social rights norms became, at best, concerned only with ensuring a subsistence minimum.

…

16.3.1 Material Inequality

Moyn's first theme concerns the silence of human rights about material inequality. The key issues here are definitional. They relate to 'human rights', 'inequality' and 'ceilings'. He uses the terms 'human rights', 'human rights law' and 'human rights movement' almost interchangeably, but, in fact, there are important distinctions that need to be drawn. In terms of the last, he relies on what comes close to a caricature of the approach taken by human rights advocates based on a limited understanding of the work of Amnesty International and Human Rights Watch, but he neither goes into any detail on the work of either of those groups nor acknowledges that the human rights movement encompasses a far more heterogeneous set of actors with very different agendas, normative priorities, constituencies and methods of work.

Despite the book's preoccupation with 'equality', Moyn avoids any systematic definition … . Instead, his analysis glides seamlessly across phrases like 'material equality', 'distributive equality', 'absolute equality of material outcomes' and 'distributional equality'. …

The third definitional issue relates to his critique of human rights (whether norms or organisations) for paying no heed to the need for a 'ceiling' on inequality. The term 'ceiling' … is never defined, beyond a reference to 'a ceiling on wealth and a constraint on material hierarchy'. For example, he laments that neo-liberals have obliterated 'whatever ceiling on inequality national welfare states had imposed', but this begs the question … as to whether welfare states ever actually imposed such ceilings.

… [F]or all of the emphasis on egalitarianism, he suggests at one stage that what is required is merely a 'modicum of equality in the distribution of the good things in life', and that it is not necessary to seek 'absolute equality of material outcomes'. At the other end of the spectrum is his suggestion that socialism is in fact the way to achieve material equality. He calls for it to be elevated 'to the global project it has rarely been but must become'. But socialism too is never defined.

…

16.3.2 Egalitarian Citizenship

A second main theme of Not Enough is that social rights, as they were understood in the post-war era, reflected a commitment to egalitarian citizenship that was later abandoned. It is not clear where this commitment was to be found. Moyn asserts that, in this founding period, 'human rights partook of the ideal of distributive equality within nations'. This is then contrasted with the sorry state of play today in which 'the spirit of human rights … has shifted from nationally framed egalitarian citizenship to a globally scaled subsistence minimum'. And he asks whether there is 'any way for human rights to return to their original relationship with distributive equality'. But … [he] presents the slimmest of evidence for the existence of any such ideal. …

…

16.3.3 The UDHR as a Welfare State Charter

A central pillar of Moyn's contrast between the late 1940s and today is the way in which he consistently characterises the 'welfare state' of the earlier era. Again, no definition is offered, despite the fact that scholars of the welfare state are united in the view that the term is notoriously difficult to pin down and has a variety of connotations. In fact, the term 'welfare state' was used only very occasionally before 1950, even in the UK, with which it is, in retrospect, most commonly associated. Moreover, in that context its content and its relationship to a more robust and demanding redistributive state were a matter of deep political contention, even among those on the left of the political spectrum who supported the various elements that would come to make up the welfare state. But this occurred well after the adoption of the UDHR. Nevertheless, the 'welfare state' takes centre stage in Moyn's retelling:

> When the United Nations canonized economic and social rights in the Universal
> Declaration of Human Rights of 1948, it consecrated the democratic welfare state that
> had emerged victorious from World War II. It thereby did more than simply enshrine the
> ideal of distributive sufficiency that the declaration explicitly defined in its series of basic
> entitlements; it also reflected the ambitious political enterprise of distributive equality.

Unless he is extrapolating entirely from wartime developments in the United States and the United Kingdom, neither of which could accurately be characterised as seeking to achieve distributive equality, it may be that he has in mind the origins of the Swedish welfare state, but these were hardly significant in the UDHR context. Or perhaps it is the Soviet model of the socialist state, but that too would seem to be a very different proposition. It is thus unclear what he means when he laments the demise of the 'ceiling on inequality national welfare states had imposed'. One might surmise that he is thinking of the strongly progressive personal income tax system that was in place in countries like the United States and the United Kingdom, partly as a result of the need to raise vast amounts of money to fight the war, and which remained an important part of the scene until the late 1970s, but there is no discussion in the book of these issues.

So when Moyn ruefully recalls the UDHR as a 'charter or template for national welfare states', it is not clear which states at that time constituted the models that others were supposed to follow. Which states embodied in the late 1940s what Moyn saw as the Declaration's 'ambitious political enterprise of distributive equality', and which states expressed such a vision as a central part of the Declaration? It certainly would not have been the Latin American states, although they were the strongest and most numerous proponents of the inclusion of social rights in the Declaration. It might have been the United States, although by 1948 it was moving away from the New Deal model. It is unlikely to have been the Union of Soviet Socialist Republics (USSR).

…

16.3.4 Social Rights as Minimum Subsistence Norms

Another central theme in *Not Enough* is that existing social rights provisions aspire only to promote 'sufficient provision' or 'a globally scaled subsistence minimum'. Because of this minimalism, 'human rights do not necessarily call for a modicum of distributive equality'. Behind this conclusion is the assumption that it would be possible to achieve a universal minimum level of living without involving any form of redistribution, a proposition that would be very difficult to show empirically.

In explaining the significance of his analysis, Moyn notes that 'social rights haven't provided us with the right language and tools to oppose rising inequality'. There is nothing in those rights that 'allow[s] us to mount a direct attack on inequality'. In this formulation, he is addressing the shortcomings of the rights themselves, not of the movements that have ignored or promoted them. The normative language, he says, is simply not up to it. But there is no analysis at all of the most expansive and capacious social rights such as the 'right to an adequate standard of living' and 'the right of everyone to the enjoyment of the highest attainable standard of physical and mental health'. [And there is only one reference to the voluminous body of work of the UN Committee on ESCR.]

* * *

Another response to Moyn's thesis comes from Nehal Bhuta, in 'Recovering Social Rights', in *ibid* (ed.), *Human Rights in Transition* (2024) 1:

> This chapter responds to a fundamental challenge made against social rights: that they are an inadequate legal and political language to address widening income and wealth inequality. …
>
> I argue that these claims reflect a great deal of truth about the present of social rights, but do not accurately characterize their past. … I recover a different register of social rights … which infused the … drafting of the [UDHR]. [Specific rights claimed in this register include the right to work, the right to subsistence, and the right to the product of one's labour.] I call these "natural social rights" or "collective natural rights," and trace their lineages through English Radical thought, French Physiocratic thought, Jacobin and Neo-Jacobin thinking, to early twentieth century state theories and constitutional social rights. The essential insight gained from recovering these repertoires of social rights is the surprising extent to which social rights ideas laid the conceptual foundations for the social state. Rather than understanding social rights as nothing more than the weak offspring of a social welfare state brought into being by social conflict, we can seem them as a historically-powerful political-ethical discourse that helped *articulate and motivate* the concept of the state as a public power that must *organize* the economy in order to ensure a "society of equals."[143] At the heart of nineteenth century ideas of social right was the demand for the creation of equal social citizens and the construction of social democracy, through the creation of a social democratic state. Recovering these ideas helps us better understand the ways that social rights *could be* a germane response to the challenge of inequality in the present.

3. Philosophical Perspectives

Much of the literature on ESR tends to overlook the philosophical dimensions of the issue. But, in practice, those aspects are rarely far below the surface in debates about ESR. It is thus necessary to have at least a general sense of philosophical arguments for and against ESR. In the readings that follow, Neier and Kelley reflect the influence of Hayek in arguing that ESR should not properly be viewed as 'rights',[144] while Griffin and Nickel outline different but related justifications for such rights. Sen responds to two major critiques of ESR.

---

[143] See the rich history of the concept of political and economic equality recounted in P. Rosanvallon, *The Society of Equals* (2013, trans. Goldhammer).
[144] For a careful analysis, see R. Plant, *The Neo-liberal State* (2010).

FRIEDRICH HAYEK, JUSTICE AND INDIVIDUAL RIGHTS
LAW, LEGISLATION AND LIBERTY (1982) APPENDIX TO CHAPTER NINE

...

... [N]ew positive 'social and economic' human rights ... demand as their counterpart a decision that somebody (a person or organization) should have the duty of providing what the others are to have. It is, of course, meaningless to describe them as claims on 'society' because 'society' cannot think, act, value, or 'treat' anybody in a particular way. If such claims are to be met, the spontaneous order which we call society must be replaced by a deliberately directed organization: the cosmos of the market would have to be replaced by a taxis [i.e. an order] whose members would have to do what they are instructed to do. They could not be allowed to use their knowledge for their own purposes but would have to carry out the plan which their rulers have designed to meet the needs to be satisfied. From this it follows that the old civil rights and the new social and economic rights cannot be achieved at the same time but are in fact incompatible; the new rights could not be enforced by law without at the same time destroying that liberal order at which the old civil rights aim.

...

It is evident that all these 'rights' are based on the interpretation of society as a deliberately made organization by which everybody is employed. They could not be made universal within a system of rules of just conduct based on the conception of individual responsibility, and so require that the whole of society be converted into a single organization, that is, made totalitarian in the fullest sense of the word. ... [R]ules of just conduct ... can never take the form of 'everybody must have so and so.' In a free society what the individual will get must always depend in some measure on particular circumstances which nobody can foresee and nobody has the power to determine. Rules of just conduct can ... can bring about only opportunities for the acquiring of such claims.

...

... If we wish everybody to be well off, we shall get closest to our goal, not by commanding by law that this should be achieved, or giving everybody a legal claim to what we think he ought to have, but by providing inducements for all to do as much as they can that will benefit others. To speak of rights where what are in question are merely aspirations which only a voluntary system can fulfil, not only misdirects attention from what are the effective determinants of the wealth which we wish for all, but also debases the word 'right', the strict meaning of which it is very important to preserve if we are to maintain a free society.

ARYEH NEIER, SOCIAL AND ECONOMIC RIGHTS: A CRITIQUE[145]
13 HUM. RTS. BRIEF (2006) 1

... I favor a fairer distribution of the world's resources; [but] through the political process. For the most part, ... it cannot take place through the assertion of rights ... . Rights only have meaning if it is possible to enforce them. But there has to be some mechanism for that enforcement, and adjudication seems to be the mechanism that we have chosen. ...

... [A]lthough there certainly will be economic ramifications of efforts to enforce [civil and political rights such as access to counsel for accused persons, and decent prisons], they do not involve a broad redistribution of society's resources or its economic burdens. Therefore, I would distinguish the incidental costs of protecting civil and political rights from the much more substantial costs of economic redistribution.

Furthermore, there will always be, in unfair economic distribution, elements of invidious discrimination, discrimination on grounds of race or gender, or denials of due process. In these circumstances, I believe it is appropriate to invoke rights. For example, if a town provides roads and sewage collection, or water and electricity, to people of one race and not to those of another ... . But I think of these matters in terms of race discrimination, which involves a denial of civil and political rights, and not economic redistribution. Finally, I want to make it clear that certain constitutions incorporate some things that could be called economic and social rights with a certain degree of legislative specificity. For example, a constitution may provide that every child shall be entitled to a free primary school or a free secondary school education. When a constitution provides that level of legislative specificity, I think it is certainly appropriate to use the judicial mechanism to enforce one's rights accordingly.

---

[145] Neier was one of the founders of Human Rights Watch and the architect of its approach to ESR.

Social/economic rights and the democratic process

The concern I have with [ESR] is when there are broad assertions ... of a right to shelter or housing, a right to education, a right to social security, a right to a job, and a right to health care. There, I think, we get into territory that is unmanageable through the judicial process and that intrudes fundamentally into an area where the democratic process ought to prevail.

In my view, the purpose of the democratic process is essentially to deal with two questions: public safety and the development and allocation of a society's resources ... . Economic and security matters ought to be questions of public debate. To withdraw either of them from the democratic process is to carve the heart out of that process.

Everybody has an opinion on what should be done to protect the public's safety, and ... as to what is appropriate in the allocation of a society's resources and its economic burdens ... . These issues ought to be debated by everyone in the democratic process, with the legislature representing the public and with the public influencing the legislature in turn. To suggest otherwise undermines the very concept of democracy by stripping from it an essential part of its role.

Indeed, whenever you get to these broad assertions of shelter or housing or other economic resources, the question becomes: What shelter, employment, security, or level of education and health care is the person entitled to? It is only possible to deal with this question through the process of negotiation and compromise ... . [A] court is not the place where it is possible to engage in [the necessary] sort of negotiation and compromise ... . That is the heart of the political process ... .

Consider the question of health care ... . If you are allocating the resources of a society, how do you deal with the person who says they need [a] kidney transplant or [a] bypass or ... anti-retroviral drugs to save their life when the cost of these procedures may be equivalent to providing primary health care for a thousand children? Do you say the greater good for the greater number, a utilitarian principle, and exclude the person whose life is at stake if they do not get the health care that they require? I do not believe that is the kind of thing a court should do ... .

Consider next the question of education. What if a constitution talks about a right to an education but is silent as to the type of education people should be entitled to? A society may say that it needs a certain elite — scientists, engineers, and brain surgeons — as well as people who are going to able to work effectively in factories and service jobs. Does someone have a right to say they are entitled to an elite education ...? Can you deal with these questions through the adjudicatory process? Again, I do not believe it is possible.

Finally, consider the question of jobs. Suppose that a decision is made through the legislative process that we have to spend a certain amount on building roads because we want peasants to be able to take their goods to market for sale. Suppose further that we have to build a port to export those goods ... . Can the judicial process deal with the question of the short-term need for jobs and social security as opposed to that of long-term socio-economic growth? Again, can you deal with a society's decision to spend some of its resources on these matters rather than provide jobs at a certain level for every single person? ...

Civil and political rights

... I am a believer in very strong civil and political rights: the right to free speech, the right to assemble, the right not to be tortured, etc. Those rights have to mean exactly the same thing every place in the world. With social and economic "rights," however, it is inevitable that they are going to be applied differently in different places. That is, if you are talking about one country with extensive resources and one that is very poor, there is not going to be the same right to shelter or to health care ... .

But suppose that one takes that same idea — that different stages of development mean different things for each country — and applies it to the concept of civil and political rights. Suppose China or Zimbabwe says it is not a developed country and therefore cannot provide the same civil and political rights as a developed country ... .

Another way in which the idea of social and economic rights is dangerous is that you can only address economic and social distribution through compromise, but compromise should not enter into the adjudication of civil and political rights. I do not want a society to say that it cannot afford to give individuals the right to speak or publish freely, or the right not to be tortured ... .

...

DAVID KELLEY, A LIFE OF ONE'S OWN: INDIVIDUAL RIGHTS AND THE WELFARE STATE
(1998) 15

... America remains unique in the role that rights play in the national culture. ... [W]hile government is necessary to secure ... freedom, it is also the greatest danger to it. Thus, the concept of rights served two functions in the political theory of the Enlightenment: to legitimate government and to control it ... .

... [T]he concept of welfare rights, a concept that reflects a more expansive view of the role of government than anything envisioned by the classical liberals of the Enlightenment. 'For Jefferson, ... the poor had no right to be free from want', observes legal scholar Louis Henkin. 'The framers saw the purposes of government as being to police and safeguard, not to feed and clothe and house' ... . They differ in what is being claimed as a right, in the obligations that they impose, and in the way they are implemented.

...

Welfare rights differ from the classical rights to life, liberty, and property in the nature of the claim that they embody ... .

... The classical rights guarantee freedom from interference by others — and may thus be referred to as liberty rights — whereas welfare rights guarantee freedom to have various things that are regarded as necessities. What that means, in essence, is that the classical liberty rights are concerned with processes, whereas welfare rights are concerned with outcomes.

Liberty rights set conditions on the way in which individuals interact. Those rights say that we cannot harm, coerce, or steal from each other as we go about our business in life, but they do not guarantee that we will succeed in our business ... .

...

... [L]iberty rights impose on other people only the negative obligation not to interfere, not to restrain one forcibly from acting as he chooses ... .

But welfare rights impose positive obligations on others ... . A welfare right is by nature a right to a positive outcome, not contingent on the success of one's own efforts. It must therefore impose on others the obligation to ensure that outcome.

On whom does the obligation fall [to provide what welfare rights require]? ... One person's liberty rights impose on every other human being the obligation to respect them. I am obliged not to murder or steal from other individuals, even those I have never encountered and with whom I have no relationship. But am I obliged to respect their welfare rights? ... The obligation to supply those goods does not fall upon me as a particular individual; it falls upon all of us indifferently, as members of society ... . Insofar as welfare rights are implemented through government programs, for example, the obligation is distributed among all taxpayers.

...

To implement the liberty rights of individuals, government must protect them against incursions by other individuals ... . The laws involved are relatively simple; they essentially prohibit specific types of actions. The government apparatus required is relatively small, the 'night-watchman state' of classical liberalism. The only significant expense involved is that of the military, to protect against foreign aggression.

The implementation of welfare rights requires a much more activist form of government. The welfare state typically involves large-scale transfer programs ... through which wealth is transferred from taxpayers to those on whom the state confers entitlements to various goods.

...

... [T]he administration of the transfer programs is enormously complex by contrast with the relatively simple prohibitions involved in protecting the rights to life, liberty, and property. The welfare state involves government in running large-scale business enterprises: pension plans, health insurance, and so on. A complex set of regulations ... and a large bureaucracy [are] required to enforce those regulations ... .

JAMES GRIFFIN, THE PRESIDENTIAL ADDRESS: DISCREPANCIES BETWEEN THE BEST PHILOSOPHICAL ACCOUNT OF HUMAN RIGHTS AND THE INTERNATIONAL LAW OF HUMAN RIGHTS 101 PROCEEDINGS OF THE ARISTOTELIAN SOCIETY (2001) 1

...

According to my account, there are two grounds for human rights ... . Personhood initially generates the rights; practicalities give them, where needed, a sufficiently determinate shape.

The way to understand personhood more fully is to distinguish the various strands of agency ... . The first stage of agency is our taking our own decisions for ourselves, not being dominated or controlled by someone else (autonomy). To be more than empty tokens, our decisions must be informed; we must have basic education, access to information and to other people's views. And then, having formed a conception of a good life, we must be able to pursue it. So we need enough in the way of material provisions to support ourselves. And if we have all that, then we need others not to stop us (liberty). Whenever the word 'basic' appears here, it means the base needed not just to keep body and soul together but to live as an agent.

From this ... we should be able to derive all human rights. We have a right to autonomy. In private life, this means ... those in authority ... must not make us, or keep us, submissive to their wills ... .We have a right to life and to some form of security of person. We have a right not to be tortured ... . We have rights to education, free expression, peaceful assembly. And we have various rights to basic material provision; these so-called welfare rights are much challenged, but for all my inclination to keep the class of human rights tight, it seems to me impossible to exclude them. So there must be a large range of rights to certain necessary conditions of agency.

Then, we must be free from interference in the pursuit of our major ends ... . [T]here must be a large range of liberty rights, because liberty is the other essential component of agency.

This, of course, is the merest start of a list. There are many more human rights ... .

...

Twentieth century lists: economic, social, and cultural rights. ... [S]ome writers are deeply sceptical about the whole class of welfare rights ... . What seems to me undeniable is that there is a human right to the minimum resources needed to live as an agent. That is more than the resources needed simply to keep body and soul together, but it is a good deal less than the lavish provision that many of the international documents have in mind. So I think that there are acceptable claims to (human) welfare rights in the major international documents. But, on my account, there is also a vast number of unacceptable and debatable claims, many more than in the case of civil and political rights.

(a) *Unacceptable Cases*: Some of the claims to welfare rights are hardly credible. Article 7c of the *Additional Protocol to the American Convention* asserts that there is a right of every worker to promotion or upward mobility in his employment. But some perfectly good jobs have no career structure ... .

...

... The *Universal Declaration* of 1948 proclaims ... a right to work ... . Yet on my account, there is no right to work. There is certainly a right to the resources needed to live as an agent, but those resources do not have to come from work. If in an advanced technological society there were not enough work for everyone, and those without it were adequately provided for, then, on the face of it, no one's human rights would be violated ... .

...

[Then in the ICESCR, there is] a right to 'the highest attainable standard of physical and mental health'. On my account, there is no such right. [This] is not even a reasonable social aim. Societies *could* mount crash programmes ... in the case of illnesses for which cures are attainable, but they often do not. They regard themselves as free to decide when they have spent enough on health, even if they are still short of the highest attainable standards, and may devote their inevitably limited resources to [other social goals] ... .

...

JAMES W. NICKEL, POVERTY AND RIGHTS
55 THE PHILOSOPHICAL Q. (2005) 385

Human rights are not ideals of the good life for humans; rather they are concerned with ensuring the conditions, negative and positive, of a minimally good life ... .

Some philosophers have followed this line of thought to the conclusion that the main economic and social right is 'subsistence'. Henry Shue, John Rawls and Brian Orend[146] make subsistence the centrepiece of their concern for economic and social rights. Shue defines subsistence as 'unpolluted air, unpolluted water, adequate food, adequate clothing, adequate shelter, and minimal preventative health care' ... . Rawls includes 'subsistence' on his very short list of human rights, treating it along with security as part of the right to life. He interprets 'subsistence' as including 'minimum economic security' or 'having general all-purpose economic means'.

The idea of subsistence alone offers too minimal a conception of economic and social rights. It neglects education, gives an extremely minimal account of health services, and generally gives too little attention to people's ability to be active participants and contributors. It covers the requirements of having a life, but neglects the conditions of being able to lead one's life.

If Shue, Rawls and Orend err by making economic and social rights too minimal, international human rights documents make them excessively grandiose ... .

... I advocate a conception [that] suggests that economic and social rights focus on survival, health and education. It requires governments to govern in such a way that the following questions can be answered affirmatively:

1. Subsistence: Do conditions allow all people to secure safe air, food and water as well as environmentally appropriate shelter and clothing if they engage in work and self-help in so far as they can, practise mutual aid through organizations such as families, neighbourhoods and churches, and procure help from available government assistance programmes? Do people enjoy access to productive opportunities that allow them to contribute to the well-being of themselves, their families and their communities?

2. Health: Do environmental conditions, public health measures and available health services give people excellent chances of surviving childhood and childbirth, achieving physical and mental competence and living a normal lifespan?

3. Education: Do available educational resources give people a good chance of learning the skills necessary for survival, health, functioning, citizenship and productivity?

...

II. The Justification of Economic and Social Rights

It is sometimes alleged that economic and social rights do not have the importance that civil and political rights have. If the objection is ... that economic and social rights do not protect fundamental interests or are too burdensome to be justifiable, very plausible rebuttals are available.

...

---

[146] Eds.: see H. Shue, *Basic Rights* (2nd edn., 1996); B. Orend, *Human Rights: Concept and Context* (2002); and J. Rawls, *The Law of Peoples* (1999).

[Contrary to Griffin's argument], autonomy by itself does not seem likely to be able to generate economic and social rights, due process rights, or rights to non-discrimination and equality before the law. To compensate, Griffin accordingly relies heavily on 'practicalities' in allowing these rights. The result is to make the justification of rights other than liberties appear shaky and derivative. This could have been avoided by introducing some other fundamental values or norms, particularly a requirement of fair treatment when very important interests are at stake ... . A fairness norm would be no more controversial than autonomy as a starting-point for human rights, and it would allow due process rights to be as central and non-derivative as liberty rights.

[Nickel then proposes] a framework that suggests that people have secure, but abstract, moral claims on others in four areas: a secure claim to have a life; a secure claim to lead one's life; a secure claim against severely cruel or degrading treatment; and a secure claim against severely unfair treatment.

All four principles protect aspects of human dignity

The UDHR speaks of the 'inherent dignity ... of all members of the human family', and declares that 'All human beings are born free and equal in dignity and rights. They are endowed with reason and conscience.' The four grounds of human rights that I have proposed provide an interpretation of these ideas. We respect a person's dignity when we protect his life and agency and when we prevent others from imposing treatment that is severely degrading or unfair.

...

AMARTYA SEN, THE IDEA OF JUSTICE
(2009) 379

The Plausibility of Economic and Social Rights
...
Two of the most powerful rejections [of ESR by theorists and philosophers] have come from Maurice Cranston and Onora O'Neill ... .

There are ... two specific lines of reproach, which I shall call the 'institutionalization critique' and the 'feasibility critique'. The institutionalization critique, which is aimed particularly at economic and social rights, relates to the belief that real rights must involve an exact correspondence with precisely formulated correlate duties. Such a correspondence, it is argued, would exist only when a right is institutionalized. Onora O'Neill has presented the following criticism with clarity and force:

> Unfortunately much writing and rhetoric on rights heedlessly proclaims universal rights to goods or services, and in particular 'welfare rights', as well as to [ESCR], without showing what connects each presumed right-holder to some specified obligation-bearer(s), which leaves the content of these supposed rights wholly obscure ... . Some advocates of universal economic, social and cultural rights go no further than to emphasize that they can be institutionalized, which is true. But the point of difference is that they must be institutionalized: if they are not there is no right.

In responding to this criticism, we have to invoke the understanding ... that obligations can be both perfect and imperfect. Even the classical 'first-generation' rights, like freedom from assault, can be seen as imposing imperfect obligations on others ...[147]

Indeed, the supportive activities of social organizations are often aimed precisely at institutional change, and the activities are plausibly seen as part of imperfect obligations that individuals and groups have in a society where basic human rights are violated ... . To deny the ethical status of these claims would be to ignore the reasoning that fires these constructive activities, including working for institutional changes ... .

The 'feasibility critique' ... proceeds from the argument that even with the best of efforts, it may not be feasible to realize many of the alleged economic and social rights for all ... . Maurice Cranston puts the argument thus:

---

[147] For more detail on 'imperfect' obligations, see *ibid,* 373-74.

> The traditional political and civil rights are not difficult to institute. For the most part, they require governments, and other people generally, to leave a man alone ... . The problems posed by claims to economic and social rights, however, are of another order altogether. How can the governments of those parts of Asia, Africa, and South America, where industrialization has hardly begun, be reasonably called upon to provide social security and holidays with pay for millions of people who inhabit those places and multiply so swiftly?

Is this apparently plausible critique persuasive? I would argue that it is based on a confounding of the content of what an ethically acknowledged right must demand ... . [H]uman rights advocates want the recognized human rights to be maximally realized. The viability of this approach does not crumble merely because further social changes may be needed at any point of time to make more and more of these acknowledged rights fully realizable and actually realized.

Indeed, if feasibility were a necessary condition for people to have any rights, then not just social and economic rights, but all rights — even the right to liberty — would be nonsensical, given the infeasibility of ensuring the life and liberty of all against transgression ... . Non-realization does not, in itself, make a claimed right a non-right. Rather, it motivates further social action. The exclusion of all economic and social rights from the inner sanctum of human rights, keeping the space reserved only for liberty and other first-generation rights, attempts to draw a line in the sand that is hard to sustain. ... .

QUESTIONS

1. The position outlined by Neier seems to track existing United States domestic policy approaches closely. Does this make it more or less convincing from a human rights perspective? Does he effectively exclude the recognition of all ESR?

2. Based on the preceding readings, how would you identify the salient distinctions between civil and political and ESR? How useful is it to think in terms of rights versus needs, negative versus positive, individual versus collective, determinate versus open textured, law versus policy?

3. Does Griffin's theory of agency provide a satisfactory basis for a theory of ESR? What about Nickel's reliance upon subsistence and human dignity?

C. THE RELATIONSHIP BETWEEN THE TWO SETS OF RIGHTS

The interdependence of the two categories of rights has always been part of UN doctrine. The UDHR of 1948 included both categories without any sense of separateness or priority. The Preamble to the ICESCR, in terms mirroring those used in the ICCPR, states that 'in accordance with the Universal Declaration ..., the ideal of free human beings enjoying freedom from fear and want can only be achieved if conditions are created whereby everyone may enjoy his [ESCR], as well as his [CPR]'. The 1993 Vienna World Conference expressed the relationship by saying that all rights are 'indivisible and interdependent and interrelated'.

The interdependence principle, apart from its use as a political compromise between advocates of one or two covenants, reflects the fact that the two sets of rights can neither logically nor practically be separated in watertight compartments. Similarly, a given right might fit equally well within either covenant, depending on the purpose for which it is declared. Some illustrations follow:

(1) The right to form trade unions is contained in the ICESCR, while the right to freedom of association is recognized in the ICCPR.

(2) The ICESCR recognizes various 'liberties' and 'freedoms' in relation to scientific research and creative activity.

(3) While the right to education and the parental liberty to choose a child's school are dealt with in the ICESCR (Art. 13), the liberty of parents to choose their child's religious and moral education is recognized in the ICCPR (Art. 18).

(4) The prohibition of discrimination in relation to the provision of, and access to, educational facilities and opportunities can be derived from both Article 2 of the ICESCR and Article 26 of the ICCPR.

(5) Even the European Convention on Human Rights, which is generally considered to cover only CPR issues, states (in Art. 2 of Protocol 1) that 'no person shall be denied the right to education'.

While the claim of 'indivisibility' is not easy to prove empirically,[148] demonstrating 'interdependence' is more straightforward. The following report highlights some of the links between the denial of ESR and of CPR.

PHILIP ALSTON, REPORT OF THE SPECIAL RAPPORTEUR ON EXTREME POVERTY AND HUMAN RIGHTS ON HIS MISSION TO THE UNITED STATES OF AMERICA UN DOC. A/HRC/38/33/ADD.1 (2018)

...

7. [The International Monetary Fund's assessment of the United States economy in 2017 was that] it "is delivering better living standards for only the few", and that "household incomes are stagnating for a large share of the population, job opportunities are deteriorating, prospects for upward mobility are waning, and economic gains are increasingly accruing to those that are already wealthy".

...

19. In a democracy, the task of government should be to facilitate political participation by ensuring that all citizens can vote and that their votes will count equally. However, in the United States there is overt disenfranchisement of more than 6 million felons and ex-felons, which predominantly affects Black citizens since they are the ones whose conduct is often specifically targeted for criminalization. In addition, nine states currently condition the restoration of the right to vote after prison on the payment of outstanding fines and fees. A typical outcome is that seen in Alabama, where a majority of all ex-felons cannot vote.

20. Then there is covert disenfranchisement, which includes the dramatic gerrymandering of electoral districts to privilege particular groups of voters, the imposition of artificial and unnecessary voter identification requirements, the blatant manipulation of polling station locations, the relocation of Departments of Motor Vehicles' offices to make it more difficult for certain groups to obtain identification, and the general ramping up of obstacles to voting, especially for those without resources. The net result is that people living in poverty, minorities and other disfavoured groups are being systematically deprived of their right to vote.

21. It is thus unsurprising that the United States has one of the lowest turnout rates in elections among developed countries ... .

...

33. Calls for welfare reform take place against a constant drumbeat of allegations of widespread fraud in the system. Government officials warned the Special Rapporteur that individuals are constantly coming up with new schemes to live high on the welfare hog, and that individual states are gaming the welfare system to cheat the federal Government. The contrast with tax reform is instructive. In the tax context, immense faith is placed in the goodwill and altruism of the corporate beneficiaries, while with welfare reform the opposite assumptions apply. The reality, of course, is that there are good and bad corporate actors and there are good and bad welfare claimants. But while funding for the Internal Revenue Service to audit wealthy taxpayers has been reduced, efforts to identify welfare fraud are being greatly intensified. Revelations of widespread tax avoidance by companies and high-wealth individuals draw no rebuke, only acquiescence and the maintenance of the loopholes

---

[148] See J. Nickel, 'Rethinking Indivisibility: Towards A Theory of Supporting Relations between Human Rights', 30 Hum. Rts. Q. (2008) 984.

and other arrangements designed to facilitate such arrangements. But revelations of food stamps being used for purposes other than staying alive draw howls of outrage from government officials and their media supporters. …

44. In many cities, homeless persons are effectively criminalized for the situation in which they find themselves. Sleeping rough, sitting in public places, panhandling, public urination and myriad other offences have been devised to attack the "blight" of homelessness. The criminalization of homeless individuals in cities that provide almost zero public toilets seems particularly callous. …

45. Ever more demanding and intrusive regulations lead to infraction notices for the homeless, which rapidly turn into misdemeanours, leading to warrants, incarceration, unpayable fines and the stigma of a criminal conviction that in turn virtually prevents subsequent employment and access to most housing. Yet the authorities in cities such as Los Angeles and San Francisco often encourage this vicious circle. … Homelessness on this scale … reflects political choices to see the solution as law enforcement rather than adequate and accessible low-cost housing, medical treatment, psychological counselling and job training. …

…

47. In many cities and counties, the criminal justice system is effectively a system for keeping the poor in poverty while generating revenue to fund not only the justice system but many other programmes. The use of the legal system to raise revenue, not to promote justice, as was documented so powerfully in a 2015 report on Ferguson, Missouri by the Department of Justice, is pervasive around the country.

48. So-called fines and fees are piled up so that low level infractions become immensely burdensome, a process that affects only the poorest members of society, who pay the vast majority of such penalties. Driving licences are also commonly suspended for a wide range of non-driving related offences, such as a failure to pay fines. This is a perfect way to ensure that the poor, living in communities that have steadfastly refused to invest in serious public transport systems, are unable to earn a living that might have helped to pay the outstanding debt. Two paths are open: penury, or driving illegally, thus risking even more serious and counterproductive criminalization.

…

52. Solutions to major social challenges in the United States are increasingly seen to lie with privatization, especially in the criminal justice system. Bail bond corporations, which exist in only one other country in the world, precisely because they distort justice, encourage excessive and often unnecessary levels of bail, and lobby for the maintenance of a system that by definition penalizes the middle class and the poor.

53. In some states, minor offences are routinely punished by placing the offender on probation, overseen by a for-profit corporation, entirely at the expense of the usually poor offender. Those who cannot pay are subject to additional fees, supervision and testing. Similarly, in 26 states judges issue arrest warrants for alleged debtors at the request of private debt collectors, thus violating the law and human rights standards. The practice affects primarily the poor by subjecting them to court appearances, arrest warrants that appear on background checks, and jail time, which interfere with their wages, their jobs, their ability to find housing and more.

54. The United States remains a chronically segregated society. Blacks are 2.5 times more likely than Whites to be living in poverty, their infant mortality rate is 2.3 times that of Whites, their unemployment rate is more than double that for Whites, they typically earn only 82.5 cents for every dollar earned by a White counterpart, their household earnings are on average well under two thirds of those of their White equivalents, and their incarceration rates are 6.4 times higher than those of Whites. These shameful statistics can only be explained by long-standing structural discrimination on the basis of race, reflecting the enduring legacy of slavery.

55. Ironically, politicians and mainstream media portrayals distort this situation in order to suggest that poverty in America is overwhelmingly Black, thereby triggering a range of racist responses and encouraging Whites to see poverty as a question of race. Too often the loaded and inaccurate message that parts of the media want to convey is "lazy Blacks sponge off hard-working Whites".

…

57. … The United States has the highest maternal mortality ratio among wealthy countries, and black women are three to four times more likely to die than White women. In one city, the rate for Blacks was 12 times higher than that for Whites.

…

66. In terms of welfare, the main responses [to the opioid crisis] have been punitive. States increasingly seek to impose drug tests on recipients of welfare benefits, with programmes that lead to expulsion from the programme for repeat offenders. Others have introduced severe punishments for pregnant women who abuse drugs. Medical professionals recognize that such policies are counterproductive, highly intrusive and misplaced. The urge to punish rather than assist the poor often also has racial undertones, as in the contrast between the huge sentences handed down to those using drugs such as crack cocaine (predominantly Black) and those using opioids (overwhelmingly White).

D. 'AVAILABLE RESOURCES'

As already noted, one of the major distinctions between ESR and CPR is that obligations in relation to the former are limited to steps that can be taken within 'available resources'. No equivalent limitation is mentioned in the ICCPR, leading many experts to suggest that the realization of CPR is therefore not resource contingent. As a result, it is often argued that while wealthy industrialized countries may be able to afford policies designed to protect ESR, most developing countries cannot. For example, Maurice Cranston has written that: '[f]or a government to provide social security ... it has to have access to great capital wealth ... . The government of India, for example, simply cannot command the resources that would guarantee' each Indian an adequate standard of living.[149] A closely related issue concerns trade-offs. It is argued that more money spent on health inevitably means less for education, or water, or food etc. For many critics it follows that, in the absence of large-scale international aid or of rapid domestic economic growth (or both), the government's hands are tied and little can be expected of it in response to its obligations under the Covenant. Pressures to reduce the size of the public sector, to privatize various functions previously performed by governments, and to stimulate growth by reducing taxes, all render governments less able to accept responsibility for ESR.

Before focusing only on ESR, it is useful to reflect further on the resource dimensions of CPR. In principal, the issue does not arise because the relevant obligation — to respect and ensure — is not made subject to any qualifications as to resources. But in reality, resources are always relevant in at least some respects. As noted earlier, Roth argues that ESR 'shortcomings [are] largely a problem of distributive justice', unless there is arbitrary or discriminatory government conduct. He cites a government's failure to provide universal primary education as a classic case, because 'there is not enough money to go around, so governments cannot provide education to all children.' But he also notes (at 65) that:

> ... similar tradeoffs of scarce resources can arise in the realm of [CPR]. Building prisons or creating a judicial system can be expensive. However, my experience has been that international human rights organizations implicitly recognize these tradeoffs by avoiding recommendations that are costly. For example, Human Rights Watch in its work on prison conditions routinely avoids recommending large infrastructure investments. Instead, we focus on improvements in the treatment of prisoners that would involve relatively inexpensive policy changes.

But what Roth terms 'distributive justice' problems also arise in relation to CPR. Consider the question of how much funding to put into a judicial system, or a police service, or how elaborate and accessible arrangements for voting will be. Each of these can be funded more or less generously, and the decision will generally be made in light of the available resources, rather than being determined solely in light of an evaluation of the ideal level of supply. Moreover, treating 'distributive justice' issues as off-limits for human rights analysis effectively locks in the status quo and makes it impossible for deep-rooted issues of economic and social injustice to be addressed within the human rights framework.[150]

---

[149] 'Human Rights: Real and Supposed', in D. Raphael (ed.), *Political Theory and the Rights of Man* (1967) 43, at 51.
[150] See generally, E. Pribytkova, 'Are There Global Obligations to Assist in the Realization of Socio-Economic Rights?', 54. *N.Y.U. J. Int'l L. & Pol.* (2022) 379.

The Response of the UN Committee on ESCR

The debates over available resources and progressive realization have been central to much of the work of the Committee on ESCR. In 1990, it adopted a broad-ranging General Comment that laid the groundwork for its overall approach. This General Comment No. 3 has subsequently been invoked by many courts around the world. In 1999, the Committee elaborated upon the steps that should be taken by a state in a situation in which available resources are clearly inadequate to enable implementation of the right to primary education. And in 2007 the Committee, in response to calls that it should reassure governments and others that it would adopt a measured approach to the question of available resources if a complaints procedure were to be adopted in the form of an Optional Protocol, laid out the factors that it would take into account. Excerpts from these three statements, and another on social security, follow.

COMMITTEE ON ECONOMIC, SOCIAL AND CULTURAL RIGHTS, GENERAL COMMENT NO. 3: THE NATURE OF STATES PARTIES OBLIGATIONS, 1990

1. Article 2 ... describes the nature of the general legal obligations undertaken by States parties to the Covenant. Those obligations include both what may be termed (following the work of the International Law Commission) obligations of conduct and obligations of result ... .[W]hile the Covenant provides for progressive realization and acknowledges the constraints due to the limits of available resources, it also imposes various obligations which are of immediate effect. Of these, two are of particular importance in understanding the precise nature of States parties obligations. One of these, ... is the 'undertaking to guarantee' that relevant rights 'will be exercised without discrimination ...'.

2. The other is the undertaking in article 2(1) 'to take steps', which in itself, is not qualified or limited by other considerations ... . [W]hile the full realization of the relevant rights may be achieved progressively, steps towards that goal must be taken within a reasonably short time after the Covenant's entry into force for the States concerned. Such steps should be deliberate, concrete and targeted as clearly as possible towards meeting the obligations recognized in the Covenant.

3. The means which should be used in order to satisfy the obligation to take steps are stated in article 2(1) to be 'all appropriate means, including particularly the adoption of legislative measures'. The Committee recognizes that in many instances legislation is highly desirable and in some cases may even be indispensable. ...

4. ... [H]owever, the adoption of legislative measures ... is by no means exhaustive of the obligations of States parties. Rather, the phrase 'by all appropriate means' must be given its full and natural meaning ... . [T]he ultimate determination as to whether all appropriate measures have been taken remains for the Committee to make.
...
7. Other measures which may also be considered 'appropriate' ... include, but are not limited to, administrative, financial, educational and social measures.
...
9. ... The concept of progressive realization constitutes a recognition of the fact that full realization of all [ESCR] will generally not be able to be achieved in a short period of time. In this sense the obligation differs significantly from that contained in article 2 of the [ICCPR] which embodies an immediate obligation to respect and ensure all of the relevant rights. Nevertheless, the fact that realization over time, or in other words progressively, is foreseen under the Covenant should not be misinterpreted as depriving the obligation of all meaningful content. It is on the one hand a necessary flexibility device, reflecting the realities of the real world and the difficulties involved for any country in ensuring full realization of economic, social and cultural rights. On the other hand, the phrase must be read in the light of the overall objective, indeed the *raison d'être* of the Covenant which is to establish clear obligations for States parties in respect of the full realization of the rights in question. It thus imposes an obligation to move as expeditiously and effectively as possible towards that goal. Moreover, any deliberately retrogressive measures in that regard would require the most careful consideration and would need to be fully justified ... .

10. ... [T]he Committee is of the view that a minimum core obligation to ensure the satisfaction of, at the very least, minimum essential levels of each of the rights is incumbent upon every State party. Thus, for example, a State party in which any significant number of individuals is deprived of essential foodstuffs, of essential primary health care, of basic shelter and housing, or of the most basic forms of education is, prima facie, failing to discharge its obligations under the Covenant. If the Covenant were to be read in such a way as not to establish such a minimum core obligation, it would be largely deprived of its *raison d'être*. By the same token, it must be noted that any assessment as to whether a State has discharged its minimum core obligation must also take account of resource constraints applying within the country concerned. Article 2(1) obligates each State party to take the necessary steps 'to the maximum of its available resources'. In order for a State party to be able to attribute its failure to meet at least its minimum core obligations to a lack of available resources it must demonstrate that every effort has been made to use all resources that are at its disposition in an effort to satisfy, as a matter of priority, those minimum obligations.

11. ... [T]he obligations to monitor the extent of the realization, or more especially of the non-realization, of economic, social and cultural rights, and to devise strategies and programmes for their promotion, are not in any way eliminated as a result of resource constraints ... .

12. Similarly, the Committee underlines the fact that even in times of severe resource constraints whether caused by a process of adjustment, of economic recession, or by other factors, the vulnerable members of society can and indeed must be protected by the adoption of relatively low-cost targeted programmes.
...

COMMITTEE ON ECONOMIC, SOCIAL AND CULTURAL RIGHTS, GENERAL COMMENT NO. 11: PLANS OF ACTION FOR PRIMARY EDUCATION, 1999

1. Article 14 of the [ICESCR] requires each State party which has not been able to secure compulsory primary education, free of charge, to undertake within two years, to work out and adopt a detailed plan of action for the progressive implementation, within a reasonable number of years, to be fixed in the plan, of the principle of compulsory primary education free of charge for all ... .
...
6. *Compulsory*. The element of compulsion serves to highlight the fact that neither parents, nor guardians, nor the State is entitled to treat as optional the decision as to whether the child should have access to primary education ... .

7. *Free of charge*. The nature of this requirement is unequivocal. The right is expressly formulated so as to ensure the availability of primary education without charge to the child, parents or guardians. Fees imposed by the Government, local authorities or the school, and other direct costs, constitute disincentives to the enjoyment of the right and may jeopardize its realization. They are also often highly regressive in effect. Their elimination is a matter which must be addressed by the required plan of action. Indirect costs, such as compulsory levies on parents (sometimes portrayed as being voluntary, when in fact they are not), or the obligation to wear a relatively expensive school uniform, can also fall into the same category. Other indirect costs may be permissible, subject to the Committee's examination on a case-by-base basis ... .

8. *Adoption of a detailed plan*. The State party is required to adopt a plan of action within two years ... .

9. *Obligations*. A State party cannot escape the unequivocal obligation to adopt a plan of action on the grounds that the necessary resources are not available. If the obligation could be avoided in this way, there would be no justification for the unique requirement contained in article 14 which applies, almost by definition, to situations characterized by inadequate financial resources. By the same token, and for the same reason, the references to 'international assistance and cooperation' in articles 2.1 and 23 of the Covenant are of particular relevance in this situation. Where a State party is clearly lacking in the financial resources and/or expertise required to 'work out and adopt' a detailed plan, the international community has a clear obligation to assist.

10. *Progressive implementation* ... . Unlike the provision in article 2.1, however, article 14 specifies that the target date must be 'within a reasonable number of years' and moreover, that the time-frame must 'be fixed in the

plan'. In other words, the plan must specifically set out a series of targeted implementation dates for each stage of the progressive implementation of the plan ... .

COMMITTEE ON ECONOMIC, SOCIAL AND CULTURAL RIGHTS, AN EVALUATION OF THE OBLIGATION TO TAKE STEPS TO THE 'MAXIMUM OF AVAILABLE RESOURCES' UNDER AN OPTIONAL PROTOCOL TO THE COVENANT: STATEMENT UN DOC. E/C.12/2007/1 (2007)

...

8. In considering a communication concerning an alleged failure of a State party to take steps to the maximum of available resources, the Committee will examine the measures that the State party has effectively taken, legislative or otherwise. In assessing whether they are "adequate" or "reasonable", the Committee may take into account, inter alia, the following considerations:

(a) The extent to which the measures taken were deliberate, concrete and targeted towards the fulfilment of economic, social and cultural rights;

(b) Whether the State party exercised its discretion in a non-discriminatory and nonarbitrary manner;

(c) Whether the State party's decision (not) to allocate available resources was in accordance with international human rights standards;

(d) Where several policy options are available, whether the State party adopted the option that least restricts Covenant rights;

(e) The time frame in which the steps were taken;

(f) Whether the steps had taken into account the precarious situation of disadvantaged and marginalized individuals or groups and, whether they were nondiscriminatory, and whether they prioritized grave situations or situations of risk.

9. The Committee notes that in case of failure to take any steps or of the adoption of retrogressive steps, the burden of proof rests with the State party to show that such a course of action was based on the most careful consideration and can be justified by reference to the totality of the rights provided for in the Covenant and by the fact that full use was made of available resources.

10. Should a State party use "resource constraints" as an explanation for any retrogressive steps taken, the Committee would consider such information on a country-by-country basis in the light of objective criteria such as:

(a) The country's level of development;

(b) The severity of the alleged breach, in particular whether the situation concerned the enjoyment of the minimum core content of the Covenant;

(c) The country's current economic situation, in particular whether the country was undergoing a period of economic recession;

(d) The existence of other serious claims on the State party's limited resources; for example, resulting from a recent natural disaster or from recent internal or international armed conflict.

(e) Whether the State party had sought to identify low-cost options; and

(f) Whether the State party had sought cooperation and assistance or rejected offers of resources from the international community for the purposes of implementing the provisions of the Covenant without sufficient reason.

...

COMMITTEE ON ECONOMIC, SOCIAL AND CULTURAL RIGHTS, GENERAL COMMENT NO. 19: THE RIGHT TO SOCIAL SECURITY (ART. 9), 2008

[While this statement is directed specifically at possible cuts in social security benefits, the Committee also applies the same approach in relation to other ESR under the Covenant.]

...

42. There is a strong presumption that retrogressive measures taken in relation to the right to social security are prohibited under the Covenant. If any deliberately retrogressive measures are taken, the State party has the burden of proving that they have been introduced after the most careful consideration of all alternatives and that they are duly justified by reference to the totality of the rights provided for in the Covenant, in the context of the full use of the maximum available resources of the State party. The Committee will look carefully at whether: (a) there was reasonable justification for the action; (b) alternatives were comprehensively examined; (c) there was genuine participation of affected groups in examining the proposed measures and alternatives; (d) the measures were directly or indirectly discriminatory; (e) the measures will have a sustained impact on the realization of the right to social security, an unreasonable impact on acquired social security rights or whether an individual or group is deprived of access to the minimum essential level of social security; and (f) whether there was an independent review of the measures at the national level.[151]

QUESTIONS

1. Could it reasonably be argued that virtually every country could afford to provide universal primary education and access to primary health care if it wished to do so?

2. Do the ESCR Committee's General Comments reflect a workable balance that resolves the objections of ESR critics to the effect that such rights are unaffordable if taken seriously and almost meaningless if the emphasis is placed on resources which will never be sufficiently 'available'? How workable are the criteria that the Committee proposes to apply in examining a complaint alleging that available resources have not been used to achieve respect for a given right?

E. CONSTITUTIONS, COURTS AND OTHER REMEDIES

Since the 1990s, ESR have assumed major constitutional significance in many countries through: (1) explicit constitutional recognition; (2) judicial interpretation of CPR to encompass at least some ESR; and (3) judicial willingness to treat previously non-justiciable ESR provisions as being justiciable.

A survey by Evan Rosevear, Ran Hirschl and Courtney Jung, in 'Justiciable and Aspirational Economic and Social Rights in National Constitutions', in Katharine Young (ed.), *The Future of Economic and Social Rights* (2019) 37, concluded that:

> ... Nearly all new democracies, and several established ones, have included some form of ESRs in their constitutions ... . Almost all constitutions also include a generic protection of 'the right to life' or 'human dignity', either in lieu of, or in addition to, a set of concrete ESRs. More than three-quarters of the world's constitutions now contain at least one formally justiciable ESR, only 17 do not incorporate at least one justiciable or aspirational ESR, and the majority of constitutions include nine or more. Indeed, such rights are now so commonly enshrined that they may reasonably be seen as a defining characteristic of third wave constitutions.

---

[151] For the Committee's approach to social security under the Optional Protocol, see Communication No. 1/2013 *López Rodríguez v. Spain*, Communication No. 1/2013 (November 2013).

...

Only four constitutions – those of Kyrgyzstan, Myanmar, Sierra Leone and Thailand – had fewer ESRs in 2016 than they did in 2000, while 51 constitutions had more.

...

The rights ... [to] education, health, child protection and social security ... were the most commonly enshrined rights in 2000 ... . All four ... are now present in at least two-thirds of all national constitutions. These rights are also much more likely to be justiciable in 2016 than they were in 2000.

Rights to a healthy environment and environmental protection have also increased disproportionately since 2000 [and] ... are now present in more than two-thirds of national constitutions. ...

...

... Whereas a right to housing is now present in 42 percent of constitutions, a right to land is present in only 14 percent. ...

...

... Civil law constitutions have been significantly more likely to entrench ESRs than common law constitutions, and recent changes confirm the distinction. ...

Despite these impressive statistics, the authors acknowledge that 'there are multiple paths and trajectories to the realization (or neglect) of ESRs, of which constitutionalization is only one aspect.' This is borne out by the fact that while an increasingly rich ESR case law has emerged, it has come mainly from just a handful of jurisdictions such as Brazil, Colombia, India, Kenya and South Africa.

The accountability of governments and other entities, as well as the availability of a remedy in cases of a violation, are indispensable elements of international human rights law. Under Article 8 of the UDHR, '[e]veryone has the right to an effective remedy by the competent national tribunals for acts violating the fundamental rights granted him by the constitution or by law.' The Declaration recognizes ESR and there is nothing to indicate that this provision was intended to apply only to CPR. There is, however, nothing in the ICESCR that is equivalent to the requirement in the ICCPR that states parties 'develop the possibilities of judicial remedy' (Art. 2(3)(b)). This lacuna seems to have encouraged many governments and commentators to assume that traditional legal remedies such as court actions are either inappropriate or at best impracticable for the vindication of ESR.

This section looks at ESR in constitutions and considers the types of remedies considered by courts. A key issue is justiciability (i.e., the ability of courts to provide a remedy for aggrieved individuals claiming a violation of those rights) which many observers continue to see as the essential hallmark of a 'real' human right. First, we consider the extent to which states are required by international law to provide constitutional recognition of ESR or specific types of remedies in relation to them.

COMMITTEE ON ECONOMIC, SOCIAL AND CULTURAL RIGHTS, GENERAL COMMENT NO. 9:
DOMESTIC APPLICATION OF THE COVENANT, 1998

A. The duty to give effect to the Covenant in the domestic legal order

1. ... The central obligation in relation to the Covenant is for States parties to give effect to the rights recognized therein. By requiring governments to do so 'by all appropriate means', the Covenant adopts a broad and flexible approach which enables the particularities of the legal and administrative systems of each State, as well as other relevant considerations, to be taken into account.

2. But this flexibility co-exists with the obligation upon each State Party to use *all* the means at its disposal to give effect to the rights recognised in the Covenant. In this respect, the fundamental requirements of international human rights law must be borne in mind. Thus the norms themselves must be recognised in appropriate ways within the domestic legal order, appropriate means of redress, or remedies, must be available to any aggrieved individual or group, and appropriate means of ensuring governmental accountability must be put in place.

...

C. ... Legal or judicial remedies?

9. The right to an effective remedy need not be interpreted as always requiring a judicial remedy. Administrative remedies will, in many cases, be adequate ... . Any such administrative remedies should be accessible, affordable, timely, and effective ... . [But] whenever a Covenant right cannot be made fully effective without some role for the judiciary, judicial remedies are necessary.

Justiciability

10. In relation to [CPR], it is generally taken for granted that judicial remedies for violations are essential. Regrettably, the contrary presumption is too often made in relation to [ESCR]. This discrepancy is not warranted either by the nature of the rights or by the relevant Covenant provisions. The Committee has already made clear that it considers many of the provisions in the Covenant to be capable of immediate implementation. Thus in General Comment No. 3 it cited, by way of example: articles 3, 7(a)(i), 8, 10(3), 13(2)(a), 13(3), 13(4) and 15(3).[152] It is important in this regard to distinguish between justiciability (which refers to those matters which are appropriately resolved by the courts) and norms which are self-executing (capable of being applied by courts without further elaboration). While the general approach of each legal system needs to be taken into account, there is no Covenant right which could not, in the great majority of systems, be considered to possess at least some significant justiciable dimensions. It is sometimes suggested that matters involving the allocation of resources should be left to the political authorities rather than the courts. While the respective competences of the different branches of government must be respected, it is appropriate to acknowledge that courts are generally already involved in a considerable range of matters which have important resource implications. The adoption of a rigid classification of economic, social and cultural rights which puts them, by definition, beyond the reach of the courts would thus be arbitrary and incompatible with the principle that the two sets of human rights are indivisible and interdependent. It would also drastically curtail the capacity of the courts to protect the rights of the most vulnerable and disadvantaged groups in society.

ESR Litigation in Specific Constitutional Settings

When reading these cases from different jurisdictions, keep in mind the following questions:
  (a) are ESR formulated in a manner that is sufficiently precise to enable judges to apply them in concrete cases?;
  (b) to the extent that such cases will involve decisions about public spending priorities, should such decisions remain the exclusive domain of the executive and legislature?;
  (c) are judges well suited in terms of their expertise, social and political background and the facilities available to them to make such decisions?; and
  (d) are there creative approaches to remedies that courts could, and should, develop in relation to ESR?

---

[152] These refer respectively to: equal rights of men and women (Art. 3), equal pay for equal work (Art. 7(a)(i)), the right to form and join trade unions and the right to strike (Art. 8), the right of children to special protection (Art. 10(3)), the right to free, compulsory, primary education (Art. 13(2)(a)), the liberty to choose a non-public school (Art. 13(3)), the liberty to establish schools (Art. 13(4)), and the freedom for scientific research and creative activity (Art. 15(3)).

1. India: Public Interest Litigation

In the Indian Constitution of 1950 the concept of 'directive principles of state policy', first used in the 1937 Irish Constitution, was used in contra-distinction to that of 'fundamental rights'. They were considered to be distinct from, and usually inferior in status to, rights that appear in the constitution without the qualification 'directive'. They appear in different forms in diverse constitutions worldwide, [153] although the Indian approach is the most significant. The Constitution contains a chapter dealing with 'fundamental rights' which consists largely of civil and political rights enforceable in the courts, and another chapter dealing with 'directive principles of state policy'. Some illustrations from the Constitution follow.

Part III. Fundamental Rights

...

Article 21. No person shall be deprived of his life or personal liberty except according to procedure established by law.

...

Part IV. Directive Principles of State Policy

...

Article 37. The provisions contained in this Part shall not be enforced by any court, but the principles therein laid down are nevertheless fundamental in the governance of the country and it shall be the duty of the State to apply these principles in making laws.

Article 39. The State shall, in particular, direct its policy towards securing:

(a) that the citizens, men and women equally, have the right to an adequate means of livelihood;

(b) that the ownership and control of the material resources of the community are so distributed as best to subserve the common good;

(c) that the operation of the economic system does not result in the concentration of wealth and means of production to the common detriment;

(d) that there is equal pay for equal work for both men and women;

(e) that the health and strength of workers, men and women, and the tender age of children are not abused and that citizens are not forced by economic necessity to enter avocations unsuited to their age or strength;

(f) that children are given opportunities and facilities to develop in a healthy manner and in conditions of freedom and dignity and that childhood and youth are protected against exploitation and against moral and material abandonment.

...

Article 41. The State shall, within the limits of its economic capacity and development, make effective provision for securing the right to work, to education and to public assistance in cases of unemployment, old age, sickness and disablement, and in other cases of undeserved want.

...

---

[153] See generally T. Khaitan, 'Constitutional Directives: Morally-Committed Political Constitutionalism', 82 *Modern L. Rev.* (2019) 603.

Article 47. The State shall regard the raising of the level of nutrition and the standard of living of its people and the improvement of public health as among its primary duties ... .

Over the years the Indian courts have redefined the relationship between fundamental rights and directive principles by integrating the two categories and making the latter potentially enforceable. This has largely been done in the context of so-called 'Public Interest Litigation' (PIL). PIL was pioneered by the Supreme Court, partly to regain popular legitimacy in the wake of its initial failure to reign in the emergency declared by Indira Gandhi in 1975, which involved severe repression of civil liberties:

> ... the court relaxed the rules of standing and pleading before the court. Thus, any public-spirited individual or entity could bring a case ... for the enforcement of a fundamental right. In addition, the court dispensed with the procedural formalities required to bring a petition, and converted all sorts of instruments (including letters written to the judges, postcards addressed to the court, and newspaper articles highlighting rights violations) to writ petitions. The court also expanded its own powers to develop a range of remedies that at times involved taking control over the activities of other agencies.[154]

The following materials provide a sampling of some landmark PIL cases.

OLGA TELLIS V. BOMBAY MUNICIPAL CORPORATION
SUPREME COURT OF INDIA, AIR 1986 SC 18 (10 JULY 1985)

CHANDRACHUD CJ (FOR THE COURT):

1. These Writ Petitions portray the plight of lakhs [hundreds of thousands] of persons who live on pavements and in slums in the city of Bombay. They constitute nearly half the population of the city ... . Those who have made pavements their homes exist in the midst of filth and squalor, which has to be seen to be believed. Rabid dogs in search of stinking meat and cats in search of hungry rats keep them company ... .

It is these men and women who have come to this Court to ask for a judgment that they cannot be evicted from their squalid shelters without being offered alternative accommodation. They rely for their rights on Art. 21 of the Constitution which guarantees that no person shall be deprived of his life except according to procedure established by law. They do not contend that they have a right to live on the pavements. Their contention is that they have a right to live, a right which cannot be exercised without the means of livelihood ... .

...

32. ... For purposes of argument, we will assume the factual correctness of the premise that if the petitioners are evicted from their dwellings, they will be deprived of their livelihood. Upon that assumption, the question which we have to consider is whether the right to life includes the right to livelihood. We see only one answer to that question, namely, that it does. The sweep of the right to life conferred by Art. 21 is wide and far-reaching ... . That, which alone makes it possible to live, leave aside what makes life livable, must be deemed to be an integral component of the right to life. Deprive a person of his right to livelihood and you shall have deprived him of his life. Indeed, that explains the massive migration of the rural population to big cities ... .

33. Article 39(a) of the Constitution, which is a Directive Principle of State Policy, provides that the State shall, in particular, direct its policy towards securing that the citizens, men and women equally, have the right to an adequate means of livelihood. [Reference is made to Arts. 41 and 37, noted above] ... The Principles contained in Arts. 39(a) and 41 must be regarded as equally fundamental in the understanding and interpretation of the meaning and content of fundamental rights. If there is an obligation upon the State to secure to the citizens an adequate means of livelihood and the right to work, it would be sheer pedantry to exclude the right to livelihood from the content of the right to life ... .

...

35 ... It would be unrealistic on our part to reject the petitions on the ground that the petitioners have not adduced evidence to show that they will be rendered jobless if they are evicted from the slums and pavements.

---

[154] N. Jain, 'The Democratizing Force of International Law: Human Rights Adjudication by the Indian Supreme Court', in A. Roberts et al. (eds.), *Comparative International Law* (2018) 319.

Commonsense, which is a cluster of life's experiences, is often more dependable than the rival facts presented by warring litigants.

...

37. Two conclusions emerge from this discussion: one, that the right to life which is conferred by Art. 21 includes the right to livelihood and two, that it is established that if the petitioners are evicted from their dwellings, they will be deprived of their livelihood. But the Constitution does not put an absolute embargo on the deprivation of life or personal liberty. By Art. 21, such deprivation has to be according to procedure established by law ... .

...

57. To summarise, ... pavement dwellers who were censused or who happened to be censused in 1976 should be given, though not as a condition precedent to their removal, alternate [sites] at Malavani or at such other convenient place as the Government considers reasonable but not farther away in terms of distance; slum dwellers who were given identity cards and whose dwellings were numbered in the 1976 census must be given alternate sites for the resettlement: slums which have been in existence for a long time, say for twenty years or more, and which have been improved and developed will not be removed unless the land on which they stand or the appurtenant land, is required for a public purpose, in which case, alternate sites or accommodation will be provided to them ... . In order to minimise the hardship involved in any eviction, we direct that the slums, wherever situated, will not be removed until one month after the end of the current monsoon season ... .

Later Indian Cases

In subsequent cases the Court expanded its interpretation of Article 21 in relation to a wide range of social sectors, including health. In *Rakesh Chandra Narayan v. State of Bihar* (1989 AIR 348) a PIL complaint alleged abusive conditions at a mental hospital in Bihar. At the Court's request, a Chief Judicial Magistrate, visited and reported that only nine out of 16 medical officers had been appointed, that there was an acute water shortage, none of the toilets functioned, there was no additional light or ventilation provided, there were 300 beds for 1,580 patients, that meals were wholly inadequate and medicines were in very short supply. In response the Court requested the Bihar authorities to put forth a 'definite scheme for improving the working of the Institution'. The Health Secretary of Bihar subsequently filed a report that the Court found to be entirely inadequate. It then ordered that a series of specific measures be taken. Eighteen months later it observed that the responses of the authorities 'have not given us the satisfaction of the touch of appropriate sincerity in action' and that they had been 'half-hearted'. It concluded that it could not, 'with any sense of confidence ... leave the management to the Health Department of the State of Bihar'. While recognizing the difficulty involved in managing a hospital located 1,000 kilometres away, the Court nonetheless appointed a Committee of Management 'with full powers to look after all aspects of the institution', prescribed its exact composition, scheduled its meetings and kept the case open.

In *Consumer Education & Research Centre v. Union of India* ((1995) 3 SCC 42) the Court examined a PIL petition complaining of the hazards faced by workers in asbestos-related industries. The petition cited International Labour Organization standards and detailed the medical consequences of the exposure. The Court took the opportunity to expand its definition of the right to life and to make a detailed remedial order:

> 26. The right to health to a worker is an integral facet of meaningful right to life to have not only a meaningful existence but also robust health and vigour without which worker [sic] would lead life of misery ... .

> 27. Therefore, we hold that right to health, medical aid to protect the health and vigour to a worker while in service or post retirement is a fundamental right under Article 21, read with Articles 39(e), 41, 43, 48A and all related Articles and fundamental human rights to make the life of the workman meaningful and purposeful with dignity of person.

> ...

> 33. The writ petition is, therefore, allowed. All the industries are directed (1) To maintain and keep maintaining the health record of every worker up to a minimum period of 40 years ...; (2) The Membrane Filter test, to detect asbestos fibre should be adopted by all the factories ...; (3) All the factories ... are directed to compulsorily insure health coverage to every worker; (4) The Union and the State Governments are directed to review the

standards of permissible exposure ... in tune with ... international standards ...; (6) [all the relevant workers shall be medically examined and, if found to be suffering from an occupational health hazards, shall be compensated 100,000 rupees.]

In *Paschim Banga Khet Mazdoor Samity v. State of West Bengal* ((1996) 4 SCC 37) the petitioner fell off a train and suffered serious head injuries. He was taken by ambulance to a succession of hospitals and turned away, either because the hospital did not have the necessary facilities, or because no free beds were available. He ended up at an expensive private hospital. The Court found a violation of Article 21:

> The Constitution envisages the establishment of a welfare state at the federal level as well as at the state level. In a welfare state the primary duty of the Government is to secure the welfare of the people [which includes providing] adequate medical facilities ... by running hospitals and health centres ... . Article 21 imposes an obligation on the State to safeguard the right to life of every person. Preservation of human life is thus of paramount importance. The Government hospitals run by the State and the medical officers employed therein are duty bound to extend medical assistance for preserving human life. Failure on the part of a Government hospital to provide timely medical treatment to a person in need of such treatment [violates] Article 21 ... .

The Court ordered measures specific to the applicant, but also remedial measures designed to ensure that in future 'proper medical facilities are available for dealing with emergency cases'. They included ordering additional emergency facilities at Primary Health Centres, the upgrading of local hospitals, improved ambulance facilities and preparation to ensure that medical personnel 'are geared to deal with larger number of patients needing emergency treatment on account of higher risk of accidents on certain occasions and in certain seasons.' In considering the financial implications of these orders, it stated:

> It is no doubt true that financial resources are needed for providing these facilities. But at the same time it cannot be ignored that it is the constitutional obligation of the State to provide adequate medical services to the people. Whatever is necessary for this purpose has to be done. In the context of the constitutional obligation to provide free legal aid to a poor accused this Court has held that the State cannot avoid its constitutional obligation in that regard on account of financial constraints ... . The said observations would apply with equal, if not greater, force in the matter of discharge of constitutional obligation of the State to provide medical aid to preserve human life. In the matter of allocation of funds for medical services the said constitutional obligation of the State has to be kept in view. It is necessary that a time-bound plan for providing these services should be chalked out ... and steps should be taken to implement the same ... .

Three areas in which the Court's activism bore important constitutional and legislative fruit are education, food and the environment. In 1992-93 the Court derived the right to education from the right to life and recognized a fundamental right to free education for children up to 14 years old.[155] This in turn led to an amendment to the Constitution (the 86th), recognizing such a right for children between six and 14 years. Some commentators have stressed the importance of these developments,[156] while others have noted that 'educational indicators remain dismal'.[157]

Similar ambivalence can be found in the literature relating to the use of PIL in relation to environmental issues. Arpitha Kodiveri, in 'Biodiversity Litigation in India: A Typology of Cases and Varieties of Environmentalism' in Guillaume Futhazar et al. (eds.), *Biodiversity Litigation* (2022) 177 acknowledges that PIL 'reshaped the nature of environmental jurisprudence in India and infused it with many international legal principles, such as the polluter pays principle, public trust doctrine, and international biodiversity law. These cases also changed the legal landscape on which future environmental laws were made.' But some of the cases came at the expense of those living in poverty, whose rights were 'placed on the backburner and ... replaced by bourgeois environmentalism and exclusionary conservation' orders.

---

[155] Mohini Jain v. State of Karnataka (1992) AIR 1858 and J P Unnikrishnan v. State of Andhra Pradesh, 1993 SCC (1) 645.
[156] F. Matthey-Prakash, The Right to Education in India: The Importance of Enforceability of a Fundamental Right (2019)
[157] A. Sengupta et al., 'Legislating Human Rights: Experience of the Right to Education Act in India', in K. Young (ed.), *The Future of Economic and Social Rights* (2019) 158.

Perhaps the most consequential PIL case was *People's Union for Civil Liberties v. Union of India & Ors.* ((2004) 12 SCC 108) which started with a PIL Writ Petition (No. 196 of 2001) invoking Articles 21 and 47 of the Constitution. It followed deaths from starvation in Rajasthan state, even though the government held ample grain supplies at the time. The Court issued a series of orders over many years, deriving a right to food from the right to life, and obtaining regular factual updates from Commissioners it appointed for this purpose. It ordered the activation of the Famine Code for three months; a doubling of the grain allocation under the food for work scheme; required ration shops to stay open and provide the grain to families below the poverty line at the set price; and the implementation of a mid-day meal scheme in schools.[158]

The 2013 National Food Security Act reflected the extent to which the People's Union for Civil Liberties (PUCL) litigation had affected mainstream political discourse, although the Act assiduously avoided any specific reference to 'the right to food'. Its stated aim is 'to provide for food and nutritional security in human life cycle approach, by ensuring access to adequate quantity of quality food at affordable prices to people to live a life with dignity'. Although the Act's impact has been mixed,[159] the ramifications of the PUCL litigation continue.

DIPIKA JAGATRAM SAHANI V. UNION OF INDIA AND OTHERS
SUPREME COURT OF INDIA (13 JANUARY 2021)

ASHOK BHUSHAN, J.

1. This writ petition has been filed as a Public Interest Litigation under Article 32 of the Constitution of India questioning the closure of the Anganwadi Centres across the country. ... [These] Centres [provide] supplementary nutrition to pregnant women, lactating mothers, adolescent girls and children up to the age of 6 years [as well as growth monitoring and counseling, pre-school education, immunization and referral services.] ... [The petitioners sought, inter alia]:

> a) [A] writ of mandamus directing the Union of India and all States and Union Territories to forthwith reopen all the Anganwadi Centres in the country and provide Anganwadi services as before the lockdown and in accordance with Sections 4 to 7 of the National Food Security Act, 2013.

...

2. ... Article 47 of the Constitution ... provides that the State shall regard the raising of the level of nutrition and the standard of living of its people and the improvement of public health as among its primary duties. The Government of India with the above objective launched a welfare scheme, namely, Integrated Child Development Services Scheme in the year 1975. ... This Court in [the 2001 PUCL case], had issued various directions for protection of right to food of the poor and the underprivileged sections including children and women. ...

3. The Parliament enacted the National Food Security Act, 2013 ... .

...

7. After spread of ... COVID-19, Anganwadi Centres were closed throughout the country in March, 2020. The distribution of special nutrition and other benefits to be provided for beneficiaries being essential services were permitted to be conducted by Anganwadi staff by resorting to Take Home Ration.

...

14. Shri Colin Gonsalves, ... counsel ... for the petitioner contends that ... after lockdown came to an end [and] due to non-opening of Anganwadi in various States beneficiaries, children pregnant women and lactating mothers are suffering. The pandemic has caused severe strain on the employment and means of livelihood of a large sections of the society especially marginal sections, who require immediate extension of all benefits as envisaged in the Scheme. ... [D]ue to non-providing of hot cooked meals to children up to the age of six years and children who are affected of malnutrition .. are suffering which needs immediate attention and remedial action.

---

[158] L. Birchfield and J. Corsi, 'Between Starvation and Globalization: Realizing the Right to Food in India', 31 *Mich. J. Int'l L.* (2010) 691.

[159] G. Dandurand, 'The Techno-politics of Human Rights: The Case of the National Food Security Act in India', 144 *Geoforum* (2023) 103819.

...

18. ... Government has a constitutional obligation to preserve human life. Good health of its citizens is its primary duty. International covenants also aim at highest attainable standards of physical and mental health. This is in interest of social justice. Inadequate supply of nutritious food to the citizens, more particularly to the children and the women shall affect their health. Therefore, the same shall be in violation of their fundamental right to health/right to live with dignity guaranteed under Article 21 of the Constitution of India.

19. The Centre as well as States are statutorily obliged to implement statutory obligation as imposed under Sections 4,5 and 6 of the Act, 2013. ...

...

24. ... [S]everal States have taken decision to open Anganwadi Centres. ...

...

26. On the other hand, there are few States who have taken decision not to reopen Anganwadi Centres. ...

...

33. It is the obligation of the State to ensure that pregnant women, lactating mothers and children in the age of 3 to 6 years and children who suffer from malnutrition are provided their dues. ... All States/Union Territories should evolve an appropriate mechanism for supervision so that dues are received by beneficiaries for whom schemes are in place. It is for the State to secure health to its citizens as its primary duty. ...

34. ... We are of the view that unless there are any specific reasons for not opening of Anganwadi Centres, all Anganwadi Centres beyond the containment zones should be made functional by all the States/Union Territories at an early date. All States may review the situation and take positive decisions on or before 31.01.2021 ... ...

RESPONSES TO INDIA'S PIL

Even *The Economist* magazine, long critical of ESR, was hesitant in 2010 to dismiss entirely the Indian Supreme Court's foray into social rights.[160] It drew attention to the risk of overburdening the state in areas where it has already failed, pointing out that '[o]ver 80% of health-care spending in India is in the private sector, ... yet any "right-to-health" legislation is likely to focus on non-functioning public clinics.' It conceded, however, that 'India's appetite for rights is the expression of a young democracy's hopes' which led them to conclude that 'India's crusading judges sometimes take on too much, but they have often held the government to account— and Indians like them for it.' It added, 'where it encourages the introduction of concrete reforms, rights talk means something'.

But much of the recent literature has been somewhat critical of the Court's approach. For example, Tarunabh Khaitan, in 'The Supreme Court as a Constitutional Watchdog' (2019) at 721 *Seminar* (2019) 22, at 23, suggests that India's is 'arguably the world's most powerful apex court' with 'power to seriously impact the lives of a billion-plus Indians'. He acknowledges that through PIL 'it has made decisions of far-reaching import in the areas of housing, environment, food security, corruption, transparency, sexual harassment, urban pollution, forest rights, and economic policy.' But he is critical of the way in which the Court has done this:

> The SCI's approach to legal reasoning and interpretation ... is astonishingly undisciplined. Relevant, even binding, precedent is far too often simply ignored. Relevant legislative or even constitutional provisions are sometimes not even discussed in the judgement. ...

> [A recent] study shows that a vast majority of the SCI's judgments neither cite previous cases, nor are they cited by later cases. All too frequently, the actual prayers of the litigants are ignored, and the court gives orders that no party before it prayed for – sometimes against persons who weren't even heard by the court.

> ...

---

[160] 'The Rights Approach: India's Rights-based Activism is Bound to Yield Less than it Promises', *The Economist* (18 March 2010).

> ... [P]oorly reasoned decisions create multiple, mutually contradictory, precedents. ...
> [B]y making judicial outcomes extremely unpredictable [the Court] incentivizes parties to
> try their luck and litigate rather than settle out of court. ... It is inevitable that the system
> will, sooner or later, implode.

Pritam Baruah, in 'Human Dignity in Indian Constitutional Adjudication', in J. Chia-Shin Hsu (ed.), *Human Dignity in Asia: Dialogue between Law and Culture* (2022) 21 argues that relying upon the concept of dignity 'was almost axiomatic for any discussion on the right to life' by the Court. Relatedly, 'every violation of liberty, equality, or dignity perhaps involves all three' in its analyses. To justify its 'uninhibited' reliance on the concept, the Court cites 'a wide range of academic literature on dignity that has emerged in law and philosophy'. Baruah warns that this approach has failed to clarify how the Court understands or applies 'dignity', and may encourage judges to rely overmuch on extra-legal concepts, such as moral and political values, in their decision-making. He attributes the problem to the Court's heavy workload, the convenient indeterminacy of the relevant concepts, and the judges' lack of philosophical training.

Finally, Neha Jain, above, is especially critical of the Court's invocation of international law:

> The court has taken up the causes of the oppressed and the voiceless, but always with an
> eye to its own political aspirations and authority. Thus, its decisions "seek to provide a
> workable *modus vivendi* rather than to articulate high values." The court has cultivated an
> image of itself as an organ for establishing government accountability while embracing
> political accommodation. It has carefully avoided upsetting any major political players,
> and concentrated on political issues that are unlikely to directly threaten their interests.
>
> ...
>
> ... [T]he court's innovative invocations of international law for myriad purposes—gap
> filling, interpretation, enlargement of the content of rights, chastisement of the other
> organs of government, supervision and monitoring of executive and legislative
> functions—may be inspired by distinctively domestic, and not entirely benevolent, aims.
> ...
>
> ... [The court] has expended little effort in explaining its judicial philosophy or the logic
> behind controversial uses of international law. Moreover, its pronouncements on the
> nature and derivation of customary international norms and on the effect of reservations
> to treaties betray a worrying incomprehension of international legal sources. ...

QUESTIONS

1. Does the Supreme Court's expansion of the scope of Article 21 and its transformation of the legal status of the directive principles go too far? In what respects? Against which criteria would you assess the success of the 'right to food' case law?

2. In defending the Court's approach, Gauri argues that critiques based on separation of powers arguments tend to assume that only one model is appropriate rather than recognizing 'that courts may play a variety of roles in different settings.'[161] And Landau concludes that in a society such as India, 'more aggressive, unconventional enforcement strategies — especially the judicious use of structural injunctions — can more effectively target social rights interventions towards the poor' than 'weak-form' or dialogue-based approaches to judicial review.[162] What do you think makes India special in this regard, and does this mean that its experience is unhelpful for determining how other societies should approach ESR?

---

[161] V. Gauri, 'Fundamental Rights and Public Interest Litigation in India: Overreaching or Underachieving', 1 *Indian J. L. & Econ.* (2010) 71.
[162] D. Landau, 'The Reality of Social Rights Enforcement', 53 *Harv. Int'l. L. J.* (2012) 402, at 404.

3. What approach has the Indian Court taken in determining the 'available resources'? Does *The Economist*'s estimate that over 80 percent of health care spending in India occurs in the private sector suggest that the Court is effectively imposing ever-more burdens on a sector that is already failing?

4. In 2012, the Indian Supreme Court held that there is a right to sleep.[163] It did so in a case in which over 1,000 police had forcibly evicted a group of more than 20,000 persons involved in what the police had deemed to be an unlawful assembly, protesting against government corruption. The police chose to act after midnight when all of the protesters had gone to sleep for the night. On what basis and under what circumstances do you think a right to sleep might reasonably be grounded in human rights law?

5. Are the critiques of PIL necessarily also a critique of the Court's social rights activism?

2. South Africa and Kenya

When South Africa's post-apartheid constitution was being debated, consideration was given to following the directive principles approach in relation to ESR. This was rejected, however, and full constitutional recognition was accorded to them. In the decades since, the South African jurisprudence has had a major impact on discussions of ESR globally, with many commentators arguing that the *Grootboom* and *TAC* cases in particular show the way forward for an effective and manageable approach to making these rights justiciable.[164]

Kenya followed a similar road. When the country was under considerable pressure from highly divisive ethnic conflicts, it turned to the adoption of a 'transformative constitution', as the South African model has long been described. While the Kenyan Supreme Court was relatively slow to engage on ESCR issues, recent judgments have been important.

The materials below focus on some of the key cases from South Africa and an important Kenyan case on housing rights. They focus especially on questions relating to 'progressive realization, the 'availability of resources' and the most appropriate remedies in such cases.

Section 1

The Republic of South Africa is one sovereign democratic state founded on the following values:

(a) Human dignity, the achievement of equality and the advancement of human rights and freedoms.
...

Section 7

(1) This Bill of Rights is a cornerstone of democracy in South Africa. It enshrines the rights of all people in our country and affirms the democratic values of human dignity, equality and freedom.

(2) The state must respect, protect, promote and fulfil the rights in the Bill of Rights.

(3) The rights in the Bill of Rights are subject to the limitations contained or referred to in section 36, or elsewhere in the Bill.
...

Section 10

Everyone has inherent dignity and the right to have their dignity respected and protected.

---

[163] *In Re: Ramlila Maidan Incident Dt.4/5.06.2011 v. Home Secretary, Union of India & Ors*, Judgment of 23 February 2012.
[164] Two other notable ESR cases are **Khosa** v. *Minister for Social Development* 2004 (6) BCLR 569 (social security for non-citizens) and *Port Elizabeth Municipality v. Various Occupiers* 2004 (12) BCLR 1268 (housing rights).

Section 11

Everyone has the right to life.

...

Section 26

(1) Everyone has the right to have access to adequate housing.

(2) The state must take reasonable legislative and other measures, within its available resources, to achieve the progressive realisation of this right.

(3) No one may be evicted from their home, or have their home demolished, without an order of court made after considering all the relevant circumstances. No legislation may permit arbitrary evictions.

Section 27

(1) Everyone has the right to have access to –

    (a) health care services, including reproductive health care;

    (b) sufficient food and water; and

    (c) social security, including, if they are unable to support themselves and their dependants, appropriate social assistance.

(2) The state must take reasonable legislative and other measures, within its available resources, to achieve the progressive realisation of each of these rights.

(3) No one may be refused emergency medical treatment.

Section 28

(1) Every child has the right:

...

    (b) to family care or parental care, or to appropriate alternative care when removed from the family environment;

    (c) to basic nutrition, shelter, basic health care services and social services;

...

Section 39

(1) When interpreting the Bill of Rights, a court, tribunal or forum:

    (a) must promote the values that underlie an open and democratic society based on human dignity, equality and freedom;

    (b) must consider international law; and

    (c) may consider foreign law.

(2) When interpreting any legislation, and when developing the common law or customary law, every court, tribunal or forum must promote the spirit, purport, and objects of the Bill of Rights.

...

SOOBRAMONEY V. MINISTER OF HEALTH (KWAZULU-NATAL)
CONSTITUTIONAL COURT OF SOUTH AFRICA, CASE CCT 32/97 (27 NOVEMBER 1997)

CHASKALSON P.:

[1] The appellant, a 41 year old unemployed man, is a diabetic who suffers from ischaemic heart disease and cerebro-vascular disease which caused him to have a stroke during 1996. In 1996 his kidneys also failed. Sadly his condition is irreversible and he is now in the final stages of chronic renal failure. His life could be prolonged by means of regular renal dialysis. He has sought such treatment from the renal unit of the Addington state hospital in Durban. The hospital can, however, only provide dialysis treatment to a limited number of patients. The renal unit has 20 dialysis machines available to it, and some of these machines are in poor condition ... . Because of the limited facilities that are available for kidney dialysis the hospital has been unable to provide the appellant with the treatment he has requested.

[2] ... Additional dialysis machines and more trained nursing staff are required to enable it to do this, but the hospital budget does not make provision for such expenditure. The hospital would like to have its budget increased but it has been told by the provincial health department that funds are not available for this purpose.

[3] Because of the shortage of resources the hospital follows a set policy in regard to the use of the dialysis resources. Only patients who suffer from acute renal failure, which can be treated and remedied by renal dialysis are given automatic access to renal dialysis at the hospital. Those patients who, like the appellant, suffer from chronic renal failure which is irreversible are not admitted automatically to the renal programme. A set of guidelines has been drawn up and adopted to determine which applicants who have chronic renal failure will be given dialysis treatment ... .

[The opinion noted that the appellant did not qualify under the guidelines. He alleged that he could not afford treatment at private hospitals, and he sought a judicial order directing Addington Hospital to provide the necessary treatment. His application was dismissed, and he then applied for leave to appeal to the Constitutional Court. His claim was based on sections 27(3) and 11 of the 1996 Constitution. The Court stressed the great disparities in wealth in South Africa, and the deplorable conditions and poverty in which millions of people lived, including lack of access to adequate health facilities.]
...

[11] What is apparent from these provisions is that the obligations imposed on the state by sections 26 and 27 in regard to access to housing, health care, food, water and social security are dependent upon the resources available for such purposes, and that the corresponding rights themselves are limited by reason of the lack of resources. Given this lack of resources and the significant demands on them that have already been referred to, an unqualified obligation to meet these needs would not presently be capable of being fulfilled. This is the context within which section 27(3) must be construed.

[14] Counsel for the appellant argued that section 27(3) should be construed consistently with the right to life entrenched in section 11 of the Constitution and that everyone requiring life-saving treatment who is unable to pay for such treatment herself or himself is entitled to have the treatment provided at a state hospital without charge.

[15] This Court has ... not yet been called upon to decide upon the parameters of the right to life or its relevance to the positive obligations imposed on the state under various provisions of the bill of rights. In India the Supreme Court has developed a jurisprudence around the right to life so as to impose positive obligations on the state in respect of the basic needs of its inhabitants ... . Unlike the Indian Constitution ours deals specifically in the bill of rights with certain positive obligations imposed on the state, and where it does so, it is our duty to apply the obligations as formulated in the Constitution and not to draw inferences that would be inconsistent therewith.

...

[17] The purposive approach [to constitutional interpretation] will often be one which calls for a generous interpretation to be given to a right to ensure that individuals secure the full protection of the bill of rights, but

this is not always the case, and the context may indicate that in order to give effect to the purpose of a particular provision 'a narrower or specific meaning' should be given to it.

[18] In developing his argument on the right to life counsel for the appellant relied upon ... *Paschim Banga Khet Mazdoor Samity and others v. State of West Bengal and another* ... [See above. The Court drew a strong distinction between the two cases. It concluded that the circumstances in that case made it] precisely the sort of case which would fall within section 27(3). It is one in which emergency treatment was clearly necessary. The occurrence was sudden, the patient had no opportunity of making arrangements in advance for the treatment that was required, and there was urgency in securing the treatment in order to stabilize his condition. The treatment was available but denied.

[19] In our Constitution the right to medical treatment does not have to be inferred from the nature of the state established by the Constitution or from the right to life which it guarantees. It is dealt with directly in section 27. If section 27(3) were to be construed in accordance with the appellant's contention it would make it substantially more difficult for the state to fulfill its primary obligations under sections 27(1) and (2) to provide health care services to 'everyone' within its available resources. It would also have the consequence of prioritising the treatment of terminal illnesses over other forms of medical care and would reduce the resources available to the state for [non-life threatening medical needs]. In my view much clearer language than that used in section 27(3) would be required to justify such a conclusion.

[20] Section 27(3) itself is couched in negative terms — it is a right not to be refused emergency treatment. The purpose of the right seems to be to ensure that treatment be given in an emergency, and is not frustrated by reason of bureaucratic requirements or other formalities ... . What the section requires is that remedial treatment that is necessary and available be given immediately to avert that harm.

[21] The applicant suffers from chronic renal failure. To be kept alive by dialysis he would require such treatment two to three times a week. This is not an emergency which calls for immediate remedial treatment. It is an ongoing state of affairs resulting from a deterioration of the applicant's renal function which is incurable. In my view section 27(3) does not apply to these facts.

[22] The appellant's demand to receive dialysis treatment at a state hospital must be determined in accordance with the provisions of sections 27(1) and (2) and not section 27(3). These sections entitle everyone to have access to health care services provided by the state 'within its available resources'.
...
[24] At present the Department of Health in KwaZulu-Natal does not have sufficient funds to cover the cost of the services which are being provided to the public ... . There are many more patients suffering from chronic renal failure than there are dialysis machines to treat such patients. This is a nation-wide problem and resources are stretched in all renal clinics throughout the land. Guidelines have therefore been established [and] ... were applied in the present case.

[25] … It has not been suggested that these guidelines are unreasonable or that they were not applied fairly and rationally ... .
...
[28] ... It is estimated that the cost to the state of treating one chronically ill patient by means of renal dialysis provided twice a week at a state hospital is approximately R60,000 per annum. If all the persons in South Africa who suffer from chronic renal failure were to be provided with dialysis treatment ... the cost of doing so would make substantial inroads into the health budget. And if this principle were to be applied to all patients claiming access to expensive medical treatment or expensive drugs, the health budget would have to be dramatically increased to the prejudice of other needs which the state has to meet.

[29] The provincial administration which is responsible for health services in KwaZulu-Natal has to make decisions about [health care] funding ... . These choices involve difficult decisions to be taken at the political level in fixing the health budget, and at the functional level in deciding upon the priorities to be met. A court will be slow to interfere with rational decisions taken in good faith by the political organs and medical authorities whose responsibility it is to deal with such matters.

[30] ... The dilemma confronting health authorities faced with such cases was described by Sir Thomas Bingham MR in R v. Cambridge Health Authority, ex parte B:[165]

> ... health authorities of all kinds are constantly pressed to make ends meet ... . Difficult and agonising judgments have to be made as to how a limited budget is best allocated to the maximum advantage of the maximum number of patients. That is not a judgment which the court can make.

[31] One cannot but have sympathy for the appellant and his family ... [b]ut the state's resources are limited and the appellant does not meet the criteria for admission to the renal dialysis programme. Unfortunately, this is true not only of the appellant but of many others who need access to renal dialysis units or to other health services. There are also those who need access to housing, food and water, employment opportunities, and social security ... .

The state has to manage its limited resources in order to address all these claims. There will be times when this requires it to adopt a holistic approach to the larger needs of society rather than to focus on the specific needs of particular individuals within society.

[37] ... The appeal ... is dismissed.

GOVERNMENT OF SOUTH AFRICA V. GROOTBOOM[166]
CONSTITUTIONAL COURT OF SOUTH AFRICA, CASE CCT 11/00 (4 OCTOBER 2000)

[Irene Grootboom and most other respondents (390 adults and 510 children) lived in a squatter settlement called Wallacedene. Their living conditions were 'lamentable': very low income population, overcrowded shacks (95 percent of which lacked electricity), no water or sewage or refuse removal services, the area partly waterlogged and dangerously close to a main thoroughfare. Many inhabitants who had applied for subsidized low-cost housing from the municipality had been on the waiting list for up to seven years.

Facing the prospect of indefinitely long and intolerable conditions, respondents began to move out of Wallacedene in September 1998, putting up shacks on vacant privately owned land (named 'New Rust') that was earmarked for eventual low-cost housing. Court proceedings brought by the owner resulted in an order of May 1999 instructing the sheriff to evict respondents and dismantle their shacks. The magistrate also ordered the parties and municipality to identify alternative land for permanent or temporary occupation by the New Rust residents. No mediation occurred, and respondents were evicted, their houses bulldozed and possessions destroyed. They then took shelter on the Wallacedene sports fields under such temporary structures as were feasible, at the time when winter rains began.

The High Court ordered the appellants to provide the respondents who were children and their parents with shelter. Its judgment stated that 'tents, portable latrines and a regular supply of water (albeit transported) would constitute the bare minimum.' The appellants, representing all spheres of government responsible for housing (central government, province of the Western Cape and municipality), brought the present appeal to challenge that order.]

JUSTICE YACOOB [FOR THE COURT]:

[6] The cause of the acute housing shortage lies in apartheid.

[The High Court concluded that the respondents' challenge under section 26 failed, because the appellant had taken 'reasonable legislative measures and other measures within its available resources to achieve the progressive realisation of the right to have access to adequate housing.' The Constitutional Court interpreted

---

[165] [1995] 2 All ER 129 (CA) at 137d–f.
[166] On *Grootboom* as a canonical case, see K. Young, 'The Canons of Social and Economic Rights', in S. Choudhry et al. (eds.), *Global Canons in an Age of Uncertainty: Debating Foundational Texts of Constitutional Democracy and Human Rights* (2024) Ch. 21.

section 26 to impose certain obligations in this case. The following excerpts from Justice Yacoob's opinion concern only section 26.]

...

[20] ... Section 7(2) of the Constitution requires the state "to respect, protect, promote and fulfil the rights in the Bill of Rights" and the courts are constitutionally bound to ensure that they are protected and fulfilled. The question is therefore not whether socio-economic rights are justiciable under our Constitution, but how to enforce them in a given case ... .

...

ii) The relevant international law and its impact

[26] During argument, considerable weight was attached to the value of international law in interpreting section 26 ... .

[The Court turned to a discussion of the ICESCR and the work of the UN Committee on ESCR. The opinion emphasized Art. 11 (the right of everyone to an adequate standard of living ..., including adequate food, clothing and housing) and Art. 2 (States parties will take appropriate steps to ensure the realization of this right ... to the maximum of available resources etc.). The opinion drew particular attention to para. 10 of General Comment No. 3 (Sec. A, above) in relation to a minimum core obligation.]

[31] ... Each right has a "minimum essential level" that must be satisfied by the states parties ... . Minimum core obligation is determined generally by having regard to the needs of the most vulnerable group that is entitled to the protection of the right in question. It is in this context that the concept of minimum core obligation must be understood in international law.

[32] It is not possible to determine the minimum threshold for the progressive realisation of the right of access to adequate housing without first identifying the needs and opportunities for the enjoyment of such a right. These will vary according to factors such as income, unemployment, availability of land and poverty. The differences between city and rural communities will also determine the needs and opportunities for the enjoyment of this right. Variations ultimately depend on the economic and social history and circumstances of a country. All this illustrates the complexity of the task of determining a minimum core obligation for the progressive realisation of the right ... .

[33] ... [T]he real question in terms of our Constitution is whether the measures taken by the state to realise the right afforded by section 26 are reasonable. There may be cases where it may be possible and appropriate to have regard to the content of a minimum core obligation to determine whether the measures taken by the state are reasonable ... .

iii) Analysis of section 26

...

[34] ... Subsections (1) and (2) are related and must be read together ... . Although the subsection does not expressly say so, there is, at the very least, a negative obligation placed upon the state and all other entities and persons to desist from preventing or impairing the right of access to adequate housing. The negative right is further spelt out in subsection (3) which prohibits arbitrary evictions. ...

[35] ... A right of access to adequate housing also suggests that it is not only the state who is responsible for the provision of houses, but that other agents within our society, including individuals themselves, must be enabled by legislative and other measures to provide housing. The state must create the conditions for access to adequate housing for people at all economic levels of our society ... .

[36] ... For those who can afford to pay for adequate housing, the state's primary obligation lies in unlocking the system, providing access to housing stock and a legislative framework to facilitate self-built houses through planning laws and access to finance. Issues of development and social welfare are raised in respect of those who cannot afford to provide themselves with housing. State policy needs to address both these groups. The poor are particularly vulnerable and their needs require special attention. It is in this context that the relationship between sections 26 and 27 and the other socio-economic rights is most apparent. If under section 27 the state has in place programmes to provide adequate social assistance to those who are otherwise unable to support

themselves and their dependants, that would be relevant to the state's obligations in respect of other socio-economic rights.

[37] The state's obligation to provide access to adequate housing depends on context, and may differ from province to province, from city to city, from rural to urban areas and from person to person. Some may need access to land and no more; some may need access to land and building materials; some may need access to finance; some may need access to services such as water, sewage, electricity and roads ... .

...

Reasonable legislative and other measures
[39] What constitutes reasonable legislative and other measures must be determined in the light of the fact that the Constitution creates different spheres of government: national government, provincial government and local government ... . A reasonable programme therefore must clearly allocate responsibilities and tasks to the different spheres of government and ensure that the appropriate financial and human resources are available.

...

[41] The measures must establish a coherent public housing programme directed towards the progressive realisation of the right of access to adequate housing within the state's available means ... . The precise contours and content of the measures to be adopted are primarily a matter for the legislature and the executive. They must, however, ensure that the measures they adopt are reasonable ... . A court considering reasonableness will not enquire whether other more desirable or favourable measures could have been adopted, or whether public money could have been better spent. The question would be whether the measures that have been adopted are reasonable ... .

[42] ... Mere legislation is not enough ... .

...

[43] Those whose needs are the most urgent and whose ability to enjoy all rights therefore is most in peril, must not be ignored ... . It may not be sufficient to meet the test of reasonableness to show that the measures are capable of achieving a statistical advance in the realisation of the right ... .

...

[46] ... Section 26 does not expect more of the state than is achievable within its available resources ... . The measures must be calculated to attain the goal expeditiously and effectively but the availability of resources is an important factor in determining what is reasonable.

...

[52] ... [T]here is no express provision [in the national housing programme] to facilitate access to temporary relief for people who have no access to land, no roof over their heads, for people who are living in intolerable conditions and for people who are in crisis because of natural disasters such as floods and fires, or because their homes are under threat of demolition. These are people in desperate need. Their immediate need can be met by relief short of housing which fulfils the requisite standards of durability, habitability and stability encompassed by the definition of housing development in the [Housing] Act.

...

[66] ... The nationwide housing programme falls short of obligations imposed upon national government to the extent that it fails to recognise that the state must provide for relief for those in desperate need. They are not to be ignored in the interests of an overall programme focussed on medium and long-term objectives. It is essential that a reasonable part of the national housing budget be devoted to this, but the precise allocation is for national government to decide in the first instance.

...

[68] Effective implementation requires at least adequate budgetary support by national government. This, in turn, requires recognition of the obligation to meet immediate needs in the nationwide housing programme. Recognition of such needs in the nationwide housing programme requires it to plan, budget and monitor the fulfilment of immediate needs and the management of crises. This must ensure that a significant number of desperate people in need are afforded relief, though not all of them need receive it immediately ... .

[69] In conclusion ... the programmes adopted by the state fell short of the requirements of section 26(2) in that no provision was made for relief to the categories of people in desperate need identified earlier ... .

...

H. *Evaluation of the conduct of the appellants towards the respondents*

...

[88] ... The state had an obligation to ensure, at the very least, that the eviction was humanely executed. However, the eviction was reminiscent of the past and inconsistent with the values of the Constitution. The respondents were evicted a day early and to make matters worse, their possessions and building materials were not merely removed, but destroyed and burnt ... .

...

[92] This judgment must not be understood as approving any practice of land invasion for the purpose of coercing a state structure into providing housing on a preferential basis to those who participate in any exercise of this kind. Land invasion is inimical to the systematic provision of adequate housing on a planned basis. It may well be that the decision of a state structure, faced with the difficulty of repeated land invasions, not to provide housing in response to those invasions, would be reasonable. Reasonableness must be determined on the facts of each case.

I. Summary and conclusion

...

[94] I am conscious that it is an extremely difficult task for the state to meet these obligations in the conditions that prevail in our country. This is recognised by the Constitution ... . I stress however, that despite all these qualifications, these are rights, and the Constitution obliges the state to give effect to them. This is an obligation that courts can, and in appropriate circumstances, must enforce.

[95] ... [S]ection 26 does oblige the state to devise and implement a coherent, coordinated programme designed to meet its section 26 obligations. The programme that has been adopted ... fell short of the obligations imposed ... .

...

TREATMENT ACTION CAMPAIGN V. MINISTER OF HEALTH
CONSTITUTIONAL COURT OF SOUTH AFRICA, CASE CCT 8/02 (5 JULY 2002)

[The Treatment Action Campaign (TAC) was the lead applicant among various other civil society groups working on HIV/AIDS. The respondents were the national Minister of Health and the various provincial authorities. The Court noted that the applicants' affidavits addressed the issues raised 'from a variety of specialised perspectives, ranging from paediatrics, pharmacology and epidemiology to public health administration, economics and statistics'.]

The Issues
[In their affidavit, the Applicants made various points, including: the catastrophic nature of the HIV/AIDS epidemic; mother-to-child HIV transmission had infected 70,000 children every year since 1998; Nevirapine significantly reduces the risk and 'is safe, of acceptable quality, and therapeutically efficacious'; the manufacturers have offered it free of charge to the South African government for five years; and while it is widely used in the private sector, the government has limited its availability to a few pilot sites, which number two per province. There follows a summary of the applicants' case.]

22.11 There is no rational or lawful basis for allowing doctors in the private sector to exercise their professional judgment in deciding when to prescribe Nevirapine, but effectively prohibiting doctors in the public sector from doing so.

22.12 ... [T]he government has failed over an extended period to implement a comprehensive programme for the prevention of mother-to-child transmission of HIV.

...

22.14 This conduct of the government is irrational, in breach of the Bill of Rights, and contrary to the values and principles prescribed for public administration in section 195 of the Constitution. Furthermore, government conduct is in breach of its international obligations ... ."

...

[23] In their argument counsel for the government raised issues pertaining to the separation of powers. This may be relevant in two respects — (i) in the deference that courts should show to decisions taken by the

executive concerning the formulation of its policies; and (ii) in the order to be made where a court finds that the executive has failed to comply with its constitutional obligations ... .

Enforcement of socio-economic rights
...
Minimum core

[26] [T]he first and second amici ... contended that section 27(1) of the Constitution establishes an individual right vested in everyone. This right, so the contention went, has a minimum core to which every person in need is entitled. The concept of "minimum core" was developed by the United Nations Committee on [ESCR in its General Comment No. 3] ... .

...

[34] Although Yacoob J [in *Grootboom*] indicated that evidence in a particular case may show that there is a minimum core of a particular service that should be taken into account in determining whether measures adopted by the state are reasonable, the socio-economic rights of the Constitution should not be construed as entitling everyone to demand that the minimum core be provided to them. Minimum core was thus treated as possibly being relevant to reasonableness under section 26(2), and not as a self-standing right conferred on everyone under section 26(1).

[35] A purposive reading of sections 26 and 27 does not lead to any other conclusion. It is impossible to give everyone access even to a "core" service immediately. All that is possible, and all that can be expected of the state, is that it act reasonably to provide access to the socio-economic rights identified in sections 26 and 27 on a progressive basis ... .

...

[37] ... [T]he courts are not institutionally equipped to make the wide-ranging factual and political enquiries necessary for determining what the minimum-core standards called for by the first and second amici should be, nor for deciding how public revenues should most effectively be spent. There are many pressing demands on the public purse ... .

[38] Courts are ill-suited to adjudicate upon issues where court orders could have multiple social and economic consequences for the community. The Constitution contemplates rather a restrained and focused role for the courts ... . [D]eterminations of reasonableness may in fact have budgetary implications, but are not in themselves directed at rearranging budgets. In this way the judicial, legislative and executive functions achieve appropriate constitutional balance.

[39] We therefore conclude that section 27(1) of the Constitution does not give rise to a self-standing and independent positive right enforceable irrespective of the considerations mentioned in section 27(2). ...
...

The applicants' contentions
[44] It is the applicants' case that the measures adopted by government ... were deficient in two material respects: first, because they prohibited the administration of nevirapine at public hospitals and clinics outside the research and training sites; and second, because they failed to implement a comprehensive programme for the prevention of mother-to-child transmission of HIV.

...

The policy confining nevirapine to the research and training sites
...

[51–55. In substance, four reasons were advanced in the affidavits for confining the administration of nevirapine to the research and training sites. (1) Where the comprehensive package was unavailable, the benefits of nevirapine would be counteracted by the transmission of HIV from mother to infant through breast-feeding. But delivery of that package is costly and problematic in some contexts. (2) The administration of nevirapine to the mother and her child might lead to the development of resistance to the efficacy of nevirapine and related antiretrovirals in later years. (3) In safety terms, the hazards of using nevirapine are unknown. (4) It is unclear if the public health system has the capacity to provide the package.]

...

[56] We deal with each of these issues in turn.

Efficacy

[57] ... It is clear from the evidence that the provision of nevirapine will save the lives of a significant number of infants even if it is administered without the full package ... .

[58] ... [T]he wealth of scientific material produced by both sides makes plain that sero-conversion of HIV takes place in some, but not all, cases and that nevirapine thus remains to some extent efficacious in combating mother-to-child transmission even if the mother breastfeeds her baby.

Resistance

[59] ... The prospects of the child surviving if infected are so slim and the nature of the suffering so grave that the risk of some resistance manifesting at some time in the future is well worth running.

Safety

[60] The evidence shows that safety is no more than a hypothetical issue ... . That is why [nevirapine's] use is recommended without qualification for this purpose by the World Health Organization ... .

Considerations relevant to reasonableness

[67] The policy of confining nevirapine to research and training sites ... fails to distinguish between the evaluation of programmes for reducing mother-to-child transmission and the need to provide access to health care services required by those who do not have access to the sites.

[68] ... A programme for the realisation of socio-economic rights must "be balanced and flexible and make appropriate provision for attention to ... crises and to short, medium and long term needs. A programme that excludes a significant segment of society cannot be said to be reasonable." [*Grootboom*]

...

Children's rights

[77] While the primary obligation to provide basic health care services no doubt rests on those parents who can afford to pay for such services, it was made clear in *Grootboom* that "[t]his does not mean ... that the State incurs no obligation in relation to children who are being cared for by their parents or families."

[78] The provision of a single dose of nevirapine to mother and child for the purpose of protecting the child against the transmission of HIV is, as far as the children are concerned, essential ... . Their rights are "most in peril" as a result of the policy that has been adopted and are most affected by a rigid and inflexible policy that excludes them from having access to nevirapine.

[79] The state is obliged to ensure that children are accorded the protection contemplated by section 28 that arises when the implementation of the right to parental or family care is lacking. Here we are concerned with children born in public hospitals and clinics to mothers who are for the most part indigent and unable to gain access to private medical treatment which is beyond their means. They and their children are in the main dependent upon the state to make health care services available to them.

...

The powers of the courts

[96] Counsel for the government contended that even if this Court should find that government policies fall short of what the Constitution requires, the only competent order ... that a court can make is to issue a declaration of rights to that effect. That leaves government free to pay heed to the declaration made and to adapt its policies in so far as this may be necessary to bring them into conformity with the court's judgment. This, so the argument went, is what the doctrine of separation of powers demands.

[97] In developing this argument counsel contended that under the separation of powers the making of policy is the prerogative of the executive and not the courts, and that courts cannot make orders that have the effect of requiring the executive to pursue a particular policy.

[98] This Court has made it clear on more than one occasion that although there are no bright lines that separate the roles of the legislature, the executive and the courts from one another, there are certain matters that are pre-

eminently within the domain of one or other of the arms of government and not the others. All arms of government should be sensitive to and respect this separation. This does not mean, however, that courts cannot or should not make orders that have an impact on policy ... .

[99] The primary duty of courts is to the Constitution and the law ... . The Constitution requires the state to "respect, protect, promote, and fulfil the rights in the Bill of Rights". Where state policy is challenged as inconsistent with the Constitution, courts have to consider whether in formulating and implementing such policy the state has given effect to its constitutional obligations. If it should hold in any given case that the state has failed to do so, it is obliged by the Constitution to say so. In so far as that constitutes an intrusion into the domain of the executive, that is an intrusion mandated by the Constitution itself. ...

...

[102] ... Particularly in a country where so few have the means to enforce their rights through the courts, it is essential that on those occasions when the legal process does establish that an infringement of an entrenched right has occurred, it be effectively vindicated. The courts have a particular responsibility in this regard and are obliged to 'forge new tools' and shape innovative remedies, if needs be, to achieve this goal ... .

...

[106] We thus reject the argument that the only power that this Court has in the present case is to issue a declaratory order. Where a breach of any right has taken place, including a socio-economic right, a court is under a duty to ensure that effective relief is granted. The nature of the right infringed and the nature of the infringement will provide guidance as to the appropriate relief in a particular case ... .

...

[112] [After reviewing cases from the United States, India, Germany, Canada and the United Kingdom, the Court concludes] that in none of the jurisdictions surveyed is there any suggestion that the granting of injunctive relief breaches the separation of powers. ...

...

Orders
[135] ... 3. Government is ordered without delay to:

> a) Remove the restrictions that prevent nevirapine from being made available ... .
>
> b) Permit and facilitate the use of nevirapine ...
>
> ...
>
> d) Take reasonable measures to extend the testing and counselling facilities at hospitals and clinics throughout the public health sector to facilitate and expedite the use of nevirapine ... .

...

MAZIBUKO V. CITY OF JOHANNESBURG
CONSTITUTIONAL COURT OF SOUTH AFRICA, CASE CCT 39/09 [2009] ZACC 28 (8 OCTOBER 2009)

[Section 27 of the South African Constitution provides that 'everyone has the right to have access to ... sufficient food and water ...'. The new government adopted a highly innovative example of a rights-based water policy. The Water Services Act (1997) recognized everyone's 'right of access to basic water supply and basic sanitation' and required every water services institution to 'take reasonable measures to realise these rights'. It defined a 'basic water supply' as 'the prescribed minimum standard of water supply services necessary for the reliable supply of a sufficient quantity and quality of water to households, including informal households, to support life and personal hygiene.' It authorized the Minister to prescribe 'compulsory national standards'. Regulation 3 (2001) provides that the minimum standard for basic water supply services is:

(b) … a minimum quantity of potable water of 25 litres per person per day or 6 kilolitres per household per month

(i) at a minimum flow rate of not less than 10 litres per minute;

(ii) within 200 metres of a household; and

(iii) with an effectiveness such that no consumer is without a supply for more than seven full days in any year.

In 1994, 12 million people did not have adequate access to water. By the end of 2006 the figure was down to 8 million, of whom 3.3 million had no access at all.

The applicants lived in Phiri, in Soweto, a township set up in the apartheid era. It was next to Johannesburg, a city with 3.2 million people living in about a million households, half of which are very poor and almost one-fifth of which are located in informal settlements. Almost 20 percent of households had no access to basic sanitary services and 10 percent had no access to a tap providing clean water within 200 metres of their home.

The respondents were the City of Johannesburg, Johannesburg Water (Pty) Ltd, and the national Minister for Water Affairs and Forestry. Since the water company was wholly owned by the City, no issue arose concerning the responsibilities of private actors.

The pipes to Soweto were badly corroded and extensive leakage occurred. Sowetan households consumed an average of 67 kilolitres per month, but were charged a flat rate based on a deemed consumption of 20 kilolitres. But less than 10 percent of households actually paid their bills and the water company derived 1 percent of its revenue from the one-quarter to one-third of its total water sales that went to Soweto. Seventy-five percent of water pumped into Soweto was thus not accounted for.

The company introduced Operation *Gcin'amanzi* (to save water), initiated in Phiri. It abandoned the flat rate system of deemed consumption and introduced three service levels: (1) a tap within 200 metres of each dwelling; (2) a tap in the yard of a household with a water flow of only 6 kilolitres per month; and (3) a metered connection. Phiri residents had to choose between (2) and (3) with the latter involving a pre-paid meter.

In 2008 the High Court rejected the pre-paid meters as being unauthorized by the City's by-laws, procedurally unfair and racially discriminatory. It also held the free water allowance to be inadequate and ordered the provision of 50 litres per person per day. In 2009 the Supreme Court of Appeal gave the City two years to amend its by-laws and set the free water allocation at 42 litres.]

O'REGAN J. [FOR THE COURT]:

…

The role of courts in determining the content of social and economic rights …

…

[50] [Reading] section 27(1)(b) [together] with section 27(2), it is clear that the right does not require the state upon demand to provide every person with sufficient water without more; rather it requires the state to take reasonable legislative and other measures progressively to realise the achievement of the right of access to sufficient water, within available resources.

…

[56] The applicants' argument [is] that the Court should adopt a quantified standard determining the content of the right not merely its minimum content. The argument must fail for the same reasons that the minimum core argument failed in *Grootboom* and *Treatment Action Campaign No 2*.

[57] Those reasons are essentially twofold. [First, the Constitution] requires the state to take reasonable legislative and other measures progressively to achieve the right of access to sufficient water within available resources. It does not confer a right to claim "sufficient water" from the state immediately.

…

[59] … Social and economic rights empower citizens to demand of the state that it acts reasonably and progressively to ensure that all enjoy the basic necessities of life. In so doing, the social and economic rights

enable citizens to hold government to account for the manner in which it seeks to pursue the achievement of social and economic rights.

[60] Moreover, what the right requires will vary over time and context. Fixing a quantified content might, in a rigid and counter-productive manner, prevent an analysis of context. The concept of reasonableness places context at the centre of the enquiry and permits an assessment of context to determine whether a government programme is indeed reasonable.

[61] Secondly, ordinarily it is institutionally inappropriate for a court to determine precisely what the achievement of any particular social and economic right entails and what steps government should take to ensure the progressive realisation of the right. This is a matter, in the first place, for the legislature and executive, the institutions of government best placed to investigate social conditions in the light of available budgets and to determine what targets are achievable in relation to social and economic rights. Indeed, it is desirable as a matter of democratic accountability that they should do so for it is their programmes and promises that are subjected to democratic popular choice.

[62] ... [T]his case illustrates that the obligation in relation to the right of access to sufficient water will vary depending upon circumstance. As emerges from research by the World Health Organisation in 2003 ... the expert evidence on the record provides numerous different answers to the question of what constitutes "sufficient water". Courts are ill-placed to make these assessments for both institutional and democratic reasons. ...

[66] The Constitution envisages that legislative and other measures will be the primary instrument for the achievement of social and economic rights ... .

[67] Thus the positive obligations imposed upon government by the social and economic rights in our Constitution will be enforced by courts in at least the following ways. If government takes no steps to realise the rights, the courts will require government to take steps. If government's adopted measures are unreasonable, the courts will similarly require that they be reviewed so as to meet the constitutional standard of reasonableness. From *Grootboom*, it is clear that a measure will be unreasonable if it makes no provision for those most desperately in need. If government adopts a policy with unreasonable limitations or exclusions, as in *Treatment Action Campaign No 2*, the Court may order that those are removed. Finally, the obligation of progressive realisation imposes a duty upon government continually to review its policies to ensure that the achievement of the right is progressively realised.

[68] These considerations were overlooked by the High Court and the Supreme Court of Appeal which ... found it appropriate to quantify the content of the right, ... they erred in this approach and the applicants' argument that the Court should set 50 litres per person per day as the content of the section 27(1)(b) right must fail.

The relevance of regulation 3(b) of the National Water Standards Regulations

[69] ... [The] minimum standard for basic water supply [contained in Regulation 3(b)] is the basis of the policy adopted by the City and Johannesburg Water. ...

[70] National government should set the targets it wishes to achieve in respect of social and economic rights clearly ... . The minimum standard set by the Minister informs citizens of what government is seeking to achieve. In so doing, it enables citizens to monitor government's performance and to hold it accountable politically if the standard is not achieved. This also empowers citizens to hold government accountable through legal challenge if the standard set is unreasonable.

[71] A reasonableness challenge requires government to explain the choices it has made. To do so, it must provide the information it has considered and the process it has followed to determine its policy. This case provides an excellent example of government doing just that ... . If the process followed by government is flawed or the information gathered is obviously inadequate or incomplete, appropriate relief may be sought ... .

[76] [I]t will in most circumstances be difficult for an applicant who does not challenge the minimum standard set by the legislature or the executive for the achievement of social and economic rights to establish that a policy based on that prescribed standard is unreasonable ... .

The reasonableness of the City's Free Basic Water policy

...

Rich and Poor

[83] The first question is whether it is unreasonable for the City to provide the 6 kilolitres of free water to rich and poor alike ... . First, [the City] asserts that the rising block tariff structure means that wealthier consumers, who tend to use more water, are charged more for their heavier water usage. The effect of this is that the original 6 kilolitres that is provided free is counterweighed by the extent to which heavy water users cross-subsidise the free allocation. Secondly, the City points to the difficulty of establishing a method to target those households who are deserving of free water. ... In my view, these reasons are persuasive and rebut the charge of unreasonableness on this ground.

Per household versus per person allowance

[84] Secondly, the applicants argue that the policy is unreasonable because it is formulated as 6 kilolitres per household (or accountholder) rather than as a per person allowance. Again the City presents cogent evidence that it is difficult to establish how many people are living on one stand at any given time; and that it is therefore unable to base the policy on a per person allocation. This evidence seems indisputable. ... The applicants' argument on this basis too must fail.

Policy based on a misconception

[85] The third argument, which the Supreme Court of Appeal upheld, is that the policy is unreasonable because the City considered that it was not under an obligation to provide a specified amount of free basic water. What is clear from the discussion above is that the City is not under a constitutional obligation to provide any *particular* amount of free water to citizens per month. It is under a duty to take reasonable measures progressively to realise the achievement of the right. This the City accepts ... . The applicants' argument on this score must also fail.

Insufficient for large households

[86] The fourth argument is that the 6 kilolitres per month per household is not sufficient in that it does not provide 50 litres per person per day across the board. There is a welter of evidence on the record indicating that household sizes in Johannesburg vary markedly ... .

[87] The picture is further complicated, however, by the fact that there is often more than one household relying on one water connection. This is especially so in townships ... . There are many water connections where there is only one resident, but there are some with as many as 20.

[88] Where the household size is average, that is 3.2 people, the free basic water allowance will provide approximately 60 litres per person per day ... . The difficulty is that many households are larger than the average ... . Yet, to raise the free basic water allowance for all so that it would be sufficient to cover those stands with many residents would be expensive and inequitable, for it would disproportionately benefit stands with fewer residents.

[89] Establishing a fixed amount per stand will inevitably result in unevenness because those stands with more inhabitants will have less water per person than those stands with fewer people. This is an unavoidable result of establishing a universal allocation. Yet it seems clear on the City's evidence that to establish a universal per person allowance would administratively be extremely burdensome and costly, if possible at all. The free basic water allowance established is generous in relation to the average household size in Johannesburg. Indeed, in relation to 80% of households (with four occupants or fewer), the allowance is adequate even on the applicants' case. In the light of this evidence, coupled with the fact that the amount provided by the City was based on the

prescribed national standard for basic water supply, it cannot be said that the amount established by the City was unreasonable.

…

Indigent registration policy

[98] The applicants also challenge the reasonableness of the City's indigent registration policy on two main grounds: the first is that it is demeaning for citizens to have to register as indigents; and the second is that because only approximately one-fifth of the households who are eligible to register are registered, the policy is unreasonable because it is under-inclusive.

…

[101] Although a means-tested policy requires citizens to apply for benefits and so disclose that they are poor, to hold a means-tested policy to be constitutionally impermissible would deprive government of a key methodology for ensuring that government services target those most in need. Indeed, nearly all social security benefits afforded by the national government are based on means-testing … . Means-testing may not be a perfect methodology [but] it seeks to ensure that those most in need benefit from government services. In their affidavits, the applicants proposed no third way as an alternative … .

[102] … The dilemma is not readily solved … . [I]t cannot be said that the policy as formulated … was unreasonable. The applicants' argument in this regard must fail.

…

Litigating social and economic rights

[159] The outcome of the case is that the applicants have not persuaded this Court to specify what quantity of water is "sufficient water" within the meaning of section 27 of the Constitution. Nor have they persuaded the Court that the City's policy is unreasonable. The applicants submitted during argument that if this were to be the result, litigation in respect of the positive obligations imposed by social and economic rights would be futile. It is necessary to consider this submission.

[160] The purpose of litigation concerning the positive obligations imposed by social and economic rights should be to hold the democratic arms of government to account through litigation. In so doing, litigation of this sort fosters a form of participative democracy that holds government accountable and requires it to account between elections over specific aspects of government policy.

[161] When challenged as to its policies relating to social and economic rights, the government agency must explain why the policy is reasonable. Government must disclose what it has done to formulate the policy: its investigation and research, the alternatives considered, and the reasons why the option underlying the policy was selected. The Constitution does not require government to be held to an impossible standard of perfection. Nor does it require courts to take over the tasks that in a democracy should properly be reserved for the democratic arms of government … .

…

CITY OF JOHANNESBURG METROPOLITAN MUNICIPALITY V. BLUE MOONLIGHT PROPERTIES 39 (PTY) LTD AND ANOTHER
CONSTITUTIONAL COURT OF SOUTH AFRICA, CASE CCT 37/11 [2011] ZACC 33 (1 DECEMBER 2011)

VAN DER WESTHUIZEN J (FOR THE COURT):

Introduction

[1] This matter concerns the fate of 86 people (Occupiers), who are poor and unlawfully occupy a property … in the City of Johannesburg (property). The property comprises old and dilapidated commercial premises with office space, a factory building and garages. The case deals with the rights of the owner of the property, Blue Moonlight Properties 39 (Pty) Ltd (Blue Moonlight) and with the obligation of the City of Johannesburg Metropolitan Municipality (City) to provide housing for the Occupiers if they are evicted. …

[2] Seventeen years into our democracy, a dignified existence for all in South Africa has not yet been achieved. The quest for a roof over one's head often lies at the heart of our constitutional, legal, political and economic discourse on how to bring about social justice within a stable constitutional democracy. ... An estimated 423,249 households in Johannesburg alone are, for example, without adequate housing. ...

[3] The practical questions to be answered in this case are whether the Occupiers must be evicted to allow the owner to fully exercise its rights regarding its property and, if so, whether their eviction must be linked to an order that the City provide them with accommodation. ...

...

Resources

...

[71] The Supreme Court of Appeal rejected the City's submission that it lacked resources. It observed that the City spoke "in the vaguest terms" about the affordability of meeting demands for housing. It noted that the record showed that the City had been operating in a financial surplus for the past year. Furthermore, the City did not state that it was unable to reallocate funds or to meet the temporary housing needs of the Occupiers. Finally, it observed that the Occupiers sought only temporary housing, whereas the City's affidavits mainly set out its inability to meet the Occupiers' permanent housing needs. This, coupled with the fact that the City had three years of prior knowledge of the Occupiers' circumstances, led the Court to find that to a great extent the City had itself to blame for its unpreparedness to deal with the Occupiers' plight.

...

Constitutional validity of the differentiation in the City's policy on emergency housing

[76] It is now necessary to determine the constitutional validity of the differentiation in the City's housing policy. That policy distinguishes between those relocated by the City itself and those evicted by private landowners. ...

...

[87] The present challenge deals with section 9(1) [equality before the law] and section 26(2) of the Constitution. The concepts of rationality and reasonableness are thus central. A policy which is irrational could hardly be reasonable. ...

[88] In the area of the right of access to adequate housing ... the question is essentially one of *reasonableness*. The availability of resources is an important factor ... .

[89] A policy that, for example, differentiates between general housing needs and emergency situations might well be understandable. The question is whether it is reasonable to differentiate within the category of emergencies between people relocated by the City and those evicted by private landowners and inflexibly to include the first but exclude the second group.

[90] In *Grootboom* this Court held that a reasonable housing programme cannot disregard those who are most in need. ...

[91] The City argues that the needs of those who live on properties it has designated as "bad buildings" are greater than those rendered homeless through eviction by a private landowner. ...

[92] By drawing a rigid line between persons relocated by the City and those evicted by private landowners, the City excludes from the assessment, whether emergency accommodation should be made available, the individual situations of the persons at risk and the reason for the eviction. Affected individuals may include children, elderly people, people with disability or women-headed households, for whom the need for housing is particularly great or for whom homelessness would result in particularly disastrous consequences. ... [I]t cannot necessarily be assumed that the City evicts or relocates mainly for reasons of safety whilst private property owners do so only for commercial reasons. Once an emergency of looming homelessness is created, it in any event matters little to the evicted who the evictor is. The policy does not meaningfully and reasonably allow for the needs of those affected to be taken into account.

[93] The City rightly argues that "queue jumping" must not be permitted. ... [But] queue jumping is not in issue in this case. The Occupiers do not claim permanent housing, ahead of anyone else in a queue. ... What they ask is not to be excluded from the City's provision of temporary housing ... simply because they are being evicted by a private landowner and not by the City.

...

[95] ... I find that whereas differentiation between emergency housing needs and housing needs that do not constitute an emergency might well be reasonable, the differentiation the City's policy makes is not. ...

...

Just and equitable remedy

...

[99] A remedy must be formulated. The order of the Supreme Court of Appeal requires the Occupiers to vacate the premises on a specific date. It also declares the City's policy unconstitutional. It orders the City to provide "temporary emergency accommodation" to the Occupiers. ...

[100] ... The date of eviction must be linked to a date on which the City has to provide accommodation. Requiring the City to provide accommodation 14 days before the date of eviction will allow the Occupiers some time and space to be assured that the order to provide them with accommodation was complied with and to make suitable arrangements for their relocation. Although Blue Moonlight cannot be expected to be burdened with providing accommodation to the Occupiers indefinitely, a degree of patience should be reasonably expected of it and the City must be given a reasonable time to comply. ...

...

GENERAL COMMENTS ON THE RIGHT TO HOUSING

Before considering two important cases from the Kenyan Supreme Court in relation to the right to housing, note should be taken of two General Comments by the Committee on ESCR. The first, General Comment No. 4, on the right to adequate housing (1991) provides:

7. ... [T]he right to housing should not be interpreted in a narrow or restrictive sense which equates it with, for example, the shelter provided by merely having a roof over one's head or views shelter exclusively as a commodity. Rather it should be seen as the right to live somewhere in security, peace and dignity. ...

8. Thus the concept of adequacy is particularly significant ... . While adequacy is determined in part by social, economic, cultural, climatic, ecological and other factors, [certain aspects must be taken into account, including:]

...

(b) *Availability of services, materials, facilities and infrastructure.* An adequate house must contain certain facilities essential for health, security, comfort and nutrition [including] safe drinking water, energy for cooking, heating and lighting, sanitation and washing facilities ... ;

...

(d) *Habitability.* [This includes] adequate space and protecting [inhabitants] from cold, damp, heat, rain, wind or other threats to health, structural hazards, and disease vectors. [P]hysical safety ... must be guaranteed as well. ...;

(e) *Accessibility.* ...;

(f) *Location.* Adequate housing must be in a location which allows access to employment options, health-care services, schools, child-care centres and other social facilities. ...

...

The second, General Comment No. 7 (1997) addresses forced evictions, defined as:

3. ... the permanent or temporary removal against their will of individuals, families and/or communities from the homes and/or land which they occupy, without the provision of, and access to, appropriate forms of legal or other protection. ...

...

9. ... [L]egislation should include measures which (a) provide the greatest possible security of tenure to occupiers of houses and land, (b) conform to the Covenant and (c) are designed to control strictly the circumstances under which evictions may be carried out. The legislation must also apply to all agents acting under the authority of the State or who are accountable to it. Moreover, ... States parties must ensure that legislative and other measures are adequate to prevent and, if appropriate, punish forced evictions carried out, without appropriate safeguards, by private persons or bodies. ...

...

15. ... [P]rocedural protections which should be applied in relation to forced evictions include: (a) an opportunity for genuine consultation with those affected; (b) adequate and reasonable notice for all affected persons prior to the scheduled date of eviction; (c) information on the proposed evictions, and, where applicable, on the alternative purpose for which the land or housing is to be used, to be made available in reasonable time to all those affected; (d) especially where groups of people are involved, government officials or their representatives to be present during an eviction; (e) all persons carrying out the eviction to be properly identified; (f) evictions not to take place in particularly bad weather or at night unless the affected persons consent otherwise; (g) provision of legal remedies; and (h) provision, where possible, of legal aid to persons who are in need of it to seek redress from the courts.

16. Evictions should not result in individuals being rendered homeless or vulnerable to the violation of other human rights. Where those affected are unable to provide for themselves, the State party must take all appropriate measures, to the maximum of its available resources, to ensure that adequate alternative housing, resettlement or access to productive land, as the case may be, is available.

...

* * *

The *Mitu-Bell* case below engages specifically with the second of these General Comments and the issue of remedies known as 'structural interdicts'. Inspired by U.S. cases like *Brown v. Board of Education*, these orders have frequently been used by the South African Constitutional Court. Their purpose is to eliminate:

> systemic violations existing especially in institutional or organisational settings. Rather than compensate for past wrongs, [a structural interdict] seeks to adjust future behaviour, and is deliberately fashioned rather than logically deduced from the nature of the legal harm suffered. Its most prominent feature is the creation of a complex ongoing regime of performance ... . [This] is facilitated by the court's retention of jurisdiction, and sometimes by the court's active participation in the implementation of the decree.[167]

MITU-BELL WELFARE SOCIETY V. THE KENYA AIRPORTS AUTHORITY ET AL.
SUPREME COURT OF KENYA, [2021] KESC 34, KLR (11 JANUARY 2021)

[The 15,325 residents of Mitumba Village, near Wilson airport in Nairobi, petitioned the High Court on 21 September 2011 in response to a notice published in the newspapers on 15 September giving them seven days to vacate the land on which they lived. Despite a restraining order issued on 22 September, the respondents demolished the village on 19 November 2011. In September 2013 the High Court concluded that the appellants' constitutional rights had been violated and ordered a 'structural interdict' which required the government and the appellants to engage in a dialogue, based on documentation provided by the former and with the participation of other interested parties and experts. However, on 1 July 2016, the Court of Appeal overturned most of the High Court judge's findings, leading to a further appeal to the Supreme Court. That Court identified the following issues for consideration:]

[115] ... 1. What is the place of Structural Interdicts (if any) as forms of relief in human rights litigation under the Constitution?
2. What is the effect of Article 2 (5) and 2 (6) of the Constitution regarding the applicability of international law in general and international human rights in particular?

---

[167] C. Mbazira, 'From Ambivalence to Certainty: Norms and Principles for the Structural Interdict in Socio-Economic Rights Litigation in South Africa', 24 *S. Af. J. Hum. Rts.* (2008) 1, at 4.

3. To what extent are Guidelines by UN bodies relevant ...?
4. Under what circumstances may a Right to Housing accrue ...?
...

(i) Structural Interdicts

...

[117] ...Article 23 (1) of the Constitution provides that:

"The High Court has jurisdiction, in accordance with Article 165, to hear and determine applications [for] redress of a denial, violation, or infringement of, or threat to, a right or fundamental freedom in the Bill of Rights" ... .

Article 23 (3) of the Constitution provides that:

> "In any proceedings brought under Article 22, a Court may grant appropriate relief, including:
>
> (a) a declaration of rights
>
> (b) an injunction
>
> (c) a conservatory order
>
> (d) a declaration of invalidity of any law that denies, violates, infringes, or threatens a right or fundamental freedom in the Bill of Rights and is not justified under Article 24;
>
> (e) an order for compensation
>
> (f) an order of judicial review

....

[121] We [consider] ... that Article 23 (3) ... empowers the High Court to fashion appropriate reliefs, even of an interim nature, in specific cases, so as to redress the violation of a fundamental right. ...

[122] ... [W]e hasten to add that, interim reliefs, structural interdicts, supervisory orders or any other orders that may be issued by the Courts, have to be specific, appropriate, clear, effective, and directed at the parties to the suit or any other State Agency vested with a Constitutional or statutory mandate to enforce the order. Most importantly, the Court in issuing such orders, must be realistic, and avoid the temptation of judicial overreach, especially in matters policy. ...

(ii) Applicability of International Law under Articles 2(5) and 2(6) of the Constitution

...

[132] ... Article 2(5) and (6) of the Constitution, recognizes international law (both customary and treaty law) as a source of law in Kenya. By the same token, a Court of law is at liberty, to refer to a norm of international law, as an aid in interpreting or clarifying a Constitutional provision ... .

[133] ... [T]he expression "shall form part of the law of Kenya" ... does not transform Kenya from a dualist to a monist state ... . [G]iven the developments in contemporary treaty making, the argument about whether a state is monist or dualist, is increasingly becoming sterile, given the fact that, a large number of modern-day treaties, conventions, and protocols are Non-Self Executing, which means that, they cannot be directly applicable in the legal systems of states parities, without further legislative and administrative action.

(iii) The Role of UN Guidelines in the Interpretation and Clarification of the Bill of Rights

...

[141] ... [W]e must ... determine whether the UN Guidelines, [General] Comment No. 7 can be regarded as general rules of international law within the context of Article 2(5) of the Constitution. ... [S]uch resolutions, declarations, and comments do not ordinarily amount to norms of international law. At best they constitute

what is called in international jurisprudence, Soft Law. However, it is also accepted that certain UN General Assembly Declarations and Resolutions can ripen into a norm or norms of customary international law, depending on their nature and history leading to their adoption. ...

[142] The UN Guidelines, General Comment No. 7 do not in our view qualify as general rules of international law, which have a binding effect on members of the international community. However, the Guidelines are intended to breathe life into the Right to Dignity and the Right to Housing under the ICCPR and the ICESCR respectively. They therefore constitute soft law in the language of international jurisprudence. In the instant case, while the trial Judge cannot be faulted for having referred to the Guidelines per se, being soft law, as opposed to general rules of international law, the learned Judge ought not to have elevated them to the status of Article 2 (5) of the Constitution.

... [T]he Guidelines actually do fill the existing lacuna as to how the Government ought to carry out evictions.

[143] ... [T] he UN Guidelines ... are tools or aids directed to states parties to help the latter in implementing the treaty or better fulfilment of their obligations there-under. Each state party is free to make use of the Guidelines, to the extent that is practicable under its legal system. The guidelines are not "binding" upon the states parties, nor are they part of the law of Kenya in the language and meaning of Article 2 (6) of the Constitution, unless they have ripened into a norm of customary international law ... .

(iv) The Reality of the Right to Housing under Article 43 (1) of the Constitution

[144] ... The appellants herein, were uprooted from their habitation by the Government, on grounds that their settlements lay on the flight path to Wilson Airport, thus posing danger to the security of the public and air travelers. By this action, the appellants were deprived of their right to shelter (read "housing") for however informal, however decrepit, these settlements had been home to their existence, their aspirations, and their very humanity. The appellants case is that the State, through its duty-bearing organs, had an obligation to respect and protect their right to housing under Article 21 (1) of the Constitution.

[145] The respondents ... argue that the appellants, had no recognizable title to the land from which they had been justifiably evicted, on security grounds. It is their case that a right to housing, cannot accrue from an illegal occupation of land by the claimants. ...

[146] The crucial question ... is when does the right to accessible and adequate housing accrue? In the language of Article 21, the right to housing, being an economic and social right, can only be realized progressively. In determining the import of the expression "progressive realization" in the *Matter of the Principle of Gender Representation in the National Assembly and Senate* ..., the Supreme Court opined:

> "... [T]he expression "progressive realization" is neither a stand-alone nor a technical
> phrase. It simply refers to the gradual or phased-out attainment of a goal-a human rights
> goal which by its very nature, cannot be achieved on its own, unless first, a certain set of
> supportive measures are taken by the State. The exact shape of such measures will vary,
> depending on the nature of the right in question, as well as the prevailing social,
> economic, cultural and political environment. Such supportive measures may involve
> legislative, policy or programme initiatives including affirmative action."

[147] ... Article 20 (5) provides that:

> "In applying any right under Article 43, if the State Claims that it does not have the
> resources to implement the right, a Court, tribunal or other authority shall be guided by
> the following principles—
>
> (a) It is the responsibility of the State to show that the resources are not available
>
> (b) In allocating resources, the State shall give priority to ensuring the widest possible
> enjoyment of the right or fundamental freedom having regard to prevailing
> circumstances, including the vulnerability of particular groups or individuals and

(c) The Court, tribunal or other authority may not interfere with a decision by a State organ concerning the allocation of available resources, solely, on the basis that it would have reached a different conclusion.

...

[149] ... [T]he question as to when the right to housing accrues ... is not dependent upon its progressive realization. The right accrues to every individual or family, by virtue of being a citizen of this Country. It is an entitlement guaranteed by the Constitution under the Bill of rights. The persistent problem is that its realization depends on the availability of land and other material resources. Given the fact that our society is incredulously unequal, with the majority of the population condemned to grinding poverty, the right to accessible and adequate housing remains but a pipe-dream for many. What with each successive government erecting the defence of "lack of resources? The situation is compounded by the fact that, for reasons incomprehensible, the right to housing in Kenya is predicated upon one's ability to "own" land. In other words, unless one has "title" to land under our land laws, he/she will find it almost impossible to mount a claim of a right to housing, even when faced with the grim possibility of eviction.

[150] This scenario has inevitably led to the emergence of the so called "informal settlements", an expression that describes a habitation by the "landless". In their struggle to survive, many Kenyans do occupy empty spaces and erect shelters thereupon, from within which, they eke their daily living. Some of these settlements sprout upon private land, while others grow on public land. It is these "settlers" together with their families who face the permanent threat of eviction either by the private owners or State agencies. The private owners will raise 'the sword of title', while the State agencies will raise 'the shield of public interest'. So where does this leave the right to housing guaranteed by Article 43 of the Constitution?

[151] While we ... [agree that] an illegal occupation of private land, cannot create prescriptive rights over that land in favour of the occupants, we don't think the same can be said of an "illegal occupation" of public land. To the contrary, we are of the considered opinion, that where the landless occupy public land and establish homes thereon, they acquire not title to the land, but a protectable right to housing over the same. Why, one may wonder, should the illegal occupation of public land give rise to the right to shelter, or to any right at all? ... The 2010 Constitution has radically transformed land tenure in this country by declaring that all land in Kenya belongs the people of Kenya collectively as a nation, communities and individuals. It also now creates a specific category of land known as public land. Therefore, every individual as part of the collectivity of the Kenyan nation has an interest, however indescribable, however unrecognizable, or however transient, in public land.

[152] The right to housing over public land crystallizes by virtue of a long period of occupation by people who have established homes and raised families on the land. This right derives from the principle of equitable access to land under Article 60 (1) (a) of the Constitution. Faced with an eviction on grounds of public interest, such potential evictees have a right to petition the Court for protection. The protection, need not necessarily be in the form of an order restraining the State agency from evicting the occupants, given the fact that, the eviction may be entirely justifiable in the public interest. But, under Article 23 (3) of the Constitution, the Court may craft orders aimed at protecting that right, such as compensation, the requirement of adequate notice before eviction, the observance of humane conditions during eviction (UN Guidelines), the provision of alternative land for settlement, etc.

[153] The right to housing in its base form (shelter) need not be predicated upon "title to land". Indeed, it is the inability of many citizens to acquire private title to land, that condemns them to the indignity of "informal settlement". Where the Government fails to provide accessible and adequate housing to all the people, the very least it must do, is to protect the rights and dignity of those in the informal settlements. The Courts are there to ensure that such protection is realized, otherwise these citizens, must forever, wander the corners of their country, in the grim reality of "the wretched of the earth".

...

[156] ... [Orders made by lower courts] ought not to have involved non- state actors, who were not parties to the suit. ... [However,] the eviction ... was carried out in contravention of a court order. ... Actions by state organs, carried out in flagrant disregard of court orders, do undermine our constitutional order, more so, if they

result in the violation of citizens' rights. If a trial Court is so moved, there is no reason why it cannot grant relief to the aggrieved.

...

WILLIAM MUSEMBI V. THE MOI EDUCATIONAL CENTRE CO. LTD.
SUPREME COURT OF KENYA (16 JULY 2021)

The petitioners (336 adults and 90 children) stated that they had resided in two informal settlements in Nairobi since 1968, on what was then public land. Their villages were officially supplied with electricity and water. In 2013, 300 armed people, accompanied by police, invaded the villages without any advance notice. They destroyed all of the property and evicted the residents. The main question before the Supreme Court was whether the right to housing applied between two private parties and whether the State had respected its 'negative obligation not to abuse or violate' the relevant rights.

...

[56] ... [T]he eviction of the Petitioners was violent and did not accord with the expected constitutional obligation of the State ... .

[57] In *Satrose Ayuma*, the High Court laid out certain principles that an evicting party must comply with. The Court, in doing so, applied international principles of law ... .

[58] The principles include the duty to give notice in writing; to carry out the eviction in a manner that respects the dignity, right to life and security of those affected; to protect the rights of women, the elderly, children and persons with disabilities and the duty to give the affected persons the first priority to demolish and salvage their property. [General Comment No.7.] ...

[59] [As to whether the eviction violated the Petitioners' rights:] Even the ordinary man in the street, confronted with the facts..., would answer the question in the affirmative. ...

...

[64] ... [I]t is manifestly evident in the present context that the mandate to ensure the realization and protection of social and economic rights does not extend to the 1st Respondent, a private entity. Even though the 1st Respondent has a negative obligation to ensure that it does not violate the rights of the Petitioners, it is not under any obligation to ensure that those rights are realized, either progressively or immediately. ...

THE RELATIONSHIP BETWEEN HOUSING AND PROPERTY RIGHTS

The ESCR Committee has received many communications on the right to housing, especially from Spain. For example, in *El Goumari and Tidli v. Spain,* Communication No. 85/2018 (2021) the domestic court failed to take account of the consequences of eviction for a family as part of a proportionality determination. The Committee found a violation of the right to adequate housing. Consider the following reflections on some of the case law emerging at the domestic and international levels.

(i) Gautam Bhatia, 'The Kenyan Supreme Court on Land, Evictions, and Horizontal Rights', *Notes from a Foreign Field* (16 July 2021), responding to *Musembi*:

> [A] distinction must be drawn between the obligation to provide alternative accommodation, and the obligation not to evict until alternative accommodation is available. The former is indeed a positive obligation and ... not binding on private parties. The latter, however, is a classic non-interference obligation, as it is just another pre-condition for when you can evict (like notice, participation, a court order etc.). ... It is thus not far-fetched to argue that it must follow from this judgment that if a private party proposes to evict people from private land, then it is for the State to take on the positive obligation of securing alternative accommodation before that eviction can take place ... .

(ii) Stuart Wilson, 'Making Space for Social Change: Pro-Poor Property Rights Litigation in Post-Apartheid South Africa', in Jason Brickhill (ed.), *Public Interest Litigation in South Africa* (2018) 159, at 182:

> Property law is one of the most important sources from which spaces of social action are constructed and reshaped. It sets the terms on which people may access and exploit material goods. Through reforms to property law, South Africa has embarked on a fundamental re-imagining of those terms. Unlawful occupiers of land have gained temporary, limited and circumscribed rights to remain where they have no common law entitlement to be. Tenants can insist that their landlords act fairly, even where their leases specify otherwise; and can hold out against a landlord who wants to repossess his property by arguing that the landlord has acted unfairly. Debtors who have failed to repay their debts can stave off debt recovery, restructure their obligations, and even prevent some forms of execution altogether, even though they have borrowed money that they have not given back.
>
> These important amendments to South African property law are reshaping social and economic relationships across a wide range of geographical and social contexts. They are driving social change. But the change that is being wrought is subtle, complex, contingent and takes time to reveal itself. ...
>
> ...
>
> [T]he principle that evictions should not lead to homelessness may drive, and has often driven, widespread community-based legal resistance to eviction. If every community under threat of homelessness by eviction responded in this way, there can be little doubt that property relations in South Africa would be transformed overnight. Not every community responds to a threat of eviction in this way. However, to detect and begin to describe a relationship between law and social change, it is enough that some communities do respond in this way, and that the law creates, expands or helps protect the space in which this is possible.
>
> ...

(iii) Mandisa Shandu and Michael Clark, 'Towards a Values-Based Approach to Property Relations in South Africa', 11 *Const. Ct. Rev. 2021* (2022) 39:

> *Abstract*: In recent decades, there has been growing dissatisfaction with the dominant theories of property law systems, founded on notions of exclusion and individualism, these systems have increasingly become associated with an unsustainable and inequitable distribution of resources. This inequitable distribution has largely been attributed to these property law systems that offer wholly disproportionate protection to the rights and interests of property owners while providing little to no recognition or protection for wider social, environmental and humanitarian concerns. These constructions of property overemphasise a single set of values – values that are largely economic, exclusionary and exploitative. Through an analysis of public land, particularly municipal land, we advocate for a rethinking of current property law relations to prioritise a more varied set of values, including social, ecological, emotional and humanist values, with the ultimate aim of realising a more social conception of property law. This is urgently required in the South African context, where access to land, tenure security and housing was historically dictated by colonialism and apartheid, and which remains influenced by deep-seated inequality. ...
>
> *Conclusion: Towards a Values-Based Approach*
>
> ...
>
> ... [T]he narrow focus of viewing municipal land as a capital asset ... limits the possibilities for municipal land to serve a societal function, such as affordable housing,

and ... this has the effect of maintaining an unequal status quo. The demands by housing activists for golf-courses on well-located parcels of public land to be redistributed is illustrative of the need to interrogate the systems and decision-making processes that protect and reproduce spatial inequality through, among other things, the economic value paradigm. An appropriate rationalisation would entail establishing a comprehensive set of principles to guide the use of public land so that decision makers are required to objectively consider broader values (that are informed and shaped by history and the current reality of unequal access to land), and to justify their decisions about a municipality's immovable property portfolio against these principles.

...

(iv) Consider this approach to legislative recognition of the right to housing in Portugal's Housing Basic Law, of 3 September 2019:
...

Article 2: Scope

1 Everyone has the right to housing, for themselves and their family, regardless of ancestry or ethnic origin, sex, language, territory of origin, nationality, religion, creed, political or ideological beliefs, education, economic situation, gender, sexual orientation, age, disability or health status.

Article 3: General principles

1 The State is the guarantor of the right to housing.

2 ... [T]he State shall programme and implement a housing policy ... .
...
4 The promotion and protection of housing are pursued through public policies, as well as through private, cooperative and social initiatives subordinated to general interest.

5 Public housing policies obey the following principles:

> a) Universality of the right to an appropriate housing unit to all individuals and their families;
>
> b) Equal opportunities ..., with positive discrimination measures when necessary;
>
> c) Social, economic and environmental sustainability ...;
>
> d) Administrative decentralization, subsidiarity and cooperation ...;
>
> e) Transparency of public procedures;
>
> f) Citizen participation and support of initiatives by local communities and populations.

...

Article 5: Effective use of housing

1 Any housing unit that is, unjustified and continuously, during the period defined by law, without effective housing use, for reasons imputable to the owner, is considered vacant.

2 Owners of vacant housing units are subject to the sanctions provided by law ... .

3 Second homes, emigrant housing and the housing units of displaced persons for occupational or health reasons are not considered vacant.
...

Article 6: …

The right to housing implies access to essential public services, as defined by specific legislation and to a suitable network of transport and social facilities … .
…

Article 9: Housing conditions

1 A housing unit is considered of adequate size for its residents if the area, the number of rooms and the water supply, sanitation and energy solutions are sufficient and do not cause situations of insalubrity, overcrowding or promiscuity-risk.
…

Article 11: Right to choose the place of residency

1 The State respects and promotes the citizens' right to choose the place of residency, according to their needs, means and preferences, without prejudice of urban planning restrictions.

2 In case of resettlement by public entities, the consultation of those involved is mandatory and, whenever possible, the permanence of persons and families to be resettled shall be promoted in the vicinity of the place where they previously resided.

3 In case of resettlement by private entities, determined by legal requirement, the consultation of those involved is mandatory and, whenever possible, the permanence of tenants or assignees of dwellings shall be promoted in the vicinity of the place where they previously resided.

4 In the allocation of adequate housing in public resettlement processes in neighbourhoods and adjoining areas, pre-existing neighbourhood and community ties shall be taken into consideration.

Article 12: Right to an address

1 The State promotes and guarantees to all citizens, namely homeless persons, the right to a postal address, inherent to the exercise of citizenship rights, including the mail delivery service.

2 Local authorities ensure toponymic identification of all dwellings in their area, including recent urban areas, urban settlements of illegal origin, precarious housing sites, dispersed housing or isolated dwellings.
…

Article 13: Eviction protection and accompaniment

…

4 The State, autonomous regions and local authorities cannot promote the administrative eviction of vulnerable individuals or families without prior guarantee of resettlement solutions, as defined by law, without prejudice to the following paragraph.

…

3. ESR in the Inter-American Convention

The Inter-American Court of Human Rights (see Chapter 11 B, below) was initially reluctant to address ESCR, but that has changed very significantly in recent years.[168] The following case addresses two important, but often neglected, dimensions of ESCR: the right to cultural identity, and freedom from discrimination on the basis of economic status.

THE MAYA KAQCHIKEL INDIGENOUS PEOPLES OF SUMPANGO ET AL. V. GUATEMALA INTER-AMERICAN COURT OF HUMAN RIGHTS, SER. C, NO. 440 (6 OCTOBER 2021)

…

---

[168] See generally R. Gargarella, 'Economic and Social Rights in Latin America: A Long and Unfinished March', in M. Langford and K. Young (eds.), *The Oxford Handbook of Economic and Social Rights* (2023) 000.

62. The instant case concerns the alleged existence of legal obstacles that prevent Guatemala's indigenous peoples ... from having access to radio frequencies. The case also concerns the alleged absence of affirmative actions by the State aimed at ensuring such access, and an alleged policy of criminalization of community radio stations operated without a license in Guatemala, which has resulted in the criminal prosecution of members of indigenous communities and raids on their community radio stations.
...

c) The right of indigenous peoples to participate in cultural life ...

119. The Court has reiterated its authority to determine violations of Article 26 of the American Convention ... .

[*Note*: ESCR are dealt with in Chapter III of the Convention, and Article 26 is headed 'Progressive Development':

> The States Parties undertake to adopt measures ... with a view to achieving progressively, by legislation or other appropriate means, the full realization of the rights implicit in the economic, social, educational, scientific, and cultural standards set forth in the [OAS Charter].]

...

125. This Court has pointed out that cultural identity is a "basic human right, and one of a collective nature in indigenous communities, which must be respected in a multicultural, pluralist and democratic society." The Court understands that the right to cultural identity "protects the freedom of individuals, including when they are acting together or as a community, to identify with one or several societies, communities or social groups, to follow a way of life connected to the culture to which they belong and to take part in its development. Thus, this right protects the distinctive features that characterize a social group without denying the historical, dynamic and evolving nature of culture."

...

128. The Court has also referred to the instrumental nature of certain rights, such as freedom of expression, to realize other rights such as the right to take part in cultural life. From this perspective, indigenous people's access to their own community radio stations, as vehicles of freedom of expression, is an indispensable element to promote the identity, language, culture, self-representation and the collective and human rights of indigenous peoples. ...

...

130. ... [In terms of] obligations of an immediate nature ..., States must ensure that this right is exercised without discrimination, and adopt effective measures for its full realization. ... [In terms of] obligations of a progressive nature ..., progressive realization means that States Parties have the specific and constant obligation to move as expeditiously and efficiently as possible toward the full realization of this right, subject to available resources, by legislation or other appropriate means. Likewise, the obligation of non-retrogression is imposed with respect to the realization of the rights achieved. Consequently, the obligations to respect and guarantee rights established in the Convention, as well as the adoption of provisions of domestic law (Articles 1(1) and 2), are essential to achieve their effectiveness.

... d) *Alleged violations of the right ... to equality before the law* ...

132. The Court has reiterated that States must refrain from carrying out actions that in any way are aimed, directly or indirectly, at creating situations of discrimination de jure or de facto. ...

133. In this regard, while the general obligation under Article 1(1) refers to the State's obligation to respect and ensure the rights contained in the American Convention "without any discrimination," Article 24 protects the "right to equal protection of the law." ... [T]aking into account the situation of poverty that affects a large part of the indigenous population in Guatemala, the Court will examine the alleged violation of Article 24 of the Convention in relation to the category of "economic status." In this sense, the Court has already established that poverty is a category protected under the Convention, since "poverty may well be understood to fall within

the category of "economic status" to which the said article expressly refers, or in relation to other categories of protection such as "social origin" or "any other social condition," in view of its multidimensional nature."

...

135. ... Article 24 of the Convention also establishes an obligation to ensure material equality. ... [It] has two dimensions. The first is a formal dimension that establishes equality before the law; the second is a material or substantial dimension that requires the adoption of affirmative measures in favor of groups that have historically been discriminated against or marginalized due to the factors mentioned in Article 1(1) of the American Convention. Thus, the Court considers that the right to equality before the law also entails the obligation to adopt measures to ensure that the equality is real and effective; in other words "to correct existing inequalities, to promote the inclusion and participation of historically marginalized groups, and to guarantee to disadvantaged individuals or groups the effective enjoyment of their rights and, in short, to provide individuals with the real possibility of achieving material equality. To this end, States must actively combat situations of exclusion and marginalization."

...

154. ... [T]he Court finds that the operation of community radio stations by indigenous peoples is an essential vehicle for their cultural survival. ... [The] broadcasting regulations in Guatemala ... in practice [prevent] indigenous peoples ... from exercising their right to participate in cultural life through their community radio stations."

[The Court required Guatemala to adapt its domestic regulations accordingly, to establish a simple procedure for obtaining licenses, and to reserve part of the radio spectrum for indigenous community radio stations.]

4. Assessing ESR Litigation

For all that it has achieved, litigation to uphold ESR has also been the subject of important critiques. Consider the following:

David Landau and Rosalind Dixon, 'Constitutional Non-Transformation?', in Katharine Young (ed.), *The Future of Economic and Social Rights* (2019) 110:

> ... [A]cross a number of different systems, judicial enforcement of social rights is often targeted at middle-class groups, rather than the poor ... .
>
> One set of explanations focuses on notions of judicial capacity, and the degree to which courts may lack the institutional tools or mechanisms to achieve the kind of broad social and economic transformation necessary for social rights to benefit the poor. ... [But] with the right degree of creativity, and potentially also supportive legal and political culture – courts may be able to overcome at least some of these institutional limitations. ...
>
> A second explanation focuses on the idea of legal and judicial 'capture,' or the degree to which courts are ultimately co-opted by the middle class as a tool for furthering their own interests and objectives. ... [I]n many cases what may appear to be capture in fact can be better understood as a form of pro-majoritarian judicial review by courts, which seek to promote the effectiveness of majority understandings of, or commitments to, social rights – in the face of either international pressures to adopt a more limited role in the protection of social rights, or blockages in domestic legislative and administrative processes that undermine the responsiveness of the state to democratic majority demands for social protection and economic redistribution.
>
> Third, ... a pro-middle-class social rights jurisprudence may in some circumstances be complementary with a more pro-poor, transformative social rights agenda: it may create the political support for such an agenda necessary to ensure adequate resources for its realization, and also support for the court, when faced with the inevitable pushback from an executive faced with budgetary pressures. ...

Farrah Ahmed and Tarunabh Khaitan, 'Constitutional Avoidance in Social Rights Adjudication', 35 *Oxford J. Leg. Stud.* (2015) 607:

> In his important book *Judging Social Rights* [2012], Jeff King offers an account of how judges should adjudicate social rights claims. ...
>
> ... [He] defends the constitutionalisation and consequent judicialisation of social rights, provided that judges adjudicate these rights in an incremental fashion. ... [He] endorses an incrementalist agenda which demands constitutional avoidance, particularisation, cautious expansion and analogical reasoning, vague rather than specific legal standards, focus on procedural rights, non-intrusive remedies and ready revisitation of precedents in social rights cases. Incrementalism, King argues, preserves a valuable, if limited, role for courts in social rights litigation, while respecting his four principles of judicial restraint: democratic legitimacy, polycentricity, expertise and flexibility.
>
> ...
>
> ... King mainly understands constitutional avoidance as a rule of last resort ...:
>
>> Where a claim may succeed on constitutional or non-constitutional grounds (which typically means choosing statutory interpretation or administrative law instead of constitutional remedies), the court should, under circumstances of serious uncertainty, prefer the non-constitutional remedy.
>
> ... King uses 'constitutional avoidance' interchangeably with a preference for administrative over constitutional grounds for judicial decisions. In other contexts, the law of torts is likely to be a more plausible alternative to constitutional law. ... [He says]:
>
>> One of the better ways to give effect to an avoidance canon is to give rights-friendly readings to statutes and soft law policies in the welfare state. And a way of extending common law protections is to use a heightened standard of judicial review when constitutional rights are 'engaged', a process that will allow the domestic court to issue a remedy in the case at hand while leaving the question of whether the constitutional rights are 'violated' open for another day.
>
> ... Ordinary statutes, common law doctrines and soft law policies should therefore be interpreted or developed in a 'rights-friendly' manner. King mainly recommends the rights-sensitive development of administrative law grounds of review including illegality, procedural impropriety, rationality (including heightened rationality) and legitimate expectations to protect social rights. King also calls for a more intense standard of judicial review when a constitutional right is 'engaged', and favours a more robust judicial approach to the enforcement of social rights through non-constitutional means, rather than the (often more deferential) enforcement through constitutional means. ...
>
> ...
>
> ... [W]e examined the potential for constitutional avoidance in landmark Indian Supreme Court cases on social rights. Of the 19 cases we examined, the claimant was successful in obtaining some remedy in 18 cases. In 15 out of these ..., at least some of the remedies granted (whether substantive access to shelter, education, medical care, or procedural safeguards protecting such access) could have been granted without invoking constitutional guarantees. There was always a statute, a policy, administrative law, common law or (in a few cases) private law provision upon which some of these remedies could have rested. ...
>
> ...

… For instance, the orders in *Olga Tellis* … did not require an appeal to constitutional rights. Rather, a robust administrative law review to protect legitimate expectations and procedural fairness was all that was required to justify the Court's orders… .

…

Kent Roach, 'Remedies and Accountability for Economic and Social Rights', in Malcolm Langford and Katharine Young (eds.), *The Oxford Handbook of Economic and Social Rights* (2023) 000:

> The challenges of devising effective remedies for ESRs are considerable. Those who ask for remedies that courts may find unmanageable, illegitimate, or too expensive risk having courts reject the merits of the ESRs claim. This danger of remedial deterrence is also complicated by the rise of populism, which means that even competent governments may not always respond promptly and in good faith to judicial rulings. The mix of remedies will change with the context. Populist resistance may make dialogic remedies less successful in the future. Environmental, migration, and public health crises may result in an increased emphasis on interim remedies designed to prevent irreparable harm. Case-specific remedies designed for specific individuals may be a means to convince reluctant courts not to abandon their remedial role and to become more comfortable with finding ESRs violations. Damage remedies may fail fully to restore victims or to prevent the reoccurrence of violations, but they may provide some tangible relief to those who have been denied ESRs rights. Damages may also provide much needed resources to finance continued mobilization and in the case of Indigenous peoples continued efforts to maximize self-determination. The award of both interim remedies and damages may also demonstrate some remedial success and promote greater awareness in civil society and governments about the dramatic harms and costs of not recognizing ESRs. Those who seek better compliance with ESRs in the future should be open to the possibility that some defeats in court could lead to political victories. Even when they win in court, it may still be necessary to continue civil society and political awareness and engagement. They may be able to use some of the instruments of populism—such as social media, consumer boycotts of corporations, and mobilization of protests—to turn a spotlight on violations of ESRs that, alas, may become even more widespread in the future.

Kira Tait and Whitney Taylor, 'The Possibility of Rights Claims-Making in Court: Looking Back on Twenty-Five Years of Social Rights Constitutionalism in South Africa', 48 *Law Soc. Inq.* (2023) 1023:

> … Our findings reveal skepticism [among ordinary South Africans] about the feasibility and efficacy of [turning to the law for social rights]. … [S]kepticism … [stems from] the disconnect in how citizens expect the state and its institutions to work and the way they experience them working. … [C]itizens' expectations of the post-apartheid state have failed to materialize. People are told they have rights, but having rights has not resulted in their anticipated outcome, whether that is being able to voice a complaint or gain access to basic services. People are told they can get help from courts, but the legal system works in ways that make accessing justice difficult. Against this backdrop, ordinary South Africans have developed doubts about the benefits of rights and the law as meaningful institutions, at times rendering it impossible for them to turn to the courts for redress. These doubts create significant challenges for state accountability, institutional development, and citizenship in postapartheid South Africa's project of democratic state building.

QUESTIONS

1. Compare the approaches taken by the Court in *Soobramoney*, *Grootboom* and *TAC*. Is the approach consistent or does the Court shift the goalposts significantly from one case to the next?

---

2. 'In the *TAC* case, the Court rolls out all the classic statements of deference to the legislature before it engages in an aggressive demolition of the government's policy choices and replaces them with its own.' Comment.

3. 'In administrative law there is generally a detailed legislative standard to apply or interpret, whereas in constitutional law the provisions are, almost by definition, open-ended. By applying a reasonableness test that is shaped by administrative law notions in interpreting constitutional provisions the Court avoids the sort of deep inquiry that is essential if ESR are to be given substantive, as opposed to merely procedural, content.' Comment.

4. Consider this assessment by Jackie Dugard, one of Mazibuko's lawyers:

"… human rights litigation might not be able to immediately dismantle structural racism especially when concretised as residential segregation and rationalised within a neoliberal cost-recovery paradigm.

But this narrow view of the value of human rights as determined by whether a case wins or loses in court, misses two critical points. First, many 'losing' cases result in direct gains for the litigants and other similarly situated people. … [D]espite losing in court, *Mazibuko* resulted in the City of Johannesburg responding politically to the grievances raised in the case by providing increased access to free basic water and halting the rollout of PPMs in poor Black residential areas.

Second … arguably the real power of rights lies 'beyond the courtroom' in the realm of the 'politics of rights'. It is here where … rights act to expose the dynamics of domination and question the existing order by providing a counter-veiling narrative to the dominant ones. … [H]uman rights-based mobilisation beyond the courtroom is a form of resistance capable of influencing discourse and shifting power relations – both likely precursors to social change. …
…
… [H]uman rights litigation is not unique in its inability thus far to have dismantled structural inequality. The global neoliberal order has proven stubbornly resistant to egalitarian socio-economic change by whatever means. …[169]"

Do you agree with Dugard's assessment?

F. ESR: BEYOND CONSTITUTIONS AND LITIGATION

It is increasingly accepted that more attention needs to be given to approaches to the implementation of ESR that do not rely largely on litigation and courts. Various commentators cited above emphasize the importance of social movements and community activism, but that approach still leaves open the question of what approaches should be pursued in legal and institutional terms. Amartya Sen has counselled against an unduly legalistic approach:

> Human rights are best viewed as pronouncements in social ethics, sustainable by open public reasoning. They may or may not be reflected in a legal framework through, say, specific "human rights legislation," but there are also other ways of implementing human rights (including public recognition, agitation, and monitoring). The viability and universality of human rights are dependent on their ability to survive open critical scrutiny in public reasoning. The corresponding obligations are both perfect and imperfect in character. Where imperfect, they ground a firm duty to reasonably consider undertaking actions which can defend or promote the relevant freedom, both in process and

---

[169] J. Dugard, 'Racial Segregation, Water Disconnection and Human Rights Litigation: An Examination of the Use of Law to Challenge Structural Racism in Detroit and Johannesburg', in D. Lupin (ed.), *A Research Agenda for Human Rights and the Environment* (2023) 81.

opportunity terms. Such obligations place implicit and explicit pressure on all who are in a plausible position to prevent the violation of economic and social rights.[170]

One starting point is to ask why the language of rights needs to be used at all, as long as the focus is on education, health, housing and so on. This is rarely a question asked in relation to CPR but it often arises in relation to ESR, with organizations such as the World Bank suggesting that they pursue ESR-compatible outcomes without needing to characterize them as such.[171] This is one response to the question of whether it really matters if ESR are treated as human rights:

> ... [The reality is that] the use of rights terminology is avoided so assiduously by governments and others precisely because it does matter very much and makes a big difference. How so? First, the use of the human rights framework ensures that in the midst of programmes designed to ensure collective well-being, the rights of the individual and not just the overall goals of the programme and the interests of the collectivity are taken into account. Second, in contrast to generic social justice language which has no defined content or agreed meaning, human rights discourse directs policymakers and others back to the internationally agreed formulations of [ESR] and the jurisprudence that has painstakingly evolved. Third, treating [ESR] as human rights rather than long-term goals introduces an element of immediate salience which might otherwise not be present. Fourth, and perhaps most importantly, the language of rights recognizes and insists on the dignity and agency of all individuals (regardless of race, gender, social status, age, disability or any other distinguishing factor) and it is intentionally empowering. Whether in the home, village, school or workplace, or in the political marketplace of ideas, it makes a difference if one is calling for the realization of collectively agreed and internationally recognized and defined rights to housing or education, rather than merely making a general request or demand. Moreover, as noted earlier, the legal conception of human rights presupposes and demands accountability, whereas characterizing [ESR] in terms of desirable goals or development challenges leaves them hostage to a great many other considerations.[172]

The same analysis suggests that a human rights approach to ESR would focus especially on the dimensions of recognition, institutionalization, and accountability. Constitutional recognition is all too rarely accompanied by specific recognition of say the '*right to* education' in the relevant legislative and administrative arrangements:

A. Legal recognition

27. ... [I]t is difficult to understand how the obligations to "recognize" the rights, and to "guarantee" non-discrimination, could possibly be achieved in the absence of targeted legislative or equivalent measures. ... [T]he general principle is that States shall, as required under international law, ensure that their domestic law is consistent with their international legal obligations by, inter alia, incorporating norms of international human rights law into their domestic law, or otherwise implementing them in their domestic legal system. The key element here is the recognition of the norm itself, not merely the adoption of measures that are pertinent to the subject-matter of the norm.

B. Obligation to establish institutions

28. Human rights are often expressed with great brevity and little or no elaboration as to their content or corresponding obligations. The relevant treaties simply recognize that there is a right to life, a right to social security or a right to recognition as a person before the law. But the assumption underpinning this approach is that institutions will be created and will help to develop the normative content of the relevant right, promote its implementation and facilitate its realization. In Spanish, the term *institucionalidad* is sometimes used to denote the institutional arrangements that are needed to underpin the rule of law and human rights. Where no

---

[170] A. Sen, 'Obligations and Economic and Social Rights', in Malcolm Langford and Katharine Young (eds.), *The Oxford Handbook of Economic and Social Rights* (2023) 000.
[171] J. Wolfensohn, 'Some Reflections on Human Rights and Development', in P. Alston and M. Robinson (eds.), *Human Rights and Development: Towards Mutual Reinforcement* (2005) 19.
[172] P. Alston, Report of the Special Rapporteur on extreme poverty and human rights (UN Doc. A/HRC/32/31 (2016)), para. 8.

institutions are designated to take the lead in implementing a particular human right, the likelihood is that little will be done to treat it as a human right per se. This is especially the case in relation to [ESR].

C. Obligation to promote accountability

29. The principle of accountability provides the overarching rationale for the establishment of an international human rights regime. It operates at two levels. One involves State accountability to the international community ... . The other involves ensuring that governments are accountable to their citizens and other rights holders. The right to a remedy is recognized in the [UDHR] and [in general] international human rights law [as well as in General Comment No. 9 of the Committee on ESCR.

Accountability

As noted above, one of the most effective mechanisms for monitoring states' compliance with their ESR obligations, apart from the Committee on ESCR, has been the Special Procedures system, described in detail in Chapter 8 below. In addition to preparing reports once or twice a year on specific themes, and sending communications (allegation letters) to governments, these independent experts also undertake country visits, at the invitation of the relevant government. In relation to ESR, the most broadly focused of the Special Procedures mandates is the Special Rapporteur on extreme poverty and human rights. The following are two examples of such reports:

SPAIN
(A/HRC/44/40/ADD.2 (2020))

10. The Special Rapporteur visited areas that many Spaniards would not recognize as a part of their country. A shanty town with far worse conditions than a refugee camp, without running water, electricity or sanitation, where migrant workers have lived for years ... . Closed-off neighbourhoods of concentrated poverty, where families are raising children with a dearth of State services, health clinics, employment centres, security, paved roads or legal electricity. A segregated school in a poor neighbourhood with a 100 per cent Roma student body and a 75 per cent rate of early leaving.

11. The single word heard most over the two-week visit was "abandoned." People felt abandoned in a rural town without public transportation to visit the doctor and no money to pay for private transport. Abandoned in a stigmatized low-income suburb that the police avoid. Abandoned to unscrupulous landlords, unconscionable rent raises or unmaintained public housing and abandoned to an arbitrary bureaucratic system that denies vital support without explanation. The common thread was an absence of government support to ensure that people do not needlessly experience the worst effects of poverty, a situation many face because of phenomena largely beyond their control, such as job loss, structural discrimination or illness.

12. People feel abandoned for good reason. The benefits of the economic recovery have largely flowed to corporations and the wealthy, while many of the public services and protections that were severely curtailed after 2008 have not been restored. Income growth has been primarily captured by those at the top ... .

13. In comparison, people in poverty have been largely failed by policymakers. ... [ESR] are rarely taken seriously, even if they are frequently invoked rhetorically. People face skyrocketing housing costs, privatization of apartment blocks and aggressive evictions, yet low cost social housing is almost non-existent, despite widespread agreement on the necessity for it. The system for providing social assistance is broken. ... [W]ealthy families [benefit] more from cash transfers than poor families. The system is fragmented, impossible to navigate and is not reaching the poor people who need it most.

...

UNITED KINGDOM
(A/HRC/41/39/ADD.1 (2019))

3. ... [O]ne fifth of its population (14 million people) live in poverty. Four million of those are more than 50 per cent below the poverty line and 1.5 million experienced destitution in 2017, unable to afford basic essentials. Following drastic changes in government economic policy beginning in 2010, the two preceding decades of progress in tackling child and pensioner poverty have begun to unravel and poverty is again on the rise. ...

4. But statistics alone cannot capture the full picture of poverty in the United Kingdom, much of it the direct result of government policies ... . There has been a shocking increase in the number of food banks and major increases in homelessness and rough sleeping; a growing number of homeless families – 24,000 between April and June of 2018 – have been dispatched to live in accommodation far from their schools, jobs and community networks; life expectancy is falling for certain groups; and the legal aid system has been decimated, thus shutting out large numbers of low-income persons from the once-proud justice system. Government reforms have often denied benefits to people with severe disabilities and pushed them into unsuitable work, single mothers struggling to cope in very difficult circumstances have been left far worse off, care for those with mental illnesses has deteriorated dramatically, and teachers' real salaries have been slashed. The number of emergency admissions to hospitals of homeless people ("of no fixed abode") increased sevenfold between 2008–2009 and 2017–2018.

5. In the past, the worst casualties of these "reforms" would have received at least minimal protection from the broader social safety net. But austerity policies have deliberately gutted local authorities and thereby effectively eliminated many social services, reduced policing services to skeletal proportions, closed libraries in record numbers, shrunk community and youth centres, and sold off public spaces and buildings including parks and recreation centres. It is hardly surprising that civil society has reported unheard-of levels of loneliness and isolation, prompting the Government to appoint a Minister for Suicide Prevention. The bottom line is that much of the glue that has held British society together since the Second World War has been deliberately removed and replaced with a harsh and uncaring ethos.
...

11. ... [T]he driving force has not been economic but rather a commitment to achieving radical social re-engineering – a dramatic restructuring of the relationship between people and the State. Successive Governments have brought revolutionary change in both the system for delivering minimum levels of fairness and social justice to the British people, and especially in the values underpinning it. ...

12. Far-reaching changes to the role of Government in supporting people in distress are almost always "sold" as part of an unavoidable fiscal "austerity" programme needed to save the country from bankruptcy. In fact, the ... many billions extracted from the benefits system since 2010 have been offset by additional resources required, by local government, by doctors and hospital accident and emergency centres, and even by the ever-shrinking, overworked and underfunded police force to fund the increasing need for emergency services.

13. The Government has made no secret of its determination to change the value system to focus more on individual responsibility, to place major limits on government support and to pursue a single-minded focus on getting people into employment. Many aspects of this programme are legitimate matters for political contestation, but it is the mentality informing many of the reforms that has brought the most misery and wrought the most harm to the fabric of British society. British compassion has been replaced by a punitive, mean-spirited and often callous approach apparently designed to impose a rigid order on the lives of those least capable of coping, and elevate the goal of enforcing blind compliance over a genuine concern to improve the well-being of those at the lowest economic levels of British society. ...

Reactions to the Special Rapporteur's United Kingdom Report

Following the rapporteur's visit, demands on UK food banks more than doubled over the next five years (Trussell Trust, *Hunger in the UK* (2023)). The Trust found that '14% of all UK adults (or their households) [had] experienced food insecurity in the 12 months to mid-2022, equating to an estimated 11.3 million people. ... [M]ore than two thirds of those experiencing food insecurity have not received food aid.'

Responses to the UN report varied, perhaps predictably, and it was the subject of more than 4,000 separate media stories.[173] The Prime Minister responded in Parliament to the report on several occasions. The Chancellor (Finance Minister) told the BBC: 'I reject the idea that there are vast numbers of people facing dire poverty in this country. I don't accept the UN rapporteur's report at all. I think that's a nonsense.' The Leader of the Opposition called the findings a 'wake-up call about the rising levels of poverty and destitution that exist in Britain today,' and the report was debated in both Houses of Parliament. The editors of *The Guardian* (Editorial, 18 November 2018) stated that the Special Rapporteur's:

> position and plain speaking have exposed this country before the world's gaze. His scathing analysis is a call not only to conscience but to Britain's self-respect. ... It is unpardonable that the costs of austerity have fallen so disproportionately upon the poor, women, ethnic minorities, children, single parents, and people with disabilities ... .
>
> ...
>
> ... It is a national embarrassment that we needed a UN poverty envoy to spell out what is so evident. It will be a greater one if we refuse to pay heed.

The Times Editorial on the report (25 May 2019) stated that:

> ... This tendentious and frivolous document says more about the weaknesses of the UN's system of monitoring human rights than it does about [the situation in Britain].
>
> Real violations of human rights are a pressing issue in many parts of the world. ... Unfortunately, partisan attacks on democratic governments, and on democratic societies generally, are what the UN's purported mechanisms of scrutiny all too often produce.
>
> The failings of Mr Alston's report are legion. As he spent only 11 days in Britain conducting his research on welfare policy since 2010, perhaps he should be commended for managing to write a document that extends as far as 21 pages.
>
> ...
>
> It is legitimate to debate the mix of private and public sector, or the right level for the public debt or deficit relative to GDP, but these issues have no bearing on Mr Alston's brief. Amber Rudd, the work and pensions secretary, has indicated that she will lodge a complaint with the UN about the report. She should do so, not to defend the reputation of the government but to force the UN to confront the politicised inadequacies of its reporting.

The Archbishop of Canterbury (*The Guardian*, 2 December 2018) said, 'I think it's really important for the government to respond carefully to that [report], not to dismiss it.' And Human Rights Watch subsequently produced its first ever report focused specifically on the right to food: *Nothing Left in the Cupboards: Austerity, Welfare Cuts and the Right to Food in the UK* (May 2019).

The reports on Spain and the United Kingdom include a focus on broader economic policies such as austerity, privatization, and inequality, which have a major impact on the availability of resources for ESR.

QUESTIONS

1. Does it really make a difference if social justice policies are formulated in terms of rights discourse?

2. What are the principal constituencies for country reports on ESR prepared by Special Rapporteurs?

---

[173] See P. Alston, B. Khawaja, and R. Riddell, 'Much ado about poverty: the role of a UN Special Rapporteur', 27 *J. Pov. and Soc. Just.* (2019) 423; M. Adler, 'The Alston Report on extreme poverty and human rights in the UK: a review', 28 *J. Pov. and Soc. Just.* (2020) 265; and F. Hill, *There Is Nothing for You Here: Finding Opportunity in the 21st Century* (2021) 158-160.

G. THE POLITICAL ECONOMY OF HUMAN RIGHTS

Although this chapter focuses on ESR, the issues raised in the following materials are of crucial importance for all human rights. In recent years, there has been a much more concerted focus in the human rights field on the root causes of violations and the underlying structures that help to maintain various forms of injustice.[174] These approaches reflect many different conceptual and theoretical streams of thought. One is the concept of 'structural violence', introduced by Johan Galtung, in 'Violence, Peace, and Peace Research, 6 *J. Peace Res.* (1969) 167. Galtung viewed social justice as a form of 'positive peace', or the absence of structural violence. He observed that 'law and order' approaches often emphasize personal or bodily violence and neglect the deeper economic and social structures that actually constrain the opportunities for individuals to perhaps an even greater extent.

Iris Marion Young, in *Responsibility for Justice* (2011), criticized the pre-occupation of philosophers like John Rawls with just 'a small subset of [society's] institutions' at the expense of focusing on those 'social-structural processes' that produce so much injustice. For Young (at 52):

> Structural injustice … exists when the social processes put large groups of persons under systematic threat of domination or deprivation of the means to develop and exercise their capacities, at the same time that these processes enable others to dominate or to have a wide range of opportunities for developing and exercising capacities available to them. Structural injustice is a kind of moral wrong distinct from the wrongful action of an individual agent or the repressive policies of a state. Structural injustice occurs as the consequence of many individuals and institutions acting to pursue their particular goals and interests, for the most part within the limits of accepted rules and norms.

In some respects, this approach is the opposite of that pursued by organizations like Human Rights Watch. As its Executive Director from 1993 to 2022 explained (in Sec. B, above), 'naming and shaming' requires the identification of a 'violator' responsible for the problem. In the case of structural violence, this might well be difficult or impossible, because the culprit could be society, the tax system, social mores, or even the market. But human rights obligations fall principally upon governments, and their obligations are not only to refrain from violations themselves or to punish known violators, but also to take whatever measures are needed to facilitate and, as far as possible ensure, conditions in which the populace is able to enjoy the full range of their rights.

The readings below touch, all too briefly, on some of the principal structural impediments to the realization of ESR. In the years ahead, proponents of human rights will need to devote far greater attention to these issues than has been the case to date.

1. Austerity[175]

The International Monetary Fund and other financial actors have replaced the terms 'austerity' or 'structural adjustment' with the more technical and obscure notion of 'fiscal consolidation'. Wolfgang Streeck, in 'A New Regime', in D. King and P. Le Galès (eds.), *Reconfiguring European States in Crisis* (2017) 139 explains that this establishes public austerity as a fundamental principle, to be achieved in part:

> by a redefinition of the responsibilities of government and the purposes of public policy, in the direction of a smaller state and an expanded market, less public and more private provision, privatization of state activities and assets, and a substitution of individual effort for collective solidarity. Ultimately, the construction of a consolidation state implies a far-

---

[174] See, e.g., V. Mantouvalou, *Structural Injustice Workers' Rights* (2023); D. Birchall, 'Reconstructing State Obligations to Protect and Fulfil Socio-Economic Rights in an Era of Marketisation', 71 *ICLQ* (2022) 227; Z. Manfredi, 'Radicalizing Human Rights', *The Boston Review*, (21 June 2022); M. McKeown, 'Structural Injustice', 16 *Phil. Compass* (2021) 1; M. Powers and R. Faden, *Structural Injustice: Power, Advantage, and Human Rights* (2019); and A. Nuti, *Injustice and the Reproduction of History* (2019).

[175] See generally, A. Nolan and J. P. Bohoslavsky (eds.), Human Rights and Economic Policy Reform (2023); G. MacNaughton and D. Frey, Economic and Social Rights in a Neoliberal World (2019); and D. Kinley, Necessary Evil: How to Fix Finance by Saving Human Rights (2018).

reaching rationalization, or 'economization', of politics and society. In the process states become less like sovereigns and more like firms: instead of overriding markets, they have to be responsive to them. Whereas the politics of democratic capitalism was to protect society from the 'vagaries of the market' (Polanyi), the politics of the consolidation state protects financial markets from what are for them the vagaries of democratic politics.

[Streeck identifies four 'lasting political-economic consequences' of fiscal consolidation:]

1. Budget balancing, if achieved by spending cuts rather than tax increases, and even more so if accompanied by tax cuts, comes at the expense of discretionary as distinguished from mandatory spending. As public budgets approach balance, a growing share of government expenditure goes to cover comparatively rigid, legally fixed expenditures, such as wages for public sector workers, public pensions, and, of course, debt service. As the final element is untouchable in a consolidation state, it is public investment, both in the physical infrastructure and in education, families, active labour market policy, and the like … that must give. Over the longer term, this will also produce pressures on 'entitlements' like social security, making them more politically vulnerable and less mandatory in effect. …

2. Budget balancing allows no new debt … . Public investment will therefore have to be financed out of what will very likely be shrinking current revenue. Regaining and retaining the confidence of financial markets may therefore require governments to cut public investment, even if real interest rates on government debt approach zero. Resulting deficiencies in physical and social infrastructures have to be attended to by private investors assuming what had previously been public responsibilities. One outcome is likely to be a growing number of public–private partnerships (PPPs) of various sorts, with returns on private investment insured by the state, and governments or individual citizens paying user fees to private firms. … [S]tates and citizens will be paying more under such arrangements than they would have paid had the investment remained in public hands. …

3. Cutting discretionary expenditure inevitably involves cuts in social services such as education and especially in universal services benefiting all citizens. As the range and quality of state-provided services deteriorate, the middle class will look for complementary or alternative private provision, and governments will be urged to allow private firms to compete with public authorities. In the process, the better-to-do will get habituated to more customized private provision, which will make them demand (further) tax cuts so they can pay for them—tax cuts that will drive further spending cuts. As the welfare state loses growing segments of its middle-class constituency, public programmes will turn into programmes for the poor which … will make them poor programmes.

4. Privatization of investment in physical and social infrastructures gives rise to a growing private industry operating in what used to be the public sector. While typically subject to regulation, private providers are likely soon to become powerful players in the political arena, where they will ally with the upwardly mobile middle class and its liberal-conservative political parties. The evolving connections of the new firms with the government—often taking the form of a revolving-door exchange of personnel—and their campaign contributions will further cement the shift from a redistributive towards a neoliberal state that abandons providing for social equity and social cohesion to civil society and the market.

Another study documented the extent to which policies demanding austerity were especially prominent in the aftermath of COVID-19:

A decade of fiscal consolidation increased poverty and inequality, especially for women, undermined progress on human rights and sparked social conflict. During 2010-20, prior to the COVID-19 pandemic, millions were pushed into poverty by the jobs crisis and by regressive austerity policies. Women were particularly affected by job losses and cuts in social protection and public services, while austerity was imposed with the implicit assumption that women would act as the shock absorbers by providing (unpaid) care at home. A vast array of social protection benefits, such as child allowances, disability benefits, gender equality programs, childcare services, services to victims of violence or housing support were rationalized as cost-saving measures … .[176]

One documented effect of austerity policies was:

Slower improvements, or deteriorations, in life expectancy and mortality trends were seen in the majority of countries, with the worst trends in England & Wales, Estonia, Iceland, Scotland, Slovenia, and the USA, with generally worse trends for females than males.[177]

International human rights bodies have tentatively begun to address the human rights implications of austerity measures,[178] although the courts will often defer to the legislature in such matters. One such example is the UK Government's 'two-child policy' which eliminated benefits otherwise payable to families for any third or subsequent child born after 6 April 2017. The policy was designed to save money and to incentivise parents with more than two children to move into work, or work more hours to make up the difference. But a 2023 report found 'no evidence that capping child benefits increases employment. Labour market activity among larger families seem to be particularly [unresponsive] to reductions in benefits income, likely due to parents' commitment to unpaid care, the scale of caregiving responsibilities and barriers to paid work.'[179]

R (ON THE APPLICATION OF SC, CB AND 8 CHILDREN) V. SECRETARY OF STATE FOR WORK AND PENSIONS AND ORS
[2021] UKSC 26

LORD REED: (with whom Lord Hodge, Lady Black, Lord Lloyd-Jones, Lord Kitchin, Lord Sales and Lord Stephens agree)
…
[The Supreme Court considered whether the policy constituted indirect discrimination against women, in contravention of the European Convention on Human Rights.]

193. … [W]omen constitute 90% of single parents bringing up children, as well as 50% of parents jointly bringing up children. … Since women are disproportionately represented among parents bringing up children, it is inevitable that they will be disproportionately affected by legislation … making changes to child-related benefits paid to parents.
…
195. … There is no suggestion that that is itself the result of discrimination on the ground of sex.

196. The differential impact on women is not, therefore, a special feature of this measure. It is inherent in any general measure which limits expenditure on child- related benefits. …

197. Once it is understood that the legitimate aims of the measure could not be achieved without a disproportionate impact on women, … the only remaining question … in relation to proportionality, is whether

[176] Isabel Ortiz and Matthew Cummins, End Austerity: A Global Report on Budget Cuts and Harmful Social Reforms in 2022-25 (2022) 6.
[177] G. McCartney et al., 'Is austerity a cause of slower improvements in mortality in high-income countries? A panel analysis', 313 Soc. Sci. & Med. (2022) 115397.
[178] P. Alston, 'The Impact of Austerity on the Protection of Human Rights', in K. Lenaerts et al (eds.), An Ever Changing Union? Perspectives on the Future of EU Law in Honour of Allan Rosas (2019) 261.
[179] M. Reader et al., Making Work Pay? The Labour Market Effects of Capping Child Benefits in Larger Families (2023).

the inevitable impact on women outweighed the importance of achieving the aims pursued. Parliament decided that the importance of the objectives pursued by the measure justified its enactment, notwithstanding its greater impact on women. I see no basis on which this court could properly take a different view.

Discrimination against children living in households containing more than two children

198. There remains the argument that the legislation discriminates against children living in households containing more than two children, by comparison with children living in households containing one or two children … .

199. Parliament's aims in enacting the legislation … [were] first, to promote the economic well-being of the country by reducing excessive public expenditure on welfare benefits, with spending on child tax credit being a particular concern; and secondly, to address what was regarded as an unfair and unreasonable aspect of the child tax credit system, namely that recipients were guaranteed a rise in income for every additional child they might choose to have, without limit. … [T]he decision … ensured that the measure would not affect families of average or below-average size.

200. … [T]he objective of protecting the economic well-being of the country is undoubtedly a legitimate aim for the purposes of the Convention. …

201. … Since the legislation is a general measure of social and economic strategy, involving an assessment of priorities in the context of the allocation of limited state resources, it follows that Parliament's assessment that the difference in treatment is justified should be treated by the courts with the greatest respect. …

…

204. … How far the welfare system should go to protect families against the vicissitudes of life is a matter on which opinions in our society differ greatly, and of which Parliament is the best judge. …

205. It is also argued that the legislation is not in the best interests of children living with persons whose entitlement to child tax credit is affected by the limitation. … But Parliament was told that reducing spending on welfare benefits would allow the Government to protect other expenditure of benefit to children: on education, childcare and health. Furthermore, the difficult question is not so much what would be in the best interests of children, but the extent to which it is fair, economically desirable and socially acceptable to impose the cost of supporting children, whose parents lack the means to do so themselves, on other members of society. Parliament must have considered that the impact of the limitation upon the interests of the children who would be affected by it was outweighed by the reasons for introducing it.

206. The assessment of proportionality, therefore, ultimately resolves itself into the question as to whether Parliament made the right judgment. That was at the time, and remains, a question of intense political controversy. It cannot be answered by any process of legal reasoning. There are no legal standards by which a court can decide where the balance should be struck between the interests of children and their parents in receiving support from the state, on the one hand, and the interests of the community as a whole in placing responsibility for the care of children upon their parents, on the other. The answer to such a question can only be determined, in a Parliamentary democracy, through a political process which can take account of the values and views of all sections of society. Democratically elected institutions are in a far better position than the courts to reflect a collective sense of what is fair and affordable, or of where the balance of fairness lies.

[The appeal against the policy was dismissed.]

2. Privatization

Governments worldwide have increasingly sold public assets to private entities and integrated the private sector into the delivery of public services, including healthcare, education, housing, and water.[180] As argued by Julien Mercille and Enda Murphy, in 'What is Privatization? A Political Economy Framework', 49 *Environ. Plan A*

---

[180] See A. Dorfman and A. Harel (eds), *The Cambridge Handbook of Privatization* (2021); C. Cordelli, *The Privatized State* (2020); and P. Alston, Report of the Special Rapporteur on extreme poverty and human rights on privatization, UN Doc. A/73/396 (2018).

(2017) 1040 privatization "restructures economies in fateful directions: ownership of public assets and goods and services provision are transferred away from collective control and into the hands of private interests. This implies not only a reduction of democratic input and accountability in economic practices and institutions but a widening of inequality."[181]

Various Special Rapporteurs have documented the ESR impacts of privatization, as has the ESCR Committee. General Comment No. 24 on ICESCR obligations in the context of business activities outlines the Committee's approach:

2. Obligation to protect

> ...

> 21. ... Privatization is not per se prohibited by the Covenant, even in areas ... where the role of the public sector has traditionally been strong. Private providers should, however, be subject to strict regulations that impose on them so-called "public service obligations":
> ...

> 22. The Committee is particularly concerned that goods and services that are necessary for the enjoyment of basic [ESCR] may become less affordable [when] provided by the private sector, or that quality may be sacrificed for the sake of increasing profits....States thus retain at all times the obligation to regulate private actors to ensure that ... services they provide are accessible to all, are adequate, are regularly assessed ... and are adapted to [the public's] needs ... .

The African Commission on Human and Peoples' Rights, in General Comment 7 (2022) on State obligations with regard to social services, also addressed the issue.

B. General human rights standards applicable to social service provision

> (11) This trend towards commercialization [of public services] undermines the object and purpose of the African Charter, which views social services not as commercial products, but as essential preconditions for the enjoyment of human rights.

> ...

(15) ... States must impose public service obligations to ensure that social services, at minimum, are:

> (a) available to all individuals on an equal basis and without discrimination;

> (b) accessible, even in times of emergency;

> (c) acceptable to the users;

> (d) of the highest attainable quality;

> (e) effectively regulated;

> (f) and subject to democratic public accountability.

C. The State obligation to ensure the provision of public social services

> (31) ... Although States have reasonable discretion when designing their systems for social service provision, there should always be a quality public option. This system should be adequately funded, democratically controlled, and non-commercial in nature.

---

[181] See J. Mercille and E. Murphy, "What is privatization? A political economy framework", 49 *Environment and Planning A: Economy and Space* (2017) 1040.

Domestic courts have also considered the permissibility of privatization. The High Court of Israel, for instance, held that a law establishing a privately operated prison was unconstitutional, reasoning:

> When the state transfers power to manage a prison, with the invasive powers that go with it, to a private profit-making corporation, it violates the human dignity of the inmates of that prison, since the public purposes that give imprisonment legitimacy are undermined and the inmates becomes a means for the private corporation to make profits.[182]

3. Inequality

One of the most troubling phenomena today is the rapid acceleration in inequality. Reports by the World Inequality Lab and Oxfam describe the trajectory. Thomas Piketty looks at the justifications often proffered to defend such vast differences.

Abhijit Banerjee and Esther Duflo, in 'Foreword' to the *World Inequality Report 2022* (at 3), observe that:

> In every large region of the world with the exception of Europe, the share of the bottom 50% in total earnings is less than 15% (less than ten in Latin America, Sub-Saharan Africa and MENA region) while the share of the richest 10% is over 40% and in many of the regions, closer to 60%. ... [E]ven more striking is what is happening to wealth. The share of the bottom 50% of the world in total global wealth is 2% ..., while the share of the top 10% is 76%. Since wealth is a major source of future economic gains, and increasingly, of power and influence, this presages further increases in inequality. Indeed, at the heart of this explosion is the extreme concentration of the economic power in the hands of a very small minority of the super-rich. The wealth of the top 10% globally ... is actually growing slower than the world average, but the top 1% is growing much faster: between 1995 and 2021, the top 1% captured 38% of the global increment in wealth, while the bottom 50% captured a frightening 2%. The share of wealth owned by the global top 0.1% rose from 7% to 11% over that period ... .

In one of its annual reports on inequality, (*Survival of the Richest: How We Must Tax the Super-Rich Now to Fight Inequality* (2023)), Oxfam notes that the world is living through an unprecedented moment of multiple crises involving widespread hunger and energy poverty, climate breakdown, COVID-19, and increasing poverty:

> ... At the same time, these multiple crises all have winners. The very richest have become dramatically richer and corporate profits have hit record highs, driving an explosion of inequality.
>
> • Since 2020, the richest 1% have captured almost two-thirds of all new wealth – nearly twice as much money as the bottom 99% of the world's population.
>
> ...
>
> • Food and energy companies more than doubled their profits in 2022, paying out $257bn to wealthy shareholders, while over 800 million people went to bed hungry.
>
> • Only 4 cents in every dollar of tax revenue comes from wealth taxes, and half the world's billionaires live in countries with no inheritance tax on money they give to their children.
>
> • A tax of up to 5% on the world's multi-millionaires and billionaires could raise $1.7 trillion a year, enough to lift 2 billion people out of poverty, and fund a global plan to end hunger.

Thomas Piketty, in *Capital and Ideology* (2020) 1, argues that:

---

[182] Academic Center of Law and Business v. Minister of Finance, HCJ 2605/05 (19 November 2009).

Every human society must justify its inequalities: unless reasons for them are found, the whole political and social edifice stands in danger of collapse. Every epoch therefore develops a range of contradictory discourses and ideologies for the purpose of legitimizing the inequality that already exists or that people believe should exist. …

In today's societies, these justificatory narratives comprise themes of property, entrepreneurship, and meritocracy: modern inequality is said to be just because it is the result of a freely chosen process in which everyone enjoys equal access to the market and to property and automatically benefits from the wealth accumulated by the wealthiest individuals, who are also the most enterprising, deserving, and useful. …

…

… Nearly everywhere a gaping chasm divides the official meritocratic discourse from the reality of access to education and wealth for society's least favored classes. The discourse of meritocracy and entrepreneurship often seems to serve primarily as a way for the winners in today's economy to justify any level of inequality whatsoever while peremptorily blaming the losers for lacking talent, virtue, and diligence. …

…

From this historical analysis one important conclusion emerges: what made economic development and human progress possible was the struggle for equality and education and not the sanctification of property, stability, or inequality. The hyper-inegalitarian narrative that took hold after 1980 was in part a product of history, most notably the failure of communism. But it was also the fruit of ignorance and of disciplinary division in the academy. The excesses of identity politics and fatalist resignation that plague us today are in large part consequences of that narrative's success. By turning to history from a multidisciplinary perspective, we can construct a more balanced narrative and sketch the outlines of a new participatory socialism for the twenty-first century. By this I mean a new universalistic egalitarian narrative, a new ideology of equality, social ownership, education, and knowledge and power sharing. …[183]

…

4. Fiscal Policy Responses

Schumpeter famously observed that 'nothing shows so clearly the character of a society and of a civilization as does the fiscal policy that its political sector adopts'.[184] And Murphy and Nagel have noted that while '[n]othing could be more mundane than taxes, … they provide a perfect setting for constant moral argument and possible moral progress.'[185] For them, taxation has two primary functions:

> (1) It determines how much of a society's resources will come under the control of government, for expenditure in accordance with some collective decision procedure, and how much will be left to the discretionary control of private individuals, as their personal property … . (2) It plays a central role in determining how the social product is shared out among different individuals, both in the form of private property and in the form of publicly provided benefits.[186]

As Streeck indicated above, mainstream neoliberal policy prescriptions are almost entirely predicated upon reducing taxes to the greatest extent possible. The result is that in many countries, including the United States and the United Kingdom, vibrant debates about the need for radical fiscal reforms proceed with little if any

---

[183] On meritocracy and taxation, see M. Sandel, The Tyranny of Merit: What's Become of the Common Good? (2020).
[184] J. Schumpeter, History of Economic Analysis (1954), at 769.
[185] L. Murphy and T. Nagel, The Myth of Ownership: Taxes and Justice (2002), at 188.
[186] ibid, at 76.

mention of higher tax rates. Yet tax is central to the ability of any government to protect and promote human rights.[187]

Consider the following overview:

ALEX COBHAM, FARIYA MOHIUDDIN AND LIZ NELSON, GLOBAL TAX JUSTICE AND HUMAN RIGHTS
GILLIAN MACNAUGHTON AND DIANE FREY (EDS.), HUMAN RIGHTS AND ECONOMIC INEQUALITIES (2021) 168

I. Introduction

… Estimates of the global revenue losses due to international tax avoidance (and tax evasion) are in the region of $700 billion each year, with lower-income countries bearing disproportionate costs. The ramifications for human rights obligations are both local and international. In equal measure, domestic tax policy and practice, and international approaches and cooperation can be instrumental in supporting national governments to maximize available resources. The prospect that states with available resources will choose to use these to meet their human rights obligations – put simply, through redistribution of income, or by providing a program of publicly funded services – also depends, in a more complex but equally fundamental way, on the role of tax and the social and fiscal policies governments choose to adopt. Tax provides a key point in the relationship between people and their States, and nurtures the accountability of States, which in turn results in long-term improvements in governance and the effectiveness of political representation. In short, tax contributes to the necessary resources to support governments in developing national poverty mitigation strategies and in establishing social protections, public services and infrastructure. …

…

II. Human Rights and the Four Rs of Tax

… State bodies are, indeed, key duty bearers and are required to act to ensure the fulfilment of human rights. Government, as agent of the State, therefore must develop economic policies, including a fiscal environment, to realize these rights. Tax plays a pivotal role in doing this. It provides the means to raise revenue and effect the redistribution of income and wealth and thereby address economic inequalities. …

This section explores … the "four Rs" of tax – revenue, redistribution, repricing and representation … .

A. Revenue

Financial resources enable governments to meet their human rights obligations. Taxes can be both regressive and progressive, but even individually regressive taxes, such as a consumption tax, can play an important role in raising revenue for progressive expenditure. The critical assessment is that of the overall incidence of the tax system and of the associated public expenditure, including benefits and credits, in order to reflect the whole distributional change. Tax justice makes the emphatic case that tax revenue is central to raising required resources for the realization of human rights.

…

B. Redistribution

… Within a tax justice normative framework, redistribution should target unearned income (that which is generated from capital gains, dividends, stocks and shares, and other financial assets such as real estate and land) and inherited wealth. These measures both broaden a country's tax base and reflect the progressive principle of taxing based on the ability to pay. …

…

---

[187] P. Alston and N. Reisch (eds.), *Tax, Inequality, and Human Rights* (2019).

Overall, the potential for progressive redistribution of wealth and income provides a powerful counterpoint to the emergence of fiscal austerity policies where national debt has been compounded by conflict in many countries throughout the world; or where an ideological response has driven regressive cuts to both expenditure and tax, as in the UK and Spain. ...

C. Repricing

There are often social costs to private behavior, and these may not be fully reflected in market prices. For example, ... a failure to tax carbon emissions can lead to societies bearing the costs of companies' production decisions. Behaviors that are associated with social or public harms or benefits can be addressed using tax as a tool to reprice market goods and services where the private and social costs or returns diverge. In other words, a progressive tax regime can intercede on behalf of public interest. ...

...

D. Representation

While often overlooked, the channel linking taxation and political representation is critical in ensuring that States are able financially to meet their obligations, including through funding public services and curtailing economic and social inequalities, and that there is sufficiently strong and broad public accountability so that inequalities of influence too can be overcome (to ensure, for example, that economic elites do not prevent effective, progressive taxation).

...

... A state operating an effective taxation system upon which it relies for most of its relatively high public expenditure is likely, over time, to become or remain responsive to its people – raising tax morale and compliance, and further supporting the quality of representation and effectiveness of spending. ... [A] State with persistently low tax-funding of its expenditures is likely to see lower levels of public spending, and deteriorating quality of governance and political representation – ultimately undermining its own legitimacy to tax.

...

The Impact of Tax Avoidance and Evasion on ESR

Each State Party to the ICESCR is required to use 'the maximum of its available resources' to meet its obligations. We have seen that the stumbling block in some of the discussions about these rights is the claim that states simply do not have the necessary resources. Yet the relevant resources can only result from appropriate fiscal policies, including the rates of taxation; how tax liabilities are structured and on whom or what they are imposed; and how much effort will be made to collect taxes due and to close loopholes or other arrangements that enable certain groups to avoid taxation. Tax 'evasion' involves a violation of the law, whereas tax 'avoidance' is legal. But the latter might rely on laws that are patently unfair and even designed to let certain groups off the hook.

Tax policies raise complex and multi-dimensional issues, but they cannot be avoided if the idea of State responsibilities for the realization of ESR are to be taken seriously. While most of the materials in this section focus on the situation in developed countries, it is important to note that the same dynamics often apply in relation to countries in the Global South. Other relevant factors in the Global South tax context include states' inability to tax multinational corporations on their operations, widespread corruption, and failures to prevent tax evasion or to address tax avoidance. The following materials are no more than snapshots of existing arrangements designed to provide a basis for discussions.

Vanessa Ogle provides historical background to the unevenness of global tax policies in 'Archipelago Capitalism: Tax Havens, Offshore Money, and the State, 1950s-1970s', 122 *Am. Hist. Rev.* 122 (2017) 1431:

> ... Tax codes as they applied to Europeans and other non-natives in colonies were extremely varied, laced with exemptions, and often simply hard to enforce. Tax rates were much lower in colonies ... .

… [W]hen Europeans retreated from the colonial world abroad in the 1950s and 1960s, some returnees sought to prolong the favorable tax arrangements that had come with empire. In comparison, the high tax rates now intended to finance the welfare state at home seemed excessive. But the former colonies were no longer set up to securely serve in their former capacity as tax shelters. … "[R]eturnees from empire," British merchant banks soon discovered, could be a lucrative source of tax haven business. Malta and Jersey began offering tailored solutions to such clientele. Similarly, to French observers at the time, it was clear that Monaco's fortunes as a burgeoning tax haven from the late 1950s on had to do with French returnees, especially from Indochina, Algeria, Tangier, and Morocco. Decolonization and the end of empires created something of a money panic and a clientele eager to move assets out of the colonial world to havens that would shelter them from [taxation]. …

Such demand for more and better tax havens had to be met by both governments and an army of avoidance assistants. Between 1945 and 1970, some of the most important new or improved tax havens and offshore markets were set up, and older ones expanded, with government involvement from London and Washington, D.C. Even where governments were not directly involved, they at least tolerated these developments. …

Money laundering is one factor which can erode a country's tax base, as described by Jack Blum, Charles Davidson, and Ben Judah in 'Offshore, National Security and Britain's Role', 11 *Tax Justice Focus* (2020), at 2:

Some estimates put the share of the UK's GDP derived from money laundering as high as 15%. London is both one of the critical nodes of the world financial system and a gateway to the offshore world: with countless financial and legal service providers ready to shuttle their clients' wealth to secrecy jurisdictions under British sovereignty like the British Virgin Islands or the Cayman Islands which have become hubs of illegal activity. All this has helped London become a favoured location for oligarchs, whose needs and wants have become a staple of the professional services sector.

Even where no illegal activity is involved, 'tax shifting', as identified by Katarzyna Anna Bilicka, in 'Comparing UK Tax Returns of Foreign Multinationals to Matched Domestic Firms', 109 *Am. Econ. Rev.* (2019) 2921, remains a problem:

… [F]oreign multinational subsidiaries shift a large proportion of their taxable profits out of the United Kingdom. Specifically, the baseline propensity score estimates suggest that foreign multinational subsidiaries underreport their taxable profits by about 50 percent relative to domestic standalones. …

…

… [P]otential revenue gains from equalizing the tax payments of foreign multinational subsidiaries and domestic standalones would vary from £3 billion at the beginning of the sample to £25 billion in 2014. Relative to the total UK corporate tax revenue, which was £30 billion in 2000 and £40 billion in 2014, this would imply that a full elimination of the differences in the reported taxable profits between domestic standalones and foreign multinational subsidiaries would lead to revenue gains of 10 percent in 2000 and 62 percent in 2014, absent behavioral changes.

Since 2015, banks and other financial intermediaries have been required to report on foreign financial assets and accounts under the U.S. Foreign Account Tax Compliance Act. On the basis of this data, Niels Johannesen et al., in 'The Offshore World According to FATCA: New Evidence on the Foreign Wealth of U.S. Households', (*NBER Working Paper* 31055, 9 March 2023) at 3, conclude that:

… [A]round 1.5 million U.S. taxpayers held foreign financial accounts with aggregate assets of around $4 trillion in tax year 2018. By comparison, the total financial assets of U.S. households totaled roughly $80 trillion according to official financial accounts. Around half of the assets in foreign accounts, just below $2 trillion, were held in jurisdictions usually considered tax havens, such as Switzerland, Luxembourg and the Cayman Islands. Just 14% of accounts are located in tax havens compared to nearly half the total wealth, which reflects that accounts in havens were on average larger.

Tax havens are central to many of the challenges in this area. The Tax Justice Network has ranked countries in its *Corporate Tax Haven Index - 2021 Results* on the basis of their complicity 'in helping multinational corporations underpay corporate income tax'. Beside each country in the list below is its 'Haven Score' which measures the scope for corporate tax abuse allowed by its tax and financial systems, and its 'Share', reflecting the percentage of the world's corporate tax abuse for which TJN calculates it is responsible:

> 1. British Virgin Islands (100; 6.4%); 2. Cayman Islands (100; 6.0%); 3. Bermuda (100; 5.7%); 4. Netherlands (80; 5.5%); 5. Switzerland (89; 5.1%); 6. Luxembourg (74; 4.1%); 7. Hong Kong (78; 4.1%); 8. Jersey (100; 3.9%); 9. Singapore (85; 3.9%); 10. United Arab Emirates (98; 3.8%); 11. Ireland (77; 3.3%); 12. Bahamas (100; 3.3%); 13. United Kingdom (69; 3.1%); ... 18. France (67; 2.1%); 19. China (63; 2.0%); ... 25. USA (47; 1.2%).

The same network, in its *State of Tax Justice 2022* report, estimates that:

> ... [A]t least 1 of every 4 tax dollars lost to multinational corporations using tax havens can be prevented by publishing government-collected transparency data that has been held from the public since at least 2016 ... [d]ue to the OECD's failure to publish aggregated country by country reporting data ... .

A path breaking study by Annette Alstadsæter, Niels Johannesen, and Gabriel Zucman, 'Who Owns the Wealth in Tax Havens? Macro Evidence and Implications for Global Inequality', 162 *J. Pub. Econ.* (2018) 89, estimated total offshore wealth kept in tax havens to be about 10 percent of world GDP, or $5.6 trillion in 2007. Almost half was in Switzerland. They also estimated the ratio of offshore wealth to GDP by country. It ranged from a very small amount in Scandinavia, to as much as 60 percent in Russia, the Gulf states, and Latin America. About 80 percent of those funds belonged to the top 0.1 percent of households.

Finally, Thomas Tørsløv et al., 'The Missing Profits of Nations', 90 *Rev. Econ. Stud.* (2023) 1499 underscores the impact of profit-shifting by multinational corporations on average tax rates:

> One of the most striking development [sic] in global tax policy since the 1980s has been the decline in corporate income tax rates. Between 1985 and 2018, the global average statutory corporate tax rate fell by about half, from 49% to 24%. One reason for this decline is international tax competition. By cutting their tax rates, countries can attract profits and capital from abroad.
>
> ...
>
> 36% of multinational profits—defined as profits made by multinationals outside of the country where their parent is located—were shifted to tax havens globally in 2015. We establish that US multinationals shift comparatively more profits: in 2015, US firms shifted more than half of their multinational profits, as opposed to about a quarter for other multinationals.

Even when multinational corporations are taxed by the states in which they are headquartered, they can often take advantage of 'business-friendly' policies to shrink their taxable income. These policies include allowable deductions of many kinds, some inserted in tax codes precisely to benefit particular categories of taxpayers. In the United States, for example, hedge fund managers have various options for ensuring that they pay perhaps 40 percent less than otherwise applicable tax rates. Major technology companies have historically paid very low tax rates: Amazon, for example, according to Just Taxes Blog (7 February 2022):

... reported a record $35 billion in U.S. pretax income for fiscal year 2021 ... . [With a federal tax bill of $2.1 billion, its] effective federal income tax rate of 6 percent means it avoided about $5.2 billion of federal income tax in 2021. If Amazon had paid the statutory 21 percent tax rate … without any tax breaks, that would have meant a tax bill of more than $7.3 billion.

The Role of International Law

The picture that emerges from the preceding materials is that there are many ways in which fiscal policies could be reformed that would result in a much higher tax yield for governments, thereby providing additional resources that could, in principle, be spent to enhance the realization of ESR.[188] The final remaining issue is what role international law plays and could play in this regard.

Lorena Bachmaier Winter and Donato Vozza, in 'Corruption, Tax Evasion, and the Distortion of Justice: Global Challenges and International Responses', 85 *Law & Contemp. Prob.* (2022) 75, contrast the extensive work that has been done to reign in some forms of corruption with the longstanding reticence to tackle tax fraud:

> Despite the common harms that countries face from corruption and from fraudulent tax practices, a notable gap exists in international legal responses to these two related but distinct global crimes. Although characterized by weaknesses or ineffectiveness, anti-corruption strategies are governed and advanced through a multilevel approach. Indeed, international conventions provide a common legal framework on anticorruption for state parties. In contrast, there is no international legal instrument to counter serious tax evasion and tax avoidance behaviors from a criminal law perspective, apart from some pieces of legislation adopted within the European Union. Given that national responses to tax evasion are marked by differences that enable tax dodging and hinder international cooperation, the absence of binding international legal responses to tax crime can precipitate serious distortions of justice and warrants further attention.

Arthur Cockfield, in 'Secrets of the Panama Papers: How Tax Havens Exacerbate Income Inequality', 13 *Colum. J. Tax L.* (2021) 45, considers possible policy reforms that might inhibit tax haven abuses. One is to create 'a cross-border withholding tax on global investments [which] could assist tax authorities in enforcing their tax laws'. A second is to establish a 'global financial registry' which would make it easier for governments to identify the ultimate (or beneficial) human owners of cross-border investments, which are often very carefully hidden. Governments would thus be better able to determine 'if their resident firms had paid tax on worldwide income'. A third option is for governments to eliminate 'onshore' laws that offer tax-haven-like benefits via domestic law. These are common in many countries, including the United States.

Cockfield also suggests some more technical fixes, including:

> the need for whistleblower protections for any individual who provides information leading to tax and financial crime prosecutions; the need to embed lawyers within tax authority audit teams to ensure proper evidence is provided to prosecutors; the need for prosecutorial incentives to pursue significant penalties against "white collar" criminals who have often attracted lenient sentences; better information sharing among government agencies when each agency sees only one part of the overall criminal financial scheme; and bureaucratic incentives to retain police, tax officials, and prosecutors in the long run, so they can gain a necessary understanding of the complexities.

> Many of these proposals necessarily implicate financial privacy. For instance, a greater sharing of information among government agencies may violate existing prohibitions against such sharing … under the view they unduly inhibit privacy interests. These privacy interests in turn must necessarily be protected within a free and democratic society for reasons that include the need to protect freedom of expression and freedom to engage in political dissent. Moreover, in an age of big data, government use of opaque

---

[188] See EU Tax Observatory, Global Tax Evasion Report 2024.

algorithms to scrutinize taxpayers, and increasing data collection, taxpayer privacy rights arguably need stronger protection.

Nevertheless, … from a distributional justice perspective, the granting of strong privacy protections to corporations or offshore bank accounts protects the interests of wealthy individuals and criminals at the expense of ordinary citizens who cannot take advantage of the benefits offered by the offshore world. In other words, the current system of strong financial privacy protection harms the public interest and contributes to income inequality.

A long-running debate concerns whether international tax reforms are best negotiated within the universal framework of the United Nations or in the 'rich countries' club', the Organisation for Economic Co-operation and Development (OECD). Tove Maria Ryding, in 'Proposal for a United Nations Convention on Tax', *Eurodad* (March 2022), argues that many developing countries have been unable to participate in that forum and that there has been a serious lack of transparency. Progress has been very slow, although in 2021 there was agreement in principal on a global minimum tax of 15 percent applicable to multinational enterprise groups with a global turnover of at least €750 million. As of mid-2023, this has yet to be implemented.

Finally, in December 2022, the UN General Assembly adopted Resolution 77/244. This records an agreement to begin intergovernmental discussions within the UN 'on ways to strengthen the inclusiveness and effectiveness of international tax cooperation through the evaluation of additional options, including the possibility of developing an international tax cooperation framework or instrument that is developed and agreed upon through a United Nations intergovernmental process, taking into full consideration existing international and multilateral arrangements'.[189]

QUESTIONS

1. Why is it important to consider the political economy of rights in general and ESR in particular, and what are the main risks of such a focus?

2. Compare the ESCR Committee's approach to privatization with the approaches of the African Commission and the High Court of Israel. Are 'public service obligations' sufficient to mitigate the risks posed by privatization?

3. How should human rights and tax justice respond to strong resistance by conservatives to more effective tax policies? Consider the situation in the United States, for example. In December 2018, *ProPublica* reported that people claiming the earned income credit in their U.S. tax returns, most of whom earn under $20,000 a year, were more likely to be audited by the Internal Revenue Service than those earning $400,000. This is consistent with a zero-tolerance approach to possible welfare fraud, and a much more lenient approach to tax fraud by high earners. Between 2010 and 2018, research by the Center on Budget and Policy Priorities[190] showed that IRS enforcement funding, adjusted for inflation, was cut by 24 percent, although the number of tax returns grew by 9 percent; operations staff were reduced by 31 percent; there were 51 percent fewer audits of corporations with more than $1 billion in assets; and the audit rate for filers earning over $1 million decreased by 61 percent. In April 2021, the IRS Commissioner told Congress that the 'tax gap', or the difference between taxes owed and taxes paid, averaged $441 billion per year, mostly as a result of evasion by the wealthy and large corporations. In 2022, Congress greatly increased future funding for the IRS, but in June 2023 the Republican Party only agreed to extend the national debt ceiling on condition that one quarter of that increase was rescinded. The nonpartisan Congressional Budget Office reported that the $21.4 billion in cuts to the IRS would result in $40.4 billion in lost revenue.

---

[189] See UN Doc. A/78/235 (2023).
[190] https://www.cbpp.org/research/federal-tax/depletion-of-irs-enforcement-is-undermining-the-tax-code.

Chapter 5. National Security, Terrorism and International Humanitarian Law

The relationship between national security and human rights is a long and troubled one. This chapter explores the subject through the prism of twenty-first century counter-terrorism law and practice. International organizations and courts have developed considerable experience over many decades in dealing with situations involving terrorism, armed conflict, and states of emergency. A rich body of legal rules and principles has developed in response to the interests and strategic goals of the various actors.

The materials raise important considerations about the distribution of interpretative and regulatory authority in times of public emergency. They also demonstrate the sweeping changes brought by the counterterrorism regime implemented after the terrorist attacks of 11 September 2001. Recurring questions include whether the proper balance is being struck between security and rights, and which rules and which institutions are best equipped to strike that balance. Some have argued that the challenge is not to achieve a balance but to manage co-dependency.

The attacks on 11 September 2001 constituted a turning point in the relationships between international law, global institutions and terrorism. It was one of the deadliest days in American history, totaling more deaths — nearly 3,000 — than the attack on Pearl Harbor and rivalling, if not exceeding, the number of Americans killed on D-Day. Nineteen members of Al Qaeda hijacked four commercial jets, two of which crashed into the 110-story twin towers of the World Trade Center, one into the Pentagon and one in a field in Pennsylvania. Almost two hours passed between the first collision and the collapse of the second World Trade Center tower, with the loss of life and panic televised around the world as the events unfolded. The near simultaneous attacks exposed major vulnerabilities in the security system of the world's superpower. Al Qaeda cells had resided within US territory. They had converted commercial transportation into catastrophic weapons. Their members' willingness to embrace suicide represented a unique strategic threat, one less susceptible to traditional modes of deterrence. With the demonstrated willingness of Al Qaeda to massacre thousands of people, intelligence agencies in the United States and elsewhere began considering with special intensity the prospect of a terrorist organization acquiring and employing weapons of mass destruction.

International institutions responded in a swift and extraordinary manner. In a resolution passed on 12 September, the UN Security Council determined that the attacks constituted a 'threat to international peace and security' and recognized the 'inherent right of individual or collective self-defence in accordance with the Charter' (Res. 1368). Accordingly, the resolution implicitly recognized that the acts of 11 September constituted an 'armed attack' under Article 51 of the UN Charter. Although the United States and other countries had experienced and responded to terrorist attacks with force in the past, the Council had never before issued such a finding. Also unprecedented, both the North Atlantic Treaty Organization and the Organization of American States formally considered 11 September an 'armed attack' and invoked the collective self-defence provisions of their respective treaties.

9/11 represented a turning point in the strategic approach of the United States to terrorism. After invading Afghanistan in 2001, the United States spent $2.313 trillion on the war through 2022.[191] This was one part of the Bush Administration's 'Global War on Terrorism' which posited that the United States was in a global 'armed conflict', of unlimited potential scope and duration, with Al Qaeda and its affiliates. This strategic posture entailed the adoption of a 'war model' in dealing with terrorism in contrast with an exclusively 'criminal law model'. A war model employs the instruments of warfare such as armed interventions, armed forces and military violence. A criminal law model employs the instruments of law enforcement, policing and prosecutions.

Choosing to adopt a war model may have a greater effect on political discourse and psychological frames than on rights and obligations under international human rights law. As will be discussed below, international human rights law adjusts state obligations regardless of whether a public emergency is designated a war or another type of threat to public order and national security. The nature of the threat — its gravity and probability — is the critical variable. That said, domestic legal questions, such as constitutional presidential powers, may turn on the classification of a situation as a war or something else. We also consider the implications of the fact that the

---

[191] Watson Institute, Brown University, *Cost of War* (2022), cited by President Biden in August 2021.

existence of an armed conflict triggers the application of international humanitarian law (IHL), which is also known as the law of armed conflict (LOAC).

A. TERRORISM: DEFINITIONS AND INSTITUTIONAL RESPONSES

At the international level, states have shown limited willingness to find a generally, if not universally, acceptable definition of terrorism. Two separate elements have contributed to this reluctance. The first is encapsulated in the adage that 'one person's terrorist is another person's freedom fighter'. While competent lawyers should be capable of classifying specific acts as illicit under any circumstance and without regard to the motivation of fighting forces, at different points in history various states have employed legal craft to create exceptions for their favoured political groups or ideological struggles. The second is that the absence of an agreed definition leaves states to craft their own approaches and to adapt counter-terrorism laws to serve more subjective purposes.

In the second half of the twentieth century, and in the absence of a strong political consensus, states interested in outlawing terrorism through international treaties had to make do with codifying the definition and prohibition of specific acts — such as hostage taking and seizure of civilian aircraft. The UN began this piecemeal approach with the adoption of the 1963 Tokyo Convention on Offences and Certain Other Acts Committed on Board Aircraft. Eight conventions of a similar character were adopted in the 1970s and 1980s, and two more before 1999. As early as 1996, India proposed a draft international convention on the suppression of terrorism. Considerable progress was made by 2002, but since then continuing negotiations in a Working Group of the Sixth Committee of the General Assembly have yielded little.

During this period, efforts at reaching a general definition of terrorism and a categorical outlawing of the practice were stymied by divergent political interests. Some argued that any definition and accompanying regulatory regime ought to recognize the legitimacy of armed struggle by national liberation groups, such as the Palestine Liberation Organization and the African National Congress, and groups resisting colonial domination. In contrast, others argued that no definition of terrorism would be acceptable if it implied that attacks on civilians could be excused in the case of armed resistance or insurgencies waged for particular purposes. Another political impasse involved the regulation of 'state terrorism'. That is, some proposed definitions of terrorism faced stiff opposition because they focused on actions by non-state actors and failed to address violence that governments employed against civilians. Finally, a nagging legal question was whether crimes against humanity — a widespread or systematic attack against a civilian population — already covered significant acts of terrorism.

Steps towards defining terrorism include the International Convention for the Suppression of the Financing of Terrorism, agreed to by the UN General Assembly in December 1999. It contains the first general definition of terrorism in an international treaty:

> Any other act intended to cause death or serious bodily injury to a civilian, or to any other person not taking an active part in the hostilities in a situation of armed conflict, when the purpose of such act, by its nature or context, is to intimidate a population, or to compel a Government or an international organization to do or to abstain from doing any act.

By mid-2001, only four states had ratified the Convention – far short of the 22 required for the treaty to enter into force. In the days following the attacks on 11 September, the Security Council called on states to join the Convention 'as soon as possible'. Within five years, 155 states had done so, and by 2024 there were 190 parties.

Another significant step towards achieving a universal definition was spurred by the Security Council. In August 2004, the government of Russia introduced Resolution 1566 on terrorism. The previous month, Russia had experienced one of the worst hostage crises in its history. A Chechnyan armed group seized a Russian school in the town of Beslan, and the standoff ended in the deaths of over 300 civilians, most of them children. The resolution was intended, in part, to expand the work of a Security Council committee beyond its existing focus on Al Qaeda and the Taliban. The Council broke new ground with a unanimously adopted resolution that effectively provided a general definition of terrorism:

> The Security Council ... acting under Chapter VII ... [r]ecalls that criminal acts, including against civilians, committed with the intent to cause death or serious bodily injury, or taking of hostages, with the purpose to provoke a state of terror in the general public or in a group of persons or particular persons, intimidate a population or compel a government or an international organization to do or to abstain from doing any act, and all other acts which constitute offences within the scope of and as defined in the international conventions and protocols relating to terrorism, are under no circumstances justifiable by considerations of a political, philosophical, ideological, racial, ethnic, religious or other similar nature ... .

These developments, however, did not resolve the legal ambiguities and political controversy surrounding a definition. Upon ratifying the Terrorism Financing Convention, three states (Egypt, Jordan and Syria) submitted a reservation to the definition of terrorism. Jordan's reservation, for example, stated that its government 'does not consider acts of national armed struggle and fighting foreign occupation in the exercise of people's right to self-determination as terrorist acts within the context of paragraph 1(b) of Article 2 of the Convention.' Two dozen states formally objected to the reservation. Most of them contended that the reservation was incompatible with the object and purpose of the treaty. None of the objections were made by an Islamic or African country. Similar cleavages emerged with respect to Security Council Resolution 1566.

In 2006, Martin Scheinin, the first Special Rapporteur on counter-terrorism proposed that:

> 'Terrorist offences' should be confined to instances where the following three conditions cumulatively meet: (a) acts committed with the intention of causing death or serious bodily injury, or the taking of hostages; (b) for the purpose of provoking a state of terror, intimidating a population, or compelling a Government or international organization to do or abstain from doing any act; and (c) constituting offences within the scope of and as defined in the international conventions and protocols relating to terrorism. Similarly, any criminalization of conduct in support of terrorist offences should be restricted to conduct in support of offences having all these characteristics (UN Doc E/CN.4/2006/98, para. 72).

It has been argued that a 'one-size fits all' approach is unworkable and should be replaced by 'a multi-definitional approach to the concept of terrorism in legal terms, with the definition used being determined by the powers exercisable in respect of it. This would work as a sliding scale: the more intrusive, repressive and oppressive the powers the narrower the definition.'[192] Another scholar has proposed distinguishing two different classes of 'especially violent' criminal activities. The first is core terrorism, involving 'actions which undermine civilians' essential rights (... such as life, physical integrity, freedom, and dignity)', which has an organizational dimension, and an intent to spread terror among the population. The second is subversion and relates to widely but not universally condemned acts which are pursued for political ends.[193] For its part, the UN continues to address terrorism per se, but has also added other phenomena such as 'racially and ethnically motivated violent extremism'.[194]

But most commentators have been strongly critical of the absence of an agreed definition.

BEN SAUL, THE LEGAL BLACK HOLE IN UNITED NATIONS COUNTERTERRORISM INTERNATIONAL PEACE INSTITUTE, GLOBAL OBSERVATORY, 2 JUNE 2021[195]

It is remarkable that two decades of extensive global counterterrorism law and cooperation have proceeded from a normative black hole: the absence of a common definition of terrorism. Security Council Resolution 1373 and successive resolutions have deliberately omitted any definition, despite requiring states to take far-reaching legislative and executive action.

---

[192] A. Greene, 'Defining Terrorism: One Size Fits All?', 66 *Int. Comp. Law Q.* (2017) 411.

[193] M. Di Filippo, 'The definition(s) of Terrorism in International Law', in R. Kolb, G. Gaggioli and P. Kilibarda (eds.), *Research Handbook on Human Rights and Humanitarian Law: Further Reflections and Perspectives* (2022) 2, at 15.

[194] For a UN overview of its activities, see UN Doc. A/77/718 (2023).

[195] See also B. Saul, *Defining Terrorism in International Law* (2008).

... [T]he Council's approach was tactically brilliant. ... [Any precise definition] would have been unlikely to reflect or attract an international consensus, triggering serious compliance problems in national implementation.

... Legal definition was instead devolved to states in national implementation. ... [They] were generally content to retain their sovereign discretion to identify and legislate for themselves the meaning of terrorism.

Much valuable and principled counterterrorism law and cooperation has occurred based on the Council's suite of resolutions, despite the lack of a definition. The failure to define terrorism continues, however, to seriously impede the effectiveness of counterterrorism, its consistency with human rights law and international humanitarian law, and the legitimacy and legality of the Council's exercise of its international security powers under the United Nations Charter.
...
[F]rom a practical standpoint, the inevitable divergence between national definitions impairs inter-state cooperation to "bring to justice" terrorists ... ...

... In the absence of an agreed international definition, one state is not required to criminalize the same "terrorist" conduct as another state by asserting extraterritorial quasi-"universal" jurisdiction over it. Instead, different domestic counterterrorism laws sail by like ships passing in the night. The legal differences are also fertile ground for political tensions ... .

... [D]ivergent national definitions equally impair cooperation across the spectrum [in matters such as] the duty on states to themselves refrain from supporting terrorism and to counter terrorist financing, prevent terrorism and support for it, prevent the movement of terrorists, address abuse of refugee status, and prevent and suppress the travel of "foreign terrorist fighters." ...

... ... [I]t is difficult for [states] to know whether there is any minimum or core "soft" concept of terrorism ... . This matters ... [because they] are subject to continuing international monitoring by the Counter-Terrorism Committee Executive Directorate (CTED) and the Financial Action Task Force (FATF) whose listing of high-risk jurisdictions can bring economic costs. ...

Stung by human rights criticisms, the Council belatedly offered a non-binding definition of terrorism in Resolution 1566. That definition has been welcomed on human rights grounds because it is so narrow. ...

The advantages of that definition include that it links terrorism to the existing convention offenses, which are widely agreed upon ... . The addition of the personal violence and specific intent elements in Resolution 1566 also reduces the overbreadth of some convention offenses ... . Many of the conventions also capture not only "public" (that is, political, religious, or ideological) violence but also "private" violence, which may be more like ordinary crime than terrorism.

The obvious defect in this definition is that it would exclude many acts commonly regarded as "terrorism." In part this is because the resolution covers only harm to people, not other targets of terrorism such as property, resources, infrastructure or utilities, communications, financial systems, the environment, or endangerment of public health and safety in general.

More pressingly, it is too narrow because it confines terrorism to the scope of the existing convention offenses. ... Many are also limited to transnational not domestic terrorism, yet the Council also requires action on the latter.

These limitations are precisely why many states have enacted more general definitions of terrorism ... .

... Resolution 1566 has not appreciably influenced national practice, and there is little evidence that the Council or CTED has sought to influence states to restrain or amend their definitions according to it. CTED's Technical Guidance (2020) to states encourages enactment of the counterterrorism convention offenses, and acknowledges simply that other definitions of terrorism should comply with human rights law. However, the opaque nature of CTED assessments—most of the time, they are not publicly released—makes it difficult to know what precisely CTED expects of national definitions in practice.

Conclusion …

… How can the Council – credibly, and with a straight face – designate all "terrorism" as a threat to international peace and security, and require legal measures to be taken against it, without explaining what it is? How is all domestic (as opposed to transnational) terrorism a threat to international security, when its effects by definition are contained entirely within a single state? It may be acceptable to identify a general category of threat, but it can hardly be a valid exercise of Charter power if that threat comprises a black hole. The Council may be an expert in politics and security, but law requires certainty and precision – or it is not law at all, just politics and arbitrariness disguised as law.

The Role of the UN Security Council

The United States mobilized the Security Council immediately after 9/11 and the Council has since been instrumental in promoting a global counter-terrorism agenda which has received enthusiastic backing from countries such as China, India, Russia, and Saudi Arabia. Council action has pursued two main tracks. The first is a 'legislative' one, which has combined measures binding upon states, pursuant to Chapter VII of the UN Charter, with a highly productive practice of supplementing those measures through soft law processes.

The second track has involved the adoption of an expansive counter-terrorism sanctions regime.[196] This has also given rise to the so-called global Magnitsky sanctions considered in Chapter 12 below. Gavin Sullivan provides an in-depth analysis of the terrorism sanctions system in *The Law of the List: UN Counterterrorism Sanctions and the Politics of Global Security Law* (2020). He characterizes the processes by which the UN produces lists of sanctioned individuals as 'a "structure making site" for identifying, calculating and stabilising "global terrorism" as a novel field of intervention by the Security Council, whilst avoiding the critical problem of having to actually define in law what terrorism is.' The procedure 'transforms complex, diffuse and localised threats into a simplified, optically consistent and commensurable set of individual list entries that can be readily manipulated by the Council and implemented with worldwide effect.'

The following Security Council documents provide an overview of the principal policies that states have been urged or required to adopt.

SECURITY COUNCIL RESOLUTION 2462
(2019)

…

Acting under Chapter VII of the Charter of the United Nations,

1. *Reaffirms* its resolution 1373 (2001) and in particular its decisions that all States shall prevent and suppress the financing of terrorist acts and refrain from providing any form of support, active or passive, to entities or persons involved in terrorist acts, including by suppressing recruitment of members of terrorist groups and eliminating the supply of weapons to terrorists;

2. *Emphasizes* its decision in resolution 1373 that all Member States shall criminalize the wilful provision or collection, by any means, directly or indirectly, of funds by their nationals or in their territories with the intention that the funds should be used, or in the knowledge that they are to be used, in order to carry out terrorist acts; and its decision in resolution 2178 [2014] that all Member States shall establish serious criminal offenses regarding the travel, recruitment, and financing of foreign terrorist fighters;

…

---

[196] See Chapter 12, below; A. Lang, 'Alternatives to Adjudication in International Law: A Case Study of the Ombudsperson to the ISIL and Al-Qaida Sanctions Regime of the UN Security Council', 117 Am. J. Int'l L. (2023); and D. Hovell, *The Power of Process: The Value of Due Process in Security Council Sanctions Decision-Making* (2016).

4. *Strongly urges* all States to implement the comprehensive international standards embodied in the revised FATF Recommendations on Combating Money Laundering, and the Financing of Terrorism and Proliferation and its interpretive notes;

5. *Decides* that all States shall, in a manner consistent with their obligations under international law, including international humanitarian law, international human rights law and international refugee law, ensure that their domestic laws and regulations establish serious criminal offenses sufficient to provide the ability to prosecute and to penalize in a manner duly reflecting the seriousness of the offense the wilful provision or collection of funds [etc.] … .

6. *Demands* that Member States ensure that all measures taken to counter terrorism, including measures taken to counter the financing of terrorism as provided for in this resolution, comply with their obligations under international law, including international humanitarian law, international human rights law and international refugee law;

…

13. *Calls on* States to invest resources in the implementation of sanctions regimes pursuant to resolutions …;

14. *Urges* all States to assess specifically their terrorist financing risk and to identify economic sectors most vulnerable to terrorist financing, including but not limited to non-financial services, such as, inter alia, the construction, commodities and pharmaceutical sectors, in line with FATF standards and *welcomes* guidance issued by the United Nations, including the "UNODC Guidance manual for Member States on terrorist financing risk assessments" and the FATF in that regard;

…

18. *Encourages* Member States to build the capacity of their financial oversight and regulatory systems in order to deny terrorists the space to exploit, raise and move funds, including by ensuring an effective implementation of reporting and disclosure requirements by the private sector as well as by taking into account the dedicated country assessments of relevant entities such as the Counter-Terrorism Committee Executive Directorate (CTED) and the FATF and its Global Network;

…

22. *Encourages* competent national authorities, in particular financial intelligence units and intelligence services, to continue to establish effective partnerships with the private sector …;

23. *Recognizes* the vital role played by non-profit organizations in national economies and social systems, *calls on* Member States to periodically conduct a risk assessment of its non-profit sector or update existing ones to determine the organizations vulnerable to terrorist financing and to inform the implementation of a risk based approach, *encourages* Member States to work cooperatively with the non-profit sector in order to prevent abuse of such organizations including front organizations by and for terrorists, while recalling that States must respect human rights and fundamental freedoms and *recalls* the relevant recommendations and existing guidance documents of the FATF in that regard, in particular its recommendation 8;

…

35. *Requests* CTED, in accordance with resolution 2395, to strengthen its assessment process relating to countering the financing of terrorism, including through targeted and focused follow-up visits as complements to its comprehensive assessments …;

…

37. *Requests* CTED and the Analytical Support and Sanctions Monitoring Team to prepare, ahead of the joint special meeting, a report on actions taken by Member States to disrupt terrorist financing and in this regard, and *invites* Member States to submit to them in writing, by the end of 2019, information on actions taken to disrupt terrorist financing;

…

STATEMENT BY THE PRESIDENT OF THE SECURITY COUNCIL
UN DOC. S/PRST/2022/7, 15 DECEMBER 2022

[Note: Presidential Statements are regularly adopted by the Security Council. Although they are not binding, because they are not adopted under Chapter VII of the Charter, they are heavily negotiated and reflect a strong degree of consensus.]

The Security Council reaffirms that terrorism in all forms and manifestations constitutes one of the most serious threats to international peace and security and that any acts of terrorism are criminal and unjustifiable regardless of their motivations, whenever, wherever and by whomsoever committed, and remains determined to contribute further to enhancing the effectiveness of the overall effort to fight this scourge on a global level.

The Security Council condemns in the strongest terms terrorism in all its forms and manifestations, and all terrorist acts, including those on the basis of xenophobia, racism and other forms of intolerance, or in the name of religion or belief, and further reaffirms that terrorism should not be associated with any religion, nationality, civilization, or group.

The Security Council strongly condemns attacks by terrorist groups or individuals on civilians, critical infrastructure and soft targets, including transnational and cross-border attacks, and demands the immediate cessation of such attacks, and calls on all Member States to summon the requisite political will to denounce all acts of terrorism.

The Security Council expresses its deep concerns as terrorist groups continue to make efforts to destabilize governments.
...
The Security Council underlines that acts of terrorism can seriously impair the enjoyment of human rights and threaten the social and economic development of all States and undermine global stability and prosperity and emphasizes that the threat of terrorism is continuing, affecting an increasing number of Member States across most regions, which may exacerbate conflicts in affected regions, and contributes to undermining affected States, specifically their security, stability, governance, social and economic development.

The Security Council further reaffirms that Member States must ensure that any measures taken to counter terrorism comply with all their obligations under international law, in particular, the UN Charter, international human rights law, international refugee law and international humanitarian law, underscores that effective counterterrorism measures and respect for human rights, fundamental freedoms and the rule of law are complementary and mutually reinforcing ... .

The Security Council underscores the importance of a whole of government and whole of society approaches, recognizes the importance of cooperation with all relevant stakeholders, such as civil society, including community-based civil society, grassroots organizations, the private sector, academia, think tanks, media, youth, women, and cultural, educational, and religious leaders in increasing awareness about the threats of terrorism and violent extremism conducive to terrorism and effectively tackling them, and in this regard urges Member States to continue efforts to ensure the full, equal and meaningful participation and leadership of women and inclusion of youth in all counter-terrorism and violent extremism conducive to terrorism approaches and strategies.

The Security Council notes with concern that terrorist groups craft distorted narratives that are based on the misinterpretation and misrepresentation of religion to justify violence, and that terrorist groups further seek to use names or religion or religious symbols, in order to manipulate followers and for propaganda or recruitment purposes.

The Security Council, in this regard, recognizes the importance of conducting outreach to entities with expertise and experience in crafting counter-narratives and promoting tolerance and coexistence, including religious actors, to counter terrorist propaganda and narratives.
...
The Security Council calls upon all Member States to implement the comprehensive international standards of the Financial Action Task Force (FATF) on Combating Money Laundering and the Financing of Terrorism and Proliferation ... .

The Security Council reiterates the obligation of Member States to prevent the movement of terrorists or terrorist groups by, inter alia, effective border controls, and, in this context, urges Member States to exchange information expeditiously, improve cooperation among competent authorities to prevent the movement of terrorists and terrorist groups to and from their territories, the supply of weapons for terrorists and financing that would support terrorists and terrorist groups, and underlines that safe havens provided to terrorists continue to be a significant concern and urges Member States to cooperate fully in the fight against terrorism, especially with those States where or against whose citizens terrorist acts are committed, in order to find, deny safe haven to, and bring to justice, extradite or prosecute, in accordance with applicable international law, any person who supports, facilitates, participates or attempts to participate in the financing, planning, preparation or commission of terrorist acts or provides safe havens.

The Security Council reaffirms its resolution 2664 (2022) and urges Member States, when designing and applying measures to counter the financing of terrorism, to take into account the potential effect of those measures on exclusively humanitarian activities, including medical activities, that are carried out by impartial humanitarian actors in a manner consistent with international humanitarian law.

…

The Security Council underlines the need to address the conditions conducive to the spread of terrorism, as outlined in Pillar I of the United Nations Global Counter Terrorism Strategy and recognizes that a comprehensive approach to defeating terrorism requires national, regional, subregional and multilateral action.

The Security Council notes with concern the increased use of the Internet, and other information and communications technologies, including social media, virtual assets and new financial instruments for terrorist purposes, and the increasing global misuse of unmanned aerial systems (UAS) by terrorists … .

…

The Security Council expresses deep concern that the threat of terrorism, in all its forms and manifestations, has increased and become more diffuse, in various regions of the world, aided by the use of new and emerging technologies for terrorist purposes, while recognizing that innovations in technology may also offer significant opportunities to use technology to counter terrorism and in this regard welcomes the adoption of Delhi Declaration on Countering the Use of New and Emerging Technologies for Terrorist Purposes by the Counter Terrorism Committee (CTC), and calls on CTC to consider developing, with the support of CTED, within a reasonable period, a set of non-binding guiding principles, as provided in the Declaration.

The Security Council recognizes the need for adequate funding for programs, technical assistance, and capacity building provided by the entities the UN Counterterrorism Global Compact, including the Office of Counter Terrorism (UNOCT) for counter terrorism to effectively support counterterrorism efforts of Member-States, especially developing ones, and encourages Member States to contribute voluntary funding in this regard.

FIONNUALA NÍ AOLÁIN, 'SOFT LAW', INFORMAL LAWMAKING AND 'NEW INSTITUTIONS' IN THE GLOBAL COUNTER-TERRORISM ARCHITECTURE
32 EUR. J. INT'L L. (2021) 919

…

2 The Sources, Status and Process of Making Soft Law

…

The concept of 'soft' law is viewed by some legal scholars as controversial. … First is the instinct that the very expression 'soft' law may appear to be an oxymoron … . The second relates to long-standing disputes over agreed definitions of the term …, most particularly that 'soft' can relate to the comparison between written versus unwritten norms, [to] the status of the norm or … to [its] normative content … . The most uncontroversial definition of soft law is that it constitutes those international norms, principles and procedures that are outside the formal sources of international law enumerated in Article 38 of the [ICJ] Statute and that lack the requisite degree of normative content to create enforceable rights and obligations but are still able to produce certain legal effects. …

'Soft' law comes in multiple forms. It can include General Assembly resolutions, declarations, guidelines, technical manuals, opinions from quasi-judicial bodies … . … [It] is produced and driven by states through a variety of mechanisms including in bilateral, multilateral and institutional settings. Increasingly, non-state actors produce, shape, contribute to and drive the enforcement and recognition of 'soft' law. …

Recognition and validation for the legal effects of 'soft' law has been increasing over many decades ... [although the] ICJ's approach has been restrained ... .

... [In the regional human rights courts] soft-law standards have played an important role in expounding and augmenting the applicable treaty standards. Soft law ... functions as a 'gap-filler' in the absence of treaty agreement or customary international law consolidation. Soft law gives guidance to states and other stakeholders in the absence of specifically formulated norms, providing useful and necessary legal frames to state action and cooperation. A key aspect of soft law is the interaction between hard and soft-law standards to shape the substance of obligations. In particular, a number of soft-law norms develop and augment binding standards and authoritatively interpret them. ... [Soft law's advantages] include access by a variety of stakeholders, informality in process as well as in negotiation, innovative modalities of engagement and analysis and a variety of pathways to produce legal norms in new and challenging global contexts.

3 From General to Specific: Soft Law's Deepening Role in Counter-terrorism

A key feature of the post-9/11 legal landscape has been the proliferation of multi-level terrorism-related regulation. This is enabled by an augmented UN internal architecture, complimented by the creation of external specialized entities responding to perceived counter-terrorism regulatory gaps and by augmented capacity at regional and national levels. A noticeable element of that legal terrain is a shift from a primary focus on treaty agreements to other forms of law-making and norm enforcement by states. ...

After 9/11, ... Security Council resolutions have developed a distinct and problematic 'legislative' character engaging in regulatory action across a range of substantive areas including sanctions, foreign fighters, regulation of travel between states, organized crime, biometrics, data collection and data sharing. Normative developments were fast-tracked ..., leading towards multilateral institutionalization, specifically the creation and reinvigoration of subsidiary organs, including ... special Committees (e.g. the Counter Terrorism Committee, CTC) and the procedurally circumscribed Office of the Ombudsperson which constitute unprecedented institutional innovations. The creation of the UN Counter-Terrorism Committee Executive Directorate (CTED) and the CTC provided new fora and entities (an inter-institutional machinery) whose production of a variety of 'soft' instruments, including standards, compendiums, sanction instructions, technical information and guidance, proceeded apace. These norms range from formal legal and capacity-building engagements, to highly informal advice, and lots in between. Central to the normative landscape has been counter-terrorism soft law.

... [There are] some unique features to counter-terrorism soft-law production. These include, first, the scale of norm proliferation ... . It is bolstered by the normative outputs of a plethora of new counter-terrorism entities at global and regional levels, including, but not limited to, the Global Counter-Terrorism Forum (GCTF) and the Financial Action Task Force (FATF). ...

Second, the nomenclature of 'soft' law appears to understate the extent to which many of these normative guidelines, declarations, 'good practices' and technical rules function as distinctly hard in counter-terrorism practice. ... [D]elegations [take] extreme care in the negotiation of provisions, exactly as if they were negotiating treaty provisions. ...

Third, ... the institutional landscape for counter-terrorism is quite unique. As a primarily coercive regulator of behaviour, counter-terrorism soft law has a repressive quality distinct from other soft-law arenas. Thus, ... states have reporting requirements to the UN Counter-Terrorism Committee, which de facto operates to leverage a portion of these norms into domestic law and oversee their practical implementation. The CTED functions as the supervision entity with an array of capacities including country visits, technical assistance in the form of 'deep dives' on national practice and assessments to enable its oversight role. Many counter-terrorism soft-law norms come with capacity building, technical expertise and support on a scale not found in other legal domains, precisely because there is a powerful UN architecture to aid their direct implementation.

...

... Terrorism resolutions are quickly followed by a rush to produce guidance, technical advice, manuals, principles and addendums for states by OCT, the Global Compact, CTED and the GCTF. ... [O]ne observes cross-fertilization, cross-referencing, message duplication and recurrent invocations of the same rules, formulated in processes that are non-transparent and non-accessible to all states, in order to present as regular conduct practices that would previously have been considered an overt challenge to state sovereignty. In almost all of these arenas, human rights are visibly side-lined ... .

...

* * *

An illustration of the impact of these international initiatives is provided by the case of Australia. Keiran Hardy and George Williams observe in 'Two Decades of Australian Counterterrorism Laws', 46 *Melb. U. L. Rev.* (2022) 34, that Australia adopted 92 counter-terrorism laws, amounting to 5,559 pages of legislation, between 2001 and 2021. Between 2002 and 2007 alone, the conservative government enacted 48 laws, averaging more than one every seven weeks:

> These include laws providing for broad preparatory offences, enhanced surveillance powers, preventative detention, warrantless access to metadata, enforceable decryption, citizenship stripping, continuing detention and many more. ... The laws have often been pushed through Parliament on tight timelines, with little time for scrutiny and debate. Once ... on the statute books, they are very rarely amended or removed. The story of these laws is one of state power continually expanding, and rarely, if ever, contracting.

> In the second decade, the main catalyst for new laws was the threat from IS and foreign fighters. However, legal responses to that threat went much further. Intelligence disclosure offences signalled a crackdown on whistleblowers, a trend confirmed by police raids on journalists and media outlets, and multiple investigations into government insiders and their lawyers. The metadata and encryption laws have a much wider scope again in affecting every Australian who uses a smartphone or the internet. Extensive lawmaking has continued since in response to threats of espionage, foreign interference, and right-wing extremism, and shows no sign of abating. ...

> The number and scope of Australia's counterterrorism laws has been heavily influenced by the politics of being 'tough on terrorism'. Even where laws have clear and recognised problems, the pressure for bipartisanship means that they can pass through Parliament with minimal scrutiny. ...

> Without enforceable protection for human rights [Australia lacks a federal Bill of Rights], there is little that courts can do to limit the scope or impact of these laws. ...

Selected Issues

The Security Council has adopted dozens of lengthy, detailed, and highly demanding resolutions and statements on counter-terrorism since 2001. The two preceding texts serve to identify many of the principal areas of action. The texts warrant careful reading and analysis. In order to assist that process, we outline below some of the human rights concerns that have been highlighted, including by successive UN Special Rapporteurs on human rights and counter-terrorism (Martin Scheinin (2005-11), Ben Emmerson (2011-17), Fionnuala Ní Aoláin (2017-23), and Ben Saul (2023-).

(a) The role of human rights

In the early years after 9/11, proponents struggled to ensure that reference was made to human rights in the resolutions, strategies, and policies adopted. But in recent years, there is almost always a clear statement affirming the importance of human rights. However, commentators have suggested that these are often tokenistic, lacking in detail, and without follow up.

Consider this assessment by Kim Lane Scheppele and Arianna Vedaschi, in *9/11 and the Rise of Global Anti-Terrorism Law: How the UN Security Council Rules the World* (2021) 245:

> The Security Council has required states to monitor terrorist finances and to halt transfers of money to and from named parties as soon as they appear on Security Council terrorism watch lists. But it never guaranteed basic due process protections for those who

appeared on these lists. The Security Council has required states to act affirmatively to prevent terrorist plots from hatching on their territory and therefore to increase the surveillance of and ability to gather information from domestic populations. But it never provided any protection for the right to data privacy. The Security Council has required states to share information with other states, encouraging the security services of states around the world to work with each other, regardless of whether these security services had reputations for working under the rule of law or its opposite. But it never set minimum human rights standards for security services. And the Security Council has required states to monitor the system of transnational travel, refugee claims, and asylum applications to make sure that terrorists are not moving around under cover of human rights protections. But it has never acknowledged that important rights are at stake – rights of travel, association, and asylum, to say nothing of general personal liberty. The concentration on the effective tracking and interception of terrorists has taken priority over any obligation to observe basic rights.

A similar perspective is provided by Fionnuala Ní Aoláin, in 'Human Rights Advocacy and the Institutionalization of U.S. "Counterterrorism" Policies Since 9/11', *Just Security*, 9 September 2021:

> [The result of post 9/11 counterterrorism policies] has been the stifling of human rights, the choking of civil society, and the weakening of the rule of law on every continent. It is not by accident that counterterrorism regulation has expanded and deepened across the globe in the past 20 years, with tranches of national legalization efforts which are broad, imprecise, and highly opaque on what precisely constitutes terrorism. In this vein, defending women's rights has been defined as terrorism, arguing for the protection of the environment is terrorism, pro-democracy movements are terrorists, humanitarian protection supports terrorists, and civil society actors are engaged in terrorism when they call their governments to account.

(b) Incitement

The Preamble to Security Council Res. 1624 (2005) condemns 'the incitement of terrorist acts' and repudiates 'attempts at the justification or glorification (*apologie*) of terrorist acts that may incite further terrorist acts'. Helen Duffy and Larissa van den Herik, in 'Terrorism and the Security Council', in Robin Geiß and Nils Melzer (eds.), *The Oxford Handbook on the International Law of Global Security* (2021) 193 observe that this resolution 'has triggered a plethora of regional standards, national laws, and prosecutorial practices directed against myriad forms of expression deemed to constitute direct or "indirect" incitement.' They note, for example, that the EU Directive on Combating Terrorism (2017/541) covers 'anyone who "makes available" in any way (re-posting, lending, distributing) a message or images which might prove "dangerous"':

> Under the shadow of [Security Council mandates], some States have incorporated new forms of 'indirect incitement' into hastily passed legislation, while others have subjected pre-existing laws to expansive interpretations. The result is a broad spectrum of offences, and prosecutions, based on diverse forms of 'dangerous' expression, such as encouragement, glorification, justification, apology, possession, dissemination or making available prohibited information or materials, or professing to be a member of or associated with prohibited organisations.

(c) Crafting counter-narratives

Because terrorist groups are seen to popularize distorted narratives 'based on misinterpretation and misrepresentation of religion', the Council regularly calls upon states to generate 'counter-narratives'. Consider the assessment (UN Doc. A/HRC/43/46 (2020)) by Special Rapporteur Ní Aoláin:

> … [D]espite recent research indicating that it remains an unproven assumption that messages, myths, promises, objectives, glamour and other enticements propagated through violent extremism can be replaced with, or dismantled by, an alternative set of communications, many national and international measures to prevent and counter violent extremism are focused on counter-narratives. … [T]here is no robust data showing that that approach works, absent a meaningful commitment to and the delivery of transformed material conditions on the ground. Without that, counter-narratives are

little more than exaggerations and are perceptively recognized as such by their target communities. ... [The UN's approach] may be counterproductive, given that it can both appear as a defence of the status quo and contribute to a loss of trust in civil society and in government, in particular where opacity with regard to the genuine nature of the countering voices is tolerated. ... [The resulting focus on] content regulation ... is directly translated in multiple national contexts into broad, indiscriminate and overreaching limitations on freedom of expression.

(d) The role of religion

While the Security Council insisted in 2022 that 'terrorism should not be associated with any religion', Special Rapporteur Ní Aoláin (UN Doc. A/HRC/43/46 (2020)) provides a different perspective:

> ... [Many counter-terrorism] programmes and policies have discriminately targeted certain groups and communities, particularly based on religious grounds ... . The widespread references [to groups such as] ISIL, Al-Qaida and Boko Haram ... have gone a long way towards colouring the debate ... ... In certain countries, the agenda ... is focused exclusively on violent Islamist extremism, obscuring other forms of extremism and leading to stigmatization and polarization. [This] ... focus ... belittles the severity of the danger posed by other groups. ...
>
> ...
>
> ... [C]omplex factors [contribute to and dovetail] with what is viewed as religious violence, including the loss of trust in public institutions caused by endemic corruption and cronyism, policies of exclusion, as well as impunity, trivialization and legal impunity. [The Special Rapporteur] affirms the broader analysis concerning the known factors conducive to terrorism and extremism and encourages States to use the resources they have to address deficits in governance, the rule of law and corruption ... .

(e) Gender

The gendered dimensions of terrorism and counter-terrorism have long been recognized. In many cases, however, the approach suggested has called for more attention to be given to women as potential leaders and executors of terrorism, or as victims of terrorism in need of protection.[197] Special Rapporteur Scheinin pushed back against such narratives in a 2009 report (UN Doc. A/64/211) that examined the complex relationships between gender equality and countering terrorism. He emphasized that 'gender is not synonymous with women, but rather it encompasses the social constructions that underlie how women's and men's roles, functions and responsibilities, including in relation to sexual orientation and gender identity, are defined and understood.'[198] His report drew strong resistance from some states.

Aleksandra Dier and Gretchen Baldwin, in *Masculinities and Violent Extremism* (2022) vii argue that gender mainstreaming efforts have failed to critically examine the structural gendered and racialized hierarchies, inequalities, and assumptions implicit in much counterterrorism analysis:

> Violent extremist and terrorist groups across the ideological spectrum exploit masculinities in their efforts to recruit and retain members. For example, many so-called "Islamist" violent extremists use a sense of victimization by the state, expectations around masculine roles, pushback against changing gender roles, and idealization of warrior masculinities to drive recruitment, retention, and broader strategic decisions. This may involve constructing masculinities based on violence and the subjugation of women or the protection of the Islamic community from outside "villains."
>
> ... Extreme right-wing discourse has traditionally focused on the gendering of spaces and hierarchical boundaries based on assumptions about masculinity and femininity. Right-wing extremists have also increasingly promoted hypermasculine violence as a way to

---

[197] For example, M. Sutten, *The Rising Importance of Women in Terrorism and the Need to Reform Counterterrorism Strategy* (2009).
[198] See M. Satterthwaite and J. Huckerby (eds.), *Gender, National Security, and Counter-Terrorism: Human Rights Perspectives* (2013).

defend against perceived outside threats, including immigrants and the feminist, lesbian, gay, bisexual, transgender, and queer (LGBTQ+), and racial justice movements. Some right-wing extremists even position themselves as "enlightened" on women's rights compared to their view of Islam while simultaneously relegating women to traditional, conservative gender roles. ...

...

... [C]ounterterrorism actors often view Muslim masculinity as violent, misogynistic, and homophobic, in contrast with a benevolent, tolerant, and protective Western masculinity. Such narratives affect their decision making, impacting policy priorities, approaches, and resource allocation. This can lead counterterrorism actors to prioritize highly securitized and militarized policies that further radicalize communities and undermine human rights. The masculinities produced by state actors can also feed into and mutually reinforce those produced by violent extremists.

(f) 'Whole-of-society'

The Council regularly calls for the adoption of 'whole of society' approaches to counter-terrorism. Compare the response of Special Rapporteur Ní Aoláin (UN Doc. A/HRC/43/46 (2020)):

> Many practices ... involve targeting particular people, communities and groups, giving rise to ... profiling, ... compounding structural discrimination and exclusion, [and] surveillance and harassment. ... [Of particular concern is] the so-called "whole of society" approach, in which responsibilities to detect "signs of radicalization" fall upon various actors in society, including teachers, social workers, medical staff and other health-care professionals, prison staff, neighbours and family members, community leaders and members of faith-based groups. ... [T]he securitization of care professions ... [impinges] on the unique ethical obligations of professionals in those fields to those they serve. [It creates] an environment in which the threat of violent extremism is ubiquitous and pervasive ... . [T]hose measures break the fragile trust that individuals and communities place in those professionals ... . Such policies lead to overselection and overreporting, largely on prohibited discriminatory grounds, having an impact on the rights to freedom of religion and expression and privacy. Furthermore, the lack of transparency about the use of the information generated and its often underregulated sharing across government entities lends credence to a perception that preventing and countering violent extremism is yet another tool of a State intelligence entity's counter-terrorism efforts, rather than a genuine effort at building resistance to the threat of violent extremism.

(g) Non-profit organizations ('NPOs')

Counter-terrorism policies now focus heavily on the need to ensure that NPOs are not used as, in the Security Council's words, 'front organizations by and for terrorists'. The lead role on this has been taken by the Financial Action Task Force (FATF), a stand-alone group of 37 states, whose extensive influence is magnified by the Council's consistent invocation of its work. The FATF states that its 'recommendations are recognised as the global anti-money laundering (AML) and counter-terrorist financing (CFT) standard'. It defines an NPO as: 'a legal person or arrangement or organisation that primarily engages in raising or disbursing funds for purposes such as charitable, religious, cultural, educational, social or fraternal purposes, or for the carrying out of other types of "good works"' (FATF, Terrorist Financing Risk Assessment Guidance (2019) 43). But many governments have used the pretext of seeking to implement such standards to crack down on their opponents within civil society. The Venice Commission (Opinion No. 1028/2021 of 18 June 2021), in reviewing Turkish legislation designed to implement FATF standards, noted that 'the obligatory auditing of [122,000] NGOs raises serious doubts about the authorities stated [counter-terrorism] objective ... . Under the pretext of conducting a "risk assessment", the measures introduced are overly far-reaching and will have a chilling effect on any NGO ... .'

(h) New technologies[199]

The Council's 2022 Presidential Statement, promoted during India's Council presidency, 'welcomes the adoption of [sic] Delhi Declaration on Countering the Use of New and Emerging Technologies for Terrorist Purposes … and calls on CTC [the Counter Terrorism Committee] to consider developing … a set of non-binding guiding principles, as provided in the Declaration'. Paragraph 32 of the Delhi Declaration envisages that such principles would assist states 'to counter the threat posed by the use of new and emerging technologies for terrorist purposes, including by compiling good practices on the opportunities offered by the same set of technologies to counter the threat, consistent with international human rights and international humanitarian law'.

Consider this report on the Delhi meeting provided by Tomaso Falchetta and Anna Oosterlinck, in 'UN Counterterrorism and Technology: What Role for Human Rights in Security?', *Just Security*, 23 November 2022:

> … The focus of the debate in most of the panels was on the real and perceived threats of abuses of ICT by terrorists; human rights got short shrift, as did even legitimate questions about the credibility of evidence cited for the alleged terrorist abuses.
>
> …
>
> … [The topic of] abuse of ICT and emerging technologies by terrorists … could be interpreted to cover a vast range of measures — anything from content moderation to social media monitoring, from limiting the use of encryption to resorting to hacking for surveillance – all in the name of countering terrorism. It essentially encourages governments to introduce counterterrorism measures with a view to addressing abuses of ICT that will likely end up undermining human rights, particularly the right to privacy and the right to freedom of expression.
>
> … Privacy International expressed its concerns at the expansion of new technologies employed for the surveillance of public spaces, whether online or offline, in the name of countering terrorism. It noted that social media monitoring is often justified as a form of content moderation for counterterrorism purposes, but that it is also abused to surveil peaceful assemblies and profile people's social conduct. Privacy International also noted how attempts by governments to access encrypted communications to identify potential terrorist threats risk introducing vulnerabilities into the systems; the result could be indiscriminate surveillance of digital communications, compromising the privacy and security of potentially all users of digital communication services.
>
> [Another NGO,] ARTICLE 19 … [noted that]: 1) security without rights is meaningless …; and 2) international human rights law dictates that the same rights apply online as offline. States can only restrict free speech on the basis of national security if the principles of legality, legitimacy, proportionality, and necessity have all been met. …
>
> Unsurprisingly, given that the text was negotiated by the 15 CTC member States behind closed doors and well ahead of the meeting in India, the Delhi Declaration does not seek to address these or other concerns raised by civil society organizations and human rights experts.

(i) Border controls

In its 2022 Presidential Statement, the 'Security Council reiterates the obligation of Member States to prevent the movement of terrorists or terrorist groups by, inter alia, effective border controls'. But there are now many accounts of the discriminatory and deeply problematic ways in which counter-terrorism-driven border controls are being used.[200] E. Tendayi Achiume, UN Special Rapporteur on racism, has documented (UN Doc. A/75/590 (2020)) how:

---

[199] For a comprehensive overview by the Special Rapporteur, see UN Doc. A/HRC/52/39 (2023).

[200] See P. Molnar, Technological Testing Grounds: Migration Management Experiments and Reflections from the Ground Up (2020); European Commission and Deloitte, Opportunities and Challenges for the Use of Artificial Intelligence in Border Control, Migration and Security (2020); and A. Shachar, *The Shifting Border: Legal Cartographies of Migration and Mobility* (2020).

Governments and United Nations agencies are developing and using emerging digital technologies in ways that are uniquely experimental, dangerous and discriminatory in the border and immigration enforcement context. By so doing, they are subjecting refugees, migrants, stateless persons and others to human rights violations, and extracting large quantities of data from them on exploitative terms that strip these groups of fundamental human agency and dignity.

… [D]igital technologies are being deployed to advance the xenophobic and racially discriminatory ideologies that have become so prevalent, in part due to widespread perceptions of refugees and migrants as per se threats to national security. In other cases, discrimination and exclusion occur in the absence of explicit animus, but as a result of the pursuit of bureaucratic and humanitarian efficiency without the necessary human rights safeguards. … [V]ast economic profits associated with border securitization and digitization are a significant part of the problem.[201]

And Niku Jafarnia, in 'The United Nations Security Council's Counterterrorism Resolutions and the Resulting Violations of the Refugee Convention and Broader International Law', 35 *Harv. Hum. Rts J* (2022) 255, describes the impact on the law relating to refugees:

… [The Security Council's] counterterrorism resolutions contravene the Refugee Convention [and other human rights protections]. The Refugee Convention [already has] built-in exceptions … [that] work to strike a balance between states needing to protect themselves and the need to grant protection to those fleeing persecution. …

…

… Beyond the possible violations of international law that the UNSC resolutions have prompted, the practical impacts of the resolutions cannot be ignored. First and foremost, the resolutions have resulted in EU counterterrorism policies that have barred large swaths of legitimate refugees from the Middle East from pursuing asylum in Europe. Because of the resolutions' over-expansive definitions of terrorism, entire groups of individuals may be deemed terrorists, and therefore will be barred from protection that they should be given by law. Under the material support provisions and the lack of exception made for humanitarian assistance, the resolutions also have impacts on the ability of NGOs to provide vulnerable communities and areas with humanitarian aid. …
[202]

Finally, consider the US Supreme Court's review of what was widely termed President Trump's 'Muslim ban'. In *Trump v. Hawaii* (138 S. Ct. 2392 (2018)) several states challenged a Presidential Proclamation (No. 9645 of September 24, 2017) that restricted entry into the United States of nationals of eight states (Chad, Iran, Libya, North Korea, Somalia, Syria, Venezuela, and Yemen) whose systems for managing and sharing information about their nationals was deemed inadequate. The list was said to have been the result of in-depth scrutiny by the Department of Homeland Security. The underlying Congressional legislation authorizes the President to suspend the entry of any aliens whose entry he deems 'would be detrimental to the interests of the United States.'

Chief Justice Roberts wrote the opinion for the 5-4 majority:

… [P]laintiffs' request for a searching inquiry into the persuasiveness of the President's justifications is inconsistent with the broad statutory text and the deference traditionally accorded the President in this sphere. …

…

---

[201] See generally E. T. Achiume, 'Racial Borders', 110 *Georgetown L. J.* (2022) 445.

[202] See also S. Graber, 'Teaching Terrorists: How United States Counterterrorism Law Violates International Humanitarian Law', 48 Yale. J. Int'l L. (2023) 153.

... [P]laintiffs allege that the primary purpose of the Proclamation was religious animus and that the President's stated concerns about vetting protocols and national security were but pretexts for discriminating against Muslims.

At the heart of plaintiffs' case is a series of statements by the President and his advisers casting doubt on the official objective of the Proclamation. ... [While running for office], the President published a "Statement on Preventing Muslim Immigration" that called for a "total and complete shutdown of Muslims entering the United States ... ." Then-candidate Trump also stated that "Islam hates us" and asserted that the United States was "having problems with Muslims coming into the country." ...

... [As President, he] retweeted links to three anti-Muslim propaganda videos. ...

... [T]he issue before us is not whether to denounce the statements. It is instead the significance of those statements in reviewing a Presidential directive, neutral on its face, addressing a matter within the core of executive responsibility. In doing so, we must consider not only the statements of a particular President, but also the authority of the Presidency itself.

... The Proclamation . . . is facially neutral toward religion. Plaintiffs therefore ask the Court to probe the sincerity of the stated justifications for the policy by reference to extrinsic statements—many of which were made before the President took the oath of office. ...

... Any rule of constitutional law that would inhibit the flexibility of the President to respond to changing world conditions should be adopted only with the greatest caution, and our inquiry into matters of entry and national security is highly constrained. ...

It cannot be said that it is impossible to "discern a relationship to legitimate state interests" or that the policy is "inexplicable by anything but animus." Indeed, the dissent can only attempt to argue otherwise by refusing to apply anything resembling rational basis review. But because there is persuasive evidence that the entry suspension has a legitimate grounding in national security concerns, quite apart from any religious hostility, we must accept that independent justification.

... The text says nothing about religion. ...

[The Court concluded that] the Government has set forth a sufficient national security justification to survive rational basis review.

Justice Sotomayor, joined by Justice Ginsburg, dissented.

... The Court's decision today fails to safeguard that fundamental principle [of religious liberty]. It leaves undisturbed a policy first advertised openly and unequivocally as a "total and complete shutdown of Muslims entering the United States" because the policy now masquerades behind a facade of national-security concerns. But this repackaging does little to cleanse Presidential Proclamation No. 9645 of the appearance of discrimination that the President's words have created. ...

...

... [T]he Court, without explanation or precedential support, limits its review of the Proclamation to rational-basis scrutiny. That approach is perplexing, given that in other Establishment Clause cases, including those involving claims of religious animus or discrimination, this Court has applied a more stringent standard of review. . . . But even under rational-basis review, the Proclamation must fall. [It] is "'divorced from any factual context from which we could discern a relationship to legitimate state interests,' and 'its sheer breadth [is] so discontinuous with the reasons offered for it'" that the policy is "'inexplicable by anything but animus.'"

QUESTIONS

1. "'[T]errorist" is a word that cleanses nuance: It suggests that there are good and bad people, and the bad ones are irredeemable enough to warrant a fixed label.'[203] If you agree with this observation, what might the consequences be in terms of applicable legal regimes?

2. Does the 'scourge of terrorism' constitute such a grave threat to international peace and security that the upending of many previously accepted norms is justified?

3. Although the Special Rapporteur on counter-terrorism, and various UN treaty bodies have regularly been highly critical of the policies pursued by states and by the UN in this area, their comments are often dismissed on the grounds that they are merely opinions and are not binding. Compare this assessment by José Alvarez:

A panoply of UN experts and assorted others — from human rights treaty bodies to the special rapporteur on torture — now routinely make ever more specific legal pronouncements — about such things as the propriety or consequences of "invalid" treaty reservations, specific interrogation techniques, or states' reliance on diplomatic assurances when engaging in the foreign rendition of suspects. While our Executive contests many of these pronouncements, even the 100 plus lawyers of the U.S. State Department are no match for the sheer quantity and variety of this institutionalized output, which, as amplified by the voice of organizations like Human Rights Watch, may achieve a legitimacy greater than the views of any single nation, including our own.[204]

4. In the view of Special Rapporteur Ní Aoláin, '[t]he conditions that give rise to sustained violence in many societies … include climate change, grinding inequality, unresolved questions of self-determination, meaningful political participation and adequate representation in fragile, complex and disputed sovereignties. None of these issues have been adequately addressed by a counter-terrorism framework, whether sequentially or intersectionally' (A/77/345 (2022) para. 30). Discuss.

5. The use of soft law is proliferating in many areas of international law. Emily Crawford, in *Non-Binding Norms in International Humanitarian Law* (2021) 254, argues that because of the importance attached to soft law norms, they need to possess a degree of legitimacy, which in turn requires 'that there is some accountability, transparency, and a lack of bias'. She adds that this 'may mean more transparency during the drafting process (such as more systematic engagement with civil society and States); more assiduous attempts to ensure broad geographical representation among participants; more extensive State consultations before and during the drafting process; more open communication regarding participants and drafting procedures; and perhaps even ongoing efforts to revise and update documents in light of State and non-State practice.' Are such 'remedies' likely to work in the counter-terrorism field? If not, what does this say about the legitimacy of the relevant processes?

6. Security concerns have led governments to justify the widespread use of new technologies using biometric data and artificial intelligence. Are UN counter-terrorism mechanisms the best placed to take the lead on regulating these uses?

---

[203] O. El Akkad, Review of V. V. Ganeshananthan, *Brotherless Night (2022), New York Times*, 1 Jan. 2023.
[204] J. E. Alvarez, 'The Internationalization of U.S. Law', 47 *Colum. J. Transnat'l L.* (2009) 537.

B. THE LEGAL FRAMEWORK

In response to terrorism or other threats to 'the life of the nation', such as armed conflict, natural disasters, or climate change-driven upheavals, governments have several options in terms of the legal framework under which they will shape their response. The first is to respond on the basis of standard constitutional and administrative law powers, including use of police powers and the criminal law. This also includes the right to impose limitations upon the enjoyment of certain rights, in line with international human rights law. The second is to declare a state of emergency (sometimes formulated as a state of exception, or state of siege) and, in effect, to suspend the enjoyment of certain rights, through derogation from the relevant obligations. The third is to treat the situation as one involving an armed conflict, whether internal or international, and thus make use of IHL.

1. Emergencies and Derogation

International law permits states to limit or suspend part of their legal obligations, and thus restrict some rights, under certain circumstances. To that end, the legal recourse available to states includes limitation clauses (discussed in the context of civil and political rights in Chapter 3, and economic, social and cultural rights in Chapter 4) and derogations systems codified in various treaties or available through norms of customary international law.

Limitation and derogation clauses in treaties have a similar function in the sense that both provide legal avenues for states to avoid obligations that would ordinarily constrain their actions. They are also similar in that neither permits states to ignore their human rights obligations altogether. However, one significant difference between the two is that derogations were designed to be applicable only in the exceptional case of a grave threat to the survival and security of a nation. The implication is that derogations were intended to be invoked as temporary measures. In contrast, limitation clauses apply across the spectrum, from everyday public order maintenance and policing strategies, to national security and large-scale military actions.

Limitation clauses are commonplace in human rights instruments. The Universal Declaration of Human Rights (UDHR), as discussed in Chapter 3, contains a general limitation clause in Article 29. The general limitation clause in Article 4 of the International Covenant on Economic, Social and Cultural Rights (ICESCR) permits state parties to subject the rights contained in the Covenant 'only to such limitations as are determined by law only in so far as this may be compatible with the nature of these rights and solely for the purpose of promoting the general welfare.' The International Covenant on Civil and Political Rights (ICCPR), by contrast, does not contain a general limitation clause. Instead, limitation clauses are included in various rights provisions such as those pertaining to freedom of association (Art. 22), freedom of movement (Art. 12), expulsion of foreign nationals (Art. 13) and access of the press and public to criminal trials (Art. 14). Several provisions in the ICCPR, such as those prohibiting torture (Art. 7) and slavery (Art. 8), are subject to no limitation.

Article 4 of the ICCPR codifies the rules for states to derogate from obligations during a state of emergency. Specific conditions are attached to a state's exercise of this option. For example, governmental measures must generally be prescribed and determined by law, shown to be necessary and designed to protect particular public interests. These conditions are designed to strike a balance between security and human rights, but they also do more than just balance. Some of the rules, for example, preclude any relaxation of obligations with respect to core rights. The prohibition on genocide is a prime example. The categorical prohibition on genocidal acts is subject to no qualification. In addition to balancing competing interests, the rules are also designed to ensure that governments do not restrict rights that have no rational or reasoned connection to meeting national concerns during a time of emergency.[205]

The following readings examine the derogation system in contrast with the protections (and limitations) that ordinarily apply.

---

[205] See generally C. Douzinas, *States of Exception: Human Rights, Biopolitics, Utopia* (2023); G. Agamben, *State of Exception* (2007); and D. Dyzenhaus, 'States of Emergency', in M. Rosenfeld, and A. Sajó (eds), *The Oxford Handbook of Comparative Constitutional Law* (2012) 442.

JOAN FITZPATRICK, HUMAN RIGHTS IN CRISIS:
THE INTERNATIONAL SYSTEM FOR PROTECTING RIGHTS DURING STATES OF EMERGENCY
(1994)

Approaching [the law on derogations] chronologically, the first legally significant standard is Article 3 common to the four Geneva Conventions of 1949, also known as "Common Article 3." Applicable during periods of internal armed conflict, a frequent setting for the invocation of emergency powers in the past several decades, Common Article 3 prescribes a set of minimal protections that must be afforded even under these dire circumstances. The guarantees of Common Article 3 are further elaborated in Articles 4 to 6 of Protocol II [to the Geneva Conventions, adopted in 1977], particularly with respect to non-derogable fair trial standards. Indeed, the entire body of international humanitarian law, both customary and codified, is highly relevant to protection of human rights during states of emergency, especially in defining non-derogable rights. International humanitarian law by nature is designed to apply in full force during the subset of emergencies involving armed conflict, so in a sense it is all emergency law. And because situations of armed conflict tend to be among the direst of emergencies, protections available then should logically be available in any other emergency context.

Two crucial sets of treaty standards were also drafted at approximately the same time as Common Article 3. Article 15 of the European Convention was drafted primarily during early 1950 with the benefit of almost three years of discussion by drafters of the Covenant on Civil and Political Rights within the United Nations. The derogation article of the European Convention served as a focal point for the debate between two alternate approaches to treaty drafting, which might be called "general enumeration" and "precise definition." The proponents of general enumeration favored drafting a document with positive definitions of rights and no exceptions or restrictions other than a single general limitations clause, similar to Article 29 of the Universal Declaration. The proponents of precise definition, on the other hand, wanted not only specific limitations clauses in many provisions defining particular rights but also a derogation article for emergencies, arguing that these clauses would actually prevent abusive suspension or denial of rights. During the final stages of the drafting process, the attraction of entrenching a list of non-derogable rights swayed a majority to favor inclusion of the derogation article.

... Article 4 [of the ICCPR] became the focus of the division of opinion between the general-enumeration and precise-definition camps ... . Another key division, leading to an awkward compromise, developed on the question whether the clause on non-derogable rights should include only those rights most important and central to human dignity and most at risk during typical emergencies, or should be expanded to include all rights that no reasonable government would need to limit substantially in any conceivable emergency.

The drafters of the American Convention on Human Rights, who began work in earnest in the 1960s, had the benefit of earlier-drafted human rights treaties as a model and began with an apparent consensus on the precise-definition approach ... . The special interest developed within the OAS on protecting human rights during states of emergency may help explain the rather different form the derogation article takes in the American Convention ... .

A brief comparison of the three derogation articles in the human rights treaties to the relevant portions of the major humanitarian law instruments reveals some interesting similarities and differences, as well as "lacunae," that have attracted ongoing efforts to formulate additional, more complete standards. ...

...

Along with the threshold of severity, the principle of proportionality is the most important and yet most elusive of the substantive limits imposed on the privilege of derogation... . The principle of proportionality embodied in the derogation clauses has its roots in the principle of necessity, which also forms one of the key pillars of international humanitarian law. The existence of competent active, and informed organs of supervision, both at the national as well as at the international level, is vital if the proportionality principle is to have meaning in practice. ... [B]oth logistical (access to information and ability to act promptly) and attitudinal (deference to national authorities, e.g., by extension of a "margin of appreciation") factors affect the functioning of the various treaty implementation organs.

The Covenant and the American Convention include clauses specifying that derogation measures may not be imposed in a manner that discriminates on the grounds of race, color, sex, language, religion, or social origin ... .

Article 15 of the European Convention is silent on the issue of discrimination in the application of emergency measures ... . Nevertheless, arbitrary discrimination against disfavored groups of various types would be difficult to justify as being "strictly required." Thus, there may be no substantive difference between the silence of the European Convention and the explicit non-discrimination clauses of the other two treaties, if only arbitrary distinctions are outlawed by the latter.

Draft non-discrimination provisos to the Covenant's derogation article were proposed by the United States (in 1948) and by France (in 1949), but adding the element of non-discrimination was not easily accomplished. The Commission on Human Rights voted in May 1950 on the basis of an oral amendment during debate to add Article 20, the non-discrimination article to the list of non-derogable rights in Article 4. Objections were immediately raised that disparate treatment of enemy aliens would be necessary during wartime, and the decision was reversed the following day. A way around this impasse was found in 1952 when a non-discrimination clause not including the classification of national origin was added to the draft derogation article.

The idea that only arbitrary discrimination is outlawed by Article 4(1) is underlined by the deliberate inclusion of the word "solely" in its text.[206] Even without this term, however, the reference to discrimination in Article 4 conveys the implication that only arbitrary and unjustifiable distinctions in the application of emergency measures would be outlawed. Thus, where an identifiable racial or religious group poses a distinct security threat not posed by other members of the community, presumably, emergency measures could be deliberately targeted against the group, despite the non-discrimination clause.

The absence of the word "solely" from the non-discrimination clause in Article 27(1) of the American Convention on Human Rights apparently has no intended significance. ...

The three treaties diverge dramatically with respect to defining absolute rights never subject to suspension. The process of defining non-derogable rights has been a markedly progressive one, with each later drafted instrument expanding the core of non-derogable rights. The European Convention begins with just four, sparely defined: the right to life, excepting deaths resulting from lawful acts of war (Article 2); the ban on torture or inhuman or degrading treatment or punishment (Article 3); the prohibition on slavery or servitude (Article 4(1)); and the prohibition on retroactive criminal penalties (Article 7).

HUMAN RIGHTS COMMITTEE, STATES OF EMERGENCY, GENERAL COMMENT 29 (ON ARTICLE 4) (24 JULY 2001)

1. ... The restoration of a state of normalcy where full respect for the Covenant can again be secured must be the predominant objective of a State party derogating from the Covenant ... .

2. ... Before a state moves to invoke Article 4, two fundamental conditions must be met: the situation must amount to a public emergency that threatens the life of the nation, and the state party must have officially proclaimed a state of emergency. The latter requirement is essential for the maintenance of the principles of legality and rule of law at times when they are most needed. When proclaiming a state of emergency with consequences that could entail derogation from any provision of the Covenant, States must act within their constitutional and other provisions of law that govern such proclamation and the exercise of emergency powers; it is the task of the Committee to monitor the laws in question with respect to whether they enable and secure compliance with Article 4. ...

---

[206] A separate vote was taken on the UK proposal to frame the clause in terms of discrimination 'solely' on one of the forbidden grounds. Support of the inclusion of 'solely' was premised on the notion that wartime measures aimed at a particular nationality, for example, might predominantly affect persons of a particular race without being race-based.

3. Not every disturbance or catastrophe qualifies as a public emergency which threatens the life of the nation...
. If States parties consider invoking Article 4 in other situations than an armed conflict, they should carefully
consider the justification and why such a measure is necessary and legitimate in the circumstances. ...

4. ... [The requirement that derogation measures are limited to the extent strictly required by the exigencies of
the situation] relates to the duration, geographical coverage and material scope of the state of emergency and
any measures of derogation resorted to because of the emergency. Derogation from some Covenant obligations
in emergency situations is clearly distinct from restrictions or limitations allowed even in normal times under
several provisions of the Covenant. Nevertheless, the obligation to limit any derogations to those strictly
required by the exigencies of the situation reflects the principle of proportionality which is common to
derogation and limitation powers. Moreover, the mere fact that a permissible derogation from a specific
provision may, of itself, be justified by the exigencies of the situation does not obviate the requirement that
specific measures taken pursuant to the derogation must also be shown to be required by the exigencies of the
situation. In practice, this will ensure that no provision of the Covenant, however validly derogated from will
be entirely inapplicable to the behaviour of a State party ... .

5. The issues of when rights can be derogated from, and to what extent, cannot be separated from the provision
in Article 4, paragraph 1, of the Covenant according to which any measures derogating from a State party's
obligations under the Covenant must be limited 'to the extent strictly required by the exigencies of the situation'.
This condition requires that States parties provide careful justification not only for their decision to proclaim a
state of emergency but also for any specific measures based on such a proclamation. If States purport to invoke
the right to derogate from the Covenant during, for instance, a natural catastrophe, a mass demonstration
including instances of violence, or a major industrial accident, they must be able to justify not only that such a
situation constitutes a threat to the life of the nation, but also that all their measures derogating from the
Covenant are strictly required by the exigencies of the situation. In the opinion of the Committee, the possibility
of restricting certain Covenant rights under the terms of, for instance, freedom of movement (Article 12) or
freedom of assembly (Article 21) is generally sufficient during such situations and no derogation from the
provisions in question would be justified by the exigencies of the situation.
...
7. ... Conceptually, the qualification of a Covenant provision as a non-derogable one does not mean that no
limitations or restrictions would ever be justified. The reference in Article 4, paragraph 2, to Article 18, a
provision that includes a specific clause on restrictions in its paragraph 3, demonstrates that the permissibility
of restrictions is independent of the issue of derogability. Even in times of most serious public emergencies,
States that interfere with the freedom to manifest one's religion or belief must justify their actions by referring
to the requirements specified in Article 18, paragraph 3... .

8. According to Article 4, paragraph 1, one of the conditions for the justifiability of any derogation from the
Covenant is that the measures taken do not involve discrimination solely on the ground of race, colour, sex,
language, religion or social origin. Even though Article 26 or the other Covenant provisions related to
nondiscrimination (Articles 2, 3, 14, paragraph 1, 23, paragraph 4, 24, paragraph 1, and 25) have not been listed
among the non-derogable provisions in Article 4, paragraph 2, there are elements or dimensions of the right to
non-discrimination that cannot be derogated from in any circumstances.
...
10. Although it is not the function of the Human Rights Committee to review the conduct of a State party
under other treaties, in exercising its functions under the Covenant the Committee has the competence to take
a State party's other international obligations into account when it considers whether the Covenant allows the
State party to derogate from specific provisions of the Covenant. ...
...
12. In assessing the scope of legitimate derogation from the Covenant, one criterion can be found in the
definition of certain human rights violations as crimes against humanity. If action conducted under the authority
of a State constitutes a basis for individual criminal responsibility for a crime against humanity by the persons
involved in that action, Article 4 of the Covenant cannot be used as justification that a state of emergency
exempted the State in question from its responsibility in relation to the same conduct. Therefore, the recent

codification of crimes against humanity, for jurisdictional purposes, in the Rome Statute of the International Criminal Court is of relevance in the interpretation of Article 4 of the Covenant.[207]

13. In those provisions of the Covenant that are not listed in Article 4, paragraph 2, there are elements that in the Committee's opinion cannot be made subject to lawful derogation under Article 4. Some illustrative examples are presented below.
(a) All persons deprived of their liberty shall be treated with humanity and with respect for the inherent dignity of the human person ... a norm of general international law not subject to derogation ... .

(b) The prohibitions against taking of hostages, abductions or unacknowledged detention ... justified by their status as norms of general international law.

(c) ... [T]he rights of persons belonging to minorities includes elements that must be respected in all circumstances ... .

(d) ... [D]eportation or forcible transfer of population without grounds permitted under international law ... .

(e) No declaration ... may be invoked as justification for a State party to engage itself, contrary to Article 20, in propaganda for war, or in advocacy of national, racial or religious hatred that would constitute incitement to discrimination, hostility or violence.

14. Article 2, paragraph 3, of the Covenant requires a State party to the Covenant to provide remedies for any violation of the provisions of the Covenant. This clause is not mentioned in the list of non-derogable provisions in Article 4, paragraph 2, but it constitutes a treaty obligation inherent in the Covenant as a whole. Even if a State party, during a state of emergency, and to the extent that such measures are strictly required by the exigencies of the situation, may introduce adjustments to the practical functioning of its procedures governing judicial or other remedies, the State party must comply with the fundamental obligation, under Article 2, paragraph 3, of the Covenant to provide a remedy that is effective.

15. It is inherent in the protection of rights explicitly recognized as non-derogable in Article 4, paragraph 2, that they must be secured by procedural guarantees, including, often, judicial guarantees. The provisions of the Covenant relating to procedural safeguards may never be made subject to measures that would circumvent the protection of non-derogable rights. Article 4 may not be resorted to in a way that would result in derogation from non-derogable rights. Thus, for example, as Article 6 of the Covenant is non-derogable in its entirety, any trial leading to the imposition of the death penalty during a state of emergency must conform to the provisions of the Covenant, including all the requirements of Articles 14 and 15.

16. Safeguards related to derogation, as embodied in Article 4 of the Covenant, are based on the principles of legality and the rule of law inherent in the Covenant as a whole. As certain elements of the right to a fair trial are explicitly guaranteed under international humanitarian law during armed conflict, the Committee finds no justification for derogation from these guarantees during other emergency situations. The Committee is of the opinion that the principles of legality and the rule of law require that fundamental requirements of fair trial must be respected during a state of emergency. Only a court of law may try and convict a person for a criminal offence. The presumption of innocence must be respected. In order to protect non-derogable rights, the right to take proceedings before a court to enable the court to decide without delay on the lawfulness of detention, must not be diminished by a State party's decision to derogate from the Covenant.
...

Other Responses to Emergencies
If the ICCPR contained no derogation clause, could states parties lawfully suspend particular treaty obligations in the event of a public emergency? Two areas of international law are relevant to answering this question: rules governing the suspension of treaties and rules governing circumstances precluding wrongfulness. As to the former, the Vienna Convention on the Law of Treaties sets forth default rules for treaty interpretation. Article

---

[207] [T]he category of crimes against humanity as defined in [the Rome Statute] covers . . . violations of some provisions of the Covenant that have not been mentioned in the said provision of the Covenant. For example, certain grave violations of Article 27 may at the same time constitute genocide under Article 6 [genocide] of the Rome Statute, and Article 7 [crimes against humanity], in turn, covers practices that are related to, besides Articles 6, 7 and 8 of the [ICCPR], also Articles 9, 12, 26 and 27.

62 provides that a state can suspend its treaty obligations due to a 'fundamental change in circumstances'. The suspension may apply to the treaty as a whole or to a single clause or provision. See Vienna Convention, Article 44. In the drafting process, states can elect to modify the default rules with respect to a specific treaty. For example, treaty drafters could narrow (or expand) the scope of conditions that permit a state to suspend its obligations. Likewise, treaty drafters could condition the ability to suspend a treaty obligation on the satisfaction of procedural criteria.

Second, the Articles on Responsibility of States for International Wrongful Acts drafted by the International Law Commission describe rules for 'circumstances precluding wrongfulness'. The draft articles of state responsibility define conditions under which a state may justify its failure to perform an international legal obligation. In the preceding analysis of derogation clauses, Joan Fitzpatrick alludes to one such justification: necessity. According to the articles of state responsibility, '[n]ecessity may not be invoked by a State as a ground for precluding the wrongfulness of an act unless the act [i]s the only way for the State to safeguard an essential interest against a grave and imminent peril.'

Another justification that may be relevant is *force majeure*. This principle excuses a state from legal responsibility if 'the occurrence of an irresistible force or of an unforeseen event, beyond the control of the State, mak[es] it materially impossible in the circumstances to perform the obligation', according to the draft articles. The practice of the International Labour Organization, for example, suggests that states can derogate from ILO conventions in the event of an armed conflict by invoking *force majeure* — whether or not the convention contains an explicit suspension clause.

In addition to the substantive scope of the right to derogate, consider the specific procedures a state is supposed to follow in derogating from its treaty obligations. Article 4 contains two procedural elements: official proclamation of a public emergency and notification to other states parties. In *Silva v. Uruguay*, Communication No. 34/1978 (1981), the Human Rights Committee observed that while 'the sovereign right of a State party to declare a state of emergency is not questioned ... by merely invoking the existence of exceptional circumstances [a State] cannot evade' its Covenant obligations. 'If the ... Government does not furnish the required justification ... [the] Committee cannot conclude that valid reasons exist to legitimize a departure from the normal legal regime prescribed by the Covenant.'

While questions relating to the justification of states of emergency have been before the European Court of Human Rights since its inception, cases from Turkey have been especially prominent in recent years, particularly in response to the failed *coup d'état* in 2016. Commentators have been critical of the actual functioning of the derogations system under the European Convention,[208] and the following materials illustrate some of the challenges involved.

VENICE COMMISSION, OPINION ON EMERGENCY DECREE LAWS NOS. 667-676 ADOPTED FOLLOWING THE FAILED COUP OF 15 JULY 2016 (10 DECEMBER 2016)

[The Monitoring Committee of the Parliamentary Assembly of the Council of Europe requested the Venice Commission's opinion on the overall compatibility of the implementation of the state of emergency in Turkey with Council of Europe standards.]

II. Factual background
6. On 15 July 2016 a group of officers within the Turkish armed forces tried to seize power in the country and overthrow President Erdoğan. The conspirators bombed the Parliament, attacked other public buildings, blocked roads and bridges in major towns, and seized a TV station. ... Hundreds of civilians were injured or killed. However, the Turkish armed forces and the population resisted, and the coup failed. The conspirators within the Army, police and other armed forces were disarmed and arrested.

7. The Venice Commission strongly and resolutely condemns ... the ruthlessness of conspirators, and expresses solidarity with the Turkish society ... .

---

[208] S. Wallace, 'Derogations from the European Convention on Human Rights: The Case for Reform', 20 *Hum. Rts L. Rev.* (2020) 769.

8. On 20 July 2016 the Government declared a state of emergency for three months. Following the approval of that declaration by Parliament, the Government started to legislate through emergency decree laws. The first was Decree Law no. 667, which entered into force on 23 July 2016.

[Note: The state of emergency was subsequently renewed seven times for a total of 24 months until it was lifted in July 2018. In all, 37 emergency decrees were issued.]

9. ... During the state of emergency, over 100.000 civil servants, military officers, judges, teachers and academics have been dismissed from their jobs. Tens of thousands have been arrested and prosecuted. Private institutions allegedly linked to the conspiracy have been closed down and their property confiscated.

10. According to Turkish official sources, there is strong evidence that the conspiracy has been organised by the supporters of Mr Fethullah Gülen, an Islamic cleric living in the US. In the Turkish official documents the Gülenist network is denoted as "FETÖ/PDY" ("Fethullah Terror Organization/Parallel State Structures").

11. Originally, the Gülenist network consisted of a large number of educational institutions, charity foundations, business entities, etc. According to the Government, in addition to being largely present in the public education, business sphere and in the third sector, the Gülenists also started secretly penetrating into State institutions.

12. According to the Turkish authorities, in December 2013 the Gülenists tried to destabilize the AKP Government by accusing some of its members of corruption. Now this incident is considered by the Government as a first coup attempt by the Gülenists. Following the events of December 2013 the Government started closing down some key entities of the Gülenist network (such as the Asya bank and the Zaman newspaper).

13. In addition, a large number of civil servants, military officers and judges suspected of Gülenist sympathies were subjected to disciplinary investigations, or transferred to other places of service. However, these measures were of a limited effect, allegedly because of hidden obstruction from the Gülenists who by then had already infiltrated various State institutions.
...
16. ... [T]he Venice Commission takes into account certain factual allegations made by the Turkish authorities, for the purpose of building its legal analysis. The first allegation is that the failed coup was prepared and implemented by a coordinated group composed at least partly of supporters of Mr Gülen within the army and other State institutions. The Turkish authorities called the Gülenist network a "terrorist organisation"; the Organisation of Islamic Cooperation is of the same opinion. There are different definitions of "terrorism". Regardless of the propriety of these characterisations, those who were directly involved in the planning and implementation of the coup definitely formed a criminal organisation.

17. The second factual allegation is that, even before the coup, a number of members of the Gülenist network were involved in certain illegal acts, which arguably qualify as crimes under the Turkish Criminal Code. ... However, this does not mean that everybody who has ever had contacts with the organisations or projects associated with Mr Gülen may be automatically considered as aiding and abetting the commission of those crimes.
...
103. The criteria used to assess the links of the individuals to the Gülenist network have not been made public, at least not officially. The Venice Commission rapporteurs were informed that dismissals are ordered on the basis of an evaluation of a combination of various criteria, such as, for example, making monetary contributions to the Asya bank and other companies of the "parallel state", being a manager or member of a trade union or association linked to Mr Gülen, using the messenger application ByLock and other similar encrypted messaging programmes. In addition, the dismissals may be based on police or secret service reports about relevant individuals, analysis of social media contacts, donations, web-sites visited, and even on the fact of residence in student dormitories belonging to the "parallel state" structures or sending children to the schools associated with Mr Gülen. Information received from colleagues from work or neighbours and even continuous subscription to Gülenist periodicals are also mentioned amongst those many criteria which are used to put names on the "dismissals lists".

…

119. Disciplinary liability, or any other similar measure, should be foreseeable; a public servant should understand that he/she is doing something incompatible with his/her status, in order to be disciplined for it. Hence, it is important to establish a moment in time at which a reasonable and well-informed person … must have understood that their continued connections with the Gülenist network were clearly unacceptable.

…

IV. Conclusions

…

225. There is no doubt that the Turkish authorities were confronted with a dangerous armed conspiracy, and that they had good reasons to declare a state of emergency and give extraordinary powers to the Government. … Nevertheless, the state of emergency regime should remain within the limits set by the Constitution and domestic and international obligations of the State.

226. The provisions of the Turkish Constitution on the declaration of a state of emergency appear to be in line with common European standards in this area. However, the Government interpreted its extraordinary powers too extensively and took measures that went beyond what is permitted by the Turkish Constitution and by international law.

227. The main concerns of the Venice Commission related to the current constitutional situation in Turkey may be summarised as follows:

- Following the declaration of a state of emergency, for over two months, the Government was de facto permitted to legislate alone, without any control by Parliament or the Constitutional Court;
- The Government took permanent measures, which went beyond a temporary state of emergency. Civil servants were dismissed, not merely suspended, organisations and bodies were dissolved and their property confiscated instead of being put under temporary State control. In addition, the Government made a number of structural changes to the legislation, which should normally be done through the ordinary legislative process outside of the emergency period;
- The Government implemented its emergency powers through ad hominem legislation. In particular, tens of thousands of public servants were dismissed on the basis of the lists appended to the emergency decree laws. Such collective dismissals were not individualised, i.e. they did not refer to verifiable evidence related to each individual and described in the decisions;
- Basic rights of administrative due process of the public servants dismissed by the decree laws or on their basis have not been respected;
- Collective dismissals were ordered because of the alleged connections of public servants to the Gülenist network or other organisations considered "terrorist", but this concept was loosely defined and did not require a meaningful connection with such organisations …;
  …
- In the area of criminal procedures, extension of the time-limit for pre-trial detention without judicial control up to 30 days is highly problematic … .
- The Government has removed crucial safeguards that protect detainees from abuses, which increases the likelihood of ill-treatment;

…

228. The Venice Commission is particularly concerned by the apparent absence of access to justice for those public servants who have been dismissed directly by the decree laws, and those legal entities which have been liquidated by the decree laws. …

…

PIŞKIN V. TURKEY,
EUROPEAN COURT OF HUMAN RIGHTS, SECOND SECTION,
APPLICATION NO. 33399/18 (15 DECEMBER 2020)

[Based on Emergency Legislative Decree No. 667, the applicant was dismissed from his job as an expert at the Ankara Development Agency, a 'public law entity'. He claimed that no valid reason had been given and that appropriate procedures had not been followed. He categorically denied any kind of link with the FETÖ/PDY and said he too considered it to be a 'terrorist organisation'. The Labour Court dismissed his claim on the grounds that his determination was lawfully carried out under Decree No. 667. On appeal, the Ankara Regional Court and the Constitutional Court also dismissed the application.]

33. The relevant parts of Emergency Legislative Decree No. 667, which came into force on 23 July 2016, read as follows:

Article 4
(1) Persons considered as belonging, affiliated or linked to terrorist organisations or structures, formations or groups which the National Security Council has determined are involved in activities prejudicial to the national security of the State:
...

(g) personnel employed in all kinds of posts, positions and status (including workers) in institutions affiliated or related to a ministry, are dismissed from the civil service upon the proposal of the head of unit, with the approval of the director of the recruitment department.
...

(2) Persons dismissed in accordance with the first paragraph cannot be employed in the civil service again ... .
...

[Under the heading of 'relevant international materials, the Court took very detailed note of the Venice Commission's Opinion (p. 000 above), and of the UN Human Rights Committee's General Comment No. 29.]
...

55. On 21 July 2016 the Permanent Representative of Turkey to the Council of Europe sent the Secretary General of the Council of Europe the following notice of derogation:

... On 15 July 2016, a large-scale coup attempt was staged in the Republic of Turkey to overthrow the democratically-elected government and the constitutional order. This despicable attempt was foiled by the Turkish state and people acting in unity and solidarity. The coup attempt and its aftermath together with other terrorist acts have posed severe dangers to public security and order, amounting to a threat to the life of the nation in the meaning of Article 15 of the [ECHR]. The Republic of Turkey is taking the required measures as prescribed by law, in line with the national legislation and its international obligations. ...
...

[Article 6]
131. ... [In relation to fair trial rights under Article 6 of the Convention, the] issue before the Court is whether the applicant benefited from a genuine assessment of his submissions during the proceedings before the domestic courts. ...
...

133. [T]he Convention is designed to "guarantee not rights that are theoretical or illusory but rights that are practical and effective" ... .

134. Moreover, Article 6 of the Convention obliges the courts to give reasons for their judgments, but cannot be understood as requiring a detailed answer to every argument put forward by the plaintiff. ...
...

140. The Court observes that ... the applicant had access to a tribunal which had full jurisdiction to hear and determine the case ..., [and the first instance] court decided to supplement the case file, heard witnesses called by the applicant and held a public hearing. Furthermore, the applicant had not been prevented from accessing any decisive piece of evidence provided to the domestic courts by the employer. In the light of the foregoing, the Court is prepared to accept that the judicial process sufficiently satisfies the requirements of adversarial proceedings and equality of arms without prejudice to its subsequent examination of the applicant's allegations concerning the effectiveness of judicial review.
...

147. ... [A]t no stage in the proceedings before the different trial benches did the domestic courts consider the question whether the termination of the applicant's employment contract for presumed links with an illegal structure had been justified by his conduct or any other relevant evidence or information. ... [I]t does not

transpire from the impugned decisions that the arguments put forward by the applicant had ever really been heard, that is to say had been duly examined by the trial courts.

148. As regards the Constitutional Court, ... by giving a summary inadmissibility decision, the latter failed to conduct any analysis of the legal and factual issues in question.

149. ... [T]he conclusions set out in the judicial decisions given ... do not demonstrate that the domestic courts conducted an in-depth, thorough examination of the applicant's arguments, that they based their reasoning on the evidence presented by the applicant and that they validly reasoned their dismissal of the latter's challenges.
...
...
150. [In conclusion], whereas the domestic courts theoretically held full jurisdiction to determine the dispute between the applicant and the administrative authorities, they deprived themselves of jurisdiction to examine all questions of fact and law relevant to the dispute before them, as required by Article 6 § 1.

151. The Court concludes therefore that the applicant was not actually heard by the domestic courts. ...
...
153. ... [E]ven in the framework of a state of emergency, the fundamental principle of the rule of law must prevail. It would not be consistent with the rule of law in a democratic society or with the basic principle underlying Article 6 § 1 ... if a State could, without restraint or control by the Convention enforcement bodies, remove from the jurisdiction of the courts a whole range of civil claims or confer immunities from civil liability on large groups or categories of persons ... There has accordingly been a violation of Article 6 § 1 of the Convention.

[Article 8]
154. The applicant ... stated that because of his dismissal he was now labelled a "terrorist" and "traitor". ... [T]he Court will examine the present case under Article 8 ...:

1. Everyone has the right to respect for his private ... life ...
2. There shall be no interference by a public authority with the exercise of this right except such as is in accordance with the law and is necessary in a democratic society in the interests of national security, public safety or the economic well-being of the country, for the prevention of disorder or crime, for the protection of health or morals, or for the protection of the rights and freedoms of others.

...
207. ... [T]he Court notes ... the general character of the wording of ... Decree No. 667, with terms such as "belonging to" and "affiliated or linked with" an illegal structure. ... [T]he Government did not cite any criteria concerning the definition of [these] concepts ... .. Moreover, the Court takes note of the Venice Commission's considerations on the foreseeability of the criteria used to assess a person's links with an illegal structure.

Nevertheless, the Court takes the view that ... the *actus reus* of such offences should be worded in general language. Otherwise, the statute may not deal with the issue comprehensively and will require constant review and updating ... .
...
209. ... Having regard to the particular circumstances of the state of emergency and to the fact that the domestic courts had full jurisdiction to review the measures adopted ..., the Court is prepared to proceed on the assumption that the impugned interference was prescribed by law.
...
222. ... [T]he Court can accept, in keeping with its findings under Article 6, that the simplified procedure established under Legislative Decree No. 667 enabling civil servants and other civil-service employees to be dismissed might be considered as having been justified in the light of the very specific circumstances of the situation ..., given that the measures taken during the state of emergency had been subject to judicial review. Consequently, it considers that no further assessment is required of the procedure ... .

223. As regards the … thoroughness of the judicial review of the impugned measure, the Court reiterates the principle that any individual subject to a measure for reasons of national security must have safeguards against arbitrary action.

224. The Court is prepared to accept that membership of structures organised along military lines or establishing a rigid, irreducible form of solidarity among their members, or else pursuing an ideology contrary to the rules of democracy, a fundamental element of "European public order", could raise an issue vis-à-vis national security and prevention of disorder where the members of such bodies are called upon to discharge public duties.
…

227. … [E]ven where national security is at stake, the concepts of lawfulness and the rule of law in a democratic society require that measures affecting fundamental human rights must be subject to some form of adversarial proceedings before an independent body competent to review the reasons for the decision and relevant evidence. If it were impossible to contest effectively a national security concern relied on by the authorities, the police or other State authorities would be able to encroach arbitrarily on rights protected by the Convention.

228. … [T]he domestic courts failed to determine the real reasons why the applicant's employment contract had been terminated … . Consequently, the judicial review of the impugned measure in the present case was inadequate.

229. … [T]he impugned measure cannot be said to have been strictly required by the special circumstances of the state of emergency. There has accordingly been a violation of Article 8 of the Convention.
…

CONCURRING OPINION of JUDGE KOSKELO

1. … I am in full agreement with the judgment in terms of the outcome, … however, I have reservations concerning the reasoning … .

Article 6
…
4. In my view, … the … requirements [of] full jurisdiction, adversarial procedure and equality of arms … were only satisfied in a purely formal sense, as a matter of abstract theory. This is hardly consonant with … upholding rights that are real and not only illusory … . [The majority] stated that the applicant was not prevented from having access to the case file regarding evidence submitted [but] … the file lacked anything that could have served to elucidate the specific facts or the evidence relied on to justify the dismissal, and thus to help the applicant discern what exactly he should challenge and how.

5. … [The Court should] dispense with the statements set out in paragraph 140. In the specific circumstances, they are more or less void of substance. The crux of matter is the actual weakness of the judicial review that took place.

Article 8
…
7. [T]he Court has consistently held that for domestic law to meet the qualitative requirements, it must afford a measure of legal protection against arbitrary interference by public authorities with the rights guaranteed by the Convention. In matters relating to fundamental rights, it would be contrary to the rule of law … for the legal discretion granted to the executive to be expressed in terms of an unfettered power. Consequently, the law must indicate with sufficient clarity the scope of any such discretion and the manner of its exercise. …
…
10. … [T]he relevant provision of … Decree No. 667 is worded very vaguely … . … It is difficult to see how such a legal basis for measures that entailed dramatic and, in principle, permanent consequences for the individuals concerned could be considered consonant with the standards developed in the Court's case-law.

11. … [T]he Venice Commission … also expressed concerns regarding the formulation of the relevant provisions, and recommended that they should be amended so that a dismissal could only be ordered on the

basis of a combination of factual elements which clearly indicated that the public servant had acted in a way which objectively cast serious doubts on his or her loyalty to the democratic legal order.

...

13. [A]s regards the judicial review and the relevant requirements of independence, one should not lose sight of the fact that all the members of the judiciary were themselves subject to the threat of dismissal under the same emergency measures. In sum, the quality of the legal framework, including the relevant safeguards, appears highly problematic from the point of view of the established Convention standards.

...

COVID-19

Around 90 percent of constitutions contain explicit provisions for dealing with states of emergency and, between 1985 and 2014, at least 137 countries made such a declaration at least once.[209] Some states are said to have 'routinized' states of emergency.[210] While counter-terrorism has been a key driver in this area, the COVID-19 pandemic, starting in early 2020, led to a flood of emergency measures, although many fewer formal derogations.[211] The following materials provide contrasting perspectives on the impact of these developments.

As noted by Tom Ginsburg and Mila Versteeg, in 'The Bound Executive: Emergency Powers During the Pandemic', 19 *Int'l J. Con. L.* (2021) 1498, COVID-related measures included 'nationwide stay-at-home orders, military-enforced curfews, suspended religious services, cellphone monitoring, the suspension of schools and other government services, restricted travel, and the censoring of news.' Some have been controversial, others have not:

> ... [T]he pandemic response has produced massive debates about the role of government power during times of crisis ... . It is conventional wisdom that emergencies require massive delegation of power to the executive, which is the only branch of government with the information, decisiveness, and speed to respond to crises. Therefore, the executive cannot be effectively constrained by the other branches of government, and may even need to operate outside the law entirely. Checks and balances that ordinarily constrain constitutional governance thus cease to exist during times of crisis. While this view, associated most prominently with Carl Schmitt, has numerous critics, it remains popular, with high-profile proponents such as Eric Posner and Adrian Vermeule, who [have articulated] a theory of an "unbound executive" ... . [They] characterize crisis governance as "Schmittian" and "post-Madisonian," because they believe that the Madisonian scheme of checks and balances, wherein different branches and levels of government have the incentives to keep each other in check, fails to operate under such circumstances. ...
>
> [The authors present] data from an original global survey ... [of] the legal basis for the early pandemic response as well as the extent to which there has been judicial oversight, legislative involvement, and whether the executive's pandemic response has encountered pushback from subnational units. ...
>
> [The] key finding is that, in many countries, checks and balances have remained robustly in place ... . Perhaps most surprising is that, in over half of the democracies we surveyed, courts have played a visible role in monitoring the executive. ... Of course, the fact that courts attempt to monitor executive power does not mean that they actually succeed. Court orders can be defied, and implementation might be lacking, especially when courts dictate complex policy responses. ...
>
> ... [I]n roughly two-thirds of countries in our survey, legislatures have been directly involved in the pandemic response, either because they had to declare or extend a state of

[209] C. Bjørnskov and S. Voigt, 'The Architecture of Emergency Constitutions', 16 *Int'l J. Con. L.* (2018) 101.

[210] S. Hennette Vauchez, 'Taming the Exception: Lessons from the Routinization of States of Emergency in France', 20 *Int'l J. Con. L.* (2022) 1793.

[211] R. R. Rubins and G. Barzilai, 'Only Sovereignty: Global Emergencies between Domestic and International Law', 55 *Cornell Int'l L. J.* (2022) 139; and R. G. Teshome, 'Derogations to Human Rights During a Global Pandemic: Unpacking Normative and Practical Challenges', 37 *Am. U. Int'l L. Rev.* (2022) 307.

emergency or because they passed new legislation. The vast majority of legislatures that passed new legislation have also attempted to provide safeguards against abuse by making these new laws specific to the current crisis and temporary in nature. ...

Finally, in a number of countries, ... subnational authorities have been more aggressive than national governments, demanding greater restrictions for their particular localities; and in some places, they have pushed back against national leaders who have been perceived as over-reaching. ...

A different picture emerges, however, when the focus is specifically on the human rights impact of COVID-related measures, as illustrated by this UN report based on civil society information (UN Doc. A/HRC/51/13 (2022)):

> 7. Between 1 January 2020 and 13 April 2022, the Secretary-General received at least 111 official depositary notifications from 24 Member States instituting states of emergency and derogations, pursuant to [the ICCPR], including extensions or introductions of new restrictions specifically related to COVID-19.

> 8. More than 175 countries reportedly adopted legal or other forms of pandemic response measures that limited civic freedoms, including freedom of assembly, association and expression. ... COVID-19 restrictions affected a wide range of civil society actors, changing how they were able to reach the communities they serve, to engage with State and other counterparts and to influence policymaking. In many countries, measures were based on outdated emergency laws, decrees and regulations or on repurposed security-related legislation, and were enacted for prolonged periods or without termination dates. Civil society responses ... also indicated that, overwhelmingly, emergency measures were adopted without any consultations with communities. Efforts to involve civil society in reviewing the measures' effectiveness were also scarce.

> 18. During the pandemic, the United Nations human rights mechanisms repeatedly raised concerns ... in relation to unequal access to COVID-19 vaccines, medicines, health technologies and diagnostics ... .

> 19. In many countries COVID-19 measures also granted increased powers to the executive branch, weakening other branches of Government and the critical oversight functions they provide, for example, by suspending judicial proceedings and thus undermining civil society's ability to bring lawsuits to challenge COVID-inspired laws and practices that infringed rights. Many Governments also defined "essential workers" narrowly, excluding lawyers, for example, and thereby effectively preventing them from providing their clients essential legal services and from accessing courts and justice, including in the context of COVID-19 curfews.

The UN report indicates that, by April 2022, only 24 of 193 UN Member States registered COVID-19-related derogations. For the Council of Europe, ten of 46 States had done so by 2023. And these numbers alone tell only part of the story. Laurence Helfer, in 'Rethinking Derogations from Human Rights Treaties', 115 *Am. J. Int'l L.* (2021) 20 calls attention to the weaknesses in the derogations system, as illustrated by the COVID-19 experience:

> The emergency measures engendered by the COVID-19 pandemic differ in several respects [from those taken in earlier decades, which focused especially on political unrest and terrorism]. For one, ... the number of derogating states ... is far lower than the more than one hundred countries that have imposed pandemic-related restrictions on individual rights.

> A second difference concerns the number and diversity of rights affected. Most COVID-19 derogations unsurprisingly focus on freedom of movement, assembly, and association. But states have also restricted the rights to liberty, to respect for private and family life, to a fair trial, to the protection of property, to freedom of expression, and to education.

Some COVID-19 controls have also infringed nonderogable rights—including the right to life, the prohibition of torture and cruel, inhuman or degrading treatment, and forced labor—and implicated a state's positive human rights obligations, including those relating to economic and social guarantees.

A third difference concerns governments that have invoked the pandemic as an excuse to repress dissent. Many of these violations relate to public health—such as arbitrary arrests and extrajudicial killings during lockdowns or censorship of information about COVID-related infections or deaths. Others range much further afield, perhaps the most infamous being Hungarian emergency laws that give the executive virtually unfettered power to rule by decree.

…

In sum, the use of derogations in response to COVID-19 is only one facet of a much broader set of restrictions and violations of human rights during the pandemic. For a mechanism designed to constrain the suspension of individual liberties during emergencies through international disclosure and oversight, the derogations regime appears to be having only a modest impact.

Fionnuala Ni Aoláin, in 'Exceptionality: A Typology of Covid-19 Emergency Powers', 26 *UCLA J. Int'l L. & Foreign Aff.* (2022) 49, reinforces that picture and expresses particular concern about the accompanying 'trend toward normalizing the exceptional and avoiding the constraints of exceptionality and oversight that follow from treaty derogation.' Consider, for example, the following legislation, adopted with minimal debate less than two weeks after the first two cases of COVID-19 were discovered in Ghana.[212]

GHANA, IMPOSITION OF RESTRICTIONS ACT, 2020
(21 MARCH 2020)

1.   The object of this Act is to provide for powers to impose restrictions on persons, to give effect to [the emergency provisions] … of the Constitution in the event or imminence of an emergency, disaster or similar circumstance to ensure public safety, public health and protection.

Imposition of restrictions

2.   (1) The President may, acting in accordance with the advice of relevant person or body, by Executive Instrument, impose restrictions specified [in the Constitution.]

(2) An Instrument made under subsection (1) should include provisions in respect of

(a) the specific restriction to be imposed;
(b) the duration of the restriction;
(c) the person to whom the restriction applies;
(d) the geographic area to which the prescription applies;
(e) the facts and circumstances for the provisions in paragraphs (a) to (d), and
(f) any other matter incidental to the attainment of the object of this Act.

3.   (l) The President may impose a restriction under subsection 1 of section 2 where the restriction

(a) is reasonably required in the interest of defence, public safety, public health or the running of essential services;
(b) is reasonably required on the movement or residence within Ghana of any person or persons generally, or any class of persons;

---

[212] For an analysis, see B. Nkrumah, 'The (Il)Legality of Ghana's Covid-19 Emergency Response: A Commentary', in E. Durojaye and D, Powell (eds.), *Constitutional Resilience and the COVID-19 Pandemic* (2022) 311; and A. Fellmeth, 'Human Rights Derogations in National Emergencies: Lessons from Africa', 28 *Sw. J. Int'l L.* (2023) 640.

(c) is required to restrict the freedom of entry into Ghana, or movement in Ghana, of a person who is not a citizen of Ghana; or

(d) is reasonably required for the purpose of safeguarding the people of Ghana against the teaching or propagation of a doctrine which exhibits or encourages disrespect for the nationhood of Ghana, the national symbols and emblems, or incites hatred against other members of the community.

(2) The imposition of the restriction under subsection (1) shall be reasonably justified in accordance with the spirit of the Constitution.

4.   (1) A restriction impose [sic] under subsection (1) of section 2 shall be for a period of not more than three months.

...

6.   A person who fails to comply with a restriction imposed under the Executive Instrument issued under subsection (1) of section 2 commits an offence and is liable on summary conviction to a fine ... or to a term of imprisonment of not less than four years and not more than ten years or to both.

7.   In this Act, unless the context otherwise requires,

"disaster" includes an occurrence [sic] by which there is serious disruption of general safety endangering the life and health of many people or large material interests which require co-ordinated action by services of different disciplines and flood, earthquake, drought, rainstorm, war, civil strife or industrial accident; and

"essential services" include
   (a) water supply services;
   (b) electricity supply services;
   (c) health and hospital services;
   (d) waste management services;
   (e) air traffic and civil aviation control services;
   (f) meteorological services;
   (g) fire services;
   (h) air transport services;
   (i) supply and distribution of fuels;
   (j) telecommunications services; and
   (k) public and private commercial transport services.

QUESTIONS

1. All *jus cogens* norms are non-derogable under Article 4, but not all non-derogable rights under Article 4 are *jus cogens* norms. In other words, there is a residual category in Article 4: ICCPR provisions that do not reflect *jus cogens* norms but nevertheless may not be suspended due to a public emergency. What are the general features of such provisions? What is the logic behind their receiving this extraordinary protection if they do not implicate peremptory norms?

2. In General Comment 29, the Committee provides an expanded list of non-derogable rights beyond those explicitly enumerated in Article 4(2). Did the Committee go too far or not far enough? What would you exclude or include?

3. In 2017, Turkey held a constitutional referendum which, in the view of one observer, put in place a system 'organized around sweeping new presidential powers including many powers equivalent to those under the state of emergency on a permanent basis'. The new system 'perpetuated the executive aggrandizement and dismantled the key checks and balances that form an integral part of any

functioning democracy'.[213] Does Judge Koskelo's gloss on the European Court's decision in *Pişkin v. Turkey* suggest that the court has adopted an overly permissive response to Turkey's state of emergency, in which over 100,000 persons were dismissed from their jobs?

4. What do you see as the key shortcomings in Ghana's Restrictions Act?

5. On three days in late March 2022, 87 people were murdered by criminal gangs in El Salvador. The government of President Nayib Bukele immediately imposed a 30-day 'state of exception', subsequently renewed every month, that increased detention without charge from three to fifteen days, restricted freedom of assembly and the right to a legal defence in court, and authorized the rounding up of alleged gang members. Within a year, 65,000 gang members were in detention, often in overcrowded, unhygienic and dangerous conditions, thus giving El Salvador the world's highest incarceration rate.[214] The Justice Minister said the suspected gang members would never return to the streets. In January 2023, the Defense Minister announced a 56.8 percent decrease in homicides between 2021 and 2022, which he attributed to the crackdown. In 2023, President Bukele's approval ratings were above 80%. How would you evaluate this situation in terms of the ICCPR, to which El Salvador is a party?

2. International Humanitarian Law and its Relationship to Human Rights

International law protects the rights of individuals during wartime. A potential difficulty in securing such protection, however, is determining how two areas of international law — the law of armed conflict (also called 'international humanitarian law') and human rights law — interrelate. Also, which institutions should have the power to interpret and apply these bodies of law? For example, should human rights institutions have the authority and competence to interpret IHL? For the moment we focus on the content of IHL and the first set of concerns, namely, the relationship between the two legal regimes. Once we better understand those issues, we can consider questions about the appropriate role of various institutions in interpreting the law.

The Structure and Content of IHL[215]

IHL is certainly a specialized body of law. It regulates, often in exacting detail, the methods of conducting hostilities and the treatment of victims of warfare. At the outset, it is important to understand three parameters that define the scope of the regime's application. First, the regime applies only in situations of armed conflict and military occupation. Second, an important distinction involves the classification of a conflict as either international (i.e., between two or more states) or non-international (e.g., between a state and a non-state group; or between two non-state groups). In general, a broader and more demanding set of IHL rules applies to international armed conflict, and only a subset of those obligations applies to non-international armed conflict. A primary reason for that normative hierarchy is that the legal authority of the state is generally at its zenith in dealing with matters within its sovereign territory; and state authority is more constrained when acting abroad in direct confrontation with the sovereign interests of another state. Third, the obligations of IHL are meant to apply equally to all parties involved in a conflict. That is, the rights and responsibilities of actors do not change according to the purported justness of one side's cause. The rules are neither more stringent for a state that aggressively invades another state, nor more relaxed for a state acting in self-defence against an aggressor. In other words, the rules that apply to conduct during an armed conflict (*jus in bello*) are separate from the rules that apply to the initial reasons for going to war (*jus ad bellum*).

IHL is governed by overarching principles and a set of specific rules. The former includes three general principles. First is the principle of necessity: an obligation to use only the amount of force needed to obtain a military objective. Second is the principle of distinction: an obligation to attack only legitimate military targets

---

[213] See E. Turkut, 'The Turkish Post-Coup Emergency and European Responses: Shortcomings in the European System Revisited', *Eur. Yb. Hum. Rts* (2022) 445.

[214] International Crisis Group, *A Remedy for El Salvador's Prison Fever* (2022).

[215] See generally A. Clapham, *War* (2021).

and never deliberately attack civilians or civilian objects. Third is the principle of proportionality: an obligation to ensure an acceptable relationship between the legitimate destructive effect and undesirable collateral effects of a military attack. The principle of proportionality may, alternatively, be formulated as an obligation to ensure any incidental loss or injury to civilian life is not excessive in relation to the military objective of an attack.

IHL is often divided into two domains, though these boundaries have merged in more recent years. One domain concerns legal obligations related to the methods and means of warfare in the conduct of military operations. This domain has historically been called 'Hague Law' — due to the city in which the principal treaties on this subject were initially adopted. Its rules are codified, for example, in The Hague Conventions concluded in 1899 and 1907. And, customary international law currently plays a significant role in defining its content, as an International Court of Justice advisory opinion on the use of nuclear weapons demonstrates. Examples of Hague Law include prohibitions on specific weapons, on the infliction of superfluous injury and unnecessary suffering, on assassination and on perfidious conduct. Contemporary issues in this domain include the use of cluster bombs, the use of remote controlled drones, the tactics of cyber attacks and cyber warfare more generally, and the definition of acts of terrorism in the context of an armed conflict.

In contrast with Hague Law, the second domain of IHL concerns the treatment of civilians and combatants who have laid down their arms and are subject to the effective authority of an opposing party to the conflict. This domain has historically been called 'Geneva Law' due as well to the treaty conferences that initially codified this area of law. The principal instruments are the four Geneva Conventions of 1949. The conventions were drafted in the aftermath of the Second World War, during the same period in which war crimes trials were taking place on the European continent and in East Asia. Collectively, the 1949 Conventions provide rules for the wounded, sick and shipwrecked (the First and Second Geneva Conventions), prisoners of war (the Third Geneva Convention) and civilians (the Fourth Geneva Convention). Contemporary controversies involving the application of Geneva Law include the definition of persons who are lawfully subject to detention and the composition of military trials in non-international armed conflict.

Most of the rules in the 1949 Conventions apply to international armed conflicts — war between two or more states. However, Article 3 common to all four Conventions, which has been called a 'convention in miniature', contains rules that apply to non-international conflicts such as civil wars. Common Article 3 imposes direct legal obligations on all parties to a conflict — including non-state actors. These obligations include the most basic rights of individuals such as freedom from torture, murder, mutilation and cruel treatment; the right to a fair trial, and the general right 'in all circumstances [to] be treated humanely'. The International Court of Justice famously referred to the rules in Common Article 3 as 'a minimum yardstick' for all armed conflicts because they reflect 'elementary considerations of humanity'.

In the midst of the Cold War, states reconvened in Geneva to negotiate two additional protocols to the 1949 Conventions. Finalized in 1977, the two Protocols involve a convergence of Hague Law and Geneva Law. That is, each Protocol contains rules pertaining to the two domains in a relatively undifferentiated organizational structure. Additional Protocol I elaborates the rules that apply in international armed conflicts. It also defines 'international armed conflict' to include national liberation and other armed struggles in exercise of the right of self-determination. Additional Protocol II contains a more modest set of rules for internal armed conflicts.

In terms of their status, the 1949 Geneva Conventions and the 1977 Protocols have secured widespread ratification. In 2006, the 1949 Conventions became the first treaties in modern history to achieve ratification by every state in the world. Their rules are also generally considered binding as a matter of customary international law. As of 2024, 174 states are party to Protocol I, and many of its provisions are considered customary international law applicable in all armed conflicts. The United States is one of the few states not to ratify the Protocol (along with India, Indonesia, Iran, Israel, Myanmar (Burma), Nepal, Pakistan, Sri Lanka and Turkey). The U.S. Government, however, considers much of the Protocol binding customary international law. When the United Kingdom ratified the Protocol in 1998, it attached a reservation stating that 'the term "armed conflict" of itself and in its context denotes a situation of a kind which is not constituted by the commission of ordinary crimes including acts of terrorism whether concerted or in isolation.' Additional Protocol II has been ratified by 169 states. Its states parties include all permanent members of the Security Council except the United States, which has signed but not ratified the agreement.

The most recent international instrument to include a broad range of IHL prohibitions is the 1998 Rome Statute for the International Criminal Court. The drafters of the Rome Statute considered it their task to produce a treaty reflecting the existing IHL regime, not to develop new law. As a consequence, Article 8 is widely understood to codify customary IHL and thus serves as a useful reference point. The Rome Statute is, however, limited to rules that incur international criminal liability. State obligations under IHL conflict, of course, encompass far more than war crimes. In 2005, the International Committee of the Red Cross (ICRC) finalized a study on customary international humanitarian law. This vast set of materials provides the ICRC's views on the rules that have acquired the status of custom in international and non-international armed conflict. The study, however, was not completed without controversy. The U.S. Government, for example, objected to parts of the methodology used to ascertain rules and some substantive conclusions of the study.[216]

The Relationship Between the Two Bodies of Law[217]

A principle familiar to many legal systems, public international law included, is *lex specialis derogat legi generali*. That is, a specific or special rule should take precedence over a general rule. This principle raises an important challenge for the legal regulation of warfare: should IHL supplant human rights law in defining the rights and obligations of individuals and states during an armed conflict?

In contrast with IHL, international human rights law applies during peacetime and wartime. The first formal recognition of the application of human rights law to armed conflict is often dated back to the 1968 International Conference on Human Rights at Teheran. That world conference also spurred a series of annual UN General Assembly Resolutions entitled 'Respect for Human Rights in Armed Conflicts', and those resolutions were a prelude to the 1977 Geneva Protocols. The recognition of the interconnections between human rights law and armed conflict, however, was a growing trend that began before the Teheran conference. Human rights instruments, some finalized before 1968 and some after, clearly contemplate situations of warfare and military matters. The European Convention on Human Rights (ECHR) (1950) and the Inter-American Convention (1969) both contain derogation clauses referring to 'time of war'. The European Convention also lists the right to life as nonderogable 'except in respect of deaths resulting from lawful acts of war'. The derogation clause in the ICCPR (1966) uses the phrase 'public emergency which threatens the life of the nation' and is well understood to encompass armed conflicts. Article 2 of the Torture Convention (1984) states: 'No exceptional circumstances whatsoever, whether a state of war or a threat of war ... may be invoked as a justification of torture.' The Convention on the Rights of the Child (1989) commits states to promoting the recovery and reintegration of 'child victim[s] of ... armed conflicts' and prohibits the recruitment and use of child soldiers. Article 30 of the Declaration on the Rights of Indigenous Peoples (2006) places restrictions on 'military activities' in the lands and territories of indigenous peoples. And Article 43 of the 2006 Convention for the Protection of All Persons from Enforced Disappearance states that the 'Convention is without prejudice to the provisions of international humanitarian law'.

In corresponding fashion, conventions related to IHL indicate the applicability of human rights norms to situations of armed conflict. The 1949 Geneva Conventions might have referred to universal human rights in preambular language, but disputes over unrelated language culminated in dropping the idea of having a preamble. As the historian Geoffrey Best explains, '[w]hat seems beyond doubt is that the human rights affiliation expressly claimed by the original, minimal preambles was in itself accepted by all parties to the 1949 diplomatic conference to the point even of being taken for granted.'[218] The most readily apparent influence of human rights norms is perhaps Common Article 3, which regulates practices within states' sovereign borders. According to the ICRC Commentaries, the article reflects 'the few essential rules of humanity which all civilized nations consider as valid everywhere and under all circumstances and as being above and outside war itself.'

---

[216] See J. Bellinger III and W. J. Haynes II, 'A US Government Response to the International Committee of the Red Cross Study on Customary International Humanitarian Law', 89 *Int'l. Rev. Red Cross* (2007) 443; and M. Milanovic and S. Sivakumaran, 'Assessing the Authority of the ICRC Customary IHL Study', 104 *Int'l Rev. Red Cross* (2022) 1856.
[217] See generally H. Duffy, 'Trials and Tribulations: Co-Applicability of IHL and Human Rights in an Age of Adjudication', in Z. Bohrer, J. Dill and H. Duffy (eds.), *Law Applicable to Armed Conflict* (2020) 15.
[218] G. Best, *War and Law Since 1945* (1994) 72.

The 1977 Additional Protocols to the Geneva Conventions continued this trend. For example, Article 72 of Additional Protocol I, which delineates some of the convention's field of application, acknowledges the relevance of human rights law: 'The provisions of this Section are additional to the rules concerning humanitarian protection of civilians and civilian objects in the power of a Party to the conflict contained in the Fourth Convention ... as well as to other applicable rules of international law relating to the protection of fundamental human rights during international armed conflict.' Protocol II contains a preamble, which notes that 'international instruments relating to human rights offer a basic protection to the human person'. More fundamentally, the 1977 Protocols represented a significant shift toward the convergence of human rights and humanitarian law norms. One of the leading commentators on the subject, G. I. A. D. Draper, voiced a series of cautions at the time. He advised that actors engaged in promoting such a fusion should consider the divergent interests and distinct structural concerns that animate the two domains of law. In a controversial essay that retains some influence, Draper explained his position:

> ... [International human rights] are neither intended nor adequate to govern an armed conflict between two states in a condition of enmity. The relevance of war to a human-rights regime is that the regime determines what happens to those human rights in that event. The regime in no way purports to regulate the conduct of the war between two states even assuming that both were subject to that human-rights regime. Hostilities and government-governed relationships are different in kind, origin, purpose, and consequences. ... Human-rights regimes and the humanitarian law of war deal with different and distinct relationships. ... It is not possible to have a regional law of war. It is possible to have a regional regime of human rights... .
>
> ...
>
> The attempt to confuse the two regimes of law is insupportable in theory and inadequate in practice. The two regimes are not only distinct but are diametrically opposed... .
>
> ... [T]he law of human rights seeks to reflect the cohesion and harmony in human society and must, from the nature of things, be a different and opposed law to that which seeks to regulate the conduct of hostile relationships between states or other organized armed groups, and in internal rebellions. The humanitarian nature of the modern law of war neither justifies the confusion with, nor dispels the opposition to, human rights.[219]

More recently a different version of Draper's points has emerged: some commentators and a few states (the United States included) have argued that, in addressing particular issues during an armed conflict, IHL should displace or supplant the application of human rights law. For example, Yoram Dinstein, in 'The Recent Evolution of the International Law of Armed Conflict: Confusions, Constraints, and Challenges', 51 *Vand. J. Transnat'l L.* (2018) 701, at 704, acknowledges 'some synergy and even a degree of overlap' between the law of armed conflict (LOAC) and international human rights law (IHL), but insists that they also 'collide head-on in certain critical areas.' In such situations, 'LOAC must prevail over human rights law because ... it is the *lex specialis*.' The problem, in his view, 'is that zealous advocates of human rights law are not willing to yield the moral high ground. They behave like the high priests of a Holy Gospel who regard any deviation from their received dogma as apostasy. ... They think that, by rejecting military necessity, they will lead us to utopia. But what they are liable to bring about is dystopia. If international law were to ignore military necessity, military necessity would ignore international law. Belligerent Parties would simply shed off any inhibitions in the conduct of hostilities.'

The International Court of Justice provided one of the most influential statements on this matter in an Advisory Opinion, *Legality of the Threat or Use of Nuclear Weapons*. The Court was faced with various opposing arguments. One argument maintained that the possession, threat or use of nuclear weapons violated the right to life under the ICCPR, a position supported by a General Comment of the Human Rights Committee in 1984. Another position held that the ICCPR protects human rights only in peacetime. And some states (including the Netherlands, the United Kingdom and the United States) took the position that IHL provides a safe harbour for parties to an armed conflict: if deaths result from actions that comply with IHL, those actions cannot be

---

[219] G.I.A.D. Draper, 'Humanitarian Law and Human Rights', Acta *Juridica* (1979) 193.

considered 'arbitrary' deprivations of the right to life. The British Government, for example, stated, 'The only sensible construction which can be placed on the term "arbitrary" in this context is that it refers to whether or not the deliberate taking of life is unlawful under that part of the international law which was specifically designed to regulate the conduct of hostilities, that is the laws of armed conflict.' In an oft-quoted passage, the ICJ stated:

> [T]he protection of the International Covenant of Civil and Political Rights does not cease in times of war, except by operation of Article 4 of the Covenant whereby certain provisions may be derogated from in a time of national emergency. Respect for the right to life is not, however, such a provision. In principle, the right not arbitrarily to be deprived of one's life applies also in hostilities. The test of what is an arbitrary deprivation of life, however, then falls to be determined by the applicable *lex specialis*, namely, the law applicable in armed conflict which is designed to regulate the conduct of hostilities.

As with many judicial opinions, the meaning of this statement has been subject to different, and sometimes conflicting, interpretations. Consider the following articulation of the Court's analysis and the rationale behind a broad application of the *lex specialis* doctrine:

> Confronted with two legal regimes – human rights law and humanitarian law – containing rules on the taking of lives, the ICJ resorted to the principle that *lex specialis derogat lex generali* to reconcile them, holding that the ICCPR provision on the right to life must be construed by making a *renvoi* to humanitarian law. *Lex specialis derogat lex generali*, or, the specific provision overcomes the general provision, is a canon of construction that is widely considered to be a general principle of law, as applicable in the international legal system as it is in national legal systems. Koskenniemi [in a 2003 paper] provides the principle's rationale: a 'special rule is more to the point ("approaches more nearly the subject in hand") than a general one and it regulates the matter more effectively ("are ordinarily more effective") than general rules do'. The thinking goes that because many of the same states have negotiated and acceded to the human rights law and humanitarian law treaties, we should presume that these treaties are consistent with one another. We should not think, for example, that it violates the right to liberty under the ICCPR or ECHR to hold a combatant as a prisoner of war until the end of active hostilities when, after all, the same states that negotiated the ICCPR and ECHR also negotiated an entire treaty on prisoners of war that allows exactly that. Because general rules ('No one shall be subjected to arbitrary arrest or detention.') may be interpreted in more than one way, we should interpret them in light of specific rules ('Prisoners of war shall be released and repatriated without delay after the cessation of hostilities.') rather than vice versa.[220]

The ICJ issued two more recent opinions involving the application of human rights in armed conflict and military occupation. The first, in 2004, concerned Israel's construction of a physical barrier in occupied Palestinian territory. The second, in 2006, involved an armed conflict between the Democratic Republic of the Congo and Uganda. On both occasions, the Court provided the following formulation:

> … [T]he protection offered by human rights conventions does not cease in case of armed conflict, save through the effect of provisions for derogation of the kind to be found in Article 4 of the International Covenant on Civil and Political Rights. As regards the relationship between international humanitarian law and human rights law, there are thus three possible situations: some rights may be exclusively matters of international humanitarian law; others may be exclusively matters of human rights law; yet others may be matters of both these branches of international law.[221]

Vaios Koutroulis, in 'Are IHL and HRL Still Two Distinct Branches of Public International Law?', in Robert Kolb, Gloria Gaggioli, and Pavle Kilibarda (eds.), *Research Handbook on Human Rights and Humanitarian Law: Further Reflections and Perspectives* (2022) 29, at 56, begins his analysis with a reference to Robert Kolb's assessment in 2010 that:

---

[220] W. Abresch, 'A Human Rights Law of Internal Armed Conflict: The European Court of Human Rights in Chechnya',16 *Eur. J. Int'l L.* (2005) 741.

[221] *Legal Consequences of the Construction of a Wall in the Occupied Palestinian Territory, Advisory Opinion*, I. C. J. Reports 2004, para. 106.

All logically possible positions concerning the relationship between the two poles of IHL and HRL [human rights law] have been defended in legal writings. First it has been said that IHL and HRL are completely separate and should remain so. Second, it has been affirmed that IHL and HRL entertain specific relations of complementarity. Third, it has been held that IHL and HRL are but two branches of the same tree and that they largely merge into one another. ... Today [these debates] appear to belong to a bygone age. The close ties between both branches are now universally recognized.

But Koutroulis's own analysis injects an element of political reality when he concludes that:

... [N]othing prevents the distinct character of IHL and HRL from being used for the benefit of HRL, helping it deploy its full effects, even in situations of armed conflict. The fact that the majority of States have not until now chosen this path speaks volumes about how strongly they want to preserve IHL, and, probably, the prerogatives that they (wish to) draw from it.

In the same volume, Walter Kälin and Jörg Künzli, in 'Human Rights Bodies: A Comparative Approach', show that there has been a clear and continuous convergence of the two bodies of law in the jurisprudence of the UN treaty bodies and of the regional courts, but they suggest that '[i]rreconcilable peculiarities of specific guarantees as well as the fact that ultimately human rights bodies are only competent to find violations of IHRL and not of IHL arguably set intrinsic limits to their full merger' (at 208).

In *The Use of Force against Individuals in War under International Law* (2022), Ka Lok Yip contrasts two prominent approaches that reflect concern at the consequences of conflating the two branches of law:

[Modirzadeh][222] ... sees the practical effect of their conflation as the transformation of LOAC into 'human rights policy' and IHRL into 'war governance', diluting the clarity of both and undermining the moral resonance of IHRL.

...

Attributing this 'blend of vague IHL concepts and human rights standards' to US-based IHRL lawyers' attempts to 'maintain a meaningful role in the policy discussion', she criticizes it as 'jumping over the question of whether the overall framing of the war against al Qaeda is anathema to human rights law and entering into the regulation of the killing itself'.

Both Modirzadeh and Moyn[223] are concerned about the imperialistic implications of the introduction of IHRL into cross-border armed conflicts, though from slightly different angles. For Modirzadeh the 'confusing admixture of IHL-like language, human rights rhetoric, and conduct-of-hostilities principles', most often used in transnational conflicts involving US attacks on non-state actors in a state with which the US is not, or at least does not acknowledge that it is, in conflict, helps sidestep its interventionist dimension. 'It becomes possible to say that IHRL can be utilized to allow for one state to invade another state's territory in order to murder individuals without an attempt to arrest, detain, charge, and try these individuals'. For Moyn, the chief concern has been 'the agenda of humanizing war while letting slip our more ambitious hopes for its eradication', referencing especially 'the Americans' situation today as we find ourselves in a "forever war" — one that has continued for almost two decades at least in part because of how humane it has been made to seem'. ... [T]he convergence of the two could entail a corrupting effect on IHRL. Not only would the compliance with LOAC be used to create the impression of a 'humane war', which masks the destructive aspect of war and dampens the urge to prevent aggression, but IHRL would also be drafted in to accentuate this illusion of the 'humaneness' of war.

---

[222] N. Modirzadeh, 'Folk International Law: 9/ 11 Lawyering and the Transformation of the Law of Armed Conflict to Human Rights Policy and Human Rights Law to War Governance', 5 *Harv. Nat' Sec. J.* (2014) 225, at 228.
[223] S. Moyn, *Humane: How the United States Abandoned Peace and Reinvented War* (2021).

By way of conclusion, Marko Milanovic, in 'The Lost Origins of *Lex Specialis*: Rethinking the Relationship between Human Rights and International Humanitarian Law', in Jens Ohlin (ed.), *Theoretical Boundaries of Armed Conflict and Human Rights* (2016) 78, at 114, emphasizes the complexity of the various regimes that are being merged, argues that the *lex specialis* principle needs to be critically re-examined and perhaps abandoned, and suggests a pragmatic way forward:

> The appeal of *lex specialis* lies in the veneer of antiquity of its Latin formula, in its apparent formality, simplicity, and objectivity. But all it really does is disguise a series of policy judgments about what outcomes are the most sensible, realistic, and practicable in any given situation. The strong variant of *lex specialis* is neither old, nor established, nor formally sound.
>
> I would thus favor dropping the *lex specialis* language … [and saying] that IHL and IHRL should be taken into account when interpreting one another, in accordance with Article 31(3)(c) [of the Vienna Convention on the Law of Treaties], without having to inquire into which one is special and which general. …
>
> … [N]ot everyone will agree with my critique … . How then to move forward …? …
>
> … [B]oth camps must acknowledge that the adherents of the other camp make some valid arguments … .
>
> Second, … applying human rights in armed conflict involves striking a balance between the universality of human rights on the one hand and considerations of effectiveness on the other, just like IHL itself embodies a balance between humanitarianism and military necessity. In particular, the corpus of human rights law, developed over decades by courts and treaty bodies primarily in times of normalcy, must be adjusted and applied more flexibly in extraordinary situations in order to avoid imposing excessive, unrealistic burdens on states. … [T]he really difficult question is how far do normal tools of interpretation allow us to go in order to achieve this flexibility. The watering down of human rights during armed conflict certainly must not go too far, so as to render them completely ineffectual or to compromise the integrity of the regime as a whole. We must also arrive at specific rules applying to specific problems that are clear and predictable, rather than endlessly ruminate on the relationship between IHL and IHRL as a whole. Derogations have the potential of being a powerful (if under-utilized) tool for achieving these goals of flexibility, regime integrity, and clarity.

NOTE

An important question that is not addressed in the materials above concerns the consequences of defining a situation neither in armed conflict nor in straightforward human rights terms. Consider this analysis by Special Rapporteur Ní Aoláin (UN Doc. A/77/345 (2022), para. 29):

> … First, international humanitarian law has an undisputed set of treaty and customary law standards which frame both State and non-State actor obligations in situations of armed conflict, including but not limited to detention, protection of civilians, status of combatants, methods and means of warfare and impartial humanitarian action. Terrorism lacks an agreed international law definition and is characterized by significant imprecision in its use and application. Applying a vague, inexact and State-subjective set of regulations to a highly complex phenomenon means that we lack consistency in standards applied to State conduct; we do not have a clear consensus on what a breach of these standards might look like, and with so much inbuilt ambiguity there is an ongoing risk of abuse. Second, as a conceptual matter the fundamental logic of terrorism discourse and practice is focused on destroying the terrorist group, targeting and extinguishing its means of support and breaking up the leadership and structures that enable the production of violence. The mantra of "not negotiating with terrorists", common across multiple

political contexts, means that once a situation or group is framed in terms of "terrorism", dialogue and negotiation is often formally prohibited and politically unacceptable. Armed conflict does not prohibit or preclude negotiation with the "enemy", and in practice has multiple pathways to bring an end to conflict, whether by amnesty … negotiation … or exchange of prisoners … . Third, the acceptance of a counter-terrorism framework generally brings a number of its regulatory preferences into play, including proscription of groups and individuals, sanctions, emergency powers that impact due process, legal proceedings and freedom of movement, countering terrorism finance measures and limitations on freedoms of expression (e.g., Internet shutdowns). Many of these measures function to exacerbate fundamental grievances that drive violence and are consistently identified with systematic human rights violations in multiple countries. These measures restrict the capacity to resolve the violence or address grievance through a more comprehensive approach, such as by way of ceasefire or peace agreements.

C. RENDITIONS

Following the 11 September attacks and the Security Council recognition of the U.S. right to self-defence, US and British forces invaded Afghanistan on 7 October 2001. By January 2002, the United States began transporting alleged Taliban and Al Qaeda members to its military base at Guantánamo Bay, Cuba. Individuals linked to Al Qaeda were apprehended not only in Afghanistan, but in other countries as well including Bosnia-Herzegovina, Egypt, Gambia, Mauritania, Pakistan and Thailand, and then transferred to Guantánamo.

The U.S. Government contended that all Taliban and Al Qaeda members were 'unlawful combatants' who, therefore, failed to qualify as prisoners of war (POW) under the Third Geneva Convention. What was at stake? As a legal matter, according POW status to detainees would require the Government to guarantee specific trial rights not necessarily provided by U.S. military commissions. POW status would also provide combatant immunity for membership in an enemy armed force (though no immunity applies to the commission of acts of terrorism, perfidy or other war crimes). Furthermore, POW status would oblige the United States to provide for certain conditions of detention, though these conditions are not clearly far superior to conditions of detention required under the Civilians (Fourth Geneva) Convention.[224] As a more general matter, according POW status might lend a form of legitimacy to these organizations.

Article 5 of the POW Convention states that '[s]hould any doubt arise as to whether persons, having committed a belligerent act and having fallen into the hands of the enemy, belong to any of the categories enumerated in Article 4, such persons shall enjoy the protection of the present Convention until such time as their status has been determined by a competent tribunal.'

The United States declared that the Geneva Conventions applied to the international armed conflict with Afghanistan. But it also contended that the Taliban and Al Qaeda and other associated groups failed to satisfy the POW criteria, that as a non-state actor (and especially as a terrorist group) Al Qaeda could not receive the protections of the Geneva Conventions, and because there was no doubt about status, an Article 5 tribunal was unnecessary.

A wide range of intergovernmental and nongovernmental organizations contested the U.S. position, including the Inter-American Commission on Human rights, the European Parliament, the International Committee of the Red Cross, the UN High Commissioner for Human Rights, and a number of foreign governments. In response, the United States pursued an inconsistent but self-serving set of legal approaches, revolving around the central question of whether or not the U.S. was involved in an armed conflict with Al Qaeda. Ryan Goodman traces some of the twists and turns:

---

[224] D. Jinks, 'The Declining Significance of POW Status', 45 *Harv. Int'l L. J.* (2004) 367.

RYAN GOODMAN, THE LAWS OF WAR IN THE AGE OF TERROR
28 J. TRANSNAT'L L. & POL'Y (2018-2019) 1

...

A. Turn 1.

Not an "Armed Conflict": Militarization

In the weeks following September 11, many experts argued that the U.S. could not be, as a matter of international law, in an armed conflict with al-Qaeda.

What was at stake? ... Accepting the armed conflict paradigm would lead to a highly militarized response ... and expansive executive and governmental power. Accordingly, arguing that the situation did not constitute an armed conflict could potentially restrain the war machine internationally and limit excessive state power at home.

... Alain Pellet ... wrote an essay entitled, "No, This Is Not War!" [contending] that the idea that the U.S. could be in an armed conflict was "legally false" [and] could lead to a "spiral of hate" and violence, "create more 'martyrs[,]'" and cost "thousands of lives of those who are already victims of the Taliban."

B. Turn 2.

Is an "Armed Conflict": Combatant Status-Determinations

Once U.S. forces began apprehending detainees in Afghanistan and elsewhere, some experts argued that the United States was in a standard armed conflict that included the Taliban and al-Qaeda.

What was at stake? The debate centered on whether the U.S. had an obligation under Article 5 of the Prisoners of War Convention to establish an independent tribunal to determine the status of individuals detained in Afghanistan and elsewhere (e.g., Bosnia). The Geneva Conventions apply only if an armed conflict exists. ... John Cerone, contended, "It is arguable that the law of international armed conflict should also govern relations between the [U.S.] and Al-Qaeda," and he suggested that Article 5 applied to members of al-Qaeda. ... [I]f the situation did not constitute an armed conflict, one could not invoke those provisions of the law of armed conflict to provide procedural protections.

C. Turn 3.

Not an "Armed Conflict": Indefinite Military Detention

Once long-term and indefinite military detention of individuals became a reality, many experts argued that the U.S. could not be in an armed conflict with al-Qaeda.

What was at stake? The Bush administration invoked the war model to argue that the law of armed conflict permits the U.S. to hold combatants in military detention "until the cessation of hostilities." In response, many experts argued [including in an amicus brief submitted to the Supreme Court in *Al-Marri v. Spagone*] that the U.S. was not in an armed conflict. ...

D. Turn 4.

Not an "Armed Conflict": Military Commission Jurisdiction

Following a Presidential Military Order establishing military commissions to try those responsible for September 11, many experts argued that such commissions were unlawful because the U.S. was not in an armed conflict with al-Qaeda.

What was at stake? ... [I]ndividuals could be tried before a military commission only for violations of the law of armed conflict. Arguing that the attacks on September 11 did not take place in an armed conflict could potentially stop military commissions in their tracks. ...

E. Turn 5.

Is an "Armed Conflict": Fair Trial Rights and Torture

Once military commissions were underway, many experts argued that such trials were unlawful because the law of armed conflict applied. ... [M]any of the same experts (myself included) also took the position that torture of detainees was prohibited by the laws of war.

What was at stake? Common Article 3 of the Geneva Conventions applies to armed conflicts between state and nonstate actors. It requires that any trials meet international standards of fairness and that all detainees be treated humanely. If Common Article 3 applies, the commissions could be held unlawful under the Geneva Conventions and CIA interrogation practices would be invalid. As a matter of customary international law, the rule reflected in Article 75 of ... Additional Protocol I could also potentially invalidate the trials and inhumane treatment of detainees. However, to apply Common Article 3 and Article 75 of Additional Protocol I requires the existence of an armed conflict.

...

F. Turn 6.
Not an "Armed Conflict": Extrajudicial Killings

Once attention became focused on the use of lethal force (e.g., targeted killings), many experts argued that the United States was not in an armed conflict with al-Qaeda.

What was at stake? The law of armed conflict is significantly more permissive than international human rights law in regulating the conditions under which individuals can be killed. Accordingly, many of the targeted killings and signature strikes carried out by the U.S. arguably would be illegal if they did not take place in an armed conflict. Professor Mary Ellen O'Connell ... has repeatedly argued that the legality of U.S. lethal force depended on this distinction; she has argued that the United States could not be in an armed conflict with al-Qaeda and therefore the U.S.' use of lethal force is illegal.

G. Final Turns.
Is an "Armed Conflict": The Future?

Other turns in the designation of the law of armed conflict have occurred with respect to the release of detainees from Guantanamo Bay. These turns include acceptance of the law of armed conflict model and calling for the release of wounded and sick detainees consistent with those provisions of the Geneva Conventions. More dramatically, they also include the call for the release of detainees on the ground that the armed conflict, or at least the condition of active hostilities, is now over.

...

In [the future], the United States will likely maintain, in step with presidential administrations over the past three decades, that international human rights law either does not apply or does not impose any additional restrictions in important situations. It is a familiar three-step move in which (1) the United States contests whether certain human rights law applies extraterritorially; (2) even if human rights law applies extraterritorially, the United States then contests whether certain human rights rules apply to some matters of armed conflict; and (3) even if human rights law applies extraterritorially and to matters of armed conflict, the United States then contests whether certain human rights rules apply when the United States does not exercise effective control on the ground. In short, the United States may disclaim that either the law of armed conflict or important international human rights obligations apply.

Under these circumstances, there will be strong pressures for experts to argue that the United States remains in an armed conflict as long as the government undertakes lethal military actions against organized armed groups--and that law of armed conflict should thus regulate the exercise of violence as a matter of law. In other words, there will be a reason to flip back again, this time in support of the application of the law of armed conflict. ...

* * *

Responding to renditions

Another way for the United States to avoid inconvenient legal constraints in prosecuting the 'war on terror' was to resort to secret detentions and clandestine transfers. The term 'rendition' is a euphemism to describe the practice of covertly sending a suspect for interrogation in a country where less rigorous, or no, human rights standards would be applied. Another alternative was to detain prisoners in Guantánamo, which was assumed to be beyond the reach of established systems of justice.

A range of UN human rights special procedures mechanisms sought to engage with the U.S. Government, over both renditions and Guantánamo, but to no avail. In 2005, the United States agreed to a one-day visit to Guantánamo by a group of these experts but refused to permit private meetings with detainees. The group rejected such terms as being incompatible with standard fact-finding procedures. In 2010, four mechanisms (dealing with torture, counter-terrorism, arbitrary detention, and disappearances) took the unprecedented step of issuing a 186-page 'joint study on global practices in relation to secret detention' (UN Doc. A/HRC/13/42). In 2022, the Special Rapporteur on human rights and counter-terrorism submitted a follow-up to that report (UN Doc. A/HRC/49/45), concluding that current practices:

> … [C]ontinue to be marked by an abject lack of adherence to fundamental human rights norms, thin lines of judicial oversight, meagre to non-existent legal and/or political accountability, targeting of religious and ethnic minorities, and a high degree of tolerance by democratic and non-democratic States alike for the subversion of the rule of law to enable persons to be rendered to jurisdictions where they have a high likelihood of being subjected to arbitrary detention, surveillance, and torture and other cruel, inhuman and degrading treatment or punishment. The permissive environment created for human right "lite" counter-terrorism since 11 September 2001, the growth of the global counter-terrorism architecture, the privatization of counter-terrorism and the weakening of national oversight mechanisms have all contributed to the current status quo. …

The following materials illustrate some of the responses within the international human rights regime by focusing on the example of one individual whose detention has been the subject of extensive litigation. Zayn al-Abidin Muhammad Husayn, consistently known as Abu Zubaydah, is a stateless Palestinian who continues to be imprisoned as an 'enemy combatant' at the U.S. detention facility in Guantánamo Bay, Cuba. An accurate overview of his treatment is provided by Joseph Margulies, one of his attorneys, in an amicus curiae brief to the U.S. Supreme Court on 11 February 2021:[225]

> For several years after his capture, Abu Zubaydah was held in various CIA "black sites" in foreign countries, where he was subjected to a relentless regime of "enhanced interrogations." On 83 different occasions in a single month of 2002, he was strapped to an inclined board with his head lower than his feet while CIA contractors poured water up his nose and down his throat, bringing him within sight of death. He was handcuffed and repeatedly slammed into walls, and suspended naked from hooks in the ceiling for hours at a time. He was forced to remain awake for eleven consecutive days, and doused again and again with cold water when he collapsed into sleep. He was forced into a tall, narrow box the size of a coffin, and crammed into another box that would nearly fit under a chair, where he was left for hours. He was subjected to a particularly grotesque humiliation described by the CIA as "rectal rehydration."

> In ostensible justification of this torture, the CIA initially took the position that Abu Zubaydah had been, inter alia, the "third or fourth man" in al Qaeda, and that he was "involved in every major terrorist operation carried out by al Qaeda," including as "one of the planners of the September 11 attacks." The CIA also maintained that Abu Zubaydah had some unique ability to resist interrogations and that he had authored the al Qaeda manual on resistance techniques. But a 2014 report of the Senate Select Committee on Intelligence determined that all these allegations were either false or unsupported by any CIA record. The CIA eventually concluded, for instance, that Abu Zubaydah had been telling the truth when he protested that he was not a member of al Qaeda. Moreover, "CIA records [did] not support" the assertion that Abu Zubaydah helped plan the September 11 attacks or any other "major terrorist operation," or that he

[225] For a personal account, see Abu Zubaydah, '"I didn't know who I was any more": how CIA torture pushed me to the edge of death', *The Guardian* (29 January 2022). See also H. Duffy, 'Dignity Denied: A Case Study', in C. Paulussen and M. Scheinin (eds.), *Human Dignity and Human Security in Times of Terrorism* (2020) 67.

had any expertise in resisting interrogations. And the most inflammatory allegation—that he had been a senior officer in al Qaeda—had been based on "single-source reporting that was recanted." The Government's contrary statement in its Petition – that Abu Zubaydah "was an associate and longtime terrorist ally of Osama bin Laden" – is categorically false.

HUSAYN (ABU ZUBAYDAH) V. POLAND
EUROPEAN COURT OF HUMAN RIGHTS, CHAMBER OF THE FOURTH SECTION, APPLICATION NO. 7511/13 (24 JULY 2014)

[Note: Because the judgment runs to 225 pages, the original headings have been omitted below.]

[National security or confidentiality concerns]

360. [In *Al Nashiri v. Poland*, Application no. 28761/11, 24 July 2014, a case with similar facts to, and decided at the same time as, the present case] the Court was mindful that the evidence requested from the Government was liable to be of a sensitive nature or might give rise to national-security concerns. For that reason, already at the initial stage of the proceedings, it gave the Government an explicit guarantee as to the confidentiality of any sensitive materials they might have produced. ...

361. However, no national-security related arguments have ever been invoked by the Government in response to the Court's evidential requests and none of the requested documents have materialised. The Government justified their failure to produce the relevant evidence by the need to ensure the secrecy of the investigation into the applicant's allegations of torture and secret detention in Poland. ... [T]hey suggested that the Court should conform to the rules of their national law. ...

...

365. ... [T]he respondent State's refusal to submit evidence based on an alleged lack of sufficient procedural safeguards guaranteeing the confidentiality of the material that they were asked to provide cannot be justified in terms of Article 38 of the Convention [the duty to furnish all necessary facilities for the Court's examination of a case].

366. Nor can ... the respondent Government ... refuse to comply with the Court's evidential request by relying on their national laws or domestic legal impediments; ... .

...

368. ... Given the exceptional difficulties involved in the obtaining of evidence by the Court owing to the high secrecy of the US rendition operations, the limitations on the applicant's contact with the outside world, including his lawyers, and his inability to give any direct account of the events complained of, those documents were also important for the examination of his complaints under other provisions of the Convention. The Polish Government have had access to information capable of elucidating the facts as submitted in the application. Their failure to submit information in their possession must, therefore, be seen as hindering the Court's tasks ... . [T]he Court is entitled to draw inferences from the Polish Government's conduct ... .

...

[Poland's cooperation]
435. ... [T]he Court finds that in the course of the relevant international inquiries the Polish authorities displayed conduct that can be characterised as denial, lack of cooperation with the inquiry bodies and marked reluctance to disclose information of the CIA rendition activities in Poland.

[Poland's knowledge and complicity]
...
444. ... [T]he Court finds that there is abundant and coherent circumstantial evidence, which leads inevitably to the following conclusions:

(a) that Poland knew of the nature and purposes of the CIA's activities on its territory at the material time and that, by enabling the CIA to use its airspace and the airport, by its complicity in disguising the movements of rendition aircraft and by its provision of logistics and services, including the special security arrangements, the special procedure for landings, the transportation of the CIA teams with detainees on land, and the securing of the Stare Kiejkuty base for the CIA's secret detention, Poland cooperated in the preparation and execution of the CIA rendition, secret detention and interrogation operations on its territory;

(b) that, given that knowledge and the emerging widespread public information …, Poland ought to have known that, by enabling the CIA to detain such persons on its territory, it was exposing them to a serious risk of treatment contrary to the Convention.

445. Consequently, Poland was in a position where its responsibility for securing "to everyone within [its] jurisdiction the rights and freedoms defined …. in [the] Convention" set forth in Article 1 was engaged in respect of the applicant at the material time.

…

[Article 3 – substantive obligations]

499. Article 3 of the Convention enshrines one of the most fundamental values of democratic societies. … [It] makes no provision for exceptions and no derogation from it is permissible … . Even in the most difficult circumstances, such as the fight against terrorism and organised crime, the Convention prohibits in absolute terms torture and inhuman or degrading treatment or punishment, irrespective of the conduct of the person concerned.

…

508. … The 2007 ICRC report gives a shocking account of the cruel treatment to which the applicant was subjected in CIA custody, from the waterboarding, through beating by the use of a collar and confinement in a box, to exposure to cold temperature and food deprivation. …

…

511. The CIA documents state that this treatment was inflicted on the applicant with the aim of obtaining information – in particular, "actionable intelligence of future threats to the United States". … [The measures] were used in a premeditated and organised manner, on the basis of a formalised, clinical procedure, setting out a "wide range of legally sanctioned techniques" and specifically designed to elicit information or confessions or to obtain intelligence from captured terrorist suspects. Those – explicitly declared – aims were, most notably, "to psychologically 'dislocate' the detainee, maximize his feeling of vulnerability and helplessness, and reduce or eliminate his will to resist … efforts to obtain critical intelligence"; "to persuade High-Value Detainees to provide threat information and terrorist intelligence in a timely manner"; "to create a state of learned helplessness and dependence"; and their underlying concept was "using both physical and psychological pressures in a comprehensive, systematic and cumulative manner to influence [a High-Value Detainee's] behaviour, to overcome a detainee's resistance posture".

… [T]he Court concludes that the treatment to which the applicant was subjected by the CIA during his detention in Poland at the relevant time amounted to torture … .

512. … [T]he Polish State, on account of its "acquiescence and connivance" in the HVD Programme must be regarded as responsible for the violation of the applicant's rights under Article 3 of the Convention committed on its territory.

…

* * *

In 2016, the European Parliament adopted a resolution (2016/2573(RSP)) in which it criticized the apathy of EU governments and institutions in response to the US Senate study, welcomed the 2016 European Court of Human Rights judgment in *Nasr and Ghali v Italy* (44883/09) 'which found that the Italian authorities had been aware of the torture perpetrated [by CIA agents] against Egyptian imam Abu Omar, and had clearly made use of the principle of 'state secrecy' to ensure that those responsible were granted de facto impunity', and called on the USA 'to investigate and prosecute the multiple human rights violations resulting from the CIA rendition and secret detention programmes'.

UNITED STATES V.. HUSAYN, AKA ZUBAYDAH, ET AL.
SUPREME COURT OF THE UNITED STATES, 595 U. S. ____ (2022), 3 MARCH 2022

JUSTICE BREYER delivered the opinion of the Court ... .*

Abu Zubaydah, a detainee in the Guantánamo Bay Naval Base, [sought] to subpoena two former Central Intelligence Agency contractors. Zubaydah sought to obtain information (for use in Polish litigation) about his treatment in 2002 and 2003 at a CIA detention site, which Zubaydah says was located in Poland. ... The Government intervened. It moved to quash the subpoenas based on the state secrets privilege. That privilege allows the Government to bar the disclosure of information that, were it revealed, would harm national security.

The Court of Appeals for the Ninth Circuit mostly accepted the Government's claim of privilege. *Husayn v. Mitchell*, 938 F. 3d 1123, 1134 (2019). But it concluded that the privilege did not cover information about the location of the detention site, which ... had already been publicly disclosed and that the state secrets privilege did not bar disclosure of information that was no longer secret ... .

I A

...

... [Various] publicly available sources say that, in 2002 and 2003, Zubaydah was detained at a CIA facility in Poland. But, the Government states, the CIA itself has never confirmed that one or more of its clandestine detention sites was located in any specific foreign country. Neither, as far as we can tell from the record, have the contractors Mitchell and Jessen [who designed and implemented much of the interrogation program] named the specific foreign countries in which CIA detention sites were located. ... Finally, although at least one former Polish government official has stated that Poland cooperated with the CIA, to our knowledge, the Polish government itself has never confirmed such allegations.

B 1

In 2010, lawyers representing Zubaydah filed a criminal complaint in Poland asking prosecutors there to hold ac- countable any Polish nationals who were involved in his alleged mistreatment in that country. Invoking a Mutual Legal Assistance Treaty, the Polish prosecutors asked American authorities for information. The United States Department of Justice refused their request on the ground that providing the information would adversely affect our national security.

In response [to the ECHR judgment, above], the Polish prosecutors reopened their investigation. They again requested information from the United States [and it was again denied].

2

... Zubaydah asked for permission to serve the contractors, Mitchell and Jessen, with subpoenas commanding them to appear for depositions and to produce "documents, memoranda and correspondence" regarding an alleged CIA detention facility in Poland and Zubaydah's treatment there. ...
... The Government claimed that disclosure of the information Zubaydah sought would violate the state secrets privilege. ...

To support its privilege claim, the Government submitted a declaration from the Director of the CIA. The Director said that Mitchell and Jessen's response to Zubaydah's subpoenas would, in this case, confirm or deny whether Poland had cooperated with the CIA. And that confirmation, the Director explained, would significantly harm our national security interests.
...

II A

The state secrets privilege permits the Government to prevent disclosure of information when that disclosure would harm national security interests. ...

---

* Various justices joined different parts of the plurality opinion.

JUSTICE GORSUCH agrees that the Government must show a reasonable danger of harm to national security, that a court must decide for itself whether the occasion is appropriate for claiming the privilege, and that in camera review is not always required to make that determination. ... We diverge from the dissent on how those principles should apply to the specific discovery requests Zubaydah has made in this litigation. Of course, our answer to that question is not a judgment of Zubaydah's alleged terrorist activities, nor of his treatment at the hands of the United States Government. Obviously the Court condones neither terrorism nor torture, but in this case we are required to decide only a narrow evidentiary dispute.

B

...

Because any response to Zubaydah's subpoenas allowed by the Ninth Circuit's decision will have the effect of confirmation or denial (by the Government or its former contractors) of the existence of a CIA facility in Poland, the primary question for us must be whether the existence (or non-existence) of a CIA detention facility in Poland falls within the scope of the state secrets privilege. For the reasons that follow, we conclude that it does.

1

We agree with the Government that sometimes information that has entered the public domain may nonetheless fall within the scope of the state secrets privilege. But see 938 F. 3d, at 1133 ("[I]n order to be a 'state secret,' a fact must first be a 'secret' "). The Government here has provided a reasonable explanation of why Mitchell and Jessen's confirmation or denial of the information Zubaydah seeks could significantly harm national security interests, even if that information has already been made public through unofficial sources.

The CIA Director stated in his declaration that the Agency's counterterrorism efforts rely on "clandestine" relationships with foreign intelligence services. The Director explained that foreign intelligence services "are a critical intelligence source," whose help is "vital to our world-wide efforts to collect intelligence and thwart terrorist attacks." He further explained that these "sensitive" relationships with other nations are "based on mutual trust that the classified existence and nature of the relationship will not be disclosed." To confirm the existence of such a relationship would "breach" that trust and have "serious negative consequences" ... . In a word, to confirm publicly the existence of a CIA site in Country A, can diminish the extent to which the intelligence services of Countries A, B, C, D, etc., will prove willing to cooperate with our own intelligence services in the future.

JUSTICE GORSUCH believes that the Government has failed to meet its "burden of showing that a 'reasonable danger' of harm to national security would follow from sharing the information sought." ... We disagree. It stands to reason that a former CIA insider's confirmation of confidential cooperation between the CIA and a foreign intelligence service could damage the CIA's clandestine relationships with foreign authorities. Confirmation by such an insider is different in kind from speculation in the press or even by foreign courts because it leaves virtually no doubt as to the veracity of the information that has been confirmed. ...

...

3

The Court of Appeals also believed that, because Mitchell and Jessen are "private parties," their "disclosures [were] not equivalent to the United States confirming or denying anything." We do not agree with this conclusion. Mitchell and Jessen worked directly for the CIA as contractors. Zubaydah contends (without contradiction) that Mitchell and Jessen "devised and implemented" the CIA's enhanced-interrogation program and that they personally interrogated Zubaydah. Given Mitchell and Jessen's central role in the relevant events, we believe that their confirmation (or denial) of the information Zubaydah seeks would be tantamount to a disclosure from the CIA itself. ...

4

At the same time, Zubaydah's need is not great. At oral argument Zubaydah suggested that he did not seek confirmation of the detention site's Polish location so much as he sought information about what had happened there. ...

5

For these reasons, we conclude that in this case the state secrets privilege applies to the existence (or nonexistence) of a CIA facility in Poland. It therefore precludes further discovery ... [since] such discovery will inevitably confirm or deny the existence of such a facility.

...

JUSTICE GORSUCH, with whom JUSTICE SOTOMAYOR joins, dissenting.

There comes a point where we should not be ignorant as judges of what we know to be true as citizens. ...

...

The government invoked the state secrets privilege only 16 times be-tween 1961 and 1980. ... Yet it has done so at least 49 times between 2001 and 2021. ...

...

...The record before us is stark. Zubaydah's detention in Poland took place 20 years ago. The location of the CIA's detention site has been acknowledged by the former Polish President, investigated by the Council of Europe, and proven "beyond reasonable doubt" to the European Court of Human Rights. Doubtless, these disclosures may have done damage to national security interests. But nothing in the record of this case suggests that requiring the government to acknowledge what the world already knows to be true would invite a reasonable danger of additional harm to national security. The government's only evidence is a declaration couched in conclusory terms ... .

...

... [For the plurality] A bare expression of national security concern becomes reason enough to deny the ancient right to every man's evidence.

...

In the end, only one argument for dismissing this case at its outset begins to make sense. ... [T]he government wants this suit dismissed because it hopes to impede the Polish criminal investigation and avoid (or at least delay) further embarrassment for past misdeeds. Perhaps at one level this is easy enough to understand. The facts are hard to face. ... But as embarrassing as these facts may be, there is no state secret here. This Court's duty is to the rule of law and the search for truth. We should not let shame obscure our vision.

QUESTIONS

1. Is the U.S. Government's position on the relationship between the two bodies of law — IHL and human rights law — persuasive? Do human rights bodies have the necessary expertise and competence to interpret and apply IHL? What factors should determine the appropriate role for such an institution?

2. Does the special threat posed by terrorism suggest that older, more protective rules are less applicable in this new context? Or is the nature of the conflict so vague and open-ended such that greater judicial safeguards are needed?

3. How would you account for the very different approaches to the practice of rendition reflected in the judgments of the European Court and the US Supreme Court?

D. DETENTION

Prior to 11 September, the UK Parliament passed the Terrorism Act 2000. The law provides a general definition of terrorism, which serves as the backbone of British anti-terrorism laws and practices. Section 1 of the legislation reads:

1 Terrorism: interpretation

(1) In this Act 'terrorism' means the use or threat of action where –

(a) the action falls within subsection (2),

(b) the use or threat is designed to influence the government or to intimidate the public or a section of the public, and

(c) the use or threat is made for the purpose of advancing a political, religious or ideological cause.

(2) Action falls within this subsection if it –

(a) involves serious violence against a person,

(b) involves serious damage to property,

(c) endangers a person's life, other than that of the person committing the action,

(d) creates a serious risk to the health or safety of the public or a section of the public, or

(e) is designed seriously to interfere with or seriously to disrupt an electronic system.

(3) The use or threat of action falling within subsection (2) which involves the use of firearms or explosives is terrorism whether or not subsection (1)(b) is satisfied.

(4) In this section –

(a) 'action' includes action outside the United Kingdom,

(b) a reference to any person or to property is a reference to any person, or to property, wherever situated,

(c) a reference to the public includes a reference to the public of a country other than the United Kingdom, ...
...

(5) In this Act a reference to action taken for the purposes of terrorism includes a reference to action taken for the benefit of a proscribed organisation.

In the aftermath of 11 September, the United Kingdom took two significant steps. First, Parliament passed the Anti-terrorism, Crime and Security Act 2001 (ATCSA). The Act provides broad powers to detain foreign nationals who cannot be deported, for example due to the threat of torture on their return or the lack of agreement with their home country. Section 23(1) states:

(1) A suspected international terrorist may be detained ... despite the fact that his removal or departure from the United Kingdom is prevented (whether temporarily or indefinitely) by –

(a) a point of law which wholly or partly relates to an international agreement, or

(b) a practical consideration.

Second, the government submitted a detailed Derogation Order under the European Convention on Human Rights and the ICCPR in contemplation of the new detention rules.

Under the ATCSA, the UK Home Secretary certified a total of 17 foreign nationals as 'suspected international terrorists'. These individuals were detained without the prospect of a criminal trial. They were alleged by the Home Secretary to have engaged in various activities including maintaining 'extensive contacts to senior terrorists worldwide', being 'at the centre in the UK of terrorist activities associated with al-Qaeda', being an 'active supporter of various international terrorist groups, including those with links to Osama Bin Laden's terrorist network ... [and engaging in] activities on their behalf include[ing] fund raising', and being 'an active supporter of the Tunisian Fighting Group, a terrorist organisation with close links to al-Qaeda ... [and having] provided direct assistance to a number of active terrorists.'

In a case brought before the UK's highest court, the then House of Lords, the petitioners had been certified as suspected international terrorists between December 2001 and early 2002. They could not be deported to their home countries because they faced a risk of torture or inhuman or degrading treatment. The Home Secretary accordingly detained the petitioners pursuant to section 23(1) of the ATCSA. Two of the detainees exercised their right to leave the United Kingdom: one went to Morocco and the other to France. One detainee was released on bail on strict conditions in April 2004. The Home Secretary revoked the certification of another detainee in September 2004. Due to the significance of the case, the House of Lords convened a panel of nine rather than the ordinary five judges, an action that had occurred only once since the Second World War. The court held that the detention measures were incompatible with the European Convention on Human Rights. Only one Law Lord dissented in the case.[226] On appeal to the European Court of Human Rights, the case was allocated to a Grand Chamber.

A AND OTHERS V. UNITED KINGDOM
EUROPEAN COURT OF HUMAN RIGHTS, GRAND CHAMBER, APPLICATION NO. 3455/05
(19 FEBRUARY 2009)

10. The Government contended that the events of 11 September 2001 demonstrated that international terrorists, notably those associated with al'Qaeda, had the intention and capacity to mount attacks against civilian targets on an unprecedented scale... . In the Government's assessment, the United Kingdom, because of its close links with the United States, was a particular target. They considered that there was an emergency of a most serious kind threatening the life of the nation. Moreover, they considered that the threat came principally, but not exclusively, from a number of foreign nationals present in the United Kingdom, who were providing a support network for Islamist terrorist operations linked to al'Qaeda. A number of these foreign nationals could not be deported because of the risk that they would suffer treatment contrary to Article 3 of the Convention in their countries of origin.

11. On 11 November 2001 the Secretary of State made a Derogation Order ... [and] lodged the derogation with the Secretary General of the Council of Europe. The derogation notice provided as follows:
...
As a result of the public emergency, provision is made in the [ATCSA], inter alia, for an extended power to arrest and detain a foreign national which will apply where it is intended to remove or deport the person from the United Kingdom but where removal or deportation is not for the time being possible ... The extended power to arrest and detain will apply where the Secretary of State issues a certificate indicating his belief that the person's presence in the United Kingdom is a risk to national security and that he suspects the person of being an international terrorist. That certificate will be subject to an appeal to the Special Immigration Appeals Commission ('SIAC').... . In addition, the certificate will be reviewed by SIAC at regular intervals. SIAC will also be able to grant bail, where appropriate, subject to conditions. It will be open to a detainee to end his detention at any time by agreeing to leave the United Kingdom.

The extended power of arrest and detention ... is a temporary provision which comes into force for an initial period of 15 months and then expires unless renewed by the Parliament. Thereafter, it is subject to annual renewal by Parliament... .
...

---

226 S. Shah, 'The UK's Anti-Terror Legislation and the House of Lords: The First Skirmish', 6 *Hum. Rts. L. R.* (2006) 416.

It is well established that Article 5(1)(f) permits the detention of a person with a view to deportation only in circumstances where 'action is being taken with a view to deportation' (*Chahal v United Kingdom* (1996)). In that case the European Court of Human Rights indicated that detention will cease to be permissible under Article 5(1)(f) if deportation proceedings are not prosecuted with due diligence... . In some cases, where the intention remains to remove or deport a person on national security grounds, continued detention may not be consistent with Article 5(1)(f) as interpreted by the Court in the *Chahal* case. This may be the case, for example, if the person has established that removal to their own country might result in treatment contrary to Article 3 of the Convention... . If no alternative destination is immediately available then removal or deportation may not, for the time being, be possible even though the ultimate intention remains to remove or deport the person once satisfactory arrangements can be made. In addition, it may not be possible to prosecute the person for a criminal offence given the strict rules on the admissibility of evidence in the criminal justice system of the United Kingdom and the high standard of proof required.

... To the extent, therefore, that the exercise of the extended power [to detain] may be inconsistent with the United Kingdom's obligations under Article 5(1), the Government has decided to avail itself of the right of derogation conferred by Article 15(1) of the Convention and will continue to do so until further notice.
...

i. The Court's approach

173. The Court recalls that it falls to each Contracting State, with its responsibility for "the life of [its] nation", to determine whether that life is threatened by a "public emergency" and, if so, how far it is necessary to go in attempting to overcome the emergency. ... [T]he national authorities are in principle better placed than the international judge to decide ... . Accordingly, in this matter a wide margin of appreciation should be left to the national authorities.

Nonetheless, Contracting Parties do not enjoy an unlimited discretion. It is for the Court to rule whether, *inter alia*, the States have gone beyond the "extent strictly required by the exigencies" of the crisis. The domestic margin of appreciation is thus accompanied by a European supervision. ...

174. ... It is fundamental to the machinery of protection established by the Convention that the national systems themselves provide redress for breaches of its provisions, with the Court exercising a supervisory role subject to the principle of subsidiarity. Moreover, the domestic courts are part of the "national authorities" to which the Court affords a wide margin of appreciation under Article 15. In the unusual circumstances of the present case, where the highest domestic court has examined the issues relating to the State's derogation and concluded that there was a public emergency threatening the life of the nation but that the measures taken in response were not strictly required by the exigencies of the situation, the Court considers that it would be justified in reaching a contrary conclusion only if satisfied that the national court had misinterpreted or misapplied Article 15 or the Court's jurisprudence under that Article or reached a conclusion which was manifestly unreasonable.

ii. Whether there was a "public emergency threatening the life of the nation"

175. The applicants argued that there had been no public emergency threatening the life of the British nation, for three main reasons: first, the emergency was neither actual nor imminent; secondly, it was not of a temporary nature; and, thirdly, the practice of other States, none of which had derogated from the Convention, together with the informed views of other national and international bodies, suggested that the existence of a public emergency had not been established.

176. ... [In] *Lawless* [the Court] held that [the words in] Article 15 ... referred to "an exceptional situation of crisis or emergency which affects the whole population and constitutes a threat to the organised life of the community of which the State is composed". In the *Greek Case* (1969), the Commission held that, in order to justify a derogation, the emergency should be actual or imminent; that it should affect the whole nation to the extent that the continuance of the organised life of the community was threatened; and that the crisis or danger should be exceptional, in that the normal measures or restrictions, permitted by the Convention for the maintenance of public safety, health and order, were plainly inadequate. In *Ireland v United Kingdom*, ... the Article 15 test was satisfied, since terrorism had for a number of years represented "a particularly far-reaching and acute

danger for the territorial integrity of the United Kingdom, the institutions of the six counties and the lives of the province's inhabitants". ...

177. Before the domestic courts, the Secretary of State adduced evidence to show the existence of a threat of serious terrorist attacks planned against the United Kingdom. Additional closed evidence was adduced before SIAC. All the national judges accepted that the danger was credible (with the exception of Lord Hoffmann, who did not consider that it was of a nature to constitute "a threat to the life of the nation"). Although when the derogation was made no al'Qaeda attack had taken place within the territory of the United Kingdom, the Court does not consider that the national authorities can be criticised, in the light of the evidence available to them at the time, for fearing that such an attack was "imminent", in that an atrocity might be committed without warning at any time. The requirement of imminence cannot be interpreted so narrowly as to require a State to wait for disaster to strike before taking measures to deal with it. Moreover, the danger of a terrorist attack was, tragically, shown by the bombings and attempted bombings in London in July 2005 to have been very real. ... [T]he existence of the threat to the life of the nation must be assessed primarily with reference to those facts which were known at the time of the derogation. ...

178. While the United Nations Human Rights Committee has observed that measures derogating from the provisions of the ICCPR must be of "an exceptional and temporary nature", the Court's case-law has never, to date, explicitly incorporated the requirement that the emergency be temporary, although the question of the proportionality of the response may be linked to the duration of the emergency. Indeed, the cases cited above, relating to the security situation in Northern Ireland, demonstrate that it is possible for a "public emergency" within the meaning of Article 15 to continue for many years. The Court does not consider that derogating measures put in place in the immediate aftermath of the al'Qaeda attacks in the United States of America, and reviewed on an annual basis by Parliament, can be said to be invalid on the ground that they were not "temporary".

179. The applicants' argument that the life of the nation was not threatened is principally founded on the dissenting opinion of Lord Hoffman, who interpreted the words as requiring a threat to the organised life of the community which went beyond a threat of serious physical damage and loss of life. It had, in his view, to threaten "our institutions of government or our existence as a civil community". However, the Court has in previous cases been prepared to take into account a much broader range of factors ... .

180. ... [T]he national authorities enjoy a wide margin of appreciation under Article 15 ... . While it is striking that the United Kingdom was the only Convention State to have lodged a derogation in response to the danger from al'Qaeda, although other States were also the subject of threats, the Court accepts that it was for each Government, as the guardian of their own people's safety, to make their own assessment on the basis of the facts known to them. Weight must, therefore, attach to the judgment of the United Kingdom's executive and Parliament on this question. In addition, significant weight must be accorded to the views of the national courts, who were better placed to assess the evidence relating to the existence of an emergency.

181. On this first question, the Court accordingly shares the view of the majority of the House of Lords that there was a public emergency threatening the life of the nation.

iii. Whether the measures were strictly required by the exigencies of the situation

182 ... As previously stated, the Court considers that it should in principle follow the judgment of the House of Lords on the question of the proportionality of the applicants' detention, unless it can be shown that the national court misinterpreted the Convention or the Court's case-law or reached a conclusion which was manifestly unreasonable. ...

183. The Government contended, first, that the majority of the House of Lords should have afforded a much wider margin of appreciation to the executive and Parliament to decide whether the applicants' detention was necessary. A similar argument was advanced before the House of Lords, where the Attorney General submitted that the assessment of what was needed to protect the public was a matter of political rather than judicial judgment.

184. ... [Despite the] wide margin of appreciation ... it is ultimately for the Court to rule whether the measures were "strictly required". In particular, where a derogating measure encroaches upon a fundamental Convention right, such as the right to liberty, the Court must be satisfied that it was a genuine response to the emergency situation, that it was fully justified by the special circumstances of the emergency and that adequate safeguards were provided against abuse. The doctrine of the margin of appreciation has always been meant as a tool to define relations between the domestic authorities and the Court. It cannot have the same application to the relations between the organs of State at the domestic level. As the House of Lords held, the question of proportionality is ultimately a judicial decision, particularly in a case such as the present where the applicants were deprived of their fundamental right to liberty over a long period of time. In any event, having regard to the careful way in which the House of Lords approached the issues, it cannot be said that inadequate weight was given to the views of the executive or of Parliament.

...

186. The Government's third ground of challenge to the House of Lords' decision was directed principally at the approach taken towards the comparison between non-national and national suspected terrorists. The Court, however, considers that the House of Lords was correct in holding that the impugned powers were not to be seen as immigration measures, where a distinction between nationals and non-nationals would be legitimate, but instead as concerned with national security. Part 4 of the 2001 Act was designed to avert a real and imminent threat of terrorist attack which, on the evidence, was posed by both nationals and non-nationals. The choice by the Government and Parliament of an immigration measure to address what was essentially a security issue had the result of failing adequately to address the problem, while imposing a disproportionate and discriminatory burden of indefinite detention on one group of suspected terrorists. As the House of Lords found, there was no significant difference in the potential adverse impact of detention without charge on a national or on a non-national who in practice could not leave the country because of fear of torture abroad.

187. Finally, the Government advanced two arguments which the applicants claimed [were new]. ...

188. The first ... was that it was legitimate for the State, in confining the measures to non-nationals, to take into account the sensitivities of the British Muslim population in order to reduce the chances of recruitment among them by extremists. However, the Government has not placed before the Court any evidence to suggest that British Muslims were significantly more likely to react negatively to the detention without charge of national rather than foreign Muslims reasonably suspected of links to al'Qaeda. In this respect the Court notes that the system of control orders, put in place by the Prevention of Terrorism Act 2005, does not discriminate between national and non-national suspects.

189. The second ... was that the State could better respond to the terrorist threat if it were able to detain its most serious source, namely non-nationals. In this connection, again the Court has not been provided with any evidence which could persuade it to overturn the conclusion of the House of Lords that the difference in treatment was unjustified. Indeed, the Court notes that the national courts, including SIAC, which saw both the open and the closed material, were not convinced that the threat from non-nationals was more serious than that from nationals.

190. In conclusion, therefore, the Court, like the House of Lords, and contrary to the Government's contention, finds that the derogating measures were disproportionate in that they discriminated unjustifiably between nationals and non-nationals. It follows there has been a violation of Article 5 § 1... .

...

THE HOUSE OF LORDS JUDGMENT IN *A AND OTHERS*

As the Grand Chamber mentioned, the House of Lords similarly invalidated the detention measures on the ground that they were disproportionate. However, in its proportionality analysis, the House of Lords not only concluded that the law was under-inclusive because it failed to cover British nationals. They also concluded that the law was: (1) under-inclusive in the use of coercive power because it allowed foreign nationals to leave for another country; and (2) over-inclusive in its coverage because it extended beyond Al Qaeda to target terrorist groups that posed no threat to the United Kingdom. The House of Lords explained:

[S]ections 21 and 23 [of the ATCSA] do permit a person certified and detained to leave the United Kingdom and go to any other country willing to receive him, as two of the appellants did when they left for Morocco and France respectively. Such freedom to leave is wholly explicable in terms of immigration control: if the British authorities wish to deport a foreign national but cannot deport him to country "A" because of *Chahal* their purpose is as well served by his voluntary departure for country "B". But allowing a suspected international terrorist to leave our shores and depart to another country, perhaps a country as close as France, there to pursue his criminal designs, is hard to reconcile with a belief in his capacity to inflict serious injury to the people and interests of this country. It seems clear from the language of section 21 of the 2001 Act, read with the definition of terrorism in section 1 of the 2000 Act, that section 21 is capable of covering those who have no link at all with Al-Qaeda (they might, for example, be members of the Basque separatist organisation ETA), or who, although supporting the general aims of Al-Qaeda, reject its cult of violence... .

Some of these features of the 2001 Act were the subject of comment by the European Commissioner for Human Rights in his Opinion 1/2002 (28 August 2002):

> The proportionality of the derogating measures is further brought into question by the definition of international terrorist organisations provided by section 21(3) of the Act. The section would appear to permit the indefinite detention of an individual suspected of having links with an international terrorist organisation irrespective of its presenting a direct threat to public security in the United Kingdom and perhaps, therefore, of no relation to the emergency originally requiring the legislation under which his Convention rights may be prejudiced.
>
> ...
>
> It would appear, therefore, that the derogating measures of the [ATCSA] allow both for the detention of those presenting no direct threat to the United Kingdom and for the release of those of whom it is alleged that they do. Such a paradoxical conclusion is hard to reconcile with the strict exigencies of the situation.

The House of Lords independently considered a claim of discrimination under Article 14 of the European Convention. The Grand Chamber decided not to reach that question on the ground that the Chamber's reasoning and conclusion in relation to Article 5 rendered that determination unnecessary. The House of Lords' opinion, however, is an important judicial landmark in analyzing non-discrimination principles in the context of combating terrorism. An excerpt of the lead opinion by Lord Bingham follows:

The appellants complained that in providing for the detention of suspected international terrorists who were not UK nationals but not for the detention of suspected international terrorists who were UK nationals, section 23 unlawfully discriminated against them as non-UK nationals in breach of Article 14 of the European Convention... .

Jackson J reflected this belief in his well-known judgment in *Railway Express Agency Inc v New York* 336 US 106, 112–113 (1949), when he said:

> I regard it as a salutary doctrine that cities, states and the Federal Government must exercise their powers so as not to discriminate between their inhabitants except upon some reasonable differentiation fairly related to the object of regulation. This equality is not merely abstract justice. ... [N]othing opens the door to arbitrary action so effectively as to allow those officials to pick and choose only a few to whom they will apply legislation and thus to escape the political retribution that might be visited upon them if larger numbers were affected. Courts can take no better measure to assure that laws will be just than to require that laws be equal in operation.
>
> ...

The United Kingdom did not derogate from Article 14 of the European Convention (or from Article 26 of the ICCPR, which corresponds to it) ... .

...

... [T]he appellants' chosen comparators were suspected international terrorists who were UK nationals. The appellants pointed out that they shared with this group the important characteristics (a) of being suspected international terrorists and (b) of being irremovable from the United Kingdom. Since these were the relevant characteristics for purposes of the comparison, it was unlawfully discriminatory to detain non-UK nationals while leaving UK nationals at large.

Were suspected international terrorists who were UK nationals, the appellants' chosen comparators, in a relevantly analogous situation to the appellants? ... The Court of Appeal thought not because (per Lord Woolf, para 56) "the nationals have a right of abode in this jurisdiction but the aliens only have a right not to be removed". This is, however, to accept the correctness of the Secretary of State's choice of immigration control as a means to address the Al-Qaeda security problem, when the correctness of that choice is the issue to be resolved. In my opinion, the question demands an affirmative answer. Suspected international terrorists who are UK nationals are in a situation analogous with the appellants because, in the present context, they share the most relevant characteristics of the appellants.

... The undoubted aim of the relevant measure, section 23 of the 2001 Act, was to protect the UK against the risk of Al-Qaeda terrorism. As noted above that risk was thought to be presented mainly by non-UK nationals but also and to a significant extent by UK nationals also. The effect of the measure was to permit the former to be deprived of their liberty but not the latter. The appellants were treated differently because of their nationality or immigration status... .

...

The Court of Appeal differed from SIAC on the discrimination issue: [2004] QB 335. Lord Woolf CJ referred to a tension between Article 15 and Article 14 of the European Convention. He held that it would be "surprising indeed" if Article 14 prevented the Secretary of State from restricting his power to detain to a smaller rather than a larger group ... .

I must respectfully differ from this analysis... . Any discriminatory measure inevitably affects a smaller rather than a larger group, but cannot be justified on the ground that more people would be adversely affected if the measure were applied generally. What has to be justified is not the measure in issue but the difference in treatment between one person or group and another. What cannot be justified here is the decision to detain one group of suspected international terrorists, defined by nationality or immigration status, and not another... .

Following *A and Others*, the Prevention of Terrorism Act 2005 provided for two types of control order to be introduced: 'derogating' and 'non-derogating' orders. The former required a derogation before they could be imposed, and have never been used. The latter enabled various restrictions to be imposed on individuals, including house arrest, limitations on freedom of movement, electronic tagging and forced relocation. Following various court challenges to this regime, the Terrorism Prevention and Investigation Measures (TPIM) Act 2011 was adopted, partly in an effort to increase compliance with Article 5 of the ECHR, although it has been described as achieving 'covert derogation' and normalising extraordinary measures.[227] In a parliamentary debate on 30 November 2021, which preceded the extension of the Act through 2026, Baroness Jones of

---

[227] H. Fenwick, 'Terrorism and the Control Orders/TPIMs Saga: A Vindication of the Human Rights Act or a Manifestation of "Defensive democracy"?', *Public Law* (2017) 609.

Moulsecoomb recalled the views that the then Prime Minister, Boris Johnson had expressed in 2005 when the Conservative Party opposed the original Bill. He said:

> It is a cynical attempt to pander to the many who think the world would be a better place if dangerous folk with dusky skins were just slammed away, and never mind a judicial proceeding; and, given the strength of this belief among good Tory folk, it is heroic of the Tories to oppose the Bill. We do so because the removal of this ancient freedom is not only unnecessary, but it is also a victory for terror.

In 2021, the Home Secretary, Priti Patel, certified that the provisions of the legislation were compatible with the rights recognized in the ECHR. In the same year, the Counter-Terrorism and Sentencing Act was adopted after attacks in 2019 and 2020 by 'known terrorist offenders'. It lowered the standard of proof required from 'the balance of probabilities' to 'reasonable belief;' extended the maximum duration of a TPIM from two to five years, and introduced drug and polygraph testing requirements. Between 2011 and 2021, 24 TPIM orders were imposed. A prominent British law firm describes these orders as having 'a draconian impact on a person's life, not only restricting the freedom of the individual but also the freedoms of any family members who live with them.'[228]

QUESTIONS

1. Is the definition of terrorism in the Terrorism Act 2000 excessively vague? Which provisions are most vulnerable to criticism along those lines? What purposes might be served by the use of ambiguity? Is this vagueness more acceptable in the context of administrative law (e.g., immigration and nationality law) than in other legal domains such as criminal law? For example, should the state retain greater power and discretion in the regulation of its borders? Are the interests in avoiding vagueness strongest for criminal defendants than for other subjects of the law?

2. In *A and Others v United Kingdom*, the Grand Chamber announced a relaxed standard of review '[i]n the unusual circumstances ... where the highest domestic court has examined the issues ...' Do you agree with the logic behind this approach? Why should the European Court relax its scrutiny only when state action is invalidated, rather than upheld, by an apex court? Should this approach be limited to the situation of derogations?

3. Consider the proportionality analysis by the Grand Chamber in *A and Others*. Are there other plausible reasons that could justify treating the class of individuals subject to detention differently than British nationals? The Court suggests that the level of threat posed by the two groups is essentially indistinguishable. Do you agree? Could British nationals generally pose a greater threat than foreign nationals? Are there other factors the Court should have used to compare the two classes of individuals? Is this decision compatible with the war model for combating terrorism discussed previously?

E. FAIR TRIALS

The right to a fair trial ranks among the most basic protections in humanitarian and human rights law. Three provisions of the 1949 Geneva Conventions and their Protocols deserve special mention. First, Common Article 3 outlaws 'the passing of sentences and the carrying out of executions without previous judgment pronounced by a regularly constituted court, affording all the judicial guarantees which are recognized as indispensable by civilized peoples.' The ICRC Commentaries explain that this provision calls for extension of the general law concerning fair trials to the arena of warfare: 'All civilized nations surround the administration of justice with safeguards aimed at eliminating the possibility of judicial errors. The Convention has rightly

---

[228] https://www.bindmans.com/knowledge-hub/blogs/tpims-what-you-need-to-know/

proclaimed that it is essential to do this even in time of war.' Second, the Civilians Convention contains a 'security proviso' permitting states to suspend treaty obligations when dealing with unlawful combatants such as spies and saboteurs; yet it too requires that 'such persons shall nevertheless be treated with humanity and, in case of trial, shall not be deprived of the rights of fair and regular trial prescribed by the present Convention.' Third, Article 75 (entitled 'Fundamental Guarantees') of Additional Protocol I is generally recognized, including by the United States, as binding customary law. It specifies elements of the right to a fair trial that are guaranteed to all individuals who do not benefit from more favourable treatment under the 1949 Conventions or the Additional Protocol. These three IHL provisions establish a floor of fair trial rights below which no state may pass. Recall that the Human Rights Committee's General Comment 29 relies on such fundamental protections in reasoning that, if certain elements of a fair trial cannot be lawfully transgressed in war, they can never be subject to derogation under the ICCPR. A difficulty is defining the content of those core fair trial rights.

IBRAHIM AND OTHERS V. THE UNITED KINGDOM
EUROPEAN COURT OF HUMAN RIGHTS, GRAND CHAMBER,
APPLICATION NOS. 50541/08, 50571/08, 50573/08 AND 40351/09 (13 SEPTEMBER 2016)

[The following description of the facts is taken from the Court's Information Note on the case: On 21 July 2005, two weeks after 52 people were killed as the result of suicide bombings in London, further bombs were detonated on the London public transport system but, on this occasion, failed to explode. The perpetrators fled the scene. The first three applicants were arrested but were refused legal assistance for periods of between four and eight hours to enable the police to conduct "safety interviews". During the safety interviews, they denied any involvement in or knowledge of the events of 21 July. At trial, they acknowledged their involvement in the events but claimed that the bombs had been a hoax and were never intended to explode. The statements made at their safety interviews were admitted in evidence against them and they were convicted of conspiracy to murder. The Court of Appeal refused them leave to appeal.

The fourth applicant was not suspected of having detonated a bomb and was initially interviewed by the police as a witness. However, he started to incriminate himself by describing his encounter with one of the suspected bombers shortly after the attacks and the assistance he had provided to that suspect. The police did not, at that stage, arrest and advise him of his right to silence and to legal assistance, but continued to question him as a witness and took a written statement. He was subsequently arrested and offered legal advice. In his ensuing interviews, he consistently referred to his written statement, which was admitted as evidence at his trial. He was convicted of assisting one of the bombers and of failing to disclose information about the bombings. His appeal against conviction was dismissed.

In their applications to the European Court of Human Rights, the applicants complained that their lack of access to lawyers during their initial police questioning and the admission in evidence at trial of their statements had violated their right to a fair trial ... .]

251. Compliance with the requirements of a fair trial must be examined in each case having regard to the development of the proceedings as a whole ...

252. The general requirements of fairness contained in Article 6 apply to all criminal proceedings, irrespective of the type of offence in issue. There can be no question of watering down fair trial rights for the sole reason that the individuals in question are suspected of involvement in terrorism. In these challenging times, ... it is of the utmost importance that the Contracting Parties demonstrate their commitment to human rights and the rule of law by ensuring respect for, inter alia, the minimum guarantees of Article 6 of the Convention. Nevertheless, when determining whether the proceedings as a whole have been fair the weight of the public interest in the investigation and punishment of the particular offence in issue may be taken into consideration. Moreover, Article 6 should not be applied in such a manner as to put disproportionate difficulties in the way of the police authorities in taking effective measures to counter terrorism ... . However, public interest concerns cannot justify measures which extinguish the very essence of an applicant's defence rights. ...
...
257. ... [A]ssessing whether a restriction on access to a lawyer is compatible with the right to a fair trial [involves] two stages. [First], the Court must assess whether there were compelling reasons for the restriction. [Second],

it must evaluate the prejudice caused to the rights of the defence by the restriction in the case in question. In other words, the Court must ... decide whether the proceedings as a whole were fair. ...

...

259. The Court accepts that where a respondent Government have convincingly demonstrated the existence of an urgent need to avert serious adverse consequences for life, liberty or physical integrity in a given case, this can amount to compelling reasons to restrict access to legal advice .... In such circumstances, there is a pressing duty on the authorities to protect the rights of potential or actual victims ... . However, ... a non-specific claim of a risk of leaks cannot constitute compelling reasons so as to justify a restriction on access to a lawyer.

...

276. ... The Court has accepted above that compelling reasons may exist where an urgent need to avert serious adverse consequences for life, liberty or physical integrity has been convincingly made out. It is in no doubt that such a need existed at the time when the safety interviews of the first three applicants were conducted. [Given what happened,] it was inevitable that the police would conclude that the United Kingdom had become the target of a wave of terrorist attacks. ... The police were operating under enormous pressure and their overriding priority was, quite properly, to obtain as a matter of urgency information on any further planned attacks and the identities of those potentially involved in the plot. ...

...

281. [In terms of the fairness of the overall process] the possibility of restricting access to legal advice was set out in law and in spite of the pressures under which the police were operating, ... the police adhered strictly to the legislative framework ... [and] the purpose of the safety interviews – to obtain information necessary to protect the public – was strictly observed ... .

...

293. Finally, there can be no doubt that there was a strong public interest in the investigation and punishment of the offences in question. Indiscriminate terrorist attacks are, by their very nature, intended to strike fear into the hearts of innocent civilians, to cause chaos and panic and to disrupt the proper functioning of everyday life. In such circumstances, threats to human life, liberty and dignity arise not only from the actions of the terrorists themselves but may also arise from the reaction of the authorities in the face of such threats. ... The public interest in preventing and punishing terrorist attacks of this magnitude, involving a large-scale conspiracy to murder ordinary citizens going about their daily lives, is of the most compelling nature.

294. In conclusion, ..., the proceedings as a whole in respect of each [of the first three applicants] were fair. There has therefore been no violation of Article 6 §§ 1 and 3 (c) of the Convention.

...

295. The fourth applicant complained that the self-incriminating statement he made as a witness, and therefore without having been notified of his privilege against self-incrimination or having been provided with access to a lawyer, was admitted at his trial.

...

298. ... The question is whether these exceptional circumstances were sufficient to constitute compelling reasons in the fourth applicant's case for continuing with his interview without cautioning him or informing him of his right to legal advice.

...

300. ... [T]the Court finds that the Government have not convincingly demonstrated ... compelling reasons in the fourth applicant's case, taking account of the complete absence of any legal framework enabling the police to act as they did, the lack of an individual and recorded determination, on the basis of the applicable provisions of domestic law, of whether to restrict his access to legal advice and, importantly, the deliberate decision by the police not to inform the fourth applicant of his right to remain silent.

...

311. ... While the offences for which [the fourth applicant] was indicted were not of the magnitude of the offences committed by the first three applicants, the threat posed by terrorism can only be neutralised by the effective investigation, prosecution and punishment of all those involved in terrorism. However, taking into account the high threshold which applies where the presumption of unfairness arises and having regard to the cumulative effect of the procedural shortcomings in the fourth applicant's case, the Court considers that the Government have failed to demonstrate why the overall fairness of the trial was not irretrievably prejudiced by the decision not to caution him and to restrict his access to legal advice. There has therefore been a violation of Article 6 §§ 1 and 3 (c) in the case of the fourth applicant.

...

JOINT PARTLY DISSENTING, PARTLY CONCURRING, OPINION OF JUDGES SAJÓ AND LAFFRANQUE

1. We understand the primary importance of protecting societies from terrorism. ... However, ... in striking the right balance between security needs and [human rights for States to] show due regard for the requirements of the rule of law and avoid straying from human-rights and rule-of-law principles. ...

2. ... [In this case,] the Court itself waters down rights, by failing to adhere to the guarantees of Article 6 ..., and without expressly stating it, de facto departs from that earlier well-established case-law ... . A human-rights court must not relinquish a level of protection that it has already granted.
...
19. ... [T]he existence of an urgent need to avert serious adverse consequences for life, liberty or physical integrity in a given case is an essential consideration in finding compelling reasons to restrict access to legal advice. ... In such circumstances one need not wait for a lawyer to be present before an interrogation starts. Is this urgent need a good enough reason not to admit access to an available lawyer? ...

20. The Court's approach relies explicitly on *New York v. Quarles* 467 U.S. 649 (1984), which recognised a "public safety exception" to the Miranda rule, permitting questioning to take place in the absence of a lawyer and before a suspect has been read his rights where there is a threat to public safety. The reference to the American approach is misplaced ... . The case-law ... clearly indicates that it applies to actual threat. ... The public-safety exception has never been used in the context of preventing future terrorist attacks which are deemed likely. In the recent terrorism case of Dzhokhar Tsarnaev, the prosecution refrained from including admissions made in the absence of a lawyer. ...

21. The fact that there is an urgent need to save lives does not explain why and how the advice and presence, in particular, of a lawyer, that is, of a right, would, as a matter of principle, be detrimental to saving lives. (Again, assuming that it does not cause delay). Are we assuming that the psychological comfort derived from a lawyer's presence is of such comfort to terrorists that it undermines the prevention of calamities? The specific status of lawyers gives them a central position in the administration of justice as intermediaries between the public and the courts. They therefore play a key role in ensuring that the courts, whose mission is fundamental in a State based on the rule of law, enjoy public confidence. Or is the Court of the view (as the Chamber seemed to concede) that the lawyer will help the cause of terrorists by precluding certain police tactics?
...
30. ... Even assuming that there were compelling reasons for not allowing access to counsel at the crucial investigative moment, the Court should have applied heightened scrutiny to determine whether the absence of the lawyer did, or did not, unduly prejudice the rights of the accused under Article 6. ...

31. There is no sign of counterbalancing by the judicial authorities in the present case. Moreover, the Court has conducted a very deferential analysis of the overall fairness and the actions of the trial judge. ... The strong public interest in a conviction cannot overrule the Convention guarantees ..., contrary to what the Court claims, namely that "the public interest in preventing and punishing terrorist attacks of this magnitude ... is of the most compelling nature". If punishment is of the "most compelling nature", then what is the role of all the safeguards granted by the Convention? If a State is of the view that such a compelling public interest exists, then the Convention provides the proper mechanism in Article 15. Derogation is possible, under the supervision of the Court. ...
...

JOINT PARTLY DISSENTING OPINION OF JUDGES HAJIYEV, YUDKIVSKA, EMMENS, MAHONEY, SILVIS AND O'LEARY

1. ... [W]e are unable to agree with the view of the majority that the fourth applicant's defence rights were violated ... .

2. ... [I]t would be a mistake to present the basic Convention issue at the heart of the four applicants' cases as being solely one of fixing the limits on the inroads that the security interests of the State may make into individual human rights ... . That would be an excessively narrow focus ... . [T]he present case directly

involve[s] the human rights of many other people than the four applicants. ... [T]his Court [is] required to identify the appropriate relationship between the fundamental procedural right to a fair trial of persons charged ... and the right to life and bodily security of the persons affected by the alleged criminal conduct. ...

3. ... The Contracting States are ... duty-bound under the Convention to act, both preventively and repressively, with a view to diminishing the threats that terrorism at its current levels and in its current forms represents for the life and bodily security of each individual coming within their jurisdiction. ...

4. ... [T]he majority focuses its analysis too narrowly on the purely procedural aspects of the fourth applicant's case, to the detriment of the wider-angled assessment of the overall picture, including the impact on the interests of other holders of Convention rights ... .

...

13. ... The police had a difficult choice to make: whether, in the absence of other direct information from or connected with the suspected bombers – only one was in custody, but was not talking to the police; and the others were still at large –, to continue obtaining from the applicant information capable of saving lives and protecting the public or to comply with the applicable police code by cautioning the applicant, with the attendant risk of stopping the flow of valuable security information. ...

...

15. ... [T]he majority ... attach ... decisive, importance ... to the question whether the police decision not to caution him and grant access to a lawyer had a basis in domestic law. ... [The essential question is:] were the authorities justified in thinking at the relevant time that cautioning the witness as a suspect would have frustrated fulfilment of the urgent need to avert the serious consequences which would result from a successfully executed terrorist attack? This question of factual substance goes to the heart of the compelling-reasons analysis but is passed over by the majority, who prefer instead to concentrate on the procedural issue ... .

...

17.... [N]on-compliance with the applicable police code of practice cannot obliterate the objective assessment of the dangerousness and volatility of the circumstances which the police and general public were facing. ...

18. ... [W]e consider that there were indeed "compelling reasons", at that crucial time in the investigation of the failed bomb attack, for the police not to caution the fourth applicant and to delay temporarily his access to legal advice on the basis of an individual assessment of the specific facts before them. ...

...

35. Contrary to the suggestion of the majority judgment, the fourth applicant's conviction was not substantially based on his initial statement. While it could be said to have played an important part in the prosecution case, its importance was significantly conditioned by the fourth applicant's decision not to retract it but rather to repeat and rely on it after he had been arrested and received legal advice, as well as his decision to remain silent at his trial ... .

...

36. ... The atrocities perpetrated in recent years ... amply demonstrate the key part that logistical and other support plays in the commission of modern-day terrorist offences involving, as they do, indiscriminate mass murder. What follows from this is, firstly in time, urgent action by the police to limit to the maximum the continuing imminent danger to the public once a terrorist attack has occurred or is under way (primarily an issue of "compelling reasons") and, thereafter, the need to prosecute wherever possible, in proceedings where fair trial rights are respected, those reasonably suspected of being part of a support network of a terrorist group. ... [T]here is a risk of "failing to see the wood for the trees" if the analysis is excessively concentrated on the imperatives of criminal procedure to the detriment of wider considerations of the modern State's obligation to ensure practical and effective human rights protection to everyone within its jurisdiction. ... [P]ublic-interest concerns, including the fight against terrorism, cannot justify measures which extinguish the very essence of a suspect's or an accused person's defence rights. A parallel consideration, however, is that neither can the imperatives of criminal procedure extirpate the legitimacy of the public interest at stake, based as it is on the core Convention rights to life and to bodily safety of other individuals.

...

Military Tribunals

One of the most vexing issues in defining the right to a fair trial in the national security context involves military tribunals. Can a military tribunal provide a fair trial and, if so, under what conditions? The following readings address this set of concerns. A report by the Inter-American Commission on Human Rights sets the stage by discussing the broader legal and normative framework. The Inter-American Commission took up the general subject of human rights law and terrorism, and issued a lengthy report in 2002. The report provides, *inter alia*, one of the most comprehensive formal pronouncements on the content of derogable and nonderogable fair trial rights. The Commission developed these legal principles partly in response to the use of military courts by Latin American governments in the 1980s and early to mid-1990s. Governmental practices that sparked international criticism included Colombia's use of 'faceless' prosecutors, judges, witnesses and attorneys in cases of terrorism and subversion; Peru's trials of civilians accused of treason and terrorism in closed proceedings before a military court and with defence counsel prohibited from accessing the government's evidence or questioning military and police witnesses; Guatemala's Special Courts for subversive activities which operated in secret locations, relied on confessions from the accused taken without counsel present and provided little time for the accused to prepare a defence; and Uruguay's secret hearings, materially ineffective appeals process for objecting to an indictment, and inadequate access of defence counsel to evidentiary files.

INTER-AMERICAN COMMISSION ON HUMAN RIGHTS, REPORT ON TERRORISM AND HUMAN RIGHTS (22 OCTOBER 2002)

Right to a Hearing by a Competent, Independent and Impartial Tribunal previously established by Law.

229. Underlying this aspect of the right to a fair hearing are the fundamental concepts of judicial independence and impartiality... . The requirement of independence in turn necessitates that courts be autonomous from the other branches of government, free from influence, threats or interference from any source and for any reason, and benefit from other characteristics necessary for ensuring the correct and independent performance of judicial functions, including tenure and appropriate professional training... . These requirements in turn require that a judge or tribunal not harbor any actual bias in a particular case, and that the judge or tribunal not reasonably be perceived as being tainted with any bias.

230. In the context of these fundamental requirements, the jurisprudence of the inter-American system has long denounced the creation of special courts or tribunals that displace the jurisdiction belonging to the ordinary courts or judicial tribunals and that do not use the duly established procedures of the legal process. This has included in particular the use of ad hoc or special courts or military tribunals to prosecute civilians for security offenses in times of emergency, which practice has been condemned by this Commission, the Inter-American Court and other international authorities. The basis of this criticism has related in large part to the lack of independence of such tribunals from the Executive and the absence of minimal due process and fair trial guarantees in their processes.

231. It has been widely concluded in this regard that military tribunals by their very nature do not satisfy the requirements of independent and impartial courts applicable to the trial of civilians, because they are not a part of the independent civilian judiciary but rather are a part of the Executive branch, and because their fundamental purpose is to maintain order and discipline by punishing military offenses committed by members of the military establishment. In such instances, military officers assume the role of judges while at the same time remaining subordinate to their superiors in keeping with the established military hierarchy.

232... . Military tribunals are also precluded from prosecuting civilians, although certain human rights supervisory bodies have found that in exceptional circumstances military tribunals or special courts might be used to try civilians but only where the minimum requirements of due process are guaranteed. During armed conflicts, a state's military courts may also try privileged and unprivileged combatants, provided that the minimum protections of due process are guaranteed. ...

...

Fair Trial, Due Process of Law and Derogation

...

246... . [N]o human rights supervisory body has yet found the exigencies of a genuine emergency situation sufficient to justify suspending even temporarily basic fair trial safeguards... .

249. Without detracting from the above standards, prevailing norms suggest that there may be some limited aspects of the right to due process and to a fair trial from which derogation might in the most exceptional circumstances be permissible. Any such suspensions must, however, comply strictly with the principles of necessity, proportionality and non-discrimination, and must remain subject to oversight by supervisory organs under international law.

250. Due process and fair trial protections that might conceivably be subject to suspension include the right to a public trial where limitations on public access to proceedings are demonstrated to be strictly necessary in the interests of justice. Considerations in this regard might include matters of security, public order, the interests of juveniles, or where publicity might prejudice the interests of justice. Any such restrictions must, however, be strictly justified by the state concerned on a case by case basis and be subject to on-going judicial supervision.

251. The right of a defendant to examine or have examined witnesses presented against him or her could also be, in principle, the subject of restrictions in some limited instances. It must be recognized in this respect that efforts to investigate and prosecute crimes, including those relating to terrorism, may in certain instances render witnesses vulnerable to threats to their lives or integrity and thereby raise difficult issues concerning the extent to which those witnesses can be safely identified during the criminal process. Such considerations can never serve to compromise a defendant's non-derogable due process protections and each situation must be carefully evaluated on its own merits within the context of a particular justice system... .

252. Similarly, the investigation and prosecution of terrorist crimes may render judges and other officials involved in the administration of justice vulnerable to threats. As noted above, states are obliged to take all necessary measures to prevent violence against such persons. Accordingly, states may be compelled by the exigencies of a particular situation to develop mechanisms to protect a judge's life, physical integrity and independence ... subject to such measures as are necessary to ensure a defendant's right to challenge the competence, independence or impartiality of his or her prosecuting tribunal ... .

...

International Humanitarian Law

...

256. As noted above, while international human rights law prohibits the trial of civilians by military tribunals, the use of military tribunals in the trial of prisoners of war is not prohibited ...

261... . [M]ost fundamental fair trial requirements cannot justifiably be suspended under either international human rights law or international humanitarian law ... includ[ing] the following:

... The right to be tried by a competent, independent and impartial tribunal in conformity with applicable international standards. In respect of the prosecution of civilians, this requires trial by regularly constituted courts that are demonstrably independent from the other branches of government and comprised of judges with appropriate tenure and training, and generally prohibits the use of ad hoc, special, or military tribunals or commissions to try civilians. A state's military courts may prosecute members of its own military for crimes relating [to] the functions that the law assigns to military forces and, during international armed conflicts, may try privileged and unprivileged combatants, provided that the minimum requirements of due process are guaranteed.

...

HUMAN RIGHTS COMMITTEE, ARTICLE 14: RIGHT TO EQUALITY BEFORE COURTS AND TRIBUNALS AND TO A FAIR TRIAL, GENERAL COMMENT 32 (2007)

... The Committee notes the existence, in many countries, of military or special courts which try civilians. While the Covenant does not prohibit the trial of civilians in military or special courts, it requires that such trials are in full conformity with the requirements of article 14 and that its guarantees cannot be limited or modified because of the military or special character of the court concerned. The Committee also notes that the trial of civilians in military or special courts may raise serious problems as far as the equitable, impartial and independent administration of justice is concerned. Therefore, it is important to take all necessary measures to ensure that such trials take place under conditions which genuinely afford the full guarantees stipulated in article 14. Trials of civilians by military or special courts should be exceptional, i.e. limited to cases where the State party can show that resorting to such trials is necessary and justified by objective and serious reasons, and where with regard to the specific class of individuals and offences at issue the regular civilian courts are unable to undertake the trials.

İNCAL V. TURKEY
EUROPEAN COURT OF HUMAN RIGHTS, GRAND CHAMBER, APPLICATION NO. 22678/93 (9 JUNE 1998)

[İbrahim İncal, a member of the local executive committee of a pro-Kurdish political party (the People's Labour Party), was convicted for participating in the preparation of a leaflet that attempted to incite hatred and hostility through racist words. The leaflet criticized the local government's restrictions on small-scale illegal trading and squatter camps, which it said were part of a larger campaign to drive Kurds back to their own regions; stated that 'passivity as a form of defence against this devastation has encouraged the State'; and that the Kurdish population should organize themselves into 'neighbourhood communities ... to assume their responsibilities and oppose this special war being waged.']

The National Security Court, composed of three judges, one of whom was a member of the military, refused to apply the Prevention of Terrorism Act but otherwise found the applicant guilty of the offences charged and sentenced him to nearly seven months' imprisonment and a fine of 55,555 Turkish lira. Following is the decision of the Grand Chamber of the ECtHR.]

63. [The Grand Chamber first analyzed and decided that İncal's criminal conviction infringed his right to freedom of expression under the Convention. The Chamber then turned to the right to a fair trial under Article 6.] The Government submitted that the ... arguments concerning these judges' responsibility towards their commanding officers and the rules governing their professional assessment were overstated; their duties as officers were limited to obeying military regulations and observing military courtesies. They were safe from any pressure from their hierarchical superiors, as such an attempt was punishable under the Military Criminal Code. The assessment system applied only to military judges' non-judicial duties. In addition, they had access to their assessment reports and could even challenge their content in the Supreme Military Administrative Court.

In the present case, neither the colleagues or hierarchical or disciplinary superiors of the military judge in question nor the public authorities who had appointed him had any connection with the parties to Mr İncal's trial or any interest whatsoever in the judgment to be delivered.
...
65. The Court reiterates that in order to establish whether a tribunal can be considered "independent" for the purposes of Article 6 § 1, regard must be had, *inter alia*, to the manner of appointment of its members and their term of office, the existence of safeguards against outside pressures and the question whether it presents an appearance of independence.
...
66... . National Security Courts ... are composed of three judges, one of whom is a regular officer and member of the Military Legal Service. ...

67. The Court notes that the status of military judges sitting as members of National Security Courts provides certain guarantees of independence and impartiality. For example, military judges undergo the same professional training as their civilian counterparts, which gives them the status of career members of the Military Legal Service. When sitting as members of National Security Courts, military judges enjoy constitutional safeguards identical to those of civilian judges; in addition, with certain exceptions, they may not be removed from office or made to retire early without their consent; as regular members of a National Security Court they sit as individuals; according to the Constitution, they must be independent and no public authority may give them instructions concerning their judicial activities or influence them in the performance of their duties.

68. On the other hand, other aspects of these judges' status make it questionable. Firstly, they are servicemen who still belong to the army, which in turn takes its orders from the executive. Secondly, they remain subject to military discipline and assessment reports are compiled on them by the army for that purpose. Decisions pertaining to their appointment are to a great extent taken by the administrative authorities and the army. Lastly, their term of office as National Security Court judges is only four years and can be renewed.

...

70. At the hearing before the Court the Government submitted that the only justification for the presence of military judges in the National Security Courts was their undoubted competence and experience in the battle against organised crime, including that committed by illegal armed groups. For years the armed forces and the military judges — in whom, moreover, the people placed great trust — had acted, partly under martial law, as the guarantors of the democratic and secular Republic of Turkey, while assuming their social, cultural and moral responsibilities. For as long as the terrorist threat persisted, military judges would have to continue to lend their full support to these special courts, whose task was extremely difficult.

... [The Court's] ... task is ... to ascertain whether the manner in which one of them functioned infringed the applicant's right to a fair trial.

71. In this respect even appearances may be of a certain importance. What is at stake is the confidence which the courts in a democratic society must inspire in the public and above all, as far as criminal proceedings are concerned, in the accused. ... What is decisive is whether his doubts can be held to be objectively justified.

72. ... [T]he Court attaches great importance to the fact that a civilian had to appear before a court composed, even if only in part, of members of the armed forces. It follows that the applicant could legitimately fear that because one of the judges of the Izmir National Security Court was a military judge it might allow itself to be unduly influenced by considerations which had nothing to do with the nature of the case ... .

73. In conclusion, the applicant had legitimate cause to doubt the independence and impartiality of the İzmir National Security Court.

There has accordingly been a breach of Article 6 § 1.

joint partly dissenting opinion of judges thór vilhjálmsson, gölcüklü, matscher, foighel, sir john freeland, lopes rocha, wildhaber and gotchev

...

In a number of cases the Court has acknowledged that a special court whose members include "experts" may be a "tribunal" within the meaning of Article 6 § 1. The domestic legislation of the Council of Europe member States provides many examples of courts in which professional judges sit alongside specialists in a particular sphere whose knowledge is desirable and even necessary in deciding certain cases, provided that all the members of the court can offer the required guarantees of independence and impartiality.

As to military judges who are members of the National Security Courts, paragraph 67 of the judgment describes the constitutional safeguards they enjoy, and paragraph 68 goes on to say that certain aspects of their status make it questionable. We consider the conclusions the Court drew from these aspects ... unconvincing.

In that connection we would observe that it is possible for ordinary judges too to be subject to assessment and to disciplinary rules and for decisions pertaining to their appointment to be taken by the administrative authorities, and that the Court has held even a three-year term of office to be sufficient. In addition, at the end of their term of office as National Security Court judges, where that term is not renewed, the judges in question remain military judges for the whole duration of their careers.

As to the argument that the composition of the court may have caused the applicant to harbour doubts about its impartiality and independence, from the point of view of "appearances", we consider that, in view of the constitutional safeguards enjoyed by military judges, doubts about their independence and impartiality cannot be regarded as objectively justified.

The logical consequence of asserting the contrary would be to cease to consider that even specialised courts can be "tribunals" for the purposes of Article 6 § 1, thus departing from the Court's well-established case-law.

ÖCALAN V. TURKEY
EUROPEAN COURT OF HUMAN RIGHTS, GRAND CHAMBER, APPLICATION NO. 46221/99 (12 MAY 2005)

In a high-profile case and one of the first international court decisions following 11 September, the Grand Chamber reaffirmed its ruling in *İncal v. Turkey*. The case involved the capture and trial of Abdullah Öcalan, the leader of the militant separatist group, Kurdistan Workers Party. In early 1999, Turkish forces captured Öcalan in Kenya and transferred him to Turkey where he was subject to prosecution before a State Security Court. A 139-page indictment accused him of founding an armed group to secede from Turkey's national territory and of instigating numerous terrorist acts.

Öcalan's trial before the Ankara State Security Court, composed of two civilian judges and one military judge, began in late March 1999. Following the *İncal* judgment, Turkey started to amend its Constitution and national legislation to permit only civilian judges to sit on state security courts. The legislative amendments passed on 22 June 1999 and went into immediate effect. The next day, a civilian judge replaced the military judge in Öcalan's trial court. The replacement judge had been present throughout the proceedings and attended all the hearings of the State Security Court from the beginning of the trial. On 29 June, the security court found Öcalan guilty.

A majority of the Grand Chamber of the ECtHR held that the presence of the military judge violated Öcalan's right to be tried by an independent and impartial tribunal:[229]

113. It is understandable that the applicant — prosecuted in a State Security Court for serious offences relating to national security — should have been apprehensive about being tried by a bench which included a regular army officer belonging to the military legal service. On that account he could legitimately fear that the State Security Court might allow itself to be unduly influenced by considerations which had nothing to do with the nature of the case.

114. As to whether the military judge's replacement by a civilian judge in the course of the proceedings before the verdict was delivered remedied the situation, the Court considers, firstly, that the question whether a court is seen to be independent does not depend solely on its composition when it delivers its verdict. In order to comply with the requirements of Article 6 regarding independence, the court concerned must be seen to be independent of the executive and the legislature at each of the three stages of the proceedings, namely the investigation, the trial and the verdict (those being the three stages in Turkish criminal proceedings according to the Government).

…

116. In its previous judgments, the Court attached importance to the fact that a civilian had to appear before a court composed, even if only in part, of members of the armed forces (see, among other authorities, *İncal*). Such a situation seriously affects the confidence which the courts must inspire in a democratic society.

Then-President of the ECtHR, Judge Luzius Wildhaber, together with five other judges, issued a dissenting opinion disagreeing strongly with the majority's view on the independence and impartiality of the trial court. The dissenting opinion stated:

6… . To say that the presence of a military judge, who was replaced under new rules (that were introduced to comply with the case-law of the European Court of Human Rights) made the State Security Court appear not to be independent and impartial is to take the "theory" of appearances very far. That, in our opinion at least, is neither realistic, nor even fair.

…

---

[229] The Court also held, *inter alia*, that the government violated the right of Öcalan to be brought promptly before a judge following his arrest, the right to initiate proceedings to determine the lawfulness of his detention and the right to legal assistance.

8. In addition, in Mr Öçalan's case [sic], and without departing from the principles established in the *İncal* judgment itself, it is hard to agree with what is said in paragraph 116 of the judgment. The applicant is there described as a civilian (or equated to a civilian). However, he was accused of instigating serious terrorist crimes leading to thousands of deaths, charges which he admitted at least in part. He could equally well be described as a warlord, which goes a long way to putting into perspective the fact that at the start of his trial one of the three members of the court before which he appeared was himself from the military.

U. S. Military Commissions

The United States government determined within two months of 9/11 that detainees would be tried by military commissions.[230] An early case involved Salim Ahmed Hamdan, Osama bin Laden's driver, who had been captured in Afghanistan, transferred to Guantánamo and selected for trial. In *Hamdan v. Rumsfeld* (126 S. Ct. 2749 (2006)) the US Supreme Court invalidated the commissions on the ground that they were not properly authorized by Congress. It held that they violated a congressional statute requiring the President to adhere to IHL, but it left open the possibility that Congress could subsequently authorize such commissions.

A majority of the Court ruled that Common Article 3 applies to the conflict between the United States and Al Qaeda and that the military commissions violated the fair trial provisions of the article. The majority held that the US commissions did not constitute a 'regularly constituted court', because the government failed to justify setting up special ad hoc tribunals outside the existing courts martial system. The majority thus implicitly accepted that a courts martial — a standing US military tribunal — would constitute a regularly constituted court. A plurality of the Supreme Court went on to conclude that particular procedures of the military commission — precluding the defendant from seeing classified evidence — failed to 'afford ... all the judicial guarantees which are recognized as indispensable by civilized peoples'. Following are excerpts from *Hamdan*:

... While the term "regularly constituted court" is not specifically defined in either Common Article 3 or its accompanying commentary, other sources disclose its core meaning. The commentary accompanying a provision of the Fourth Geneva Convention, for example, defines "'regularly constituted'" tribunals to include "ordinary military courts" and "definitely exclud[e] all special tribunals." GCIV Commentary 340 (defining the term "properly constituted" in Article 66, which the commentary treats as identical to "regularly constituted"); see also *Yamashita*, 327 U.S., at 44, 66 S. Ct. 340 (Rutledge, J., dissenting) (describing military commission as a court "specially constituted for a particular trial"). And one of the Red Cross' own treatises defines "regularly constituted court" as used in Common Article 3 to mean "established and organized in accordance with the laws and procedures already in force in a country." Int'l. Comm. of Red Cross, 1 Customary International Humanitarian Law 355 (2005); see also GCIV Commentary 340 (observing that "ordinary military courts" will "be set up in accordance with the recognized principles governing the administration of justice").

... At a minimum, a military commission "can be 'regularly constituted' by the standards of our military justice system only if some practical need explains deviations from court-martial practice."[231] ...

[A plurality of the Court continued.]

Inextricably intertwined with the question of regular constitution is the evaluation of the procedures governing the tribunal and whether they afford "all the judicial guarantees which are recognized as indispensable by civilized peoples." Like the phrase "regularly constituted court," this phrase is not defined in the text of the Geneva Conventions. But it must be understood to incorporate at least the barest of those trial protections that have been recognized by customary international law. Many of these are described in Article 75 of [Protocol I]. Although the United States declined to ratify Protocol I, its objections were not to Article 75 thereof. Indeed, it appears that the Government "regard[s] the provisions of Article 75 as an articulation of safeguards to which all persons in the hands of an enemy are entitled." Taft, The Law of Armed Conflict After 9/11: Some Salient

---

[230] Military Order governing the Detention, Treatment, and Trial of Certain Non-Citizens in the War Against Terrorism (13 November 2001).
[231] Further evidence of this tribunal's irregular constitution is the fact that its rules and procedures are subject to change mid trial, at the whim of the Executive. See Commission Order No. 1, ß 11 (providing that the Secretary of Defense may change the governing rules 'from time to time').

Features, 28 *Yale J. Int'l. L.* 319, 322 (2003). Among the rights set forth in Article 75 is the "right to be tried in [one's] presence." Protocol I, Art. 75(4)(e).[232]

… [V]arious provisions of Commission Order No. 1 dispense with the principles, articulated in Article 75 and indisputably part of the customary international law, that an accused must, absent disruptive conduct or consent, be present for his trial and must be privy to the evidence against him. That the Government has a compelling interest in denying Hamdan access to certain sensitive information is not doubted. But, at least absent express statutory provision to the contrary, information used to convict a person of a crime must be disclosed to him.

Subsequent to the Supreme Court decision, Congress passed the Military Commission Acts of 2006 and 2009. Notably the statute expressly embraces the application of Common Article 3 to the conflict between the United States and Al Qaeda. It authorizes the President to prosecute 'unprivileged enemy belligerent' before military commissions.[233]

Guantánamo

A detailed report by a Working Group led by Claire Finkelstein and Harvey Rishikof, entitled *Beyond Guantánamo: Restoring The Rule of Law to the Law of War* (2022) provided an overview of the impact of these long-running military commissions:

… [Guantánamo] is a highly inefficient operation, one that costs taxpayers $540 million per year to operate, or $13 million per prisoner annually … .

…

As of … July 1, 2022, Guantánamo is home to thirty-six detainees: … nineteen are recommended for transfer, ten are in the military commission prosecution process, five are being held in indefinite law-of-war detention and not recommended for transfer, and two are serving penal sentences as the result of conviction by the military commissions. Many of these individuals suffer from the psychological and physical consequences of abusive treatment, practices that federal judges, convening authorities, and even two U.S. presidents have referred to, or characterized as "torture."

The Working Group unanimously concludes that the military commissions are dysfunctional, and that the system is unlikely ever to produce meaningful trials and impartial verdicts. Whatever the original intention, the military commissions have failed to provide either the promised transparency or justice, and most of the pending cases continue to languish in pretrial proceedings, showing little hope of resolution. The start of the earliest trial is at least a year off, and the Department of Defense is building a new courtroom at the facility, both of which suggest that the Biden administration is not planning to close Guantánamo any time soon. A number of factors have conspired to produce the delays in trial: the geographic location, the lack of a governing body of law, the involvement of multiple bureaucracies and agencies that render procedures cumbersome and inefficient, multiple judges, the felt need on the part of the U.S. government to maintain high levels of secrecy, and repeated instances of governmental misconduct and interference with the process. These factors, and the delays they have produced, have created an indelible taint that calls into question the likelihood these tribunals will be capable of producing impartial verdicts or outcomes perceived as legitimate.

A report by Letta Tayler and Elisa Epstein, of Human Rights Watch, entitled *Legacy of the "Dark Side": The Costs of Unlawful U.S. Detentions and Interrogations Post-9/11* (9 January 2022) provides another highly critical perspective:

No U.S. government officials have been held accountable for creating, authorizing, or implementing the CIA's secret detention and torture programs. All but a heavily redacted summary of the landmark 2014 U.S. Senate Intelligence Committee report on the covert CIA program (the "Torture Report") remains classified. The portions that have been released make clear that the torture was as useless in producing actionable intelligence as it was brutal. Like Presidents Obama and Donald J. Trump before him, President Joseph R. Biden has shown

---

[232] Other international instruments to which the United States is a signatory include the same basic protections set forth in Art. 75. See, e.g., ICCPR, Art. 14(3)(d) (setting forth the right of an accused '[t]o be tried in his presence, and to defend himself in person or through legal assistance of his own choosing'). Following the Second World War, several defendants were convicted by military commission for violations of the law of war for failing to afford fair trials to captives, including not apprising accused individuals of all evidence against them. See 5 UN War Crimes Commission 30 and 75.

[233] For details, including the 2019 *Edition of the Manual for Military Commissions*, see
https://www.mc.mil/legalresources/MilitaryCommissionsDocuments.aspx

no appetite for releasing the Torture Report, much less criminally investigating the architects of the Rendition, Detention, and Interrogation (RDI) program or other post-September 11 abuses. Biden also opposes allowing the International Criminal Court to include abuses by U.S. nationals in its investigation on grave human rights crimes in Afghanistan.

Abroad, the U.S. has continued abusive practices against terrorism suspects including transferring them to countries that torture, and, in at least some cases, unlawfully detaining them at U.S.-run sites abroad or at sea. Although such U.S. detention-related counterterrorism violations have dramatically decreased, Washington has replaced capture with kill, conducting air strikes—often with armed drones that have killed thousands of civilians, including outside recognized battlefields. Its counterterrorism campaign has spread to 85 countries with scant transparency or oversight.

…

… U.S. extraordinary renditions, unlawful detentions, and torture after September 11 [have involved massive costs,] including to the victims and suspects, to U.S. taxpayers, and to U.S. moral authority and counterterrorism efforts worldwide, ultimately jeopardizing universal human rights protections for everyone. [The report] argues that significant counterterrorism reforms, including closing the prison at Guantánamo, strengthening measures to protect civilians from death and harm, increasing transparency and accountability for the crimes the U.S. has committed, and addressing religious and racial biases, are critical steps toward mitigating the damage.

QUESTIONS

1. Which of the three approaches articulated in the judgments in *Ibrahim v. United Kingdom* strike the most appropriate balance between upholding security and protecting the rights of both the citizenry and the defendants?

2. What aspect, if any, of the European Court of Human Rights' analysis in *İncal* turns on the status of the defendant (civilian versus military) or on the nature of the offence? Do those distinctions explain the source of disagreement between the majority and dissenting opinions? Why should the test for an independent and impartial tribunal turn on such considerations? Should it matter whether a conflict is between a government and an internal separatist movement, a state and a transnational terrorist organization, or two states?

3. Why does the Inter-American Commission suggest that any trial of a civilian by a military court is categorically prohibited? Should that rule apply as well in international and transnational armed conflicts?

4. Should the presence of a single military judge on a three-judge panel, as in *İncal*, be a sufficient reason to invalidate the proceedings? Does the presence of civilian judges help counteract potential bias? How might military judges be different from other 'expert' judges that the dissenters in *İncal* suggest are permitted under the Court's case law? Would modifying other aspects of the proceedings — a different number and ratio of civilian and military judges, weighted voting rules, or appellate review — make the presence of military judges acceptable in your view?

5. Within three months of Russia's invasion of Ukraine, in February 2022, Ukraine's Prosecutor General had opened over 13,000 cases. On May 23, a 21-year-old Russian soldier, Vadim Shishimarin, was sentenced to life imprisonment for shooting a civilian. Governments supporting Ukraine have not raised significant concerns about this development, but commentators have been troubled: 'War crime trials are fraught affairs in general, but they're especially tricky when held against enemy soldiers in the midst of a conflict. Domestic judges' impartiality and ability to dispense justice to the adversary accused of atrocities are bound to be questioned. The other side will always vilify the proceedings as vicious propaganda, show trials, or lawfare.'[234] Discuss.

---

[234] S. Vasiliev, 'The Reckoning for War Crimes in Ukraine Has Begun', *Foreign Policy* (17 June 2022).

PART C: RIGHTS, DUTIES AND DILEMMAS OF UNIVERSALISM

The preceding chapters conveyed no sense of a uniform, coherent, uncontested human rights regime. From the controversies over capital punishment in Chapter 1, the dispute over permitted methods for interrogating prisoners in Chapter 3, the challenges to the very concept of economic and social rights in Chapter 4, and the competing conceptions of national security in Chapter 5, we have seen major differences in understandings of human rights both among legal orders of different states and within states. Such contests within and about the human rights regime are both predictable and appropriate. The struggle to define and uphold human rights is inevitably an ongoing one that is never definitively won (or lost).

Part C concentrates on notions of rights and of contests and disputes about them, exploring the very idea of rights more systematically than did the prior materials. Chapter 6 examines the nature of rights and rights discourse, and the character and consequences of duty-oriented rather than rights-oriented social systems. Chapter 7 begins with exploration of the opposition between universalism and cultural relativism in understanding the character of the human rights regime.

Chapter 6. Rights versus Duties

Thus far the materials have described, but barely commented on, the fundamental characteristic of the UDHR and ICCPR: their foundation in the rhetoric and concept of rights. Many view that rhetoric as unproblematic, as the central and inevitable component of a universal discourse about human dignity and humane treatment of individuals by governments. Others, to the contrary, view a discourse about rights as alien and harmful to their states or cultures, disruptive of traditional social structures, or subversive of authority. Consider the following queries:

(1) Why does the language of rights dominate the texts of the declarations and treaties as well as many new constitutions and even the slogans and polemics of political debate?

(2) Is that language intrinsically superior to other possible ones — for example, the language of duties, which might lead to a Universal Declaration of Human Duties, or the language and methods of utility? Is rights language essential to the values and goals of the human rights regime? Or is the currency of that language a matter of historical contingency, in that the postwar movement to protect human dignity found its roots in liberal political cultures in which rights had long ago taken root?

(3) Does a particular substantive content necessarily attach to the language of rights? For example, do 'rights' necessarily express the principles of the liberal political tradition, as with respect to non-discrimination, due process, or freedom of religion or speech? Are the same questions equally relevant to the language of duties? Are either rights or duties empty receptacles that are open to many different types of values and ideas, some of which might be antagonistic to the liberal tradition?

(4) Universality informs the discourse and content of rights in the UDHR and the basic treaties. But why should we accept that the stated norms are universal? Are arguments about their universal character accepted worldwide? Or do some parts of the world view many important provisions in the basic human rights instruments as particular to the Western liberal tradition, hence inapplicable to radically different states and cultures? Would the same criticism be as applicable to a duty-based Universal Declaration?

A. RIGHTS AND RIGHTS RHETORIC

We here consider different understandings, historical and contemporary, of the notion of 'rights' and inquire whether rights have inherent implications for a society's moral, political and socio-economic order. For example, does rights rhetoric in a constitution and statutes, or in a dominant moral and political theory, point to an individualistic, communitarian, or other type of society? Does it necessarily assume certain institutional arrangements for government, such as a constitutional separation of powers and an independent judiciary? Are the answers to questions such as these most likely to be found through philosophical reflection, deeper understanding of the history of rights, or in looking to human rights in practice in today's world.

The twenty-first century has witnessed a remarkable explosion of writing and debate over both the philosophical and historical dimensions of human rights. It is impossible for a casebook of this type to do justice to the richness of the increasingly specialized and sophisticated debates, although elements of them are spread throughout the book as a whole. The same applies to non-Western approaches to the theory of rights, with a wide range of Global South perspectives being captured in different chapters. But the largely theoretical or conceptual writings on theories of rights that are excerpted below emanate largely from the Global North and engage largely with Western traditions. Rights as a fundamental language of law, politics and morals grew within and are associated with the Western liberal tradition. This is not, however, to say that the claims, interests, values and ideals expressed through rights language in the basic human rights instruments are exclusive to the Western liberal tradition. Many of them, as we have seen, may be expressed through other languages as well — for example, the language of duty and responsibility of the state, government and individuals.

The various authors whose writings follow have been selected because they illustrate very different and often incompatible perspectives, ranging from the sceptical (Koskenniemi), liberal (Steiner), pragmatic (Beitz),

Marxist (O'Connell), feminist (Brown), and critical (Kennedy), to the non-anthropocentric (Mégret), and iterative/engaged (Cotulo). The goal of the materials is not to arrive at any single theory or understanding of the nature, origins, or significance of rights or rights-talk, but to gain an understanding of the complexity and richness of the notions involved.

MARTTI KOSKENNIEMI, RIGHTS, HISTORY, CRITIQUE
ADAM ETINSON (ED.), HUMAN RIGHTS: MORAL OR POLITICAL? (2018) 41

What are human rights? Where do they come from? How can we know them, or know if we "have" them? (And what does "having a right" mean?) Any discussion of the nature or role of rights tends very rapidly to lead to questions that seem soluble only by taking a stand on some pretty tough issues that have been debated for at least 2,000 years of Western political thought. Although some do suggest, or at least imply, that we are now finally in a position to give good responses to questions such as these, most would think it ridiculous to expect that we may have legitimate recourse to right-talk only once this has actually taken place. Surely it is possible to talk meaningfully of rights even in the absence of any firm philosophical founding. ... There is much in the world that we do although we cannot quite explain why we do so. Perhaps all we can say about rights, at least for now, is that something like them needs to be supposed for the other things we do in or think about the world to make sense. This would make them articles of a pragmatic faith, referring back to nothing grander than the effortless intimacy we have with our practices. But why would this be wrong? Is not asking those grander questions just to have missed the postmodern boat?

... Rights-language has distributive consequences. In an otherwise utilitarian policy-environment, rights indicate preferences that, we believe, should not be overridden by whatever net benefits a policy might offer. This is why everyone has a great interest in translating their preferences into rights. Without an authoritative list of such preferences, however, there is no limit to the translation process. In the end, all social conflict will appear as rights-conflict. At that point, it begins to seem imperative to find an answer to questions such as: "What really is a 'right' (in contrast to a mere 'preference')? How do we know them? Do they exist in some hierarchy? What values determine their position?" ...

A return to philosophy will hardly prove helpful. The twentieth century has not been kind to the idea that the resolution of social conflicts should take place by abstract reasoning. ... Speaking in a universal language has come to appear as an effort to exercise hegemony. Hence, I think, the increasing recourse to anthropology and sociology in rights-analysis. Hence also the impressive recent surge of histories of rights. ... Perhaps, if rights cannot be grounded on faith or philosophy, we might at least think of them historically, as part of the normative organization of a period. Much new historical work has looked for the origin of our present obsession with individual (human) rights. That origin has been found in different periods. Were "human rights" part of Roman (civil) law? Or did they only emerge in the process or recovery of that law in the twelfth and thirteenth centuries? Did they belong to Canon law or emerge only with the nominalist attack upon Thomistic rationalism? Should the first significant articulation of the idea of human rights be credited to the Spanish scholastics? Or would it be more appropriate to focus on Protestant ideas about resistance to authority in the sixteenth century? Should Hobbes or Grotius be heralded—for good or ill—as the intellectual fathers of the idea of individual (natural) rights? Or did the idea of such rights emerge only with eighteenth-century Enlightenment, the American Bill of Rights (1776), or the French *Déclaration des droits de l'homme et du citoyen* (1789)? What about the connection between the emergence of human rights and the abolition of slavery, or the rise of the various humanitarian movements in the nineteenth century?

Others have argued that there is no such long trajectory of "rights" passing through history at all. They have suggested that rights should be seen as part of twentieth-century institutional politics—perhaps that it "began" in the debates on minority protection within the League of Nations, or the passing of the 1948 Universal Declaration on Human Rights (UDHR), and as a reaction to Hitlerite racial aggression. Others have claimed that our present rights talk should be seen in even more recent light—as part of an effort to marry free market liberalism and religious conservatism in the postwar era, an offshoot of 1970s cold war strategies or the ideological foundation for 1990s institutional developments in international human rights law.

The turn to history in order to understand rights today is surely useful, though not as an effort to search for the origin of our present rights-practices. That would presuppose the self-evidence of our present rights—the very starting-point that was questioned—and reduce the past into its immature "predecessor". History is useful not because it "originates" or "foreshadows" present practices but because it provides illustrations of the ways in which a political vocabulary (such as rights-language) can be used for the accomplishment of different tasks. There are serious interpretative questions about the meaning and relations of "natural rights", "individual rights", "subjective rights", and "human rights" in different periods. They resemble each other, but are also different. While political philosophy seeks to clarify the differences and resemblances in its pursuit of a good rights-vocabulary, history, or at least conceptual history, seeks to locate rights in the contexts of contestation where they have been used to defend or attack distributive schemes and claims of jurisdiction. History does not resolve today's problems. But it may relieve us from the anxiety that a loss of faith in rights as providing a ready-made set of answers to social conflict may engender. It brings them down from a conceptual heaven and shows them as parts of a human world where they give shape and meaning to our agendas and pursuits. What we should think of them, or how they might be implemented in a world of scarce resources will still remain a matter of political judgement.

…

II. The Power and Weakness of Rights: Some Conclusions

… Rights have both supported and challenged the power of religious institutions. They have been a key ideological instrument to support private property against extractions by the king or public power, as well as a basis to challenge the inequality of property and the power of money. In early modern Germany, rights were invoked to defend individual liberty but also to retrench a firm central power assigned to look after the security and happiness of the citizens. During the European Enlightenment rights supported revolution but also state-building and then, as now, the two things have often gone together. As much as rights have defended individuals against their communities, they have also underwritten the community's power to demand that individuals respect its traditions: liberalism, republicanism, and even socialism have thrived on rights.

…

… [T]he common discourse about rights being "universal, inalienable and indivisible" is an intellectual stopgap and a political dead end. It looks towards a world of harmony where the right of all humans—that is to say the preferences of all—would organize themselves harmoniously and in a coterminous way. Neither conceptual logic nor historical experience supports such a view. Since Kant, and perhaps earlier, the view that rights exist in harmony has been an aspect of rationalist imagination whose political force may have been formidable, but which has lent itself to assist whatever cause and agenda. Because it denies the reality of conflicts, explaining them as misunderstandings about everyone's real preferences, it has complicated, instead of facilitated, their resolution.

No doubt, rights theorists have long since recognized that the way to utopia is not opened by assuming a pre-existing harmony where none exists. The process of redescribing some interests or preferences as "rights" has been and continues to be about struggle and compromise in which some claimants win, others lose. … The massive translation of "interests" into "rights" in the late twentieth century was occasioned precisely by the hope that in this way they could be made untouchable, lifted outside politics altogether. But there is no limit to this translation, which is why the world of politics became saturated by rights-claims. For every claim of right, the burden that is to fall upon somebody for honouring it may be seen as a violation of the rights of the latter. Every increase of the right to freedom of somebody is felt as an encroachment on the right to security of someone else. And so on. There is no social conflict in which both sides could not, with some plausibility, invoke their interest as a "right". The result has been the rise of the bureaucratic management of rights through ubiquitous practices of "balancing" whose criteria are received from an institutional bias that cannot be articulated by the rights whose limit and content it sets.

…

… [Rights-talk focuses] on things we "have" or (to follow Grotius) "faculties" we "possess" [and] seems obsessively concerned with identities rather than the structural determination of those identities. Rights-talk may support our capacity to exercise a religion we profess, to express an opinion or to support a party we prefer, or to use a property we have—that is to say, to be "true" to ourselves and our life projects. But it is blind to the conditions within which we come to think of ourselves as "religious" in a particular way, members of a party, property-owners or persons with specific opinions. This, I think, is an important aspect of the intellectual dead end that rights bring with them. They claim to protect our (person, group) identities and preferences without ever questioning how we came to have them. They are so close, so intimate with our assumed selfhood that they make it impossible for us to situate ourselves in any larger context—especially the context of an ubiquitous identity-producing power.

...

HENRY STEINER, SOME CHARACTERISTICS OF THE LIBERAL POLITICAL TRADITION HENRY STEINER AND PHILIP ALSTON, INTERNATIONAL HUMAN RIGHTS IN CONTEXT (1996) 187

Observers from different regions and cultures can agree that the human rights movement, with respect to its language of rights and the civil and political rights that it declares, stems principally from the liberal tradition of Western political and legal thought. That observation lies at the core of argument by states from non-Western parts of the world that some basic provisions in instruments like the UDHR or ICCPR are inappropriate and inapplicable to their circumstances. Those instruments, the argument goes, purport to give a genuinely universal expression to certain tenets of liberal political culture, and advocates basing their criticism of counties in the developing world on the human rights movement are effectively advancing a contemporary form of imperialism. Thus liberal thought and practices inform much contemporary debate ... about the meaning and relevance of cultural relativism.

For the purpose of facilitating some comparisons between liberalism and the human rights movement, this Comment sketches characteristics that observers would associate with the different expressions of the liberal tradition during the twentieth century. The Comment has a limited historical scope. It does not reach back to the origins of liberal thought in the seventeenth century and Age of Enlightenment, or to changes in that body of thought in the nineteenth century.

The liberal political tradition has never been and surely is not today a monolithic body of thought requiring one and only one form of government. The very term 'liberal' has assumed different meanings, from the liberal economics associated with the laissez faire school of the nineteenth century to contemporary associations of liberalism in a country like the United States with a more active and engaged state concerned with the general welfare of the population and with regulation of the market and nongovernmental actors — the modern regulatory and welfare state so familiar to Western states.

The contemporary expressions of liberal thought by theorists like Dworkin or Rawls depart significantly from the writings of the classical theorists influencing its development, like Bentham, Kant, Locke, Mill, Rousseau and Tocqueville. The differences among such classical writers are reflected in the distinct versions of liberal ideology and the varied structures and practices of self-styled liberal democracies. This variety and ongoing transformation suggest caution in making inclusive and dogmatic comparisons between, say, liberalism and the human rights movement, which has during the last six decades generated its own internal conflicts and has itself undergone significant change.

No characteristic of the liberal tradition is more striking than its emphasis on the individual. Liberal political theory and the constitutive instruments of many liberal states frequently employ basic concepts or premises like the dignity and autonomy of the individual, and the respect that is due to all individuals. The vital concept of equality informs these terms: the equal dignity of all human beings, the equal respect to which individuals are entitled, the equal right for self-realization. It is not then surprising that equal protection and equal opportunities without repressive discrimination constitute so cardinal a value of contemporary liberalism. In general, the protection of members of minorities against invidious discrimination continues to be a central concern for the liberal state.

Such stress on the individual informs basic justifications for the state. The liberal state rests on, its very legitimacy stems from, the consent of the people within it. Within liberal theory, that consent is both hypothetical, as in the notion of a social contract among the inhabitants of a state of nature to create the political state, and institutionalized through typical practices such as periodic elections. Such ideas are explicit in the basic human rights instruments. Note Article 21 of the UDHR ('The will of the people shall be the basis of the authority of government') and Article 25 of the ICCPR (the importance of elections 'guaranteeing the free expression of the will of the electors').

From the start, liberal theory has been attentive to the risk of abuse of the individual by the state. The rights language that is found in constitutional bills of rights, statutory provisions for basic rights, political traditions not expressed in positive law and writings of theorists and advocates respond to this need for protection against the state. The rights with which the individual is endowed limit governmental power — the right not to be tortured, not to be discriminated against on stated grounds. Until the early twentieth century, liberal theory and the liberal state were far less attentive to violations of rights by non-state actors, corporations or individuals, but heightened regulation of the non-state (private) sector and the growth of international human rights have brought significant change, particularly since World War II.

Historically the protection of the property right against interference by the state and others played a major role in liberal theory. Indeed, questions of the relationships between liberalism and free enterprise or capitalism have long been debated. They take on a particular pungency in the post-Cold War world of spreading markets, spreading democracy and globalization.

Sometimes the types of rights just referred to are described as 'negative': the hands-off or non-interference rights (don't touch), or the right to be interfered with (as by arrest, imprisonment) only pursuant to stated processes. It is partly the prominence of the rights related to notions of individual liberty, autonomy and choice and the right related to property protection that produces the sharp division in much liberal thought between the state and individual, between government and nongovernmental sectors, between what are often referred to as the public and private realms or spheres of action.

This conception of negative rights, and of negative freedom as the absence of external constraints, together with the historical alliance of political liberalism with conceptions of a free market and laissez faire, led to liberalism's early emphasis on sharply limited government. The tension between that early ideology and background, and the growing emphasis over more than a century on the welfare and regulatory functions of the modern liberal state, remain central to much political and moral debate today.

That debate is related to an opposition that has developed in liberal thought between negative rights or negative liberty (freedom), and positive or affirmative rights or liberty (freedom). Those terms have acquired different meanings. For example, 'positive rights' have been described as entitlements of individuals to the effect that the state should not simply respect the 'private' sphere of inviolability of the individual (the negative rights), but should also 'act' in particular ways to benefit the individual, perhaps by providing education or health care. In this sense, the 'positive rights' of individuals such as the right to education or health care impose duties on the state to provide the necessary institutions or resources.

In a different and more ample sense, positive liberty has been described as 'liberty to' as opposed to 'liberty from' — for example, the liberty to realize oneself, to satisfy one's real interests, to achieve individual self-determination. One form of such positive liberty facilitated by the state would be governmental policies and institutions fostering the active political participation of citizens in electoral and other processes that help to determine the exercise of public power. Through such positive liberty, the individual can participate in the creation and recreation of self and state. The state readily and naturally becomes involved in this search of individuals for positive liberty, characteristically by creating the conditions that make the individual quest more likely to succeed, but at the dangerous authoritarian extreme by attempting to define the content of genuine self-realization and by coercing individuals to achieve it.

What an individual should seek in life, what idea of the good in life that individual holds, how the individual seeks self-realization, remain in the liberal state matters of individual choice to which both negative and positive conceptions of rights and freedom are relevant. That state must be open to a variety of ends, a variety of conceptions of the good, that individuals will express. The liberal state must then be a pluralist state. Its structure of rights, going beyond the rights to personal security and equal protection to include rights of conscience and speech and association, facilitates and protects the many types of diversity within pluralism, as well as ongoing argument in the public arena about the forms and goals of social and political life.

Precisely what governmental structures best realize such liberal principles is among the disputed features of the liberal tradition. The liberal state is closely associated with the ideal of the rule of law, hence with some minimum of separation of government powers such as an independent judiciary that can protect individual rights against executive abuse. The fear of tyranny of the majority lies at the foundation of the argument for restrictions on governmental power through a constitutional bill of rights limiting or putting conditions on what government can do. How to enforce that bill of rights against the executive and legislature has never achieved a consensus among liberal states. They vary in the degree to which they subject legislative action to judicial review, hence in the degree to which governmental power, even if supported by a freely voting majority of the population, can abridge or transform or abolish rights. The trend among liberal democracies over the last few decades has been toward judicial review of legislative as well as executive action.

The liberal tradition continues to be subjected to deep challenges from within and without, and thus continues its process of evolutionary change. During and particularly after the Cold War, its interaction with states of the developing world posed complex issues in relation to efforts of some of those states to develop new forms of government and economy. For example, the relationships in the former Communist states of Central and East Europe between liberalism, privatization and property rights, markets and regulation thereof, and the provision of welfare remain ambiguous and in flux. More generally, questions of the relationship between liberalism and a market economy, or liberalism and ethnic nationalism, have assumed heightened prominence. In a Western country such as the United States, liberalism responds to challenges from diverse perspectives such as communitarian ideas, civic republicanism, and multiculturalism (cultural particularism).

Some of these contemporary challenges underscore a continuing debate within liberalism, the two sides to which can lead to significantly different political and social orders: individual or group identity as primary. The group may be — to use the conventional porous and overlapping terms — national, linguistic, religious, cultural, ethnic. At the extreme, it is not compatible with a liberal creed for a governing order to subordinate individuals fully to the demands of such kinds of groups. With respect to the core values of liberalism, individual rights remain lexically prior to the demands of a culture or group, to the claims of any collective identity or group solidarity.

Nonetheless, the liberal state is hardly hostile to groups as such. It is not blind to the influence of groups (religious, cultural, ethnic) or of group and cultural identity in shaping the individual. Indeed, the political life of modern liberal democracies is largely constituted by the interaction, lobbying and other political participation of groups, some of which are natural in their defining characteristic (race, sex, elderly citizens), and some formed out of shared interests (labour unions, business associations, environmental groups). The liberal state, by definition committed to pluralism, must accommodate different types of groups, and maintain the framework of rights in which they can struggle for recognition, power and survival.

Such issues indicate how much is open and debated within liberalism about the significance of the priority of the individual in the contemporary liberal state — or different types of liberal states. Should we, for example, understand the 'individual' abstractly, as similar in vital respects everywhere, both within the same state and universally? Or do we understand the individual contextually, as influenced or even determined by ethnic, cultural, national, religious and other traditions and communities? Should we even phrase the question in such dramatic contrasts, or should we rather assume that the answers are too complex for any clear choice between them?

Since the birth of the human rights movement, ... such issues about the individual and the collective have taken on great pungency in the contradictions bred, on the one hand, by the spread of both liberal ideology with its emphasis on the individual and of market ideology with its stress on private initiative, and on the other hand, by the often savage bursts of ethnic nationalism in many parts of the world with their stress on collective rather than individual identity.

... Rights are no more determinate in meaning, no less susceptible to varying interpretations and disputes among states, than any other moral, political or legal conception — for example, 'property', or 'sovereignty', or 'consent', or 'national security'. Within liberal states, different institutional solutions have been brought to the question of who should determine and develop the content of rights, and who should resolve the many and puzzling conflicts among rights. In the international arena, this problem becomes all the more complex. What mechanisms, what institutional framework, what allocation or separation of powers, what blend of overtly political and judicial resolution of these issues, will we find in the international human rights movement?

CHARLES BEITZ, THE IDEA OF HUMAN RIGHTS
(2009) 7

... Some philosophers have conceived of human rights as if they had an existence in the moral order that can be grasped independently of their embodiment in international doctrine and practice—for example, as "natural rights" or their secular successors, as fundamental moral rights possessed by all human beings "as such" or "solely in virtue of their humanity," or as conditions for social institutions about which all the world's social moral codes agree. These possibilities are not mutually exclusive. The usual view is that international human rights ... express and derive their authority from some such deeper order of values. For those who accept some variation of this kind of view, the task of a theorist of international human rights is to discover and describe the deeper order of values and judge the extent to which international doctrine conforms to it.

I shall argue that it is a mistake to think about international human rights in this way. These familiar conceptions are question-begging in presuming to understand and criticize an existing normative practice on the basis of one or another governing conception that does not, itself, take account of the functions that the idea of a human right is meant to play, and actually does play, in the practice. ... [T]hey are also at odds with the historical development of international human rights doctrine. Its authors disowned the thought that human rights are the expression of any single conception of human nature or human good or of any but the most general understanding of the purposes of human social organization. They took it as an ineliminable fact that people would differ about these matters. They therefore aspired to a doctrine that could be endorsed from many contemporary moral, religious, and cultural points of view and that was suited to be implemented by means distinctive to characteristically modern forms of social organization. The approach that takes human rights as the expression of a received philosophical idea risks missing this feature of international human rights.

... [T]he human rights enterprise is a global practice. The practice is both discursive and political. As a first approximation, we might say that it consists of a set of norms for the regulation of the behavior of states together with a set of modes or strategies of action for which violations of the norms may count as reasons. The practice exists within a global discursive community whose members recognize the practice's norms as reason-giving and use them in deliberating and arguing about how to act. These norms are expressed in the [UDHR and the major treaties, though] these formulations are open to interpretation and revision within the practice. The discursive community in which the practice resides is global and consists of a heterogeneous group of agents, including the governments of states, international organizations, participants in the processes of international law, economic actors such as business firms, members of nongovernmental organizations, and participants in domestic and transnational political networks and social movements. The approach I shall explore tries to grasp the concept of a human right by understanding the role this concept plays within the practice. Human rights claims are supposed to be reason-giving for various kinds of political action which are open to a range of agents. We understand the concept of a human right by asking for what kinds of actions, in which kinds of circumstances, human rights claims may be understood to give reasons.

... I note two qualifications. First, in holding that the practice consists of norms which are widely recognized within a discursive community, I do not mean to say that there is agreement within the community about the scope and content of the system of norms taken as a whole, about the weights that should be attached to the reasons for action supplied by these norms, or about how conflicts among human rights, or between human rights and other values, should be resolved. Indeed, ... it is not only an inevitable but also a functionally significant aspect of the practice of human rights that its norms serve as much to frame disagreement as agreement. ... We rely on the practice for an understanding of the discursive roles of human rights, not (or anyway not directly) to delineate their scope or content.

The other qualification is that the practice of human rights is emergent. It is ... not a mature social practice. There is disagreement about all its main elements—for example, about the content of its norms, the eligible means for their application and enforcement, the distribution of responsibilities to support them, and the weight to be accorded to considerations about human rights when they come into conflict with other values. International human rights institutions lack capacities for authoritative adjudication of disputes and coercive enforcement of the practice's norms. The division of labor between public human rights institutions and nongovernmental organizations that participate in international institutional processes is unstable. Most importantly for our purposes, there is no unambiguous basis for establishing the boundaries of the discursive community within which the practice takes place. I have said that the meaning of the idea of a human right can be inferred from its role in a discursive practice, but if the boundaries of the discursive community are indistinct—for example, if there is no authoritative basis for ruling participants in or out—then there may be unavoidable indeterminacy in our understanding of the idea. All of these features reflect the practice's emergent character and all complicate a practical analysis. Notwithstanding the complications, ... the practice of human rights ... organizes much of the normative discourse of contemporary world politics and commands the energy and commitment of large numbers of people and organizations.

... [A] practical approach ... [calls] into question ... two familiar conceptions ... —the idea of human rights as entitlements that belong to people "by nature" or "simply in virtue of their humanity" and the distinct idea of human rights as objects of agreement among diverse moral and political cultures. ...

...

[This approach does not suggest that it is necessary] to accept the contents of existing human rights doctrine as binding on us or to agree that the practice as we find it is the best way to realize the hope one might see in it as a matter of first impression. These are questions to be examined in their own right. But neither question can be rendered coherently without a clear grasp of the idea of human rights. To achieve such a grasp we do not suppose that human rights must express or derive from a single basic value or that they constitute a single, fundamental category of moral concern. Instead, we treat international human rights as a normative practice to be grasped *sui generis* and consider how the idea of a human right functions within it.

PAUL O'CONNELL, ON THE HUMAN RIGHTS QUESTION
40 HUM. RTS. Q (2018) 965

...

A. Marx on Rights

... Marx's ... 1843 essay *On the Jewish Question* ... was written as a response to Bruno Bauer's argument that if Jewish people in Germany were to receive political emancipation, the same civil and political rights as other Germans, they must first renounce (or, from Bauer's perspective, emancipate themselves) from Judaism. In an excoriating critique of Bauer's argument, Marx also engaged in a general reflection on the nature of rights as such. Crucial to Marx's analysis of rights, and their limitations, is the distinction he draws between *political* emancipation and *human* emancipation. The former can be achieved by the conferral of civil and political rights, but is formal and limited; the latter is substantive, genuine, and can only be achieved through transcending existing social relations (capitalism), and collapsing the division between political citizens active in and through the state and private individuals who exist in "civil society."

Starting from this premise, Marx argues that "the so-called *rights of man*, as distinct from the *rights of the citizen*, are simply the rights of a *member of civil society*, that is, of egoistic man, of man separated from other men and from the community." To demonstrate this, Marx identifies what he sees as the core rights in the *French Declaration of the Rights of Man and the Citizen* (equality, liberty, security, and property) and sets out to show the necessarily truncated nature of each of these rights within the capitalist system. So, for example, he argues that "liberty as a right of man is not founded upon the relations between man and man, but rather upon separation of man from man. It is the right of such separation. The right of the *circumscribed* individual, withdrawn into himself."

In a similar vein, he argues that property is "the right of self-interest" which "leads every man to see in other men, not the *realization*, but rather the *limitation* of his own liberty." Equality, in this context, is merely the guarantee that "every man is equally regarded as a self-sufficient monad," while security is the guarantee of each selfish, isolated individual's property. In light of this, Marx concludes that:

None of the supposed rights of man, therefore, go beyond the egoistic man, man as he is, as a member of civil society; that is, an individual separated from the community, withdrawn into himself, wholly preoccupied with his private interest and acting in accordance with his private caprice. Man is far from being considered, in the rights of man, as a species-being; on the contrary, species-life itself—society—appears as a system which is external to the individual and as a limitation of his original independence. The only bond between men is natural necessity, need and private interest, the preservation of their property and their egoistic persons.

In sum, Marx argues that the rights of man do not, in substance, reflect genuine human emancipation. Instead, while purporting to emancipate individuals they are, in fact, constitutive of a set of social relations that denies individuals the capacity to realize their true nature (species-being) as social beings. Real emancipation will only take place when the social relations of capitalism are transcended, and the distinctions between formal political freedom and action in the "private" sphere are replaced by genuine community.

...

... [I]n his *Critique of the Gotha Program* ... Marx criticizes the limitations of "bourgeois right"—in particular the inability of formal, legal equality to account for substantive real world differences between individuals and classes. This, in turn, means that the language of equality, and formal guarantees of equal right, in fact serve to conceal and entrench substantive inequality. Marx concludes his critique of the Gotha Program by dismissing the idea of equal rights as "dogmas, ideas which in a certain period had some meaning but have now become obsolete verbal rubbish" and been reduced to mere "ideological nonsense."

Though highly critical of the concept of right as used in the Gotha Program, Marx also acknowledges that right "can never be higher than the economic structure of society and its cultural development conditioned thereby," or, in other words, that equal rights, as such, can never challenge the inherent inequalities produced by the capitalist system. Marx concludes by noting that only when capitalism is transcended and a truly new form of society has begun to consolidate itself "can the narrow horizon of bourgeois right be crossed in its entirety and society inscribe on its banner: From each according to his ability, to each according to his needs!" As with *On the Jewish Question*, Marx could be read here as rejecting rights, or, he can be seen as engaging in a thorough and necessary critique of blind faith in rights. Bringing to the fore the ways in which the un-freedom produced by capitalism structurally and necessarily frustrates the high ideals contained in appeals to human rights, without necessarily constituting a rejection of rights *tout court*.

...

... Clearly, then, Marx's stated views on rights throughout his life can best be described as "critical, differentiated, underdeveloped and, in more than a few instances, ambiguous." All of which is to say that while Marx was certainly critical of human rights as lauded, liberal abstractions, he was also aware of their value and importance in political struggles to advance the interests of the working class. ...

...

WENDY BROWN, SUFFERING THE PARADOXES OF RIGHTS
WENDY BROWN AND JANET HALLEY (EDS.), LEFT LEGALISM/LEFT CRITIQUE (2002)
420[235]

This essay does not take a stand for or against rights, but rather, seeks to map some of the conundrums of rights for articulating and redressing women's inequality and subordination in liberal constitutional regimes. ...

Speaking for the disenfranchised in loose cross-cultural fashion, Gayatri Spivak depicts liberalism (and other modernist emancipatory formations) as "that which we cannot not want." This from a Derridean Marxist postcolonial feminist critic keenly aware of what liberalism cannot deliver, what its hidden cruelties are, what unemancipatory relations of power it conceals in its sunny formulations of freedom and equality. Indeed, Spivak's grammar suggests a condition of constraint in the production of our desire so radical that it perhaps even turns that desire against itself, foreclosing our hopes in a language we can neither escape nor wield on our own behalf. Patricia Williams refigures this condition of entrapment as one that might be negotiated through dramatic catachresis. Forcing rights out of their usual ruses of abstraction that mystifies and universalism that excludes, she insists that we procure them for "slaves . . . trees . . . cows . . . history . . . rivers and rocks . . . all of society's objects and untouchables." Albeit in a very different register, Drucilla Cornell argues in parallel with Williams, insisting that women's right to "minimum conditions of individuation," and in particular to an imaginary domain in which a future anterior is not beyond women's grasp, is the surest way to finesse the tradeoff between liberty and equality that liberal rights discourse is generally thought to force. Yet even in Williams's and Cornell's critical yet ultimately utopian rapprochements with rights discourse, there is a tacit confession that recalls Spivak's own weary recognition of the historical limits of our political imagination. If we are constrained to need and want rights, do they inevitably shape as well as claim our desire without gratifying it?

---

[235] In response, see A. Lever, 'The Politics of Paradox: A Response to Wendy Brown', 7 *Constellations* (2000) 242.

...

... [A] provisional answer to the question of the value of rights language for women is that it is deeply paradoxical: rights secure our standing as individuals even as they obscure the treacherous ways that standing is achieved and regulated; they must be specific and concrete to reveal and redress women's subordination, yet potentially entrench our subordination through that specificity; they promise increased individual sovereignty at the price of intensifying the fiction of sovereign subjects; they emancipate us to pursue other political ends while subordinating those political ends to liberal discourse; they move in a transhistorical register while emerging from historically specific conditions; they promise to redress our suffering as women but only by fracturing that suffering—and us—into discrete components, a fracturing that further violates lives already violated by the imbrication of racial, class, sexual, and gendered power.

...

Paradox may be distinguished from contradiction or tension through its emphasis on irresolvability: multiple yet incommensurable truths, or truth and its negation in a single proposition, or truths that undo even as they require each other. But paradox also signifies a doctrine or opinion that challenges received authority, goes against the doxa. In *Only Paradoxes to Offer*, a study of nineteenth-century French feminists, Joan Wallach Scott parlays this definition into a political formation: "Those who put into circulation a set of truths that challenge but don't displace orthodox beliefs create a situation that loosely matches the technical definition of paradox." Scott then suggests that the paradoxical utterances and strategies of the feminists she studied emerged as a consequence of arguing on behalf of women's rights, and of women's standing as individuals, in a discursive context in which both individuals and rights were relentlessly identified with masculinity. Thus, feminists were arguing for something that could not be procured without simultaneously demanding a transformation in the nature of what they were arguing for, namely, the "rights of man" for women. This rendered paradox the structuring rather than contingent condition of their political claims.

Scott's insight into nineteenth-century French feminism may be of help in understanding our own circumstances. First, the problem she identifies persists into the present, namely, that women's struggle for rights occurs in the context of a specifically masculinist discourse of rights, a discourse that presumes an ontologically autonomous, self-sufficient, unencumbered subject. Women both require access to the existence of this fictional subject and are systematically excluded from it by the gendered terms of liberalism, thereby making our deployment of rights paradoxical. Second, moving beyond Scott's focus, even as invocations of rights for a particular subject (e.g., women) on a particular issue (e.g., sexuality) in a particular domain (e.g., marriage), all of which have been historically excluded from the purview of rights, may work to politicize the standing of those subjects, issues, or domains, rights in liberalism also tend to depoliticize the conditions they articulate. Rights function to articulate a need, a condition of lack or injury, that cannot be fully redressed or transformed by rights, yet within existing political discourse can be signified in no other way. Thus rights for the systematically subordinated tend to rewrite injuries, inequalities, and impediments to freedom that are consequent to social stratification as matters of individual violations and rarely articulate or address the conditions producing or fomenting that violation. Yet the absence of rights in these domains leaves fully intact these same conditions.

If these are the conditions under which rights emerge as paradoxical for women, as simultaneously politically essential and politically regressive, what are the possibilities for working these paradoxes in politically efficacious fashion? Unlike contradictions, which can be exploited, or mystification, which can be exposed, or disavowal, which can be forced into confrontation with itself, or even despair, which can be negated, the politics of paradox is very difficult to negotiate. Paradox appears endlessly selfcanceling, as a political condition of achievements perpetually undercut, a predicament of discourse in which every truth is crossed by a countertruth, and hence a state in which political strategizing itself is paralyzed.

... How might attention to paradox help formulate a political struggle for rights in which they are conceived neither as instruments nor as ends, but as articulating through their instantiation what equality and freedom might consist in that exceeds them? In other words, how might the paradoxical elements of the struggle for rights in an emancipatory context articulate a field of justice beyond "that which we cannot not want"? And what form of rights claims have the temerity to sacrifice an absolutist or naturalized status in order to carry this possibility?

DAVID KENNEDY, THE INTERNATIONAL HUMAN RIGHTS MOVEMENT: PART OF THE PROBLEM?
15 HARVARD HUM. RTS J. (2002) 101

...

II.   A Short List of Pragmatic Worries and Polemical Charges

...

A. Human Rights Occupies the Field of Emancipatory Possibility

Hegemony as resource allocation. The claim here is that this institutional and political hegemony makes other valuable, often more valuable, emancipatory strategies less available. This argument is stronger, of course, when one can say something about what those alternatives are - or might be. But there may be something to the claim that human rights has so dominated the imaginative space of emancipation that alternatives can now only be thought, perhaps unhelpfully, as negations of what human rights asserts- passion to its reason, local to its global, etc. As a dominant and fashionable vocabulary for thinking about emancipation, human rights crowds out other ways of understanding harm and recompense. This is easiest to see when human rights attracts institutional energy and resources that would otherwise flow elsewhere. But this is not only a matter of scarce resources.

Hegemony as criticism. Human rights also occupies the field by implicit or explicit delegitimation of other emancipatory strategies. ... Where this is so, pursuing a human rights initiative or promoting the use of human rights vocabulary may have fully untended negative consequences for other existing emancipatory projects. ...

Hegemony as distortion. To the extent emancipatory projects must be expressed in the vocabulary of "rights" to be heard, good policies that are not framed that way go unattended. This also distorts the way projects are imagined and framed for international consideration. For example, it is often asserted that the international human rights movement makes an end run around local institutions and strategies that would often be better - ethically, politically, philosophically, aesthetically. ... A "universal" idea of what counts as a problem and a solution snuffs out all sorts of promising local political and social initiatives to contest local conditions in other terms. But there are other lost vocabularies that are equally global - vocabularies of duty, of responsibility, of collective commitment. Encouraging people concerned about environmental harm to rethink their concerns as a human rights violation will have bad consequences if it would have turned out to be more animating, for example, to say there is a duty to work for the environment, rather than a right to a clean environment.

The "right to development" is a classic-and well known-example. Once concerns about global poverty are raised in these terms, energy and resources are drawn to developing a literature and an institutional practice at the international level of a particular sort. Efforts that cannot be articulated in these terms seem less legitimate, less practical, less worth the effort. ...

B. Human Rights Views the Problem and the Solution Too Narrowly

Narrow in many ways. People have made many different claims about the narrowness of human rights. Here are some: the human rights movement foregrounds harms done explicitly by *governments* to individuals or groups - leaving largely unaddressed and more legitimate by contrast harms brought about by governments indirectly or by private parties. Even when addressing private harms, human rights focuses attention on *public* remedies - explicit rights formalized and implemented by the state. One criticizes the *state* and seeks *public* law remedies, but leaves unattended or enhanced the powers and felt entitlements of private actors. ...

Insulating the economy. ... Human rights foregrounds problems of *participation* and *procedure*, at the expense of distribution, implicitly legitimating the existing distributions of wealth, status and power in societies once rights have been legislated, formal participation in government achieved, and institutional remedies for violations provided. ...

... [T]he imbalance between civil/political and social/economic rights is neither an accident of policies nor a matter that could be remedied by more intensive commitment. It is structural, to the philosophy of human rights, to the conditions of political possibility that make human rights an emancipatory strategy in the first place, to the institutional character of the movement, or to the ideology of its participants and supporters.

Foregrounding form. The strong attachment of the human rights movement to the legal formalization of rights and the establishment of legal machinery for their implementation makes the achievement of these forms an end in itself. ...

Backgrounding the background. The effects of a wide array of laws that do not explicitly condone violations but nevertheless affect the incidence of violation in a society are left unattended. ...

...

C. Human Rights Generalizes Too Much

Universal goods and evils. The vocabulary and institutional practice of human rights promotion propagates an unduly abstract idea about people, politics and society. A one-size-fits-all emancipatory practice underrecognizes and reduces the instance and possibility for particularity and variation. This claim is not that human rights are too "individualistic." Rather, the claim is that the "person," as well as the "group," imagined and brought to life by human rights agitation is both abstract and general in ways chat have bad consequences.

...

Becoming free only as an instance of the general. To come into understanding of oneself as an instance of a pre-existing general – "I am a 'person with rights" - exacts a cost, a loss of awareness of the unprecedented and plastic nature of experience, or a loss of a capacity co imagine and desire alternative futures. ...

Not just bad for victims. The articulation of concrete good and evil in abstract terms is not only limiting for victims. The human rights vocabulary makes us think of evil as a social machine, a theater of roles, in which people are "victims," "violators," and "bystanders." At its most effective, human rights figures victims as passive and innocent, violators as deviant, and human rights professionals as heroic. Only the bystanders are figured in ambivalent or uncertain terms. ...

D. Human Rights Particularizes Too Much

Emancipating the "right holders." The specific way human rights generalizes is to consolidate people into "identities" on the basis of which rights can be claimed. There are two issues here: a focus on *individuals* and a focus, whether for individuals or groups, on *right-holding identity*. The focus on individuals and people who come to think of themselves as individuals blunts articulation of a shared life. The focus on discrete and insular right holding identities blunts awareness of diversity, of the continuity of human experience, of overlapping identities. Together these tendencies inhibit expression of the experience of being part of a community.

...

* * *

A decade later, David Kennedy concluded, in 'The International Human Rights Regime: Still Part of the Problem?', in Rob Dickinson et al. (eds.), *Examining Critical Perspectives on Human Rights* (2012) 19 at 34, that:

> Human rights is no longer the way forward – it focuses too longingly on the perfection of a politics already past its prime. Like constitutional orders before it, a new global governance regime will be imagined and built through collective hope, struggle, and disappointment. It took a long time to invent and civilize a national politics, to organize the world in nation states, and to subject them to one another's ethical judgment. Building a national politics across the planet had a strong emancipatory dimension – slaves, women, workers, peasants, colonial dominions obtained citizenship in relationship to the new institutional machinery of a national politics. We can see human rights as the apogee and epitaph for that politics. Building a new politics for a global society and a global economy will be every bit as difficult. Let us hope it does not take as long; and does not require as much violence in order to be born.

PAUL O'CONNELL, ON THE HUMAN RIGHTS QUESTION
40 HUM. RTS. Q (2018) 975

III. Critiques of Rights

…

A. Critical Legal Studies and the Critique of Rights

In the early 1980s, the Critical Legal Studies (CLS) movement engaged in a sustained critique of the concept of rights. Some of the key aspects of the various CLS critiques were that rights, and rights talk, tended: (i) to insulate and valorize subordination in the private sphere; (ii) to legitimate, perpetuate, and conceal greater injustice than they addressed; and (iii) that the language of rights tended to be atomistic and to alienate people from one another. A further, central element of the CLS critique was that human rights, as with all legal discourse, were inherently indeterminate. All of this stemmed from a "loss of faith in rights" on the part of sections of the American left.

…

B. The Critique of Rights Today

… [In the early 2000s] a new wave of human rights critiques emerged. One prominent account was articulated by David Kennedy. …

…

Similar misgivings about human rights have been expressed by … Martti Koskenniemi. … With Kennedy and Koskenniemi we have a restatement of key elements of the earlier CLS critique, namely that rights are indeterminate and do not touch the real, material causes of injustice and inequality. From Wendy Brown, and others, we also get a restatement of the idea that human rights are problematic because they entrench forms of individuality and subjectivity which, on balance, tend to sustain the status quo. Likewise, Zizek and others argue that the language of human rights mainly provides an ideological apologia for Western imperial interventions around the world. In this way, "human rights practice essentially results in both the reproduction and strengthening of the very state-governing apparatuses it confronts, and as a result ultimately undermines its own aims." From all of this, it follows, that movements for fundamental social change should be skeptical of and eschew the language of human rights, and instead should focus on other emancipatory discourses.

C. The Limits of Critique

The first thing that needs to be said about these critical accounts of human rights is that they raise crucially important and valid critiques of dominant liberal discourses of human rights. With that said, these critiques also fall short in several important ways. Three of the main shortcomings in these critiques are: (i) the overemphasis on the dominant narrative of human rights; (ii) the idealistic nature of the critiques (in the sense that they are, in the first instance, an engagement with and critique of ideas and concepts in the abstract); and (iii) the divorce of this critique from concrete struggles. Each of these shortcomings, more pronounced in some cases than others, reduces these critical accounts to a sort of radical quietism; a stance which decries the extant order, without conceiving or countenancing any meaningful alternative.

The indeterminacy critique, highlighting the atavistic forms of individuality at the heart of mainstream accounts of human rights and the cynical deployment of human rights to justify imperialist depredations, are all valid. The problem, however, is when these legitimate critiques of liberal/dominant rights discourses evolve into a rejection of rights as such. It is undeniable, as Blackburn puts it, that human rights are cynically deployed for "great-power ends," that liberal rights discourse entrenches a truncated form of individuality, and that rights are not the neutral, determinate rules that liberal legalism pretends they are. All of this, however, merely demonstrates the inaccuracy of the self-perception of dominant human rights discourses, and says little or nothing about how movements striving for fundamental social change can or should engage with the language and concept of rights as such.

Tied to this one-sidedness is the idealistic character of these rights critiques. … Anthony Chase highlighted this shortcoming …:

Nothing is more striking about the literary criticism approach than the unwillingness or inability of its practitioners to provide concrete historical and sociological studies of instances where the "self-confidence" or "self-activity" of radical social movements … have actually been "crushed", not by arduous working conditions or impoverization, not by the inability of civil society to impose civil rights and liberties against state power, not by police surveillance or death squads, not by famine or inadequate public health services, not by the dull necessity of economic reproduction, not by armed invasions, prison and torture cells, or "surgical air strikes" against villages and cities, but, rather extraordinarily, by the central target of CLS critique: appellate judicial reasoning in the liberal mode. The enormous emphasis upon and exclusive focus given to the rhetoric of judges in (apparently) maintaining empires, civilizations, and the fabric of societies, has made CLS a unique form of social theory (if one may call it that), in existence hardly anywhere outside of the cloistered legal academy.

… Critiques of rights in the broad CLS tradition routinely lose sight of this, and become trapped in a hall of mirrors where the enemy is a discourse, rather than the material relationships that structure discourses one way or another.

Finally, then, these critiques are lacking because they are divorced from concrete struggles and the ideas which animate such struggles. So, for example, it is true to say that rights can have myriad different meanings in the abstract, but in concrete cases they are given a specific meaning. This meaning is fought over and determined in and through social struggles, which sometimes make their way to the rarefied environs of the courtroom, but are not limited to this. The critique of rights, in the abstract, loses much of its veracity and efficacy when the messiness of political and social struggles have to be accounted for. …

…

V. Conclusion

Critiques of human rights highlight crucial shortcomings in the dominant, liberal discourse. However, shifting the frame of reference and situating discussions of human rights within a Marxist tradition that emphasizes contradiction, social struggle, and the need to transcend the system which structurally undermines human flourishing, opens a way of understanding human rights that can support movements for radical social change. Of course, the assertion of human rights will not bring about fundamental transformation in and of itself, but they can play an important role in broader struggles to do that. …

**FRÉDÉRIC MÉGRET, THE ANTHROPOCENTRISM OF HUMAN RIGHTS
VINCENT CHAPAUX, FRÉDÉRIC MÉGRET AND USHA NATARAJAN (EDS.), THE
ROUTLEDGE HANDBOOK OF INTERNATIONAL LAW AND ANTHROPOCENTRISM
(2023) 35**

Introduction

… By anthropocentric I mean a philosophy of centring the human, based on the idea that humans have primary moral standing and are the only measure of justice. That human rights are anthropocentric may strike one as precisely the point. After all, human rights are the rights of humans and, therefore, how could they be anything other than anthropocentric?

…

… I make the case that the human rights project is, in fact, more deeply, centrally, and problematically anthropocentric than the focus on intra-human justice suggests; that it is, in fact, only exclusively focused on intra-human justice because it has fundamentally bracketed and excluded questions of relations to other animal species and, more broadly, to the environment. I suggest that, by contrast, much can be gained from a reading of human rights as not so much a political arrangement inter se (as suggested, for example, by the anthropocentric focus of the language of social contract) but at least in part as much as a political arrangement from which nature, including non-human animals, is specifically and deliberately – if implicitly and covertly – excluded.

... I will argue that there could not be a 'human' in international human rights law without the human encounter with its radical (animal, natural) other.

...

The key question ... is not so much whether non-human animals or nature should have rights, but what it might mean for the human rights project itself if they were to have such rights. In turn, that debate hinges on the degree to which protections of non- human animals or nature should be anthropocentric or ecocentric. Closely related is the notion of whether the foundation for rights protection is deontological or utilitarian and, ultimately, what the basis for humans having rights is in the first place. ...

...

Defining the Human Rights Project in Opposition to Nature

...

First, the human rights project is premised on a fundamental intuition about the distinction of the human subject from nature and not simply, as is conventionally understood, about the equality of humans between themselves. ... [T]he modern discourse of human rights was in fact preceded by eighteenth-century efforts to distinguish humanity from both God and animals ... . The claim that only humans have rights is, in turn, tied to ideas about the distinctiveness and, indeed, the superiority of human animals. ...

Second, the human rights project, having proclaimed the fundamental distinguishability of humans from nature doubles down on that intuition by defining freedom as the fundamental right in a liberal order. Freedom involves the right to pursue one's uniquely human goals, to self- determine unhindered. ...

Lurking within that familiar political definition of freedom, however, is an underlying claim that does not even need to be mentioned, namely that there are no worthwhile non-human limitations to freedom – that humans, in short, should have complete freedom from nature itself. Human freedom is the freedom to continuously emancipate oneself from nature and, in the process, further cement one's humanity as fundamentally distinct from nature. ...

Third and logically, claims about human rights quickly lead to claims of dominion over nature as the natural consequence of freedom from nature. Nature does not have dominion over itself. ...

A fortiori, this means that humans can engage in killing non-human animals. Just as the end of society is self-preservation, killing 'wild savage beasts' such as lions and tigers amidst which 'men can have no society nor security' (Locke) is fundamental to human freedom. More fundamentally, this means that humanity can 'remake the world' in its image ... .

...

A Crisis of Humanism?

... [T]he model on which ideas of human rights and the legal institutional machinery of international human rights law are premised has been subjected to a triple crisis of Western modernity. ...

First, a relative normalisation of 'humanity'. If the shiny specificity of human rights was based on ideas about the incommensurability of the human to other living and inanimate categories and a sense of 'human exceptionalism', that myth has been deeply challenged. ...

...

The second crisis involves a major rediscovery in the West of the vulnerability of humans to nature, following centuries of an inflated notion of human dominion over it. Amidst increasing panic about global ecological catastrophe, resource depletion, and even the possibility of human extinction, an overarching sense of doom is projected. ...

...

Third, a late modern disenchantment with humanity. The Holocaust proved beyond doubt humans' cruelty to humans, but also that cruelty's specific enabling at the heart of modernity. In a sense, moreover, that failed promise of modernity had already long been the ordinary experience of victims of slavery or colonisation. ... [C]limate change and the emergence of the Anthropocene, by suggesting both the finitude of planetary resources and the ultimately self-destructive nature of human freedom alongside capitalism's deep complicity in racism, may precipitate an even deeper crisis of Western modernity. Where the Holocaust could be dismissed as a perversion of modernity, the colossal harm wreaked by the pursuit of material accumulation arises in a context where modernity is working exactly as it was supposed to.

…

The Problem of Integration with the Human Rights Project

…

The dominant thinking within the human rights community seems to be one of benevolent indifference or agnosticism about the rights of non-humans, without a sense of the intellectual crisis that such extension should evoke or thinking about what an overall post- humanist rights project might mean for the classical human rights project. At worst, the siloed conception to rights may lead to a kind of separatism wherein the internal integrity of the human rights project is not challenged but merely leads to a deferral of much-needed critical synthesis. What is currently lacking are theories that would integrate both human rights, animal rights, and nature rights. It seems as if the latter two have been deployed as counter- fires to the first but with little recognition of how they might have to cede to or override each other, leaving the impression of a disjointed patchwork that skirts some of the difficult questions.

One can wonder, in particular, whether proclamations of rights of non-humans alone can offset the hegemonic propensities of an anthropocentric conception of human rights. Although the image of a triangle between human animal, non-human animal, and nature might give the impression that the three are equal poles, in truth by far the more ambitious pole if one is willing to let go of the tyranny of the anthropocentric mindset is the biocentric one (focusing on nature), in that it stands to encompass others into a theory of all beings. Non-human animal rights, particularly those traditions focusing on mammals and sentient animals, are extremely wedded to a certain view of their proximity to human-ness. Only rights of nature potentially offer a radical and holistic decentring from not just the human subject, but any sense that the particular qualities of humans (distributed and found in other near-species as they may be) ought to be the sole measure of rights.

…

Conclusion

…

In practise, some kind of reconciliation of bio-centric and anthropo-centric theories of rights is unavoidable, perhaps one that emphasises their eco-centric commonalities from some kind of meta-normative standpoint. Whatever non-anthropocentric line of argument may be available to challenge environmental disruptions, there will often be an anthropocentric one as well. …

The possibility remains, it is true, that some harms are either not captured by human rights violations or at such a level of generality (e.g., global warming) as to create insolvable problems of juridical standing and of collective action. Deep ecological philosophies of rights at least caution against the temptation of technological quick fixes (e.g., geoengineering) for the exclusive benefit of humans and more generally about the continuing value of that which is beyond humans. …

Still, that environmental degradation and animal cruelty are simply another facet of 'man's inhumanity to man' is hard to resist as a conclusion. It calls into question the very 'colonial matrix' of modernity as it has expressed both in relation to nature and the dispossessed. It sug- gests that the search for environmental harmony may paradoxically be a much more agonistic process than bland UN appeals to the compatibility of human rights and the environment suggest ('we are all in this together'), one deeply implicated in class, gender, race, and colonial struggles. And it suggests a re-energising of the human rights project in conditions of global environmental degradation … .

Finally, although much of the emphasis on nature and non-human animals is on how the human is called upon to continuously reframe the rights of both, it is important to note the extent to which both then retroact on the very intellectual project of humanity … ….

…

… [N]on-anthropocentric conceptions of human rights might reinstate a sense that Humanity rather than the traditional individual human subjects of rights is the appropriate framework for conceptualising inter-realm relations – indeed, that the focus on individuals is what has led human rights into some of the dead ends from which global environmental degradation is born. Instead of a self-knowing, self-referring, and self-empowering

Humanity, the move to nature and to a lesser extent non-human animal rights prompts a renewed framing of the human species' destiny and, in fact, an embrace of human diversity as it expresses itself in a pluralist patchwork of conceptions of nature and legacies of differentiated responsibilities towards it.

Whereas modernity, imperfectly universalised among others through the international law of human rights, emphasised an untrammelled right to frame nature in one's image, the Anthropocene may yet highlight conditions in which a wounded humanity's role is framed not so much by itself than by the obligations imposed upon it by its immersion into forms of existence beyond it and how those stand to be affected by continuing inequities between humans. ...

The proclamation of non-human rights might thus help spell out anew the specificity of the human rights project. Indeed, projects of non-human rights do not give up on a sense of human specificity; they arguably merely reframe it, except as a specificity that does not cut humans from the world through a relationship of dominion as much as one that reinscribes nature within the human and the human within nature. In that respect, not so much ecocentrism itself, but the ecocentric critique of rights and, as the case may be, the rights' reception of that critique could be in the best tradition of critiques of rights that have, since at least Marx and extending to contemporary feminist and communitarian thinkers, underscored the poverty of liberal conceptions of rights framed around the atomistic and desocialised nature of the human.

LORENZO COTULA, BETWEEN HOPE AND CRITIQUE: HUMAN RIGHTS, SOCIAL JUSTICE AND RE-IMAGINING INTERNATIONAL LAW FROM THE BOTTOM UP
48 GA. J. INT'L & COMP. L. (2020) 473

This Article reflects on the place of human rights, particularly international human rights law, in strategies to advance social justice. It argues that, while some critique takes aim at an encompassing human rights "project," the contested nature of human rights calls for more granular analyses that consider the diverse constellations of actors, agendas, arenas, and approaches connecting human rights to social justice. And while much public debate has focused on institutionalized human rights actors and frameworks, the article identifies human rights' primary emancipatory promise in the agency of the social actors— indigenous peoples, agrarian movements, trade unions, non-governmental organizations (NGOs), grassroots groups—that have appropriated and in some cases reconfigured human rights from the bottom up.

Examples include international litigation to validate new interpretations of long-recognized rights; public campaigning for new international instruments to shift the contours of human rights; and invoking internationally recognized rights to change public discourses in local to global policy arenas. This recentring of the discussion around how social actors mobilize internationally recognized human rights is part of a wider shift in the way international law is conceived of, not just as a practice located in the global centers of international diplomacy, but as a phenomenon that is both experienced and to some extent shaped at the grassroots as well.
...

... [The article examines] two case studies of "reactive" and "constitutive" forms of rights-claiming to distil qualitative insights on the place of human rights in social justice strategies. ...

The first case study ... concerns the "reactive" use of human rights in indigenous peoples' struggles to challenge the award of commercial natural resource concessions in their ancestral territories. This case study relies particularly heavily on human rights litigation and jurisprudential developments that occurred within the regional human rights systems of Africa and the Americas. The second case study considers the use of human rights in "constitutive" strategies to transform the economic paradigm that underpins the global food system. This part focuses on the longstanding and ultimately successful advocacy of international agrarian movements for the adoption, by the United Nations General Assembly, of the United Nations Declaration on the Rights of Peasants and Other People Working in Rural Areas [General Assembly Res. 73/165 (2018)].
...

V. Discussion

A. Human Rights: Intellectual Histories, Legal Configurations, and Social Practices

... Both [case studies] reflect significant "wins," whether in the form of public interest litigation or international (soft) law making. Yet both also beg difficult questions about the real scale of the advances made, and whether these advances can ultimately transform socioeconomic relations.

The issue is not just that it is difficult for social actors to secure international judgments or declarations, or to properly enforce or implement them once they have been obtained, particularly in the face of powerful vested interests. The more probing question is whether even a properly implemented ruling or instrument would meaningfully reshape socio-economic ordering. Taken alone, a few judgments do not reverse the long history of mass dispossession affecting indigenous lands, and an international soft-law instrument does not alter entrenched patterns of land ownership, the international protection of intellectual property rights affecting the governance of seed systems, or the structure of agricultural value chains. By resorting to the instruments of positive law, social actors must translate their demands into conceptual categories— such as the right to property—that are associated with dominant economic and political organization.

In harnessing such hegemonic concepts in counter-hegemonic terms, and in locating social justice advocacy within institutionalized human rights processes, strategies to "juridify" inherently political disputes must operate "within the system." They may entail advocated-for and even actually observed reforms, as illustrated by the jurisprudential reconfiguration of the right to property in the light of legal categories that resonate with indigenous conceptions. But they do not necessarily challenge the foundational parameters of the system. Indeed, the mobilizing and even the reconfiguring ultimately rest on the acceptance of the very state-centric international system of control over natural resources and development pathways that is instrumental to advancing commercial modes of production and to the dispossession of peasants and indigenous peoples in many parts of the world. While the two case studies illustrate bottom-up agency by indigenous and agrarian movements, states played important roles in both, whether as bearers of human rights obligations and respondents in human rights litigation, or as negotiators and adopters of international soft law.
...
... [T]he use of internationally recognized human rights in discursive strategies and social processes can transcend the juristic limitations of the legal concepts at play. ...

[W]here activists appropriate human rights to catalyse public mobilization, the scope of the resulting action is not necessarily restricted to the perimeter delineated by jurisprudential interpretations of international human rights law. The experience of the Sawhoyamaxa community occupying its traditional lands now under commercial operations exemplifies how social actors can shift registers—moving from legal proceedings to direct action—in different times and places, while also using the human rights register to legitimize land occupations that would otherwise contravene positive law.

In these regards, any assessments of the emancipatory potential of human rights in social justice struggles cannot be limited to a discussion of the ways in which those rights have been construed by drafters, tribunals and jurists, or of the intellectual origins and cultural matrices that have affected the historical development of human rights law. While legal experts will be primarily concerned with the techniques of legal drafting and interpretation, emancipatory potential is a function of a wider range of socio-political as well as juridical variables.

Therefore, those assessments would also need to consider how human rights are appropriated in socio-political arenas, where discursive practices may create ruptures with established ideational matrices and departures from the traditional canons of juristic interpretation. Considering these practices would require broadening the methods of inquiry to pursue a more grounded understanding of rights in their social context. To different extents and in different ways, both the indigenous rights jurisprudence and the United Nations Declaration on the Rights of Peasants indicate that this "activist" use of human rights can ultimately sustain evolutions in normative configurations, via jurisprudential interpretations and international (soft) law making, thereby intersecting with, and cross-fertilizing, the traditional purview of doctrinal analyses.

In these respects, the two case studies call for expanding the horizons of current debates about the relation between human rights and social justice. While public debates have often focused on the work of mainstream human rights organizations based in the global North, both examples highlight the prominent role that social movements that are at least partly located in the global South—including actors that do not primarily identify themselves as human rights organizations—have played in developing distinctive modes to invoke and reshape human rights in pursuit of social justice.

B. From Human Rights Frameworks to Rights-Claiming as a Practice of Contestation

...

This harnessing of human rights by indigenous and agrarian movements illustrates the need to re-center the debates about the emancipatory potential of human rights from institutionalized human rights actors and frameworks to rights-claiming as a practice of contestation. In this perspective, invoking human rights may constitute a channel for social actors to articulate a rupture with aspects of socio-political ordering, as much as a juridical avenue for producing legally enforceable outcomes to change a given material situation. Human rights are therefore viewed as both vehicles and outcomes of political struggle, and their development is, at least in part, the story of how social actors—including groups that do not primarily define their institutional mandates in human rights terms—have appropriated rights language and instruments to advance their agendas.

This perspective outlines a different set of dimensions in the practice of human rights, one where legal forms are embedded in social processes and where human rights are advanced, at least in part, through the vision, resolve and action of social groups. In addition, the import and effectiveness of rights-claiming are to be assessed not only in terms of judicial, legislative, or even material outcomes, but also in relation to the ways in which advocacy can use human rights to legitimize counter-hegemonic worldviews and catalyse collective action.

These considerations apply in different ways to reactive and constitutive strategies, and failure to disaggregate the discussion can lead to analytical confusion. In reactive modes, the main concern may be about addressing a specific situation or pattern of human rights abuse. In many situations, this reactive rights-claiming will reflect a principled position that fundamentally espouses the framing of the human rights being invoked. But recourse to human rights in reactive mode can also be instrumental and even opportunistic. ...

...

In constitutive modes, on the other hand, recourse to human rights may have more foundational and normative connotations, there may be more space for more explicit ruptures with prevailing juridical arrangements. This does not necessarily mean that the substantive social justice demands are themselves qualitatively more radical than in reactive modes, and if the advocacy translates into formalised inter-governmental processes it may have to come to terms with the compromises that tend to characterise international negotiations and law making. But when articulating social justice demands in constitutive human rights modes, advocates are less constrained by established human rights forms, and they may enjoy greater latitude in aligning human rights concepts with their own social justice goals.

C. Rights-Claiming in Contested Socio-Political Terrains

...

Critique is the engine of change, so it is essential that social justice (and human rights) thinkers and practitioners continuously interrogate their assumptions and approaches and, where necessary, reorient them accordingly. Critiques of rights both old and new have exposed human rights' limitations— whether structural or contingent—in promoting more just socio-economic relations. They have established a challenge for advocates to develop ever more ambitious and effective human rights practices, and to explore alternative or complementary strategies to comprehensively address social justice challenges. At the same time, there is a need to broaden current debates to more plural perspectives that recognize the diversity of human rights actors, agendas, arenas and approaches, and to open spaces for more fully engaging with the practices of actors located outside the human rights mainstream. By seeking to understand how diverse social actors have appropriated and reimagined human rights from the bottom up, it might become possible to ask different questions about whether and how human rights can sustain emancipatory action.

NOTE

A number of different understandings about rights — their derivation, nature, content and consequences — appear in the readings above. Consider the following binaries, with the characterizations on the left reflecting natural rights-type approaches, and those on the right more flexible, policy-oriented approaches:

inalienable	socially constructed
absolute	qualified, contingent, context dependent
universal	particular, culturally specific
eternal, ahistorical	historicist, evolving, open to change
based on human dignity	based on utility, power

QUESTIONS

1. With respect to David Kennedy's arguments, consider:

(a) What illustrations could you offer of situations where reliance on rights rhetoric to advance popular claims crowded out other 'emancipatory vocabularies' and strategies — for example, mass political action — that could possibly or even likely have achieved more? Consider, for example, earlier materials examining the struggles for 'women's rights', the arguments against torture, and arguments in favour of economic/social rights like health care or housing. Is mass political action — electoral campaigns, marches by protestors to a capital city, boycotts — necessarily independent of rights rhetoric embedded in such action?

(b) Suppose that a human rights advocate argued to a minister of education in a developing country that giving schoolgirls equal educational opportunities would improve talent, energy, productivity and the level of economic well-being within the family and the country — that is, benefits will far exceed costs. Is the 'hegemony' of rights rhetoric apt to block such argument? Could both modes of argument be used together? What of using simultaneously several different modes of argument — utilitarian, fairness-based, rights-based — with respect to environmental degradation?

(c) Do this book's earlier materials support the author's argument that human rights directs so much attention to the public sector (that is, the state as the only identified violator of human rights in the conventions and in human rights discourse) that many violations occurring in the non-state sector (employment discrimination, family violence) are apt to remain hidden and untouched?

(d) The author several times characterizes human rights as claims and arguments based on reason, whereas other emancipatory languages and strategies rely on faith and passion. Do you agree with this distinction, which tends to characterize 'rights' as cerebral and abstract, while other languages/strategies are more basic, emotional, appealing, stimulating to people?

B. DUTY-BASED SOCIAL ORDERS

1. Duties

The following readings describe and analyse duty-oriented, rather than rights-oriented, social ordering through law and cultural tradition. Robert Cover comments on the legal culture of Judaism, which stresses obligations imposed by God rather than rights. He suggests historical reasons why Western states and Judaism developed in these different ways. Jomo Kenyatta describes aspects of the education of the young in the Gikuyu people in Kenya, particularly the inculcation of elements of social obligations and duty. Finally, Christopher Roberts recounts Mahatma Gandhi's emphasis on duties rather than rights. Although the cultural and religious contexts and the content of the duties referred to are radically different in these readings, they suggest important consequences of an orientation towards duty/obligation and the gap between such an orientation and the liberal political culture that influenced the human rights regime.

Note that the duties/obligations referred to in these readings are *not* the same as duties within a *scheme of rights* that correlate to the described rights. For example, the individual's basic right to be free from torture imposes a correlative (corresponding) duty on the state not to torture. The following readings talk of duties imposed on *individuals* rather than on the state or some other collective entity. That is, they are not correlative duties to others' rights, but imposed on the individual from the outset. Article 29(1) of the UDHR offers an analogy to such use of duties, as does the preamble to the ICCPR. But explicit language of individual duty to other individuals (other than the implied, traditional correlative duties), to society, or to the state in the universal human rights system is rare. A closer analogy to the present readings, particularly the excerpts from Kenyatta, is provided by the African Charter on Human and Peoples' Rights, examined at Sec. B3, below.

ROBERT COVER, OBLIGATION: A JEWISH JURISPRUDENCE OF THE SOCIAL ORDER 5 J. OF L. AND RELIG. (1987) 65

I. Fundamental Words

Every legal culture has its fundamental words. When we define our subject this weekend as human rights, we also locate ourselves in a normative universe at a particular place. The word 'rights' is a highly evocative one for those of us who have grown up in the post-enlightenment secular society of the West. ...

Judaism is, itself, a legal culture of great antiquity. It has hardly led a wholly autonomous existence these past three millennia. Yet, I suppose it can lay as much claim as any of the other great legal cultures to have an integrity to its basic categories. When I am asked to reflect upon Judaism and human rights, therefore, the first thought that comes to mind is that the categories are wrong. I do not mean, of course, that basic ideas of human dignity and worth are not powerfully expressed in the Jewish legal and literary traditions. Rather, I mean that because it is a legal tradition Judaism has its own categories for expressing through law the worth and dignity of each human being. And the categories are not closely analogous to 'human rights'. The principal word in Jewish law, which occupies a place equivalent in evocative forcsectioe to the American legal system's 'rights', is the word 'mitzvah' which literally means commandment but has a general meaning closer to 'incumbent obligation'.

Before I begin an analysis of the differing implications of these two rather different key words, I should like to put the two words in a context — the contexts of their respective myths. For both of us these words are connected to fundamental stories and receive their force from those stories as much as from the denotative meaning of the words themselves. The story behind the term 'rights' is the story of social contract. The myth postulates free and independent if highly vulnerable beings who voluntarily trade a portion of their autonomy for a measure of collective security. The myth makes the collective arrangement the product of individual choice and thus secondary to the individual. 'Rights' are the fundamental category because it is the normative category which most nearly approximates that which is the source of the legitimacy of everything else. Rights are traded for collective security. But some rights are retained and, in some theories, some rights are inalienable. In any event the first and fundamental unit is the individual and 'rights' locate him as an individual separate and apart from every other individual.

I must stress that I do not mean to suggest that all or even most theories that are founded upon rights are 'individualistic' or 'atomistic'. Nor would I suggest for a moment that with a starting point of 'rights' and social contract one must get to a certain end. Hobbes as well as Locke is part of this tradition. And, of course, so is Rousseau. Collective solutions as well as individualistic ones are possible but, it is the case that even the collective solutions are solutions which arrive at their destination by way of a theory which derives the authority of the collective from the individual. ...

The basic word of Judaism is obligation or mitzvah. It, too, is intrinsically bound up in a myth — the myth of Sinai. Just as the myth of social contract is essentially a myth of autonomy, so the myth of Sinai is essentially a myth of heteronomy. Sinai is a collective — indeed, a corporate — experience. The experience at Sinai is not chosen. The event gives forth the words which are commandments. In all Rabbinic and post Rabbinic embellishment upon the Biblical account of Sinai this event is the Code for all Law. All law was given at Sinai and therefore all law is related back to the ultimate heteronomous event in which we were chosen-passive voice. ...

What have these stories to do with the ways in which the law languages of these respective legal cultures are spoken? Social movements in the United States organize around rights. When there is some urgently felt need to change the law or keep it in one way or another a 'Rights' movement is started. Civil rights, the right to life, welfare rights, etc. The premium that is to be put upon an entitlement is so coded. When we 'take rights seriously' we understand them to be trumps in the legal game. In Jewish law, an entitlement without an obligation is a sad, almost pathetic thing. ...

Indeed, to be one who acts out of obligation is the closest thing there is to a Jewish definition of completion as a person within the community. A child does not become emancipated or 'free' when he or she reaches maturity. Nor does she/he become sui juris. No, the child becomes bar or bat mitzvah, literally one who is of the obligations. Traditionally, the parent at that time says a blessing. Blessed is He that has exonerated me from the punishment of this child. The primary legal distinction between Jew and non-Jew is that the non-Jew is only obligated to the 7 Noachide commandments ... .

The Uses of Rights and Obligations

The Jewish legal system has evolved for the past 1900 years without a state and largely without much in the way of coercive powers to be exercised upon the adherents of the faith. I do not mean to idealize the situation. The Jewish communities over the millennia have wielded power. Communal sanctions of banning and shunning have been regularly and occasionally cruelly imposed on individuals or groups. Less frequently, but frequently enough, Jewish communities granted quasi-autonomy by gentile rulers, have used the power of the gentile state to discipline dissidents and deviants. Nonetheless, there remains a difference between wielding a power which draws on but also depends on pre-existing social solidarity, and, wielding one which depends on violence. ...

In a situation in which there is no centralized power and little in the way of coercive violence, it is critical that the mythic center of the Law reinforce the bonds of solidarity. Common, mutual, reciprocal obligation is necessary. The myth of divine commandment creates that web. ... It was a myth that created legitimacy for a radically diffuse and coordinate system of authority. But while it created room for the diffusion of authority it did not have a place for individualism. One might have independent and divergent understandings of the obligations imposed by God through his chosen people, but one could not have a world view which denied the obligations.

The jurisprudence of rights, on the other hand, has gained ascendance in the Western world together with the rise of the national state with its almost unique mastery of violence over extensive territories. Certainly, it may be argued, it has been essential to counterbalance the development of the state with a myth which a) establishes the State as legitimate only in so far as it can be derived from the autonomous creatures who trade in their rights for security — i.e., one must tell a story about the State's utility or service to us, and b) potentially justifies individual and communal resistance to the Behemoth. It may be true as Bentham so aptly pointed out that natural rights may be used either apologetically or in revolutionary fashion, and there is nothing in the concept powerful enough analytically to constrain which use it shall be put to. Nevertheless, it is the case that natural right apologies are of a sort that in their articulation they limit the most far-reaching claims of the State, and the revolutionary ideology that can be generated is also of a sort which is particularly effective in countering organic statist claims.

Thus, there is a sense in which the ideology of rights has been a useful counter to the centrifugal forces of the western nation state while the ideology of mitzvoth or obligation has been equally useful as a counter to the centripetal forces that have beset Judaism over the centuries.

...

... [T]he Maimonides system contrasts the normative world of mitzvoth with the world of vanity — hebel. It seems that Maimonides, in this respect, as in so many others has hit the mark. A world centered upon obligation is not, really cannot be, an empty or vain world. Rights, as an organizing principle, are indifferent to the vanity of varying ends. But mitzvoths because they so strongly bind and locate the individual must make a strong claim for the substantive content of that which they dictate. The system, if its content be vain, can hardly claim to be a system. The rights system is indifferent to ends and in its indifference can claim systemic coherence without making any strong claims about the fullness or vanity of the ends it permits.

...

JOMO KENYATTA, FACING MOUNT KENYA: THE TRIBAL LIFE OF THE GIKUYU (1965) 109

[These excerpts are taken from a description by Kenyatta, who later became the first post-colonial president of Kenya, of the Gikuyu people (often rendered from Swahili into English as 'Kikuyu') in that country.]

[The children] are also taught definitely at circumcision the theory, as it were, of respect to their parents and kinsfolk. Under all circumstances they must stay with them and share in their joys and sorrows. It will never do to leave them and go off to see the world whenever they take the notion, especially when their parents are in their old age. They must give them clothes, look after their garden, herd their cattle, sheep and goats, build their grain stores and houses. It thus becomes a part of their outlook on life that their parents shall not suffer want nor continue to labour strenuously in their old age while their children can lend a hand and do things to give them comfort.

...

The teaching of social obligations is again emphasised by the classification of age-groups to which we have already referred. This binds together those of the same status in ties of closest loyalty and devotion. Men circumcised at the same time stand in the very closest relationship to each other. When a man of the same age-group injures another it is a serious magico-religious offence. They are like blood brothers; they must not do any wrong to each other. It ranks with an injury done to a member of one's own family. The age-group (riika) is thus a powerful instrument for securing conformity with tribal usage. The selfish or reckless youth is taught by the opinion of his gang that it does not pay to incur displeasure. He will not be called to eat with the others when food is going. He may be put out of their dances, fined, or even ostracised for a time. If he does not change his ways he will find his old companions have deserted him.

...

Owing to the strength and numbers of the social ties existing between members of the same family, clan and age-group, and between different families and clans through which the tribe is unified and solidified as one organic whole, the community can be mobilised very easily for corporate activity. House-building, cultivation, harvesting, digging trap-pits, putting up fences around cultivated fields, and building bridges, are usually done by the group; hence the Gikuyu saying: 'Kamoinge koyaga ndere', which means collective activities make heavy tasks easier. ...

...

The selfish or self-regarding man has no name or reputation in the Gikuyu community. An individualist is looked upon with suspicion and is given a nickname of mwebongia, one who works only for himself and is likely to end up as a wizard. He may lack assistance when he needs it. ...

In the Gikuyu community there is no really individual affair, for everything has a moral and social reference. The habit of corporate effort is but the other side of corporate ownership; and corporate responsibility is illustrated in corporate work no less than in corporate sacrifice and prayer.

...

CHRISTOPHER N.J. ROBERTS, THE CONTENTIOUS HISTORY OF THE INTERNATIONAL BILL OF HUMAN RIGHTS
(2014) 140

...

... Nearly forty years before the UDHR was adopted, [Mahatma Gandhi] wrote that under British law, those living in dependencies "have never got and never can get their rights until they have performed their corresponding duties." For Gandhi, the path to rights – that is, rights to be invoked and relied on with full certainty – was through one's duties. He applied this philosophical and practical orientation to all types of political and social dilemmas. For example, when he spoke in 1921 to a gathering of laborers on strike in the Indian city of Madras about the rights they had to living wages, to education, and to the "same fresh water and fresh air as [their] employers," he also went to lengths to admonish the workers that they had corresponding duties and obligations that must be performed to effect such rights. What was essential in obtaining one's rights was, for Gandhi, to become an integral part of a broader system of human relationships. It was only through a relationship of mutual dependence that an individual could demand the rights that corresponded to the nature and strength of the relationship already formed. When in 1940 he wrote to H. G. Wells about his new book on the rights of man, Gandhi suggested that Wells would be better off thinking less about rights. "Begin with a charter of Duties of Man . . . and I promise the rights will follow as spring follows winter." And by 1946 he had virtually abandoned the quest for rights. ...

So in 1947 when the seventy-seven-year-old leader of the independence movement was asked to present his views on human rights for the UNESCO compendium, his response would have come as no surprise to any of his devotees. Gandhi's contribution was inseparable from his larger struggle against the institutions and practices of colonialism. ... While other contributors provided detailed and lengthy philosophical tomes, Gandhi's three-paragraph contribution captured in a few, short sentences the powers and illusions of human rights.

> I learnt from my illiterate but wise mother that all rights to be deserved and preserved came from duty well done. Thus the very right to live accrues to us only when we do the duty of citizenship of the world. From this one fundamental statement it is easy enough to define the duties of Man and Woman and correlate every right to some corresponding duty to be first performed. Every other right can be shown to be a usurpation hardly worth fighting for.

QUESTIONS

1. 'A duty-based social order seems inherently less subject to universalization (with respect to the duties imposed on individuals) than a rights-based social order (with respect to the rights attributed to individuals). That is, the content of duties (obligations toward elders, toward the community, toward God) seems to be very particular and bound to a given context, a product of a given religion or political or social culture or history, whereas individuals' rights seem to be more divorced from a particular context and can therefore be stated more abstractly.' Do you agree? Can you suggest any examples?

2. '"Individual rights" necessarily imply equality among all rights holders, which is to say among all members of society. This in fact is what the contemporary human rights instruments declare. To the contrary, duties can be (and frequently are) defined so as to impose hierarchy, status, and discrimination in a given social order.' Do you agree? Can you suggest examples?

3. 'Different from a regime of rights, a regime of duties intrinsically exerts an inward, centripetal force. It draws individual duty-bearers into the society, connects them intricately with other individuals and the community in a variety of ways, blurs the separate identity of the individual from society, and leads to a more communal and collective structure of life.' Do you agree?

4. Note that Article 2(3) of the ICCPR requires states to provide all persons whose rights have been violated with 'an effective remedy', and to develop particularly the possibilities of 'judicial remedy'. Do

rights imply a preference for or even require individual (judicial or other) remedies against the state, whereas a regime of individual duties is less likely to provide such remedies?

2. Duty Provisions of National Constitutions

In modern constitutions, as in human rights treaties, provisions conferring rights on individuals far outnumber those imposing duties. Nevertheless, many state constitutions in force in 2024 contain provisions expressing duties. Consider the following examples:

CHINA

Article 42: Citizens … have the right as well as the duty to work.

Work is a matter of honour for every citizen who is able to work. …The State encourages citizens to take part in voluntary labour. …

…

Article 46: Citizens … have the duty as well as the right to receive education.

…

Article 49: … Both husband and wife have the duty to practise family planning. …

Parents have the duty to rear and educate their children who are minors, and children who have come of age have the duty to support and assist their parents.

…

Article 52: It is the duty of citizens of the People's Republic of China to safeguard the unification of the country and the unity of all its nationalities.

ECUADOR

Article 69: To protect the rights of persons who are members of a family: …

> 5. The State shall promote the joint responsibility of both mother and father and shall monitor fulfillment of the mutual duties and rights between mothers, fathers, and children.

Article 83: Ecuadorians have the following duties and obligations …: …

> 2. To not be lazy, not lie, not steal. …

> 5. To respect human rights and to fight for their enforcement.

> 6. To respect the rights of nature, preserve a healthy environment and use natural resources rationally, sustainably and durably.

> 7. To promote public welfare and give precedence to general interests over individual interests, in line with the good way of living. …

> 14. To respect and recognize ethnic, national, social, generational, and gender differences and sexual orientation and identity. …

> 16. To help, feed, educate and raise one's children. …

UGANDA

Objective XXIX: Duties of a citizen.

The exercise and enjoyment of rights and freedoms is inseparable from the performance of duties and obligations; and, accordingly, it shall be the duty of every citizen—

    (a) to be patriotic and loyal to Uganda and to promote its well-being;

    (b) to engage in gainful work for the good of that citizen, the family and the common good and to contribute to national development;

    (c) to contribute to the well-being of the community where that citizen lives;

    (d) to promote responsible parenthood;

    (e) to foster national unity and live in harmony with others;

    (f) to promote democracy and the rule of law; …

QUESTIONS

1. Are any of the preceding provisions inconsistent with international human rights law?

2. Would you support the inclusion in your own country's constitution of duties relating to work, environment, care of children and parents, and voting?

---

3. Rights and Duties in the African Charter

The African Charter on Human and Peoples' Rights was adopted in 1981, entered into force in 1986, and as of 2024 had been ratified by 54 of the African Union's 55 member states. The application of the Charter is examined in Chapter 11C below. The focus here is on those of its provisions that distinguish it from other international human rights treaties, especially its emphasis on African values and duties. It is also distinctive in recognizing a range of collective or peoples' rights, such as peoples' rights to 'economic, social and cultural development', 'to national and international peace and security', and 'to a generally satisfactory environment favourable to their development' (Articles 22-24).

In terms of African values, consider first the following provisions in the Preamble to the Charter:

The African States … parties to the present convention …,

…

Reaffirming the pledge they solemnly made in Article 2 of the [Charter of the Organization of African Unity] to eradicate all forms of colonialism from Africa …;

Taking into consideration the virtues of their historical tradition and the values of African civilization which should inspire and characterize their reflection on the concept of human and peoples' rights;

…

> Considering that the enjoyment of rights and freedoms also implies the performance of duties on the part of everyone;
>
> ...
>
> Conscious of their duty to achieve the total liberation of Africa, the peoples of which are still struggling for their dignity and genuine independence, and undertaking to eliminate colonialism, neo-colonialism, apartheid, zionism and to dismantle aggressive foreign military bases and all forms of discrimination ...;
>
> Reaffirming their adherence to the principles of human and peoples' rights and freedoms contained in the declarations, conventions and other instrument adopted by the Organization of African Unity, the Movement of Non-Aligned Countries and the United Nations;
>
> Firmly convinced of their duty to promote and protect human and people' rights and freedoms taking into account the importance traditionally attached to these rights and freedoms in Africa;
>
> ...

Chapter I of Part I of the Charter lists the specific 'human and peoples' rights'. While many of the rights address the same themes as in the ICCPR, there are important language differences which can be seen by comparing, for example, Article 7 of the Charter on criminal procedure with Articles 14 and 15 of the ICCPR, or Article 13 of the Charter on political participation with Article 25 of the ICCPR. Similarly, permissible limitations are stated differently. Thus, Article 6 assures the right to liberty 'except for reasons and conditions previously laid down by law'; Article 8 subjects freedom of conscience and religion 'to law and order'; and Article 10 recognizes the right to free association 'provided that [the individual] abides by the law'. Article 14 protects the right to property, but provides for 'encroachments' that differ from standard approaches.

Some provisions explicitly recall Africa's experience with the slave trade and colonization. Thus, Article 20 states that:

> ...
>
> 2. Colonized or oppressed peoples shall have the right to free themselves from the bonds of domination by resorting to any means recognized by the international community.
>
> 3. All peoples shall have the right to the assistance of the States parties to the present Charter in their liberation struggle against foreign domination, be it political, economic or cultural.

Article 12(5) responds to the expulsion of tens of thousands of Ugandan citizens of Asian descent by President Idi Amin in 1972. It prohibits the 'mass expulsion of non-nationals', defined as measures 'aimed at national, racial, ethnic or religious groups'. The Charter has no provision for derogation of rights in situations of national emergency equivalent to Article 4 of the ICCPR.

The Charter includes an abbreviated list of economic and social rights in Articles 15-17. Unlike the ICESCR, no qualification is included in relation to progressive realization or available resources. But, for present purposes, our focus is on Chapter II of Part I which deals with 'individual duties'.

References to 'duties' are not alien to human rights instruments. Consider Article 29 of the UDHR, the preambles to the UN Charter and the two Covenants, and the American Declaration of the Rights and Duties of Man. Nonetheless, the African Charter is the first human rights treaty, as opposed to a declaration, to include an enumeration of or to give forceful attention to individuals' duties. In this respect, it goes well beyond the conventional notion that duties may be correlative to rights, such as the obvious duties of states that are correlative (corresponding) to individual rights — for example, states' duties not to torture or to provide a structure for voting in political elections. The Charter also goes beyond correlative duties of individuals that many human rights instruments explicitly or implicitly impose — for example, an individual's right to bodily security imposes a duty on other individuals not to invade that right. The Charter differs by defining duties that are not simply the 'other side' of individual rights, and that run from individuals to the state as well as to other groups and individuals. Hence the Charter directly raises the issues of universalism and cultural relativism that are addressed in Chapter 7.

Article 27

1. Every individual shall have duties towards his family and society, the State and other legally recognised communities and the international community.

2. The rights and freedoms of each individual shall be exercised with due regard to the rights of others, collective security, morality and common interest.

Article 28

Every individual shall have the duty to respect and consider his fellow beings without discrimination, and to maintain relations aimed at promoting, safeguarding and reinforcing mutual respect and tolerance.

Article 29

The individual shall also have the duty:

1. To preserve the harmonious development of the family and to work for the cohesion and respect of the family; to respect his parents at all times, to maintain them in case of need.

2. To serve his national community by placing his physical and intellectual abilities at its service.

3. Not to compromise the security of the State whose national or resident he is.

4. To preserve and strengthen social and national solidarity, particularly when the latter is strengthened.

5. To preserve and strengthen the national independence and the territorial integrity of his country and to contribute to his defence in accordance with the law.

6. To work to the best of his abilities and competence, and to pay taxes imposed by law in the interest of the society.

7. To preserve and strengthen positive African cultural values in his relations with other members of the society, in the spirit of tolerance, dialogue and consultation and, in general, to contribute to the promotion of the moral well being of society.

8. To contribute to the best of his abilities, at all times and at all levels, to the promotion and achievement of African unity.

Consider the following analysis of duties and their relationships both to rights and to African tradition and culture.

MAKAU MUTUA, HUMAN RIGHTS AND THE AFRICAN FINGERPRINT
MAKAU MUTUA, HUMAN RIGHTS: A POLITICAL AND CULTURAL CRITIQUE (2002) 71

...
... [M]uch of the criticism of the Charter has been directed at its inclusion of duties on individuals. ... This criticism ... should [lead us to] examine the concept of duty in precolonial African societies and demonstrate

its validity in conceptualizing a unitary, integrated conception of human rights in which the extreme individualism of current human rights norms is tempered by the individual's obligation to the society.

Capturing the view of many Africans, B. Obinna Okere has written that the 'African conception of man is not that of an isolated and abstract individual, but an integral member of a group animated by a spirit of solidarity.'...
...
In practical terms, this philosophy of the group-centered individual evolves through a series of carefully taught rights and responsibilities. At the root were structures of social and political organization, informed by gender and age, which served to enhance solidarity and ensure the existence of the community into perpetuity. ... Relationships, rights, and obligations flowed from these organizational structures, giving the community cohesion and viability. Certain obligations, such as the duty to defend the community and *its* territory, attached by virtue of birth and group membership. ...
...
Defense of the community, a state-type right exacted on those who came under its protection, was probably the most serious positive public obligation borne by young men. ... [M]ost individual duties attached at the family and kinship levels. ...
...
This conception, that of the individual as a moral being endowed with rights but also bounded by duties, proactively uniting his needs with the needs of others, was the quintessence of the formulation of rights in precolonial societies. It radically differs from the liberal conception of the individual as the state's primary antagonist. ... Moreover, it provides those concerned with the universal conception of human rights with a basis for imagining another dialectic: the harmonization of duties and rights. ... This African worldview, [Cobbah] writes, "is for all intents and purposes as valid as the European theories of individualism and the social contract." Any concept of human rights with pretensions of universality cannot avoid mediating between these two seemingly contradictory notions.

The Duty/Rights Conception

... [T]he African Charter is the first human rights document to articulate the concept [of duty] in any meaningful way. ...
...
Ironically, colonialism, though a divisive factor, created a sense of brotherhood or unity among different African nations within the same colonial state, because they saw themselves as common victims of an alien, racist. and oppressive structure. Nevertheless, as the fissures of the modern African state amply demonstrate, the unity born out of anticolonialism has not sufficed to create an enduring identity of nationhood in the context of the postcolonial state. ...
...
... While acknowledging that it is impossible to recapture and reinstitute precolonial forms of social and political organization, this chapter nonetheless asserts that Africa must partially look inward, to its precolonial past, for possible solutions. Certain ideals in precolonial African philosophy, particularly the conception of humanity, and the interface of rights and duties in a communal context as provided for in the African Charter, should form part of that process of reconstruction. ...
...
The series of explicit duties spelled out in articles 27 through 29 of the African Charter could be read as intended to recreate the bonds of the precolonial era among individuals and between individuals and the state. They represent a rejection of the individual "who is utterly free and utterly irresponsible and opposed to society." In a proper reflection of the nuanced nature of societal obligations in the precolonial era, the African Charter explicitly provides for two types of duties: direct and indirect. A direct duty is contained, for example, in article 29(4) of the Charter which requires the individual to "preserve and strengthen social and national solidarity, particularly when the latter is threatened." There is nothing inherently sinister about this provision; it merely repeats a duty formerly imposed on members of precolonial communities. If anything, there exists a heightened need today, more than at any other time in recent history, to fortify communal relations and defend national solidarity. ...

The African Charter provides an example of an indirect duty in article 27(2), which states that "The rights and freedoms of each individual shall be exercised with due regard to the rights of others, collective security, morality and common interest." This duty is in fact a limitation on the enjoyment of certain individual rights. It merely recognizes the practical reality that in African societies, as elsewhere in the world, individual rights are not absolute. Individuals are asked to reflect on how the exercise of their rights in certain circumstances might adversely affect other individuals or the community. ...

Duties are also grouped according to whether they are owed to individuals or to larger units such as the family, society, or the state. Parents, for example, are owed a duty of respect and maintenance by their children. Crippling economic problems do not allow African states to contemplate some of the programs of the welfare state. The care of the aged and needy falls squarely on family and community members. This requirement — a necessity today — has its roots in the past: it was unthinkable to abandon a parent or relative in need. ...

Some duties are owed by the individual to the state. These are not distinctive to African states; many of them are standard obligations that any modern state places on its citizens. ... Such duties are rights that the community or the state, defined as all persons within it, holds against the individual. ...

The duties that require the individual to strengthen and defend national independence, security, and the territorial integrity of the state are inspired by the continent's history of domination and occupation by outside powers over the centuries. The duties represent an extension of the principle of self-determination, used in the external sense, as a shield against foreign occupation. ... Likewise, the duty to place one's intellectual abilities at the service of the state is a legitimate state interest, for the "brain drain" has robbed Africa of massive intellect. In recognition of the need for the strength of diversity, rather than its power to divide, the Charter asks individuals to promote African unity, an especially critical role given arbitrary balkanization by the colonial powers and the ethnic animosities fostered within and between the imposed states.

... [T]he Charter also requires the state to protect the family, which it terms "the natural unit and basis of society," and the "custodian of morals and traditional values." There is an enormous potential for advocates of equality rights to be concerned that these provisions could be used to support the patriarchy and other repressive practices of precolonial social ordering. It is now generally accepted that one of the strikes against the precolonial regime was its strict separation of gender roles and, in many cases, the limitation on, or exclusion of, women from political participation. ...

However, these are not the practices that the Charter condones when it requires states to assist families as the "custodians of morals and traditional values." Such an interpretation would be a cynical misreading of the Charter. The reference is to those traditional values which enhanced the dignity of the individual and emphasized the dignity of motherhood and the importance of the female as the central link in the reproductive chain; women were highly valued as equals in the process of the regeneration of life. The Charter guarantees, unambiguously and without equivocation, the equal rights of women in its gender equality provision by requiring states to "eliminate every discrimination against women" and to protect women's rights in international human rights instruments." ...

...

The most damaging criticism of the language of duties in Africa sees them as "little more than the formulation, entrenchment, and legitimation of state rights and privileges against individuals and peoples." However, critics who question the value of including duties in the Charter point only to the theoretical danger that states might capitalize on the duty concept to violate other guaranteed rights. The fear is frequently expressed that emphasis on duties may lead to the "tramping" of individual rights if the two are in opposition. ...

...

* * *

For all of the concerns expressed by commentators when the Charter was first adopted, the duties provisions have played a surprisingly minor role in practice, as explained by Rachel Murray, in *The African Charter on Human and Peoples' Rights: A Commentary* (2019) 576:

> ... [A]n interpretation of perhaps what one may have considered to be the crux of
> individual duties, namely that individuals, rather than the State, have responsibilities
> towards fellow human beings, one's family, community and the country in which one

lives, [has] not been the focus of the African Commission's attention, nor yet, that of the African Court. It is possible that both the African Commission and Court and those litigating before them have shied away from advancing these duties, save those instances where a State has, unsuccessfully, attempted to use them to limit rights. ... It is a shame that the opportunity that the ACHPR offers in Articles 27–29 to influence a 'new direction in the thinking of human rights', has not been fully exploited. ...

...

While others have attempted to clarify the content of the provisions, suggesting that they can be divided into 'general duties' and 'special duties', or 'direct and indirect' duties, or indeed that Article 27 'introduces the legal edifice relating to individual duties, as a general statement of the duties and the following Articles as providing an exhaustive enumeration and explanation of them', the fact remains that there has been little analysis from the African Commission and African Court which confirms or denies whether these specific duties are legal or simply moral.

One of the consequences of this relative silence on these provisions, beyond Article 27(2), is evidence of a lack of clarity among States at least as to what the duties actually entail. An analysis of the State reports under Article 62 reveal differing interpretations of the duties, and it has not gone unnoticed by the African Commission that some States have omitted them entirely from their reports. Indeed, Malila's analysis of the coverage of individual duties in State reports is insightful, citing a question from Lesotho that it would 'appreciate guidance of the African Commission ... on [Articles 27, 28 and 29] as we do not seem to comprehend exactly what is required of us'.

It has been argued that the duties are so vague as to be unenforceable. Further, even on the few occasions where obligations or recommendations have been addressed in specific instances to individuals and non-State actors, the African Commission has no means to enforce their implementation beyond inclusion in its resolutions, press releases and other statements.

...

... [T]he presumption is that such duties may be enforced at the domestic level and thereby 'their enshrinement in the African charter does not therefore place any additional burden on the individual'. As to whether they should be provided for in national legislation, Malila cautions against an obligation on States to 'replicate these duties in their domestic law', given that there is no express requirement in the ACHPR on them to do so.

QUESTIONS

1. How does the emphasis in Article 29 of the African Charter on 'harmony', 'cohesion', 'community', 'security', 'social and national solidarity', 'territorial integrity', 'positive African cultural values', the 'moral well-being of society' and 'African unity' fit with the relatively traditional human rights recognized earlier in the Charter?

2. Does Mutua's article (a) explain and seek to justify in terms of African history and culture the relevant provisions of the Charter, or (b) seek to reconcile those provisions with the human rights regime, or (c) both? Does he succeed in the second task? Does he suggest that the West and Africa should in some respects go their separate ways, or that Africa has indeed much to teach the West about the directions of its own rights-oriented thought?

4. Recent Debates over Duties and Responsibilities

Over the past two decades there has been a revival in the Global North of debates over rights and duties amid claims that the latter have been neglected, thereby impoverishing the former and facilitating the emergence of a deeply problematic culture of rights. These debates are different from the earlier examples explored in this Chapter. Ben Saul, in 'In the Shadow of Human Rights: Human Duties, Obligations, and Responsibilities', 32 *Colum. Hum. Rts. L. Rev.* (2001) 565 gives a sense of some of the motivating concerns:

> Over the past decade, critics ... have become concerned, even alarmed, by a supposed "imbalance between rights and responsibilities." ... [C]ommentators have argued that the discourse of human and civil rights has become "characterized by hyper-individualism, exaggerated absoluteness, and silence with respect to personal, civic, and collective responsibilities." A questionable explosion of individual rights has supposedly conspired to compromise the general welfare and the public good, overshadow corresponding human responsibilities, and impoverish political life. People no longer ask what they can do for their country, only what their country can do for them.
>
> On this view, a "flight from individual responsibility" has produced an expectant citizenry that feels entitled to government services, without any sense of obligation to pay taxes, perform jury service, or undertake national service. Many irresponsible people, for example, depend blissfully on welfare--as if by choice rather than economic necessity. Rights consciousness has allegedly led to a surge of self-interested litigation, creating a moral culture of highly atomistic individuals motivated by advocacy; "a society driven by [responsibilities] ... promotes service, tolerance, compromise, and progress, whereas a society driven by [rights] ... is preoccupied with acquisition, confrontation, and advocacy."

The traditional response to such concerns has been that democratically elected governments are limited only by the need to respect human rights in their ability and entitlement to impose obligations, duties, or responsibilities upon the citizenry. Whereas international human rights standards are designed to hold governments to account for their inevitable failures to respect or ensure rights, there is no equivalent need for international standards to empower governments to impose duties. But this has not quieted the debate. What is surprising is that calls for a greater emphasis on duties have come from commentators across the political spectrum. The following excerpts provide a sampling:

(i) Samuel Moyn, Reclaiming the Language of Duty in an Age of Human Rights, ABC [Australian Broadcasting Corporation] Religion and Ethics portal, 30 Oct 2019:

> Today ..., liberal emphasis on duties is a distant memory at every scale. Political theory lost track of the concept in the second half of the twentieth century. ... In the public sphere, duties are similarly absent. Neither liberals in their domestic projects, nor the Universal Declaration and subsequent international movements, have successfully offered powerful public visions of social interdependence, collective agency, or planetary responsibility.
>
> Our age of rights, lacking a public language of duties, is an historical outlier. The consequences are significant. Human rights themselves wither when their advocates fail to cross the border into the language of duty; insofar as compliance with norms on paper is sought, the bearers of duties have to be identified and compelled to assume their burden.
>
> ...
>
> But duties may have an even larger role to play than simply completing the circuit of rights fulfilment. ... Gandhi's cosmopolitan responsibility, ... might help to confront these global-scale menaces. ... [I]nternational law in particular beckons for duties corresponding to the human rights established by the last generation's work. Specifically,

one might call for cosmopolitan responsibilities for the sake of the many to balance the transnational commercial freedoms that currently redound to the benefit of a few.

Another forgotten tradition asserts cosmopolitan duties of states … [through] … the proposition that rich states owe duties to the world's poor and the global commons. …

Of course, it would be a grievous mistake to insist, as … Gandhi apparently did, that enjoyment of rights ought to depend on assumption of duties first. And it is undeniable that the rhetoric of duties has often been deployed euphemistically by those whose true purpose is a return to tradition won by limiting the rights of others.

…

… [R]ejecting duty entirely means rejecting a public vocabulary that might save a range of values from continuing neglect, whether socioeconomic equality, global justice or environmental welfare.

Further, duties could matter precisely because many of our most intractable problems are global. … Gandhi's call to prioritise duties reflected a self-conscious cosmopolitanism: duties are at the core of a worthy citizenship of the world. It is highly doubtful that human rights alone will address these public dilemmas in either theory or practice. In fact, they have already failed to do so.

…

The anxious sense that to legitimate talk of duty is to flirt with disaster – that, all things considered, it is best to stick exclusively to the vindication of hard-won rights – is understandable but indefensible. …

… There is a growing realisation among activists that talking the talk of other people's rights may lead inexorably to experiences of solidarity that, in turn, affect how claims are made. A self-styled human-obligations movement … would not only better capture some aspects of existing activism. It also would help dispel worries about its libertarian associations, particularly since northern activists have a continuing penchant for demoting economic and social rights and distributive justice … .

(ii) Nigel Biggar, *What's Wrong with Rights?* (2020) 334:

> … [Those] of us in the rights-saturated West need to get beyond whatever it is that is tying our tongues over duty and virtue. Rights-talk is just not enough. It implies as much, of course, since legal rights must have correspondent legal duties. But legal right-holders are also subject to moral duties that determine how they should exercise their rights, and whether they should exercise them at all; and all legal duty-bearers need moral virtues that enable them to carry out their duties. … [F]or too long we have suppressed [these ideas], acquiescing in the lazy notion that law suffices to structure our public relations and that morality can and should be left at home. But this is not true. We cannot out-source all responsibility for governing relations between citizens to the police, the courts, and penal institutions. … [I]n addition to law and legal rights, we need common moral norms that civil social bodies own, promote, and enforce. For the sake of the plausibility of rights-talk, the prudence of rights, and the possibility of respecting them, we need to muster the courage to own and affirm duty and virtue in public … . [We need] a sustainable, morally realist form of modernity—one that recognises *right* before it asserts and multiplies *rights*.

(iii) Kathryn Sikkink, *The Hidden Face of Rights: Toward a Politics of Responsibilities* (2020) 1:

> … We who believe in human rights need to begin talking and thinking explicitly about the politics and ethics of responsibility. A rights-and-responsibilities approach is a framework, not a recipe for action. It requires us to think strategically about the networked responsibilities of many state and non-state actors, including individuals, to

work collectively to implement human rights. There are risks and discomforts in emphasizing responsibilities, but the risks of inaction and complacency are worse.

...

- To address environmental crises, it is necessary to emphasize not only our rights to a clean environment, but also the obligations of states, corporations, institutions, and individuals to protect the environment. ...

- To protect digital privacy and combat digital disinformation, we must demand that our government do more. But unless other organizations—especially corporations like Facebook and Google—take action, implementation will be radically incomplete. There is also a role for schools, universities, and individuals to step up digital training ... .

- To strengthen our political system, it is not enough to stress our right to vote; we also need to practice our responsibility to vote and to help others vote. ...

- To confront economic inequality, it is necessary to stress both the economic rights of individuals to an adequate standard of living and the duties of corporations and individuals to pay taxes ... .

- We need to protect our right to free speech and protest not only by exercising it, but also by practicing the responsibility not to drown out the speech of others.

- ... The state can and should use incentives or sanctions to compel responsibility, but these are costly and crude tools. The voluntary acceptance of mutual responsibilities by a variety of actors is the key to full implementation of rights. ...

(iv) United Kingdom Ministry of Justice, *Human Rights Act Reform: A Modern Bill of Rights – consultation* (updated 12 July 2022), Chapter 3:

> A 'rights culture' that displaces personal responsibility and the public interest
>
> 124) The international human rights framework recognises that not all rights are absolute and that an individual's rights may need to be balanced, either against the rights of others or against the wider public interest. ...
>
> 125) The idea that rights come alongside duties and responsibilities is steeped in the UK tradition of liberty, but is also reflected in the qualifications in the [European Convention and the UDHR]. The increasing reliance on human rights claims over the years has, however, led to a culture of rights decoupled from our responsibilities as citizens, and a displacement of due consideration of the wider public interest.
>
> 126) Since 2000, human rights claims have been brought by many people who have themselves showed a flagrant disregard for the rights of others. We have seen, for example, the right to respect for a family and private life used to avoid deportation by foreign offenders who have committed serious crimes. The case against the UK on prisoner voting [the government introduced a blanket ban on voting by those in prison] was originally brought by John Hirst, convicted of manslaughter for killing his landlady with an axe.... We have also seen the right to a family life used to challenge the separation of sexual partners in prison, and to challenge the refusal of all telephone contact and inter-prison visits between a couple who married in one prison but were later separated.
>
> ...

130) These claims were unsuccessful, but often the fact that they can be brought at public expense serves to undermine public confidence in the Human Rights Act. ...

131) Whilst human rights are universal, a Bill of Rights could require the courts to give greater consideration to the behaviour of claimants and the wider public interest when interpreting and balancing qualified rights. More broadly, our proposals can also set out more clearly the extent to which the behaviour of claimants is a factor that the courts take into account when deciding what sort of remedy, if any, is appropriate. This will ensure that claimants' responsibilities, and the rights of others, form a part of the process of making a claim based on the violation of a human right.

(v) InterAction Council, Universal Declaration of Human Responsibilities (1997):

[The Council is a group of former Presidents and Prime Ministers. They proposed that this declaration be adopted by the UN General Assembly, as the UDHR had been.]

Fundamental Principles for Humanity

Article 1

Every person ... has a responsibility to treat all people in a humane way.

Article 2

No person should lend support to any form of inhumane behavior, but all people have a responsibility to strive for the dignity and self-esteem of all others.

Article 3

No person, no group or organization, no state, no army or police stands above good and evil; all are subject to ethical standards. Everyone has a responsibility to promote good and to avoid evil in all things.

Article 4

All people, endowed with reason and conscience, must accept a responsibility to each

and all ... in a spirit of solidarity: What you do not wish to be done to yourself, do not do to others.

Non-Violence and Respect for Life

Article 5

Every person has a responsibility to respect life. ...

Article 6

Disputes between states, groups or individuals should be resolved without violence. ... Every

citizen and public official has a responsibility to act in a peaceful, non-violent way.

...

Justice and Solidarity

Article 8

Every person has a responsibility to behave with integrity, honesty and fairness. ...

Article 9

All people, given the necessary tools, have a responsibility to make serious efforts to overcome poverty, malnutrition, ignorance, and inequality. …

Article 10

All people have a responsibility to develop their talents through diligent endeavor; they should have equal access to education and to meaningful work. Everyone should lend support to the needy, the disadvantaged, the disabled and to the victims of discrimination.

Article 11

All property and wealth must be used responsibly in accordance with justice and for the advancement of the human race. …

…

(vi) Anne Peters, *Beyond Human Rights: The Legal Status of the Individual in International Law* (2016) 112:

> The idea of fundamental duties owed to the State encounters misgivings. A first problem results from the fact that … the assumption of fundamental duties in reality often constitutes a pretext for the State to limit fundamental rights. Secondly, there is a risk of circumvention: According to current law, limitations of international human rights must satisfy the requirements set out in treaties in accordance with the rule of law, and they must especially be based on a sufficient legal foundation and be proportionate. An undifferentiated invocation of "fundamental duties" risks circumventing precisely these limits on limitations of human rights set out in positive international law.
>
> Thirdly and generally speaking, the assertion of fundamental duties vis-à-vis the State constitutes an attempt to provide additional legitimation of State power. …
>
> Finally, the conception of fundamental duties owed to the State as a corollary to fundamental rights is misleading at a basic level. It suggests that the State in turn has "fundamental rights" and "claims" vis-à-vis individuals. This is misguided, because the State is in a superior position in light of its instruments of power. It is not in need of protection like the individual. It is not an end in itself and does not enjoy any rights, only powers.
>
> …
>
> … Fundamental duties in the sense of hard legal obligations legally owed to the State are not a component of universal international law, nor should they be.

QUESTIONS

1. What understandings of duties emerge from these different analyses? Are the commentators talking only about a change of strategy or emphasis, or would some of the proposals bring fundamental change?

2. Moyn and Sikkink both emphasize the potential of a duties-based approach to rescue values such as 'socioeconomic equality, global justice, or environmental welfare' from neglect. How would this be transformative?

3. Is an emphasis on 'cosmopolitan responsibilities' just a way of acknowledging that because human rights obligations do not extend directly to corporate and other private actors, the only recourse available is to moral conceptions?

Chapter 7. Conflict in Culture, Tradition and Practices: Challenges to Universalism

A. UNIVERSALISM AND CULTURAL RELATIVISM

The question of the 'universal' or 'relative' character of human rights has been a source of debate and contention from the outset. These divergent understandings of the nature of human rights have sometimes been cast as alternatives, as polar visions with no intermediate ground between them, and sometimes as allowing for a more complex view that understands some norms as universal and others as relative to context and culture. The generally antagonistic positions have borne a number of descriptions — for example, 'absolute' ('universal') as opposed to 'contingent' ('relative'), or imposed ('universal') as opposed to self-determined ('relative') rights. The contest between these positions took on renewed vigour as the human rights regime slowly developed, and in important respects weakened, earlier more robust understandings of the scope of national sovereignty and of domestic jurisdiction. Indeed, significant links have developed over the decades between some of the claims associated with cultural relativism and claims of sovereign autonomy for a state to follow its own path.

Put simply, the partisans of universality claim that international human rights — like rights to equal protection, physical security, fair trials, free speech, freedom of religion and free association — are and must be the same everywhere. This claim applies at least to the rights' general content, for advocates of the position that rights are universal of course recognize that many basic rights (such as the right to a fair criminal trial) allow for historically and culturally influenced forms of implementation or realization (i.e., states are not required to use the Anglo-American jury to assure a fair trial; states need not follow any one particular voting system to meet the requirement of a government that represents the will of the people).

Advocates of cultural relativism claim that (most, some) rights and rules about morality are encoded in and thus depend on cultural context. They often use the term 'culture' in a broad and diffuse way that reaches beyond indigenous traditions and customary practices to include political and religious ideologies and institutional structures. Hence notions of right and wrong, and moral rules based on them, necessarily differ throughout the world because the cultures in which they take root and inhere themselves differ. This relativist position can thus be understood simply to assert the empirical claim that the world contains an impressive diversity in views about right and wrong which is linked to the diverse underlying cultures.

But the strong relativist position goes beyond arguing that there is — as a matter of fact, empirically — an impressive diversity of rights and moralities. It attaches an important consequence to this diversity: that no transcendent or transcultural ideas of right can be found or agreed on, and hence that no culture or state (whether or not in the guise of enforcing international human rights) is justified in attempting to impose on other cultures or states what must be understood to be ideas associated particularly with the imposing culture. In this strong form, cultural relativism necessarily contradicts a basic premise of the human rights regime. Its core values are respect for diversity and the related local autonomy.

Mayanthi Fernando, in 'Cultural Relativism', *Oxford Bibliographies in Anthropology* (2013) gives an overview of the different forms of relativism:

> In a 1580 essay called "On the Cannibals," early Enlightenment thinker Michel de Montaigne posited that men are by nature ethnocentric and that they judge the customs and morals of other communities on the basis of their own particular customs and morals, which they take to be universally applicable. Montaigne's essay foreshadowed the emergence in early 20th-century American anthropology of the principle of cultural relativism in a more robust and programmatic form, as a descriptive, methodological, epistemological, and prescriptive approach to human diversity. Franz Boas and his students, especially Melville J. Herskovits, were at the forefront of this new development, one that became foundational to modern anthropology. Against the biological and racial determinism of the time, they held that cultures develop according to the particular circumstances of history rather than in a linear progression from "primitive" to "savage" to "civilized," that culture (rather than race or biology) most affects social life and human

behavior, and that culture shapes the way members of a particular cultural group think, act, perceive, and evaluate. This new theorization of the culture concept led to a multifaceted approach to studying human diversity called cultural relativism. Cultural relativism is an umbrella term that covers different attitudes, though it relies on a basic notion of emic coherence: Each culture works in its own way, and beliefs and practices that appear strange from the outside make sense when contextualized within their particular cultural framework. More specifically, descriptive relativism holds that cultures differ substantially from place to place. Methodological relativism holds that the ethnographer must set aside his or her own cultural norms in order to understand another culture and explain its worldview. Epistemological relativism holds that because our own culture so mediates our perceptions, it is often impossible to fully grasp another culture in an unmediated way. Prescriptive or moral relativism holds that because we are all formed in culture, there is no Archimedean point from which to evaluate objectively, and so we must not judge other cultures using our own cultural norms. Recently, cultural relativism has become a straw man term, defined pejoratively as the strongest form of moral relativism; namely, that we cannot make any kind of moral judgments at all regarding foreign cultural practices. At the turn of the 20th century, cultural relativism was a progressive anthropological theory and methodological practice that sought to valorize marginalized communities in an inegalitarian world. Now cultural relativism is criticized as doing precisely the opposite: allowing repressive and inegalitarian societies to hide behind the cloak of cultural difference.

On their face, human rights instruments (which in their treaty form impose legal obligations, and convert moral rules into legal rules) are surely on the 'universalist' side of this debate. The landmark instrument is the *Universal Declaration of Human Rights*, much of which has clearly become customary international law. The two Covenants, with states parties from all the world's regions and covering a large percentage of the global population, also speak in universal terms: 'everyone' has the right to liberty, 'all persons' are entitled to equal protection, 'no one' shall be subjected to torture, 'everyone' has the right to an adequate standard of living. Neither in the definitions of rights nor in the limitation clauses (which permit states parties to restrict the enjoyment of rights because of public order, policy or health) does the text of these basic instruments make any explicit concession to cultural variation.

To the relativist, these instruments and their pretension to universality may suggest primarily the arrogance or 'cultural imperialism' of the West, given the West's traditional urge — expressed, for example, in political ideology (liberalism) and in religious faith (Christianity) — to view its own forms and beliefs as universal, and to attempt to universalize them. Moreover, some relativists argue that the push to universalizing norms destroys the diversity of cultures and hence amounts to another path towards cultural homogenization in the modern world — itself a contradiction of the value of cultural survival stressed in, for example, Article 27 of the International Covenant on Civil and Political Rights (ICCPR). But the debate between these two positions follows no simple route. It is open to a range of views and strategies.

During the Cold War, such debates (sometimes no more than highly politicized accusations and routine polemics) took place dominantly between the Communist world and its sympathizers on the one hand, and the Western democracies on the other. The Western democracies charged the Communist world with violating many basic rights, particularly those of a civil and political character. The latter replied both by charging the West with violations of the more important economic and social rights, and by asserting that the political ideology of Communism pointed towards a different understanding of rights.

That particular debate died more-or-less together with the Soviet Union, though some of its themes survive in different form, such as in disagreements between China and the United States. Today the universal-relative debate takes place primarily across Global North-Global South lines, or in a religious (West-Islam) framework. It also includes non-state actors, such as indigenous peoples.

The principle that norms are universal, which permeates the main human rights instruments starting with the Universal Declaration, rests on a few basic postulates, beliefs and assumptions. Perhaps the fundamental one is equal human dignity. Denial of that principle, at least with respect to the regulation of action and behaviour, itself shatters universalism, without even reaching the divisive issues posed by cultural relativism. That denial has been a commonplace in world history, strikingly evident in the history of the twentieth century. Consider the following observations of a philosopher, Richard Rorty, in 'Human Rights, Rationality and Sentimentality', in Obrad Savić (ed.), *The Politics of Human Rights* (1999) 67, at 74:

> … For most white people, until very recently, most Black people did not so count. For most Christians, up until the seventeenth century or so, most heathens did not so count. For the Nazis, Jews did not so count. For most males in countries in which the average annual income is under four thousand dollars, most females still do not so count. Whenever tribal and national rivalries become important, members of rival tribes and nations will not so count. Kant's account of the respect due to rational agents tells you that you should extend the respect you feel for people like yourself to all featherless bipeds. This is an excellent suggestion, a good formula for secularizing the Christian doctrine of the brotherhood of man. But it has never been backed up by an argument based on neutral premises, and it never will be. Outside the circle of post-Enlightenment European culture … most people are simply unable to understand why membership in a biological species is supposed to suffice for membership in a moral community. This is not because they are insufficiently rational. It is, typically, because they live in a world in which it would be just too risky — indeed, would often be insanely dangerous — to let one's sense of moral community stretch beyond one's family, clan, or tribe.

> To get whites to be nicer to Blacks, males to females, Serbs to Muslims, or straights to gays, to help our species link up into what Rabossi calls a 'planetary community' dominated by a culture of human rights, it is of no use whatever to say, with Kant: notice that what you have in common, your humanity, is more important than these trivial differences. For the people we are trying to convince will rejoin that they notice nothing of the sort. Such people are *morally* offended by the suggestion that they should treat someone who is not kin as if he were a brother. … They are offended by the suggestion that they treat people whom they do not think of as human as if they were human. …

> … The identity of these people, the people whom we should like to convince to join our Eurocentric human rights culture, is bound up with their sense of who they are *not*. …

The introductory readings below come out of the rich anthropological literature on culture and cultural relativism. Anthropologists have long had to wrestle with these issues, in the context of their ethnographic writings about diverse cultures whose practices and values depart radically from the West. Often those practices would be open to serious moral criticism from the perspectives of Western thought. The anthropological writings have sought primarily to describe, explain and understand the alien culture, within the framework of one or another theoretical perspective or methodology. They have not historically sought to pass judgement, to condemn or praise, the practices they describe.

Thus the role of the anthropologist has traditionally been very different from that of the human rights investigator who monitors and reports and the human rights advocate who works to arrest the described violations. To be sure, investigators and advocates may also seek to understand and to describe the cultural contexts in which they are operating. But those working with the large international human rights organizations characteristically combine their description with moral and legal assessment of a given state's conduct against international human rights standards. They will, in appropriate cases, condemn the state's conduct and urge the state or others to take corrective or coercive measures. Their work is inherently judgmental and normatively based. They seek to vindicate and advance respect for human rights.

Mark Goodale observes, in *Anthropology and Law: A Critical Introduction* (2017) 96, that the 'anthropology of human rights has developed innovative approaches in methodology, epistemology, and ethics such that an anthropological perspective is now a common presence within academic debates over human rights, within international institutional policy making, and among human rights practitioners.' This is all the more surprising given that the initial engagement between the two fields came in the form of the following statement issued in the name of the American Anthropological Association, which staked out a determinedly sceptical view. When reading it, keep in mind that the human rights regime addresses primarily states, whereas ethnographic writings involve primarily peoples or tribes or societies. The latter may be non-state entities, and in any event are objects of study distinct from the political organization and political acts of the state itself.

AMERICAN ANTHROPOLOGICAL ASSOCIATION, STATEMENT ON HUMAN RIGHTS
49 AMER. ANTHROPOLOGIST (1947) 539

[In 1947, the UN Commission on Human Rights had begun drafting what ultimately became the UDHR of 1948. The Statement below was submitted as a contribution to the debate by the Executive Board of the American Anthropological Association, although in fact it was written entirely by Melville Herskovits and not subjected to scrutiny or debate by the AAA membership.[236] It uses several designations to refer to the pending document that became the UDHR.]

The problem faced by the Commission on Human Rights of the United Nations in preparing its Declaration on the Rights of Man must be approached from two points of view. The first, in terms of which the Declaration is ordinarily conceived, concerns the respect for the personality of the individual as such and his right to its fullest development as a member of his society. In a world order, however, respect for the cultures of differing human groups is equally important.

These are two facets of the same problem, since it is a truism that groups are composed of individuals, and human beings do not function outside the societies of which they form a part. The problem is thus to formulate a statement of human rights that will do more than just phrase respect for the individual as an individual. It must also take into full account the individual as a member of the social group of which he is a part, whose sanctioned modes of life shape his behavior, and with whose fate his own is thus inextricably bound.

… How can the proposed Declaration be applicable to all human beings and not be a statement of rights conceived only in terms of the values prevalent in the countries of Western Europe and America? …

If we begin, as we must, with the individual, we find that from the moment of his birth not only his behavior, but his very thought, his hopes, aspirations, the moral values which direct his action and justify and give meaning to his life in his own eyes and those of his fellows, are shaped by the body of custom of the group of which he becomes a member. … [I]f the essence of the Declaration is to be, as it must, a statement in which the right of the individual to develop his personality to the fullest is to be stressed, then this must be based on a recognition of the fact that the personality of the individual can develop only in terms of the culture of his society.
…
… Doctrines of the 'white man's burden' have been employed to implement economic exploitation and to deny the right to control their own affairs to millions of peoples over the world, where the expansion of Europe and America has not meant the literal extermination of whole populations. Rationalized in terms of ascribing cultural inferiority to these peoples, or in conceptions of their backwardness in development of their 'primitive mentality', that justified their being held in the tutelage of their superiors, the history of the expansion of the western world has been marked by demoralization of human personality and the disintegration of human rights among the peoples over whom hegemony has been established.

The values of the ways of life of these peoples have been consistently misunderstood and decried. Religious beliefs that for untold ages have carried conviction and permitted adjustment to the Universe have been attacked as superstitious, immoral, untrue. And, since power carries its own conviction, this has furthered the process of demoralization begun by economic exploitation and the loss of political autonomy. …

We thus come to the first proposition that the study of human psychology and culture dictates as essential in drawing up a Bill of Human Rights in terms of existing knowledge:

1. The individual realizes his personality through his culture, hence respect for individual differences entails a respect for cultural differences.

---

[236] Goodale, at 99.

There can be no individual freedom, that is, when the group with which the individual identifies himself is not free. There can be no full development of the individual personality as long as the individual is told, by men who have the power to enforce their commands, that the way of life of his group is inferior to that of those who wield the power. ...

2. Respect for differences between cultures is validated by the scientific fact that no technique of qualitatively evaluating cultures has been discovered.

This principle leads us to a further one, namely that the aims that guide the life of every people are self-evident in their significance to that people. ...

3. Standards and values are relative to the culture from which they derive so that any attempt to formulate postulates that grow out of the beliefs or moral codes of one culture must to that extent detract from the applicability of any Declaration of Human Rights to mankind as a whole.

Ideas of right and wrong, good and evil, are found in all societies, though they differ in their expression among different peoples. What is held to be a human right in one society may be regarded as anti-social by another people, or by the same people in a different period of their history. The saint of one epoch would at a later time be confined as a man not fitted to cope with reality. Even the nature of the physical world, the colors we see, the sounds we hear, are conditioned by the language we speak, which is part of the culture into which we are born.

The problem of drawing up a Declaration of Human Rights was relatively simple in the eighteenth century, because it was not a matter of *human* rights, but of the rights of men within the framework of the sanctions laid by a single society. ...

Today the problem is complicated by the fact that the Declaration must be of worldwide applicability. It must embrace and recognize the validity of many different ways of life. It will not be convincing to the Indonesian, the African, the Indian, the Chinese, if it lies on the same plane as like documents of an earlier period. ...

* * *

In the following reading, Sally Engle Merry provides a very different understanding of 'culture' and how it should be understood in the context of human rights. One question is: what is being asserted by the claim that a given state or region must be free to follow its own 'cultural tradition', even if thereby violating norms in universal treaties? Many meanings of the term appear and disappear in this debate; often 'culture' as a justification for difference is not referred to as such, but is implicit in a state's argument. Or that broad term is disaggregated into some of its complex components, such as language, religion, traditions, rituals and other practices.

Meanings of culture may also differ across the divides of different languages. Consider some definitions for 'culture' in the *American Heritage Dictionary of the English Language* (1969):

> ... 4. Intellectual and social formation. 5. The totality of socially transmitted behavior patterns, arts, beliefs, characteristic of a community or population. 6. A style of social and artistic expression peculiar to a society or class. 7. Intellectual and artistic activity.

SALLY ENGLE MERRY, HUMAN RIGHTS AND GENDER VIOLENCE (2006) 2

Chapter 1: Culture and Transnationalism

... Human rights ideas, embedded in cultural assumptions about the nature of the person, the community, and the state, do not translate easily from one setting to another. If human rights ideas are to have an impact, they need to become part of the consciousness of ordinary people around the world. Considerable research on law and everyday social life shows that law's power to shape society depends not on punishment alone but on becoming embedded in everyday social practices, shaping the rules people carry in their heads. Yet, there is a great distance between the global sites where these ideas are formulated and the specific situations in which they are deployed. We know relatively little about how individuals in various social and cultural contexts come to see themselves in terms of human rights.

Nor do ideas and approaches move readily the other way from local to global settings. Global sites are a *bricolage* of issues and ideas brought to the table by national actors. But transnational actors, and even some national elites, are often uninterested in local social practices or too busy to understand them in their complicated contexts. ... Transnational reformers must adhere to a set of standards that apply to all societies if they are to gain legitimacy. ...

The division between transnational elites and local actors is based less on culture or tradition than on tensions between a transnational community that envisions a unified modernity and national and local actors for whom particular histories and contexts are important. Intermediaries such as NGO and social movement activists play a critical role in interpreting the cultural world of transnational modernity for local claimants. ... [T]hey take local stories and frame them in ... human rights language. ...

... [H]uman rights create a political space for reform using a language legitimated by a global consensus on standards. But this political space comes with a price. Human rights promote ideas of individual autonomy, equality, choice, and secularism even when these ideas differ from prevailing cultural norms and practices. Human rights ideas displace alternative visions of social justice that are less individualistic and more focused on communities and responsibilities, possibly contributing to the cultural homogenization of local communities. ...

...

There are several conundrums in applying human rights to local places. First, human rights law is committed to setting universal standards using legal rationality, yet this stance impedes adapting those standards to the particulars of local context. This perspective explains why local conditions often seem irrelevant to global debates. Second, human rights ideas are more readily adopted if they are packaged in familiar terms, but they are more transformative if they challenge existing assumptions about power and relationships. Activists who use human rights for local social movements face a paradox. Rights need to be presented in local cultural terms in order to be persuasive, but they must challenge existing relations of power in order to be effective. Third, to have local impact, human rights ideas need to be framed in terms of local values and images, but in order to receive funding, a wider audience, and international legitimacy, they have to be framed in terms of transnational rights principles. ...

Theorizing the Global-Local Interface

The global-local divide is often conceptualized as the opposition between rights and culture, or even civilization and culture. Those who resist human rights often claim to be defending culture. For example, male lineage heads in the rural New Territories of Hong Kong claimed that giving women rights to inherit land would destroy the social fabric. ... [T]hese arguments depend on a very narrow understanding of culture and the political misuse of this concept. ...

Even as anthropologists and others have repudiated the idea of culture as a consensual, interconnected system of beliefs and values, the idea has taken on new life in the public sphere, particularly with reference to the global South. ...

...

Seeing culture as contested and as a mode of legitimating claims to power and authority dramatically shifts the way we understand the universalism-relativism debate. It undermines those who resist changes that would benefit weaker groups in the name of preserving "culture," and it encourages human rights activists to pay attention to local cultural practices. This view of culture emphasizes that culture is hybrid and porous and that the pervasive struggles over cultural values within local communities are competitions over power. More recent anthropological scholarship explores processes by which human rights ideas are mobilized locally, adapted, and transformed and, in turn, how they shape local political struggles. As Cowan, Dembour, and Wilson point out,

"Rather than seeing universalism and cultural relativism as alternatives which one must choose, once and for all, one should see the tension between the positions as part of the continuous process of negotiating ever-changing and interrelated global and local norms". Culture in this sense does not serve as a barrier to human rights mobilization but as a context that defines relationships and meanings and constructs the possibilities of action.

Deconstructing Culture

Although culture is a term on everyone's lips, people rarely talk about what they mean by it. The term has many meanings in the contemporary world. It is often seen as the basis of national, ethnic, or religious identities. Culture is sometimes romanticized as the opposite of globalization, resolutely local and distinct. ... In international human rights meetings, culture often refers to traditions and customs: ways of doing things that are justified by their roots in the past. There is a whiff of the notion of the primitive about this usage of the term culture. It is not what modern urbanites do but what governs life in the countryside. ... Culture was often juxtaposed to civilization during the civilizing mission of imperialism, and this history has left a legacy in contemporary thinking.
...
There is a critical need for conceptual clarification of culture in human rights practice. Insofar as human rights relies on an essentialized model of culture, it does not take advantage of the potential of local cultural practices for change. ...

... Cultures consist of repertoires of ideas and practices that are not homogeneous but continually changing because of contradictions among them or because new ideas and institutions are adopted by members. They typically incorporate contested values and practices. Cultures are not contained within stable borders but are open to new ideas and permeable to influences from other cultural systems, although not all borders are equally porous. Cultural discourses legitimate or challenge authority and justify relations of power.

Of the myriad ways culture is imagined in transnational human rights discussions, two of the most common ones reflect an essentialized concept of culture. ...

[1] Culture as Tradition

Within the discourse of human rights activism, culture is often used as a synonym for tradition. Labeling a culture as traditional evokes an evolutionary vision of change from a primitive form to something like civilization. ... So-called traditional societies are at an earlier evolutionary stage than modern ones, which are more evolved and more civilized. Culture in this sense is not used to describe the affluent countries of the global North but the poor countries of the global South, particularly isolated and rural areas. ...

Although some human rights activists refer to "good" cultural practices and "harmful" cultural practices and a few feminist scholars examine cultural practices that protect women from violence, many who write about women's right to protection from violence identify culture and tradition as the source of the problem. ... [T]he human rights process seeks to replace cultural practices that are discriminatory with other cultural practices rooted in modern ideas of gender equality. Thus, like the colonial state, they seek to move ethnically defined subjects into the realm of rights-bearing modernity. This effort sometimes demonizes culture as it seeks to save individuals from its oppressive effects.

Female genital cutting (also called female genital mutilation) is the poster child for this understanding of culture.
...

[2] Culture as National Essence

A second common understanding of culture is as national essence or identity This concept of culture grows out of the German romantic tradition of the nineteenth century. Confronted with the claims to universal civilization of England and France, Germans began to draw a distinction between the external trappings of civilization and the inward, spiritual reality of culture. German romantics asserted the importance of a distinct culture, or Kultur, which formed the spiritual essence of their society. Each people, or Volk, has its own history and culture that expresses its genius. This includes its language, its laws, and its religion. The cosmopolitan elite corrupts it, while foreign technological and material values undermine it. ...

Culture as national essence is fundamental to claims to indigenous sovereignty and ethnonationalism, often in resistance to human rights. In 1993, when Lee Kuan Yew of Singapore claimed that human rights failed to incorporate Asian values, he drew on this understanding of culture. With support from several other Asian leaders, he argued that Asian values differed from Western conceptions of human rights. In some ways, the Asian values argument replays the German romantic resistance to French and English claims to civilization. Indeed, one critic of the Asian values argument notes that it falls into Orientalist notions of a communitarian East, with communal values, and an individualistic West.

Although the Asian values argument is less often articulated now, it represents one of many ways that leaders assert that human rights violate the fundamental cultural principles of a nation or a religion and therefore cannot be adopted.[237] Women's rights are often opposed by those who claim to defend culture. ...

Culture as Contentious

... Over the last two decades, anthropology has elaborated a conception of culture as unbounded, contested, and connected to relations of power, as the product of historical influences rather than evolutionary change. Cultural practices must be understood in context, so that their meaning and impact change as their context shifts. ... [Cultures] include institutional arrangements, political structures, and legal regulations. As institutions such as laws and policing change, so do beliefs, values, and practices. Cultures are not homogeneous and "pure" but produced through hybridization or creolization.

... These different perspectives on culture affect policies concerning women. For example, in Uruguay's country report to the committee monitoring the Women's Convention, the government expressed regret that more women were not involved in politics but blamed cultural traditions, women's involvement in domestic tasks, and the differences in wages by gender. In contrast, facing the same absence of women politicians, Denmark offered funds to offset babysitting expenses when women attended meetings. In the first case, the barrier to change is theorized as cultural tradition; in the second case, as institutional arrangements of child care. The first model sees culture as fixed; the second assumes that the meanings of gender will change as institutional and legal arrangements change.

...

... [C]ulture is as important in shaping human rights conferences as it is in structuring village mortuary rituals. Thinking of those peoples formerly labeled "backward" as the only bearers of culture neglects the centrality of culture to the practice of human rights. UN meetings are deeply shaped by a culture of transnational modernity, one that specifies procedures for collaborative decision-making, conceptions of global social justice, and definitions of gender roles. Human rights law is itself primarily a cultural system. Its limited enforcement mechanisms mean that the impact of human rights law is a matter of persuasion rather than force, of cultural transformation rather than coercive change. Its documents create new cultural frameworks for conceptualizing social justice. It is ironic that the human rights system tends to promote its new cultural vision through a critique of culture.

Vernacularization

In 1999, the American Anthropological Association adopted a Declaration on Anthropology and Human Rights that marked a deep change from its earlier position:

> As a professional organization of anthropologists, the AAA has long been, and should continue to be, concerned whenever human difference is made the basis for a denial of

---

[237] For a more recent analysis, see M. Thompson, 'What's Asia Got to Do with It? "Asian Values" as Reactionary Culturalism', in G. Facal, E. Lafaye de Micheaux, and A. Norén-Nilsson (eds.), *The Palgrave Handbook of Political Norms in Southeast Asia* (2024) 277.

basic human rights, where "human" is understood in its full range of cultural, social, linguistic, psychological, and biological senses.

[The AAA, in its working definition of principles of respect for difference, 'builds on' the UDHR and other basic human rights covenants and conventions.] The AAA definition thus reflects a commitment to human rights consistent with international principles but not limited by them. Human rights is not a static concept. Our understanding of human rights is constantly evolving as we come to know more about the human condition. It is therefore incumbent on anthropologists to be involved in the debate on enlarging our understanding of human rights on the basis of anthropological knowledge and research.[238]

In the years since, the concept of 'vernacularization' has come to prominence in the anthropological literature.[239] In the readings below, Sally Engle Merry and Peggy Levitt explain their understanding of the concept and how it works in practice. Harri Englund then describes the distortions introduced through linguistic translation in some African contexts.[240]

SALLY ENGLE MERRY AND PEGGY LEVITT, THE VERNACULARIZATION OF WOMEN'S HUMAN RIGHTS
STEPHEN HOPGOOD, JACK SNYDER AND LESLIE VINJAMURI (EDS.), HUMAN RIGHTS FUTURES (2017) 213

How do human rights travel around the world? They are created through diverse social movements in many parts of the world and crystallized into a form of symbolically universal law under the supervision of the UN and its human rights organizations. This law-like form is then reappropriated by myriad civil society organizations and translated into terms that make sense in their local communities. This is the process of vernacularization: the extraction of ideas and practices from the universal sphere of international organizations, and their translation into ideas and practices that resonate with the values and ways of doing things in local contexts. Local places are not empty, of course, but rich with other understandings of rights, the state, and justice. ...

The process of vernacularization converts universalistic human rights into local understandings of social justice. While considerable scholarship on human rights sees universalism and relativism as oppositional, vernacularization bridges this divide. A focus on this process follows the trend in the anthropology of law to examine human rights in practice, exploring how they circulate, how they are adopted and used, and what forms of resistance and opposition they encounter when they come into contact with other national or religious ideologies of social justice. In contrast to scholarship on the dissemination of human rights in other disciplines, anthropology offers insights into the transformation of meanings and practices within small social settings, highlighting aspects of its circulation and use that can be obscured by the focus on the state in international relations and legal scholarship. ...

...

Conclusions

... Human rights are only one set of ideas and approaches available to them. Some groups are deeply embedded in other justice ideologies, such as liberation theology or the feminist violence against women movement, and make only fleeting and indirect references to human rights. ...

... External funding, including international funding, offers more space to move into challenging issues and to engage in work that is relatively unsupported by local and national women's organizations and ideologies ... .
... The funding allows them greater latitude ... [but] comes with strings attached. ...

---

[238] www.aaanet.org/stmts/humanrts.htm.
[239] See generally, P. Alston (ed.), *Capturing the Complexity of Human Rights: From Vernacularization to Quantification* (2024).
[240] For an account of how the widely-used Chinese translation of the International Covenants changed the meaning of key terms by comparison with the original text, see J. Seymour and P. Yuk-tung Wong, 'China and the International Human Rights Covenants', 47 *Crit. Asian Stud.* (2015) 514.

What does the human rights framework offer in situations in which it does not have a strong resonance or a close fit with existing ideologies? It offers the legitimation of a transnational set of standards, the magic of a universal moral code, and technologies of building cases through reporting and documentation. But perhaps the most important contribution is access to allies outside the local community. By phrasing issues in the language of human rights, they become understandable to other organizations and individuals participating in this transnational ideological system. The human rights framework itself helps ideas travel. ...

...

Vernacularization is a process in which issues, communication technologies, and modes of organization and work are appropriated and translated, sometimes in fragmented and incoherent ways, at the interface of transnational, national, and local ideologies and practices. It is often a pragmatic strategy for mobilizing political, cultural, and financial resources. For some leaders, of course, human rights is a matter of faith and morality. Vernacularization is not a form of cultural homogenization since human rights ideas are substantially transformed by the organizations that use them. It is not a clash between universal principles and cultural relativist assertions of difference but a pragmatic process of negotiation and translation. When organizations talk little about human rights, this reflects a lack of political traction for human rights, not cultural relativist resistance. The process is a dimension of the partial, pragmatic, and unstable nature of the transnational circulation and adoption of ideas and practices that Tsing refers to as "friction," shaped by the structural conditions under which adoption and resistance take place.

However, the need to vernacularize human rights in a way that is resonant with local cultural practices serves as a limitation on the transformative power of human rights. ...

... Understanding the role of vernacularization in the human rights process highlights two dilemmas for human rights practitioners: the process of vernacularization may so attenuate the core principles of human rights that they no longer carry the meaning that is embedded in the system as a whole. Moreover, human rights as a frame of reference can be appropriated in a variety of ways, including those that violate the core principles of the human rights system itself. Nevertheless, such active appropriation and redefinition of human rights is an inevitable dimension of the global circulation of ideas and practices.

HARRI ENGLUND, PRISONERS OF FREEDOM: HUMAN RIGHTS AND THE AFRICAN POOR
(2006) 47

Translation in an African context presents a set of salient empirical problems, not least because the vast majority of Africans depend on national and vernacular languages for efficient communication. Human rights discourse, as a relatively recent phenomenon associated with the post-Cold War wave of democratization, has arrived through official languages inherited from colonial rulers. [M]ajor political and cultural issues are raised by the way in which the discourse is translated ... . Of fundamental importance is that translation in [Malawi and Zambia] has taken place as a "top-down" exercise, with no evidence of attempts to consult a broad cross-section of native speakers before launching a translation for human rights. "[L]ocal cultures of human rights" have been allowed little space to develop and to influence the introduction of a new discourse. Instead, activists, politicians, journalists, and others spearheading the translation have taken their particular interest in democratization as a universal concern. They have, accordingly, translated rights as freedoms, with a particular emphasis on political and civil liberties.

... Contemporary discussions about human rights, whatever the country or society in which they are held, are remarkable for the extent to which they presuppose abstraction, the ability to apply the same notions and principles across a wide variety of actual situations. ...

[T]he introduction of legal language ... replaces relationships with rules; situational considerations, with abstract principles. The distinction between the jural and the moral in some African languages is subverted in the post-Cold War preoccupation with human rights. The preoccupation has assumed a decisively legalist content. In contrast to the Kiswahili and Luganda understandings of rights as things that are associated with moral authority, itself unevenly distributed in society, the legalist discourse on human rights asserts universal equality before the law. As the supreme arbiter of conflicts and disputes, the law is regarded as being above any actual political and cultural factor influencing those conflicts and disputes. Interestingly, a similar process of abstraction has been observed among those who seek to oppose human rights discourse by appealing to cultures and traditions. Rather than situating culture in shifting everyday practices, "culture talk" often revolves around an abstraction that is claimed to define a people's essential characteristics. More often than not, and in postcolonial no less than in colonial Africa, such an abstraction serves elite privileges rather than the democratic expectations of rights talk.

[H]uman rights discourse even when asserting all individuals as equals can be deprived of its democratizing potential and made to serve particular interests in society. The problem, patently, is intrinsic not to particular words themselves but to translation as a cultural and political process, its own situational characteristics obscured by human rights activists' commitment to abstraction and universalism. In Chichewa, which is the sole national language of Malawi and, known as Chinyanja, one of the seven national languages of Zambia, the established translation summons up rights as individual freedoms a highly consequential, albeit scarcely premeditated, move. *Ufulu wachibadwidwe* hinges on the meanings of *ufulu* as "freedom," "liberty," and "independence," defined by the recent Chichewa/Chinyanja monolingual dictionary as "an opportunity to live freely, happily and witl1out fear'." The adjectival *wachibadwidwe* uses the verb *kubadwa*, "to be born," to specify such freedom as the individual's birth right.

Pascal Kishindo, a Malawian linguist, has suggested that, despite being offered as a translation of "human rights," *ufulu wachibadwidwe* is actually a new coinage. As such, the way in which Malawians and Zambians arrived at this particular coinage offers insights into the politics of translation, as do its appearances in the Chichewa/Chinyanja versions of international human rights documents and national laws. While pursuing such insights, one must keep in mind that *ufulu*, like most lexical items, has multiple connotations and can be used to advance competing interests. Kishindo has analyzed the shift in its primary connotations from national independence to personal freedom and liberty. Although *ufulu* continues to be used for independence from colonial rule, the transition to multiparty politics in the early 1990s made freedom from postcolonial dictatorship a more urgent topic in political discourse, with the plural form *maufulu*, "freedoms," gaining wider currency. Its equivalent in Kiswahili, *uhuru*, has had a similar trajectory, evident in its application by some women for transformed gender relations. Later in this chapter I examine, however, how the emancipatory potential of *ufulu* is qualified by, among other things, another central concept in the Chid1ewa/Chinyanja discourse on human rights *udindo*, translating as "responsibility:'

The idea of responsibility merits attention, because it has proven a convenient construct for human rights activists, politicians, and journalists to counter the criticisms of their excessive emphasis on individual freedoms. Just as the idea of freedom can be conjured up to advance different political agendas, so too is it necessary to ask what kind of responsibility a particular human rights discourse exhorts. Several generations of political philosophers have understood rights and responsibilities to be entwined, and liberal egalitarianism has not been confined to individual freedoms. It has involved a commitment to securing positive rights to economic justice.
…

…

Poor Translations for Poor People

… Translations into so-called local languages have provided one justification for many NGOs' existence, since the translations by government departments have generally been confined to very few documents. Translations have not, however, been a priority for most donors of aid, and the work of translation has often been linked to broader programs of civic education or, in the case of some organizations, abandoned in favor of other activities. One consequence of the lack of resources is the rather haphazard manner in which translations have been commissioned and carried out. …

By granting to themselves the tasks of both translation and its quality control, activists and officers risked producing inaccurate translations. Their assumed expertise, moreover, mitigated fears of a backlash, because those who were expected to receive the translations were rarely in a position to voice public criticism. In Malawi and Zambia, no mechanism existed to ensure that the translations were not as poor as the people who were supposed to read them. …

...

A comparison between different translations of the [UDHR] reveals even more clearly how Chichewa/Chinyanja speakers can be disempowered by inaccurate translation. In the absence of coordination, at least two very different translations of the declaration exist, one provided by the United Nations Information Centre in Zambia and the other by the Malawi Human Rights Resource Centre, an NGO. While somewhat abridged and simplified translations may be inevitable in a document meant for wide circulation, interesting questions are what translators omit from the original and how inaccurate translations may compromise readers' capacity for emancipatory interpretations. For instance, the subsection 4 of Article 23 reads,

> Everyone has the right to form and to join trade unions for the protection of his interests.

[The author's translation back into English of the Malawian translation is:]

> Everyone has the freedom to start or to join an organization that represents workers.

[His translation of the Zambian version is:]

> Every person has the opportunity to be a member of any organization that assists in his/her well-being.

...

[Article 22 UDHR reads:]

> Everyone, as a member of society, has the right to social security and is entitled to realization, through national effort and international co-operation and in accordance with the organization and resources of each State, of the economic, social, and cultural rights indispensable for his dignity and the free development of his personality.

[The author's translation back into English of the Malawian translation is:]

> Everyone has the freedom to get assistance from the state when well-being is undermined in accordance with the extent to which the state can assist, as well as the freedom of economic activity and of what helps him/her to foster respect, development in life and his/her humanity.

The Zambian version [translates as:]

> Every person as a citizen of a country has the opportunity to receive protection in improving his/her life, and he/she must understand his/her freedom in the economy, entertainment and customs, a thing that is very important in the good-ness and development of his/her life.

...

Controlling Freedoms

...

For ruling politicians and human rights activists in democratic Malawi, nostalgia for the one-party era was not an option. Instead, and despite major differences among themselves, they sought to dominate the public discourse by educating the populace on the concept of human rights. When she launched the Malawi Human Rights Youth Network in 2002, the presidential adviser on NGOs and civil society instructed her audience that "where one's rights end is where another one's rights begin. There is a tendency among the people to claim rights while impinging on other people's rights." Responsibility, *udindo* in Chichewa, came to complement the emphasis on rights as freedoms. ...

...

... By establishing a discourse confined to rights as freedoms, activists, politicians, and other self-proclaimed experts made it extremely difficult to express and pursue alternatives to the current disempowerment of the majority. As a proposed limitation to excess freedom, the concept of responsibility failed to provide an alternative, because it made individuals the responsible partners. As in abstract legalism in general, solutions to structural inequalities were thought to lie in the particular encounters of two or more aggrieved parties, preferably in a court of law. The solutions were, in brief, piecemeal, however profound and widespread the abuses.

Political history is a key context for the preoccupation with rights as freedoms. A tacit alliance between politicians and politically independent activists, as improbable as it was real, was a consequence of this history, centered on a public discourse on freedoms. The discourse was introduced to the general public through inaccurate translations, sometimes omitting those notions and provisions that could qualify the single-minded focus on freedoms. This process of disempowerment was, at least for most human rights activists, entirely unforeseen. Activists' own interest in political and civil rights, understandable for historical reasons, was instrumental to the way in which freedoms came to dominate the public discourse, never quite qualified by the notion of responsibility.

… [A] further factor in the entrenchment of the new discourse [was] the thinly veiled patronizing approach that enabled self-proclaimed experts to discount popular responses to their interventions. … [D]espite their personal frustrations with politics and the economy, young people were usually the ones who spread this disempowering discourse through so-called civic education. … [An] important factor in the entrenchment of the new discourse [was] the avoidance of overtly political issues by those donor agencies that fund NGOs and programs of civic education.

∗ ∗ ∗

The following materials explores cultural relativism from the perspective of Islam.[241] An-Na'im argues that 'human rights advocates in the Muslim world must work within the framework of Islam to be effective … [and] should struggle to have their interpretations of the relevant [Islamic] texts adopted as the new Islamic scriptural imperatives for the contemporary world.' Those interpretations would be broadly consistent with the norms of international human rights. An-Na'im is then attentive to the relation between the international system and a given religious tradition, and to the possibility of reconciliation through reinterpretation of the tradition, rather than through identification of cross-cultural values among different systems that in some sense transcend or trump aspects of the religious tradition that defy or are otherwise inconsistent with them. Adnan Zulfiqar, in 'Human Rights Norms from Below', 48 *Yale J. Int'l L.* (2023) 55, at 102, develops the link between Merry's approach and that of An-Na'im by suggesting that Islamic jurists use 'Islamic law as a local vernacular and … indigenize human rights norms by giving them greater moral credibility with target societies.'

ABDULLAHI AHMED AN-NA'IM, HUMAN RIGHTS IN THE MUSLIM WORLD
3 HARV. HUM. RTS. J. (1990) 13

Introduction

Historical formulations of Islamic religious law, commonly known as Shari'a, include a universal system of law and ethics and purport to regulate every aspect of public and private life. The power of Shari'a to regulate the behavior of Muslims derives from its moral and religious authority as well as the formal enforcement of its legal norms. As such, Shari'a influences individual and collective behavior in Muslim countries through its role in the socialization processes of such nations regardless of its status in their formal legal systems. For example, the status and rights of women in the Muslim world have always been significantly influenced by Shari'a, regardless of the degree of Islamization in public life. Of course, Shari'a is not the sole determinant of human behavior nor the only formative force behind social and political institutions in Muslim countries.
…
I conclude that human rights advocates in the Muslim world must work within the framework of Islam to be effective. They need not be confined, however, to the particular historical interpretations of Islam known as Shari'a. Muslims are obliged, as a matter of faith, to conduct their private and public affairs in accordance with

---

[241] See generally A. M. Ibrahim, 'A Not-So-Radical Approach to Human Rights in Islam', 96 *J. of Relig.* (2016) 346; and M. Bak McKenna, 'Feminism in Translation: Reframing Human Rights Law through Transnational Islamic Feminist Networks', in R. Gould and K. Tahmasebian (eds.), *The Routledge Handbook of Translation and Activism* (2020) 317.

the dictates of Islam, but there is room for legitimate disagreement over the precise nature of these dictates in the modern context. Religious texts, like all other texts, are open to a variety of interpretations. Human rights advocates in the Muslim world should struggle to have their interpretations of the relevant texts adopted as the new Islamic scriptural imperatives for the contemporary world.

A. Cultural Legitimacy for Human Rights

The basic premise of my approach is that human rights violations reflect the lack or weakness of cultural legitimacy of international standards in a society. Insofar as these standards are perceived to be alien to or at variance with the values and institutions of a people, they are unlikely to elicit commitment or compliance. While cultural legitimacy may not be the sole or even primary determinant of compliance with human rights standards, it is, in my view, an extremely significant one. Thus, the underlying causes of any lack or weakness of legitimacy of human rights standards must be addressed in order to enhance the promotion and protection of human rights in that society.

… This cultural illegitimacy, it is argued, derives from the historical conditions surrounding the creation of the particular human rights instruments. Most African and Asian countries did not participate in the formulation of the Universal Declaration of Human Rights because, as victims of colonization, they were not members of the United Nations. When they did participate in the formulation of subsequent instruments, they did so on the basis of an established framework and philosophical assumptions adopted in their absence. For example, the pre-existing framework and assumptions favored individual civil and political rights over collective solidarity rights, such as a right to development, an outcome which remains problematic today. Some authors have gone so far as to argue that inherent differences exist between the Western notion of human rights as reflected in the international instruments and non-Western notions of human dignity. In the Muslim world, for instance, there are obvious conflicts between Shari'a and certain human rights, especially of women and non-Muslims.

… In this discussion, I focus on the principles of legal equality and nondiscrimination contained in many human rights instruments. These principles relating to gender and religion are particularly problematic in the Muslim world.
…

II. Islam, Shari'a and Human Rights
…

A. The Development and Current Application of Shari'a

To the over nine hundred million Muslims of the world, the Qur'an is the literal and final word of God and Muhammad is the final Prophet. During his mission, from 610 A.D. to his death in 632 A.D., the Prophet elaborated on the meaning of the Qur'an and supplemented its rulings through his statements and actions. This body of information came to be known as Sunna. He also established the first Islamic state in Medina around 622 A.D. which emerged later as the ideal model of an Islamic state. …

While the Qur'an was collected and recorded soon after the Prophet Muhammad's death, it took almost two centuries to collect, verify, and record the Sunna. Because it remained an oral tradition for a long time during a period of exceptional turmoil in Muslim history, some Sunna reports are still controversial in terms of both their authenticity and relationship to the Qur'an.

Because Shari'a is derived from Sunna as well as the Qur'an, its development as a comprehensive legal and ethical system had to await the collection and authentication of Sunna. Shari'a was not developed until the second and third centuries of Islam. …
…
Shari'a is not a formally enacted legal code. It consists of a vast body of jurisprudence in which individual jurists express their views on the meaning of the Qur'an and Sunna and the legal implications of those views. Although most Muslims believe Shari'a to be a single logical whole, there is significant diversity of opinion not only among the various schools of thought, but also among the different jurists of a particular school. …

Furthermore, Muslim jurists were primarily concerned with the formulation of principles of Shari'a in terms of moral duties sanctioned by religious consequences rather than with legal obligations and rights and specific temporal remedies. They categorized all fields of human activity as permissible or impermissible and recommended or reprehensible. In other words, Shari'a addresses the conscience of the individual Muslim, whether in a private, or public and official, capacity, and not the institutions and corporate entities of society and the state.

...

Whatever may have been the historical status of Shari'a as the legal system of Muslim countries, the scope of its application in the public domain has diminished significantly since the middle of the nineteenth century. Due to both internal factors and external influence, Shari'a principles had been replaced by European law governing commercial, criminal, and constitutional matters in almost all Muslim countries. Only family law and inheritance continued to be governed by Shari'a. ...

Recently, many Muslims have challenged the gradual weakening of Shari'a as the basis for their formal legal systems. Most Muslim countries have experienced mounting demands for the immediate application of Shari'a as the sole, or at least primary, legal system of the land. These movements have either succeeded in gaining complete control, as in Iran, or achieved significant success in having aspects of Shari'a introduced into the legal system, as in Pakistan and the Sudan. Governments of Muslim countries generally find it difficult to resist these demands out of fear of being condemned by their own populations as anti-Islamic. Therefore, it is likely that this so-called Islamic fundamentalism will achieve further successes in other Muslim countries.

The possibility of further Islamization may convince more people of the urgency of understanding and discussing the relationship between Shari'a and human rights, because Shari'a would have a direct impact on a wider range of human rights issues if it became the formal legal system of any country. ...

I believe that a modern version of Islamic law can and should be developed. Such a modern 'Shari'a' could be, in my view, entirely consistent with current standards of human rights. These views, however, are appreciated by only a tiny minority of contemporary Muslims. To the overwhelming majority of Muslims today, Shari'a is the sole valid interpretation of Islam, and as such *ought* to prevail over any human law or policy.

B. Shari'a and Human Rights

In this part, I illustrate with specific examples how Shari'a conflicts with international human rights standards.
...
...

The second example is the Shari'a law of apostasy. According to Shari'a, a Muslim who repudiates his faith in Islam, whether directly or indirectly, is guilty of a capital offense punishable by death. This aspect of Shari'a is in complete conflict with the fundamental human right of freedom of religion and conscience. The apostasy of a Muslim may be inferred by the court from the person's views or actions deemed by the court to contravene the basic tenets of Islam and therefore be tantamount to apostasy, regardless of the accused's personal belief that he or she is a Muslim.

The Shari'a law of apostasy can be used to restrict other human rights such as freedom of expression. A person may be liable to the death penalty for expressing views held by the authorities to contravene the official view of the tenets of Islam. Far from being an historical practice or a purely theoretical danger, this interpretation of the law of apostasy was applied in the Sudan as recently as 1985, when a Sudanese Muslim reformer was executed because the authorities deemed his views to be contrary to Islam.

A third and final example of conflict between Shari'a and human rights relates to the status and rights of non-Muslims. Shari'a classifies the subjects of an Islamic state in terms of their religious beliefs: Muslims, *ahl al-Kitab* or believers in a divinely revealed scripture (mainly Christian and Jews), and unbelievers. In modern terms, Muslims are the only full citizens of an Islamic state, enjoying all the rights and freedoms granted by Shari'a and subject only to the limitations and restrictions imposed on women. *Ahl al-Kitab* are entitled to the status of *dhimma*, a special compact with the Muslim state which guarantees them security of persons and property and a degree of communal autonomy to practice their own religion and conduct their private affairs in accordance with their customs and laws. In exchange for these limited rights, *dhimmis* undertake to pay *jizya* or poll tax and submit to Muslim sovereignty and authority in all public affairs. ...

According to this scheme, non-Muslim subjects of an Islamic state can aspire only to the status of *dhimma*, under which they would suffer serious violations of their human rights. *Dhimmis* are not entitled to equality with Muslims. [Economic and family law illustrations omitted.]

...

IV. A Case Study: The Islamic Dimension of the Status of Women ...

The present focus on Muslim violations of the human rights of women does not mean that these are peculiar to the Muslim world. As a Muslim, however, I am particularly concerned with the situation in the Muslim world and wish to contribute to its improvement.

The following discussion is organized in terms of the status and rights of Muslim women in the private sphere, particularly within the family, and in public fora, in relation to access to work and participation in public affairs. This classification is recommended for the Muslim context because the personal law aspects of Shari'a, family law and inheritance, have been applied much more consistently than the public law doctrines.[242] The status and rights of women in private life have always been significantly influenced by Shari'a regardless of the extent of Islamization of the public debate.

A. Shari'a and the Human Rights of Women

... The most important general principle of Shari'a influencing the status and rights of women is the notion of *qawama*. *Qawama* has its origin in verse 4:34 of the Qur'an: 'Men have *qawama* [guardianship and authority] over women because of the advantage they [men] have over them [women] and because they [men] spend their property in supporting them [women]'. According to Shari'a interpretations of this verse, men as a group are the guardians of and superior to women as a group, and the men of a particular family are the guardians of and superior to the women of that family.

... For example, Shari'a provides that women are disqualified from holding general public office, which involves the exercise of authority over men, because, in keeping with the verse 4:34 of the Qur'an, men are entitled to exercise authority over women and not the reverse.

Another general principle of Shari'a that has broad implications for the status and rights of Muslim women is the notion of *al-hijab*, the veil. This means more than requiring women to cover their bodies and faces in public. According to Shari'a interpretations of verses 24:31, 33:33,[243] 33:53, and 33:59[244] of the Qur'an, women are supposed to stay at home and not leave it except when required to by urgent necessity. When they are permitted to venture beyond the home, they must do so with their bodies and faces covered. *Al-hijab* tends to reinforce women's inability to hold public office and restricts their access to public life. They are not supposed to participate in public life, because they must not mix with men even in public places.

... In family law for example, men have the right to marry up to four wives and the power to exercise complete control over them during marriage, to the extent of punishing them for disobedience if the men deem that to be necessary.[245] In contrast, the co-wives are supposed to submit to their husband's will and endure his

---

[242] The private/public dichotomy, however, is an artificial distinction. The two spheres of life overlap and interact. The socialization and treatment of both men and women at home affect their role in public life and vice versa. While this classification can be used for analysis in the Muslim context, its limitations should be noted. It is advisable to look for both the private and public dimensions of a given Shari'a principle or rule rather than assume that it has only private or public implications.

[243] [O Consorts of the Prophet ... .] And stay quietly in your houses, and make not a dazzling display, like that of the former Times of Ignorance; and establish regular prayer, and give regular charity; and obey God and His Apostle. And God only wishes to remove all abomination from you, ye Members of the Family, and to make you pure and spotless.

[244] O Prophet! Tell thy wives and daughters, and the believing women, that they should cast their outer garments over their persons (when abroad): that is most convenient, that they should be known (as such) and not molested. And God is Oft-Forgiving, Most Merciful.

[245] Polygamy is based on verse 4:3 of the Qur'an. The husband's power to chastise his wife to the extent of beating her is based on verse 4:34 of the Qur'an.

punishments. While a husband is entitled to divorce any of his wives at will, a wife is not entitled to a divorce, except by judicial order on very specific and limited grounds. Another private law feature of discrimination is found in the law of inheritance, where the general rule is that women are entitled to half the share of men.

In addition to their general inferiority under the principle of *qawama* and lack of access to public life as a consequence of the notion of *al-hijab*, women are subjected to further specific limitations in the public domain. For instance, in the administration of justice, Shari'a holds women to be incompetent witnesses in serious criminal cases, regardless of their individual character and knowledge of the facts. In civil cases where a woman's testimony is accepted, it takes two women to make a single witness. *Diya*, monetary compensation to be paid to victims of violent crimes or to their surviving kin, is less for female victims than it is for male victims.

... These overlapping and interacting principles and rules play an extremely significant role in the socialization of both women and men. Notions of women's inferiority are deeply embedded in the character and attitudes of both women and men from early childhood.
...

C. Muslim Women in Public Life

A similar and perhaps more drastic conflict exists between reformist and conservative trends in relation to the status and rights of women in the public domain. Unlike personal law matters, where Shari'a was never displaced by secular law, in most Muslim countries, constitutional, criminal, and other public law matters have come to be based on secular, mainly Western, legal concepts and institutions. Consequently, the struggle over Islamization of public law has been concerned with the re-establishment of Shari'a where it has been absent for decades, or at least since the creation of the modern Muslim nation states in the first half of the twentieth century. In terms of women's rights, the struggle shall determine whether women can keep the degree of equality and rights in public life they have achieved under secular constitutions and laws.
...

... Educated women and other modernist segments of society may not be able to articulate their vision of an Islamic state in terms of Shari'a, because aspects of Shari'a are incompatible with certain concepts and institutions which these groups take for granted, including the protection of all human rights. To the extent that efforts for the protection and promotion of human rights in the Muslim world must take into account the Islamic dimension of the political and sociological situation in Muslim countries, a modernist conception of Islam is needed.

V. Islamic Reform and Human Rights
...
Islamic reform needs must be based on the Qur'an and Sunna, the primary sources of Islam. Although Muslims believe that the Qur'an is the literal and final word of God, and Sunna are the traditions of his final Prophet, they also appreciate that these sources have to be understood and applied through human interpretation and action. ...

A. An Adequate Reform Methodology

... The basic premise of my position, based on the work of the late Sudanese Muslim reformer *Ustadh* Mahmoud Mohamed Taha, is that the Shari'a reflects a historically-conditioned interpretation of Islamic scriptures in the sense that the founding jurists had to understand those sources in accordance with their own social, economic, and political circumstances. In relation to the status and rights of women, for example, equality between men and women in the eighth and ninth centuries in the Middle East, or anywhere else at the time, would have been inconceivable and impracticable. It was therefore natural and indeed inevitable that Muslim jurists would understand the relevant texts of the Qur'an and Sunna as confirming rather than repudiating the realities of the day.

In interpreting the primary sources of Islam in their historical context, the founding jurists of Shari'a tended not only to understand the Qur'an and Sunna as confirming existing social attitudes and institutions, but also to emphasize certain texts and 'enact' them into Shari'a while de-emphasizing other texts or interpreting them in ways consistent with what they believed to be the intent and purpose of the sources. Working with the same primary sources, modern Muslim jurists might shift emphasis from one class of texts to the other, and interpret the previously enacted texts in ways consistent with a new understanding of what is believed to be the intent and purpose of the sources. This new understanding would be informed by contemporary social, economic, and political circumstances in the same way that the 'old' understanding on which Shari'a jurists acted was informed by the then prevailing circumstances. The new understanding would qualify for Islamic legitimacy, in my view, if it is based on specific texts in opposing the application of other texts, and can be shown to be in accordance with the Qur'an and Sunna as a whole.

For example, the general principle of *qawama*, the guardianship and authority of men over women under Shari'a, is based on verse 4:34 of the Qur'an.

… This verse presents *qawama* as a consequence of two conditions: men's advantage over and financial support of women. The fact that men are generally physically stronger than most women is not relevant in modern times where the rule of law prevails over physical might. Moreover, modern circumstances are making the economic independence of women from men more readily realized and appreciated. In other words, neither of the conditions — advantages of physical might or earning power — set by verse 4:34 as the justification for the *qawama* of men over women is tenable today.

The fundamental position of the modern human rights movement is that all human beings are equal in worth and dignity, regardless of gender, religion, or race. This position can be substantiated by the Qur'an and other Islamic sources as understood under the radically transformed circumstances of today. For example, in numerous verses the Qur'an speaks of honor and dignity for 'humankind' and 'children of Adam', without distinction as to race, color, gender, or religion. By drawing on those sources and being willing to set aside archaic and dated interpretations of other sources, such as the one previously given to verse 4:34 of the Qur'an, we can provide Islamic legitimacy for the full range of human rights for women.

Similarly, numerous verses of the Qur'an provide for freedom of choice and non-compulsion in religious belief and conscience.[246] These verses have been either de-emphasized as having been 'overruled' by other verses which were understood to legitimize coercion, or 'interpreted' in ways which permitted such coercion. For example, verse 9:29 of the Qur'an was taken as the foundation of the whole system of *dhimma*, and its consequent discrimination against non-Muslims. Relying on those verses which extol freedom of religion rather than those that legitimize religious coercion, one can argue now that the *dhimma* system should no longer be part of Islamic law and that complete equality should be assured regardless of religion or belief. The same argument can be used to abolish all negative legal consequences of apostasy as inconsistent with the Islamic principle of freedom of religion. [Discussion omitted of mechanisms and methods within Islam for development and reform.]

… The ultimate test of legitimacy and efficacy is, of course, acceptance and implementation by Muslims throughout the world.

B. Prospects for Acceptance and Likely Impact of the Proposed Reform …

… Governments of Muslim countries, like many other governments, formally subscribe to international human rights instruments because, in my view, they find the human rights idea an important legitimizing force both at home and abroad … .

Nevertheless, the proposed reform will probably be resisted because it challenges the vested interests of powerful forces in the Muslim world and may upset male-dominated traditional political and social institutions. These forces probably will try to restrict opportunities for a genuine consideration of this reform methodology. …

---

[246] See, for example, verse 2:256 of the Qur'an which provides: 'Let there be no compulsion in religion: Truth stands out clear from error … .' In verse 18:29 God instructs the Prophet: 'Say, the Truth is from your Lord. Let him who will, believe, and let him who will, reject [it]'.

Consequently, the acceptance and implementation of this reform methodology will involve a political struggle within Muslim nations as part of a larger general struggle for human rights. I would recommend this proposal to participants in that struggle who champion the cause of justice and equality for women and non-Muslims, and freedom of belief and expression in the Muslim world. Given the extreme importance of Islamic legitimacy in Muslim societies, I urge human rights advocates to claim the Islamic platform and not concede it to the traditionalist and fundamentalist forces in their societies. I would also invite outside supporters of Muslim human rights advocates to express their support with due sensitivity and genuine concern for Islamic legitimacy in the Muslim world.

...

* * *

In a recent comment, Mohammad Fadel, in 'Muslim Modernism, Islamic Law, and the Universality of Human Rights', 36 *Emory Int'l L. Rev.* (2022) 713 characterizes An-Na'im's work:

> ... as an attempt to reconcile one's specific commitments ... arising out of being a Sudanese, African-Arab Sunni male-with the universal commitments arising out of being a member of humanity. At different times, An-Na'im offered various strategies to accomplish this reconciliation. One strategy was to propose a radical inversion of those elements of Quranic and Islamic teachings that Muslims should deem universally authoritative ... . [Another took] an institutional perspective: a secular state, committed to religious neutrality, could create the political space within which individual Muslims could work out freely for themselves different ways to reconcile their particular commitments with universal ones.

> ... [His] call for a cross-cultural approach to human rights remains salient more than a quarter century after he first articulated it. Muslims, in particular, find their human rights threatened by both non-Muslim states, whether authoritarian (e.g., China) or militantly secular/democratic (e.g., France), and authoritarian Muslim-majority states (e.g., Egypt). Despite the disparate political and economic systems of these different regimes, they are united by a profound hostility to assertions made by Muslims of rights that others take for granted; such hostility rests on the claim that by exercising their rights in a manner inconsistent with the state's wishes, Muslims are acting in a manner contrary to the public order. Some of this hostility could be mitigated by a clearer articulation of Islamic legal principles and their presentation in a language that does not make them seem incommensurate with the rules of international human rights law. ...

Abdullahi Ahmed An-Naim subsequently elaborated on his overall approach in *Decolonizing Human Rights* (2021) 123:

> In conclusion, [my] core propositions ... can be summarized as follows. Any expectation of legal enforcement of universal human rights (not just those that happen to be protected under domestic law as the civil rights of citizens) by any nation-state is a ruthless mirage. Any outcome that can be expected of the legal protection of human rights by the state is unsustainable in practice unless it is accepted and internalized as an indigenous norm by the people concerned. Conversely, any human rights norms that are accepted and internalized by people in their communities will be predominantly upheld in their own daily practice, and states can enjoy the voluntary cooperation of their populations when enforcing the right in exceptional cases of violation. This is already happening for many human rights norms in the daily practice of communities everywhere, but the current international advocacy regime is exclusively focused on violations because the survival of the current system of institutionalized monitors is totally dependent on the existence of violations, not the reality of compliance.

> The paradigm shift and strategy I am calling for is to focus on making compliance with human rights the constant daily norm in our interpersonal and intracommunal relations, the socialization of our children, and the organization of our social institutions. There is simply no alternative to reliance on habitual conformity if we are to have the human and

material resources and political will to enforce human rights norms in the rare and exceptional instances of their violation. This strategy may sound difficult or time-consuming, but it is in fact the fastest, most effective, and most sustainable way of protecting human rights as the rights of every human being, everywhere, all the time. Whoever seeks to protect any human right among any people should immediately begin to work within that community to promote that norm through cultural transformation and political mobilization. That is how norms that can produce the spontaneous practice of gender equality and religious pluralism can be entrenched and expanded.

Comments on Cultural Relativism

Consider the following observations:

Rosalyn Higgins, *Problems and Process: International Law and How We Use It* (1994), at 96:

> It is sometimes suggested that there can be no fully universal concept of human rights, for it is necessary to take into account the diverse cultures and political systems of the world. In my view this is a point advanced mostly by states, and by liberal scholars anxious not to impose the Western view of things on others. It is rarely advanced by the oppressed, who are only too anxious to benefit from perceived universal standards. The non-universal, relativist view of human rights is in fact a very state-centred view and loses sight of the fact that human rights are human rights and not dependent on the fact that states, or groupings of states, may behave differently from each other so far as their politics, economic policy, and culture are concerned. I believe, profoundly, in the universality of the human spirit. Individuals everywhere want the same essential things: to have sufficient food and shelter; to be able to speak freely; to practise their own religion or to abstain from religious belief; to feel that their person is not threatened by the state; to know that they will not be tortured, or detained without charge, and that, if charged, they will have a fair trial. I believe there is nothing in these aspirations that is dependent upon culture, or religion, or stage of development. They are as keenly felt by the African tribesman as by the European city-dweller, by the inhabitant of a Latin American shanty-town as by the resident of a Manhattan apartment.

Louise Arbour, UN High Commissioner for Human Rights, Statement to the UN Commission on Human Rights (14 March 2005):

> I am ... concerned that we have unduly embroiled our normative discourse in unnecessary clashes of vision, creating competing images, each incomplete and ineffective without the addition of the other. Are human rights universal or culturally specific? Are they collectively or individually held? Should we promote them, or protect them? Which is the more effective: technical cooperation or naming and shaming; country analysis or thematic debates? Which comes first: peace or justice; economic, social and cultural rights, or civil and political rights; development or democracy?
>
> Such questions serve, in practice, as little more than a series of diversions to the real task in hand. They become the theoretical playground within which we demonstrate our irrelevance and justify our inaction, whether than inaction is borne of indifference, shrewd calculation, or despair.

Judge Bonello, Concurring Opinion in *Al-Skeini v. United Kingdom* (European Court of Human Rights, Grand Chamber, Application No. 55721/07 (7 July 2011)), which concerned the issue of whether UK obligations under the European Convention on Human Rights applied to certain actions of its troops in Iraq:

> 37. I confess to be quite unimpressed by the pleadings of the United Kingdom Government to the effect that exporting the European Convention on Human Rights to Iraq would have amounted to "human rights imperialism". It ill behoves a State that

imposed its military imperialism over another sovereign State without the frailest imprimatur from the international community, to resent the charge of having exported human rights imperialism to the vanquished enemy. It is like wearing with conceit your badge of international law banditry, but then recoiling in shock at being suspected of human rights promotion.

38. Personally, I would have respected better these virginal blushes of some statesmen had they worn them the other way round. Being bountiful with military imperialism but bashful of the stigma of human rights imperialism, sounds to me like not resisting sufficiently the urge to frequent the lower neighbourhoods of political inconstancy. For my part, I believe that those who export war ought to see to the parallel export of guarantees against the atrocities of war. And then, if necessary, bear with some fortitude the opprobrium of being labelled human rights imperialists.

QUESTIONS

1. What are the advantages and risks of understanding human rights promotion as a process of vernacularization?

2. An-Na'im suggests an approach to the questions of how to understand divergences among cultures with respect to human rights issues and how to go about finding common ground. How would you describe that approach? Exogenous, endogenous, or some mix? Does it appear helpful in resolving contemporary disputes over, say, gender discrimination or capital punishment? Do Merry's observations about culture and modes of cultural change support or call into question An-Na'im's project?

B. DISSONANCE AND CONFLICT: ILLUSTRATIONS

Against the background of Chapters 6 and 7(A), with their examination of rights discourse and presentation of different perspectives on universalism and cultural relativism, this Part explores four human rights issues now in contention and active debate among and within countries.

In the illustrations below, two different phenomena become central to the debate: (1) The asserted universal norm *itself* may be challenged, perhaps on the ground that it lacks universal validity, or that it conflicts with ultimate religious commands, or that it violates long-standing tradition that assures cultural integrity and survival. This chapter's illustrations contain examples of these kinds of arguments to further develop the theme of cultural relativism. (2) The second phenomenon involves a conflict among different rights that are each recognized to some extent in the leading human rights instruments. The dispute is sometimes related to cultural relativism and sometimes distinct, but is formally internal to the human rights corpus. What, for example, are the respective boundaries of rights that in given contexts squarely conflict with each other? Freedom of religious belief and practice may conflict with non-discrimination norms; freedom of speech may conflict with the protection of minority groups. As materials in Chapter 6(A) made clear, such types of conflict are endemic to rights discourse, as they are to law in general.

Several of the following illustrations concern family, gender and religion — interrelated topics that have characterized much discussion of the last decade about cultural relativism and that often involve conflicting rights. Thus the studies examine gender and family in relation to a state's or ethnic group's internal custom, or in relation to religion.

The problems discussed in this chapter have become acute within many developing countries. In recent decades, such countries experienced strong external and internal pressures to rethink and revise, sometimes radically, their traditional beliefs and practices. The relentless assault of the developed world on other cultures, the penetration of those cultures by trade, investment, high-tech media and tourism, as well as the universalization of ideas and values like human rights, have launched transformative processes that are often referred to under the broad rubric of globalization. The challenge to a state or region's traditional ways and to other state practices that depart from the universal human rights instruments increasingly comes from internal groups as well as from international advocates and organizations. The upheavals in Arab countries following the Arab Spring provide but one striking illustration in that regard. Women played an important part in the demonstrations that brought down the Mubarak government, but it has been estimated that 90 percent of married women in Egypt have been subjected to female genital mutilation. Virginity tests were applied to women arrested in the pro-democracy demonstrations, and the Egyptian Criminal Code (Section 60) states that 'no punitive damages can be obtained if the woman has been beaten by her husband with good intentions'. In 2019, the Grand Imam of al-Azhar, the highest religious law authority in Egypt ruled that 'beating a woman is permitted, but is not obligatory. It is permitted in order to confront the rebellious woman and to break her arrogance and in order to protect the family from loss and dissolution.'

1. Gender

The potential for conflict in a large number of states between the objectives of human rights treaties, on the one hand, and customary laws and practices as well as religious beliefs on the other, is a highly contested terrain. Gender-related issues are prominent here, as many traditional norms and much local custom that retain power and influence today impose different roles and duties on men and women. To some extent, such problems stem from the increasing power and prominence in recent years of fundamentalist religious groups, many of which actively oppose the transformative impetus of human rights with respect to traditional gender roles.

Customary laws and practices may conflict with prohibitions in the text of the ICCPR and CEDAW or in action taken by the relevant treaty bodies. Recall Articles 2(f) and 5(a) of CEDAW that require states to take all appropriate measures to modify or abolish customs, practices and social and cultural patterns of conduct that constitute discrimination or that are based on the idea of inferiority or on stereotyped roles for women.

Writing almost three decades ago, Tracy Higgins, in 'Anti-Essentialism, Relativism, and Human Rights', 19 *Harvard Women's L. J.* (1996) 89, concluded that:

> Confronted with the challenge of cultural relativism, feminism faces divergent paths, neither of which seems to lead out of the woods of patriarchy. The first path, leading to simple tolerance of cultural difference, is too broad. To follow it would require feminists to ignore pervasive limits on women's freedom in the name of an autonomy that exists for women in theory only.

> The other path, leading to objective condemnation of cultural practices, is too narrow. To follow it would require feminists to dismiss the culturally distinct experiences of women as false consciousness. Yet to forge an alternative path is difficult, requiring feminists to confront the risks inherent in global strategies for change.

> Building upon women's shared experiences inevitably entails a risk of misdescription, or worse, cooptation but contains the promise of transforming and radicalizing women's understanding of their own condition. Emphasizing difference threatens to splinter women politically, undermining hard-won progress, but may simultaneously uncover new possibilities for re-creating gender relations. Forging a combined strategy that respects both commonality and difference requires feminists to acknowledge that we cannot eliminate the risk of coercion altogether, but the risk of inaction is also ever present.

This section begins with two readings that consider the complexity of developing feminist perspectives on human rights related to gender, problems that bear on the following case studies. It then explores a practice that is variously referred to, with strikingly different political and moral innuendo and sometimes agendas, as female circumcision, female genital cutting, or female genital mutilation.

SINDISO MNISI AND ANINKA CLAASSENS, RURAL WOMEN REDEFINING LAND RIGHTS IN THE CONTEXT OF LIVING CUSTOMARY LAW
25 S. AF. J. HUM. RTS. 9 (2009) 491

I Introduction

Women's rights activists and lawyers in Africa have tended to treat the customary arena as inherently dangerous to women's interests, pointing to the frequency and regularity with which the discourse of the customary is used to disempower women and bolster patriarchal interests. Anne Whitehead and Dzodzi Tsikata conclude that there are 'simply too many examples of women losing out when modern African men talk of custom'. In this context, strategies to secure women's land rights in Africa have tended to avoid the customary law arena in favour of formal legal initiatives such as the registration of joint land titles for both spouses.

However, these legal strategies have also proven to be problematic. Titling programmes are often captured by elites and used to entrench the position of those with formal rights (mostly men) at the expense of overlapping 'secondary' entitlements vesting in women, especially unmarried women. Further, strategies that focus on attaining individual ownership for women have been criticised as relevant only to small numbers of middle class women and for failing to articulate with the concerns of women whose survival is embedded within a web of reciprocal family and community relationships, for whom the protection and preservation of the land rights vesting in the family or group may be a priority. Furthermore, legal strategies that focus exclusively on the creation of a 'formal' statutory property regime separate from the customary arena fail to come to grips with the fact that in South Africa many of the most serious land-related problems facing women exist at the interface between distorted custom and past colonial and apartheid statute law. Customary entitlements to land vesting in women are rendered invisible to the formal legal system even in instances where women continue to use and occupy the land in question. For many women living in rural areas, the only means of countering threatened evictions lies in asserting use and occupation rights derived from customary entitlements that are at odds with overlaid 'formal' legal rights held by men. Legal strategies that seek to avoid the customary arena may unwittingly remove the ground from under the feet of those women for whom customary entitlements are the best or only basis on which to assert or prove land rights. Moreover, they ignore the fact that the women concerned are entitled to have their rights recognised through a system of law that the Constitution recognises as legitimate, and to demand that they have a say in how this system of law develops.

To outline the shortcomings of statutory reforms that focus on providing land titles as the 'solution' is not to deny that the discourse of the customary is fraught with serious dangers for women. ...
...

II Challenging the Assumptions Underlying the 'Rights' and 'Custom' Dichotomy

The popular discourse counter-posing rights and culture is mirrored by an academic discourse that contrasts 'universalism' and 'cultural relativism'. The two poles of universalism and cultural relativism have been debunked as false opposites which obscure more than they clarify ... .
...
International political agendas coincide with these debates. At one extreme, liberal human rights agendas are used to justify invasion of other countries. At the other is the practice of countries refusing to endorse equality provisions on the basis that they conflict with local custom or group identity which must be protected from 'western influence'. ...

[Based on relevant] studies, several critiques are particularly pertinent to our discussion of women's land rights and customary law. First, the bounded group identities and closed 'cultures' posited by the cultural relativists have been subject to recurrent challenge. This characterisation of culture leads to essentialism and belies the ongoing processes of contestation, change and adaptation that occur within and between cultures. It ignores the fact that there are no longer (if ever there were) bounded cultures circumscribing people's life experience.

Cultural relativists tend to privilege static versions of custom that deny competing, internal constructs advanced by marginalised groups who often employ rights claims in their struggles for change.

Universalists, on the other hand, are critiqued for essentialising the content of human rights. The content of rights has been shown to be variable and subject to constant re-negotiation at all levels of society, including within the jurisprudence of different countries and international instruments. Once the content of rights is recognised as the outcome of context-specific processes, claims of universalism need to be tempered by the recognition of the context- specific processes in which rights are claimed, negotiated, adjudicated, developed and re-defined.

Perhaps the most pragmatic criticism of both universalism and relativism is couched in legal pluralism. The argument here is that both sides fail to take into account the plural legal contexts in which people invoke rights claims (whether to individual or cultural rights) in most societies, and in post-colonial and post-socialist societies in particular. In the context of overlapping international instruments, state law, informal local law and customary regimes, people tend to 'mix and match', drawing on whichever authority, law or 'right' best advances their specific interests in those instances. Implicit in the pluralist position is that claims are forged at the interface between overlapping systems of law and custom which combine the 'imported' and the local, the formal and the informal. Hence, nowhere can 'rights' or custom be said to exist or operate in isolation from the other.
…

DIANNE OTTO, FEMINIST APPROACHES TO INTERNATIONAL LAW
ANNE ORFORD AND FLORIAN HOFFMANN (EDS.), THE OXFORD HANDBOOK OF THE THEORY OF INTERNATIONAL LAW (2016) 488

…
2. Visions

… [F]or many feminists, the vision of women's inclusion and equality in the existing social and legal order is inadequate. Their ambitions are more transformative, seeking to challenge the masculinist ways of thinking that are embedded in the underlying templates that determine what equality and inclusion look like, discursively and in practice. … A well-worn method of representing [feminism's multiple genealogies] is to identify various genres of feminist legal scholarship, in terms of their philosophical and political commitments. In international law, these taxonomies usually adopt 'liberal' feminism as their starting point, moving on to describe other genres generationally as, in various ways, responses to the limitations of liberalism like: 'radical' and 'cultural' feminisms which focus on women's subordination (rather than inequality) as the foundational site of oppression; 'Marxist' and 'socialist' feminisms which centre attention on the exploitation of women's economic and reproductive labour; 'critical race' and 'postcolonial' feminisms which position sex/gender as one of multiple intersecting axes of oppression in the larger context of imperial power; and 'post-structural' and 'queer' feminisms which understand the identities and practices associated with gender and sexuality as fluid and multiple, rather than naturally determined and dualistic.

Elements from several of these approaches are likely to be found in most feminist projects in international law; although there is no doubt that radical feminist ideas have been very influential in recent years. This influence has focused attention on women's sexual subordination and victimhood, making many feminists uncomfortable because it has had the paradoxical effect of granting new legitimacy to long-standing protective gender tropes, rather than challenging them. While identifying the dominant strand(s) informing any particular feminist intervention is empowering and critical knowledge, it is often more useful to think of feminist ideas in international law as operating as a network, aspects of which are drawn upon depending on politics, history, context, strategy, and goals, rather than as parallel sets of ideas that function in isolation from or opposition to each other—although they can do this as well, and sometimes with paralyzing effects, as with opposing feminist views about whether prostitution should be regulated as work or criminalized as violence against women. While such internal feminist debates foster the critical self-reflection that is part of the life-blood of feminism, it is important to work against the stasis that understanding feminism in terms of competing strands installs. It is more useful, and apt, to think of feminist approaches to international law as a shifting and contested network of ideas and allegiances that, in seeking to make sex/ gender a central analytical category, draw on multiple and sometimes competing feminist perspectives and engage with other critical traditions in law. …

My search for more detail about the feminist visions of the future—feminist utopias, if you like—that have informed feminists' engagements with international law has not been very fruitful. While the starting point is usually the desire to change women's disadvantaged position vis-à-vis men around the world, there are many ways that a feminist might go about promoting such change … . For some, the project is to realize the liberal humanist promises of universality and equality, while for others it is to struggle against neoliberal economic globalization and its deeply gendered inequitable effects. For some, the primary subject of feminist analysis is women, while for others the feminist subject includes women, men, and all other sex/gender identities, and for yet others she is an intersectionally constituted subject located in her specific history, especially her colonial history, and the many other vectors of disadvantage that have an influence on her situation, such as race, caste, indigeneity, sexuality, and economic status. However, even this does not exhaust the possible subjects of feminism, as gender is also an analytical system that attributes value to objects and ideas that have little or no relationship at all with sexed bodies and identities. In this approach, the subject of feminism is the entire discursive framework of international law, and the task is to reveal its reliance on gendered signs to order ways of thinking that legitimate and normalize an inequitable world order and then to radically reconstruct its entire conceptual framework. …

… In what ways sex/gender would matter in a reimagined feminist world is an open question. …

Female Genital Mutilation/Cutting (FGM/C)

Since the late 1970s, when an American feminist, Fran P. Hosken, published *The Hosken Report: Genital and Sexual Mutilation of Females*, and began the process of replacing discussions of female circumcision with an uncompromising condemnation of female genital mutilation, efforts to eliminate this practice have been surrounded by controversy. In 1983, for example, the Association of African Women for Research and Development endorsed a fight against FGM, but roundly criticized the 'crusade of the West' that derived from 'the moral and cultural prejudices of Judeo-Christian Western society'. '[T]he new crusaders have fallen back on sensationalism, and have become insensitive to the dignity of the very women they want to 'save'. They are totally unconscious of the latent racism which such a campaign evokes in countries where ethnocentric prejudice is so deep-rooted.'[247]

In 2012, Nigerian-American writer Teju Cole raised a similar critique in response to the efforts of Invisible Children, an American NGO, to mobilize outrage at human rights violations committed by Joseph Kony's Lord's Resistance Army in Uganda. In a series of tweets that went viral, he observed that: '… the fastest growth industry in the US is the White Savior Industrial Complex'; and that '[t]he white savior supports brutal policies in the morning, founds charities in the afternoon, and receives awards in the evening'.[248]

FGM/C first emerged on the UN agenda in 1983, when the Sub-Commission on the Prevention of Discrimination and Protection of Minorities called for a study. In the same year the Sub-Commission set up a Working Group, including participants from UNICEF, UNESCO, and WHO, to study 'traditional practices affecting the health of women and children'. In 1990, the Commission on Human Rights appointed a Special Rapporteur on traditional practices. Her final report was submitted only in 2005.[249] In 1997, WHO, UNICEF, and the United Nations Population Fund (UNFPA) adopted a policy opposing FGM. The 2024 version of WHO's policy (below) identifies four types of FGM, and this typology is now widely used around the world. The OHCHR has expressed concern that efforts to eliminate FGM have led to a major increase in instances of 'cross-border and transnational' FGM (UN Doc. A/HRC/56/29 (2024).

UN human rights treaty bodies, and notably the Special Rapporteur on violence against women, have also taken a strong stand against FGM, as illustrated below in the report by the CEDAW Committee. For its part, the UN

[247] M. Davies (ed.), *Third World-Second Sex: Women's Struggles and National Liberation* (1983), at 217.
[248] See T. Cole, 'The White-Savior Industrial Complex', *The Atlantic* (21 March 2012).
[249] See generally, J. Pace, *The United Nations Commission on Human Rights: 'A Very Great Enterprise'* (2020) 205-9; and R. Khosla et al., 'Gender Equality and Human Rights Approaches to Female Genital Mutilation: A Review of International Human Rights Norms and Standards,' 14 *Reprod. Health* (2017) 59.

Human Rights Council first condemned the practice in 2013. In its Resolution 44/16 (2020), entitled 'Elimination of female genital mutilation', the Council:

>   …
>
>   2. Urges States to condemn all harmful practices that affect women and girls, in particular protect women and girls from this form of violence;
>
>   3. Also urges States to ensure the protection of and provision of support to women and girls subjected to, or at risk of, female genital mutilation and to address the underlying systemic and structural causes in which the harmful practice is rooted …;
>
>   4. Further urges States to ensure that national action plans and strategies on the prevention and elimination of female genital mutilation are adequately resourced and include projected timelines for goals and incorporate clear targets and indicators … ;
>
>   5. Encourages States to put in place national coordination mechanisms to prevent and eliminate female genital mutilation …;
>
>   …

WORLD HEALTH ORGANIZATION, FEMALE GENITAL MUTILATION – FACT SHEET, 5 FEBRUARY 2024

Female genital mutilation (FGM) comprises all procedures that involve partial or total removal of the external female genitalia, or other injury to the female genital organs for non-medical reasons. The practice has no health benefits for girls and women and cause severe bleeding and problems urinating, and later cysts, infections, as well as complications in childbirth and increased risk of newborn deaths.

The practice of FGM is recognized internationally as a violation of the human rights of girls and women. It reflects deep-rooted inequality between the sexes and constitutes an extreme form of discrimination against girls and women. It is nearly always carried out by traditional practitioners on minors and is a violation of the rights of children. The practice also violates a person's rights to health, security and physical integrity; the right to be free from torture and cruel, inhuman or degrading treatment; and the right to life, in instances when the procedure results in death. In several settings, there is evidence suggesting greater involvement of health care providers in performing FGM due to the belief that the procedure is safer when medicalized. WHO strongly urges health care providers not to perform FGM and has developed a global strategy and specific materials to support health care providers against medicalization.

Types of FGM

Female genital mutilation is classified into 4 major types.

Type 1: … the partial or total removal of the clitoral glans …, and/or the prepuce/ clitoral hood … .
Type 2: … the partial or total removal of the clitoral glans and the labia minora …, with or without removal of the labia majora … .
Type 3: …infibulation … the narrowing of the vaginal opening through the creation of a covering seal. …
Type 4: … all other harmful procedures to the female genitalia for non-medical purposes, e.g. pricking, piercing, incising, scraping and cauterizing the genital area.

No health benefits, only harm

FGM has no health benefits, and it harms girls and women in many ways. It involves removing and damaging healthy and normal female genital tissue, and it interferes with the natural functions of girls' and women's bodies.
…

Immediate complications can include: [severe pain; excessive bleeding (haemorrhage); genital tissue swelling; fever; infections, e.g. tetanus; urinary problems; wound healing problems; injury to surrounding genital tissue; shock; death].

Long-term complications can include: [urinary, vaginal, menstrual, and sexual problems; increased risk of childbirth complications and newborn deaths; need for later surgeries; psychological problems (depression, anxiety, post-traumatic stress disorder, low self-esteem, etc.)].

Who is at risk?

FGM is mostly carried out on young girls between infancy and adolescence, and occasionally on adult women. According to available data from 30 countries where FGM is practiced in the western, eastern, and north-eastern regions of Africa, and some countries in the Middle East and Asia, more than 200 million girls and women alive today have been subjected to the practice with more than 3 million girls estimated to be at risk of FGM annually. FGM is therefore of global concern.

…

INQUIRY CONCERNING MALI UNDER ARTICLE 8 OF THE OPTIONAL PROTOCOL TO THE CONVENTION ON THE ELIMINATION OF ALL FORMS OF DISCRIMINATION AGAINST WOMEN
UN DOC. CEDAW/C/IR/MLI/1 (24 DECEMBER 2019)

[The 'sources' that requested the Committee to undertake an inquiry alleged that FGM was widespread in Mali. After the State Party consented to the inquiry, three members of the Committee visited Mali for 12 days in December 2018. That year, Mali was ranked 182nd out of 189 countries on the Human Development Index, had a literacy rate of 24.6 percent for women, compared with 44.8 percent for men. The country was also 'characterized by an upsurge in gender-based violence against women, low representation and participation of women in decision-making forums, and the absence of women from the peace process and the process of national reconciliation'.

In 2015 the prevalence of FGM stood 'at 82.7 per cent among women aged from 15 to 49 years and 76.4 per cent among girls aged from 0 to 14 years. …The prevalence among girls was the highest in West Africa in 2017 and exceeded the subregional average of 25.4 per cent.' While there was considerable variation among ethnic groups and religions, there was little difference according to urban/rural location or socioeconomic status. The breakdown according to WHO's typology was: Type II: 48.9 percent of women aged from 15 to 49 years; Type IV, 14.6 percent; and Type III, 10.6 percent. 73 percent of women were subjected to genital mutilation in early childhood and only 0.4 percent at the age of 15 years or over.]

…

2. Sociocultural context and gender stereotyping

21. In the State party, 71 per cent of women and 66 per cent of men aged from 15 to 49 years state that female genital mutilation is a practice required by religion. Religious leaders, during a debate on the subject of female genital mutilation in Mopti in 2010, condemned the most severe forms of excision and affirmed their willingness to debate the issue further with stakeholders. [The government and] the National Human Rights Commission, however, emphasized the socioeconomic nature of the practice. Nonetheless, the Committee notes the persistence among religious leaders of a tendency to defend female genital mutilation and assert the mandatory nature of the practice. It also notes that the lack of knowledge of religious texts has an impact on the belief in a link between the practice and religion.

22. In Mopti, religious leaders said that female genital mutilation was a way of controlling women's sexual activity. [Some] said that a girl who had not undergone genital mutilation was seen as bringing shame on the family, and there is a belief in some quarters that having sexual relations with a woman who has not undergone genital mutilation causes impotence in the man.

23. One victim … explained that, once she had undergone genital mutilation, her family had welcomed her as a "woman". [Some] religious leaders … said that genital mutilation was necessary in order to purify a woman in preparation for marriage. [An NGO] confirmed that families feared that their daughters would not find a husband if they had not undergone genital mutilation.

…

25. … [T]he head of the extended family, usually a man, was the one who decided whether the girls were to be subjected to genital mutilation, highlighting the fact that his authority took precedence over that of the parents, who generally went along with the decision.

…

[The Committee concluded that the State party had made many efforts to prevent FGM, including implementing policies and programmes and establishing structures and bodies focused on prevention and awareness raising. But the results had been poor, insufficient resources had been made available, awareness-raising efforts had not been well targeted, and public awareness of FGM's harmful effects was very low. Attempts to legislate against FGM had been thwarted by religious leaders and political will was lacking.]

VIII.　Legal findings

A. Obligations of the State party under the Convention in relation to female genital mutilation

53. Under the Convention and … general recommendation No. 31 … [FGM] is a harmful practice and a form of gender-based violence … … …

…

56. Under articles 2 (f), 5 (a), and 16 (1) (a), read in conjunction with article 5 (a), States parties are required to eliminate prejudices, stereotypes and customs that subordinate women to men and create gender inequality, which are at the root of female genital mutilation. They are also required to protect all women, including those who have not been subjected to genital mutilation, from the gender bias and stereotypes that make such mutilation a condition for marriage, thus depriving them of equality with men in the enjoyment of the right to enter into marriage. In addition, under article 2 of the Convention, … States parties must take measures to modify social and cultural patterns of conduct that are based on the idea of the inferiority of women and girls.

…

59. The Committee recalls that the obligations of States parties under the Convention do not cease in periods of armed conflict or in states of emergency resulting from political events. Consequently, the security crisis and the state of emergency that have been in place since 2015 do not relieve Mali of its obligations under the Convention.

…

D.　　Grave or systematic nature of the violations

…

80. The Committee finds that the State party is responsible for the following:

> (a)　Grave violations of rights under the Convention, considering the discriminatory nature of female genital mutilation and the failure to fulfil its obligation to protect the majority of women and girls from female genital mutilation and ensure that they have appropriate access to health care and justice, thereby exposing them to severe physical and psychological suffering, impeding investigations and obstructing victims' access to remedies;

> (b)　Systematic violations of rights under the Convention, considering that the State party has knowingly omitted to take effective measures to:

>> (i)　Criminalize and prohibit female genital mutilation and ensure that the crime is punished by severe penalties;
>> (ii)　Provide for measures, including legislative measures, to protect, care for and rehabilitate victims of female genital mutilation;

(iii)   Counter negative cultural attitudes and social norms that legitimize female genital mutilation and the stigmatization of women and girls who do not agree to such mutilation.

...

* * *

A Kenyan Case Study

FGM/C has been litigated in a number of states. Here we consider a case from Kenya in which the court addresses various challenges seeking to prevent the implementation of that country's Prohibition of Female Genital Mutilation Act, 2011. The 2001 Children's Act had already criminalized the subjection of children to harmful cultural practices, and the 2015 Protection against Domestic Violence Act classified FGM as violence. In 2019, a Presidential Directive called for FGM's eradication by 2022, an effort that is promoted by a semi-autonomous Anti-FGM Board. The prevalence of the practice diminished from 32 percent in 2003, to 27 percent in 2009, and 21 percent in 2014.

According to UNICEF, FGM programmes have focused on consultations, observation, and open dialogue with community members so that programmes can be tailored to specific locations. Efforts have also been made to identify 'alternative rites of passage' that substitute for FGM but are considered meaningful to the individual and the community.[250]

KAMAU V. ATTORNEY-GENERAL ET AL.,
HIGH COURT OF KENYA AT NAIROBI, CONSTITUTIONAL PETITION NO. 244 OF 2019
(17 MARCH 2021)

JUDGES ACHODE, KIMONDO, AND MUIGAI,

Introduction

1. Dr. Tatu Kamau (hereafter the Petitioner) is a medical doctor. She challenged the constitutionality of the Prohibition of Female Genital Mutilation Act ... .

...

3. The Petitioner pleaded that ... the Act contravenes ... the Constitution by limiting women's choice and right to uphold and respect their culture; ethnic identity; religion; beliefs; and, by discriminating between men and women. She opines that the Act is an "imperialist imposition from another culture that holds a different set of beliefs or norms".

4. She contended that ...the Act expressly forbids a qualified medical practitioner from performing female circumcision, thereby denying adult women access to the highest attainable standard of health, including the right to healthcare enshrined under Article 43 (1)(a) of the Constitution.

5. When the Petitioner testified, she claimed to speak on behalf of communities that practice female circumcision; and, for the women who have been jailed for carrying out the rite.

6. One of the main issues in the Petition is whether it is constitutional to prohibit an adult woman from freely choosing to undergo the rite under the hand of a trained and licensed medical practitioner.

...

Whether FGM is a harmful cultural practice

...

128. The Petitioner posited that no particular culture is superior to another. She submitted that the rights of willing women from communities that practiced the now prohibited cultural ritual of female circumcision have been violated by the Act. She was of the view that their consent has been disregarded ... .

---

[250] UNICEF, 'Case Study on the End Female Genital Mutilation (FGM) Programme in the Republic of Kenya' (April 2021).

129. To answer these issues, it is necessary to examine FGM, its causes and consequences and whether they occasion harm. ...

...

131. ... Articles 53 and 55 of the Constitution refer to harmful cultural practices in protection of children and the youth. The Maputo Protocol [Protocol to the African Charter on Human and People's Rights on the Rights of Women in Africa, 2003] in Article 1 (g) defines Harmful Practices as: all behavior, attitudes and/or practices which negatively affect the fundamental rights of women and girls, such as their right to life, health, dignity, education and physical integrity.

...

133. Article 5 of the Maputo Protocol calls for the elimination of harmful practices, by prohibiting and condemning "all forms of harmful practices which negatively affect the human rights of women and which are contrary to international standards".

134. ... [T]he commitment to eliminate harmful practices is linked not only to promoting the health and well-being of women but also to women's human rights.

135. The assumption is that anyone above the age of 18 years undergoes FGM voluntarily. However, this hypothesis is far from reality, especially for women who belong to communities where the practice is strongly supported. The context within which FGM/C is practiced is relevant as there is social pressure and punitive sanctions. From the evidence, it is clear that those who undergo the cut are involved in a cycle of social pressure from the family, clan and community. They also suffer serious health complications while those who refuse to undergo it suffer the consequences of stigma. Women are thus as vulnerable as children due to social pressure and may still be subjected to the practice without their valid consent.

136. From the evidence before us, it is clear that the rationale for FGM/C varies from one community to another. In some communities FGM/C is a rite of passage to adulthood or womanhood; it fosters virginity and modesty and makes for better marriage prospects. In other communities it is a measure to curb women's sexual desire while in others it confers social status in the community. In some cultures, if an uncircumcised woman marries into the community she is at risk of undergoing FGM/C upon being married or during her first pregnancy or labour.

137. All survivors disclosed devastating immediate, short-term and long-term effects [of] FGM/C. They underwent FGM/C at [the] young and tender age of 9 to 14 years. They told the court that they experienced excruciating pain during cutting and thereafter until the wound healed and on occasions that they undertook biological functions. They suffered bleeding, incontinence and in the long term psychological and even psychotic conditions from trauma. ...

...

139. In *Katet Nchoe & Ano v Republic*, High Court Nakuru, ... [2011] eKLR, the accused persons were charged with manslaughter arising out of FGM. ... The Court held:

> In our case, FGM is certainly harmful to the physical and no doubt psychological and
> sound well-being of the victim. It may lead to child birth complications, in this case, it led
> to premature death of a teenager. That kind of custom could be truly well discarded and
> buried in the annals of history, just as we no longer remove our 2, 4 or 6 teeth from our
> lower jaw, or adorn our faces, cheeks with healed blisters.

140. The Petitioner contended that Section 19(1) of Act expressly forbids a qualified medical practitioner from performing female circumcision thereby denying willing adult women access to the highest attainable standard of health ... .

141. Medicalization of FGM/C does not mitigate harm on the girl /woman as demonstrated by the FGM/C survivors who deposed affidavits and/or testified in Court were consistent and had similar experience after FGM/C. ...

142. … Under Article 2 (4) [of the Constitution] any law, including customary law that is inconsistent with the Constitution is void to the extent of the inconsistency and any act or omission in contravention of the Constitution is invalid.

143. Some harmful cultural practices are nonetheless valued as 'traditional cultural heritage' in some communities. Cultural rights intertwine with human rights in certain social spaces, and are not easy to separate but the Constitution offers the first most important standard against which the relevance of all other laws, religions, customs, and practices are to be measured.

144. The Constitution also restricts customary law and religions through certain other provisions whose overall effect is to rid of harmful traditional practices. …
…
148. The challenge is one of balancing the competing rights under Articles 26 (right to life), Article 27 (on equality and freedom from discrimination), Article 28 (on human dignity) Article 29 (on freedom and security of the person) and Article 43 (on the highest attainable standard of health and reproductive healthcare) against the rights in Articles 11, 32 and 44 (on culture, religion, belief and language).

149. Article 25 of the Constitution prescribes fundamental rights and freedoms that shall not be limited. The right to enjoy one's culture religion and belief as envisaged in Articles 11, 32 and 44 are derogable.

150. Article 24 prescribes that the right and fundamental freedom may be limited to the extent the limitation is reasonable and justifiable based on human dignity equality and freedom. The limitation shall be proportionate to the legitimate aim.
…
153. [D]espite the rights enshrined in Articles 11, 32 and 44 of the Constitution relating to culture, religion, beliefs and language, the rights can be limited due to the nature of the harm resulting from FGM/C to the individual's health and well-being.

154. We shall now comment briefly on the exclusion of Type IV FGM/C. Section 2 of the Act defines FGM/C Type I, II & III but excludes Type IV which the WHO includes as "unclassified". The latter includes any other procedure involving, genital pricking, piercing with tongs or scissors including razor blades, incising and stretching of the clitoris/labia.

155. Section 19 of the Act criminalizes FGM/C except where it is a surgical operation for a person's physical and mental health or at any stage of labour or birth. It further provides that culture, religion, custom or practice or consent shall not be a defence.

[Earlier in the judgment (at para. 106) the court had noted that practices omitted by the Act include cosmetic surgeries, labiaplasty, piercing and burning of female genitalia with corrosive substances and so forth. As a result, it noted (para. 107) that the Act favours a miniscule of the population who engage in such Type practices.]

156. We find that from the stand point of criminal law a lacuna is created that hampers the effective enforcement of the Act. The criminalization of the three types of FGM/C and not Type IV, which is unclassified, makes it difficult to effectively enforce the Act. There seems to be no objective or professional process to distinguish between the various types of FGM/C during investigation or prosecution.

Whether the enactment of the FGM Act violated the right of women to uphold culture and identity

157. Culture, and in particular the desire to preserve one's cultural identity, is the central plank of the Petitioner's case in support of FGM/C. … [T]he preamble to the Constitution recognizes the culture and customs of the Kenyan people … .
…
159. According to the 4th Interested Party, the enactment of the Act was necessitated by the need to shield women in communities that advocate for FGM/C and who have no say or capacity to give the consent when it comes to FGM/C. The practice prior to the enactment of the Act was that the decision of when, where and who will perform the act was decided by men. It was urged that whereas Article 44(1) and (2) of the Constitution

guarantees a person's right to participate in the cultural life of his or her choice and to enjoy his or her culture, sub-article (3) thereof prohibits a person from compelling another to perform, observe or undergo any cultural practice or rite.

160. The Petitioner however argued that consenting female adults should not be prevented or prohibited from undergoing female circumcision which she says is an age old valued tradition among certain communities. ...

161. ... [I]t is no defence to a charge under the [Act] that the person on whom the act involving female genital mutilation was performed consented to that act ... .

...

167. From the evidence of the survivors S.S.H., F.A.S.A. and those who escaped the cut like R.J.K, they all confirmed the misinformation, deception and societal pressure they were subjected to, to undergo the cut. For instance, when F.A.S.A told her parents that she did not want to go through the cut, her mother told her that no one would marry her if she missed the cut. She threatened to report her mother to the Police. Nevertheless, her father took her and her sister to the doctor and they underwent the cut. R.J.K may have escaped the cut, but she suffered beatings from irate family members and was shunned by the community and prospective suitors. She finally relocated to Nairobi.

...

170. According to the 2nd respondent, the context in which FGM/C is practiced within the various communities is a conundrum affecting not only women from communities practicing FGM/C but also women married into communities practicing FGM/C who are forced to undergo the cut in order to fully participate in the lives of the community and gain 'respect and acceptance from their loved ones and elders' in the communities into which they have married.

...

181. On discrimination, the Petitioner contended that the impugned Act overtly favours the cultural practices of one gender against the cultural practices of the other gender in contravention of Article 27 of the Constitution which provides for equality and freedom from discrimination based on gender. It was urged that while men were free to undergo a similar surgical procedure, the Act showed open intolerance to adult women who wished to undergo female circumcision to uphold their culture.

[The court then reviewed the relevant Constitutional provisions, as well as those of the UDHR, the CEDAW Convention, and the African Charter on Human and Peoples' Rights.]

...

195. The second stage of analysis is to interrogate whether the prohibition of female circumcision while allowing male circumcision resulted in unfair discrimination. Indeed, the reality of our society is that men and women are treated differently with regard to cultural rites.

196. Whereas the evidence adduced hereto points to discrimination, we are not convinced that the said discrimination was unreasonable. ...

197. The 1st and 2nd Respondents argued that FGM/C was a harmful cultural practice and was not similar to male circumcision. It was their evidence that equating FGM/C to male circumcision was flawed stating that unlike male circumcision which boasts of health benefits, female circumcision was both harmful and with no health benefits. ...

...

202. After a careful examination of the provisions of the Act against those of Article 28 of the Constitution, we are of the considered view that the impugned Act does not violate the Constitution or women's right to dignity.

203. On the main issue of whether the right to culture has been violated, the Petitioner faulted the Act for condemning and misrepresenting the age old tradition as violent and dangerous. In particular, that the Act defines 'female circumcision' as 'mutilation' which connotes an intention to incapacitate and destroy. She took the view that female circumcision is part of the national heritage and history. This, the Petitioner argued, infringed upon women's right to practice the cultural life of their choice making the Act contra-constitution.

204. Article 11(1) of the Constitution recognizes culture as the foundation of the nation and as the cumulative civilization of the Kenyan people and nation. Article 11(2)(a) obligates the state to promote all forms of national and cultural expression … .

…

207. Culture is dynamic and not static and will continue to grow responding to new factors. It is also fluid and changes from time to time. It is susceptible to be swayed by many factors such as religion, education, and influence from other communities, inter-marriage and urbanization. But there are certain aspects of culture that identify a particular group, their history, ancestry and way of life and this diversity is recognized and protected by the Constitution. See *Mohamed Ali Baadi and others vs. Attorney General & 11 others* [2018] eKLR.

…

210. The Constitution grants the freedom to exercise one's culture. However, that freedom has to be carried out in line with the other constitutional provisions. From the law we observe that culture entails various modes of expression. Therefore, what is limited is any expression that will cause harm to a person or by a person to another person. FGM/C falls into the latter category.

211. It therefore follows that while our Constitution has a general underlying value of freedom, this value of freedom is subject to limitation which is reasonable and justifiable. Additionally, it has not inscribed the freedom to inflict harm on one's self in the exercise of these freedoms. …

…

214. The evidence before us demonstrates that the practice of FGM/C implicates not only the right to practice cultural life but also the right to health, human dignity and in instances when it results in death, the right to life. The provisions of international treaties reproduced hereto are also clear that not all traditional practices are prohibited, but only those that undermine international human rights standards.

215. In sum there is no doubt that FGM/C was central to the culture of some communities in Kenya including the Kikuyu to which the petitioner belongs. However, from the medical evidence, and as discussed earlier, we are left in no doubt about the negative short term and long term effects of FGM/C on women's health. We have also discussed the absence of consent by victims who undergo the rite which violates Article 44 (3) of the Constitution. We are not persuaded that one can choose to undergo a harmful practice. From the medical and anecdotal evidence presented by the respondents, we find that limiting this right is reasonable in an open and democratic society based on the dignity of women.

Disposition and Final Orders.

216. Our final orders shall be as follows:

a)   That the Amended Petition is devoid of merit and is hereby dismissed.

b)   That the Attorney General (1st Respondent) shall forward proposals to the National Assembly to consider amendments to section 19 of the Prohibition of Female Genital Mutilation Act (No. 32 of 2011) with a view to prohibiting all harmful practices of FGM as set out in this judgment.

…

* * *

Male Circumcision

In 2012, a German court held that the religious circumcision of male children constituted the criminal offence of causing bodily injury and that the child's right to self-determination should prevail over the parent's right to freedom of religion. The case involved the circumcision of a four-year-old Muslim boy who was taken to hospital suffering extensive bleeding.

While the doctor was ultimately acquitted, the court decided that a child's right to self-determination superseded his parents' right to freedom of religion. The decision prompted widespread uproar, particularly among Jewish and Muslim groups, and as far away as Turkey, Israel and the United States. Germany's Central Council of Jews called it "an unprecedented and dramatic intrusion on the right to self-determination of religious communities." Ali Demir, the chairman of the Islamic Religious Community, argued that circumcision is a "harmless procedure, a tradition that is thousands of years old and highly symbolic."

Ultimately, the Bundestag, Germany's parliament, passed a law allowing the religious procedure. According to the new rules, specially qualified members of religious communities can perform the operation in the first six months of a boy's life, after which it must be performed by a physician.

In 2013, the issue was addressed in a resolution adopted by the Parliamentary Assembly of the Council of Europe:

> ...

> 2. The Parliamentary Assembly is particularly worried about a category of violation of the physical integrity of children, which supporters of the procedures tend to present as beneficial to the children themselves despite clear evidence to the contrary. This includes, among others, female genital mutilation, the circumcision of young boys for religious reasons, early childhood medical interventions in the case of intersex children, and the submission to, or coercion of, children into piercings, tattoos or plastic surgery.

> ...

> 7. The Assembly therefore calls on member States to:

> ...

> 7.5.1. publicly condemn the most harmful practices, such as female genital mutilation, and pass legislation banning these, thus providing public authorities with the mechanisms to prevent and effectively fight these practices, including through the application of extraterritorial "legislative or other measures to establish jurisdiction" for cases where nationals are submitted to female genital mutilation abroad ...;

> 7.5.2. clearly define the medical, sanitary and other conditions to be ensured for practices which are today widely carried out in certain religious communities, such as the non-medically justified circumcision of young boys;[251]

> ...

The characterization of male circumcision in this way drew concerted criticism from both the Jewish and Muslim communities, and the Assembly responded two years later with a new resolution:

> 9. As far as circumcision of young boys is concerned, the Assembly refers to its Resolution 1952 (2013) on children's right to physical integrity and, out of a concern to protect children's rights which the Jewish and Muslim communities surely share, recommends that member States provide for ritual circumcision of children not to be allowed unless practised by a person with the requisite training and skill, in appropriate medical and health conditions. Furthermore, the parents must be duly informed of any potential medical risk or possible contraindications and take these into account when deciding what is best for their child, bearing in mind that the child's interest must be considered the first priority.

> ...

---

[251] 'Children's right to physical integrity', Resolution 1952 (2013).

11. The Assembly is convinced that education is the key to combating ignorance, breaking down stereotypes, building trust and mutual respect and promoting sincere support for the shared values of living together.[252]

RE B AND G (CHILDREN) (CARE PROCEEDINGS)
[2015] EWFC 3

SIR JAMES MUNBY, PRESIDENT OF THE FAMILY DIVISION:

[1] These are care proceedings in relation to two children, B, a boy, born in July 2010 and G, a girl, born in July 2011 … … . [B]oth the father, F, and the mother, M, come from an African country … . The family are Muslims.
…

…

[4] The most important issue in the proceedings is whether G has been subjected to female genital mutilation (FGM) and, if she has, what the implications of that are in relation to planning for her and her brother's future.
…

[55] … FGM is a criminal offence under the Female Genital Mutilation Act 2003. It is an abuse of human rights. It has no basis in any religion. [As I said in 2004] it is a "barbarous" practice which is "beyond the pale." [Other judges have described it as "an evil practice …" and .. "a repulsive practice … deleterious to women's health." I entirely agree.

…

[59] Circumcision of the male … is the removal of some, or all, of the prepuce (foreskin) … . [It] involves the removal of a significant amount of tissue, creates an obvious alteration to the appearance of the genitals and leaves a more or less prominent scar … .

[60] It can readily be seen that although FGM of WHO Types I, II and III are all very much more invasive than male circumcision, at least some forms of Type IV, for example, pricking, piercing and incising, are on any view much less invasive than male circumcision.

[61] It is also important to recognise that comparatively few male circumcisions are performed for therapeutic reasons. Many are performed for religious reasons (as in Judaism and Islam). However, large numbers of circumcisions are performed for reasons which, as the particular prevalence of the practice in, for example, the English-speaking world and non-Muslim Africa suggests, are as much to do with social, societal, cultural, customary or conventional reasons as with anything else, and this notwithstanding the justifications sometimes put forward, that circumcision of the male is hygienic or has prophylactic benefits, for example, the belief that it reduces the incidence of penile cancer in the male, the incidence of cervical cancer in female partners and the incidence of HIV transmission.

[62] … There is nothing in the case-law to suggest that male circumcision is, of itself, such as to justify care proceedings … . On the contrary, judges in the Family Division have on occasions made orders providing for non-therapeutic circumcision … . …

[63] In the present case the point arises in striking form. The family, as I have said are Muslims. I assume, therefore, that B either has been or will in due course be circumcised. Yet … this is not a matter that has been raised before me. There is no suggestion, nor could there be, that B's circumcision can or should give rise to care proceedings. … G's FGM Type IV (had it been proved) would have been relied upon by the local authority, prior to its change of stance referred to above, as justifying the adoption of both children, even though on any objective view it might be thought that G would have subjected to a process much less invasive, no more traumatic (if, indeed, as traumatic) and with no greater long-term consequences, whether physical, emotional or psychological, than the process to which B has been or will be subjected.

[64] … … The explanation … is simply that in 2015 the law generally, and family law in particular, is still prepared to tolerate non-therapeutic male circumcision performed for religious or even for purely cultural or

---

[252] Parliamentary Assembly of the Council of Europe, 'Freedom of religion and living together in a democratic society', Resolution 2076 (2015).

conventional reasons, while no longer being willing to tolerate FGM in any of its forms … . Certainly current judicial thinking seems to be that there is no equivalence between the two … .

…

[68] … In my judgment, any form of FGM constitutes "significant harm" … . What then of male circumcision?

[69] … Given the comparison between what is involved in male circumcision and FGM WHO Type IV, to dispute that the more invasive procedure involves the significant harm involved in the less invasive procedure would seem almost irrational. In my judgment, if FGM Type IV amounts to significant harm, as in my judgment it does, then the same must be so of male circumcision.

[70] I should add that my conclusions in relation to whether FGM, including FGM Type IV, constitutes "significant harm" for the purposes of family law, is quite separate from the question of whether particular examples of FGM Type IV involve the commission of criminal offences under the Female Genital Mutilation Act 2003. As I have already pointed out, FGM Type IV comes within the ambit of the criminal law only if it involves "mutilation". The question of whether a particular case of FGM Type IV – for example, the case as presented here by the local authority in relation to G – involves mutilation is, in my judgment, not a matter for determination by the family court, and certainly not a matter I need to determine in the present case. It is a matter properly for determination by a criminal court as and when the point arises for decision in a particular case.

[71] … The fact that [FGM] may be a "cultural" practice does not make FGM reasonable; indeed, the proposition is specifically negatived by section 1(5) of the 2003 Act. And, as I have already pointed out, FGM has no religious justification. So … it can never be reasonable parenting to inflict any form of FGM on a child.
…

[72] It is at this point in the analysis, as it seems to me, that the clear distinction between FGM and male circumcision appears. Whereas it can never be reasonable parenting to inflict any form of FGM on a child, the position is quite different with male circumcision. Society and the law, including family law, are prepared to tolerate non-therapeutic male circumcision performed for religious or even for purely cultural or conventional reasons, while no longer being willing to tolerate FGM in any of its forms. There are, after all, at least two important distinctions between the two. FGM has no basis in any religion; male circumcision is often performed for religious reasons. FGM has no medical justification and confers no health benefits; male circumcision is seen by some (although opinions are divided) as providing hygienic or prophylactic benefits. Be that as it may, "reasonable" parenting is treated as permitting male circumcision.

[73] I conclude therefore that although both involve significant harm, there is a very clear distinction in family law between FGM and male circumcision. FGM in any form will suffice to establish 'threshold' in accordance with section 31 of the Children Act 1989; male circumcision without more will not.
…
[78] … Plainly, given the nature of the evil, prevention is infinitely better than 'cure'. Local authorities need to be pro-active and vigilant in taking appropriate protective measures to prevent girls being subjected to FGM. And … the court must not hesitate to use every weapon in its protective arsenal if faced with a case of actual or anticipated FGM. … Given … the distressingly great prevalence of FGM in this country even today, some thirty years after FGM was first criminalised, … the family courts [and] the criminal courts, … have an important role to play and a very much greater role than they have hitherto been able to play.
…

* * *

Scholars have had a mixed reaction to the issue raised, but left unresolved, in the *Re B and G (children)* case. Kai Möller, in 'Male and Female Genital Cutting: Between the Best Interest of the Child and Genital Mutilation', 40 *Oxf. J. Leg. Stud.* (2020) 508, provides a justification for banning both male and female genital cutting.

> … [T]he current discourse around female genital cutting has not provided a convincing
> foundation for the view that any interference with the female genitals is considered
> categorically impermissible. The reasons … usually advanced … – pointing to the harm,

lack of religious motivation, absence of medical benefits, and existence of patriarchal power structures – are valid considerations, but they do not apply to all kinds of genital cutting and in particular not the less intrusive forms. [This article proposes] a different basis for the rejection of all forms of female genital cutting, namely girls' right to physical integrity. ... [A] girl's body is not a 'resource' that the parents are free to 'trade in' for some other benefit, such as a strengthening of her female identity or the bringing about of a conviction that no pain will overwhelm her; rather, the parents are obligated to respect and protect the integrity of their daughter's body and in particular her genitals. A further advantage of this approach is that it justifies convincingly why all kinds of female genital cutting are wrong, including those that are considerably less invasive and harmful than male cutting, and it cuts off any discussion of whether some, milder, forms of genital cutting should be considered acceptable. [The author contends that] the current approach of the law, according to which male genital cutting is in principle permissible and can even be ordered by a court, is indefensible and must be changed. ... [T]he reasons commonly relied on to justify the differential treatment by the law of male and female genital cutting are unconvincing. We cannot, therefore, maintain that female genital cutting is categorically unacceptable while endorsing a balancing approach to male cutting. Furthermore, the correct way to think about the wrongness of genital cutting is to regard it as intrinsically wrong because it violates the right to physical integrity of the child; thus, the conclusion that genital cutting is wrong as a matter of principle applies equally to boys and girls.

Brian D. Earp and Sara Johnsdotter, in 'Current Critiques of the WHO Policy on Female Genital Mutilation', 33 *Your Sexual Med. J.* (2021) 196 agree that there is an element of parallelism in the two cases, but propose a rather different approach. They begin with a survey of scholarly critiques that have been made of the terminology of FGM, including claims that it is imprecise, inaccurate, misleading, harmful, ethnocentric, and sexist:

> ... it is sometimes argued that women who support, manage, oversee, and even perform FGC in their communities must be victims of brainwashing or false consciousness, having internalized their inferior status to men. However, this argument is not as straightforward as it may seem.

> To begin with, women from affected communities who endorse FGC (usually the majority), regularly report believing that modified genitalia—in both males and females—are more hygienic, more civilized/respectable, and more esthetically appealing. ... ...

> ...

> ...[I]t is typically assumed that support for FGC by affected women must be irrational, or, at best, a regrettable psychological adaptation to an unjust situation. However, this assumption has itself been argued to rest on a patriarchal stereotype that ignores, devalues, or denies women's agency despite robust evidence of its existence in the relevant spheres. ...

> ... [Other concerns raised] include the following:

> 1.   The characterization seems to reflect longstanding racist and colonial stereotypes of "primitive" African societies, in which black and brown women, constructed as passive victims of male-oriented cultural practices, need to be rescued from the men in their own villages, who are believed to be brutal and barbaric.

> This is in spite of the fact that:

> 2.   Virtually all societies that practice medically unnecessary FGC also practice medically unnecessary MGC, usually in a parallel ceremony serving similar social functions. ...

3.   Depending on the group, either the male or the female form of cutting may be more severe, risky, or potentially detrimental to sexual enjoyment. The most dangerous and deadly form of genital cutting anywhere in the world appears to be … MGC as it is practiced … among the Xhosa of South Africa.

4.   When practiced as a rite of passage into adulthood (or as part of a Muslim religious initiation), neither MGC nor FGC is typically intended to undermine the initiate's capacity for sexual pleasure. …

5.   Almost invariably, where they occur together, men are in charge of the male rites and women are in charge of the female rites, often with little or no mutual knowledge or influence over the workings of the other. …

…

As it stands, the WHO appears to be engaged in highly selective condemnation of only non-Western, female-only genital cutting, irrespective of harm, consent, or the comparability of the cutting to other medically unnecessary practices. …

In 2022, the UN Secretary-General reported (UN Doc. A/77/312, para. 75) that 'a girl is approximately one third less likely to have undergone [FGM] compared with three decades ago.' But the report also acknowledged the steady presence of FGM 'in many high-prevalence countries over several decades'. Successful interventions were said to include:

…health education and community dialogues with parents and religious leaders; advocacy and awareness-raising among key stakeholders, especially communities and the media; investment in the education of both girls and their mothers; legislation, together with political will and enforcement; and the involvement of health-care workers as key change agents in prevention.

QUESTIONS

1. In 2010 the American Academy of Pediatrics adopted a Policy Statement on 'Ritual Genital Cutting of Female Minors'. While opposing all types of FGC that pose risks of physical or psychological harm, the statement also observed that 'the ritual nick suggested by some pediatricians is not physically harmful and is much less extensive than routine newborn male genital cutting. There is reason to believe that offering such a compromise may build trust between hospitals and immigrant communities, save some girls from undergoing disfiguring and life threatening procedures in their native countries, and play a role in the eventual eradication of FGC. It might be more effective if federal and state laws enabled pediatricians to reach out to families by offering a ritual nick as a possible compromise to avoid greater harm.' An alternative approach, proposed by Norway's Children's Ombudsman in 2011 is to set a minimum age of 15 or 16 for ritual male circumcision in order to respect 'children's best interests and their right to self-determination on religious and health matters'. Comment on these proposals in light of the materials above.

2. How convincing and/or useful do you find the WHO's typology of FGM/C, noting the observations made by Earp and Johnsdotter above?

3. How would you apply a child's right to physical integrity in the context of other common cultural practices, such as ear/nose piercing or male circumcision? How might it inform medical treatment of intersex and transgender children?

4. Condemnation of FGM/C by international human rights institutions and Western NGOs has led to pushback from some communities, who view the campaign as based in cultural imperialism and fear the 'criminalisation of culture'.253 How would you respond?

2. Religion

No topic generates more controversy — or indeed more complex ideas — than relationships between (1) institutionalization of religion or religious belief or practice in the state and (2) human rights norms.[254] From one perspective, religious beliefs and human rights are complementary expressions of similar ideas, although religious texts invoke the language of duties rather than rights. Important aspects of the major religious traditions — canonical text, scholarly exegesis, ministries — provide the foundation or justification for, or reinforce, many basic human rights. Evident examples include rights to bodily security, or to economic and social provision for the needy. From another perspective, religious traditions may impinge on human rights, and religious leaders may assert the primacy of those traditions over rights. Recall the illustrations in An-Na'im's article, above. The banner of cultural relativism may here be held high. If notions of state sovereignty represent one powerful concept and force that challenges and seeks to limit the reach of the international human rights movement, religion can then represent another.

The topics in this section explore selected issues within this large theme. They involve the distinction sketched by some scholars between freedom *of* religion, and freedom *from* religion. The first freedom is threatened primarily by state conduct that prohibits public expression of religious belief and sharply restricts religious practice or ritual. Such conduct may stem from an ideologically secular state that seeks to limit the role of organized religions, or at the other extreme from fundamentalist states that will not tolerate other forms of religious expression. The second freedom *from* again is threatened primarily by the state, which may impose the beliefs or practices of an official or dominant religion on all citizens, whatever their religious community (if any, for some citizens will be secular or atheist). In such circumstances, human rights additional to the right to freedom of religion may also be implicated. Forms of gender discrimination enforced by the state may find roots in sacred religious texts. The state may repress certain speech that is widely viewed as offensive to the dominant religion. And so on.

These issues do not involve a simple dichotomy of the 'state' and 'citizens'. As the materials in Chapters 6 and 7 have illustrated, religion-based restraints or obligations may be rooted in a broad religious culture that is both closely related to and distinct from the state, and may be insisted on or enforced by a range of non-state actors. Religion and society will often be as apt a framework for discussion as religion and state. The state itself may adopt many attitudes and pursue many policies, ranging from support of the religious culture to neutrality, to active opposition to a religion's teachings and demands.

Before exploring some of the human rights dimensions, it is appropriate to note how significantly the general religious landscape is changing in the world. A 2015 report by the Pew Research Center, entitled *The Future of World Religions: Population Growth Projections, 2010-2050* provides an overview:

> The religious profile of the world is rapidly changing, driven primarily by differences in fertility rates and the size of youth populations among the world's major religions, as well as by people switching faiths. ... If current trends continue, by 2050:
>
> • The number of Muslims will nearly equal the number of Christians around the world.

---

253 B. Shell-Duncan et al., 'Legislating Change? Responses to Criminalizing Female Genital Cutting in Senegal', 47 L. *& Soc. Rev.* (2013) 803, 831.
254 N. Bhuta (ed.), *Freedom of Religion, Secularism, and Human Rights* (2019).

- Atheists, agnostics and other people who do not affiliate with any religion – though increasing in countries such as the United States and France – will make up a declining share of the world's total population.

- The global Buddhist population will be about the same size it was in 2010, while the Hindu and Jewish populations will be larger than they are today.

- In Europe, Muslims will make up 10% of the overall population.

- India will retain a Hindu majority but also will have the largest Muslim population of any country in the world, surpassing Indonesia.

- In the United States, Christians will decline from more than three-quarters of the population in 2010 to two-thirds in 2050, and Judaism will no longer be the largest non-Christian religion. Muslims will be more numerous in the U.S. than people who identify as Jewish on the basis of religion.

- Four out of every 10 Christians in the world will live in sub-Saharan Africa.

The following materials start with a comparative survey of questions of religion and state and freedom of religion. These comparisons among states highlight a vital issue that permeates this section: what are the links between religious communities, or one religious community, and the state? The spectrum is large, from notions of separation to the pervasive interrelationships in several countries between Islam and the state.

a. Comparative Perspectives among States

Consider the following examples of different national approaches to the relationship between the state and religious groups.

W. COLE DURHAM, PATTERNS OF RELIGION STATE RELATIONS
JOHN WITTE AND M. CHRISTIAN GREEN (EDS.), RELIGION AND HUMAN RIGHTS: AN INTRODUCTION (2011) 360

The configurations of religion-state relations across the world's legal systems are remarkably diverse, reflecting differences of history, philosophy, religious demography, culture, constitutional and political systems, and numerous other factors. Moreover, religion-state relations in every country are in constant flux. ... Yet broad patterns or types of relationships are discernible ... .
...

Theocratic States

In this pattern type, the linkage between state and religion is so close that it is virtually impossible to distinguish state from religious rule. ... [T]he theocratic state ... postulates total unity of religious and political institutions. Theocratic states typically seek to replicate their vision of what divine rule would be like or what this vision calls for ... ... The key ... factor ... is that they constitutionally subordinate all branches of government (legislative, executive and judicial) to a religious normative framework. In addition, they tend to institutionalize this subordination by providing strong linkages (if not outright merger) of religious institutions and state bodies.

The most obvious example of this type of regime is the Vatican City ... .

Historically, there have been theocratic or religious states associated with many of the world's religions ... .

The primary current examples of theocratic or religious states are found in the Muslim world. Countries that consider themselves to be Islamic states according to their constitutions or basic laws include Afghanistan, Bahrain, Brunei Darussalam, Iran, Maldives, Mauritania, Oman, Pakistan, Saudi Arabia, and Yemen. ... [T]hese countries ... affirm in various ways that the State is subordinate to Islamic law, and ... [give] religious leaders institutional supervision authority to assure compliance with Islamic law. Some go further and entrench the religious character of the State by giving it constitutionally irrevocable status. … [T]he State itself is subordinated to a particular religious system … .

Established Religions

… [This category covers] systems in which there is an official state religion [that remains] in some sense distinct from and subordinate to the state … . In its ideal form, at least according to its Eastern Orthodox advocates, this type orchestrates a "symphony" of harmony between religion and the State. There is a broad range of possible "established religions," stretching from systems in which the state religion is granted a strictly enforced monopoly in religious affairs to much more tolerant regimes such as those one finds in contemporary England, Norway, and Finland. Roman Catholicism has in the past been the state religion of a number countries where it was predominant—most notably Spain and Italy and various Latin American countries. Evangelical Lutheranism remains the state church in Norway, Denmark, and Iceland … . Various branches of Eastern Orthodoxy constitute the established churches of Armenia and Greece.

Typically, though not always, established religions are declared to be the state religion in their constitutions. In the Muslim world, this is the case with respect to Algeria, Bangladesh, Djibouti, Egypt, Iraq, Jordan, Kuwait, Libya, Malaysia, Maldives, Morocco, Qatar, Tunisia, and the United Arab Emirates. …

Religious Status Systems

In a number of countries … the State recognizes the jurisdiction of a number of religious systems, typically in areas dealing with family law and inheritance. The legal system that applies typically depends on the religion of the individual. The European Court of Human Rights has held that such "plural legal systems" cannot be squared with the [ECHR]. But such systems clearly exist, including those in Israel, India, Lebanon, and a number of Muslim countries. One of the virtues of these systems is that they respect the autonomy of different religious communities and their right to administer their own religious law. [The risk is that they may] limit exit rights of those who wish to leave the community, or to interpret its norms in distinctive ways. There is also a risk that dominant groups can exploit such autonomy to justify second-class status for minorities … and may use it to construct ghettos … .

… While marking an advance in their day, however, such systems typically fail to provide full equality of treatment when assessed from the perspective of contemporary human rights law.

Endorsed Religions

[While not] formally affirming that one particular religion is the official or state religion, [these systems] acknowledge that a particular religion has a special place in the country's history and traditions. This is now quite typical in countries with a Roman Catholic heritage … . In a similar vein, Thailand, and Sri Lanka endorse Buddhism. … The … acknowledgement of a special historical and cultural role can take different forms ranging from financial to mere symbolic support. It may take the form of a general acknowledgement of religious heritage (e.g., Christian heritage in Poland and Fiji; Eastern Orthodoxy in Georgia and Russia); a recognition of the role of a particular religion in nation's formation (e.g., Timor-Leste and Paraguay); the recognition of a predominant religion; or recognition of religious phenomena, such as the existence of God, specific characteristics of deity, creationism, God's omnipotence, omniscience and omnipresence, trinitarianism, monotheism, reference to religious founders, or other notions of sanctity. … [In some cases, this system] operates as a thinly disguised method of preserving the prerogatives of establishment and channeling significant aid to the favored religions.

Preferred Sets of Religions

This can be a variation of other forms of positive identification, except that multiple religions are favored. …

Cooperationist Regimes

... [These regimes take] a neutral but positive and "cooperative" stance toward religions in society. [They include] most European systems ... . Typical in such schemes is substantial cooperation in church finance, religious education, various humanitarian services, and so forth, though at least in theory such aid is provided on a non-discriminatory basis ... . [But] it is easy to slip from cooperation to patterns of state preference, with a tendency to favor the major religions in a country.

Accommodationist Regimes

Accommodationism might be thought of as cooperation without any direct financial subsidies. Accommodation can be seen both in allowing certain types of indirect financial and other support for different religions and in protecting the freedom to act in accordance with distinctive religious beliefs. ... Accommodationist regimes protect freedom ... by not allowing statutes to carve out exceptions to constitutional and human rights guarantees of freedom of religion or belief. ...

Separation

... [A]pproximately one-third of the nations on earth have some type of separationist regime. Some ... view separation primarily as a method for protecting religion from the State; others see the "wall of separation" as a method of protecting the state and society from excessive religious power; many ... see it as [both]. At the "benign neutrality" end, separation differs relatively little from accommodation, except that it insists on a more rigorous separation of religious and state institutions ... . [T]he mere reliance on religious premises in public argument may be deemed inconsistent with separationist principles.

Less benign forms of separationism make stronger attempts to cordon off religion from public life. ... [R]eligious differences are not viewed as an appropriate justification for differential treatment. Inadvertent insensitivity to religious needs can easily result. Regulations initially formulated without religious animus can have the incidental effect of imposing unnecessary or disproportionately heavy burdens on religious groups. ...

... From an accommodationist perspective, compulsory exclusion of religion from public life constitutes a form of discrimination. From a more rigorously separationist perspective, in contrast, separation treats all religions equally by relegating them all to the private sphere. Of course, this overlooks the fact that secular outlooks are not constrained in the same way. ... [If] the public sphere expands to fill a substantially larger share of total social space, the space available for religion can shrink substantially. ... Separation in its most objectionable guise demands that religion retreat from any domain that the State desires to occupy, but is untroubled by intrusive state regulation and intervention in religious affairs.

Laïcité

Laïcité is the specifically French model of separation, and has been retained in the legal systems of many of France's former colonies. Thirty-four constitutions characterize the relationship of religion and the state in their respective systems not by proscribing establishment or by calling explicitly for separation, but by affirming that they are secular states. ... While there are a broad range of interpretations of the notion of laïcité, it tends in general to generate systems that are at the rigid separationist end of separationism.

Secular Control Regimes

Prior to the end of the Cold War, a number of communist states pursued a course of militant atheism which was actively hostile to religion ... . [S]tates such as China, Cuba, Vietnam, and North Korea continue to assert such policies. ...

A control regime shares some surface similarities with established and historically favored religions, except that these regimes make a secular ideology the official worldview of the State, and seek to repress dissenters from that view (i.e., religious believers). ...

Abolitionist States

At the negative end of the identification continuum lie regimes with the overt goal of eliminating religion as a social factor [such as] Albania during the Soviet era ... .

* * *

The complexity of the sort of classification that Durham undertakes in the preceding reading is illustrated by the following comment by the UN Special Rapporteur on freedom of religion and belief (UN Doc. A/HRC/37/49 (2018)):

12. Studies ... have produced myriad classification models for the relationships between State and religion. [One such approach is that used by Durham.] Others assess the role of constitutional stipulations in establishing and regulating the overall relationship between religious and State authorities.

13. A 2017 study, ... of all 193 [UN Member States], concluded that some 42 per cent of States either declared official support for one religion (21 per cent) or conferred favour onto one or more religions (21 per cent). Another 53 per cent ... did not identify with any faith or belief. A small number ... (5 per cent) exerted "a very high level of control over religious institutions in their countries or hold a negative view of religion in general". An earlier study, on the other hand, ... produced 14 subcategories grouped into 4 overarching relationships between State and religion ... concluding that 41 States had official religions, 77 favoured one or more religions, 43 did not identify with any religion and 16 had a negative view of the role of religion in public life.

14. Given such complexities, there is no consensus as to either how the relationships between State and religion should be classified, or on the terminology for characterizing their nature. The Special Rapporteur does not endorse any conclusion or particular model for such relationships generated by the above-mentioned studies. ...

In other words, capturing the complexities involved is both very challenging and politically fraught. The following readings thus confine themselves to offering snapshots of how the relationship between the state and religion has operated in practice in four very different settings: Germany, the United States, Cambodia, and China.

TOBIAS CREMER, NATIONS UNDER GOD:
HOW CHURCH–STATE RELATIONS SHAPE CHRISTIAN RESPONSES TO RIGHT-WING POPULISM IN GERMANY AND THE UNITED STATES
12 RELIGIONS (2021) 254.

1. Introduction

This paper compares the cases of Germany and the United States to investigate how a country's institutional settlement of Church–State relations can shape Christian communities' responses to right-wing populist politics. Germany and the United States are representative of many western countries in having recently experienced a surge of right-wing populist movements, which prominently display Christian symbols and use Christian language. Pro-Trump rioters parading oversized crosses and Jesus flags during the storming of the Capitol in January 2021, or Germany's far-[right] Alternative for Germany (AfD) stylising itself as the defender of Germany's "Judeo-Christian heritage" are two ... recent examples ... . [T]he reactions of German and American Christian communities to such references are strikingly different. In the US, White Christians supported Donald Trump's right-wing populist campaign at record-levels in the 2016 and 2020 elections and many American Christian leaders appeared at least tacitly supportive of the Trump administration. By contrast, German Protestants and Catholics were significantly less likely to vote for the AfD than irreligious voters, and Germany's churches have emerged as some of the far right's most outspoken public critics. ...

...

5. Conclusions

… First, that even though different settlements of Church–State relations may be designed with similar intentions—that is in the German and US cases with the aim to strengthen religion as a pillar of liberal democracy—they often exercise opposing incentives and pressure structures on Christian communities as they confront right-wing populist movements. Second, that the effects of these different and pressure structures are often most directly felt by faith leaders, whose response to right-wing populism in Germany and the US appeared importantly influenced by the institutional settlement of Church–State relations. Specifically, Germany's model of benevolent neutrality, which favours clear hierarchies, centralised structures and formally includes German faith leaders in the policymaking process, seemed to give clergy greater incentives to defend the status quo against populist attacks from the AfD, while also equipping them with the institutional basis and social prestige to do so without needing to fear major repercussions. By contrast, America's formal "Wall of Separation" and unregulated religious marketplace, which is more conducive to flat hierarchies, de-centralised churches and informal access to policymaking, appears not only to have facilitated the rise of siege and victimhood narratives among some Christian leaders, thus making them less likely to publicly defend the status quo. But by making faith leaders more depended on personal relations for political access, and on donors and congregants for their livelihood, it has also raised the potential risks for faith leaders to condemn Trumpism—especially at times when Donald Trump was in office and secularisation and de-institutionalisation already undermined deference to Christian leadership in the US. Third, this research suggests that by ways of shaping faith leaders' willingness and ability to create social taboos against the populist right Church–State relations can also importantly influence the voting behaviour of Christians in the pews. Thus, Germany's centralised system of benevolent neutrality appears not only to have encouraged the leadership of the Protestant and Catholic churches to be more outspoken against the AfD, but also to have boosted their ability to maintain social taboos against the AfD by enshrining their status as foremost representatives of Christianity in German society. By contrast, America's decentralised, non-hierarchical and pluralistic system, produces less deferential authority structures. Instead, the decentralised structure of denominations, as well as the prominence of non-denominational leaders, appeared to significantly undermine the traditional religious establishments' sway over voters and their ability to create and maintain taboos around Trumpism.

…

BENJAMIN LAWRENCE, SAFFRON SUFFRAGE: BUDDHIST MONKS AND CONSTITUTIONAL POLITICS IN CAMBODIA
37 J. L. & RELIG. (2022) 259

Introduction

Shortly before the UN-administered elections that formed Cambodia's Constituent Assembly in 1993, … the leaders of the country's two Buddhist sects, both approached Yasushi Akashi, the head of the United Nations Transitional Authority in Cambodia, known as UNTAC. Their request was … that Buddhist monks be formally excluded from the vote. Akashi refused … and instead insisted on adherence to the democratic norm of universal suffrage, thus ensuring that Cambodia's Buddhist monks would, for the first time in the country's history, participate in democratic election. Meanwhile, … [it was agreed] that the country's constitution would include provisions for democratic elections based on "universal and equal suffrage" … . … [T]hese decisions created a fundamental source of constitutional contestation and debate that has rumbled on for decades, about the role of religion in Cambodian politics and the relationship between Buddhism and the state. …

It was the express wish of the two leaders of the Cambodian Buddhist community, or *sangha* … that Buddhist monks be precluded from voting. It is for this reason that Ian Harris, a scholar of Cambodian Buddhism, described the decision to allow monks to vote as an "imposition" and an act of "cultural insensitivity" by Akashi and UNTAC. …

…

Conclusion

… [These decisions] produced in Cambodia a new constitutional status quo wherein monks could actively engage in electoral politics. This new status quo has brought to the surface an underlying societal ambivalence over the role that Buddhism, and Buddhist monks, should play in politics. … [T]he country's monks and religious institutions have sought different ways of resolving this constitutional tension … . The result, at least with respect to Cambodia's otherwise largely authoritarian constitutional context, has been a peculiarly liberal compromise. Rather than overriding the precedent set by the UN-administered election of 1993, by introducing a religious exception …, Cambodia's political leaders have largely left it to the country's Buddhist *sangha* to resolve the issues of constitutional practice surrounding monkish politics on its own. … [While] Cambodia's various opposition parties have undoubtedly been more vociferous in their support of monks seeking to register to vote (perhaps reflecting their belief that they have the sympathy of much of the *sangha*, at least in its more populous lower ranks), the ruling Cambodian People's Party has nonetheless rebuffed calls for government intervention.

For their part, Cambodia's *sangha* authorities have clearly and repeatedly attempted to discourage and inhibit monks from voting or engaging in politics. Yet, they have largely refrained from formally preventing them from doing so. In the process, members of the Buddhist clergy have publicly contested the meaning of the Constitution, and actively employed constitutional arguments, as a way to further their cause. Of course, opposition to monks being allowed the right to vote has been explained in terms of religious doctrine, wherein political engagements are seen to risk corrupting the monks who are supposed to have assumed the role of "world renouncer" and delegitimizing the *sangha* as a set of supposedly politically neutral institutions. However, calls from the Supreme Patriarchs of both sects of the Cambodian *sangha* for state intervention to introduce and enforce a prohibition through constitutional or legislative amendments have also been articulated in constitutional terms, with clear reference frequently being made to Buddhism's special status and the implicit responsibility this is considered to bestow on the government to protect the state religion. This has been countered by Buddhist monks, meanwhile, who have similarly insisted on their engagement in electoral politics, justifying it on both religious and constitutional grounds. As such, monks assert a sense of dual-identity … in which they can be both a secular, right-bearing citizen on the one hand, and a religious figure on the other. For some, the latter identity extends so far as to supplement the constitutionally grounded right to vote with an additional duty to do so in the interest of religiously infused conceptions of justice and goodness. The decision to vote need not always be part of a more general commitment to the pursuit of justice in the secular world through the practice of engaged Buddhism. Nonetheless, it is clear that—at least for some Cambodian monks— the philosophical foundations and ultimate aims of the two (the decision to go to the polls and the adoption of engaged Buddhism) often intersect.

SONGFENG LI, FREEDOM IN HANDCUFFS: RELIGIOUS FREEDOM IN THE CONSTITUTION OF CHINA
35 J. L. & RELIG. (2020) 113

[This analysis focuses mainly on Article 36 of the Constitution of China, which states:

Citizens of the People's Republic of China enjoy freedom of religious belief.

No State organ, public organization or individual may compel citizens to believe in, or not to believe in, any religion; nor may they discriminate against citizens who believe in, or do not believe in, any religion.

The State protects normal religious activities. No one may make use of religion to engage in activities that disrupt public order, impair the health of citizens or interfere with the educational system of the State.

Religious bodies and religious affairs are not subject to any foreign domination.]

…

The question arises as to why the Chinese Constitution says that freedom of religion is protected when, in reality, it does not allow people to enjoy this right. It is easy to conclude that China's constitution is not enforced and plays little role in China's legal system, being only a symbolic document.

…

Taking the Chinese Constitution Seriously

... Why enshrine constitutional guarantees for the right to religious freedom, among others, when the CCP [Chinese Communist Party] obviously opposes such rights? Actually, the Chinese government attaches great importance to what the Constitution does and does not provide. ...

Second, both the Chinese Constitution and the CCP's constitution require the CCP to abide by the Constitution. ...

Third, Chinese leaders have come to realize the importance of the Constitution and have increasingly stressed the importance of implementing it.

Fourth, China has recently organized a Constitution Day, and established a constitutional oath system to promote respect for and implementation of the Constitution. ... Both the setting up of a National Constitution Day and the establishing of a constitutional oath system are aimed at promoting the rule of law and highlighting the importance of upholding China's Constitution.

Unlike the US Constitution, the Chinese Constitution is not a social contract that limits the power of government. Rather, it was formulated under the leadership of the CCP and represents the institutionalization and legalization of the party's position and policies. ... In short, the Chinese Constitution does not so much protect the fundamental rights and freedoms of every citizen as define the future direction of the whole country. ... [T]he CCP and the Chinese government are under increasing pressure to implement the Constitution. Returning to the initial question, since the Constitution purports to protect freedom of religion and the Chinese government has stressed the implementation of the Constitution, why are there a large number of cases in which religious freedom has been violated? The answer is that the Chinese Constitution provides only a very limited protection for religious practice. Article 36 of the Constitution protects freedom of religious belief and "normal" religious activities. The government has the power to decide which activities are "normal" and which are "abnormal." This leaves open the possibility that the government can deem various religious practices "abnormal" and thus outside the sphere of legal protection. ...

...

Conclusion

... On the basis of the Chinese Constitution, citizens are free to believe what they want, but the government reserves the right to set the boundaries as to how the beliefs are practiced. And, more importantly, the limitations the government sets are dependent upon the Chinese Constitution. The Constitution establishes multiple limitations on religious freedom. First, [it] establishes state atheism as an official ideology, rather than remaining secular and neutral. All Chinese citizens, whether religious believers or not, are required to be educated by the atheistic government and under the leadership of the CCP. Second, religious freedom ... is a legal right, rather than a fundamental right, which means that these so-called rights and freedom are vested by the Constitution, and since they are not inalienable, they are subject to legal restrictions. The NPC [National People's Congress] can and does pass legislation, to a certain extent, limiting individuals' religious freedom. Third, the Chinese Constitution stipulates basic obligations of citizens that limit religious freedom. Fourth, Article 36 ... protects only the inner freedom of religious belief, not the freedom of religious practice. And the second half of Article 36 places restrictions on religious freedom. In sum, religious freedom in the Chinese Constitution is an exceedingly limited form of freedom.

...

b. International Law Perspectives

Here we turn to the universal human rights instruments. Note the limited degree to which those instruments have developed ideas about religion and state or religion and human rights, at least in relation to their far greater development of human rights ideas in fields like race, gender or democratic participation. But, as in many other areas of human rights, the space left open increases the importance of the role played by other actors such as treaty bodies and UN Special Rapporteurs. Indeed, the first major UN survey of the field was Arcot Krishnaswami's 1960 *Study of Discrimination in the Matter of Religious Rights and Practices* (UN Doc. E/CN.4/Sub.2/200/Rev.1). He proposed 16 'basic rules' to guide practice, and recommended their adoption by the UN. But, since the ICCPR was then only in draft form and the United States was still blocking progress on it, nothing was done.

A starting point is Article 18 of the ICCPR, adopted in 1966:

1. Everyone shall have the right to freedom of thought, conscience and religion. This right shall include freedom to have or to adopt a religion or belief of his choice, and freedom, either individually or in community with others and in public or private, to manifest his religion or belief in worship, observance, practice and teaching.

2. No one shall be subject to coercion which would impair his freedom to have or to adopt a religion or belief of his choice.

3. Freedom to manifest one's religion or beliefs may be subject only to such limitations as are prescribed by law and are necessary to protect public safety, order, health, or morals or the fundamental rights and freedoms of others.

4. The States Parties to the present Covenant undertake to have respect for the liberty of parents and, when applicable, legal guardians to ensure the religious and moral education of their children in conformity with their own convictions.

For the most part, with the exception of paragraph 4, the ICCPR followed the relevant content of the UDHR on this issue. It was widely assumed that a separate treaty on religious intolerance, as called for by the UN General Assembly in 1960, would later be drafted.[255] But this soon became politically contentious and it took nine years of drafting before a non-binding declaration could be adopted:

DECLARATION ON THE ELIMINATION OF ALL FORMS OF INTOLERANCE AND OF DISCRIMINATION BASED ON RELIGION OR BELIEF
GA RES. 36/55 (1981)

The General Assembly
...
Considering that the disregard and infringement of human rights and fundamental freedoms, in particular of the right to freedom of thought, conscience, religion or whatever belief, have brought, directly or indirectly, wars and great suffering to mankind, especially where they serve as a means of foreign interference in the internal affairs of other States and amount to kindling hatred between peoples and nations,

Considering that religion or belief, for anyone who professes either, is one of the fundamental elements in his conception of life and that freedom of religion or belief should be fully respected and guaranteed,

Considering that it is essential to promote understanding, tolerance and respect in matters relating to freedom of religion and belief ...,
...
Proclaims this Declaration on the Elimination of All Forms of Intolerance and of Discrimination Based on Religion or Belief:

Article 1

1. Everyone shall have the right to freedom of thought, conscience and religion. This right shall include freedom to have a religion or whatever belief of his choice, and freedom, either individually or in community with others and in public or private, to manifest his religion or belief in worship, observance, practice and teaching.

---

[255] C. Evans, 'Time for a Treaty? The Legal Sufficiency of the Declaration on the Elimination of All Forms of Intolerance and Discrimination', 2007 *BYU L. Rev.* 617.

2. No one shall be subject to coercion which would impair his freedom to have a religion or belief of his choice.

3. Freedom to manifest one's religion or belief may be subject only to such limitations as are prescribed by law and are necessary to protect public safety, order, health or morals or the fundamental rights and freedoms of others.

Article 2

1. No one shall be subject to discrimination by any State, institution, group of persons, or person on the grounds of religion or other belief.

2. For the purposes of the present Declaration, the expression 'intolerance and discrimination based on religion or belief' means any distinction, exclusion, restriction or preference based on religion or belief and having as its purpose or as its effect nullification or impairment of the recognition, enjoyment or exercise of human rights and fundamental freedoms on an equal basis.

Article 3

Discrimination between human being on the grounds of religion or belief constitutes an affront to human dignity and a disavowal of the principles of the Charter of the United Nations, and shall be condemned as a violation of the human rights and fundamental freedoms proclaimed in the Universal Declaration of Human Rights and enunciated in detail in the International Covenants on Human Rights, and as an obstacle to friendly and peaceful relations between nations.

Article 4

1. All States shall take effective measures to prevent and eliminate discrimination on the grounds of religion or belief in the recognition, exercise and enjoyment of human rights and fundamental freedoms in all fields of civil, economic, political, social and cultural life.

2. All States shall make all efforts to enact or rescind legislation where necessary to prohibit any such discrimination, and to take all appropriate measures to combat intolerance on the grounds of religion or other beliefs in this matter.

Article 5

1. The parents or, as the case may be, the legal guardians of the child have the right to organize the life within the family in accordance with their religion or belief and bearing in mind the moral education in which they believe the child should be brought up.

2. Every child shall enjoy the right to have access to education in the matter of religion or belief in accordance with the wishes of his parents or, as the case may be, legal guardians, and shall not be compelled to receive teaching on religion or belief against the wishes of his parents or legal guardians, the best interests of the child being the guiding principle.

...

Article 6

In accordance with article 1 of the present Declaration, and subject to the provisions of article 1, paragraph 3, the right to freedom of thought, conscience, religion or belief shall include, inter alia, the following freedoms:

...

(d) To write, issue and disseminate relevant publications in these areas;

(e) To teach a religion or belief in places suitable for these purposes;

(f) To solicit and receive voluntary financial and other contributions from individuals and institutions;

(g) To train, appoint, elect or designate by succession appropriate leaders called for by the requirements and standards of any religion or belief;

(h) To observe days of rest and to celebrate holidays and ceremonies in accordance with the precepts of one's religion or belief;

(i) To establish and maintain communications with individuals and communities in matters of religion and belief at the national and international levels.

Article 7

The rights and freedoms set forth in the present Declaration shall be accorded in national legislation in such a manner that everyone shall be able to avail himself of such rights and freedoms in practice.

...

Article 8

Nothing in the present Declaration shall be construed as restricting or derogating from any right defined in the Universal Declaration of Human Rights and the International Covenants on Human Rights.

* * *

The Declaration has been criticized for its lack of ambition and failure to address key issues, but in the absence of the political will or a propitious international environment for agreement on religious issues, it has been generally acknowledged as the best available platform:

> We need to work on it as the basis (albeit an incomplete basis) of activism in an arena where few international platforms and standards actually exist. The Declaration makes a tenuous but welcome start in a field where much progress remains necessary – in elaborating legal standards, focusing on implementation of protected rights, and acknowledging the need to respond effectively to violations.[256]

Commenting on the Declaration, Donna Sullivan, in 'Advancing the Freedom of Religion or Belief Through the UN Declaration on the Elimination of Religious Intolerance and Discrimination', 82 *Am. J. Int. L.* (1988) 487 noted some of its shortcomings. The Declaration is directed at governments, so that '[i]nteractions among members of the same religious groups are ... not easily analyzed under the Declaration.' It is also premised upon a typical 'Western model of religion, in which religious institutions and authority are structurally separable from political and other social institutions'. Sullivan observes that the Declaration omitted explicit reference to the freedom to change one's religion or belief in order 'to avoid the implicit approval of proselytizing'. But, in her view, that freedom remains implicit in the right to have a religion or belief, and that the 'savings clause' in Article 8 ensures that the standards in the UDHR and the ICCPR cannot be diminished. In relation to the concept of 'intolerance', she notes two views that have been taken of its meaning and significance in the Declaration:

> ... The view that intolerance describes the emotional, psychological, philosophical and religious attitudes that may prompt acts of discrimination or violations of religious freedoms is persuasive. Where intolerance fuels such conduct as killing or the destruction of property, these acts constitute violations of substantive international human rights, such as the right to life, and, in most cases, violations of national law. If intolerance motivates deprivations of the freedom to manifest religion or belief, these acts again constitute violations of substantive rights protected by the Declaration itself.

> ...

> A second approach to combating intolerance, which was proposed during drafting but rejected, is to prohibit the expression of ideas based on religious hatred and the incitement of hatred and discrimination based on religion or belief. [See Article 20 of the ICCPR.] ...

---

[256] N. Ghanea, 'The 1981 UN Declaration on the Elimination of All Forms of Intolerance and of Discrimination Based on Religion or Belief: Some Observations', in *ibid (ed.), The Challenge of Religious Discrimination at the Dawn of the New Millennium* (2003) 30.

In the absence of a treaty in this area, two other sources of elaboration of the content of the right have assumed particular importance. The first is a General Comment by the UN Human Rights Committee, established under the ICCPR, which adopts such documents to reflect its understanding and interpretation of the Covenant's provisions. See Ch. 9A 3, below for a discussion of the nature and purpose of General Comments. The second are reports issued by the UN Human Rights Council's Special Rapporteur on freedom of religion or belief, a mandate first created in 1986 to focus on 'religious intolerance' and changed in 2000 to its current title.

HUMAN RIGHTS COMMITTEE, GENERAL COMMENT NO. 22: THE RIGHT TO FREEDOM OF THOUGHT, CONSCIENCE AND RELIGION
(1993)

...

2. Article 18 protects theistic, non-theistic and atheistic beliefs, as well as the right not to profess any religion or belief. The terms 'belief' and 'religion' are to be broadly construed. Article 18 is not limited in its application to traditional religions or to religions and beliefs with institutional characteristics or practices analogous to those of traditional religions ... .

3. Article 18 distinguishes the freedom of thought, conscience, religion or belief from the freedom to manifest religion or belief. It does not permit any limitations whatsoever on the freedom of thought and conscience or on the freedom to have or adopt a religion or belief of one's choice. These freedoms are protected unconditionally ... .

4. The freedom to manifest religion or belief may be exercised 'either individually or in community with others and in public or private'. The freedom to manifest religion or belief in worship, observance, practice and teaching encompasses a broad range of acts. The concept of worship extends to ritual and ceremonial acts giving direct expression to belief, as well as various practices integral to such acts, including the building of places of worship, the use of ritual formulae and objects, the display of symbols, and the observance of holidays and days of rest. The observance and practice of religion or belief may include not only ceremonial acts but also such customs as the observance of dietary regulations, the wearing of distinctive clothing or head coverings, participation in rituals associated with certain stages of life, and the use of a particular language customarily spoken by a group. In addition, the practice and teaching of religion or belief includes acts integral to the conduct by religious groups of their basic affairs, such as the freedom to choose their religious leaders, priests and teachers, the freedom to establish seminaries or religious schools and the freedom to prepare and distribute religious texts or publications.

5. The Committee observes that the freedom to 'have or to adopt' a religion or belief necessarily entails the freedom to choose a religion or belief, including the right to replace one's current religion or belief with another or to adopt atheistic views, as well as the right to retain one's religion or belief. Article 18.2 bars coercion that would impair the right to have or adopt a religion or belief, including the use of threat of physical force or penal sanctions to compel believers or non-believers to adhere to their religious beliefs and congregations, to recant their religion or belief or to convert ... .

6. The Committee is of the view that article 18.4 permits public school instruction in subjects such as the general history of religions and ethics if it is given in a neutral and objective way ... . The Committee notes that public education that includes instruction in a particular religion or belief is inconsistent with article 18.4 unless provision is made for non-discriminatory exemptions or alternatives that would accommodate the wishes of parents and guardians.

7. In accordance with article 20, no manifestation of religion or belief may amount to propaganda for war or advocacy of national, racial or religious hatred that constitutes incitement to discrimination, hostility or violence ... .

8. Article 18.3 permits restrictions on the freedom to manifest religion or belief only if limitations are prescribed by law and are necessary to protect public safety, order, health or morals, or the fundamental rights and freedoms of others. The freedom from coercion to have or to adopt a religion or belief and the liberty of parents and guardians to ensure religious and moral education cannot be restricted. In interpreting the scope of

permissible limitation clauses … limitations may be applied only for those purposes for which they were prescribed and must be directly related and proportionate to the specific need on which they are predicated … .

9. The fact that a religion is recognized as a state religion or that it is established as official or traditional or that its followers comprise the majority of the population, shall not result in any impairment of the enjoyment of any of the rights under the Covenant, including articles 18 and 27, nor in any discrimination against adherents to other religions or non-believers. In particular, certain measures discriminating against the latter, such as measures restricting eligibility for government service to members of the predominant religion or giving economic privileges to them or imposing special restrictions on the practice of other faiths, are not in accordance with the prohibition of discrimination based on religion or belief and the guarantee of equal protection under article 26 … .

10. If a set of beliefs is treated as official ideology in constitutions, statutes, proclamations of ruling parties, etc., or in actual practice, this shall not result in any impairment of the freedoms under article 18 or any other rights recognized under the Covenant nor in any discrimination against persons who do not accept the official ideology or who oppose it.

...

REPORTS OF THE SPECIAL RAPPORTEUR ON FREEDOM OF RELIGION OR BELIEF

Individual experts appointed to this office can serve for a maximum of six years. Since 1986, there have been six different mandate-holders. The following two reports were prepared by Ahmed Shaheed, Special Rapporteur from 2016 to 2022.

i. Antisemitism (UN Doc. A/74/358 (2019))257

...

II. Combating antisemitism ...

4. … [A]ntisemitism [has] received scant attention as a human rights issue. Overall, data collection worldwide is limited, and in many States antisemitic harassment is significantly underreported. Nevertheless, reports of hostility, discrimination and violence motivated by antisemitism have increased in many parts of the world. …
...

IV. Key findings

11. The Jewish population was estimated at 14,606,000 worldwide in 2018, with 15 countries in the Americas and Western and Eastern Europe being home to the largest populations outside of Israel. …

12. Aptly termed "the oldest hatred", prejudice against or hatred of Jews, known as antisemitism, draws on various theories and conspiracies, articulated through myriad tropes and stereotypes and manifested in manifold ways, even in places where few or no Jewish persons live. This includes ancient narratives promoted by religious doctrine and pseudoscientific theories offered in the latter half of the second millennium to legitimize bigotry, discrimination and genocide of Jews. More contemporary forms of antisemitism employ narratives about the role of Jews in society, frequently informing or intersecting with other forms of bigotry, misogyny and discrimination.

A. Historical narratives and tropes

13. Some of the oldest antisemitic narratives can be traced back to theologies that attributed collective guilt for the murder of Jesus to Jews, treating them as "malicious" and "evil". Such tropes, which identify Jews as descendants of Judas or Satan and depict them as "cunning, controlling and powerful", have been promoted through religious teachings and depicted in art, and they have sometimes motivated contemporary antisemitic

---

257 See generally G. Quer, 'Antisemitism and the UN', in A. Lange et al. (eds.), *Confronting Antisemitism in Modern Media, the Legal and Political Worlds*

(2021) 413; and N. Gordon, 'Between Human Rights and Civil Society: The Case of Israel's Apartheid Enablers', 48 *L. and Soc. Inquiry* (2023) 1.

acts. Other tropes reflect contempt for the Jewish religion, including the recurring false allegation that Jews engage in the ritual murder of non-Jews (the "blood libel"), and continue to pervade contemporary discourse.

14. Antisemitism is also often expressed in racialized terms, with Jewish people characterized as subhumans who must be excluded from "normal" human civilization. This pseudoscientific approach was used to justify the persecution of Jews in Nazi Germany and the subsequent acts of genocide committed by the Nazis and their accomplices against the European Jewish population, while antisemitic expressions of Holocaust denial seek to repudiate or minimize the harrowing historical facts of that systematic murder of 6 million Jews.

15. Assertions that Jews are a "wandering" people without a land or nation, whose members conspire to advance their collective interests to the detriment of their "host" countries, or that Jews constitute a "powerful, global cabal" that manipulates governments, the media, banks, the entertainment industry and other institutions for malevolent purposes, are also expressions of antisemitic attitudes. Many of those negative stereotypes were promulgated in the Protocols of the Elders of Zion, a discredited forgery published in the early twentieth century and widely disseminated in the Middle East, alleging a secret Jewish plan for world domination. Those stereotypes often underpin modern conspiracy theories attributing responsibility to Jews for everything from immigration to terrorist attacks.

B. Trends in contemporary rhetoric

16. The Special Rapporteur is alarmed by the growing use of antisemitic tropes by white supremacists, including neo-Nazis and members of radical Islamist groups, in slogans, images, stereotypes and conspiracy theories meant to incite and justify hostility, discrimination and violence against Jews.

17. The Special Rapporteur also takes note of numerous reports of an increase in many countries of what is sometimes called "left-wing" antisemitism, in which individuals claiming to hold anti-racist and anti-imperialist views employ antisemitic narratives or tropes in the course of expressing anger at the policies or practices of the Government of Israel. ... [I]t is never acceptable to render Jews as proxies for the Government of Israel.
....
18. The Special Rapporteur further notes the claims that the objectives, activities and effects of the Boycott, Divestment and Sanctions movement are fundamentally antisemitic. The movement promotes boycotts and stockholder divestment initiatives against Israeli or international corporations and institutions that supporters of the movement maintain are "complicit" in violations of the human rights of Palestinians by the Government of Israel. .... He recalls that international law recognizes boycotts as legitimate forms of political expression and that non-violent expressions of support for boycotts are, as a general matter, legitimate speech that should be protected. However, he also stresses that expression that draws on antisemitic tropes or stereotypes, rejects the right of Israel to exist or advocates discrimination against Jewish individuals because of their religion, should be condemned.
...

E. Online manifestations of antisemitism

35. Antisemitic hate speech is particularly prevalent online. Unanimous concern raised by all those engaged for this report noted that platforms like Gab (a Twitter-like platform that permits hate speech), 4chan and Twitter provide a forum for people ... to create networks in which they are able to share extreme antisemitic views. A study of online antisemitic hate speech found on Twitter in English revealed 4.2 million antisemitic tweets in one year alone, not including tweets of images or emojis. Publicly prominent Jewish individuals and organizations are also specifically targeted with antisemitic comments online.
...
39. Antisemitism online includes far-right tropes that Jews spearhead feminist, lesbian, gay, bisexual, transgender and intersex movements and immigration movements as a method of perpetrating a "white genocide", conspiracy theories that have been repeated in the online manifestos posted by far-right terrorists prior to mass shootings in synagogues. ....
...

VI. Recommendations

...

A. States and political actors

...

76. Governments must also acknowledge that antisemitism poses a threat to stability and security and that antisemitic incidents require prompt, unequivocal responses from leaders. ... [T]he commission of antisemitic hate crimes engages the obligation of the State under international human rights law to protect Jews against the violation of their fundamental rights. States must also invest in preventive security measures, compliant with international human rights law, to deter antisemitic hate crimes. They ... [also] have an affirmative responsibility to address online antisemitism, as the digital sphere is now the primary public forum and marketplace for ideas.

77. States should enact and enforce hate crime legislation that recognizes antisemitism as a prohibited bias motivation and that is clear, concrete and easy to understand. ...

ii. Islamophobia (UN Doc. A/HRC/46/30 (2021))

...

A. Key findings and conceptual framework

12. ... Islamophobia [may be characterized] as a pool of ideas or ideologies that includes two overlapping processes whereby Islam and Muslims are essentialized and "othered". While the precise character is context-specific, in its most prevalent form, the Islamophobic mindset treats Islam – a global religion with widely diverse interpretations and practices worldwide – as a monolithic and fundamentalist creed that advocates violence, sexism and homophobia. Denying Islam of its status as a religion, the Islamophobic mindset considers Islam a fixed political ideology that endangers "Western civilization" and other nations where Muslims are a minority population. In parallel, as followers of Islam, Muslims are demonized as disloyal "others" who are intent upon imposing their values on non-believers through violence, "overbreeding" and the radicalization of "good" Muslims.

13. Scholars have explored how this latter process functions as a form of "racialization", instilling the idea that Muslim identity is a fixed marker of cultural – not just religious – difference, characterizing Muslims as a foreign "other". Simultaneously drawing upon Muslims' religion, race and culture, Muslims are differentiated as a social group apart from the majority and treated as inferior on the basis of such perceived differences. As such, some recognize Islamophobia as a form of anti-Muslim racism. Scholars and human rights experts also underscore the gendered forms of the phenomenon whereby Muslim women – particularly Muslim women who wear a head covering – are cast as subordinates without agency, while Muslim men and those who look Muslim by virtue of their skin colour and facial hair, are deemed to be intrinsically violent. ...

...

B. Dissemination of intolerant narratives

Harmful stereotypes and tropes about Muslims and Islam are chronically reinforced by those working in the mainstream media, powerful politicians, influencers of popular culture and academics. Muslims are generally underrepresented and are often mispresented in the media. In one study, the European Commission against Racism and Intolerance (ECRI) reported that in over 600,000 news items published in 2016 and 2017 in the Netherlands, the adjectives most used to describe Muslims were "radical", "extremist" and "terrorist"; in contrast, people from the Netherlands were often described as "known", "average" and "beautiful". Other studies have shown that media outlets in several countries disproportionately focus on negative angles for news stories involving Muslims such as reporting on their perceived failure to integrate, and more media attention is often paid to terrorist attacks committed by Muslims than to terrorist attacks committed by far-right extremists.

...

16. ... [M]any films depict Muslims negatively and play into harmful stereotypes, with some even claiming that the "Muslim-as-terrorist" film has become a legitimate genre (or subgenre) in its own right. ...

...

C. Discrimination

Securitization

23. ... Over the past two decades, Muslim individuals and communities have borne the brunt of the use and abuse of counter-terrorism measures. ...

24. States have reportedly incorporated their essential services, including education and health care, within their national security apparatus in a way that disproportionately heightens surveillance of Muslims and potentially compounds existing inequalities, including educational and health outcomes. Doctors and other health personnel, social workers and educators are co-opted as enablers of the State's securitization apparatus by being mandated to report who is ostensibly at risk of radicalization. ...

...

V. Conclusions

70. Both conscious and unconscious bias against Muslims perpetuated by individuals, politicians, social influencers, the media and hate groups, among others, play a significant role in dehumanizing Muslims, motivating hate crimes, promoting discrimination and exacerbating socioeconomic exclusion. Scholars and rights monitors emphasize that Islamophobic attitudes often perpetuate a vicious circle whereby State policies validate private Islamophobic attitudes and actions, and the prevalence of such attitudes can propel State policies that penalize Muslims.

71. Collective blame cast on Muslims for terrorist acts purportedly carried out in the name of Islam, alongside Islamophobic attitudes that draw on negative overgeneralizations about Islam and essentializations of Muslims – which depict them as threatening and centre on constructions of irreconcilable cultural differences between Muslims and the values of majority populations – have fuelled acts of discrimination, hostility and violence against Muslim individuals and communities.

...

73. The Special Rapporteur emphasizes that international human rights law protects individuals, not religions. Nothing in the present report suggests that criticism of the ideas, leaders, symbols or practices of Islam is something that should be prohibited or criminally sanctioned. Rather, the Special Rapporteur emphasizes that the discrimination and intolerance that emanate from the ideologies of Islamophobia present a significant challenge to States' aspirations to foster democratic pluralism and respect, protect and promote all human rights. Peaceful, inclusive, pluralistic societies that endeavour to respect the human rights of all persons regardless of religious or belief identity must oppose religious bigotry and racism, but they must also avoid censoring purely discursive speech.

74. ... [I]t is essential to identify and evaluate how State structures perpetuate and legitimize Islamophobia and actively discriminate against Muslim individuals and communities.

...

DEFINING ANTISEMITISM

In 2016, the International Holocaust Remembrance Alliance (IHRA), an NGO, adopted a definition of antisemitism as a 'non-legal tool' to facilitate monitoring of relevant practices. It defines antisemitism as "a certain perception of Jews, which may be expressed as hatred toward Jews. Rhetorical and physical manifestations of antisemitism are directed toward Jewish or non-Jewish individuals and/or their property, toward Jewish community institutions and religious facilities".

The definition offers some illustrations:

 (a) Manifestations might include the targeting of the State of Israel, conceived as a Jewish collectivity. However, criticism of Israel similar to that levelled against any other country cannot be regarded as antisemitic. ...;

 (b) Contemporary examples of antisemitism ... could, taking into account the overall context, include ...:

(i) Calling for, aiding or justifying the killing or harming of Jews in the name of a radical ideology or an extremist view of religion;

(ii) Making mendacious, dehumanizing, demonizing or stereotypical allegations about Jews …;

(iii) Accusing Jews as a people of being responsible for real or imagined wrongdoing committed by a single Jewish person or group, or even for acts committed by non-Jews;

(iv) Denying the fact, scope, mechanisms (e.g. gas chambers) or intentionality of the … the Holocaust;

(v) Accusing the Jews as a people, or Israel as a State, of inventing or exaggerating the Holocaust;

(vi) Accusing Jewish citizens of being more loyal to Israel, or to the alleged priorities of Jews worldwide, than to the interests of their own nations;

(vii) Denying the Jewish people their right to self-determination, e.g. by claiming that the existence of a State of Israel is a racist endeavour;

(viii) Applying double standards by requiring of Israel a behaviour not expected or demanded of any other democratic nation;

(ix) Using the symbols and images associated with classic antisemitism (e.g. claims of Jews killing Jesus or "blood libel") to characterize Israel or Israelis;

(x) Drawing comparisons of contemporary Israeli policy to that of the Nazis;

(xi) Holding Jews collectively responsible for actions of the State of Israel.

The scope of the definition became a matter of considerable controversy. In response, the Special Rapporteur on freedom of religion or belief, Ahmed Shaheed (UN Doc. A/74/358 (2019)) provided this analysis:

53. The definition has been … endorsed by the European Parliament… and by the Secretary-General of the Organization of American States. It is used by a number of [NGOs] that monitor antisemitism and was recognized by the [UN] Secretary-General … in 2018.

54. … [Critics] have expressed concern that it can be applied in ways that could effectively restrict legitimate political expression, including criticism of policies and practices being promoted by the Government of Israel that violate the rights of Palestinians. Such concerns are focused on three of the illustrative examples … namely [vii, viii and x, above]. The Special Rapporteur notes that the definition … does not designate them as examples of speech that are *ipso facto* antisemitic and further observes that a contextual assessment is required … . Nevertheless, the potential chilling effects … on speech that is critical of policies and practices of the Government of Israel must be taken seriously … . Therefore, the use of the definition, as a non-legal educational tool, could minimize such chilling effects and contribute usefully to efforts to combat antisemitism. When public bodies use the definition in any regulatory context, due diligence must be exercised to ensure that freedom of expression within the law is protected for all. …

In 2022, the Special Rapporteur on racism, E. Tendayi Achiume (UN Doc. A/77/512) offered a different response:

71. The Special Rapporteur ... calls attention to the politically motivated instrumentalization of the fight against antisemitism, which is increasingly linked to the [IHRA definition] ... . While reiterating the urgent need for Member States to remain committed to fighting antisemitism in all its manifestations, she urges greater attention and care regarding the implications of tools used in that context. ...

72. ... [The IHRA definition] has become highly controversial and divisive owing to its susceptibility to being politically instrumentalized and the [resulting] harm done to human rights ... . [The rapporteur] cautions against reliance on the working definition as a guiding instrument for and at the [UN].

73. ... About 350 leading scholars support an alternative definition of antisemitism established in the Jerusalem Declaration on Antisemitism ... .[258]

...

75. Although the [IHRA] working definition is promoted as being "non-legally binding", its *de facto* influence on the policy and practice of governments and private actors has contributed to violations of the human rights of freedom of expression, assembly and political participation, among others. ... [I]t is precisely the "soft law" status of the working definition that effectively helps to undermine certain co-existent rights, without offering any remedy or means to legally challenge such violations. ...

76. The [definition and examples] are wielded to prevent or suppress legitimate criticisms of the State of Israel, a State that must, like any other in the [UN] system, be accountable for human rights violations that it perpetrates. ...

...

79. Precisely because the scourge of antisemitism remains an urgent issue ..., the Special Rapporteur urges the United Nations system and Member States urgently to launch an open and inclusive process to identify an enhanced response to antisemitism ... consistently rooted in and supportive of human rights. ...

QUESTIONS

1. In what respects does the General Comment of the Human Rights Committee appear to go beyond Article 18 itself with respect to notions of religious freedom, and beyond the 1981 Declaration? What implications have Article 18 and the 1981 Declaration for the issue of 'establishment'?

2. Does the Declaration reach beyond action by the state to cover conduct (that is, to require or prohibit certain conduct) by private (non-state) actors? If so, under what provisions and with respect to what kinds of conduct?

3. How do you assess the value of the reports on antisemitism and islamophobia? What role should Special Rapporteurs play in resolving the controversy over examples of antisemitism?

---

[258] https://jerusalemdeclaration.org/

c. Proselytism

KOKKINAKIS V. GREECE
EUROPEAN COURT OF HUMAN RIGHTS, 1993, SER. A, NO. 260-A (15 DECEMBER 1997)

[Minos Kokkinakis, a Greek national, was born in 1919 into an Orthodox Christian family. In 1936, he became a Jehovah's Witnesses, a Christian sect originating in the nineteenth century, and known for intense door-to-door canvassing by its members. He was arrested more than 60 times for proselytism, and on several occasions imprisoned for a period of months. In 1986, he and his wife called at the home of a Mrs Kyriakaki to engage her in discussion about religion. Her husband, cantor at a local Orthodox church, informed the police who arrested him. Kokkinakis was convicted under Law No. 1363/1938 of the crime of engaging in proselytism and was sentenced to four months' imprisonment. The Court of Appeal upheld the conviction. The Court of Cassation dismissed an appeal, rejecting the plea that the law violated Article 13 of the Greek Constitution and hence could not be applied.

Kokkinakis then brought a case against Greece before the European Commission of Human Rights, claiming that his conviction violated provisions of the European Convention on Human Rights. Greece, a party to that Convention, had accepted the jurisdiction of the Commission to hear individual complaints. The Commission found that Greece had violated Article 9 of the Convention. It then referred the case to the European Court of Human Rights, whose jurisdiction Greece had also accepted. (The jurisdiction and work of this Court are examined in Ch. 11A, below).

Section 4 of Law No.1363/1938, as later amended, made 'engaging in proselytism' a crime, and further provided:

> 2. By 'proselytism' is meant, in particular, any direct or indirect attempt to intrude on the religious beliefs of a person of a different religious persuasion, with the aim of undermining those beliefs, either by any kind of inducement or promise of an inducement or moral support or material assistance, or by fraudulent means or by taking advantage of his inexperience, trust, need, low intellect or naïvety.

The Greek Constitution of 1975 stated in Article 3 that the 'dominant religion in Greece is that of the Christian Eastern Orthodox Church'. ...

Article 13 of the Constitution provided:

> 1. Freedom of conscience in religious matters is inviolable. The enjoyment of personal and political rights shall not depend on an individual's religious beliefs.

> 2. There shall be freedom to practise any known religion; individuals shall be free to perform their rites of worship without hindrance and under the protection of the law. The performance of rites of worship must not prejudice public order or public morals. Proselytism is prohibited.

Several accounts appeared in the opinions of the Greek courts of the interaction between Kokkinakis and Kryiakaki. The trial court stated that the defendant:

> attempted to proselytise and, directly or indirectly, to intrude on the religious beliefs of Orthodox Christians, with the intention of undermining those beliefs, by taking advantage of their inexperience, their low intellect and their naïvety. In particular, they went to the home of [Mrs Kyriakaki] ... and told her that they brought good news; by insisting in a pressing manner, they gained admittance to the house and began to read from a book on the Scriptures which they interpreted with reference to a king of heaven, to events which had not yet occurred but would occur, etc., encouraging her by means of their judicious, skilful explanations ... to change her Orthodox Christian beliefs.

The Court of Appeal repeated this account, and added that Kokkinakis began to read out passages from Holy Scripture, which he:

skillfully analysed in a manner that the Christian woman, for want of adequate grounding in doctrine, could not challenge, and at the same time offered her various similar books and importunately tried, directly and indirectly, to undermine her religious beliefs. He must consequently be declared guilty of the above-mentioned offence.

One appeal judge dissented, asserting that no evidence showed that Kyriakaki was particularly inexperienced in Orthodox Christian belief or was of particularly low intellect or naïve.

There follow excerpts from the opinion of the European Court:]

[A 1953 judgment of the Greek Supreme Administrative Court had stated, with respect to the meaning of the prohibition of proselytism, that the Constitutional ban:]

> means that purely spiritual teaching does not amount to proselytism, even if it demonstrates the errors of other religions and entices possible disciples away from them, who abandon their original religions of their own free will; this is because spiritual teaching is in the nature of a rite of worship performed freely and without hindrance. Outside such spiritual teaching, which may be freely given, any determined, importunate attempt to entice disciples away from the dominant religion by means that are unlawful or morally reprehensible constitutes proselytism as prohibited by the aforementioned provision of the Constitution.

18. The Greek courts have held that persons were guilty of proselytism who ... offered a scholarship for study abroad; ... distributed 'so-called religious' books and booklets free to 'illiterate peasants' or to 'young schoolchildren'; or promised a young seamstress an improvement in her position if she left the Orthodox Church, whose priests were alleged to be 'exploiters of society'.

[The opinion noted that the Jehovah's Witnesses movement had been present in Greece for about a century, and that its membership in Greece was estimated to be between 25,000 and 70,000. Between 1975 and 1992, 4,400 members had been arrested, 1,233 committed to trial and 208 convicted, some for other offences than proselytism. It then turned to Kokinnakis's claim that Article 9 of the European Convention had been violated.]

28. The applicant's complaints mainly concerned a restriction on the exercise of his freedom of religion. The Court will accordingly begin by looking at the issues relating to Article 9, which provides:

> 1. Everyone has the right to freedom of thought, conscience and religion; this right includes freedom to change his religion or belief and freedom, either alone or in community with others and in public or private, to manifest his religion or belief, in worship, teaching, practice and observance.

> 2. Freedom to manifest one's religion or beliefs shall be subject only to such limitations as are prescribed by law and are necessary in a democratic society in the interests of public safety, for the protection of public order, health or morals, or for the protection of the rights and freedoms of others.

29. The applicant did not only challenge what he claimed to be the wrongful application to him of section 4 of Law no. 1363/1938. His submission concentrated on the broader problem of whether that enactment was compatible with the right enshrined in Article 9 of the Convention ... He pointed to the logical and legal difficulty of drawing any even remotely clear dividing-line between proselytism and freedom to change one's religion or belief and, either alone or in community with others, in public and in private, to manifest it, which encompassed all forms of teaching, publication and preaching between people.

...

Mr Kokkinakis complained, lastly, of the selective application of this Law by the administrative and judicial authorities; it would surpass 'even the wildest academic hypothesis' to imagine, for example, the possibility ... that an Orthodox Christian would be prosecuted for proselytising on behalf of the 'dominant religion'.

...

31. ... [F]reedom of thought, conscience and religion is one of the foundations of a "democratic society" within the meaning of the Convention. It is, in its religious dimension, one of the most vital elements that go to make

up the identity of believers and their conception of life, but it is also a precious asset for atheists, agnostics, sceptics and the unconcerned. The pluralism indissociable from a democratic society, which has been dearly won over the centuries, depends on it.

...

According to Article 9, freedom to manifest one's religion is not only exercisable in community with others, 'in public' and within the circle of those whose faith one shares, but can also be asserted 'alone' and 'in private'; furthermore, it includes in principle the right to try to convince one's neighbour, for example through 'teaching', failing which, moreover, 'freedom to change [one's] religion or belief', enshrined in Article 9, would be likely to remain a dead letter.

...

33. ... [The limitations clause in Article 9(2)] refers only to 'freedom to manifest one's religion or belief'. In so doing, it recognises that in democratic societies, in which several religions coexist within one and the same population, it may be necessary to place restrictions on this freedom in order to reconcile the interests of the various groups and ensure that everyone's beliefs are respected.

...

36. The sentence passed by the [criminal court and the court of appeal] amounts to an interference with the exercise of Mr Kokkinakis's right to 'freedom to manifest [his] religion or belief '. Such an interference is contrary to Article 9 unless it is 'prescribed by law', directed at one or more of the legitimate aims in paragraph 2 and 'necessary in a democratic society' for achieving them.

...

[Kokkinakis claimed that the requirement that a prohibition be 'prescribed by law' had not been met by Section 4 of the Greek Law; and that the definition of proselytism had no 'objective' base, perhaps a deliberate decision 'to make it possible for any kind of religious conversation or communication to be caught by the provision'. He referred to the risk of extension 'by the police and often by the courts too of the vague terms of the section, such as ... "indirect attempt" to intrude on the religious beliefs of others.' And he added that '[p]unishing a non-Orthodox Christian even when he was offering "moral support or material assistance" was tantamount to punishing an act that any religion would prescribe and that the Criminal Code required in certain emergencies.'

The Court noted that it was essential to avoid 'excessive rigidity' in legislation in order to keep pace with changing circumstances. Many criminal statutes 'to a greater or lesser extent are vague'. Practice under the proselytism statute and a 'body of settled national case-law' interpreting the Law were such as to 'enable Mr. Kokkinakis to regulate his conduct in the matter'. Hence the Law was 'prescribed by law' within the meaning of Article 9(2).

The Court next inquired into whether there had been a 'legitimate aim' for the Law within the meaning of Article 9(2).]

43. In the applicant's submission, religion was part of the 'constantly renewable flow of human thought' and it was impossible to conceive of its being excluded from public debate. A fair balance of personal rights made it necessary to accept that others' thought should be subject to a minimum of influence, otherwise the result would be a 'strange society of silent animals that [would] think but ... not express themselves, that [would] talk but ... not communicate, and that [would] exist but ... not coexist'.

44. Having regard to the circumstances of the case and the actual terms of the relevant courts' decisions, the Court considers that the impugned measure was in pursuit of a legitimate aim under Article 9 para. 2, namely the protection of the rights and freedoms of others, relied on by the Government.

[The Court turned to the requirement that a restrictive measure be 'necessary in a democratic society.']

45. Mr Kokkinakis did not consider it necessary in a democratic society to prohibit a fellow citizen's right to speak when he came to discuss religion with his neighbour. He was curious to know how a discourse delivered with conviction and based on holy books common to all Christians could infringe the rights of others. Mrs Kyriakaki was an experienced adult woman with intellectual abilities; it was not possible, without flouting fundamental human rights, to make it a criminal offence for a Jehovah's Witness to have a conversation with a cantor's wife. Moreover, the Crete Court of Appeal, although the facts before it were precise and absolutely clear, had not managed to determine the direct or indirect nature of the applicant's attempt to intrude on the

complainant's religious beliefs; its reasoning showed that it had convicted the applicant 'not for something he had done but for what he was'. ...

46. The Government ... pointed out that if the State remained indifferent to attacks on freedom of religious belief, major unrest would be caused that would probably disturb the social peace.

47. The Court has consistently held that a certain margin of appreciation is to be left to the Contracting States in assessing the existence and extent of the necessity of an interference, but this margin is subject to European supervision, embracing both the legislation and the decisions applying it, even those given by an independent court. The Court's task is to determine whether the measures taken at national level were justified in principle and proportionate. ...

48. First of all, a distinction has to be made between bearing Christian witness and improper proselytism. The former corresponds to true evangelism, which a report drawn up in 1956 under the auspices of the World Council of Churches describes as an essential mission and a responsibility of every Christian and every Church. The latter represents a corruption or deformation of it. It may, according to the same report, take the form of activities offering material or social advantages with a view to gaining new members for a Church or exerting improper pressure on people in distress or in need; it may even entail the use of violence or brainwashing; more generally, it is not compatible with respect for the freedom of thought, conscience and religion of others.

Scrutiny of section 4 of Law no. 1363/1938 shows that the relevant criteria adopted by the Greek legislature are reconcilable with the foregoing if and in so far as they are designed only to punish improper proselytism, which the Court does not have to define in the abstract in the present case.

49. The Court notes, however, that in their reasoning the Greek courts established the applicant's liability by merely reproducing the wording of section 4 and did not sufficiently specify in what way the accused had attempted to convince his neighbour by improper means. None of the facts they set out warrants that finding.

That being so, it has not been shown that the applicant's conviction was justified in the circumstances of the case by a pressing social need. The contested measure therefore does not appear to have been proportionate to the legitimate aim pursued or, consequently, 'necessary in a democratic society ... for the protection of the rights and freedoms of others'.

50. In conclusion, there has been a breach of Article 9 of the Convention.
...

PARTLY CONCURRING OPINION OF JUDGE PETTITI
...
The expression "proselytism that is not respectable", which is a criterion used by the Greek courts when applying the Law, is sufficient for the enactment and the case-law applying it to be regarded as contrary to Article 9.
...
... [T]he haziness of the definition leaves too wide a margin of interpretation for determining criminal penalties.
...
Proselytism is linked to freedom of religion; a believer must be able to communicate his faith and his beliefs in the religious sphere as in the philosophical sphere. Freedom of religion and conscience is a fundamental right and this freedom must be able to be exercised for the benefit of all religions and not for the benefit of a single Church, even if this has traditionally been the established Church or 'dominant religion'.

Freedom of religion and conscience certainly entails accepting proselytism, even where it is 'not respectable'. Believers and agnostic philosophers have a right to expound their beliefs, to try to get other people to share them and even to try to convert those whom they are addressing.

The only limits on the exercise of this right are those dictated by respect for the rights of others where there is an attempt to coerce the person into consenting or to use manipulative techniques.

The other types of unacceptable behaviour — such as brainwashing, breaches of labour law, endangering of public health and incitement to immorality, which are found in the practices of certain pseudo-religious groups — must be punished in positive law as ordinary criminal offences. Proselytism cannot be forbidden under cover of punishing such activities.

...

The wording adopted by the majority of the Court in finding a breach, namely that the applicant's conviction was not justified in the circumstances of the case, leaves too much room for a repressive interpretation by the Greek courts in the future, whereas public prosecution must likewise be monitored. In my view, it would have been possible to define impropriety, coercion and duress more clearly and to describe more satisfactorily, in the abstract, the full scope of religious freedom and bearing witness.

...

Let us look now at the facts of the case. On the one hand, we have a militant Jehovah's Witness, a hardbitten adept of proselytism, a specialist in conversion, a martyr of the criminal courts whose earlier convictions have served only to harden him in his militancy, and, on the other hand, the ideal victim, a naïve woman, the wife of a cantor in the Orthodox Church (if he manages to convert her, what a triumph!). He swoops on her, trumpets that he has good news for her (the play on words is obvious, but no doubt not to her), manages to get himself let in and, as an experienced commercial traveller and cunning purveyor of a faith he wants to spread, expounds to her his intellectual wares cunningly wrapped up in a mantle of universal peace and radiant happiness. Who, indeed, would not like peace and happiness? But is this the mere exposition of Mr Kokkinakis's beliefs or is it not rather an attempt to beguile the simple soul of the cantor's wife? Does the Convention afford its protection to such undertakings? Certainly not.

...

I should certainly be inclined to recommend the Government to give instructions that prosecutions should be avoided where harmless conversations are involved, but not in the case of systematic, persistent campaigns entailing actions bordering on unlawful entry.

That having been said, I do not consider in any way that there has been a breach of the Convention.

...

Comments on Kokkinakis

Kokkinakis remains the landmark judgment in this area for the European human rights regime. But it has been widely criticized, and its lack of clarity is considered by many commentators to have facilitated the complex and confusing jurisprudence followed by the European Court of Human Rights in the cases considered later in this chapter. Consider these comments:

Malcolm Evans, 'The Freedom of Religion or Belief in the European Court of Human Rights since the *Kokkinakis case*. Or "Quoting *Kokkinakis*"', in Jeroen Temperman, T. Jeremy Gunn, and Malcolm D. Evans (eds.), *The European Court of Human Rights and the Freedom of Religion or Belief: The 25 Years since* Kokkinakis (2019) 33:

> ... In *Eweida v. UK* [2013] it was said that '[r]eligious freedom is primarily a matter of individual thought and conscience. ...

> Six months later, in *Sindicatul "Păstorul cel Bun" v. Romania* [2013] the Grand Chamber said that '[t]he autonomous existence of religious communities is indispensable for pluralism in a democratic society and is an issue at the very heart of the protection which Article 9 affords. It directly concerns not only the organisation of these communities as such but also the effective enjoyment of the right to freedom of religion by all their active members. Were the organisational life of the community not protected by Article 9, all other aspects of the individual's freedom of religion would become vulnerable'.

> Whereas the quote from *Eweida* emphasises the individual nature of the right, the *Sindicatul* case highlights its collective nature. Both draw on the *Kokkinakis* statement; *Eweida* quoting it expressly, *Sindicatul* by using its language, although not directly acknowledging it. This tension lies at the heart of much of the controversy surrounding

the practical application of Article 9: is it focussed on the individual, the religious or belief communities or the broader community as a whole? Is it about the individual versus the community? Or is it about the individual in community? And if so, which community? Both cases raised precisely such questions. The problem with the *Kokkinakis* approach is that it can support outcomes based on any of these approaches – or on none.

Brett G. Scharffs, '*Kokkinakis* and the Narratives of Proper and Improper Proselytizing', in *ibid*, 153:

> Two things are worth noting. First, the Court imposes a distinction between "proper" proselyting and "improper" proselytism upon the Greek statute and Constitution, a distinction that does not exist in these laws. This has the effect of preserving a criminal law that is overbroad, vague, and leaves too much discretion to prosecutors and judges, while holding that the application of the law in this case was a violation of Article 9.

Second, the Court compounds this imposition by failing to define clearly the difference between what is proper and improper. In the various accounts of the facts of the case, we see wildly diverging versions of what actually happened as well as of the significance of those facts. Thus, the case stands as a cautionary tale not only of the hazards of judicial storytelling, but also of the power of judicial law-making. It is not surprising that with such a shaky foundation, the Court prepares the way for subsequent jurisprudence on proselytizing that is unstable, unprincipled, and inconsistent.

MAKAU MUTUA, HUMAN RIGHTS, RELIGION, AND PROSELYTISM HUMAN RIGHTS: A POLITICAL AND CULTURAL CRITIQUE (2002) 94

... With the African theater as the basic laboratory, I intend to unpack the meaning of religious freedom at the point of contact between the messianic faiths and African religions and illustrate how that meeting resulted in a phenomenon akin to cultural genocide. The main purpose here is not merely to defend forms of religion or belief but rather to problematize the concept of the right to the free exercise of messianic faiths, which includes the right to proselytize in the marketplace of religions. In societies such as those in Africa where religion is woven into virtually every aspect of life, its delegitimation can eventually lead to the collapse of social norms and cultural identities. The result, as has been the case in most of sub-Saharan Africa, is a culturally disconnected people, neither themselves nor the outsiders in Europe, North America, and the Arab world that they seek to imitate. In other words, I argue that imperial religions have necessarily violated the individual conscience and the communal expressions of Africans and their communities by subverting African religions. In so doing, they have robbed Africans of essential elements of their humanity ... .

Since the right to religious freedom includes the right to be left alone — to choose freely whether to believe and what to believe in — the rights regime by requiring that African religions compete in the marketplace of ideas incorrectly assumes a level playing field. The rights corpus not only forcibly imposes on African religions the obligation to compete — a task for which as nonproselytizing, noncompetitive creeds they are not historically fashioned — but also protects evangelizing religions in their march toward universalization. In the context of religious freedom, the privileging by the rights regime of the competition of ideas over the right against cultural invasion, in a skewed contest, amounts to condoning the dismantling of African religions.

I also argue that the playing field, the one crucial and necessary ingredient in a fair fight, is heavily weighted against Africans. Messianic religions have been forcibly imposed or their introduction was accomplished as part of the cultural package borne by colonialism. Missionaries did not simply offer Jesus Christ as the savior of benighted souls, his salvation was frequently a precondition for services in education and health, which were quite often the exclusive domain of the Church and the colonial state... . [I]n most cases, the embrace of indigenous societies by the European imperial powers was so violent and total that conformity was the only immediate option....

...

A discussion about limitations on religious rights at first blush appears to frustrate some of the major ideals of the human rights movement. It raises the question about the tension between the restriction of the right to evangelize or advocate a point of view and one of the central ideals of the human rights movement, the promotion of diversity and the right to advocate ideas or creeds. An exploration of the manner in which the human rights corpus ought to view religious rights — whether to further limit or to expand the protections they currently enjoy — raises a fundamental tension: how does a body of principles that promotes diversity and difference protect the establishment and manifestation of religious orders that seek to destroy difference and forcibly impose an orthodoxy in Africa — as both Christianity and Islam, the two major proselytizing religions, attempted, and in many cases successfully did? Precisely because of the ethos of universalization common to both, the messianic faiths sought to eradicate, with the help of the state, all other forms of religious expression and belief and close off any avenues through which other competing faiths could be introduced or sustained ...

.

...

The challenge for the human rights movement is to move beyond the singular obsession with wrongs committed directly by the state — although it remains the most important obligee of the discourse — and confront nonstate actors in order to contain and control human rights violations in the private sphere. To do so, the movement has to take on powerful private institutions in the private realm, including established religion. It is my argument that although religious human rights must be defined, secured, and protected, there is a correlative duty on the part of religions to respect the human rights of nonbelievers and adherents of other religions or faiths and not to seek their coerced conversion either directly or through the manipulation and destruction of other cultures.

...

The two most geographically diverse religions — Christianity and Islam — are also the most imperial; they are proselytizing and universalist in their attempts to convert into their faith the entire human race. Although these religions are not spread through physical violence today, they have historically been forcibly introduced. ... But central to them is the belief in the racial superiority of the proselytizers ... . It does not require a profound knowledge of history to prove that both Arab and European perceptions of Africa have been decidedly racist over the centuries ... .

...

Although human rights law amply protects the right to proselytize through the principles of free speech, assembly, and association, the pecking order of rights problematizes the right to evangelize where the result is the destruction of other cultures or the closure of avenues for other religions. It is my argument that the most fundamental of all human rights is that of self-determination and that no other right overrides it. Without this fundamental group or individual right, no other human right could be secured, since the group would be unable to determine for its individual members under what political, social, cultural, economic, and legal order they would live. Any right which directly conflicts with this right ought to be void to the extent of that conflict.

...

... Although many of the rights enumerated in human rights law attach to individuals, they only make sense in a collective, social perspective. This is the case because the creation or development of a culture or a religion are societal, not individual, endeavors. I make this point to underline the importance of culture or religion to individuals and groups. An individual's morals, attitudes toward life and death, and identity come from this collective construction of reality through history.

No one culture or religion is sovereign in relationship to any other culture or religion. Proper human rights ought to assume that all cultures are equal. This view rejects the notion that there is a hierarchy of cultures or religions; that some cultures are superior to others even though they may more technologically advanced. Belief in the contrary has led to military invasions to "civilize," colonize, and enslave, as was the case with Christianity in Africa. Cultures, however, have always interacted throughout history; there are no pure cultures, as such, although many traditions retain their distinctive personality. In many cases, the voluntary, unforced commingling of cultures has led to a more vital and creative existence. Several lessons can be drawn from this premise. The human rights movement should encourage the crossbreeding of cultures and tolerance for diversity. But it should frown upon homogenization and the imposition of uniformity.

...

Perhaps there is nothing that can be done today to reverse the negative effects of forced or coerced religious proselytization during the era of colonialism in Africa. Nor is it possible to reclaim wholly the African past as though history has stood still. This does not mean, however, that we should simply forget the past and go on as if nothing happened. The anguish and deprivation caused by that historical experience is with me and millions of other Africans today. We bear the marks of that terrible period. For those Africans who choose not to be Christians or Muslims, the past is not really an option: it was so effectively destroyed and delegitimized that it is practically impossible to retrieve as a coherent scheme of values. It is this loss that I mourn and for which I blame Christianity and Islam. The human rights corpus should outlaw those forms of proselytization used in Africa, because their purpose and effect have been the dehumanization of an entire race of people. It could do so by elaborating a treaty that addresses religious human rights but provides for the protection and mechanisms of redress for forms of proselytization that seek to unfairly assimilate or impose dominant cultures on indigenous religions.

Proselytism in India

In 1999, during a visit to India, Pope John Paul II stated that '[r]eligious freedom constitutes the very heart of human rights. ... Its inviolability is such that individuals must be recognized as having the right even to change their religion, if their conscience so demands.' Allesandra Stanley, in 'Pope Tells India His Church Has Right to Evangelize', *New York Times,* 8 November 1999, reported that this was:

> ... an argument that many religious leaders in India accept only with difficulty. Christian conversions are at the heart of a political and religious dispute that has made the ...
> pope's visit a tense one. Christian proselytizing is fuel for Muslim fundamentalists, but it is also a source of uneasiness between the pope and some of his more moderate and like-minded religious peers.

MUKESH KUMAR AND GARIMA YADAV, ANXIETIES OF THE DOMINANT: LEGAL, SOCIAL, AND RELIGIOUS IN THE POLITICS OF RELIGIOUS CONVERSION IN INDIA
11 OXFORD J. L. & RELIG. (2022) 4

Currently, 10 out of 28 Indian states and 8 union territories have anti-conversion laws that prohibit religious conversions on grounds of marriage, force, allurement, and fraud. The present-day anti-conversion laws identify the decision to change one's faith as a criminal offence until and unless prior permission is sought from the state asserting that:

> No person shall convert or attempt to convert, either directly or otherwise, any other person from one religion to another, by use or practice of misrepresentation, force, undue influence, coercion, allurement or by any fraudulent means or by marriage nor shall any person abet, convince or conspire such conversion.

All the recent anti-conversion laws are similar in their content, structure, and wording. ... These laws are held by many as contradicting constitutional values of the liberty of thought, expression, belief, and faith ... . The definition of allurement, force, and fraud in anti-conversion laws is ambiguous that gives an edge to the police and self-styled Hindu-vigilante groups to interpret any public activity of non- Hindus, including the constitutionally allowed legitimate methods of proselytizing such as peaceful public preaching, as per their political convenience. Similarly, the broad and vague definition of force impinges on all meaningful religious interactions between individuals of different denominations. Many charitable acts which are fundamental part of religions like Islam and Christianity may also be framed as tactics of religious conversion. Education offered by missionary institutions to poor children and orphans is nowadays interpreted as a sinister design of conversion.

Presently, Hindu vigilante groups encouraged and re-energized by these laws regularly attack individuals belonging to the minority, target their worship spaces, and harass Muslim and Christian clerics under the pretext of exposing ploys of 'unlawful conversions'. ...

...

Conclusion

... [R]eligious conversion is prominent in public debates because it simultaneously intersects the imagined boundaries of nation, caste, religion, and gender. Consequently, any associated legal change concerning religious conversion brings discussions on nationality, identity, community, belonging, individual rights, and the issue of freedom face to face with one another.

...

Religious conversion is not a monolithic process. Scholars have shown that various factors direct an individual towards changing one's religious belief and identification. Historically, if one thinks from the perspective of converts, religious conversion has also served as terrain of multiple possibilities of social mobility and emancipation from oppression. However, Hindu fundamentalists frame all religious conversions as achieved by exerting political pressure externally. Making constitutional provisions for religious conversion through ambiguously defined terms such as force, fraud, and allurement in response to some bogus theories of Hindu right activists is also an instance of an impending conservative pressure on the legal fabrics of Indian democracy.

Although the legality of anti-conversion laws, especially regarding interfaith marriages, is questioned from time to time by the Supreme Court, individuals, particularly Muslim youths, undergo suppression by the state. Religious conversion is totally banned under the new legal provisions in various Indian states. Any violation of these provisions is met with hostility by police forces and Hindu vigilante groups. Overall, the legality of religious conversion politics yields political benefits because it can effectively tie itself with the discourse of nation, religion, community, identity, and multiple other narratives of public significance to perpetually maintain fissures between religions to reap benefits from such divides.

QUESTIONS

1. How do you assess the Kokkinakis opinion? Do you find justification for any restriction on proselytizing other than those related to coercion, undue imposition on the listener, and similar matters?

2. How do you assess Mutua's views? Can they be limited to matters or religion, or would his arguments apply equally to other attributes of a culture, such as discrimination, or extreme forms of punishment, or authoritarian rule by priests or by elders of a community? How would you seek to resolve the tensions that Mutua underscores, such as through arguments in favour of cultural variety and survival as opposed to arguments for universal norms?

---

3. Dress and Symbols, Migration and Multiculturalism

The larger flows of immigrants in recent decades from developing countries to Europe and the United States have led to more complex and sometimes abrasive cultural mixes. Migrants carry cultural and religious beliefs and practices with them; many immigrants continue to adhere to those beliefs and seek to continue the practices accompanying them, as well as the beliefs' manifestations in routine daily behaviour. Sometimes, as in the case of female genital cutting, the practices grow out of deeply rooted culture and traditions. Sometimes, as in the issue of headscarves discussed below, they have at least in part a religious foundation. In either case, in the increasingly multicultural states of the developed world, newcomers' practices and routine behaviour — one or another form of dress is frequently at issue — stir discomfort, concern and even intense hostility in the host state. That concern and hostility will often continue after the immigrants or their children have become citizens. The issue is starkly posed: whether the immigrants or new citizens should be allowed to continue their practices, or whether they should be required to follow laws and practices of the developed country that effectively require their abolition. Severe sanctions, including expulsion from schools and criminal proceedings, may await those who refuse to surrender their beliefs and ways.

Of course, such conflicts raise serious human rights issues. The opening materials concern immigrant communities, while the later materials examine similar issues that arise in national settings among groups of citizens. The main focus is on Europe and the treatment of Muslims. In a 2017 report, the Pew Research Center noted that, from mid-2010 to mid-2016 alone, the share of Muslims in Europe rose more than 1 percentage point, from 3.8 percent to 4.9 percent (from 19.5 million to 25.8 million). By 2050, the share of the continent's population that is Muslim could more than double, rising to 11.2 percent or more, depending on how much migration is allowed into Europe.

In a 2021 report (UN Doc. A/HRC/46/30, para. 26), the UN Special Rapporteur on freedom of religion or belief noted that:

> Despite the fact that some women regard it as integral to their faith or identity, at least 11 States in Europe, Africa and South Asia impose public restrictions or bans on Muslim head coverings – predominantly worn by women – on the grounds that this type of religious dress is incompatible with a secular public space, violates the rights of Muslim women or poses a security risk. Other States reportedly permit certain institutions (e.g., schools, places of work or the courts) to exercise discretion on whether to permit Muslim dress.

Although the following analysis was written some years ago, it remains highly relevant and lays the foundation for the court cases that follow, which involve disputes arising out of the large societal changes that the author describes.

TIMOTHY SAVAGE, EUROPE AND ISLAM: CRESCENT WAXING, CULTURES CLASHING
27 WASH. Q. (2004) 25

… As the MENA [Middle East and North Africa] population doubles in the next three decades and Europe's shrinks, increased migratory flows from south to north appear unavoidable — a trend augmented by Europe's graying population, as opposed to the youthful MENA average.

...

The growing Muslim presence in Europe has tended to cluster geographically within individual states, particularly in industrialized, urban areas within clearly defined, if not self-encapsulated, poorer neighborhoods such as Berlin's Kreuzberg district, London's Tower Hamlets, and the *banlieues* (suburbs) of major French cities, further augmenting its visibility and impact yet circumscribing day-to-day contact with the general population
… .

...

The nature of the Muslim presence in Europe is also changing. No longer "temporary guest workers," Muslims are now a permanent part of western European national landscapes, as they have been for centuries in southeastern Europe. The institutionalization of Islam in Europe has begun, as has a "re-Islamization" of Muslims in Europe.

… Like European Christians and Jews, European Muslims are not a monolithic group. Nonetheless, Muslims increasingly identify first with Islam rather than with either their family's country of origin or the European country in which they now reside. Moreover, this phenomenon is significantly more pronounced among younger Muslims.

… The current generation is also modernizing and acculturating to aspects of contemporary European society at a faster rate than the first waves of Muslim immigrants did. Younger Muslims are adopting attributes of the European societies in which they were born and raised, such as language; socialization through schooling; and, in many cases, some of the secular perspectives of the country in which they reside. Yet, generally they do not feel part of the larger society nor that they have a stake in it. Conversely, even though they may be third-generation citizens, they often are not viewed as fellow citizens by the general public but are still identified as foreigners and immigrants instead.

...

Despite these trends in citizenship, younger Muslims are resisting assimilation into secular European societies even more steadfastly than the older generation did. Europe's Muslims, including the younger generation, are willing to integrate and respect national norms and institutions as long as they can, at the same time, maintain their distinct Islamic identity and practices. They fear that assimilation, that is, total immersion into European society, will strip them of this identity. Yet, this is the price many Muslims increasingly see European governments and publics demanding: to have Europe become a melting pot without accommodation by or modifications of the existing culture. Studies in France and Germany find that second- and particularly third-generation Muslims are less integrated into European societies than their parents or grandparents were. The recent headscarf affairs in France and Germany underscore and further exacerbate this basic clash.

Perceived discrimination in European societies affecting employment, education, housing, and religious practices is compelling many second- and third-generation Muslims to embrace Islam as their badge of identity. Indeed, the unemployment rate among Muslims is generally double that of non-Muslims, and it is worse than that of non-Muslim immigrants. Educational achievement and skill levels are relatively low, participation by Muslim women in the workforce is minimal, opportunities for advancement are limited, and biases against Muslims are strong. Such factors contribute to the isolation — and self-encapsulation — of Muslim communities in Europe ... .

...

The rapidly growing Muslim populations seem to be overwhelming the ability of European governments to draw the lines of tolerance rationally, consistently, and convincingly. Europeans see Muslims as a direct challenge to the collective identity, traditional values, and public policies of their societies, as demonstrated by the heated controversies over the hijab [scarf], Muslim food (halal), the construction of mosques, the teaching of Islam in schools, and Muslim burial rites. This attitude is also reflected in intense debates over women's rights, church-state relations, and Islam's compatibility with democracy. Politicians, pundits, and ordinary citizens are all seized with the "Islamic challenge."

... The threat is framed in terms of security (terrorism) and economics (jobs); yet, the core issue is identity and the perceived cultural threat Islam poses to the European way of life. Europeans have even coined a name for it: Islamophobia. Conversely, this tendency to see Muslims as a monolith has its reverse image in Muslim allegiance to the umma, which transcends other loyalties; tends to reinforce the "we/them" perspective; and is part of the reason why Muslims resist assimilation — the total loss of identity-related indicators of existing differences from European societies — and insist on integration — a reconstituted identity that stresses remaining differences — or, in some cases, recommunalization — a physical presence in Europe but no accommodation with European society ... .

[T]he challenge for Europe seems more daunting [than that of the United States with respect to racial hostility and tolerance] because it involves not only integration and tolerance but also redefining both parties' identities. Each side will have to change and move toward the other. Europe's Muslims will need to accept the norms, customs, and cultures of the states in which they live and reject efforts to establish a parallel society, while the general European population will need to broaden its horizons to embrace and accommodate diversity, accepting integration and not just complete assimilation as a valid relationship to society.

...

For their part, Muslims in Europe, who must confront poverty, bigotry, de facto segregation, and limited social mobility, are likely to find it difficult to embrace Europe's liberal democratic views on gender equality; sexual liberalization; and the principles of compromise, egalitarianism, and identification with the state. These are all issues that challenge the traditional views not only of Muslims but also of individuals with an Arab, Turkish, or South Asian heritage, as the vast majority of Europe's Muslims are. These cultural backgrounds have not included the Enlightenment as a central pillar, and the idea of a secular society is for the most part alien. Moreover, as Mustafa Malik notes, in these societies, "[Resistance] to liberalism was heightened by hatred for European colonialists, who represented liberal values." Lack of organization and political standing, diversity of views and interests, economic weakness, and the absence of clear leadership pose major complicating hurdles, all of which Europe's Muslims will need to address if they are to contribute their part to Europe's transformation.

...

Although the situation in Europe is not quite there, the tipping point may be closer than is generally realized. As intolerance toward Muslim communities grows in Europe, European Muslims are growing more self-confident but also more dissatisfied, particularly as Europe's economy continues to sputter. The percentage of Muslims in France is rapidly approaching that of African-Americans in the United States in 1950 (10 percent), and the percentage of Muslims in Europe as a whole will pass that benchmark within the next decade... .

...

Conversely, however, a success in dealing with the building clash of cultures and identities, which results in a shift of both Muslim and non-Muslim European mind-sets, and crafts a societal framework that encourages integration and respects individual as well as national identities would negate Huntington's thesis of the inevitable incompatibility of Islam and the West. It would require change in European society, to be sure. As with all change, there would be winners and losers. Yet, success holds out the hope of reinvigorating and redefining Europe, proffering a possible corrective to its projected political, economic, and demographic decline as well as moving European integration to a new level and giving it new meaning.

...

* * *

Bans on headscarves have now been considered by a range of international bodies, and the materials that follow reproduce some of the key decisions. A useful starting point is the judgment of the European Court of Human Rights in *Dahlab v. Switzerland*, Application No. 42393/98 (2001). The applicant, a Catholic woman, was a primary school teacher in the secular public school system in Geneva. She converted to Islam and soon began to 'observe a precept laid down in the Koran whereby women were enjoined to draw their veils over themselves in the presence of men.' She refused the request of the Director General of Primary Education to stop wearing a headscarf to class, and was soon dismissed. She was not given relief by the Swiss authorities, and thus brought an action before the European Court on the ground that the prohibition of the headscarf infringed her freedom to manifest her religion pursuant to Article 9 of the European Convention. The Court agreed with the conclusions of the Swiss administrative and judicial authorities, and declared the application inadmissible. It stated in part:

> The Court accepts that it is very difficult to assess the impact that a powerful external symbol such as the wearing of a headscarf may have on the freedom of conscience and religion of very young children [between 4 and 8] ... . [T]he wearing of a headscarf might have some kind of proselytizing effect, seeing that it appears to be imposed on women by a precept which is laid down in the Koran and which ... is hard to square with the principle of gender equality. It therefore appears difficult to reconcile the wearing of an Islamic headscarf with the message of tolerance, respect for others and, above all, equality and non-discrimination that all teachers in a democratic society must convey to their pupils ... . [H]aving regard, above all, to the tender age of the children for whom the applicant was responsible as a representative of the State, the Geneva authorities did not exceed their margin of appreciation and ... the measure they took was therefore not unreasonable.

In the year before the Grand Chamber decision, a French law came into force effectively banning from state primary and secondary schools the headscarf worn by many Muslim girls as well as 'conspicuous', or 'overtly manifest', clothing or symbols of other religions such as large crosses for Christians and large skullcaps for Jewish boys. Other states in Europe allowed schools to prohibit headscarves in certain cases. These developments across the European landscape were understood by the court when it issued the following judgment:

LEYLA ŞAHIN V. TURKEY
EUROPEAN COURT OF HUMAN RIGHTS, GRAND CHAMBER, APPLICATION NO. 44774/98 (10 NOVEMBER 2005)

[The applicant, a Turkish citizen, came from a traditional family of practising Muslims, and considered it her religious duty to wear the Islamic headscarf. She did so during her four years studying medicine in a Turkish university. She then transferred to Istanbul University to continue her studies. In a series of episodes beginning in 1998 she was censured by university authorities for refusing to comply with university circulars based on legislation banning students wearing headscarves from lectures and courses. After being denied enrolment and admission to lectures, she sought relief from Turkish courts, but was unsuccessful. Ultimately, the applicant abandoned her studies in Turkey and pursued her medical education at Vienna University. After failing to secure judicial relief in Turkey, she initiated proceedings against Turkey under the European Convention on Human Rights. In a 2004 judgment, a Chamber of the European Court of Human Rights held unanimously that there had been no violation of the Convention. The applicant's request that the case be referred to the Court's Grand Chamber was accepted. In its 2005 judgment, the Grand Chamber also ruled against the applicant.]

30. The Turkish Republic was founded on the principle that the State should be secular (*laik*). ...

...

32. The defining feature of the Republican ideal was the presence of women in public life and their active participation in society. Consequently, the ideas that women should be freed from religious constraints and that society should be modernised had a common origin. ... [W]omen obtained equal political rights with men.

...

35. In Turkey wearing the Islamic headscarf to school and university is a recent phenomenon which only really began to emerge in the 1980s ... . Those in favour of the headscarf see wearing it as a duty and/or a form of expression linked to religious identity. However, the supporters of secularism ... see the Islamic headscarf as a symbol of a political Islam ...

[In the Turkish Constitutional Court's opinion upholding the university's position, the judges stated that secularism had achieved so important a position among constitutional values because of the country's historical experience and the particularities of Islam compared to other religions; secularism was an essential condition for democracy and acted as a guarantor of freedom of religion and of equality before the law. Students must be allowed to work in a tolerant atmosphere without being deflected from their goals by signs of religious affiliation such as the headscarf.

The ECtHR opinion included a comparative survey about laws about headscarves across different European countries. The survey indicated that state legislation varied on many details — for example, how, if at all, the headscarf was regulated, and the level of school/university that was covered by any regulation.]

Alleged violation of Article 9 of the convention

70. The applicant submitted that the ban on wearing the Islamic headscarf in institutions of higher education constituted an unjustified interference with her right to freedom of religion, in particular, her right to manifest her religion. She relied on Article 9 of the Convention ... .

...

104. The Court reiterates that as enshrined in Article 9, freedom of thought, conscience and religion is one of the foundations of a "democratic society" ... .

105. While religious freedom is primarily a matter of individual conscience, it also implies, *inter alia*, freedom to manifest one's religion, alone and in private, or in community with others, in public and within the circle of those whose faith one shares. ... .

106. In democratic societies, in which several religions coexist within one and the same population, it may be necessary to place restrictions on freedom to manifest one's religion or belief in order to reconcile the interests of the various groups and ensure that everyone's beliefs are respected. ...

107. The Court ... also considers that the State's duty of neutrality and impartiality is incompatible with any power on the State's part to assess the legitimacy of religious beliefs or the ways in which those beliefs are expressed ...

...

109. Where questions concerning the relationship between State and religions are at stake, on which opinion in a democratic society may reasonably differ widely, the role of the national decision-making body must be given special importance. This will notably be the case when it comes to regulating the wearing of religious symbols in educational institutions, especially in view of the diversity of the approaches taken by national authorities on the issue. It is not possible to discern throughout Europe a uniform conception of the significance of religion in society and the meaning or impact of the public expression of a religious belief will differ according to time and context. Rules in this sphere will consequently vary from one country to another according to national traditions and the requirements imposed by the need to protect the rights and freedoms of others and to maintain public order. ...

110. This margin of appreciation goes hand in hand with a European supervision embracing both the law and the decisions applying it. The Court's task is to determine whether the measures taken at national level were justified in principle and proportionate. ...

...

115. After examining the parties' arguments, the Grand Chamber sees no good reason to depart from the approach taken by the Chamber [in its 2004 judgment]:

> ... The Court ... notes the emphasis placed in the Turkish constitutional system on the protection of the rights of women ... .

> ... In addition, like the Constitutional Court ..., the Court considers that, when examining the question of the Islamic headscarf in the Turkish context, there must be borne in mind the impact which wearing such a symbol, which is presented or perceived as a compulsory religious duty, may have on those who choose not to wear it. As has already been noted, the issues at stake include the protection of the "rights and freedoms of others" and the "maintenance of public order" ... . Imposing limitations on freedom in this sphere may, therefore, be regarded as meeting a pressing social need by seeking to achieve those two legitimate aims, especially since, as the Turkish courts stated ..., this religious symbol has taken on political significance in Turkey in recent years.

... The Court does not lose sight of the fact that there are extremist political movements in Turkey which seek to impose on society as a whole their religious symbols and conception of a society founded on religious precepts ... It has previously said that each Contracting State may, in accordance with the Convention provisions, take a stance against such political movements, based on its historical experience. The regulations concerned have to be viewed in that context and constitute a measure intended to achieve the legitimate aims referred to above and thereby to preserve pluralism in the university.

...

117. The Court must now determine whether in the instant case there was a reasonable relationship of proportionality between the means employed and the legitimate objectives pursued by the interference.

118. Like the Chamber ..., the Grand Chamber notes at the outset that it is common ground that practising Muslim students in Turkish universities are free, within the limits imposed by educational organisational constraints, to manifest their religion in accordance with habitual forms of Muslim observance. In addition, the resolution adopted by Istanbul University on 9 July 1998 shows that various other forms of religious attire are also forbidden on the university premises.

...

121. ... By reason of their direct and continuous contact with the education community, the university authorities are in principle better placed than an international court to evaluate local needs and conditions or the requirements of a particular course. ...

122. In the light of the foregoing and having regard to the Contracting States' margin of appreciation in this sphere, the Court finds that the interference in issue was justified in principle and proportionate to the aim pursued.

123. Consequently, there has been no breach of Article 9 of the Convention.

II. Alleged violation of Article 2 of Protocol No. 1

[The Applicant also argued that Article 2 of Protocol No. 1 of the European Convention should be interpreted to uphold her right to wear a headscarf while attending the university. That article provides:

> No person shall be denied the right to education. In the exercise of any functions which it assumes in relation to education and to teaching, the State shall respect the right of parents to ensure such education and teaching in conformity with their own religious and philosophical convictions.]

The Grand Chamber relied heavily on its reasoning with respect to freedom of religion in concluding that there had been no violation of Article 2 of Protocol No. 1....

...

DISSENTING OPINION OF JUDGE TULKENS

...

2. ... Underlying the majority's approach is the *margin of appreciation* which the national authorities are recognised as possessing and which reflects, *inter alia*, the notion that they are "better placed" to decide how best to discharge their Convention obligations in what is a sensitive area. The Court's jurisdiction is, of course, subsidiary and its role is not to impose uniform solutions, especially "with regard to establishment of the delicate relations between the Churches and the State" ... .

3. I would perhaps have been able to follow the margin-of-appreciation approach had not two factors drastically reduced its relevance in the instant case. The first concerns the argument the majority use to justify the width of the margin, namely ... the lack of a European consensus in this sphere. The comparative-law materials do not allow of such a conclusion, as in none of the member States has the ban on wearing religious symbols extended to university education ... . The second factor concerns the European supervision that must accompany the margin of appreciation ... . [O]ther than in connection with Turkey's specific historical background, European supervision seems quite simply to be absent from the judgment. ...

4. On what grounds was the interference with the applicant's right to freedom of religion through the ban on wearing the headscarf based? In the present case, ... [there were] two main arguments: secularism and equality... . In a democratic society, I believe that it is necessary to seek to harmonise the principles of secularism, equality and liberty, not to weigh one against the other.

...

7. ... The majority ... consider that wearing the headscarf contravenes the principle of secularism. ...

... [A] generalised assessment of that type gives rise to at least three difficulties. Firstly, the judgment does not address the applicant's argument — which the Government did not dispute — that she had no intention of calling the principle of secularism ... into doubt. Secondly, there is no evidence to show that the applicant, through her attitude, conduct or acts, contravened that principle ... . Lastly, the judgment makes no distinction between teachers and students, [contrary to] *Dahlab v. Switzerland* ... which concerned a teacher ... . [T]he position of pupils and students seems to me to be different.

8. Freedom to manifest a religion entails everyone being allowed to exercise that right, whether individually or collectively, in public or in private, subject to the dual condition that they do not infringe the rights and freedoms of others and do not prejudice public order.

As regards the first condition, this could have been satisfied if the headscarf the applicant wore as a religious symbol had been ostentatious or aggressive or was used to exert pressure, to provoke a reaction, to proselytise or to spread propaganda and undermined — or was liable to undermine — the convictions of others. However, the Government did not argue that this was the case and there was no evidence before the Court to suggest that Ms Şahin had any such intention. As to the second condition, it has been neither suggested nor demonstrated that there was any disruption in teaching or in everyday life at the University ... .

9. ... [T]he possible effect which wearing the headscarf, which is presented as a symbol, may have on those who do not wear it does not appear to me, in the light of the Court's case-law, to satisfy the requirement of a pressing social need ... .

10. In fact, it is the threat posed by "extremist political movements" seeking to "impose on society as a whole their religious symbols and conception of a society founded on religious precepts" which, in the Court's view, serves to justify the regulations in issue, which constitute "a measure intended ... to preserve pluralism in the university" ... .

While everyone agrees on the need to prevent radical Islamism, a serious objection may nevertheless be made to such reasoning. Merely wearing the headscarf cannot be associated with fundamentalism and it is vital to distinguish between those who wear the headscarf and "extremists" who seek to impose the headscarf as they do other religious symbols. Not all women who wear the headscarf are fundamentalists and there is nothing to suggest that the applicant held fundamentalist views ... . [T]he judgment fails to provide any concrete example of the type of pressure concerned ... .

11. Turning to *equality*, the majority focus on the protection of women's rights and the principle of sexual equality ... . By converse implication, wearing the headscarf is considered synonymous with the alienation of women. The ban on wearing the headscarf is therefore seen as promoting equality between men and women. However, what, in fact, is the connection between the ban and sexual equality? The judgment does not say ... . [W]earing the headscarf has no single meaning; it is a practise that is engaged in for a variety of reasons. It does not necessarily symbolise the submission of women to men and there are those who maintain that, in certain cases, it can even be a means of emancipating women. What is lacking in this debate is the opinion of women, both those who wear the headscarf and those who choose not to.

12. ... The applicant, ... [said] that she wore the headscarf of her own free will. In this connection, I fail to see how the principle of sexual equality can justify prohibiting a woman from following a practice which, in the absence of proof to the contrary, she must be taken to have freely adopted ... .

13. ... In these circumstances, there has been a violation of the applicant's right to freedom of religion, as guaranteed by the Convention.
...
[The dissenting opinion also disagreed on several grounds with the majority's disposition of applicant's claim based on Article 2 of Protocol No. 1.]
...

* * *

In 2008, under the leadership of Prime Minister Recep Tayyip Erdoğan and his Justice and Development Party (the *Adalet ve Kalkınma Partisi*), Turkey's Parliament passed a constitutional amendment, by an overwhelming majority, allowing women to wear headscarves on university campuses. The amendment was challenged in a case brought before the Constitutional Court. The Court invalidated the measure reasoning, in part, that it violated the Turkish Constitution's foundational commitment to secularism. In 2013 the ban was lifted, with some exceptions for the military, police force and judiciary. At the 2023 election both the re-elected government and the opposition announced strong support for official legal steps to enshrine women's right to wear Islamic headscarves.

a. Headscarves in France

The background to the developments traced below is well captured by this analysis by Roger Cohen, in 'An Embattled Public Servant in a Fractured France', *New York Times* (1 January 2021):

> France is in theory a nondiscriminatory society where the state upholds strict religious neutrality and people are free to believe, or not, in any God they wish. It is a nation, in its self image, that through education dissolves differences of faith and ethnicity in a shared commitment to the rights and responsibilities of French citizenship.
>
> This model, known as laïcité, often inadequately translated as secularism, is embraced by a majority of French people. They or their forebears became French in this way. No politician here would utter the words "In God we trust." The Roman Catholic Church was removed more than a century ago from French public life. The country's lay model supplants any deity.
>
> But, in a country with an uneasy relationship to Islam, laïcité is also contested as the shield behind which France discriminates against its large Muslim population and avoids confronting its prejudices. ...

France enacted a national law in 2004 categorically prohibiting any student attending an elementary or secondary state school from wearing 'conspicuous' religious garb and symbols, including the headscarf.[259] Previously, French law had provided state schools with discretion to prohibit Muslim girls from wearing the headscarf under certain conditions. Those conditions included a determination by school authorities that 'inherently, in the circumstances in which [religious signs] are worn, individually or collectively, or conspicuously or as a means of protest, might constitute a form of pressure, provocation, proselytism or propaganda, undermine the dignity or freedom of the pupil or other members of the educational community, compromise their health or safety, disrupt the conduct of teaching activities and the educational role of the teachers, or, lastly, interfere with order in the school or the normal functioning of the public service.' The law also designated local disciplinary authorities to determine whether an individual's breach of a dress code would result in suspension from school.

In 2008, a chamber of the European Court of Human Rights issued a judgment addressing the pre-2004 French legal regime. The case, *Dogru v. France* (Application No. 27058/05), involved an 11-year-old Muslim girl who was expelled from a state school due to her failure to obey a school rule prohibiting headscarves in physical education classes. The Court applied the Grand Chamber's framework in *Sahin* and concluded that the school's actions were consistent with the Convention:

> 73. … [T]he Court considers that the conclusion reached by the national authorities that the wearing of a veil, such as the Islamic headscarf, was incompatible with sports classes for reasons of health or safety is not unreasonable … .

> 74. The Court also notes that the disciplinary proceedings against the applicant fully satisfied the duty to undertake a balancing exercise of the various interests at stake … . [T]he authorities concerned made many unsuccessful attempts over a long period of time to enter into dialogue with the applicant and a period of reflection was granted her and subsequently extended. Furthermore, the ban was limited to the physical education class, so cannot be regarded as a ban in the strict sense of the term. Moreover, … these events had led to a general atmosphere of tension within the school … .

> …

> 76. The Court considers … that the penalty of expulsion does not appear disproportionate, and notes that the applicant was able to continue her schooling by correspondence classes … .

Following the judgment by the ECtHR, France enacted new legislation which came into force in 2011. The law specifically addresses full-face coverings such as burqas and niqabs.[260] Women are forbidden from wearing such garments in public spaces, defined very broadly to include streets, markets, private stores, government buildings, train stations and public transit. Belgium adopted a very similar prohibition which also came into force in 2011. Unlike the French law, Belgium's included the possibility of imprisonment (up to seven days) for women who violate the law. Some municipalities in other European countries (e.g., Italy and Spain) have also enacted laws prohibiting burqas and niqabs in public institutions or have interpreted existing law to effectuate such a prohibition.

Belgium has been second only to France in enacting restrictive legislation in this area. Consider the following case, which has been subjected to considerable criticism.[261]

SAMIRA ACHBITA V. G4S SECURE SOLUTIONS NV
COURT OF JUSTICE OF THE EUROPEAN UNION, C-157/15 (14 MARCH 2017)

Facts

G4S is an undertaking that provides reception services. G4S employees are not permitted to wear any religious, political or philosophical symbols while on duty. On 12 February 2003, Ms Achbita joined G4S as a receptionist

---

[259] S. Hennette-Vauchez, 'Religious Neutrality, Laïcité and Colorblindness: A Comparative Analysis', 42 *Cardozo L. Rev.* (2021) 539.

[260] The burqa is a full-body garment that hides a woman's face by a mesh screen. The niqab is a garment that includes a veil covering the entirety of a woman's hair and face except for her eyes.

[261] See, for example, J. Weiler, 'Je Suis Achbita!', 28 *Eur. J. Int'l L.* (2017) 989.

without objecting to that company rule. However, in April 2006, she announced that, in future, she intended to wear a headscarf during working hours as well, for religious reasons. On 12 June 2006, on account of her firm intention to wear the Islamic headscarf, Ms Achbita was dismissed.

Procedural history

[Between 2007 and 2010, the Antwerpen Labour Court and an appeals court both dismissed a claim by Ms Achbita on the grounds that there had been no discrimination.]

Judgment

29. It is necessary... to determine whether the internal rule at issue in the main proceedings gives rise to a difference in treatment of workers on the basis of their religion or their belief and, if so, whether that difference in treatment constitutes direct discrimination within the meaning of Article 2(2)(a) of [European Council] Directive 2000/78.

30. ... [T]he internal rule at issue in the main proceedings refers to the wearing of visible signs of political, philosophical or religious beliefs and therefore covers any manifestation of such beliefs without distinction. The rule must, therefore, be regarded as treating all workers of the undertaking in the same way by requiring them, in a general and undifferentiated way, inter alia, to dress neutrally, which precludes the wearing of such signs.

[Based on the evidence, the Court found that the internal rule had not been applied differently to Ms Achbita as compared to any other worker, and that there was thus no difference of treatment that is directly based on religion or belief.]

...

34. ... [The] difference of treatment [might be considered to be] indirectly based on religion or belief ... [thus putting] persons adhering to a particular religion or belief ... at a particular disadvantage.

35. ... [The question is whether the] difference of treatment ... is objectively justified by a legitimate aim and if the means of achieving that aim are appropriate and necessary.

...

37. ... [T]he desire to display, in relations with both public and private sector customers, a policy of political, philosophical or religious neutrality must be considered legitimate.

38. An employer's wish to project an image of neutrality towards customers relates to the freedom to conduct a business that is recognised in Article 16 of the Charter and is, in principle, legitimate, notably where the employer involves in its pursuit of that aim only those workers who are required to come into contact with the employer's customers.

...

40. ... [T]he fact that workers are prohibited from visibly wearing signs of political, philosophical or religious beliefs is appropriate for the purpose of ensuring that a policy of neutrality is properly applied, provided that that policy is genuinely pursued in a consistent and systematic manner.

41. In that respect, it is for the referring court to ascertain whether G4S had, prior to Ms Achbita's dismissal, established a general and undifferentiated policy of prohibiting the visible wearing of signs of political, philosophical or religious beliefs in respect of members of its staff who come into contact with its customers.

42. As regards ... the question whether the prohibition ... was necessary, it must be determined whether the prohibition is limited to what is strictly necessary. In the present case, what must be ascertained is whether the prohibition on the visible wearing of any sign or clothing capable of being associated with a religious faith or a political or philosophical belief covers only G4S workers who interact with customers. If that is the case, the prohibition must be considered strictly necessary for the purpose of achieving the aim pursued.

...

44. Having regard to all of the foregoing considerations, the answer to the question put by the referring court is as follows:

–   Article 2(2)(a) of Directive 2000/78 must be interpreted as meaning that the prohibition on wearing an Islamic headscarf, which arises from an internal rule of a private undertaking prohibiting the visible wearing of any political, philosophical or religious sign in the workplace, does not constitute direct discrimination based on religion or belief within the meaning of that directive.

— By contrast, such an internal rule of a private undertaking may constitute indirect discrimination within the meaning of Article 2(2)(b) of Directive 2000/78 if it is established that the apparently neutral obligation it imposes results, in fact, in persons adhering to a particular religion or belief being put at a particular disadvantage, unless it is objectively justified by a legitimate aim, such as the pursuit by the employer, in its relations with its customers, of a policy of political, philosophical and religious neutrality, and the means of achieving that aim are appropriate and necessary, which it is for the referring court to ascertain.

* * *

In a subsequent case, also from Belgium, *OP v. Commune d'Ans* (Case C-148/22, 28 November 2023), the CJEU considered a claim to wear a headscarf from a municipal worker who had no contact with the public. It held that:

> an internal rule of a municipal authority prohibiting, in a general and indiscriminate manner, the members of that authority's staff from visibly wearing in the workplace any sign revealing, in particular, philosophical or religious beliefs may be justified by the desire of the said authority to establish, having regard to the context in which it operates, an entirely neutral administrative environment provided that that rule is appropriate, necessary and proportionate in the light of that context and taking into account the various rights and interests at stake.

S.A.S. V. FRANCE
EUROPEAN COURT OF HUMAN RIGHTS, GRAND CHAMBER, APPLICATION NO. 43835/11 (1 JULY 2014)

The Facts

I. The Circumstances of the Case

…

10. The applicant is a French national who was born in 1990 and lives in France.

11. In the applicant's submission, she is a devout Muslim and she wears the burqa and niqab in accordance with her religious faith, culture and personal convictions. According to her explanation, the burqa is a full-body covering including a mesh over the face, and the niqab is a full-face veil leaving an opening only for the eyes. The applicant emphasised that neither her husband nor any other member of her family put pressure on her to dress in this manner.

12. The applicant added that she wore the niqab in public and in private, but not systematically: she might not wear it, for example, when she visited the doctor, when meeting friends in a public place, or when she wanted to socialise in public. She was thus content not to wear the niqab in public places at all times but wished to be able to wear it when she chose to do so, depending in particular on her spiritual feelings. There were certain times (for example, during religious events such as Ramadan) when she believed that she ought to wear it in public in order to express her religious, personal and cultural faith. Her aim was not to annoy others but to feel at inner peace with herself.

13. The applicant did not claim that she should be able to keep the niqab on when undergoing a security check, at the bank or in airports, and she agreed to show her face when requested to do so for necessary identity checks.

14. Since 11 April 2011, the date of entry into force of Law no. 2010-1192 of 11 October 2010 throughout France, it has been prohibited for anyone to conceal their face in public places.

The Law

...

3. The Court's assessment

(a) Alleged violation of Articles 8 and 9 of the Convention

106. The ban on wearing, in public places, clothing designed to conceal the face raises questions in terms of the right to respect for private life (Article 8…) of women who wish to wear the full-face veil for reasons related to their beliefs, and in terms of their freedom to manifest those beliefs (Article 9 …).

107. … [P]ersonal choices as to an individual's desired appearance, whether in public or in private places, relate to the expression of his or her personality and thus fall within the notion of private life. …

108. [I]n so far as that ban is criticised by individuals who, like the applicant, complain that they are consequently prevented from wearing in public places clothing that the practice of their religion requires them to wear, it mainly raises an issue with regard to the freedom to manifest one's religion or beliefs … . …

...

(i) Whether there has been a "limitation" or an "interference"

110. … [T]he Law of 11 October 2010 confronts the applicant with a dilemma …: either she complies with the ban and thus refrains from dressing in accordance with her approach to religion; or she refuses to comply and faces criminal sanctions. … There has therefore been … an "interference" with or a "limitation" of the exercise of the rights protected by Articles 8 and 9 … .

...

(iii) Whether there is a legitimate aim

[The Court focused on whether the measure was justified by reference to "protection of the rights and freedoms of others".]

118. Firstly, the Court is not convinced by the Government's submission in so far as it concerns respect for equality between men and women.

119. … [A] State Party cannot invoke gender equality in order to ban a practice that is defended by women – such as the applicant – in the context of the exercise of the rights enshrined in those provisions, unless it were to be understood that individuals could be protected on that basis from the exercise of their own fundamental rights and freedoms. …

120. Secondly, … respect for human dignity cannot legitimately justify a blanket ban on the wearing of the full-face veil in public places. The Court is aware that the clothing in question is perceived as strange by many of those who observe it. It would point out, however, that it is the expression of a cultural identity which contributes to the pluralism that is inherent in democracy….

121. Thirdly, the Court finds, by contrast, that under certain conditions the "respect for the minimum requirements of life in society" referred to by the Government – or of "living together" … – can be linked to the legitimate aim of the "protection of the rights and freedoms of others".

122. The Court … [is] able to accept that the barrier raised against others by a veil concealing the face is perceived by the respondent State as breaching the right of others to live in a space of socialisation which makes living together easier. That being said, in view of the flexibility of the notion of "living together" and the resulting risk of abuse, the Court must engage in a careful examination of the necessity of the impugned limitation.

...

(iv) Whether the measure is necessary in a democratic society
(a) General principles concerning Article 9 of the Convention

...

124. As enshrined in Article 9, freedom of thought, conscience and religion is one of the foundations of a "democratic society" within the meaning of the Convention. …

125. While religious freedom is primarily a matter of individual conscience, it also implies freedom to manifest one's religion, alone and in private, or in community with others, in public and within the circle of those whose faith one shares. ... . Article 9 does not, however, protect every act motivated or inspired by a religion or belief and does not always guarantee the right to behave in the public sphere in a manner which is dictated by one's religion or beliefs ... .

126. In democratic societies, in which several religions coexist within one and the same population, it may be necessary to place limitations on freedom to manifest one's religion or beliefs in order to reconcile the interests of the various groups and ensure that everyone's beliefs are respected ... .

127. The Court has frequently emphasised the State's role as the neutral and impartial organiser of the exercise of various religions, faiths and beliefs, and has stated that this role is conducive to public order, religious harmony and tolerance in a democratic society. ...

128. Pluralism, tolerance and broadmindedness are hallmarks of a "democratic society". Although individual interests must on occasion be subordinated to those of a group, democracy does not simply mean that the views of a majority must always prevail ... .

129. It is also important to emphasise the fundamentally subsidiary role of the Convention mechanism. The national authorities have direct democratic legitimation and are, as the Court has held on many occasions, in principle better placed than an international court to evaluate local needs and conditions. In matters of general policy, on which opinions within a democratic society may reasonably differ widely, the role of the domestic policy-maker should be given special weight ... .

...

131. This margin of appreciation, however, goes hand in hand with a European supervision ... .

...

(γ) Application of those principles to the present case

...

139. As regards the question of necessity ..., the Court understands that a State may find it essential to be able to identify individuals in order to prevent danger for the safety of persons and property and to combat identity fraud. It has thus found no violation of Article 9 ... in cases concerning the obligation to remove clothing with a religious connotation in the context of security checks and the obligation to appear bareheaded on identity photos for use on official documents. However, in view of its impact on the rights of women who wish to wear the full-face veil for religious reasons, a blanket ban on the wearing in public places of clothing designed to conceal the face can be regarded as proportionate only in a context where there is a general threat to public safety. The Government have not shown that the ban ... falls into such a context. ...

...

141. The Court observes that [the aim of ensuring the observance of the minimum requirements of life in society as part of the "protection of the rights and freedoms of others"] is an aim to which the authorities have given much weight. ... [T]he explanatory memorandum accompanying the bill ... indicates that "[t]he voluntary and systematic concealment of the face ... is quite simply incompatible with the fundamental requirements of 'living together' in French society" and that "[t]he systematic concealment of the face in public places, contrary to the ideal of fraternity, ... falls short of the minimum requirement of civility that is necessary for social interaction". It indeed falls within the powers of the State to secure the conditions whereby individuals can live together in their diversity. Moreover, the Court is able to accept that a State may find it essential to give particular weight in this connection to the interaction between individuals and may consider this to be adversely affected by the fact that some conceal their faces in public places.

142. Consequently, the Court finds that the impugned ban can be regarded as justified in its principle solely in so far as it seeks to guarantee the conditions of "living together".

143. It remains to be ascertained whether the ban is proportionate to that aim.

144. Some of the arguments put forward by the applicant and the intervening non-governmental organisations warrant particular attention.

145. Firstly, it is true that only a small number of women are affected. ... [A]bout 1,900 women wore the Islamic full-face veil in France at the end of 2009 ... ... It may thus seem excessive to respond to such a situation by imposing a blanket ban.

146. In addition, there is no doubt that the ban has a significant negative impact on the situation of women who, like the applicant, have chosen to wear the full-face veil for reasons related to their beliefs. ... [T]he ban may have the effect of isolating them and restricting their autonomy, as well as impairing the exercise of their freedom to manifest their beliefs and their right to respect for their private life. ... [T]he women concerned may perceive the ban as a threat to their identity.

147. ... [A] large number of actors, both international and national, in the field of fundamental rights protection have found a blanket ban to be disproportionate ... .
...
149. ... [T]he Court is very concerned ... that certain Islamophobic remarks marked the debate which preceded the adoption of the Law of 11 October 2010. It is admittedly not for the Court to rule on whether legislation is desirable in such matters. ... [R]emarks which constitute a general, vehement attack on a religious or ethnic group are incompatible with the values of tolerance, social peace and non-discrimination ... .

150. The other arguments put forward in support of the application must, however, be qualified.

151. Thus, while ... the scope of the ban is broad, [the Law] does not affect the freedom to wear in public any garment or item of clothing – with or without a religious connotation – which does not have the effect of concealing the face. ... [T]he ban is not expressly based on the religious connotation of the clothing in question but solely on the fact that it conceals the face. ...

152. As to the ... criminal sanctions ... attached to the ban, ... [they] are among the lightest that could be envisaged, since they consist of a fine at the rate applying to second-class petty offences (currently EUR 150 maximum), with the possibility for the court to impose, in addition to or instead of the fine, an obligation to follow a citizenship course.

153. ... [T]he ban prevents certain women from expressing their personality and their beliefs by wearing the full-face veil in public. However, for ... the Government ... it was a question of responding to a practice that the State deemed incompatible ... [with] the requirements of "living together". From that perspective, the respondent State is seeking to protect a principle of interaction between individuals, which in its view is essential for the expression not only of pluralism, but also of tolerance and broadmindedness without which there is no democratic society. It can thus be said that the question whether or not it should be permitted to wear the full-face veil in public places constitutes a choice of society.

154. In such circumstances, the Court has a duty to exercise a degree of restraint in its review of Convention compliance, since such review will lead it to assess a balance that has been struck by means of a democratic process within the society in question. ... [I]n matters of general policy, on which opinions within a democratic society may reasonably differ widely, the role of the domestic policy-maker should be given special weight.

155. In other words, France had a wide margin of appreciation in the present case.

156. This is particularly true as there is little common ground among the member States of the Council of Europe as to the question of the wearing of the full-face veil in public. ... [T]here is no European consensus against a ban. Admittedly, from a strictly normative standpoint, France is very much in a minority position in Europe: except for Belgium, no other member State of the Council of Europe has, to date, opted for such a measure. ... [H]owever, ... the question ... is or has been a subject of debate in a number of European States.
...

157. Consequently, having regard in particular to the breadth of the margin of appreciation afforded to the respondent State in the present case, the Court finds that the ban imposed ... can be regarded as proportionate to the aim pursued ... .

...

(b) Alleged violation of Article 14 of the Convention taken in conjunction with Article 8 or Article 9

160. The Court notes that the applicant complained of indirect discrimination. It observes in this connection that, as a Muslim woman who for religious reasons wishes to wear the full-face veil in public, she belongs to a category of individuals who are particularly exposed to the ban in question and to the sanctions for which it provides.

161. ...[W]hile it may be considered that the ban imposed by the Law of 11 October 2010 has specific negative effects on the situation of Muslim women who, for religious reasons, wish to wear the full-face veil in public, this measure has an objective and reasonable justification for the reasons indicated previously ... .

162. Accordingly, there has been no violation of Article 14 of the Convention taken in conjunction with Article 8 or Article 9.

...

[The Court, by 15-2, found no violation of Article 8, and also by 15-2, no violation of Article 9.]

JOINT PARTLY DISSENTING OPINION OF JUDGES NUSSBERGER AND JÄDERBLOM

A. Sacrificing of individual rights to abstract principles

...

2. ... [T]he opinion of the majority ... sacrifices concrete individual rights guaranteed by the Convention to abstract principles. ...

B. No legitimate aim under the Convention

...

4. [T]he majority see a legitimate aim in ensuring "living together" ... . We have strong reservations about this approach.

5. ... The very general concept of "living together" does not fall directly under any of the rights and freedoms guaranteed within the Convention. ... [T]he concept seems far-fetched and vague.

6. It is essential to understand what is at the core of the wish to protect people against encounters with others wearing full-face veils. The majority speak of "practices or attitudes ... which would fundamentally call into question the possibility of open interpersonal relationships". ... It seems to us, however, that such fears and feelings of uneasiness are not so much caused by the veil itself, ... but by the philosophy that is presumed to be linked to it. Thus the recurring motives for not tolerating the full-face veil are based on interpretations of its symbolic meaning. ... [A] French parliamentary commission ... saw in the veil "a symbol of a form of subservience". The explanatory memorandum to the French bill referred to its "symbolic and dehumanising violence". The full-face veil was also linked to the "self-confinement of any individual who cuts himself off from others whilst living among them". Women who wear such clothing have been described as "effaced" from the public space.

7. All these interpretations have been called into question by the applicant, who claims to wear the full-face veil depending only on her spiritual feelings and does not consider it an insurmountable barrier to communication or integration. ... [T]here is no right not to be shocked or provoked by different models of cultural or religious identity, even those that are very distant from the traditional French and European lifestyle. In the context of freedom of expression, the Court has repeatedly observed that the Convention protects not only those opinions "that are favourably received or regarded as inoffensive or as a matter of indifference, but also ... those that offend, shock or disturb", pointing out that "[s]uch are the demands of pluralism, tolerance and broadmindedness without which there is no 'democratic society'". The same must be true for dress codes demonstrating radical opinions.

8. ... [T]he right to respect for private life also comprises the right not to communicate and not to enter into contact with others in public places – the right to be an outsider.

9. It is true that "living together" requires the possibility of interpersonal exchange. It is also true that the face plays an important role in human interaction. But this idea cannot be turned around, to lead to the conclusion that human interaction is impossible if the full face is not shown. This is evidenced by examples that are perfectly rooted in European culture, such as the activities of skiing and motorcycling with full-face helmets and the wearing of costumes in carnivals. Nobody would claim that in such situations (which form part of the exceptions provided for in the French Law) the minimum requirements of life in society are not respected. People can socialise without necessarily looking into each other's eyes.

...

12. [I]t is doubtful that the French Law pursues any legitimate aim under ... the Convention.

C. Proportionality of a blanket ban on the full-face veil

1. Different approaches to pluralism, tolerance and broadmindedness

13. ... [It is] difficult to argue that the rights protected outweigh the rights infringed. This is especially true as the Government have not explained or given any examples of how the impact on others of this particular attire differs from other accepted practices of concealing the face, such as excessive hairstyles or the wearing of dark glasses or hats. In the legislative process, the supporters of a blanket ban on the full-face veil mainly advanced "the values of the Republic, as expressed in the maxim 'liberty, equality, fraternity'". The Court refers to "pluralism", "tolerance" and "broadmindedness" ... .

14. However, all those values could be regarded as justifying ... on the contrary, the acceptance of such a religious dress-code and the adoption of an integrationist approach. In our view, the applicant is right to claim that the French legislature has restricted pluralism... .. ... In its jurisprudence the Court has clearly elaborated on the State's duty to ensure mutual tolerance between opposing groups and has stated that "the role of the authorities ... is not to remove the cause of tension by eliminating pluralism, but to ensure that the competing groups tolerate each other". By banning the full-face veil, the French legislature has done the opposite. ...

2. Disproportionate interference

15. ... [W]e cannot ... agree with the majority that the ban is proportionate to the aim pursued.

(a) Margin of appreciation

16. ... [W]e are unable to conclude that in this particular situation the respondent State should be accorded a broad margin of appreciation.

17. Firstly, the prohibition targets a dress-code closely linked to religious faith, culture and personal convictions and thus, undoubtedly, an intimate right related to one's personality.

18. Secondly, it is not convincing to draw a parallel between the present case and cases concerning the relationship between State and religion. ... [T]he Law was deliberately worded in a much broader manner, generally targeting "clothing that is designed to conceal the face" and thus going far beyond the religious context ... .

19. Thirdly, it is difficult to understand why the majority are not prepared to accept the existence of a European consensus ... . The fact that forty-five out of forty-seven member States of the Council of Europe, and thus an overwhelming majority, have not deemed it necessary to legislate in this area is a very strong indicator for a European consensus. ...

20. The arguments drawn from comparative and international law militate against the acceptance of a broad margin of appreciation and in favour of close supervision by the Court. … [I]t still remains the task of the Court to protect small minorities against disproportionate interferences.

(b) Consequences for the women concerned

21. … In our view, the restrictive measure cannot be expected to have the desired effect of liberating women presumed to be oppressed, but will further exclude them from society and aggravate their situation.

22. With regard to the majority's assumption that the punishment consists of mild sanctions only, … the multiple effect of successive penalties has to be taken into account.

23. … [O]nly a small number of women … are affected by the ban. That means that it is only on rare occasions that the average person would encounter a woman in a full-face veil … .

(c) Less restrictive measures

24. Furthermore, the Government have not explained why it would have been impossible to apply less restrictive measures, instead of criminalising the concealment of the face in all public places. No account has been given as to whether or to what extent any efforts have been made to discourage the relatively recent phenomenon of the use of full-face veils, by means, for example, of awareness-raising and education. …

D. Conclusion

25. … [W]e find that the criminalisation of the wearing of a full-face veil is a measure which is disproportionate to the aim of protecting the idea of "living together" – an aim which cannot readily be reconciled with the Convention's restrictive catalogue of grounds for interference with basic human rights.
…

YAKER V. FRANCE
HUMAN RIGHTS COMMITTEE, COMMUNICATION NO. 2747/2016, FINAL VIEWS (17 JULY 2018)

The facts as submitted by the author

2.1   The author is a Muslim and wears a niqab (full face veil). On 6 October 2011, she was stopped for an identity check while wearing her niqab on the street in Nantes. She was then prosecuted and convicted of the minor offence of wearing a garment to conceal her face in public.

2.2   Consequently, the author was convicted on 26 March 2012 and was ordered by the community court in Nantes to pay a fine of 150 euros, the maximum penalty for the offence in question, which was established by Act No. 2010-1192 of 11 October 2010. …
…
2.4   The author is challenging, on the basis of article 18 of the Covenant, the prohibition against concealing the face in public areas, which deprives those wishing to wear a full-face veil of the possibility to do so.
…

Issues and proceedings before the Committee

Consideration of the merits

8.2   … The Committee notes the State party's argument that … the Act does not specially treat religious clothing. The Committee notes, however, that article 2 (II) broadly exempts from the Act clothing worn for "health reasons" or on "professional grounds", or that is "part of sporting, artistic or traditional festivities or events", including "religious processions", or clothing that is prescribed or legally authorized by legislative or regulatory provisions. The Committee further notes … that fewer than 2,000 women wear the full-face veil in

France, and that the vast majority of checks under the Act have been performed on women wearing the full-face veil.

8.3   The Committee ... considers that the ban introduced under the Act constitutes a restriction or limitation of the author's freedom to manifest her beliefs or religion — by wearing her niqab — within the meaning of article 18 (1) of the Covenant.

...

8.5   ... It is therefore incumbent upon the Committee to assess whether the restriction, which is prescribed by law, pursues a legitimate objective, is necessary for achieving that objective, and is proportionate and non-discriminatory.

8.6   The Committee notes that the State party has indicated two objectives that the Act is intended to pursue, namely the protection of public order and safety, and the protection of the rights and freedoms of others.

8.7   With respect to protection of public order and safety, the State party contends that it must be possible to identify all individuals when necessary to avert threats to the security of persons or property and to combat identity fraud. ... [H]owever, ... the Act is not limited to such contexts, but comprehensively prohibits the wearing of certain face coverings in public at all times, and that the State party has failed to demonstrate how wearing the full-face veil in itself represents a threat to public safety or order that would justify such an absolute ban. Nor has the State party provided any public safety justification or explanation for why covering the face for certain religious purposes — i.e., the niqab — is prohibited, while covering the face for numerous other purposes, including sporting, artistic, and other traditional and religious purposes, is allowed. ...

8.8   Even if the State party could demonstrate the existence of a specific and significant threat to public safety and order in principle, it has failed to demonstrate that the prohibition contained in Act No. 2010-1192 is proportionate to that objective, in view of its considerable impact on the author as a woman wearing the full-face veil. Nor has it attempted to demonstrate that the ban was the least restrictive measure necessary to ensure the protection of the freedom of religion or belief.

8.9   With regard to the second objective presented by the State party, understood as the protection of the fundamental rights and freedoms of others under article 18 (3), the Committee notes the State party's argument based on the concept of "living together" ... .

8.10   ... [T]he Committee observes that the concept of "living together" is very vague and abstract. The State party has not identified any specific fundamental rights or freedoms of others that are affected by the fact that some people present in the public space have their face covered, including fully veiled women. Nor has the State party explained why such rights would be "unfairly" obstructed by wearing the full-face veil, but not by covering the face in public through the numerous other means that are exempted from the Act. The right to interact with any individual in public and the right not to be disturbed by other people wearing the full-face veil are not protected by the Covenant and therefore cannot provide the basis for permissible restrictions within the meaning of article 18 (3).

8.11   Even assuming that the concept of living together could be considered a "legitimate objective" ... the State party has failed to demonstrate that the criminal ban ... is proportionate to that aim, or that it is the least restrictive means that is protective of religion or belief.

8.12   ... The Committee ... concludes that the ban ... and the conviction ... violated the author's rights under article 18 of the Covenant.

8.13   As to the author's claims under article 26 of the Covenant, namely that the law in question had the effect of indirectly discriminating against the minority of Muslim women who wear the full-face veil, the Committee notes the State party's argument that the prohibition introduced by the Act is not based on the religious connotation of the clothes in question, but on the fact that they conceal the face. ... [F]rom the text of the Act, the debate preceding its adoption and its implementation in practice, the Committee observes that the Act is applied mainly to the full-face Islamic veil, which is a form of religious observance and identification for a minority of Muslim women.

...

8.15   The Committee notes that the State party has provided no explanation why the blanket prohibition on the author's veil is reasonable or justified, in contrast to the exceptions allowable under the Act. The Committee further notes that the blanket ban on the full-face veil introduced by the Act appears to be based on the assumption that the full veil is inherently discriminatory and that women who wear it are forced to do so. While acknowledging that some women may be subject to family or social pressures to cover their faces, the Committee observes that the wearing of the full veil may also be a choice — or even a means of staking a claim — based on religious belief, as in the author's case. The Committee further considers that the prohibition, rather than protecting fully veiled women, could have the opposite effect of confining them to their homes, impeding their access to public services and exposing them to abuse and marginalization. ...

8.16   Finally, although the State party contends that the sanctions imposed on women who decide to wear the full veil in public are "measured", the Committee notes that the penalties have a criminal nature and have been applied against some women, including the author, on multiple occasions. Such sanctions necessarily negatively impact the author's right to manifest her religion through wearing the veil and potentially other rights.

8.17   ... [T]he Committee considers that the criminal ban ... disproportionately affects the author as a Muslim woman who chooses to wear the full-face veil, and introduces a distinction between her and other persons who may legally cover their face in public that is not necessary and proportionate to a legitimate interest, and is therefore unreasonable. The Committee hence concludes that this provision and its application to the author constitutes a form of intersectional discrimination based on gender and religion, in violation of article 26 of the Covenant.

* * *

A 2022 report by the Open Society Justice Initiative, entitled *Restrictions on Muslim Women's Dress in the 27 EU Member States and the United Kingdom*, traced the evolution of these policies:

> Such restrictions were considered unacceptable for most of the post-World War II era in Europe, where respect for the religious liberties of minorities formed an essential component of European liberal democracy. Things started to change in the 1980s and 1990s, as Muslim youth came of age and expected to participate in European societies on equal footing. Geopolitical developments in the Middle East accelerated the change and gave rise to the bogeyman of the suspicious Muslim. After 9/11, policymakers declared a global war on terror premised on this stereotype. A popular narrative proclaimed the discordance of Islam and the West, with Muslim women's religious dress—allegedly always imposed by Muslim men—rising as the ultimate symbol of incompatibility. The burqa forced on Afghan women by the Taliban served as the dominant reference. The idea that Muslims as a group were the new "enemy within," with beliefs and practices reflecting values and norms inferior to those of Europe, acquired legitimacy across the political spectrum. Echoing Orientalist prejudices and stereotypes about Muslims already prevalent in Europe, it served to justify banning the visible presence of Muslim women and Islam from various spaces.[262]

The report found that only twelve of the 28 states had 'no legal bans, or cases or reports about institutional or private bans.' It notes that 'in most cases it was mainstream political parties that actually enacted religious dress restrictions', although these had also been supported by far-right political parties. It notes that, although the ECHR and the CJEU had 'given states and private actors more leeway in instituting bans', litigation at the national level had been more successful in achieving rulings against bans.

---

[262] Open Society Justice Initiative, 'Restrictions on Muslim Women's Dress in the 27 EU Member States and the United Kingdom: Policy Report', (March 2022) 5.

<hr>

QUESTIONS

1. Turkey's situation showed some similarities to the French situation and some dramatic differences. Do you believe that, as a matter of policy or law, the ban of headscarves in public educational institutions was equally justified or unjustified in France and Turkey or more justified in one country than the other?

2. How might we account for the very different approaches taken by the European Court and the Human Rights Committee in these cases?

<hr>

b. Crucifixes in Italian Classrooms

In a major controversy involving religious symbolism, the ECtHR decided *Lautsi v. Italy*, which concerned the presence of crucifixes in state school classrooms in Italy. In a unanimous opinion, a chamber of seven judges held that the practice was incompatible with the freedom of religion. Relying in part on *Dahlab*, the Court reasoned:

> Ms Lautsi's convictions also concern the impact of the display of the crucifix on her children, who at the material time were aged 11 and 13. The Court acknowledges that, as submitted, it is impossible not to notice crucifixes in the classrooms. In the context of public education they are necessarily perceived as an integral part of the school environment and may therefore be considered "powerful external symbols" (see *Dahlab v. Switzerland* (2001)).

> The presence of the crucifix may easily be interpreted by pupils of all ages as a religious sign, and they will feel that they have been brought up in a school environment marked by a particular religion. What may be encouraging for some religious pupils may be emotionally disturbing for pupils of other religions or those who profess no religion. That risk is particularly strong among pupils belonging to religious minorities. Negative freedom of religion ... extends to practices and symbols expressing, in particular or in general, a belief, a religion or atheism. That negative right deserves special protection if it is the State which expresses a belief and dissenters are placed in a situation from which they cannot extract themselves if not by making disproportionate efforts and acts of sacrifice.

Dominic McGoldrick, below, called the political response to the Chamber's judgment in *Lautsi* 'without precedent in European human rights terms', and noted widespread opposition, including from 20 countries that supported 'Italy in the defence of the crucifix'. The judgment continues to resonate in Italy many years later.[263]

LAUTSI V. ITALY
EUROPEAN COURT OF HUMAN RIGHTS, GRAND CHAMBER, APPLICATION NO. 30814/06 (18 MARCH 2011)

[T]he second sentence of Article 2 of Protocol No. 1 does not prevent States from imparting through teaching or education information or knowledge of a directly or indirectly religious or philosophical kind ... .

... [I]t requires the State, in exercising its functions with regard to education and teaching, to take care that information or knowledge included in the curriculum is conveyed in an objective, critical and pluralistic manner, enabling pupils to develop a critical mind particularly with regard to religion in a calm atmosphere free of any

<hr>

[263] Sebastián Guidi, 'Law Over Legalism: International Court Legitimacy in *Lautsi v. Italy*', 33 *Duke J. Comp. & Int'l L.* (2023) 45

proselytism. The State is forbidden to pursue an aim of indoctrination that might be considered as not respecting parents' religious and philosophical convictions. That is the limit that the States must not exceed.

...

There is no evidence before the Court that the display of a religious symbol on classroom walls may have an influence on pupils and so it cannot reasonably be asserted that it does or does not have an effect on young persons whose convictions are still in the process of being formed.

However, it is understandable that the first applicant might see in the display of crucifixes in the classrooms of the State school formerly attended by her children a lack of respect on the State's part for her right to ensure their education and teaching in conformity with her own philosophical convictions. Be that as it may, the applicant's subjective perception is not in itself sufficient to establish a breach of Article 2 of Protocol No. 1.

The Government ... explained that the presence of crucifixes in State-school classrooms, being the result of Italy's historical development, a fact which gave it not only a religious connotation but also an identity-linked one, now corresponded to a tradition which they considered it important to perpetuate. They added that, beyond its religious meaning, the crucifix symbolised the principles and values which formed the foundation of democracy and western civilisation, and that its presence in classrooms was justifiable on that account.

The Court takes the view that the decision whether or not to perpetuate a tradition falls in principle within the margin of appreciation of the respondent State. The Court must moreover take into account the fact that Europe is marked by a great diversity between the States of which it is composed, particularly in the sphere of cultural and historical development. It emphasises, however, that the reference to a tradition cannot relieve a Contracting State of its obligation to respect the rights and freedoms enshrined in the Convention and its Protocols.

...

... [T]he decision whether crucifixes should be present in State-school classrooms is, in principle, a matter falling within the margin of appreciation of the respondent State. Moreover, the fact that there is no European consensus on the question of the presence of religious symbols in State schools speaks in favour of that approach.

This margin of appreciation, however, goes hand in hand with European supervision ... .

In that connection, it is true that by prescribing the presence of crucifixes in State-school classrooms — a sign which, whether or not it is accorded in addition a secular symbolic value, undoubtedly refers to Christianity — the regulations confer on the country's majority religion preponderant visibility in the school environment.

That is not in itself sufficient, however, to denote a process of indoctrination ... .

...

... [A] crucifix on a wall is an essentially passive symbol and this point is of importance in the Court's view, particularly having regard to the principle of neutrality. It cannot be deemed to have an influence on pupils comparable to that of didactic speech or participation in religious activities.

[The Grand Chamber next describes the passages of the ECtHR's lower chamber opinion (reproduced above) relying on *Dahlab*, but determined that that case] cannot serve as a basis in this case because the facts of the two cases are entirely different.

... *Dahlab* concerned the measure prohibiting the applicant from wearing the Islamic headscarf while teaching, which was intended to protect the religious beliefs of the pupils and their parents and to apply the principle of denominational neutrality in schools enshrined in domestic law. After observing that the authorities had duly weighed the competing interests involved, the Court held, having regard above all to the tender age of the children for whom the applicant was responsible, that the authorities had not exceeded their margin of appreciation.

Moreover, the effects of the greater visibility which the presence of the crucifix gives to Christianity in schools needs to be further placed in perspective by consideration of the following points. Firstly, the presence of crucifixes is not associated with compulsory teaching about Christianity. Secondly, according to the indications provided by the Government, Italy opens up the school environment in parallel to other religions. The Government indicated in this connection that it was not forbidden for pupils to wear Islamic headscarves or other symbols or apparel having a religious connotation; alternative arrangements were possible to help schooling fit in with non-majority religious practices; the beginning and end of Ramadan were "often celebrated" in schools; and optional religious education could be organised in schools for "all recognised religious creeds". Moreover, there was nothing to suggest that the authorities were intolerant of pupils who believed in other religions, were non-believers or who held non-religious philosophical convictions. In addition, the applicants did not assert that the presence of the crucifix in classrooms had encouraged the development of teaching practices with a proselytising tendency ... .

* * *

Consider the following reactions to *Lautsi*.

Joseph Weiler, who represented eight intervening states before the Grand Chamber, argues in 'State and Nation; Church, Mosque and Synagogue', 8 *Int'l. J. Con. L.* 157 (2010):

> ... There are those who truly believe that laïcité is a primordial condition — sine-qua-non for a good liberal democracy and that, at least implicitly, the non-laïque position is sub-optimal at best and aberrational at worst. Consequently, it is morally imperative for good democrats and liberal pluralists to attempt to clip the wings of religious manifestations of the non-laïque state as far as possible — a principled and consistent position.
>
> There are others (myself included) who hold the view that, even more in today's world than before, the European version of the non-laïque state is hugely important in the lesson of tolerance it forces on such states and its citizens towards those who do not share the "official" religions and in the example it gives the rest of the world of a principled mediation between a collective self-understanding rooted in a religious sensibility, or religious history, or religiously-inspired values and the imperative exigencies of liberal democracy. That there is something inspiring and optimistic by the fact that even though the Queen is the Titular Head of the Church of England, the many Catholics, Muslims and Jews, not to mention the majority of atheists and agnostics, can genuinely consider her as "their Queen" too, and equal citizens of England and the UK. I think there is intrinsic value of incalculable worth in the European pluralism which validates both a France and UK as acceptable models in which the individual right to and from religion may take place.
>
> ...
>
> ... [S]urely Freedom FROM Religion is not absolute, and its vindication has to be so balanced, and the principle collective good against which it should be balanced would, in my view, be the aforementioned collective freedom of a self-understanding, self-definition and determination of the collective self as having some measure of religious reference. Freedom OF Religion surely requires that no school kid be obligated to chant God's name, even in, say, God Save the Queen. But does Freedom FROM Religion entitle such to demand that others not so chant, to have another national anthem? How does one negotiate the individual and the collective rights at issue here?
>
> ... [B]oth to understand the new debates and to arrive at meaningful, ethical, deontological, identitarian and pragmatic results may profit by this reframing.

Stanley Fish, in 'Crucifixes and Diversity: The Odd Couple', *New York Times* (28 March 2011):

> The question is not what can a crucifix possibly mean in all the settings the world might offer, but what does it in mean in this setting, hanging on the wall of every classroom with a state imprimatur? What is a non-Christian student likely to think — "Aha, a

symbol of pluralism and universal acceptance" or "I get it; this is a Catholic space and I'm here on sufferance?" ...

...

Exclusion would be the result, we are told, if the students had been the objects of indoctrination, but because the crucifixes just hang there without saying anything, they were not: "[A] crucifix on a wall is an essentially passive symbol" and "it cannot be deemed to have an influence on pupils comparable to that of didactic speech." Judge Bonello [in concurrence] glosses and drives home the point: "The mere display of a voiceless testimonial of a historical symbol ... in no away amounts to teaching." Actually, it does: the lesson (of official authority) is enhanced by not being voiced; the absence of didactic speech itself says "you don't have to be told what this means; you know." The effect is the one produced in a country where a king or leader-for-life has his picture hung everywhere. Nothing need be said.

Julie Ringelheim, in 'State Religious Neutrality as a Common European Standard? Reappraising the European Court of Human Rights Approach', 6 *Oxford J. L. and Relig.* (2017) 24:

> ... [D]etermining what state denominational neutrality means exactly and what it entails in specific contexts raises special challenges for the Court. First of all, neutrality is not a straightforward concept. It can be subject to different interpretations. Second, when elaborating this principle, the Court must take into consideration the diversity of existing state–religion arrangements across Europe. ...
>
> ...
>
> ... As references to neutrality have multiplied, the meaning afforded to this notion has become blurred. It has come to mean different things in different rulings. And there are clear tensions between some of these interpretations. This ambiguity is problematic. ...
>
> ...
>
> ... In effect, the Court balances between three different understandings of the concept that need to be disentangled. They are characterized here as 'neutrality as absence of coercion', 'neutrality as absence of preference', and 'neutrality as exclusion of religion from the public sphere'. *Lautsi and Others v Italy* (2011), *Folgerø and Others v Norway* (2007), and *Ebrahimian v France* (2015) exemplify each of these models of neutrality. It will be argued that 'neutrality as absence of preference' provides the most adequate model for an ECHR-based concept of state religious neutrality.
>
> ...
>
> ... [T]he Court's approach to the principle of state neutrality has become increasingly blurred and fragmented. Where religious instruction at school is at stake, it sticks to the second model of neutrality, that is, respect for conscientious and religious freedom implies that the state should not manifest a preference for a religion. But where the display of religious symbols by the state at school is concerned, the Court retreats to a lower standard of protection. Neutrality here merely means 'absence of coercion'. At the same time, where states officially opt for the 'neutrality as exclusion of religion' model, the Court allows them a wide margin of appreciation to impose restrictions on an individual's right to manifest their religion when they are in a public institution. ... [A]lthough they are very different, the latter two visions of neutrality both entail a weakening of the protection of the individual's rights if compared with the 'neutrality as absence of preference' approach.

Malcolm Evans, in 'State Neutrality and Religion in Europe: What's the Prospect?', 11 *Oxford J. L. and Relig.* (2022) 4, at 16:

... [T]he tensions inherent in the developing jurisprudence are best exemplified in the judgments of the Chamber and Grand Chamber [in *Lautsi*]. ... [F]or the Chamber, the presence of the cross ... embodied the State endorsement of Roman Catholicism and so its presence breached the rights of the applicant; for the Grand Chamber the cross was just 'there', passively doing nothing other than just being there, and so its presence did not amount to a violation of the applicant's rights. ... [I]t was in fact doing both. It literally depends on who was looking at it. Ultimately, the Grand Chamber is telling the applicant that it does not see what they are seeing. And like it or not, that is taking sides.

...

The problem with the Chamber decision in *Lautsi* was that it seemed to suggest that neutrality and impartiality involved cleansing the public space of the trappings of religion on the grounds that those trappings might cause offense. This has only to be stated to be seen to be untenable. There is no right to be insulated from things which cause offence; indeed, the Court has made it very clear for very many years that there is freedom to say things which may cause offense. If causing offense alone is not sufficient to require someone not to speak, how can it be sufficient alone to justify the removal of a cross, or of a statue? One cannot have a classroom in which there both is and is not a cross; a plinth on which there both is and is not a statute. There must be a choice as to which it is to be. ...

Dominic McGoldrick, in 'Religion in the European Public Square and in European Public Life: Crucifixes in the Classroom?', 11 *Hum. Rts. L. Rev.* 451 (2011), at 487:

There was no evidence before the GC [Grand Chamber] that the display of a religious symbol on classroom walls might have an influence on pupils ... . The GC's reliance on the lack of evidence is particularly interesting. In previous religious clothing cases the Court either ignored evidence that the wearing had not actually caused any problems or made its own assertions about their possible effects (*Dahlab*, *Şahin*).

...

Even engaging in a relative approach to the assessment of symbols was inevitably going to leave the GC open to criticism. Islamic headscarves, worn by a minority, may be powerful external symbols that challenge neutrality. However, Christian crucifixes, a symbol of the majority religion, are somehow merely passive and do not challenge neutrality. It may have been better for the GC to have simply accepted that the assessment of the meaning and effect of religious symbols was complex and would be left to the national authorities to assess within the normal bounds of the margin of appreciation.

...

As noted, the GC's view was that the decision whether or not to perpetuate a tradition fell in principle within the margin of appreciation of the State. Historically, those traditions have been dominated by Christianity. The inevitable consequence is that non-dominant traditions (i.e. minority, non-Christian ones) will not be equally represented or perpetuated in the public reasoning and public visual squares. Added to that, the ECtHR has accepted that, in the defence of a secular order, a state can prohibit the wearing of Islamic headscarves in schools, and even in universities ... .

It has been suggested that Christianity and Christian values have been defended even at the expense of trampling on fundamental individual freedoms, because the ECtHR does not perceive them as conflicting with the core values of the Convention system. Islam, on the other hand, even when it is the vast majority's religion (as with Turkey), has been restrictively regulated on the ground that it threatens the democratic basis of the State. Assessing the value of the ECHR to Muslims is a complex task. However, the problem is also one of public and political perception ... . It has been argued that the GC's decision in *Lautsi*, 'confirms the Christian-centric outlook of European institutions and it will confirm many Turks' perceptions that as Muslims, they are inevitably viewed with suspicion'.

QUESTIONS

1. Is the logic of the ECtHR ruling in Dahlab consistent with the Chamber's or the Grand Chamber's decision in Lautsi?

2. Does the presence of the crucifix in Italian classrooms constitute, in itself, an injury to minority groups that is incompatible with the freedom of religion or is the real threat the prospective risk of a slippery slope?

3. Are you persuaded by Weiler that all citizens of England see the Queen as 'their Queen'? Do you agree with Weiler's framing of that claim:

[I]t is this special combination of private and public liberties, reflecting a particular spirit of tolerance, which explains how in countries such as, say, Britain or Denmark to give but two examples, where there is an established state church no less — Anglican and Lutheran, respectively — Catholics, Jews, Muslims and, of course, the many citizens who profess no religious faith, can be entirely 'at home,' play a full role in public life including the holding of the highest office, and feel it is 'their country' no less than those belonging to the established church.

4. McGoldrick states that the Grand Chamber perhaps should have 'simply accepted that the assessment of the meaning and effect of religious symbols was complex and would be left to the national authorities to assess within the normal bounds of the margin of appreciation.' Would applying his criticism result in a different outcome in the Lautsi case or simply a different rationale for the same holding?

5. Neville Cox, in 'Pejorative Assertions, Human Rights Evaluation, and European Veiling Laws', 71 *Am. J. Comp. L.* (2023) 1, reinforces McGoldrick's emphasis on the importance of actual evidence. He argues that the European Court, in contrast to the UN Human Rights Committee, 'accepts assertions of facts from states as to why their laws are justified in the absence of any demonstrable supporting evidence' and characterizes this as 'an irresponsible abdication of responsibility'. How might a more demanding approach in requiring evidence to support governments' assertions about impact, affect the outcome in such cases?

---

4. Freedom of Speech

Freedom of speech forms one of the obvious boundary lines between relatively open and closed societies, between liberal democracies and different types of authoritarian states. Whatever the form of authoritarian regime, a liberal value like speech and its related rights such as assembly and association will bow to one or another degree to censorship and other repressive controls. In some instances, the explanations for different understandings of this human right would stress factors like an authoritarian regime's guiding ideology and its rulers' concern about resistance or subversion. Relatively free speech may pose too great a danger for the survival of the existing political system. In other cases, different conceptions of free speech and its relation to other rights and state interests may reflect religious beliefs, cultural patterns or long-standing traditions and practices.

But free speech is not only at risk in authoritarian states. Even states with strong human rights traditions might struggle to find an appropriate balance between robust free speech protections and respect for the rights of others. In recent years, the boundaries of the right to free speech in a liberal society have been tested by hate speech in its many different forms, as well as calls to prohibit speech (including offensive texts and cartoons) deemed blasphemous or defaming of a religion. It is these latter issues that are examined below.

Hate Speech

The heterogeneity generated within many countries by large-scale migration has led to increased racial, religious and cultural tensions and backlash, which have in turn been exploited and exacerbated by populist and nationalist political responses. The ubiquity of social media and other novel forms of communication has enabled hate speech to proliferate, made it harder to define and regulate, and given it a greater international reach and salience.

The ICCPR Committee's views in the 1996 *Faurisson* case below concern a 'Holocaust-denial law' that has a close affinity with laws making 'hate speech' a criminal offence (that may also be subject to civil sanctions). While the subsequent materials emphasize the definitional challenges involved, the term covers abusive, denigrating, or harassing speech based on a group or individual's national, religious, racial or ethnic identity. In some but not all definitions, such speech must incite violence or discrimination.[264]

The laws imposing criminal and other sanctions on hate speech clearly impinge on freedom of speech, a core value protected under the major universal and regional human rights instruments:

> *Article 19, UDHR:* Everyone has the right to freedom of opinion and expression; this right includes freedom to ... impart information and ideas through any media and regardless of frontiers.

> *Article 19, ICCPR:* ...

(2) Everyone shall have the right to freedom of expression; this right shall include freedom to ... impart information and ideas of all kinds, regardless of frontiers ... .

(3) The exercise of the right provided for in paragraph 2 of this article carries with it special duties and responsibilities. It may therefore be subject to certain restrictions, but these shall only be such as are provided by law and are necessary:

  (a) For respect of the rights or reputations of others;

  (b) For the protection of national security or of public order (*ordre public*), or of public health or morals.

Note also the following ICCPR articles, each of which has a comparable UDHR article: (1) the equal protection clause in Article 26; (2) the provision in ICCPR Article 5 that nothing in the Covenant should be interpreted as implying 'for any group or person any right to engage in any activity ... aimed at the destruction of any of the rights and freedom recognized herein ... .'; and (3) the provision in Article 17 that no one shall be subject to 'arbitrary or unlawful interference with his privacy ... nor to unlawful attacks on his honour and reputation'.

The arguments in favour of free speech are broadly familiar, for example: its contribution to the full realization of the individual human personality; the challenge to existing beliefs (the 'marketplace of ideas') and the related stimulus to inquiry, debate and development of knowledge; its relation to principles of democratic government and pluralism; and its close functional association with other human rights like freedoms of belief, religion and association. But are these arguments sufficient to justify the protection of hate speech directed at particular racial, ethnic, religious, gender identity or other groups or their members? Such speech itself attacks basic premises of the human rights system, premises as deep as equal human dignity, respect for others and equal protection. Hate speech may deny that the targeted group is entitled to benefit together with the rest of the population from human rights protections. It may advocate, indeed passionately urge, discriminatory or even

---

[264] J. Waldron, *The Harm in Hate Speech* (2012).

violent action against members of the targeted group. It may pose threats of a greater or lesser immediacy of such violence.

The quoted provisions above of the ICCPR include qualifications to free speech that bear generally on these types of restrictive laws. Several human rights instruments are more explicit on these issues — for example, Article 20(2) of the ICCPR: 'Any advocacy of national, racial or religious hatred that constitutes incitement to discrimination, hostility or violence shall be prohibited by law.' Manfred Nowak, in *U.N. Covenant on Civil and Political Rights: CCPR Commentary* (2nd edn. 2005), observes (at 474–5) that the 'legal formulation of this provision is not entirely clear'. The wording of paragraph (2):

> literally means that incitement to discrimination without violence must also be prohibited ... . Particularly inexplicable is the insertion of the word 'discrimination'... .
>
> ... It is most difficult to conceive of an advocacy of national, racial or religious hatred that does not simultaneously incite discrimination ... . Art. 20(2) ... may be sensibly interpreted only in light of its object and purpose, i.e., taking into consideration its *responsive character* with regard to the Nazi racial hatred campaigns ... . Thus, despite its unclear formulation, Art 20(2) does not require States parties to prohibit advocacy of hatred in private that instigates non-violent acts of racial or religious discrimination. What the delegates ... had in mind was to ... prevent the public incitement of racial hatred and violence within a State or against other States and peoples.

Some states have forbidden political groups or parties that are based on racism, and hence employ hate speech, from participating in elections. In Israel, for example, Amendment No. 9 to the Basic Law on the Knesset (Parliament) provides: 'A candidate's list shall not participate in elections to the Knesset if its objects or actions, expressly or by implication, include one of the following: ... (3) incitement to racism'. In late 2022, the newly elected coalition government announced its intention to eliminate that provision.

THE *JERSILD* AND *JALLOW* DECISIONS

Consider the approach of the European Court of Human Rights in *Jersild v. Denmark*, (Application No. 15890/89) (1994). The question was whether Jersild, a Danish journalist, was criminally liable for aiding and abetting three youths who made racist remarks on interviews conducted by Jersild on a television programme on matters of public interest. The youths were members of the Greenjackets, a group that engaged in hate speech, in this case against Danish residents of African descent. In the course of the interview, which had been sharply edited by Jersild from an initial length of hours to a few minutes, the men made numerous ugly and denigrating remarks about black people. There was no allegation that Jersild or the broadcasting station shared those views. On the other hand, since the point of the programme was to convey information to the Danish public about atypical, small racist groups, there was no effort by Jersild or the broadcasting station to challenge or oppose the racist views expressed.

A Danish penal statute, responsive to obligations of Denmark under the Convention on the Elimination of All Forms of Racial Discrimination, imposed a fine or imprisonment on '[a]ny person who, publicly or with the intention of disseminating it to a wide circle of people, makes a statement, or other communication, threatening insulting or degrading a group of persons on account of their race, colour, national or ethnic origin or belief ...'. The three youths were found guilty of violating the statute, and did not appeal. Jersild was found guilty of aiding and abetting the three youths. His conviction was affirmed by the Danish appellate courts, and he then instituted proceedings before the European Court of Human Rights.

The Court decided that the conviction — that is, not the hate-speech statute abstractly, but the statute as here applied to Jersild for aiding and abetting — violated the free expression provisions (including freedom of media) of Article 10 of the ECHR. Its opinion stressed the need to protect freedom of the press, and that news reporting through interviews was an important means of informing the public. Conviction of a journalist in these circumstances could hamper discussion of matters of public interest. It concluded that the limitation on Jersild's freedom of expression was not 'necessary in a democratic society', a requirement of Article 10. The prosecution and conviction were disproportionate to the state's interest, also expressed in Article 10, of protecting the reputation or rights of others.

A joint dissenting opinion by Judges Ryssdal, Bernhardt, Spielmann and Loizou observed:

> ... The applicant has cut the entire interview down to a few minutes, probably with the consequence or even the intention of retaining the most crude remarks. That being so, it was absolutely necessary to add at least a clear statement of disapproval. The majority of the Court sees such disapproval in the context of the interview, but this is an interpretation of cryptic remarks. Nobody can exclude that certain parts of the public found in the television spot support for their racist prejudices.
>
> And what must be the feelings of those whose human dignity has been attacked, or even denied, by the Greenjackets? Can they get the impression that seen in context the television broadcast contributes to their protection? A journalist's good intentions are not enough in such a situation, especially in a case in which he has himself provoked the racist statements.

Another dissenting opinion by Judges Gölcüklü, Russo and Valticos noted:

> While appreciating that some judges attach particular importance to freedom of expression, the more so as their countries have largely been deprived of it in quite recent times, we cannot accept that this freedom should extend to encouraging racial hatred, contempt for races other than the one to which we belong, and defending violence against those who belong to the races in question. It has been sought to defend the broadcast on the ground that it would provoke a healthy reaction of rejection among the viewers. That is to display an optimism, which to say the least, is belied by experience. Large numbers of young people today, and even of the population at large, finding themselves overwhelmed by the difficulties of life, unemployment and poverty, are only too willing to seek scapegoats who are held up to them without any real word of caution; for — and this is an important point — the journalist responsible for the broadcast in question made no real attempt to challenge the points of view he was presenting, which was necessary if their impact was to be counterbalanced, at least for the viewers.

Consider also a 2022 Opinion by the UN Committee on the Elimination of All Forms of Racial Discrimination in a case involving Denmark:

JALLOW V. DENMARK
COMMITTEE ON THE ELIMINATION OF RACIAL DISCRIMINATION, OPINION ADOPTED REGARDING COMMUNICATION NO. 62/2018, UN DOC. CERD/C/108/D/62/2018 (1 DECEMBER 2022)

1. The author... is Momodou Jallow, born in 1977. He is a Swedish national, former spokesman for the National Association of Afro-Swedes and national coordinator for the European Network Against Racism in Sweden. ...

Factual background

2.1 On 23 October 2014, an exhibition of pictures by the controversial Swedish artist D.P. was held on the premises of the Danish Parliament in Copenhagen, under the auspices of the Danish People's Party. ...

2.2 The pictures exhibited included the following:

(a) An image of Adolf Hitler with the text: "NOT ONLY [N*****S] HAVE DREAMS";

(b) An image of the author, in which he is hung by the neck from a bridge, along with two other black persons, with the text: "HANG ON, Afrofobians";

(c) An image of the author, in which he appears as a slave who runs away from his owner, with the text: … (Our negro slave has run away) [and] (He disappeared / last Saturday 16 April and goes by the name of Mamadou Jallow …;

(d) A cartoon showing a black person with a liquorish pipe in his or her mouth, with the text: "this is not a crack[N****R] or is it?";

(e) A picture of two Roma community leaders, including their names, with the text: … (Gypsy crime is a good thing).

2.3 The artist D.P. has been convicted in Sweden of defamation and inciting hatred against an ethnic group, for creating and exhibiting those images. In Copenhagen, the images were exhibited with an explanatory text based on interviews given by the artist, explaining the content of the relevant picture, its background and purpose, and the decisions by the Swedish courts concerning each of them.

2.4 The explanatory text presented with the picture described in paragraph 2.2 (a) above indicated that, given the media attention given to the fiftieth anniversary of Martin Luther King Junior's "I have a dream" speech, D.P. made the work to draw attention to the fact that Hitler also had a dream and that not all dreams deserved being celebrated. The explanatory text presented with the picture in paragraph 2.2 (b) above indicated that the artwork was related to an incident that had occurred in 2013, when a black man had been ill-treated and almost pushed off a bridge in Sweden. The author, who was at that time the spokesman for the National Association of Afro-Swedes, had indicated that the incident was related to "white Swedish racism". However, it was later determined that the perpetrators of the attack were of Kurdish origin. … The explanatory text displayed with the picture described in paragraph 2.2 (d) above indicated that the artwork had been in response to the attempt by the European Union to prohibit liquorish pipes. In addition, it was indicated that the picture was related to the decision of a liquorice manufacturer to stop using a black face as a logo, to avoid stereotyping black people. The artist, emulating René Magritte's painting The Treachery of Images, in which the text under the image of a pipe reads "Ceci n'est pas une pipe" (This is not a pipe), "drew a liquorice pipe, as it was not a 'crack[n****r]', but only a liquorice pipe". …

…

Complaint

3.1 The author alleges that the State party has violated his rights under articles 4 (a) and (c) and 6 of the International Convention on the Elimination of Racial Discrimination [ICERD], by allowing the exhibitions to take place and by refusing to prosecute the organizers.

3.2 According to the author, the decision to stop the investigation constitutes a violation of article 4 (a), because it reveals that, in practice, the authorities prevent the effective investigation of hate crimes falling under article 266 of the Criminal Code. …

…

Consideration of the merits

7.5 … In order to qualify as racist hate speech as encompassed by article 4 (a) of the Convention, … it does not suffice … that the expressions in question contain a racist content. … [T]he Convention requires, in addition, that the speech act in question amounts to the dissemination of ideas based on racial or ethnic superiority or hatred, incitement to hatred, contempt or discrimination, threats or incitement to violence and expressions of insults, ridicule or slander or justification of hatred, contempt or discrimination, when it clearly amounts to incitement to hatred or discrimination. The racist content of a speech act must be accompanied by one of these additional factors … . …

…

7.7 … [T]he Committee concludes that the five pictures referred to in the communication fall within the scope of article 4 (a) of the Convention. The Committee notes the racist depictions and wording that, in different ways, express ideas of racial superiority. They compare the Civil Rights Movement with the ideology of National Socialism, use racial slurs and depict images of slavery to degrade a person. Some of the pictures do not only display a racist content, but also depict individual persons and portray them in a degrading manner, reproducing racist stereotypes in a way that can incite racial hatred, discrimination and violence. ...

7.8 The Committee takes note of the State party's assertion that the exhibition ... [was intended] to start an essential social debate about the limits of the freedom of expression in a democratic society. ...

7.9 ... [T]he expression of ideas and opinions made in the context of academic debates, political engagement or similar activity, and without incitement to hatred, contempt, violence or discrimination, should be regarded as legitimate exercises of the right to freedom of expression, even when such ideas are controversial. ... The Committee notes that the context of an exhibition cannot be used as a pretext in order to display pictures which would otherwise be understood as racist hate speech. The ... explanatory texts of the pictures did not show that the organizers of the exhibitions distanced themselves from the racist content of the pictures. ... [R]eprints of the pictures were sold in the exhibition hall, thereby facilitating [their] dissemination ... . Against this background, the Committee does not agree that the purpose of the exhibitions was solely to start a debate ... but that it also served the purpose to disseminate the pictures and their racist content. ...

...
7.12 ... The Committee takes note of the decision of the State Prosecutor, in which she analysed each picture and the text accompanying it ... [and of the fact that] the Director of Public Prosecutions confirmed this assessment.

7.13 The Committee notes with appreciation that the Prosecution Service of the State party took the allegations of racist hate speech seriously and conducted a thorough analysis ... . The mere conduct of an investigation does not suffice. In this context, the Committee also recalls its recommendation that the criminalization of forms of racist expression should be reserved for serious cases, to be proven beyond reasonable doubt, while less serious cases should be addressed by means other than criminal law, taking into account, inter alia, the nature and extent of the impact on targeted persons and groups. In the light of the qualification of the pictures as racist hate speech, however, the Convention required an appropriate and proportional response from the State party in an effort to combat this incident of racial discrimination. The absence of an effective response by the State party to the incident that qualifies as racist hate speech was not in conformity with the requirements of the Convention.

8. The ... facts ... disclose a violation of article 4 (a), read in conjunction with article 6, of the Convention. ...

* * *

Betül Durmuş, in 'The CERD stands firm against racist hate speech: *Jallow v. Denmark*', *EJIL: Talk!*, (2 June 2023) criticized the decision for not having engaged sufficiently with the role of satire:

> ... [T]he ECtHR famously held that "satire is a form of artistic expression and social commentary and, by its inherent features of exaggeration and distortion of reality, naturally aims to provoke and agitate" and "any interference with an artist's right to such expression must be examined with particular care". ... [T]he ECtHR also noted later that satire is not always a mitigating factor: "the blatant display of a hateful and anti-Semitic position disguised as an artistic production is as dangerous as a fully-fledged and sharp attack". It is unfortunate that the Committee did not provide further guidance as to how it understands the role of satirical art under Article 4.

QUESTION

What criteria would enable the CERD Committee or any other human rights body to assess whether the conduct in the Jallow case should be classified as satire deserving of more leeway?

HATE SPEECH IN CONFLICT SITUATIONS

Recall the 1946 Judgment of the International Military Tribunal at Nuremberg (Ch. 2D, above), which makes sparse reference to the Holocaust but includes the following observation:

> The persecution of the Jews at the hands of the Nazi Government has been proved in the greatest detail before the Tribunal. It is a record of consistent and systematic inhumanity on the greatest scale. Ohlendorf, Chief of Amt III in the RSHA from 1939 to 1943, and who was in command of one of the Einsatz groups in the campaign against the Soviet Union testified as to the methods employed in the extermination of the Jews ... . When the witness Bach Zelewski was asked how Ohlendorf could admit the murder of 90,000 people, he replied: 'I am of the opinion that when, for years, for decades, the doctrine is preached that the Slav race is an inferior race, and Jews not even human, then such an outcome is inevitable' ... . The Nazi Party preached these doctrines throughout its history, *Der Stürmer* and other publications were allowed to disseminate hatred of the Jews, and in the speeches and public declarations of the Nazi leaders, the Jews were held up to public ridicule and contempt ... .

Consider the following observations about Rwanda by Bill Berkeley, 'Radio in Rwanda: The Sounds of Silence', *San Diego Union-Tribune* (18 August 1994):

> ... Human rights groups, the United Nations and even, reluctantly, the U.S. State Department have described [the] systematic slaughter [in Rwanda] as 'genocide', yet no one has explained how thousands of peasants who say they had never killed before could have been lured, incited or coerced into participating in mass murder on par with this century's worst massacres. One answer ... lies in the sinister propaganda broadcast by radio stations affiliated with the now-deposed Rwandan government. This was the match that started the fire ... .

> ...

> ... The Tutsis were demonized ... Radio Rwanda and a station owned by members of [the former Hutu President] Habyarimana's inner circle, Radio Milles Collines, had been terrorizing the Hutus with warnings about the evil Tutsi-led RPF and Hutu oppositionists, who were labeled 'enemies' or 'traitors' and who 'deserved to die'. Endless speeches, songs and slogans demonized the Tutsis ... .

> Throughout the terror, Radio Rwanda and Radio Milles Collines have systematically blurred the distinction between rebel soldiers and Tutsi civilians. On May 23, for example, Radio Rwanda warned its listeners of what it called the 'means and clues that the Inyenzi [cockroaches] use to infiltrate in a given zone'. It said RPF soldiers 'change their clothing appearance most of the time, trying to be confused with ordinary people who till the soil and go to the market'.

> Hutus were urged to 'guard seriously the roadblock', a reference to the checkpoints where Tutsis were selected for slaughter. On June 1 Radio Milles Collines described the rebels as 'criminals' responsible for a series of harrowing massacres, a fact it claimed had been 'confirmed by international sources'... . [T]he broadcast concluded: 'This is the real face of the RPF. These people are not Rwandans, they are revengeful Ugandans. We hate them; we are disgusted with them, and nobody will accept that they take power ... .'

> ...

> 'All the Westerners who come here ask us this question', says Sixbert Musangamfura, a Hutu journalist. 'They forget the evil of Hitler's propaganda. The propaganda heard here resembles the propaganda made by Joseph Goebbels. People received this propaganda all day long. It is the propaganda that is at the base of this tragedy.' ...

In relation to the mass killings and displacement in Myanmar, noted in Ch. 2D above, Jenifer Whitten-Woodring et al., in 'Poison If You Don't Know How to Use It: Facebook, Democracy, and Human Rights in Myanmar', 25 *Int'l J. Press/Pol.* (2020) 407 describe the role of social media:[265]

> ... In 2014, the price of SIM cards dropped to about $1. By 2015, mobile phone penetration reached 56 percent ...

> ... Facebook became synonymous with the Internet and an important source for news ... in part due to Facebook's ... "free basics" program, which ... allowed many cellphone customers to sign up for a free, albeit limited, version of Facebook ... By 2017 ... more than 30 percent of the population had Internet access. ... [T]he government mostly does not regulate the Internet.

> Violence toward the Rohingya coincided with a proliferation in extreme speech and disinformation appearing on Facebook, much of it targeting Muslims and the Rohingya in particular. Fink argues that Facebook's wide reach, its interactivity, and viral potential created an atmosphere of "heightened anxiety" and that "in at least one case," a Facebook post appeared to connect directly to mob violence directed at the Rohingya. ...

> The conflict escalated in August 2017. At that time, there were more than 150 highly influential accounts, pages, and groups that routinely spread hateful messages against Muslims and the Rohingya, available on Facebook. ... [The military's] "clearance operations" ... prompted more than 750,000 Rohingya to flee. [In 2018,] the U.N. Fact-Finding Mission called ... for an investigation into the military's use of Facebook in the spread of hate speech and disinformation.

> ...

> ... Facebook gained influence at a time when government publications seemed to condone extreme speech and when trust in foreign media was declining. ... [C]onditions ... were ripe for online extreme speech to occur and for disinformation to remain unchallenged. ...

SEXUAL ORIENTATION HATE SPEECH

In *Vejdeland & Ors v. Sweden* (Application No. 1813/07) (2012) the four applicants were convicted for distributing some 100 leaflets left in or on pupils' lockers in an upper secondary school. They contained anti-homosexual messages that the Swedish Supreme Court found to constitute agitation against a national or ethnic group, defined at the time to include contempt for a group of people with reference to their sexual orientation.

Having found that the convictions did interfere with the applicants' Article 10(1) freedom of expression, the European Court examined whether that interference was 'necessary in a democratic society', in terms of Article 10(2). It reiterated its long-standing jurisprudence according to which freedom of expression protects ideas, even if they offend, shock or disturb, but that necessary restrictions can be imposed.

> 54. The Court notes that the applicants distributed the leaflets with the aim of starting a debate about the lack of objectivity of education in Swedish schools ... . [E]ven if this is an acceptable purpose, regard must be paid to the wording of the leaflets. [A]ccording to the leaflets, homosexuality was "a deviant sexual proclivity" that had "a morally destructive effect on the substance of society" [and] was one of the main reasons why HIV and AIDS had gained a foothold and that the "homosexual lobby" tried to play down paedophilia. In the Court's

---

265 See also N. Morada' 'Hate Speech and Incitement in Myanmar before and after the February 2021 Coup', 15 *Global Responsibility to Protect* (2023)107.

opinion, although these statements did not directly recommend individuals to commit hateful acts, they are serious and prejudicial allegations.

55. [I]nciting to hatred does not necessarily entail a call for an act of violence, or other criminal acts. Attacks on persons committed by insulting, holding up to ridicule or slandering specific groups of the population can be sufficient for the authorities to favour combating racist speech in the face of freedom of expression exercised in an irresponsible manner ... . [D]iscrimination based on sexual orientation is as serious as discrimination based on "race, origin or colour" ... .

56. The Court also takes into consideration that the leaflets were left in the lockers of young people who were at an impressionable and sensitive age and who had no possibility to decline to accept them ... . Moreover, the distribution of the leaflets took place at a school which none of the applicants attended and to which they did not have free access.

57. ... The Supreme Court acknowledged the applicants' right to express their ideas while at the same time stressing that along with freedoms and rights people also have obligations; one such obligation being, as far as possible, to avoid statements that are unwarrantably offensive to others, constituting an assault on their rights. [It] ... found that the statements in the leaflets had been unnecessarily offensive. It also emphasised that the applicants had left the leaflets in or on the pupils' lockers, thereby imposing them on the pupils. Having balanced the relevant considerations, [it] found no reason not to apply the relevant Article of the Penal Code.

58. Finally, ... [the] Court notes that the applicants were not sentenced to imprisonment ... [but instead] three of them were given suspended sentences combined with fines ranging from approximately EUR 200 to EUR 2,000, and the fourth applicant was sentenced to probation. The Court does not find these penalties excessive in the circumstances.

59. ... [T]he Court considers that the conviction ... and the sentences ... were not disproportionate to the legitimate aim pursued and that the reasons given by the Supreme Court in justification of those measures were relevant and sufficient. The interference with the applicants' exercise of their right to freedom of expression could therefore reasonably be regarded by the national authorities as necessary in a democratic society for the protection of the reputation and rights of others.

60. ... [T]he application does not reveal a violation of Article 10 of the Convention.

CONCURRING OPINION OF JUDGE SPIELMANN, JOINED BY JUDGE NUSSBERGER:

1. ... [I]t is with the greatest hesitation that I voted in favour of finding no violation ... .

2. As my colleague, Judge András Sajó, pointed out [in dissent] in *Féret v. Belgium* [16 July 2009]:

> "Content regulation and content-based restrictions on speech are based on the assumption that certain expressions go "against the spirit" of the Convention. But "spirits" do not offer clear standards and are open to abuse. Humans, including judges, are inclined to label positions with which they disagree as palpably unacceptable and therefore beyond the realm of protected expression. However, it is precisely where we face ideas that we abhor or despise that we have to be most careful in our judgment, as our personal convictions can influence our ideas about what is actually dangerous."

...

4. ... [The Swedish Supreme Court relied, inter alia, on an obligation] "to avoid, as far as possible, statements that are unwarrantably offensive to others, constituting an assault on their rights"... .

5. It is submitted that this is a rather vague test which seems to me to be inconsistent with the traditional and well-established case-law of our Court ... .

6. Still, I agreed, albeit very reluctantly, to find no violation because the distribution of the leaflets took place at a school ... in the lockers of young people who were at an impressionable and sensitive age and who had no possibility to decline to accept the leaflets. ...

7. It should also not be forgotten that a real problem of homophobic and transphobic bullying and discrimination in educational settings may justify a restriction of freedom of expression under [Article 10(2)] ...

.

...

CONCURRING OPINION OF JUDGE BOŠTJAN M. ZUPANČIČ:

1. It was with some hesitation that I voted for no violation of Article 10 ... .

...

3. [T]he American Supreme Court takes a very liberal position concerning the contents of the controversial messages. That the statement is arguably of inappropriate or controversial character "... *is irrelevant to the question of whether it deals with a matter of public concern*" ... "*Speech on public issues occupies the highest rank of the hierarchy of First Amendment values, and is entitled to special protection*".

4. Moreover, the American Supreme Court has set a higher standard for the applicable law in such cases to be facially constitutional. First, it must avoid *content* discrimination (i.e., the State cannot forbid or prosecute inflammatory speech only on *some* "disfavoured" subjects) and, second, it must avoid *viewpoint* discrimination (i.e., forbidding or prosecuting inflammatory speech that expresses one particular view on the subject) ... . [I]f this American double test were applied to the present case, the [Swedish law] would not pass muster on either count, especially the second: had the applicants defended homosexuality and railed against "wicked homophobes" in their leaflets, they would probably not have been convicted.

5. In our case we have relied on a different kind of logic as did the Swedish Supreme Court ... .

...

9. ... School grounds [are] a non-public place, requiring an intrusion in order to distribute any information of whatever kind that has not been previously approved by the school's authorities. Coming back to the [US] Supreme Court ..., it has held that "*the undoubted freedom to advocate unpopular and controversial views in schools and classrooms must be balanced against the society's countervailing interest in teaching students the boundaries of socially appropriate behavior*".

...

12. ... [W]e seem to go too far in the present case — on the grounds of proportionality and considerations of hate speech — in limiting freedom of speech by over-estimating the importance of what is being said. In other words, if exactly the same words and phrases were to be used in public newspapers ..., they would probably not be considered as a matter for criminal prosecution and condemnation.

GENDERED HATE SPEECH

Gendered hate speech has been voluminous in recent years, especially on social media. Consider the following response by Irene Khan, UN Special Rapporteur on the right to freedom of opinion and expression (UN Doc. A/76/258 (2021)):

> 68.   As misogyny proliferates on social media platforms, there are increasing calls to prohibit or criminalize gendered hate speech. ...
>
>   ...

70.   Although gender and sex are not mentioned in [ICCPR] article 20 (2), they can and should be considered grounds for protection in view of the gender equality clauses elsewhere in the Covenant and the broader intersectional approach to non-discrimination … . In addition … the Rabat Plan of Action on the prohibition of advocacy of national, racial or religious hatred that constitutes incitement to discrimination, hostility or violence,[266] six elements are proposed as a threshold test for hate speech: the context; the speaker; the intent; the content and form of the speech; the extent of the speech act; and the likelihood, including the imminence, of harm. Providing all these elements are satisfied, gendered hate speech can be prohibited under international law. However, it should not be criminalized except in the most egregious cases of real and imminent danger with a clear intention to cause serious harm.

71.   The Rabat Plan of Action … sets out three categories: harmful speech that constitutes a crime because it presents real and imminent danger; harmful speech that does not reach that threshold but may justify civil action; and offensive speech that raises concerns in terms of tolerance, hostility or discrimination and should be addressed through non-legal measures, such as condemnation, awareness-raising and education.

72.   Such a graduated approach could provide an international benchmark for defining gender-based hate speech in a way that protects both women's safety and freedom of expression.

REGULATION OF HATE SPEECH

The broader question of how to respond to online hate speech was considered by a previous Special Rapporteur on freedom of opinion and expression, David Kaye (UN Doc. A/74/486 (2019)). He emphasized that approaches in international law to 'hate speech' involve a 'double ambiguity'. On one hand, many governments use it in a similar manner to the 'way in which they use "fake news", to attack political enemies, non-believers, dissenters and critics.' But, on the other hand, the perception that it is 'just speech' 'seems to inhibit Governments and companies from addressing genuine harms. He concluded that all companies in the ICT sector should:

(a) Evaluate how their products and services affect the human rights of their users and the public, through periodic and publicly available human rights impact assessments;

(b) Adopt content policies that tie their hate speech rules directly to international human rights law, indicating that the rules will be enforced according to the standards of international human rights law, including the relevant United Nations treaties and interpretations of the treaty bodies and special procedure mandate holders and other experts, including the Rabat Plan of Action;

(c) Define the category of content that they consider to be hate speech with reasoned explanations for users and the public and approaches that are consistent across jurisdictions;

(d) Ensure that any enforcement of hate speech rules involves an evaluation of context and the harm that the content imposes on users and the public, including by ensuring that any use of automation or artificial intelligence tools involve human-in-the-loop;

(e) Ensure that contextual analysis involves communities most affected …;

(f) As part of an overall effort to address hate speech, develop tools that promote individual autonomy, security and free expression, and involve de-amplification, de-monetization, education, counter-speech, reporting and training as

---

[266] UN Doc. A/HRC/22/17/Add.4 (2013), Appendix.

alternatives, when appropriate, to the banning of accounts and the removal of content.

In light of Kaye's recommendations, consider Facebook's Community Standards on Hate Speech (June 2023):[267]

> We believe that people use their voice and connect more freely when they don't feel attacked on the basis of who they are. That is why we don't allow hate speech on Facebook. It creates an environment of intimidation and exclusion, and in some cases may promote offline violence.
>
> We define hate speech as a direct attack against people — rather than concepts or institutions— on the basis of what we call protected characteristics: race, ethnicity, national origin, disability, religious affiliation, caste, sexual orientation, sex, gender identity and serious disease. We define attacks as violent or dehumanizing speech, harmful stereotypes, statements of inferiority, expressions of contempt, disgust or dismissal, cursing and calls for exclusion or segregation. We also prohibit the use of harmful stereotypes, which we define as dehumanizing comparisons that have historically been used to attack, intimidate, or exclude specific groups, and that are often linked with offline violence. We consider age a protected characteristic when referenced along with another protected characteristic. We also protect refugees, migrants, immigrants and asylum seekers from the most severe attacks, though we do allow commentary and criticism of immigration policies. Similarly, we provide some protections for characteristics like occupation, when they're referenced along with a protected characteristic. Sometimes, based on local nuance, we consider certain words or phrases as frequently used proxies for PC groups.
>
> We also prohibit the usage of slurs that are used to attack people on the basis of their protected characteristics. However, we recognize that people sometimes share content that includes slurs or someone else's hate speech to condemn it or raise awareness. In other cases, speech, including slurs, that might otherwise violate our standards can be used self-referentially or in an empowering way. Our policies are designed to allow room for these types of speech, but we require people to clearly indicate their intent. If the intention is unclear, we may remove content.

The *Faurisson* opinion that follows deals with 'Holocaust denial laws' that have been enacted by many states.[268] As noted in Dominic McGoldrick and Thérèse O'Donnell, 'Hate-Speech Laws: Consistency with National and International Human Rights Law', 18 *Leg. Stud.* 453 (1997), at 457, these laws vary a great deal:

> The essential feature of the laws which attracts the label of holocaust denial is that they make it a criminal offence to deny certain things in a certain way ... . [F]or the French law it is 'crimes against humanity as defined by the Nuremberg International Military Tribunal'. The German law is wider, as it refers to 'persecution under National Socialism or any other form of despotism or tyranny'. The Israeli law is even wider again: 'acts committed in the period of the Nazi regime, which are crimes against the Jewish people or crimes against humanity'. The Austrian law extends to denial of the 'nationalist socialist genocide or other national socialist crimes against humanity'. The Austrian law extends to cover the gross trivialisation, approval or justification of the same. The German law is similar.

In a twist on such laws, Poland adopted an Amendment to the Act on the Institute of National Remembrance of 2018 that criminalized public speech attributing responsibility for the Holocaust to Poland or the Polish nation. Following international criticism of the impact on freedom of speech, academic freedom, and the capacity to debate alleged Polish collaboration with the Nazi authorities, the relevant provisions were repealed in less than a year.

---

[267] https://transparency.fb.com/policies/community-standards/hate-speech/
[268] See generally L. Hennebel and T. Hochmann (eds.), *Genocide Denials and the Law* (2011); G. Lewy, *Outlawing Genocide Denial: The Dilemmas of Official Historical Truth* (2014); and R. Bilali, Y. Iqbal and S. Freel, 'Understanding and Counteracting Genocide Denial', in L. Newman (ed.), Confronting Humanity at its Worst: Social Psychological Perspectives on Genocide (2019) 284.

The following excerpts from Frederick Schauer, 'The Exceptional First Amendment', in Michael Ignatieff (ed.), *American Exceptionalism and Human Rights* (2005), at 32, underscore the breadth of the concept.

> ... Although the label "hate speech" tends to be applied capaciously, the phrase can be understood as encompassing four distinct but interrelated freedom of speech issues. First, there is the question of the legitimacy of prohibiting various racial, ethnic, and religious epithets — [*n******], *wog, kike, paki, kaffir,* and the like — words whose use, except as ironic self-reference by members of those groups, is invariably intended to harm, to offend, and to marginalize. Second, the question of hate speech sometimes involves the issue of restrictions on circulating certain demonstrably false factual propositions about various racial or religious groups, with prohibitions on Holocaust denial being the most common example. A third hate speech issue arises with respect to laws prohibiting the advocacy of or incitement to racial or religious intolerance, hatred, or violence, as with explicit calls to race-based violence, explicit appeals for racial exclusion, and explicit calls for repatriation of members of racial or religious minorities to the countries of their ancestry. Finally, hate speech questions are presented, especially in the context of gender when it is argued that epithets, and occasionally pictures, create a hostile, and therefore marginalizing or excluding, workplace or educational or cultural environment.

> ... The precise form of attempting to control hate speech by law varies considerably among the nations of the world. Germany and Israel, among other countries, ban the Nazi Party and its descendants, as well as prohibiting other political parties whose programs include racial hatred, racial separation, and racial superiority.' ... Germany, Israel, and France are among the nations that prohibit the sale and distribution of various Nazi items, including swastikas, Nazi flags, and, on occasion, images of Adolph Hitler and copies of *Mein Kampf.*' ... Canada, Germany, and France, along with others, permit sanctions against those who would deny the existence of the Holocaust.' ... The Netherlands outlaws public insults based on race, religion, or sexual preference." ... And South Africa, New Zealand, Australia, Canada, the United Kingdom, and all of the Scandinavian countries, among many others, follow the mandates of Article 20(2) of the [ICCPR], and Articles 4(a) and 4(b) of the [ICERD], by making it a crime to engage in the incitement to racial, religious, or ethnic hatred or hostility.

FAURISSON V. FRANCE
VIEWS OF THE HUMAN RIGHTS COMMITTEE, COMMUNICATION NO. 550/1993, UN DOC. CCPR/C/58/D/550/1993 (8 NOVEMBER 1996)

[Robert Faurisson, author of the communication and a former professor of literature, was removed from his university chair in 1991. He had expressed doubt about or denial of the accuracy of conventional accounts of the Holocaust, including (1) his conviction that there were no homicidal gas chambers for the extermination of Jews in Nazi concentration camps, (2) his doubts over the number of people killed, and (3) his disbelief in the records and evidence of the Nuremberg trial that were used to convict Nazis.

In 1990, the French legislature passed the so-called 'Gayssot Act'. It amended the 1881 law on Freedom of the Press by adding Article 24 *bis*, which made it an offence to contest (*contestation*) the existence of the category of crimes against humanity as defined in the London Charter of 1945, on the basis of which Nazi leaders were convicted by the International Military Tribunal at Nuremberg in 1945–1946. For the relevant provision of the Charter and excerpts from the Nuremberg judgment, see Ch. 2D, above.

Faurisson attacked the 1990 law as a threat to academic freedom, including freedom of research and expression. He claimed that the Gayssot Act raised to the rank of infallible dogma the proceedings and verdict at Nuremberg, and endorsed forever the orthodox Jewish version of the Second World War. Arguing that the Nuremberg records could not be treated as infallible, he cited examples of historical revision such as the Katyn massacre in Poland of Polish army officers that was initially attributed to Germans but that was later shown to be of Soviet responsibility. Faurisson described as 'exorbitant' the 'privilege of censorship' from which the representatives of the Jewish community in France benefitted.

The state party noted that anti-racism legislation adopted by France in the 1980s was considered insufficient to bring legal action against the trivialization of Nazi crimes. There was governmental concern over 'revisionism' by individuals justifying their writing through their status as historians. The French Government viewed these revisionist theses as a 'subtle form of contemporary anti-semitism'. The Gayssot Act was meant to fill a legal vacuum while defining the new criminal conduct as precisely as possible.

Associations of French resistance fighters and of deportees to German concentration camps filed a private criminal action against Faurisson, who was convicted in 1991 of violating the Gayssot Act. The Court of Appeal of Paris upheld the conviction and imposed a fine. Faurisson took the position that further appeal to the Court of Cassation would be futile and filed the present communication. He argued that the Act violated the ICCPR, although his communication did not invoke specific provisions.

In addition to the Final Views of the ICCPR Committee itself, there were five individual opinions signed by seven Committee members.]

9.4 Any restriction on the right to freedom of expression must cumulatively meet the following conditions: it must be provided by law, it must address one of the aims set out in paragraph 3(a) and (b) of article 19, and must be necessary to achieve a legitimate purpose.

9.5 ... [T]he Committee concludes ... that the finding of the author's guilt [in the French proceedings] was based on his following two statements: '... I have excellent reasons not to believe in the policy of extermination of Jews or in the magic gas chambers ... I wish to see that 100 per cent of the French citizens realize that the myth of the gas chambers is a dishonest fabrication'. His conviction therefore did not encroach upon his right to hold and express an opinion in general. Rather the court convicted Mr. Faurisson for having violated the rights and reputation of others. For these reasons the Committee is satisfied that the Gayssot Act, as read, interpreted and applied to the author's case by the French courts, is in compliance with the provisions of the Covenant.

9.6 To assess whether the restrictions ... were applied for the purposes provided for by the Covenant, the Committee ... [notes that permissible] restrictions ... may relate to the interests of other persons or to those of the community as a whole. Since the statements made by the author, read in their full context, were of a nature as to raise or strengthen anti-semitic feelings, the restriction served [sic] the respect of the Jewish community to live free from fear of an atmosphere of anti-semitism. [They were therefore permissible.]

9.7 Lastly the Committee needs to consider whether the restriction of the author's freedom of expression was necessary. The Committee noted the State party's argument contending that the introduction of the Gayssot Act was intended to serve the struggle against racism and anti-semitism. It also noted the statement of ... the then Minister of Justice, which characterized the denial of the existence of the Holocaust as the principal vehicle for anti-semitism ... . [T]he Committee is satisfied that the restriction of Mr. Faurisson's freedom of expression was necessary within the meaning of article 19, paragraph 3, of the Covenant.

10. [The Committee found there had been no violation by France of Article 19(3).]

STATEMENT OF THOMAS BUERGENTHAL

As a survivor of the concentration camps of Auschwitz and Sachsenhausen whose father, maternal grandparents and many other family members were killed in the Nazi Holocaust, I have no choice but to recuse myself from participating in the decision of this case.

INDIVIDUAL OPINION BY NISUKE ANDO (CONCURRING)

... In my view the term 'negation' ('contestation'), if loosely interpreted, could comprise various forms of expression of opinions and thus has a possibility of threatening or encroaching the right to freedom of expression, which constitutes an indispensable prerequisite for the proper functioning of a democratic society.

In order to eliminate this possibility it would probably be better to replace the Act with a specific legislation prohibiting well-defined acts of anti-semitism or with a provision of the criminal code protecting the rights or reputations of others in general.

INDIVIDUAL OPINION BY ELIZABETH EVATT AND DAVID KRETZMER, CO-SIGNED BY ECKART KLEIN (CONCURRING)

...

3 ... . While we entertain no doubt whatsoever that the author's statements are highly offensive both to Holocaust survivors and to descendants of Holocaust victims (as well as to many others), the question under the Covenant is whether a restriction on freedom of expression in order to achieve this purpose may be regarded as a restriction necessary for the respect of the rights of others.

...

7. The Committee correctly points out, as it did in its General Comment 10, that the right for the protection of which restrictions on freedom of expression are permitted by article 19, paragraph 3, may relate to the interests of a community as a whole. This is especially the case in which the right protected is the right to be free from racial, national or religious incitement ... . It appears ... that the restriction on the author's freedom of expression served to protect the right of the Jewish community in France to live free from fear of incitement to anti-semitism ... .

8. The power given to States parties under article 19, paragraph 3, to place restrictions on freedom of expression, must not be interpreted as license to prohibit unpopular speech, or speech which some sections of the population find offensive. Much offensive speech may be regarded as speech that impinges on one of the values mentioned in article 19, paragraph 3(a) or (b) (the rights or reputations of others, national security, *ordre public*, public health or morals). The Covenant therefore stipulates that the purpose of protecting one of those values is not, of itself, sufficient reason to restrict expression. The restriction must be necessary to protect the given value. This requirement of necessity implies an element of proportionality. The scope of the restriction imposed on freedom of expression must be proportional to the value which the restriction serves to protect ... .

9. The Gayssot Act is phrased in the widest language and would seem to prohibit publication of bona fide research connected with matters decided by the Nuremburg Tribunal. Even if the purpose of this prohibition is to protect the right to be free from incitement to anti-semitism, the restrictions imposed do not meet the proportionality test. They do not link liability to the intent of the author, nor to the tendency of the publication to incite to anti-semitism. Furthermore, the legitimate object of the law could certainly have been achieved by a less drastic provision that would not imply that the State party had attempted to turn historical truths and experiences into legislative dogma that may not be challenged, no matter what the object behind that challenge, nor its likely consequences. In the present case we are not concerned, however, with the Gayssot Act, *in abstracto*, but only with the restriction placed on the freedom of expression of the author by his conviction for his statements in the interview in Le Choc du Mois. Does this restriction meet the proportionality test?

10. The French courts examined the author's statements in great detail. Their decisions, and the interview itself, refute the author's argument that he is only driven by his interest in historical research. ... While there is every reason to maintain protection of bona fide historical research against restriction, even when it challenges accepted historical truths and by so doing offends people, anti-semitic allegations of the sort made by the author, which violate the rights of others in the way described, do not have the same claim to protection against restriction. The restrictions placed on the author did not curb the core of his right to freedom of expression, nor did they in any way affect his freedom of research ... . It is for these reasons that we joined the Committee ... .

* * *

In a 2015 ECtHR Grand Chamber case, *Perinçek v. Switzerland* (Application No. 27510/08, Judgment of 15 October 2015), a Turkish politician had been convicted in Switzerland for publicly asserting that the mass deportations and massacres of Armenians in the Ottoman Empire in 1915 had not amounted to genocide.[269] The Swiss courts held that Perinçek's motives were racist and nationalistic and that his statements did not

---

[269] See generally, M. D. Baer, *Sultanic Saviors and Tolerant Turks: Writing Ottoman Jewish History, Denying the Armenian Genocide* (2020).

contribute to the historical debate. The European Court found that freedom of expression (Article 10) had been violated. It found that the dignity of the victims and the dignity and identity of modern-day Armenians were protected by the right to respect for private life (Article 8), but that a balance had to be struck with Article 10, taking into account the specific circumstances of the case and the proportionality between the means used and the aim sought to be achieved. It concluded that it had not been necessary, in a democratic society, to subject the applicant to a criminal penalty in order to protect the rights of the Armenian community at stake in the case. In particular, the Court took into account that: the applicant's statements bore on a matter of public interest and did not amount to a call for hatred or intolerance; the context in which they were made had not been marked by heightened tensions or special historical overtones in Switzerland; the statements could not be regarded as affecting the dignity of the members of the Armenian community to the point of requiring a criminal law response in Switzerland; there was no international law obligation for Switzerland to criminalise such statements; the Swiss courts appeared to have censured the applicant simply for voicing an opinion that diverged from the established ones in Switzerland; and the interference with his right to freedom of expression had taken the serious form of a criminal conviction.

In *Pastörs v. Germany* (Application No. 55225/14, Judgment of 3 October 2019) the ECtHR considered a case brought by a Member of Parliament in Mecklenburg-Western Pomerania against his criminal conviction in Germany for a speech he gave in parliament on 28 January 2010, one day after Holocaust Remembrance Day. He said, *inter alia*:

> "… [P]people can sense that the so-called Holocaust is being used for political and commercial purposes … Since the end of the Second World War, Germans have been exposed to an endless barrage of criticism and propagandistic lies – cultivated in a dishonest manner primarily by representatives of the so-called democratic parties … . Also, the event that you organised here in the castle yesterday was nothing more than you imposing your Auschwitz projections onto the German people in a manner that is both cunning and brutal. You are hoping … for the triumph of lies over truth."

The European Court upheld the conviction:

46. The Court attaches fundamental importance to the fact that the applicant planned his speech in advance, deliberately choosing his words and resorting to obfuscation to get his message across: a qualified Holocaust denial showing disdain towards the victims of the Holocaust and running counter to established historical facts … . …

47. While interferences with the right to freedom of expression call for the closest scrutiny when they concern statements made by elected representatives in Parliament, utterances in such scenarios deserve little, if any, protection if their content is at odds with the democratic values of the Convention system. …

48. … [T]he applicant intentionally stated untruths in order to defame the Jews and the persecution that they had suffered during the Second World War. Reiterating that it has always been sensitive to the historical context of the High Contracting Party concerned when reviewing whether there exists a pressing social need for interference with rights under the Convention and that, in the light of their historical role and experience, States that have experienced the Nazi horrors may be regarded as having a special moral responsibility to distance themselves from the mass atrocities perpetrated by the Nazis, the Court therefore considers that the applicant's impugned statements affected the dignity of the Jews to the point that they justified a criminal-law response. Even though the applicant's sentence of eight months' imprisonment, suspended on probation, was not insignificant, the Court considers that the domestic authorities adduced relevant and sufficient reasons and did not overstep their margin of appreciation. The interference was therefore proportionate to the legitimate aim pursued and was thus "necessary in a democratic society".

In response to the Faurisson case, consider the following views of Christopher Caldwell, in 'Historical Truth Speaks for Itself', *Financial Times* (18 February 2006):

> Madeleine Reberioux, the late leftist historian, warned of the biggest danger of the Gayssot law as soon as it was passed. "One day", she wrote, "it's going to lead into other areas besides the genocide against the Jews — other genocides and other assaults on what will be called 'historical truth'." She was right. A law declaring the Turkish killings of Armenians early last century to be a "genocide" was passed in 2001; later that year, another law defined the slave trade as a "crime against humanity"; a year ago, legislation mandated that teachers stress the "positive role" of the French presence in North Africa. Each new officialisation of remembrance calls into being more "moral lobbies", which press their claims with ever more insistence in ever more obscure corners of political life and with ever more legal clout.
>
> ...
>
> Mr Dworkin's case [below] for abolishing laws against Holocaust denial on grounds of political legitimacy is the right one. Of course, no one should be under the illusion that being able to go out and deny the Holocaust will add much to any "debate". The official truth of western governments about the Holocaust happens to be the truth. Allowing delusions or anti-Semitic propaganda to masquerade as "opinions" will not change that. So those western countries with laws against Holocaust denial are now in a tricky position. They must undo laws that have proved unworkable and counterproductive — and at a moment when some of those laws' most vocal detractors are violent people of ill will.

The difficulty of developing international standards in this area has been analysed in terms of five internal features of the right:

MONA ELBAHTIMY, THE RIGHT TO BE FREE FROM THE HARM OF HATE SPEECH IN INTERNATIONAL HUMAN RIGHTS LAW
(2021) 179

... [The first is an 'emotive' component. The] right obliges states to make their national laws intolerant of an extreme emotion – *hatred* – if its advocacy incites, inter alia, the emotional harm of *hostility* towards targeted groups. In this sense, the key terms 'hatred' and 'hostility' construct the meaning of the right. However, both terms are unrelated to concrete practice, being concerned instead with intangible states of mind, attitudes, and psychological states of abhorrence, detestation, and enmity. ...

The right's second feature relates to the nature of the causal or likelihood-based relationship between advocacy of hatred and its alleged harms, which is indirect, cumulative, and mentally and emotionally mediated. ... [P]roving the inciting nature of hate advocacy [is complex], given the difficulties in precisely or empirically establishing and measuring incitement ... .

[Third,] ... a very delicate balance [must] be struck between the equality and liberty rights of speakers and members of targeted groups ... . The interaction of the two values ... is multifaceted and complex. The right takes effect by restricting speakers' freedom of expression. Yet liberty as a value is not enhanced only through the protection of a wider range of expressions; liberty can be at risk for members of targeted groups if they are not provided with protection against the harms of hate speech, as this can have a 'silencing effect' on them. ...

[The fourth feature] is its 'group identity' aspect. ... The right is integral to the promotion of collective goals, the prevention of communal harms, and the protection of group identities. It therefore adds another source of tension between individual and group rights. Drawing a sharp dividing line between the two categories of protection (the individualized and the collective) is inherently difficult, given that hate speech targets individuals based on their group-defining characteristics or identity. ...

The ... fifth feature [is the religion component. A] delicate, and often very difficult, balance has to be struck between freedom of religious expression, on the one hand, and protection for targeted religious adherents, on the other. This further complicates the precise determination of the threshold beyond which advocacy of religious hatred should be prohibited ... .

...

... The way ahead

... It does not appear possible to secure broad agreement on an approach that moves beyond the current level of abstraction by adding specificity to the content and effects of proscribed advocacy of hatred. ...

... [T]o overcome such paralysis, one strategy is [to focus on procedures] ... This approach would not answer the difficult question of *what* the precise legal threshold of Article 20(2) is; rather, it would address *how* to determine such threshold within different national contexts. National authorities need sufficient guidance in implementing their obligations under IHRL to prohibit incitement to hatred. Such guidance is an important factor in the avoidance of excessively prohibitive laws that suppress legitimate speech, inconsistent implementation of laws, and restrictive interpretations of laws in ways that thwart the obligation's preventive function – its central value from a policy perspective. Rather than legal or textual development, the efforts of the international community might instead be directed towards the provision of such guidance to states in the form of a *procedural manual* for enforcement of the right to protection from incitement to hatred. This would allow states to take into consideration their own national contexts when seeking to resolve the threshold dilemmas and inherent tensions underlying the five internal features of the right.

Procedural development ... provides a jurisdiction-specific response to that phenomenon. This can best be described as *regulatory relativism*, in which the means of achieving protection of the right is best determined in accordance with the particular context involved.

[Relativist challenges arise in relation to each of the five internal features of the right.]

Accordingly, despite the fact that hate speech is generally recognized as a universal problem, it is a problem in which particularized political, cultural, and historical national contexts play a crucial role. The hate speech phenomenon is not a static problem, but one which needs to be seen as a dynamic social process involving context. ...

There are striking variations, even among liberal democracies, when it comes to the hate speech legal landscape. Different criteria are applied to define the threshold between free speech and hate speech. The legislative patterns and judicial practices related to the resolution of the hate speech problem are predicated upon different conceptions of the content of prohibited expressions, the scope of recognized harms of hate speech, the extension of protection to groups and to group-defining characteristics, the range of groups protected, and the standards of causality between advocacy of hatred and its alleged harms. The prohibition of hate advocacy that constitutes clear and unambiguous incitement to immediate violence or illegal acts is the aspect of the norm that enjoys most transnational resonance, since it easily crosses cultural and ideological boundaries. However, legal regulation of hate advocacy that falls short of incitement to violence but creates a social climate conducive to hostility and discrimination does not enjoy the same universal resonance. ...

QUESTIONS

1. Two of the concurring opinions in *Vejdeland* acknowledge hesitation in agreeing with the Court's opinion. How convincing do you find the Court's analysis? Is it a major victory for the rights of the LGBTQI community or a slippery slope for inroads against freedom of expression in relation to contested issues?

2. As a legislator, would you have voted for the Gayssot Act? How would you have reacted to the following argument in general, or as applied to the passage of that Act?

... [I]f there is any right which enjoys primacy among rights, it is arguably the principle of equality and non-discrimination ... . The goal of hate mongers is to convince others that the members of the target group are not entitled to equal protection of the law; the hate mongers seek a society of discrimination ... . They should not be entitled to claim protection under the right to freedom of expression for their abuse of speech rights to achieve that goal.270

3. Would a conviction by French courts be likely to be upheld under the Committee's approach? Under the concurring opinion by Elizabeth Evatt and David Kretzmer? How do these opinions differ, and which do you view as the better one?

4. Does Elbahtimy's 'regulatory relativism' approach provide an appropriate solution, or might it risk the proliferation of contextually justified bans that would undermine aspirations to achieve a common approach internationally?

NOTE ON THE UNITED STATES

The United States ratified the ICCPR in 1992. In giving its consent to ratification, and acting consistently with proposals made to it by the Bush Administration, the Senate entered a reservation: 'Article 20 does not authorize or require legislation or other action by the United States that would restrict the right to free speech and association protected by the Constitution and laws of the United States.'

Compare with Article 20 an equivalent provision, Article 4 of the Convention on the Elimination of All Forms of Racial Discrimination (CERD). In that article, the states parties 'condemn all propaganda ... based on ideas or theories of superiority of one race or group of persons or one colour or ethnic origin'. They undertake to declare a punishable offence 'all dissemination of ideas based on racial superiority or hatred, incitement of racial discrimination, as well as all acts of violence' against such a race or group. Article 1 defines 'racial discrimination' to mean any distinction based on 'race, colour, descent, or national or ethnic origin' that has the purpose or effect of impairing equal enjoyment of rights 'in the political, economic, social, cultural or any other field of public life'. When the United States ratified the CERD Convention, it reserved as to Article 4.

The primary constitutional provision referred to in these two reservations by the United States is the First Amendment: 'Congress shall make no law ... abridging the freedom of speech ... .' Consider the following analysis by Fredrick Schauer, in 'The Exceptional First Amendment', in Michael Ignatieff (ed.), *American Exceptionalism and Human Rights* (2005), at 29:

> ... [A]lthough a constitutional or quasi-constitutional right to freedom of expression is the international norm, the contours of that right vary widely even among ... liberal democracies ... . [T]he American First Amendment, as authoritatively interpreted, remains a recalcitrant outlier to a growing international understanding of what the freedom of expression entails. In numerous dimensions, the American approach is *exceptional* ... .
>
> ...
>
> ... [T]he American understanding is that principles of freedom of speech do not permit government to distinguish protected from unprotected speech on the basis of the point of view espoused. Specifically, this prohibition on what is technically called "viewpoint discrimination" extends to the point of view that certain races or religions are inferior, to the point of view that hatred of members of minority races and religions is desirable, and to the point of view that violent or otherwise illegal action is justified against people

---

270 S. Farrior, 'Moulding the Matrix: The Historical and Theoretical Foundations of International Law Concerning Hate Speech', 14 *Berkeley J. Int'l. L.* 1 (1996), at 6, 98.

because of their race, their ethnicity, or their religious beliefs. ... [The government may not] prohibit public denials of the factuality of the Holocaust just because of the demonstrable falsity of that proposition and the harm that would ensue from its public articulation.

... [*Brandenburg v. Ohio*, 395 U.S. 444 (1969)] stands for the proposition that in the United States restrictions on the incitement of racial hatred can be countenanced under the First Amendment only when they are incitements to *violent* racial hatred, and even then only under the rare circumstances in which the incitements unmistakably call for immediate violent action, and even then only under the more rare still circumstances in which members of the listening audience are in fact likely immediately to act upon the speaker's suggestion... . Jean Le Pen could not be sanctioned in the United States, as he was in France, for accusing Jews of exaggerating the Holocaust ... .

...

... Where in the rest of the world freedom of expression appears to be understood as an important value to be considered along with other important values of fairness, equality, dignity, health, privacy, safety and respect, among others, in the United States the freedom of expression occupies pride of place, prevailing with remarkable consistency in its conflicts with even the most profound of other values and the most important of other interests.

Blasphemy

In *Otto-Preminger-Institut v. Austria*, Ser. A, No. 295-A (20 September 1994), the European Court of Human Rights decided 6-3 that the seizure and forfeiture of a blasphemous film did not violate the freedom of expression guaranteed by Article 10. The applicant association had advertised the screening of the film, *Das Liebeskonzil*, based on an 1894 play, which:

> ... portrays the God of the Jewish religion, the Christian religion and the Islamic religion as an apparently senile old man prostrating himself before the devil with whom he exchanges a deep kiss and calling the devil his friend ... . Other scenes show the Virgin Mary permitting an obscene story to be read to her and the manifestation of a degree of erotic tension between the Virgin Mary and the devil. The adult Jesus Christ is portrayed as a low grade mental defective and in one scene is shown lasciviously attempting to fondle and kiss his mother's breasts, which she is shown as permitting.

The film was presented by the association as a 'satirical tragedy'. 'Trivial imagery and absurdities of the Christian creed are targeted in a caricatural mode and the relationship between religious beliefs and worldly mechanisms of oppression is investigated.' The Innsbruck Regional Court in Austria ordered seizure and forfeiture of the film under Section 188 of the Austrian Penal Code for the criminal offence of 'disparaging religious precepts'. The criminal proceedings against the association were eventually dropped.

Since there was no dispute that the seizure constituted an interference with the association's freedom of expression, the European Court considered whether the seizure was permissible under the conditions set by of Article 10, paragraph 2. The Court concluded that the interference had the 'legitimate aim' of protecting the rights of others to freedom of religion. Interpreting Article 9 of the Convention to include the right to respect for one's religious feelings, the Court found that such considerations outweighed the film's contribution to public debate. The Court reasoned:

> The respect for the religious feelings of believers as guaranteed in Article 9 can legitimately thought to have been violated by provocative portrayals of objects of religious veneration; and such portrayals can be regarded as malicious violation of the spirit of tolerance, which must also be a feature of democratic society. The Convention is to be read as a whole and therefore the interpretation and application of Article 10 in the

present case must be in harmony with the logic of the Convention ... . [T]he Court accepts that the impugned measures pursued a legitimate aim under Article 10 para. 2, namely 'the protection of the rights of others'.

The Court stressed that freedom of expression applies not only to ideas that are favourably received, but also to those 'that shock, offend or disturb the State or any sector of the population. Such are the demands of that pluralism, tolerance and broadmindedness without which there is no "democratic society."' Nonetheless, people exercising their rights under Article 10 were subject to duties, among which could legitimately be included 'an obligation to avoid as far as possible expressions that are gratuitously offensive to others and thus an infringement of their rights, and which therefore do not contribute to any form of public debate capable of further progress in human affairs'.

The Court determined that the seizure could be considered 'necessary in a democratic society'. There was no 'uniform conception of the significance of religion in society' throughout Europe, 'even within a single country'. A 'certain margin of appreciation is therefore to be left to the national authorities in assessing the existence and extent of the necessity of such interference'. It is 'for the national authorities, who are better placed than the international judge, to assess the need for such a measure in the light of the situation obtaining locally'. Given that the Tyrolean population was 87 percent Roman Catholic, the Court found that the Austrian authorities had acted within their margin of appreciation 'to ensure religious peace in that region and to prevent that some people should feel the object of attacks on their religious beliefs in an unwarranted and offensive manner.'

Three judges dissented. Given the precautions against offence to viewers taken by the association through a warning announcement, the showing of the film to a paid audience only, and the restriction of viewing to those over 17 years of age, the dissent found the seizure and forfeiture to be disproportionate to the aim pursued, and thus not necessary in a democratic society.

* * *

In *Wingrove v. United Kingdom*, European Court of Human Rights (Application No. 17419/90, Judgment of 25 November 1996), a film director who was a British national alleged that the United Kingdom had violated Article 10 by interfering with the director's freedom of expression through refusing to grant a distribution certificate for his 18-minute video work, *Visions of Ecstasy*. The work involved visions of St Teresa about the crucified Christ, and in the view of the British Board of Film Classification, drew Christ graphically into the erotic desire of St Teresa. The refusal to grant the certificate was based on the Board's conclusion that the video constituted blasphemy, defined in a recent case as 'any contemptuous, reviling, scurrilous or ludicrous matter related to God, Jesus Christ or the Bible'. The decision was upheld by the Video Appeals Committee.

The European Commission voted 14–2 that there had been a violation of Article 10. The Commission and the United Kingdom brought the case before the European Court, which concluded by a 7–2 vote that there had been no violation of Article 10. Some of its observations about the requirement in Article 10 that a restriction be 'necessary in a democratic society' follow:

> 57. The Court observes that the refusal to grant *Visions of Ecstasy* a distribution certificate was intended to protect 'the rights of others', and more specifically to provide protection against seriously offensive attacks on matters regarded as sacred by Christians ... .

> ... [B]lasphemy legislation is still in force in various European countries. It is true that the application of these laws has become increasingly rare and that several States have recently repealed them altogether ... . Strong arguments have been advanced in favour of the abolition of blasphemy laws, for example, that such laws may discriminate against different faiths or denominations ... . However, the fact remains that there is as yet not sufficient common ground in the legal and social orders of the member States of the Council of Europe to conclude that a system whereby a State can impose restrictions on the propagation of material on the basis that it is blasphemous is, in itself, unnecessary in a democratic society and thus incompatible with the Convention ... .

58. … [A] wider margin of appreciation is generally available to the Contracting States when regulating freedom of expression in relation to matters liable to offend intimate personal convictions within the sphere of morals or, especially, religion. Moreover, … there is no uniform European conception of the requirements of 'the protection of the rights of others' in relation to attacks on their religious convictions. What is likely to cause substantial offence to persons of a particular religious persuasion will vary significantly from time to time and from place to place, especially in an era characterised by an ever growing array of faiths and denominations. By reason of their direct and continuous contact with the vital forces of their countries, State authorities are in principle in a better position than the international judge to give an opinion on the exact content of these requirements with regard to the rights of others as well as on the 'necessity' of a 'restriction' intended to protect from such material those whose deepest feelings and convictions would be seriously offended … .

This does not of course exclude final European supervision. Such supervision is all the more necessary given the breadth and open-endedness of the notion of blasphemy and the risks of arbitrary or excessive interferences with freedom of expression under the guise of action taken against allegedly blasphemous material … . Moreover the fact that the present case involves prior restraint calls for special scrutiny by the Court … .

The Court (para. 50) also considered the fact that the English law of blasphemy 'only extends to the Christian faith'. It was not, however, for the European Court 'to rule *in abstracto*' about the compatibility of British law with the Convention. 'The extent to which English law protects other beliefs is not in issue before the Court which must confine its attention to the case before it … . The uncontested fact that the law of blasphemy does not treat on an equal footing the different religions practised in the United Kingdom does not detract from the legitimacy of the aim pursued in the present context.' A concurring opinion of Judge Pettiti observed that the Convention left 'scope for review under Article 14. In the present case no complaint had been made to the European Court under that article.'

A dissenting opinion of Judge Lohmus noted that the law of blasphemy 'only protects the Christian religion and, more specifically, the established Church of England … . This in itself raises the question whether the interference was (in the language of Article 10) "necessary in a democratic society".'

QUESTION

Do these opinions resolve the question of who in the liberal state must show tolerance to whom? Must the majority put up with the minority's views and modes of expression (at least where those views and expressions are not 'forced' on the majority through unavoidable public acts)? Or is it the minority that must take account of the majority's sensibility and refrain from offending it?

THE DANISH CARTOONS AND DEFAMATION OF RELIGION

In 2005, a Danish newspaper named *Jyllands-Posten* published cartoons that proved to be offensive to many Muslims. They consisted of unflattering and mocking notions about Muslims and caricatures of the Prophet Mohammed, including a cartoon portraying Mohammed wearing a turban in the shape of a bomb ready to explode — an obvious reference to terrorist acts committed in the name of Islam. The controversy led to widespread protests and riots, the severing of diplomatic relations between an Arab state and Denmark, death threats against the cartoonists and others involved and far-reaching trade boycotts by some states of Danish goods. The cartoons were republished by newspapers in several European countries, including France, Germany, Italy, the Netherlands, Spain and Switzerland. By contrast, most major newspapers in the United

States, Canada and the United Kingdom refrained from republication, although the cartoons were rapidly available on the internet.

The protests were the stronger because many Muslims understand that Islam bans any image, let alone caricature, of the Prophet; such images are often viewed as blasphemous. As Ruti Teitel noted at the time:

> Many people saw the cartoons as ... exhibiting intolerance toward those whose religion is Islam ... . To understand why so many Muslims were so gravely offended, it is important to see that the cartoons don't stand alone, but rather were published against a backdrop of political and legislative action that, to many Muslims, reflects a repeated pattern of disparagement of Islam in the public sphere. At present, Europe is struggling with issues of identity ... . The crisis arises because of new demographics, at the same time as new regionalism. Many Muslims feel they are being relegated to second-class citizenship in Europe. And they relate the publication of the cartoons — by a newspaper they feel would not consider publishing anti-Christian or anti-Jewish cartoons — to this wrongful sense that they are not full citizens.[271]

In the wake of the diplomatic outcry the Danish Prime Minister refused to meet with a group of eleven ambassadors from Muslim-majority countries. The government responded that 'freedom of expression has a wide scope and the Danish government has no means of influencing the press.' It added that blasphemy was, however, prohibited under Danish law and that offended parties could bring suit if they wished. A subsequent complaint was dismissed by the public prosecutor. The Egyptian Minister of Foreign Affairs called for 'an official Danish statement underlining the need for and the obligation of respecting all religions and desisting from offending their devotees to prevent an escalation which would have serious and far-reaching consequences.' No such statement was forthcoming. The following year, the Organization of the Islamic Conference (OIC), representing 57 states with significant Muslim populations, established an OIC Observatory on Islamophobia. It tracked developments worldwide including, for example, the 2008 movie, *Fitna*, in which a Dutch politician, Geert Wilders, interspersed excerpts from the Qur'an with media images of acts of hatred or violence attributed to Muslims, and the March 2011 burning by a Florida pastor of a Qur'an. The Observatory's 2011 report stated that '[t]he scourge of Islamophobia continued unabated, despite all efforts to raise awareness of its dangers and the need to contain it' and concluded that 'Islamophobia remains a matter of transcendental priority for the OIC.'

The OIC's principal response to the problem at the international level took the form of a campaign begun in 1999 to combat the 'defamation of religions'. Over a number of years, resolutions were adopted by contested votes in the UN Human Rights Council and the General Assembly. GA Resolution 62/154 (18 December 2007), adopted by a vote of 108 in favour, 51 against and 25 abstentions, is representative:

> The General Assembly,
>
> ...
>
> 2. Expresses its deep concern about the negative stereotyping of religions and manifestations of intolerance and discrimination in matters of religion or belief still in evidence in the world;
>
> 3. Strongly deplores physical attacks and assaults on businesses, cultural centres and places of worship of all religions as well as targeting of religious symbols;
>
> 4. Expresses its deep concern about programmes and agendas pursued by extremist organizations and groups aimed at the defamation of religions and incitement to religious hatred, in particular when condoned by Governments;

---

[271] R. G. Teitel, 'No Laughing Matter: The Controversial Danish Cartoons Depicting the Prophet Mohammed, and Their Broader Meaning for the Europe 's Public Square', *New York Law School Digital Commons* (15 February 2006).

5. Also expresses its deep concern that Islam is frequently and wrongly associated with human rights violations and terrorism;

6. Notes with deep concern the intensification of the campaign of defamation of religions and the ethnic and religious profiling of Muslim minorities in the aftermath of the tragic events of 11 September 2001;

7. Recognizes that, in the context of the fight against terrorism and the reaction to counter-terrorism measures, defamation of religions and incitement to religious hatred becomes an aggravating factor that contributes to the denial of fundamental rights and freedoms of members of target groups, as well as their economic and social exclusion;

8. Deplores the use of the print, audio-visual and electronic media, including the Internet, and any other means to incite acts of violence, xenophobia or related intolerance and discrimination against Islam or any other religion, as well as targeting of religious symbols;

9. Stresses the need to effectively combat defamation of all religions and incitement to religious hatred, against Islam and Muslims in particular;

10. Emphasizes that everyone has the right to hold opinions without interference and the right to freedom of expression, and that the exercise of these rights carries with it special duties and responsibilities and may therefore be subject to limitations as are provided for by law and are necessary for respect of the rights or reputations of others, protection of national security or of public order, public health or morals and respect for religions and beliefs;

11. Urges States to take action to prohibit the advocacy of national, racial or religious hatred that constitutes incitement to discrimination, hostility or violence;

12. Also urges States to provide, within their respective legal and constitutional systems, adequate protection against acts of hatred, discrimination, intimidation and coercion resulting from defamation of religions, to take all possible measures to promote tolerance and respect for all religions and beliefs and the understanding of their value systems and to complement legal systems with intellectual and moral strategies to combat religious hatred and intolerance;

13. Urges all States to ensure that all public officials, including members of law enforcement bodies, the military, civil servants and educators, in the course of their official duties, respect people regardless of their different religions and beliefs and do not discriminate against persons on the grounds of their religion or belief, and that any necessary and appropriate education or training is provided;

14. Underscores the need to combat defamation of religions and incitement to religious hatred by strategizing and harmonizing actions at the local, national, regional and international levels through education and awareness-raising; ...

The concept that a religion could be defamed was subsequently hotly debated in various UN fora. In April 2009, for example, three UN Special Rapporteurs (dealing with racism, freedom of religion and freedom of expression) issued a joint statement:

> We have repeated time and again that all human rights are universal, indivisible and interdependent and interrelated. Yet nowhere is this interdependence more obvious than in the discussion of freedom of expression and incitement to racial or religious hatred. The right to freedom of expression constitutes an essential aspect of the right to freedom of religion or belief and therefore needs to be adequately protected in domestic

legislation. Freedom of expression is essential to creating an environment in which a critical discussion about religion can be held. While the exercise of freedom of expression could in some extreme cases affect the right to manifest the religion or belief of certain identified individuals, it is conceptually inaccurate to present "defamation of religions" *in abstracto* as a conflict between the right to freedom of religion or belief and the right to freedom of opinion or expression.

In recent years, there have been challenges with regard to the dissemination of expressions which offend certain believers ... . [A] clear distinction shall be made between three types of expression: (1) expressions that constitute an offence under international law; (2) expressions that are not criminally punishable but may justify a civil suit; and (3) expressions that do not give rise to criminal or civil sanctions but still raise a concern in terms of tolerance, civility and respect for the religion or beliefs of others ... .

Whereas the debate concerning the dissemination of expressions which may offend certain believers has throughout the last ten years evolved around the notion of "defamation of religions", we welcome the fact that the debate seems to be shifting to the concept of "incitement to racial or religious hatred", sometimes also referred to as "hate speech".

Indeed, the difficulties in providing an objective definition of the term "defamation of religions" at the international level make the whole concept open to abuse. At the national level, domestic blasphemy laws can prove counter-productive, since this could result in the de facto censure of all inter-religious and intra-religious criticism. Many of these laws afford different levels of protection to different religions and have often proved to be applied in a discriminatory manner. There are numerous examples of persecution of religious minorities or dissenters, but also of atheists and non-theists, as a result of legislation on religious offences or overzealous application of laws that are fairly neutral.

Whereas some have argued that "defamation of religions" could be equated to racism, we would like to caution against confusion between a racist statement and an act of "defamation of religion". We fully concur with the affirmation from the ICERD that any doctrine of superiority based on racial differentiation is scientifically false, morally condemnable, socially unjust and dangerous. However, there is not necessarily an analogy to be drawn with regard to religious issues. Indeed, several religions are characterized by truth claims — or even by superiority claims — which have been traditionally accepted as part of their theological grounds. Consequently, the elements that constitute a racist statement may not be the same as those that constitute a statement "defaming a religion" as such. To this extent, the legal measures, and in particular the criminal measures, adopted by national legal systems to fight racism may not necessarily be applicable to "defamation of religions" ... .[272]

In 2010, the Special Rapporteur on freedom of religion welcomed the fact that the United Kingdom had recently abolished the offences of blasphemy and blasphemous libel, but also noted that the Indonesian Constitutional Court had upheld an anti-blasphemy law 'which imposes criminal penalties of up to five years imprisonment on individuals who deviate from the basic teachings of the official religions.'[273]

In 2011, the UN Human Rights Committee adopted General Comment No. 34 on Article 19: Freedoms of opinion and expression, in which it observed (in para. 48) that:

Prohibitions of displays of lack of respect for a religion or other belief system, including blasphemy laws, are incompatible with the Covenant, except in the specific circumstances envisaged in article 20, paragraph 2, of the Covenant. Such prohibitions must also comply with the strict requirements of article 19, paragraph 3, as well as such articles as 2, 5, 17,

---

[272] http://www2.ohchr.org/english/issues/racism/rapporteur/docs/Joint_Statement_SRs.pdf.
[273] UN Doc. A/65/207 (29 July 2010), para. 44.

18 and 26. Thus, for instance, it would be impermissible for any such laws to discriminate in favour of or against one or certain religions or belief systems, or their adherents over another, or religious believers over non-believers. Nor would it be permissible for such prohibitions to be used to prevent or punish criticism of religious leaders or commentary on religious doctrine and tenets of faith.

In response to these debates, in 2011 the UN Human Rights Council adopted by consensus a resolution (Res. 16/18 of 24 March 2011) that omitted all references to defamation and drew directly upon proposals put forward by the OIC. It called on states 'to foster a domestic environment of religious tolerance, peace and respect, by':

(a) Encouraging the creation of collaborative networks to build mutual understanding, promoting dialogue and inspiring constructive action towards shared policy goals and the pursuit of tangible outcomes ...;

(b) Creating an appropriate mechanism within Governments to, inter alia, identify and address potential areas of tension between members of different religious communities, and assisting with conflict prevention and mediation;

(c) Encouraging training of Government officials in effective outreach strategies;

(d) Encouraging the efforts of leaders to discuss within their communities the causes of discrimination, and evolving strategies to counter these causes;

(e) Speaking out against intolerance, including advocacy of religious hatred that constitutes incitement to discrimination, hostility or violence;

(f) Adopting measures to criminalize incitement to imminent violence based on religion or belief;

(g) Understanding the need to combat denigration and negative religious stereotyping of persons, as well as incitement to religious hatred, by strategizing and harmonizing actions at the local, national, regional and international levels through, inter alia, education and awareness-building;

(h) Recognizing that the open, constructive and respectful debate of ideas, as well as interfaith and intercultural dialogue at the local, national and international levels, can play a positive role in combating religious hatred, incitement and violence;

...

In Ireland, a common law offence of blasphemous libel was reflected in the 1937 Constitution. It was applicable only to Christianity and in 1999 the Irish Supreme Court found it incompatible with the guarantee of religious equality. New legislation, the Defamation Act of 2009, sought to amend the approach but was never enforced. The prohibition of blasphemy was repealed in 2020 following a referendum in 2018 which was supported by 65 percent of those who voted.

RONALD DWORKIN, EVEN BIGOTS AND HOLOCAUST DENIERS MUST HAVE THEIR SAY
THE GUARDIAN (14 FEBRUARY 2006)

The British media were right, on balance, not to republish the Danish cartoons that millions of furious Muslims protested against in violent and terrible destruction around the world. Reprinting would very likely have meant more people killed and more property destroyed. It would have caused many British Muslims great pain ... . [T]he public does not have a right to read or see whatever it wants no matter what the cost, and the cartoons are in any case widely available on the internet.

There is a real danger, however, that the decision of British media not to publish, though wise, will be wrongly taken as an endorsement of the widely held opinion that freedom of speech has limits, that it must be balanced against the virtues of multiculturalism, and that the government was right after all to propose that it be made a crime to publish anything "abusive or insulting" to a religious group. Freedom of speech is not just a special and distinctive emblem of western culture that might be generously abridged or qualified as a measure of respect for other cultures that reject it, the way a crescent or menorah might be added to a Christian religious display. Free speech is a condition of legitimate government. Laws and policies are not legitimate unless they have been adopted through a democratic process, and a process is not democratic if government has prevented anyone from expressing his convictions about what those laws and policies should be. Ridicule is a distinct kind of expression; its substance cannot be repackaged in a less offensive rhetorical form without expressing something very different from what was intended. That is why cartoons and other forms of ridicule have for centuries, even when illegal, been among the most important weapons of both noble and wicked political movements.

So in a democracy no one, however powerful or impotent, can have a right not to be insulted or offended. That principle is of particular importance in a nation that strives for racial and ethnic fairness. If weak or unpopular minorities wish to be protected from economic or legal discrimination by law — if they wish laws enacted that prohibit discrimination against them in employment, for instance — then they must be willing to tolerate whatever insults or ridicule people who oppose such legislation wish to offer to their fellow voters, because only a community that permits such insult may legitimately adopt such laws. If we expect bigots to accept the verdict of the majority once the majority has spoken, then we must permit them to express their bigotry in the process whose verdict we ask them to respect. Whatever multiculturalism means — whatever it means to call for increased "respect" for all citizens and groups — these virtues would be self-defeating if they were thought to justify official censorship.

Muslims who are outraged by the Danish cartoons point out that in several European countries it is a crime publicly to deny, as the president of Iran has denied, that the Holocaust ever took place. They say that western concern for free speech is therefore only self-serving hypocrisy, and they have a point. But of course the remedy is not to make the compromise of democratic legitimacy even greater than it already is but to work toward a new understanding of the European convention on human rights that would strike down the Holocaust-denial law and similar laws across Europe for what they are: violations of the freedom of speech that that convention demands.

It is often said that religion is special, because people's religious convictions are so central to their personalities that they should not be asked to tolerate ridicule in that dimension, and because they might feel a religious duty to strike back at what they take to be sacrilege. Britain has apparently embraced that view because it retains the crime of blasphemy, though only for insults to Christianity. But we cannot make an exception for religious insult if we want to use law to protect the free exercise of religion in other ways. If we want to forbid the police from profiling people who look or dress like Muslims for special searches, for example, we cannot also forbid people from opposing that policy by claiming, in cartoons or otherwise, that Islam is committed to terrorism, however silly we think that opinion is. Religion must be tailored to democracy, not the other way around. No religion can be permitted to legislate for everyone about what can or cannot be drawn any more than it can legislate about what may or may not be eaten. No one's religious convictions can be thought to trump the freedom that makes democracy possible.

QUESTIONS

1. What provisions of the ICCPR could you have relied on to seek relief for the publication in a European country of the cartoons? Would it be relevant if you were a resident Muslim in such a country or were a national and resident of a Middle Eastern country?

2. Consider the following critique of General Comment No. 34:

... Article 19(3) expressly permits freedom of expression to be restricted in the name of public morals ... .

No doubt, blasphemy laws do not sit easily with a secular public moral vision. But the reality is that for millions of people (and dozens of countries), religion, and religious devotion is at the heart of their moral compass. Insofar as the public moralities of these countries is concerned, unacceptable irreverence (blasphemy) may be as morally unsayable as hate speech or the "n-word" is in Western Europe or as Holocaust denial is in Germany. De facto then, in these countries, blasphemous speech does offend, in a unique way, against public morality.[274]

3. Do you agree with the views expressed by Dworkin?

---

[274] N. Cox, 'Justifying Blasphemy Laws: Freedom of Expression, Public Morals, and International Human Rights Law', 35 *J. L. and Relig.* (2020) 33, at 58.

Made in the USA
Monee, IL
07 January 2025

76236000R00304